COMPREHENSIVE HANDBOOK
OF
PSYCHOTHERAPY

COMPREHENSIVE HANDBOOK OF PSYCHOTHERAPY

VOLUME 1

PSYCHODYNAMIC/OBJECT RELATIONS

Editor-In-Chief   **FLORENCE W. KASLOW**

Volume Editor   **JEFFREY J. MAGNAVITA**

John Wiley & Sons, Inc.

This book is printed on acid-free paper. ∞

Copyright © 2002 by John Wiley & Sons, Inc.. All rights reserved.

Published by John Wiley & Sons, Inc., Hoboken, New Jersey.
Published simultaneously in Canada.

No part of this publication may be reproduced, stored in a retrieval system or transmitted in any form or by any means, electronic, mechanical, photocopying, recording, scanning or otherwise, except as permitted under Sections 107 or 108 of the 1976 United States Copyright Act, without either the prior written permission of the Publisher, or authorization through payment of the appropriate per-copy fee to the Copyright Clearance Center, 222 Rosewood Drive, Danvers, MA 01923, (978) 750-8400, fax (978) 646-8600, or on the web at www.copyright.com. Requests to the Publisher for permission should be addressed to the Permissions Department, John Wiley & Sons, Inc., 111 River Street, Hoboken, NJ 07030, (201) 748-6011, fax (201) 748-6008.

Limit of Liability/Disclaimer of Warranty: While the publisher and author have used their best efforts in preparing this book, they make no representations or warranties with respect to the accuracy or completeness of the contents of this book and specifically disclaim any implied warranties of merchantability or fitness for a particular purpose. No warranty may be created or extended by sales representatives or written sales materials. The advice and strategies contained herein may not be suitable for your situation. The publisher is not engaged in rendering professional services, and you should consult a professional where appropriate. Neither the publisher nor author shall be liable for any loss of profit or any other commercial damages, including but not limited to special, incidental, consequential, or other damages.

This publication is designed to provide accurate and authoritative information in regard to the subject matter covered. It is sold with the understanding that the publisher is not engaged in rendering professional services. If legal, accounting, medical, psychological or any other expert assistance is required, the services of a competent professional person should be sought.

Designations used by companies to distinguish their products are often claimed as trademarks. In all instances where John Wiley & Sons, Inc. is aware of a claim, the product names appear in initial capital or all capital letters. Readers, however, should contact the appropriate companies for more complete information regarding trademarks and registration.

For general information on our other products and services please contact our Customer Care Department within the United States at (800) 762-2974, outside the United States at (317) 572-3993, or fax (317) 572-4002.

Wiley also publishes its books in a variety of electronic formats. Some content that appears in print may not be available in electronic books. For more information about Wiley products, visit our web site at www.wiley.com.

Library of Congress Cataloging-in-Publication Data:

Comprehensive handbook of psychotherapy / [editor-in-chief] Florence W. Kaslow.
    p. cm.
  Includes bibliographical references and index.
  Contents: v. 1. Psychodynamic/object relations / [edited by] Jeffrey J. Magnavita — v. 2. Cognitive-behavioral approaches / [edited by] Terence Patterson — v. 3. Interpersonal/humanistic/existential / [edited by] Robert F. Massey, Sharon Davis Massey — v. 4. Integrative/eclectic / [edited by] Jay Lebow.
  ISBN 0-471-01848-1 (set) — ISBN 0-471-38263-9 (cloth : alk. paper : v. 1); ISBN 0-471-65325-X (pbk.) — ISBN 0-471-65332-2 (set : pbk.)
  1. Psychotherapy—Handbooks, manuals, etc. 2. Cognitive therapy—Handbooks, manuals, etc. 3. Behavior therapy—Handbooks, manuals, etc. I. Kaslow, Florence Whiteman. II. Magnavita, Jeffrey J. III. Patterson, Terence. IV. Massey, Robert F. V. Massey, Sharon Davis. VI. Lebow, Jay.

RC480 .C593 2002
616.89'14—dc21
                                      2001045636

Printed in the United States of America.

10 9 8 7 6 5 4 3 2 1

Contributors

Jacques P. Barber, PhD, is associate professor and associate director at the Center for Psychotherapy Research, Department of Psychiatry and Psychology, University of Pennsylvania School of Medicine in Philadelphia, Pennsylvania. Dr. Barber has published more than 100 articles, chapters, and books in the area of psychotherapy research.

Helen E. Benedict, PhD, is professor of psychology at Baylor University and a registered play therapist supervisor for Association for Play Therapy. She is a frequent leader of national and international workshops on play therapy, especially object-relations play therapy and play therapy for children with attachment disorders and children who have experienced interpersonal trauma. She also leads an active research program on play therapy process using children's play themes.

M. Sue Chenoweth, MS, PsyD, is in private practice in Hartford, Connecticut. She is affiliated with the Institute of Living–Hartford Hospital Mental Health Network in Hartford. She is a consultant for the Women's Sexual Health Program–Connecticut Surgical Group, P.C., Urology Division in Hartford.

John F. Clarkin, PhD, is a professor of clinical psychology in psychiatry at the Joan and Sanford I. Weill Medical College of Cornell University, the codirector of the Personality Disorders Institute, and the director of psychology at the Cornell Medical Center. Dr. Clarkin is on the research faculty and is a lecturer at Columbia University's Psychoanalytic Center.

Gerhard W. Dammann, MD, Dipl.-Psych., is attending psychiatrist, clinical psychologist, and psychoanalyst (IPA) at the Psychiatric University Hospital in Basel, Switzerland, and Department of Psychosomatic Medicine and Psychotherapy, Technical University Medical School in Munich, Germany.

Ellen A. Dornelas, PhD, is director of Behavioral Health Programs, Preventive Cardiology, at Hartford Hospital and assistant professor of medicine at the University of Connecticut School of Medicine. Her research interests are focused on health psychology with special emphasis on psychological factors related to heart disease.

Scott C. Duncan, PhD, is clinical lecturer, Department of Psychiatry, at the University of Alberta, Edmonton, Canada. He is a therapist in the Psychiatric Treatment Clinic of the Department and also maintains a private psychotherapy practice.

Peter Fonagy, PhD, FBA, is Freud Memorial Professor of Psychoanalysis and director of the Sub-Department of Clinical Health Psychology at University College in London. He is director of the Clinical Outcomes Research and Effectiveness Centre and the Child and Family Centre, both at the Menninger Foundation in Kansas. He is also director of research at the Anna Freud Centre, London, a clinical psychologist, and a training and supervising analyst in the British Psycho-Analytical Society in child and adult analysis.

Diana Fosha, PhD, is associate clinical professor of psychology at Adelphi University's Derner Institute of Advanced Psychological Studies. She is the author of *The Transforming Power of Affect: A Model of Accelerated Change* (Basic Books, 2000) and of recent articles that integrate emotion theory, affective neuroscience, and attachment research into the theory and technique of accelerated experiential-dynamic psychotherapy. She maintains a private practice in New York City.

Cheryl Glickauf-Hughes, PhD, is a licensed psychologist, an adjunct professor at Emory University Department of Psychiatry, and a private practitioner in Atlanta, Georgia. She has co-authored two books and numerous book chapters and articles.

Paul A. Grayson, PhD, is director of New York University Counseling Service and clinical assistant professor of psychiatry at New York University Medical School. Dr. Grayson is coauthor of *Beating the College Blues,* a self-help guide for students, and coeditor of *College Psychotherapy,* a volume for college psychotherapists.

Stanley I. Greenspan, MD, is clinical professor of psychiatry and pediatrics at George Washington University Medical School, supervising child psychoanalyst at Washington Psychoanalytic Institute, and chairman of the Interdisciplinary Council for Developmental and Learning Disorders.

José Guimón, MD, PhD, is professor of psychiatry at Geneva University Medical School in Switzerland, director of the World Health Organization Collaborative Center for Research and Training in Mental Health, and author of more than 150 papers and 30 books.

Mary F. Hall, PhD, LICSW, is currently an associate professor at the Smith College School for Social Work where she teaches the *Human Behavior in the Social Environment* and *Clinical Practice* sequences. Major administrative assignments have included service as director of Continuing Education, clinical coordinator of the school's doctoral program, and area coordinator in the Field Work Department for MSW interns. She has also held prior faculty appointments at the Shirley Ehrenkrantz New York University School of Social Work and the Boston University School of Social Work. Her current research interest is the interface between race and gender in pregnant substance abusers.

Lara Hastings was trained at Baylor University and is currently completing a postdoctoral at the Child and Family Guidance Center in Dallas, Texas.

Cecile Rausch Herscovici, Lic, is a full professor of psychology at the Universidad del Salvador and codirector of the Institute of Systems Therapy in Buenos Aires, Argentina. She is an approved supervisor of the American Association for Marriage and Family Therapy, member of the American

Family Therapy Academy, of the Academy for Eating Disorders, and of the European Council for Eating Disorders. She is also editor of the Ediciones Granica Series in Eating Disorders.

Michael D. Kahn, PhD, ABPP, is professor emeritus of clinical psychology at the University of Hartford in West Hartford, Connecticut, where he recently retired as director of academic affairs for the Graduate Institute of Psychology. He is a fellow in the American Psychological Association, the American Orthopsychiatric Association, and an approved supervisor of the American Association of Marital and Family Therapy. He is a charter member of the American Family Therapy Academy, member of several editorial boards, and author of more than 40 publications on sibling relations and integrative therapies. Dr. Kahn maintains an active private practice in Hartford, Connecticut, and is also a professional jazz musician in New England.

Rosemarie LaFleur Bach, PsyD, is a psychologist with The Institute of Living, Hartford Hospital's Mental Health Network, and school clinician at the Chesire School System, contracted through Hartford Hospital and the Grace Webb School, The Institute of Living. She is also in private practice.

Kenneth N. Levy, PhD, is assistant professor of the Clinical Psychology Doctoral Program, Graduate School and University Center, and Department of Psychology at Hunter College, City University of New York. He is also adjunct assistant professor, Psychology Section, Department of Psychiatry, Joan and Sanford I. Weill Medical College of Cornell University. Dr. Levy also has a private practice in New York, New York.

Leslie M. Lothstein, PhD, ABPP, is director of psychology at The Institute of Living, Hartford Hospital's Mental Health Network, and has academic appointments at Case Western Reserve University, University of Hartford, and UCONN Farmington Health Center. Dr. Lothstein serves as consultant on risk assessment for sex offenders for the Department of Mental Health and Addiction Services, Connecticut, and as vice chair of the Advisory Board, Whiting Forensic Division, Connecticut Valley Hospital.

Rita E. Lynn, PsyD, has been a senior member of the Institute of Group Analysis (London) for more than 30 years. She worked with Dr. Robin Skynner as his cotherapist. She was a teaching fellow at St. Bartholomew's Hospital (London) and held a post at the Medical College of the London Hospital, where she taught and consulted for 10 years. Until moving to the United States, she supervised and trained the Institute's trainee analysts. She now lives in Los Angeles, where she is a professor at the American Behavioral Studies Institute. She has authored numerous articles on the British Object Relations approach to treatment.

Jeffrey J. Magnavita, PhD, ABPP, is a fellow of the American Psychological Association and is both a licensed psychologist and marriage and family therapist. He is the founder of the Connecticut Center for Short-Term Dynamic Psychotherapy and an adjunct professor of clinical psychology at the University of Hartford's Graduate Institute of Professional Psychology. He is the author of three books: *Restructuring Personality Disorders, Relational Therapy for Personality Disorders,* and *Theories of Personality: Contemporary Approaches to the Science of Personality,* as well as numerous professional publications.

J. Christopher Muran, PhD, is chief psychologist and director of the Brief Psychotherapy Research Program at Beth Israel Medical Center, associate professor of psychiatry at Albert Einstein College of Medicine, and associate editor for psychotherapy research. He has coedited *The Therapeutic Alliance in Brief Psychotherapy*, coauthored *Negotiating the Therapeutic Alliance: A Relational Treatment Guide*, and edited *Self-Relations in the Psychotherapy Process*.

John S. Ogrodniczuk, PhD, is a clinical assistant professor in the Department of Psychiatry at the University of British Columbia. His research interests include identifying matches between patient characteristics and types of short-term, time-limited psychotherapies (group, individual, partial hospitalization). Other interests include the use of psychotherapy for medically ill patients.

Ferruccio Osimo, MD, is a psychiatrist in Milan, Italy. He is adjunct professor of Dynamic Psychotherapy, Università Statale di Milano; president of IESA (International Experiential STDP Association), New York; a fellow of the American Academy of Psychoanalysis; and treasurer of OPIFER (Organization of Italian Psychoanalysts-Federation and Roster).

Jeree H. Pawl, PhD, was the director of the Infant-Parent Program at the University of California, San Francisco, for twenty years following her work with Selma Fraiberg at the Child Development Project at the University of Michigan. She is also a current member of the board of directors of Zero to Three, The National Center for Infants, Toddlers and Families, and a past president of that organization.

William E. Piper, PhD, is a professor in the Department of Psychiatry at the University of British Columbia, Vancouver, Canada. He was president of the Society for Psychotherapy Research and of the Canadian Group Psychotherapy Association, and is currently editor of the International Journal of Group Psychotherapy.

Jeremy D. Safran, PhD, is professor of psychology at the New School for Social Research and Senior Research Scientist at Beth Israel Medical Center. He has authored *Widening the Scope of Cognitive Therapy*, coauthored *Emotion in Psychotherapy*, *Interpersonal Process in Cognitive Therapy*, and *Negotiating the Therapeutic Alliance: A Relational Treatment Guide*. He has also coedited *Emotion, Psychotherapy, and Change* and *The Therapeutic Alliance in Brief Psychotherapy*.

Lynne R. Siqueland, PhD, is currently an adjunct assistant professor at the University of Pennsylvania Medical School in the Center for Psychotherapy Research, where she has been involved in training and supervision of supportive expressive dynamic therapy. She is also in private practice at the Children's Center for OCD and Anxiety specializing in the treatment of anxiety disorders.

Marion F. Solomon, PhD, is on the Senior Extension Faculty at UCLA, Department of Humanities, Sciences and Social Sciences, and a professor at the American Behavioral Studies Institute in Los Angeles. She is author of two books, *Narcissism and Intimacy,* and *Lean on Me: The Power of Positive Dependency in Intimate Relationships*. She is coauthor of *Short Term Therapy for Long Term Change,* and has coedited two books, *Countertransference in Couples Therapy,* and *The Borderline Patient*.

Maria St. John, MA, MFT, has been a senior therapist and clinical supervisor at the Infant-Parent Program at the University of California, San Francisco, for nine years. She is currently a doctoral candidate in the Department of Rhetoric at the University of California, Berkeley, studying the rhetorics of psychoanalysis.

Mary Target, PhD, is a senior lecturer in psychoanalysis at University College London and an associate member of the British Psychoanalytic Society. She is deputy director of research at the Anna Freud Centre, member of the Curriculum and Scientific Committees, chairman of the Research Committee of the British Psychoanalytic Society, and chairman of the Working Party on Psychoanalytic Education of the European Psychoanalytic Federation.

Paul D. Thompson, MD, is director of Preventive Cardiology and director of Cardiovascular Research at Hartford Hospital and professor of medicine at the University of Connecticut School of Medicine. His research interests include the effects of exercise training in preventing and treating heart disease and risk of sudden death during exercise.

Manuel Trujillo, MD, is director of psychiatry at Bellevue Hospital and professor of clinical psychiatry and vice chair, Department of Psychiatry, at New York University School of Medicine. Dr. Trujillo is a distinguished academic clinician, psychiatric administrator, innovator, and researcher. He has been involved extensively in the fields of urban, cross-cultural, and community psychiatry.

Marolyn Wells, PhD, is director, professor, and licensed psychologist at Georgia State University Counseling Center; joint appointment with the Department of Counseling and Psychological Services; and private practitioner in Atlanta, Georgia. Dr. Wells has coauthored two books and numerous book chapters and articles, and is a fellow of the Georgia Psychological Association.

Foreword

Dr. Magnavita has collected a broad-ranging group of contributions, providing an open-minded but critical, enthusiastic yet realistic educational experience. We are in good hands.

As the book illustrates, psychodynamic approaches to psychotherapy have proliferated, stimulated by the limitations of traditional psychoanalysis and by infusions of existential thought, with its emphasis on selfhood and being with the other, as in Kohut's self psychology, and of interpersonal or social concepts, centering on relationship patterns and their reoccurrence in therapy, as in object relations and intersubjective analysis. There is also the now widely accepted body of evidence linking change in psychotherapy to the quality of the relationship between patient and therapist.

What is the conscientious reader to do with the many ideas celebrated here? They are a wonderful challenge to efforts of selection and digestion.

For example, central to much clinical thinking are concepts of development. But what are we to do with the problem of individual uniqueness, the unpredictable outcome of the myriad factors shaping development? We need concepts of growth, but they must not constrain us. So often, the most remarkable people emerge from the most difficult circumstances.

How do we select the unit to work with? Is it the traditional one-to-one, couples, or group work, or even the home-bound therapy eloquently described here?

Bodies and urges have long been central concerns. There is also the brain as the organ of mental representation, and affects that now rival ideas as the medium of change.

And how much pathological emphasis should we give, perhaps particularly, to the most frightening presentations? The redemption of a pedophile is described in one of these chapters as partly the result of his therapist's inspired remark, "Anyone who loves kids that much can't be all bad." By the patient's own testimony, this changed his life.

Critical in these chapters is a contest between the usual subjects of therapeutic attention—id, ego, and superego (plus the ego ideal that self psychology has made central)—and the intersubjective field, in which the goal is to create a space where both parties can freely exchange what occurs to each and where the two can arrive at understanding and change.

Patterns of sexuality are an age-old topic. Today, the ground has partly shifted to concerns with power, respect, and equality.

And the problems of marriage, without which many of us might well be unemployed, seem increasingly to have become an educational tool for the long-term study of one self in relation to another.

Here is perhaps as close to a practical answer as we are likely to get: Keep as much as we can put into the back of our minds for those occasions that may prompt retrieval. Let our intuitive responses guide us. Or the deeper, perhaps wiser, reflection offered here: Ours is an effort to plumb a depth of thought untouched by words and a gulf of formless feelings untouched by thought! We work in the dark. Our doubts should be cherished.

Meanwhile, neuroscience is teaching that the human brain is significantly a creation of each individual's experience, the individual self being formed by interaction with the world and others, including our therapeutic selves. Rather than replacing these chapters, neuroscience is confirming and may someday be extending them.

The challenge of the work is immense, needing the lifetime that, often, we can give it. Let us celebrate the diversity of our efforts and the opportunities they provide. We have the chance, seldom matched, to make lives better.

LESTON HAVENS, MD
Professor of Psychiatry
Harvard Medical School
and The Cambridge Hospital

Preface

The world of psychotherapy theory and practice has changed markedly in the past 30 years. During this time, many forces have converged, leading to major alterations in the therapeutic landscape. Therefore, it seemed essential to produce this four-volume *Comprehensive Handbook of Psychotherapy* to illuminate the state of the art of the field, and to encompass history, theory, practice, trends, and research at the beginning of the twenty-first century.

These volumes are envisioned as both comprehensive in terms of the most current extant knowledge and as thought provoking, stimulating in our readers new ways of thinking that should prove generative of further refinements, elaborations, and the next iteration of new ideas. The volumes are intended for several audiences, including graduate students and their professors, clinicians, and researchers.

In these four volumes, we have sought to bring together contributing authors who have achieved recognition and acclaim in their respective areas of theory construction, research, practice, and/or teaching. To reflect the globalization of the psychotherapy field and its similarities and differences between and among countries and cultures, authors are included from such countries as Argentina, Australia, Belgium, Canada, Italy, Japan, and the United States.

Regardless of the theoretical orientation being elucidated, almost all of the chapters are written from a biopsychosocial perspective. The vast majority present their theory's perspective on dealing with patient affects, behaviors or actions, and cognitions. I believe these volumes provide ample evidence that any reasonably complete theory must encompass these three aspects of living.

Many of the chapters also deal with assessment and diagnosis as well as treatment strategies and interventions. There are frequent discussions of disorders classified under the rubric of Axis I and Axis II in the fourth edition of the *Diagnostic and Statistical Manual of Mental Disorders* with frequent concurrence across chapters as to how treatment of these disorders should be approached. There are other chapters, particularly those that cluster in the narrative, postmodern, and social constructivist wing of the field, that eschew diagnosis, based on the belief that the only reality of concern is the one being created in the moment-to-moment current interaction: in this instance, the therapeutic dialogue or conversation. In these therapies, goals and treatment plans are coconstructed and coevolved and generally are not predicated on any formal assessment through psychological testing. Whereas most of the other philosophical/theoretical schools have incorporated the evolving knowledge of the brain-behavior connection and the many exciting and illuminating findings emanating from the field of neuroscience, this is much less true in the postmodern wing of the field, which places little value on facts objectively verified by consensual validation and replication.

One of the most extraordinary developments in the past few decades has been that barriers between the theoretical schools have diminished, and leading theoreticians, academicians, researchers, and clinicians have listened to and learned from each other. As a result of this cross-fertilization, the *move toward integration* among and between theoretical approaches has been definitive. Many of the chapters in Volumes 1, 2, and 3 also could fit in Volume 4. Some of the distance between psychodynamic/object-relations therapies and cognitive-behavioral therapies has decreased as practitioners of each have gained more respect for the other and incorporated ideas that expand their theory base and make it more holistic. This is one of the strongest trends that emerges from reading these volumes.

A second trend that comes to the fore is the recognition that, at times, it is necessary to combine judicious psychopharmacological treatment with psychotherapy, and that not doing so makes the healing process more difficult and slower.

Other important trends evident in these volumes include greater sensitivity to issues surrounding gender, ethnicity, race, religion, and socioeconomic status; the controversy over empirically validated treatments versus viewing and treating each patient or patient unit as unique; the importance of the brain-behavior connection mentioned earlier; the critical role assigned to developmental history; the foci on outcome and efficacy; and the importance of process and outcome research and the use of research findings to enhance clinical practice. There is a great deal of exciting ferment going on as our psychotherapeutic horizons continue to expand.

These volumes would not have come to fruition without the outstanding collaboration and teamwork of the fine volume editors, Drs. Jeffrey Magnavita, Terrence Patterson, Robert and Sharon Massey, and Jay Lebow, and my gratitude to them is boundless. To each of the contributing authors, our combined thank you is expressed.

We extend huge plaudits and great appreciation to Jennifer Simon, Associate Publisher at John Wiley & Sons, for her guidance, encouragement, and wisdom. Thanks also to Isabel Pratt, Editorial Assistant, for all her efforts. It has been a multifaceted and intense enterprise.

We hope the readers, for whom the work is intended, will deem our efforts extremely worthwhile.

FLORENCE W. KASLOW, PhD, ABPP
Editor-in-Chief

Palm Beach Gardens, Florida

Contents

FOREWORD xi
Leston Havens, MD

PREFACE xiii
Florence W. Kaslow, PhD, ABPP

CHAPTER 1
PSYCHODYNAMIC APPROACHES TO PSYCHOTHERAPY: A CENTURY OF INNOVATIONS 1
Jeffrey J. Magnavita

SECTION ONE

PSYCHOTHERAPY WITH CHILDREN

CHAPTER 2
THE DEVELOPMENTAL BASIS OF PSYCHOTHERAPEUTIC PROCESSES 15
Stanley I. Greenspan

CHAPTER 3
OBJECT-RELATIONS PLAY THERAPY 47
Helen E. Benedict and Lara Hastings

CHAPTER 4
INFANT MENTAL HEALTH 81
Jeree H. Pawl and Maria St. John

CHAPTER 5
PSYCHODYNAMIC APPROACHES TO CHILD THERAPY 105
Peter Fonagy and Mary Target

SECTION TWO

PSYCHOTHERAPY WITH ADOLESCENTS AND YOUNG ADULTS

CHAPTER 6
EATING DISORDERS IN ADOLESCENCE 133
Cecile Rausch Herscovici

Chapter 7
Psychodynamic Psychotherapy with Undergraduate and Graduate Students — 161
Paul A. Grayson

SECTION THREE

Psychotherapy with Adults

Chapter 8
Supportive-Expressive Psychotherapy — 183
Lynne R. Siqueland and Jacques P. Barber

Chapter 9
Brief Psychodynamic Therapy — 207
Ferruccio Osimo

Chapter 10
An Object-Relations Approach to the Treatment of Borderline Patients — 239
John F. Clarkin, Kenneth N. Levy, and Gerhard W. Dammann

Chapter 11
A Relational Approach to Psychotherapy — 253
J. Christopher Muran and Jeremy D. Safran

Chapter 12
Mastering Developmental Issues through Interactional Object-Relations Therapy — 283
Cheryl Glickauf-Hughes and Marolyn Wells

Chapter 13
The Activation of Affective Change Processes in Accelerated Experiential-Dynamic Psychotherapy (AEDP) — 309
Diana Fosha

Chapter 14
Short-Term Dynamic Psychotherapy of Narcissistic Disorders — 345
Manuel Trujillo

Chapter 15
A Relational-Feminist Psychodynamic Approach to Sexual Desire — 365
M. Sue Chenoweth

SECTION FOUR

Psychotherapy with Families and Couples

Chapter 16
Object-Relations Couples Therapy — 387
Marion F. Solomon and Rita E. Lynn

CHAPTER 17
SELF-OBJECT RELATIONSHIP THERAPY WITH COUPLES 407
  Michael D. Kahn

CHAPTER 18
RELATIONAL PSYCHODYNAMICS FOR COMPLEX CLINICAL SYNDROMES 435
  Jeffrey J. Magnavita

SECTION FIVE

GROUP PSYCHOTHERAPY

CHAPTER 19
PSYCHODYNAMICALLY ORIENTED GROUP THERAPY 457
  William E. Piper, John S. Ogrodniczuk, and Scott C. Duncan

CHAPTER 20
PSYCHODYNAMIC/OBJECT-RELATIONS GROUP THERAPY WITH SCHIZOPHRENIC PATIENTS 481
  José Guimón

CHAPTER 21
GROUP THERAPY TREATMENT OF SEX OFFENDERS 501
  Leslie M. Lothstein and Rosemarie LaFleur Bach

SECTION SIX

SPECIAL TOPICS

CHAPTER 22
GROUPS IN THERAPEUTIC COMMUNITIES 529
  José Guimón

CHAPTER 23
PSYCHODYNAMIC TREATMENT FOR CARDIAC PATIENTS 549
  Ellen A. Dornelas and Paul D. Thompson

CHAPTER 24
RACE, GENDER, AND TRANSFERENCE IN PSYCHOTHERAPY 565
  Mary F. Hall

CHAPTER 25
CONTEMPORARY PSYCHODYNAMICS: MAJOR ISSUES, CHALLENGES, AND FUTURE TRENDS 587
  Jeffrey J. Magnavita

AUTHOR INDEX 605

SUBJECT INDEX 614

CHAPTER 1

Psychodynamic Approaches to Psychotherapy: A Century of Innovations

JEFFREY J. MAGNAVITA

The first century of modern psychotherapy began with Freud's "discovery" of the unconscious and use of free association. We are at an auspicious time at the turn of the century in the field of psychotherapy; much has been achieved over the past century and many new developments are occurring. Although some believe that psychoanalysis has outlived its usefulness (Dumont, 1993), the discoveries of Freud and his followers have continued to spawn remarkable developments that have created an ever stronger amalgam of psychodynamic psychotherapy. It is true that some aspects of psychoanalytic theory have not been empirically supported or clinically validated, most notable, the psychosexual theory of development and the view that wishes rather than trauma account for some forms of psychopathology. However, many constructs remain vital and central to present-day clinical practice (Magnavita, 1993b). Many of these constructs have evolved and continue to evolve as other clinicians/theorists have expanded, altered, and blended them, and as new breakthroughs in other disciplines have been made and incorporated. For example, the incorporation of von Bertalanffy's (1948) general systems theory has greatly expanded the range of psychodynamic conceptualization and treatment. The twentieth century saw various groundbreaking theoretical innovations.

Many of the cutting-edge theoretical and technical developments in the field today are presented in this volume. Schafer (1999), himself an analytic pioneer, comments: "In the second half of the 20th century, we have been witness to remarkable changes in psychoanalytic theory and practice" (p. 339). Prior to Freud's discovery of free association, the use of hypnosis was the major technique for exploring and mapping the unconscious. With the advent of the technique of free association, a remarkable window into the unconscious process was opened. In this chapter, I review some of the essential developments and advances that have occurred in psychoanalysis and psychodynamic psychotherapy during the past century. Now, the beginning of the twenty-first century, the field of psychoanalysis can be seen to be enormous and its influence on popular culture and lexicon widespread. This chapter refers to only a small fraction of the diversity of work that has evolved from Freud's original conceptualization and approach to treatment.

THE ORIGINS OF THE TERM PSYCHOTHERAPY

In the first chapter of this four-volume work, a mention of the origins of the word psychotherapy is in order. "Long before terms such as *psychotherapeutics* and *psychotherapy* were coined, methods were employed for treating or ministering to various forms of suffering—whether those were thought of as diseases, illnesses, ailments, disorders, syndromes, or other forms of sickness—through the use of psychological rather than physical measures" (Jackson, 1999, p. 10). The origins of the term psychotherapy suggest that it appeared "toward the end of the 1880's, and had its roots in the Liebeault-Bernheim school of suggestive therapeutics at Nancy" (pp. 7–8). According to Jackson, it first appeared in a work by Hippolyte Bernheim entitled *Hypnotisme, suggestion, psychotherapie* in 1891. Essential to early "healer-sufferer" relationships were factors such as hope, sympathy/compassion, and the influence of the mind on the body.

THE FIRST COMPREHENSIVE THEORETICAL MODEL OF HUMAN PSYCHIC FUNCTIONING

The discovery of the unconscious and the development of psychoanalytic methods ushered in a new form of scientific inquiry that may be considered to be the birth of modern scientific psychology. This is not to minimize the other paradigmatic shifts that occurred in other areas of psychology, such as the application of empirical methods to the study of various psychological topics, for example, Pavlov's (1927) work with classical conditioning, which set the stage for the development of behaviorism. Freud's work stands as one of the intellectual milestones of the twentieth century (Schwartz, 1999). His theory of psychoanalysis is considered by many to be equivalent to the genius of Einstein's theory of relativity and Darwin's theory of evolution (Bischof, 1970). Freud offered remarkable new ways of understanding the mind, psychopathology, and methods of ameliorating human emotional suffering. It is important to remember from a historical perspective that "there was a profound awareness of an unconscious realm" prior to Freud's work and that "there is an impressive 19th century literature that deals with unconscious *psychic structures*" (Dumont, 1993, p. 195). Freud and his followers were "large system builders" and "beneficiaries of a vast literature that provided them with virtually all the insights bearing on the unconscious" (p. 196).

Psychoanalysis was born when Freud abandoned hypnosis in favor of the technique of free association (Magnavita, 2002). Freud originally was very taken with hypnosis and was influenced by Charcot, who pioneered the technique. Breuer also stoked his interest in hypnosis, but S. Freud (1966) became frustrated with it:

> Originally Breuer and I myself carried out psychotherapy by means of hypnosis; Breuer's first patient was treated throughout under hypnotic influence, and to begin with I followed him in this. I admit that at that period the work proceeded more easily and pleasantly, and in a much shorter period of time. Results were capricious and not lasting; and for that reason I finally dropped hypnosis. And I then understood that an insight into the dynamics of these illnesses had not been possible so long as hypnosis was employed. (p. 292)

According to Havens (1973): "Breuer's *method*, however, remained very close to Charcot's. It was symptom-centered, hypnotic, and objective" (p. 90). Freud's method was a radical departure from Breuer's and Charcot's approaches.

"Fundamental to Freud's thinking about the mind was a simple assumption: If there is a discontinuity in consciousness—something the person is doing but cannot report or explain—then the relevant mental processes necessary to 'fill in the gaps' must be unconscious" (Westen & Gabbard, 1999, p. 59). Freud's technique of free association allowed him and others who followed to explore the dark recesses of the human psyche and to provide a map of the unconscious. He outlined the topographical contours with his delineation of the regions of unconscious, preconscious, and conscious zones. He proposed a tripartite model of human psychic functioning with three structural components, now taught in every introductory psychology course: the id, the ego, and the superego. He offered an explanation of how the instinctual sexual and aggressive forces were modulated and channeled either neurotically into symptom formations or characterologically into personality disturbance. His emphasis on psychosexual development, much of which has not been validated, represented one of the first credible stage theories of human development. Key concepts of repression and resistance offered psychoanalysts a way to understand how unacceptable impulses and painful affects are lost to the conscious mind but are expressed in a variety of symbolic ways. Current-day psychotherapists of just about every ilk have incorporated the concept of repression into their theoretical systems.

DERIVATIVE THEORETICAL SYSTEMS

Psychoanalysis and psychodynamic concepts are in constant evolution; they are reinterpreted, transformed, and revitalized. A static system never could have provided the field with such a wealth of raw material that could be mined for over a century and still continue to be vital for each new generation. The following four models all have an important place in psychodynamic theory and are reviewed in more detail throughout this volume.

EGO PSYCHOLOGY: THE EMPHASIS ON ADAPTATION

The ego psychologists were especially interested in the functioning of the ego and emphasized the importance of adaptation (Hartmann, 1958, 1964). Ego psychology set out to elaborate the various aspects of healthy functioning or ego-adaptive capacity. This aspect of psychodynamic theory was expanded by Horner (1994, 1995) and is an extremely valuable component of psychodynamic assessment, especially when conducting brief dynamic therapy.

OBJECT-RELATIONS THEORY: THE EMPHASIS ON ATTACHMENT

Winnicott viewed aggression as emerging from the disruption of attachment rather than emanating from an instinctual drive, as Freud suggested (Winnicott, Shepherd, & Davis, 1989). This was the beginning of the object-relations model, advanced by Melaine Klein (1975), W. R. D. Fairbairn (1954), Margaret Mahler (Mahler, Pine, & Bergman, 1975), Annie Reich (1960), and others (Buckley, 1986). Object relations recognized the primacy of attachment. Winnicott did not believe the infant could be studied outside the maternal-child dyad; he went so far to say "There is no such thing as a baby," suggesting that when you describe the baby, you describe the dyad (Rayner, 1991, p. 60). This theoretical development heralded the move away from the emphasis on the intrapsychic to a *dyadic* model. One of Winnicott's best-known concepts is the "good-enough mother," which implies that although one doesn't need perfect parenting, there must be at least a critical level of parental function for uncomplicated developmental progression (Winnicott, Shepherd, & Davis, 1989, p. 44).

Self Psychology: The Study of Narcissism

Kohut's (1971, 1977) groundbreaking work expanding Freud's concept of narcissism enabled clinicians to begin to understand and treat another form of pathological adaptation that was not effectively treated with standard psychoanalysis. Stolorow, Atwood, and Orange (1999) describe some of the inherent difficulties:

> As useful and pathbreaking as his contextualization of narcissism may have been, Kohut's (1977) subsequent elevation of his psychology of narcissism to a metatheory of the total personality—a psychoanalytic psychology of the self—has created some knotty problems. For one thing, self psychology's unidimensionality, the exclusive focus on the narcissistic or selfobject dimension of experience and of transference—its establishment, disruption, and repair—has tended to become reductive, neglecting and failing to contextualize other important dimensions. Even more problematic has been the insidious movement from phenomenology to ontology, from experience to entities—a movement reminiscent of Freud's (1923/1961) shift from the centrality of unconscious emotional conflict to the trinity of mental institutions presumed to explain it. (p. 384)

Kohut's major contribution was in his emphasis on the development of the self from the fragile infant state to the cohesive adult personality. He added much to our understanding of patients who have disorders in their basic sense of self-esteem. This branch of psychoanalytic theory then began to provide a clearer differentiation between those with emotional disturbances based on intrapsychic conflict who had sufficient attachment experience and those patients with deficits in their self-structure. The patients with deficit have not had the necessary experiences that lead to a solid intrapsychic structure, as reflected by adaptive defenses and a stable sense of oneself. Traditionally, these preoedipal or, in many cases, prelanguage trauma patients have disturbances in primary attachments. This may be the result of injuries that occurred from insufficient mirroring of the primary attachment figure or severe attachment insufficiency or disruption (Frank, 1999).

Interpersonal Psychiatry: The Dyadic Relationship

Harry Stack Sullivan (1953) developed an interpersonal theory of psychoanalysis from his object-relational perspective. Havens (1973) writes: "Harry Stack Sullivan is the most original figure in American psychiatry, the only American to help found a major school" (p. 183). Sullivan was not so concerned with what transpired inside people but rather focused on what occurred in the relational field. This represented the most radical departure to that time from Freud's structural drive theory of repressed emotions and intrapsychic forces. Sullivan believed that needs were interpersonal and that the therapeutic process was based not on detached observation but on being a participant-observer. In other words, the therapeutic matrix included two people who mutually contributed to the interpersonal experience. He coined the term "self-system" to account for the process of gaining satisfaction and avoiding anxiety in interpersonal relations.

Intersubjectiveness

Many theorists and clinicians challenged Freud's position that the therapist should be a detached observer of the patient's unconscious process. In their book *Faces in a Cloud: Subjectivity in Personality Theory*, Stolorow and Atwood (1979) began to explore the issue of subjectivity and laid the groundwork for the study of intersubjectivity (Stolorow et al., 1999). They state: "To be an experiencing subject is to be positioned in the intersubjective contexts of past, present, and future" (p. 382). This theory of intersubjectivity emphasizes what many current workers believe is vital: affect. "The shift from drive to affect, one of the hallmarks of our intersubjective perspective, is of great theoretical importance, because unlike drives, which originate deep within the interior of an isolated mental apparatus, affectivity is something that from birth onwards is regulated, or misregulated, within an ongoing intersubjective system" (Stolorow et al., 1999, p. 382). Affective theory (Ekman & Davidson, 1994) has only fairly recently been considered a topic worthy of scientific focus.

THE CATALOGUING AND EMPIRICAL SUPPORT OF DEFENSES

In Freud's structural drive model, defensive functioning was accorded a prominent role in protecting a person against anxiety and continues to represent a major conceptual leap in understanding intrapsychic and interpersonal functioning. Freud considered defenses to be used both adaptively and in pathological form, and his original conceptualization continues to spawn new developments (Holi, Sammallahti, & Aalberg, 1999). Key concepts in understanding the function of defenses include repression and resistance. Defenses allow for repression of painful conflict in many patients and lead to patterns of reenactment in others. Defenses also turn into resistance to the therapist's effort to relieve the suffering. Higher-level defenses serve to enrich and strengthen the ego organization (Schafer, 1968).

Anna Freud (1936; Sandler, 1985) continued the process her father began of enumerating and cataloguing defenses. Although for a time, academic psychologists eschewed the construct of defense as being irrelevant, it has proven to be quite robust and has continued to demonstrate tremendous clinical utility and prominence in most current psychodynamic conceptual systems. Researchers such as George Vaillant (1992) and Phebe Cramer (1987, 1991, 1998, 1999) have empirically documented the validity of many of these defenses and their developmental progression from lower to higher levels. This "stage-related fashion" has been validated by Cramer's (1991, p. 39) research. For example, *projection*, a higher-level defense than *denial*, seems to increasingly predominate during adolescence. Also, the research shows that anxiety does increase defensive functioning (Cramer & Gaul, 1988).

PERSONALITY THEORY, PERSONALITY DISORDER, AND CONTEMPORARY PSYCHOPATHOLOGY

Freud's metapsychology was a theory both of personality and of psychopathology, as well as a method of treatment for emotional disorders. Many conceptual elements of Freud's model and subsequent developments continue to be useful to current personality theorists and their contemporary models of personality (Magnavita, 2002).

Psychoanalytic theorists/clinicians were very interested in and contributed vast amounts of clinical case material and insight into an understanding of character development, which serve as the basis for current diagnostic systems. Current psychopathologists and personality theorists draw from over a century of conceptual developments, many of which are presented in this volume. Psychodynamic constructs have shown remarkable explanatory power, "including characteristic ways of coping with and defending against impulses and affects; perceiving the self and others; obtaining satisfaction of one's wishes and desires; responding to environmental demands, and finding meaning in one's activities, values, and relationships" (Westen & Gabbard, 1999, p. 82). Contemporary theorists such as Millon (1999) and Kernberg (1996) recognize what the early character analysts such as W. Reich (1949), Horney (1937), and Fenichel (Fenichel & Rapaport, 1954) came to see as crucial: that personality configuration should guide treatment.

Personality disorders are endemic in contemporary society, most likely the result of the Industrial Revolution and the fragmentation of social structure and extended family units due to the mobility of members of modern society (Magnavita, 2002). Clinicians are faced with the fact that approximately half of those receiving mental health treatment are diagnosed either with a primary or comorbid personality disorder (Merikangas & Weissman, 1986; Weissman, 1993). Furthermore, 1 in 10 Americans qualify for this diagnosis. "Personality Disorders (PDs) are a topic of considerable interest to both clinicians and researchers alike, in part because of the high prevalence in the general population, and because of the difficulty in treating these conditions with standard forms of therapy" (Magnavita, 1999b, p. 1). New applications of psychodynamic treatment as well as cognitive, cognitive-behavioral, interpersonal, and integrative approaches have been developed expressly for treating personality disorders and complex clinical syndromes, a combination of a number of clinical syndromes and personality disturbance (Magnavita, 2000a). Most models of psychotherapy have integrated or expanded to include the construct of unconscious processing. The effective treatment of these personality disorders and complex clinical syndromes requires comprehensive treatment integration and, often, multiple models and combinations of treatment (Magnavita, 1999a; Millon, 1999).

It is interesting to note that neuroscientific theory provides some support for the clinical methods of Ferenczi's and Reich's approaches to treating personality pathology (Grigsby & Stevens, 2000). "Here is where Sandor Ferenczi's 'active' therapy may be useful. If one wants to change one's character, it is not simply enough to become aware of an unconscious schema—one also must make an effort not to engage it" (p. 322). Based on their neurodynamic model of personality, Grigsby and Stevens conclude:

> If the therapist repeatedly points out character traits of which the patient is ordinarily unaware, their automatic performance is disrupted and learning (in other words, a change in the neural networks subserving the schema) may occur. The habitual behavior in a sense is "unlearned" as one tends to become increasingly aware of the behavior during its performance. . . . The process is not easy, however, and the individual may be reluctant to go against the grain of character, since it is uncomfortable and may require great effort. (p. 322)

THE FOUNDATION AND ASCENDANCE OF AFFECTIVE SCIENCE

Darwin (1998) demonstrated the importance and function of affect, and Freud offered a theory about the place of affect in human psychopathology. The emphasis on repressed affect as a source of anxiety and symptom formation laid the foundation for today's affective science. The importance of affective functioning was emphasized by Silvan Tomkins (1962, 1963, 1991) who advanced our understanding of the centrality of emotional experience (Ekman & Davidson, 1994). For the most part, however, "The topic of emotion was downplayed until the 1960's, a decade characterized by the advent of neobehaviorism and social learning theory, a movement toward cognitivism, and greater interest in systems theory" (Lazarus, 1991, p. 40). Neuroscientists have also recognized the importance of emotion in understanding consciousness and brain structuralization and organization. Emotion primes the neuronal networks and assists in learning. We have come to understand why the intense emotional activation that occurs from trauma, particularly when the trauma occurs early in development, has a significant impact on personality formation. The universality of emotion seems to be a cross-cultural phenomenon, although there is still some debate between the cultural relativists and Darwinians. Nevertheless, it is fairly well established that there are six primary emotions—anger, fear, sadness, disgust, happiness/joy, and surprise—and secondary emotions, which include guilt, shame, and pride. Emotion is considered by many contemporary theorists and clinicians to be the lifeblood of the therapeutic process. For example, rage and its mobilization can be a powerful transformative experience. Cummings and Sayama (1995) write about a requirement they believe is important:

> Just as one would not trust a surgeon who fears the sight of blood, why trust a therapist who cannot stand the sight of "psychic blood" when an intervention that might be termed psychological surgery is in the best interest of the patient. Mobilization of rage in the interest of health is a powerful technique in the hands of a compassionate therapist. It is deadly in the hands of a noncompassionate therapist. Similarly, the surgeon's scalpel in the wrong hands would be inappropriate, sadistic, or fatal. (p. 54)

Affective science, like cognitive science, is becoming a component part of understanding personality, psychopathology, and psychotherapy (Magnavita, 2002).

THE DEVELOPMENT OF SUPPRESSION AND REDISCOVERY OF TRAUMA THEORY

Freud believed that hysteria derived from child sexual abuse. In fact, he believed that he had discovered the "causative agent in all the major neuroses" (Schwartz, 1999, p. 73). This finding about the prevalence of child sexual abuse by fathers and others, which has held up in current time as a factor for Dissociative Identity Disorder and Borderline Personality Disorder, may have been too much for Freud to accept. Some believe that he experienced a personal crisis and worried about the impact that publishing these findings might have on his career. He has been harshly criticized and condemned by some modern-day writers (Masson, 1984, 1990). According to Masson, the field of psychoanalysis suppressed the truth and did not take seriously patient reports of incest and abuse. Rachman (1997) writes:

> Psychoanalysis has had a love/hate relationship with the seduction theory and the treatment of the incest trauma. In point of fact, the origins of psychoanalysis are based upon Freud's discovery that neurosis (hysteria) was caused by the sexual seduction of mostly female patients by their fathers (and secondarily by surrogated father figures). This was a remarkable discovery and established psychoanalysis on a phenomenological basis—that is to say, the data for the analysis were generated from the subjective report of the patient. (p. 317)

Freud's abandonment of this seduction/trauma theory was a major setback for him and the field of psychoanalysis. His replacement, wish fulfillment, had the aura of blaming the victim. Even though Freud abandoned trauma theory as the cause of many forms of psychopathology when he replaced the seduction theory with an Oedipal one, others, most notably Ferenczi (1933), continued to work along the original line. Rachman (1997) suggests that Ferenczi's early findings and model of trauma are remarkably consistent with contemporary trauma models (Herman, 1992): "On the basis of his work with difficult cases, Ferenczi verified Freud's original seduction theory and emphasized a return to the original findings" (p. 317). The suppression of Ferenczi's findings is a dark spot in the history of psychoanalysis.

LONG-TERM PSYCHOANALYTIC PSYCHOTHERAPY AND PSYCHOANALYSIS

As Freud's psychoanalytic technique began to crystallize, his original experimentation and interest in brief treatment waned. The development of his technique of free association and the emphasis on the development of the transference neurosis lengthened the course of psychoanalysis. Psychoanalytic treatment provided Freud with the method he needed to probe further the unconscious and begin the process of organizing his observations and mapping the intrapsychic terrain. This led to the development of metapsychology.

Traditional psychoanalysis, consisting of three to five psychotherapy sessions per week over the course of many years, has greatly receded as a form of treatment due to the cost and time required. However, for those who are interested in becoming psychoanalysts, a training analysis is still required by some psychoanalytic institutes (Havens, 2001). This can be extremely beneficial for those who want to pursue a career as a "depth" therapist or to conduct psychoanalysis. At the turn of this century, most practitioners who conduct long-term therapy are highly influenced by the psychodynamic model, with its emphasis on unconscious processes, transference/countertransference, and establishing conditions where the patient can freely speak what comes to mind. This model of treatment offered a compendium of technical advances that have been well articulated in major works, such as *The Technique of Psychoanalytic Psychotherapy* (Langs, 1989).

Efforts to Accelerate Psychodynamic Treatment

From the very beginning, efforts were made to accelerate the course of psychoanalysis. The major innovator and father of short-term dynamic psychotherapy, Ferenczi, was rejected for his challenge to orthodox psychoanalysis (see Osimo, this volume). Ferenczi (Ferenczi & Rank, 1925) and generations of clinician-theorists after him developed innovative technical interventions. The analytic community tended to discredit them and reject their pioneering efforts, though others, such as Alexander and French (1946), rediscovered them later (Magnavita, 1993a). The field of short-term dynamic psychotherapy is one example of how psychodynamic metapsychology continues to revitalize and shape the field of psychotherapy. In the past 20 years there has been a major resurgence of interest in this evolutionary branch of psychodynamic therapy. Many of the cutting-edge theorists/clinicians are included in this volume. As cost-effectiveness has become a major concern in the delivery of mental health treatment, contemporary clinicians increasingly revisit the works of the pioneering figures in short-term therapy (Cummings & Sayama, 1995).

APPLICATION OF PSYCHOANALYSIS AND PSYCHODYNAMIC THERAPY TO CHILDREN

The twentieth century witnessed another major phenomenon when psychotherapeutic techniques were modified for the treatment of childhood disorders. Although Freud treated a few children, it was not until his daughter Anna's pioneering work at the Hamptead Child-Therapy Clinic was disseminated that the field of child therapy emerged. Melanie Klein (1975), another pioneering figure in theories and techniques of child therapy, also contributed much to the field and modified analytic techniques in the treatment of psychotic disorders (Sayers, 1991). Many techniques of current-day play therapy have their origins in the works of these two pioneering women of psychoanalysis.

A TREND TOWARD INTEGRATIVE THEORY AND A MULTIPERSPECTIVE APPROACH TO PSYCHOTHERAPY

Many theorists have recognized the need for integration in the field of personality theory and psychotherapy (Magnavita, 2002). In fact, William James (1890), the father of modern psychology, was one of the original proponents of integrating seemingly disparate systems. He believed that human nature was far too complex to be reduced to a theoretical, consistent system. His clarion call did herald a movement, which gained credibility in the last quarter of the twentieth century. However, before integration could occur, a variety of models had to be developed and tested over time.

Gordon Allport (1968) also called for systematic eclecticism. He realized that eclectic was a word of "ill-repute" (p. 3), but he believed that theoretical assimilation offered promise. Theorists and clinicians had to wait until there were sufficiently developed discrete theories or models that could be integrated. The topic of psychotherapy integration is covered extensively in volume 4 of the *Comprehensive Handbook of Psychotherapy* and will not be recapitulated here. It is important to note, however, that modern psychodynamic theory and practice have been shaped by integration within psychodynamic schools.

Pine (1985) and Mann and Goldman (1982) have suggested a multiperspective approach using the main theoretical perspectives as lenses, each offering a different view of a clinical phenomenon. Theoretical blending occurs as well when other theoretical constructs outside psychoanalysis, such as systems theory, have been assimilated (Messer, 1992). Dollard and Miller (1950) presented a major effort in the classic volume *Personality and Psychotherapy: An Analysis in Terms of Learning, Thinking, and Culture*. This groundbreaking volume represented a new integrative theory of personality and psychotherapy (Magnavita, 2002). The domain and scope of psychodynamic psychotherapy has been broadened even further with the incorporation of triadic theory (Bowen, 1978) and a relational-systemic component (Magnavita, 2000b).

CRITICISM AND CONTROVERSY

Numerous criticisms have been leveled against the field of psychoanalysis, some justified and others less so. One of the major problems of the past century has been the isolation of psychoanalysis from other disciplines although there have been exceptions such as the interdisciplinary work of Erik Erikson (Coles, 2000). This is beginning to shift, although much potential was lost for interdisciplinary cross-fertilization, which would have strengthened and further evolved the field. Another problem for which the field has been justly criticized is the relative lack of interest in providing empirical support for treatment effectiveness. Admittedly, this is an onerous task, but nevertheless a vital one. Popular notions about psychodynamic treatment have been difficult to dislodge. One important assumption made by many regards the sanctity of the therapeutic relationship. This has been reified to the point of not allowing the process to be studied, except third-hand. With the advent of low-cost audiovisual equipment, the process of psychotherapy is now capable of being readily studied by clinicians. Inspired by the trendsetting and courageous work of pioneering practitioners who videotaped their treatment sessions, a new generation of clinicians is using this technology to advance the field and provide more intensive training for psychotherapists. Clearly, there are potential pitfalls and a possible downside to using videotape for research and training, but the advances in knowledge seem to outweigh potential difficulties.

SUMMARY

Psychoanalytic concepts, theories, and techniques continue to have a strong influence on current psychodynamic psychotherapy, as well as many other schools presented throughout this *Comprehensive Handbook of Psychotherapy*. Psychoanalysis offered the first comprehensive metapsychology of personality function, psychopathology, and methods of psychological healing. Many of the main evolutionary theoretical models of psychoanalysis continue to offer multiple perspectives for understanding the vast variations in human suffering confronted in clinical practice by mental health clinicians. Useful methods and techniques of treatment have derived from these theoretical systems and offer the clinician at the start of the second century of modern psychotherapy an array of approaches with which to assist those who come with the hope of being healed.

REFERENCES

Alexander, F. G., & French, T. M. (1946). *Psychoanalytic therapy: Principles and application.* New York: Ronald Press.

Allport, G. W. (1968). *The person in psychology: Selected essays.* Boston: Beacon Press.

Bernheim, H. (1891). *Hypnotisme, suggestion, psychotherapie: Etudes nouvelles.* Paris: Octave Doin.

Bischof, L. J. (1970). *Interpreting personality theories* (2nd ed.). New York: Harper & Row.

Bowen, M. (1978). *Family therapy in clinical practice.* New York: Aronson.

Buckley, P. (Ed.). (1986). *Essential papers on object relations.* New York: New York University Press.

Coles, R. (Ed.). (2000). *The Erik Erikson reader.* New York: Norton.

Cramer, P. (1987). The development of defense mechanisms. *Journal of Personality, 55*(4), 597–614.

Cramer, P. (1991). Anger and the use of defense mechanisms in college students. *Journal of Personality, 59*(1), 39–55.

Cramer, P. (1998). Freshman to senior year: A follow-up study of identity, narcissism, and defense mechanisms. *Journal of Research in Personality, 32,* 156–172.

Cramer, P. (1999). Personality, personality disorders, and defense mechanisms. *Journal of Personality, 67*(3), 535–554.

Cramer, P., & Gaul, R. (1988). The effect of success and failure on children's use of defense mechanisms. *Journal of Personality, 56,* 729–741.

Cummings, N., & Sayama, M. (1995). *Focused psychotherapy: A casebook of brief, intermittent psychotherapy throughout the life cycle.* New York: Brunner/Mazel.

Darwin, C. (1998). *The expression of the emotions in man and animal* (3rd ed.). New York: Oxford University Press.

Dollard, J., & Miller, N. E. (1950). *Personality and psychotherapy: An analysis in terms of learning, thinking, and culture.* New York: McGraw-Hill.

Dumont, F. (1993). The forum: Ritualistic evocation of antiquated paradigms. *Professional Psychology: Research and Practice, 25*(3), 195–197.

Ekman, P., & Davidson, R. J. (Eds.). (1994). *The nature of emotion: Fundamental questions.* New York: Oxford University Press.

Fairbairn, W. R. D. (1954). *An object-relations theory of the personality.* New York: Basic Books.

Fenichel, H., & Rapaport, D. (Eds.). (1954). *The collected papers of Otto Fenichel* (2nd ed.). New York: Norton.

Ferenczi, S. (1933). The confusion of tongues between adults and children: The language of tenderness and passion. In M. Balint (Ed.), *Final contributions to the problems and methods of psychoanalysis* (Vol. 3, pp. 156–167). New York: Brunner/Mazel.

Ferenczi, S., & Rank, O. (1925). *The development of psychoanalysis.* New York: Nervous and Mental Diseases.

Frank, G. (1999). The deficit model of psychopathology: Another look. *Psychoanalytic Psychology, 16*(1), 115–118.

Freud, A. (1936). *The ego and the mechanisms of defense.* New York: International Universities Press.

Freud, S. (1961). The ego and the id. In J. Strachey (Ed. and Trans.), *The standard edition of the complete psychological works of Sigmund Freud* (Vol. 19, pp. 3–66). London: Hogarth Press. (Original work published 1923)

Freud, S. (1966). *The complete introductory lectures on psychoanalysis* (J. Strachey, Ed. and Trans.). New York: Norton.

Grigsby, J., & Stevens, D. (2000). *The neurodynamics of personality.* New York: Guilford Press.

Hartmann, H. (1958). *Ego psychology and the problem of adaptation.* New York: International Universities Press.

Hartmann, H. (1964). *Essays on ego psychology: Selected problems in psychoanalytic theory.* New York: International Universities Press.

Havens, L. L. (1973). *Approaches to the mind: Movement of the psychiatric schools from sects toward science.* Boston: Little, Brown.

Havens, L. L. (2001). Personal communication.

Herman, J. L. (1992). *Trauma and recovery.* New York: Basic Books.

Holi, M. M., Sammallahti, P. R., & Aalberg, V. A. (1999). Defense styles explain psychiatric symptoms: An empirical study. *Journal of Nervous and Mental Diseases, 187*(11), 654–660.

Horner, A. J. (Ed.). (1994). *Treating the neurotic patient in brief psychotherapy.* Northvale, NJ: Aronson.

Horner, A. J. (1995). *Psychoanalytic object relations therapy.* Northvale, NJ: Aronson.

Horney, K. (1937). *The neurotic personality of our time.* New York: Norton.

Jackson, S. W. (1999). *Care of the psyche: A history of psychological healing.* New Haven, CT: Yale University Press.

James, W. (1890). *The principles of psychology* (Vols. 1–2). New York: Henry Holt.

Kernberg, O. F. (1996). A psychoanalytic theory of personality disorders. In J. F. Clarkin & M. F. Lenzenweger (Eds.), *Major theories of personality disorders* (pp. 106–140). New York: Guilford Press.

Klein, M. (1975). *The writings of Melanie Klein* (Vols. 1–4). London: Hogarth Press.

Kohut, H. (1971). *The analysis of the self.* Madison, CT: International Universities Press.

Kohut, H. (1977). *The restoration of the self.* Madison, CT: International Universities Press.

Langs, R. (1989). *The technique of psychoanalytic psychotherapy* (Vols. 1–2). Northvale, NJ: Aronson.

Lazarus, R. S. (1991). *Emotion and adaptation.* New York: Oxford University Press.

Magnavita, J. J. (1993a). The evolution of short-term dynamic psychotherapy. *Professional Psychology: Research and Practice, 24*(3), 360–365.

Magnavita, J. J. (1993b). On the validity of psychoanalytic constructs in the 20th century. *Professional Psychology: Research and Practice, 25*(3), 198–199.

Magnavita, J. J. (1999a). Challenges in the treatment of personality disorders: When the disorder demands comprehensive integration. *In Session: Psychotherapy in Practice, 4*(4), 5–17.

Magnavita, J. J. (1999b). Advancements in the treatment of personality disorders: Introduction [Special issue]. *In Session: Psychotherapy in Practice, 4*(4), 1–4.

Magnavita, J. J. (2000a). Integrative relational therapy of complex clinical syndromes: Ending the multigenerational transmission process. *Journal of Clinical Psychology/In Session: Psychotherapy in Practice, 56*(8), 1051–1064.

Magnavita, J. J. (2000b). Introduction: The growth of relational therapy. *Journal of Clinical Psychology/In Session: Psychotherapy in Practice, 56*(8), 999–1004.

Magnavita, J. J. (2002). *Theories of personality: Contemporary approaches to the science of personality.* New York: Wiley.

Mahler, M. S., Pine, F., & Bergman, A. (1975). *The psychological birth of the human infant: Symbiosis and individuation.* New York: Basic Books.

Mann, J., & Goldman, R. (1982). *A casebook in time-limited psychotherapy.* New York: McGraw-Hill.

Masson, J. M. (1984). *The assault on truth: Freud's suppression of the seduction theory.* New York: Farrar, Straus and Giroux.

Masson, J. M. (1990). *Final analysis: The making and unmaking of a psychoanalyst.* New York: Addison-Wesley.

Merikangas, K. R., & Weissman, M. M. (1986). Epidemiology of *DSM-III* Axis II personality disorders. In A. J. Frances & R. E. Hales (Eds.), *Psychiatric update: The American Psychiatric Association annual review* (Vol. 5). Washington, DC: American Psychiatric Press.

Messer, S. B. (1992). A critical examination of belief structures in integrative and eclectic psychotherapy. In J. C. Norcross & M. R. Goldfried (Eds.), *Handbook of integrative psychotherapy* (pp. 130–165). New York: Basic Books.

Millon, T. (1999). *Personality-guided therapy.* New York: Wiley.

Pavlov, I. P. (1927). *Conditioned reflexes: An investigation of the physiological activity of the cerebral cortex* (G. V. Anrep, Trans.). New York: Oxford University Press.

Pine, F. (1985). *Developmental theory and clinical process.* New Haven, CT: Yale University Press.

Rachman, A. W. (1997). *Sandor Ferenczi: The psychotherapist of tenderness and passion.* Northvale, NJ: Aronson.

Rayner, E. (1991). *The independent mind in British psychoanalysis.* Northvale, NJ: Aronson.

Reich, A. (1960). Pathologic forms of self-esteem regulaton. *Psychoanalytic study of the child, 15,* 215–232.

Reich, W. (1949). *Character analysis* (3rd ed.). New York: Farrar, Straus and Giroux.

Sandler, J. (with Freud, A.). (1985). *The analysis of defense.* New York: International Universities Press.

Sayers, J. (1991). *Mothers of psychoanalysis: Helen Deutsch, Karen Horney, Anna Freud and Melanie Klein.* New York: Norton.

Schafer, R. (1968). *Aspects of internalization.* New York: International Universities Press.

Schafer, R. (1999). Recentering psychoanalysis: From Heinz Hartmann to the contemporary British Kleinians. *Psychoanalytic Psychology, 6*(3), 339–354.

Schwartz, J. (1999). *Cassandra's daughter: A history of psychoanalysis.* New York: Viking/Penguin.

Stolorow, R. D., & Atwood, G. E. (1979). *Faces in a cloud: Subjectivity in personality theory.* Northvale, NJ: Aronson.

Stolorow, R. D., Atwood, G. E., & Orange, D. M. (1999). Kohut and contextualism: Toward a post-Cartesian psychoanalytic theory. *Psychoanalytic Psychology, 16*(3), 380–388.

Sullivan, H. S. (1953). *The interpersonal theory of psychiatry.* New York: Norton.

Tomkins, S. S. (1962). *Affect imagery consciousness: Volume I. The positive affects.* New York: Springer.

Tomkins, S. S. (1963). *Affect imagery consciousness: Volume II. The negative affects.* New York: Springer.

Tomkins, S. S. (1991). *Affect imagery consciousness: Volume III. The negative affects anger and fear.* New York: Springer.

Vaillant, G. E. (Ed.). (1992). *Ego mechanisms of defense: A guide for clinicians and researchers.* Washington, DC: American Psychiatric Press.

von Bertalanffy, L. (1948). *General systems theory.* New York: Braziller.

Weissman, M. M. (1993). The epidemiology of personality disorders: A 1990 update. *Journal of Personality Disorders, 7,* 44–63.

Westen, D., & Gabbard, G. O. (1999). Psychoanalytic approaches to personality. In L. A. Pervin & O. P. John (Eds.), *Handbook of personality: Theory and research* (2nd ed., pp. 57–101). New York: Guilford Press.

Winnicott, C., Shepherd, R., & Davis, M. (Eds.). (1989). *Psychoanalytic exploration: D. W. Winnicott.* Cambridge, MA: Harvard University Press.

SECTION ONE

PSYCHOTHERAPY WITH CHILDREN

Chapter 2   The Developmental Basis of Psychotherapeutic Processes
Chapter 3   Object-Relations Play Therapy
Chapter 4   Infant Mental Health
Chapter 5   Psychodynamic Approaches to Child Therapy

CHAPTER 2

The Developmental Basis of Psychotherapeutic Processes

STANLEY I. GREENSPAN

Through clinical work and observations with infants and young children, we have been able to more fully identify and describe the early stages of ego development. We have also been able to describe stage-specific affective interactions and relationship patterns and individual motor and sensory processing differences that influence these early capacities. Taken together, these elements constitute the Developmental, Individual-Difference, Relationship-Based (DIR) model (Greenspan, 1997a, 1997b). This model provides a developmental framework for conceptualizing the psychotherapeutic process. The DIR framework, which can be applied to both children and adults, includes an individualized developmental approach to assessment and diagnosis and the practice of psychotherapy and psychoanalysis. It also includes developmental insights into a range of disorders (e.g., anxiety, depression, character, and personality disorders, autism, mental retardation, learning disorders) and informs a comprehensive intervention program for children with autistic spectrum disorders and other special needs.

The DIR model is based on relatively recent insights about three interrelated processes that contribute to a child's development. The first process involves early stages in a child's presymbolic *functional emotional development* (the building blocks of ego functioning and intelligence). These capacities include regulation and shared attention; relating with intimacy; gestural, affective reciprocal and social interactions; and creating and connecting symbols. The second process involves each child's *individually different underlying processing capacities*, such as sensory modulation, auditory and visual-spatial processing, and motor planning. Infants and young children differ significantly in their sensory reactivity, auditory and visual-spatial processing, and motor planning and sequencing, and these differences are important contributors to ego structure, character, and symptom formation. The third process involves the *role of relationships and affective interactions* in facilitating a child's intellectual and emotional growth. For example, the earliest cognitive structures and sense of causality do not, as Piaget believed, first arise from early sensorimotor (cognitive) explorations. They arise from even earlier affective interactions between a baby and his or her caregiver (e.g., a smile begetting a smile). At each stage of early cognitive development, emotional interactions lead the way. The meaning of words, early quantity concepts ("a lot" to a 2½-year-old is more than he expects; "a little" is less than he wants), logical and abstract thinking, and even important components of grammar depend on specific types of emotional interactions (Greenspan, 1997b; Greenspan & Wieder, 1999). Similarly, early ego development can now be traced to specific types of early emotional interactions. For example, complex reciprocal affective interactions in the second year of life enable children to begin integrating affective polarities and form a more integrated sense of self.

THE DIR MODEL AND CONSTRUCTING THE DEVELOPMENTAL PROFILE

In the DIR model of development, there are three dynamically related influences on development. Biological, including genetic, influences affect what the child brings into his or her interactive patterns. They do not act directly on behavior, but on part of the child-caregiver interactive process. Cultural, environmental, and family factors influence what the caregiver or interactive partner brings into the interactions. The resultant child-caregiver interactions then determine the relative mastery of six core developmental processes (e.g., regulation, relating, preverbal affective reciprocity). Symptoms or adaptive behaviors are the result of these stage-specific affective interactions.

The DIR model enables the clinician to construct a detailed developmental profile based on these dynamic processes. A special feature of the profile is its focus on early presymbolic levels of ego functioning. Higher levels of ego functioning are explored through an elaboration of the content of the patient's mental life; presymbolic levels often involve basic structure-building, affective interactions. In considering different types of problems and personalities, one is often tempted to go where the action is, getting caught up in the conflict of the moment (the family drama or, understandably, the patient's anguish). However, a full developmental profile includes early presymbolic structures as well as dynamic contents (i.e., a full profile includes the "drama" and the "stage" on which the drama takes place).

The profile begins with a description of individuals' regulatory capacities: the ability to remain calm, attentive, and process and respond in an organized way to the variety of sensations around them. Next is a rich description of their style and capacity for engaging, followed by their capacity to enter into reciprocal affective gesturing in a full range of emotional and thematic realms. Then comes their ability to organize their behavior and affects into purposeful patterns that constitute a presymbolic sense of self and take into account the expectations of their environment. These presymbolic capacities are followed by the ability to represent wishes, affects, and ideas, use them imaginatively, and then create bridges between different represented experiences as a basis for a representational sense of self and other, a differentiated sense of time and space, and affect proclivities, the capacity to construct a sense of reality and to move toward abstract and reflective thinking.

In each area of the profile, one looks for competencies as well as deficits (where the ability is not attained at all). One also looks for constrictions (where the ability is there but not at its full, robust, and stable form). Constrictions may involve a narrowing of the thematic or affective range (only pleasure, no anger), a lack of stability (the child can engage, but loses this capacity and becomes self-absorbed whenever anxious), or a lack of motor, sensory, cognitive, or language support for that capacity (e.g., the child can be assertive with words, but not with motor patterns).

After an individual's profile is constructed, two contributions to the challenges or strengths of that profile are explored. These are the biologically based regulatory contributions (i.e., motor and sensory processing differences) and the family, cultural, and interactive contributions.

CASE EXAMPLE OF THE DIR DEVELOPMENTAL PROFILE

To illustrate the importance of constructing such a profile, consider the following example. A 6-year-old girl presented with an inability to talk in school and an ability to talk only to her mother. She had always been a dependent, clingy, quiet, and passive little girl, had a lot of separation anxiety in going to school, and always had difficulty interacting with other children. However, her difficulties were getting worse over the prior two years. It will be instructive now to look at the profile that was constructed for this little girl from numerous play sessions. She took a long time to connect with the therapist doing the evaluation. She would initially fiddle with toys or other objects in a seemingly self-absorbed way and only with many vocal overtures would she enter into a state of shared attention, where she was paying attention to the therapist. The therapist had to maintain a fairly high level of activity to keep this state of shared attention. Similarly, although she had some warmth and the therapist found herself looking forward to seeing the child, the therapist kept feeling she had to work hard to maintain the sense of engagement. There was some emotional expressiveness and some back-and-forth smiling and smirking, suggesting some capacity for emotional reciprocity, but often, the emotional responses were either very inhibited (lacking) or global, with seemingly inappropriate giggling or repetitive, tense, discharge-oriented play (such as banging a doll). Often, the content of the play, such as banging the doll, was not connected to the affect (which might be a smile as she banged the doll aggressively). She was purposeful and organized in her interactions and play, but during times of transitions, going from one activity to another, she would seem to get lost in her own world again, and the therapist would have to work to regain a sense of organized interaction. She used lots of ideas and was able to build bridges between her ideas (answering "what" and "why" questions), but her imaginative play was focused on only a few themes in a very intense, repetitive manner. She had dolls undressing and had one doll doing aggressive things to the genital areas of the other dolls. In one scene, she had monsters blocking some of the dolls from getting their clothes back, with sadistic fights ensuing. In this profile, then, we see a child who has marked constrictions at the presymbolic areas of development around attention, engagement, and reciprocal affective gesturing and cuing, as well as a preoccupation and constriction at the symbolic or representational level.

In cases like this, with a little child who can elaborate themes, I found that many therapists would focus predominantly on the content of the child's themes (in this case, her preoccupation with sexual and aggressive themes) and obviously want to explore the family dynamics that were contributing, including questions of sexual abuse, sexual play with other children or babysitters, or overstimulation due to exposure to sexual materials or witnessing sexual scenes. But our profile, in addition to alerting us to these factors, also alerts us to the fact that there is a lack of mastery of critical early phases of development, including an ability for consistent attention, engagement, and the earliest types of affective reciprocity. When, for example, children cannot match the content of their interests to their affects, it often suggests that early in life, a caregiver was unable to enter into reciprocal gesturing around certain affective inclinations. For example, the way children learn to match content with affect is by demonstrating different affects as an infant in association with different kinds of behavior, perhaps knocking the food off the table with a look of defiance or surprise. In return, they get a reciprocal affect or gesture back from Mommy or Daddy. If the parent freezes or withdraws at that moment, however, there is no return affective gesture and the child's content (i.e., throwing the food on the floor) now has no reciprocal affects associated with it. As a consequence, the child doesn't develop the rich connections between interactive affects and content. Obviously, various types of processing problems can also contribute.

In terms of regulatory patterns in this case, the child did have some overreactivity to touch and sound and some mild motor planning problems, but was quite competent in her auditory and visual-spatial processing abilities. There were both physical and interactive differences contributing to her profile.

As we looked at her developmental profile, we were therefore alerted to the fact that there were a number of prerepresentational issues that need to be worked on in therapy as well as issues involved in her emerging symbolic world. As we were speculating from her profile, we wondered whether there were some profound difficulties ongoing in the early relationship between this child and her caregivers as well as some current experiences that were leading to her preoccupation with sex and aggression. We also wondered about current trauma severe enough to disrupt basic presymbolic abilities (if, for example, they were formerly attained).

As a result of this profile, the therapist who had started with twice-a-week sessions to work on the content of the child's play and once-a-month sessions with the parents shifted her approach. It was decided that it was important to develop a deeper alliance with this family to explore the nature of this little girl's preoccupation with sexual and aggressive content and, therefore, they needed to be seen at least once a week. It was also determined that because there were a number of constrictions of the prerepresentational capacities, the therapist needed to work with the parents' interactions with their daughter to foster mastery of these basic interactive capacities around attention, engagement, and reciprocal affective interchange. She also began working on the issues directly in therapy, paying more attention to affects and gestures, the tone of the relationship itself, and the understanding of verbal content.

A developmental profile systematically done will help the therapist look in a balanced way at the whole individual and, most important, will help the therapist raise hypotheses about where the challenges may lie and even some potential reasons for the challenges. The profile enables the therapist to develop a therapeutic strategy to further explore the initial hypothesis. Without such a systematic profile, it's easy for the therapist to get lost in the content or symptoms of the moment without a full appreciation of all the areas of challenge and the likely experiences that might be associated with them.

In some respects, by focusing on the patient's fundamental capacities, the developmental profile may reveal aspects of the patient's developmental history that the patient's "memories" are unable to reveal. The processes that the developmental perspective helps us observe reveal where the patient has been and, even more important, where he or she needs to go.

THE DEVELOPMENTALLY BASED PSYCHOTHERAPEUTIC PROCESS WITH CHILDREN AND ADULTS

The individualized profile and the DIR model can inform the practice of psychotherapy and psychoanalysis. Most therapists use a developmental framework in their clinical work. Many recent developmental discoveries, however, have not yet found their way into this evolving frame of reference. See *Developmentally Based Psychotherapy* (Greenspan, 1997a) for a detailed description of this approach.

OBSERVING AND WORKING WITH FUNDAMENTAL DEVELOPMENTAL PROCESSES

The overarching principle of a developmentally based approach to psychotherapy is mobilization of the developmental processes associated with an adaptive progression of the personality throughout childhood and adulthood. The therapeutic relationship is the vehicle for mobilizing developmental processes in the therapy sessions and for helping the patient create developmentally facilitating experiences outside the therapy situation. The critical difference between the developmentally based approach to the psychotherapeutic process and other approaches is the degree to which early stages in development are observed and worked with. Typically, most therapists work with verbal material with adults and verbal and play themes with children. If earlier levels are worked with (e.g., separation-individuation), they are worked with in terms of verbal or symbolic elaborations. Early stages can be worked with more directly in terms of critical structural features. These involve the capacity to self-regulate; relate to others; process, comprehend, and use preverbal affective gestures to define a sense of intent and form a preverbal sense of self and integrate basic emotional polarities; and learn to represent affects and experiences and broaden and differentiate one's inner affective, symbolic life.

To mobilize these fundamental developmental processes, however, we must be able to identify them in children and adults. Brief descriptions of these processes appear below. (For more complete discussion, including clinical observations and developmental studies, see Greenspan, 1989, 1992, 1997a, 1997b.)

Level 1
The first level of development involves regulation and shared attention, that is, self-regulation and emerging interest in the world through sight, sound, smell, touch, and taste. Children and adults build on this early developing set of capacities when they act to maintain a calm, alert, focused state and organize behavior, affect, and thoughts.

We have observed individual differences in constitutional-maturational characteristics that contribute to one's regulating capacities. They begin in infancy and then can be observed in older children and adults. These maturational patterns may change as one develops, however. The following list may prove helpful in observing regulatory differences:

1. Sensory reactivity, including hypo- and hyperreactivity in each sensory modality (tactile, auditory, visual, vestibular, olfactory).
2. Sensory processing in each sensory modality (e.g., the capacity to decode sequences, configurations, or abstract patterns).
3. Sensory affective reactivity and processing in each modality (e.g., the ability to process and react to degrees of affective intensity in a stable manner).
4. Motor tone.
5. Motor planning.

Sensory reactivity (hypo or hyper) and sensory processing can be observed clinically: Is the child or adult hyper- or hyposensitive to touch or sound? Do sounds of motors or of a noisy party overwhelm the individual? Is a gentle touch on the hand or face reacted to by a startled withdrawal? The same questions must be asked in terms of vision and movement in space. In addition, in each sensory modality, processing of sensations occurs. Does the 4-month-old "process" a complicated pattern of information input or only a simple one? Does the 4½-year-old have a receptive language problem and therefore is unable to sequence words together or follow complex directions? Is the young adult prone to get lost in his own fantasies because he has to work extra hard to decode the complex verbal productions of others? Is the 3-year-old an early comprehender and talker, but slower in visual-spatial processing? If spatial patterns are poorly comprehended, a child may be facile with words, sensitive to every emotional nuance, but have no context, never see the "forest"; such children get lost in the "trees." In the clinician's office, they may forget where the door is or have a hard time picturing that mother is only a few feet away in the waiting room. Similarly, adults may find it difficult to follow instructions or easily get lost in new settings. They may also have difficulty seeing the emotional big picture. If the mother is angry, the child may think the earth is opening up and he is falling in; he cannot comprehend that she was nice before and will probably be nice again. Similarly, adults may be overwhelmed by the emotion of the moment, losing sight of the past or future.

It is also necessary to look at the motor system, including motor tone, motor planning (fine and gross), and postural control. A picture of the motor system will be provided by observing how a person sits or runs, maintains posture, holds a crayon or pen, hops or draws, and makes rapid alternating movements. Security in regulating and controlling one's body plays an important role in how one uses gestures to communicate. Motor planning and sequencing (i.e., the ability to initiate and carry out a series of actions to solve problems) is an especially important component of initiative, problem-solving, executive functions (planning, judgment, etc.) and many ego functions. Motor planning influences the ability to regulate dependency (being close or far away), the confidence in regulating aggression ("Can I control my hand that wants to hit?"), and the ability to comprehend social sequences and follow through on tasks.

The constitutional and maturational variables may be thought of as regulatory factors. When they contribute to difficulties with attending, remaining calm and organized, or modulating affect or behavior and therefore are a prominent feature of a disorder of behavior, affect, or thought, such a disorder may be considered a regulatory disorder (Greenspan, 1992). Regulatory differences sometimes are attributed to "lack of motivation" or emotional conflicts. Observing carefully and obtaining a history of regulatory patterns will make it possible to separate maturational variations from other factors and also determine how many factors often operate together.

In addition, there are feelings and themes that emanate from the processes of self-regulation, attention, and interest in the world. Children and adults get a sense of confidence in their ability to be calm, regulated, and interested in the world. They also may have a feeling of basic security in the way their body works, especially their perceptual and motor equipment. A sense of control often goes along. When difficulties during this stage arise, we not infrequently see themes concerned with being overwhelmed and falling apart and, at times, attempts at omnipotent overcontrol to create order and manipulate select sensory or motor experiences.

We are finding that when certain processing patterns are coupled with certain environmental patterns, they can intensify each other. We can observe, therefore, what Freud had anticipated: the ways in which the biological influences on character structure and the selection of defenses operate (Greenspan, 1989). For example:

- Individuals who are overreactive to touch or sound and have stronger auditory processing abilities and relatively weaker visual-spatial ones tend toward the hysterical, depressive, and anxiety disorders. Those who have difficulty with movement in space tend toward phobic disorders.
- Individuals who are underreactive to sensations and have low motor tone tend toward more withdrawn behavior. They tend to escape into fantasy and, in the extreme, evidence more schizoid and autistic patterns.
- Individuals with hyporeactivity to sensations along with stimulus-craving patterns, coupled with high activity levels and organized gross motor patterns, tend toward

risk taking and, if there is emotional deprivation, antisocial patterns.
- Individuals with relatively stronger visual-spatial processing and overreactivity to certain sensations tend toward patterns characterized by negativism, stubbornness, and compulsiveness.
- Individuals with marked motor planning and sequencing challenges tend toward attentional problems.

When environmental conditions enhance flexibility rather than pathology, we tend to see healthy character formation, but with a tendency toward one or another of these characteristics. For example, instead of panic or anxiety or depression, we see a sensitive person who is reactive and alert to others' moods and behaviors.

Level 2
The second level of development involves forming relationships. Relationship patterns, once formed, continue and further develop throughout the course of life. Most clinicians have a great deal of experience in monitoring the quality of relatedness. But sometimes, the clinician ignores the quality of engagement while working on specific ideas or thoughts, so that indifference, negative feelings, or impersonal or aloof patterns continue longer than necessary.

For example, the child who walks in and goes right for the toys, ignoring the clinician, is different from the child who looks at the clinician with a twinkle in his eye and points to the toys, waiting for a warm accepting smile. The adult who strides in the office and makes a beeline for the new painting on the wall with nary a wave or a nod in the therapist's direction may be eschewing any initial sense of engagement to cement a relationship. One observes if there is a range of affects used to try to establish a sense of connectedness and relatedness: warmth, pleasure, intimacy, and trust.

In addition, with this stage, there are often feelings and themes of positive nurturance and optimism. In contrast, difficulties with this stage and its processes can be associated with feelings and themes of isolation, emptiness, greed, preoccupation with inanimate objects, and overreaction to expectable relationship challenges, such as temporary losses or disappointments. At times, one also sees compensatory themes centered around grandiosity and the need for unconditional love.

Level 3
The third level involves purposeful communication: intentional, preverbal affective communications or gestures. These gestures include facial expressions, arm and leg movements, vocalizations, and spinal posture. From the middle of the first year of life onward, individuals rely on gestures to communicate. Initially, during the stage of purposeful communication, simple reciprocal gestures such as head nods, smiles, and movement patterns serve a boundary-defining role. The "me" communicates a wish or intention and the "other" or "you" communicates back some confirmation, acknowledgment, or elaboration on that wish or intention.

When there have been distortions in the emotional communication process, as occurs when a mother responds in a mechanical, remote manner or projects some of her own dependent feelings onto her infant, the infant and, later, the child and adult may not learn to appreciate causal relationships between people at the level of compassionate and intimate feelings. This situation can occur even though causality seems to be developing in terms of the inanimate world and the impersonal human world.

During an interview, a child or adult demonstrates mastery of this stage by using purposeful gestures, such as facial expressions, motor gestures (showing you something), or vocalization. Aimless behavior, misreading of the other person's cues, or fragmented islands of purposeful interaction together with aimless or self-absorbed behavior indicate challenges at this level. The ability to be purposeful around some affects but not others (e.g., around love but not assertiveness) also indicates limitations.

Themes that characterize this level can include a "can do" sense of mastery. Difficulties with this stage may be associated with the sense that interactions can be chaotic and fragmented, helplessness about one's ability to have impact on others, passivity, fears of unpredictability, and lack of an emerging differentiation of different feeling states, wishes, and intentions.

This stage of two-way, causal, intentional communication (or somatopsychologic differentiation) indicates processes occurring at the somatic (sensorimotor), affective, and emerging psychological levels. It is a foundation for self and other boundaries and, therefore, for basic ego functioning and reality testing.

Level 4
The fourth stage, behavioral organization or a complex sense of self, involves more complex affective and social patterns involving many circles of intentional communication with the aim of solving problems (e.g., a child taking an adult to the shelf to get help in getting a book or toy). Patterns that began with these early capacities can be seen in many behaviors in older children and adults, including comprehending simple gestural cues, such as eye contact, finger pointing, interjections or vocalizations, facial expressions, motor gestures, and different subtle affect expressions. The therapist should note whether patients initiate such gestures and in turn respond to the clinician's countergesturing with a further gesture of their own.

The different emotions patients reveal suggest the range and type of affect gestures they can communicate. The range and degrees of specific affects can be very broad. In the aggressive domain, for instance, there are gradations that run from assertive, competitive, and mildly aggressive behavior to explosive and uncontrolled rage. The same is true for the affectionate and caring domain, which ranges from promiscuous emotional hunger, to mild affection, a sincere sense of warmth, and compassion to the developmentally advanced emotion of empathy. Affects can be combined with verbal themes, showing a pattern during a session.

How does the person begin the session? What happens as he or she moves through the first third to the middle of the session, and then from the last third to saying good-bye? Follow the change in affect. For example, an individual may come in showing apprehension and tentativeness, become warm and then competitive; show concern with issues of sibling or spousal jealousy and rivalry; and then express concern about separating from the therapist toward the end of the interview. Another patient may show only one or two affects during the entire interview.

The basic emotional messages of life—safety and security versus danger, acceptance versus rejection, approval versus disapproval—can all be communicated through facial expressions, body posture, movement patterns, and vocal tones and rhythm. Words enhance these more basic communications, but most of us form split-second judgments regarding a new person's dangerousness or approachability from his or her gestures before the conversation even gets started. In fact, if a person looks threatening and says "You know, I'm your friend," we tend to believe the gestures and discount the words.

At a more subtle level, gestural communication also relays to us what aspects of our own emotions are being accepted, ignored, or rejected. The raised eyebrows and head nods we perceive quickly tell us whether the person hearing our message is reacting with excitement, anger, curiosity, or detachment. More important, our ever emerging definition of the uniqueness of our very self is dependent on how others react to our own special tendencies with preverbal gestures. Differential responses stir different affects and are part of the process that refines and defines our maturing behavior and sense of self. How is our mischievous behavior and devilish grin responded to: with an accepting smile or a head-shaking frown? Our natural inclinations toward mischievousness, laziness, and a whole host of other personality traits are in part accepted and supported or refined or squelched as a result of the impact of this nonverbal communication system. The nonverbal, gestural communication system is therefore a part of every dialogue contributing to our sense of who we are and what we perceive.

In fact, it is through this system that we first integrate different affective polarities such as love and hate. One may observe whether a person can integrate, as part of one long interactive pattern, different affective states or if each state is a separate island.

The clinician who focuses only on a person's words may miss an underlying, critical lack of organized gestural communication ability. The "spacey" child who floats in and out of the room, or misreads the implied social rules of the playroom and hides toys, ignoring the therapist's facial expressions and sounds; the adult who misreads the intentions of others, seeing, for example, assertiveness as anger or dependence as rejection—both betray an inability to fully process organized gestural communications.

Complex, self-defining gestures (such as opening and closing 30 or 40 circles of communication in a row) emerge in the second year of life and are further developed and seen in increasingly complex, nonverbal interactions, where patterns are communicated and comprehended. As one observes gestures expressing a complex sense of self, one should take note not only of the range of affects but the richness and depth of affects observed. Are they superficial, as if the person is simply playacting or imitating someone? Or do they convey a sense of personal depth? In other words, is one able to empathize with the way the patient is feeling? One also observes the complexity and organization of gestures. Are there many gestures that work together to convey an emotional theme such as competitiveness or a wish for closeness and dependency or both?

Feelings and themes emanating from this stage include assertiveness, exploration and curiosity, pleasure and excitement, anger and aggression, a beginning sense of gender (in an infant or child), and an initial capacity for self-limit setting. In contrast, if there are challenges at this level, the child or adult may experience patterns such as narcissistic self-absorption or preoccupation with polarized feeling states and themes such as grandiosity, suspiciousness, somatic concerns, and global self-deprecation. One may also see preoccupation with fragmented partial needs and wishes, for example, certain types of limited pleasures.

Level 5
The fifth level involves the elaboration and sharing of ideas and meanings. The individual's ability to represent or symbolize experience is illustrated in the pretend play of a child or the verbal expression of the adult's worries and anxieties.

Building on the capacities of this level, children and adults use ideas to indicate their wishes, intentions, and expectations. For example, children may indicate a certain degree of trust or cautiousness about trying to define what is going to happen in the clinical interview. They may stage pretend play sequences, featuring hurricanes and disasters or children getting injections. They may be indicating their expectations of this new relationship. Children whose play focuses on dolls being fed and everyone being happy may be indicating a different set of expectations about the emerging relationship with the clinician. The adult who talks about relationships in the past that have led to disappointment is giving different messages than the patient who talks of satisfying relationships.

This level in relating not only involves using representations or symbols in play and/or verbal communication, but sometimes is evidenced by the use of subtle spatial communications, such as building complicated towers or houses with passages in them. Older children and adults sometimes use a picture to convey a feeling or complex meaning. Adults often use descriptions of visual imagery from dreams or free associations. One can observe the depth and range of themes developed at the representational level. Are there only shallow, repetitive dramas or rich, deep ones with a range of emotions?

From this fifth stage, we often observe the construction of a rich pattern of imagery concerning inner wishes, ideas, and feelings. Fantasies emerge that are part of an elaborate imaginative capacity. Fantasies can embrace most of the major themes of life, from dependency and separation anxiety to curiosity, assertiveness, and aggression. In short, a rich, intrapsychic symbolic life is created. In contrast, challenges at this level can be associated with a paucity of emotionally rich ideation, fears of separation, concerns with danger, and a tendency to experience and rely on action patterns or somatization, rather than ideas or symbols.

Level 6
The sixth level involves creating logical bridges between representations or ideas. Shared meanings are used both to elaborate wishes and feelings and to categorize meanings and solve problems. As logical bridges between ideas are established, various types of reasoning and appreciation of reality emerge, including dealing with conflicts and distinguishing what is pretend from what is believed to be real. As children become capable of emotional thinking, they begin to understand relationships between their own and others' experiences and feelings. They begin to elaborate and eventually differentiate those feelings, thoughts, and events that emanate from within and those that emanate from others, and they begin to differentiate the actions of others from their own. This process gradually forms the basis for the differentiation of self representations from the external world, animate and inanimate. It also provides the basis for such crucial personality functions as knowing what is real and unreal, regulating impulse and mood, and the capacity to focus attention and concentrate to learn and interact. The capacity for differentiating internal representations becomes consolidated as object constancy is established (Mahler, Pine, & Bergman, 1975). As the capacity for a differentiated internal symbolic world is consolidated, children become capable of progressing into higher levels of ego development. Briefly, as children move into latency and become more concerned with peers, they begin to appreciate emotional complexity such as gray area feelings.

At the sixth level, children can make connections between different ideas and feelings ("I am mad because you took my toy") and balance fantasy and reality. Adults similarly can hold logical conversations about wishes and feelings and make connections ("I feel lonely and needy, and I get helpless when I feel that way. Sometimes I get mad because I can't stand being so vulnerable").

Shared differentiated meanings involve the communication of ideas to another person and building on the other person's responses, not just having ideas. Some people communicate only their own ideas, never building on the responses of the other person. In both childhood dramas and adult conversations, they talk but do not easily absorb or reply to someone else's ideas and comments. For example, when a 4-year-old girl came home from preschool, she played out scene after scene of being a princess, letting her mother hold her imaginary ermine robe, while her mother's casual questions, such as "What does the princess want me to do next?" and "Who did you play with today?" were ignored. Similarly, a 40-year-old businessman seen in therapy could elaborate about how "No one satisfies me." He was unable to wrench his thoughts away from this theme and would obsessively return to it, regardless of the therapist's comments or questions. Without the ability to form bridges between various feelings states, including his own and someone else's, that patient was incapable of exploring a fuller range of feelings. Other individuals are just the opposite, diligently following instructions, listening to every word, but rarely elaborating their own feelings about or understanding of events.

Children operating at the level of creating logical bridges between different islands of symbolic or representational communication do not negotiate only via pretend dramas. They also begin to negotiate the terms of their relationship with the clinician in a more reality-based way. "Can I do this?" or "Can I do that?" the child may say. "What will you do if I kick the ball into the wall?" the child may inquire. Children may also want to know if they and the clinician can play after the session is over because they enjoy the playroom so much (and seem to yearn for a little extra contact with other people). A child's negotiations about bringing parents into the playroom, wanting either to continue or to end the session early, or curiosity about where the clinician lives and what his or her family is like, clearly indicate a use of symbols or words in a logical, interactive way. These logical bridges between one thought and another suggest that this more advanced level of negotiating relationships has been mastered. The adult who shifts between free associations and logical reflection, or who wonders about how two feelings are connected, or who makes such connections, also reveals this level.

The fifth and sixth stages of representational elaboration and differentiation can be observed and further assessed as one looks at the way individuals organize the content of their communications and deal with anxiety. Thematic development (i.e., the content of the communication) helps one assess the individual's representational level. Look first at the overall organization in terms of the presence or absence of logical links connecting the thematic elements. A certain minimum capacity to organize thinking can be expected with adults. With a child, however, the standards vary according to age, and the organization of themes must be weighed against the age-appropriate standard.

Here, too, themes may cover the broad range of human dramas, from dependency to aggression. We also may see a more integrated sense of gender emerging along with interests in different aspects of sexuality and pleasure. Often emanating from this stage are themes of power, being admired, and being respected. Some degree of concern with shame, humiliation, loss of love, and fear of injury to self and others is also expected. When there are challenges, one may see symbolic somatic expressions (preoccupation with one's own body functioning), symbols used in the service of action rather than reflection, and polarized rather than integrated themes (preoccupation with things being all bad or all good). We may see massive preoccupation with order, control, or limited types of pleasure or sexuality. In addition, we may see paralyzing preoccupations with shame, humiliation, loss of love, and injury or harm to self or others.

There are also advanced stages of representational differentiation. The sixth functional developmental capacity keeps growing and includes a number of substages reflecting the progress of development as it advances. These include expanding perception and reasoning capacities to include triadic and then multiple social groups. It also includes the internalization of a sense of self as a reference for a stable sense of reality and the capacity to broaden one's sense of reality into an integrated picture of past and present, as well as future possibilities in the context of expanding interpersonal, family, and group experiences. These substages can be observed to see what level of advanced ego development an individual has attained. It is important to note that if the basic stage of representational differentiation is not stable and broad, there invariably will be difficulties at these higher levels. These basic levels of representation and the advanced levels or substages are outlined in Table 2.1.

26 Psychotherapy with Children

Table 2.1 Developmental levels of representation.

Basic Levels
- *Representational elaboration and differentiation*
  —Action level: Person uses ideas to convey action and discharge rather than as a true symbol (e.g., "I hit him").
  —Somatic level: Person uses ideas to describe body sensations (e.g., "My stomach hurts" or "is exploding").
  —Global level: Person uses ideas to describe global affect states (e.g., "feel good" "feel bad").
  —Polarized level: Person uses ideas to polarize affects into all-or-nothing states.
  —Differentiated, Abstracted, Affective Representational level: Person uses ideas to describe specific affects and elaborate them and reasons about them.

Advanced Levels
- *Triangular thinking:* Triadic interactions among feeling states ("I feel left out when Susie likes Janet better than me").
- *Relativistic thinking (playground politics):* Shades and gradations among differentiated feeling states (ability to describe degrees of feelings around anger, love, excitement, disappointment; "I feel a little annoyed").
- *Internalized sense of self (the world inside me):* Reflecting on feelings in relationship to an internalized sense of self ("It's not like me to feel so angry"; "I shouldn't feel this jealous").
- *Extending representational capacity to new realms of biological, psychological, and social experience:* Expanding reflective feeling descriptors into sexuality, romance, closer and more intimate peer relationships, school, community, and culture, and emerging sense of identity ("I have such an intense crush on that new boy that I know it's silly. I don't even know him").
- *Extending representational capacities in time and space:* Using feelings to anticipate and judge future possibilities in light of current and past experience ("I don't think I would be able to really fall in love with him because he likes to flirt with everyone and that has always made me feel neglected and sad"). Broadening reflective capacities to include the larger community and culture.
- *Extending representational capacities into the stages of adulthood, middle age, and the aging process:* Expanding feeling states to include reflections and anticipatory judgment with regard to new levels and types of feelings associated with the stages of adulthood, middle age, and the aging process, including:
  —Ability to function independently from and yet remain close to and internalize many of the capacities initially provided by one's nuclear family.
    - Inner sense of security.
    - Judgment and self-limitation of behavior and impulse.
    - Regulation of mind.
    - Reality-based organized thinking.
  —Intimacy (serious long-term relationships).
  —The ability to nurture and empathize with one's children without overidentifying with them.
  —The ability to broaden one's nurturing and empathetic capacities beyond one's family and into the larger community.
  —The ability to experience and reflect on the new feelings of intimacy, mastery, pride, competition, disappointment, and loss associated with family, career, and intrapersonal changes of midlife and the aging process. (See Greenspan, 1989, 1997b for further discussion and review of the research related to these stages.)

Summary of Developmental Levels

The organizational levels discussed above are not difficult to observe, and are often taken for granted. When a child comes into the playroom ready to play or talk, there is often some rapport or emotional relatedness that soon develops between therapist and child. As soon as the therapist opens the door and the child makes eye contact or perhaps follows a few facial or arm gestures indicating where the toys are kept, we have an intentional, preverbal communication system going. Therapist and child are engaged and intentional with each other.

As the child begins complex play, staging mock battles with appropriate sound effects or making noises and pointing to indicate "Get me that!", more complex intentional communication is occurring. When the child puts feelings into words and elaborates pretend play themes, the level of shared meanings or representational elaboration is reached. The next level is reached when the child not only elaborates themes, but constructs bridges between domains of experience: "I'm scared when I'm mad." The ability to categorize experience indicates emotional thinking (i.e., representational differentiation). A symbolic "me" and a symbolic "you" are now in evidence: "I always get so scared of everything." Most important, the capacity for categorizing experience helps an individual elaborate feelings and build on another's communications. The patient can have a logical two-way dialogue and tell the difference between fantasy and reality.

Individuals may have clear compromises in their attainment of these organizational levels, such as patients who come to therapy and can only partially engage. When anxious or frightened, they typically disengage and become aloof or withdrawn. Not infrequently, they also get disorganized and cannot even gesture purposefully and intentionally. Their gestures and speech become disjointed. Their capacity for representational elaboration is limited to either disorganized emotional communications or organized descriptions of impersonal events. There is little capacity for balancing subjective elaborations and an appreciation of reality. They use words in a fragmented way, tend to be concrete and impersonal in their descriptions of the world, gesturally signal in a disorganized and chaotic way, and, although capable of engaging with others, easily disengage and become aloof.

As clinicians look at the tendency to use verbal descriptions of behavior, and organize these descriptions rather than put them into acting-out behaviors,* they further look to see if the person can represent global, somatically based affects and can represent simple, general affects or more differentiated, abstracted affects. Clinicians also look for the ability to make connections between different affective domains and categories of feelings and behaviors, and the ability for self-observation and reasoning about one's emotional inclinations and tendencies. One can further look at this last category in terms of the ability to observe oneself and reason in different dimensions: in the here-and-now, which is the easiest in a historical sense; to anticipate the future; and to do all of the above as part of an active exploration, and finally, to integrate them.

As clients are capable of more differentiated self-observing capacities, they can apply this to different types of relationship patterns. Therefore, in terms of comprehending relationships, various levels of representational differentiation can also be noted. At an early level, one is able to explore feelings that occur in dyadic relationship patterns; at a later level, one is able to test triangular relationship patterns. A still later level involves group patterns that have many different dyads and triads as well as the relationship between members of the group and the group as a whole. Finally, signposts of higher levels of organization can be seen in the ability to move into explorations of feelings having to do with stable internal values and principles and being able to look at an emerging sense of self against these aspirations and principles.

---

*Acting-out behaviors are usually characteristic of the person who hasn't yet mastered the complex interchange of behavioral intentions and expectations and who is somewhat arrested between the simple gestural and complex gestural stages.

PRINCIPLES OF DEVELOPMENTALLY BASED PSYCHOTHERAPY

The developmental approach to the psychotherapeutic process builds on an understanding of and ability to work with all the critical developmental levels at the same time. A number of principles summarize this approach.

PRINCIPLE 1

Build on the patient's natural inclinations and interests to try to harness all the core developmental processes the patient is capable of at the same time. These core processes have to do with self-regulation, forming intimate relationships, engaging in simple boundary-defining gestures, and complex preverbal, self-defining communication. They also have to do with representing internal experience, including representing and abstracting wishes, intentions, and affects, and becoming able to differentiate these internal representations and build bridges between them. Where the patient has not reached a certain level, the therapist engages him or her at the levels that have been mastered, and begins the process of working toward experiences that will facilitate reaching the new levels.

In many psychoanalytic and psychodynamic therapies, it is mistakenly assumed that many patients can use a highly differentiated representational system to perceive, interpret, and work through earlier experiences and conflicts. Most patients, however, evidence either deficits or constrictions at prerepresentational as well as representational levels, and these levels need to be worked with directly.

PRINCIPLE 2

The therapist should work with the patient at the patient's developmental level. It is essential not to make the mistake of communicating with the patient in a manner that is inappropriately abstract or basic. For example, some individuals do not have the capacity for verbal expression of emotions. They may operate on a more basic, earlier level where affect spills over immediately into behavior. They stomp and yell and scream when they are angry; they cling when they are needy. They commonly don't say, "I feel angry" or "I miss you so much that I think about you all the time." We often put those words in a patient's mouth, yet they really may not be able to abstract affect in that way. If such patients begin to act out aggressively or withdraw after the therapist's vacation, for example, offering them an interpretation like "Gee, you must have missed me and are showing me your anger by stubbing out your cigarettes on my couch" will go right over their heads. Patients may nod, but if they are operating at a more primitive level, they simply won't get it. It won't be a meaningful intervention because the patient is not at the level to process that kind of interpretation. For such an intervention to be effective, patients need to be able to represent affect, to see connections between different affects ("I missed you, and therefore I'm mad"), and to self-observe while seeing this connection.

PRINCIPLE 3

Engage the patient in the context of his or her individual processing differences (regulatory profile). For example, the sensory-hypersensitive individual requires soothing; the underreactive, self-absorbed individual requires animated dynamic interaction. (See discussion of Developmental Level 1, above, for more examples.)

PRINCIPLE 4

Therapists should aim to effect change by helping patients negotiate the developmental levels they have not mastered and strengthen vulnerable or limited processing capacities. These levels may have been bypassed earlier in life, which at present is in evidence as a deficit or constriction. In facilitating the negotiation of a developmental level or processing limitation, the therapist is not simply a commentator or insight giver, but a *collaborator in the construction of experience.* The therapist does this within the traditional boundaries of the therapeutic relationship, and not by role-playing or reenacting "real" relationships. Collaborating in the construction of experience should not be confused with historical tactics, such as a "corrective emotional experience," where the therapist may deliberately take an extra vacation to stimulate certain feelings in the patient. Such contrived strategies can undermine the naturally occurring affects that will characterize the therapeutic relationship.

Rather, therapists use the tools of communication available within the confines of the therapeutic role of following and dealing with the patient's spontaneous communications, verbal and nonverbal. As collaborative constructors of experience, therapists are aware of the different developmental levels of the therapeutic relationship. They do not limit themselves to exploring only the more representational levels. They also are aware of the importance of the interactive experience, guided by the patient's natural inclinations and communications. Therapists must be especially aware of their own countertransference tendencies so that the therapeutic explorations reflect the patient's natural, spontaneous inclinations and communications at multiple developmental levels. Therapists listen, empathize, and offer developmentally useful communications, while patients explore their experiences as best they can. In maintaining the integrity of the therapeutic relationship, therapists allow for future transference configurations.

A brief illustration may help illuminate this point. Consider a patient who tends to withdraw during the sessions and become aloof and mechanical in his affect. Traditionally, the therapist might be very patient and comment once or twice about the patient's aloofness or tendency to withdraw, but not do anything to alter that state of withdrawal directly other than comment on it intellectually. Months, even years, may go by with a relatively mechanical therapist and an equally mechanical patient, with little or no affect exchange taking place. If the patient were at an advanced representationally differentiated level and could abstract affect and see connections, the therapist might be able to effect change by this approach. For example, the therapist might muse "Every time you seem mad at me, you tend to withdraw." Such a comment may help open up the patient's associations.

But with the patient who is not representationally differentiated, who is instead primitively organized and tends to withdraw when he feels intensity of affect of any kind, the therapist must pay attention to and focus on subtleties in the patient's nonverbal behavior and affective tone. Let us postulate, for example, that this person's mother was intrusive and his father was emotionally removed. Neither parent successfully found a way to woo this sensory-sensitive person into a more intimate pattern of relating. The therapist pays careful attention to his mood and physical sensations while the patient is in various states of attention and relatedness. Rather than using the tone he uses with other patients, the therapist needs to find a particular tone and rhythm (e.g., using voice tone and rhythm and facial gestures to maintain a sense of relatedness) that will work with this particular patient. The establishment of this pattern may be a critical first therapeutic step. Rather than comment that the patient is afraid of his direct gaze, the therapist maintains the rhythms that increase relatedness and wonders what voice tone or look the patient finds most comforting. For example, the therapist notes that when he talks assertively and looks directly at the patient, the patient becomes more aloof; when he talks softly and looks slightly to the side of the patient, only periodically looking directly at him, the patient is more engaged.

Therapist and patient then observe and experience different states of relatedness together; they explore at the same time. Initially, they do not explore historical or even current complex patterns of wishes and feelings. They explore, in a supportive manner, aspects of their interaction (e.g., the patient may be helped to see that he finds the therapist's voice soothing or irritating). The therapist uses the boundaries of the therapeutic relationship in a new way, but still maintains those boundaries.

In general, the therapist attempts to first broaden the range of experiences dealt with at the patient's developmental level. For example, if the patient avoids assertion or aggression or intimacy, the therapist's initial goal is to facilitate a full range of feelings at his or her current level. The next goal is to help the patient move up to the next level.

Principle 5

Therapists should always promote the patient's self-sufficiency and assertiveness. This principle, though generally accepted in most dynamic therapies, is often ignored. Learning occurs in life, and particularly in the psychotherapeutic process, through a person's own active discovery in the context of the relationship he or she develops with the therapist. For example, it is often not helpful to make comments on the person's behavior or affects, while the person nods acceptingly and then goes on free associating. It is the active learning done by patients themselves, as opposed to the passive nodding acceptance of what the therapist says and does, that proves to be more helpful. Always promote patients' own assertiveness, self-sufficiency, and active construction of their experiences, as opposed to the more passive, compliant acceptance of what we may have to offer them. Not infrequently, in the enthusiasm of the moment, we assume that the patient's nod or compliant free associations along the lines we suggest is proof of the value of our insight.

Part of individuals' self-sufficiency is rooted in their ability to create growth-producing experiences in other relationships in addition to the therapeutic one. As a particular issue is being mastered, the therapist needs to actively explore factors that might be interfering with the patient taking this step.

Principle 6

The representational system, including unconscious symbols, are only the tip of the iceberg. Of special importance to better understanding the developmental basis of psychotherapy is the fact that the representational system, so central to most dynamic therapies, deals only with the most surface aspects of ego functioning. The ability to represent experience and elaborate representations, and the ability to differentiate among representations, are the two levels of ego functioning acquired in later stages of ego development (i.e., when children are already verbal and symbolic). There are four earlier levels that must also be dealt with, which deal with the way experience is organized prerepresentationally. They include how regulation (sensory reactivity and processing) occurs; the way early engagements and relationships are formed and elaborated; and how early simple and complex, intentional, gestural communication becomes a part of a prerepresentational pattern of mental organization.

By being aware of early stages of ego development, therapists have greater empathetic range. They can go beyond empathy to be an actual facilitator of new ego development. While intuitive therapists have always been able to empathize with early affective states, most therapists will be aided by a theoretical road map indicating the sensory, regulatory, gestural, behavioral, and affective signposts to look out for. Limitations due to countertransference phenomena and the therapist's own experiences naturally limit one's empathetic range to some degree.

PRINCIPLE 7

Affect and interaction are the basis for ego development and, more generally, intelligence. The therapist's role is based on the critical notion that development occurs from affective interactions. This notion emerged from our observation that both emotional and intellectual growth depend on affective interactions and that these interactions can be harnessed in various contexts. In this model, interactions are, in a sense, the fuel that mobilizes the mind's various functions. These interactions create opportunities for affective interchange, and these affects are then vital to the way the mind organizes itself and functions.

Each interaction gives rise to affects such as pleasure, annoyance, surprise, sadness, anger, and curiosity. Variations in the quality and intensity of these and other affects make for an almost infinite variety of affect patterns. The affects, in many respects, operate as the orchestra leader, organizing and differentiating the mind's many functions. Affects stemming from interactions become the foundation for both ego growth and differentiation and, more broadly, for intelligence (Greenspan, 1979a, 1997b).

Ego growth is not a surprising concomitant of affective interchanges, but cognitive or intellectual abilities are not usually thought of as stemming from interactive and affective patterns. To see why they do, consider the following. A child is learning to say "hello," a seemingly simple cognitive task. Does the child learn to say hello only to close friends, relatives, and those who live within a quarter-mile of his house? When he meets a stranger, does he think to himself, "Where does this person live in relationship to me?" Or is the decision of when to say hello mediated by an affective cue, such as a warm feeling when seeing a familiar, friendly face, which, without even thinking, leads to the smile, the hello, and an extended hand. If it's the latter, we would promote it by creating opportunities for interactions where the child could link his affects, thoughts, and behaviors.

Intellectual activity requires two components: the affectively mediated creation of personal experience and the logical analysis of that experience. Almost every intellectual experience an infant, young child, or adult has involves these two components: an affective as well as a more purely cognitive one. This process begins early in development. The earliest experiences are double-coded according to both their physical and affective properties. The affects, in fact, appear to work like a sensory organ, providing critical information. For example, the ball is red, but looking at it also feels nice, scary, or interesting. The food is yellow and firm and affectively is delightful or annoying. As a child learns about size, shape, and quantity, each of these experiences are also both emotional and cognitive. For example, "a lot" is more than you expected; "a long time" is the rest of your life. The ability to count or formalize these quantities is simply the formal classification of what you already affectively know.

The earliest sense of causality and ego differentiation emerges not from sensorimotor explorations, as Piaget (1962) thought, but from earlier affective interactions (e.g., a smile causing a smile back; Greenspan, 1997b). At each stage of cognition, affects lead the way. Complex abstract concepts, such as love, honor, and justice, are also the products of these same processes. The concepts have a formal, cognitive definition, but to comprehend or create this definition requires a range of personal affective experience. Love, for example, is pleasure and excitement, but it is also commitment and loyalty, as well as the ability to forgive and recover from anger. Taken together, these affective experiences associated with the word give it its full abstract meaning. We have observed that children and adults who remain concrete have difficulty integrating multiple affective experiences into a word or concept.

Affects are also, as indicated earlier, at the foundation of our most basic ego functions. Our sense of self and other differentiates out of an infinite number of subtle affective interchanges at each of the stages of ego development. In addition, the selection of defenses or coping strategies is often mediated by affects. When a child avoids an angry encounter and becomes compliant and sweet, often the affect of fear mediates this change in the child's behavior, feeling tone, and ideas. When an adult avoids intimacy or competition, there are sometimes unpleasant affects associated with these types of interactions mediating the avoidance. There is a hierarchy of ways in which the ego copes with underlying affects. These include disorganized behavioral patterns, states of self-absorption, intentional impulsive patterns, somatically experienced affects, polarized, global emotions and beliefs, and represented, symbolized feelings and experiences (from fragmented to cohesive integrated forms).

In our developmental model, therefore, interactions and their associated affects mobilize all aspects of development, emotional as well as cognitive. A wise person is both intellectually and emotionally wise; the two cannot be separated. There are, of course, individuals who have isolated areas of cognitive skill (perhaps in science, math, or the arts), and there are individuals who have highly differentiated ego structures who lack some of these areas of skill. But overall intelligence, wisdom, and emotional maturity are part of one and the same process. An integrated and differentiated human being is one who can negotiate all the areas of age-expected functioning: emotional, social, and intellectual.

The affects, as they come into place and as therapeutic experiences harness them, not only differentiate and develop our personalities, they also serve as the orchestra leader for our many ego functions and capacities. When we are trying to remember something quickly or figure out which cognitive operation to use, we don't logically explore all the various alternatives; we quickly come to the strategy or memory through our emotional orchestra leader. Similarly, when we automatically use a particular defense coping strategy or regressive route, these same affects determine the selected operations.

Another important dimension of reciprocal, affective interactions is that they lead to the capacity for an individual to use affect as a signal, which fosters anticipation and consideration of alternatives rather than direct discharge, shutdown, or withdrawal. The regulation made possible by back-and-forth affective exchanges leads to symbolization, and the symbolization of affect makes it possible to use affect as a signal.

CASE EXAMPLE OF A LATENCY-AGE CHILD

This is a case of a latency-age child, Andy, who tended to be either agitated or depressed. The goals of his psychotherapy were to help him progress to higher levels in his functional emotional capacities (i.e., ego development). Specifically, one of the goals was to enable him to engage in longer chains of regulated, reciprocal affective exchanges. During longer and longer exchanges, the therapist would help Andy better regulate his affective and behavioral expressions through critical preverbal as well as verbal responses. For example, when Andy would begin to evidence more agitation in his voice and body movements, the therapist would deliberately move toward a more soothing, comforting tone to attempt to down-regulate the intensity of affect. When Andy became more apathetic and self-absorbed, the therapist would deliberately move toward a more energized rhythm of preverbal and verbal exchange (e.g., more animated facial expressions and faster tempo) to up-regulate. At the same time that the therapist was working at the preverbal level, he would also periodically explore how Andy felt during these shifts of affective rhythm and intensity. He was attempting to help Andy symbolize and reflect on the subtle feeling states he was experiencing when either agitated or apathetic.

Over a period of six months, Andy was able to make progress toward both of these goals. He gradually responded to the therapist's soothing, comforting tone of voice and interactive rhythm by becoming more regulated (less agitated) when talking, for example, about his father being unfair or kids at school picking on him. He was also able to begin verbalizing more abstracted feeling states, shifting from somatic descriptions and descriptions of actions he was going to carry out to true descriptions and reflections on inner feelings. For example, instead of talking about his exploding insides or how he was going to punch so-and-so, he began describing "feeling like my insides were shouting... like I was so mad."

Interestingly, as Andy was able to symbolize affect, he began to use affect as a signal (i.e., to both unconsciously and consciously anticipate next steps). For example, when his brother came into his room uninvited, Andy became aware of feeling angry and then considered alternative actions. It is important to note that his capacity to use affect as a signal was based on his first learning to regulate reciprocal affective exchanges and then describe his affective states symbolically. Both steps appear to be important. Without the regulation, affective states tend to be intense and, therefore, are often experienced in an overwhelming or catastrophic manner, and there is a tendency toward discharge, somatization, or interpersonal withdrawal. The regulation of the affective interchanges enables shifts toward symbolization (i.e., greater awareness and description of subtle affective states); in turn, the symbolization enables the affects to serve as intrapsychic signals.

Therapeutic interactions, which generate affects, are at the foundation of developmentally based psychotherapy. Each component of ego development requires certain types of interactions and affective experience. The challenge of the therapeutic process is to figure out ways to harness these as part of the therapeutic relationship. Therapists must always remember, however, that the therapeutic relationship is only a component of patients' overall set of relationships and, therefore, one needs to help patients create opportunities for interactive and affective experiences in other sectors of their life. The therapeutic relationship that attempts to provide the critical experiences in the patient's life, rather than assist the patient in orchestrating such life experiences, many limit necessary and healthy age-expected interactions.

A CASE EXAMPLE OF DEPRESSION

Consider another example to illustrate the developmental approach to the psychotherapeutic process. A middle-aged depressed woman had grown up with an extremely intrusive, controlling mother and a very available but passive father who deferred to mother. As near as can be reconstructed (some of it intellectually from mother's behavior), even as an infant and toddler, this woman's every reach for any sort of dependency gratification or for closeness was met by her mother's intrusive, controlling, and sometimes rejecting responses. The patient later came to feel that her mother's behavior was aimed at humiliating her. Much of her latency, adolescence, and now adulthood were geared to never showing weakness, vulnerability, or neediness in regard to her mother.

In addition, this patient had a history from her own recollection, as well as from her parents' descriptions of her, of overreactivity to basic sensations, such as touch and sound. She was gifted in her use of language but had relatively weaker visual-spatial processing capacities. These patterns continued into adulthood, leaving her prone to feeling "overloaded," "fragmented," or "falling apart." She would experience overload when in a noisy room or in a group of people brushing up against her. She was much better at recalling details than "seeing the big picture"; her "loud," forceful, "top sergeant" mother, for example, made her "cringe" when she would surprise her and walk into her room.

The patient's tendency to become overloaded and fragmented and her difficulty in visual-spatial abstracting, in terms of regulating patterns, would have made it hard, under any circumstances, for her to engage as a toddler in the full range of organized behavioral and emotional patterns. Fragmented, piecemeal patterns would be more likely to occur. Likewise, it would have been difficult for her to conduct organized and integrated mental representations as a preschooler. Again, fragmented patterns would be more likely from the combination of overreactivity and relatively weak integrating capacities. With an intrusive, overwhelming mother, however, what might have been difficult to master became almost an impossibility. The relationship with the mother, therefore, accentuated her constitutional and maturational weaknesses. A soothing, comforting mother might have helped her overcome her vulnerabilities. At the same time, the dynamics of her relationship with her mother were intensified by her regulatory patterns. A child with excellent self-calming and self-soothing abilities and strong integrating capacity might have been able to deal with an intrusive mother by becoming a little stubborn or negative or, simply, strong-willed. This patient's degree of rage and humiliation and sense of fragmentation were all quite intense, in part because of the regulatory pattern.

As she progressed into her representational phase, she was, therefore, unable to fully represent nurturing, caring interactions in a stable manner because they weren't occurring at the behavioral interaction level.

Contributing to this woman's depression in adulthood was an inability to represent longing feelings for anyone in her life, including her child, the therapist, or her husband, who was thoughtful and very devoted to her. During the therapist's vacation times, the patient would get agitated and uncomfortable, but could never picture the therapist away on vacation or experience longing or angry feelings. All she experienced was "a vague sense of anxiety, tension in my muscles, and a feeling like I'm going to fall down." Intellectually, being a sophisticated individual, she said, "I'm probably missing you, but I'll be honest, I don't feel a shred of it, although I feel physically lousy when you're away." Interestingly, she felt similarly when she had an urgent work project and needed to talk with her husband when he was away on a business trip. During the day, she would get agitated, headachy, and dizzy and experience patterns of disorganized thinking. When she was having a big meeting with her bosses, she could never imagine being soothed by her husband or calling him up for a pep talk beforehand: "The image just never occurred to me."

This person, like many who are prone to depression, may lack the ability to represent, in the most fundamental sense, wishes and affects having to do with longing feelings. They are, in fact, better at representing anger or aggression than longing. They have conflicts with aggression, but an even more fundamental issue is the very lack of ability to represent critical affects. This type of difficulty has been observed in patients with psychosomatic and substance abuse difficulties (Nemiah, 1977).

The ability to represent certain longing feelings can be viewed metaphorically as each individual's ability to create a personal internal Linus-type security blanket. Early in development, children initially are at a level where their own real behavior and the behavior of their caregivers as well as the presence of specific concrete objects serve security and communicative purposes. Around 18 to 24 months, however, under optimal circumstances, they develop the ability to create internal images, as Mahler and others (1975) described so well. These internal images become invested with certain wishes and feelings. Once children can create images, these can obviously be used for self-soothing as well as for fantasizing about anger. Once individuals have the flexibility to create representational images, they can create a temporary sense of security and experiment with anger while embraced in the safety of real relationships. Many individuals, for a variety of reasons, cannot create aspects of mental representations, often because of early conflicts in their prerepresentational stage and/or certain regulatory patterns. I believe this scenario holds true for the woman discussed here, where the seeking of dependency and support was involved in behavioral-level conflicts with her mother. Such people cannot chance creating the representational image of these wishes. This patient may have given up those types of seeking behaviors before she was even 2 years of age. Her only memories were those told to her, for example, that she either ran around without purpose or withdrew and was sometimes defiant. She never sought out her mother to cuddle or hug; she always treated her mother as a person who could give her things. She was more warm and nurturing with her father, and could seek support from him, albeit in concrete ways.

In our developmental model, an important aspect of certain types of depression is not necessarily the loss of the real object, but the loss of, or never having the ability to create, the internal representation of the object, particularly in its soothing and dependency-oriented patterns. This leaves the person at the mercy of direct, concrete behavioral patterns. A sense of internal self-esteem, based on representations of the object, in terms of soothing, admiration, respect, and reassurance, is not present. It is not the loss of the real object but the internal representation that may be a critical aspect of certain types of depression. Interestingly, the biological components of depression may be mediated through the regulatory patterns (hyperreactivity and/or visual-spatial integration), rather than as a direct effect on mood. Therefore, there is an interaction between experience and biology.

These considerations play out in the treatment of this patient. Simply clarifying and interpreting these patterns would not be sufficient, and might be counterproductive. First, the therapist must always meet patients at the developmental level of their ego structure. For this patient, it meant dealing directly with her regulatory patterns, not only by helping her describe them, but creating in the office a regulatory environment (e.g., not talking too fast or intrusively and finding soothing vocal rhythms and tones). Second, attention should be paid to behavioral expectations. In this case, the patient expected intrusion and her countertendencies were to withdraw or become fragmented in speech or behavior. It was insufficient to simply point out that whenever she felt needy, she expected the analyst to intrude and overwhelm her, as she felt her mother had done in the past. Because this was a behavioral rather than representational expectation, it was experienced not as "I *feel* as though you will control me," but as "You *are* going to control me" and, with regard to her withdrawn or fragmented behavior, "You are *overloading* me."

The therapist was verbally interactive to maintain a sense of relatedness when the patient was withdrawing. His counterbehavior was geared to increase the patient's behavioral and affective range. He attempted to help the patient organize communications when she became fragmented (e.g., "I lost your last idea"). When she became very fragmented, he increased visual and behavioral interchange through gestures to maintain organization. When there were gestural indications in terms of tone of voice, motor gestures, or affect cues of dependency feelings, the therapist would attempt to maintain and further elaborate these through the interactive dialogue, which provided an experience of nonintrusive comfort. As the patient withdrew or became hostile in anticipation of intrusiveness, initially the therapist did not clarify or interpret underlying feelings or wishes. Such comments would have been at a different developmental level than the patient's level at that point. Instead, the therapist maintained the dialogue with the behavioral descriptions: "You see me as doing this to you, rather than being comforting."

As the patient became more flexible, the therapist helped her identify those affects that led to withdrawal or fragmentation, which were initially at a somatic, physical level: "My muscles are tense"; "My heart is beating fast." Detailed somatic descriptions led to abstracted affect descriptions and representational-type patterns: "I feel like I'm falling apart"; "I feel empty"; "I feel lonely and isolated." Eventually, states of longing and need could be communicated in terms of "missing feelings," and the capacity to represent dependency and longing emerged, perhaps for the first time in the patient's experience.

Once she could represent experience, it was possible to use clarifying and interpretive comments to help her deal with pathologic defenses and work through her conflicts. She could then further develop her capacities for representational differentiation and self-observation. There are a number representational levels (from concrete to more abstract and reflective) that are described elsewhere in this text.

Some of these strategies are no different from approaches that many intuitive therapies have been following for years. But often they are viewed as "intuitive" and not systematic or central to therapeutic growth. The developmental perspective can help systematize them and open up new areas for inclusion, such as constitutional and maturational differences and the different developmental levels that are not always intuitive.

SCHEMATIC OUTLINE OF THE FUNCTIONAL DEVELOPMENTAL LEVELS

To assist in visualizing the developmental approach to mental health and illness, the schematic outline in Table 2.2 may be useful. For each fundamental capacity, there are a range of possibilities, from very adaptive and healthy to maladaptive and disordered. This type of approach may prove more useful than narrow-based, symptom-oriented approaches and could even be used for research applications. Clinically, each capacity can be rated on a 20-point scale, for example, and the totals summed for a more global picture. Reliability studies based on rating videotapes of children and validity studies as well as a manual are available (Greenspan, DeGangi, & Wieder, 2001).

APPLICATION OF DIR MODEL TO CHILDREN WITH AUTISTIC SPECTRUM DISORDERS

Although a number of intervention and educational strategies have been developed for children with autistic spectrum disorders (Bristol et al., 1996; Rogers, 1996), there has not been sufficient emphasis on working with individual processing patterns and different functional developmental capacities.

In contrast to limited educational models that focus on isolated cognitive skills and behavioral models that isolate and work with selective discrete behaviors, the DIR model focuses on underlying developmental processes and structures. It extends traditionally helpful relationship approaches (Carew, 1980; Feuerstein, Rand,

Table 2.2 Functional developmental levels.

	Self-Regulation		
0–5 Points	6–13 Points	14–19 Points	20 Points
Attention is fleeting (a few seconds here or there) and/or very active or agitated or mostly self-absorbed and/or lethargic or passive.	When very interested or motivated or captivated, can attend and be calm for short periods (e.g., 30 to 60 seconds).	Focused, organized, and calm except when overstimulated or understimulated (e.g., noisy, active, or very dull setting); challenged to use a vulnerable skill (e.g., a child with weak fine motor skills asked to write rapidly), or ill, anxious, or under stress.	Focused, organized, and calm most of the time, even under stress.
	Engagement		
Aloof, withdrawn, and/or indifferent to others.	Superficial and need-oriented, lacking intimacy.	Intimacy and caring are present but disrupted by strong emotions, like anger or separation (e.g., person withdraws or acts out).	Deep, emotionally rich capacity for intimacy, caring, and empathy, even when feelings are strong or under stress.
	Intentionality		
Mostly aimless, fragmented, unpurposeful behavior and emotional expressions (e.g., no purposeful grins or smiles or reaching out with body posture for warmth or closeness).	Some need-oriented, purposeful islands of behavior and emotional expressions. No cohesive larger social goals.	Often purposeful and organized, but not with a full range of emotional expressions (e.g., seeks out others for closeness and warmth with appropriate flirtatious glances, body posture, and the like, but becomes chaotic, fragmented or aimless when very angry).	Most of the time purposeful and organized behavior and a wide range of subtle emotions, even when there are strong feelings and stress.
	The Preverbal Sense of Self: Comprehending Intentions and Expectations		
Distorts the intents of others (e.g., misreads cues and, therefore, feels suspicious, mistreated, unloved, angry, etc.).	In selected relationships can read basic intentions of others (such as acceptance or rejection) but unable to read subtle cues (like respect or pride or partial anger).	Often accurately reads and responds to a range of emotional signals, except in certain circumstances involving selected emotions, very strong emotions, or stress or due to a difficulty with processing sensations, such as sights or sounds (e.g., certain signals are confusing).	Reads and responds to most emotional signals flexibly and accurately even when under stress (e.g., comprehends safety vs. danger, approval vs. disapproval, acceptance vs. rejection, respect vs. humiliation, partial anger, etc.).

(continued)

Table 2.2 *(Continued)*

0–5 Points	6–13 Points	14–19 Points	20 Points
Creating and Elaborating Emotional Ideas			
Puts wishes and feelings into action or into somatic states ("My tummy hurts"). Unable to use ideas to elaborate wishes and feelings (e.g., hits when mad, hugs or demands physical intimacy when needy, rather than experiencing idea of anger or expressing wish for closeness).	Uses ideas in a concrete way to convey desire for action or to get basic needs met. Does not elaborate idea of feeling in its own right (e.g., "I want to hit but can't because someone is watching" rather than "I feel mad").	Often uses ideas to be imaginative and creative and express range of emotions, except when experiencing selected conflicted or difficult emotions or when under stress (e.g., cannot put anger into words or pretend).	Uses ideas to express full range of emotions. Is imaginative and creative most of the time, even under stress.
Emotional Thinking			
Ideas are experienced in a piecemeal or fragmented manner (e.g., one phrase is followed by another with no logical bridges).	Thinking is polarized, ideas are used in an all-or-nothing manner (e.g., things are all good or all bad. There are no shades of gray.).	Thinking is constricted (i.e., tends to focus mostly on certain themes like anger and competition). Often thinking is logical, but strong emotions, selected emotions, or stress can lead to polarized or fragmented thinking.	Thinking is logical, abstract, and flexible across the full range of age-expected emotions and interactions. Thinking is also relatively reflective at age-expected levels and in relationship to age-expected endeavors (e.g., peer, spouse, or family relationship). Thinking supports movement into the next stages in the course of life.
Additional Functional Developmental Stages			

Throughout the life cycle, these stages build on emotional thinking.
- *Triangular thinking.* Triadic interactions among feeling states ("I feel left out when Susie likes Janet better than me").
- *Relativistic thinking (playground politics).* Shades and gradations among differentiated feeling states (ability to describe degrees of feelings around anger, love, excitement, love, disappointment—"I feel a little annoyed").
- *Internalized sense of self (the world inside me).* Reflecting on feelings in relationship to an internalized sense of self ("It's not like me to feel so angry" or "I shouldn't feel this jealous").
- *Extending representational capacity to new realms of biological, psychological, and social experience.* Expanding reflective feeling descriptors into new realms, including sexuality, romance, closer and more intimate peer relationships, school, community, culture, and emerging sense of identity ("I have such an intense crush on that new boy that I know it's silly; I don't even know him").
- *Extending representational capacities in time and space.* Using feelings to anticipate and judge future possibilities in light of current and past experience ("I don't think I would be able to really fall in love with him because he likes to flirt with everyone and that has always made me feel neglected and sad"). Broadening reflective capacities to include larger community and culture.

Table 2.2 *(Continued)*

- *Extending representational capacities into the stages of adulthood, middle age, and the aging process.* Expanding feeling states to include reflections and anticipatory judgment with regard to new levels and types of feelings associated with the stages of adulthood, including:
  —Ability to function independently from, and yet remain close to and internalize many of the capacities initially provided by one's nuclear family.
  - Inner sense of security.
  - Judgment and self monitoring of behavior and impulses.
  - Regulation of mood.
  - Reality-based, organized thinking.
  —Intimacy (serious long-term relationships).
  —The ability to nurture and empathize with one's children without over-identifying with them.
  —The ability to broaden one's nurturing and empathetic capacities beyond one's family and into the larger community.
  —The ability to experience and reflect on the new feelings of intimacy, mastery, pride, competition, disappointment, and loss associated with the family, career, and intrapersonal changes of mid-life and the aging process.

Hoffman, & Miller, 1979; Feuerstein et al., 1981; Greenspan, 1979a, 1979b, 1989, 1997b; Klein, Wieder, & Greenspan, 1987; Rogers & Lewis, 1989). It does this through an understanding of three unique features: children's functional developmental level, their individual processing differences, and the affective interactions likely to broaden their functional developmental capacities and enable them to move to higher developmental levels.

In this approach, children's affect or intent is harnessed by following their lead or natural interests. However, they are not followed into aimless or perseverative behavior. Their affective interests are used as a guide to mobilize attention, engagement, purposeful interactions, and preverbal problem solving and, eventually, to create ideas and build bridges between them. Focusing on these fundamental functional developmental processes rather than specific behaviors or skills (which are often part of these broader processes) helps to reestablish the developmental sequence that went awry. For example, rather than trying to teach a child who is perseveratively spinning the wheels on a car to play with something else or to play with the car appropriately, the caregiver uses the child's interest and gently spins the wheel in the opposite direction to get reciprocal, affective interactions going. These affective interactions, however, are tailored to the child's individual differences; soothing or energetic interactions, visual or auditory patterns, complex or simple motor patterns may be emphasized, depending on the child's profile. Consider the following examples of individual developmental profiles guiding the interaction.

The first child, a 3½-year-old, was fleetingly engaged, capable only occasionally of purposeful gestures. He had very weak motor planning and sequencing capacities and was underreactive to sensation. He required an intervention program that provided a great deal of sensory input (because of his sensory underreactivity), animated affective interaction (to woo him into engagement), and highly motivating yet simple challenges (a favorite perseverative toy was put on the caregiver's head) to draw him into more engagement and purposeful interactions (e.g., reaching for the toy). He was working at mastering the early functional developmental capacities of engagement and simple purposeful gestures.

A very different approach was required for a second case. This 4-year-old child could engage and be purposeful some of the time, but became easily overloaded because of sensory hypersensitivity to touch and sound. As a consequence, he would become self-absorbed and perseverative. At other times, he could use purposeful gestures to problem-solve (take a caregiver to the door to try to go outside), and imitate simple gestures, including sounds, and, on occasion, use a word meaningfully (e.g., "Open") and feed a doll. He was, however, significantly delayed in social skills and functional language (and most of the time would memorize scripts and randomly repeat phrases). In contrast to the first case, this child, because of his sensory hypersensitivities, required extra soothing, not animation or sensory play. He also needed opportunities to turn perseveration into interactions and problem-solving activities (e.g., instead of letting him simply open and close the play garage door when the toy car made too much noise, we challenged him to put the car inside the garage and tell it to "stop" by having a gesturing and talking car driver insist on parking the car). Functional language was further encouraged by challenging him to connect words like "open" and "stop" to intent or emotional interests by setting up situations where he would want to imitate "open" to open a door to get his favorite toy. Similarly, scripted or echolalic language was turned into purposeful problem-solving interactions by challenging him with highly motivating, meaningful choices, such as choosing between two objects he might be labeling in a rote manner. He was wooed into a continuous flow of problem-solving interactions even when overloaded (with soothing but compelling interactions). Based on his unique profile, this child worked at a different functional developmental level than the first child—the level of complex, purposeful, social problem solving and the early use of ideas—and required a more soothing approach.

Case 3 was similar to Case 2 except that this child was underreactive to touch and sound, had slightly weaker auditory processing, significantly weaker articulation (oral-motor) and expressive language, and relatively stronger visual-spatial capacities. Therefore, instead of soothing, the interactions needed to be very animated. Pictures were used to augment symbolic communication, not simply to convey needs or choices, but to enable characters in pretend play to amplify their action dramas with dialogue and elaborate a sequence of back-and-forth communication. Interestingly, this child learned to read and write faster than she learned to speak. Therefore, we used reading and writing to maintain both pretend and reality-based dialogues while she was improving her speaking. Interactions using her strengths increased two-way gestural and symbolic communication and enabled her to develop the capacity to build bridges between ideas and think.

COMPONENTS OF A COMPREHENSIVE PROGRAM

A comprehensive program often includes interactive speech therapy (three to five times per week), occupational therapy (two to five times per week), appropriate biomedical approaches, a developmentally appropriate education program, and a home-based program of developmentally appropriate interactions, which includes consultations working on caregiver-child interactions and, if needed, direct therapeutic work with the child. It also includes regular family consultations and team meetings for reviewing the overall therapeutic and educational program and coordination of relevant biomedical interventions.

The home-based program of developmentally appropriate interactions is especially important. It is related to the National Association for the Education of Young Children recommendation of developmentally appropriate practices for all children (Bredekamp & Copple, 1997). Such practices, however, are difficult for a child with severe processing problems who may spend hours perseverating and self-stimulating, including repetitively watching the same videotapes. To help such a child become involved in developmentally appropriate interactions requires tailoring the interactions to the child's natural interests (mood and mental state), functional developmental level, and individual processing differences. This often includes three types of interactions: (1) spontaneous, follow-the-child's-lead interactions geared to enable the child to work on the six functional developmental levels; (2) semistructured problem-solving interactions to work on specific cognitive, language, and social skills as determined by the team of parents and educators (e.g., helping the child to say "open" when a toy is put outside the door); and (3) motor, sensory, and spatial activities geared to improve these typically vulnerable processing capacities. These developmentally appropriate types of interactions are needed during the child's waking hours to mobilize growth. What children do most of the time determines their pattern of progress; without these interactions, they often will shift into perseverative, self-stimulatory, or aimless patterns.

When a child develops some capacity for relating, gesturing, and imitating, including imitating words, an important component of the overall program during the preschool years is an integrated preschool (i.e., 25% children with special needs and 75% children without special needs). Here, teachers are especially gifted in interacting with challenging children and working with them on interactive gesturing, affective cuing, and early symbolic communication. The preschool enables children with special needs to interact with children who are interactive and communicative (e.g., as a child reaches out for relationships and communication, there are peers who reach back). Four or more play sessions with a peer who is interactive and verbal are also essential at this point, so that the child can practice emerging abilities with a friend. To minimize self-absorption and perseveration and to enable children and their parents to be reengaged, it is important for the therapeutic program to begin as soon as possible.

The DIR intervention approach, which focuses on the delayed child's developmental level and individual differences, is different from psychotherapy or play therapy. What often occurs in traditional play therapy with children with autism is a type of parallel play, rather than true developmentally based interactions.

Steps in the DIR Intervention Process

For children with autistic spectrum patterns, initial therapeutic goals often need to focus on four essential presymbolic capacities. The first is to foster regulation, focus, and concentration (shared attention) through gearing interactive experiences to the child's processing profile (e.g., very energetic and challenging for the underreactive child and soothing and gradual for the oversensitive child). The second is to promote engagement with the human world through following the child's lead and working with his or her pleasurable interests. The third is creating opportunities for two-way intentional communication through enticing the child to take initiative and use gestures purposefully, such as taking a desired toy from the top of dad's head.

When children are perseverative, aimless, avoidant, or negative, we treat every behavior as though it is purposeful. We might "get stuck" in a door they are opening and closing (a kind of cat-and-mouse game). As they try to get us out of the way, gestural interactions occur and behavior becomes purposeful. For children who are aimless or wandering, a clinician might follow them to a corner of the room and try to interest them in what "we" are looking at or playfully obstruct their path, pretending to be a horse. It is important to soothe and comfort when being playfully obstructive, though after a few minutes, children often find these types of interactions amusing.

As children become more interactive and purposeful, they are ready to work on the fourth presymbolic capacity: to interact continuously (i.e., open and close many circles of communication in a row) to solve problems, such as taking dad to the toy area to get the horse. Many children, even as they become verbal, lack mastery of continuous social problem-solving interaction, leaving them vulnerable to intermittent self-absorption and perseveration and the limited use of ideas.

With sufficient practice on continuous problem-solving interactions, children learn to incorporate imitation into their social dialogue and may copy feeding a doll, or repeating "mine" or "open" to get the door open or get her doll back. Through "copycat" games, they may gradually learn to use ideas creatively and begin to pretend, for example, feeding the dolly.

With lots of interactive pretend play and pulling for words when the child's affects or interests are high, the child gradually may become symbolic. However, it is often much easier for children to pay attention to their own ideas rather than the ideas of others because of auditory processing difficulties. The caregiver or therapist enters the child's symbolic world with back-and-forth exchanges of emotionally meaningful ideas, including debates and opinions rather than facts (in both pretend play and logical conversations). These symbolic exchanges encourage emotional differentiation, reality testing, and higher levels of abstract and logical thinking.

The common practice of teaching thinking through scripting dialogue for the child does not work. Children learn to think and abstract and generalize by connecting more and more affectively meaningful experiences to the concepts, words, and behavior they are using. Over time, imaginative play and emotionally meaningful negotiations, not memorized scripts, become the foundations for higher-level social and cognitive abilities.

Case Example of a Child with an Autistic Spectrum Disorder

Alex, a 2½-year-old, was seen because of parental concerns of extreme self-absorption, perseveration, and self-stimulation. There was no language and only intermittent ability to relate to parents around concrete needs, such as getting juice or a cookie. History revealed delayed motor milestones (e.g., walking at 16 months) and a pattern of some moderate ability to engage in the first year, but a gradual movement toward self-absorption and repetition from the middle of the second year on. A diagnosis of autism had been made by a developmental pediatrician; a biomedical and neurological workup was negative.

We conducted a comprehensive evaluation, which includes detailed history, observations of child-caregiver interactions, and exploration of family patterns, as well as assessments of all areas of development. In observing Alex, we saw that there was some fleeting eye contact and a quick turn away toward perseverative play with a toy.

This child was preoccupied with wheels on cars and would spin them around and around. His father, who took the lead in playing with him, quickly got impatient and tried to hold his son's hand and direct him to other toys, which resulted in tantrumming and more intense self-stimulatory activity. Mother tended to talk to Alex about what he was doing and try to be supportive, but was unable to get any engagement going as he was unable to understand what she was saying.

Our systematic developmental profile revealed that Alex had only fleeting capacity for shared attention and engagement and was purposeful only with objects, although he could purposefully turn away from and avoid his caregivers. He was unable to engage in complex problem solving or multicircle interactions using gestures, and there were no indications of symbolic capacities in terms of either elaboration or building logical bridges. In other words, he seemed to have some very limited capacities at the first three levels, with no evidence of capacities at the fourth, fifth, and sixth levels.

Alex's processing profile revealed severe deficits in auditory processing and language, as well as marked deficits in motor planning and sequencing; even with his interest in toys, he could carry out only one-step actions, such as spinning a wheel, banging a toy, or pressing against something. His visual-spatial processing looked like it might hold some relative strengths for him, but would require further observation. For example, he seemed to flit around to multiple objects in the room; once, when his father took away something he was playing with, he appeared to begin to walk behind his father to try to find it. He quickly became self-stimulatory, and it wasn't possible to be sure he was embarking on a search (when motor planning is impaired, it can be hard to assess visual-spatial processing). He was very sensory underreactive and also evidenced low muscle tone.

With this profile in hand, we were able to begin a comprehensive intervention program. It included three individual speech therapy sessions per week and three individual occupational therapy sessions a week. It also included an intensive home program involving the three types of interactions described earlier. In the home program, we took advantage of Alex's interest in objects to help him become more engaged, purposeful, and intentional. For example, instead of trying to change his activity, we coached father to join him in spinning wheels and try to entice Alex into spinning father's bigger and faster car wheel. Alex generally ignored this enticing overture, so we coached father to get his hand stuck on Alex's wheel (playful obstruction). This worked better. Alex would look at his father and push his wheel a little harder or try to pull it away. Dad was helped to supportively let Alex win for a second and then get his hand stuck again. Their first interactions occurred around these types of playful obstructions.

We also coached the parents to be very energetic to compensate for Alex's underreactivity. He needed highly energized caregivers for him to even notice them, let alone interact. Animated voices, exaggerated facial expressions, and gentle but clear gestures were the rule of the day. Lots of visual support to take advantage of relatively stronger visual-spatial processing was provided through brightly colored toys, well-lit rooms, and interesting visual designs and visual challenges in the play (e.g., hiding things).

Mother was helped to combine her verbal dialogue with gestures and actions. Alex tended to accept another car with better wheels from her, in comparison to his father. She could move the car with big fancy wheels away from him and he would come after her to get it. Over time, these beginnings led to more engagement and more purposeful interaction.

Space precludes describing the next steps in this case in detail. Over time, Alex was able to string together many purposeful interactions in a row and eventually problem-solve and imitate. After about a year of intensive work, he was able to imitate sufficiently to start copying words and, eventually, phrases.

Once Alex became more related and able to use many gestures in a row as part of a long chain of reciprocal interactions, to problem-solve, and to use a few words, we recommended a regular preschool program with an aide so that he could practice his new skills with peers. Over the next few years, progress sped up because Alex was now engaged and interactive with his environment and, therefore, learning all the time; there was only occasional self-stimulatory and perseverative activities and he could easily be drawn into patterns of engagement when he became self-absorbed.

The key to his program was the comprehensiveness and intensity of the intervention, which enabled him to practice his new skills in a nurturing and joyful manner, rather than spend lots of time in states of self-absorption. At present (Alex is now 10 years old), he is a bright, verbal child with a sense of humor and some close friends. He's doing well in his family and in a regular grade school. He still has challenges in motor planning and sequencing (penmanship and writing), but is rather gifted in his verbal insights about the world. Most important, he's a very warm and loving child.

Alex is one of a subgroup of children who have done very well and exceeded our expectations. There appears to be a subgroup of children with autistic spectrum diagnoses who can do exceedingly well. Other subgroups we've identified make much slower progress (Greenspan & Wieder, 1997, 1999). Children who make rapid progress have the ability to become engaged and purposeful and to problem-solve in the early phases of intervention and quickly move on to imitative capacities and the beginnings of symbolic communication. Even though Alex's initial profile showed many more challenges than most of the children in this subgroup who do well, he was able to make consistent progress in the critical areas of engagement, reciprocal interactions, problem solving, and imitation early in his program. He may have presented looking more challenging in part because his parents weren't able to intuitively figure out how to work with his biologically based processing challenges and, as indicated earlier, they tended to accentuate his difficulties. Their capacity to learn quickly as well as his and their ability together to participate in an intensive, comprehensive program were significant factors.

SUMMARY

New insights into the early stages of the development of the mind have the potential to advance our understanding of the psychotherapeutic process. In this chapter, we have presented the developmental structuralist framework and its associated DIR model. We showed how this developmental model can deepen and broaden psychotherapeutic work with children and adults with a range of challenges. We also showed how it could be used as the basis for constructing individualized comprehensive programs for children with special needs.

REFERENCES

Bredekamp, S., & Copple, C. (Eds.). (1997). *Developmentally appropriate practices in early childhood programs*. Washington, DC: National Association for the Education of Young Children.

Bristol, M., Cohen, D., Costello, J., Denckla, M., Eckberg, T., Kallen, R., et al. (1996). State of the science in autism: Report to the National Institutes of Health. *Journal of Autism and Developmental Disorders, 26*, 121–154.

Carew, J. V. (1980). Experience and the development of intelligence in young children at home and in day care. *Monographs of the Society for Research in Child Development, 45*(607), 1–115.

Feuerstein, R., Miller, R., Hoffman, M., Rand, Y., Mintsker, Y., Morgens, R., et al. (1981). Cognitive modifiability in adolescence: Cognitive structure and the effects of intervention. *Journal of Special Education, 150*(2), 269–287.

Feuerstein, R., Rand, Y., Hoffman, M., & Miller, R. (1979). Cognitive modifiability in retarded adolescents: Effects of instrumental enrichment. *American Journal of Mental Deficiency, 83*(6), 539–550.

Greenspan, S. I. (1979a). Intelligence and adaptation: An integration of psychoanalytic and Piagetian developmental psychology. *Psychological Issues, Monograph 47/68*. New York: International Universities Press.

Greenspan, S. I. (1979b). Psychopathology and adaptation in infancy and early childhood: Principles of clinical diagnosis and preventive intervention. *Clinical Infant Reports, No. 1*. New York: International Universities Press.

Greenspan, S. I. (1989). *The development of the ego: Implications for personality theory, psychopathology, and the psychotherapeutic process.* Madison, CT: International Universities Press.

Greenspan, S. I. (1992). *Infancy and early childhood: The practice of clinical assessment and intervention with emotional and developmental challenges.* Madison, CT: International Universities Press.

Greenspan, S. I. (1997a). *Developmentally based psychotherapy.* New York: International Universities Press.

Greenspan, S. I. (1997b). *The growth of the mind and the endangered origins of intelligence.* Reading, MA: Addison-Wesley Longman.

Greenspan, S. I., DeGangi, G., & Wieder, S. (2001). *The Functional Emotional Assessment Scale (FEAS) for infancy and early childhood: Clinical and research applications.* Bethesda, MD: Interdisciplinary Council on Developmental and Learning Disorders.

Greenspan, S. I., & Wieder, S. (1997). Developmental patterns and outcomes in infants and children with disorders in relating and communicating: A chart review of 200 cases of children with autistic spectrum diagnoses. *Journal of Developmental and Learning Disorders, 1,* 87–141.

Greenspan, S. I., & Wieder, S. (1999). A functional developmental approach to autism spectrum disorders. *Journal of the Association for Persons with Severe Handicaps, 24*(3), 147–161.

Klein, P. S., Wieder, S., & Greenspan, S. I. (1987). A theoretical overview and empirical study of mediated learning experience: Prediction of preschool performance from mother-infant interaction patterns. *Infant Mental Health Journal, 89*(2), 110–129.

Mahler, M. S., Pine, F., & Bergman, A. (1975). *The psychological birth of the human infant.* New York: Basic Books.

Nemiah, J. C. (1977). *Alexithymia: Theories and models.* Proceedings of the eleventh European conference on psychosomatic research. Basel, Switzerland: Karger.

Piaget, J. (1962). The stages of intellectual development of the child. In S. Harrison & J. McDermott (Eds.), *Childhood psychopathology* (pp. 157–166). New York: International Universities Press.

Rogers, S. (1996). Brief report: Early intervention in autism. *Journal of Autism and Developmental Disorders, 26,* 243–246.

Rogers, S. J., & Lewis, H. (1989). An effective day treatment model for young children with pervasive developmental disorders. *Journal of the American Academy of Child and Adolescent Psychiatry, 28,* 207–214.

CHAPTER 3

Object-Relations Play Therapy

HELEN E. BENEDICT AND LARA HASTINGS

HISTORY OF THERAPEUTIC APPROACH

The model of object-relations play therapy to be presented in this chapter developed out of three major traditions: object-relations therapy with adults, play therapy, and developmental psychopathology. Whereas the first two traditions have often intersected to some degree, a fully elaborated play therapy approach has been lacking. The first application of the emerging object-relations theories to children is found in the work of Melanie Klein (1932). However, both play therapy and object-relations therapy, though building on some of Klein's revolutionary concepts, moved away from each other. Both departed from the therapy model of Klein, with each tradition developing independently. Only recently have there been significant attempts to integrate play therapy methods and current object-relations theories (Prior, 1996). Integrating an object-relations play therapy approach with current research findings from developmental psychopathology provides a powerful frame of reference for approaching relationally based child assessment and treatment.

Play therapy first began to be a significant factor in psychotherapy with children during the 1930s in the parallel development of the three psychoanalytically based but quite different play therapy approaches of Anna Freud (1936), Melanie Klein (1932), and Margaret Lowenfield (1939). All three approaches continued to develop, although Freud's work was ultimately more influential for play therapy than either Klein's or Lowenfield's. Another thread in the emergence of play therapy as it is practiced today is the structured therapy of Levy (1939) and Solomon (1938) that also first appeared in the 1930s. The structured approach has continued to develop through the work of Hambridge (1955), Gardner (1971), Jernberg (1979), and, more recently, Brody (1993).

Increasingly, two other major traditions have influenced the practice of play therapy. The first of these to develop, nondirective play therapy, grew out of relationship therapies, the work of Allen (1942) and applications of Carl Rogers's (1951) ideas by Virginia Axline (1947). Directive play therapies, representing a diversity of theoretical stances, emerged as a strong contrast to the Rogerian approach. These include Gestalt play therapy (Oaklander, 1988), filial therapy (Guerney, 1964), cognitive-behavior play therapy (Knell, 1993), Adlerian play therapy (Kottman, 1993), and ecosystemic play therapy (O'Connor, 1991).

By the early 1990s, there existed a rich tradition of play therapies, ranging from psychoanalytic to structured to nondirective and directive approaches. However, no single approach has emerged. Object-relations play therapy, while drawing its theoretical base from object-relations therapy with adults, has incorporated many techniques from various play therapy approaches including those from the psychoanalytic tradition (Prior, 1996) but also several from Axline (1964), Brody (1993), and O'Connor (1991).

THEORETICAL CONSTRUCTS

Object-relations theories center on two fundamental assumptions: First, the core of psychological functioning is believed to be the relationship between the self and significant others (Glickauf-Hughes & Wells, 1997); second, as development proceeds, interactions between the infant and significant others and the infant's emerging perception of those interactions become internalized as concepts or templates of the self, other, and self in relation to other. These "internal working models," which are essentially cognitive-affective structures, filter perceptions and shape the attitudes and reactions of the developing child's and eventually the adult's interpersonal relationships (Bowlby, 1988; Siegel, 1999). Internal working models thus first emerge in the context of experience of the earliest relationships in life, and interrelate as "object relations" that animate a person's understanding of and functioning in relationships. Throughout the life span, internal object relations not only influence but also are influenced by experience in relationships.

Many theorists have developed models that have contributed to the understanding of how "an individual's mental representations of self and others become enduring psychic structures" (Glickauf-Hughes & Wells, 1997, p. 18). These models started from a basic psychoanalytic viewpoint but often have been informed by the ego psychologist's emphasis on coping resources and experiential influences on psychological development, in contrast to traditional drive theory (Blanck & Blanck, 1986). The approach to object-relations play therapy presented here places particular emphasis on the works of Mahler and associates (Mahler, 1968; Mahler, Pine, & Bergman, 1975) and on concepts derived from the British object-relations school (Bowlby, 1988; Fairbairn, 1952; Winnicott, 1965, 1971a, 1971b), as well as Prior (1996), whose model integrates the trauma literature with concepts drawn from Kernberg (1966). Recent work in both neuroscience and developmental psychology, especially the works of Stern (1985), Schore (1994), and empirical studies of early attachment (Kraemer, 1992), have also contributed to the model presented.

Mahler, who based her model on detailed observations of young children in therapy and on mother-child pairs followed longitudinally over the first three years of life, proposed that the early development of object relations proceeded through three stages, culminating in the emergence of emotional object constancy around 3 years of age (Mahler, 1968; Mahler et al., 1975). These three stages, modified by the empirical work of Stern and others, provide the basic framework for conceptualization of the object-relations play therapy presented here. Mahler's first stage, normal autism, occurs over the first month of life. Whereas Mahler assumed the infant was objectless, Stern (1985) found evidence that infants are born with rudimentary object-relatedness. We want to avoid confusion with infantile autism as a disorder and adequately capture this rudimentary relatedness, and replace autism with the term *presymbiosis* here. The second stage is *normal symbiosis,* in which the infant functions as if the caregiver and infant form a dual unity, occurring from about 2 to 4 months of age. The third stage, *separation-individuation,* has been divided by Mahler into subphases: differentiation (about 4 to 11 months), in which the infant shifts from an inward-directed focus to outward-directed tension and alertness; practicing (about 11 to 17 months), in which the newly mobile infant moves away from the symbiotic orbit to explore the world, returning to the mother periodically for "refueling"; rapprochement (about 18 to 24 months), in which the toddler becomes increasingly aware of his or her vulnerability and thus seeks closeness with the mother, yet simultaneously has a strong need for separateness and autonomy; and "on the way to object constancy" (about 24 to 36 months), in which the toddler increasingly separates from the mother while integrating the good and bad parts of both the self and the object.

In the model presented here, we argue that when progress through Mahler's stages and substages is arrested or distorted, it results in characteristic patterns of relating and behaving depending on when the problem arises. Each point of arrest has a pattern of psychopathological functioning with unique dynamics that warrant particular therapeutic goals and techniques. Moreover, these behavioral patterns differ in important ways from presentations of pathology at the adult end of the developmental trajectory, presumed to have originated in unsuccessful negotiation of Mahler's stages.

Several representatives of the British object-relations school, notably Winnicott, Bowlby, and Fairbairn, have contributed concepts that we have incorporated in our model to clarify either the dynamics of object-relations development or therapeutic goals and techniques. Winnicott's (1971a) concept of the transitional object, a phenomenon that can be experienced or employed when the object is experienced as separate but not yet constant, is often consciously introduced in object-relations play therapy to facilitate constancy in the therapeutic relationship or to promote progress in separation-individuation. His notions of "good-enough mothering" and holding environment both emphasize the child's need, developmentally and within therapy, to be protected from impingement while also experiencing acceptance and having needs me (Abram, 1996). Winnicott's concept of attunement, where the caregiver is sensitive to the infant's needs and meets those needs accurately, describes an essential feature of the therapeutic relationship in this approach (Glickauf-Hughes & Wells, 1997). Finally, Winnicott (1965) describes a false self, where the child's compliance in an attempt to gain approval leads the child to lose ready access to the true self, which we propose is a key feature of arrested development at the time the child emerges from the rapprochement crisis. Fairbairn (1952) contributed the concept of obstinate attachment, which helps explain the paradox of young children remaining intensely attached to an abusive or nonattuned caregiver.

Bowlby (1988) articulated the concept of attachment as a neurologically based innate drive to seek security in relationships. Schore (1994) elaborates on the interface of neurological development in the attachment process and the evolution of object relations during the first three years of life. Increasingly, evidence is mounting that the mother-child relationship influences and is influenced by neurological development (Stern, 1985; Siegel, 1999). For example, the absence of what Schore calls the "mother-infant dance" has profound ramifications for neurological development as well as the development of attachment, particularly in the orbitofrontal cortex.

Another concept from Bowlby (1988), which has been empirically demonstrated in the work of Ainsworth and her students (Cicchetti, Toth,

& Lynch, 1995), is that of a secure base. In the presence of a secure base, the caregiver is perceived as safe, stable, and caring, enabling the infant to feel free to move away from the caregiver and explore the environment. As will be seen in the presentation of the actual therapy, establishing a secure base relationship is central to effective therapy.

Prior (1996) contributed to this approach in three ways. First, he applied Kernberg's (1966) concept of "unmetabolized object parts" to explain mechanisms of splitting in relationally traumatized children and account for episodes of rage in his object-relations model of child therapy for sexual abuse victims. His notion of relational trauma has significantly influenced our view of the types of psychopathology most appropriate for treatment using our approach. Prior also elaborates on Fairbairn's concept of obstinate attachment when he argues that through splitting, the child comes to attach all of the "bad" feelings and emerging object representations to the self to maintain the "good" parent representation needed for psychological survival in an abusive environment.

Thus, this model of object-relations play therapy integrates Mahler's stages of development of emotional object constancy with recent behavioral and neuropsychological research on early relationship development. This approach places central importance on the biological pathways for attachment and relationship development as they interface with the caregiving environment to direct neurological development of cognitive-affective structures called internal working models. These internal working models emerge early in life and continually evolve over the lifetime and serve to guide perceptions of and interactions with others. Although object relations theoretically can be modified throughout life, their plasticity is greatest in the first years of life. In experiences of relational trauma, internal working models and the neural networks they reflect become more rigid with ongoing development and can ultimately result in adult personality disorders that are resistant to treatment. The object-relations play therapy model thus argues that interventions based on developmentally sensitive understanding of object-relations dynamics and needs should be conducted in childhood, when the potential for change is greatest.

METHODS OF ASSESSMENT AND INTERVENTION

Assessment

Effective object-relations play therapy requires careful assessment of the child and the child's world. This assessment needs to focus on four major areas: developmental assessment, dynamic and object-relations evaluation, clinical diagnosis, and systems assessment. Only by understanding the child's developmental level for each of the ego functions, the dynamics of the child's emerging object relations, the child's clinical presentation, and the types of experiences the child has within the family and, when applicable, the school system can the therapist determine appropriate therapeutic goals for the child and broader systems.

Determining developmental level for a child requires observation and data gathering for each of the ego functions: language, cognition, perception, emotional, social, psychosexual, play, and motor development. Several sources of information can be used for this assessment, including observation, interviews with parents and teachers, and standardized instruments such as tests of adaptive, intelligence, achievement, neuropsychological or language functioning. (For an overview of developmental assessment, see O'Connor, 2001.) In this part of the assessment, it is crucial to be constantly aware of uneven development, as many children appropriate for object-relations play therapy may have cognitive and intellectual development far in advance of their social and emotional development or some other pattern of vastly uneven ego functions.

Assessing the dynamics of emerging objects relations for the child requires familiarity with each of the six object-relations presentations, which are detailed later in this chapter. Information relevant to determining the child's internal working models and interpersonal dynamics must come from several sources. The two primary sources for this part of the assessment are the parent history/interview and the child play assessment and interview. In the parent interview, which is also used to obtain information relevant to a formal diagnosis, historical information, especially on any interpersonal or attachment stress, should be combined with clinical judgment about the parents' personality functioning, parenting, and relationship to the child. Many types of information are accessible in a diagnostic play/interview session with the child. By examining the play themes and interpersonal relationships presented in the play as well as the relationship with the examiner during the assessment, the assessor often can gain a good understanding of the child's object relations. In addition, children over age 5 often provide quite direct information about how they approach the world and relationships and how they understand themselves in an interview.

Clinical evaluation requires obtaining a picture of the symptoms shown by the child leading to a *Diagnostic and Statistical Manual of Mental Disorders (DSM-IV)* diagnosis (American Psychiatric Association [APA], 1994). Again, many sources of data are available to complete this part of the assessment. In obtaining a formal diagnosis, historical information as well as the observations, interviews, and developmental assessment described above provide much needed information. Other tools that should be used include behavior checklists, such as the Child Behavior Checklist (Achenbach, 1991a, 1991b), formal diagnostic interviews, such as the Diagnostic Interview Scale for Children (Costello, Edelbrock, Duncan, Kalas, & Klaric, 1987), and projective testing, such as drawing tests (Allan, 1988), storytelling tasks, and the Rorschach (Kelly, 1999).

Finally, the assessment of the child requires an evaluation of the broader systems in which the child functions, family and school being most important. At the immediate family level, such techniques as Marshak Interaction Method (Lindaman, Booth, & Chambers, 2000), interviews of adult attachment status, direct observation of unstructured parent-child interaction, and home visits can be extremely helpful when combined with the history interview. The school environment can be assessed using teacher behavior checklists and questionnaires, interviews with the teacher, and school visits. Both for school and for the broader family system, sources of strength for the child and factors that appear to maintain the less adaptive child behaviors should be assessed (O'Connor, 2000).

Intervention planning is the ultimate goal of assessment. In object-relations play therapy, the clinical and object-relations presentation level is determined and therapeutic goals and techniques are chosen that are appropriate to the child's developmental level and diagnostic formulation. Possible interventions in addition to play therapy, such as interventions at the family or school level, are determined through the same assessment process.

INTERVENTION

When utilizing an object-relations approach, establishing the therapist-child relationship first initiates and then centers the entire therapeutic process. When distortions or disruptions in the development of object relations occur, trust becomes the central issue in establishing the therapeutic relationship. For many of the children most in need of object-relations play therapy, establishing such trust can be an extended process. The therapist should foster this "secure base" relationship through several means. First, the therapist must show a warm, caring, and accepting attitude toward the child. Second, the therapist must be sensitive to the child's needs. In essence, the therapeutic relationship should mimic the attunement characteristic of the "good-enough" caregiver's behavior across the first few years of life needed to develop a strong attachment between child and caregiver. Such attunement requires both understanding the child's current situation as well as anticipating the child's future needs. This can be achieved through matching the child's affect or mood, using reflections to track the child's activities, imitating the child, or accepting the child's requests to imitate him or her. In addition, attunement is demonstrated when the therapist helps the child meet his or her needs.

There are several additional ways to foster the "secure base" relationship in play therapy. Consistency on the part of the therapist helps provide a sense of safety within which trust can develop. Consistency of contact (e.g., weekly sessions) may be supplemented by consistent routines for beginning and ending the session and consistency of space. It is important that the office/playroom remain as constant as possible. This requires that the toys be stored in predictable places from week to week, that children not be allowed to take toys away from the room, and that when new toys are added, the child is told so there are no surprises.

The therapist is responsible for providing a sense of safety, both physical and psychological, throughout the therapeutic process. Physical safety would seem quite easy to provide. However, many children with attachment disorders or a history of interpersonal trauma play dangerously and take many risks, making the assurance of physical safety something requiring deliberate attention from the therapist. A sense of safety can include stating the playroom rules in terms of making sure both child and therapist are safe, maintaining physical proximity when the child chooses to jump or climb on furniture, and even holding the child if necessary to keep the child safe.

Psychological safety builds on the warmth, attunement, consistency, and provision of physical safety described above. In addition, it requires that the therapist be able to comfortably handle the child's expected attempts to control the therapist as well as the child's distortions around anger. Because children who have experienced interpersonal trauma typically have difficulties with anger, either expressing it in out-of-control ways or inhibiting it when it should be expressed, the therapist must be able to challenge such distortions in understanding of anger. This includes encouraging expression of anger while providing containment of its excesses through limit setting. In addition, allowing and containing expressions of anger without either withdrawing emotionally from the child or returning anger with anger shows the child that anger does not have to destroy relationships.

Once the secure base relationship is established, the working phase of therapy begins. The therapeutic goal of this phase of treatment is to modify the child's internal working model of the self, other, and self in relation with other through stimulating, challenging, and encouraging the development of alternatives to the existing model. The therapist accomplishes this goal by integrating child-responsive and invitational play therapy techniques based on themes and relationships encoded in the child's play with a theoretical formulation based on the child's developmental object-relations presentation.

Object-Relations Play Therapy Technique
Object-relations play therapy technique involves three essential components for effective intervention. First, this approach requires that the therapist be child-responsive: Each intervention by the therapist occurs in attuned responsiveness to the child's play and patterns

of interaction with the therapist (Benedict & Mongoven, 1997). The therapist participates actively in the therapeutic relationship, moving between nondirective and directive interventions as needed in response both to the specific therapeutic goals for the child and the child's ongoing play content and interactions with the therapist.

Second, object-relations play therapy requires the therapist to be centered on the developmental level and needs of the child. As discussed earlier, the therapist's understanding of the child's developmental level, both in terms of the child's progress in achieving object constancy and the child's ego functions, including language, cognition, emotional, and social development, serves to guide each intervention. Only when the therapist adjusts interactions to the child's developmental level can the therapist be fully "attuned" to the child.

The third aspect of this approach concerns the interventions made by the therapist. To maintain the secure base relationship while challenging the child's internal working models, each actual intervention of the therapist must be "invitational" in nature (Gil, 1991). Essentially, the therapist offers to the child new directions for play and new possible ways of interacting with the therapist (and, by extension, others) through open-ended overtures within the play. These invitations can be accepted and used by the child or ignored and even rejected with no negative consequences to the relationship with the therapist or to the child's sense of safety in the play room. For example, a young boy might be playing a scene where the "good guy" is trying to control the "scary monster" that is imagined to be in the room. The therapist might offer the child an invitation, such as "Maybe the good guy can build a wall to keep the monster away." In response, the child might look for blocks to build a wall, even asking the therapist to help with the building, or the child might ignore the invitation or shift play to some other theme. Any of these or other possible responses from the child is fully acceptable to the therapist.

Child-responsive, developmentally sensitive, and invitational play therapy relies heavily on the therapist's understanding of the child's play. That understanding is facilitated by awareness of the possible meanings of various common themes seen in therapeutic play. When engaging in imaginative or fantasy play, children tend to play certain easily identified themes having to do with such important broad content areas as aggressive and power concerns, family and nurturance, safety and control, exploration and mastery, and sexuality. A specific example of one of these themes is "nurturing" play, where a character within the play is offering some sort of nurturance by cooking for, feeding, giving gifts to, or caregiving another character. Another theme is "fixing," where one character "repairs" a "broken" object or "doctors" a sick or hurt (that is, broken in some way) character.

Recent research by the authors and their associates has codified the commonly seen play themes and examined the typical themes in play for children with differing interpersonal histories and different presentations of object-relations development (Benedict & Shelton, 1996; Benedict et al., 1966; Holmberg, Benedict, & Hynan, 1998; McClain, 1998; McGee, 1998; Narcavage, 1998; Wooley, 1998). By attending to these themes, the therapist can understand the child's metaphoric presentation of concerns, confusions, and interpersonal relationship issues. The therapist thus observes, and interacts, in the child's play in such a way that the therapist forms hypotheses about possible meanings each theme has for the child. The therapist uses these hypotheses, in conjunction with his or her understanding of the child's object-relations presentation, to issue invitations within the play metaphor that serve to challenge or stimulate the child to modify existing object relations in healthier directions. Play themes thus function as a major tool for the therapist. Understanding the themes the child plays spontaneously provides a window to the child's object relations, and issuing invitations within the themes enables the child to understand the therapist's communications and use them to facilitate growth in an environment of safety.

A second tool important to effective object-relations play therapy focuses not on the content of the play but on the affects and interactional patterns demonstrated through the play. Our laboratory has codified these into an interpersonal relations and affect coding system, which can also be reliably used to understand the child's object relations (Benedict, Hastings, Ato, Carson, & Nash, 1998). Some of the interactional patterns so coded are boundary setting and boundary violation, control, imitation, helping, sharing, and protecting. Some of the affective expressions coded are anger, sadness, and rejection. By observing the interaction patterns and affects in the child's play, the therapist gains insight into the object relations of the child. By then offering child-responsive invitations, the therapist can sensitively challenge and modify those object relations for that child.

Finally, two "process" codes, which essentially codify relationships between themes or interpersonal codes, have been identified that greatly facilitate the therapist's understanding of the child's object relations. The first of these, called *doing and undoing*, draws attention to the expression of ambivalence. Children who experience attachment disorders or interpersonal traumas at a young age and thus show delays and distortions in development of object constancy and healthy object relations often feel intensely ambivalent about the important people or objects in their world. Yet, developmental research by Susan Harter (1983) and others shows that children's cognitive understanding and direct verbal expression of ambivalent feelings develop slowly and do not appear consistently until children are between 8 and 10 years old. Thus, young children express ambivalence by rapidly shifting the valence of the interaction during play. For example, a child might alternately kill and then hug the mommy figure. Similarly, a 4-year-old boy fed the therapist soup and, just as the therapist began eating, calmly said it was "poison."

A second type of process code important in object-relations play therapy is *stage mix*. In this play, the child has a character simultaneously play two distinct developmental stages at the same time. This type of play suggests a lack of boundaries between roles and is frequently seen when the child is "parentified" or "burdened" by needing to take care of a parent (Chase, 1999). An example of this is a child who put on the "wedding dress" in the playroom and walked around the room in the dress sucking on a baby bottle (Grigoryev, personal communication, 1996). Trina, whose therapy is described at the end of this chapter, used stage mix in her play, where it seemed to reflect her confusion about roles in her relationship with both her mother and her custodial grandmother.

Conceptualizations of Developmental Level of Disordered Object Relations

Disordered object relations can occur at several points in the development of object constancy, as proposed by Mahler et al. (1975). The nature of the child-caregiver relationship, including the contributions of the child's temperament and biological givens and the contributions from the caregiver, determines whether the child develops healthy, distorted, or arrested object relations. Disturbed object relations color the child's negotiation of subsequent developmental tasks and relationships. Six characteristic patterns of disordered object relations have been proposed by Glickauf-Hughes and Wells (1997) as a framework for understanding adult psychopathology. In our clinical practice, we have identified a parallel set of clinical presentations that appear to represent the early manifestations of disturbed object relations in young children.

The six childhood presentations, although similar in dynamics to the proposed origins of adult personality problems, differ from the adult patterns in significant ways. Whereas adult patterns represent fully internalized object relations, children's patterns are a combination of early, incompletely developed object relations and actual interaction patterns occurring in real time in the child's life with significant attachment figures. Such emerging object relations are more plastic than those seen in adults and more open to clinical intervention. Therefore, the relationship between child and therapist has significantly more elements of a real relationship that offers an alternative object around which object relations can be formed or modified than has the relationship between adult and therapist. Although the child may show some transference-like elements, much of the therapeutic work occurs within the actual relationship between child and therapist. The ongoing contributions of the current caregiver-child system to the child's emerging object relations place an additional challenge for the therapist, requiring intervention where possible in that system as an adjunct to therapy with the child.

Each of the six presentations can be characterized in terms of the probable early experiences in the child-caregiver relationship that set the stage for the emergence of disturbed object relations and the internal working models of self, other, and relationships that appear to be emerging for the child. Each of the six presentations also can be characterized in terms of the child's prominent play themes, with their probable meanings for the child and the interpersonal relationships expressed in play. From these, one can create a dynamic formulation that in turn guides therapeutic goals and interventions.

The presymbiotic and early symbiotic presentation, the earliest presentation to develop, has its roots in the first few months of life, when the infant requires an engaged, attuned caregiver to develop a basic sense of trust. When such a caregiver is not available, whether because of maternal pathology, such as severe depression, substance abuse, or personality disorder, or the child's inability to respond to the world because of prematurity, neurological problems, or sensory deficits, or some combination of both, the infant's emerging object relations show distortions in trust, interpersonal connections, ability to accept nurturing, and poor self-regulation. Table 3.1 outlines these dynamics and presents the prominent play themes and interpersonal relationships with their meanings, as well as therapeutic goals and appropriate therapeutic techniques to meet those goals.

The second presentation to emerge developmentally focuses on problems occurring during two of Mahler's stages and is called a practicing and rapprochement presentation. The caregiver-child system for this presentation appears unable to negotiate the child's attempts to separate and individuate, resulting in a lack of self-constancy, self-fragmentation, splitting between negative and positive thoughts and negative and positive part objects, and intense expression of ambivalence. Table 3.2 outlines the characteristics of this presentation. As can be seen from this table, a practicing and rapprochement problem will produce quite different dynamics, play themes, relationship patterns, and therapeutic goals than those characteristic of presymbiotic and symbiotic presentations.

The third presentation seen clinically, called compromised rapprochement, emerges during or just after Mahler's rapprochement phase. Here, the child seems to have resolved the ambivalence in a way that severely compromises the child's emerging internal working model of the self, others, and relationships. Table 3.3 outlines the characteristics of this presentation. These children present as estranged from genuine feelings and needs, relating to others as part objects to fill needs, with the result that they appear both pseudomature and pseudoautonomous. It is this group that most clearly demonstrates the false self of Winnicott (1965).

Table 3.1 Dynamics and treatment of presymbiotic and early symbiotic presentations.

Probable early experiences and relationships:	Neglect, rejection, invalidation of child's being, attunement failure.
Internal working model of self and other:	Lack of basic trust of others.
	Self that resists interpersonal connection and nurturing.
	Minimal self-regulation or ability to modulate affect.
Internal working model of relationships:	Withdrawal from others; largely defensive.
Dynamic formulation:	Self is detached, with rigid boundaries between self and other; underlying fear of self-fragmentation if needs and feelings are expressed or acknowledged.

Prominent Play Themes	*Meanings of Play Themes*
Aggression: Any general aggression or aggression where there is an "aggressor" and a "victim."	Child may have angry feelings without any clear sense of why feeling angry; child may be affectively stimulated, which leads to an explosion of feeling; child may have strong angry feelings expressed in role of aggressor; victim role may indicate a sense of no control over daily life.
Constancy: Hide-and-seek, mirror play, and other activities that seem to focus on establishing the child's identity or the constancy of others' identity.	Child has tenuous sense of trust and is using games to test therapist's trustworthiness; child has difficulty maintaining a constant image of important adults and uses separation and reunion to help build such an image; child has difficulty maintaining a constant image of self and is fascinated by representations of self-constancy (e.g., mirrors, self-naming).
Nurturing: Positive nurturing activities such as feeding, giving, or holding.	Child may need nurturance but feel unsafe expressing dependency needs.
Self-nurturing: Nurturing directed at self, as when the child, as "baby," feeds or comforts self.	Child needs nurturance but doesn't trust the world to provide it so self-nurtures; child is pseudoautonomous because of lack of confidence in others to provide care and protection.
Instability: Play in which people or things are falling off surfaces or are precariously balanced as if to fall, or when things fall apart, such as the walls of a house falling down.	Child may see danger in the world; child may feel fragmented and "unstable" in the world, especially when the child is the one about to fall.

Interpersonal/Process Codes	*Meanings of Interpersonal/Process Codes*
Roughhousing: Child seeks to engage the therapist in positively toned toddlerlike physical play, such as tickling or being picked up.	Child may be regressing to toddler-type interactions in the service of reworking symbiosis stage; child may be seeking physical comfort but needs to request it indirectly; child may have limited sense of "bodily self" and seeks roughhousing to establish boundaries and closeness with therapist.

Table 3.1 *(Continued)*

Interpersonal/Process Codes	Meanings of Interpersonal/Process Codes
Fusion: Child directly plays out a lack of boundary between self and therapist (e.g., drawing self and therapist's faces within a single head outline).	Child may be returning to the symbiosis stage as a secondary presymbiosis-symbiosis reworking; suggests progress.
Imitation-control: Child demands that the therapist imitate the child's verbalizations or behaviors.	Child uses projective identification to facilitate a symbiotic transference with the therapist; suggests progress.
Doing and undoing: Child plays a theme immediately followed by a theme with opposite meaning or valence, such as aggression followed by a display of affection.	Change in meaning or valence suggests conflict and mixed feelings around issues expressed in play or interpersonal behavior.
(a) *Boundary setting/boundary violation:* Establishing and then violating boundaries, such as when a character closes a house door against a monster who then breaks down the door and comes into the house.	(a) Child is uncertain about the integrity of own boundaries.
(b) *Anger/affection:* Directly expressed anger or hostility toward a character or the therapist, followed by expressed affection.	(b) Child has feelings of anger toward caregiver related to perceived deprivation, and feels expression of anger is unacceptable, so tries to undo it with affection.

Therapeutic Goals	Therapeutic Techniques toward Goals
Facilitate receptivity to nurturance, and then connectedness.	Create safe holding environment by emphasizing emotional and physical safety.
Establish symbiotic transference from which client can separate adaptively.	Show attunement by mirroring and reflecting child's feelings. Provide context of constancy by providing transitional pictures, verbalizing shared memories, and preserving traces of child's play.
Establish cohesive, nondefensively based sense of self.	Provide safety for child's recognition and expression of needs.
Facilitate self-regulation skills.	Invite body expression of feelings and relate to verbal expressions. Provide structure around physical contact to establish boundaries, encourage self-awareness, and facilitate self-regulation.
Promote ability to tolerate, label, and verbalize feelings.	Contain, reflect, and provide safety around feelings.
Probable developmental trajectory:	Schizoid personality.

Table 3.2 Dynamics and treatment of practicing and rapprochement presentations.

Probable early experiences and relationships:	Caregiver withdraws attention, support, and/or approval as child attempts to separate and individuate; likely to be personality problems or severe psychopathology in caregiver.
Internal working model of self and other:	Lack of self-constancy, with splitting of negative and positive thoughts, perceptions, and feelings.
	Self-fragmentation and regression likely.
	Objects not constant and fragmented with splitting between positive and negative part objects, leading to rapid shifts in mood and behavior.
Internal working model of relationships:	Extremely ambivalent close relationships that alternate between clinging and rage; moving into and away from relationship.
	Separation-individuation process incomplete; often arrested at rapprochement crisis.
Dynamic formulation:	Anxiety related to conflicts around engulfment and abandonment; strong fear of both self-fragmentation and loss of object.

Prominent Play Themes	*Meanings of Play Themes*
Constancy: Hide-and-seek, mirror play, and other activities that seem to focus on establishing the child's identity or the constancy of others' identity.	Child has difficulty maintaining a constant mental image of important adults and uses the separation and reunion to help build such an image; child has difficulty maintaining a constant image of self and is fascinated by representations of self constancy (e.g., mirrors, self-naming).
Separation: Child plays out someone leaving or separating from another character.	Child is reenacting separation/individuation through play typical of toddlers either at the practicing or rapprochement stage; child has an anxious attachment to the caregiver and practices controlling who moves away; child may view separation from caregiver as punishment.
Good guy versus bad guy: Aggressive play in which good/bad characters are clearly identified.	Child is engaging in splitting as a defense against simultaneous awareness of contradictory feelings about self or others; child may not have made developmentally appropriate progress in ability to accept and integrate both good and bad parts of self and others.
Sorting: Child lines thing up or sorts them into categories, such as nice animals and mean animals.	Child sorts in an attempt to separate good from bad things as part of defensive splitting or ambivalence about important relationships; sorting can represent the emergence of compulsive defenses to manage out-of-control internal experience.

Table 3.2 *(Continued)*

Interpersonal/Process Codes	Meanings of Interpersonal/Process Codes
Control: Child or character is bossy or directive, ordering either therapist or another character around.	Child may feel world is chaotic, and attempts to gain security by means of controlling others.
Stage mix: Child plays two different stages of the life span simultaneously within one character (e.g., a baby doing an adult activity such as driving a car).	Child may be living in an environment where roles are unclear, such as a parent enacting projective identification with the child; child may not have developed stable object constancy and shifts roles rapidly because of uncertainty about role boundaries.
Doing and undoing: Child plays a theme immediately followed by a theme with opposite meaning or valence, such as aggression followed by a display of affection.	Change in meaning or valence suggests conflict and mixed feelings around issues expressed in play or interpersonal behavior.
(a) *Fusion/separation:* Child fuses with and then separates from therapist.	(a) Suggests conflict involving wish to fuse (and internalize good object) and simultaneous fear of engulfment.
(b) *Boundary setting/boundary violation:* Establishing and then violating boundaries, such as when a character closes a house door against a monster who then breaks down the door and comes into the house.	(b) Child is uncertain about the integrity of own boundaries.
(c) *Anger/affection:* Directly expressed anger or hostility toward a character or the therapist, followed by expressed affection.	(c) Child has feelings of anger toward caregiver related to perceived deprivation, and feels expression of anger is unacceptable, so tries to undo it with affection.

Therapeutic Goals	Therapeutic Techniques toward Goals
Facilitate separation and individuation.	Be a "secure base" from which child can explore.
Integrate split representations of self and other.	Function as a container for child's ambivalence by providing safety, empathy, and validation during play; remain constant despite child's changeable affect and behavior.
Help develop object constancy.	Foster constancy through facilitating memories and preserving play traces, and providing constant therapeutic setting.
Foster integrated sense of self.	Encourage and support genuine self-expression, and awareness and definition of boundaries, through labeling motives, affect, and behaviors and their interconnections in play.
Increase frustration tolerance.	Set appropriate limits but give choices; verbalize limits and anticipate consequences of dangerous or inappropriate behavior.
Probable developmental trajectory:	Borderline personality.

Table 3.3 Dynamics and treatment of compromised rapprochement presentations.

Probable early experiences and relationships:	Rejection of child's expression of needs and feelings; use of child to meet caregiver's needs; admiration and approval of child as reflection of caregiver, rather than love and acceptance of child as own person.
Internal working model of self and other:	Self estranged from genuine needs and feelings, with little ability to self-soothe or be playful or spontaneous.
	Relates to others more as part objects to fill needs than as integrated people with needs and feelings of their own.
Internal working model of relationships:	May manipulate or control others (as in controlling caregiving), frequently idealizing or devaluing aspects of others.
Dynamic formulation:	Child presents a false self that is pseudomature and pseudoautonomous, with little awareness of needs and feelings. There is the illusion that separation-individuation has been resolved, but this "resolution" is based on maintaining connection to a good internal object by compromising authentic needs and feelings. Anxiety relates to fears of loss of object or approval. Lack of playfulness reveals inhibition and anxiety about play and self-exploration, as knowing self is perceived as unsafe. Obstinate attachment, where child defensively identifies with a bad object to maintain connection to the good object, is often present.

Prominent Play Themes	*Meanings of Play Themes*
Self-nurturing: Nurturing directed at self, as when the child, as "baby," feeds or comforts self.	Child has been parentified and thus is hyperresponsible; suggests child does not trust others to meet needs and must do it alone.
Nurturing: Positive nurturing activities such as feeding, giving, or holding.	Child has been parentified and tries to gain acceptance from therapist by nurturing or taking care of him or her.
Constancy: Hide-and-seek, mirror play, and other activities that seem to focus on establishing the child's identity or the constancy of others' identity.	Hiding things may be hinting that there are parts of the self hidden; child hides as a way of maintaining connection and constancy from a distance.
Store/shopping: Child sets up a store where child or therapist shops or a character goes shopping.	Child wants to be in control of how needs are met.
Mastery: Child builds something or shows ability to perform some skill or ability.	Child may need to be able to do more adult things to feel safe, especially if child has been parentified; child may show mastery at the beginning of therapy to mask fear and anxiety, or to prove to the therapist that the child is somehow not "bad" or needing help.

Table 3.3 (*Continued*)

Interpersonal/Process Codes	Meanings of Interpersonal/Process Codes
Control: Child or character is bossy or directive, ordering either therapist or another character around.	Child is trying to order world and empower self; child may feel internal world is chaotic and controls others in an effort to feel more secure.
Independence: Child refuses help and insists on doing something alone in a context where child is realistically dependent on adult for help.	Child may be parentified and feel he or she must take care of things by self; child may show a false or pseudoautonomy as a defense against feelings of vulnerability; child is so threatened by unmet intense dependency needs that he or she has resolved not to need anyone.
Teasing: One character playfully tricks or teases another (not hostile).	Child may be teasing to test the therapist's psychological safety; child may use teasing to keep the therapist at a distance, especially when difficult issues are being approached.
Imitation-control: Child demands that the therapist imitate the child's verbalizations or behaviors.	Child may use imitation as a way of controlling others (see Control).
Stage mix: Child plays two different stages of the life span simultaneously within one character (e.g., a baby doing an adult activity such as driving a car).	Child may have developed a false self and show both false mature self and unmet needs of infantile self simultaneously; child may be parentified.

Therapeutic Goals	Therapeutic Techniques toward Goals
Develop ability to connect with others in an authentic way.	Model healthy boundaries and verbally address boundary issues within context of genuine relationship where therapist avoids "blank slate" in favor of sharing selective appropriate parts of therapist's real self.
Help child understand needs and feelings of others and relinquish need to control others through caretaking.	Show attunement and respect boundaries, enabling rather than challenging child's controlling play.
Encourage child's capacity for age-appropriate play.	Provide a safe holding environment offering external source of safety (e.g., invite rescue), and assure child's safety during play.
Increase child's awareness of genuine self, both needs and feelings.	Encourage labeling and verbalization of hidden feelings; support strengths and empathize with vulnerabilities by affirming abilities, encouraging problem solving, and identification of child's coping and behavior patterns.
Help child develop ability to self-soothe.	Model soothing and self-care with characters and identify needs of characters in play; show ways they can gratify needs adaptively.
Probable developmental trajectory:	Narcissistic personality.

Table 3.4 Dynamics and treatment of "On the Way to Object Constancy" presentations.

Probable early experiences and relationships:	Abuse and/or neglect, with inconsistent meeting of dependency needs; scapegoating and/or parentification; control of child by a caregiver lacking in self-control; disempowerment of the child.
Internal working model of self and other:	Self shows some constancy with at least some awareness of needs and feelings, but overall self lacks integration.
	Uneven ego strength, so will show difficulty with one or more of the following: self-regulation, delay of gratification, anticipation of consequences, or stress tolerance.
	Hidden self, where child is caught between the wish to be found and the terror of being discovered.
	Sees others as not constant, alluring but unreliable in meeting child's needs.
Internal working model of relationships:	Alternating anxious attachment and counterdependence.
	Overtly compliant but defiant in covert, passive ways.
	General passivity in relationships.
Dynamic formulation:	A basic failure to identify with caregiver, and thus lack of appropriate internalization of caregiver's self-soothing capacities, empathy, or auxiliary ego functions, which at this stage of development should be part of self-representations and functions. Anxiety relates to fear of loss of approval and/or autonomy. Child lacks ability to self-soothe.

Prominent Play Themes	*Meanings of Play Themes*
Safety: Focus is on establishing safety for the child or an identified character; can involve keeping something inside/outside a particular space, and keeping characters out of danger.	Child may feel it is important to keep feelings contained, particularly angry feelings; child may come from a home where it is not acceptable to talk about things, and uses containers to carefully enclose loaded issues; child may feel a need to protect important others (including their feelings); child is seeking to protect self from dangers.
Nurturing: Positive nurturing activities such as feeding, giving, or holding.	Child has been parentified and tries to gain acceptance from therapist by nurturing or taking care of him or her; child may show self-nurturance because he or she does not trust others to meet needs and must do it alone.
Danger: Potential danger is identified and needs to be addressed; can include dangerous characters and dangerous places.	Child may be indicating a sense that world is unsafe; indication of "dangerous" feelings inside, which cannot be revealed, as well as perceived threat of exposure; can represent perceptions of underground family tensions.
Aggression: Any general aggression or aggression where there is an "aggressor" and a "victim."	Child may be expressing formerly repressed anger about previous victimization in real life.

Table 3.4 *(Continued)*

Prominent Play Themes	Meanings of Play Themes
Good guy versus bad guy: Aggressive play in which good/bad characters are clearly identified.	Child is engaging in splitting as a defense against simultaneous awareness of contradictory feelings about self or others; child may not have made developmentally appropriate progress in ability to accept and integrate both good and bad parts of self and others; child may be preoccupied with questions of good and badness, being "super good" to win approval of others; child must be constantly vigilant in play so that "bad" behavior doesn't occur.
Broken: A character is broken, sick, or hurt and needs to be fixed.	Child may be indicating broken relationships in own life; suggests feelings that world is broken and thus unsafe; broken house suggests that home is perceived as unsafe, unstable, or breaking apart (as in divorce); child's developing self-representation may be fragmented or not yet integrated.
Fixing: Something broken is fixed by repairs.	May be an attempt to "undo" previous aggressive play that child fears is unacceptable.
Interpersonal/Process Codes	*Meanings of Interpersonal/Process Codes*
Positive connection: Play that emphasizes a positive connection between two characters but is not openly affectionate.	Child is "refueling" on positive play before returning to major issues that are difficult to play about.
Boundary setting: Where play imposes a physical boundary between two people or characters.	Child may use boundaries to establish a sense of personal safety; represents an attempt to rework rapprochement, with setting boundaries as part of the struggle to individuate.
Protect: Play where a stronger (or adult) character acts to protect weaker (or child) character.	Child may be showing that a character needs protection.
Doing and undoing: Child plays a theme immediately followed by a theme with opposite meaning or valence, such as aggression followed by a display of affection.	Change in meaning or valence suggests conflict and mixed feelings around issues expressed in play or interpersonal behavior.
(a) *Safety/danger:* Child establishes safe place and then danger intrudes.	(a) Child worries about lack of safety and vulnerability to danger, suggesting child is uncertain whether he or she will be able to be safe in a threatening environment.
(b) *Broken/fixing:* Something is hurt or broken, and then fixed.	(b) Child is concerned with perceptions of injury, damage, or vulnerability in the self, caregiver, or family; fixing suggests either hope or emerging empowerment.
(c) *Boundary setting/boundary violation:* See Table 3.1.	(c) Child is uncertain about the integrity of own boundaries.

(continued)

Table 3.4 *(Continued)*

Therapeutic Goals	Therapeutic Techniques toward Goals
Resolve ambivalent attachment to caregiver and/or grieve separation and loss.	Be emotionally available without being either controlling or infantilizing.
Build child's trust in those who can meet the child's needs.	Provide constancy and attunement to child, reflecting child's feelings and preserving child's play traces and memories.
Foster appropriate levels of assertiveness.	Model healthy boundary setting for child and verbalize child being in charge of own boundaries and rights to feel differently from others.
Increase frustration and stress tolerance, focusing on self-soothing and self-esteem.	Help child anticipate consequences and verbally connect distress and anxiety to sources of frustration and stress. Encourage developmental body play for enhancing self-soothing.
Encourage child's valuing of own needs as much as the needs of others so child loses need to have a hidden self.	Provide safe holding environment for expression of needs and feelings and serve as a container for negative affects.
Foster an integrated, stable sense of self.	Encourage genuine self-expression, validate needs and feelings, and affirm value of child's hidden self.
Probable developmental trajectory:	Dependent, passive, avoidant features.

When a child experiences attachment or interpersonal trauma following relatively successful negotiation of the rapprochement phase within Mahler's stages, the resulting dynamics and internal working models are generally less impaired than when trauma occurs before this point. The fourth presentation occurs during the phase Mahler calls "on the way to object constancy" and is outlined in Table 3.4. In some ways, these children present like children showing compromised rapprochement, but the estrangement from feelings is much less complete. Thus, although these children do have some self-awareness, they lack an integrated self and show uneven ego strength with some difficulty with self-regulation, delay of gratification, anticipation of consequences, or stress tolerance. Often passive in relationships, these children tend to vacillate between overt compliance and covert resistance.

The final presentation prior to the development of object constancy occurs in the late separation-individuation phase. Children with this presentation are typically oppositional and tend to be preoccupied with feelings of shame and doubt and a sense of being unable to meet high internal standards for behavior. The dynamics, themes, interpersonal relationships, and therapeutic goals and techniques of this presentation are outlined in Table 3.5. Play during therapy for these children is often inhibited or stereotyped, with intense need to be in control of the situation, again requiring differing goals and techniques during treatment.

The final presentation to emerge developmentally is a post-Oedipal presentation, which is presented in Table 3.6. Although these children appear to have self and object constancy and generally good ego functions, they also tend to act out conflicts and fail to rely on the ego functions they have developed. They tend to work to gain approval of others through an exaggerated dependency and/or seductiveness with a limited sense of initiative and often considerable confusion about affectional and sexual needs.

Table 3.5 Dynamics and treatment of late separation-individuation presentations.

Probable early experiences and relationships:	Overcontrolling caregiver, restricting the child's impulses, affects, and autonomous behaviors.
Internal working model of self and other:	Self preoccupied with feelings of shame and doubt, with a restricted sense of autonomy.
	Self-presentation is self-contained or inhibited with a pseudoautonomous stance; sees self as unable to meet high internal standards for behavior.
	Sees others as potentially out of control or dangerous and a threat to child's sense of control.
Internal working model of relationships:	Relationships focus on power struggles with considerable oppositionality, sometimes to the point of little genuine connection outside of the need for control.
Dynamic formulation:	Child has stable sense of self but lacks integration of affective experience into core self. Child is preoccupied with need to keep the world organized and manageable to compensate for feelings of being out of control; the result is compulsiveness and rigidity with feelings of shame when control isn't maintained. Child often engages in stereotyped, repetitive, or inhibited play and lacks spontaneity. Any sense of losing control leads to anxiety, as does failure to meet internal standards, which are often excessively high and/or rigid.

Prominent Play Themes	*Meanings of Play Themes*
Instability: Play in which people or things are falling off surfaces or are precariously balanced as if to fall, or when things fall apart, such as the walls of a house falling down.	Child may feel or fear world is falling apart; child may see danger in the world.
Cleaning: Cleaning spontaneously or talking about cleaning something dirty or nasty.	May indicate a child who manages anxiety by keeping everything clean and perfect.
Sorting: Child lines thing up or sorts them into categories; such as nice animals and mean animals.	Child feels or fears that world is chaotic and is trying to establish a sense of order.
Danger: Potential danger is identified and needs to be addressed; can include dangerous characters and dangerous places.	Child may be indicating a sense that the world is unsafe.
Power: Involves power relationships, with emphasis on strength and differential power.	Child is feeling weak and wants to feel strong; child may be identifying with strong person.
Fail: Lack of ability to master tasks undertaken, or lack of confidence in ability (e.g., giving up easily, apparent frustration).	Child may set unrealistically high internal standards that engender anxiety, shame, self-doubt if/when not met.

(continued)

Table 3.5 *(Continued)*

Interpersonal/Process Codes	Meanings of Interpersonal/Process Codes
Control: Child or character is bossy or directive, ordering either therapist or another character around.	Child may feel internal world is chaotic and controls others in an effort to feel more secure; child is trying to order the world and empower the self; child may need to control the interpersonal interaction to maintain an appropriate level of personal safety; maintains connection with distance so that relationship is less threatening and basic conflict stays out of awareness.
Boundary violation: Violation or overstepping of literal or figurative boundaries, whether interpersonally or in play.	Child may feel endangered physically or psychologically, as if boundaries are at risk of intrusions.
Refusal to cooperate: Child or character in play refuses to cooperate when such cooperation would normally occur in the play.	Child may be focused on establishing independence and autonomy; child may use oppositionality to test the therapist's willingness to give the control in the therapy setting to the child.
Doing and undoing: Child plays a theme immediately followed by a theme with opposite meaning or valence, such as aggression followed by a display of affection.	Change in meaning or valence suggests conflict and mixed feelings around issues expressed in play or interpersonal behavior.
(a) *Independence/dependence:* Child insists on doing alone a task where help is realistically needed and then insists on help on another task where none is needed.	(a) Child feels compelled to strive for self-sufficiency because of perceived inability of caregivers to meet needs; conflict suggests that the child feels unequipped to achieve self-sufficiency, though perceives self-sufficiency as the safest, surest route to getting needs met.
(b) *Danger/escape:* Child plays about a danger from which the character escapes.	(b) Child worries about danger but sees self as responsible for avoiding or escaping danger.
(c) *Mastery/failure:* Child alternately succeeds and fails to mastery an activity.	(c) Child vacillates between successful mastery and a sense of failure because of impossibility of meeting internal standards.

Therapeutic Goals	Therapeutic Techniques toward Goals
Increase value of relationship itself over value of being in control.	Provide attunement, empathy, and validation. Mirror feelings and acceptance of feelings as part of self.
Encourage greater sense of genuine autonomy and move away from reliance on power struggles and reactivity.	Accommodate child's need for control, asking child to teach, encouraging child in making choices; accept child's demands while maintaining safety.
Facilitate an increase in sense of safety within both connection and autonomy.	Model appropriate risk taking while maintaining physical and psychological safety of the room.
Increase affective expression and spontaneity.	Encourage expression of feelings and model warmth coupled with emotional expressiveness and spontaneity. As about feelings, affirm and label feelings, especially ones child is uncomfortable expressing.
Lessen impact of overly harsh self-expectations.	Acknowledge, take responsibility for, and accept mistakes. Model self-acceptance and realistic expectations by reacting appropriately to own mistakes.
Probable developmental trajectory:	Obsessive-compulsive personality.

Table 3.6 Dynamics and treatment of post-oedipal presentations.

Probable early experiences and relationships:	Seductive opposite-sex parent, or need of opposite-sex parent for child to align against same-sex parent; disallows any aggressive impulses and fosters passivity and helplessness.
Internal working model of self and other:	Sees self as unable to take initiative.
	Guilty about sexual and aggressive impulses; confusion of affectional and sexual needs.
	Sees others as demanding approval from the child.
Internal working model of relationships:	Child uses exaggerated dependency to please and gain the approval of significant others, often with a highly seductive quality.
Dynamic formulation:	Child has self and object constancy with generally good ego functions, but tends to act out conflict rather than reflect and rely on these ego functions, at the same time acting helpless and passive.

Prominent Play Themes	*Meanings of Play Themes*
Aggression: Any general aggression or aggression where there is an "aggressor" and a "victim."	Child may have angry feelings without any clear sense of why; may lose control because play touches on a difficult issue and is angry that the feelings or events have been recalled; child may feel powerless in daily life and acts as aggressor to gain sense of control; aggressive role may indicate way child is in daily life (may include significant feelings of being unable to control angry feelings).
Power: Involves power relationships, with emphasis on strength and differential power.	Child is feeling weak and wants to feel strong; child is showing how it feels to be controlled by a power figure in the child's life.
Seek: Character consults a power figure such as a parent, judge, or supernatural/mystical power like a wizard or God.	Child is showing a pattern of pseudodependency, turning to a power figure to please the power figure.
Adult: Child assumes adult roles and activities, such as going on a date or going steady.	Child has identified with older siblings or adults and wants to be like them either to receive their approval or to magically provide safety or comfort to self as if the other is present.
Fail: Lack of ability to master tasks undertaken, or lack of confidence in ability (e.g., giving up easily, apparent frustration).	Child may have a fear of taking the initiative and attempting to be competent.
Sexual activities: Play that shows or alludes to direct sexual behavior either between characters or between child and therapist. In the latter case, the child makes overtly sexually seductive overtures toward the therapist.	Child may have learned that sexual activities garner the immediate attention of adults and may be seeking the therapist's attention; child may be in a covertly seductive relationship (e.g., with opposite sex parent) and engage in seductive behavior to gain affection.

(continued)

Table 3.6 *(Continued)*

Interpersonal/Process Codes	Meanings of Interpersonal/Process Codes
Help: A character helps through teaching, guiding, or rescuing another character.	Child may be seeking help in a pseudodependent fashion to engage therapist.
Protect: Play where a stronger (or adult) character acts to protect weaker (or child) character.	Child may be pseudodependent and elicit protection through "helpless" behavior, as a way to engage therapist.
Control: Child or character is bossy or directive, ordering either therapist or another character around.	Child may need to control the interpersonal interaction to maintain an appropriate level of personal safety; maintains connection with distance so that relationship is less threatening and basic conflict stays out of awareness.
Doing and undoing: Child plays a theme immediately followed by a theme with opposite meaning or valence, such as aggression followed by a display of affection.	Change in meaning or valence suggests conflict and mixed feelings around issues expressed in play or interpersonal behavior.
(a) *Broken/fixing:* See Table 3.4.	(a) Child is concerned with perceptions of injury, damage, or vulnerability in self, caregiver, or family; fixing suggests either hope or emerging empowerment.
(b) *Independence/dependence:* See Table 3.5.	(b) Child feels compelled to strive for self-sufficiency because of perceived inability of caregivers to meet needs; conflict suggests that child feels unequipped to achieve self-sufficiency, though perceives self-sufficiency as the safest, surest route to getting needs met.
(c) *Safety/danger:* See Table 3.4.	(c) Child worries about lack of safety and vulnerability to danger, suggesting child is uncertain whether he or she will be able to be safe in a threatening environment.
(d) *Anger/affection:* Directly expressed anger or hostility toward a character or the therapist, followed by expressed affection.	(d) Child has feelings of anger toward caregiver related to perceived deprivation, and feels expression of anger is unacceptable, so tries to undo it with affection.

Therapeutic Goals	Therapeutic Techniques toward Goals
Develop self-assertion and appropriate levels of initiative.	Provide warmth and avoid directing child's play, fostering too much dependency, or responding to child's seductiveness; affirm child's efforts at initiative and mastery.
Help child learn to differentiate sexuality and dependency needs to gain needed affection without seductiveness.	Clarify emotions and help verbalize when child seems to confuse affection with seductiveness. Connect child behaviors with others' perceptions of seductiveness.
Encourage child to use ego functions to self-regulate and self-monitor.	Encourage child's positive self-statements and affirm the child when he or she makes accurate self-perceptions and observations.
Increase frustration tolerance and decrease acting-out.	Help child anticipate consequences of actions and encourage child to actively solve problems encountered. Provide clear limits and provide choices around limits so child will rely more on ego functions.
Probable developmental trajectory:	Hysterical personality.

Object-relations play therapy begins with an understanding of the specific developmental presentation of the child, including the dynamic picture, characteristic play themes and interpersonal relationships, therapeutic goals, and specific therapeutic techniques. This understanding is then integrated with the phases of treatment described earlier: establishing a secure base relationship, challenging the internal working models through invitations based on hypotheses emerging from the child's play and relationship themes, and finally through a carefully planned termination phase, where the goal is to promote object constancy and extension of new internal working models into the wider world.

MAJOR SYNDROMES, SYMPTOMS, AND PROBLEMS TREATED

Object-relations play therapy is a relationship-focused approach. It is the treatment of choice for a particular spectrum of child emotional and behavior problems. Child problems best treated by this therapy primarily result from chronic interpersonal trauma experienced in parent-child or significant other-child relationships. Often, such children present as identified patients with diagnoses secondary to parent-child relational pathology that is characterized by some degree of abandonment, impingement, or both. The child's emotional and behavioral problems reflect attempts to cope with or adapt to an environment (and/or the relationships within it) perceived as overwhelmingly threatening, unstable, unpredictable, or inconsistent (Prior, 1996). Object-relations play therapy uses the therapeutic relationship to reshape pathological internal working models of self and others in ways that promote more faith in caregivers, encourage respect for limits, and develop more adaptive strategies for relating interpersonally and for coping with frustration and stress.

In the extreme, parental abandonment or impingement may occur in the form of abuse or neglect. However, less extreme forms of parental abandonment or impingement, particularly when chronic and/or unpredictable, are also likely to precipitate maladaptive coping strategies (Lee & Gotlib, 1996; Levoy, Rivinus, Matzko, & McGuire, 1991). A child is likely to feel abandoned under any circumstances in which the parent is perceived as unwilling or unable to provide support or protection when the child is feeling overwhelmed. For example, an emotionally unavailable parent (such as a depressed mother who is regaining equilibrium after an episode of domestic violence, or a mother anxiously preoccupied with her current romantic relationship) is likely to be perceived as abandoning (Canino, Bird, Rubio-Stipec, & Bravo,1990; Hall, 1996; Kolbo, Blakely, & Engleman, 1996; Lee & Gotlib, 1991; Radke-Yarrow & Klimes-Dougan, 1997).

Feelings of being overwhelmed are intensified when the parent is perceived as a threat, as when a parent is prone to outbursts or unpredictability, such as a substance abusing parent or one with a personality disorder (Levoy et al., 1991; Wooley, 1998). A child may feel overwhelmed not only when a parent is intrusive or the home environment is chaotic, but also when a parent in compromised in his or her ability to effectively and consistently set limits. Conversely, an anxiously overprotective parent may be experienced as intrusive, at the same time promoting the development of perceptions that the environment is threatening. Feeling chronically overwhelmed contributes to the development of an internal model of self perceived as alone and unprotected in dealing with the environment, and thus vulnerable, easily disorganized, and disempowered (Hamilton, 1990).

Internal models of others that develop based on experience with others perceived as abandoning and/or impinging are associated with intense affects (e.g., rage, shame) that are not easily metabolized or integrated in a child's experience without the development of mature and effective coping mechanisms (Prior, 1996). The child's development of coping strategies is arrested at a primitive level, stunted by the experience of feeling chronically overwhelmed (Levoy et al., 1991). Such primitive coping strategies include avoidance (which builds tension and results in periodic outbursts), externalization (e.g., disruptive behavior), oppositionality or defiance (an attempt to feel empowered by means of demonstrating counterdependence), compulsivity (an attempt to impose order on chaotic internal and external environments), controlling interpersonal style (to regulate distance and exercise rigid interpersonal boundaries), role-reversed or parentified caretaking, inhibition of needs and feelings in an effort to accommodate caregivers, and shutting down. In reliance on primitive coping strategies, which are developed in adaptation to a chronic "state of emergency," the child becomes extremely vulnerable to stress and inflexible in coping and, as a result, often develops maladaptive interpersonal strategies (i.e., controlling behavior, whether in terms of oppositional defiance or overaccommodation). The child acts out internal conflicts interpersonally in an effort to establish control over chaos in both internal and external environments (Prior, 1996).

Self-regulation problems also often arise in connection with parent-child relational pathology. Compromised ability to modulate needs and feelings has its origins in parental lack of attunement, which is invariably associated with abandonment and/or impingement in the parent-child relationship. When a parent is unattuned, the child's needs and feelings go unreflected, much less unmodulated by the caregiver. The child does not experience responsiveness, which would promote awareness of needs and feelings that need to be managed, and has no model for internalizing the ability to soothe self when such needs and feelings arise (Hamilton, 1990). A child's inability to modulate needs and feelings exacerbates perceptions of internal chaos in a way that strains inadequate coping resources, insidiously escalating anxiety that may be manifested in either internalizing (e.g., anxiety or mood disorders) or externalizing (e.g., hyperactivity or disruptive behavior) symptoms.

These dynamics of disordered object relations that underlie the development of primitive, ineffective coping strategies, in combination with self-regulation problems, characterize a number of child emotional and behavior problems for which the object-relations play therapy approach is suitable. For example, Reactive Attachment Disorder of Infancy or Early Childhood (RAD), as defined in *DSM-IV*, includes criteria relating to both pathogenic caregiving and disturbance in child social relatedness (e.g., compulsive need to control others, interpersonal ambivalence, inhibition or disinhibition in social relations). Additional symptoms often associated with RAD include lying, lack of empathy, hypervigilance, and oppositionality. Attachment disordered children can be viewed as arrested at the presymbiotic or early symbiotic developmental stage of object relations, in which the child has never established enough basic trust to attach to, much less separate from, the caregiver. Attachment disorder subtypes as described by Zeanah and colleagues (Zeanah & Boris, 2000; Zeanah, Mammen, & Lieberman, 1993) characterize stages of developmental progress that may be achieved despite ongoing unresolved disorder in object relations (e.g., self as vulnerable and counterdependent, other as untrustworthy and/or threatening). Attachment disordered children need relationship-focused treatment to address distortions in object relations to rebuild capacity for trust, which underlies nurturing interpersonal connection, empathy for others, and prosocial respect for limits and provides a basis for development of adaptive coping strategies.

The diagnosis of so-called regulatory disorder, as defined by the 0–3 diagnostic classification system proposed as an alternative to *DSM-IV* for use in early childhood (Zero to Three, 1994), most adequately captures the self-regulation problems associated with interpersonal trauma. In *DSM-IV* terms, such self-regulation problems are often captured in diagnoses such as disruptive behavior disorders, Attention-Deficit/Hyperactivity Disorder (ADHD), and, increasingly, Bipolar Disorder. Among children with such diagnoses, it is useful to evaluate whether development of symptoms was influenced by adaptation to a chaotic environment in which it was not possible to develop self-regulation skills. In such cases, problems that seem primarily to require medication and/or behavior management also would benefit from being addressed by object-relations play therapy, to reshape disordered object relations and resultant maladaptive coping strategies that underlie problems that look primarily behavioral. Self-regulation problems may be observed at any developmental stage of object relations.

Disruptive behavior disorders, such as Oppositional Defiant Disorder and Conduct Disorder, have their roots in attachment problems, though this is often overlooked. Underneath the tough exterior of a defiant child with conduct problems is a traumatized child who is acting out to cope with internal and external chaos. Such children can be understood as arrested at the practicing and rapprochement developmental stage of object relations.

Mood and anxiety disorders may emerge at any development stage of object relations. Dysthymic Disorder is widespread among chronically overwhelmed children who struggle with coping deficits and ongoing perceptions of lack of support. Depression may result from perceptions of abandonment associated with parental emotional unavailability. In addition, children with disordered object relations may experience pervasive generalized anxiety that is rooted in fundamental perceptions that the environment is not safe and people in it are either unavailable or present a threat. Depression and anxiety may be more subjectively felt, as opposed to being acted out in hyperactivity or disruptive behavior, among children in the later developmental stages of object relations. When depression or anxiety is the presenting problem, it is useful to consider whether disordered object relations may be a contributing factor.

Abuse and neglect constitute extremes in parent-child relational pathology. Under such circumstances, interpersonal trauma is likely to be experienced as more pronounced. Regardless of the developmental stage in which trauma is experienced, the intensification of trauma can be expected to contribute to increased rigidity of distortions in object relations, inflexibility in coping, and vulnerability to disorganization (e.g., either disorganized behavior or "shutting down" under stress).

Many childhood disorders result from multiple contributing factors. It is useful to consider whether disordered object relations may be involved when identifying treatment issues and formulating interventions. Although object-relations play therapy is ideally indicated for treatment of disorders arising from the dynamics described above, in its promotion of healthy models of self, others, and relationships and encouragement of respect for boundaries and limits, elements of object-relations play therapy can be gainfully employed to enhance any child's treatment plan.

CASE EXAMPLES

Object-relations play therapy can be illustrated by examining briefly the therapy for two children, one who initially presented as presymbiotic and early symbiotic (Ann, age 10), and one who initially presented as compromised rapprochement (Trina, age 4). Each case presentation is organized in keeping with the appropriate table, beginning with the history that describes the child's early experiences and relationships, continuing with a dynamic formulation, including the therapist's understanding of the child's internal working models, followed by a description of the child's play and relationships within therapy. The therapeutic goals and treatment techniques used are described as well.

Case 1: Ann

Diagnosis and Assessment
Ann's was a difficult and complex case and cannot be fully summarized here. Instead, the description focuses on the major shifts in object relations seen during the first three phases of therapy (see Table 3.1). Ann, age 10 at the time of referral and the only child of divorced parents, lived with her mother during the school year and her maternal grandparents in a nearby city during the summer. Her parents divorced when she was just 1 year old because her mother had discovered that the father was both physically and sexually abusive of Ann. The mother reported that Ann would cover her head with her arms in her crib if her father came near. Ann and her mother continued to have contact with the father intermittently, and these visits, where the father stayed in their home, were rather loosely supervised by the mother. It became evident during therapy that this contact had been quite sexualized by the father, with the mother essentially unaware of his behavior. The father had significant alcohol problems, difficulty holding a job, and a probable diagnosis of Schizophrenia. He had spent some time in jail for molesting a girl about Ann's age and again for indecent exposure, both jail terms occurring when Ann was between 6 and 11 years of age. Thus, Ann's early experience with her father was one of rejection, abuse, and attachment failure. The mother, who reported being afraid of the father and therefore unable to limit or control visits, had significant borderline features and only reluctantly entered therapy when Ann was 10 years of age at the insistence of Ann's therapist. Like the father, the mother appeared quite limited, at least for Ann's first eight to nine years of life, in her ability to attach and attune to Ann's needs. Recent diagnosis of the mother with hypoglycemia when Ann was nearly 10 seemed to provide her with an explanation of previous failures to meet Ann's needs and an openness to therapy. The mother's therapist and Ann's therapist had only occasional contact, and the two therapies proceeded relatively independently. The mother made good progress in this therapy and it is believed that her increased psychological availability contributed to Ann's progress.

Ann had been referred for evaluation and play therapy at age 5. She received several months of treatment, which were terminated when the therapist moved out of the area. Ann appeared to form a strong attachment to this therapist, which she recalled in surprising detail for the current therapist. It appears from the first therapist's description that Ann found in that relationship many of the things missing with her parents and she began to attach and move toward object constancy and healthier object relations, progress that was halted by the relatively abrupt departure of the therapist. The mother rejected a referral for continued treatment at that time despite clear indications that Ann needed it. Ann's early history included frequent ear infections with significant hearing loss that was corrected surgically at age 4. It was only after the surgery that she began to speak.

At age 10, Ann's presentation, which was quite similar to that seen at age 5, suggested at first a pervasive developmental disorder such as autism or Asperger's Disorder, as she avoided eye contact, was extremely rigid in her play, and was impaired in social relating, alternately indiscriminately friendly or extremely aloof and stiff in interactions. Extremely immature, she seemed much more like a preschooler than a 10-year-old. She seemed related to her mother, but she had difficulties with peers and other adults and had been placed in a self-contained classroom for the emotionally impaired within special education. Despite appearing autistic-like, there were several signs that this diagnosis did not actually describe her accurately. Careful assessment showed that she lacked the cognitive disruptions and sensory sensitivities often seen with such children. Ann was doing age-appropriate academic work in school and related quite well to preschool children. Projective testing and play assessment both revealed intense ambivalence about relationships, considerable anger and sad affect below the surface, and a complex of issues around separation-individuation, sexuality, and safety. Based on the impaired social relatedness and frequent indiscriminate friendliness as well as the history of severe infant abuse by the father and probable emotional neglect by the mother, the diagnosis was Reactive Attachment Disorder of Infancy and Early Childhood, Disinhibited subtype (*DSM-IV*). Although not usually diagnosed at such a late age, anecdotal information from the first therapist suggests this was an appropriate diagnosis at age 5, and Ann appeared to be frozen at that level of functioning.

Case Formulation
The object-relations formulation for Ann suggested that she was currently showing presymbiotic-symbiotic functioning, which appeared in some ways to be a retreat from intense distress encountered when she attempted the separation-individuation steps in practicing and rapprochement. She had some elements of a symbiotic bond with her mother, but it was fragile and failed to offer sufficient support for her to engage in relationships meaningfully. It appears that Ann formed a strong attachment to her first therapist, and when that person left, she retreated into a secondary autistic stance. Thus, her withdrawal from others was defensive in nature and she actively resisted interpersonal connection and nurturing. She was limited in her ability to express affect openly, although projective tests revealed considerable strong negative affects and unmet needs. This can be seen in an incident that occurred early in treatment. Ann was transported to therapy by her school and one day she was brought early; the therapist was not at the door of the building to greet her, as was usually the case. Ann made no comments about this but seemed particularly detached from the therapist. Her play became much more sterile, mostly lining up toys and separating them into groups and playing a highly ritualized game about several puppets deciding whether or not to go on a picnic. When the therapist, after most of the session with Ann detached, reflected that Ann might be angry about the incident, Ann began to play again in the ways she had played in earlier sessions.

Treatment Approach and Rationale for Its Selection
Ann's play in the early sessions confirmed both the presymbiotic-symbiotic dynamic with some elements of practicing and rapprochement. Therefore, the therapeutic goals selected were initially those from the presymbiotic and symbiotic presentation (Table 3.1), with a plan to shift goals once a therapeutic symbiosis was achieved to the goals for practicing and rapprochement (Table 3.2).

Much of Ann's play was stereotyped and appeared directed at keeping the therapist at a distance. Her early play also had dolls hiding, with the therapist as a mother doll trying to find them (constancy play), several dolls falling off the roof or falling and hitting their heads (instability play), and preparing food for several dolls (nurturing play). Constancy play was also seen in Ann's giving names to all of the dolls in the playroom (and all of her dolls at home as well), which she remembered and used consistently through the course of therapy. Other early play suggested the ambivalence about separation. The most striking feature of this play involved a small doll she named Angie, who ran away from the mother doll (held by the therapist) repeatedly. When the mother doll was close to finding Angie, Ann would have Angie disappear by claiming that the mother had really found a balloon that looked like Angie, which then popped, or a chalk drawing of Angie, which was then erased. Whenever Angie moved away from the mother in the play, Angie somehow disintegrated. Her intense ambivalence about identity (and individuation) was seen in her designating several dolls as pairs of twins whom the mother could not distinguish.

The initial challenge of therapy was to establish a secure base relationship by facilitating Ann's receptivity to nurturance and connectedness. This was a prolonged phase of therapy, as Ann had become quite rigid in her defensive withdrawal. This relationship was slowly developed primarily through the therapist's providing consistency, remaining attuned despite Ann's frequent detachment, and continual invitations to recognize Ann's feelings and needs in a context of safety.

Once a relationship has been established, the goal of therapy is to foster a symbiotic transference that can lead to adaptive separation and individuation. Ann required a prolonged phase of symbiosis with the therapist before she began the separation-individuation process. This symbiosis could be seen in several ways. Ann learned everything she could about the therapist and incorporated it into the play, for example, having a character that looked like the therapist and had the same birthday with a last name that matched the street name of the therapist's home. On one occasion, Ann drew the letters of her name superimposed on the letters of the therapist's name, as though Ann-Helen were a single entity. She also engaged in imitation-control play, where she demanded that the therapist imitate her own verbalizations and behaviors. Thus, the goal of forming a strong symbiotic transference was met in the second phase of therapy.

During the work to establish a symbiotic transference, work focused on two other goals: facilitating self-regulation and promoting ability to tolerate, label, and verbalize feelings. Ann showed poor self-regulation in two ways. First, she seemed to need to continually check on her activities in the mirror (a large observation window that covered one wall of the playroom), as if she wasn't sure of where she was and what she was doing without checking in the mirror. The mirror was left uncovered during therapy and the therapist verbalized Ann's activities as she watched herself in the mirror. Second, Ann, a tall child for her age, often sat in a preschool-size chair in the playroom and she frequently fell off the chair (which did not hurt her, given how low the chair was). Falling off the chair almost always occurred when she was talking about feelings or difficult subjects, as if she couldn't both handle feelings and regulate her body activity. Both behaviors were intimately tied to feelings issues. Work progressed in this area through reflections by the therapist of Ann's feelings and needs and invitations by the therapist to talk about the feelings of Ann's play characters. Over time, Ann was increasingly able to minimize both behaviors, showing increased trust of the therapist and an increased ability to recognize and express her feelings directly.

In some ways, the most interesting phase of Ann's treatment occurred as she began to separate and individuate from the therapist. At this point, the therapy had moved to the practicing and rapprochement goals for therapy. Ann engaged in two distinct play themes at this time. First, she engaged in what can be called "elevator therapy." Ann came to therapy directly from school; her mother was firmly convinced, based on her own history of hypoglycemia, that Ann needed a snack at the beginning of therapy. So Ann had established a pattern of going on the elevator with the therapist to get a drink and snack from vending machines on another floor of the building. Ann was quite afraid of the elevator, especially if other people were on it, and never had used it without the therapist being present.

One day, Ann decided she could get on the elevator alone. At first, she hopped on and off again before the door closed. Soon, she would let the door close and go to the vending machines on her own. Finally, she would spend nearly half of each session getting on the elevator, going to one floor after another and exploring, each time returning to talk to or wave at the therapist. By remaining outside the elevator on the playroom floor of the building, the therapist served as a "secure base" for the separation process. In essence, Ann found a safe way to engage in the exploring and returning for refueling seen by toddlers in the practicing phase.

The second way Ann proceeded with separation-individuation was through a set of paintings she did each time she entered the playroom following "elevator therapy." She began each painting with a red vertical line down the center of the paper. On top of this, in the middle of the page, she painted a filled circle on the line. This drawing, by her verbal report, was a cross-section of a "flea-flea germ-germ." Then, on the right side of the paper, she painted a yellow sun. Next to the sun would be a small figure that looked like a small animal lying on its back with feet up in the air. On the left side of the paper, she drew an ill-defined blob, either in red or blue, with an identical upside-down "animal" next to it. Ann would announce that the first animal was a "dead flea-flea germ-germ" that died from getting too close to the sun. She would then point to the other figure and say it was also a "dead flea-flea germ-germ," only this one died because it got too close to the cold place or too far away from the sun. Finally, Ann would put identical numbers above each side of the paper (usually either 350 or 500) to indicate the body count of "dead flea-flea germ-germs" for the day. The paintings were highly predictable and stylized. Taken together with the elevator therapy, the "flea-flea germ-germ" paintings seemed to graphically demonstrate Ann's ambivalence about separating and individuating from the therapist and, by extension, from her mother. She would begin each session by separating and reconnecting with the therapist several times using the elevator, then come into the room and paint one or more "flea-flea germ-germ" paintings.

After allowing both types of play for several sessions, the therapist worked to foster an integrated sense of self by facilitating awareness of boundary issues. She chose to interpret the boundary issues conveyed by the paintings by saying that the "flea-flea germ-germ" was like Ann. When she got too close to people, she felt like she would burn up and die but if she got too far away, she would also die. The "flea-flea germ-germ" and, by extension, Ann could not seem to find the middle. She had portrayed vividly the sense that she was vacillating between fusion and extreme withdrawal, both of which prevented an integrated sense of self with appropriate boundaries.

Ann accepted the interpretation and ended both types of play. She seemed to be much calmer and more comfortable with the therapist, and therapeutic work in the final phase of therapy moved toward the goal of object constancy. Increasingly, Ann was able to identify her own needs, be assertive about meeting those needs in therapy, and show a more integrated sense of self. A detailed presentation of this final phase is not possible given the limited space, yet the first three phases illustrate the use of object-relations play therapy with a severely disturbed child.

CASE 2: TRINA

Diagnosis and Assessment
Case 2 demonstrates object-relations play therapy with a child initially presenting with compromised rapprochement. Trina, nearly 5 years of age at the time of referral, had experienced considerable interpersonal trauma in her first four years of life. She was born to a young single mother, Angela, whose other child was in the permanent care of the paternal grandparents, with no contact with the mother. Angela partially abandoned Trina at age 2 months,

leaving her with her new boyfriend's parents, with a promise to return and get her. Angela's mother intervened and got the infant, who began to live with her and her current husband (step-grandfather to Trina) when Trina was about 4 months of age. Angela was in and out of the home over the next several months, sometimes caring for the baby, but usually leaving that to the grandmother. When Trina was 18 months of age, her maternal grandmother went to prison for 18 months and Trina was cared for exclusively by the step-grandfather. By this time, Angela had largely abandoned Trina, moved to a nearby city, and had a third child by a new boyfriend. The step-grandfather would not allow Angela to see Trina on the few times she tried to visit. The grandmother returned when Trina was 3, and both grandparents cared for her. However, the marriage was marked by conflict and violence (each grandparent significantly injured at least once), and they divorced when Trina was nearly 4. Trina was now in the care of the maternal grandmother with frequent visits by both her mother, who would take Trina for a few weeks and then return and disappear for several months, and the step-grandfather, who appeared strongly attached to Trina. By the time of referral, the grandmother was in a new relationship and living with Trina in a "communal" arrangement with several college-age adults in addition to her boyfriend.

All three major adults in Trina's life had significant psychological problems. The mother, Angela, had severe personality problems and seemed minimally invested in Trina except to "show her off" to others as an example of her "mothering." Angela also lost custody of her third child, who lived with his father but made several week-long visits to Angela. She would often have long visits with Trina at the same time that she had the younger brother, so the two played together, although Trina and her brother fought more than played. The grandfather, a Vietnam veteran with Posttraumatic Stress Disorder and intermittent Explosive Disorder, was consistently caring of Trina but also demanding of her and frighteningly violent with the grandmother in front of the child. The maternal grandmother showed good self-awareness (the apparent result of several years of psychotherapy) and was generally attuned to Trina but had a history of experiencing severe abuse during her childhood and Dissociative Identity Disorder. Thus, Trina had experienced numerous changes in her primary caregiver, and each of these individuals appeared limited in some ways in their ability to accept and love Trina without using her to meet their own psychological needs.

Trina showed few overt symptoms at the time of referral by her day care teacher. She was described as overly attached to the teacher, unable to let her be out of sight while at school, and also overly attached to her transitional object, a much-repaired Raggedy Ann doll she had had since birth. She also showed separation anxiety with her grandmother and a tendency to tantrums much like those of a far younger child. Trina met the criteria for a formal diagnosis of Separation Anxiety Disorder (*DSM-IV*).

Case Formulation
In terms of her object-relations development, Trina appeared to match the compromised rapprochement presentation seen in Table 3.3. She came to the evaluation session showing an unusual combination of immature and pseudomature behaviors. She seemed quite adultlike, continually monitoring the mood of her grandmother and declaring more than once that she could take care of everything and did not need any help from anyone (independence). At the same time, she pretended to be a baby, talking baby talk and sucking on a baby bottle. Although she explored the room fully, she showed almost no spontaneous play. She denied any problems or bad feelings, even during a later session when the grandmother was late returning to get her and Trina appeared

extremely anxious and upset in her nonverbal behavior.

Treatment Approach and Rationale for Its Selection
The specific object-relations play therapy approach used in this case derived from the treatment goals and techniques outlined in Table 3.3 for compromised rapprochement. As treatment began, Trina was slow to form a trusting relationship. Initially, she was extremely cooperative and well behaved, with a parallel lack of spontaneity in her play. When she did play, Trina typically played out the themes and interpersonal relationships expected with this presentation. She frequently showed a strong need to make and build things (mastery) and then show them to both the therapist and her grandmother. At other times, she would draw and then insist the therapist copy her drawing exactly (imitation-control). She often set up a store where she sold toys to the therapist (store/shopping). In all of her play at this time, Trina was very controlling (control). She would sometimes care for the baby or pretend to be a baby herself. When she was baby, she was "queen baby" (stage mix), who fed herself and took care of herself (self-nurturing). Another frequent interaction pattern was to "trick" the therapist (or her grandmother, who sometimes joined her play sessions), usually in the context of surprising them at a birthday party, set up with the sandbox serving as the cake.

The therapy proceeded with the therapist's working toward the goals in Table 3.3, especially using reflection of hidden feelings, relinquishment of therapist control of the setting except for reasons of physical safety, and modeling good and soothing care with the babies. Whenever Trina played with the babies, the therapist would talk about what babies needed and what good caretakers should do. As Trina's trust developed, she allowed herself to be the baby and be directly nurtured by the therapist. She also began asking questions about why her mother did not take good care of her. These questions were stimulated by the arrival of the mother's fourth child when Trina was 5½. Angela, supported by her new husband's family, seemed to be more attached to and able to care for her fourth child than she had been with her other three children (although this interest and effort waned considerably as the baby began to crawl), and Trina would ask why her mother could take care of the baby but hadn't known how to take care of her.

Once Trina began playing a baby who could be cared for by the therapist, her play in general became more spontaneous. She played over and over a scene where the baby wasn't safe (climbing unsafely, or taking "medicine," or cooking on a "hot" stove), while requiring the therapist to make the baby safe. She also played many scenes where the mother figure (played by Trina using the doll as her baby) was angry and abusive or neglectful of the baby, eliciting invitations from the therapist to talk about or demonstrate the care babies need.

Trina's relationship with the grandmother changed during this time. She was more trusting, more comfortable separating from the grandmother, and appeared to be more securely attached. At the same time, she began actively resisting contact with her mother. It became clear that Angela was often abusive of Trina, yelling at her, spanking her unusually hard and often, hitting her at times or slapping her face, and failing to supervise her and keep her safe when she visited. It is noteworthy that Angela would take for herself any locket or other jewelry of Trina's that she liked. Angela had to be reported to protective services and ultimately was required to relinquish all custody of Trina. Having made a strong attachment to her grandmother, Trina worked extensively in play to establish the baby as good whether the mother could care for it or not. She made a good adjustment to the termination of her mother's parental rights and actually seemed relieved that she was now protected. The therapeutic relationship had evolved to one in which Trina expressed genuine feelings and healthy boundaries. It served as a safe holding environment for Trina to strengthen her attachment to her grandmother and facilitate the development of object constancy and a positive internal working model of the self.

POSTTERMINATION SYNOPSIS AND EFFECTIVENESS DATA

Object-relations play therapy has been used with numerous cases in therapy lasting between six months and two to three years, depending on the severity of the problems encountered. To date, no controlled empirical studies of effectiveness have been completed. However, clinical follow-up data have been available for many of the children seen, including Ann and Trina. The typical therapeutic pattern was the formation of a therapeutic relationship followed by work shifting the object relations developmentally closer to full object constancy. As their object relations changed, their symptoms often ameliorated. Ann was more socially appropriate and by age 13, was able to be mainstreamed at school, where she continued to make progress in relating to her peers. Trina, who had begun therapy with a pattern of frequent tantrums in school, ended the tantrums after about a year, when she had entered the phase of therapy working on the mother-daughter relationship and what babies need. Children less severely traumatized than Ann or Trina tend to make changes in their object relations more easily and require less extensive treatment before they show significantly improved interpersonal relationships indicative of more mature and healthy object relations.

SUMMARY

We have presented an object-relations model of play therapy based on Mahler's developmental stages of separation/individuation supplemented by concepts drawn from Fairbairn, Winnicott, and Bowlby's attachment theory. Six distinct clinical presentations were examined in terms of their dynamics, typical play, therapeutic goals, and therapeutic techniques. This model is particularly appropriate for children who have experienced attachment problems or interpersonal trauma, such as abuse, neglect, family violence, or parents with severe psychopathology, in the first several years of life.

REFERENCES

Abram, J. (1996). *The language of Winnicott: A dictionary and guide to understanding his work*. Northvale, NJ: Aronson.

Achenbach, T. M. (1991a). *Manual for the Child Behavior Checklist/4–18 and 1991 profile*. Burlington: University of Vermont, Department of Psychiatry.

Achenbach, T. M. (1991b). *Manual for the Teacher's Report Form and 1991 profile*. Burlington: University of Vermont, Department of Psychiatry.

Allan, J. (1988). *Inscapes of the child's world: Jungian counseling in schools and clinics*. Dallas: Spring.

Allen, F. (1942). *Psychotherapy with children*. New York: Norton.

American Psychiatric Association. (1994). *Diagnostic and statistical manual of mental disorders* (4th ed.). Washington, DC: Author.

Axline, V. M. (1947). *Play therapy: The inner dynamics of childhood*. Boston: Houghton Mifflin.

Benedict, H. E., Chavez, D., Holmberg, J., McClain, J., McGee, W., Narcavage, D., et al. (1966). *Benedict play therapy theme code*. Unpublished working paper, Baylor University, Waco, TX.

Benedict, H. E., Hastings, L., Ato, G., Carson, M., & Nash, M. (1998). *Revised Benedict play therapy theme code and interpersonal relationship code*. Unpublished working paper, Baylor University, Waco, TX.

Benedict, H. E., & Mongoven, L. B. (1997). Thematic play therapy: An approach to treatment of attachment disorders in young children. In H. Kaduson, D. Cangelosi, & C. E. Schaefer (Eds.), *The playing cure: Individualized play therapy for specific childhood problems*. New York: Aronson.

Benedict, H. E., & Shelton, L. E. (1996, October). *Disorders of attachment: Themes in play therapy and treatment implications.* Workshop presented at the 13th annual Association for Play Therapy conference, Chicago.

Blanck, R., & Blanck, G. (1986). *Beyond ego psychology: Developmental object relations theory.* New York: Columbia University Press.

Bowlby, J. (1988). *A secure base: Parent-child attachment and healthy human development.* New York: Basic Books.

Brody, V. (1993). *The dialogue of touch: Developmental play therapy.* Treasure Island, FL: Developmental Play Training Associates.

Canino, G. J., Bird, H. R., Rubio-Stipec, M., & Bravo, M. (1990). Children of parents with psychiatric disorder in the community. *Journal of the American Academy of Child and Adolescent Psychiatry, 29,* 398–406.

Chase, N. D. (Ed.). (1999). *Burdened children: Theory, research, and treatment of parentification.* Thousand Oaks, CA: Sage.

Cicchetti, D., Toth, S. L., & Lynch, M. (1995). Bowlby's dream comes full circle: The application of attachment theory to risk and psychopathology. In T. H. Ollendick & R. J. Prinz (Eds.), *Advances in clinical child psychology* (Vol. 17, pp. 1–75). New York: Plenum Press.

Costello, A. J., Edelbrock, C. S., Duncan, M. K., Kalas, R., & Klaric, S. (1987). *Diagnostic Interview Scale for Children.* Pittsburgh, PA: University of Pittsburgh, School of Medicine, Western Psychiatric Institute and Clinic.

Fairbairn, W. R. D. (1952). *An object-relations theory of the personality.* New York: Basic Books.

Freud, A. (1936). *The ego and the mechanisms of defense.* New York: International Universities Press.

Gardner, R. A. (1971). Mutual storytelling: A technique in child psychotherapy. *Acta Paedopsychiatrica, 38,* 253–262.

Gil, E. (1991). *The healing power of play.* New York: Guilford Press.

Glickauf-Hughes, C., & Wells, M. (1997). *Object-relations psychotherapy: An individualized and interactive approach to diagnosis and treatment.* New York: Aronson.

Guerney, B. (1964). Filial therapy: Description and rationale. *Journal of Consulting Psychology, 28,* 304–310.

Hall, H. (1996). Parental psychiatric disorder and the developing child. In M. Gopfert, J. Webster, & M. V. Seeman (Eds.), *Parental psychiatric disorder: Distressed parents and their families* (pp. 17–41). Cambridge, England: Cambridge University Press.

Hambridge, G. (1955). Structured play therapy. *American Journal of Orthopsychiatry, 25,* 601–617.

Hamilton, N. G. (1990). *Self and others: Object relations theory in practice.* Northvale, NJ: Aronson.

Harter, S. (1983). Cognitive-developmental considerations in the conduct of play therapy. In C. E. Schaefer & K. J. O'Connor (Eds.), *Handbook of play therapy* (pp. 95–127). New York: Wiley.

Holmberg, J., Benedict, H., & Hynan, L. (1998). Gender differences in children's therapy themes: Comparisons of children with a history of attachment disturbance or exposure to violence. *International Journal of Play Therapy, 7,* 67–92.

Jernberg, A. M. (1979). *Theraplay: A new treatment using structured play for problem children and their families.* San Francisco: Jossey-Bass.

Kelly, F. D. (1999). *The psychological assessment of abused and traumatized children.* Mahwah, NJ: Erlbaum.

Kernberg, P. (1966). Structural derivatives of object relations. *International Journal of Psychoanalysis, 47,* 236.

Klein, M. (1932). *The psycho-analysis of children.* London: Hogarth Press.

Knell, S. M. (1993). *Cognitive-behavioral play therapy.* Northvale, NJ: Aronson.

Kolbo, J. R., Blakely, E. H., & Engleman, D. (1996). Children who witness domestic violence: A review of empirical literature. *Journal of Interpersonal Violence, 11,* 281–293.

Kottman, T. (1993). The king of rock and roll: An application of Adlerian play therapy. In T. Kottman & C. Schaefer (Eds.), *Play therapy in action* (pp. 133–167). Northvale, NJ: Aronson.

Kraemer, G. W. (1992). A psychobiological theory of attachment. *Behavioral and Brain Sciences, 15,* 493–541.

Lee, C. M., & Gotlib, I. H. (1991). Family disruption, parental availability and child adjustment. In R. J. Prinz (Ed.), *Advances in behavioral assessment of children and families: A research annual* (Vol. 5, pp. 171–199). London: Jessica Kingsley.

Levoy, D., Rivinus, T. M., Matzko, M., & McGuire, J. (1991). Children in search of a diagnosis: Chronic trauma disorder of childhood. In T. M. Rivinus

(Ed.), *Children of chemically dependent parents: Multiperspectives from the cutting edge* (pp. 153–170.). New York: Brunner/Mazel.

Levy, D. (1939). Trends in therapy: Release therapy. *American Journal of Orthopsychiatry, 9,* 713–736.

Lindaman, S. L., Booth, P. B., & Chambers, C. L. (2000). Assessing parent-child interactions with the Marschak Interaction Method (MIM). In K. Gitlin-Weiner, A. Sandgrund, & C. Schaefer (Eds.), *Play diagnosis and assessment* (2nd ed.). New York: Wiley.

Lowenfield, M. (1939). The world pictures of children. *British Journal of Medical Psychology, 18,* 65–101.

Mahler, M. S. (1968). *On human symbiosis and the vicissitudes of individuation.* New York: International Universities Press.

Mahler, M. S., Pine, F., & Bergman, A. (1975). *The psychological birth of the human infant: Symbiosis and individuation.* New York: Basic Books.

McClain, J. M. (1998). *An exploration of death themes within preschool children's play therapy.* Unpublished doctoral dissertation, Baylor University, Waco, TX.

McGee, W. A. (1998). *Children exposed to domestic violence: An analysis of their play in therapy.* Unpublished doctoral dissertation, Baylor University, Waco, TX.

Narcavage, C. J. (1998). *Child-responsive therapy: Treatment of choice for reactive selective mutism.* Unpublished doctoral dissertation, Baylor University, Waco, TX.

Oaklander, V. (1988). *Windows to our children: A Gestalt therapy approach to children and adolescents.* Highland, NY: Center for Gestalt Development.

O'Connor, K. (1991). *The play therapy primer: An integration of theories and techniques.* New York: Wiley.

O'Connor, K. (2000). *The play therapy primer* (2nd ed.). New York: Wiley.

Prior, S. (1996). *Object relations in severe trauma: Psychotherapy of the sexually abused child.* Northvale, NJ: Aronson.

Radke-Yarrow, M., & Klimes-Dougan, B. (1997). Children of depressed mothers: A developmental and interactional perspective. In S. S. Luthar, J. A. Burack, D. Cicchetti, & J. R. Weisz (Eds.), *Developmental psychopathology: Perspective on adjustment, risk, and disorder* (pp. 374–389). Cambridge, England: Cambridge University Press.

Rogers, C. (1951). *Client-centered therapy.* Boston: Houghton Mifflin.

Schore, A. (1994). *Affect regulation and the origin of the self: The neurobiology of emotional development.* Hillsdale, NJ: Erlbaum.

Siegel, D. J. (1999). *The developing mind: Toward a neurobiology of interpersonal experience.* New York: Guilford Press.

Solomon, J. (1938). Active play therapy. *American Journal of Orthopsychiatry, 18,* 402–413.

Stern, D. N. (1985). *The interpersonal world of the infant: A view from psychoanalysis and developmental psychology.* New York: Basic Books.

Winnicott, D. W. (1971a). *Playing and reality.* London: Tavistock.

Winnicott, D. W. (1971b). *Therapeutic consultations in child psychiatry.* New York: Basic Books.

Winnicott, D. W. (1965). *The maturational processes and the facilitating environment: Studies in the theory of emotional development.* New York: International Universities Press.

Wooley, L. M. (1998). *An exploration of the play therapy themes of children who have a parent with a personality disorder.* Unpublished doctoral dissertation, Baylor University, Waco, TX.

Zeanah, C. H., Jr., & Boris, N. W. (2000). Disturbances and disorders of attachment in early childhood. In C. H. Zeanah Jr. (Ed.), *Handbook of infant mental health* (2nd ed.). New York: Guilford Press.

Zeanah, C. H., Jr., Mammen, O. K., & Lieberman, A. F. (1993). Disorders of attachment. In C. H. Zeanah Jr. (Ed.), *Handbook of infant mental health* (pp. 322–349). New York: Guilford Press.

Zero to Three. (1994). *Diagnostic classification: 0–3. Diagnostic classification of mental health and developmental disorders of infancy and childhood.* Arlington, VA: Zero to Three: National Center for Clinical Infant Programs.

CHAPTER 4

Infant Mental Health

JEREE H. PAWL AND MARIA ST. JOHN

What emerged... was a form of "psychotherapy in the kitchen," so to speak, which will strike you as both familiar in its methods and unfamiliar in its setting. The method, a variant of psychoanalytic psychotherapy, made use of transference, the repetition of the past in the present, and interpretation. Equally important, the method included continuous developmental observations of the baby and a tactful, non-didactic education of the mother in the recognition of her baby's needs and her signals.

—Fraiberg, S., Adelson, E., and Shapiro, V. (1980, p. 171)

HISTORY OF THERAPEUTIC APPROACH

EARLY ROOTS OF INFANT-PARENT PSYCHOTHERAPY: THE FIELD OF INFANT MENTAL HEALTH

Children's likelihood of survival and every aspect of their experience are shaped by the qualities of the social structures in which they live. These include the nature of their family, their immediate culture and community, and their society's health, and educational, legal, and political systems. Children's well-being, importance, and value rest on the attitudes expressed through these very complex systems.

It seems appropriate to begin by sketching briefly the various perspectives on mental health in infancy that have been expressed within different disciplines over time. This includes representative contributions from psychologists, psychoanalysts, and psychiatrists, child development researchers, investigators interested in infant capacities, and those who are active in mental health intervention. Although we cannot be comprehensive, we hope to give some sense of the different perspectives and their mutual influences that have resulted in a clinical focus on the emotional development of infants and toddlers.

The Primary Caregiving Relationship
Interest in the "mental health" of infants emerged most dramatically around the systematic recognition of the effects of the deprivation of stimulation and interaction between caregivers and infants housed in institutions. Early on,

Skeels and Dye (1939) had experimented with providing greater and more personal care to orphans by having institutionalized young women with retardation act as surrogate parents. The positive effects on the infants' development were clearly documented.

Much of the literature on deprivation was summarized by Provence and Lipton (1962) in their own study of institutionalized infants. They drew on the work of Chapin (1915), Levy (1947), Spitz (1945, 1946), and Bowlby (1960), as well as discussions of Bowlby's theories by Anna Freud (1960), Shure (1960), and Spitz (1960). Their investigation provided a more detailed analysis of the nature of the deprivation itself and the differing effects on the infants than had characterized prior efforts. They focused on discerning what processes in development were most vulnerable to this deprivation by closely analyzing the details of the infants' responses. By adopting this careful, clinical observational approach, Provence and Lipton not only supported previous findings that the absence of focused, emotionally charged, responsive care (referred to as "maternal deprivation") had an adverse impact on development, but also drew a general conclusion that synthesized their findings in an important way:

> Human development, even in infancy, is complex and multi-determined. The effects of maternal deprivation on an infant in the first year of life depend upon the degree of deficit in both the quantity and quality of maternal care, upon the infant's biological endowment and upon age and length of time he is subjected to the deprivation. Many individual combinations of these factors are possible and produce a variety of clinical pictures in terms of severity of symptoms. (Provence & Lipton, 1962, p. 162)

Recognizing the multiple determinants of the developmental process, Provence and Lipton (1962) catalogued the affected areas of development (different in individual children) that were observed both during institutionalization and after placement. These included motor development, language, reactions to people, control of impulses and capacity to defer gratification, difficulty making transitions, and impairments of thinking (i.e., thinking through and anticipating, generalizing, overcoming obstacles, and concreteness of thought). They went on to clarify that the permutations of strengths and vulnerabilities they observed also could occur in any mother-child pair, again recognizing the salient consideration of individual differences in both, but particularly in the child. They acknowledged the singular contributions of Escalona (1950, 1953) and Escalona and Leitch (1953) to their understanding and appreciation of these differences.

Coleman, Kris, and Provence (1953) pointed to both the variations in parental attitudes and the development of the mother-child relationship as important variables in infant development. Ten years later, a volume in honor of Milton Senn, the developmental pediatrician who helped establish the Yale Child Study Unit in 1948, addressed the biological aspects of development, and included a variety of contributions by pediatricians, child psychologists, and psychoanalysts that served to expand the horizon of medical education to include the healing of mind as well as body, and to remind physicians of their power and privilege as well as the importance of helping parents to understand their young children (Solnit & Provence, 1963).

Concurrently, Winnicott (1945, 1953, 1957) expanded on the subtleties and vicissitudes of development, culminating in his use of the often-quoted phrase "an ordinary devoted mother," to acknowledge the importance of the mother (or consistent mother substitute), the need for maternal devotion, and the fact that the skills and sensibilities of the ordinary mother are extremely complex and wholly "good enough." (Many of Winnicott's papers addressing these issues were collected in the

1975 volume *Through Paediatrics to Psychoanalysis: Collected Papers*.) Additionally, Erikson's (1950a, 1950b) contributions outlining the stages of development around their central tasks, the interactions associated with each, and the central outcome to be achieved were widely influential. Through all of these contributions, infants were beginning to be viewed in two important new ways. First, the young child's intrinsic, influential role in his or her own development was recognized. Second, the infant's demand to be heard and responded to in supportive, positive, and growth-promoting ways was registered.

Infant Capacities
Another important contributing stream of great influence to the understanding of early childhood development flowed from the growing investigation of infant capacities. Bower (1974), drawing on his own work (Bower, 1970; Bower, Broughton, & Moore, 1970, 1971; Bower & Wishart, 1972) and that of others, such as Cruickshank (1941), Fantz (1961), and Lipsett (1969), utilized studies of intentional reaching in neonates, coordination of vision and touch, the development of object concept and object permanence, and infant motivation to create a portrait of the infant as vigorously involved in a dynamic, interactive process of development. He maintained that the infant's intrinsic pleasure in problem solving and the dramatic role of experience in development meant that infancy was the critical period in cognitive development—the time when the greatest gains and the greatest losses can occur. Simultaneously, it became clear that the infant had more skills, and had them earlier, than anyone but parents could have imagined.

Lewis and Rosenblum's (1974) seminal work, "The Effect of the Infant on Its Caregiver," addressed deliberately what was felt to be previous neglect of the significance of the interaction between mothers and infants in terms of the infant's contributions in shaping those ongoing transactions.

Intervention in the Social Environment
Gradually, the probable usefulness of therapeutic intervention with children and families at earlier ages had emerged. Caplan (1951, 1955) introduced the concept of a "public health approach" to child psychiatry. This was well represented by a number of observers (e.g., Langford, 1955; Lindemann, Vaughn, & McGinnis, 1955; Rosenfeld & Brandt, 1955), who argued against a focus of attention on only the individual patient and advocated for the inclusion of all the emotional forces operating in smaller or larger sections of the community. From his work in child guidance clinics, Caplan came to see the troubled child as embedded in the environment and drew two important conclusions. One focused on the need to support treatment of the parents of a troubled child, using "child-centered" therapy or "focused case work" as an important and effective endeavor. This was understood as an effort to remove children from the role of serving as a costly solution to their parents' unaddressed problem, an attempt to interrupt the dynamic misperception of the child, and to free the child to be a "separate person." A second conviction was that it is highly likely that a child comes to be in the center of family conflict because of a previous parental crisis, and that, following Lindemann et al.'s (1955) bereavement work in which the object is to achieve healthy coping as an outcome of loss, it is important to track and intervene at points of ordinary or extraordinary crisis. This is the perspective adopted by Brazelton in his book, *Touchpoints* (1992).

Finally, Caplan urged that community workers (i.e., nurses, physicians, teachers) should be equipped with "necessary knowledge" so that they can swing the delicate equilibrium toward healthy coping and away from disturbance for the benefit of both family and child. This unspecified necessary knowledge was designed to give community practitioners the tools to administer crucial "mental health first aid." Caplan felt that consultation with mental health specialists should be regarded as the "essential element" in all programs of prevention, no matter what the expertise or discipline of the provider. Simultaneously, E. Furman (1957) provided treatment for children under 5 years of age by way of their parents. R. Furman and Katan (1969) followed the same model in a nursery school setting, essentially the model utilized by S. Freud (1909/1955a) in his treatment of phobia in a 5-year-old boy. At one end of the parent/child treatment continuum, parents were instructed on how to understand and respond to their child; at the other, the understanding of conflictual, personal dynamics of the parents was included as a factor in child treatment.

In 1976, a collection of articles by experts in the field of child psychiatry and child development drawn from 14 years of publication in the *Journal of the American Academy of Child Psychiatry* were brought together in one volume by Rexford, Sander, and Shapiro. In this volume, Shapiro issued a call for greater activity, within psychiatry, in the area of infancy. He pointed to the increasing interest in early childhood as a natural outgrowth of adult retrospective reconstruction utilizing the developmental point of view, and noted that the psychiatric vantage point promotes an appreciation of the impact of early interpersonal relationships, supports a holistic view of the child, and attempts to honor the role of the child in his or her own development.

CONTEMPORARY APPROACHES

Knowledge has continued to proliferate and theories have emerged that creatively utilize psychoanalytic theory and a range of infancy research. Investigators working in this area include Stern (1977, 1985, 1989, 1994, 1995, 2000), Emde (Emde, 1983; Emde & Hewitt, 2001; Emde, Gaenbauer, & Harmon, 1976, 1982), Trevarthen (1995, 1996, 2001; Trevarthen & Aitken, 2001), Beebe (2000), Beebe and Lachmann (1988, 1998; Beebe, Lachmann, & Jaffe, 1997); each has made important contributions from specific areas of interest and expertise. Greenspan (1981, 1994, 1997, 2000; Greenspan & Levis, 1999; Greenspan, Nover, Lourie, & Robinson, 1987) has conceptualized a widely influential developmental model that integrates the infant's constitutional-maturational patterns and the environment as mediated through the parent-child relationship. He has organized his conceptualization of developmental levels and their tasks around meaningful engagement, communication, and shared meaning. This organization has been utilized by Greenspan to suggest what to observe about children and how, as well as how to provide appropriate clinical treatment, specifically with children on the autistic continuum.

Emde (Emde 1983; Emde & Hewitt, 2001; Emde et al., 1976, 1982), utilizing data on infant capacities and research on adult-child interaction in the context of psychoanalytic theory, has developed theories regarding the internal experience and resulting structures related to self in infancy. His work on the nature and role of affect and the complexity of interpersonal impact is subtle and complex.

Stern (1977, 1985, 1989, 1994, 1995, 2000), also utilizing infant research in the area of capacities and mother-child interaction, created a vivid construction of the internal, developing world of the infant embedded in an interpersonal perspective. He also pursued some of the links between the understanding of mother-child interaction and clinical treatment, and explored a number of models of infant-parent psychotherapy. The most recent perspective now included stems from attempts of investigators to understand the significance of current work on brain development. Research in this area has been conducted by Schore (2001a, 2001b), Emde and Hewitt (2001), and others.

The complexity of what contributors have come to consider, the respect for environment and for the intrinsic qualities of the child, are embedded in the work of many contemporary researchers and theoreticians. They are representative of many who have utilized the earlier efforts of those interested in infancy, added to those efforts and continue, with others, to explore the intricacies and complexities of human development.

Though current investigators proceed in different ways and are personally captured by different aspects of development, the majority embrace a common point of view that honors the uniqueness of the infant and the parents, the mutual impact of the infant and its caregivers, and the power of biology, interpersonal relationships, and the widest environmental context. These are the basic understandings that they have inherited and on which knowledge continues to build. Perhaps the most important outcome has been the steadily increasing interest in the first three years of life and an awareness of their important and shaping influence.

THE INFANT-PARENT PROGRAM: PARAMETERS OF INFANT-PARENT PSYCHOTHERAPY

Although there are many different infant mental health programs that vary greatly in terms of setting, scope, and style of service delivery, it is our intention to focus on the one with which we are the most familiar. It was within and as part of the above broader context, that Selma Fraiberg (Fraiberg & Fraiberg, 1980) and her colleagues developed the model of infant-parent psychotherapy, one of the earliest and most influential programs in infant mental health intervention. This was developed at the University of Michigan in the Department of Psychiatry (1973–1979). (Many of the papers describing the work of the program during the University of Michigan years are collected in the *Clinical Studies in Infant Mental Health: The First Year of Life*, Fraiberg & Fraiberg, 1980.) The program moved to the Department of Psychiatry at the University of California, San Francisco, in 1979 and continues its efforts there.

Over the course of the past 23 years, the program has continued to develop and practice infant-parent psychotherapy in a community mental health setting. The program is based at San Francisco General Hospital, and three major services are offered under its auspices: infant-parent psychotherapy, developmental neuropsychological assessment, and mental health consultation to child care. This work has been described and discussed by Kalmanson and Pekarsky (1987), Lieberman (1992), Lieberman and Birch (1985), Lieberman and Pawl (1984), Lieberman, Silverman, and Pawl (2000), Pawl (1993), Pawl, Ahern, Grandison, Johnston, St. John, and Waldstein (2000), Pekarsky (1992), Seligman (1994), and Seligman and St. John (1995).

The Infant-Parent Program serves families with infants or toddlers in which there are difficulties in the relationship between the parents and child. Families are referred by obstetric and pediatric professionals, child care providers, child welfare workers, and others working with vulnerable parent populations, such as adolescent mothers, chronically mentally ill adults, and parents in recovery from chemical dependency. The concerns that prompt referrals focus primarily, though not exclusively, on the parents' capacities. Difficulties with which the parents struggle may, for example, prompt professional doubts about the parents' ability to provide for the child's physical and emotional well-being. Alternatively or simultaneously, concern may be focused on a child's behavior or condition, such as situations in which children are exhibiting a diagnosable constellation of symptoms, or when their behavior consistently interrupts the smooth running of grown-ups' lives. There are also some instances in which the infant's intrinsic capacities are of primary concern.

As St. John and Pawl (2000) wrote, however, "Most often, by the time a family enters the

Infant-Parent Program, both the parent(s) and the child are showing signs of distress" (p. 9), and it is the experience of each of the other that is the focus for treatment. As Pawl and Lieberman (1997) wrote, "One of the primary questions in infant-parent psychotherapy, and a question that renews itself in each treatment is: Who is the patient [the parent or the child]? An accurate, but less than adequate answer is 'both'" (p. 340). The parent and the baby create a relationship, and each makes potent contributions to it. Improvement in that relationship is the goal of treatment.

THEORETICAL CONSTRUCTS

Theory, Practice, and Reality: Home Visiting

Home visiting has been an inherent component of and vehicle for the practice of infant-parent psychotherapy since its inception. The delivery of this mental health service in the home setting represents both a response to a perceived community service need and a unique theoretical orientation. The perceived need is here described first; the theoretical constructs supporting the practice follow.

Most of the families with whom we meet would not be seen regularly if they needed to appear at clinic appointments. As anyone with a small baby knows, the rhythms of infancy frequently do not coincide with the clockwork schedules of most sectors of the external world. Bus schedules also can be unpredictable, and traveling by bus, especially with small children, is inconvenient enough to be daunting even when there is a clear idea of what will be gained from such efforts. When the fruits of the journey seem amorphous or the risks (e.g., exposure to scrutiny or criticism, or the threat of loss of custody of children) considerable, there is no initial motivation to expend such energy.

Furthermore, when parents' histories are such that their expectations of helping professionals are very low, their sense of their rights to competent professional service of any kind precarious, and their sense of shame, vulnerability, or futility regarding their circumstances high, the impediments to seeking or accepting mental health treatment are formidable and justifiable. Seligman and Pawl (1984) discussed the ways these factors can impede the formation of a therapeutic working alliance. They can also prevent parents facing multiple difficulties in their lives as individuals and in relation to their small children from seeking assistance at all. We offer infant-parent psychotherapy as a home-based service to make it a realistic, possible venture for families who might otherwise be completely bereft of mental health treatment at a juncture in their family life cycle when they might most sorely need it.

Beyond its necessity, however, home visiting also offers a wealth of possibility to the process of infant-parent psychotherapy, and is thus an important part of our theoretical orientation. The home visiting therapist is able to observe family life in all of its singular complex specificity, and to gain at a visceral level a sense of the material conditions that define a family's day-to-day reality. For therapists, this reality is frequently an initially painful aspect of providing treatment, because we most often treat socially and economically disadvantaged families, many of whose life circumstances are quite dire. One therapist, for example, discovered that the mother with whom she had spoken initially on the telephone who complained that her son was "hyperactive" lived in a one-room apartment with three small children. Although the 3-year-old boy in question appeared to the therapist to demonstrate a developmentally appropriate level of energy, it was clear to her that for this mother, whose depression made even trips to the neighborhood park difficult, the boy's needs were readily experienced as "too much." Furthermore, when the therapist accompanied the family to the park one day, she found that the mother's concern about broken bottles and hypodermic needles in the sandbox was justified. On another day, there was a shooting in the same park, and a neighborhood child narrowly escaped injury. Although this mother's depression was clearly an important factor in this family's dynamics, the therapist would have been unable to imagine, include, or respond as appropriately to the contextual elements of the family's circumstances if she had not seen and experienced them herself. Witnessing the injury inflicted on infants, toddlers, and their families as a result of poverty, homelessness, environmental illness, racial and sexual discrimination, anti-immigration policy, the wedded threats of chemical dependency, violence, and incarceration, and the erosion of social service support assists infant-parent psychotherapists in meaningfully appraising families' difficulties and in conveying to families their awareness and sincere interest in understanding the ways they experience their lives.

Home visiting is an important part of our theoretical framework for another reason. Often, troubles in the relationship between parents and their infants and small children are inextricable from complexities and sorrows in relation to the parents' sense of home and the child's experience of it. Whether because poverty and ghettoization prevent a parent from securing a home that offers the family a basic sense of safety, or because recent immigration to the United States has left parents feeling displaced and cut off from their own family, language, history, and culture, or because dislocation or deracination have been encoded and transmitted intergenerationally within a family that has lived with hardship in one place for a long time, it is the case that for many people, the place where they live offers few of the comforts, pleasures, or protections more typically associated with the word "home." The wish to protect and to be protected, to provide and to be provided for, to belong, the yearning for community, for relationships that have been lost or are being strained or eroded, the memory of people or states or places to which access has been lost, the wish to feel that one matters—this inchoate longing for a sense of home has long been defended against via whatever strategies a parent's personality and psychological disposition dictate.

These subterranean difficulties influence and are reflected in the material ways a family inhabits the space they occupy. Three examples come to mind. One single mother treated in our program had had Eastern European grandparents who were killed in the Holocaust. This woman hoarded, and kept her apartment so cluttered that there was literally no room for her twin sons to crawl without danger of their bringing piles of books or boxes tumbling down on them. Clearly, this is relevant on many levels. A Native American grandmother seen in our program was at risk of losing the custody of her grandson, whom she loved very much and who looked to her as the sole source of gentleness, care, and protection he had encountered in his three years of life. The placement was threatened by the condition of abject squalor in which this pair lived. It vexed county social workers that the filth resulting from pigeons who roosted inside the house, a toilet that would clog and go unfixed for weeks, and food left to decay in various rooms appeared barely to trouble this grandmother. The infant-parent therapist learned that this woman had been raised as a migrant worker by abusive, alcoholic parents. The family was homeless except during periods when they had a car and lived in that. At a very basic level, and for complex psychological reasons, this woman lived inside her house as though she were still on the streets. The third example involves a Mexican mother who was referred to our program because she had been accused of medical neglect of her infant daughter, who was sick and in need of ongoing medical attention. It became clear that for this woman, "home" was not the one-room urban apartment that she occupied with her daughter, but the Mexican village she regretted leaving and longed for desperately. She had the idea that it was only there, not in the big county hospital in the foreign city in which she found herself, that her daughter could be healed. Should her daughter get well in the United States, it would represent to this mother an unbearable breach with her true home.

Sometimes, an infant-parent psychotherapist can assist a parent in sorting through these complex issues (we might call them locopsychological) in the course of attending to the child's experience of the parent and the parent's experience of the child in the context of their literal home. Such domestic domains as sleep (e.g., whether, or for how long, an infant sleeps in the same bed or room as the parents, how a child falls asleep or is expected to fall asleep, the manner in which a small child is awakened by or awakens the parents), eating (where, when, how, what, with whom and with how much relish, fuss, strife, or ceremony), hygiene, toileting, discipline, housekeeping, and play are grist for the mill of infant-parent psychotherapy. When families experience relief from struggle in some of these domains, they are better able to enjoy and respond to each other and to live meaningfully in the place in which they dwell.

Finally, and closely connected with all of this, home visiting is important because infants are phenomenological creatures: They deal in perceptions of texture, temperature, taste; register gradations of comfort and discomfort; establish rhythms and express preferences through the body-based systems that define them; seek and organize themselves around and form their expectations of the world based on the bodies and behaviors of the people on whom their lives depend. When an infant-parent psychotherapy takes place in a small child's home, it is taking place where almost everything of significance to the child exists. As Pawl, St. John, and Pekarsky (2000) wrote, "To be a regular visitor in a small child's home is to be a figure in his or her inner world" (387).

"MATURATIONAL PROCESSES AND THE FACILITATING ENVIRONMENT": INFANT AND PARENT DEVELOPMENT WITHIN THE RELATIONAL MATRIX

The writings of the pediatrician/psychoanalyst D. W. Winnicott (1945, 1953, 1957, 1965, 1971, 1975) describe and inform many aspects of infant development as we understand and seek to support it through infant-parent psychotherapy. Winnicott is perhaps most famous for having coined the welcome phrase "good-enough mothering." He described infants' ever-present contribution to their relational matrix, the crucial and commonplace attentiveness of primary caregivers (usually mothers) to their infants' needs, and the ways this attentiveness enables the infant's increasingly differentiated participation in relationships and the world. Winnicott (1965) wrote, for example:

> Parents do not have to make their baby as the artist has to make his picture or the potter his pot. The baby grows in his or her own way if the environment is good enough. Someone has referred to the good enough provision as the "average expectable environment." The fact is that throughout the centuries mothers, parents, and parent-substitutes have in fact usually provided exactly those conditions that the infant and small child do in fact need at the beginning. (p. 96)

Winnicott (1965) distinguished between ordinary situations in which parents are able to provide in this good-enough way for their infants, and those worrisome situations in which, for some combination of reasons, they are not. The "ordinary" situations are in themselves quite complex. Winnicott wrote:

> The infant . . . is at this first and earliest stage in a state of mergence, not yet having separated out mother and "not-me" objects from the "me," so that what is adaptive or "good" in the environment is building up in the infant's storehouse of experience as a self quality, indistinguishable at first (by the infant) from the infant's own healthy functioning. (p. 97)

When we observe infants over time, we can trace the ways their repeated satisfactory experiences in the world as it is mediated for them by ordinary, reliable, devoted caregivers, in tandem with the healthy development of their own innate capacities (motor, cognitive, and social-emotional), give rise to senses of personal competence and confident interest in others. It is important to stress, as Winnicott (1965) did, that experiences of being disappointed, frustrated, and misunderstood are not only unavoidable in typical development, but crucial. He described these as necessary "failures of adaptation" of the caregiver to the infant's needs: "These failures are again a kind of adaptation because they are related to the growing need of the child for meeting reality and for achieving separation and for the establishment of a personal identity" (pp. 96-97).

These remarkable conditions of typical development may be contrasted with situations in which these processes are impeded. Winnicott (1965) wrote, "The maturational process only takes effect in an individual infant insofar as there is a [good-enough] facilitating environment" (p. 239). The institutionalized infants studied by Spitz (1945, 1946), whose physical needs were provided for but who were deprived of human connectedness, testified through their responses of abjection to the ordinary brilliance of the good-enough caregiver-infant relational matrix.

When caregivers are unable to provide sufficiently satisfactory responses to an infant's needs in a reliable, ongoing way, this unreliability can be built into the developing child's most profound sense of self, others, and the world. When infants are abandoned to states of distress, subjected to intermittent responsiveness from caregivers, or responded to in a fashion radically out of keeping with their needs, they manage these intolerable situations in costly and problematic ways. Some of these management strategies and the resulting developmental difficulties are discussed below.

Development as it is understood in infant-parent psychotherapy is a lifelong process. Clearly, the physiological processes involved in infant and child development constitute a particularly gripping and wondrous field of study. As babies grow older, they confront their parents with new attendant developmental issues. Parenting is itself a role with important implications for adult development. Stern (1995) proposed the term "the motherhood constellation" to denote the phenomenon he observed:

> With the birth of a baby, especially the first, the mother passes into a new and unique psychic organization that I call the motherhood constellation. As a psychic organizer, this "constellation" will determine a new set of action tendencies, sensibilities, fantasies, fears, and wishes. . . . It is seen as a unique, independent construct in its own right, of great magnitude in the life of most mothers, and entirely normal. (p. 171)

When things go awry in the parent-infant system, parents as well as infants suffer the consequences, and developmental opportunities are lost on all sides. But one of the most precious findings of infant-parent psychotherapy is that, although the first months and years of a child's life frequently (if not inevitably) constitute a time of special vulnerability for families, they also often represent a time of unparalleled opportunity for psychological growth and positive change. In the 23 years of practice at the Infant-Parent Program, therapists have certainly met parents who were unable to ensure their own or their children's safety and well-being or to provide a good-enough facilitating environment; we have never, however, met a parent who did not wish to, even when this wish took an inchoate form and was barely recognizable in its expression. That these infant-parent relationships are also embedded in further complicated relational matrices is also relevant.

"Ghosts in the Nursery" and the Walking Wounded: The Unharmonious Cohabitation of Conflict and Trauma

What model of the mind is assumed in infant-parent psychotherapy? The answer to this question has changed over time. The phrase that has become emblematic of infant-parent psychotherapy over the years is Fraiberg, Adelson, et al.'s (1980) image of "ghosts in the nursery." This image dramatized the psychoanalytic concept of repetition in the present of unresolved conflict from the past, but addressed the special circumstance in which this repetition is enacted not in relation to a psychoanalyst, as it was conceptualized in classical theory, but rather in relation to an infant. Fraiberg wrote:

> In every nursery there are ghosts. They are the visitors from the unremembered past of the parents, the uninvited guests at the christening. Under favorable circumstances, these unfriendly and unbidden spirits are banished from the nursery.... The baby makes his own imperative claim upon parental love and, in strict analogy with the fairy tales, the bonds of love protect the child and his parents against the intruders, the malevolent ghosts. (p. 164)

Sometimes, however, these "ghosts" persist and prevent a family from perceiving and responding to one another in spontaneous, connected, and mutually gratifying ways. Fraiberg wrote that infant-parent psychotherapy was developed to treat situations in which an infant has become:

> the representative of figures in the parental past, or a representative of an aspect of the parental self that is repudiated or negated. In some cases the baby himself seems engulfed in the parental neurosis and is showing the early signs of emotional disturbance. In treatment, we examine with the parents the past and the present in order to free them and their baby from old "ghosts" who have invaded the nursery, and then we must make meaningful links between the past and the present through interpretations that lead to insight. At the same time ... we maintain the focus on the baby through the provision of developmental information and discussion. We move back and forth, between present and past, parent and baby, but we always return to the baby. (p. 61)

In one case, for example, Dianna, a woman who had lost her own mother to a prolonged hospitalization when she was a young child, experienced her 8-month-old son Joe's newly developed ability to crawl, and specifically his exploratory forays away from her, as an abandonment. Unaware of this experience, however, and focused only on the practical difficulties her son's mobility introduced (mess and mishap), Dianna decided that she "needed a break," and she planned a trip for herself. She weaned Joe abruptly in preparation for this separation. Joe responded to this baffling and upsetting change in a much more circumscribed way than many young children would, and perhaps than he himself would had the arrangement persisted. On the first day that his mother refused to nurse him, he cried and protested. On the second day, he accepted her refusals without protest, but developed a remarkable symptom: at irregular intervals throughout the day, he hit himself on the head with his fist. The infant-parent therapist observed this startling behavior. Dianna, alarmed by Joe's self-hitting, was quick to make the connection in the conversation with the therapist between her abrupt weaning of Joe and his unusual symptom. Dianna was also able to identify her true motivation for traveling away from Joe: her experience of his moving away from her, the devastating feelings of abandonment rooted in her own history that this separation evoked for her, and her inclination to ward off these feelings by turning passive into active, by abandoning rather than being abandoned.

The case of Joe and Dianna illustrates the application in infant-parent psychotherapy of the psychoanalytic model, in which the problem is understood as repression of a parental memory (or the affect associated with it) that gives rise to repetition. The solution inheres in making the unconscious conscious, or, as S. Freud (1914/1955b) wrote, "remembering...and working through" to break from the cycle of repetition. This model continues to be useful in situations in which a parent is able and inclined to think about his or her past and, with the help of a therapist, to bring into consciousness and into words memories, ideas, and feelings that have previously been banished from consciousness. Sometimes, this process uncovers a particular memory or conviction of which the parent has been unaware and that has functioned as a lynchpin for the parent's psychological organization. More frequently, there are multiple nexuses of thought, feeling, and memory that tend to remain remote from consciousness and to influence perceptions and actions. The process of reflecting in which the parent engages with the therapist in relation to the infant *in itself* loosens unconscious convictions, challenges accustomed expectations, and opens up new possibilities of experience.

In other cases, this model is less resonant as a central vehicle of useful understanding (though all modes may be relevant at different moments within any one treatment). Often, the injuries a parent has suffered began early enough and have been pervasive and multilayered enough to have negatively shaped in the most basic ways how the parent experiences self, others, and the world. It is then not a matter of a particular memory being too painful to bring to consciousness, or even a collection of unconscious ideas, memories, and feelings that are repressed, but rather, of a severing of the ties between entire realms of experience and of the capacity for reflective thought being itself impaired. Judith Herman (1992) wrote, "Traumatic events produce profound and lasting changes in physiological arousal, emotion, cognition and memory. Moreover, traumatic events may sever these normally integrated functions from one another" (p. 34).

Herman (1992) developed the concept of complex Posttraumatic Stress Disorder to account for situations in which prolonged and repeated trauma necessitates a diagnostic model that goes beyond Posttraumatic Stress Disorder, which is tied to a circumscribed traumatic event. Herman wrote:

> Survivors of prolonged abuse develop characteristic personality changes, including deformations of relatedness and identity. Survivors of abuse in childhood develop similar problems with relationships and identity; in addition, they are particularly vulnerable to repeated harm, both self-inflicted and at the hands of others. (p. 119)

Often, the parent-child dyads and triads we treat are in the clutches of this more fundamental and pervasive kind of repetition of harm—a repetition that results not from repression, but from disassociation; not from forgetting painful thoughts and experiences, but from building a personality structure around surviving intolerable experiences that precludes the capacity to remember. These structures shape the way the world is seen and experienced.

Infant-parent psychotherapy in these instances involves identifying those aspects of the parents' manner of holding themselves and moving through the world that have been constricted or distorted as a result of known or probable historical trauma. These aspects include style of self-presentation, personality structure, ways of organizing information, characteristic modes of relating, and systems of self-regulation. Through intervention that focuses on the parent's experience of the child and the child's experience of the parent, infant-parent psychotherapy gently but persistently challenges the worldview these patterns express. The dynamic context for this is, of course, the relational matrix created.

METHODS OF ASSESSMENT AND INTERVENTION

Clinical Assessment

Assessment in infant-parent psychotherapy entails initially identifying whether difficulties of significant proportions exist in the relationship between an infant or toddler and his or her caregivers, and if so, how these are expressed and what causes them. In large measure, this information is gleaned through clinical observation and interview initially and continuing over time. When ambiguity initially exists, persists, or arises in the course of therapy, it may be appropriate in addition for the child to be seen in the program's developmental neuropsychology unit. It may also be relevant to seek an evaluation of a parent for diagnostic purposes and/or medication consultation. If clinical assessment does not result in a confident understanding of the parent or raises other issues where further knowledge seems necessary, a referral for evaluation will be initiated.

Ongoing clinical assessment entails considering development as a range of expectable capacities and dynamics. This concept is relevant to both child and parent development. It is important that clinical observations be undertaken by therapists who are knowledgeable about infant/toddler and adult development. Recognizing and understanding what typical and atypical behaviors look like in infants, toddlers, and parents is central. It is crucial to know infant and toddler capacities and also the range of capacities relevant to ordinary parenthood. It is also necessary to appreciate the levels of meaning of behaviors and to appreciate the transactions within the infant-parent relationship.

Infants express preferences and experiences from the first moments of life. These expressions become more nuanced and complex as the infant's capacities unfold and expand. It takes time and attention to get to know a particular baby, and knowledge of the range of developmentally expectable behaviors of infants in general is necessary. However, when things are going well enough with an infant, it is possible to determine a sound hypothesis regarding the meaning of his or her behaviors. When things are going well enough, parents are very good at participating in this process, and undertake it on their own. Consider, for example, a mother who knows the difference between the sound of a "hungry cry," a "sleepy cry," a "tummy hurt cry," and a "just plain fussy cry" in her 3-month-old.

When things are not going well enough for an infant, it becomes increasingly difficult to discern the meaning behind his or her behavior, although the meaning is always there, even when it is an expression of the frustration or despair experienced in rudimentary attempts to make sense of the world. Concomitantly, when things are not going well enough between a parent and child, the parent is often illiterate with respect to the infant's signals, and misreads or ignores them habitually. One axis of assessment, then, is defined by these questions: How legible is the infant's experience? How able is the parent to understand or form hypotheses about the meanings of the infant's behavior? Do parent and child engage in the mutual construction of meaning, or is meaning imposed unilaterally? These questions are answerable much of the time through observation. One watches for distortions in parental perceptions and the creation of behaviors in babies and toddlers that seem primarily responsive to negative perceptions and treatment. Sometimes, children resemble an assemblage of negative projections that serve as a framework for their own, barely discernable inclinations of self. Such understandings emerge through observation, hypothesis, and providing the necessary climate of curiosity for the voices of parent and child to emerge in all their singularity and duality.

Silverman and Lieberman (1999) have discussed some of the ways in which negative parental attributions not only prevent a parent from accurately perceiving the meaning behind a child's behavior, but can also constrict and influence the child's experience of self, such that the child may develop into conformity with the parent's distorted perceptual system. When these dynamics are underway in an infant-parent or toddler-parent dyad or triad, identifying ruptures in the system—evidence of experiences and meanings that run contrary to the dominant account—is an important part of the assessment process.

DEVELOPMENTAL NEUROPSYCHOLOGICAL ASSESSMENT

Though aimed at thoroughly understanding and including constitution and temperamental contribution to a child's apperception, this assessment embraces the understanding of this child and his or her development in the context of the child's signal relationships. This is achieved in the course of four one- to two-hour sessions that include child, parent(s), therapist, and developmental neuropsychologist. It includes parent interview, play observation, and formal testing of the child, and attends to cognition, attention, memory, motor skills, language, visual processing, and social-emotional functioning. Ahern and Grandison (2000) have described this work in detail. Most important, the parent is the ultimate recipient of what has been mutually learned and it is the parent for whom the report is written. The child is also included fully in the process. The written report has proved equally useful to other professionals with whom the family is involved.

THE ROLE OF ASSESSMENT WITH RESPECT TO FAMILIES' INVOLVEMENT WITH OTHER AGENCIES

Even when no formal developmental neuropsychological assessment has been conducted, the information and understanding acquired with the family through the process of clinical assessment can be useful to other agencies involved with the family.

The infant and toddler years are complex, action-packed, emotionally intense times for all families, and no one navigates them anything like perfectly. Sometimes, professionals working in other capacities with families of very small children (pediatricians, day care providers, social workers, public health nurses, etc.) are alarmed by the emotional pitch and intensity and the apparent vulnerability of the infant family system. When these issues are compounded by the stressors associated with poverty, racial and ethnic discrimination, and other social forces that make protecting and providing for a family difficult for parents, these professionals sometimes perceive greater individual and family pathology than exists. Birch (1994) suggested that aggressive impulses toward children are a much ignored, ordinary, and nonpathological part of the parenting experience for mothers. When a family comes under professional scrutiny, sometimes professionals allow little room for this side of what we consider to be normal parental ambivalence toward children. Even when worrisome things are clearly in evidence for everyone, a context for understanding helps other professionals to continue to work with the family in a way that emphasizes the family's strengths and supports them, rather than pathologizing their vulnerabilities.

INTERVENTION

Infant-parent psychotherapeutic intervention has been conceptualized as involving four modalities: concrete support, nondidactic developmental guidance, psychodynamic psychotherapy, and emotional support (Fraiberg & Fraiberg, 1980; Lieberman & Pawl, 1993; Lieberman, Silverman, & Pawl, 2000; Pawl & Lieberman, 1997; Pawl, St. John, & Pekarsky, 2000). Emotional support has been further conceptualized as the essential quality of the therapist-patient relationship and the overall relational matrix (Pawl, 1995b). These modalities of intervention come into focus as they are relevant to their impact on the parent or the child individually, and on the relationship among all involved.

Emotional Support

Fraiberg, Shapiro, and Cherniss (1980) initially conceptualized emotional support as a discrete modality of infant-parent psychotherapy:

> On the one hand, we provide an ongoing, nondidactic education to facilitate the development of the parent-child relationship and to lead parents into an understanding of their baby's needs, and the ways they, as parents, can promote development. On the other hand, we also address feelings and psychological stress the parents may be experiencing as they attempt to respond to the infant's developmental needs. (p. 65)

These activities were seen to constitute emotional support. This has been further conceptualized as the essential quality of the therapist-patient relationship, in which all of the other modalities are embedded (Pawl & St. John, 1998).

Nondidactic Developmental Guidance

This entails the sensitive provision of developmental information and observation as these seem relevant to the overall process.

Concrete Support

Because the needs of small dependent children often evoke feelings of need in more or less conscious and concrete ways in the adults who care for them, need is frequently a theme—either overt or covert—throughout infant-parent psychotherapies. In addition, many of the families that have been seen throughout the course of the development of infant-parent psychotherapy have been families whose concrete circumstances range from precarious financial stability to abject poverty and homelessness. To fail to attempt to assist parents in securing the necessities of life with a small child or not to acknowledge the realities of their needs would be to relegate the treatment to uselessness.

This does not mean, however, that the infant-parent psychotherapist enters a family with the intention of forming a laundry list of things to do and crossing them off one by one. On the contrary, the extent to which and the ways in which a therapist assists a family in getting their concrete needs met and ambitions realized is a matter of an evolving therapeutic contract. In some cases, parents have no hope initially that anything other than a ride to the pediatrician or the grocery store could ease the strain they experience. Such offers then represent the first token of earnestness on the therapist's part to really find ways to address the family's troubles as they experience them. Most families come to find other modalities of intervention equally or more helpful, and frequently, concrete support becomes a much less relevant mode in the course of a treatment. Conversely, some parents are uncomfortable accepting concrete support from a stranger and are prepared to consider it only after they have gotten to know the therapist and to find the therapist reliable and capable of taking care of himself or herself.

Home visiting in itself constitutes a form of concrete support. Beyond this, concrete support might involve providing rides or keeping a family company on errands or appointments; advocating on behalf of a family with landlords, social workers, day care providers, or health professionals; locating resources such as sources of diapers, formula, toys, clothes, or child equipment; making referrals to support groups, respite care, psychiatrists, pediatricians, or day care; navigating the process of their enrolling in school or job training or applying for work or child care leave; or joining a parent in folding the laundry during a visit. These activities are understood and implemented such that they fit comfortably with and can be a vital part of the complex therapeutic relationship. Vigilance and self-awareness on the part of the therapist are, of course, vitally necessary, as they are in any thoughtful treatment.

Psychodynamic Psychotherapy
Psychodynamic interventions with infant-parent dyads and triads can be remarkably powerful. The fact that babies so frequently function as transference objects for their parents—as representatives of important figures from the parents' past, including their own parents, themselves as infants, and other key people in the parents' lives—has potentially positive as well as negative consequences. Intervention directed at the infant-parent relational matrix can have resonance throughout the generations; not only can the present familial relationships be set on a more promising path, but unresolved conflicts and sorrows from the parental past can be resolved and released, and a strong and flexible foundation can be laid for the child's potential future disposition as a parent. Fraiberg, Shapiro, et al. (1980) wrote evocatively about the transformational power of the infant in infant-parent psychotherapy: "The baby can be a catalyst. He provides a powerful motive for positive change in his parents. He represents their hopes and deepest longings; he stands for renewal of the self; his birth can be experienced as a psychological rebirth for his parents" (pp. 53–54).

How might an infant-parent psychotherapist assist a family in realizing this potential for positive psychological change and growth? The standard fare of psychodynamic psychotherapy entails a verbal exchange between therapist and patient focusing on observation of experience, ideas, feelings, and behavior, and speculation regarding the origins, functions, and significance of these. These are also the ingredients of which infant-parent psychotherapeutic interventions are made, with the difference that it is not an individual psyche that is at issue, but the joint representational system of the infant-parent matrix.

Lieberman, Silverman, and Pawl (2000) applied Stern's (1995) notion of "ports of entry" into "the parent-infant clinical system." They noted that psychotherapeutic intervention in infant-parent psychotherapy is aimed at the web of mutually constructed meanings in the infant-parent relationship. They identified five commonly used ports of entry for intervention: the child's behavior, the parent-child interaction, the child's representations of the self and of the parent, the parent's representations of the self and of the child, and the parent-therapist relationship. We would add that the child-therapist relationship can also represent a port of entry for intervention, although it is always inclusive interaction among the therapeutic cluster that is the goal (St. John & Pawl, 2000). The infant is the agent of change only as the infant can be experienced differently by the parent. The baby is the final solidifier and has a role in the entire process, but the therapist's attitude and the parents' experience of the therapist, not only in relation to themselves but in relation to the baby, is the opening wedge to the baby's effectiveness. Simply experiencing the baby as the therapist sees him or her can positively affect the parental view. This is different from a primary reliance on interpretation as the central effort in clearing away debris for the new experience of the child by the parent and by the child of the parent, although this may at times be useful as well. (A more detailed perspective on the parent-therapist relationship has been described by Pawl, 1995.)

Specific techniques of psychodynamic infant-parent psychotherapy can include many things. For example, the therapist might make use of inquiry that encourages parents to verbalize their ideas about the infant, and may perhaps implicitly challenge these ideas by putting them into a question. Such a focus, however, must not be disingenuous. Whatever the therapist's hypothesis, it must be a hypothesis. Therapists ask because they are genuinely curious. They might ask, "How do you know when he's hungry?" They might use observation-out-loud: "He is trying to turn his head away from the bottle." They might use speculation-out-load: "Maybe he doesn't want any more milk right now. Maybe he is full and wants to rest." Often, observation-out-loud explores the possibility of something positive about the parent-infant relationship and brings it to light: "Look how she follows you with her eyes when you walk across the room. I think she doesn't want to lose sight of such an important person." Sometimes, it is aimed at exploring something negative and focusing on that: "When you (parents) get so angry at each other and yell so loudly, Timmy seems to make himself as little as he can." Sometimes, this kind of observation must be followed up with speculation: "I wonder whether he is afraid that you will hurt each other again?" Sometimes, a straightforward statement of conviction, with or without a piece of developmental guidance, is better than a speculation: "Children can have funny ideas about what causes what, and they sometimes feel that they are to blame even for things they had nothing to do with. I believe that Timmy thinks you hurt each other because he did something wrong." Representing a possible experience of the baby has been identified as another infant-parent psychotherapeutic technique: "I wonder if what he'd like to say is, When you disappear from day care and don't say good-bye, it scares me that you could just disappear at any moment." Sometimes, the therapist makes an observation-in-action, such as when a toddler brought a broken toy to a therapist after his father stepped on it, and the therapist in turn placed the toy in the hands of the father. This suggests that it is the father's job to repair the things that are broken between him and his son. This is, in a sense, an emblematic comment in action.

These and related psychotherapeutic techniques are aimed in general at assisting the family in symbolizing through words, actions, and interactions the issues that matter to them, rather than remaining stuck in patterns of thought and action that are unfulfilling or damaging to them. Domains that are frequently addressed via psychotherapeutic interventions include space, time, and energy. The significance of home visiting with regard to a family's situation in relation to the space they occupy has already been discussed. In addition, issues of connection, separation, and individuation are navigated across space, both physical and psychic.

The domain of time has to do with memory and repetition (past), the capacity for spontaneity, flexibility, and connectedness (present), and the ability to be planful and hopeful (future). One mother in our program had lost custody of an older child and was arrested in a state of perpetual lamentation of the loss of that child, to the extent that she would hold her new infant close, rock her, and cry "I lost my baby. I lost my baby." Stranded in a kind of timelessness, this woman was in the process of "losing" her potential connection with her present baby. The infant-parent psychotherapy involved assisting this woman in moving from melancholia to mourning (S. Freud, 1917/1957) with respect to the loss of her first child, in becoming emotionally available to her present child, and in conceiving of a future with this child that would be different from her own childhood and from the pattern she had lived out with the older girl. (This case is described in more detail later in the chapter.) Infant-parent psychodynamic intervention in the domain of time also frequently involves sorting out or establishing generational lines that are functional for a family, whether this means relieving the burden of the parentified child of a depressed mother, assisting a father in assuming a position of partnership with a mother rather than remaining in an infantile position in relation to her and a competitive relation to his child, or liberating a woman who was deprived as a child from a siblinglike rivalrous relation with her own child.

Infant-parent psychodynamic interventions in the domain of energy have to do with assisting infant-parent dyads and triads in understanding the ways their respective systems of self-regulation work in relation to one another, how their temperaments complement or challenge one another, and how the intense influx of both life force and demand introduced by the presence of the baby influences the parental system. Furthermore, through psychodynamic intervention, depression-related depletion and passivity may be lifted, trauma-related numbing may be reduced, and anxiety-related perseveration may be arrested such that new reserves of energy become available for relationships and life.

MAJOR SYNDROMES, SYMPTOMS, AND PROBLEMS TREATED

The symptoms and problems of central interest to the infant-parent psychotherapist are those embedded within the transactions of the infant-parent relationship. These are the focus of treatment. Frequently, these problems are seen as nested in ideas of abuse, deprivation, and neglect, whether emotional or more physically manifested. Although problems may exist within parent or child and clearly contribute to the troubled relationships, they are not the primary focus of the work, though they are totally relevant and involved.

Without exception, the parents treated in this program are diagnosable, and these diagnoses range widely across the entire spectrum of disturbances described in the *DSM-IV* (American Psychiatric Association [APA], 1994). Crucial as this information is, it is not that disturbance that is directly treated, although treatment will have some positive impact on those problems. Directly treating the parent's disturbance is not the main intent of infant-parent psychotherapy, even though the treatment may prove to have a main effect in improving the adult's functioning in a variety of spheres in addition to being a parent.

Infants' and toddlers' diagnoses tend to be more limited, and include Depression, Reactive Attachment Disorder, Separation Anxiety Disorder, Attention Deficit Disorder, feeding and eating disorders, sleep disorders, and syndromes that may be revealed by neurodevelopmental assessment. Outside of *DSM-IV*, the *Diagnostic Classification Zero to Three* (1994) diagnostic framework offers a useful system for discerning and describing what can go awry regarding infants' and toddlers' capacities, relational orientations, and ways of experiencing the world.

The problems treated using infant-parent psychotherapy focus on what occurs between parent and child, even as the therapist must strive to understand the internal world of each participant.

CASE EXAMPLE

DIAGNOSIS

Helen and her 1-year-old baby Angel were referred for infant-parent psychotherapy by the social worker at the halfway house where they had been living for the previous six months. The referral was made because of this worker's concerns that Helen's mental illness left her at risk of neglecting Angel. Helen carried a diagnosis of Schizoaffective Disorder, for which she received disability assistance and was prescribed Stelazine. She was followed by a psychiatrist at the county hospital, who met with her on a once-monthly basis for medication monitoring. Helen had lived on her own since she was 16 years of age, rotating between periods of precarious stability during which she managed to maintain housing, usually shared with transient friends, and periods of decompensation during which she was homeless or lived in shelters. She had suffered numerous traumas, including a rape and a stabbing, and she exhibited posttraumatic symptomotology such as derealization, disassociation, and numbing as well as the severe mood and thought disturbances present during periods of decompensation. She also suffered from pervasive depression and her thinking was extremely concrete.

Helen had had another daughter, Cathy, eight years prior to this pregnancy and had lost custody of her on grounds of neglect when she was an infant. Angel's birth had precipitated a decompensation, and Helen had received more comprehensive mental health assessment and treatment at that point because Angel's presence in her life brought her to the attention of multiple mental health and social service systems. The two lived for a time in a residential psychiatric program for mothers and babies, and then were discharged to the halfway house where they currently resided. The halfway house social worker who referred the pair for infant-parent psychotherapy reported that Helen was "so depressed she was depressing the baby," and that "all she talks about is her other kid."

Case Formulation

The infant-parent psychotherapy assessment confirmed the social worker's impression that Helen's psychological disposition was adversely affecting Angel, and that Helen was preoccupied with thoughts of her older daughter to Angel's detriment. As was described previously, Helen would clasp Angel to her and rock her with a faraway look in her eyes, repeating, "I lost my baby. I lost my baby." She rarely spoke directly to Angel, except in an inauthentic-seeming syrupy babytalk. She attended to Angel, but only in a noncontingent way. That is, she was given over completely to rituals of child tending such as feeding and bathing, but she administered to her automatically, rather than in response to perceived needs and desires on Angel's part, and treated Angel as though she were a much younger infant: a babe in arms. She tended to dress Angel (as well as herself) in multiple layers of clothing that constricted her movement and to feed her more frequently and in bigger quantities than necessary or desirable.

Helen found it anxiety-provoking to leave the house, and so the pair were confined to a small interior space that was shared with other mentally disabled adults and one other, younger infant. Angel was receiving precious little stimulation and had few arenas in which to exercise the expansion of motor, cognitive, or social-emotional developmental capacities. She had long since given up efforts to engage her mother in nuanced exchanges, and instead presented as an alarmingly placid 1-year-old. Helen experienced Angel's ability to smile on cue and her compliance with and perhaps enjoyment of the cuddling sessions Helen initiated as evidence that Angel was a "happy baby." On the contrary, we saw Angel as a depressed, deprived 1-year-old well on the way to developmental delay in many areas.

Treatment Approach and Rationale for Its Selection

We saw Helen as suffering from a mental illness that had bearing on her ability to adequately parent Angel, but that might not preclude the possibility that she could succeed in this regard. That is, it was clear that her historical vulnerability to decompensation put her at risk for again finding herself in a state in which it was impossible to care for Angel, and there were even now serious problems in her present relationship with Angel. It seemed possible that the care Helen was receiving now would enable her to maintain an adequate level of functioning such that infant-parent psychotherapy could be beneficial. Specifically, Helen was in psychiatric treatment and was medically compliant, was in a stable, assisted-living housing situation, and was receiving a number of family support services that had not been available to her in the past.

The infant-parent psychotherapy that ensued focused on two areas. First, the therapist assisted Angel in reinitiating and amplifying a signaling system that had fallen into disuse as a result of the failure of her environment to respond. Second, the therapist focused on loosening the grip of Helen's perseverative ideas about her older daughter so that she was able to perceive and respond to Angel in the here and now. Both of these processes were facilitated by the therapist's attentiveness to the immediate observable experience of both mother and child. She made use of all of the techniques of intervention described previously to bring Helen and Angel into focus for each other and to assist them in communicating with each other.

The therapist learned early on that it was necessary to be very specific and clear with Helen, whose concrete thinking and pervasive sense of ominousness conspired to make the world quite frightening for her. For example, the therapist's use on one occasion of the expression "I'll keep my eyes peeled" inspired terror in Helen, who could not keep the gruesome image this phrase evoked out of her head. Any metaphors, in other words, tended to be more baffling and unsettling than enlightening, and it was necessary to avoid them. In addition, the therapist developed a special communicative style with this pair in response to their combined difficulties. This style was characterized by a slight expansion or amplification of responses—surprise, puzzlement, amusement, consternation—as a way of enlivening the affective field and highlighting the expressive texture that most people take for granted and deploy and respond to as a matter of course. She expressed both her own experiences and her understanding of Helen's and Angel's experiences in this way. For example, once, when Helen was methodically spooning oatmeal into Angel's mouth despite the fact that Angel seemed more and more reluctant to consume it, the therapist said, "Angel, you look like you're so finished you're ready to say 'No more oatmeal!'" and stuck out her tongue. Angel laughed and stuck out her tongue too. As predicted, Helen found the therapist's antics amusing and intriguing rather than irritating or unremarkable. When Helen was treated inconsiderately by a disability clerk, the therapist registered indignation and anger in a similar, slightly intensified manner, and Helen responded with wonder that someone would "get their dukes up over me."

From these initial sparks of affectively charged exchange, a true system of signal and response caught fire between Helen and Angel. Miraculously, as the flesh-and-blood child in her care became more real and present for Helen, the older child receded to her place in the past. The therapist assisted in this process: for example, when Helen made her global statement "I lost my baby," she responded by saying "You are remembering Cathy and feeling sad about the things that happened to the two of you back then." Helen was able eventually to articulate her fear that she would inevitably lose Angel just as she had lost Cathy, and the therapist was able to reassure her "Angel is right here in your arms." Helen and the therapist retraced the events that had occurred in the past, identified the elements of Helen's life that were different now, anticipated junctures that might be difficult in the future, and planned ways of coping and securing extra help should Helen's distress increase.

But they never strayed far in their conversations from their present interactions with Angel. Angel herself became the most engaging advocate for the urgency of the present. Within a few months of the beginning of treatment, Angel became much more expressive and engaging during sessions. She demanded her mother's attention with age-appropriate insistence. It took longer for her to maintain this persistence outside of the sessions; the therapist's missing amplifications and focus resulted in less effectively rewarding responses from Helen to Angel than when in the therapist's presence. Over time, however, Helen's ability to engage on her own in enlivened, responsive interactions with Angel took hold, and she became a devoted and effective, if a somewhat odd and sometimes sad, mother.

POSTTERMINATION SYNOPSIS AND
EFFECTIVENESS DATA

The two remained in infant-parent psychotherapy for three years. At the time of termination they were living independently, and Helen still made use of the psychiatric services available to her through the county hospital. Angel attended a family day care, where she had a positive relationship with the provider and enjoyed interactions with other children. Her vulnerabilities included a tendency to withdraw into elaborate fantasy play when upset or anxious. Her strengths included her creativity and pleasure in artistic activities, an advanced vocabulary and appetite for conversation, and powerful imaginative capacities that drew certain adults and children toward her. It seemed to us a poignant picture of how this child had learned to survive in a world mediated by a mother as devoted but troubled as hers. When the going got rough, Angel retreated into a fantasy world that was perhaps a version of the mysterious world of her mother's disturbance, but she communicated its intrigues successfully enough that others were motivated to stay in touch with her when she went there. And, unlike her mother, that world was one that she symbolized, rather than one that impaired her capacity for symbolization.

Helen and Angel continue to live independently seven years after termination. Helen has continued to receive individual psychiatric treatment, but no educational or family support professional involved with the pair has seen cause to refer Angel for mental health treatment or to bring the family to the attention of the Department of Human Services.

SUMMARY

Although infant mental health programs vary greatly in the structure and specific foci of their services, many share a commitment to treating infants in the context of their family from a psychodynamic perspective, and the modality of infant-parent psychotherapy has provided a theoretical framework and a technical model for doing so. Mental health professionals specializing in infancy address clinical concerns in a broad range of areas, including the internal experiences of infants and toddlers; the internal experience of parents or primary caregivers; and the delicacy and power of expectations and experiences of interpersonal exchange, including exchanges between patients and therapists. These professionals are knowledgeable in the areas of mental health and its disturbances, human development, and the practical demands of being the parent of an infant or toddler. They are familiar with the multitude of social systems in which families routinely or occasionally become involved, such as the medical, educational, social service, and legal systems. They are committed to treating infants in the context of the *relationships* in which they are embedded, and are inclined to think in terms of the child-caregiver dyad whenever difficulties are presented by either. These professionals also are highly aware of the impact they themselves have on their clients. Tracking the vicissitudes of these relational networks is a vital aspect of the therapeutic endeavor.

REFERENCES

Ahern, C., & Grandison, C. (2000). Inclusivity in developmental neuropsychological assessment. In J. H. Pawl et al. (Eds.), *Responding to infants and parents: Inclusive interaction in assessment, consultation, and treatment in infant/family practice* (pp. 23–27). Washington, DC: Zero to Three.

American Psychiatric Association. (1994). *Diagnostic and statistical manual of mental disorders* (4th ed.). Washington, DC: Author.

Beebe, B. (2000). Constructing mother-infant distress: The microsynchrony of maternal impingement and infant avoidance in the face-to-face encounter. *Psychoanalytic Inquiry, 20*(3), 421–440.

Beebe, B., & Lachmann, F. M. (1988). Mother-infant mutual influence and precursors of psychic structure. In A. Goldberg (Ed.), *Frontiers in self psychology* (pp. 3–25). Hillsdale, NJ: Analytic Press.

Beebe, B., & Lachmann, F. M. (1998). Co-constructing inner and relational processes: Self- and mutual regulation in infant research and adult treatment. *Psychoanalytic Psychology, 15*(4), 480–516.

Beebe, B., Lachmann, F. M., & Jaffe, J. (1997). Mother-infant interaction structures and presymbolic self- and object representations. *Psychoanalytic Dialogues, 7*(2), 215–224.

Birch, M. (1994, April). *Rock-a-bye baby: Ordinary maternal hate.* Presented at the spring meetings of Division 39 of the American Psychological Association, Washington, DC.

Bower, T. G. R. (1974). *Development in infancy.* San Francisco: Freeman.

Bower, T. G. R., Broughton, J. M., & Moore, M. K. (1970). The coordination of vision and touch in infancy. *Perception and Psychophysics, 8*.

Bower, T. G. R., Broughton, J. M., & Moore, M. K. (1971). The development of the object concept as manifested by changes in the tracking behavior of infants between 7 and 20 weeks of age. *Journal of Experimental Child Psychology*(2), 11.

Bower, T. G. R., & Wishart, J. G. (1972). The effects of motor skill on object permanence. *Cognition* (2), 1.

Bowlby, J. (1960). Grief and mourning in infancy and early childhood. *Psychoanalytic Study of the Child, 15,* 9–52.

Brazelton, T. B. (1992). *Touchpoints: Your child's emotional and behavioral development.* New York: Addison-Wesley.

Caplan, G. (1951). A public health approach to child psychiatry. *Mental Hygiene, 25*(2).

Caplan, G. (1955). Recent trends in preventive child psychiatry. In G. Caplan (Ed.), *Emotional problems of early childhood.* New York: Basic Books.

Chapin, H. D. (1915). Are institutions for infants necessary? *American Medical Association Journal, 64,* 1–3.

Coleman, R. W., Kris, E., & Provence, S. (1953). The study of variations of early parental attitudes: A preliminary report. *Psychoanalytic Study of the Child, 8,* 20–47.

Cruickshank, R. M. (1941). The development of visual size constancy in early infancy. *Journal of Genetic Psychology, 5,* 327–351.

Emde, R. N. (1983). The prerepresentational self and its affective core. *Psychoanalytic Study of the Child, 38,* 165–192.

Emde, R. N., Gaenbauer, T., & Harmon, R. J. (1976). Emotional expression in infancy: A biobehavioral study. *Psychological Issues: A Monograph, 10,* 37.

Emde, R. N., Gaenbauer, T., & Harmon, R. J. (1982). Using our emotions: Principles for appraising emotional development and intervention. In M. Lewis & L. Taft (Eds.), *Developmental disabilities: Theory, assessment and intervention* (pp. 409–424). New York: SP Medical and Scientific Books.

Emde, R. N., & Hewitt, K. (Eds.). (2001). *Infancy to early childhood: Genetic and environmental influences on developmental change.* New York: Oxford University Press.

Erikson, E. H. (1950a). *Childhood and society.* New York: Norton.

Erikson, E. H. (1950b). Growth and crises of the healthy personality. In M. J. E. Senn (Ed.), *Symposium on the healthy personality, Supplement II: Problems of infancy and childhood.* New York: Josiah Macy Jr. Foundation.

Escalona, S. K. (1950). The use of infant tests for predictive purposes. *Bulletin of Menninger Clinic, 14,* 117–128.

Escalona, S. K. (1953). Emotional development in the first year of life. In M. J. E. Senn (Ed.), *Problems of infancy and childhood.* New York: Josiah Macy Jr. Foundation.

Escalona, S. K., & Leitch, M. (1953). Earliest phases of personality development: A non-normative study of infant behavior. *Monographs of the Society for Research in Child Development, 17*(1, Serial No. 54).

Fantz, R. I. (1961). The origin of form perception. *Scientific American, 204,* 66–72.

Fraiberg, S., Adelson, E., & Shapiro, V. (1980). Ghosts in the nursery: A psychoanalytic approach to the problem of impaired infant-mother relationships. In S. Fraiberg & L. Fraiberg (Eds.), *Clinical studies in infant mental health: The first year of life* (pp. 164–196). New York: Basic Books.

Fraiberg, S., & Fraiberg, L. (Eds.). (1980). *Clinical studies in infant mental health: The first year of life.* New York: Basic Books.

Fraiberg, S., Shapiro, V., & Cherniss, D. S. (1980). Treatment modalities. In S. Fraiberg & L. Fraiberg (Eds.), *Clinical studies in infant mental health: The first year of life* (pp. 49–77). New York: Basic Books.

Freud, A. (1960). Discussion of Dr. John Bowlby's paper. *Psychoanalytic Study of the Child, 15,* 53–62.

Freud, S. (1955a). Analysis of a phobia in a five-year-old boy. In J. Strachey (Ed.), *The standard edition of the complete psychological works of Sigmund Freud* (Vol. 10, pp. 1–147). London: Hogarth Press. (Original work published 1909)

Freud, S. (1955b). Remembering, repeating and working through (further recommendations on the technique of psychoanalysis-II). In J. Strachey (Ed. & Trans.), *The standard edition of the complete psychological works of Sigmund Freud* (Vol. 12, pp. 145–156). London: Hogarth Press. (Original work published 1914)

Freud, S. (1957). Mourning and melancholia. In J. Strachey (Ed.), *The standard edition of the complete psychological works of Sigmund Freud* (Vol. 14, pp. 237–258). London: Hogarth Press. (Original work published 1917)

Furman, E. (1957). Treatment of under-fives by way of their parents. *Psychoanalytic Study of the Child, 12,* 250–262.

Furman, R. A., & Katan, A. (Eds.). (1969). *The therapeutic nursery school: A contribution to the study and treatment of emotional disturbances in young children.* New York: International Universities Press.

Greenspan, S. (1981). *Psychopathology and adaptation in infancy and early childhood: Principles of clinical diagnosis and preventive intervention.* New York: International Universities Press.

Greenspan, S. (1994). *Infancy and early childhood: The practice of clinical assessment and intervention with emotional and developmental challenges.* Madison, CT: International Universities Press.

Greenspan, S. (1997). *Developmentally based psychotherapy.* Madison, CT: International Universities Press.

Greenspan, S. (2000). Children with autistic spectrum disorders: Individual differences, affect, interaction, and outcomes. *Psychoanalytic Inquiry, 20*(5), 675–703.

Greenspan, S., & Levis, N. B. (1999). *Building healthy minds: The six experiences that create intelligence and emotional growth in babies and young children.* Cambridge, MA: Perseus Books.

Greenspan, S., Nover, R. A., Lourie, R., & Robinson, M. (Eds.). (1987). *Infants in multirisk families: Case studies in preventive intervention* (Clinical Infant Reports, No. 3). Madison, CT: International Universities Press.

Herman, J. (1992). *Trauma and recovery: The aftermath of violence. From domestic abuse to political terror.* New York: HarperCollins.

Kalmanson, B., & Pekarsky, J. (1987, Winter). Infant-parent psychotherapy with an autistic toddler. *Infant Mental Health Journal, 8*(4), 382–397.

Langford, W. S. (1955). Disturbance in mother-infant relationships leading to apathy, extra-nutritional sucking and hair fall. In G. Caplan (Ed.), *Emotional problems of early childhood* (pp. 57–76). New York: Basic Books.

Levy, R. J. (1947). Effects of institutional vs. boarding home care on infants. *Journal of Personality, 15,* 233.

Lewis, M., & Rosenblum, L. A. (1974). The effect of the infant on its caregiver. In M. Lewis & L. A. Rosenblum (Eds.), *The origins of behavior series* (Vol. 1). New York: Wiley.

Lieberman, A. F. (1992). Infant-parent psychotherapy with toddlers. *Development and Psychopathology, 4*(4), 559–574.

Lieberman, A. F., & Birch, M. (1985). The etiology of failure to thrive: An interactional developmental approach. In D. Drotar (Ed.), *New directions in failure to thrive: Research and clinical practice* (pp. 259–279). New York: Plenum Press.

Lieberman, A. F., & Pawl, J. H. (1984). Searching for the best interests of the child: Intervention with an abusive mother and her toddler. *Psychoanalytic Study of the Child, 39,* 527–548.

Lieberman, A. F., & Pawl, J. H. (1993). Infant-parent psychotherapy. In C. H. Zeanah (Ed.), *Handbook of infant mental health* (pp. 427–442). New York: Guilford Press.

Lieberman, A. F., Silverman, R., & Pawl, J. H. (2000). Infant-parent psychotherapy: Core concepts and current approaches. In C. H. Zeanah (Ed.), *Handbook of infant mental health* (pp. 472–484). New York: Guilford Press.

Lindemann, E., Vaughn, W. T., Jr., & McGinnis, M. A. (1955). Preventive intervention in a four-year-old child whose father committed suicide. In G. Caplan (Ed.), *Emotional problems of early childhood* (pp. 5–30). New York: Basic Books.

Lipsett, L. (1969). Learning capacities of the human infant. In R. J. Robinson (Ed.), *Brain and early behavior*. London: Academic Press.

Pawl, J. H. (1993). A stitch in time: Using emotional support, developmental guidance, and infant-parent psychotherapy in a brief intervention. In E. Fenichel & S. Provence (Eds.), *Development in jeopardy* (pp. 203–229). New York: International Universities Press.

Pawl, J. H. (1995a). *Early intervention and the infant mental health perspective.* Plenary address presented at the National Training Institute of Zero to Three.

Pawl, J. H. (1995b). The therapeutic relationship as human connectedness: Being held in another's mind. *Zero to Three: Bulletin of the National Center for Clinical Infant Programs, 15*(4), 1–5.

Pawl, J. H., Ahern, C., Grandison, C., Johnston, K., St. John, M., & Waldstein, A. (2000). *Responding to infants and parents: Inclusive interaction in assessment, consultation, and treatment in infant/family practice.* Washington, DC: Zero to Three: National Center for Infants, Toddlers and Families.

Pawl, J. H., & Lieberman, A. (1997). Infant-parent psychotherapy. In J. Noshpitz (Ed.), *Comprehensive textbook of child psychiatry* (pp. 339–350). New York: Basic Books.

Pawl, J. H., & St. John, M. (1998). *How you are is as important as what you do in making a positive difference for infants, toddlers and their families.* Washington, DC: Zero to Three: National Center for Infants, Toddlers and Families.

Pawl, J. H., St. John, M., & Pekarsky, J. H. (2000). Training mental health and other professionals in infant mental health: Conversations with trainees. In J. D. Osofsky & H. E. Fitzgerald (Eds.), *WAIMH handbook of infant mental health* (Vol. 2, pp. 377–402).

Pekarsky, J. (1992). Supervision and mentorship of students: Scenes from supervision. *Learning through supervision and mentorship* (pp. 53–55). Washington, DC: Zero to Three: National Center for Clinical Infant Programs.

Provence, S., & Lipton, R. (1962). *Infants in institutions: A comparison of their development with family-reared infants during the first year of life.* New York: International Universities Press.

Rexford, E., Sander, L., & Shapiro, J. (Eds.). (1976). *Infant psychiatry: A new synthesis. Monograph of the Journal of the American Academy of Child Psychiatry* (No. 2). New Haven, CT: Yale University Press.

Rosenfeld, B. A., & Brandt, M. (1955). A mother whose child would not eat: Psychiatric casework in a well-baby clinic. In G. Caplan (Ed.), *Emotional problems of early childhood* (pp. 31–55). New York: Basic Books.

Schore, A. (2001a). Effects of early relationship trauma on right brain development, affect regulation, and infant mental health. *Infant Mental Health Journal, 22*(1/2), 201–269.

Schore, A. (2001b). Effects of a secure attachment relationship on right brain development, affect regulation, and infant mental health. *Infant Mental Health Journal, 22*(1/2), 7–66.

Seligman, S. (1994). Applying psychoanalysis in an unconventional context: Adapting infant-parent psychotherapy to a changing population. In A. J. Solnit, P. B. Neubauer, S. Abrams, & A. S. Dowling (Eds.), *Psychoanalytic Study of the Child: Volume 49* (pp. 487–510). New Haven, CT: Yale University Press.

Seligman, S., & Pawl, J. (1984). Impediments to the formation of the therapeutic alliance in infant-parent psychotherapy. In J. Call, E. Galenson, & R. Tyson (Eds.), *Frontiers of infant psychiatry: Volume II* (pp. 232–237). New York: Basic Books.

Seligman, S., & St. John, M. (1995). No space for baby: Pseudomaturity in an urban little girl. In E. G. Corrigan & P. E. Gordon (Eds.), *The mind object: Precocity and pathology of self-sufficiency* (pp. 155–176). Northvale, NJ: Aronson.

Shure, M. (1960). Discussion of Dr. John Bowlby's paper. *Psychoanalytic Study of the Child, 15,* 63–85.

Silverman, R., & Lieberman, A. F. (1999). Negative maternal attributions, projective identification, and the intergenerational transmission of violent relational patterns. *Psychoanalytic Dialogues: A Journal of Relational Perspectives, 9*(2), 161–186.

Skeels, H. M., & Dye, H. B. (1939). A study of the effects of differential stimulation on mentally retarded children: Proceedings. *American Association on Mental deficiency* 44(1), 114–136.

Solnit, A. J., & Provence, S. (1963). *Modern perspectives in child development.* New York: International Universities Press.

Spitz, R. A. (1945). Hospitalism: An inquiry into the genesis of psychiatric conditions in early childhood. *Psychoanalytic Study of the Child, 1,* 53–74.

Spitz, R. A. (1946). Hospitalism: A follow-up report. *Psychoanalytic Study of the Child, 2,* 113–117.

Spitz, R. A. (1960). Discussion of Dr. Bowlby's paper. *Psychoanalytic Study of the Child, 15,* 86–94.

Stern, D. N. (1977). *The first relationship: Infant and mother.* Cambridge, MA: Harvard University Press.

Stern, D. N. (1985). *The interpersonal world of the infant: A view from psychoanalysis and developmental psychology.* New York: Basic Books.

Stern, D. N. (1989). The representation of relational patterns: Developmental considerations. In A. Sameroff & R. N. Emde (Eds.), *Relationship disturbances in early childhood: A developmental approach* (pp. 52–69). New York: Basic Books.

Stern, D. N. (1994). One way to build a clinically relevant baby. *Infant Mental Health Journal, 15*(1), 9–25.

Stern, D. N. (1995). *The motherhood constellation.* New York: Basic Books.

Stern, D. N. (2000). The relevance of empirical infant research to psychoanalytic theory and practice. In J. Sandler et al. (Eds.), *Clinical and observational psychoanalytic research: Roots of a controversy* (pp. 73–90). Madison, CT: International Universities Press.

St. John, M., & Pawl, J. H. (2000). Inclusive interaction in infant-parent pssychotherapy. In J. H. Pawl et al. (Eds.), *Responding to infants and parents: Inclusive interaction in assessment, consultation, and treatment in infant/family practice* (pp. 8–14). Washington, DC: Zero to Three.

Trevarthen, C. (1995). Mother and baby: Seeing artfully eye to eye. In R. L. Gregory et al. (Eds.), *The artful eye* (pp. 157–200). New York: Oxford University Press.

Trevarthen, C. (1996). Lateral asymmetries in infancy: Implications for the development of the hemispheres. *Neuroscience and Biobehavioral Reviews, 20*(4), 571–586.

Trevarthen, C. (2001). Intrinsic motives for companionship in understanding: Their origin, development, and significance for infant mental health. *Infant Mental Health Journal, 22*(1/2), 95–131.

Trevarthen, C., & Aitken, K. J. (2001). Infant intersubjectivity: Research, theory, and clinical applications. *Journal of Child Psychology and Psychiatry and Applied Disciplines, 42*(1), 3–48.

Winnicott, D. W. (1945). *Primitive emotional development: Collected papers.* New York: Basic Books.

Winnicott, D. W. (1953). Transitional objects and transitional phenomena. *International Journal of Psycho-Analysis, 34,* 89–97.

Winnicott, D. W. (1957). *Mother and child: A primer of first relationships.* New York: Basic Books.

Winnicott, D. W. (1965). *The maturational processes and the facilitating environment: Studies in the theory of emotional development.* Madison, CT: International Universities Press.

Winnicott, D. W. (1971). *Playing and reality.* New York: Routledge.

Winnicott, D. W. (1975). *Through paediatrics to psychoanalysis: Collected papers.* New York: Basic Books.

Zero to Three: National Center for Clinical Infant Programs. (1994). *Diagnostic classification 0–3: Diagnostic classification of mental health and developmental disorders of infancy and early childhood.* Washington, DC: Author.

CHAPTER 5

Psychodynamic Approaches to Child Therapy

PETER FONAGY AND MARY TARGET

HISTORY OF THE PSYCHODYNAMIC APPROACH TO CHILD THERAPY

THE EVOLUTION OF PSYCHODYNAMIC THEORIES OF CHILD DEVELOPMENT

Freud was the first to give meaning to mental disorder by linking it to childhood experiences (Breuer & Freud, 1895) and to the vicissitudes of the developmental process (S. Freud, 1900). His original developmental formulations (S. Freud, 1905) radically altered our perception of the child from one of somewhat idealized naïveté and innocence. He suggested that children are constitutionally predisposed to an inevitably partially successful struggle to adapt their sexual and aggressive instincts to the demands of a civilized society. S. Freud (1933) painted a picture of the child as an individual in turmoil, constantly struggling to master biological needs and make these acceptable to society. He posited that the drama takes place universally in the development of every human being within the microcosm of the family (S. Freud, 1930).

Over a period of 45 years of psychoanalytic writing, Freud gradually moved from seeing psychological problems as arising out of suppressed emotions, which gained expression in the form of symptoms, to an increasingly complex view, where the counterbalance of psychological forces within the mind was seen as the critical aspect of psychological adaptation. In his last full formulation, the so-called structural model, S. Freud (1923) envisioned three psychic agencies: (1) instinctual, principally sexual and aggressive energies located in the id; (2) an internalized set of moral values encoded in the superego; and (3) adaptive mechanisms organized in the ego. In this complex model, normal adaptation could be seen as the harmonious functioning of these agencies, whereas psychological abnormality invariably reflected a breakdown of the ego's capacity to respond to the demands of the id, the superego, and the external environment.

Ego psychologists both elaborated and balanced Freud's view by focusing on the evolution of children's adaptive capacities, which they bring to bear on their struggle with their biological needs. Hartmann (1939) attempted to take a wider view of the developmental process, to link drives and ego functions, and to show how negative interpersonal experiences beyond the expectable range could jeopardize the evolution of the psychic structures essential to adaptation. He also showed that reactivation of earlier structures (regression) was the most important component of psychopathology. Hartmann (1955, p. 221) was among the first to point to the complexity of the developmental process, stating that the reasons for the persistence of a particular behavior are likely to be different from the reasons for the original appearance of the behavior earlier in development. Among the great contributions of ego psychologists are the identification of the ubiquitous nature of intrapsychic conflict throughout development (Brenner, 1982) and the recognition that genetic endowment, as well as interpersonal experiences, may have a critical influence on the child's developmental path.

Freud's daughter, Anna Freud, was strongly influenced by these psychological ideas of the North American psychoanalytic tradition, although her practice was in London. Her major contribution was linking normal emotional development to diagnosable psychopathology (A. Freud, 1965). She charted normal development along a series of "developmental lines" and made the powerful suggestion that equilibrium between developmental processes was a key aspect of normal development. Her work emphasized that symptomatology is not a fixed formation, but rather a dynamic entity superimposed on, and intertwined with, an underlying developmental process. A child whose environment selectively compromised some but not other developmental processes was thought to be at risk of maladjustment and psychopathology. Anna Freud's vision of the relationship of development and psychopathology lies, conceptually at least, at the heart of the new, integrative discipline of developmental psychopathology (see Sroufe, 1990).

Margaret Mahler (1968) drew attention to the paradox of self-development: that the achievement of a separate identity involves giving up a highly gratifying closeness with the caregiver. Her observations of the "ambitendency" of children in their second year of life assisted understanding of individuals who experienced chronic problems consolidating their individuality. Mahler's framework highlights the importance of the caregiver in facilitating separation and helps explain the difficulties experienced by children whose parents fail to perform a social referencing function for the child: evaluating for them the realistic danger associated with unfamiliar environments (Feinman, 1991; Hornik & Gunnar, 1988). A traumatized, troubled parent may hinder rather than help a child's adaptation (Terr, 1983). An abusive parent may altogether inhibit the process of social referencing (Cicchetti, 1990; Hesse & Cicchetti, 1982). The pathogenic potential of the withdrawing object, when confronted with the child's wish for separateness, was further elaborated by Masterson (1972) and Rinsley (1977) and helps to account for the transgenerational aspects of psychological disturbance (see Baron, Gruen, & Asnis, 1985; Links, Steiner, & Huxley, 1988; Loranger, Oldham, & Tullis, 1982).

Edith Jacobson (1964) and Joseph Sandler (1987) further elaborated the ego psychological model. Both theoreticians suggested a move away from the mechanistic psychological model suggested by Freud to one that was far more compatible with modern cognitive neuroscience. They de-emphasized the biologically rooted notions of drives and instincts, replacing these with constructs such as wishes and the role of representational structures in the child's mind and how these might mediate both reality and its distortion associated with internal conflict. Sandler's development of A. Freud's and Jacobson's work (e.g., Sandler & Rosenblatt, 1962) coherently integrated the developmental perspective with psychoanalytic theory. His comprehensive psychoanalytic model has permitted developmental researchers (Emde, 1983, 1988a, 1988b; Stern, 1985) to integrate their findings with a psychoanalytic formulation, which clinicians also have been able to use. At the core of Sandler's formulation lies the representational structure, which contains both reality and distortion and is the driving force of psychic life. A further important component of his model is the notion of the background of safety (Sandler, 1987), which is closely tied to Bowlby's concept of secure attachment (Bowlby, 1969).

Concurrently, in the United Kingdom, a completely different approach to psychodynamic theory grew out of the work of Melanie Klein (1946). One of Klein's fundamental postulates was the assumption of two radically different modes of mental functioning. The first, the paranoid-schizoid position, described a state of mind (prototypically in the human infant) in which loving and destructive feelings toward the love object could not simultaneously be accommodated, so that the conflict had to be dealt with by splitting, that is, creating separate images of the loved and the hated figure. With cognitive development, this inevitably leads to what Klein termed the depressive position, in which children recognize that the object they love and the one they hate are one and the same. Klein's ideas originally met with considerable skepticism because of her extravagant assumptions about the cognitive capacities of infants, which were incompatible with the state of developmental knowledge at that time. More recently, developmental research has confirmed many of Klein's claims (Gergely, 1991), such as those concerning the perception of causality (Bower, 1989) and causal reasoning (Golinkoff, Hardig, Carlson, & Sexton, 1984). Klein's ideas rapidly became popular, principally because of the helpfulness of her clinical observations. For example, she proposed the notion of projective identification, a concept that others subsequently developed to provide a means of accounting for the common experience of therapists that patients can exert a significant influence over the therapist's state of mind. Klein believed that projection was the most basic mechanism available to children to deal with destructiveness: They rid themselves of their destructive fantasies by placing them onto other persons. It is only through the therapist's interpretive work, particularly with such destructive fantasies, that children are enabled to reclaim disowned aspects of themselves and allow for the development of a less malevolent and more realistic appraisal of others.

Studies of severe character disorders by psychoanalysts in Britain focused on the early relationship with the caregiver as a critical aspect of development. Fairbairn (1952) shifted theoretical emphasis from the satisfaction of biological desires to the individual's need for the other. This helped shift psychoanalytic attention from structure to content, and profoundly influenced both British and North American psychoanalytic thinking. Working in this tradition, and also influenced by Klein, Donald Winnicott (1965) proposed a number of fundamental psychodynamic developmental notions, such as primary maternal preoccupation, the mirroring function of the caregiver, and the transitional space in development between fusion and separateness, within which symbolic thought and play were considered to be rooted. Most recent studies support Winnicott's assertions concerning the traumatic consequences of early maternal failure, particularly maternal depression (see, e.g., Cummings & Davies, 1994), and the importance of maternal sensitivity for the establishment of a secure relationship (Ainsworth, Blehar, Waters, & Wall, 1978; Belsky, Rovine, & Taylor, 1984; Bus & van Ijzendoorn, 1992; Grossmann, Grossmann, Spangler, Suess, & Unzner, 1985).

Heinz Kohut (1977), who was probably influenced by Winnicott's work, rekindled the interest of North American psychoanalysts in the interpersonal aspects of early development. He saw the caregiver as having a mirroring role and the goal of development as one of achieving a coherent sense of self. If the caregiver is able to become a "selfobject," empathically attuned to the infant's or young child's mental states, the child's sense of personhood will be firmly established. Within a self psychology, drive theory took secondary importance. Kohut (1971) suggested that the dominance of drives was itself an indication of the child's failure to have attained an integrated self structure, which normally would adequately regulate drive states. Kohut's formulations concerning narcissistic personality structures have been highly influential and helpful in extending the applicability of psychodynamic approaches from the strictly neurotic to the so-called character disorder spectrum of disorders.

Kernberg's systematic integration of structural theory and object-relations theory (Kernberg, 1976, 1982, 1987) is probably the most frequently used psychoanalytic model, particularly in relation to personality disorders. His model of psychopathology is developmental, in the sense that personality disturbance is seen to reflect the limited capacities of the young child to address intrapsychic conflict. Kernberg followed Jacobson and Sandler in seeing the mind as principally a representational organ. He postulated the existence of relationship representations consisting of self, object, and affect that characterize the specific relationship. Kernberg reconceptualized the theory of drives, seeing these as developmental achievements, integrations of multiple triadic self-object-affect representations. Whereas in neurotic cases, the integration achieved is relatively complete, in personality disorders, the self and other representations are only partial and are infused with overwhelming and extreme emotional states of both ecstasy and persecutory terror and aggression. Kernberg's ideas have been enormously influential in psychoanalytic thinking and are particularly helpful because they lend themselves relatively well to operationalization and empirical study (Clarkin, Kernberg, & Yeomans, 1999).

John Bowlby's (1969, 1973, 1980) exposition of attachment theory shares this virtue of openness to empirical scrutiny. Bowlby's work on separation and loss focused developmentalists' attention on the importance of the security (safety and predictability) of the earliest relationships. Safety and predictability must be experienced for the child to acquire a capacity for relatively problem-free later interpersonal relationships. Bowlby assumed that representational systems and internal working models evolve based on a template created by the earliest relationship of the infant to the caregiver. If the expectation that need and distress will be met by comforting is encoded into these models, the child will be able to approach relationships in a relatively undefensive way. If this is not the case, if the child's caregivers lack sensitivity (Ainsworth et al., 1978), the child's representational system will be defensively distorted to either minimize or heighten experiences of arousal and dismiss or become entangled in the response of others (Main, Kaplan, & Cassidy, 1985).

Daniel Stern (1985) took a novel approach to the psychoanalytic study of childhood. His milestone contribution to the psychoanalytic theory of development is exceptional in being normative rather than pathomorphic and prospective rather than retrospective. Like Kohut, his main concern is the development of a coherent self structure. His psychoanalytic model, however, has much in common with Sandler's representational theory as well as Kernberg's focus on the affective aspect of early relationships.

THE EVOLUTION OF PSYCHODYNAMIC TECHNIQUE WITH CHILDREN

Specific therapeutic techniques that could help psychoanalysts to address the psychiatric problems of childhood did not appear until the 1920s. S. Freud's observations concerning the psychology of young children prepared the way for the application of the insights gained from psychoanalytic treatment of adults to the treatment of children. Best known are Freud's grandson's separation game (S. Freud, 1920) and his case study of Hans (S. Freud, 1909), a 5-year-old with an animal phobia, whose treatment by his physician father was supervised by Freud. Freud used these observations principally to confirm his assumptions about infantile instinctual life through the direct observation of children and to prevent him (and other adult psychoanalysts) from making false developmental assumptions (S. Freud, 1926).

Hermine Hug-Helmuth (1920, 1921) was the first clinician to use the technique of play therapy. Her pioneering work, now largely forgotten, combined an insight-oriented technique, focused primarily on the child's unconscious sexual fantasies, with a powerful developmental perspective, whereby she saw children as needing to be "strengthened" in the mental capacities needed for their developmental tasks. This latter emphasis has echoes in present-day cognitive therapy and psychoanalytic approaches.

The other great pioneers of the field, Anna Freud (1946) and Melanie Klein (1932), independently (but frequently with reference to one another) evolved techniques to enable clinicians to take a psychoanalytic therapeutic approach to children. Working under the influence of Karl Abraham (1927), a Berlin-based psychoanalyst, Klein regarded children's play as essentially the same as the free association of adults: motivated by unconscious fantasy activated principally by the relationship with the analyst and requiring verbalization (interpretation) if the child's anxiety was to be adequately addressed. The interpretation of the child's deep anxieties concerning destructive and sadistic impulses was the principal focus of child analytic work. She advocated that therapists establish an interpretative relationship, even with preschool children, from the beginning. The emphasis placed on the relationship with the analyst meant that work with parents and other adults in the child's life (e.g., teachers) was not seen as central.

Klein saw direct interpretation of the projective processes as critical. In "Notes on Some Schizoid Mechanisms" (Klein, 1946) and "The Origins of Transference" (Klein, 1952), she discussed the importance of the common childhood unconscious fantasy of placing part of the self into another person and perceiving unwanted qualities in the other rather than in oneself to relieve oneself of unwanted feelings (such as greed or envy). She regarded this form of fragmentation of the sense of self as part of normal infantile development, but as the cause of pathology and the key focus for interpretations when it persisted beyond infancy. She assumed that although projective identification was distressing, it also helped children to create the fantasy, not only that the other was the "containers" of their own unwelcome traits, but also that (as these unattractive attributes still partly belonged to the self) the children could control the other person (object). The clinician's understanding was enriched by the assumption that children's perception of him or her gave clues about conflictual aspects of their experience of themselves. Bion (1959) showed how such projective experiences could be expected to have an impact on "the container" and how the capacity of that individual to "metabolize" (understand and accept) the projection may be critical in development as well as in the success of therapy. Thus, the therapist's subjective experience (countertransference) could be a clue to the child's unconscious fantasies, and the therapist's capacity to understand and tolerate these became the key component of successful treatment.

Modern Kleinians (e.g., DeFolch, 1988; O'Shaughnessy, 1988) have, to some degree, modified the classical Kleinian position; early interpretations of assumed deeply unconscious material are less frequently offered, and there is greater attention to the defensive qualities of many manifestations of the child's nonconscious processes. The immediate interaction with the analyst, however, remains the core focus of therapeutic work, and the underlying conceptualization continues to be based on the notion of fragmentation of the self-representational structure, which may be undone through verbalization and interpretation. The countertransference experience of the therapist is the central guide.

Drawing on the work of Klein, Winnicott (1965, 1971) reinforced Klein's emphasis on the influence of early life on childhood pathology while introducing additional techniques into child analysis. For example, specific drawing techniques were used, and Winnicott also emphasized nonverbal aspects of the therapist's stance, in particular the importance of a "holding" environment and the central role of play. One of his major contributions was the concept of a transitional area between self and object, where the subjective object and the truly objective object are simultaneously recognized (Winnicott, 1971). This insight was critical in developing an appreciation of the interpersonal nature of therapeutic interaction in child analysis (Altman, 1994).

By contrast, Anna Freud's approach placed more emphasis on the child's developmental struggle with adaptation to a social as well as an intrapsychic environment. Her training as a nursery school teacher led her to be very concerned with children's actual external circumstances, as well as their unconscious internal world. She made fewer assumptions concerning the meaning of children's play, approached therapeutic work far more gradually, recommended working in collaboration with parents and teachers (particularly in communicating understanding derived from the therapy), and focused far more on the complications and conflicts arising from children's libidinal (sexual) impulses than on innate aggression. Her focus was on children's wish to protect their fragile internal world from conflict by adopting psychological strategies (mechanisms of defense; A. Freud, 1936) such as denial, repression, or identification with the aggressor. The focus of her technique therefore was the interpretation of defenses and, through this, the anxieties that motivated them.

Her approach to child analysis invariably takes into consideration the limitations imposed by development on the child's "ego functioning," and focuses primarily on the support of the development of the ego and the restoration of the child to a normal developmental path. Pine (1985) stressed that the analyst, like the parent, creates a supportive environment for the child's incompletely developed ego. He saw such techniques as mutative in their own right and considered interpretations in the context of support to be qualitatively different from interpretations in the context of abstinence, as is recommended by Kleinian child analysts. The pressure for the analyst to be an active and "real" participant in the therapeutic situation has grown in recent years (see also Altman, 1992; Warshaw, 1992). However, many of these reconceptualizations lack coherent theoretical rationale and specific technical recommendations as to how departures from abstinence may be put to good therapeutic effect.

Freudian child psychoanalysis became popular as a treatment in the United States in the first half of this century, and was systematically described by Anna Freud and her colleagues (Sandler, Kennedy, & Tyson, 1980); it has also influenced many forms of psychodynamic treatment of children and families. Individual child psychodynamic psychotherapy, based on these principles, is frequently used and highly regarded among child psychiatrists and psychologists in the United States (Kazdin, Bass, Siegel, & Thomas, 1990). In the United Kingdom, as well as in Latin America, Melanie Klein's model proved to be more popular.

UNDERLYING THEORETICAL CONSTRUCTS

As the historical review indicates, there is no agreed upon formulation shared by all psychoanalytic schools. There are major theoretical divisions, which overlap in part with issues of technique originating from different understandings of the nature of development and psychopathology (King & Steiner, 1991). Nevertheless, there are probably a core set of assumptions to which all psychodynamic therapists would, to a greater or lesser extent, subscribe. They can be summarized as follows.

PSYCHOLOGICAL CAUSATION

Psychodynamically oriented child therapists assume that mental disturbance may be usefully studied at the level of *psychological causation*, that is, that the representation of past experience, its interpretation and meaning, largely unconscious, determines children's reaction to their external world and their capacity to adapt to it. The emphasis on psychic causation does not imply either a lack of respect for or inattention to other levels of analysis of childhood psychiatric problems, such as the biological, the family, or broader social factors. Nevertheless, psychiatric problems, whether at the root genetic or constitutional or socially caused, are seen by the psychodynamically oriented child clinician as the meaningful consequence of the child's unconscious beliefs, thoughts, and feelings, and therefore as potentially accessible in psychotherapy.

UNCONSCIOUS MENTAL PROCESSES

Psychodynamic clinicians assume that the explanation of conscious ideation and intentional behavior requires the assumption of complex *unconscious mental processes* functioning outside of awareness. Psychodynamic clinicians probably no longer think in terms of "an unconscious" in the sense of a physical space where forbidden or repudiated feelings and ideas are stored. Yet, they assume that nonconscious fantasies, associated with wishes for gratification or safety, profoundly influence children's behavior and their capacity to regulate affect and to adequately handle their social environment.

INTERPERSONAL INTERACTIONS

Like cognitive scientists, psychodynamic therapists assume that the experience of the self with others is internalized, leading to *representational structures of interpersonal interactions* that, at the simplest level, determine the child's expectations of others, and more elaborately determine the "shape" of self and other representations and the nature of the internal world of the child. Psychodynamic clinicians from different traditions formulate this general idea somewhat differently. Bowlby's (1973, 1980) concept of "internal working models" of self-other relationships based on the infant-mother relationship is perhaps the closest to formulations from other areas of clinical psychology. In essence, all so called object-relations theories posit that the emotional life of the child (and adult) is organized around mental representations, however partial, of the self in relation to an important figure, imbued with a specific affect (e.g., Kernberg, 1976).

CONFLICT

The ubiquity of intrapsychic *conflict* is assumed. It is seen as causing suffering (or a felt lack of safety; Brenner, 1982). Adverse childhood environments may create intrapsychic conflicts of overwhelming intensity and/or fail to equip the child adequately to deal with conflicts within the normal range of early experience (Winnicott, 1965). Thus, trauma (such as loss of a caregiver) or long-term abuse undermines personality development by intensifying incompatible wishes or reducing the child's capacity to resolve conflicts through mental work.

DEFENSE

The child is predisposed to modify unacceptable unconscious wishes through a range of mental mechanisms aimed at reducing the sense of conflict. *Defense* mechanisms form a developmental hierarchy, which reflects the degree of pathology experienced by the individual; developmentally early defenses, such as splitting, or projective identification, are normally associated with more severe disturbances. A neurotic symptom, such as phobic anxiety, may be understood as a result of displacement of fear from the representation of one model of interaction (e.g., father-child) to another (e.g., teacher-child). Considerably more resistant to therapy is the more primitive defense of splitting of affect, whereby a child alternately derogates and idealizes the caregiving figure. Immature or early defenses are assumed to reflect the absence of higher-level, integrative capacities (Pine, 1985).

Multiple Meanings

Psychodynamic therapists assume that children's communication in the session has meaning beyond that intended by the children and, by analogous mechanisms, that children's symptoms carry *multiple and complex meanings,* reflecting the nature of their internal representations of others and others' relationship to the children as they perceive it. The therapist is able to bring children's attention to aspects of their behavior that are ego-dystonic and hard to understand. By making appropriate links, the therapist illustrates to children that these behaviors may be seen as rational in terms of unconscious mental experience and psychic causation (Sandler et al., 1980).

Transference

It is generally accepted that internalized representations of interpersonal relationships, which determine the child's behavior with others in the outside world, also become active in the context of the therapeutic relationship. They do so by means of the process known as *transference.* The relationship to the therapist has primacy, in that it provides a window to the child's expectations of others and can come to be a vehicle for the unwanted and disowned aspects of the child's thoughts and feelings. Transference displacement may include such aspects of past relationships or past fantasies about these as well as conflictual aspects of current relationships to parents, siblings, or important others. The relative neutrality and ambiguity of the therapeutic relationship encourages externalizations of repudiated aspects of past relationships (R. L. Tyson & Tyson, 1986), but the situation becomes more complicated because the child's verbal and nonverbal behavior must naturally have an impact on the therapist's experience. However, modern psychodynamic therapists tend to make extensive use of their subjective reactions to understand the roles that the child is implicitly asking them to play. Through exploring the role they have been placed in by the child, therapists are enabled to achieve a better understanding of the child's representation of role relationships and feelings about them (Tyson & Tyson, 1986).

The Whole Person

Modern psychodynamic child psychotherapy emphasizes the current state of children in relation to their environment, history of past relationships, and adaptations to these. Psychotherapists generally recognize that the therapy they offer has an important holding or containing function in the child's life, which, beyond interpretation and consequent insight, creates the possibility of a reintegration or reorganization of the child's internal world that in turn facilitates the child's adaptive development. The child therapist thus takes a *whole person* perspective, encompassing all aspects of the child's unfolding concerns (biological, environmental, intrapsychic). The establishment of a relationship with an adult that is open and nonexploitative may serve as the basis of new internalizations, bringing about a healthier resolution of pathogenic experiences.

METHODS OF ASSESSMENT AND INTERVENTION

Assessment

Traditionally, psychodynamic therapists have worked with relatively less severely disturbed young people. Hoffman (1993), Glenn (1978), Sandler et al. (1980), and others have identified the criteria of suitability for psychodynamic psychotherapy as the following:

1. Good verbal skills and psychological-mindedness, that is, the ability to conceive of behavior as mediated by mental states (thoughts and feelings). Equally important here is the child's capacity to tolerate awareness of conflicts and anxieties, particularly those previously kept unconscious, without risking substantial disorganization or disintegration of the personality.
2. A supportive environment that is able to sustain the child's involvement in an intense and demanding long-term interpersonal relationship. Particularly important here is the willingness of parents to respect the boundaries of the child's therapy and promote the child's commitment to the treatment.
3. A diagnostic assessment that indicates the primacy of internal conflict underlying symptomatology.
4. Traditionally, psychotherapists were reluctant to treat children with major developmental deficits (ego deviations) that were not the result of unconscious conflict and therefore could not be seen as resolvable through insight.
5. As the child's motivation for treatment stems from anxiety, guilt, or other unpleasant affects, these experiences are often seen as essential to ensuring the child's commitment to the treatment as well as a sense of agency (a sense of responsibility for one's problems and actions).
6. It is assumed that a capacity to form relationships and develop trust must be present for psychodynamic therapy to operate.

There is evidently a group of children commonly treated by psychodynamic psychotherapy who do not meet the criteria discussed above. We have described this group in our retrospective examination of case records at the Anna Freud Centre (Fonagy & Target, 1996a, 1996c). Other descriptions by Cohen, Towbin, Mayes, and Volkmar (1994), Towbin, Dykens, Pearson, and Cohen (1993), and Bleiberg (1987, 1994a) have arrived at strikingly similar descriptions. This group of children appear to suffer from a variety of deficiencies of psychological capacities, indicated, for example, by lack of control over affect, lack of stable self and other representations, and diffusion of their sense of identity.

Whereas the two groups may be readily distinguished in terms of descriptive criteria, elsewhere, we have tentatively suggested a conceptual framework that may help to provide a theoretically based psychodynamic distinction (Fonagy, Edgcumbe, Moran, Kennedy, & Target, 1993). In this model, we distinguish children whose problems may be seen as a consequence of distortion in mental representations, either of others or of themselves. Such distorted representations may arise out of exceptional environmental factors or defensive distortions associated with various forms of intrapsychic conflict. Broadly speaking, these children correspond to what has traditionally been regarded as the neurotic category. By contrast, children with more severe problems, who usually present with multiple disorders, low levels of adaptation, and poor personality functioning, may be seen as suffering from defensive inhibition or distortion of mental processes rather than just the mental representations that such processes generate. Thus, for this group of children, a wide variety of situations are likely to bring about maladaptive functioning, as the very capacities that may be involved in achieving adaptive functioning are impaired. Although biological factors may play an important role in both types of pathology, in both cases, the focus on psychological causation is retained. For example, inhibitions on specific ways of thinking occur as attempts at adaptation.

METHODS OF INTERVENTION

Important considerations from the point of view of psychotherapeutic technique arise out of this distinction. Disorders of mental representation are well served by a primarily interpretive therapeutic process, which aims at addressing distorted ideas and integrating repudiated or incoherent notions of self and other. The reintegration of split-off (repressed), often infantile but troublesome ideas into the child's developmentally appropriate mental structures is the therapeutic aim (Abrams, 1988). In the more severely disturbed group of patients, this kind of approach has limited usefulness. There is a need for strengthening or disinhibiting mental processes that may have been disengaged (decoupled) or distorted for defensive or constitutional biological reasons. These patients may need assistance in labeling and verbalizing affects and ideas. Much of psychodynamic intervention aimed at the so-called neurotic patient may change the organization or the shape of the child's mental representation (Sandler & Rosenblatt, 1962). To regenerate mental processes, an alternative set of psychodynamic techniques, emphasizing a developmental approach, is necessary. Our review of current therapeutic approaches is based on this distinction.

Therapeutic Approaches Addressing Disorders of Mental Representation

It follows from the assumptions of psychodynamic psychotherapy reviewed above, that child therapists using these techniques expect children to be using distorted and/or unconscious mental representations in maladaptive ways. For example, children may unconsciously represent their father as cruel and rageful, a representation distorted by their own unconscious aggression. Further, it is anticipated that these distortions have a developmental dimension whereby ideas or feelings are more appropriate to an earlier stage of development and are likely to confuse the child's current perceptions (Abrams, 1988). The separation (repression, denial, displacement) of such early ideas is assumed to be defensive. For example, the perception of a caregiver as cruel and destructive may be based on an infantile perception of that parent. As a consequence of the pain associated with this perception of a loving father, this representation never came to be integrated into the evolving representation of the father in the child's mind. It exists as a separate yet disturbing idea. Children may react to the presence of such a representation as potentially painful and incompatible with their perception of the parent as loving and affectionate. By displacing this perception onto others whom they then perceive as frightening, children may exaggerate the subjective likelihood of burglars or other intruders attacking them and their family. Of course, if such ideas are based on the externalization of their own aggressive feelings toward the father, it is these feelings that have to be addressed in the context of the therapy.

The therapist, using the child's verbalization, nonverbal play, dream reports, or other behaviors, attempts to create a model of the child's conscious and unconscious thoughts and feelings. On the basis of this model, the therapist helps children to acquire an understanding of their irrational or at times inappropriate feelings and beliefs. This kind of understanding may, under ideal conditions, result in the integration of developmentally earlier modes of thinking into a more mature and age-appropriate framework. The structure of the treatment appears to be relatively unimportant. Some therapists use toys or games, others more readily engage children in a process of self-exploration. In most contexts, the therapist works to draw attention to possible unconscious determinants of the child's behavior. Therapists tend to use material of the child's fantasy and play in conjunction with other information they have obtained about the child (parental reports, school reports, etc.) to construct a plausible picture of the child's emotional concerns. The most common foci of psychodynamic child therapists tend to be children's concerns about their body, anxieties about conscious or unconscious destructive or sexual impulses, and concerns about relationships with or between caregivers or siblings or peers.

Psychodynamic therapists use a range of standard techniques. These have been systematized on the basis of empirical studies by Paulina Kernberg (1995), who observed a number of somewhat overlapping but reliably distinguishable categories of interventions. These include:

1. Supportive interventions aimed at reducing children's anxiety or increasing their sense of competence and mastery using suggestion, reassurance, empathy, or the provision of information.
2. Summary statements or paraphrases of children's communication to that point that support and develop the therapeutic exchange with the children.
3. Clarifications of children's verbalization or affect. These help prepare children for interpretation or simply direct their attention to noticeable aspects of their behavior, such as a repeated tendency to behave in self-defeating, self-destructive ways.
4. Interpretations attempt to identify and spell out representations of which children are likely not to be aware and which they are likely to find difficult or totally unacceptable. It is therefore expected that children will show a certain degree of resistance to such verbalizations on the part of the therapist. Interpretations have to be carefully timed to maximize their acceptability to the child. Ideally, therapists accumulate considerable evidence to support their conjectures, making their acceptance more or less automatic.

In formulating an interpretation, the therapist is well advised to concentrate attention on the therapeutic situation itself, where evidence is most likely to become available. Although the therapist often may be able to identify significant connections between the child's behavior in therapy and what the therapist knows about the child's past experience, interpretations, at least in the early phase of treatment, are best restricted to the child's current conflicts, in the immediate context brought into the therapy. The ultimate aim of the therapist is to provide the child with an emotionally meaningful, comprehensive understanding of the connections between past experiences and current methods of coping with conflict.

Kernberg (1995) distinguishes three kinds of interpretations: (1) interpretations of defenses, (2) interpretations addressing repudiated wishes, and (3) reconstructive interpretations. The first of these draws the child's attention to actual exclusion of certain ideas from awareness. This focuses attention on certain contents but also invites the child to consider alternative strategies for coping with or expressing these ideas or feelings. The second kind of interpretation generally aims to explain the child's behavior in terms of a putative nonconscious wish. Most frequently, the need for defense is explained in terms of the presence of an unconscious wish. For example, the therapist might say, "I think you tend to forget your dreams because in these dreams, you are able to think about how angry you feel with your father and about your wish to punish him in cruel ways for how he has treated you."

Reconstructive interpretations aim not only to explain a current state of affairs in the child's mind, but also to give an account of how this may have come about. The reconstruction of early experience in this context is somewhat controversial. Psychodynamically oriented psychotherapists frequently assume that the representation the child constructs of them is powerfully influenced by the child's prior experiences with caregivers, but it does not invariably follow that these experiences find direct expression in such representations. For example, a child might see the therapist as a critic who persistently undermines the child's sense of confidence and well-being. The child is thus evidently externalizing an internal representational figure who constantly bombards the self with disparagement and criticism. Such a representation may well be the product of defensive maneuvers rather than an indication of the presence of a severely critical adult figure in the child's past. Thus, the therapist might safely interpret "I think you are worried about my criticizing you because there is a voice inside your head that constantly says that you are such a naughty child that nobody could love you." It would probably be unwise to assume, however, that such a critical figure was actually part of the child's earlier experience. Such an "internal object" is more likely to be a split part of the child's self-representation, which may indeed be based on the internalization of an actually destructive and aggressive caregiver or may be a disowned destructive or aggressive part of the child, separated off precisely because the perceived kindness of the actual parent made such aggressive impulses seem totally unacceptable and intolerable to the child. In either case, what needs to be addressed in reconstructive interpretations is how unacceptable a child finds even a small amount of residual aggression and destructiveness that has remained as part of the self structure. Through verbalization of these defensive aspects, children are gradually able to modify their internal standards for acceptable ideas and feelings and take on board the destructive aggression as part of their self-representation, leading to greater integration and flexibility in their psychic functioning.

Thus, therapists' interventions mostly tend to combine a focus on defenses, wishes, and past or current experience. Such interventions have in common a focus on the child's emotional experience in relation to these domains. The therapeutic action of psychoanalytic psychotherapy is assumed to be "work in the transference" (Strachey, 1934). The child's interaction with the therapist becomes increasingly invested with affect as the therapy progresses, as internal representations of relationships find expression in the relationship with the therapist. "Working through," helping children to understand their reactions to the therapist in terms of anxieties, conflicts, and defenses, is regarded as the essence of therapeutic work.

The development of the transference is facilitated by (1) the therapist's neutrality; (2) emotional availability (attunement to the child's predicament); (3) encouragement to freely express thoughts and feelings; (4) the regularity and consistency of the therapeutic structure; and (5) the child's underlying perception of the therapist as a benign figure (Chethik, 1989). The transference relationship offers a window on both the nature of the child's relationship with the caregiver, as experienced by the child, and aspects of the child's experience of the self—particularly those aspects the child experiences as unacceptable and wishes quickly to externalize onto the figure of the therapist. This role enables the therapist to learn about the child's internal world. Distorted mental representations are identified, clarified, and understood and ideally reintegrated with the mature aspects of the child's thinking (Abrams, 1988).

For example, a shy, frightened, and withdrawn boy, age 8, who was referred because of his depression, developed an exceptionally acrimonious relationship with his therapist. The therapist frequently found herself shamed and ridiculed, endlessly failing in the tasks set by the child, and accused of being stupid. The child simultaneously bullied and patronized the therapist. The therapist gently showed the child how he often considered himself not to be good enough and placed himself in situations where this would be all too evident. Gradually, the idea was presented that being insignificant and "no good" was preferable (safer) because it avoided the even more unpleasant possibility of observing that the therapist or his parents might be disappointed with him. Eventually, the problem was traced back to his guilt feelings about his sadistic, aggressive feelings toward his younger brother, whose birth precipitated his depressive episode.

Termination of the treatment is signaled by (1) symptomatic improvement; (2) improved family and peer relationships; (3) the ability to take advantage of normal developmental opportunities; (4) the ability to deal with new environmental stressors; and (5) the ability to use the therapy more effectively (experience the therapy as helpful, allow the therapist's interpretive work to continue, express feelings more readily, show gratitude as well as criticism and anger, show insight, humor, and healthy self-mockery, etc.; Kernberg, 1995). "Traditional" psychodynamic treatment of this sort is rarely prolonged; much may be achieved in once-weekly meetings over one year, although treatment length is generally 18 months to two years (Fonagy & Target, 1996c).

Therapeutic Approaches Addressing Disorders of Mental Processes

Not all childhood disorders respond readily to psychotherapeutic intervention. Over recent decades, the psychodynamic approach has been extended to children who are categorized as narcissistic, borderline, or severely conduct disordered and delinquent as well (see, e.g., Bleiberg, 1987, 1994a, 1994b; Marohn, 1991; Rinsley, 1989). From a psychodynamic perspective, most children with so-called neurotic disorders may be understood in terms of distortions of mental representations of either self or other (Sandler & Rosenblatt, 1962). The distorted ideas with which more severely disturbed children tend to present cannot be readily addressed solely by interpretative psychotherapeutic work. Ideas that, in less severely disturbed children, appear to be repudiated (aggression or aggressive sexual ideation) are often consciously accessible for such children; insight into these seems of little therapeutic relevance. Defenses, as normally conceived, are often hard to identify. Referring to children's anxiety rarely makes them feel understood; it simply leaves them confused. Psychodynamic understanding of these children is possible if we assume that defensive operations for this group do not simply entail the modification of specific ideas and feelings but rather the mental processes responsible for generating the mental representations (Fonagy et al., 1993). For example, children traumatized by their caregiver find contemplating the caregiver's feelings and ideas intensely painful because, at least in their eyes, these must involve the caregiver's wish to harm them. Thus, they defensively inhibit the psychological functions (mental processes) responsible for generating representations of mental states, at least in the context of attachment relationships (Fonagy et al., 1995).

The therapeutic approach required to address problems of inhibited mental processes are qualitatively different from those that may be helpful in treating neurotic children. The therapist's task is to make children feel that it is once again safe to make full use of their mind. It may be assumed that most mental processes are, at least potentially, available, and the free exploration of thoughts and ideas serves to disinhibit the child's pervasive defensive stance. Therapeutic approaches with such children have increasingly emphasized the promotion of opportunities for playing with ideas (Fonagy & Target, 1996b). To some degree, the therapeutic approach is unchanged. It is the aim of therapy that is modified (Fonagy & Target, 1998). Neither the recovery of repressed memories or feelings, nor arriving at an understanding of unconscious reasons for their avoidance is relevant to therapeutic change. The very process of achieving understanding or the very act of contemplating feelings and ideas may, in itself, help severely disturbed children to recover their capacity to regulate, organize, and represent mental states. Some techniques required to achieve this end have been previously systematically excluded from psychodynamic work with neurotic children because of their expected interference with therapeutic neutrality.

Effective interventions are surprisingly simple and include strategies such as (1) the enhancement of reflective processes through observation and verbalization of the child's feelings; (2) the enhancement of impulse control through helping the child identify ways of channeling impulses into socially acceptable forms of behavior; (3) building cognitive self-regulatory strategies through symbolization and metaphor and by the demonstration of the therapist's own capacities for the modulation of experience through reflective thinking and talking; (4) generating interest in the mental states of others, often, at least initially, by focusing on the child's perception of the therapist's mental state; (5) developing the child's capacity to play, at first with objects, then with others, and finally with feelings and ideas; and (6) the demonstration to the child of multiple ways of seeing physical reality (Bleiberg, Fonagy, & Target, 1997). Looked at in this way, psychodynamic therapy is no longer considered a predominantly insight-oriented, conflict-solving psychological treatment, but rather a developmentally based mentalization-enhancing approach. It may link diverse therapeutic orientations such as systemic family therapy and cognitive-behavioral therapy (CBT). For example, both CBT and mental-process-oriented psychodynamic psychotherapy aim to enhance the child's capacity to organize and structure experiences. The difference lies in the focus of the cognitive approach on particular mental schemata, whereas the psychodynamic approach aims at promoting a broad set of capacities. We expect that an important component of the effectiveness of both therapeutic orientations may be mediated through the rekindling of the child's confidence in the self-organization of internal states. A more focused approach is likely to be more appropriate to children with less pervasive dysfunctions. As yet, there is no evidence available to substantiate this kind of distinction.

PROBLEMS FOR WHICH THE PSYCHODYNAMIC APPROACH IS EXPECTED TO BE EFFICACIOUS

The psychodynamic approach to child therapy was designed to treat what has traditionally been referred to as neurotic disturbance. P. Tyson (1992) describes neurosis as characterized by (1) a predominance of internalized conflicts producing symptoms, (2) a capacity for affect regulation, and (3) a capacity for self-responsibility. Kernberg (1975) has added to this list the predominance of repression as a mechanism of defense. However, modern descriptive psychiatry has largely discredited the term neurosis as lacking in clarity and reliability, and probably also overinclusive and based on an outmoded theory of psychological disorder.

Despite this slight, neurosis refused to disappear. Empirical studies of psychiatric symptoms in children (Achenbach, 1988, 1995) support a dichotomy between internalizing (emotional) disorders and externalizing (conduct) disorders. In an oversimplified way, this dichotomy distinguishes children who make themselves miserable (i.e., those who experience their symptoms as ego-dystonic) from children who make everyone but themselves miserable (i.e., those who experience their symptoms as ego-syntonic).

Obviously, an easy differentiation between inner suffering and outwardly directed misery does not stand up well to close clinical scrutiny. Aggressive, delinquent, and hyperactive children experience much suffering and inner turmoil (Katz, 1992; O'Brien, 1992), just as surely as anxious and inhibited youngsters can entrap their parents and teachers in a tight web of control and unhappiness.

Nonetheless, the internalizing-externalizing dichotomy captures meaningful dimensions of children's psychopathology. Clinically, children with internalizing disorders resemble the anxious, inhibited, neurotic children that constitute the primary indication for child analysis according to the child analytic literature; internalizing disorders can be roughly described as neurosis shorn of theoretical baggage.

There is little research available on the outcome of psychodynamic treatment that might guide appropriate application (Weisz, Weiss, Morton, Granger, & Han, 1992). The most extensive study of intensive psychodynamic treatment was a chart review of more than 700 case records at a psychoanalytic clinic in the United Kingdom (Fonagy & Target, 1996c; Target & Fonagy, 1994). The observed effects of psychodynamic treatment were relatively impressive, particularly with younger children and those with an emotional disorder or a disruptive disorder whose symptom profile included anxiety. Children with pervasive developmental disorders or mental retardation appeared to respond poorly to psychodynamic treatment. There was some evidence that more intensive treatment was desirable for children with emotional disorders whose symptomatology was extremely severe and pervasive.

Some smaller-scale studies demonstrated that psychodynamic therapy could bring about improvement in aspects of psychological functioning beyond psychiatric symptomatology.

Heinicke (1965; Heinicke & Ramsey-Klee, 1986) demonstrated that general academic performance was superior at one-year follow-up in children who were treated more frequently in psychodynamic psychotherapy. Moran and Fonagy (1987; Fonagy & Moran, 1990; Moran, Fonagy, Kurtz, Bolton, & Brook, 1991) demonstrated that children with poorly controlled diabetes could be significantly helped with their metabolic problems with relatively brief intensive psychodynamic psychotherapy. Lush and colleagues (Lush, Boston, & Grainger, 1991) in a naturalistic study offered preliminary evidence that psychodynamic therapy was helpful for children with a history of severe deprivation who were placed in foster homes or adopted. Improvements were noted only in the treated group. Negative findings, however, were reported by Smyrnios and Kirkby (1993). In this study, no significant differences were found at follow-up between a time-limited and a time-unlimited psychodynamic therapy group and a minimal contact control group.

All these studies suffer from severe methodological shortcomings, including (1) small sample size; (2) nonstandardized, unreliable assessment procedures; (3) nonrandom assignment; (4) nonindependent or overnarrow assessments of outcome; (5) lack of full specification of the treatment offered; and (6) the absence of measures of therapist adherence. Better evidence is available for the success of therapeutic approaches that cannot be considered as direct implementations of psychoanalytic ideas. Kolvin et al. (1981), for example, demonstrated that psychodynamic group therapy had relatively favorable effects when compared with behavior therapy and parent counseling, particularly on long-term follow-up. A sobering finding is reported by Szapocznik and colleagues (1989), who randomly assigned disruptive adolescents to either individual psychodynamic therapy, structural family therapy, or a recreational control group. Both active forms of treatment led to significant gains, but on one year follow-up, family functioning had deteriorated in the individual therapy group while the child functioning was improved for both groups.

Interpersonal psychotherapy, although not a psychodynamic treatment, (Klerman, Weissman, Rounsaville, & Chevron, 1984), nevertheless incorporates interpersonal psychodynamic principles. In a preliminary implementation of this therapy for depressed adolescents, Mufson and colleagues (Mufson, Moreau, Weissman, & Klerman, 1993) report promising results. In terms of the conceptual framework outlined above, these children would be described as suffering from disorders of mental representation. Generally, pervasive developmental disorders, psychosis, and major deficiencies in psychological capacities are regarded as negative indications. Although there have always been a number of child psychotherapists who have attempted to work with psychotic and autistic children (e.g., Alvarez, 1992; Klein, 1930), the majority have felt that they cannot help these children using psychoanalytically oriented work. More recently, however, the psychodynamic approach has been extended to apply not only to so-called neurotic disorders, but also to the understanding and treatment of borderline, narcissistic, delinquent, and conduct disordered youngsters (Bleiberg, 1987, 1994a, 1994b; Marohn, 1991; O'Brien, 1992; Rinsley, 1989), as well as schizoid and even psychotic children (e.g., Cantor & Kestenbaum, 1986). We have seen how clinical work with these more severely disturbed children quickly highlights the limitations of the "classical" analytic strategy. Bleiberg, Fonagy, and Target (1997) identified two clusters of youngsters who may be regarded as suitable for modified psychodynamic therapy, notwithstanding the severity of their disorder. They suggest that these clusters have in common the presence of at least one emotional disorder (e.g., depression, dysthymia, Generalized Anxiety Disorder, Separation Anxiety Disorder, social phobia); however, these symptoms must be seen in the context of a broader disturbance of social and emotional development, including marked impairment of peer relationships, affect regulation, frustration tolerance, and poor self-esteem.

One subgroup, designated Cluster A, are characterized by fragile reality contact and thought organization, idiosyncratic magical thinking, ideas of reference, suspiciousness, and deep discomfort in social situations. They can neither make full sense of the social world, nor communicate adequately their internal states. They resemble the Cluster A *Diagnostic and Statistical Manual of Mental Disorders (DSM-IV)* personality disorder diagnoses for adults, and children described by Cohen et al. (1994) and Towbin et al. (1993) as multiplex personality disorder. By contrast, Cluster B children (if referred below school age) show a hunger for social response, intense, often dramatic affect, clinginess, hyperactivity, and temper tantrums. School-age children may meet Axis 1 criteria for Attention-Deficit/Hyperactivity Disorder, Conduct Disorder, or Mood Disorder, but their lack of adequate affect regulation is the major feature of the picture; a sense of elation and blissful merger with others close to the child seems to alternate with rage and self-hatred. They have been linked to adult "dramatic" personality disorders (Cluster B) and have been described by Bleiberg (1994a, 1994b) and by Petti and Vela (1990). We have linked both clusters to an impairment of reflective function (Bleiberg et al., 1997). With the more severely disturbed children in these two clusters, the therapeutic approach that addresses disorders of mental processes, described above, is appropriate.

CASE STUDY

History, Diagnosis, and Assessment

A few days after his tenth birthday, David was found unconscious on the floor at school. He had refused to have breakfast and had had a hypoglycemic episode. Since the diagnosis of diabetes at the age of 7 years, he had had at least 12 hospitalizations associated with hypoglycemic episodes. David's referral for psychodynamic therapy was preceded by several attempts at behavioral intervention and two years of family therapy. David's referral was prompted by the need to improve control over his diabetes, but his violence and provocation of family members and peers was an equally grave source of concern. He was aggressive with his mother and father and was immediately abusive with the therapist as soon as he showed curiosity and interest in David. David met the *DSM-IV* diagnostic criteria for Oppositional Defiant Disorder and hyperactive-impulsive Attention Deficit Disorder, and suffered from anxiety and maladaptive health behavioral problems that affected his ability to control his diabetes.

David's mother had had considerable difficulties even before his birth. An unwanted and aggressive child, she had been sent away to boarding school at the age of 5. David, her first child, strained her meager resources. She was unable to feed him or see him for two weeks after his birth and remained on antidepressants for most of his early years. When David was 3, she was briefly hospitalized for depression. Aggression seemed to be an accepted part of life in this household. In her fights with David, mother "gave as good as she got," sometimes sitting on him, hitting him in the head, and pulling his hair. David's father was a conscientious provider who retired to the sidelines after coming home from work, leaving his wife to handle the three children, but then denigrating her for her failure to manage them.

CASE FORMULATION

David showed an unusual form of intense resistance from the very beginning of his assessment: He could not tolerate his therapist thinking about him. This intolerance manifested itself in the form of a quite generalized unwillingness to contemplate the thoughts and feelings that anyone might have about anyone else close. David appeared to be almost phobic about the thoughts and feelings that people generally could be expected to experience. He protected himself from his therapist's thinking about him just as he might have tried to blot out his mother's rejection of him through her years of depression and then active hostility. His vehement attacks on his therapist and the therapeutic process attempted to obliterate the reality of the therapist's interest and insight, maintaining an illusion of mutual lack of concern. Simply interpreting this state of affairs was of little help to David. Cases such as his highlight the limitations of conflict interpretation. They also point out that limited mentalizing abilities are rooted in various combinations of *developmental deficit*—constitutionally and/or environmentally derived—*and active defensive efforts* against the awareness of mental states.

TREATMENT APPROACH AND
RATIONALE FOR ITS SELECTION

The therapeutic situation in itself pushes children to become aware of another person's mental state. When children actively resist such awareness, the therapist may focus the children's attention on his or her own mental state rather than attempting to comment on their goals, beliefs, and desires. Clinical experience has shown that children find it helpful to focus interventions around their perceptions of the therapist's mental states, as a precursor to self-reflection. Many such children find the mental states of adults around them either confusing or frightening. The therapeutic environment provides a relatively safe context for getting to know the way they are seen by others, which can then become the core of their own self-perceptions. Therapists, of course, do not necessarily reveal to the children what they actually experience; rather, they share with the children their perception of how the children might be experiencing the therapist's state of mind at that moment. Some therapists have used guessing games along these lines (Moran, 1984), which seem to appeal to certain children, and we include an illustration of this form of technique. The approach taken here was described elsewhere as psychodynamic developmental therapy (Fonagy & Target, 1996d).

David entered treatment and wasted no time in launching vicious attacks and attempts to provoke the therapist. Although seemingly an imaginative, creative boy, his material somehow lacked the qualities of spontaneity and mutuality. David insisted on playing a stereotyped board game of his own invention. The game consisted of describing an alien culture of exceptional physical and intellectual prowess. The therapist interpreted that this helped him to feel competent in the therapeutic environment, which in so many ways felt frightening and alien. Such interventions, however, failed to alter the pattern.

Indeed, David perceived his therapist as frightening and as potentially violent. Interpretations of David's projection of his anger onto the therapist were rarely effective in curtailing his attacks, which often required direct physical restraint. The alternative to attack was retreat. Increasingly, he would withdraw form the therapeutic encounter. When it seemed relevant, the therapist commented on David's uncertainty about his identity except when angry and fighting; on his secret pleasure in the physical contact with his mother, however violent and frightening this was; on his rebellion against authority, his lack of acceptance of his illness, and many other themes. Such interpretations only led to more abusive behavior. He claimed not to care about the therapist, whom he found stupid and irrelevant. In response, the therapist talked about David's difficulty in understanding or expressing what was going on in his mind and the terrible helplessness this caused him to feel. David shrugged his shoulders, said his head was empty, and buried himself in his comic book.

David's attacks on his therapist continued. The more the therapist tried to forge links in David's mind, the more hostile or withdrawn David became. Even when David felt understood, the consequences were dire. About one year into his treatment, in an exceptionally lively session, David acknowledged feeling enslaved by his mother, his diabetes, and his therapy. This moment of rare therapeutic exchange was short-lived. Soon afterward, David was hospitalized in a ketotic state and on return to the sessions, appeared even more withdrawn.

David frequently accused the therapist of wearing a Darth Vader mask. At other times, he would look at the therapist and ask, "What's the matter? Do you want a fight?" Beyond highlighting the ever present fear of the therapist, these comments gave a clue as to the reasons David could derive little help from interpretations that went beyond reflecting his current affect. Looking at a person gave him no clear idea of the person's mental state. He could rely only on a fixed, concrete image: a cruel, vindictive other. His sense of himself as a being with a mind was so poorly established that he would not conceive of his therapist as someone trying to *understand* a mental life that he could hardly grasp himself. David's obsessive fantasies of alien figures, incapable of affect and possessing destructive mental powers, became understandable as proto-representations in which subjective experience had been replaced by mindless aggression.

David's therapist was inventive; a game emerged in the second year of treatment in which David and his therapist made notes on "what I think you think I am thinking about you today." David wished to repeat this game day after day for months. Increasingly, he would call for a round at times of heightened anxiety during his session. Taking his cue from David, the therapist focused on clarifications of David's current mental state, particularly in relation to him, rather than offering formulations of David's unconscious feelings about his past and present relationships.

During one session, the therapist and David played "tennis" on the table. David won and showed the guilty anxiety he often manifested on such occasions. He became highly excited and began to throw himself on the couch, shouting the names of tennis stars. The therapist said: "I wonder if you think I might be less disappointed if I knew I had been beaten by a great tennis player, and then you would not have to feel so uncomfortable." Rather than replying, David stood up on the couch and hit the therapist with his racquet. The therapist moved out of harm's way but did not restrain David. A few moments later, David shouted: "You don't know me!" The therapist replied: "You don't want me to know you, because then I might not like how big and strong you feel." David spun round and round on his heels making himself dizzy and collapsed in a heap on the floor. He then said he had a headache, intimating that he was dangerously hypoglycemic. The therapist assumed that David was feigning the headache both to test the therapist and to take revenge against him. Reflecting on the confusion he felt about David's possible urgent need for food, the therapist said, "One can feel very helpless when one doesn't really know how someone else feels, but it's even worse when one doesn't know how one feels oneself. I think you feel very frightened that if you become strong and powerful, I will no longer want to help you and perhaps just let you die." David, without saying a word, emptied the contents of his pockets onto the carpet. He then proceeded to stuff everything back in a careless way so that there was no room for about a third of his pieces. Before the therapist could say anything, David snapped, "Why don't you just shut up?" The therapist said, "By bullying me and shouting at me, I think you hope to get rid of all the thoughts and feelings that you feel we could not cope with." David looked at his therapist for the first time in a friendly way and suggested they play the "I think you think" game. He wrote, "frightened" as his first guess about what the therapist thought David thought, then added "get lost!" The therapist confirmed that he thought David was frightened because somehow he felt that his success would destroy the therapist and then David would get lost.

POSTTERMINATION SYNOPSIS

In this interchange, the therapist treated David's aggression as a defense against the anxiety that close mental contact engendered in him. Gradually, David became more prepared to contemplate fears, thoughts, and wishes in himself and in his therapist. In the third and fourth year of David's treatment, his terror of being seen as "bad" began to surface. His unprovoked, excessively aggressive acts could now be seen as aimed at people whom he experienced as seeing him in a negative way. Therapeutic work on David's avoidance of recognizing thoughts and feelings, and his anxieties about being shamed, helped him to establish diabetic control and settle into school. His treatment, which lasted four years, was successful in that his destructive outbursts were greatly reduced and his deliberate self-harm ceased. His relationships with others, however, remained restricted and somewhat mistrustful.

SUMMARY

Psychodynamic psychotherapy has a well-developed and helpful body of theory that has inspired many generations of clinicians. Psychodynamic ideas are applied in contexts well beyond the treatment of psychiatric disorders, such as the fields of psychology, other social sciences, literature, and the arts. Psychodynamic psychotherapy is one of the oldest theory-driven forms of psychological treatment of mental disorders (probably antedated only by hypnosis). Nevertheless, in terms of empirical investigations of either its underlying constructs or its therapeutic outcome, it is still in its infancy.

The shortcomings of psychodynamic approaches include:

1. Lack of operationalization in most descriptions of technical interventions, whose effectiveness is supported almost entirely by evocative case illustrations.
2. Inadequate specificity regarding technical interventions appropriate for children with a particular diagnosis or clinical presentation.
3. Limited evidence of efficacy, specially evidence derived from randomized, controlled trials.
4. A rather loose relationship among theory/ies of psychopathology (in turn, poorly supported by empirical data), theory of technique, and technique as actually carried out in clinical practice.
5. Lengthy treatments, with rather global goals, raising concerns about cost-effectiveness.
6. Shortage of reliable procedures for evaluating ongoing clinical progress.
7. A significant heterogeneity of therapeutic approaches within this category, defying integration and rationalization.
8. An overt as well as covert antagonism on the part of many psychodynamic practitioners to the idea of systematic evaluation and scrutiny.

Psychodynamic child therapists thus face formidable challenges to their clinical and theoretical convictions, to their professional status, and, as managed care relentlessly expands its control over reimbursement and denies payment for child therapy, to their livelihood. There are many of us, however, who, notwithstanding our awareness of the current limitations of the approach, remain convinced of its unique value, not just as a methodology for the study of the psychological difficulties of childhood, but also as a method of clinical intervention with children whom we find it hard to reach using other methods. Psychodynamic child clinicians are for the most part well aware of the tremendous challenge they face in persuading health care organizations as well as consumers of services of the unique value of their approach. Considerable work remains to be done, but a new culture of research is now emerging within the psychoanalytic community (Emde & Fonagy, 1997; Wallerstein & Fonagy, 1999). It is, we believe, a realistic hope that over the next decade, substantial evidence will emerge that will delineate the specific value of the approach for the long-term development of children with psychological disorders. Work is already underway at a number of centers internationally, and time will tell whether psychodynamic treatment works and, if so, for whom.

REFERENCES

Abraham, K. (1979). *Selected papers of Karl Abraham.* New York: Brunner/Mazel.

Abrams, S. (1988). The psychoanalytic process in adults and children. *Psychoanalytic Study of the Child, 43,* 245–261.

Achenbach, T. M. (1988). Integrating assessment and taxonomy. In M. Rutter & A. H. Tuma (Eds.), *Assessment and diagnosis in child psychopathology* (pp. 300–343). New York: Guilford Press.

Achenbach, T. M. (1995). Diagnosis, assessment, and comorbidity in psychosocial treatment research. *Journal of Abnormal Child Psychology, 23,* 45–64.

Ainsworth, M. D. S., Blehar, M. C., Waters, E., & Wall, S. (1978). *Patterns of attachment: A psychological study of the Strange Situation.* Hillsdale, NJ: Erlbaum.

Altman, N. (1992). Relational perspectives on child psychoanalytic psychotherapy. In N. J. Skolnick & S. C. Warshaw (Eds.), *Relational perspectives in psychoanalysis* (pp. 175–194). Hillsdale, NJ: Analytic Press.

Altman, N. (1994). The recognition of relational theory and technique in child treatment: Child analytic work [Special Issue]. *Psychoanalytic Psychology, 11,* 383–395.

Alvarez, A. (1992). *Live company: Psychoanalytic psychotherapy with autistic, borderline, deprived and abused children.* London: Routledge.

Baron, J., Gruen, R., & Asnis, L. (1985). Familial transmission of Schizotypal and Borderline Personality Disorders. *American Journal of Psychiatry, 142,* 927–934.

Belsky, J., Rovine, M., & Taylor, D. G. (1984). The Pennsylvania Infant and Family Development Project: III. The origins of individual differences in mother-infant attachment: Maternal and infant contributions. *Child Development, 55,* 718–728.

Bion, W. R. (1959). Attacks on linking. *International Journal of Psychoanalysis, 40,* 308–315.

Bleiberg, E. (1987). Stages in the treatment of narcissistic children and adolescents. *Bulletin of the Menninger Clinic, 51,* 296–313.

Bleiberg, E. (1994a). Borderline disorders in children and adolescents: The concept, the diagnosis, and the controversies. *Bulletin of the Menninger Clinic, 58,* 169–196.

Bleiberg, E. (1994b). Neurosis and conduct disorders. In J. M. Oldham & M. B. Riba (Eds.), *American Psychiatric Press review of psychiatry* (Vol. 13, pp. 493–518). Washington, DC: American Psychiatric Press.

Bleiberg, E., Fonagy, P., & Target, M. (1997). Child psychoanalysis: Critical overview and a proposed reconsideration. *Psychiatric Clinics of North America, 6,* 1–38.

Bower, T. R. (1989). *The rational infant: Learning in infancy.* New York: Freeman.

Bowlby, J. (1969). *Attachment and loss. Vol. 1: Attachment.* London: Hogarth Press and the Institute of Psycho-Analysis.

Bowlby, J. (1973). *Attachment and loss. Vol. 2: Separation: Anxiety and anger.* London: Hogarth Press and Institute of Psycho-Analysis.

Bowlby, J. (1980). *Attachment and loss. Vol. 3: Loss: Sadness and depression.* London: Hogarth Press and Institute of Psycho-Analysis.

Brenner, C. (1982). *The mind in conflict.* New York: International Universities Press.

Breuer, J., & Freud, S. (1895). Studies on hysteria. In J. Strachey (Ed.), *The standard edition of the complete psychological works of Sigmund Freud* (Vol. 2, pp. 1–305). London: Hogarth Press.

Bus, A. G., & van Ijzendoorn, M. H. (1992). Patterns of attachment in frequently and infrequently reading mother-child dyads. *Journal of Genetic Psychology, 153,* 395–403.

Cantor, S., & Kestenbaum, C. (1986). Psychotherapy with schizophrenic children. *Journal of the American Academy of Child Psychiatry, 25,* 623–630.

Chethik, M. (1989). *Techniques of child therapy: Psychodynamic strategies.* New York: Guilford Press.

Cicchetti, D. (1990). The organization and coherence of socioemotional, cognitive, and representational development: Illustrations through a developmental psychopathology perspective on Down syndrome and child maltreatment. In R. Thompson (Ed.), *Socioemotional development: Nebraska symposium on motivation* (pp. 259–279). Lincoln: University of Nebraska Press.

Clarkin, J. F., Kernberg, O. F., & Yeomans, F. (1999). *Transference-focused psychotherapy for Borderline Personality Disorder patients.* New York: Guilford Press.

Cohen, D. J., Towbin, K. E., Mayes, L., & Volkmar, F. (1994). Developmental psychopathology of multiplex developmental disorder. In S. L. Friedman & H. C. Haywood (Eds.), *Developmental follow-up: Concepts, domains and methods* (pp. 155–182). New York: Academic Press.

Cummings, E. M., & Davies, P. T. (1994). Maternal depression and child development. *Journal of Child Psychology and Psychiatry, 35,* 73–112.

DeFolch, T. E. (1988). Guilt bearable or unbearable: A problem for the child in analysis: Psychoanalysis of children [Special issue]. *International Review of Psychoanalysis, 15,* 13–24.

Emde, R. N. (1983). Pre-representational self and its affective core. *The Psychoanalytic Study of the Child, 38,* 165–192.

Emde, R. N. (1988a). Development terminable and interminable: I. Innate and motivational factors from infancy. *International Journal of Psychoanalysis, 69,* 23–42.

Emde, R. N. (1988b). Development terminable and interminable: II. Recent psychoanalytic theory and therapeutic considerations. *International Journal of Psychoanalysis, 69,* 283–286.

Emde, R. N., & Fonagy, P. (1997). An emerging culture for psychoanalytic research? [Editorial]. *International Journal of Psychoanalysis, 78,* 643–651.

Fairbairn, W. R. D. (1952). *An object-relations theory of the personality.* New York: Basic Books.

Feinman, S. (1991). *Social referencing and the social construction of reality in infancy.* New York: Plenum Press.

Fonagy, P., Edgcumbe, R., Moran, G. S., Kennedy, H., & Target, M. (1993). The roles of mental representations and mental processes in therapeutic action. *Psychoanalytic Study of the Child, 48,* 9–48.

Fonagy, P., & Moran, G. S. (1990). Studies on the efficacy of child psychoanalysis. *Journal of Consulting and Clinical Psychology, 58,* 684–695.

Fonagy, P., Steele, M., Steele, H., Leigh, T., Kennedy, R., Mattoon, G., et al. (1995). The predictive validity of Mary Main's Adult Attachment Interview: A psychoanalytic and developmental perspective on the transgenerational transmission of attachment and borderline states. In S. Goldberg, R. Muir, & J. Kerr (Eds.), *Attachment theory: Social, developmental and clinical perspectives* (pp. 233–278). Hillsdale, NJ: Analytic Press.

Fonagy, P., & Target, M. (1996a). A contemporary psychoanalytical perspective: Psychodynamic developmental therapy. In E. Hibbs & P. Jensen (Eds.), *Psychosocial treatments for child and adolescent disorders: Empirically based approaches* (pp. 619–638). Washington, DC: American Psychological Association and the National Institutes of Health.

Fonagy, P., & Target, M. (1996b). Playing with reality: I. Theory of mind and the normal development of psychic reality. *International Journal of Psychoanalysis, 77,* 217–233.

Fonagy, P., & Target, M. (1996c). Predictors of outcome in child psychoanalysis: A retrospective study of 763 cases at the Anna Freud Centre. *Journal of the American Psychoanalytic Association, 44,* 27–77.

Fonagy, P., & Target, M. (1996d). Psychodynamic developmental therapy for children: A contemporary application of child psychoanalysis. In E. D. Hibbs & P. S. Jensen (Eds.), *Psychosocial treatment research with children and adolescents.* Washington, DC: American Psychological Association and the National Institutes of Health.

Fonagy, P., & Target, M. (1998). Mentalization and the changing aims of child psychoanalysis. *Psychoanalytic Dialogues, 8,* 87–114.

Freud, A. (1936). *The ego and the mechanisms of defence.* New York: International Universities Press.

Freud, A. (1946). *The psychoanalytic treatment of children.* London: Imago.

Freud, A. (1965). *Normality and pathology in childhood.* London: Penguin Books.

Freud, S. (1900). The interpretation of dreams. In J. Strachey (Ed.), *The standard edition of the complete psychological works of Sigmund Freud* (Vols. 4–5, pp. 1–715). London: Hogarth Press.

Freud, S. (1905). Three essays on the theory of sexuality. In J. Strachey (Ed.), *The standard edition of the complete psychological works of Sigmund Freud* (Vol. 7, pp. 123–230). London: Hogarth Press.

Freud, S. (1909). Analysis of a phobia in a five-year-old boy. In J. Strachey (Ed.), *The standard edition of the complete psychological works of Sigmund Freud* (Vol. 10, pp. 1–147). London: Hogarth Press.

Freud, S. (1920). Beyond the pleasure principle. In J. Strachey (Ed.), *The standard edition of the complete psychological works of Sigmund Freud* (Vol. 18, pp. 1–64). London: Hogarth Press.

Freud, S. (1923). The ego and the id. In J. Strachey (Ed.), *The standard edition of the complete psychological works of Sigmund Freud* (Vol. 19, pp. 1–59). London: Hogarth Press.

Freud, S. (1926). The question of lay analysis. In J. Strachey (Ed.), *The standard edition of the complete psychological works of Sigmund Freud* (Vol. 20, pp. 77–172). London: Hogarth Press.

Freud, S. (1930). Civilization and its discontents. In J. Strachey (Ed.), *The standard edition of the complete psychological works of Sigmund Freud* (Vol. 21, pp. 57–146). London: Hogarth Press.

Freud, S. (1933). New introductory lectures on psychoanalysis. In J. Strachey (Ed.), *The standard edition of the complete psychological works of Sigmund Freud* (Vol. 22, pp. 1–182). London: Hogarth Press.

Gergely, G. (1991). Developmental reconstructions: Infancy from the point of view of psychoanalysis and developmental psychology. *Psychoanalysis and Contemporary Thought, 14,* 3–55.

Glenn, J. (1978). *Child analysis and therapy.* New York: Aronson.

Golinkoff, R. M., Hardig, C. B., Carlson, V., & Sexton, M. E. (1984). The infant's perception of causal events: The distinction between animate and inanimate objects. In L. P. Lipsitt & C. Rovee-Collier (Eds.), *Advances in infancy research* (pp. 125–165). Norwood, NJ: Ablex.

Grossmann, K., Grossmann, K. E., Spangler, G., Suess, G., & Unzner, L. (1985). Maternal sensitivity and newborn orienting responses as related to quality of attachment in Northern Germany. In I. Bretherton & E. Waters (Eds.), Growing points in attachment theory and research. *Monographs of the Society for Research in Child Development, 50*(1–2, Serial No. 209), 233–256.

Hartmann, H. (1939). *Ego psychology and the problem of adaptation.* New York: International Universities Press.

Hartmann, H. (1955). Notes on the theory of sublimation. In *Essays on ego psychology* (pp. 215–240). New York: International University Press.

Heinicke, C. M. (1965). Frequency of psychotherapeutic session as a factor affecting the child's developmental status. *Psychoanalytic Study of the Child, 20,* 42–98.

Heinicke, C. M., & Ramsey-Klee, D. M. (1986). Outcome of child psychotherapy as a function of frequency of sessions. *Journal of the American Academy of Child Psychiatry, 25,* 247–253.

Hesse, P., & Cicchetti, D. (1982). Perspectives on an integrated theory of emotional development. *New Directions for Child Development, 16,* 3–48.

Hoffman, L. (1993). An introduction to child psychoanalysis. *Journal of Clinical Psychoanalysis, 2,* 5–26.

Hornik, R., & Gunnar, M. R. (1988). A descriptive analysis of infant social referencing. *Child Development, 59,* 626–634.

Hug-Helmuth, H. (1920). Child psychology and education. *International Journal of Psychoanalysis, 1,* 316–323.

Hug-Helmuth, H. (1921). On the technique of child analysis. *International Journal of Psychoanalysis, 2,* 287–303.

Jacobson, E. (1964). *The self and the object world.* New York: International Universities Press.

Katz, C. (1992). Aggressive children. In J. O'Brien, D. J. Pilowsky, & O. Lewis (Eds.), *Psychotherapies with children and adolescents: Adapting the psychodynamic process* (pp. 91–108). Washington, DC: American Psychiatric Press.

Kazdin, A. E., Bass, D., Siegel, T., & Thomas, C. (1990). Cognitive behavioral treatment and relationship therapy in the treatment of children referred for antisocial behavior. *Journal of Consulting and Clinical Psychology, 58,* 76–85.

Kernberg, O. F. (1975). *Borderline conditions and pathological narcissism.* New York: Aronson.

Kernberg, O. F. (1976). *Object relations theory and clinical psychoanalysis.* New York: Aronson.

Kernberg, O. F. (1982). Self, ego, affects and drives. *Journal of the American Psychoanalytic Association, 30,* 893–917.

Kernberg, O. F. (1987). An ego psychology-object relations theory approach to the transference. *Psychoanalytic Quarterly, 51,* 197–221.

Kernberg, O. F. (1995). Child psychiatry: Individual psychotherapy. In H. I. Kaplan & B. J. Sadock (Eds.), *Comprehensive textbook of psychiatry* (6 ed., pp. 2399–2412). Baltimore: Williams & Wilkins.

King, P., & Steiner, R. (1991). *The Freud-Klein controversies: 1941–45.* London: Routledge.

Klein, M. (1930). The psychotherapy of the psychoses. *British Journal of Medical Psychology, 10,* 226–234.

Klein, M. (1932). *The psycho-analysis of children.* London: Hogarth Press.

Klein, M. (1946). Notes on some schizoid mechanisms. In M. Klein, P. Heimann, S. Isaacs, & J. Riviere (Eds.), *Developments in psychoanalysis* (pp. 292–320). London: Hogarth Press.

Klein, M. (1952). The origins of transference. In *The writings of Melanie Klein* (pp. 48–56). London: Hogarth Press.

Klein, M., Heimann, P., Issacs, S., & Riviere, J. (Eds.). (1946). *Developments in psychoanalysis.* London: Hogarth Press.

Klerman, G. L., Weissman, M. M., Rounsaville, B. J., & Chevron, E. S. (1984). *Interpersonal psychotherapy of depression.* New York: Basic Books.

Kohut, H. (1971). *The analysis of the self.* New York: International Universities Press.

Kohut, H. (1977). *The restoration of the self.* New York: International Universities Press.

Kolvin, I., Garside, R. F., Nicol, A. R., MacMillan, A., Wolstenholme, F., & Leitch, I. M. (1981). *Help starts here: The maladjusted child in the ordinary school.* London: Tavistock.

Links, P. S., Steiner, M., & Huxley, G. (1988). The occurrence of Borderline Personality Disorder in the families of borderline patients. *Journal of the Personality Disorders, 2,* 14–20.

Loranger, A., Oldham, J., & Tullis, E. (1982). Familial transmission of *DSM-III* Borderline Personality

Disorder. *Archives of General Psychiatry, 39*, 795–799.

Lush, D., Boston, M., & Grainger, E. (1991). Evaluation of psychoanalytic psychotherapy with children: Therapists' assessments and predictions. *Psychoanalytic Psychotherapy, 5*, 191–234.

Mahler, M. (1968). *On human symbiosis and the vicissitudes of individuation.* New York: International Universities Press.

Main, M., Kaplan, N., & Cassidy, J. (1985). Security in infancy, childhood and adulthood: A move to the level of representation. In I. Bretherton & E. Waters (Eds.), Growing points of attachment theory and research. *Monographs of the Society for Research in Child Development, 50*, 66–104. Chicago: University of Chicago Press.

Marohn, R. C. (1991). Psychotherapy of adolescents with behavioral disorders. In M. Slomowitz (Ed.), *Adolescent psychotherapy* (pp. 145–161). Washington, DC: American Psychiatric Press.

Masterson, J. F. (1972). *Treatment of the borderline adolescent: A developmental approach.* New York: Wiley.

Moran, G. (1984). Psychoanalytic treatment of diabetic children. *The Psychoanalytic Study of the Child, 38*, 265–293.

Moran, G., Fonagy, P., Kurtz, A., Bolton, A., & Brook, C. (1991). A controlled study of the psychoanalytic treatment of brittle diabetes. *Journal of the American Academy of Child and Adolescent Psychiatry, 30*, 926–935.

Moran, G. S., & Fonagy, P. (1987). Psychoanalysis and diabetic control: A single case study. *British Journal of Medical Psychology, 60*, 357–372.

Mufson, L., Moreau, D., Weissman, M. M., & Klerman, G. L. (1993). *Interpersonal psychotherapy for depressed adolescents.* New York: Guilford Press.

O'Brien, J. (1992). Children with Attention-Deficit Hyperactivity Disorder and their parents. In J. O'Brien, D. J. Pilowsky, & O. Lewis (Eds.), *Psychotherapies with children and adolescents: Adapting the psychodynamic process* (pp. 109–124). Washington, DC: American Psychiatric Press.

O'Shaughnessy, E. (1988). W. R. Bion's theory of thinking and new techniques in child analysis. In E. B. Spillius (Ed.), *Melanie Klein today: Developments in theory and practice. Vol. 2: Mainly practice* (pp. 177–190). London: Routledge.

Petti, T. A., & Vela, R. M. (1990). Borderline disorders of childhood: An overview. *Journal of the Academy of Child and Adolescent Psychiatry, 29*, 327–337.

Pine, F. (1985). *Developmental theory and clinical process.* New Haven, CT: Yale University Press.

Rinsley, D. B. (1977). An object relations view of borderline personality. In P. Hartocollis (Ed.), *Borderline personality disorders: The concept, the syndrome, the patient* (pp. 47–70). New York: International Universities Press.

Rinsley, D. B. (1989). Notes on the developmental pathogenesis of Narcissistic Personality Disorder. *Psychiatric Clinics of North America, 12*, 695–707.

Sander, L. W. (1962). Issues in early mother child interaction. *Journal of the American Academy of Child Psychiatry, 1*, 141–166.

Sandler, J. (1987). *From safety to the superego: Selected papers of Joseph Sandler.* New York: Guilford Press.

Sandler, J., Kennedy, H., & Tyson, R. (1980). *The technique of child analysis: Discussions with Anna Freud.* London: Hogarth Press.

Sandler, J., & Rosenblatt, B. (1962). The concept of the representational world. *Psychoanalytic Study of the Child, 17*, 128–145.

Smyrnios, K. X., & Kirkby, R. J. (1993). Long-term comparison of brief versus unlimited psychodynamic treatments with children and their parents. *Journal of Consulting and Clinical Psychology, 61*, 1020–1027.

Sroufe, L. A. (1990). An organizational perspective on the self. In D. Cicchetti & M. Beeghly (Eds.), *The self in transition: Infancy to childhood* (pp. 281–307). Chicago: University of Chicago Press.

Stern, D. N. (1985). *The interpersonal world of the infant: A view from psychoanalysis and developmental psychology.* New York: Basic Books.

Strachey, J. (1934). The nature of the therapeutic action of psychoanalysis. *International Journal of Psychoanalysis, 50*, 275–292.

Szapocznik, J., Rio, A., Murray, E., Cohen, R., Scopetta, M., Rivas-Valquez, A., et al. (1989). Structural family versus psychodynamic child therapy for problematic Hispanic boys. *Journal of Consulting and Clinical Psychology, 57*, 571–578.

Target, M., & Fonagy, P. (1994). The efficacy of psychoanalysis for children with emotional disorders.

Terr, L. C. (1983). Chowchilla revisited: The effects of psychic trauma four years after a school-bus kidnapping. *American Journal of Psychiatry, 140,* 1543–1550.

Towbin, K. E., Dykens, E. M., Pearson, G. S., & Cohen, D. J. (1993). Conceptualizing "borderline syndrome of childhood" and "childhood schizophrenia" as a developmental disorder. *Journal of the American Academy of Child and Adolescent Psychiatry, 32,* 775–782.

Tyson, P. (1992, December). *Neurosis in childhood and in psychoanalysis.* Paper presented at the annual meeting of the American Psychoanalytic Association, Washington, DC.

Tyson, R. L., & Tyson, P. (1986). The concept of transference in child psychoanalysis. *Journal of the American Academy of Child Psychiatry, 25,* 30–39.

Wallerstein, R. S., & Fonagy, P. (1999). Psychoanalytic research and the IPA: History, present status and future potential. *International Journal of Psychoanalysis, 80*(Pt. 1), 91–109.

Warshaw, S. C. (1992). Mutative factors in child psychoanalysis: A comparison of diverse relational perspectives. In N. J. Skolnick & S. C. Warshaw (Eds.), *Relational perspectives in psychoanalysis* (pp. 141–173). Hillsdale, NJ: Analytic Press.

Weisz, J. R., Weiss, B., Morton, T., Granger, D., & Han, S. (1992). *Meta-analysis of psychotherapy outcome research with children and adolescents.* Los Angeles: University of California.

Winnicott, D. W. (1965). *The maturational process and the facilitating environment.* London: Hogarth Press.

Winnicott, D. W. (1971). *Playing and reality.* London: Tavistock.

SECTION TWO

PSYCHOTHERAPY WITH ADOLESCENTS AND YOUNG ADULTS

Chapter 6   Eating Disorders in Adolescence

Chapter 7   Psychodynamic Psychotherapy with Undergraduate and Graduate Students

CHAPTER 6

Eating Disorders in Adolescence

CECILE RAUSCH HERSCOVICI

HISTORY OF THE THERAPEUTIC APPROACH

Eating disorders are a major health problem in most Western countries and rapidly becoming an issue of concern in the majority of Westernized cultures. They have become a frequent prototypical disorder of female adolescent development in our time and the third most prevalent chronic condition for this group. A review of the studies of mortality rates for Anorexia Nervosa shows that compared to females 14 to 24 years old in the general population, these patients are 12 times more likely to die. When comparing death rates of Anorexia Nervosa with those of female psychiatric patients for this age range, the former are twice as likely to die (Sullivan, 1995). Only 10% of those presenting with eating disorders are males. Gordon (2000) refers to eating disorders as "ethnic disorders" to emphasize the sociocultural factors that explain their increase in our time. This concept, originally proposed by Deveraux (1980) proposes that certain disorders express the contradictions and anxieties that are particular to a particular culture at a certain historical period. As is characteristic of ethnic disorders, eating disturbances express themselves in various degrees of intensity, ranging from mild to severe. They are exaggerated extensions of normal and highly valued behaviors and attitudes in a culture and thus become a widely imitated model for expressing distress.

The contemporary craze about fitness, dieting, and food control have become the vehicle by which many individuals escape from seemingly unmanageable personal suffering and thus attain an elusive sense of control. Eating disorders represent a final common pathway for expressing a wide variety of idiosyncratic problems, such as difficulty with autonomy, emancipation, self-worth, control, and refusal to comply. It is common knowledge that eating disorders generate fascination and awe, and in a sense, they seem to mirror the conflicting pressure to consume and control that is so prevalent in our society. These disturbances also become political when viewed in connection with female submission to prevailing and unrealistic standards of beauty and slimness associated with discipline, success, and acceptance. The characteristic experiences and dilemmas of anorexic patients seem to exaggerate and reflect pervasive problems of female identity in the wider culture. Cross-cultural studies of normal female development show that despite the changes that feminism has brought along, most girls are still brought up to be people pleasers, very sensitive to external demands. They are less encouraged than boys are to develop autonomous behaviors.

Baker Miller (1976) suggests that women's sense of self-worth is still determined by responding to the demand to help others, and this requires the subordination of one's own needs to those of others. Furthermore, women often feel that their achievements are not a proof to themselves of their worthiness; rather, a performance to please others is. In this frame of mind, their constant dread is not being certain of their ability to sustain that level of excellence. A consequence of this pattern of socialization is that the girl often reaches adolescence with a feeling of powerlessness and dependency, which hinders the process of leaving home. This is one of the main reasons for the emergence of eating disorders at this developmental stage in a girl's life. Her body is the only part of herself over which she feels that she has control.

Epidemiology of Eating Disorders

The most researched and well-known eating disorders are Anorexia Nervosa and Bulimia Nervosa. Anorexia Nervosa is characterized by a relentless pursuit of thinness, leading to a state of emaciation. Anorexia restrictors, reduce weight by severe dieting; anorexic bulimic patients, maintain severe weight loss by further purging. This added stress on a malnourished body often causes additional damage. Bulimia Nervosa is characterized by cycles of binge eating. The patient, in an attempt to control the feared increase in weight, follows the binge, either by purging, by severe dieting, or excessive physical activity. The prevalence of Anorexia Nervosa and Bulimia Nervosa among middle and high school girls is 0.2 to 0.5% and 1 to 2%, respectively (van Hoeken, Lucas, & Hoek, 1998). Later additions to the diagnostic categories are Eating Disorders Not Otherwise Specified, of which Binge Eating Disorder and borderline conditions are the most commonly found (Hoek, 1995; Shisslak, Cargo, & Estes, 1995). This heterogeneous category accounts for 8% of the adolescent female population and comprises individuals who struggle with body dissatisfaction and disordered eating patterns that produce significant physical, psychological, and social distress (Austin, 2000; Shisslak et al., 1995). Taken together, the disordered eating behavior spectrum affects at least 10% of adolescent girls; 8:1 is the estimate of the female-to-male ratio for the more severe syndromes (Levine, Piran, & Irving, 2001).

Due to the secrecy surrounding this problem and the few community-based studies, the true incidence of Bulimia Nervosa is not known, but surveys using questionnaires have revealed that as many as 19% of female students report bulimic symptoms. Regarding Anorexia Nervosa, it is unclear whether the increase in cases reported in health care facilities reflects an actual increase or is mostly due to improved methods of case identification. Over 40% of cases of Anorexia Nervosa are detected by general practitioners; conversely, only 11% of the community cases of Bulimia Nervosa are detected. Because of the secretiveness and shame associated with these disorders, probably many more cases go unreported. That is why studies of clinical samples probably will always reflect an underestimation of the incidence of these disorders in the community (Hoek, 1995).

Hermeneutics of Therapeutic Approach

Hermeneutics refers to how the therapist understands the patient's experience. In the case of eating disorders, this understanding often does not suffice when attempting to change a multidimensional syndrome of still enigmatic etiology; therefore, a multimodal approach is suggested (Pinsof, Wynn, & Hambright, 1996). In recent years, the therapist's understanding of the patient's dynamic psychopathology often has been clearly differentiated from the interventions needed to help the patient (Dare & Crowther, 1995). This chapter presents an integrated relational approach to eating disorders that articulates constructs from systemic and individual treatment paradigms (Magnavita, 2000).

Eating disorders occur along a continuum of severity, from mild to seriously disturbed. Symptomatic expressions can occur in a relatively intact psyche in the context of normal family development, or in a very impaired individual immersed in a family context that fails to further the process of separation and individuation (Herscovici & Bay, 1990). Such is the case of *imitative anorexics*, who have had a healthy development in a favorable family context, go on an "innocent" diet with the goal of looking better, and then become trapped in the biological vulnerabilities to food restriction and the psychopathology of starvation. Many of these cases remit spontaneously or with little therapeutic effort, if detected early. These are the ones that prove most amenable to self-help and psychoeducational strategies.

A second group is composed of those for whom *the disorder evolves in the context of a dysfunctional family* whose members are immersed in the tension derived from unresolved issues of the past. Often, their equilibrium is threatened by the exogenous striving inherent in adolescence. They will benefit most from family therapy.

The third and most serious form of presentation is an *eating disorder in the context of a dysfunctional family system where the patient has experienced a pervasive developmental impairment resulting in a personality problem and reflecting a disorder of the self* (Herscovici, 1996). It may take the form of symbolic expressions of distorted self and object representations (object-relations model) or nonsymbolic restitutional emergency measures utilized to gain cohesion of the self (self psychology model).

THE SYSTEMIC PARADIGM

The application of systems theory to psychotherapy can be seen most clearly in the general literature on theory and practice of family therapy. Moreover, in recent years, the development of family systems medicine increasingly has become the operational frame for conducting treatment of eating disorders, the epitome of a systems approach combined with a biopsychosocial model. Epistemology refers to the rules we utilize to get to know and understand the world and our experience. Cybernetic epistemology is considered to have been a turning point in the behavioral sciences (Nichols & Schwartz, 1998). This new understanding of human behavior emphasizes the role of the social context in shaping individual behavior, emotions, and ideas. General systems theory deals with the study of the relation among the parts that interact in a context, stressing that they are parts of a whole that is not equal to the sum of its components. From this relational perspective, symptomatic behavior in a family member is understood as the manifestation of interactive processes that take place in the here and now of family life. Organization refers to the consistent way in which the components of a system relate to each other and provide its structure. This psychotherapeutic approach aims at changing the family organization as a means of changing the life of its members. Changes are believed to last longer because the change in each member continues to affect the other members, thus reverberating through the system and reinforcing change (Becvar & Becvar, 1996).

In the initial stages, family therapy relied on "more scientific" disciplines such as cybernetics, physics, and biology to be considered a valid alternative to psychoanalysis. In the 1970s, when family therapy had attained a place of its own in the mental health field, the animosity with its early rival subsided. Nowadays, most family therapists agree that it is equally important to understand the forces that are behind the relationship among the family members as to understand those that are inside the individuals. In other words, to comprehend human nature, one must focus on and understand both the individual and the system he or she inhabits. A relevant caveat is the need to distinguish whether the understanding of the individual's "inner forces" assists or misleads in bringing about necessary change (Herscovici, 1999).

The family system is viewed as a network of interpersonal relationships. Haley (1987) said that to look at symptoms in individual terms is similar to imagining a stick with only one end. What we formerly thought of as emerging from an individual, in this theory is considered a response to something that is somewhere in the system. A relational perspective (Kaslow, 1996) inevitably leads to changing the focus from content to process. In other words, instead of searching for the historical explanation of the current problems, one looks for the maintaining factors that operate on the current interactions. Instead of thinking in terms of who started what, family therapy deals with human problems as a series of movements that evolve in repetitive cycles. The underlying premise is that insight per se does not bring about change. Therefore, the focus of change is on behavior rather than cognitions or emotions. One great advantage of this perspective is that in lieu of inferring underlying causes that one cannot observe and that often are not amenable to change, it focuses on observable, current interactions that perpetuate the problems. Because these can be accessed, change can take place.

Family structure includes dyads, triangles, subsystems, and boundaries. To think in *dyadic* terms implies that both members of the relationship are mutually defined. Consider, for example, a case in which the social phobia of the anorexic was related to her mother's depression. If the young girl avoids going out, she can keep the mother company and thus mitigate her depression. That the mother and daughter remain overinvolved, with blurred *boundaries*, is maintained at the expense of distance with the angry father and husband, who is kept peripheral; this reinforces the symptomatic structure. *Triangulation* is the process by which a conflicted dyad pulls in a third person to regain its balance. In the above case, the marital dyad had been through significant conflict due to an infidelity of the wife. This led to violence and threats of divorce. At that point in time, their daughter started her weight-loss program, which turned into a severe case of Anorexia Nervosa. The parents rushed to rescue their daughter, and resolution of their conflict was postponed. The subsequent social phobia kept her at home at a stage when she felt her mother needed her.

Boundaries are a crucial concept in this theory. They refer to a way of describing the distance kept among members of the system (Minuchin, 1974). In the case just described, the boundary between mother and daughter was blurred due to their enmeshment. As a result, there was an excessive closeness and a permanent intrusion into the other person's feelings and thoughts. The mother would proudly state that words were unnecessary between them, that by simply looking at her face, she would know exactly what was going on inside her daughter. Contrarily, the impermeable boundary that separated the mother from her husband kept them alienated. Consequently, the daughter became triangulated; one way of avoiding taking sides was to remain involved in her obsessive preoccupation with food and calorie counting.

Boundaries can protect the individual from outside intrusion so that autonomy can be negotiated. In families with a chronic anorexic member, it is frequent to see blurred boundaries among the members that result in overprotection and enmeshment. The family members feel very close and often create a rigid boundary separating them from the outside world. This is expressed in the suspicion and fear that permeate interactions with individuals who do not belong to the family system. One father said, "We are like a hand with five fingers; they may move separately, but they all belong to one hand."

In another case, a female patient who suffered from Binge Eating Disorder and had a long history of eating disorders was part of a Jewish Orthodox family. The family motto was that to be safe, you had to remain within the religious community. The mother was a phobic and a hypochondriac who always feared impending catastrophe. The parents' main concern was that their daughters seemed to have no interest in marriage. In fact, none of the three young women had ever become emotionally involved in a heterosexual relationship. They all studied and worked well but kept a guarded distance from the outside world. When the family overinvolvement was pointed out, the girl realized that she automatically called her home every couple of hours, "just checking to make sure everyone was all right." Leaving home seemed like an overwhelming task. Instead, she resorted to daydreaming about unavailable candidates who would live with her in the family home. Her binge eating and consequent overweight reinforced her staying at home, where she fought and cried but felt safer than "being outside in the cold."

This is a case of what Magnavita (2000) calls "the developmentally arrested dysfunctional personologic system," which thwarts individuation and maturation of its members (p. 64). These families have difficulty tolerating differences and movements toward autonomy. Not surprisingly, the entry into the adolescent peer world with the accompanying sexual awakening and decrease in family control is a challenge for these families and their members. Additionally, if the youngster is triangulated in the marital conflict and is needed to stabilize the system, the eating disorder serves to reinforce her permanence in that position. Rigid interactions commonly are seen in disturbed families. They may have been functional at an earlier stage in the family's development but have become outdated. These families often lack the flexibility to adjust to normal life crises and thus become more dysfunctional at the transition points of developmental stages. They fail to reorganize to respond to the new demands of the context (Minuchin, 1974).

In the past decade, the focus of family therapy has expanded to include the way families are affected by gender roles, race, social class, and sexual orientation. The feminist perspective (Baker Miller, 1976; Brumberg, 1988; Walker, 1996) challenges the malevolent influence of certain values and cultural practices, such as gender stereotypes and inequalities. There is tremendous social pressure for women to be concerned with social judgments about their appearance. Girls are often brought up to put the needs of the other before their own. These patriarchal structures shape gender differences, and the disproportionate gender representation of eating disorders are a dramatic expression of this bias. Nevertheless, one should be cautious not to overextend this line of thought. Pointing out oppressive cultural attitudes should not overshadow the role played by the patient and her family in the development and maintenance of problems. In essence, the therapist should strive for an inclusive both/and stance.

The goal of structural family therapy (Minuchin & Fishman, 1981) is to tackle the symptom and to attain change in the family structure. Narrative therapists (White, 1991) assist clients to emerge from therapy with a sense of empowerment that enables them to take a proactive role as an agent of change in their community context. One therapeutic formulation of this is by the Anti-Anorexia League. The purpose of this virtual organization is to educate individuals about Anorexia Nervosa by identifying and circulating among the patients knowledge and practices that counteract the culture-bound practices that contribute to fuel the spread of the disorder (White 1991, p. 39). Bowen (1978) referred to the family as a combination of emotional and relationship systems. The systemic approach involves understanding of an individual within the context of interactions and relationships. This view seems to lead to a logical link with a developmental perspective.

THE PSYCHODYNAMIC FRAME

The psychodynamic model may be oriented toward traditionally analytic, interpersonal, object-relations, or self psychology. The core of psychodynamic thinking is the *meaning* of the symptomatic behavior. It emphasizes the place of infancy and early childhood experiences in shaping the person so that when the social, familial, cultural, biological, and cognitive processes converge to render individuals vulnerable to an eating disorder, the syndrome choice and the tenacity with which they cling to it may be understood in terms of certain developmental characteristics.

In contemporary psychoanalytic thinking, eating disorders are understood in terms of disorders of personal relationships and the organization of the self. Each theoretical model has its own language and emphasizes a specific developmental phase when attempting to explain the developmental failure associated with an eating disorder. Most authors agree that there seems to be a maturational crisis inherent in eating disorders (Crisp, 1980), and the symptomatic arrangement serves the ultimate purpose of avoiding maturational fears and freezing conflicts. Nevertheless, there is no evidence of any such consistent association implicated in the etiology of eating disorders. Therefore, the main value of the psychodynamic constructs is in giving therapist and patient a common ground for a psychological rationale for the disorder, expressed in therapeutically workable concepts. Patients differ greatly at presentation in terms of personality, level of motivation for change, resources, conflict-free areas, family context, and so on. They also vary along the stages of treatment. Accordingly, our lenses for understanding and intervening should be flexible and coherent.

Attachment Theory
Bowlby's (1969) attachment theory posits that close, positive attachments are a core human necessity. The quality of the early attachment with the primary caretaker plays a leading role in determining the quality of future relationships. It is held that deprivation of early bonds with or threatened loss of an adequate attachment to the primary caretaker will render the child vulnerable to and subsequently result in adverse psychological reactions. If the innate attachment need is satisfied via positive interpersonal relationships, normal development takes place. Contrarily, if this need is frustrated due to disturbed interpersonal relationships, the individual feels unworthy of love and low self-esteem ensues. Disturbed interpersonal relationships include fear of abandonment or rejection as well as loss of approval or acceptance of affect and attachment.

Object-Relations Theory
This model, stemming from the British school of theorists such as Mahler (1968), Klein (1957), Spitz (1965), and Fairbairn (1952), has focused on showing how past childhood experience is reflected in *object relations.* This developmental theory points out that we develop our patterns of relating following those of our early relationships, particularly with the parents who are internalized as *objects.* Core issues in psychic development are the deficiencies or distortions in the development of object relationships. The human drives naturally seek connections, they are oriented toward establishing relationships, and tension results in the context of frustrated relationships. In fact, the term *object* is a misnomer that refers to the *person* toward whom the

drives are directed. Interpersonal contact is internalized as a representation of that relationship (*introject*). Understanding of the individual and his or her motivations is derived from comprehending how the relationships were internalized by that individual and transformed into a notion of *self* or *self-image.*

In this theory, the most important relationship is with the early caretaker, usually the mother or the primary parent surrogate, as a pattern for subsequent relationships in life. If the interactions of the infant with the caretaker are positive, the emotional experience will be one of satisfaction and the self will be experienced as loved and cared for. If the interactions are negative, the infant will experience the caretaker as hostile and abandoning, will feel persistent emotional hunger, and experience the self as frustrated and angry.

For a child to tolerate separateness from the caregiver who provides support, nurturance, and comfort, the provider must be perceived as reliable. In normal development, ambivalence is tolerated. Deficient early attachments will negatively influence relating style in later stages of life, not only in how but also regarding to whom one relates. The goal of object-relations therapy is to understand how these childhood patterns are repeated in adult life.

Patients with eating disorders tend to have a deficient sense of being in control of their lives and well-being, which feeds into their fear of novelty and striving for order and restraint. They feel that others have an overwhelming power over them and that they must strive to be perfect; otherwise, they are totally bad and therefore hated and abandoned. These are some of the potent forces that shape the personality problems of many eating disordered patients. According to this theory, the anorexic's attempt at separation and individuation is met with a hostile, rejecting, withdrawing maternal introject. Conversely, her clinging, regressive behavior is met with support and reward (Masterson, 1978). More recently, Masterson (1995) described the mechanism by which these patients defensively focus on others instead of themselves, thereby contributing to their impaired sense of self-worth. Sugarman and Kurash (1982), who focus on bulimic patients, state that these patients lack the ego function of object constancy. Therefore, when separated from their symbiotic mother, they are unable to soothe themselves by automatically evoking a mental representation of the mother. Bingeing becomes a means of evoking the mother or primary caretaker and thus being soothed.

For Kernberg (1994), eating disorders are a "relentless sadistic attack on the patient's body" that alternately represents conflicting pleasure, femininity, and heterosexuality. This construct is easily applicable to those patients who so often restrain from eating as a way of self-punishment and depriving themselves of the pleasure derived from their favorite foods. The symbolic component in the anorexic's attitude to food is intensified by restrictive behavior and food preoccupation. The capacity to resist eating can be felt as a victory against an intrusive desire. Food and sexuality seem to be closely intertwined in these patients' inner world. The emaciation usually also serves the purpose of blurring the adolescent body and thus postponing the desired and feared sexualization of relationships. The possibility of another person exerting sexual attraction renders the subject vulnerable to the desirable but dangerous loss of control and feared submission to the other.

Self Psychology Theory
The main author of this model is Kohut (1971, 1977), who developed self psychology based on the construct of the self. He defines the self as an organization of experience characterized by cohesiveness, vitality, and a sense of continuity in time and space. Starting in infancy, the self integrates and develops to produce either health or pathology. If caregiving is adequately responsive to the infant's needs and if early

relationships are healthy and nurturing, the result will be a healthy and mature organization of the self, capable of healthy relationships. According to this theory, what drives us is the search for those relational experiences that are required to sustain a cohesive sense of self. A stable, healthy, or true self will result in the ability to provide one's own regulation of tension, self-esteem, and self-cohesion. Conversely, if the early environment is one of emotional deprivation, these functions will be impaired and development will become derailed. The result will be structural deficits and pathological defenses that result in a vulnerability to a personality impairment, such as seen in those eating disorders associated with personality disorders. Often, this takes the shape of a painful experiential state of emptiness and numbness, a sense of being an automaton, not really living. Symptoms then represent attempts to restore cohesion or a sense of being alive.

Nevertheless, it is not only the early years that exert such a fundamental influence on development. In the childhood years, if parents are self-absorbed, overwhelmed, or depressed, they often are unavailable to supply selfobject needs. The future anorexic tends to respond to this with a facade of pseudo-self-sufficiency and believing she is the cause of burden; she may embark on a rescue mission of maintaining the well-being or narcissistic balance of those close to her. Deprived from the satisfaction of her selfobject needs, she devotes herself to the care, feeding, and narcissistic support of others, thus embodying the compliant model child so often described in families of anorexic patients.

THEORETICAL CONSTRUCTS

As we progress in the research and practice of psychotherapy, we become ever more aware of the complexity and multidetermination of all human phenomena. Patients and their contexts are unique, and therapists are constantly faced with the challenge of selecting which treatment plan is best for each stage of the therapeutic process (Beutler & Clarkin, 1990). Eating disorders, specifically Anorexia Nervosa and Bulimia Nervosa, have been studied intensely over the past three decades. As a result, we have gained in our understanding of the disorders and the accompanying treatment issues. With Anorexia Nervosa, crude mortality rates increase with longer follow-up periods, ranging from 5 to 20% over a 20-year period (Ratnasuriya, Eisler, Szmukler, & Russell, 1991). On the average, more than 40% of anorexics recover, 33% improve, and 20% have a chronic course (Gowers, Norton, Halek, & Crisp, 1994). A short interval between onset of symptoms and beginning of treatment is a favorable prognostic factor (Steinhausen, 1995). These facts underscore the importance of early intervention. In the case of Bulimia Nervosa, only 50% of patients have a favorable outcome and the associated mortality rate is uncertain but may be higher than expected when compared to the general population (Hsu, 1995).

Eating disorders remain serious and potentially lethal illnesses. Pinsof, Wynn, and Hambright (1996) have shown that a multimodal approach is required for the treatment of serious disorders such as these. When focusing on eating disorders, many therapists are led toward a systems approach while considering the convergence of biological, individual, familial, social, and cultural dimensions in the form of predisposing, precipitating, and maintenance factors (Garfinkel & Garner, 1982).

The Biopsychosocial Paradigm

Eating disorders are biopsychosocial in nature (Engle, 1980). Etiologic components include biogenetic and sociocultural factors, individual personality traits, body dissatisfaction, and dieting history as well as life stressors. The family of origin system often plays a leading role both in the development of the eating disorder and as a health resource in treatment of child and adolescent patients. Clearly, dieting and pursuit of thinness are rampant in Western society, and yet only a small proportion of those who are terrified at facing the onset of adolescence develop Anorexia Nervosa. As Strober (1997) elegantly points out and consistent with the aforementioned frame of reference, this disease is perceived as originating in inherited extremes of personality traits that severely restrict a young woman's ability to cope with the challenges of pubertal growth. Taking into account the importance of early failures in parenting and trauma or other hazards to the development of the self, this author places special emphasis on three main avenues of influence for the development of Anorexia Nervosa: personality traits, the challenges of puberty, and the family context.

Personality Traits
There is evidence that major structures of our personality are partly inherited, and these interact with experience in shaping both normal development and psychological illness (Cloninger, 1986). The notion that certain qualities of personality make a person vulnerable to Anorexia Nervosa is consistent with the recurrence of such traits in these patients. Sometimes, they are accounted for prior to the onset of the disease but are often accentuated by the weight loss and persist beyond weight recovery. The personality traits that Strober (1997, p. 233) describes for Anorexia Nervosa patients are:

- High emotional reserve and cognitive inhibition, with subsequent emotional withdrawal.
- Preference for routine, orderly, and predictable environments, with poor adaptability to change. Avoidance of novelty and need to retain control of their surroundings.
- Heightened compliance and perfectionism, with a tendency to persevere even in the absence of ostensible reward.
- Risk avoidance, including of intimacy, especially with those outside the immediate family.
- Dysphoric reactivity to stressful events with low tolerance to emotionally charged experiences.
- Excessive rumination, frequently in the form of nagging self-doubt.

These personal dispositions undoubtedly play an active role in shaping the way a youngster responds to the demands of the developmental stage he or she is facing.

Challenges of Puberty
This is a stage in which, typically, the youngster begins to withdraw from the family, feeling a pull in a different direction of belonging. The peer group is assigned greater relevance in terms of determining what is appropriate; more intimate and sexualized relationships are established; family loyalties are under scrutiny and differentiation ensues. The families of these patients often secretly share the anorexic's fear of adolescent growth. In dysfunctional family systems, with intergenerational coalitions, it is frequent to find that the patient is convinced that her physical and emotional proximity is indispensable to the allied parent's safety and well-being. The new distance introduced by adolescent peer relationships is avoided. In those families in which patients have experienced abuse, neglect, or hostile criticism, the youngster feels threatened by emotional relationships, which they are certain will be intrusive and disappointing. Additionally, there are changes in body appearance, and sexual characteristics emerge.

All of these challenge the rigidity of those girls who approach this stage with the belief that safety and esteem are tied to compliance and the ability to keep the new and threatening life changes at bay. The body, a symbol of maturity, sexuality, and pleasure, becomes a source of unrest, and its growth must be arrested at all costs. Her natural inclination to rigid discipline turns dieting into a way to gain an increasing sense of control. As the weight loss progresses, the feared emotions and needs are silenced. The biological and psychological regression that follows the increasing weight loss allows her to move from impending fear to psychological safety. Anorexia Nervosa becomes the armor that shields her from being noticed and discovered in her weaknesses and sense of inefficacy. It allows for a display of discipline and self-control. A tight grasp is kept on the disease that becomes her raison d'être.

The Family Context

An eating disorder develops in the context of a particular relationship, which is quite different from saying it is caused by it. Even though it is obvious that patients vary and so do their families, most of the characteristics that Minuchin (Minuchin, Rosman, & Baker, 1987) postulated decades ago as descriptive of psychosomatic families continue to apply, at least for many of the severe, chronic Anorexia Nervosa cases. Rather than preceding the illness, these characteristics may be a way of adapting to the grueling intricacies of the disorder.

Any attempt to distinguish the current family organization from the one clients had prior to the onset of the illness will probably be approximate and certainly hypothetical. Recent literature has cautioned against confusing observations of current family functioning with the idea of a familial etiology of the disorder. As Eisler (1995) warned, clinical observation is likely to be idiosyncratic and will probably highlight a striking aspect of family functioning that may be applicable to only most severe cases. Yet, over time, those accounts become embedded in the "professional folklore" and are mistakenly considered facts that apply to the syndrome (p. 156). Current beliefs should be scrutinized carefully when one is reviewing the role of family factors in the etiology of eating disorders. Some facts that should be kept in mind include:

- The pattern of distribution of eating disorders according to social class may have changed in recent years, and the greater aggregation of Anorexia Nervosa in higher social classes may no longer reflect the current picture. No differences have been found for anorexics or bulimics regarding birth order, family composition, or family size (Eisler, p. 157).
- Parents of adolescents with minor neurotic signs are not more psychologically disturbed than the parents of those with Anorexia Nervosa.
- The level of closeness among family members is often lower than what the subject would ideally like. Communication in general and affective expression in particular are usually reported as restricted. Overall, the differences found between eating disorder families and controls, accounted for by questionnaires, may apply only to highly select clinical samples (p. 166).
- Levels of expressed emotion (EE) are generally low in families of anorexics. The number of critical comments is small and hostility is rare. This is consistent with clinical findings of these families as conflict-avoiding. There is moderate warmth and relatively few positive remarks are made (p. 167).
- Families of bulimics have a tendency to blame and belittle, with raised levels of hostility and criticism (p. 169).
- Studies show that emotional overinvolvement, defined by EE scales of parents showing exaggerated emotional behavior in response to the child's problems, or marked overprotective behavior, is consistently low in these families. Eisler (1995) suggests that this may be part of a broader trait of subdued affective expression (p. 167). It is also possible that this difference may relate to how this feature is defined in the scales.
- Family members of bulimic patients have a higher incidence of affective disorder and alcoholism. Additionally, there is a higher

incidence of obesity and eating disorders among the mothers of binge/purge-type Anorexia Nervosa and Bulimia Nervosa patients.
- In the families of binge/purge-type Anorexia Nervosa and Bulimia Nervosa, conflict is more overt and explicit. This is probably due to the nature of the symptoms and how family members react to their secrecy. They usually feel cheated, disappointed, and impotent to make things better. This often translates into anger. The patient, in turn, feels spied on, controlled, and frustrated in failing to control the bingeing.
- When comparing families of eating disordered patients with the general population, the families that differ less are those of restrictive-type Anorexia Nervosa patients. On the other hand, families of binge/purge-type Anorexia Nervosa and Bulimia Nervosa have more similarities among each other.
- Anorexic patients tend to perceive their mothers as more empathic and understanding of their feelings. Conversely, their fathers usually are less expressive of their emotions and their daughters experience them as more distant.
- Usually, bulimic patients are less pleased with their families and report more conflict and distress in family life. This may not reflect the parents' appreciation of family life. Notably, as the patient recovers from her eating disorder, she also improves her perception of her family.

In summary, many of the differences observed when comparing families of eating disorder patients and controls are found only in clinical samples. In community-based samples, the differences are smaller or even disappear. There do not appear to be common family factors that lead to the development of an eating disorder. Furthermore, in light of recent research, there does not appear to be a particular type of family functioning style that can be consistently linked with eating disorders. This argues against the disorder's originating in a specific type of experience in the family. The difference between the clinical and community samples suggests that much of what therapists identify in the families they treat are factors associated with a more entrenched course of the illness (Eisler, 1995).

THE BODY IN EATING DISORDERS

A path often leading to eating disorders is described by Sands (1989), who notes that developing girls are encouraged to show and thus obtain exhibitionist gratification mainly in the sphere of physical appearance. In later life, the body becomes the privileged arena to reveal psychopathology.

Developmentally, the self starts out being the site of bodily sensations. When the cohesion or integrity of the self is threatened, it is experienced by these patients as a loss of control of the body. One attempt at restoring control is to focus on the shape of one's body or the amount of calories ingested. The ideas that accompany the relation between eating behavior and the body are often delusional. One patient remained awake all night because she was certain that the calories consumed at dinner would be greater if she fell asleep immediately. Another girl was so worried about her weight that she developed a stiff neck when she stepped off the weighing scale after she had taken the commitment of not looking at the scale numbers. A young boy pleaded not to be made to cry any longer, because his swollen eyes made him look fat. Yet another patient would vigorously massage her toothpick arms with reduction gel after each meal, to make sure the food wouldn't settle there. All have in common the concept of their body as a dangerous field where mysterious forces operate and they must exert a frantic attempt at control to keep these forces in check.

Other patients experience their bodies as a battlefield where the separation and individuation process is fought. Who decides what one needs to eat and how much one needs to weigh become the controversial issues. Such is the case of a young boy who had a grandiose and omnipotent self that colored his stance in the world. His e-mail address started with "superbobby@," and he demanded to be at the core of any family decisions regarding mealtimes, outings, and so on. The mealtime agreed on was never acceptable to him, and he threatened to not eat unless they yielded to serve his dinner at 11 P.M. He was a smart and sweet child, unless he wasn't getting his way; then, he would break out in a tantrum. When physical activity was restricted to save the little energy he ingested, Bobby resorted to doing push-ups vigorously to get his way.

There has been considerable attention lately on the issue of child sexual abuse and its possible impact on the individuals who develop eating disorders. Needless to say, depending on the personal vulnerabilities, the relationship to the perpetrator, and the developmental timing, sexual abuse can have a devastating impact, affecting the attitude not only toward one's body but also toward a sense of self-worth. For the anorexic, ridding herself from her female body through starvation may be seen as a way of protecting herself from further assaults. Binge eating and purging can become ways of managing intolerable levels of tension. Waller (1992) has shown that those bulimic patients who have a history of sexual abuse are more likely to engage in the most violent purging. The reported figures range from approximately 10 to 60%, depending on how stringent the definition of sexual abuse, with the highest prevalence for the operational definition of "any unwanted, unpleasant or coercive sexual event" (Palmer, Oppenheimer, Dignon, Chaloner, & Howells, 1990). Comparison of studies is difficult due to different methods and samples. Reviews indicate that, whereas most studies cluster around 30%, there is conflicting evidence as to whether bulimic patients are more likely to have experienced sexual abuse than restricting anorexics (Waller, 1992). Even though this rate is higher than in the general population, it is comparable to that found in other psychiatric disorders (Vanderlinden & Vandereycken, 1995).

Reports indicate that manifestations of physical violence are more prevalent in bulimic subjects (30%), who experience violence against themselves and/or directed at another family member, compared to 7% of anorexics, who experience violence against themselves. A thorough study comparing eating disordered patients in terms of abusive experiences (Schmidt, Tiller, Blanchard, Andrews, & Treasure, 1997) suggests that bulimics are more likely than anorexics to experience a variety of childhood adverse circumstances, including indifference, abuse, inconsistency in care arrangements, and discord. What remains unclear is to what extent these occur in their lives more frequently than in the general population.

HOSTILITY IN EATING DISORDERS

In Bulimia Nervosa cases, the impulsivity that accompanies the syndrome facilitates the expression of anger. Patients and their families tend to have a much more open expression of conflict in their interaction. In contrast, anorexic patients usually appear to be compliant and find it hard to express anger; their families are frequently conflict-avoidant. Most anorexics usually are covered with layers of clothing that not only keep them warm but also hide the body they feel embarrassed about. Sometimes, they take pleasure in exhibiting their emaciated body, as though taking pride in exposing their disorder, a way of saying "Look at how miserable I am. Look at how I suffer." Needless to say, this may be a nonverbal way of accusing significant others of causing their plight.

In one case, Lucia, a restrictive anorexic, would wake up exactly one hour and a half after falling asleep to peel and slice the fruit she was about to eat. The fruit was then laid out in strict order, matching colors, sizes, and flavors organized by gradual increases in intensity. This young woman refused to eat in the presence of any family member. Her parents begged for compliance. Lucia inwardly felt that her refusal was a way of punishing them for having made her break up a relationship with a man they disapproved of. Her Anorexia Nervosa had been active for the prior 10 years, ever since this separation had occurred. Even though other therapists had pointed out this connection, she had been unable to transcend the symbiosis with her parents. She continued to use her body and her life as a means to relate to them with all the ambivalence this entailed. She felt very guilty for being ill and causing her parents so much worry and pain and feared being the reason of their feared premature death. They, in turn, felt guilty because they had been told so often in previous treatment settings that they had caused their daughter's condition and so continued to spend a fortune on her treatments without realizing that they had inadvertently given up their own lives. The only thing that mattered to these parents during all those years was whether their daughter had gained a gram. Thus, the anorexia kept parents and daughter together in this crazy, miserable fashion.

METHODS OF ASSESSMENT AND INTERVENTION

Assessment

Usually completed in two weeks, assessment has three main goals: initial assessment, psychoeducation, and the establishment of a treatment alliance. There are a number of refined instruments (self-report and interview-based) currently in use that enable one to diagnose, score, and compare subjects and evaluate outcome (Christie, Watkins, & Lask, 2000). One recent valuable addition is the Structured Inventory on Anorexic and Bulimic Disorders, with special instructions for evaluating adolescents (Fichter & Quadflieg, 2001).

Initial evaluation is done at the individual and familial levels. The individual patient is evaluated regarding the severity of symptoms and time of onset as well as psychosocial performance and psychopathology. Once diagnosis of the eating disorder is ascertained, family and patient are instructed regarding the eating disorder, the self-perpetuating nature of food restriction and purging habits, and the probable treatment pitfalls in future stages. This psychoeducation portion of treatment is extremely relevant in helping families consolidate a rationale that supports the treatment.

From the individual stance, attention is paid to the meaning of the eating disorder at the behavioral, relational, and cognitive levels. The family system is assessed regarding its current life cycle stage and the developmental struggles the family members are dealing with or avoiding. Knowledge of the family structure in terms of boundaries, intergenerational coalitions, and alliances as well as the family's resources will guide the treatment plan.

Assessment of the family system involves the elaboration of a functional hypothesis of the eating disorder in the context of the family system. This implies exploring the role the eating disorder plays in stabilizing the family system (e.g., Does it serve the purpose of keeping family members overinvolved? Is it related to difficulty dealing with a developmental crisis regarding career choice and leaving home?) and, conversely, the ways the family contributes to stabilizing the symptom (e.g., when the girl gains weight, the father expresses his fears of her becoming chubby, as in the past). It is important to establish what the central theme is in this family that is organized by the eating disorder and its consequences. Is it an issue of power, of control? Is it an issue of separation and individuation? Is it a matter of who is to blame for bringing this about (the father's decision to divorce; the mother's new plastic surgery). Additionally, because patients usually present a therapeutic dilemma in terms of their desire to change the existing problem without having to change themselves, it is critical to explore the feared consequences of change (Papp, 1983; Vanderlinden & Vandereycken, 1989).

An important goal is the establishment of a therapeutic alliance. Of the nonspecific therapeutic factors associated with good outcome, it appears that instilling hope, defining the problem as solvable, and setting up a therapeutic alliance are the most important. Anorexia Nervosa is commonly ego-syntonic; paradoxically, patients cling to their potentially lethal symptoms as though they were lifesaving. Not surprisingly, patients seldom seek treatment but are usually referred for therapy and approach it with hesitation and suspicion. Conversely, Bulimia Nervosa is a very distressful and shame-producing disorder. Patients with both disorders share a morbid fear of fatness. The former group is totally opposed to weight restoration as a crucial goal of treatment and therefore, more often than not, come to therapy because they are brought, not because it is their choice. Therefore, the establishment of a therapeutic alliance is the critical issue at commencement of treatment and should be carefully monitored throughout. The challenge to the therapist is to assure the patient that the rewards of change will be more beneficial to her well-being than holding onto her eating disorder as an armor that protects her from the turbulence of developmental struggles.

Treatment for Anorexia Nervosa

Ideally, treatment should be tailored to the requirements of each case, with a progression from least intrusive to most intensive interventions. Inpatient care is a valid option when there is lack of positive response to or availability of outpatient care, significant weight loss, and/or medical complications and a suicide risk. So far, the best therapeutic results for treatment of Anorexia Nervosa are linked to nutritional rehabilitation accompanied by family and individual therapy.

Minuchin's (Minuchin, Rosman, & Baker, 1978) seminal insight regarding the wisdom of treating adolescent anorexics with family therapy has been further demonstrated in later research. Of the few randomized controlled studies for Anorexia Nervosa that have been carried out so far, Russell, Szmukler, Dare, and Eisler (1987) found that family therapy was superior to supportive individual therapy for those patients whose onset of illness occurred at 18 years of age or younger. At a five-year follow-up, family therapy proved to have a radically superior effect both for recovery and for abbreviating the course of the disorder (Russell, Dare, Eisler, & Le Grange, 1992). Family counseling, where parents were given advice in managing their sick child, has shown a similar effect. This option is recommended when parents have a hypercritical attitude toward the patient because evidence shows that this attitude further undermines the patient's self-esteem. Once the parents are more at ease and less angry, conjoint sessions can be resumed. The possible common positive elements for change in these approaches deserve to be looked at.

Undoubtedly, weight restoration should be the first goal of treatment for the seriously malnourished patient, not only because it is lifesaving, but because it improves personality functioning and mood and reduces obsessional thinking and body image distortion. Weight restoration is generally effective in about 85% of cases (Hsu, 1990, p. 136) if it is carried out in conjunction with family and individual therapy, when the latter is necessary. A major consideration is the patient's trust that the caring team will prevent her from becoming fat. In this sense, the creation of a safety net that protects the patient from her fear of loss of control (e.g., meal plan) has proven useful. At the beginning, therapy deals with the patient and her family regarding the conflictive aspects related to eating. Additionally, the presence of psychiatric comorbidity ought to be identified and dealt with.

Psychosocial interventions preferably should include a shared understanding of the psychodynamic conflicts underlying the disorder as much as the complexity of family relationships and developmental issues. The former are often useful constructs that contribute to enhancing the therapeutic alliance by giving meaning to the patient's plight. In this newly formulated, workable reality, alternatives become apparent and change can take place.

Family and couples therapy are useful not only for symptom alleviation, but also for dealing with problems in the family system that may be contributing to the maintenance of the disorder. Furthermore, these therapies have been found to be a cost-effective way of tapping into the therapeutic resources of the family. There has been little study of the optimal role of either individual or group psychotherapy for Anorexia Nervosa. Nevertheless, because of the enduring nature of many of the features that accompany this disorder in the most entrenched cases, it is advisable to follow these patients with some form of individual therapy for at least a year. If group therapy is an available option, it should be considered only as an adjunct, and caution should be taken regarding a careful selection and monitoring of patients to ensure that they do not get caught in competitive loops regarding who is the thinnest or sickest patient.

When the anorexia becomes a chronic condition, it tends to provide the person with a compensatory identity that allows for some significant presence in the world. That is why the initial stages of weight restoration often are sailed through rather quickly; it is when the patient approaches her target weight and envisions the crossroads of normality that she becomes terrified of what lies ahead. The sick identity has enabled her to access a seemingly safe place in the world (Herscovici, 1996). These cases benefit most from ongoing individual therapy that fosters a more realistic body image, self-assertion, self-esteem, and empowerment.

Treatment of Bulimia Nervosa

The patient with bulimia is usually in her late adolescence or early adulthood. Contrary to the patient with Anorexia Nervosa, who is brought to therapy, the person with Bulimia Nervosa is in desperate need of help to alleviate the distress of the symptoms she wants to get rid of. The weight of these patients is usually in the normal range. Nevertheless, because these patients suffer from a morbid fear of fatness, when they realize that the goal of treatment is not weight loss and they fear normal eating habits will undermine their cherished desire, they tend to have difficulty managing the anxiety derived from this. It is important to ascertain motivation status before treatment is undertaken, because dropout is frequent when this variable is not carefully considered.

Of the psychotherapeutic control studies for Bulimia Nervosa, cognitive-behavioral therapy (CBT) has been found to be the treatment of choice. Results show a significant reduction in binge eating and purging, attitudes toward body shape, and general psychological functioning. Recent studies show that early progress in therapy is the best predictor of outcome (Agras et al., 2000). This marker (70% decrease in purging by the sixth treatment session) enables clinicians to try other therapies for patients who do not respond to CBT in the first weeks of treatment. Interpersonal therapy has shown to be a good alternative (Agras, Walsh, Wilson, & Fairburn, 1999). Antidepressant medication, when combined with psychotherapy, has been shown to be effective in dealing with bulimic and depressive symptoms. Group therapy and self-help groups also have shown positive treatment effects.

The American Psychiatric Association treatment guidelines (2000) recommend "family therapy whenever possible, especially for adolescents still living with parents or older patients with ongoing conflicted interactions with parents." Additionally, they caution that "the nature and intensity of treatment depends on the symptom profile and severity of impairment, not the *DSM-IV* diagnosis" (p. 25).

THE PSYCHOTHERAPEUTIC PROCESS

The therapeutic process follows certain general stages. It must be kept in mind that patients vary, and so does the amount of time and specific interventions devoted to each stage. Research has shown that when treating youngsters with eating disorders, it is better to focus on the family context and empower the parents rather than look at the intrapsychic level alone (Russell, 1994; Russell et al., 1987). In the treatment of children and adolescents with eating disorders, it is critical to help parents move beyond the sense of blame that seems inherent in most families. This translates into two major distinctions: (1) Separate blame from responsibility, the latter creating a sense of agency while the former usually sets off a defensive and blaming spiral that fosters a malignant context; (2) Differentiate those family factors that might have precipitated the onset of an eating disorder (excessive concern with body appearance, parental abuse or negligence, or overinvolvement that discourages autonomy) from current family patterns that might perpetuate the problem. The common denominator along the entire therapeutic process is for the clinician to help family members view themselves not as guilty but as an irreplaceable resource for recovery.

THE TREATMENT FRAME

Due to the complex nature and outcome of eating disorders, it is advisable for the therapist to be specially trained in their treatment. Relying on ongoing supervision, collaboration, or consultation is always preferable. The therapist should have a collaborative frame, with the ability to negotiate strategies and interventions within a multimodal team approach. Comorbid features as well as severity of clinical condition are relevant to deciding treatment frame. It is preferable to have specialized inpatient or day hospital care as a referral option if outpatient treatment is not safe enough. Nevertheless, because recent studies support that family-based outpatient care has proven to be a good treatment for Anorexia Nervosa patients living at home (Lock, Le Grange, Agras, & Dare, 2000), this cost-effective treatment option is always preferable for this group. The number of members of the treatment team should vary according to the requirements of the given case and special care should be taken to avoid collusions. It is not uncommon for the members of the treatment team to be inadvertently drawn into the patient system and take sides with the individuals. If this divisive strategy is not acknowledged and neutralized, often it has detrimental effects on the treatment.

The feminist model of family therapy focuses on how gender issues are perpetuated through the family life. This approach emphasizes cultural factors associated with eating disorders as well as issues of power, so pervasively influential in women's everyday lives (Walters, Carter, Papp & Silverstein, 1988). These principles involve accepting and celebrating gender-related differences and also emphasizing personal responsibility for health and well-being. Enhancing autonomy, self-worth, and standing up against a sense of weakness or ineffectiveness are central tenets in feminist ideology. These principles constitute a therapeutic attitude that should prevail regardless of the gender of the patient or therapist (Bryant-Waugh, 2000).

A pragmatic approach that takes into consideration the idiosyncrasies of the presenting problem and constantly monitors effectiveness is more advisable than a stringent model. Furthermore, we have evidence from research and our clinical work that involvement of parents in treatment is absolutely crucial. Regardless of the family intervention chosen (parental counseling or family therapy), the goal is to go beyond blaming and empower the parents to feel capable of helping their children overcome and transcend such a life-threatening way of expressing their often impaired sense of ability to deal with life challenges.

STAGES OF TREATMENT FOR EATING DISORDERS

Stage 1: Symptom Management
This phase is usually completed in two to four months. During this period, it is strongly advisable to focus attention on the family context rather than the intrapsychic level. As we stated earlier, in the treatment of young people with eating disorders, it is important to enlist the parents in the treatment system. For this partnership to be viable, it is essential to move beyond blame. Treatment seeks to enable the parents to assume temporary control over the patient's eating behavior until it is normalized. A technique that favors this is the behavioral paradigm, by which the youngster's access to a normal life is contingent on weight gain. In other words, a policy of bed rest and no privileges (social visits, physical activity, entertainment, etc.) is enforced until weight recovery and normal eating habits occur (Minuchin et al., 1978). It is important that the therapist keep a critical balance so that the patient doesn't perceive therapist and parents as ganging up against her, but rather that they are all united to battle the "intruding" eating disorder. The narrative approach, with its technique of "externalizing the problem," is especially useful in safeguarding the patient's dignity and self-respect (White & Epston, 1990). It allows for detaching the problem from the person and, subsequently, the problem's establishing an identity of its own. The joint exploration of the many ways in which the problem (eating disorder) inflicts pain and suffering allows for those affected by the problem to join in fighting it. This is a very practical way of moving beyond explanations that emphasize pathology and blame and progress toward positive change, enlisting the patient in this pursuit.

To override the youngster's strongly held views regarding eating behavior, the parents need to be knowledgeable about the required changes that will ensure long-term goals of well-being. This can be achieved through *parental counseling*. The goal is to create an environment in which parents are helped to find their own solutions, what works for them, keeping a balance between acknowledging the patient's experience and enforcing her safety and health. When there is current or premorbid family dysfunction, it is advisable to embark on *family therapy*. Nevertheless, during this stage, other family conflicts are deferred and focus is kept on enhancing motivation for change of eating behavior and weight restoration.

Stage 2: Normalizing the System and Conflict Resolution
This phase has a variable duration, usually around two to four months. Once the symptomatic behavior is in check, there is a gradual restoration to the patient of control over her eating habits. This allows for other family issues to be addressed. Additionally, siblings often endure suffering and postponement of attention to their needs due to the stress of living with an eating disordered member. It is useful to have family sessions that will allow for the exploration and planning of ways to minimize the impact of the illness on their everyday lives while routines haven't yet normalized.

Another reason for moving from parental counseling to family therapy is the evidence of ongoing marital conflict that involves the identified patient. This does not imply that family therapy should turn into marital therapy, with the children as onlookers; rather, this is an opportunity for marital conflict to be identified as a stress-producing problem that the parents need to work on and for which the patient should not feel responsible. Other indicators are when we observe difficulties with the separation-individuation process that hinder the youngster's voice from being expressed and heard in the family. Another possible focus of family therapy is the enhancement of a context that facilitates any disclosure of abuse. Because one cannot underestimate the importance of the identified patient openly communicating such issues during the family sessions, it is essential that the therapist monitor this process.

In working with separated and stepfamilies, one must have a clear image of the roles played by the different adults involved. Because these contexts strongly favor splitting and coalition forming, it is likely that the patient will exploit these to her disadvantage. A helpful intervention is to acknowledge these divisions and the history of disagreements between the parents while stressing the need for joint decision making (Honig, 2000). During this stage, the developmental issues are dealt with and particular focus is placed on age-appropriate autonomy and non-eating-disorder issues. Individual sessions with the patient are often in order, specially for older adolescents.

Stage 3: Termination
At this phase, which usually lasts no more than two sessions, the goal is to enhance family members' sense of empowerment, focusing on their strengths in overcoming the eating disorder and their capacity to grow from that experience. Autonomy of the subsystems is checked and future routes of development are anticipated. Additionally, special care is taken to highlight family members' weaknesses and developmental pitfalls that might precipitate a family crisis or a relapse of the eating disorder. During this process, therapists usually are rewarded when they ask the family what they think were turning points that enabled change in the therapeutic process as well as what they learned from the experience. Follow-up at scheduled intervals is a cost-efficient safety net for preventing relapse that cannot be overestimated.

In addition to the basic treatment frame described, multidimensional disorders sometimes require an array of ancillary interventions (physiotherapy, exercise, massage, group work, and/or assertiveness training). Of special note are techniques to improve body image distortion. These are currently carried out at an experimental level because we do not have controlled trials regarding their efficacy. Because this has been shown to be a feature predictive of outcome, we should follow this development with care.

TREATMENT OUTCOME

For all age groups, eating disorders represent an extreme of psychiatric morbidity and have an adverse impact on most areas of life. Evidence shows that eating disorders tend to become refractory and autonomous over time. Therefore, early, appropriate interventions may significantly affect recovery. There is agreement in the field that a four-year span from the onset of the disorder is the minimum time required to evaluate outcome. A short duration of illness correlates with a good outcome. Dropout and response to treatment in adolescent eating disorders have been associated with high scores of family EE (van Furth, 1991). Moreover, EE levels have been shown to decrease after successful family treatment (Le Grange, Eisler, Dare, & Hodes, 1992). Additionally, a dysfunctional family environment negatively affects prognosis for all eating disorders (Herzog, Keller,

Lavori, & Ott, 1988; Steinhausen, Rauss-Mason, & Seidel, 1991; van Engeland, van der Ham, van Furth, & van Strien, 1995). Thus, family therapy counseling is the treatment of choice whenever possible and attainment of family support for treatment is a critical goal. Authors are generally in agreement that the wisest approach to multidetermined disorders such as Anorexia Nervosa and Bulimia Nervosa is multidimensional and biopsychosocial in nature.

Most studies evaluating treatment efficacy contain poor descriptions of how therapy was conducted and are thus difficult to replicate. Additionally, the majority of patients are treated outside of research settings with a variety of therapeutic approaches that differ significantly from those utilized in research. Even though, more often than not, the therapeutic approach chosen is determined more by therapist's preference than by research findings, many patients seem to improve significantly. To this date, no specific treatment factors have been found to be consistently effective. Because the silver bullet is eluding us, it is important that we attend not only to the *hard* scientific data but also to nontherapeutic factors that have been studied more recently.

MAJOR SYNDROMES TREATED USING THIS APPROACH

The treatment outlined so far has been found to be useful for most cases of Anorexia Nervosa and Bulimia Nervosa (Herscovici & Bay, 1996). A difficulty associated with the treatment of eating disorders is the fact that they so often involve personality and trait disturbances. Available data show that adolescent sufferers present a range of comorbid psychopathology that is comparable in content to that of adults. These findings are striking when considering that latent disturbances often do not become apparent during adolescence. Those most commonly seen, even in recovered patients, include depression, Obsessive-Compulsive Disorder, and Anxiety Disorder (Neiderman, 2000, p. 87). A follow-up study of adolescent-onset Anorexia Nervosa showed that after six years of presentation, 30% qualified for Affective Disorder and 43% for Anxiety Disorder (Smith, Feldman, Nasserbakht, & Steiner, 1993). A 56% rate of comorbid Major Depression was reported in a sample of adolescent bulimics (Herzog, Keller, Lavori, & Bradburn, 1991). Often, Major Depression and Anxiety Disorder develop prior to the eating disorder.

Psychometric studies assessing personality factors report purging anorexics as more disturbed and emotionally labile, and more impulsive, oppositional, and antisocial (Leon, Lucas, Colligan, Ferlinande, & Kamp, 1985). In other words, restrictive and binge/purge patients vary along personality dimensions that involve control, and often disorders coincide with personality disturbances (Steiger & Stotland, 1995, p. 52).

Evidence suggests that the patients' premorbid traits are mostly timidity and perfectionism. Rastam (1992), when studying adolescent anorexics, estimated that 67% of them showed a personality disorder (PD) prior to onset of the eating disorder and 35% showed Obsessive-Compulsive Disorder. Others report that eating disorders are associated with stable underlying personality disturbances that exist independent of the eating disorder. In fact, obsessional traits in weight-restored anorexics are strikingly stable through the years, and adult bulimic samples suggest the existence of primary characteristics that become exaggerated during the active phase of the eating disorder (Strober, 1980; Windauer, Lennerts, Talbot, Touys, & Beaumont, 1993). Still, other studies show that weight restoration in teenage anorexics leads to a normalization of disturbed traits, indicating that an active eating disorder will either color characterological features or exacerbate latent personality problems (Leon et al., 1985; Strober, 1980).

Overall, estimates of PD in mixed anorexic and bulimic samples are high and concentrate in the 50% to 75% range (Steiger & Stotland, 1995, p. 53). Restrictive Anorexia Nervosa appears to show the most consistent pattern, aligned with the anxious-fearful (Cluster C) PD. For normal-weight bulimics, borderline and histrionic PD are the most frequent; yet, compulsive, avoidant, and dependent are also common personality disorders. Studies show that eating disordered patients have been found to have heavy loadings on risk avoidance, conformity, obsessiveness, self-criticism, and narcissistic need for approval (Steiger & Stotland, 1995, p. 54).

In terms of relational diagnoses, eating disorders occur in families showing variable forms of dysfunction. Additionally, studies point to the idea that severity of family dysfunction may be a better predictor of personality disturbance in the eating disordered sufferer than of eating disorder symptom severity (Head & Williamson, 1990). Although we need more clarity as to the possible influences of individual and family processes in the development of eating disorders, we have enough knowledge about maintenance factors to pursue meaningful treatment that will enable recovery.

CASE EXAMPLE

Susana, 18, was the only daughter of a very rational, articulate set of parents, both physicians who had three older sons, also physicians. She had always been a bright student, very compliant, and socially appreciated, mainly for her helping ways. She was apparently cheerful and full of life, a disciplined ballerina who didn't mind being chubby and seemed to please everyone around her. The family tradition was that at age 18 years, the youngsters would leave home and move 1,500 miles away to Buenos Aires to attend the university. The youngsters would live in the maternal grandmother's home during those years, under the supervision of the grandmother and two aunts, whom Susana was certain were virgins.

She had always been extremely close to her mother, who confided all of her troubles, including the father's infidelities, to her daughter. Susana was brought up in an adult atmosphere and always had wise comments regarding any issue. The girl seemed to be extremely independent, traveling often as an unaccompanied minor. She led a family-centered life with cordial but few peer relationships. During the weekend, the men in the family would go to their summer home, but she would rather stay with her mother, reading at home. She had always known she was going to be a lawyer and was looking forward to moving to Buenos Aires.

The girl started her weight loss at age 16, following a mastectomy performed on her mother after she was diagnosed with cancer. The mother was cured but refused to have plastic surgery to repair the aesthetic damage. Soon, these concerns were replaced by the terror that inundated the mother when she realized that her daughter was anorexic. The father was in stark denial; in his eyes, his daughter was too smart and happy to embark on such a self-destructive enterprise. They engaged in a long-distance treatment, traveling to Buenos Aires monthly. During that time, the mother took full charge of supervising the daughter's food intake. Susana regained weight, although along with that, she became obsessively preoccupied with her body image and calorie consumption in a way that was not evident when she had been underweight.

The psychotherapeutic functional hypothesis put to the family was that Susana, due to leave home two years later, had panicked over separating from her family. The Anorexia Nervosa stunted not only the girl's bodily transformation and subsequent sexual challenges, but also her leaving home process. This fear, which may have been triggered by the danger of losing her mother due to her recent cancer, was in fact imbedded in the family structure. Mother and daughter were inseparable. Additionally, her overinvolvement with this warm and generous family left her experientially and emotionally unprepared to leave home. The family denied all this. They believed that the daughter's intelligence and the mother's tenacity at controlling her food intake would suffice to overpower the Anorexia Nervosa. What more proof than the fact that she was slowly and steadily gaining weight?

As the year ended, Susana was about to finish high school and move out of her parents' home. The day the girl reached her target weight, she broke down and embarked on a relentless pursuit of thinness, which now openly alienated her from the world. She became tyrannical and fought her mother to tears for every pea on her plate. She quickly became emaciated and was about to be hospitalized. At that point, the realization that she was in danger unleashed intense hypochondriac anxieties and served the purpose of allowing her to eat and regain weight, not because she desired food but simply to avoid death. With her nutritional rehabilitation completed, the family brought her to Buenos Aires to start her university studies and embark on a formal therapeutic endeavor. The parents went back to their home town and Susana remained with the grandmother and virgin aunts.

Susana became totally out of control. She would have panic attacks when going to the university. She felt terrified of failing at school and could not tolerate the anxiety provoked by just the thought of taking exams. Her childlike grandiosity suffered a great disappointment when she dropped out of school, unable to cope with the possibility of not being able to achieve at her A-plus level, as in the past. She was convinced that she was a total failure and would never amount to anything. Susana perceived her idealized mother as someone who had been able to overcome adversity and strive for excellence, regardless of the circumstances.

She began dating a boy her age; this was her first brush with heterosexual love. She became very excited with this novelty and feared her parents' disapproval. Her guardians became outraged that she should want to date in this condition; they thought she wasn't emotionally stable enough to handle such a volatile situation. The mother became frightened and utilized the medication for her panic attacks as an excuse to demand that Susana not be given permission to go out. This formerly most serene and predictable mother suddenly became increasingly frantic, interrogating Susana over the phone as though her daughter were a delinquent. The girl became more disorganized each day. When medication was increased, she calmed down and started to restrict her food intake, this time with a clear desire to die. Susana felt lifeless, not entitled to have a life of her own, naughty and guilty for not agreeing with her mother, who responded to her separation intent with a hostile and rejecting stance. If this was her maternal introject, it certainly became reinforced by her mother's real attitude.

The crisis that unfolded surpassed the imaginable for this rational and most proper family. The girl would make plans to go to the country for a weekend with her married brother and family, and the mother would call in a rage, demanding that the trip be canceled immediately, threatening to have the police intervene to stop her daughter from going to a carnival parade where "nude bodies were being exhibited." When this sort of conflict ensued, the girl would bang her head against the wall and crawl into a corner and refuse to eat. The parents were summoned to Buenos Aires and the family underwent intense family therapy until the symptoms were under control and the maturational crisis became manageable.

DIAGNOSIS AND ASSESSMENT

The individual diagnosis (*DSM-IV* criteria; APA, 1994) was of Anorexia Nervosa, restrictive type. Following this author's classification stated earlier, this is an eating disorder in the context of a dysfunctional family system, where the patient has experienced a pervasive developmental impairment resulting in a personality problem and reflecting a disorder of the self. Other assessment instruments utilized showed that this patient had an 85 to 95 percentile range on the body dissatisfaction, perfectionism, maturity fears, and asceticism subscales. Additionally, the somatization and paranoid ideation dimensions were significantly elevated. The former reflects distress arising from perceptions of body functioning and somatic equivalents of anxiety; the latter refers to suspiciousness, hostility, grandiosity, centrality, and fear of loss of autonomy (Derogotis, 1994). The initial family assessment, which had led to a diagnosis of developmentally arrested dysfunctional personologic system (DevDps), had missed the overlap with another category: the covertly narcissistic dysfunctional system (CNrDps; Magnavita, 2000).

In fact, Susana was not only having difficulty in the separation-individuation process because of her protective role of the parental subsystem; more important, this system was involved in an arrangement such that the offspring were serving the unmet emotional needs of the parents. The parents had always had an unhappy marriage, perhaps partly because each of them had failed to differentiate from their own family of origin. The trade-off for their financial and professional success as physicians was that they left Buenos Aires early in their marriage but remained guilty and indebted to their elders for this distance. They responded to this with implicit covert pacts. The father secretly channeled money to his mother. The mother's arrangement was more sophisticated; all their offspring were to come to Buenos Aires to further their university education, but they were to live in the grandmother's home under her strict and loving care, in an atmosphere where sex was sinful and family loyalty was the highest value. Thus, they became engulfed in the mother's world, which protected them from the father's "dangerous" influence. The father participated only in medical (professional) matters, and the couple remained hindered in their capacity to become emotionally involved. Triangulation was the interactional rule for this family. Susana, the only daughter and mother confidant, was the epitomized victim of this plight. Through her body, she expressed the conflict around sexuality and pleasure and punished herself by depriving her body of the needed nourishment and by banging her head against the wall while crying that she was useless and bad because she was ruining everyone's life. At a time when she felt totally out of control of her circumstances, the one domain she was still able to exert omnipotent power over was her food intake. In this, she was able to defeat her idealized mother and her "bitter guardians," who had attempted to control her life. Additionally, as her weight loss progressed and her adolescent body vanished, she became totally absorbed by this preoccupation; she forgot about boys, love, life, and the pain of growing up and of separating. Now she was no longer separated. Her mother opened her arms to embrace her regressive daughter, and momentarily this family regained their balance.

TREATMENT APPROACH

Interestingly, most of the above constructions were never openly shared with the family. Their main value was serving as a frame that allowed for the intense joining with each of these family members in their pain and dilemmas and to challenge them to act differently. From that vantage point, it was possible to tap into their resources to further positive change. The initial treatment stages did not follow the earlier stated outline because of the living conditions and distance of the parents. During the individual sessions with Susana, it was possible to piece together the family picture, at least from the girl's perspective. This allowed for a good joining with the therapist that enabled the new experience of relating to someone outside the family circle and feeling understood and valued. One cannot underestimate the importance of the therapist's being knowledgeable and experienced in eating disorders. Eating disordered patients are often delusional and become more inclined to trust someone who is an empathic connoisseur. During this stage, the main achievement was to motivate Susana to overcome her Anorexia Nervosa and gather the courage necessary to wander into the outside world. For this, it was imperative that she differentiate from her parents and construct her own identity. She realized there was a life beyond the family that she had not felt entitled to and that her life plan had been designed by others. In her words, "I am faced with the plight of transforming from a marionette to a young woman."

The turning points of this therapy were:

1. Defining the crisis as having reached a life-threatening point. Her safety was secured by enforcing adequate nutrition. Her clinical condition was monitored by a specialized physician.
2. Realization that the individual sessions with Susana were augmenting her triangulation (she was encouraged to move forward in her development, embracing peer-appropriate behaviors, and that was contrary to the family rule).
3. Realization that her mother was trapped beyond her will (and knowledge?) in this multigeneration pact and was unable to undo it alone.
4. The father was strongly encouraged and supported to reenter the family system. He challenged the mother in her child-rearing values and approach.
5. Both parents were helped to sort out reasonable expectations and put in charge of monitoring Susana's living arrangements while in Buenos Aires.
6. The therapeutic system was opened to include the siblings, maternal grandmother, and grandaunts.
7. The brothers' difficulties with growing up were worked through, highlighting their educational value for Susana.
8. The father was connected with Susana in new outdoor physical activities. They were able to enjoy sharing time together.

Conditions that enabled this therapeutic process were:

1. The certainty that there was no malevolent intent in this family arrangement.
2. The therapeutic alliance based on trust and respect that permeated the whole treatment, even at the most difficult times.
3. Susana's strong will and determination to succeed in this therapeutic endeavor.

OUTCOME

Soon after family therapy started, Susana began to recover her weight, eating habits, and hope. Four months later, she successfully completed her admission course and exams for entering the university. It was a very trying experience for her, and as soon as she finished, she went back to her parents' home for summer vacation. The psychometric data obtained six months after family therapy had commenced showed significant improvement in most subscales. The ones that remained stable were those of body dissatisfaction and perfectionism. The former is a known risk factor for eating disorder relapse; the latter is a personality trait characteristic of Anorexia Nervosa patients. Further therapy will focus on these issues, and individual treatment is more suitable for that work. It is important to keep in mind that a systems frame is not defined by the number of people in the therapy room, but rather by how the problem is perceived and understood. Since the last session, Susana has called on two occasions to say she was enjoying her social and family life and experimenting with finessing her parents when they tried to pull her into their issues. She trusts this will prepare her to face the next semester, living away from home and getting on with a life of her own.

SUMMARY

The case presented previously illustrates the multimodal treatment of an eating disorder in the context of a dysfunctional family system. Susana's pervasive triangular involvement in the parental conflict had resulted in a thwarted maturation and individuation. Developmentally appropriate autonomy threatened the family equilibrium and the Anorexia Nervosa not only kept her peer involvement and sexual awakening at bay; it also invited maternal intrusion and control. In her rigid mind frame, any attempt at separation and individuation that failed to coincide with the mother's expectations, was inherently terrifying. Unfortunately, reality confirmed these fears and only the process that evolved in the family therapy allowed for this to change. The psychodynamic object relation theory formulations were useful in contributing to the therapists' understanding of some of the underlying processes. Nevertheless, if they would have been utilized as interpretive interventions in lieu of family therapy, the patient's triangulation probably would have been reinforced and her outcome impaired. In other words, when considering therapeutics, one must be weary of the boundaries of such theory. The approach of choice must be guided by efficacy evidence.

Critical to this outcome was the maintenance of a solid therapeutic alliance with each one of the family members, which made it possible to move beyond blame and empower the individuals to attain the courage to strive for ageappropriate autonomy. This case clearly illustrates that when treating eating disorders, it is not a matter of knowing all or more approaches, but rather of utilizing interventions that are of clinical relevance to the specific case.

REFERENCES

Agras, W. S., Crow, S. J., Halmi, K. A., Mitchell, J. E., Wilson, G. T., & Kraemer, H. C. (2000). Outcome predictors for the cognitive-behavioral treatment of bulimia nervosa: Data from a multisite study. *American Journal of Psychiatry, 157,* 1302–1308.

Agras, W. S., Walsh, B. T., Wilson, G. T., & Fairburn, C. G. (1999, April). *A multisite comparison of cognitive behavior therapy and interpersonal therapy in the treatment of bulimia nervosa.* Session presented at the meeting of the 4th International Conference on Eating Disorders, London.

American Psychiatric Association. (1994). *Diagnostic and statistical manual of mental disorders* (4th ed.). Washington, DC: Author.

American Psychiatric Association. (2000). *Practice guidelines for the treatment of patients with eating disorders* (2nd ed.). Washington, DC: Author.

Austin, S. B. (2000). Prevention research in eating disorders: Theory and new directions. *Psychological Medicine, 30,* 1249–1262.

Baker Miller, J. (1976). *Towards a new psychology of women.* Boston: Beacon Press.

Becvar, D. S., & Becvar, R. J. (1996). *Family therapy: A systemic integration* (3rd ed.). Boston: Allyn & Bacon.

Beutler, L. E., & Clarkin, J. F. (1990). *Systematic treatment selection: Toward targeted therapeutic interventions.* New York: Brunner/Mazel Integrative Psychotherapy Series.

Bowen, M. (1978). *Family therapy in clinical practice.* New York: Aronson.

Bowlby, J. (1969). *Attachment and loss. Volume I: Attachment.* New York: Basic Books.

Brumberg, J. J. (1988). *Fasting girls: The history of anorexia nervosa.* Cambridge, MA: Harvard University Press.

Bryant-Waugh, R. (2000). Developmental-systemic-feminist therapy. In K. J. Miller & J. S. Mizes

(Eds.), *Comparative treatments for eating disorders* (pp. 160–181). New York: Springer.

Christie, D., Watkins, B., & Lask, B. (2000). Assessment. In B. Lask & R. Bryant-Waugh (Eds.), *Anorexia nervosa and related eating disorders in childhood and adolescence* (2nd ed., pp. 105–125). East Sussex, England: Psychology Press.

Cloninger, C. R. (1986). A unified biosocial theory of personality and its role in the development of anxiety states. *Psychiatric Developments, 3*, 167–226.

Crisp, A. H. (1980). *Anorexia nervosa: Let me be.* New York: Grune & Stratton.

Dare, C., & Crowther, C. (1995). Psychodynamic models of eating disorders. In G. Szmukler, C. Dare, & J. Treasure (Eds.), *Handbook of eating disorders: Theory, treatment and research* (pp. 125–139). Chichester, England: Wiley.

Derogotis, L. R. (1994). *Symptom Checklist 90–Revised. Administration, scoring and procedures manual* (3rd ed.). Minneapolis, MN: National Computer System.

Deveraux, G. (1980). *Basic problems in ethnopsychiatry* (pp. 3–71, 214–236). Chicago: University of Chicago Press.

Eisler, I. (1995). Family models of eating disorders. In G. Szmukler, C. Dare, & J. Treasure (Eds.), *Handbook of eating disorders: Theory, treatment and research* (pp. 155–176). Chichester, England: Wiley.

Engle, G. L. (1980). The clinical application of the biopsychosocial model. *American Journal of Psychiatry, 137*, 535–544.

Fairbairn, W. R. D. (1952). *Psychoanalytic studies of the personality.* London: Tavistock.

Fichter, M., & Quadflieg, N. (2001). *Structured inventory for anorexic and bulimic disorders with DSM IV and ICD-10.* Available from www.lrz-muenchen.de/~Gehrke OR www.epi.med.uni-muenchen.de

Garfinkel, P. E., & Garner, D. M. (1982). *Anorexia nervosa: A multidimensional perspective.* New York: Brunner/Mazel.

Gordon, R. A. (2000). *Eating disorders: Anatomy of a social epidemic.* Oxford, England: Blackwell.

Gowers, S., Norton, K., Halek, C., & Crisp, A. H. (1994). Outcome of outpatient psychotherapy in a random allocation treatment study of anorexia nervosa. *International Journal of Eating Disorders, 15*(2), 165–177.

Haley, J. (1987, March/April). An interview with Jay Haley: The disappearance of the individual. *Family Therapy Networker*, 39–40.

Head, S. B., & Williamson, D. A. (1990). Association of family environments and personality disturbance in bulimia nervosa. *International Journal of Eating Disorders, 9*, 667–674.

Herscovici, C. R. (1996). *La esclavitud de las dietas* [The slavery of dieting]. Buenos Aires, Argentina: Paidós.

Herscovici, C. R. (1999). Terapia sistémica. In J. E. Abadi, H. F. Alvarez, & C. R. Herscovici (Eds.), *El bienestar que buscamos: Tres enfoques terapéuticos* [Searching for well-being: Three therapeutic approaches] (pp. 89–171). Buenos Aires, Argentina: Adriana Hidalgo.

Herscovici, C. R., & Bay, L. (1990). *Anorexia nerviosa y bulimia: Amenazas a la autonomía* [Anorexia nervosa and bulimia: Threats to autonomy]. Buenos Aires, Argentina: Paidós.

Herscovici, C. R., & Bay, L. (1996). Favorable outcome for anorexia nervosa patients treated in Argentina with a family approach. *Eating Disorders Journal of Treatment and Prevention, 4*(1), 59–66.

Herzog, D. B., Keller, M. B., Lavori, P. W., & Bradburn, I. S. (1991). Bulimia nervosa in adolescence. *Developmental and Behavioral Pediatrics, 12*, 191–195.

Herzog, D. B., Keller, M. B., Lavori, P. W., & Ott, I. L. (1988). Short-term prospective study of recovery in bulimia nervosa. *Psychiatry Research, 23*, 45–55.

Hoek, H. W. (1995). The distribution of eating disorders. In K. D. Brownell & C. Fairburn (Eds.), *Eating disorders and obesity: A comprehensive handbook* (pp. 207–211). New York: Guilford Press.

Honig, P. (2000). Family work. In B. Lask & R. Bryant-Waugh (Eds.), *Anorexia nervosa and related eating disorders in childhood and adolescence* (2nd ed., pp. 187–204). East Sussex, England: Psychology Press.

Hsu, G. L. K. (1990). *Eating disorders.* New York: Guilford Press.

Hsu, G. L. K. (1995). Outcome of bulimia nervosa. In K. D. Brownell & C. Fairburn (Eds.), *Eating disorders and obesity: A comprehensive handbook* (pp. 238–244). New York: Guilford Press.

Kaslow, F. W. (1996). Recurrent themes across diagnoses. In F. W. Kaslow (Ed.), *Handbook of relational diagnosis and dysfunctional family patterns* (pp. 523–532). New York: Wiley.

Kernberg, O. F. (1994). *Technical approach to eating disorders in patients with Borderline Personality Disorder.* Paper presented at the 14th regional conference of the Chicago Psychoanalytic Society, Chicago.

Klein, M. (1957). *Envy and gratitude: A study of unconscious sources.* London: Tavistock.

Kohut, H. (1971). The analysis of the self. *Monograph series of the psychoanalytic study of the child* (4th ed.). New York: International Universities Press.

Kohut, H. (1977). *The restoration of the self.* New York: International Universities Press.

Le Grange, D., Eisler, I., Dare, C., & Hodes, M. (1992). Family criticism and self starvation: A study of expressed emotion. *Journal of Family Therapy, 14,* 177–192.

Leon, G., Lucas, A., Colligan, R., Ferlinande, R., & Kamp, J. (1985). Sexual, body-image, and personality attitudes in anorexia nervosa. *Journal of Abnormal Psychology, 13,* 245–258.

Levine, M. P., Piran, N., & Irving, L. M. (2001). Disordered eating behavior in adolescents. In T. Gullotta & M. Bloom (Eds.), *The encyclopedia of primary prevention and health promotion.* New York: Kluwer Academic/Plenum Press.

Lock, J., Le Grange, D., Agras, W. S., & Dare, C. (2000). *Treatment manual for anorexia nervosa: A family based approach.* New York: Guilford Press.

Magnavita, J. J. (2000). *Relational therapy for personality disorders.* New York: Wiley.

Mahler, M. S. (1968). *On human symbiosis and the vicissitudes of individuation.* New York: International Universities Press.

Masterson, J. F. (1978). The borderline adolescent: An object relations view. In S. C. Feinstein & P. L. Giovacchini (Eds.), *Adolescent psychiatry* (Vol. 6, pp. 344–359). Chicago: University of Chicago Press.

Masterson, J. F. (1995). Paradise lost: Bulimia, a closet narcissistic personality disorder: A developmental, self and object relations approach. In R. C. Maroh & S. C. Feinstein (Eds.), *Adolescent psychiatry* (Vol. 20, pp. 253–266). Hillsdale, NJ: Analytic Press.

Minuchin, S. (1974). *Families and family therapy.* Cambridge, MA: Harvard University Press.

Minuchin, S., & Fishman, H. C. (1981). *Family therapy techniques.* Cambridge, MA: Harvard University Press.

Minuchin, S., Rosman, B. L., & Baker, L. (1978). *Psychosomatic families: Anorexia nervosa in context.* Cambridge, MA: Harvard University Press.

Neiderman, M. (2000). Prognosis and outcome. In B. Lask & R. Bryant-Waugh (Eds.), *Anorexia nervosa and related eating disorders in childhood and adolescence* (2nd ed., pp. 81–101). East Sussex, England: Psychology Press.

Nichols, M. P., & Schwartz, R. (1998). *Family therapy: Concepts and methods* (4th ed., pp. 109–137). Needham Heights, MA: Allyn & Bacon.

Palmer, R. L., Oppenheimer, R., Dignon, A., Chaloner, D., & Howells, K. (1990). Childhood sexual experiences with adults reported by women with eating disorders: An extended series. *British Journal of Psychiatry, 156,* 699–703.

Papp, P. (1983). *The process of change* (pp. 45–46). New York: Guilford Press.

Pinsof, W. M., Wynn, L. C., & Hambright, A. B. (1996). The outcomes of couple and family therapy: Findings, conclusions and recommendations. *Psychotherapy, 33,* 321–331.

Rastam, M. (1992). Anorexia nervosa in 51 Swedish adolescents: Premorbid problems and comorbidity. *Journal of the American Academy of Child and Adolescent Psychiatry, 31,* 819–829.

Ratnasuriya, R. H., Eisler, I., Szmukler, G. I., & Russell, G. F. M. (1991). Anorexia nervosa: Outcome and prognostic factors after 20 years. *British Journal of Psychiatry, 158,* 495–502.

Russell, G. F. M. (1994, April). *Relapse prevention in the treatment of anorexia nervosa: A discussion of family, psychopharmacologic and cognitive behavioral treatments.* Workshop presented at the 6th International Conference on Eating Disorders, New York.

Russell, G. F. M., Dare, C., Eisler, I., & Le Grange, P. D. F. (1992). Controlled trials of family treatments in anorexia nervosa. In K. A. Halmi (Ed.), *Psychobiology and treatment of anorexia nervosa and bulimia nervosa.* Washington, DC: American Psychiatric Press.

Russell, G. F. M., Szmukler, G. I., Dare, C., & Eisler, I. (1987). An evaluation of family therapy in anorexia nervosa and bulimia nervosa. *Archives of General Psychiatry, 44,* 1047–1056.

Sands, S. H. (1989). Eating disorders and female development: A self-psychological perspective. In A. I. Goldberg (Ed.), *Progress in self psychology* (Vol. 5, pp. 75–103). Hilldale, NJ: Analytic Press.

Schmidt, U., Tiller, J., Blanchard, M., Andrews, B., & Treasure, J. (1997). Is there a specific trauma precipitating anorexia nervosa? *Psychological Medicine, 27,* 523–530.

Shisslak, C. M., Cargo, M., & Estes, L. S. (1995). The spectrum of eating disturbances. *International Journal of Eating Disorders, 18,* 209–219.

Smith, C., Feldman, S. S., Nasserbakht, A., & Steiner, H. (1993). Anorexia nervosa: Clinical features and long term follow-up. *Journal of Chronic Disorders, 21,* 361–367.

Spitz, R. (1965). *The first year of life.* New York: International Universities Press.

Steiger, H., & Stotland, S. (1995). Individual and family factors in adolescents with eating disorders and syndromes. In H. C. Steinhausen (Ed.), *Eating disorders in adolescence* (pp. 49–67). New York: Walter de Gruyter.

Steinhausen, H. C. (1995). The course and outcome of anorexia nervosa. In K. D. Brownell & C. Fairburn (Eds.), *Eating disorders and obesity: A comprehensive handbook* (pp. 234–237). New York: Guilford Press.

Steinhausen, H. C., Rauss-Mason, C., & Seidel, R. (1991). Follow up studies of anorexia nervosa: A review of four decades of outcome research. *Psychological Medicine, 21,* 447–451.

Strober, M. (1980). Personality and symptomatological features in young nonchronic anorexia nervosa patients. *Journal of Psychosomatic Research, 24,* 353–359.

Strober, M. (1997). Consultation and therapeutic engagement in severe anorexia nervosa. In D. M. Garner & P. E. Garfinkel (Eds.), *Handbook of treatment for eating disorders* (2nd ed., pp. 229–247). New York: Guilford Press.

Sugarman, A., & Kurash, C. (1982). The body as a transitional object in bulimia. *International Journal of Eating Disorders, 1,* 57–67.

Sullivan, P. F. (1995). Mortality in anorexia nervosa. *American Journal of Psychiatry, 152,* 1073–1074.

Vanderlinden, J., & Vandereycken, W. (1989). Family therapy within the psychiatric hospital: Indications pitfalls and specific interventions. In W. Vandereycken, E. Kog, & J. Vanderlinden (Eds.), *The family approach to eating disorders* (pp. 263–273). New York: PMA Publishing.

Vanderlinden, J., & Vandereycken, W. (1995). Sexual abuse and psychological dysfunctioning in eating disorders. In H. C. Steinhausen (Ed.), *Eating disorders in adolescence.* New York: Walter de Gruyter.

van Engeland, H., van der Ham, T., van Furth, E. F., & van Strien, D. C. (1995). The Utrecht prospective longitudinal studies on eating disorders in adolescence: Course and the predictive power of personality and family variables. In H. C. Steinhausen (Ed.), *Eating disorders in adolescence.* New York: Walter de Gruyter.

van Furth, E. F. (1991). *Parental expressed emotion and eating disorders.* Unpublished doctoral dissertation, University of Utrecht, England.

van Hoeken, D., Lucas, A. R., & Hoek, H. W. (1998). Epidemiology. In H. W. Hoek, J. L. Treasure, & M. A. Kaztman (Eds.), *Neurobiology in the treatment of eating disorders* (pp. 97–126). London: Wiley.

Walker, L. (1996). Assessment of abusive spousal relationships. In F. W. Kaslow (Ed.), *Handbook of relational diagnosis and dysfunctional family patterns* (pp. 338–356). New York: Wiley.

Waller, G. (1992). Sexual abuse and the severity of bulimic symptoms. *British Journal of Psychiatry, 161,* 90–93.

Walters, M., Carter, B., Papp, P., & Silverstein, O. (1988). *The invisible web: Gender patterns in family relationships.* New York: Guilford Press.

White, M. (1991). Deconstruction and therapy. *Dulwich Center Newsletter, 3,* 21–40.

White, M., & Epston, B. (1990). *Narrative means to therapeutic ends.* London: Norton.

Windauer, U., Lennerts, W., Talbot, P., Touys, S., & Beaumont, P. (1993). How well are "cured" anorexia nervosa patients? An investigation of 16 weight recovered anorexic patients. *British Journal of Psychiatry, 163,* 195–200.

CHAPTER 7

Psychodynamic Psychotherapy with Undergraduate and Graduate Students

PAUL A. GRAYSON

In many respects, college and graduate students are model candidates for psychodynamic psychotherapy. Young, attractive, verbal, intelligent, headed for success, they are YAVISes par excellence. Developmentally, they're at just the right stage: mature enough to reflect on their experience and see family dynamics in perspective, yet still pliable and unfettered enough to make changes in their lives. No wonder therapists delight in working with this population. Students are the sort of patients insight-oriented therapies are designed to treat.

Yet, for all they have going for them, students still can be a therapeutic challenge. One reason is their unreliability about treatment. Brief therapy is the rule at campus services anyway, but students are not fastidious about sticking to even brief therapy time schedules. A second reason is the complexity of their difficulties. Maybe at one time college psychotherapy was a cozy enclave, the treatment of the developmental struggles of emotionally healthy, ethnically homogeneous, economically privileged young people—but no longer. The work today still emphasizes developmental struggles, but thrown into the mix are also diversity concerns, "real life" stressors, and considerable psychopathology. Students' problems can be a conundrum to sort out, let alone treat, especially within such brief and uncertain time conditions.

These, then, are the defining features of student psychotherapy: gifted clients, scarce time, and complex problems. This chapter describes the therapy approach I have fashioned to work with this talented but challenging population. Unless otherwise indicated, I refer throughout to both undergraduates and graduate students, whom I see at New York University's Counseling Service (UCS) in roughly equal numbers.

HISTORY OF APPROACH

The field of college psychotherapy took off slowly. Although the first mental hygiene program was set up at Princeton in 1910, roughly half the nation's colleges and universities had no organized mental health programs in 1951 (Reinhold, 1991). Even years later, many schools still lacked such programs, leaving it to students who had personal problems to chance upon sympathetic faculty members or deans, brave off-campus treatment, or, most often, suffer in silence. At my own small, all-male liberal arts college in the late 1960s, not only was there no psychotherapy service, but nobody I knew had ever seen a therapist—or dared to admit it.

Perhaps antiwar and civil rights protests, burgeoning drug use, and the advance of coeducation convinced the laggards. Whatever the reason, by the end of the next decade, psychotherapy services had spread throughout academia, and, despite budgetary vicissitudes and occasional "outsourcing" experiments, they've remained a fixture ever since. Today, virtually all colleges in America—and many institutions overseas—provide some sort of on-campus assistance for students who have psychological concerns.

But what sort of assistance? Originally, there were two models: mental health services, which grew out of the campus health service, and counseling services, which were sponsored by psychology departments and/or student personnel programs (Archer & Cooper, 1998). Mental health services had primarily psychiatrist staffs, specialized in personal issues, and attended closely to psychopathology—even though, by all accounts, there was less of it back then. In the very physician-like words of two college psychiatrists 30 years ago, their "fundamental task [was] to prevent and treat illness" (Farnsworth & Munster, 1971, p. 1). By comparison, counseling services were more relaxed, welcoming places. Staffed mostly by counseling psychologists, they dealt with academic and vocational concerns as well as personal problems and emphasized normal student development over psychopathology.

Over time, the differences between mental health and counseling services blurred. Fewer original mental health services could afford the budgetary extravagance of all-psychiatry staffs. Fewer original counseling services bothered with vocational and academic counseling, as these areas were now normally farmed out to separate campus offices. Most important, all services sought a middle ground between the purely mental health service approach, which seemed too heavy-handed for the average case, and the purely counseling service approach, which seemed ill-equipped to deal with psychopathology. The common goal became to reach out to everyone, from the healthy student to the severely disturbed.

As for college psychotherapy's theoretical orientation, historically, the one area of general agreement, endorsed by mental health and counseling services alike, is the relevance of a developmental perspective. (With a few exceptions [see Committee on the College Student of the Group for the Advancement of Psychiatry, GAP Report, 1999], the development in question has been that of undergraduates, not graduate students.) According to the developmental perspective, college students are in a transitional stage between adolescence and adulthood. To negotiate this transition, they have to master certain developmental tasks: separating from family, living autonomously, forging a positive and coherent identity, forming friendships and intimacies, advancing toward career goals. The challenges of the college experience push them to accomplish these developmental tasks. Thus, the first-year student's move from childhood home to on-campus housing is, if all goes well, a maturational step toward separation and autonomy. Choosing courses and an academic major during the middle college years are steps toward identity formation. Making postgraduation plans during the fourth year is a step toward career choice. In many such ways, the time-ordered tests of the college years dovetail with the maturational tasks of becoming an adult (Medalie, 1981). And so the college therapist's task is, in part, to help students simultaneously manage college pressures and master developmental tasks.

Although academics have churned out many versions of student development theory, bristling with formidable professional language like "domains" and "vectors" and "modes" (Slimak, 1992), all college therapists more or less endorse the points outlined above. College therapy is unanimously deemed to be about supporting student development. On other theoretical questions, however, the unanimity disappears. Perusal of the literature shows therapists adopting a variety of theoretical positions—when, that is, they trouble with theory. There has been, and is, no consensual model of college psychotherapy.

Modified psychoanalytic approaches turn up regularly in college therapy writings. Blos (1946), a pioneer writing from an ego psychological perspective, frowned on on-campus classical psychoanalysis for neurotic conditions, recommending instead "deal[ing] with the derivatives of [unconscious infantile] conflicts in terms of ego reactions" (p. 577). May's (1988) *Psychoanalytic Psychotherapy in a College Context* draws on Freud and other main psychoanalytic theorists to apply the psychoanalytic approach to college students in the college environment. Other psychoanalytically influenced college therapists have invoked Melanie Klein's concept of projective identification (Romney & Goli, 1991), Mahler's research into the toddler (Webb & Widseth, 1988), and Kohut's self psychology (Schwitzer, 1997).

Nonpsychoanalytic approaches have been adopted too, among them cognitive-behavior therapy, solution-focused therapy, paradoxical interventions, and family systems therapy. I particularly want to pay homage to one work that does not fall in with any of the popular models, Eugenia Hanfmann's too seldom remembered *Effective Therapy for College Students* (1978), which draws on the even more overlooked theoretical and clinical contributions of Andras Angyal (1965). If I had to pick a single guide to explain the art of treating students on campus, Hanfmann's wise, humane, and jargon-free volume would be the clear choice.

Although various treatment approaches have been used, overall the literature on college psychotherapy has not stressed theory. My experience attending college psychotherapy conferences confirms this atheoretical slant. On the whole, college therapists are more concerned with special problems, like substance abuse or eating disorders, and special populations, like first-year students and women, than with applying the theories of Freud, Kernberg, Kohut, or Beck. When writings do incorporate theory, the approach tends to be integrative, as in May's (1988) broad-based psychoanalytic treatment. To me, this makes sense. Day-to-day interactions with students demand therapeutic flexibility, discouraging any inclination toward theoretical purity.

Two other recent trends remain to be discussed: the ascendance of brief therapy and the diversification of the student population. Because these topics are central to my own thinking and practice, they are reserved for the next section.

THEORETICAL CONSTRUCTS

Brief Therapy and Its Variants

College psychotherapy naturally gravitates toward brief treatment. The college semester, for one thing, permits only about 16 weeks of uninterrupted treatment, and then only for the provident few who start at the beginning of the term. Although some students return to therapy after the winter break or summer vacation, usually the semester's end is a natural stopping point.

Brief therapy is also an economic fact of life. Most colleges and universities these days simply cannot fund enough therapists for a long-term, open-ended psychotherapy program. This reality has sparked debate, some college therapists optimistically calling brief therapy the treatment of choice for many students anyway (Hersh, 1988, Steenbarger, 1992), others decrying session limits (Webb & Widseth, 1988).

Practically speaking, the debate is moot. The typical college service has no fiscal choice but to cut down on appointments by imposing a brief therapy model.

But even if the academic calendar and college finances didn't limit therapy, students themselves would. The reason is their fast-changing lives. College stressors, as we have seen, change from first year to last. On a smaller scale, something similar happens over the semester, with students early in the term adjusting to new classes and perhaps new roommates, then to a relatively tranquil but academically decisive middle period, and finally to the pressure cooker of final exams, followed by another leave-taking (Grayson, 1985). As if all these changes weren't dizzying enough, on a day-to-day basis students are forever experimenting with relationships, sex, alcohol and drugs, academic and extracurricular commitments, sleep schedules, and diet. Such a mercurial existence inevitably bollixes up treatment schedules. As stressors flare up and fade, so goes students' therapy attendance.

College therapy is therefore brief, but not uniformly brief. In reality, we can discern several basic attendance patterns, each a distinct treatment experience: traditional brief therapy, very brief contacts, abbreviated therapy, irregular therapy, and intermittent therapy. Confusingly, it's usually unclear at the beginning of treatment which attendance pattern will ensue. Therapists must dive into the work without knowing beforehand how deep or far they are destined to go.

Before we turn to the nontraditional attendance patterns, which are so characteristic of college therapy, it must be stated that many students do pursue traditional brief therapy, the kind one reads about in treatment manuals. These faithful souls show up reliably for every appointment and proceed until arriving at the semester break or the session limit. Their treatments can be understood in terms of distinct beginning, middle, and ending phases, the last phase permitting an emphasis on termination issues (Mann, 1973; Sifneos, 1979).

Nontraditional Attendance Patterns

But the majority of college treatments play out in less orderly fashion. Very brief contacts (almost one half of UCS's cases) last for only a session or two. Though their official purpose may be to get referrals or receive information, they are, in their own way, true therapy experiences. Abbreviated therapies start off like traditional brief therapy, but then come to an earlier consensual conclusion, slowly fizzle out, or stop abruptly with a dropout. Irregular therapies wend their wobbly way through cancellations, reschedules and no-shows, changes in appointment day, and requests for spaced-out appointments, emergency unscheduled appointments, and perhaps a new therapist. After a while, their unpredictability becomes the norm. Finally, intermittent therapies consist of multiple courses of brief treatment over a student's college career.

From students' standpoint, all such truncated or erratic or discontinuous therapies make perfect sense. Students show up at the psychotherapy service when they feel distressed. They miss appointments, as they miss classes, because that is the casual way on campus. And sooner or later, they leave therapy, because the latest crisis has passed, they've had enough exploration, or they're busy with other matters. Their original decision to visit the college service was not a commitment to undertake therapy but an immediate response to a pressing need.

But for therapists trained in traditional brief therapy (if trained in brief therapy at all), nontraditional patterns disrupt the game plan. One can't count on a set number of sessions to conduct an inquiry, develop a relationship, and achieve treatment goals. One certainly can't count on getting to all the issues one might like. The only recourse is to be ready for anything. Because the student may in fact continue in treatment, thought must be given to follow-up sessions and goals. But because every session may be the last, each must be a helpful experience in its own right. Treatment must be both cumulative and catch-as-catch-can.

Nontraditional attendance patterns have a double-edged influence on the therapeutic alliance. On the one hand, very brief and irregular treatments are neither conducive to nor reflective of strong student-therapist bonds. The student who flits in and out of the office may feel no stronger attachment to the therapist than to faculty advisors, academic counselors, or half a dozen others on campus—not to mention group therapists, psychiatric consultants, or other individual therapists. (One way or another, many students acquire a number of helpers.) And yet, the mere prospect of return visits—intermittent therapy—prolongs a therapist's influence; students feel attached to their therapist even when not actively in treatment, drawing consolation from the therapist's ongoing availability. What these therapy relationships may lack in intensity is made up for in staying power.

Nontraditional attendance patterns also defuse or cloud termination issues. Very brief and highly irregular cases generally have a low-key ending. Interrupted treatments may allow no discussion of ending at all. The prospect of intermittent treatment, meanwhile, renders last sessions less final, more like trial separations than a true goodbye. Throw in the fact that many treatments are overshadowed at the end by final exams anyway, and the result is therapy that often ends anticlimactically, not with a bang but a whimper.

PSYCHODYNAMIC OPPORTUNITIES

Compared to the developmental perspective, which makes students' problems seem like normal growing pains, psychodynamic explanations have a way of emphasizing what's wrong with a person. For this reason, many campus psychotherapy services call themselves Student Development Centers, dissociating themselves from anything smacking of traditional psychodynamic psychotherapy that might scare away skittish students. But although one perspective sounds benign and the other incriminating, developmental and psychodynamic explanations are really two sides of the same coin. The major psychoanalytic models are stage theories, after all, and the most renowned developmental theorist, Erik Erikson, built his conceptualization on Freud's foundation. In my own practice, it is difficult to imagine treating students' developmental struggles without thinking and responding psychodynamically.

Not that students on arrival at the psychotherapy service are necessarily ready for psychodynamic ministrations. Although they show up for all sorts of reasons, including the ever-popular "I just want to talk" and "My roommate's in counseling so I thought I'd try it too," many come in, or are coaxed in by friends and family, because something is acutely wrong that wants putting right. The issue may be an academic setback, anxiety attacks, homesickness, a romantic breakup, an unwanted pregnancy, or any of several dozen other upsets. Often, a combination of stressors, on- and off-campus, does the trick: too many sleep-deprived nights juggling job responsibilities and study pressures, family strife and roommate tensions. (Whoever imagines students have it easy doesn't know them.) Whatever the presenting concerns, what students usually want is fast relief. Crisis management or at least problem solving is where college therapy tends to begin.

But students are resilient and their crises are short-lived. They are also introspective (sometimes morbidly so), intensely curious about themselves, their relationships, and their place in the world, and even those not so inclined have a hard time avoiding self-scrutiny when so much at college shakes comfortable old assumptions. A little prompting, therefore, is all it may take to nudge therapy from crisis mode to self-reflection. Once the immediate upset calms down and before the next one erupts, opportunities arise to dig deeper and work psychodynamically.

As I apply it, the psychodynamic is an inclusive model, in the spirit of Pine's (1990) and McWilliams's (1994) integrative view of the drive, ego, object relations, and self perspectives. Sometimes, a student's fears of and defenses against experiencing affects come to the forefront, a classically psychoanalytic theme that, among brief therapy models, best fits the approaches of Malan (1976) and Davanloo (1980). Sometimes, the spotlight shifts to lifelong misperceptions of other people and associated self-defeating relationship patterns, a theme in keeping with either an object relations or interpersonal perspective and the brief therapy models of Luborsky (1984) and Strupp (Strupp & Binder, 1984). Salient too may be problems with personal agency, authenticity, and self-esteem: self psychology emphases. The challenge isn't to find plausible perspectives. It is, rather, to select an apt one for emphasis. Thus, although inevitably and almost automatically I view students through different theoretical lenses at different times, I'm always on the lookout for the one perspective, and the one core issue, to elevate in importance. In very brief therapy, a single big theme thoroughly examined packs more wallop than a dozen loosely connected insights.

In practice, this approach involves looking for a focus or, more accurately, two foci. The first, the focal problem, is a primary symptom or problem area, usually one of the student's original complaints. The focal problem not only keeps the initial inquiry from flying off in all directions, but also points to a goal: One measure of therapy's success will be progress on this problem. The second focus, the focal theme, usually evolves later. The focal theme is a deeper issue or core theme—the one big psychodynamic insight—that speaks to the student's problems and serves as the therapy's motif, tying the inquiry together. Working with the focal theme is what makes meaningful change possible: "One changes significantly in one's roots, not in one's branches" (Angyal, 1965, p. 205).

Exploring the past is important, as in any psychodynamic treatment, but because of time limitations, one must do so efficiently. The chief importance of mining the past is to illuminate the present, especially the focal problem and theme. Reviewing childhood experiences reveals to students how they unwittingly keep their histories alive in their current maladaptive perceptions and responses.

Another staple of psychodynamic therapy, attention to the therapeutic relationship, is important too—but with a caveat. Unquestionably, when a student's focal problem or focal theme comes up in relation to the therapist, gently citing this here-and-now example is therapeutically useful, bringing the issue into sharp relief. And if a student has a negative reaction toward the therapist, that reaction had better be dealt with promptly or the student may drop out of treatment. But, unlike in psychoanalysis (see Schafer, 1980), in brief therapy the study of the therapist-student relationship should not become an end in itself. When a student's dependent or flirtatious or superior manner has no apparent tie to either focus, usually it's best to sit on the information until it may prove clinically relevant.

Interpreting resistances, another standard psychodynamic activity, similarly requires caution. Certainly, it's sometimes necessary to point out how students deny, minimize, or make a joke of problems, how they hide feelings, blame other people and events, and use their formidable reasoning abilities to explain away the truth. But resistance interpretations to late adolescents risk being heard as condescending or blaming or controlling—in one dread word: parental. They are best made, therefore, in an egalitarian spirit, and then only when the student is ready to hear.

The Impact of Diversity

In recent years, college campuses have dramatically diversified in race, ethnicity, and culture, sexual lifestyles, age, and level of psychopathology. Students from these newly represented groups face the same college stressors and developmental strains as everyone else, but their adjustment is further complicated by their particular pressures. The tricky assessment task raised by diversity is teasing influences apart. When are a student's coping difficulties attributable to the burdens of being somehow "different"? When is diversity a smoke screen obscuring other factors?

The influence of race, ethnicity, and culture on student adjustment deserves a volume in itself. At the cost of oversimplification, let me offer a few observations about the three principal racial minorities. African Americans, particularly if from disadvantaged backgrounds, often shoulder major outside burdens—debt, full-time jobs, family responsibilities—and the weight of being pioneers, the first from their family to attend college. On campus, they sometimes feel alienated, viewing White classmates and professors as uncomprehending and unsupportive. Yet, they can't win, because when they do make White friends or academically shine, other African Americans may ostracize them as "too White." With all these pressures, the developmental tasks of separating from home, fitting in on campus, and forming a positive sense of identity are made that much more difficult.

The same themes crop up with Latino students, again especially those from disadvantaged backgrounds, although Latino-White student relationships, though hardly smooth, are less charged than Black-White relations. But Latinos sometimes face the additional handicaps of English-language problems and families living abroad. Asian Americans sometimes have these last handicaps too, and many also report intense family pressures to excel at studies, study only certain fields, and pass up extracurricular activities and romance. Because many Asian Americans simultaneously chafe at and deeply respect parental control, their separation and identity strivings can tie them in knots. Another common complaint is the stereotype that all of them are, or should be, academic "geeks."

Having made these broad-brush statements, let me hasten to qualify them. Not only don't the generalizations apply to many individuals, but they give no hint of the scope of ethnic and cultural diversity on campus, of all the international and first-generation students, all the unlikely biracial and bicultural, multiracial and multicultural combinations. In the week these words were written, I have seen a Nigerian student raised in England, a Japanese national new to America, an ethnic Indian raised in the Middle East, a first-generation Ecuadorian, and an Irish Korean born in the United States. Not one of their stories neatly fits broad racial generalizations.

And yet, along with the dazzling variety in experiences, one also finds an opposite phenomenon: students from dramatically different backgrounds articulating certain common themes. Time and again, minority and international students speak of the clash between family and American mainstream values (to say nothing of Greenwich Village values), the feeling of being different and an outsider on campus, and the wish for more same-group adult role models. Repeatedly, they remark that in their culture one doesn't go to therapy or talk about feelings to outsiders, or at all. The speaker may be a Turkish international student, an African American, a first-generation Korean American, or a Hasidic Jew, but the messages are remarkably alike.

One final point before leaving race, ethnicity, and culture: These influences can be crucial—or they can be therapeutically beside the point. Overestimating the ethnic factor is as much an assessment risk as missing it. A foreign-born student gave an account of her mother's harsh style of upbringing. "Was that typical of mothers from your country?" I asked, confident from something I'd read or heard that the answer would be yes. "Oh no," she said. "That was just my mother."

A second area of diversification is sexual lifestyle. These days, students matter-of-factly talk about their same-sex partners and their jaunts to late-night sex clubs, and nobody on my campus gives it a thought that there's an Office of Gay, Lesbian, Bisexual, and Transgender Students. Yet, just 30 years ago, homosexual students were threatened with expulsion from college and were viewed by comparatively tolerant college psychiatrists as having a "basic character disorder" (Farnsworth & Munster, 1971, pp. 101–108). But though the times today are relatively open and tolerant, societal and internalized homophobia are of course still realities, and students' adjustment is still a struggle. Relations with unsympathetic parents, for one thing, leaves gay, lesbian, and bisexual students two unhappy choices: either hiding their sexuality or coming out and facing estrangement. Making friends, establishing intimacies, and particularly maintaining self-esteem can be complicated. So can deciding on sexuality; students confused by erotic and sexual feelings sometimes feel pressure to prematurely declare a sexual orientation. Again, these are broad generalizations. For many students, a minority sexual orientation, like minority ethnic status, is a source of pride and identification but otherwise no big deal. They request therapy not because of their sexuality but because they have other personal problems, just like anyone else.

The influx of students today who are in their late 20s, 30s, and sometimes far older are a third, and growing, source of diversity. When I entered the field of college therapy two decades ago, I didn't expect someday to listen to a sophomore weigh the pros and cons of disciplining her teenage daughter. But so I have, as I have listened to other students describe marital affairs and troublesome ex-spouses, mortgages, career changes, and enlarged prostates. Older undergraduates obviously have different concerns from traditional-age undergraduates as graduate students have different concerns from undergraduates. Yet, certain aspects of the school experience can elicit the adolescent in anyone. Educational expenses, to choose a prime example, can oblige older students to depend on parents again for financial support, even to move back in with them. Student status brings out child-parent overtones in relationships with professors. Student activities—reading books and exchanging viewpoints, receiving grades, thinking about career choices—pulls for a quintessentially adolescent self-examination and doubt. Therapy with older students, or for that matter with graduate students, therefore involves an intriguing combination of concerns. Sometimes, it feels like talking to an older adult, sometimes, to a floundering 18-year-old.

A final area of diversity is level and type of pathology. Unlike college therapy's early days, today's student population spans the full spectrum of mental health. At one end are healthy young men and women, the ones who, when they stumble over the hurdles that college and growing up place in their path, right themselves with relatively straightforward therapeutic interventions. At the other end are a large number of chronically disturbed individuals, many more than in years past, drawn to campus partly because of laws requiring colleges to provide accommodations for psychiatric disabilities. And in the middle is the largest group of psychotherapy service consumers, whose struggles reflect some combination of traditional student concerns and demonstrable pathology. Added to the other kinds of diversity, the range and variety of pathology keeps things clinically interesting. College therapists never know who's coming into the office next. Each student poses a fresh clinical challenge calling for a distinctive therapeutic response.

METHODS OF ASSESSMENT AND INTERVENTIONS

Assessment

Although some college psychotherapy services use formal instruments (A. J. Schwartz, personal communication, 1999), most confine the assessment process to student-completed intake forms and the therapeutic interview. UCS's own three-page intake form packs in dozens of questions about treatment history, academic history, current employment, and family background. Included is a 46-item problem checklist that runs the gamut of student miseries from Academic Performance to Suicide Concerns. The Intake Form takes 15 minutes to fill out and 5 minutes to review. At the end of reading it, one already has a fair idea of what to expect from the student.

The main assessment tool, the therapeutic interview, is not much different from that in other time-limited settings. My first question is the standard query about what brings the student in for help at this time. I then ask about the history of these presenting concerns, key symptom areas (mood, sleep, etc.), and any other areas of difficulty, using the Intake Form response as a guide: "You checked off Sexual Orientation. Would you like to tell me about that?" As in any initial interview, I form impressions of the patient's overall level of mental health, psychological-mindedness, expectations of treatment, attitudes about self, and manner of relating to me.

Although the assessment interview is familiar, I stress student issues. When a student fails to mention studies, I am sure to ask. Academics, after all, are the point of college, and academic problems are often the channel through which separation and identity conflicts are expressed. Eating and body image concerns, rampant among females and not rare among male students, call for careful assessment. Alcohol and drug use can be tricky; the knee-jerk student response, "I don't have problems with drinking or drugs," too often translates to downing 12 beers at a sitting or smoking marijuana every afternoon, but it's no problem because a friend consumes more. Suicidal concerns merit careful questions, and more and more these days, so do violence and abuse—toward or by the student. Throughout the interview, I listen for difficulties in separating from (or ever attaching to) parents, establishing a coherent and positive identity, progressing toward career goals, and forming friendships and intimate relationships: the overarching tasks of late adolescent development.

Several years ago, UCS experimented with a formal intake system, assessing students first and then assigning them to an appropriately matched therapist. But after a year, this experiment was scrapped, because too many students objected to making the switch after opening up to the initial interviewer. Besides, it seemed ludicrous to separate assessment and therapy if most students came in for only one to four sessions anyway. The current system matches students and therapists based on a mutually free time; that pairing remains unless there's reason to change it. Assessment and treatment both begin in session 1 and proceed in tandem for as long as the student stays in therapy.

Treatment

The First Session
Assessment is not the only task of the first 45 minutes. Many students, especially international students and racial minorities, have never talked before to a therapist, and they're not certain how they feel about it. An early piece of business, therefore, is to educate and reassure about the process: the preparatory work that Hanfmann (1978) calls "precounseling."

The particulars of precounseling vary, depending on the student. Sometimes, I state that going to therapy does not mean one is crazy or abnormal, one is entitled to go even if a roommate's problems are worse, and I am not sitting in judgment of the student, or parents. Sometimes, I explain how talking helps, what is expected of the student (some sit quietly and obediently, as if at a medical examination), and why, despite all the hype, emotional problems are not simply "biochemical." If a student seems uncomfortable because we're somehow different, I open this up for discussion. (Fortunately, differences in ethnicity, gender, and sexual orientation are seldom fatal to the therapeutic alliance.) It goes without saying that no words at this stage can dissolve deeper resistances. All patients want both to know and not know about themselves, want to change and not change; that's the challenge of any psychotherapy. Still, sensitive early handling of a student's fears, doubts, and misconceptions can tilt the balance in favor of giving therapy a try.

Students who feel a sense of urgency about their problems need encouragement to be patient: "When you insist on ending these anxiety attacks all at once, you only make yourself more anxious." However, I do try from the very first session to relieve pressing problems, for maybe this will be my only chance with the student. At the beginning, then, I am at my most eclectic, using whatever I have in my bag of tricks to alleviate acute suffering and restore impaired functioning. In a case of panic attacks, I teach that the symptom is extreme anxiety rather than something more sinister, point out the harm of negative thoughts and the benefit of constructive thoughts, and give a quick demonstration of deep breathing and relaxation techniques. In the aftermath of a romantic breakup, I validate the painfulness of the experience (nothing wounds inexperienced young people like a breakup), review coping methods the student has tried, and may advise spending a weekend with family or close friends. Although I do not emphasize insight at this point, I do make a few gentle probes: "Do you have any ideas what may be causing you to feel so anxious?" "Have you had other losses that affected you like this?" The student may not be ready yet, but the seeds are planted for later exploration.

Toward the end of the session, I briefly summarize the main themes and open for discussion what should come next. Should the student have more sessions? (Almost always the response is yes.) If so, should the sessions be with me, or should I give a referral for time-unlimited off-campus treatment? (Most students elect on-campus therapy.) Is group therapy indicated? (Often it is, although most students initially balk at the idea.) Is a medication consult warranted? (Once anathema, medications have become, sad to say, the only treatment some students value.) With luck, the student's opinions jibe with my own. If we disagree, I generally suggest we put off final treatment decisions until we've met at least one more time.

For the majority of students who will continue to see me, the next step is to identify a focal problem (the first focus). This takes negotiation. The typical first response to my request for a focal problem is anything but focused: "Well, I'd like to work on my temper, and my relationship with my father, and self-esteem, and procrastination, and . . ." And so I try again, using follow-up questions adapted from solution-focused therapy: "But if one thing could change that would make you later feel glad you worked with me, what would that change be?" (Walter & Peller, 1992). Eventually, most students are able to name a symptom or problem as their main priority. Next, I seek a therapeutic goal: "How would you know you've made progress on this problem? What would be different?" The goal introduces the idea that therapy isn't just talk. Our sessions are to help change something in the student's approach to the focal problem.

At the end of the session, I give homework, which reinforces the focus and sends the motivating message that there's something constructive to do right away. My usual assignment is to notice examples of the focal problem:

"Why don't you be aware of times during the week when the problem happens. Pay attention to the situation and how you react. Then next time, we can explore these instances together."

Next Sessions
In contrast to the first session, I begin follow-up sessions without structure, inviting students to bring up what's on their mind. (In later sessions, the simple prompt "So" can get the ball rolling.) Given the encouragement to begin anywhere, many students strike off in unforeseen directions and show new sides of their personalities. Someone who in the first week seemed to be falling apart may now composedly muse about friendships and career options; someone else who seemed to have run-of-the-mill homesickness may now confide a horrific history of childhood sexual and physical abuse. I expect to be surprised by students and am always ready to revise early assessment conclusions and revisit the question of the most suitable focal problem.

Although subsequent sessions begin nondirectly, there is an agenda. If the student brings up previously undisclosed problems, I look for connections to the focal problem, assuming the original problem still seems to be the main priority: "How do you think this topic you're talking about now might be involved in your central concern?" If the student directly talks about the focal problem, I ask questions about it: How does the student understand that the problem happened again this week? What thoughts and feelings accompanied its occurrence? When else do these thoughts and feelings surface? How does the student feel about the problem (anxious? ashamed? defeated? guilty? secretly proud?), and how might this feeling affect its perpetuation? How do other people understand, and react to, the problem? Through this directed inquiry, I invite the student on a collaborative search, the two of us together following up leads on the nature and source of the focal problem.

Sometime in the first few sessions, I briefly but systematically ask about the past, asking for characterizations of each family member, each one's relationship with the student, and the student's role within the family. If I sense something, I also ask about early relationships with peers and teachers. If necessary, I inject immediacy into the exercise: "If you could be 10 years old again, what would you say to me about your parents divorcing?" The answers are culled for further clues about the focal problem: "So your father would blow up whenever he saw you crying. What impact do you think that has on you now, during this period of depression?" "I wonder how all those times feeling like the odd person out with your sisters is related to your social isolation now."

Throughout, I'm on the alert for changes in the student's affect, level of resistance, reactions to me, and my own reactions to the student. Sometimes, these phenomena are pronounced enough to comment on without knowing if they relate to the focal problem: "You seem to be having a strong reaction right now. What are you feeling?" I am most inclined to pounce, though, when I sense a relevance: "You've explained how you always stop yourself while writing papers. I wonder if you're not doing the same thing right now, stopping yourself from talking to me."

There quickly emerges, as can be seen, an embarrassment of therapeutic riches: the student's current life in its many aspects, the past, here-and-now reactions during the session, any reported dreams or fantasies. There's a wealth of material, but precious little time to mine it. The challenge, therefore, is to sift through it all and extract a focal theme, a dominant trend or pattern that pulls the material together and bears on the focal problem. Obviously, selecting a focal theme is a matter of judgment and simplification. The more one speaks to a student, the more connections, parallels, and explanations come to light, the more nuanced an understanding of the relative influence of external stressors, developmental strains, diversity factors, and pathological elements. Students are complicated, their problems amenable to different interpretations. Ideally, however, one theme stands out that makes sense to both of us, comes up recurrently in the clinical material, and lends itself to change. Ideally, there's a big idea around which we can organize our investigation.

The focal themes I favor are plainly observable in students' day-to-day lives and statable in simple language. They are often, at least in early formulations, rather homely ideas, which taken out of context can sound trite. But the test of a good focal theme is that it registers as true. Often, the truth is something the student already hazily knows but hasn't faced up to. A few examples will demonstrate. A student's focal problem was puzzling anger outbursts. The focal theme we arrived at, which he'd half realized before, was his sensitivity to slights; his anger boiled over whenever he felt put down. Another student's focal depressive symptoms were traced to the sweeping extent she denied herself wishes and needs, which therefore became our focal theme. With a third student, also mired in depression and at a loss to explain it, the thrust of our discussions—the focal theme—became her depression-inducing guilt and fear about breaking away from her traditional Indian family.

Once a focal theme is identified, its exploration takes center stage. The initial focal problem is by no means forgotten, other topics are fair game, and new insights accrue, but everything is tested for its relationship to the predominant theme. Exploration of the focal theme leads to ever more precise and elaborate formulations. The angry student whose focal theme was sensitivity to slights was later understood to be unconsciously getting back at anyone who reminded him of his sadistic older brother and demanding, rejecting father. The depressed student fearful of asserting her wishes and needs was later found to be trapped in her role as the strong, healthy daughter in an emotionally troubled family. These versions, in turn, were further modified as more information came to light. Refining the focal theme is an ongoing process.

The purpose of all this attention to the focal theme is to help the student break free, to change. Change, of course, is a mysterious phenomenon. Why certain students make progress, and precisely what makes it possible, is impossible to pin down. Still, the dogged investigation of a central theme surely plays a part. Once students understand their self-defeating ways and the price they pay for them, the natural tendency is to try a healthier path. And once the first step is taken, it becomes easier to take the next, and then the next.

To support change in relation to the focal theme, I look for it, scanning for even small examples of movement in the student's day-to-day life: "But you see, you actually spoke up this time. What was that like for you?" And: "How were you able to do it?" Setbacks are treated as opportunities to learn more: "So you held yourself back from speaking up. What do you think made it hard to do?" And: "If you could rewrite history, how would you handle the situation differently?" Occasionally, I assign homework inviting change, although I'm wary of pushing students before they're ready.

The general strategy, then, is as follows: Identify a focal problem, examine it from all angles, arrive at a "deeper" focal theme, then concentrate on the theme with an eye to encouraging change. That, at any rate, is the plan. In actuality, many cases take a different path. Some students, especially the very brief and irregular attenders, finish therapy without our homing in on, let alone sinking our teeth into, a viable focal theme. They still may part gratefully, whether due to improved fortunes, my supportive listening, or who knows what factor (it helps treatment outcomes when cases start in the gloomy winter and finish with the flowers in bloom), but we never arrive at that "aha" moment when their story yields a larger meaning. Other students do come away with insight into a focal theme and perhaps determination to pursue long-term treatment, no mean accomplishments for a handful of sessions, but they finish still mired in their basic struggle. But then there are the successes, when the student's surface problems yield to a deeper understanding, and deeper understanding fosters genuine change. Trainees who've slogged through slower therapies at other settings marvel at witnessing this phenomenon. Their college patients who were bogged down in problems suddenly grasp something fundamental about themselves and determine to act differently. It's a heady process to witness.

The Role of Nondirective Responses
Brief therapy requires activity and structure, particularly in directing attention to the foci. But a healing ingredient of any treatment is simply talking to an empathic listener. Active interventions must be balanced, therefore, with a softer therapeutic response: patient listening. In the same vein, I favor liberal use of mirroring responses, brief restatements (the briefer the better) that clarify students' meaning, affirm their worth, and encourage further disclosures. There's no need to say more about the universal techniques of listening or mirroring, but I do want to make clear that, focal emphasis notwithstanding, I actually spend more time in sessions patiently attending to a student's words than directing the inquiry.

Nimble balancing is also required around a possible parental role. As a rule, I take pains to avoid playing the parent, because late adolescents struggling to be free of adult control don't need controlling by me. To establish a collaborative, egalitarian relationship, I open up for discussion the decision to work together, the choice of focal problem, and the meaning of clinical material ("What are your ideas about what this means?"), and couch statements in tentative, nonauthoritarian language ("Tell me if I'm getting this right, but it sounds as if . . ."). Even so, some students hear my remarks as parentally intrusive or critical, and so I ask about that: "What does it feel like when I make an observation? You often have a pained expression on your face." Other students solicit a parental response, which also warrants comment: "It sounds as if you're asking me what to do here, as if you can't decide for yourself. What do you think that's about?" On occasion, though, a student seems so lost or bent on self-destruction that I put aside my theoretical scruples and deliberately act in loco parentis: "You're feeling so desperate now that I sense you'll only make matters worse if you try to study again tonight. Why don't you take the evening off and do something with your friends." Once students get past the rough spots, I gladly relinquish my parenting duties and return to supporting their autonomy.

Transference, Countertransference, and Termination
In addition to the child-parent undertones, other relationship themes inevitably come up with students. Late adolescents relate to therapists in all the ways adults do: warmly, hyperrationally, demandingly, placatingly, dismissively, suspiciously, seductively. College therapists in turn have a full complement of countertransference reactions, among which I would single out protective feelings (students *are* like children sometimes), exasperation (they can be like *difficult* children sometimes), overidentification (they're at a pivotal point in their lives), attraction (they're so young, good-looking, and charming), and fascination (their life stories can be the stuff of romance and drama). Although many transference and countertransference themes may enter the room, I generally do not direct attention to these currents unless they threaten the treatment alliance or clearly pertain to the focus, in which case, I tackle the issue

head-on: "We've seen how hard it is for you to confront people directly. I wonder if something like that isn't going on here today between you and me, because after I started the session late, you've seemed much quieter than usual."

Because the end of treatment is often indeterminate, there may be no opportunity to discuss it. When a case does come to a known finish, I emphasize termination to the extent that it seems emotionally salient. My sense is that many students have only mild feelings about the finish of brief treatment, and so I don't belabor its significance. For those who view termination as a repetition of past abandonments, rejections, or neglect, I do point out and ask about their reactions. As with any other aspect of treatment, I particularly stress termination reactions when they relate to the focal theme.

PROBLEM AREAS AND DIAGNOSIS

I am sometimes asked at social gatherings to name the typical problems of today's students. The expectation seems to be that there's a bumper sticker answer, the top two or three concerns defining the current college generation. In fact, users of the psychotherapy service have just about every personal difficulty imaginable, save mental retardation and senile dementia. On UCS's intake form checklist, they most frequently check off Anxiety, Stress, and Depression, but there are plenty of mentions too of Eating or Weight Concerns, Family Problems, Identity Concerns, Romantic Problems, Academic Performance, Suicide, and so on. Another popular misconception is that the undergraduate and graduate school years are a cushy respite from real-life pressures. Actually, today's students are as likely to be weighed down by full-time jobs, credit card debt, and family obligations as by homesickness, midterm exams, and roommate squabbles, and it's not as if on-campus pressures are trivial in their own right. (Who among us would want to be cooped up again with a roommate or saddled with four midterms?) Add to the equation the particular adjustment challenges faced by diverse groups and by emotionally disturbed students, and inarguably, the problems of students are both wide-ranging and substantial.

Although students fall into most Axis I and II categories, certain diagnostic trends can be noted. Adjustment disorders are prevalent, reflecting both the stressfulness of students' lives and the fluidity of their symptoms. A few students—the once common, now quaint, pure developmental cases—are most accurately described by V-codes: parent-child relational problems, partner relational problems, academic problems, and identity problems. Many others have an Axis I or Axis II feel but are hard to pigeonhole diagnostically, partly because of limitations in the diagnostic system, but also because of their puzzling variability. Sometimes, the best recourse is to create a composite diagnostic picture by putting a question mark next to several *Diagnostic and Statistical Manual of Mental Disorders* categories.

Problems and diagnoses are one factor determining which students to treat in brief therapy. All things being equal, serious eating disorders, substance abuse, Bipolar Disorder, recurrent Major Depressive Disorder, and Obsessive-Compulsive Disorder call for referral to off-campus providers. Other indications are vague, diffuse, or chronically entrenched problems, an extensive treatment history, and a history of losses or unstable relationships: negative experiences that short-term therapy might duplicate. Conversely, students who present a clear focal problem, are new to treatment, recognize their own role in their difficulties, and are motivated to change hold promise for brief therapy. But with the majority of students, I would say, one can build a case for either on-campus or off-campus treatment. Often, the inclination of student and therapist alike is to start a trial of on-campus treatment and see how it goes, reserving the possibility of referral for later. Besides, a college service serves the entire student community and can't be too fussy about selection criteria.

Some students unmistakably wrong for brief therapy flatly refuse to take a referral or arrive too late in the academic year to refer out. The only alternative is to tide them over for a time and pave the way for a future referral. Even in these cases, students are unpredictable. Sometimes, the unlikeliest patients register meaningful short-term therapeutic gains.

CASE STUDY

"Sonia" came to my attention in ominous fashion, via a phone call from a local hospital. A social worker called to ask what follow-up services we could provide for a 25-year-old French-speaking NYU graduate student from Belgium. A week earlier, Sonia had been taken unconscious to the hospital after making a serious suicide attempt. Now that she was ready to be released, could University Counseling Service treat her?

It wasn't clear from the social worker's description what to expect, beyond the assurance that Sonia was emotionally stable and willing to meet with me. Indeed, at our first meeting, Sonia spoke freely and amiably, although her shifting gaze and fluttering hands betrayed anxiety and she had some difficulty finding the right words in English. She explained that her Belgian boyfriend, Laurent, had unexpectedly called 10 days earlier to break up with her. Though she had never before seriously considered committing suicide, on hearing this news she promptly made up her mind to do it. After two days of planning, she left her roommate and off-campus apartment, checked into a hotel, at first tried to cut her wrists with a kitchen knife, and then, when that proved too painful, swallowed a half bottle of champagne and 32 over-the-counter sleeping pills. That was all she could remember, until she woke up having her stomach pumped in the emergency room.

As Sonia spoke, I had something of the experience of watching a slick and stylish European film. This sweet-looking, vivacious, smiling young woman gave enough cinematic detail that I could picture every scene, from the boyfriend's jarring phone call to her disorienting hospital stay among psychotic patients and brusque aides. The story was riveting, the teller charming. But almost entirely missing from her account was access to her inner life, her emotions and motives. How had she felt, I asked, when Laurent dropped his bombshell? She couldn't say. What went through her mind while deciding to take her life and carrying out her meticulous plans? She'd simply decided to do it; she'd always been intrigued by death. (Some of her responses had an existential flavor.) But surely she'd been thinking about Laurent during this time? No, not really; she was too busy with her plans. How did she feel now about taking her life? Oh no, she'd never do it again, she'd had that "experience" and so wouldn't repeat it. Besides, Laurent had called, it was all a big misunderstanding, and he'd just flown in to stay with her for a week.

Sonia's manner was lively, almost merry, as if therapy, like suicide, were an interesting adventure she'd happily experience. Yes, she said, she would very much like to continue meeting so we could understand her suicide attempt. And yes, she'd take my office and the Protection Service's phone numbers in case of an emergency.

Initial Diagnosis and Assessment

After the first session, I wrote down this reluctant diagnostic impression in Sonia's chart: "Adjustment Disorder (this doesn't at all do justice to the puzzle she presents, but I can't think of anything closer)." The hospital report, which arrived a week later, also settled on Adjustment Disorder with Depressed Mood, putting "none" next to the Axis II space. My diagnosis was chosen by default. At this initial session, it seemed evident that despite her suicide attempt, Sonia did not meet the criteria for a depressive disorder, let alone any other Axis I category. And although a suicide attempt following a threatened abandonment suggests Borderline Personality Disorder, there were no clear indications of instability of relationships, identity, or affect, intense anger, or other borderline signs. Nor did any other personality disorder seem to fit.

Adjustment Disorder seemed the best diagnosis available, but it revealed nothing about what was most conspicuous about Sonia: the disconnection between the events she reported and her feelings and motives. She seemed all pleasant surface, no inner life. I had no idea at this point what the disconnectedness was about, only the conviction that it was implicated in her suicide attempt and would have to be central to her treatment. As for her suicidal potential, I wasn't sure what to think. Her cheerful manner and ready assurances bespoke someone not at all at risk. Yet, this same lively young woman had methodically carried out a lethal plan that surely would have succeeded had chambermaids not happened into the bathroom where she lay unconscious. Suppose Laurent had a change of heart and left her again; how would she react? Suppose she was deceiving me—or herself—about her suicidal inclinations?

CASE FORMULATION

As might be expected, Sonia's emotional inaccessibility had a long history; she couldn't even remember reacting when at age 8 she learned of her parents' divorce. The third session brought the first clue about where this emotional blockage originated. Her mother, she said, pressured her to be productive, studious, and strong: a doer and help giver, not a feeler and help seeker. In later sessions, she periodically picked up this thread again. Her mother was moody and easily hurt, prone to depression, and, if she felt wronged or disappointed, sometimes refused to acknowledge Sonia for days afterward. The little girl did everything possible to avoid her mother's displeasure, indeed, to stay out of the mother's way. But children cannot escape or do without their mother for long. When contact was unavoidable, the girl learned to placate, cheer up, and essentially parent the mother, and mercilessly drove herself to be the academic success her mother insisted on. These strategies came at a steep price. Attentiveness to her mother's feelings, wishes, and needs had made her a stranger to her own inner life. The cheerful, stoical, and "good" false self she presented to her mother and, inevitably, to her teachers, friends, and boyfriend—and now to me—required ignoring the unfulfilled person inside. In developmental terms, this 25-year-old woman had neither separated from her mother nor consolidated her own sense of identity.

Coming to New York, I suspect, was to be an escape from her straitjacket, but it almost proved her undoing. Although out of touch with her feelings, Sonia surely missed her boyfriend and Belgian friends, and she felt lonely and isolated in a strange, anonymous city, at a disadvantage because of her language difficulties. Being far from home allowed her to question her academic direction and career plans and simply to have fun—liberating possibilities, but also threats to her lifelong adaptation. Already, then, she was feeling vulnerable and uncertain, when Laurent's abrupt long-distance rejection overwhelmed her limited coping resources. Without experience in reaching out to others or soothing herself, or even tolerating or making sense of what she was feeling, and with a philosophical view of suicide blinding her to the horror of what she was doing, she almost inevitably latched onto suicide. Sonia plotted to kill herself because at her darkest moment she was psychologically unprepared to do anything else.

The irony is that her attempt came just as her sense of self finally was awakening. Merely coming to New York was a break from the mother. Questioning her course of studies was an unprecedented look inside herself. Even the suicidal plan expressed a fledgling, if cockeyed, self-assertion. Only far from home, she explained, did she feel free and selfish enough to disregard other people's wishes and do as she pleased: end her life.

TREATMENT APPROACH

Despite her eagerness, I wasn't optimistic after our first meeting that therapy would be of much help to Sonia. The focal problem, understanding the suicide attempt, and the immediate goal, preventing another, were both clear enough. But how could we fathom her motives if she was unable or unwilling to access her inner life? As it happens, I underestimated her therapy resources. After I twice pointed out the startling discrepancy between her scary actions and her bubbly manner, she readily agreed in the second session to work on discovering her emotions. This issue, a promising focal theme, struck home. In the next sessions, she reported feeling "sad" when Laurent returned to Belgium, but "happy" to test herself by being alone again. She felt "fed up" working on a major paper, was starting to "enjoy" New York, and in a dream felt "angry" with herself for having distanced friends from home. Sonia reported these feelings in a tentative way, the usual half-anxious, half-ingratiating smile pasted on her face (which I pointed out), but something genuine seemed to be getting through. It was as if she was learning to speak the language of emotions as she was also studying to improve her English. In focusing on her inner life, we also looked for situations where she'd kept her emotions bottled up or couldn't find emotions at all, such as in her dealings with Laurent. More and more, she grasped the extent of her self-unawareness and self-denial.

The next step was to discover what blocked her from experiencing feelings. Questioned about family background in the third session, she cautiously ventured her first statements about her mother's inhibiting influence. From then on, I looked for opportunities to return to her relationship with her mother and to note similar self-inhibiting tendencies in her other relationships.

In session 5, I referred Sonia to a women's therapy group at UCS. My intention was to encourage further emotional expression and assure her of continued support, as our individual sessions were due to run out several weeks before her one-year program ended. Two weeks later, she scheduled an emergency session. She couldn't talk about herself in the group, she told me, visibly upset. Instead, she felt obligated to help out the other members, to put their concerns ahead of hers. When I commented that this confining role sounded familiar, she said yes, more and more she realized this had been true her whole life. She then launched into a full-blooded lament about her parentified relationship with her mother. Lately she'd felt angry at her mother, she said. She looked straight at me as she spoke, for once, not smiling.

Throughout the therapy, I was sensitive to calibrating the degree of structure. As I always do, I related material to our focal theme, which in her case meant drawing attention to the contents of her emotional life and the reasons for and consequences of keeping it at bay. Whatever we discussed—her mother, her studies, her manner in the session—was examined through this prism. But I also felt it crucial with this young woman who'd devoted a lifetime to obedience to allow her room to talk about whatever she pleased. Given this license, Sonia discoursed on her displeasure with the cold hospital attendants, her wish to be more affectionate with Laurent, her obstacles as a female scholar in a male-dominated field, her love of taking walking excursions in Manhattan, and her ambivalence about telling her mother about the suicide attempt. She did not delve deeply into her parents' divorce or her relationship with her father, nor did I push her to. Encouraged to say what she wanted, she seemed to get in touch with herself at her own pace.

In our ninth meeting, Sonia asked if she could conserve her remaining sessions. She wanted to meet me several times right before leaving New York to talk about dealing with her mother and readjusting to life back home. In the meantime, she would continue group sessions, which were going better now. As it turned out, she returned only once more, a week before her departure (I was pleased to see her on my schedule) to bring me up to date and say goodbye. She had decided, she said, to tell her mother about the suicide. She'd been more open and affectionate when Laurent came for a second visit, although she wondered why she didn't have stronger sexual feelings for him or for any of her prior boyfriends. She also noticed herself still feeling angry about his original phone call breaking up with her. Her plan was to continue individual therapy and consider couples therapy when she returned to Belgium. Would it be all right, she asked at the end of the session, if she let me know how things turned out? I told her I would be delighted, and squeezed her hand as she got up to leave.

POSTTERMINATION SYNOPSIS

Although I wouldn't call Sonia's therapy typical—no such case exists in my case load—it does illustrate how college treatments can stop and pick up again unpredictably, and how more than one clinician, in this case, the group leader and I, can work collaboratively with a student. Her case also exhibits the familiar jumble of diversity factors (an international student's adjustment to New York and the English language), family dynamics (the relationship with her mother), personality deficits (renunciation of her feelings and wishes) associated with stunted development (separation and identity problems), and the catalytic jolt of an unforeseen stressor (her boyfriend's phone call).

But most of all, Sonia's case illustrates college psychotherapy's characteristic lightning transition from crisis management to productive exploration. In her initial presentation, Sonia seemed a genuine suicide risk and a poor bet for psychological insight. It appeared dubious whether I could break through her merry facade and make contact with the genuine human being. But the suicidal threat never materialized, and almost from the beginning, she showed curiosity about breaking through her facade, our well-chosen focal theme. In the span of weeks, her manner in my office advanced from emotional inarticulateness and a pleasing falseness, to hesitant emotional expressiveness, to signs of genuine communicativeness. Outside the office, she became more responsive to her boyfriend, enjoyed city strolls without beating herself up for it, set her sights on a more congenial career path, and steeled herself to be real with her mother. More work remained to be done, which she recognized. But in a remarkably short time in treatment she had grasped a fundamental self-defeating pattern and promptly set off in a healthier direction—the kind of results that makes treating students such a distinctive and deeply gratifying experience.

SUMMARY

Although college and graduate students are well suited for psychodynamic psychotherapy, the work is complicated by students' erratic attendance in treatment and by their complex problems, which typically embrace late adolescent-young adult developmental struggles, college pressures, real life stressors, psychopathology, and, more and more in recent years, the particular problems of diverse groups. To bring order to the complexity, therapists should strive to home in on a focal problem area and a focal psychodynamic theme. Even in a few sessions, a directed psychodynamic inquiry can help students surmount their immediate stressors and also start to understand and change fundamental self-defeating patterns.

REFERENCES

Angyal, A. (1965). *Neurosis and treatment: A holistic theory.* New York: Wiley.

Archer, J., Jr., & Cooper, S. (1998). *Counseling and mental health services on campus.* San Francisco: Jossey-Bass.

Blos, P. (1946). Psychological counseling of college students. *American Journal of Orthopsychiatry, 16,* 571–580.

Committee on the College Student of the Group for the Advancement of Psychiatry. (1999). Helping students adapt to graduate school: Making the grade (GAP Report). *Journal of College Student Psychotherapy, 14,* 21–34.

Davanloo, H. (1980). A method of short-term dynamic psychotherapy. In H. Davanloo (Ed.), *Short-term dynamic psychotherapy* (pp. 43–71). New York: Aronson.

Farnsworth, D. L., & Munster, P. K. (1971). The role of the college psychiatrist. In G. B. Blaine, Jr. & C. C. McArthur (Eds.), *Emotional problems of the student* (pp. 1–16). New York: Appleton-Century-Crofts.

Grayson, P. A. (1985). College time: Implications for student mental health services. *Journal of American College Health, 33,* 198–204.

Hanfmann, E. (1978). *Effective therapy for college students.* San Francisco: Jossey-Bass.

Hersh, J. B. (1988). A commentary on brief therapy. *Journal of College Student Psychotherapy, 3,* 55–58.

Luborsky, L. (1984). *Principles of psychoanalytic psychotherapy.* New York: Basic Books.

Malan, D. H. (1976). *The frontier of brief psychotherapy.* New York: Plenum Press.

Mann, J. (1973). *Time-limited psychotherapy.* Cambridge, MA: Harvard University Press.

May, R. (Ed.). (1988). *Psychoanalytic psychotherapy in a college context.* New York: Praeger.

McWilliams, N. (1994). *Psychoanalytic diagnosis.* New York: Guilford Press.

Medalie, J. (1981). The college years as a mini-life cycle: Developmental facts and adaptive options. *Journal of the American College Health Association, 30,* 75–79.

Pine, F. (1990). *Drive, ego, object and self.* New York: Basic Books.

Reinhold, J. E. (1991). The origins and early development of mental health services in American colleges and universities. *Journal of College Student Psychotherapy, 6,* 3–14.

Romney, P., & Goli, M. (1991). Projective identification and eating disorders on a college campus. *Journal of College Student Psychotherapy, 6,* 53–74.

Schafer, R. (1980). *The analytic attitude.* New York: Basic Books.

Schwitzer, A. M. (1997). The inverted pyramid framework applying self psychology constructs to conceptualizing college student psychotherapy. *Journal of College Student Psychotherapy, 11,* 29–47.

Sifneos, P. E. (1979). *Short-term dynamic psychotherapy.* New York: Plenum Press.

Slimak, R. E. (1992). A student development metamodel for university and college counseling center professionals. *Journal of College Student Psychotherapy, 6,* 25–36.

Steenbarger, B. N. (1992). Intentionalizing brief college student psychotherapy. *Journal of College Student Psychotherapy, 7,* 47–62.

Strupp, H. H., & Binder, J. L. (1984). *Psychotherapy in a new key.* New York: Basic Books.

Walter, J. L., & Peller, J. E. (1992). *Becoming solution-focused in brief therapy.* New York: Brunner/Mazel.

Webb, R. E., & Widseth, J. C. (1988). Facilitating students' going into and stepping back from their inner worlds. *Journal of College Student Psychotherapy, 3,* 5–16.

Section Three

PSYCHOTHERAPY WITH ADULTS

Chapter 8   Supportive-Expressive Psychotherapy

Chapter 9   Brief Psychodynamic Therapy

Chapter 10 An Object-Relations Approach to the Treatment of Borderline Patients

Chapter 11 A Relational Approach to Psychotherapy

Chapter 12 Mastering Developmental Issues through Interactional Object-Relations Therapy

Chapter 13 The Activation of Affective Change Processes in Accelerated Experiential-Dynamic Psychotherapy (AEDP)

Chapter 14 Short-Term Dynamic Psychotherapy of Narcissistic Disorders

Chapter 15 A Relational-Feminist Psychodynamic Approach to Sexual Desire

CHAPTER 8

Supportive-Expressive Psychotherapy

Lynne R. Siqueland and Jacques P. Barber

HISTORY OF THE THERAPEUTIC APPROACH

The term supportive-expressive (SE) psychoanalytic psychotherapy was used originally to describe the open-ended, psychoanalytically oriented therapy conducted at the Menninger Foundation (Knight, 1949; Wallerstein, 1986; Wallerstein, Robbins, Sargent, & Luborsky, 1956). As a theoretical orientation, SE is rooted in Freud's work on technique (Freud, 1958a, 1958b, 1958c, 1958d, 1958e, 1958f) and that of some of Freud's main followers in the psychoanalytic tradition (e.g., Bibring, 1954; Fenichel, 1941; Stone, 1951).

SE is a succinct description of dynamic therapy as conceptualized by important theorists, such as Gabbard (1996), who wrote that "the actual interventions used in dynamic therapy and psychoanalysis can be conceptualized on an expressive-supportive continuum" (1994, p. 519). This continuum lies at the root of SE as manualized by Luborsky (1984). SE is a codification of commonly practiced dynamic therapy. In our experience, clinicians readily consider SE a form of dynamic therapy that is not very different from their own therapeutic approach. SE has had a widespread influence on modern dynamic therapy in the United States and abroad (Gabbard, 1994, 1996).

The specific codification of SE developed by Luborsky has been further defined in a series of treatment manuals (Book, 1998; Luborsky, 1984, a revised edition of Luborsky, 1984, is in preparation) that are appropriate for a wide range of patients and conditions. Additional adaptations of SE have been developed for depression (Luborsky & Mark, 1991; Luborsky, Mark, et al., 1995), generalized anxiety-disorder (GAD; Crits-Christoph, Crits-Christoph, Wolf-Palacio, Fichter, & Rudick, 1995), opiate (Luborsky, Woody, Hole, & Velleco, 1995), cocaine dependence (Mark & Faude, 1995, 1998), and avoidant and obsessive compulsive personality disorders (Barber, 1990).

SE manuals do not prescribe therapist interventions on a session-by-session basis, but provide general principles of treatment and guidelines for therapists. This degree of specification is consistent with dynamic therapy's need for the flexible use of techniques as they are relevant to the configuration of defenses and conflictual relationship patterns of each patient. The SE treatment manual for depression, for example, includes specific techniques and issues related to the treatment of depression, such as suicidal risk, helplessness and hopelessness, dealing with loss, anger, and poor capacity to recognize depression. Nevertheless, the SE treatment manual for depression is very similar to the general manual, but with an emphasis on understanding the depressive symptoms in the context of interpersonal/intrapsychic conflicts. In SE, these are called the core conflictual relationship theme (CCRT; Luborsky & Crits-Christoph, 1990, 1998).

THEORETICAL CONSTRUCTS

The CCRT method has been used to assess and study central relationship patterns in SE therapy. It refers specifically to patients' recurrent main wishes (or needs or intentions), main response of others (imagined or real; RO), and patients' response (response of self in terms of feelings, cognitions, or behaviors; RS) in interpersonal relationships. The three components of the CCRT are inferred for each interpersonal interaction the patient describes.

The CCRT, like other similar concepts in other forms of dynamic therapy (e.g., Barber & Crits-Christoph, 1993), serves as a springboard for the therapist's interventions throughout treatment and is developed separately for each patient. In this way, the CCRT is utilized to address the patient's idiosyncratic way of relating, which may or may not be similar to that of other patients. The use of the CCRT enables SE therapists, like some other therapists (e.g., cognitive therapists), to treat patients with a variety of conflicts and disorders. The SE model assumes that gains in self-understanding about the CCRT and subsequent change in the CCRT mediate symptom improvement. Furthermore, these changes are facilitated by the positive therapeutic alliance.

SE and other dynamic therapists try to help patients become aware of their central relationship patterns and how these patterns are associated with their symptoms. The CCRT (Luborsky & Crits-Christoph, 1990) refers to patients' characteristic interpersonal and intrapsychic conflicts. The CCRT has received substantial empirical support (see reviews by Barber & Crits-Christoph, 1993; Luborsky, Barber, & Crits-Christoph, 1990; Luborsky & Crits-Christoph, 1998) and has been employed for many years in clinical work. Clinicians can define a specific CCRT for each patient coming for treatment, without necessarily having a preconception of the CCRT ahead of time. Patients' self-understanding (greater insight) of their CCRT and changes in the CCRT are hypothesized to mediate changes in symptoms. The mechanism of change and treatment techniques are discussed in further detail later in this chapter.

Some of the central concepts of SE, such as transference, insight, interpretation, and the therapeutic alliance, can be traced back to earlier generations of psychoanalytic theorists and clinicians:

Luborsky (1990) has compared the Freudian (1958b) observations on *transference* and the CCRT and found that the two concepts share much in common. However, the specific operationalization of transference in the SE model in the form of the CCRT (wishes, ROs, and RSs) is original to Luborsky (1977).

With the introduction of Freud's structural model, the goal of psychoanalysis, *insight,* changed from making the unconscious conscious to emphasizing the integration of intrapsychic structure. In SE therapy, understanding the interrelations of the CCRT components and the connections between these components and symptoms in current and past relationships is the main focus of treatment.

Insight or self-understanding is achieved by therapists' repetitive *interpretations* of interpersonal themes across situations and across relationships (working through). Especially important in SE, but not necessary, is the interpretation of the transference. Working through of the transference is used to help patients understand how early relationships distort their present relationships, including the relationship with the therapist. SE therapists follow traditional short-term dynamic therapists' (e.g., Malan, 1976) recommendations of interpreting components of the interpersonal themes in the three apexes of the triangle of insight (present relationships, transference, and past or parental relationships). In SE, interpretations are guided by the CCRT formulation and the interpretations target the components. Studies have explored the accuracy of therapists' interpersonal interventions (i.e., the extent to which the therapist addresses the interpersonal patterns that have been identified by independent judges to be salient for each patient). Crits-Christoph, Cooper, and Luborsky (1988) showed that accurate interpretation of the primary CCRT wishes (W) and ROs was significantly related to good outcome in a sample of neurotic patients treated with SE, even after controlling for the effects of general errors in technique and the quality of the therapeutic alliance. Delivering expressive techniques (i.e., interpretations) in a competent manner (Barber, Crits-Christoph, & Luborsky, 1996) was associated with lower depression in SE, controlling for patient severity, quality of the therapeutic alliance, and delivery of supportive techniques. More recent research indicates that accurate interpretations of the CCRT predict change in depression over the first eight weeks of cognitive therapy for depression, and also predict retention in cognitive therapy for opiate addiction (Crits-Christoph et al., 1996). Considering another aspect of the impact of accurately interpreting the CCRT, Crits-Christoph, Barber, and Kurcias (1993) showed that therapist accuracy in addressing interpersonal themes facilitated the development or maintenance of a positive therapeutic alliance (another variable central to change in SE) over the course of treatment. These findings are particularly important because they document that the alliance is not an unchangeable patient characteristic, but that therapists' actions do indeed impact the alliance, opening the door for further research on specific attempts to improve the alliance through altering therapist actions. In addition, this research suggests that supportive and expressive techniques do not conflict with each other but instead enrich each other.

The concept of the alliance used in SE has a rich history in psychoanalytic writings. For example, Greenson's (1965) concept of the working alliance and Zetzel's (1958) concept of the therapeutic alliance contributed to Luborsky's (1976) concept of the helping alliance. But, in contrast to many Freudians who saw the alliance as a background for transference interpretation, Luborsky views the alliance as curative. There is a substantial body of empirical evidence indicating that a good alliance predicts positive treatment outcome (Horvath & Symonds, 1991).

METHODS OF ASSESSMENT AND INTERVENTION

Assessment

Assessment is usually done through clinical interview, as in standard practice. The therapist collects information in the first sessions about the patient's background, current living and social situation, presenting problem, history of psychological difficulties, and past treatment. The case formulation also evolves over the course of the first few sessions by reviewing patient narratives to develop the CCRT. Either therapist notes, case material, or transcripts can be used to develop the CCRT. The case formulation based on the CCRT serves as the basis for intervention and is modified as new data are provided by the patient over the course of therapy.

When SE therapy is used in research settings, a patient typically receives a full structured diagnostic interview with a separate clinical evaluator prior to meeting with the therapist. Luborsky and Crits-Christoph (1990) have described the Relationship Anecdotes Paradigm (RAP), a semistructured interview used to gather narratives from which a CCRT can be created. Patients are asked to tell about specific and meaningful events that involved them with another person; they are asked to provide specific information about the place and time of the event and what happened and was said during that incident. Patients are asked to tell 10 of these interactions involving diverse people. It has been found that RAP narratives told prior to treatment are very similar to narratives told in the first sessions of therapy (Barber, Luborsky, Crits-Christoph, & Diguer, 1995).

INTERVENTION

What Changes in SE Therapy?
The Principles of Psychoanalytic Psychotherapy: A Manual of Supportive-Expressive Therapy (Luborsky, 1984) serves as the foundation for CCRT-based therapy or SE psychodynamic psychotherapy. This general manual is currently under revision by Luborsky; other authors have expanded or modified the work for specific patient populations (see below). In the general manual, Luborsky (1984) suggests that there are specific changes that occur in SE therapy. First, the patient comes to an increased understanding of the core conflictual relationship problems and symptoms. This understanding leads to changes in symptoms and "greater mastery over deleterious expressions of the CCRT and changes in some components of the CCRT (e.g., responses of other or self)" (p. 16). Second, the patient has an increased sense of an ally in the struggle to overcome aspects of self-defeating CCRT problems through the helping alliance with the therapist. Third, the patient leaves therapy with an internalized mastery of the CCRT patterns by both internalizing the image of the supportive therapist and internalizing and being able to use the understanding of the CCRT outside of the therapy room.

Beginning Phase of Treatment
The beginning stage involves setting the goals and establishing the therapy arrangements. The therapist works with patients over the first few sessions to establish the goals of treatment, which usually focus on the alleviation of symptoms. Some patients start with an interpersonal focus, seeking help specifically for difficulties in interpersonal relationships. The therapist works to ground the symptoms within an interpersonal framework by summarizing recent or past interactions when symptoms arose.

Another therapist task is to explain the treatment process or how treatment works. A number of researchers have found that informing or even educating patients about the treatment process can aid in retention in or satisfaction with treatment (e.g., Hoehn-Saric et al., 1964). Many patients are uncertain of what therapy entails and often expect advice or more directive treatment than is offered in dynamic therapy. Patients need to be advised that they will take the lead in determining the course and content of the session. In addition, a therapist goal is to aid patients in developing their own understanding of their problems, leading to patient-generated solutions rather than telling the patient what to do. The therapist can also tell patients that they will be focusing on interpersonal relationships. The Luborsky (1984) manual contains a socialization script that can be used for these purposes. Finally, the therapist clarifies the treatment arrangements as to where, when, and how frequently sessions will occur. It is crucial in short-term treatment that the patient understands the number of sessions and time constraints for the treatment. This needs to be stated clearly in the first session, and the patient needs to be reminded throughout treatment about the time and sessions remaining.

Early and Middle Phases of Treatment
  Eliciting Narratives. The CCRT provides the basis for the interpretive work and requires that patients be able to tell stories about their interpersonal relationships and to come to understand their stories. Some patients tell clear and rich stories of their interpersonal interactions. With other patients, many details and depth are missing. With each narrative, the therapist is listening for what the patient wished, needed, or wanted out of the interaction (Wish-W), how the patient perceived that the other person responded to this need (RO), and what the patient's response was in the interaction or afterward (RS). The therapist needs to listen for what is missing. Patients' narratives can have deficits in a number of areas that are related to their current difficulties and these give therapists cues to targets of intervention. Does the therapist know or understand what the patient wished to get out of the interaction? Does the patient even know what he or she wished for? Does the patient have conflicting or even irreconcilable wishes (e.g., to be close, and to not open self up for fear of hurt)?

The RO focuses on what the patient perceived about the others' response, not what actually happened. When the patient describes what the other person did or said, does the therapist have the same interpretation of the RO as the patient? Was the other person rejecting, as the patient describes, or distracted or not attentive? The level of discrepancy in interpretations is indicative of the patient's difficulties and might lead to different treatment strategies. Are the other people in the patient's life hurtful or rejecting, and does the therapist need to help the patient question why he or she stays engaged with these people? Or is the patient actually receiving positive responses from others but unable to recognize this or take it in? Is it clear how the RS follows from the described interaction? For example, does the patient internalize the rejection of others by deciding that he or she is no good, becoming self-critical and depressed? Or does the patient become either appropriately angry or assertive about his or her needs not being met? Or does the patient externalize and blame others, rather than recognizing his or her part in the interaction? Each of these areas would lead to potential different foci of intervention.

Therapists can help patients tell better stories with the goal that patients come to a clearer understanding of what is happening in their interpersonal interactions. Books by Mark and Faude (1998) and Book (1998) provide helpful suggestions on working with patients to develop narratives. Some of this is quite straightforward and is described here. The therapist can explicitly ask the patient: What were you hoping would happen in this situation? What did you want from this person? What were you expecting would happen? If there is a lack of detail, the therapist can help by asking these kinds of questions: What did you say or do? Then what happened? The therapist works with the patient to generate both curiosity and a level of reflection about interpersonal interactions. For a very anxious patient, the therapist may have to help slow the patient down. The therapist can say: "It is really important that I understand both what you were feeling and what happened, so I am going to ask you some questions to be sure I have it right." The therapist can ask about the ROs: "What did the other person do or say that let you know he or she was not interested or didn't care? How could you tell?" For the RS, the therapist can ask patients how they got to that particular mood or state: "You say that your boss inappropriately said you did something wrong that was not your responsibility. How did you end up depressed and down on yourself?" Many times, the links between events are missing. The therapist notices that the story does not make sense and can gently point out these missing pieces to patients.

Supportive Techniques of Treatment. Luborsky (1984) discusses the importance of establishing a relationship of rapport and trust with clients and lists several techniques or strategies for creating and maintaining this helping alliance. These techniques include conveying a sense of understanding and acceptance of the patient and developing a liking for the patient. The supportive element forms the foundation of trust that allows for the expressive work and, as research suggests, is curative on its own.

The importance of a focus on patient's goals as part of the alliance is also stressed by Luborsky (1984). He suggests that therapists can build a strong alliance through a number of different approaches related to goals of treatment:

(1) Convey through words and manner support for the patient's wish to achieve the goals of treatment. (2) Communicate a realistically hopeful attitude that the treatment goals are likely to be achieved. (3) Recognize, on appropriate occasions, that the patient has made some progress toward the goals. (pp. 82–89)

Further, he suggests that maintaining an awareness of patient goals, checking in regularly with patients about their goals for treatment, and noting steps in progress toward goals are part of providing a supportive environment.

Luborsky (1984) highlights the importance of establishing a "we bond," creating a sense that therapist and patient are a team to help the patient address the difficulties that brought the patient to treatment. The therapist promotes this bond by the techniques described above as well as the following: "(1) Convey recognition of patient's growing ability to do what the therapist does in using the basic tools of treatment. (2) Refer to experiences that the patient and therapist have been through together" (pp. 88–89).

The therapist points out instances in which patients use their growing understanding in and outside of therapy. Early in treatment, this can simply be a growing awareness of problematic ways of relating. This awareness often first arises after interactions are over; later, patients become aware of their responses during the interaction. This ability to recognize both typical feelings and behavior "at the moment" allows patients more opportunity for control and alternative ways of coping.

Expressive Techniques of Treatment. The primary purpose of the CCRT is to provide a case formulation that guides therapist interpretations. The interpretations follow directly from the CCRT. The therapist listens for and responds to narratives from the "relationship triad": current relationships, family of origin, and the therapist. The therapist determines from the current material what aspect of the CCRT is most relevant. Often, early in treatment, interpretations simply relate two components of the CCRT formulation. The interpretation could include a wish-RO; for example, "You went to your husband hoping he would validate your feelings, but you experienced that he was not even interested in hearing what you had to say." In contrast, a RO-RS example might be: "When you felt your husband ignored you, you became depressed and withdrew from talking to him." Later, the therapist could put these pieces together in one interpretation: "You went to your husband hoping for validation, and when he did not seem to be listening, you became sad and decided not to try to continue to talk to him." The therapist might also help the patient to make the link between RO and RS; for example, "It sounds like when he wasn't paying attention, you decided your feelings weren't important enough without his acknowledgment, so you just sort of gave up but then felt quite alone." Many times, patients have two conflicting wishes, for example, wanting to be close and wanting to protect themselves from hurt.

The therapist tries to help the patient understand how the symptom is linked to the core conflictual relationship pattern. The symptom is usually one of the RSs. Especially early in treatment, symptoms are framed as coping attempts. The symptoms may have been the way the patient learned to master relationship conflicts. One of the goals of therapy is to explore whether these coping strategies are still needed and to consider other solutions that may be less painful and self-defeating or more helpful.

The therapist is also gauging how complex an interpretation should be made based on the patient's responsiveness. As in all dynamic treatment, either patient agreement/recognition or the production of more material or emotion guides whether the therapist proceeds or pulls back. From the first session on, the therapist can offer "trial interpretations" to assess the patient's level of awareness or understanding and ability to use the therapist's interpretations. Some patients have a clear and pervasive pattern that affects most relationships. Others may have one pattern that is most clearly linked to the symptoms for which they seek treatment. Others may do quite well in certain contexts, such as work or friendships, and have a problematic interaction only in their intimate relationships. Indeed, Crits-Christoph and Luborsky (1990a) have shown a significant decrease in the degree of pervasiveness of the relational themes by the end of treatment. Interestingly, the pervasiveness of wishes remained unchanged, while the pervasiveness of ROs and RSs decreased. Furthermore, change in pervasiveness was associated with change in symptoms.

The goals of SE are an increased understanding of problematic interpersonal patterns as well as mastery over these cycles. These two outcomes are believed to lead to change in symptoms because problematic cycles are maintaining symptoms. Change is believed to come about by mastery of the CCRT in a number of ways. Patients become more explicit and clear about their wishes and needs, becoming aware and asking for what they want; therefore, the ROs are more likely to be positive and congruent with the patient's wishes. Book (1998) has expanded discussion of the wish component by differentiating between regressive and progressive wishes: "Regressive wishes have to do with desires to destroy, mutilate or be sadistic, or they represent desires to be overly dependent or retreat and isolate oneself from others" (p. 51). The therapist does not help patients actualize such wishes; instead, Book suggests that regressive wishes need to be reframed as a RS, and the therapist needs to work with the patient to identify the unarticulated progressive wish. The progressive wish can take many forms but often involves the wish to make contact, to be in control, and to be respected; the regressive wish is a response to not having the progressive wish met.

Change also occurs in many treatments related to the ROs. For some patients, the expected ROs are clearly transferential because they are based on or biased by early childhood experiences. The therapist helps the patient to elucidate the connection between past and current experiences. Patients can become lost in trying to repair past relationships that are unlikely to change because loyalty keeps them trapped in deleterious patterns. Patients often may wait and continue to wish that significant others in their life will finally care, understand, or respond in a particular way. Instead, patients may need to grieve over these missed opportunities or experiences and understand how these experiences impact their current relationships. Other patients need to become aware that they are choosing people who cannot respond positively or meet their needs. At times, patients provoke others to respond to them as their parents responded in the past.

Much of the therapy work involves patients becoming aware and taking responsibility for self-defeating patterns. The therapist works with the patient to understand whether the expected RO and RS are still necessary or useful.

What is most likely to change is patients' RSs, either because patients become clearer about what they want, or they understand how others' interactions affect them. This understanding either leads to change in the interactions themselves or to change in how patients perceive themselves related to the interactions. RSs have both affective and behavioral components; patients come to either feel differently, behave differently, or both. They begin to differentiate themselves from others' perceptions or question others' perceptions if these conflict with their own experience. They learn to hold onto what they know or understand of themselves in the face of others' reactions. Research in SE treatment (Crits-Christoph & Luborsky, 1990a) has suggested that wishes do not change significantly with treatment perhaps because some of the most common wishes are fundamental to the human experience (wishes to be close, to be accepted). However, RSs do change, as do perceived ROs (Crits-Christoph & Luborsky, 1990a).

Identifying the Level of Supportive and Expressive Techniques. An SE approach attempts to be flexible and adaptive to most types of patients by determining the level of supportive versus expressive techniques that are optimal for each patient. Rather than using an exclusively interpretive or confrontational model, the therapist actually helps patients to maintain useful defenses or coping techniques that bolster their level of functioning. With most patients, a therapist expects, at least in theory, to move from using more supportive techniques in earlier sessions to employing more expressive techniques as trust and rapport develop over time. The therapist always tries to point out when patients ignore or do not discuss certain topics or emotions and to understand the discomfort associated with expressing oneself. However, patients' ability to make use of interpretive or expressive techniques evolves and changes over the course of treatment and sometimes even within sessions. Therefore, the therapist is continually evaluating and assessing how much the patient can take in. Indeed, tact and timing of dynamic therapy are the most difficult aspects to articulate and teach.

We have found Wachtel's (1993) discussion of accusatory and facilitative interpretations very helpful in both teaching SE therapy and defining good expressive or interpretive work. Wachtel suggests that patients become "defensive" or unable to respond positively to interpretations because so many times, interpretations seem to convey that the patient has been caught doing or saying something he or she should not. Wachtel suggests that instead, interpretations should be permission-granting, giving patients the message that it is okay to be more accepting of a part of their experience that they have been afraid to acknowledge. These permission-granting interpretations address the patient's fear about the expression of feelings and help the patient to question whether hiding or denial is necessary. In his book, Wachtel gives examples of both types of interpretations and offers examples of how to say things differently.

Finally, Connolly, Crits-Christoph, Shappell, Barber, and Luborsky (1998) have provided one of the first descriptions of SE treatment in practice and how it differs from traditional psychoanalytic therapy. They examined therapist interventions in sessions 2 to 4 of a short-term (16 sessions) SE treatment for depression. In general, therapists were quite active, averaging 125 statements per session, indicating that they were speaking about half the time. On average, 5 therapist statements per session were interpretations focused primarily on the patient's parents, significant others, and self. Here, interpretations had a relatively broad definition that included both statements that linked past and current experiences and statements that explain possible reasons for thoughts, feelings, or behaviors. Only 5% of interpretations focused on the patient's childhood past, and only one interpretation per session focused on the therapist-patient relationship. Therefore, in the time-limited version of SE, the treatment is focused more on the present and intensive exploration of the therapist-patient transference is limited.

Termination

Termination has different implications and course in an open-ended versus time-limited treatment format. Often in open-ended treatment, the patient has control over when termination occurs and it usually coincides with improvement in symptoms or presenting problem. In time-limited treatment, however, patients may feel that therapy stops before they are ideally ready. In either format, the goal of termination of treatment is for the patient to internalize both the image of the therapist as helper and the tools of treatment so that progress can continue after active treatment ends.

In addition, termination often leads to working through the CCRT as it pertains to the therapist (the transference), if this has not occurred previously in the treatment. Whereas the therapist may have been perceived as caring and supportive for most of the treatment, the therapist can be viewed, if not worked through, during this phase as another person who abandons or disappoints (ROs) the patient. The therapist helps by linking the feelings of termination to the CCRT pattern that has been addressed in its other forms. Luborsky, Mark, et al. (1995) suggest that termination is about attachment and separation. As these authors suggest, " The first part of treatment shows the fears and satisfactions of making an attachment; the second part shows the fears and satisfactions of the impending separation" (p. 30). The concern is that the patient will not be able to cope with the loss of the therapist and that all gains of therapy will be erased as well. Often, there is an exacerbation of symptoms around the time of termination, as if patients were testing their ability to manage independently. The therapist can help normalize this experience. The goal of termination is for patients to realize that they possess the tools of therapy, and they use these tools to work through the likely resurgence of symptoms during the termination period.

In short-term treatments, patients may have to accept that only some of the goals they had for treatment have been achieved or that they now have the tools to continue the therapy work on their own. Often, the time limit of short-term treatment motivates patients to progress faster than with open-ended work. The goal of the termination is to help patients summarize the work that has come before, understand their CCRT pattern, and review how they have broken the cycle of the pattern.

MAJOR SYNDROMES, SYMPTOMS, AND PROBLEMS TREATED

There is evidence supporting the efficacy of SE in its open-ended form (Luborsky, Crits-Christoph, Mintz, & Auerbach, 1988) with a diverse sample of patients. Modifications to the basic SE model and treatment manuals have been designed for depression, anxiety, and substance abuse. A chapter describing the modifications made to the original SE treatment and basic dynamic themes for each type of patient can be found in Barber and Crits-Christoph (1995) on dynamic therapies for Axis I disorders. Luborsky's writings on depression (Luborsky, Mark, et al., 1995) focus on nine themes that are the focus of treatment: patient's sense of helplessness, vulnerability to disappointment and loss, states of anger turned inward, vulnerability of self-esteem, suicidal ideation and intention, pessimistic explanatory style, poor capacity to recognize the state of depression, and events that trigger depression, and inclination to expect negative responses from self and other. The chapter on GAD (Crits-Christoph et al., 1995) targets the role of insecure/conflicted attachment and past traumas in the development of the disorder. In addition, this treatment targets the role of worry, hypothesized to be a defensive reaction that allows patients to avoid more difficult emotional and interpersonal issues. Data supporting the efficacy of SE for depression (Diguer, Barber & Luborsky, 1993; Luborsky, Diguer, et al., 1996) and GAD are available (Crits-Christoph, Connolly, Azarian, Crits-Christoph, & Shappell, 1996), with recent randomized data directly comparing GAD to a reflective listening (supportive therapy) recently completed (Crits-Christoph, personal communication). Two additional open trials of SE were conducted by Barber, Morse, Krakauer, Chittams, & Crits-Christoph (1997) over a period of 52 once-a-week sessions for patients with avoidant and obsessive-compulsive personality disorders. Treatment emphasized the explorations of the CCRT and focused on defense analysis, transference interpretations, and increasing the ego-dystonicity of dysfunctional ego-syntonic behaviors. Preliminary results of these trials indicated that patients with obsessive-compulsive disorder were more likely than the avoidant patients to not meet personality diagnosis at the end of treatment.

The modifications of SE for substance abuse have been tested in three randomized clinical trials. Luborsky, Woody, et al. (1995) describe its modifications for opiate dependence. Two psychotherapies, SE and cognitive therapy (CT), were added to methadone maintenance for opiate addicts. Patients receiving SE and CT showed greater improvement and benefit in more areas than patients receiving standard drug counseling. Patients with comorbid psychiatric problems benefited most from the addition of the psychotherapies (Woody, Luborsky, McLellan, & O'Brien, 1990; Woody et al., 1983). These benefits were found mostly in areas of functioning other than drug use. The efficacy for SE for opiate addicts was also replicated in a community sample (Woody, McLellan, Luborsky, & O'Brien, 1995).

SE therapy has been modified for cocaine-dependent patients (Mark & Faude, 1995, 1998). The primary modifications include a more active role for the therapist, helping the patient develop complete and coherent narratives, addressing the patient's diminished capacity to experience and reflect due to continued drug use, interpreting the drug use as both a RS and a wish, and working with enactments between patient and therapist (Mark & Faude, 1995). SE for cocaine dependence was tested in the NIDA Cocaine Collaborative Treatment Study, a multisite psychotherapy outcome study. All treatments significantly reduced cocaine use, and SE was not significantly different in efficacy from CT. However, in this study, both psychotherapies were less effective on drug use outcome than individual drug counseling (Crits-Christoph et al., 1999).

Manualized standardized clinical trials of SE without control conditions are ongoing in several places in the world for both Axis I and Axis II conditions. These include Toronto, Sydney, and Stockholm in addition to the United States.

CASE EXAMPLE

Diagnosis and Assessment

Presenting Problem
Lori was a 25-year-old white female who sought treatment due to feeling inhibited and uncomfortable in her sexual relationship with her husband. (Some details of patient history have been modified to protect confidentiality.) She felt little desire for sex and while engaged in sexual activities felt "far away and distant" (RS). She had hoped these feelings would have disappeared with time; however, she had been with her husband for three years and the feelings had not changed. Interestingly, there were few problems in the sexual relationship when the couple first became sexually intimate, but difficulties increased as they began a more serious, committed relationship. Lori had only been married three months at the time of intake but had been living with her now husband for

about three years, and they had a 2-month-old daughter.

In addition to the sexual difficulties, Lori described struggling with an eating disorder, restricting food to maintain a set weight and being "fixated on not getting fat." She had lost a good deal of weight and was once hospitalized at an eating disorders program. This was complicated by an undiagnosed gastrointestinal disorder that caused severe pain. Once diagnosed and put on medication, she did not lose more weight and ate more appropriately, but Lori still had body preoccupation and restricted her intake. In addition, she described a long-standing coping style of not dealing with issues, not wanting to think about feelings, and avoiding conflict (wishes), especially anger, by blocking it out.

Background Information
Lori was the youngest of four children. Her father was a successful businessman who also suffered from bipolar disorder and alcoholism. At the time of intake, he was quite ill with cancer. Her father was described as very critical and "mean" to all family members, especially when intoxicated. Her mother was a homemaker; Lori described her as passive and trying to please her father. She described the family as close, all living within a few blocks of each other. Lori lived 30 minutes away and the family commented on "how far away" she was. Her parents were in their 60s, and Lori had some caretaking responsibilities, such as handling their legal and other paperwork. None of the other siblings was reported to suffer from depression or any other mental health problems. Lori's husband was a professional and 16 years older than she. She had met him while working as his assistant and continued to work with him in his business. At the time of their meeting, he was married; they began dating when he separated from his wife.

Lori related her current sexual difficulties to an experience of sexual molestation when she was age 10 by her father's best friend, who was also the family doctor. She had been invited over to play with her doctor's son, who was not there when she arrived. The family doctor took her to a room and fondled her and penetrated her with his finger and asked/made her to fondle him. Lori told her mother about the incident (it was unclear whether she did so at the time or several months later), who believed her enough to never leave her alone again with the doctor. However, the mother asked that Lori continue to see him as the family doctor because her mother thought it would be too upsetting to Lori's father to hear what his friend had done. Lori's father was not told about the molestation at the time of the incident.

Approximately one year prior to starting treatment, Lori, with the support of her brother and husband, confronted this doctor about what he had done. She went to his office and read him a letter she had drafted discussing the impact of his actions on her and his responsibility for hurting her. The doctor did not deny her allegations, but she did not wait to hear his reply after reading her letter aloud. When her father was finally told of the incident, he was totally supportive of his daughter and cut off all contact with his long-time friend. After this confrontation, Lori felt less angry about the incident and thought about it less, but her sexual life remained affected. At session 4, she brought in a newspaper article stating that this doctor had lost his license because of medical malpractice due to fraud. She reported satisfaction that he was no longer practicing and was publicly humiliated.

Previous Treatment
Lori had sought therapy twice before. She claimed to remember nothing about the first therapy that lasted one or two sessions. The second therapy was with a female therapist she had starting seeing two years before this therapy. She was in therapy for about five months, but then stopped because she didn't feel she was "getting much response or suggestions" from the therapist. She returned six months

later for another six months and then stopped when she had her baby. Lori was due to return after the birth of her baby but never called the therapist back. She decided she needed to seek another therapist because she felt her prior therapist was uncomfortable talking about her sexuality and the past abuse experience and this was inhibiting her progress.

Diagnosis

Hypoactive Sexual Desire Disorder.

Anxiety Disorder Not Otherwise Specified.

Rule out eating disorder (Anorexia or Bulimia).

TREATMENT

Beginning Treatment and Establishing Treatment Goals

As part of orienting the patient to treatment, Lori and her therapist reviewed the expectations and parameters for treatment, including weekly sessions. Given Lori's past history in therapy and her ambivalence, the therapist and she made a contract for 10 sessions. They agreed to the goal of a focus on Lori's discomfort in the sexual relationship with her husband and to gaining understanding of the relation of these difficulties to the past trauma. Despite these preparations, Lori had a difficult time engaging in treatment. She came to the first two sessions, but a month elapsed between the second and third sessions because of cancellations.

Establishing the Alliance and Supportive Component

Given Lori's concerns about her past therapy, the therapist attempted to provide a warm, supportive environment where Lori had control about what was discussed and when. Lori was clearly anxious in the sessions, talked very rapidly, rarely allowing the therapist a chance to comment. She also shared quite a lot of very personal information about sexuality in the first sessions. This was uncomfortable for her, but she felt "she had to get it out." The therapist encouraged Lori to set her own pace and to decide what she felt comfortable sharing. Lori reported "frustration" at having to start over in therapy and the impact of this problem on her life. The therapist empathized with her frustration and provided encouragement and hope that their work together would lead to improvement.

As part of the alliance-building portion, the therapist also checked in with Lori regularly on two issues: Did Lori perceive the therapist as open and receptive to discussing the sexual difficulties and did she feel able to discuss her problems with the therapist? Was treatment addressing the issues and goals she had for the therapy? Lori reported feeling much more comfortable with the current therapist and felt the therapist could "handle" what she had to say. Lori said she had already found talking to the therapist helpful.

Lori seemed even more anxious in session 3, in which she read aloud the letter she had written to the doctor when she confronted him a year earlier. Despite Lori's anxiety, the therapist viewed this willingness to share the letter as a sign of her growing trust in the therapist. However, Lori reported that she often could not remember what was talked about in session and sometimes had an upset stomach after it was over. Lori was aware of her confusion and tendency to block out thinking about difficult issues. She asked to come to sessions every two weeks rather than weekly. The therapist agreed to this arrangement after discussing her concerns that Lori was having difficulty getting started in treatment and Lori's reported frustration that things were not progressing quickly enough.

Expressive Element

The therapist also used these initial sessions to gather relationship episodes to formulate the CCRT. Lori told stories about her current relationship with her husband, past and current relationship with her mother and father, and her experience with the doctor who molested her. In general, Lori had difficulty identifying and articulating her wishes and paying attention to how she felt or responded to other people's actions. Early sessions then focused on elucidating her wishes and helping her attend to her internal states and reactions to others. However, a preliminary CCRT was identified that could be modified as treatment progressed and as Lori provided more detailed narratives (see Table 8.1). In general, she viewed her husband as very supportive and understanding. Her husband asked her to tell him what she liked or disliked in their sexual relationship and said he would honor her wishes and work with her. However, Lori had decided to never say no to her husband's requests for sex. She was afraid if she began to do so, she and her husband would never have sex because she never wanted it. Lori reported a long history of criticism by her father and feeling that nothing was ever good enough. By contrast, she currently felt quite close to and supported by her mother. However, Lori also saw her mother sacrifice her own and her daughter's needs for the father, most obviously regarding the abuse incident. Lori claimed that her mother was the one who taught her how to block out what she felt or to pretend things were okay because her mother was an expert at doing this.

Case Formulation and Treatment Approach Selected

As stated, the case formulation is based on the CCRT. In turn, the CCRT provides the targets for intervention. The SE approach was chosen based on the interpersonal nature of the presenting problem and the patient's wish for increased understanding of this problematic interpersonal cycle and her own feelings.

Initial Phase of Treatment. The therapist made the first CCRT interpretations from narratives told thus far. The therapist discussed Lori's wish to be close and to trust but also reviewed important experiences where Lori felt that her

Table 8.1 Preliminary CCRT based on early narratives.

	Wish	Response of Other	Response of Self
Husband	To be close, intimate.	Wants and provides intimacy.	Close and loving in many ways.
	To provide for husband's needs.	Insists needs met (sex) despite wife's lack of desire.	Passive compliance.
			Withdrawal, distance.
Doctor	To trust.	Betray trust.	Anger.
	To be cared for.	Abuse and molest her.	Withdrawal.
			Forget or block out.
			Experience self as damaged.
			Intrusive memories.
Father	To be close.	Keep at distance.	Withdrawal.
	To be accepted.	Critical.	Argues back.
			Guilt at distance.
Mother	To be close.	Also close, available.	Feels close, connected.
	To be cared for.	Loving.	Loving.
		Sacrificed daughter's needs to husband.	Anger.
			Model's mother's style of "blocking out."

trust had been betrayed (most obviously, by her doctor). Even when she did not feel betrayed, Lori experienced others (mother and past therapist) as not understanding her or putting their own needs before hers. In general, Lori coped by withdrawing and pretending everything was okay, or by not clearly stating what she needed and sacrificing to others' needs. The therapist suggested that these experiences might make therapy difficult for Lori despite her desires to be involved in treatment. Lori and her therapist discussed ways these past experiences were impacting her intimate relationship with her husband based on expectations Lori now brought to her relationships about intimacy and control. Therapy was offered as a place of her own that was private, and the goal was to focus on herself in contrast to most of her experiences.

Lori came to sessions regularly for the next two sessions but then two months elapsed between the fifth and sixth session. She had gone on vacation for one to two weeks and her father had been in and out of the hospital, with uncertainty each time about whether he would recover from cancer. With both her father's illness and her sexual difficulties, Lori was trying to cope with blocking her feelings out, stating that she was "sick of thinking so much." She reported that with all that was happening, she could not make a commitment to come regularly. The therapist and she discussed her usual style of coping by shutting down when overwhelmed and her tendency to sacrifice herself to others' needs. The therapist recommended that she continue to come to treatment regularly but also stated that Lori would have to decide what she needed. In the sessions that she did attend, Lori began to talk about feeling anger at her husband regarding sexual issues. She did not understand how she could feel that way about him when he was not doing anything. During these sessions, Lori would often lose her train of thought or not be able to remember what the therapist had said. This was particularly noticeable when asked about her feelings of anger.

Middle Phase of Treatment. After treatment had been going on for six months with only about eight sessions, Lori asked if her husband could come in too. She wanted her therapist to meet her husband and she wanted him to give his perspective on the situation. Given the interpersonal nature of the presenting problem and Lori's request, the therapist agreed to meet with him for one session with Lori also attending. Prior to the session, the therapist discussed what Lori felt comfortable sharing about herself and about the therapy work. In the session, Lori's husband spoke about his growing frustration with the sexual problem and his concern about his wife's commitment to treatment. He clearly seemed to care about his wife and have empathy about the impact of her past trauma and experiences with her family of origin on her current difficulties. He expressed his willingness to help. However, one of the husband's other goals was clearly to "check out the therapist" and express his feelings about lack of progress. He also talked about his concerns about the viability of the relationship if problems did not improve. The therapist stressed that Lori was working in treatment, that the problem was interpersonal, and that it would be important for the husband to allow some time to address the issue without his threatening to leave the relationship.

Lori began coming regularly after this session with her husband, although she was often late. She had felt fine about how the joint session had gone and thanked the therapist for her willingness to have the session. She stated that she had been anxious throughout the session that the therapist might share something she considered private. In many ways, this session served to build the helping alliance and enact the CCRT. Lori was able to express her wish for the therapist to meet with her husband and the therapist met this request. In addition, the therapist proved trustworthy about respecting her privacy and not sacrificing Lori's needs to her husband. (Lori had a positive RO to her more explicit wish and the therapist did not react in the expected negative RO by abusing Lori's trust or sacrificing her needs.) Perhaps not surprisingly given her usual coping style, Lori had not remembered that her husband said he considered leaving the relationship. The therapist and Lori discussed the possible parallel between feeling forced to be in therapy by her husband as she felt forced to have sex even though she did not desire it (repetition of the issue in the transference). At the conclusion of the tenth session, Lori stated that she felt comfortable with the relationship, had found therapy helpful, and wanted to continue without a set contract for number of sessions.

Lori became more engaged in and committed to therapy. She began to talk in sessions specifically about not wanting to enjoy sex, began to remember what was talked about in sessions, and related things week to week more frequently. She also began to talk about some decrease in anger and tension in the sexual relationship. Lori began to talk about the disadvantage inherent in her coping style of blocking things out, in that she had trouble remembering good things as well as bad. Below, we provide some excerpts from session 15 to illustrate the expanded CCRT for this patient and ways of working with the CCRT in session. To begin, Lori and the therapist discuss Lori's father being in the hospital ill with cancer:

LORI: Yeah um, um, my father in the hospital again on Monday and again on Friday and it's so screwed up. I mean it gets you in such a turmoil because this is a man you love and he has his pants on backwards and all this other stuff got to put him in the hospital and can't talk. But they said, you know we're concerned that he's not going to come out of this. And it's like you know you go, okay is this something you'd prepared for, is this something's going to happen and then he comes home he's fine. It's funny because it's solely true that if he's calling me sweetie he's still sick and if he's miserable he's back.

THERAPIST: You were telling me about that.

LORI: It's like so backwards and you know like the doctor had said to me, well how does he seem to you? And I said well he's still calling her sweetie, my mom, or honey, so that's a pretty given answer right there that you know he's still not better. Oh, yeah, he's so loveable when he's sick, very sweet very you know, he needs help to do this and you feel like helping him.

THERAPIST: That must be so confusing when you feel closer to him when he is ill than . . .

LORI: And it's like, when I first found out he was in the hospital I didn't go over to see him until like Thursday and then I was going over this tremendous guilt by not going to see him but I didn't want to face all that because I knew he wasn't getting any better. I just didn't want to deal with it but then I was overloaded with guilt. You know I called him every day but then I was overloaded with guilt that I didn't go and see him. So I only ended up seeing him once he got out yesterday but because I can't.

Here is the CCRT for the father derived from this segment. This CCRT is similar to the working CCRT, with the added dimension of Lori dealing with her father's likely death.

W: Desire closeness and interaction with father.

To avoid contact or conflict.

RO: Father will act in way that will make her angry.

Be critical or cruel.

Not recognize her being there because of illness.

Father is nice to her only when he is sick.

RS: Avoid interaction.
Denial of feelings.
Guilt.
Confusion.

The therapist then tries to help Lori articulate the feelings guiding her interactions, to clarify what she is concerned about in terms of response from her father and what her RS is. The therapist articulates a pattern to her way of coping with this situation based on previous material.

THERAPIST: How do you feel when you think about going to see him or go see him?

LORI: I distance myself; it's almost like I'm unable to open up that door because if you open it up he's going to go home the next day. And then you are going to go, okay where does this leave me now. He was real sick but he's good now . . .

THERAPIST: And if you open it up you are worried you'd get really upset . . .

LORI: Not necessarily to start crying because there wasn't actually anything to start crying about but the reality of the situation will set in. I mean, thinking of him now, I know that he's not well. I know that, but I don't have to open up the door to find that out either.

THERAPIST: So that's another place you feel you have to keep up a wall to keep those feelings at bay. (*The putting up and breaking down walls is a metaphor the patient had used in a previous session. The therapist is labeling the most prominent RS: avoidance and denying feelings.*)

LORI: Yeah, yeah and that's why I didn't go and visit him and then and then one day I didn't even call him at all but he doesn't remember anything. And I kind of took advantage of that because the one time I didn't call you know I felt. I mean I carry this tremendous guilt that I didn't call him to see how he was doing but even if I did he wouldn't remember me calling anyway. So it kind of fucks with your head. I don't want to deal with this . . .

THERAPIST: So sometimes you don't deal with him because he's going to be angry and critical, but when he's sick like that, it's not that your trying to avoid him. Is it more seeing him so, so weak?

LORI: Yeah, and having it real, because when he's up and walking around you don't constantly think, man is he sick. I mean I can be sweet to him, I mean I like him, when he's sick because I can be sweet from my heart, it's not a show or anything, um, but it's screwy because then once he gets better really better he becomes an S.O.B. You know and it's like fluctuation in feelings.

The therapist asks about the anticipated RO. The pattern is for Lori to expect her father to become angry or critical. However, in this situation, it is not clear that this anticipated reaction is what is leading to the avoidance. Here, it appears that she does not want to accept the possibility of his dying. She actually wants to be sincere and loving with him but feels she can only be that way if he is very sick. If he is well, she fears he will be his usual angry self, and she does not want to let herself be vulnerable to being hurt.

THERAPIST: Do you worry what would happen if he did die and you hadn't been to see him or were not able to say something to him. Would that be harder on you, do you think?

LORI: Um, no because I mean I'm sure to a degree it may, but I'm content with the way I feel. I mean I'm, I feel justified I guess. It's not like I'm doing this for, I guess maybe it is a selfish reason.

THERAPIST: But it feels like you have to kind of protect yourself from him?

LORI: Yeah, I mean if it's going to happen it's going to happen. I'll deal with it when it happens but this in and out of the hospital bit. It's just confusing. So, um . . .

THERAPIST: Well, you know, you've talked about a number of situations that you try to deal with by pushing your feelings away, try to compartmentalize things like . . .

LORI: I can't deal with the uncertainty of everything, you know. If I knew what was going to happen, maybe I would open that door.

Later in the same session, the therapist and Lori were talking about her feelings about her husband. The therapist asks about whether anger comes when he wants sex and she does not feel like it. At first, one can see that Lori moves to complete denial and goes to lengths to say how positive her feelings are for her husband. However, Lori tries to bring up the theme that the therapist and she had started to discuss in a previous session, about her conflicting wishes with her husband.

LORI: I feel completely comfortable, very loving, very, um, and a lot of times, a lot of times I'll just look at him and I really am, I feel so fortunate. And hopefully like you are in the same position. I love this man so much and he loves me so much. We get along so well. I mean we work together every day from the minute we're together, from the minute we wake up in the morning till we go to bed at night. . . .

We were talking about how I want to make him happy and then I get confused because I don't want to make him happy. It's still extremely confusing to me because I love him. I mean we just have, I mean I'm not like overdoing it or anything like that and living in a fairy tale or anything like that but we just have a reciprocity. He doesn't take advantage of me because I'm younger than him or he doesn't put me down. I mean he's very good for me, and I'm very good for him and yet I still feel this way. So I say don't feel this way because you love this person—this is your everything this is your whole life. I mean I'm sure that if this was somebody who really got on my nerves or he abused me or we didn't get along or we constantly fought, then I might not have as much drive or this anger. I want to get to the point where I get rid of the anger. Where it goes from there I have no idea.

THERAPIST: We've talked about it a few times in various parts of your life, and I think it happened in your sexual life too. One of the ways you learned to cope with strong feelings is to kind of compartmentalize. Like we were talking about with your dad, about seeing him. You try to put walls between your different feelings. You talk a lot about wanting to break down the walls sexually—let yourself experience your feelings.

LORI: That's the walls I'm talking about knocking down, I just want to be wall-free, you know.

THERAPIST: I think what the problem is, what's happening to you now is that you have these loving, caring, totally real feelings for your husband and there's no denying the truth of them, they exist. But then this anger comes up in sexual relationship that is very real too. I think by your trying to keep the walls up, you can never integrate the fact that you feel both so loving about him and that there is something about what's going on there that makes you so angry and rage-filled that you can't feel the love at the moment.

The therapist feels that she needs to affirm that she heard and believes the positive feelings Lori has for her husband. She validates these feelings. However, she is working with Lori to articulate her two, often conflicting wishes about her husband to be close and to not please him. In addition, Lori's usual RS is to avoid these feelings, pretend they don't exist, or be able to acknowledge that she feels both things. Therefore, the therapist is working to more clearly articulate the patient's wishes and her RSs.

LORI: Yeah, yeah, that's exactly right. I mean we love each other—I have peripheral vision, I mean . . .

THERAPIST: So, rather than convincing yourself out of what you are feeling—telling yourself, I shouldn't feel this about your husband because he's not doing anything and he's a nice guy. We have to understand where that anger is coming from. Trying to keep those two feelings separated or convince yourself out of it rather than understanding it, is what I think is making it stay longer. No matter how loving a relationship you have with someone, there are moments where your rage-filled with somebody. It sounds as if something comes up when your husband is initiating or pushing you. There's some reaction like Fuck you—you will not do this to me, and I think we need to understand what that's about. (Again, the therapist is using the patient's expression or language from previous sessions to label her feelings or reactions.)

LORI: Yeah, like, who do you think you are?

THERAPIST: Like, who's this pushy dick, right?

LORI: Yeah, exactly, it's just like I'm not a cocky person, I'm not uh, um. I'm a very friendly person. And I, I don't cop attitudes easily. I mean, I just get like really pissed, you know. Not that I could hurt anybody or anything like that, but it's just like, you know, who do you think you are?

I don't know whether it's necessarily what he wants me to do to him or to myself or whether he's just talking to me. I don't know, but like I say, if I have something in my mind that I would want him to do I'd never tell him. I'd never tell him, because I don't feel comfortable telling him what would feel good, even though I should tell him what makes me feel good because then it will make me feel good, it will put me in a comfortable position, you know.

The patient begins to recognize the nature of her reaction and to try to understand the reason for her self-defeating behavior (RS).

THERAPIST: Is there an issue of not wanting him to have information about you, like not letting him have some of your secrets?

LORI: I might do just enough just to make him react on his own but not obviously enough where he'll go, oh, is that what you want me to do?

THERAPIST: Is there some way he has some power or control over you?

LORI: I don't know. Say that again.

The therapist is trying to articulate Lori's conflicting wishes for closeness and control. Here, as at other times, the patient seems to forget what the therapist said when she talks about the patient's wish for control. However, in this session, the patient is able to stay with the discussion and expand on this wish.

THERAPIST: I was wondering if there was any way that it feels like, if you gave away that information or something like that, he'd have some power or control over you that feels scary to let go of.

LORI: Yeah, yeah, I guess in a sense that would be right and then he would know, it's like giving away my cards or something like that—I don't like him getting that satisfaction of pleasing me.

THERAPIST: Do you know why?

LORI: No, I have no fricken idea and I can't believe I actually got that out of my mouth, because two minutes from now I'll ask you what did I say.

THERAPIST: Because I think the minute you start to feel some of that anger, you feel there is no justification. It feels illogical and so bad for you to think that way about your husband, who's somebody you love. It seems that you are using all your energy to convince yourself you are not angry and instead try to distance yourself or go away. But the anger feels very powerful anyway.

LORI: I don't know how I get it away um. I mean, it's almost like sometimes when I do feel angry I'll want to just lay there and not move at all and just be like a board.

THERAPIST: Because in that way you show your anger?

LORI: And that's like kind of getting it out, you know; it's kind of like lashing out at him.

THERAPIST: Because your being unresponsive feels bad to him, I mean . . .

LORI: Because I'm being, I'm not responding to him, it's almost like I'm getting even.

THERAPIST: So you kind of know at that moment that your anger is one way to express that somehow . . .

LORI: Yeah, because I never want to verbally express it.

THERAPIST: How would it come out?

LORI: I'd probably just push him away. You know, I don't think that there's too many words to follow, like you know, how can you do this to me or anything like that. It's just more like, knock it off, what do you think your doing?

THERAPIST: Well, it's so interesting. There's a way that the level of intimacy or closeness in your relationship with your husband challenges and confronts you in a way other relationships have not. But also, your husband's style, which is quite assertive and dominating, probably provokes this more than other men. You picked someone who will make you address these issues of control.

Again, the CCRT, once elaborated, is similar to the CCRT with the father set out earlier. The therapist makes the link in the session between the two patterns:

W: To be intimate (sexually), close, and spontaneous.
(To be in control).
RO: Supportive and loving.
To be controlling or dominant.
RS: Confusion.
Reaction formation.

Passive-aggression (not give self or take in what offered, deny pleasure).
Avoidance of anger.

The CCRT with the therapist can be inferred from the patient's behavior in this session, even though it is not directly discussed in this transcript. Early in the session, Lori often interrupted the therapist and did not let her comment on what she was saying. Again, the struggle regarding intimacy and closeness versus control was playing itself out in the patient-therapist relationship. As the session progressed and Lori came to a clearer understanding of what was happening, she was able to slow down and let the therapist in. The end of the session was really much more of a reciprocal dialogue. Here is the CCRT based on Lori's behavior with the therapist this session:

W: To be close, to disclose, to address conflict.
RO: Offer closeness and reflection.
Also guide or control session.
RS: Frustration.
Not want to take in what given or offered because of loss of control.
Distance self.
Confusion.

The therapist and Lori addressed the CCRT with the therapist at a number of different points in the treatment. Early on in treatment, Lori felt forced to "get it all out" or work at a frantic pace in session, and the therapist encouraged Lori to set her own pace. They discussed Lori's tendency to interrupt the therapist or to not let her speak. At first, Lori suggested that she would interrupt because she was afraid of forgetting her thoughts or what she had to say. As time passed, they discussed this in the context of protecting herself from getting too close by not letting the other person in. Later in treatment, the pattern was discussed as a struggle for control. Lori did not report experiencing the therapist on the surface as controlling; however, the therapist often pushed Lori to acknowledge feelings or needs that she tried to avoid. From about the tenth session on, the therapist and Lori could notice when the struggle was happening in session and discuss together how to stop that cycle.

Final Phase of Treatment. Treatment continued for another 12 sessions after this fifteenth session and focused primarily on the conflicting wishes of closeness and control. The therapist and Lori worked on ways for her to accept these feelings and to more directly express her needs. As she began to address her wishes and feelings, Lori reported feeling more spontaneous and free in her sexual relationship. Prior to therapy, she reported few sexual fantasies or little exploration of her own pleasure. She began to have very vivid sexual dreams that involved both her husband as well as an attraction to women. These dreams also focused around issues of closeness and control. She became concerned and frightened at first that her fantasies must reflect what she wanted to do in her behavior. However, as the therapist helped her clarify this distinction, she began to enjoy the freedom to explore that she experienced in her dreams. Lori was able to cope with a number of major life changes over these next few months that were both positive (buying a new house, pregnancy) and negative (death of her father). She was more able to be present with her father before his death and to come to some resolution about the positive and negative aspects of their relationship.

Termination Issues
Lori continued in therapy until the birth of her second child about a year and a half after she initiated treatment. The therapy focused on termination issues because she would be off for a few months after the baby was born, even though she said she planned to return. Prior to the baby's birth, Lori was feeling that the sexual problem was much improved and that she was enjoying sex. She became more aware of her feelings and her pattern of responding or coping and actively tried to change interactions with others, especially her husband and her family.

POSTTERMINATION SYNOPSIS AND EFFECTIVENESS DATA

Lori contacted the therapist about four months after the birth of her child and scheduled a number of appointments that were always cancelled. Her second child suffered some medical complications that required frequent doctor's appointments. About six months after the birth, Lori did come in for a final session. She reported continued improvements in her sexual relationship, saying that she really wanted sex now. Lori seemed to be a very good mother, confident, not intrusive, and connected with her children. It seemed as if the issues she struggled with in her other relationships were not impacting the relationship with her children at this time.

Even though Lori seemed to be in some ways repeating her pattern from the previous therapy of not returning as planned after the birth of her baby, she did handle this termination in a different way. She came to a final session to summarize and provide some closure to the work. In addition, by her report, she felt connected to her therapist, able to express when the therapist was not meeting her needs, and felt she received what she had wanted from therapy. Lori reported that she would feel positive about returning to therapy if she needed to at a later time.

SUMMARY

We have presented very briefly the main constructs of SE therapy, a form of relatively structured dynamic therapy that has received some empirical validation. In the amount of space allotted, we decided to provide the large picture of where we are now in working in SE and in researching its efficacy and its mechanisms of change. Thus, we have also limited the more in-depth discussion of the applications of SE. We recommend interested readers to the Luborsky (1984) manual and Book's (1998) excellent *How to Practice Brief Psychodynamic Psychotherapy: The Core Conflictual Relationship Theme Method*, which provides rich, clinical detail about working with this approach.

REFERENCES

Barber, J. P. (1990). *Outline of treatment manuals for SE for avoidant personality and obsessive-compulsive personality disorders*. Philadelphia: University of Pennsylvania Press.

Barber, J. P., & Crits-Christoph, P. (1993). Advances in measures of psychodynamic formulations. *Journal of Consulting and Clinical Psychology, 61*, 574–585.

Barber, J. P., & Crits-Christoph, P. (Eds.). (1995). *Dynamic therapies for psychiatric disorders (Axis 1)*. New York: Basic Books.

Barber, J. P., Crits-Christoph, P., & Luborsky, L. (1996). Effects of therapist adherence and competence on patient outcome in brief dynamic therapy. *Journal of Consulting and Clinical Psychology, 64*, 619–622.

Barber, J. P., Luborsky, L., Crits-Christoph, P., & Diguer, L. (1995). A comparison of core conflictual relationship themes before psychotherapy and during early sessions. *Journal of Consulting and Clinical Psychology, 63*, 145–148.

Barber, J. P., Morse, J. Q., Krakauer, I., Chittams, J., & Crits-Christoph, K. (1997). Change in obsessive-compulsive and avoidant personality disorders following time-limited supportive-expressive therapy. *Psychotherapy, 34*, 133–143.

Bibring, E. (1954). Psychoanalysis and the dynamic psychotherapies. *Journal of the American Psychoanalytic Association, 2*, 745–770.

Book, H. E. (1998). *How to practice brief dynamic psychotherapy: The CCRT method*. Washington, DC: American Psychological Association.

Connolly, M. B., Crits-Christoph, P., Shappell, S., Barber, J. P., & Luborsky, L. (1998). Therapist interventions in early sessions of brief supportive-expressive psychotherapy for depression. *Journal of Psychotherapy Practice and Research, 7*(4), 290–300.

Crits-Christoph, P., Barber, J. P., & Kurcias, J. S. (1993). The accuracy of therapists' interpretations and the development of the therapeutic alliance. *Psychotherapy Research, 3*, 25–35.

Crits-Christoph, P., Connolly, M. B., Azarian, K., Crits-Christoph, K., & Shappell, S. (1996). An open trial of brief supportive-expressive psychotherapy in the treatment of generalized anxiety disorder. *Psychotherapy, 33*, 418–430.

Crits-Christoph, P., Cooper, A., & Luborsky, L. (1988). The accuracy of therapists' interpretations and the outcome of dynamic psychotherapy. *Journal of Consulting and Clinical Psychology, 56*, 490–495.

Crits-Christoph, P., Crits-Christoph, K., Wolf-Palacio, D., Fichter, M., & Rudick, D. (1995). Brief supportive-expressive psychodynamic therapy for generalized anxiety disorder. In J. P. Barber & P. Crits-Christoph (Eds.), *Dynamic therapies for psychiatric disorders (Axis I)* (pp. 43—83). New York: Basic Books.

Crits-Christoph, P., & Luborsky, L. (1990a). Change in CCRT pervasiveness during psychotherapy. In L. Luborsky & P. Crits-Christoph (Eds.), *The core conflictual relationship theme* (pp. 133–146). New York: Basic Books.

Crits-Christoph, P., & Luborsky, L. (1990b). The measurement of self-understanding. In L. Luborsky & P. Crits-Christoph (Eds.), *The core conflictual relationship theme* (pp. 189–196). New York: Basic Books.

Crits-Christoph, P., Siqueland, L., Blaine, J., Frank, A., Luborsky, L., Onken, L. S., et al. (1999). Psychosocial treatments for cocaine dependence: Results of the National Institute on Drug Abuse Collaborative Cocaine Treatment Study. *Archives of General Psychiatry, 57*, 493–502.

Diguer, L., Barber, J. P., & Luborsky, L. (1993). Three concomitants: Personality disorder, psychiatric severity, and outcome of dynamic psychotherapy of major depression. *American Journal of Psychiatry, 150*, 1246–1248.

Fenichel, O. (1941). Problems of psychoanalytic technique. *Psychoanalytic Quarterly, 7.*

Freud, S. (1953). Fragment of an analysis of a case of hysteria. In J. Strachey (Ed. and Trans.), *The standard edition of the complete psychological works of Sigmund Freud* (Vol. 7, pp. 15–22). London: Hogarth Press. (Original work published 1905)

Freud, S. (1958a). On beginning the treatment (further recommendations on the technique of psychoanalysis-I). In J. Strachey (Ed. and Trans.), *The standard edition of the complete psychological works of Sigmund Freud* (Vol. 12, pp. 112–144). London: Hogarth Press. (Original work published 1913)

Freud, S. (1958b). The dynamics of transference. In J. Strachey (Ed. and Trans.), *The standard edition of the complete psychological works of Sigmund Freud* (Vol. 12, pp. 97–108). London: Hogarth Press. (Original work published 1912)

Freud, S. (1958c). The handling of dream interpretation in psychoanalysis. In J. Strachey (Ed. and Trans.), *The standard edition of the complete psychological works of Sigmund Freud* (Vol. 12, pp. 81–96). London: Hogarth Press. (Original work published 1911)

Freud, S. (1958d). Observations on transference-love (further recommendations on the technique of psychoanalysis-III). In J. Strachey (Ed. and Trans.), *The standard edition of the complete psychological works of Sigmund Freud* (Vol. 12, pp. 157–171). London: Hogarth Press. (Original work published 1915)

Freud, S. (1958e). Recommendations to physicians practicing psychoanalysis. In J. Strachey (Ed. and Trans.), *The standard edition of the complete psychological works of Sigmund Freud* (Vol. 12, pp. 109–120). London: Hogarth Press. (Original work published 1912)

Freud, S. (1958f). Remembering, repeating and working through (further recommendations on the technique of psychoanalysis-II). In J. Strachey (Ed. and Trans.), *The standard edition of the complete psychological works of Sigmund Freud* (Vol. 12, pp. 145–156). London: Hogarth Press. (Original work published 1914)

Gabbard, G. O. (1994). *Psychodynamic psychiatry in clinical practice: The DSM-IV edition.* Washington, DC: American Psychiatric Press.

Gabbard, G. O. (1996). Psychodynamic psychotherapies. In G. O. Gabbard & S. D. Atkinson (Eds.), *Synopsis of treatments of psychiatric disorders* (2nd ed., pp. 515–521). Washington, DC: American Psychiatric Press.

Greenson, R. R. (1965). The working alliance and the transference neurosis. *Psychoanalytic Quarterly, 34,* 155–181.

Hoehn-Saric, R., Frank, J., Imber, S., Nash, E., Stone, A., & Battle, C. (1964). Systematic preparation of patients for psychotherapy: I. Effects on therapy behavior and outcome. *Journal of Psychiatric Research, 2,* 267–281.

Horvath, A. O., & Symonds, B. D. (1991). Relation between working alliance and outcome in psychotherapy: A meta-analysis. *Journal of Counseling Psychology, 38,* 139–149.

Knight, R. P. (1949). A critique of the present state of the psychotherapies. *Bulletin of the New York Academy of Medicine, 25,* 100–114.

Luborsky, L. (1976). Helping alliances in psychotherapy: The groundwork for a study of their relationship to its outcome. In J. L. Claghorn (Ed.), *Successful psychotherapy* (pp. 92–116). New York: Brunner/Mazel.

Luborsky, L. (1977). Measuring a pervasive psychic structure in psychotherapy: The core conflictual relationship theme. In N. Freedman & S. Grand (Eds.), *Communicative structures and psychic structures* (pp. 367–395). New York: Plenum Press.

Luborsky, L. (1984). *Principles of psychoanalytic psychotherapy: A manual for supportive-expressive (SE) treatment.* New York: Basic Books.

Luborsky, L. (1990). The convergence of Freud's observations about transference and the CCRT evidence. In L. Luborsky & P. Crits-Christoph (Eds.), *Understanding transference: The core conflictual relationship theme method* (pp. 251–266). New York: Basic Books.

Luborsky, L, Barber, J. P., & Crits-Christoph, P. (1990). Theory based research for understanding the process of dynamic psychotherapy. *Journal of Consulting and Clinical Psychology, 58,* 281–287.

Luborsky, L., & Crits-Christoph, P. (Eds.). (1990). *Understanding transference: The CCRT method.* New York: Basic Books.

Luborsky, L., & Crits-Christoph, P. (Eds.). (1998). *Understanding transference: The CCRT method* (2nd ed.). Washington, DC: American Psychiatric Press.

Luborsky, L., Crits-Christoph, P., Mintz, J., & Auerbach, A. (1988). *Who will benefit from psychotherapy?* New York: Basic Books.

Luborsky, L., Diguer, L., Cacciola, J., Barber, J. P., Moras, K., Schmidt, K., et al. (1996). Factors in outcome of short-term dynamic psychotherapy for chronic vs. nonchronic major depression. *Journal of Psychotherapy, Practice and Research, 5,* 152–159.

Luborsky, L., & Mark, D. (1991). Dynamic time-limited supportive-expressive psychotherapy. In P. Crits-Christoph & J. P. Barber (Eds.), *Handbook of short-term dynamic therapies* (pp. 110–136). New York: Basic Books.

Luborsky, L., Mark, D., Hole, A. V., Popp, C., Goldsmith, B., & Cacciola, J. (1995). Supportive-expressive dynamic psychotherapy of depression: A time-limited version. In J. P. Barber & P. Crits-Christoph (Eds.), *Psychodynamic psychotherapies for psychiatric disorders (Axis I)* (pp. 13–42). New York: Basic Books.

Luborsky, L., Woody, G., Hole, A. V., & Velleco, A. (1995). Supportive-expressive dynamic psychotherapy for treatment of opiate drug dependence. In J. P. Barber & P. Crits-Christoph (Eds.), *Dynamic therapies for psychiatric disorders (Axis I)* (pp. 131–160). New York: Basic Books.

Malan, D. H. (1976). *Toward the validation of dynamic psychotherapy.* New York: Plenum Press.

Mark, D., & Faude, J. (1995). Supportive-expressive therapy for cocaine abuse. In J. P. Barber & P. Crits-Christoph (Eds.), *Dynamic therapies for psychiatric disorders (Axis I)* (pp. 294–331). New York: Basic Books.

Mark, D., & Faude, J. (1998). *The demonization of addicts and their drugs.* New York: Aronson.

Stone, L. (1951). Psychoanalysis and brief psychotherapy. *Psychoanalytic Quarterly, 20,* 215–236.

Wachtel, P. L. (1993). Accusatory and facilitative comments: Criticism and permission in the therapeutic dialogue. In P. L. Wachtel (Ed.), *Therapeutic communication: Principles and effective practice* (pp. 68–86). New York: Guilford Press.

Wallerstein, R. S. (1986). *Forty-two lives in treatment: A study of psychoanalysis and psychotherapy.* New York: Guilford Press.

Wallerstein, R. S., Robbins, L., Sargent, H., & Luborsky, L. (1956). The psychotherapy research project of the Menninger Foundation: Rationale, method, and sample use. *Bulletin of the Menninger Clinic, 20,* 221–280.

Woody, G. E., Luborsky, L., McLellan, A. T., & O'Brien, C. P. (1990). Corrections and revised analyses for psychotherapy in methadone maintenance programs. *Archives of General Psychiatry, 47,* 788–789.

Woody, G. E., Luborsky, L., McLellan, A. T., O'Brien, C. P., Beck, A. T., Blaine, J., et al. (1983). Psychotherapy for opiate addicts: Does it help? *Archives of General Psychiatry, 40,* 639–645.

Woody, G. E., McLellan, T., Luborsky, L., & O'Brien, C. (1995). Psychotherapy in community methadone programs: A validation study. *American Journal of Psychiatry, 152,* 1302–1308.

Zetzel, E. (1958). Therapeutic alliance in the analysis of hysteria. In E. Zetzel (Ed.), *The capacity for emotional growth* (pp. 182–196). London: Hogarth Press.

CHAPTER 9

Brief Psychodynamic Therapy

FERRUCCIO OSIMO

HISTORY OF THE THERAPEUTIC APPROACH

Short-term dynamic psychotherapies can be divided into three groups, according to which factor is mainly responsible for their brevity (Osimo, 1991). In the first group, the abbreviating factor is *time* itself; that is, the therapy's duration is established rigidly beforehand. In *focal* approaches, the working area is circumscribed beforehand; once a *focus*, or the conflict area regarded as being pivotal, has been selected, all interpretations or other interventions are formulated in that direction. The third group, based on an *acceleration* of the therapeutic process, aims to resolve the significant symptom and character issues, but more rapidly than in longer methods. The approach described here, according to Fosha (2000), is an experiential short-term dynamic psychotherapy (E-STDP). Davanloo's (1986, 1990) approach and those by Alpert (1992), Fosha (1992, 2000), Sklar (1992), Coughlin Della Selva (1996), McCullough Vaillant (1997), and Magnavita (1997) are part of the same group. These models are more efficient than those in the first and second groups, as they can be effective in a relatively short time with people who show more complex problems and a stronger resistance to change.

The idea of accelerating the therapeutic process is not new in the field of psychodynamics. Ferenczi, in the first lines of his essay "The Further Development of an Active Therapy in Psycho-analysis" (1920, p. 199), wrote: "Psychoanalysis, as we employ it to-day, is a procedure whose most prominent characteristic is *passivity*." Another of Freud's most brilliant disciples, Rank (1924), was also deeply concerned with the *healing* side of psychoanalysis, thus with *emotional experiencing*, rather than with theoretical speculation: "Therapeutic possibilities do not conform, in any expected degree, to the increase of our knowledge, and ... even simple therapeutic action can be arrested by too much knowledge and too much [cognitive] insight" (p. 202). In 1933, Reich published *Character Analysis*, in which he outlined a new dynamic approach to personality disorders. Reich questioned the "basic rule" of free association, in that the character of an individual "is usually expressed in a specific *attitude* or *mode of existence* ... [representing] ... an expression of the patient's entire past" (p. 48). These theoretical and technical points, and Reich's emphasis on the freeing of emotions from the body, are highly relevant to the present approach of short-term psychotherapy. The first systematic, and indeed highly productive, clinical trials explicitly aimed at making psychoanalysis "briefer and more effective" are those reported in the milestone book by Alexander and French (1946). A brief summary of their clinical evidence demonstrated the following:

- Intense reexperiencing of the conflicting emotions in the transference, that is, in the actual relation with an emotionally responsive therapist, brings about therapeutic change. This is what Alexander (Alexander & French, 1946, p. 22) called "corrective emotional experience," which is pivotal to dynamic change.
- If such reexperiencing can be brought about rapidly, dynamic change will also be rapid. The phase of consolidation of change or "working through" is not a question of time, but of adequate emotional experience.
- When an effective approach is used, no matter the length, frequency, and total number of sessions, even relatively early traumas can be reactivated and solved.

Balint (1955) founded the Brief Psychotherapy Workshop (BPW) at the Tavistock Clinic, consisting of a group of selected and gifted clinicians, one of whom was David Malan. Their initial idea was to identify a conflict area on which to concentrate dynamic work, for which Balint coined the term *focus*. Malan has reported that the therapies supervised at the BPW were never *really* focal, because interpretations actually addressed all the meaningful material (Malan, 2001, personal communication). The term "focal" applied to brief therapy, however, became widespread. In the mid-1960s, Malan started his own Brief Psychotherapy Workshop, and the first for trainees, at the Tavistock Clinic.

Malan postulated the unavoidable connection among selection criteria, therapeutic technique used, and the *quality* of results obtained. His elucidation of the dynamic process and of change mechanisms in brief psychotherapy is invaluable. Malan (1963, 1976, 1979) was actually able to disprove the "hypothesis of superficiality" which claims that brief psychotherapy is a *superficial treatment*, applicable only to *superficially ill* patients, and bringing about *superficial results*. His own selection criteria, however, are fulfilled by fewer than 10% of patients.

During the past 25 years, short-term psychotherapy has made remarkable progress, especially due to the technical improvements introduced by Davanloo (1990) and theoretically explained by Malan (1986a, 1986b). In the early 1980s, Davanloo was the first to demonstrate, in his video presentations, that even severe character problems can be dealt with in under 40 sessions. This revolutionary approach has been technically challenging to master. Moreover, there always is a strong connection between a therapeutic methodology and the personality of its proponents (Osimo, 1994). Other therapists, after receiving Davanloo's teaching and supervision, have thus devised approaches that are attuned to and enriched by their own personalities.

Magnavita (1997) developed a flexible approach to the restructuring of personality disorders that facilitates the planning and tailoring of treatment according to each patient's needs. The research work carried out in New York by the Beth Israel Research Program (McCullough, Winston, et al., 1991) empirically validated Alexander's intuition. Experimental evidence demonstrates that transference interpretations followed by an emotional response bear a significant correlation with improvement at termination, whereas an intervention followed by a defensive response correlates negatively with outcome. Also in connection with this research, a group of colleagues, Alpert, Fosha, and Sklar (Fosha, 1992), developed accelerated empathic therapy. They are especially concerned with the sharing of emotions with the patient as a means of accelerating the dynamic process. An important evolution is described by Fosha (2000). Finally, an integrative approach was developed by McCullough Vaillant (1997) called short-term anxiety-regulating therapy. Her approach "creates a strong connection between research data and clinical methodology and integrates the [effective] aspects of different theories, such as dynamic, behavioral, cognitive, and gestalt therapeutic approaches" (Osimo, 1998, p. 98).

THEORETICAL CONSTRUCTS ON WHICH E-STDP IS BASED

The theoretical and clinical foundation of E-STDP is represented mainly by the discoveries and research work of Balint, Ornstein, and Balint (1972), Malan (1963, 1976), Davanloo (1986, 1990), and McCullough Vaillant (1997) and, before them, by Ferenczi (Ferenczi & Rank, 1925/1987), Reich (1933), and Alexander (Alexander & French, 1946). Malan, in particular, has been the driving force in this field for the past 50 years, carrying out outstanding research. E-STDP can be regarded as an evolution of Malan's brief psychotherapy, integrating new elements that make it suited to a wider range of patients, including many of those with neurotic syndromes and personality disorders. The main components of E-STDP are (1) Malan's triangles, (2) mirroring function, and (3) dynamic activities, which include defense restructuring (DA), anxiety regulation (AA), and emotional maieutics (XA), aiming to bring about a rapid access to the unconscious conflicting emotions.

E-STDP is characterized by the following:

1. A psychodynamic foundation and the adoption of the two Triangles as its main conceptual frame. It incorporates Freud's theory of human conflict, rooted in the conscious-unconscious and id-ego-superego systems.
2. Equal emphasis given to the actual experiencing of emotions, which are felt through the body and are regarded as the most genuine and meaningful expression of conscious and unconscious human inner life.
3. The therapist's active mirroring of the patient's nonverbal and verbal expressions is regarded as pivotal. Various other analysts emphasized aspects of the connection between mirroring and psychoanalysis, among them Mahler (1967), Winnicott (1971), and Kohut (1971). The mirroring function taken on by the therapist in E-STDP (Osimo, 2001b) consists of repeated and frequent description to the patient of his or her defensive attitudes, feelings, and anxieties.
4. A real interpersonal relationship between therapist and patient is seen as the only basis on which therapeutic techniques can build.
5. Operational ways in which this interpersonal relation can be used psychotherapeutically. This includes three distinct dynamic activities, each of which should be implemented when required, depending on the moment-to-moment patient-therapist interaction. DA, AA, and XA are regarded as equally important and effective, but should be timed and dosed depending on (1) the moment-to-moment patient-therapist interaction, (2) the patient's personality structure and presenting problems, and (3) the therapist's personal inclination and ability as regards each dynamic activity.
6. No rigid scheme or operational sequence can be formulated using the E-STDP approach. On the contrary, all choices of how to intervene stem from the patient-therapist rapport, as well as from the clinical feedback coming from the patient. The ability to recognize and make use of

these can be achieved only by means of systematic viewing of the videorecorded sessions together with supervision by an experienced clinician specializing in this approach.

THE TWO TRIANGLES

Malan (1963; Malan & Osimo, 1992) was the first to develop the idea of putting these two triangles together as a graphic representation of all possible intrapsychic and interpersonal dynamics (see Figure 9.1).

The *Triangle of Person* divides the patient's interpersonal relationships into three categories: (1) those that are current or belong to the recent past (**C**); (2) the relationship with the therapist (**T**); and (3) those of the past (**P**), that is, mainly with the primary attachment figures (Bowlby, 1982). This last corner of the Triangle of Persons is placed at the bottom, signifying that it is "deeper" and tends to be reached after the other two. The *Triangle of Conflict* represents the three elements on which psychodynamic theory is based: (1) defenses (**D**); (2) unconscious feelings, desires, representations, and impulses (**X**); and (3) anxiety (**A**). Again, the **X** corner of the triangle is placed at the bottom because feelings and impulses that are excluded from consciousness are regarded as "deeper," as they tend to be reached after the anxieties and defenses that were mobilized for the purpose of excluding them. The Triangle of Person represents the other people in the patient's life, and the Triangle of Conflict represents the patient's dynamic self. Alternative names for the two triangles are therefore Triangle of Self and Triangle of Others. Thus, the relationship between the self and others is also represented in the scheme.

By virtue of this scheme, it is possible to divide the therapist's interventions according to what part of the dynamic self they address and in connection with what category of others. A therapist addressing the **D** corner will say, for example, "You are detached." But if a therapist says "You seem anxious (**A**) because I detected your anger (**X**), and therefore you detach yourself from me (**D**)," the three corners of the Triangle of Conflict are all addressed. This is termed a **D-A-X** interpretation. If we focus on the therapist's saying "because *I* detected . . . you detach . . . *from me*," thus calling attention to what is happening in connection with himself or herself, the therapist has given a **D-A-X** interpretation in the **T** (transference). Similarly, a therapist might inquire: "Is this anger (**X**) you felt at your boss reminding you of any (= **C**, **P**, or **T**) other time in your life when you got angry at somebody?" In this case, the therapist's question links a current angry feeling or fantasy with a feeling that may have been mobilized in the patient in different moments of his or her life and in connection with different

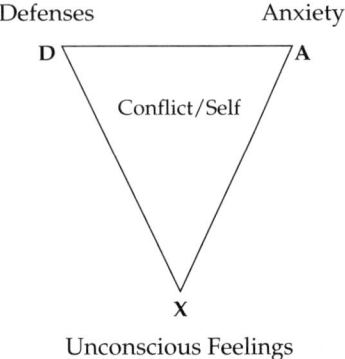

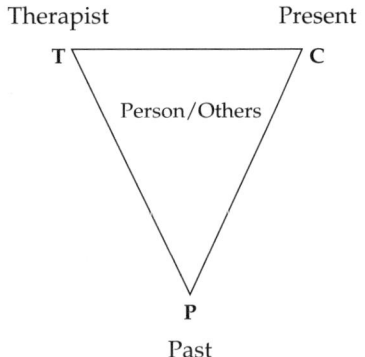

Figure 9.1 The two triangles.

people. According to the two triangles, this intervention would be called an interpretation of **X** aiming toward a **T-C-P** link.

There are many ways of including or excluding one or more corners of the triangle(s). Theoretically speaking, the most complete interpretation is one comprising, linking together, and making sense of all the elements represented by all the corners of both triangles. This amounts to interpreting the conflict **D-A-X** in its entirety and as experienced in connection with all of the three categories of people—**T, C,** and **P**—representing the patient's others. On practical grounds, this degree of exhaustiveness is not always necessary or appropriate, and the therapist's intervention will be best represented using *some of* the corners of the two triangles. These distinctions, based on the dynamic function of what the patient "brings in" moment by moment, have an important practical application, especially when making a decision about the right move on the therapist's part, and, using a concept from the present approach, a decision about which activity is most appropriate at any given moment of the interaction with the patient. This type of decision, however, does not rely solely on the *here and now* of the relationship with the therapist. It also involves the technical-methodological approach employed. As regards E-STDP, this aspect is further elaborated in the following sections and by means of an illustrative case.

The Mirroring Function

One factor that undoubtedly favors an acceleration of the dynamic process in E-STDP is the *mirroring* function of the therapist. This is the therapist's ability to function as a mirror, reflecting aspects of the patient's self onto him or her, especially those aspects of which the patient is less aware, that can convey emotions, fears, and defensive attitudes. Their "restitution" to the patient often mobilizes that sense of wonder characteristic of the process of discovering something new and revealing. In the actual framework of the interaction with the patient, the mirroring function may give rise to clarifications and interpretations, but the essence of it is *providing the patient with constant feedback about what he or she is conveying*. This is achieved by *frequent*, repeated interventions conveying to the patient what the therapist sees or otherwise perceives. Mirroring is never administered with a neutral attitude; rather, it is used in connection with one of the three dynamic activities. This is why it is called a "function" and not an activity of its own.

Activation of Unconscious Conflicting Emotions

Research supports the view that, to start a therapeutic process bringing about dynamic change, patients need to be enabled to *experience* their conflicting emotions with a *sufficient* intensity. Sufficiency is obviously a relative measure, varying in different cases and circumstances. Research does confirm, however, that Alexander's emphasis on emotional experience as a crucial requirement for change is entirely justified. For this reason, the sooner this *good-enough emotional experience* (Osimo, 2001a) takes place and the dynamic process gets started, the briefer psychotherapy will be. If one aims to make this possible, one needs to rapidly reduce or neutralize the forces blocking this experience. Emotional activation amounts to bringing about a *sufficient increase in the intensity* with which the *conflicting emotions* are experienced by the patient.

Because we need to activate the unconscious emotions that are an expression of the patient's self (represented by **X** in the Triangle of Conflict), and because these are kept unconscious by the defences (**D**) and are counteracted by inhibitory feelings (**A**), we need to alter the complex balance existing among the three forces. The most efficient way to alter this balance is to have ways of acting on *all* the corners of the Triangle of Conflict and to know when to make use of each of these ways. This is what the dynamic activities are meant for, each of them aiming for the dynamic element represented at the corresponding corner of the Triangle of Conflict. They may be represented by the capitals at the three corners of the Triangle of Conflict followed by a capital **A**, standing for "activity"; thus, **DA** for defense restructuring, **AA** for anxiety regulation, and **XA** for emotional maieutics. What follows is a description of each of the three activities. A way of assessing which activity should be used at a given moment (i.e., the operational manual of E-STDP; Osimo, 2001b) is summarized in the next section.

*Defense Restructuring (**DA**)*

Theory. Anna Freud (1937/1966) described approximately ten *defense mechanisms* of the ego, producing a clear conceptual analysis of the methods that humans use to defend themselves from emotional suffering. Though still accepted for diagnostic purposes, this framework has no great operational value. Vaillant carried out far-reaching longitudinal studies of the ways various **D**s are used in attempting to adapt to life's changing needs. Vaillant's research (1977, 1993) provides strong evidence that **D**s are distributed along a hierarchy that moves from a very low level of adaptation to an optimal level. In the attempt to confront the complex reality of our conscience, or superego, of our desires, or id, and our relationship with others and reality, the ego negates, distorts, or represses part of the external or internal reality. This *hierarchy of defenses* has remarkable diagnostic value because the analysis of the **D**s, carried out during the evaluation sessions or the trial relationship (next section), provides crucial information regarding the level of maturity/immaturity of the **D**s used. This, in turn, is highly relevant to the rapidity with which **D**s can be restructured, and hence to the degree of acceleration that is possible and desirable in the therapeutic process.

Practice. Whatever the degree of maturity of the predominant **D**s a patient uses, what the therapist is met with is the patient's interactive style. Some of these ways are in fact ingrained patterns of behavior that a person habitually employs in connection with others in his or her daily attempts to perform a successful interchange without being exposed to intolerable emotional suffering (**X**) or overwhelming anxiety (**A**). They are the basic building blocks of a person's character and can be broadly referred to as *character* defenses. Because a patient uses them to take certain attitudes with others, including the therapist, they may be called *position defenses*. To give a few examples: *Facial expressions* and *glances* can be indicative of distance or proximity; *posture* might indicate openness or lack thereof, as it might also indicate the presence of both together; striated or voluntary *muscle tone* is an indicator of anxiety (Coughlin Della Selva, 1996, p. 10). Even *tone of voice* will reveal anxiety and suggest one's overall attitude; it can be circumspect or arrogant, joyous or angered, open or timid, leaning toward idealizing or sweetening or pessimistic, plaintive or sarcastic, seductive or childish, according to the case. Finally, the content of the communication may reveal, hide, or distort certain important aspects of the self. All these levels together represent position defenses, whose combination forms the individual's character.

Besides position **D**s, there is another way a therapist encounters the patient's defenses from the very beginning of their interaction. Whereas structural and position **D**s represent an individual's consolidated internal functioning and interpersonal patterns, other **D**s are more fluid and are activated to maintain emotional distance. Their degree of activation is thus proportional to the extent to which a patient feels threatened by a therapist's attempts to create a close relationship.

The theory of these **D**s arose from the close collaboration of Malan (1986a, 1986b) and Davanloo (1986, 1990), who named them "tactical defenses." They are "operating in the human psyche, or, as it is more correct to say, in the psyche of a patient when he/she is interacting with the therapist" (Osimo, 1991, p. 44). Such **D**s include vagueness, approximation, evasiveness, diversions, and retractions (Osimo, 1991) as well as some nonverbal **D**s that have similar effects, such as avoiding glances, frequent smiles, giggles, or whimpers and an air of detachment (Coughlin Della Selva, 1996, p. 9).

Before Davanloo (1986–1990) understood their importance, these **D**s were often overlooked. In fact, they play an important role, in that they enable a patient to communicate apparently important information while remaining minimally involved. Statements such as "I think I'm angry," "I have the sensation of sadness," and "I think that I'm satisfied with my marriage" are so void of emotional content that they constitute a pure dialectical exercise. If therapists are not aware of this, they may take such statements as acquired facts, whereas the patient has stated them in a noncommitting way, without taking on any emotional ownership of them. Simple but direct clarifications by the therapist, such as "Are you or aren't you angry?", "Are you sad or not?", and "Are you really happy or is that something that you are simply telling me?", force patients to define their emotional stance, communicating to their unconscious the therapist's intention of confronting all the issues in depth. On the one hand, this message leads to *resistance* in patients, sometimes causing them to defend even more. At the same time, however, patients realize that the therapist is determined, knows what he or she wants, and is strong enough to accept patients' feelings (**X**), even if these may be unconsciously frightening. As a result of this, patients feel reassured and the *therapeutic alliance* is strengthened. An efficient management of the interactive **D**s, therefore, can reduce the patient's distance, thereby increasing therapist's and patient's emotional involvement in the relationship. This emotional involvement is a prerequisite for a rapid activation of the greatest possible dynamic interaction between patient and therapist and for the creation of a strong *therapeutic alliance.*

There is another important element of the **D**s, involving the degree to which the individual is aware of using them. It often happens that a person makes constant use of position and tactical **D**s, without being aware of their defensive function. In such cases, it can be said, using a term that I find contorted, that the defenses are ego-syntonic or even that the defensive barrier is "cemented with the ego" (Davanloo, 1986, 1990). Essentially, this means that a patient completely identifies with his or her own **D**s and, as a consequence, cannot *see* them. To the therapist's observation "Do you realize how you speak of everything in generalizations and in a monotone?", an ego-syntonic patient would respond by saying "Yes, yes, that's how I am" or "That's my personality," as if this were an unchangeable fact, like the color of one's eyes.

At any given time in the session, each patient brings some resistance and some therapeutic alliance. It is the prime responsibility of the therapist, who is involved in restructuring the **D**s, to render all of them visible and recognizable to the patient. This is carried out by calling patients' attention to the **D** modes that they use, describing them, and, if necessary, clarifying their use as **D**s. Such mirroring interventions must be repeated each time, until the patient is able to clearly see and understand the **D**s. The more ego-syntonic the **D**s are, the more it will be necessary to draw attention to them repeatedly. As this mirroring continues, patients become increasingly aware of their own defensive mechanisms and the therapist thus will be able to move on to the second part of the restructuring. This involves helping patients to renounce those **D**s that, instead of helping, are hindering the therapeutic process and limiting patients' adaptation to their social environment.

Two powerful techniques capable of obtaining this renunciation are the *challenge to the defenses* (Davanloo, 1986, 1990) and the *validation of the defenses in the past but not in the present* (McCullough Vaillant, 1997). Suffice it to say here that a therapist might feel more comfortable or more suited to one or the other. Whereas the challenge technique implies a daring attitude and tone, an active confrontation, **D** validation requires an equal amount of specificity and relentlessness but a more welcoming attitude and tone. The therapist's perception of a given patient's personality structure may also influence this technical option, in that the more the defensive system is seen as presenting with a rigid, tough resistance to change, the more a therapist may feel it appropriate to give a powerful shock, thus resorting to the challenge technique. The illustrative clinical case discussed later is basically an example of this kind. If, on the other hand, the defensive system of a patient is perceived by the therapist as a malfunctioning system needing highly active modification and healing, the corresponding attitude will be in the direction of **D** validation.

Anxiety Regulation (AA)

In the psychodynamic paradigm, anxiety (**A** in the Triangle of Conflict) is the prototype emotion mobilized in response to deep feelings (**X**) whose expression would be adaptive but is made impossible by their intensity and conflicting nature. According to McCullough Vaillant's (1997) functional view, the main function of **A** is *inhibitory*. Practically all other feelings can play an inhibitory role, but those most often having this effect, besides **A**, are shame, guilt, and emotional pain. **A** is typically experienced both psychologically and physically. Its most frequent manifestations are sensations in the abdomen or stomach, accelerated heartbeat, sweating, and a subjective experience similar to fear.

Not all of the **A**, however, is experienced at a conscious level. Like Coughlin Della Selva (1996, pp. 10–11), Davanloo identified three principal channels to the depth of the conscious and unconscious **A**: (1) through the striated musculature, (2) through the smooth musculature, and (3) by producing an alteration of the cognitive processes. When most **A** takes the way of the striated musculature, **A** is nearer to consciousness and patients "tend to associate their physical tension with **A** and to have a fairly accurate idea of what they are anxious about" (p. 10). When, instead, most of the **A** and its causes are unconscious, either the smooth musculature or the cognitive processes will be affected. Smooth musculature is involuntary and can involve most of the internal organs as well as the neuroendocrine system. Essentially, this is the case with people who tend to somaticize, often remaining unaware of the connection between their physical ailments, such as headaches, diarrhea, gastritis, and their state of nervousness. In such cases, too rapid a freeing of **A** is damaging because it is released directly on the organs involved, a potentially dangerous consequence in the case of organic pathologies such as asthma, ulcerative colitis, and duodenal ulcers. These situations must be nurtured with time so that patients can gradually become accustomed to the knowledge of their own **A** and can thus develop increasing tolerance toward it. Finally, when **A** alters the cognition, the body is not the victim, the ego function is. Mobilizing **A** could result in losing one's train of thought; sudden sensations of weakness, dizziness, or drowsiness, an urgent and sudden need for motor activity; and thought dissociation.

In the relationship between patient and therapist, **A** is mobilized in response to deep feelings coming nearer to consciousness. This usually happens as a consequence of the therapist's activities (**DA** or **XA**; see below). But within the session, it is crucial that, as McCullough Vaillant (1997, p. 13) states, the level of **A** must be "bearable and not overwhelming." Otherwise, **A** would act as a cloud covering all other emotions. The desirable level of **A** is one that does not exceed the patient's tolerance threshold.

The essence of the concept of **AA** (McCullough Vaillant, 1997) lies in not limiting oneself to merely making anxiety-laden material surface, but also in helping the patient to confront the **A** that derives from it. If, because of a gradual **AA**, deep emotion (**X**) continues to be perceived within tolerable intensity levels, this experiencing can continue uninterrupted for as long as necessary without inhibitory interference. This is likely to provide a *corrective emotional experience* (Alexander & French, 1946). Various effective techniques for **AA** are described by McCullough Vaillant (1997); see her book (for clinical illustrations). Suffice it to say here that patients must be helped to recognize the ways they *experience* **A**. Another element of **AA** consists of making patients aware of the *connection* between their **A** and the underlying conflicting feelings (**X**). Finally, all interventions are to be carried out in an atmosphere of emotional presence and sharing between therapist and patient. The therapist is thus perceived as strong and allied to the patient, and this has a powerful supportive effect, which increases the patient's tolerance of **A**.

Fear of Expression and Emotional Maieutics (XA)
The *Oxford English Dictionary* defines "maieutic" as: "Pertaining to intellectual midwifery, i.e. to the Socratic process of helping a person to bring into full consciousness conceptions previously latent in his mind." When applied to E-STDP, this definition can be paraphrased: "Pertaining to *emotional* midwifery, i.e., to the process of helping persons to *experience fully emotions* previously latent in *themselves*." A midwife (*maia*, in ancient Greek) helps the mother to give birth and to withstand the pain of delivery. The parallel with what a therapist can do is not just metaphorical. Emotions are in fact felt through the body, and moving them out (in Latin, *e-movere* means "move out" or "move from") can indeed be painful. **XA** serves to catalyze the expression of emotions, experiences, or impulses that have not entered consciousness because of the fear, also unconscious, of releasing them or experiencing them for what they really are. The purpose of this activity is to attenuate this specific fear, help the *coalescing* of an emotion and the *experiencing* of it, make emotional *expression* possible, and *accept* what is expressed (Osimo, 2001b).

What led the author to realize the importance of this aspect was the observation that in some cases, even after **D**s were restructured and the level of **A** and emotional contact were adjusted to a satisfactory degree, the expected unconscious emotions did not emerge, and this was puzzling. Taped sessions were reviewed many times, seeking possible errors or omissions. Which of the patient's **D**s had been overlooked? Which **D**s was the patient not able to overcome despite his or her commitment and the therapist's help? The author realized that there is a varying degree of resistance in each patient, directly *deriving from the fear of expression in and of itself*. Thus, when the patient is theoretically ready and even actually willing to express, but is simultaneously paralyzed by the fear of doing so, there is resistance.

It is useful to keep this fear, so closely connected with the act of expressing, distinct from other types of **A** in that it has an intense, primordial quality and is not accessed by consciousness for the very reason that it *precedes* emotional expression. With some patients, a holding or generally accepting attitude is insufficient, and acting on their **D**s is even less useful. They need the therapist's *active support of their expression* because they are not able to sustain the emotional impact themselves. Of course, there are other individuals for whom this particular fear is negligible. With such individuals, **XA** is not really necessary. In a number of cases, however, it is necessary to facilitate access into their innermost emotions.

The ways of carrying out **XA** are simple and almost as primordial as the fear of expression. Obviously, the purpose of **XA** is to attenuate fear and, therefore, to provide a highly specific support of emotional expression. Verbal interaction is not always necessary, and is usually very limited, aiming to directly support expression or diminish the fear of it. Generally, it is limited to short phrases such as "A feeling seems to be coming," "Is there an emotion stirring within you now?", and even "You seem frightened/terrified of something that is moving inside you." Because the verbal component is the least important, describing **XA** solely with words is very difficult. It is best to work with the videotaped material to make the interaction between therapist and patient directly observable. In fact, the fundamental aspect, whether accompanied by statements such as those above or not, is the therapist's whole disposition toward the patient. This involves the therapist's *presence,* which includes the spirit of willingness to accept the patient's emotions. An openness, which is expressed through looks and tone of voice, empathically reflects expressions and posture.

Fostering the springing out of emotions involves presence, containment, and contact. It must serve to alleviate pain, to give strength without rejecting, thus making patients feel that their attempt to "let go" and the fear that accompanies it are balanced with a sufficient amount of understanding support. To express, patients may need additional strength, which can be derived from the emotional connection formed with the therapist. This overall attitude helps the experience of emotions and strengthens the relationship with the therapist, who is then perceived as a living human being, truly involved in the relationship and capable of closeness. It also catalyzes the therapeutic process, avoiding excessive cognitive efforts and rationalization. To achieve this it is crucial to be open and to participate and connect as much as possible. This involves actively getting close to the other person, whereas the fact of deliberately limiting communication to a verbal level notably reduces the possibility of carrying out **XA**, increasing the **Ds** and leading to the detachment and freezing of emotions in both patient and therapist. A frequent omission by therapists is failure to observe, support, and facilitate everything that is expressed through the body. As a result, many aspects of the expression are lost, especially in cases where most or a considerable part of the expression takes place through the body.

METHODS OF ASSESSMENT AND INTERVENTION

The Trial Relationship

Trial relationship (**TR**) derives from Davanloo's (1990) trial therapy, with a number of modifications and more emphasis on the interpersonal aspect. It takes place during the first therapeutic session and subsequently can be completed in one or two sessions. In this phase, it is preferable to conduct longer, two- to three-hour sessions, as this is a complex intervention that fulfills a variety of needs.

1. To establish an emotional contact with the other person.
2. To try out the three activities, **DA**, **XA**, and **AA**, and, on the basis of the patient's responsiveness to each of them and combinations of them, to determine the possibility of a *more or less* rapid access to the unconscious emotions and conflicts.
3. To make a psychodynamic formulation of the patient's problems.
4. To collect a thorough history, paying particular attention to the psychoemotional development and the quality of relational experiences in the patient's life. Physical pathology will also have to be detected and recorded because of its importance and possible connection with emotional problems. A psychiatric or descriptive diagnosis will be formulated.
5. To evaluate the results of the **TR** itself, that is, the motivation of both therapist and patient to work together and the feasibility of this type of psychotherapy, including an estimate of its duration.

Flexible Format

In general, the **TR** lasts between one and six hours over one or two sessions. The higher the patient's *resistance* and the greater the complexity of his or her problems, the longer the **TR** will have to be. Another reason for the extended duration of the **TR** session(s) is that it often mobilizes **A** and arouses emotions that must be allowed first to be experienced and then to settle, avoiding a sudden interruption of the session while the patient is in contact with very intense emotions.

The E-STDP approach requires that therapists use all of their relational skills in establishing an open rapport with the patient. Therefore, it is important that therapists "be themselves" and act naturally. Everything counts: the way one looks at the other, facial expression, body position, emotional attitude; willingness to respond to the most common requests for clarification, such as those concerning the session, the face-to-face position of the chairs, videorecording, payment arrangements, and so on. Therapists can introduce themselves by saying their name and shaking hands with the patient, which is repeated at the beginning and end of every session.

Therapists cannot always be readily open and attentive. They may have gone to bed too late the night before or be distracted by their own personal happiness or worries. Certainly, it is essential to feel "well enough" to be able to conduct a session, because pretending to feel well will hinder the creation of a good connection. It must be clear from the onset that in making themselves available to develop a relationship with the patient, therapists expect a similar commitment in return. Generally, the most efficient way of conveying this message is to start immediately to mirror the tactical **D**s used by the patient. These are used by the patient with an unconscious aim to create an emotional distance from the therapist. As soon as they appear, patients must be made aware of their tendency to engage in diffuse discourse, to retract, divert, indulge in stereotypical smiles or facile whimpers, to leave everything vague, and to always weigh words. By making patients immediately aware of these maneuvers and of their effect on the relationship, it gradually becomes possible to:

- Mirror the defenses (**DA**) and determine patients' responsiveness to this.
- Evaluate patients' initial motivation to work with this approach, on the basis of their willingness to cooperate, to a lesser or greater degree, in seeking to avoid reliance on tactical **D**s after they have been mirrored.
- Observe even the slightest signs of **A** or any other feeling (**X**).
- Speed up the taking of personal history.

It is not always best to start by mirroring the tactical **D**s. If a patient is charged with **A**, it first is necessary to carry out **AA**, bringing it down to levels that will make satisfactory communication possible. This also represents a way of *taking care of the relationship with the patient*, showing interest in his or her experience of the interaction with the therapist. Finally, it can occur, though more rarely, that patients arrive at a session under the influence of a prior feeling. For example, they may be irritated by earlier having explained their problems to other therapists or by having to fill in boring questionnaires and take projective tests. Or patients may be in a state of acute grief. In such cases, it is best to begin the session by facilitating these emotions by means of **XA**.

Regardless of how the session has begun, throughout the **TR**, there will be a repeated succession of passages from one dynamic activity to another. The result will be an activation of the patient's unconscious conflicting emotions. This means a rapid uncovering of the relevant dynamics, as well as an acceleration of history taking and the creation of a relationship with the patient. As a result of this, in a relatively short time, the **TR** will answer a few crucial questions: (1) Is this patient responding sufficiently well to the E-STDP approach? (2) Is he or she working with sufficient rapidity to make it realistic to undertake an accelerated therapeutic process? (3) Is E-STDP powerful and specific enough for this patient's type of problem, or are other approaches likely to be more effective? When the answers to these questions are affirmative, a therapeutic contract will be agreed on with the patient and standard-length therapeutic sessions will follow on a weekly basis.

MAJOR SYNDROMES, SYMPTOMS, AND PROBLEMS TREATED WITH E-STDP

The inclusion or exclusion of possible candidates to E-STDP rests, ultimately, is the outcome of the **TR**. No scale, no questionnaire, no diagnostic classification of patients can make up for direct clinical judgment and provide an accurate enough prediction of the answers to the three crucial questions mentioned at the end of the preceding section. This does not mean, though, that diagnosis, projective testing, and other measures or indicators are useless or irrelevant. Nevertheless, their resolving power is insufficient for this purpose, in that the descriptive recognition and classification of a syndrome or "disturbance" says too little about the extent to which the profound forces behind it can be permanently modified. Three indicators are regarded as valuable aids and are considered here: descriptive diagnosis, prevailing defensive style, and Global Assessment of Functioning (GAF; American Psychiatric Association [APA], 1994, p. 32).

Patients with personality disorders and most neuroses are the major target of E-STDP. Treatment, as well as its length, is always patient-tailored in E-STDP, but Avoidant, Dependent, Passive-Aggressive, Depressive, Antisocial, and some Obsessive-Compulsive, Borderline, and Histrionic Personality Disorders tend to require up to 40 sessions, the same as a number of other Axis I disturbances, such as depressive, anxiety, somatoform, and sexual disorders due to psychological factors, and Bulimia Nervosa. Patients with Narcissistic, Paranoid "traits of" (McCullough Vaillant, 1997, p. 408) Schizoid and Schizotypal Personality Disorders, and the remaining types of Obsessive-Compulsive, Borderline, and Histrionic Personality Disorders will more often need a higher number of sessions, ranging from 40 to 80.

As regards the *prevailing defensive style*, Vaillant's hierarchy of defenses (Vaillant, 1977) is extremely useful. Vaillant served as a *DSM-IV* advisor on defense levels and individual defense mechanisms (APA, 1994, Appendix B). The distinction made there between neurotic and immature defensive styles provides an excellent indicator. The more that projection, schizoid fantasy, hypocondriasis, and other immature **Ds** are woven into the structure of the patient's defensive system, the greater the therapeutic task that lies ahead.

The GAF also represents a useful index. A GAF > 60 is likely to allow for a rapid activation of the unconscious conflicting emotions and, consequently, for a shorter therapy, whereas a GAF between 50 and 60 generally requires a more gradual pace. With a GAF between 40 and 50, the application of a longer format of E-STDP, over 80 sessions, is often required.

CASE EXAMPLE: AN EVER-WAITING YOUNG WOMAN

DIAGNOSIS AND ASSESSMENT

This patient, a woman 22 years of age, had been seen a few times prior to the **TR**, by a psychiatric resident at the Psychiatric Clinic, Universitá

Statale di Milano, Italy.* The *DSM-IV* diagnosis was Panic Disorder Without Agoraphobia, 300.01 on Axis I, and Dependent Personality Disorder, 301.6 on Axis II. She had had panic attacks for the prior 2½ years, which were unsuccessfully treated with fluoxetine and benzodiazepines.

CASE FORMULATION

Her history included her father's death from a sudden heart attack when her mother was two months pregnant with the patient. She spent many years with her maternal grandparents, with whom, apparently, she got on well. She saw her mother mainly on weekends. Then she moved in with her mother and brother. Recently, she had had problems concerning work, having been fired, and this seemed in some way relevant to the precipitation of her problems, even though it was unclear exactly how. Besides the panic symptoms, the patient had strong inner feelings of being different from her peers; she felt inferior, easily dismissed, and not cared about. She was highly compliant with others' needs and demands (mother, boyfriend, boss), which resulted in a tendency to let herself be used. She was unable to achieve the closeness she craved.

TREATMENT APPROACH AND RATIONALE FOR ITS SELECTION

The case was discussed at weekly case conference, where the resident emphasized the stubbornness with which the patient was constantly complaining about her panic attacks (PA). It was understandable that she needed to call attention to this symptom, which she perceived as very frightening and paralyzing, but, at the same time, the patient's monotonous and repetitive complaints made it arduous to address other meaningful aspects of her life. As a result of the case discussion, we decided to offer her a **TR**, in the hope that a direct approach to the patient would elicit a good response and that this would improve our understanding of the underlying dynamics. It was expected beforehand that we would be faced with a patient who was at the same time very anxious *and* using her symptoms as a defensive barrier, opposing all attempts to get to the deeper issues involved. The emphasis placed on the rigidity of the patient's character in the case conference called for a challenging stance on the therapist's part. It must also be observed that:

- According to a more organic, but equally respectable, vision of things, PA might arise from a biological predisposition, in which case, there would be little sense in looking for a psychodynamic explanation and cure.
- Even in cases where there is or may be a psychodynamic etiology or explanation, this would not necessarily imply that a given patient is willing to have it addressed and that he or she is capable of using this understanding constructively.

There was an implied twofold mandate in this **TR**: first, to try to go beyond the patient's defensive anxiety and stubbornness; and second, to explore the patient's dynamics and see if they were amenable to psychotherapy, and, if not, to refer the patient for an alternative approach that has proven useful for anxiety disorders in other cases, such as cognitive therapy, psychotropic drugs, or autogenic training.

One of the advantages of the extended format of the **TR** is that it can answer a number of questions in a single session, which saves time. Of

---

*A few vignettes from this clinical case, in much less detail and without the 5 years 8 months follow-up material, are included in an article published by the *Journal of the American Academy of Psychoanalysis* (Osimo, 1998).

course, the time required for such an interview is generally longer than the ritual 50 minutes. In this case, total time was 2 hours and 15 minutes. The following version is abridged, but remarkably detailed, to convey how far-reaching a **TR** can be, both in terms of the areas covered and the depth of the emotional response. This richness of data and the possibility of starting up the therapeutic process do indeed justify the session's long duration.

TRIAL RELATIONSHIP

The Symptom Used as a Defense against the Relationship
Predictably, the patient started off with her favorite subject: anxiety and PA.

THERAPIST: What seems to be your problem?
PATIENT: Panic attacks: out of the blue, with really no reason, a lot of anxiety . . . it practically paralyzes me.
THERAPIST: Uhm, uhm.
PATIENT: That is, when a bad panic attack occurs, I must do something because . . . otherwise, if I think about it, I get worse. A mounting terror takes hold of me and . . . I am afraid of something. (Puts her left hand on her chest.)
THERAPIST: You mean you have a physical sensation right where you pointed?
PATIENT: Yes, my heart beats right here. As though something made me anxious.

As usually happens in this type of syndrome, there is anticipatory anxiety. Moreover, after 2½ years, PA have become a "natural" or familiar aspect of the patient's life, as though, rather than arising in one way or another from the patient, they had an independent reality of their own that is totally out of the patient's control, the same as would apply to an epileptic fit. This aspect adds to the seemingly organic origin of this syndrome. Nevertheless, the patient is *really* anxious and the ways in which her **A** is manifested need to be explored. If **A** is too intense, it can work like a cloud, preventing any other aspect from being seen, so it will need to be regulated (see above). The patient describes her **A**:

PATIENT: Here it's like having a weight on my stomach, my hands start sweating, I start going cold, pale, that is, it feels like a knot in my throat, at times I get palpitations . . . at times instead I only have these . . . but I am afraid of fainting, of falling ill.

This patient feels taken over by her attacks of **A**, as though she is made totally powerless by them. The feeling she is conveying is: There is nothing anyone can do about it! She cannot see the *defensive* use she constantly makes of her symptom; that is, her defense is ego-syntonic, it is felt as being a part of her ego. The therapist starts to challenge this conviction:

THERAPIST: Uhm, uhm, I understand. Then this is just a physical problem you have.
PATIENT: Well, physical . . . I went for blood testing . . . and I've got nothing physically . . . I happen to get up in the morning feeling well, I get up; in the night, after supper, I throw myself on the sofa, I don't know, I start getting anxious, anxiety starts and so forth.

The patient explains that it comes about more often in the night, either at home, especially if she is alone, or at the store (where she used to work) or in the street.

THERAPIST: Do you often happen to be home on your own?
PATIENT: No, well, not really. There's my mother and my brother; I don't know, perhaps when my mum goes to the mountains on weekends, and my brother goes out . . . at times I am left alone, I may watch TV, so I don't think about it . . .

THERAPIST: Your mother goes to the mountains. Do you never go with her?
PATIENT: No, I prefer staying home. There's my boyfriend there. On Sunday I go out, so . . . it comes in the night when I am alone.
THERAPIST: Uhm, uhm.
PATIENT: I get scared to feel ill. I start thinking I'm feeling ill, that something will happen, all this comes about and I start feeling shaky.
THERAPIST: So the idea of feeling ill . . .
PATIENT: Scares me.

This indicates the need for further exploration of her anxiety.

THERAPIST: What is your idea of what might occur?
PATIENT: I don't know, that something is about to come. That is, when I start feeling my heart pounding, Oh God, now something is happening to me.
THERAPIST: What is happening?
PATIENT: Ah, that I will faint, or I will get a heart attack, or I get dizzy . . . I start being shaky, I'm afraid of falling down, of feeling ill, that something will happen to me, and of fainting.
THERAPIST: Uhm and also of dying. (This comment is based on what the patient said in previous interviews.)
PATIENT: Yeah, yeah, that goes in phases, I mean, at times, I often think I will die there and then, at other times instead, I use my head and I say: Well once you've died, that's it! But at times it hinders and weakens me.

Here the therapist makes a tentative interpretation, with no response whatsoever:

THERAPIST: Your inner experience, then, is that you might die and nobody would come to your rescue.
PATIENT: That is, more than dying I am afraid of feeling ill, especially among people . . . I am afraid something will happen to me among people . . . also when I am alone at home and none of the family is around . . . I am scared that something will happen to me and nobody can help.
THERAPIST: Did this ever happen?
PATIENT: No, it's 2½ years now I've been going on like that. Last year, worse; this year, a bit better. Last year, right horrible: every night at a given time . . .

By now, the interviewer has realized what the resident must have experienced while she was interacting with this patient, and that unless one is prepared to go on forever talking about panicking and anxiety, this **D** needs to be put aside. That is, it is crucial to break down this barrier hiding whatever else is meaningful in the patient's emotional life. From now on, the patient's defense of putting forward her symptom as a shield is challenged again and again with a view to making a better and freer emotional connection with the therapist possible, instead of continuing to confine their interaction to that single theme.

THERAPIST: Now then, when I ask you What's your problem, what do you answer?
PATIENT: Well, that . . .
THERAPIST: No, because it isn't a physical problem, no?
PATIENT: Not in my opinion, no.
THERAPIST: So, what is the problem you think you have *in your life*?
PATIENT: In my life?
THERAPIST: Yes, because by now, we know everything about your symptom.
PATIENT: It is hindering me . . .
THERAPIST: Do you notice you keep on talking about that?
PATIENT: To me, this is the main problem.
THERAPIST: So, why is it that you are coming here? Your doctor would certainly prescribe you a new sedative if you ask him.
PATIENT: Am I supposed to be on sedatives all my life?

THERAPIST: Why have you come here?
PATIENT: To get help.
THERAPIST: But the point is, What kind of help? Because I don't know if you notice it, but you are saying nothing about your life . . . and if you go on like this, we'll never understand why the symptoms came about. What's the problem in your life?

It is remarkable how, as the therapist is trying to corner the patient's defensive use of her symptom, the patient's unconscious starts to release just a bit of information about her life. Initially, however, this happens in homeopathic dosage, and in a doubtful, tentative way.

PATIENT: Well, maybe . . . partly about work . . . I liked that job, but they fired me . . . I was left at home and it was . . . I started with this symptom thing, because I could not have the job I wanted. I had many interviews, but . . . nothing. (The patient seems sad while saying this.)

Breaking through the Defensive Barrier
Now the patient is providing an important link between her symptoms and "not managing to have the job I wanted." In a different framework, such as a less active psychodynamic therapy or psychoanalysis, this communication by the patient could and should be interpreted, for example, by inquiring about the patient's feelings about that incident, or about other situations in her life when she felt similarly disappointed or left out. But the therapist here chooses to carry on with his challenge to the **D**s, which will actually bring about a faster surfacing of emotions (**X**) in the patient. Another consequence of this rapid weakening of the patient's defense will be that a notable part of the derepressed feelings will be felt in connection with the therapist, who has been "guilty" of having disabled the patient's defensive system. In the triangles' language, there is an activation of **X** at the **T**. The next intervention by the therapist is ruthlessly unsupportive, but what he says is accurate and, again, refers the patient to the emotional part of herself:

THERAPIST: So, we are getting nearer to something [meaningful]. At the same time, this is not an employment agency, just as it isn't a drug dispensary, and you haven't come here to find a job.
PATIENT: Sure. (Voice changes, eyes are looking around.)
THERAPIST: So, what's happened, your job ended and . . .
PATIENT: (Choked.) And nothing.

Now the patient is visibly emotionally aroused. It is crucial for the therapist to realize this and to shift from **DA** to helping the patient to express what she is feeling using **XA**.

THERAPIST: What is your feeling right now?
PATIENT: There is anger, more than anything else.
THERAPIST: Anger, at whom?
PATIENT: That is . . . at myself, that is, I'm unable to . . .

Frequently patients suddenly getting in touch with an intense feeling (**X**) react with **A** and try to protect the therapist from what they feel. This patient, under the impact of her emotion, stops looking at the therapist and seems unable to direct her anger at a specific person.

THERAPIST: You say you feel anger. You don't look at me and say it is at yourself.
PATIENT: No, I mean to say . . . (Again looks away.)
THERAPIST: And you keep on looking away . . . there, do you notice that?
PATIENT: (Defiant.) Have I to look you in the face?

THERAPIST: Do you notice you tend to *avoid* my face? (The patient nods.) That is, when you say you feel anger, and we still don't know at whom, you start avoiding my eyes.
PATIENT: I'm not doing it on purpose.
THERAPIST: I didn't say that. So, can we look at this anger you have?
PATIENT: Okay.
THERAPIST: It is what kind of anger, is it strong or . . .
PATIENT: Strong.

The patient has now admitted to her rage and to her avoidance of the therapist's eyes, but she will immediately resort to a sequence of other **D**s: She first generalizes, then tries to retract what she said and to deny her feeling, and finally she starts rationalizing about not wanting to blame it on anybody. It would *seem* that she is angry, but not at anybody in particular. We take up the interview after a few lines.

THERAPIST: Uhm, do you notice that you have this tendency to remain vague? When you say "at people." (The patient nods.) Can we look at it more closely?
PATIENT: Yes.
THERAPIST: Because this rage came about, sure, it can be at more than one person, but, to start with, at whom? There must be someone in particular.
PATIENT: No, not as far as that. That is, I have rage in a general sense, meaning that . . .
THERAPIST: But this is general.
PATIENT: Ah, that is, I am not angry at somebody.
THERAPIST: Do you notice the way you avoid focusing on the target of your anger?
PATIENT: The point is that I don't know. That is, I *think* I am angry.
THERAPIST: Now you *think* you are angry. You're not sure anymore?
PATIENT: Okay, I am sure, with somebody, in that I didn't expect they would leave me . . .

THERAPIST: With somebody?
PATIENT: Since it is a firm, it cannot be just one person to tell me: You stay home.
THERAPIST: This is a nice piece of reasoning, but are you angry at the wall? At the world?
PATIENT: No.
THERAPIST: Then you are angry at somebody.
PATIENT: (Again trying to rationalize.) I am not angry at someone, I am angry in the sense . . .
THERAPIST: (Extremely direct.) Are you saying that I am being unclear or that I am mad?
PATIENT: No, I am not saying that . . .
THERAPIST: Because if I am, I won't be able to help you.

The therapist is conveying, by implication, that the decision about whether to disclose emotionally charged information rests entirely with the patient. Only if she will disclose, however, will the therapist be able to help her. The patient ends up admitting to her anger:

PATIENT: Yes, I have rage, I did not expect this decision.
THERAPIST: Someone is likely to have made you think differently.
PATIENT: Yes, in the office, voices . . .
THERAPIST: Some *people's* voices?
PATIENT: Correct.

After some further resistance, the patient admits her anger at her floorwalker. The patient got on pretty well in that job, and she describes Mr. R. as a kind and lenient man, trying to be helpful. She worked there for two years on a time-limited contract. As this is being said, the patient gets a bit sad, which the therapist mirrors back to her, using **XA** to facilitate the feeling:

THERAPIST: And you get a lump again (The patient smiles.) when I say it is a time-limited contract. How come?

PATIENT: I don't know. Today this is the way it goes.

Last Resistance and Surfacing of Deep Emotion
The patient resorts to vagueness again, but sadness is coming, and she needs just a bit of further **XA**. The therapist mirrors to the patient what he is seeing.

THERAPIST: When you say "Today this is the way it goes," again you tend to leave things vague. But you are here out of your own free choice, aren't you? Because you have a problem you want to solve, because these problems are hindering you and make your life a misery and . . . uhm, pitiful. And you said "Today it's the way it goes." Not today only, but yesterday and the day before as well . . . and in a way also tomorrow, unless we do something today. And there is a lot of feeling in you. In a way, I have in front of me a young woman who seems to me to have a great need to share with me what she feels; at the same time, she avoids looking at me and she seems afraid to let me see, even if she desires it, she seems to be afraid . . . and it seems that you have much sadness and not only anger. (**XA**, **AA**, and **DA**.)
PATIENT: Uhm. (Starts sobbing.)
THERAPIST: Uhm, what does it mean?
PATIENT: That you are right.
THERAPIST: That this is true?
PATIENT: (Nods, already sobbing for some time.)

For some time, the therapist helps the patient to sustain the experience of her feeling, using **XA**. Because such an intense sadness is being freed in the patient, it is a good moment for getting to understand something regarding the *origin* of this sadness, helping the patient to stay with her feeling and express thoughts or memories coming on its wave.

THERAPIST: What are the sad thoughts coming to your mind and that accompany this sadness of yours?
PATIENT: (Sobbing more and more, with a broken voice.) That is, *all* that I *ever* had was failures.
THERAPIST: So there is much sadness, there is much more that needs to come out. When you say that, in a way, all that you had was failures—which is quite a statement—what is the first thing that comes to mind?
PATIENT: Ah, that I was born, that is, since I was born . . .
THERAPIST: Go on.
PATIENT: (Cannot speak.)
THERAPIST: You are overwhelmed with sadness.
PATIENT: I can't manage to stop sobbing.
THERAPIST: Uhm, so there must be plenty of things to say, ah? (**AA + XA**.)
PATIENT: In my opinion, it's been since I was born . . . (Sobs.) Well, I am unlucky. Everything I decide to do . . .
THERAPIST: Mmmh. You see, in this moment, what you are saying may well be true, but it is very general, isn't it? "From when I was born to date: all wrong."
PATIENT: It's also to do with my character, whenever I start something . . .
THERAPIST: Blaming it all on yourself is not helping you.
PATIENT: Ah, I know . . .
THERAPIST: (Continuing to help the patient's expression.) Because there is much sadness, but there is also much anger, as we know. So, unless you want to keep on avoiding, even here with me, to share with me your most genuine thoughts and feelings—which would be a self-destructive thing to do, no? Because you come here in order to solve a problem you have. We know this problem of yours has to do with these feelings you have inside. It would be counterproductive if they don't come out.

PATIENT: Yes, you are right.
THERAPIST: Then you would leave the place with your fear, your symptoms, and all the rest that we know by heart, everybody knows that by heart, but it is not what you want.
PATIENT: I am fed up even mentioning it. (Goes on sobbing.)
THERAPIST: Since you are fed up, let's look at where all this feeling there is in you comes from, okay? If you wish the two of us to get somewhere together.
PATIENT: Yes.
THERAPIST: Can you afford leaving this place without getting anywhere?
PATIENT: I don't believe so. (Whispered.)
THERAPIST: Then let's see where all this sadness and this anger come from, uhm?
PATIENT: (Pause, sobbing.) Well . . .
THERAPIST: Where do you want to start?

Mourning of Father's Death

PATIENT: When I was little, that my daddy died, that my mother was pregnant with me when he died. (Sobs.) And then . . .
THERAPIST: Hang on . . . wait before saying "and then." Clearly, there's already a very intense feeling about this (The patient keeps on sobbing, but more intensely.) and you are defending against it because it is very painful.
PATIENT: There are times when I feel almost calm, at other times I think about it . . .
THERAPIST: Do you see there is a very great pain?
PATIENT: Mmmh?
THERAPIST: It seems to me that there is something very painful that you are feeling.
PATIENT: Yes, I told you. At times, when somebody asks, I, quietly, say "He died." At times, I think of it and anguish comes. (Broken voice.)
THERAPIST: What is tormenting you? Be honest with yourself.

PATIENT: At times, I might have wished he was near me. I don't even know, let's say, the way he was. Yet, I would have liked . . .
THERAPIST: (Implicitly linking the patient's desire to look at her father with the **T**.) And you are not looking at me!
PATIENT: I would have liked to get to know him, that is . . .

It turns out that, in spite of never having seen her father, she saw pictures of him, keeps one in her wallet, and often looks at it. There are a number of meaningful feelings concerning her father, which are now explored together by patient and therapist. Since the moment the patient got in touch with her profound sadness, she has been in a "core state," in which there is no resistance, and she is going through a "visceral experience of deep affect" (Fosha, 2000, 2001). This makes it possible to weave together the inner emotional life of the patient, her desires, and her conflicts. By the end of this **TR** session, therapist and patient will have put together a "dynamic map," enabling them to make a decision about type of treatment and its planning. The doubts about whether the patient is responsive to dynamic psychotherapy are resolved. A very rich inner life involving the father is now unfolding. From her youth and adolescence, the patient had always had a longing to do things with her father, to go around with him, to get to know him, his character. She often thinks of him, imagining his facial expression, his eyes.

THERAPIST: First of all, do you imagine his eyes would look at you or avoid looking?
PATIENT: No, they look at me!

Father's expression would convey that he is willing to help her, that he is close. This dead father is very much alive in the patient's mind and has kept her company through the years.

This says much about the patient's emotional life and, moreover, suggests some difficulty or inadequacy in her relationships with her mother and, possibly, with other parental figures. All this will need to be investigated before the end of the **TR**.

When she was a girl, she spent time with her male cousin, who is her age, and her uncle. She remembers she felt different from her cousin as well as from other children, whose families would get together on weekends. As the patient is recalling all this and describing her inner life, there are waves of emotion coming. She is at times sobbing in sadness, and at other times angry, as when she says:

PATIENT: It does not feel just to me that I was not able to know him . . . . nor that he, automatically, could see me. He hasn't seen his daughter, do you understand?

She loved her cousin, but felt envious of his closeness with his father. She starts feeling compassion for herself and gradually comes to other painful feelings of both pity and anger at her father for having died. All these feelings are tangled together and are also often conflicting with each other. The patient's desire for her father and her need to mourn his death are thoroughly understandable, but, at the same time, her enormous emphasis on this suggests that other important relations in her life may be missing some crucial element and this might be the reason that she needs to overinvest her inner images and memories of father, thus using a mechanism of *displacement.*

PATIENT: But now more than before. Now I would perhaps need my father, even if there is my mother. I don't know, at times I'd really wish . . . (Sobs.) I think of him, I'd really wish to see him, you see?
THERAPIST: As though the picture could come to life . . .

PATIENT: Exactly.
THERAPIST: This is what you intensely desire. A poignant desire, this one. That is, I mean, it is painful.
PATIENT: (Sobs.) And yet, I'd love that. That is, in my fantasy, I would want something like that to happen.
THERAPIST: So, in your life, you are still very connected with this father you never met. You long for him. You want him. You never stopped wanting him . . . and in a way, you go as far as thinking that you will die from a heart attack. Quickly. Out of the blue. Which is what happened to your father, mmh?
PATIENT: I am afraid of ending like him. Without managing to live all my life. Enjoy my children . . .

Various aspects of the defensive identification of the patient with her father are highlighted, and further anger is uncovered. As the therapist points out, however, if she really were to die from a heart attack:

THERAPIST: Somebody else would suffer then.
PATIENT: If something happened to me? Of course, there would be my mother. At times I think of that, though.

Precipitating Event
For the first time, the patient's mother and brother come into the dynamic picture. The patient, metaphorically speaking, needs to be with her father, but she is starting to admit other important people on the scene of her unconscious life. Before getting to all this, we may observe that one of the deep desires mentioned by the patient was that her father could have seen her having a job for the first time in her life. This accounts for the fact that being let down by her floorwalker had such a disproportionate impact on her and precipitated her symptoms.

PATIENT: I think of my father more often now.

THERAPIST: Excellent. Then let's see a specific time you remember.

PATIENT: Thinking of him? When I was happy, when I had my job, and I felt settled, let's say, I thought of him; my thought was that he might, well, feel satisfied, had he been here.

THERAPIST: When did this happen, when you started working?

PATIENT: Yes, when I worked. I had my independence, I saw that my mum was happy about me. I thought that if my father had been there, surely he would have felt satisfied with me. That is... (Pause. The patient sobs and cannot speak. She bends forward in pain.)

THERAPIST: Is it very strong, this pain?

PATIENT: Rather so. I believe I missed out some moments in life which a father and a son can share. Like feeling a protection...

Brother

The patient said "son" and not "daughter" (the Italian for these differ by just one vowel), and the therapist takes this chance to explore the patient's feelings in connection with her brother. It turns out that there is some envy of the brother, who had a father for seven years and was "recognized" by him. As will emerge, other sources of this envy are that her mother is more attentive to him than to the patient.

THERAPIST: But you've been the one who was not recognized?

PATIENT: Sure, I have been unlucky. I am not aware of whether he knew my mother was pregnant before he died. Apart from that, I would have liked it if we'd seen each other, if we'd had a rapport, like father and child.

THERAPIST: Would you have looked at him in his eyes?

PATIENT: That is my remorse.

THERAPIST: When you say "remorse," you feel guilty about something.

PATIENT: Yeah, I mean: I could have been born one year earlier. (Smiles.)

THERAPIST: You see that, in a way, there is rage because your father didn't conceive you one year before! Because, of course, it rested with him, no? Not with you.

Here, in an utterly spontaneous way, the patient depicts her ability to use detachment as a defense, pretending indifference. As will appear later, this defense is also closely connected with her relationship with her mother.

PATIENT: Of course! Not with me, at last! Let's say it is a burden; that is, when I think about it. At other times, instead, even when I talk about it I don't care... At times, when I talk with friends, they may ask—like at school, you know, when they get to know each other—I am peaceful. There is no rage as I speak.

THERAPIST: Are you detached?

PATIENT: Yes, I am detached. That is, I say: He died, that's it. He died from infarction, the end. Instead, maybe, when I talk like this, I get a lump in my throat. Probably I am...

THERAPIST: But did you happen to talk about this with someone else?

Mother: The Missing Closeness

PATIENT: With my mum, no. I refrain; that is, because I feel ashamed. We may talk about it when she brings up the subject... and I think to myself: I would have enjoyed seeing him. Then maybe I get a lump. And I go, because I don't want my mum to see me crying about that.

THERAPIST: Let's look at it, because clearly, nobody can give you back your father, that's for sure. But when someone dies, he leaves memories, and regarding your mother, he left her you, your brother, a number of memories, part of which are nice,... I don't know if you are aware of them or not, because if you never talked about it, you can't know!

PATIENT: We don't often face this subject, at home.
THERAPIST: It seems to me that you never face it!
PATIENT: As a child, clearly, I was told that he died. But it is not the case that I go and ask my mum about the way he was, the way he behaved. That is, it feels absurd to me, and shame comes!
THERAPIST: We have already learned about this ability of yours to detach yourself, leave things vague, to say "couldn't care less"; yet, one of the things your father left, on his death, are the memories of him. And he left feelings in you, that we partially saw, and who knows how many feelings he may have left in your mother, brother, or other people! But many of these memories are preserved in your mother...
PATIENT: It's true!
THERAPIST: And your mother is alive.
PATIENT: We never talked about it.
THERAPIST: Let's see, because it is curious, in a way, if we think about it.
PATIENT: Yes, curious. I live with her everyday, and... we don't...
THERAPIST: This huge gap that there is in your life—and that you feel so intensely—your mother could partly fill it both by being a good mother (this we will look at later, we cannot put all together) and, regarding your father, also telling you about him, and sharing your feelings for this husband/father. That is, this man did exist. He is not here anymore, but he was. It's not the case that he's never been there, which would be a different situation.
PATIENT: I don't know. To me it is as though he'd never been there.

The father comes to the forefront again: He smoked cigarettes, he liked station wagons for the family and often changed cars, but the patient finds it very difficult to talk about all this with her mother. This shows that in the relationship with her mother, there must be some difficulty about closeness. In the session, this gives rise to some resistance, which, in turn, will need to be dealt with.

PATIENT: But at the same time, I don't feel like asking my mother. That is, it's almost like... I don't want my mother to see me crying or... to talk about this... (Sobs, broken voice.) Neither do I want her to know that I suffer because of this.
THERAPIST: Then you are without a father and without a mother!
PATIENT: No, I talk to my mother, I am not saying...
THERAPIST: Talk about the weather?
PATIENT: Of all the problems I have, but not of this one.
THERAPIST: Certainly not of all.... It seems to me that there is a lot you don't talk about with your mother. I don't know. This is my impression.
PATIENT: My mother is like a friend.
THERAPIST: What kind of a friend? A seaside friend? Let's see.
PATIENT: But I talk to my mother all the time, but not about this.
THERAPIST: Yes, yes, let's see. Because I think this is crucial. The first crucial thing in your life.

At this point in the **TR** interview, because the patient's conflicting emotions have already been activated, the simple fact of having stated that her mother is important to her and that it is unclear whether this relationship is fulfilling or not, is enough to trigger the patient's feelings. What comes out is that there is some good communication about daily life events. The patient can talk to her mother about job problems and if she and her boyfriend had a row. The latter usually happens when the patient feels neglected by him.

The patient is again sobbing and the therapist wonders if it is her fate to be always neglected.

Her answer confirms this, as she lists other neglecting people (e.g., her relatives). Feelings of shame about being neglected emerge, as though it was her fault. This aspect of the patient's character is explored carefully; she tends to be underdemanding with everybody, in terms of her emotional needs, which makes her feel a bit of a victim. Actually, she is not victimized about her real needs and wishes; rather, she calls attention to her symptoms or to her job problems, with a complaining but ineffective attitude, without managing to get the help and affection she wants. With some further help from the therapist, the patient is capable of overcoming her resistance: She admits to her jealousy of a previous boyfriend of her mother's, as well as to her anger and pain about never having felt that her mother's love was exclusive and unconditional. All this takes up a large part of the **TR** interview; it is summarized here for reasons of space. The relationship with her mother turns out to play a big part in the patient's character problem: her compliance and lack of assertion, her avoidance of what really matters, and her (consequent) detachment. Her feelings of shame and guilt block her desires and cripple her self-affirmation. As a consequence of this, she developed a dependent, underdemanding personality, and the only way she can call attention to her needs is through her panic symptoms. The careful and exhaustive exploration of the nuances of the patient's feelings and defenses is made possible only by a constant monitoring and mirroring of her attitude, posture, and expression in an atmosphere of closeness with the therapist. We take up the interview after about 45 minutes of constructive, cooperative, and emotionally charged exploration of all this.

A Corrective Emotional Experience

THERAPIST: You see, then, that there is a paralysis in you, in your life? Because you would need to talk about this and more than this with your mother, but this rage is still there! And as a result of not expressing it, you are crippled! You don't manage to do what you need to do, you can't talk to your mother, you take a detached position, and a wall of coldness gets built between you and your mother.

PATIENT: (Sobbing.) Yes.

THERAPIST: And you play a part in this. As we saw here, you can put up this wall, but you can also break it down.

PATIENT: But I can't. I don't really feel I can go to my mother and talk about these things. What do I tell her: I am enraged with you . . . ?

THERAPIST: You can talk about these issues, since here with me you seem to be talking about them.

PATIENT: But not with her.

THERAPIST: I mean, can you do it here?

PATIENT: Yes, but I feel ashamed.

THERAPIST: Do you feel ashamed here with me?

PATIENT: No, but I do with my mother. I would never speak of this with my mother.

THERAPIST: Do you see that this is self-destructive?

PATIENT: I know, but what could I tell her: I am angry with you because . . . I wouldn't know where to start!

THERAPIST: What to say is something you will decide that moment. What I want you to reflect on is that when you are in front of your mother, you tend to take a detached, distant position, and this is the opposite of what you need. This way you cut your own throat. This is what I want you to reflect on. Do you agree with what I said?

PATIENT: Yes.

THERAPIST: I mean, does it feel far-fetched or clear?

PATIENT: Clear. It is the truth.

THERAPIST: In a way, you tried to create this distance even with me. I am no exception, it is something you do with others as well.

PATIENT: Sure, yes.

THERAPIST: So it is unthinkable that you do this only with me. This inability to open up and instead to close down is something you have with others too, no?

PATIENT: Yes. (Pause.)
THERAPIST: How do you feel in this moment?
PATIENT: Calm. Now I do. (Pause.)

This relational problem with her mother is certainly crucial. It erodes the quality of the patient's affective life, leaving her dissatisfied in relation to most people, including her mother, brother, and boyfriend. The therapist now wishes to try to complete the picture by exploring the other important relationships.

Brother, Grandparents, and Close of the Interview
The patient's brother is older than she by eight years. There is a distance with him as well. He is "different" from the patient, meaning that he is able to open up and ask for advice, either from their mother or from the patient. She is pleased with this, but never asks for support or advice in her own turn, and ends up feeling neglected.

PATIENT: I always decide everything on my own. I do what I want. If something comes to mind, I do that. I ask nobody.
THERAPIST: Are you stubborn?
PATIENT: Stubborn.
THERAPIST: But you defeat your own interests... because it seems to me that you have a few strong desires, like, for instance, the one about closeness... You have this capacity to do everything on your own... but this is keeping you far from satisfying your need for closeness.
PATIENT: So it is. That is, I laugh and I joke, but... I've always been a shy, shut-in girl, but I've always adjusted, also with my friends... But even with them, it is not that kind of friendship...
THERAPIST: Is it a bit superficial?
PATIENT: Exactly! With many people. On the other hand, there are two women friends with whom there is real attachment.
THERAPIST: Really?
PATIENT: Yes, but regarding these things, I do not talk of my problems.
THERAPIST: Not even with them?
PATIENT: I happen to see others who have a rapport, with friends, they joke and laugh. I, I mean, I joke, I talk, but not a lot. I don't let them very close... as though I didn't care, which is not the case.
THERAPIST: When you say so, I do not understand in this moment what position you take.
PATIENT: What?
THERAPIST: When you say you cannot do as the others do, with that kind of despondent air, I don't understand if it is something you'd want to be able to achieve, or if you like being the victim.

Here, the therapist is exploring the patient's motivation to work hard in therapy to change her character. A therapist can be available and provide help and competence, but he or she would be unable to carry out the work in the absence of a patient willing to change. In this particular case, as in many others in this respect, one of the things to check is the possibility of working *together*. The majority of personality-disordered people do, in fact, have either a defiant or an overcompliant attitude.

PATIENT: No, I would like to be able to do that.
THERAPIST: There are times when you say "I cannot" with such a beaten attitude, as to let one think that it is something that cannot change. What is the way things are?
PATIENT: (Smiles.) I'd like to be different from how I am.
THERAPIST: I don't know... these things we said, about your stubbornness and the fact that you put a distance... You may well make a different decision.
PATIENT: I know one could behave differently, but how does one do it?
THERAPIST: What counts here is not how, because there is therapy for this. The thing is what you want, I mean... this is a choice.
PATIENT: I'd prefer to be a different person.
THERAPIST: And, as you say, there is no magic wand for changing character.
PATIENT: It's true.

THERAPIST: It involves work.
PATIENT: Yes quite!
THERAPIST: Do you feel you want to face this work or not?
PATIENT: Yes. (Pause, looks away.)
THERAPIST: Yes or no? Because you say yes looking away.
PATIENT: I have tried at times.
THERAPIST: By yourself, you mean?
PATIENT: Yes.
THERAPIST: Right! That's the way you are used to! But this is a type of work that one cannot do alone. It has taken the two of us to do it.

The patient is clearly willing to get the help she needs, and now she is able to see into her defense of proud self-sufficiency. Before bringing the TR to a close, the therapist inquires about her relationship with the maternal grandparents, because as a child, the patient lived with them for many years. A few highly meaningful words by the patient:

PATIENT: ... my grandparents... Well nothing, they brought me up... and
THERAPIST: With whom was the relationship stronger?
PATIENT: With my grannie. In fact, she was like a mother to me.

The patient, assisted by the therapist, reviews her attachment to her grandmother until the moment of her death, when the patient was 12. Her grannie also died from heart problems, like her father. The patient says there was a lot of closeness between them and, at the therapist's comment about how painful it must have been when she died, the patient starts sobbing again. She did not want to see her grannie's body, but she went to the funeral. The grandfather died shortly after.

THERAPIST: So, there is this big emotional involvement with those who died: your father...
PATIENT: And my grandparents.

THERAPIST: Your grandparents. Your grannie more, but also your grandpa.
PATIENT: Well, my grannie more because I was closer to her, but with my grandpa as well. He was with me all the time, our connection was really strong.
THERAPIST: And for some reason, with people who are alive—whether it is your mother, your brother, your boyfriend—part of your affection does not flow, it remains... it doesn't...
PATIENT: (Pause, sigh.)

By this time, there is enough evidence about the following:

1. The patient presents with panic attacks and a character problem, with elements of overcompliance, low self-assertion, low self-esteem, difficulty expressing disagreement, need for reassurance, feeling helpless when alone.
2. She is responsive to a highly active and challenging but also empathic dynamic approach.
3. The psychodynamic picture is clear enough to confirm the descriptive diagnosis and to exclude other, more severe problems that might require a different approach.
4. Hence, she is a good candidate for E-STDP.

THERAPIST: Do you think that the points we touched on are relevant to your life and to your problems?
PATIENT: Yes, they are.
THERAPIST: And regarding your feelings of fear, of dying from a heart attack or from something else... do you think there may be a connection... between these symptoms and the fact that the people you most loved have died?
PATIENT: Yes, yes.
THERAPIST: And there is rage because they died and, in a way, a part of you would like to take revenge and end up the same way!
PATIENT: It's not that I want to die!

THERAPIST: I know you don't want to. But, in a way, you do. I mean: you don't go as far as dying, but you manage very well to spoil your life, in a way!

PATIENT: I am realizing that.

It is now possible to propose a short-term psychotherapy to the patient, and to make plans for the 50-minute therapeutic sessions. The **TR** session can come to a close.

THE OTHER NINE SESSIONS

Session 1 was scheduled three months after the **TR**. During that time she had three major PA, with a strong component of fear of dying. The first session centered on her conflict between her longing for emotional closeness and feeling cared about, and her keeping others distant out of rage at not being understood and respected. She ended up not really saying the important things to anybody.

In session 2, other people's problems continued being more important than hers. She felt and behaved in a self-dismissive way. She mentioned having always slept in bed with her mother. When she was alone, she was afraid and needed to turn on the lights and TV. During the prior week, however, breaking her usual habit, she was able to speak with her mother about her state of suffering.

Session 3 threw light on a number of crucial aspects, providing further dynamic understanding. The patient said her symptoms were improving; she did not feel anxious either outside or at home and was generally calmer inside, more contained. However, she missed her boyfriend, Marco, whom she had recently left. She used to meet with him every day. At the same time, as a result of leaving him, she now felt more self-assured and independent. Two important new elements arose in this session:

1. The patient recalled that, at age 16, when the relationship with Marco started, her mother had to be admitted to the hospital, where she spent 20 days. Her condition seemed potentially severe, even though later she was completely cured.

2. In that same period, the patient started high school. She remembered having felt extremely anxious the night prior to the first day of school lest she would not be able to wake up in time the following morning. Her mother was in the hospital, and she was home alone. The habit of sleeping with mother had always provided *physical* closeness to the patient, which might have been positive in itself, had it not been the *only* type of closeness the patient felt she could have with her mother. Finally, one of the patient's symptoms, her need to turn on all the lights and TV when she is alone in the house, is starting to make sense as a way of making up for the lack of mother's physical presence in the house.

In session 4, the patient reported that she had been symptom-free during the prior week and that she felt more relaxed. She went out with two women friends and spoke about her present difficulties, giving up her usual falsely self-assured attitude. A meaningful series of incidents that she addressed in this session concerned her mother's behavior regarding food. This turned out to be an excellent illustration of the different attitudes the mother had from the patient and from the brother. The patient reported that when they were having fish or rice, of which the brother is fond but which the patient dislikes, her mother "forgets or pretends to forget that I don't like it," and this behavior triggers the patient's rage. This problem clearly goes beyond food: It highlights some real difficulty the mother must have always had with the patient, who, it is worth remembering, was born seven months after the husband's death.

The patient began session 5 by saying, "Coming here, which makes me think about things, I understood that, actually . . . I do not want to take things in anymore... so I thought about these things which I kept inside, since my mother never talked of them... Now I am aware of what I could do." Asked for clarification, she added: "Yes, I mean that I could be different... more open, even if... it is difficult for me! But let's say that I am aware of this, that I should open up, not keep things inside, at least with my mother." This spontaneous opening is meaningful in that it marks the moment when the patient feels it is in her power to change her character. The session is concerned with consolidating the patient's recent insights: (1) which of her mother's behaviors are likely to make her anxious or to trigger an angry reaction; (2) what exactly are the patient's desires (i.e., to feel that she can *talk to a mother* who *does really take into account* what she says, wants, and feels, and to feel, at least once in her life, that she is the *most important person* for her mother; and (3) what are the patient's feelings about not having her desires noticed or satisfied (i.e., raging inside). The final realization is that *she doesn't really need her mother so badly,* because she is able to relate well to other figures, such as her women friends.

Session 6 gave way to the patient's intense anger. When the therapist asked where the anger came from, the surprising answer was: "It goes back to when I was born," followed by "It was not worth being born." The essence of all this was the patient's thought that, because her father died when her mother was two months pregnant, she might well have decided to abort her.

This session began as a partial relapse into anxiety and passivity, and ended with a deepening of the patient's conflicting feelings of anger, love, and compassion for her mother. These dynamics were further elucidated in session 7, which started out with the patient being highly resistant, detached, nervously biting her nails, and seemingly having nothing to say. Over the weekend, she "did something different," she "enjoyed herself," she said, not very convincingly. At the therapist's question whether she felt disturbed or annoyed, the patient started to cry, an angry crying, and said she was worried lest she disturbed the women friends with whom she had gone out. The therapist, with an implicit reference to what had emerged in the previous session, pointed out that she was not sure if they really enjoyed her company or were just tolerating her out of pity. She felt that the latter applied, and a sad account started of her feeling "different" in the years of her primary school. Her mother worked full time, even on Saturdays then (a schoolday in Italy), and there was an arrangement with the teacher, who caught the bus with the patient and put her off at the right stop. She cried a lot, feeling different from the other children and not really cared for by her mother. This last impression was fostered by the mother's forgetfulness when, a number of times, she forgot to collect the patient from school. This made her feel ashamed and at the center of a pitiful scene. The therapist, making a link with the transference and giving the patient a corrective emotional experience (Alexander & French, 1946), commented that the two of them, patient and therapist, would have to make sure that, before concluding treatment, she had come to feel really ready to go on independently, so as not to feel dumped by the therapist the way she felt abandoned by her mother.

With the aim of testing the patient's self-esteem, in session 8 the therapist inquired about any lack of confidence she might feel as a woman in relation to men. She felt she was not particularly beautiful, but knew that boys could feel attracted to her, so that was not a worry. The therapist tried to explore as much as possible before fixing a termination date. Considering the patient's multiple experiences of feeling neglected and let down, this also represented a corrective emotional experience (Alexander & French, 1946). The patient's reassuring response to this was that, as therapy progressed, she got to discover a number of unsuspected connections among the way she is, her relationship with her mother, and her symptoms. She would never have guessed that all her anxiety arose from such connections. Moreover, she said she would try to "go on like this . . . not to pity myself in a harsh way" and to "take part more in things."

PATIENT: It all seems different. When I am here, I am capable of thinking about what I have inside, I manage to get it out . . . of course, it is not something I can do with people I don't know . . . but I am not even disturbed, that is, when I talk about these things with somebody else, this doesn't bring about . . . Here, instead, it has brought about . . . it shook me a bit, that is . . . perhaps it was my true feelings . . .
THERAPIST: Uhm, perhaps?
PATIENT: No, these were my true feelings (Laughs.), my true feelings, the ones I have . . . I think I got out all of my feelings in all the sessions we had. I don't know what else . . . there is nothing left to get out.
THERAPIST: (Eventually convinced.) In this case, this is a good reason to terminate fairly soon.

Session 9 provided a confirmation of what emerged in the previous session. Some degree of character change was detectable, in terms of a stronger sense of "being herself" and an increase in self-esteem and in the ability to assert herself and to participate emotionally. Also, the fits of rage seemed to belong to the past. There were positive feelings for the therapist, and she stated she would come back if she has problems.

POSTTERMINATION SYNOPSIS AND
EFFECTIVENESS DATA

The patient was given three follow-up interviews: 6 months, 2 years 10 months, and 5 years 8 months after termination. By the first follow-up, her life was transformed, and this dynamic change persisted over time. She was much more in touch with her wishes and desires and assertive enough to have them fulfilled in a realistic way. Her feelings of inferiority had substantially subsided and there was more closeness with her mother. Here is a brief quotation from the 2 years 10 months interview, which reflects this: "I am happy and I am, like, trying to convey it to my mother, who knows me . . . I can be affectionate with her, with my women friends. Not that previously there was a wall, but . . ." She had found a new job that was satisfactory to her, and felt grateful to the therapist. She had taken up again with Marco, but now she felt they were on the same level. At times, she would go out with friends without Marco. She was studying to take her baccalaureate. Once (in almost three years) she started developing the premonitory signals of a PA. This was during the funeral of a close friend who had died in a car accident; she had had to leave the church. Later that night, she was home alone, and she thought "Now it comes," but it did not. What follows is a summary of the last follow-up, 5 years 8 months after termination.

PATIENT: (Warm smile.)
THERAPIST: Are you well?
PATIENT: Now I am. A number of changes took place over these last two years.
THERAPIST: For better or for worse?

Relationships with Others
PATIENT: For better. I left my previous boyfriend, with whom I had stayed for 10 years . . . and since I made that decision, I feel better.
THERAPIST: Three years ago you said you got on much better with him.
PATIENT: Yes, but in the end it was too tying. It all started when I was attending my evening classes to get my baccalaureate. I met a number of people and this gave me a push. I realized I was doing something for myself. I wasn't valued enough when I was with him. Now I realize it, even if it's difficult to leave someone, after 10 years. . . . I met another

man, he's totally different. So I said to myself: Well, there are different people!

THERAPIST: Yes, because you started your relation with Marco at 16...

PATIENT: I've gone out with him [the present boyfriend] for one year now. I get on well. I don't have the problems I had. He's more understanding, not stifling. I feel well, I don't have that anxiety that I had before. I feel well.

THERAPIST: Any plans for the future?

PATIENT: Not yet.

THERAPIST: In general what is the way you experience your relationships with others, including your mother and brother? Did these change?

PATIENT: Yes.

THERAPIST: Can you give me an example?

PATIENT: Before, I had problems of putting forward my opinion. Now I feel a mastery over myself, and I can sustain a dialogue.

THERAPIST: Do you see others differently?

PATIENT: They hindered me more, before.

THERAPIST: Are they more benign now?

PATIENT: Not benign, but I can express my opinion without being afraid of being wrong.

THERAPIST: They scare you less.

PATIENT: Yes.

THERAPIST: And when there is something you want or need from someone?

PATIENT: Perhaps because I feel better with myself, I also feel that others understand me more. Previously I was more shut in.

THERAPIST: Can you give an example?

PATIENT: When I talk to my mother, dialogue is more spontaneous. It's difficult to explain... I make myself understood.

THERAPIST: And then you feel understood.

PATIENT: Yes, in that respect. Maybe before, I saw too many negative things. Now I see the positive side and I react better. I feel better inside, honestly, and I come to see others too in a more positive way.

THERAPIST: And with your mother?

PATIENT: We get on better, even though, at times, she's a bit nagging.

THERAPIST: Can you give an example?

PATIENT: She tends to stifle me a bit, but it is something I can handle.

THERAPIST: Your brother?

PATIENT: No problem with him.

Work

She took her baccalaureate and has a steady job. She was promoted and is fairly satisfied, but would like to be paid more.

Symptoms

THERAPIST: Do you still have anxiety attacks?

PATIENT: Not strong ones, I can control them... strangely enough, it sometimes happens, last time a month ago, I was with my mother...

THERAPIST: How was it?

PATIENT: I'd got home from work, we were chatting and preparing for supper, I felt giddy and a bit anxious.

THERAPIST: With palpitations?

PATIENT: No, just a bit anxious. Then, differently from before, I think of something else, and it goes.

THERAPIST: Did you think of any possible trigger?

PATIENT: No, I didn't think of it, it is not a problem that I feel to be important... because it goes away. Differently from before. I am not afraid of it coming back again. Honestly, I don't think of something that worries me during the day. One thing is that nowadays, I happen to be home on my own, something I previously feared. It's happened even for many days, and I get on well. I didn't expect this because, at the idea of being alone I used to get a bit agitated and scared. Now it is demonstrated that it is not so. I am very satisfied about this. I put myself to the test on this and...

THERAPIST: Excellent, it was a pleasure to see you, thank you for coming.

PATIENT: Thank you for calling me, I am happy to come.

Comment about Follow-Up Interviews

In this case, which exemplifies the course of treatment utilizing this approach, the patient's life and her relations have changed, becoming much more fulfilling for her. Symptoms are much improved. There is some residual anxiety that does not worry or hinder her, which might be connected with her relationship with her mother. She is pleased with her progress and appears much more vital and alive.

SUMMARY

The idea of accelerating the course of psychotherapy has a long lineage that begins with Freud but was advanced by Ferenczi. An emphasis on emotional experiencing, instead of cognitive insight, was encouraged by Rank. These two trends have laid the groundwork for contemporary experientially based short-term dynamic therapy. Many other pioneering workers have elaborated and evolved theoretical and technical components of brief psychodynamic therapy (BPT) to create an ever stronger amalgam that can be used for a broad spectrum of symptom and character disturbances. The main components of these models include the use of theoretical triangles to conceptualize and guide treatment, emphasis on mirroring, and rapid access to the unconscious with technical interventions aimed toward emotional activation. The emphasis on emotional maieutics entails the process whereby the patient enjoys a full emotional experience brought to the surface by the emotional midwifery of the therapist. BPT relies on the use of a trial relationship ranging from one to three hours to determine the suitability for treatment with this approach. Regardless of the degree of pathology, it is the patient's response to treatment that best determines suitability.

REFERENCES

Alexander, F., & French, T. M. (1946). *Psychoanalytic therapy.* New York: Ronald Press.

Alpert, M. (1992). Accelerated empathic therapy: A new short-term dynamic psychotherapy. *International Journal of Short-Term Psychotherapy, 7,* 133–156.

American Psychiatric Association. (1994). *Diagnostic and statistical manual of mental disorders* (4th ed.). Washington, DC: Author.

Balint, M., Ornstein, P., & Balint, E. (1972). *Focal psychotherapy: An example of applied psychoanalysis.* London: Tavistock.

Bowlby, J. (1982). *Attachment and loss. Volume I: Attachment* (2nd ed.). New York: Basic Books.

Coughlin Della Selva, P. (1996). *Intensive short-term dynamic psychotherapy.* New York: Basic Books.

Davanloo, H. (1986). Intensive short-term psychotherapy with highly resistant patients: I. Handling resistance. *International Journal of Short-Term Psychotherapy, 1,* 107–133.

Davanloo, H. (1990). *Unlocking the unconscious.* Toronto, Canada: Wiley.

Ferenczi, S. (1920). The further development of an active therapy in psycho-analysis. In *Further contributions to the theory and technique of psychoanalysis* (pp. 198–217). London: Karnac Books.

Ferenczi, S., & Rank, O. (1987). The development of psychoanalysis. In G. H. Pollack (Ed.) & C. Newton (Trans.), *Classics in psychoanalysis monograph series* (Series No. 4). Madison, CT: International Universities Press. (Original work published 1925)

Fosha, D. (Ed.). (1992). Accelerated empathic therapy (AET): History, development and theory [Special issue]. *International Journal of Short-Term Psychotherapy, 7*(3), 127–198.

Fosha, D. (2000). *The transforming power of affect.* New York: Basic Books.

Fosha, D. (2001, May 10–12). *Core affect and its dyadic regulation.* Acta of the conference Core Factors for Effective Short-Term Dynamic Psychotherapy, Milano, Italy.

Freud, A. (1966). *The ego and the mechanisms of defense.* New York: International Universities Press. (Original work published 1937)

Kohut, H. (1971). *The analysis of self.* London: Hogarth Press.

Magnavita, J. J. (1997). *Restructuring personality disorders: A short-term dynamic approach.* New York: Guilford Press.

Mahler, M. (1967). On human symbiosis and the vicissitudes of individuation. *Journal of the American Psychoanalytic Association, 15,* 740–763.

Malan, D. H. (1963). *A study of brief psychotherapy.* London: Tavistock.

Malan, D. H. (1976). *Toward the validation of dynamic psychotherapy.* New York: Plenum Press.

Malan, D. H. (1979). *Individual psychotherapy and the science of psychodynamics.* Oxford, England: Butterworth-Heinemann, Arnold.

Malan, D. H. (1986a) Beyond interpretation: Initial evaluation and technique in short-term dynamic psychotherapy: Part I. *International Journal of Short-Term Psychotherapy, 1,* 59–82.

Malan, D. H. (1986b) Beyond interpretation: Initial evaluation and technique in short-term dynamic psychotherapy: Part II. *International Journal of Short-Term Psychotherapy, 1,* 83–106.

Malan, D. H., & Osimo, F. (1992). *Psychodynamics, training, and outcome in brief psychotherapy.* Oxford, England: Butterworth-Heinemann, Arnold.

McCullough, L., Winston, A., Farber, B., Porter, F., Pollack, J., Laikin, M., et al. (1991). The relationship of patient-therapist interaction to outcome in brief psychotherapy. *Psychotherapy, 28,* 525–522.

McCullough Vaillant, L. (1997). *Changing character.* New York: Basic Books.

Osimo, F. (1991). Time limit, focality and intensive short-term dynamic psychotherapy. *International Journal of Short-Term Psychotherapy, 6,* 35–51.

Osimo, F. (1994). Method, personality and training in short-term psychotherapy. *International Journal of Short-Term Psychotherapy, 9,* 173–187.

Osimo, F. (1998). The unexplored complementarity of short-term and long-term analytic approaches. *Journal of the American Academy of Psychoanalysis, 26*(1), 95–107.

Osimo, F. (2001a, May 10–12) *The good-enough emotional experience.* Acta of the conference Core Factors for Effective Short-Term Dynamic Psychotherapy, Milano, Italy.

Osimo, F. (2001b) *Parole, emozioni e videotape. Manuale di Psicoterapia Breve Dinamico Esperienziale [Words, emotions, and videotape. Manual of experimental STDP].* Franco Angeli Editore.

Rank, O. (1924). *The trauma of birth.* Mineola, NY: Dover.

Reich, W. (1933). *Character analysis.* New York: Noonday Press.

Sklar, I. (1992). *Issues of loss and AET.* Paper presented at the conference on brief therapy approaches: The sequelae of trauma, STDP Institute, Denville, NJ.

Vaillant, G. E. (1977). *Adaptation to life.* Boston: Little, Brown.

Vaillant, G. E. (1993). *Wisdom of the ego.* Cambridge, MA: Harvard University Press.

Winnicott, D. W. (1971). Mirror-role of mother: Family in child development. In *Playing and reality.* London: Tavistock.

CHAPTER 10

An Object-Relations Approach to the Treatment of Borderline Patients

JOHN F. CLARKIN, KENNETH N. LEVY, AND GERHARD W. DAMMANN

Treatment research and subsequent clinical guidelines for practitioners are, with a few exceptions, designed around specific symptom constellations and diagnoses as defined in the *Diagnostic and Statistical Manual of Mental Disorders*, third edition (*DSM-III;* American Psychiatric Association [APA], 1980, and its successors). Research has focused on manualized treatments of brief duration, often cognitive-behavioral in orientation, with the goal of reducing symptoms of specific Axis I *DSM* disorders. At the other extreme are those clinicians who perceive each patient as unique, who must be treated by a creative and intuitive therapist unhindered and unencumbered by a manualized treatment. The treatment to be described in this chapter, transference focused psychotherapy (TFP), can be placed between these two extremes. TFP is a principle-driven treatment that calls on the creativity of the therapist given certain principles and structure of treatment. TFP is not focused on a *DSM-IV* (APA, 1994) symptom disorder. It addresses a group of patients selected and assessed for a level of personality organization called borderline personality organization (BPO). BPO is defined by Kernberg (1976) as a severely disturbed level of personality organization characterized by identity diffusion (e.g., an incoherent and contradictory sense of self and others), the use of primitive defenses (e.g., splitting and denial), and deficits in reality testing. Patients diagnosed with BPO often meet *DSM-IV* Axis II criteria for Borderline Personality Disorder (BPD) as well as other Axis II personality disorders such as paranoid, narcissistic, and antisocial.

Seen in this context, TFP is unique in a number of ways. It is treatment based on a specific theory of etiology and psychopathology rather than an atheoretical *DSM*-based category. TFP is detailed in a manual for the long-term treatment of these patients (Clarkin, Yeomans, & Kernberg, 1999). There have been only a few attempts to manualize psychodynamic treatments, and these are for the brief treatment of patients with mixed Axis I and II disorders (Luborsky, 1984; Strupp & Binder, 1984). TFP does not micromanage the therapist and spell out the treatment for each session before the treatment begins. Rather, it is an articulation of a structured treatment in terms of principles of intervention that are applied carefully by a therapist to an individual patient. The principles of the treatment are articulated at three levels of intervention: (1) strategies that infuse the whole treatment, (2) tactics that guide decisions in each session, and (3) techniques that are used in the moment-to-moment interaction between patient and therapist.

In this chapter, we examine the theory of object relations as it applies to people in general and to patients with BPO specifically. We describe TFP and examine our preliminary efforts to empirically study it. As psychotherapeutic treatment is the focus of this volume, we then apply object-relations theory to the modified psychodynamic treatment of an individual with BPO.

OBJECT-RELATIONS THEORY

Object Relations Beginning with Freud

Freud's early writings contained references or implied the notion of internal objects and their representation. For instance, in *On Aphasia*, Freud (1891/1953) proposed a new model of speech and was interested in what manner the body is reproduced in the cerebral cortex. It was in this paper that Freud first dealt with how *Objektvorstellung*, or object representations, come into existence, proposing that object representations are constructed in the process of perceiving and standing for something in the real world. One year later, in *Studies on Hysteria* (Breuer & Freud, 1895), Freud referred to transference as a "false connection" between someone who had been the object of the patient's earlier wishes and the doctor now treating the patient. Freud did not explicitly use the concept of object representation. He did believe that to have such a false connection between the past and the present, the object of the earlier wishes must have been internalized and represented. In his monumental work *The Interpretation of Dreams* (1900), Freud referred to unconscious memory traces and implied that they had the power to perpetuate the feelings involved in the forgotten early experience, to attract attention to themselves in the course of dream and symptom formation, and to press for conscious expression, dream representation, and symbolic representation in symptomatic behavior and character pathology. In the same book, Freud also discussed "hysterical identifications" and posited that many of his patients' symptoms were an unconscious likening of themselves to significant persons in their lives, most often perhaps to their character flaws and actual transgressions.

In 1914, Freud introduced the idea that unconscious fantasies about objects may, under certain circumstances, take the place of actual relationships. Three years later, in *Mourning and Melancholia* (1917/1957), probably his most seminal work in terms of object relations, identification is the means by which one not only remembers, but in part emotionally replaces a lost external object with an aspect of oneself that has been modeled after the lost external object. Freud described how, in melancholia, a relationship with an external object is "transformed . . . into a cleavage between the critical activity of the ego and the ego as altered by identification" (p. 249). In other words, an external relationship is replaced by an internal one that involves an interplay of two active aspects of the person that have resulted from a splitting of the ego. Here, identification was understood as a defense against the bereaved person's anger at or aggression toward the lost, abandoned, and ambivalently regarded object, already too fragile in being either dead or otherwise gone. Identification with the figure's negative qualities engaged patients in relentless self-reproach and loathing. The ego's development occurs through several stages of awareness, as well as the incremental differentiation and integration of self and object representations. In addition, Freud seemed to be suggesting that the melancholic individual's object relations result from a failure to achieve the differentiation of the self from the other.

Following Freud, Melanie Klein (1984a, 1984b) and her student, Rado, increasingly emphasized internal relationships. Rado (1928) suggested that the melancholic absorbs in the lost other a split, dyadic "good object" and "bad object," the former symbolic of the beloved but potentially punitive parent surrogates. Rado's concept of the split good-bad introject became the basis for later contributions by Klein, Fairbairn, and Kernberg. Klein (1984a, 1984b) noticed that the internal images of objects were much more ferocious than the actual parents appeared to be. She proposed that these internal figures were distorted by sadistic fantasies. For Klein, internal objects and an inner world were not replicas of the external world, but were built up through the mechanisms of introjection and projection from the beginning of life. She pointed out that the newborn may be generating mental representations from birth in the form of bodily representations or instinctual/drive representations. Klein proposed that infants attempt to protect their own integrity as an organism and that of the primary object of attachment (which they experience as a part of themselves) by projecting their innate destructiveness onto the environment and introjecting its good aspects or, reciprocally, by projecting the good aspects of themselves onto the good object and experiencing themselves removed from discomfort or danger. Thus, the first object, the mother's breast, is split into a bad or frustrating breast and a good and gratifying breast, each of which may be projected and introjected. Klein emphasized that the ego must also be split in a way that corresponds with the object, thus creating what was later viewed by Kernberg (1976) as a self-object-affect unit. Klein proposed that the integration of these split representations is dependent on the mothering person's ability to hold, contain, and metabolize toxic projections for the child to reintroject. As splitting resolves, whole object relations become central to mature functioning in normal development. Maturing children learn that their loving wishes are directed toward the same object as their destructiveness. The mother whom the child hates and wishes to destroy for depriving him or her is the same mother the child loves for nurturing him or her. Children then develop remorse and guilt and wish to restore or repair the object they previously wanted to diminish. As they work through their guilt, they come to recognize their loving and destructive impulses as their own, and their mother's nurturing and depriving qualities as her own. Of course, the self is loving and also somewhat destructive. The object is loving and also a bit destructive. Whole object-relatedness is achieved as the self and object are increasingly differentiated and integrated.

Kernberg's Reformulation

Following Freud (1900), Klein (1984a, 1984b), and Jacobson (1964), Kernberg (1976) postulated that representational models derived from attachment relationships to caregivers through a process called internalization (the taking in of what is in the environment into one's own mind) can be conceived as personality. Kernberg proposed that early experiences with others in relation to oneself are stored in memory (internalized) and that these memories consist of three parts: (1) a self-representation, (2) a representation of others, and (3) the affective state characteristic of these interactions. For Kernberg, the degree of differentiation and integration of these representations of self and other, along with their affective valance, constitutes personality organization. The basic logic of Kernberg's model is that as development proceeds, representations of self and others become increasingly more differentiated and integrated. These mature, integrated representations allow for the integration of good and bad, positive and negative, and for the tolerance of ambivalence, difference, and contradiction in oneself and others.

For Kernberg, personality organization can range from extremely disturbed, that is, psychotic, through relatively reality-oriented and adaptive levels, to high-level neurotic functioning. Kernberg (1976) coined the term borderline personality organization as a broad construct, encompassing severe forms of serious personality disturbances, including *DSM*'s (APA, 1994) conception of BPD, Antisocial, Narcissistic, and Histrionic Personality Disorders. For Kernberg, borderline personality can be thought of as a severely disturbed level of personality organization, characterized by the defense mechanism of splitting. Splitting is the dividing of people and things into two categories, good and bad, with no middle ground nor understanding of the complex nature of people and things. This does not allow the person to see the self or others at a particular time with much richness or complexity.

GENERAL MODEL OF OBJECT-RELATIONS THEORY

There are shared hypotheses and issues of concern that unite those who espouse the object-relations point of view. These shared issues have been summarized (Kernberg, 1995) as follows: (1) integration of drives with object relations; each drive derivative is constituted by a self representation and a related object representation linked by an affect disposition; (2) focus on the early, pre-Oedipal stages of development; (3) impulse-defense equilibrium, seen as impulsively and defensively activated object relations; (4) focus on the structural characteristics of the early ego-id matrix before the consolidation of the tripartite structure; and (5) the importance of the internalization of "bad" object relations (i.e., aggressively invested and dissociated representations of self and others).

Among the theorists who hold an object-relations point of view, there are some identifiable issues that distinguish and separate them (Kernberg, 1995): (1) the extent to which the theory is consistent with or runs counter to Freud's drive theory; (2) the origin and role of aggression as a motivator of behavior; (3) the process by which actual experiences of infancy and childhood are transformed by unconscious fantasy; and (4) in treatment technique, the interpretation of transference enactments in terms of the activation of the patient's intrapsychic conflicts versus the view that transference and countertransference are shaped by the analyst's personality.

TREATMENT WITH AN OBJECT-RELATIONS APPROACH

Object-relations theory provides the TFP therapist with an organized theory of the development of the patient's personality pathology, a cognitive map for the clinical assessment of the patient, and a guide for organizing the interventions in the here-and-now therapeutic interaction with the patient.

ASSESSMENT

A psychoanalytic and object-relations assessment of the patient for treatment planning highlights two aspects: the personality organization of the patient, with an important distinction between neurotic organization and borderline organization, and a careful assessment of the patient's current symptoms. The assessment is concerned with symptoms and personality organization as the essentials in treatment planning and does not overemphasize conflicts or psychodynamics.

Kernberg (1981) has described a clinical interview, called the structural interview, for this assessment. The structural interview addresses the symptoms that the patient is experiencing and the level of personality organization. The interview attends predominantly to the current situation(s) in the patient's life. It begins with an invitation for the patient to describe in detail and exhaustively all current symptoms (depression, anxiety, etc.) and problem areas (work, intimate relations, etc.). In the second part of the interview, the clinician invites patients to describe their sense of self and their sense of important others in their life; for example, "Please describe for me in as rich detail as you can how you see yourself and what makes you unique." From the patient's description of self and others, one begins to arrive at a diagnosis of the structural organization of the particular patient. Normal and neurotic level organizations have a clear conception of self and a consistent and clear conception of others, without identity diffusion. These conceptions of self and others operate in a functional pattern of neurotic defenses, such as humor and rationalization, but in the context of an accurate sense of the social reality. In borderline organization, there is identity diffusion; that is, there is a chaotic, confused, and at times contradictory sense of self, with an accompanying inability to conceive of others as separate and complicated.

Intervention

Strategies of TFP

The strategies of TFP are the overall goals of the treatment as guided by the psychodynamic and object-relations conceptualization of the pathology. The first strategy of TFP is to define the dominant object relations that unfold in the interaction between patient and therapist. There are a number of steps in this process. First, the therapist must experience and tolerate the confusion of the patient's inner world as it unfolds in the transference. Patients at a borderline level of organization often enter treatment with early and intense transference reactions and with intense need for immediate attention from the therapist. Patients with BPO not only tend to have intense and rapid transference reactions, but these transference reactions can shift rapidly according to the different internalized relationships that are being experienced in the moment and according to which role within the patient-therapist relationship is being assigned, often out of awareness, to the patient and to the therapist. To understand this transference situation, the therapist must constantly be asking, Why is the patient telling me this? Who am I to the patient at this point? The patient is treating me as if I am whom? The question often arises of what is transference and what is simply the perception of the patient at the moment. A helpful operational definition is that transference may be involved in any behavior or response of the patient that differs from the average expectable response in a given situation.

As a second step, the therapist identifies the dominant object relations in the room. In the third step, the therapist metaphorically names the actors in the room. For example, the therapist might say, "You are quite angry that I was five minutes late for the session. Your discussion of this suggests that you experience yourself, at the moment, as an angry, needy child who is being neglected by an inattentive parent." This is an attempt to verbalize the patient's internal object-relations world that is being manifested in the here-and-now interaction in the room. The patient experiences himself or herself as unattended and projects onto the therapist an opposing internal object of a neglectful parent.

The second strategy of TFP is to observe and interpret patient role reversals. Because the borderline patient has an internal world composed of unintegrated opposing objects that are both idealized and persecutory, the objects will be experienced by the patient in alternating and contradictory ways, sometimes in rapid succession. The therapist's strategy is to observe these reversals and bring them to the attention of the patient. Thus, "At the beginning of this session, you were suggesting that I am an ideal therapist who is better than those you have had in the past. And now you are saying that I am a terrible therapist who does not understand you. How are these two views connected or reconcilable?"

We have emphasized the discrete and discontinuous nature of the internal representations of self and other in the patient with BPO. These representations are not static. The characteristics that are attributed to the self can abruptly shift to the other, and those attributed to the other can shift to the self. This oscillation and abrupt change is related to the confusion the therapist often experiences with BPO patients. It is the task of the therapist to expect and be alert to these rapid oscillations and be ready to put them into words.

The third strategy of TFP is to observe and interpret linkages between object-relations dyads that defend against each other. The internal representations of a patient organized at a borderline level include dyads that are opposites, although one of the dyadic pairs may be closer to consciousness than the other. The dissociation between dyads serves a defensive function of protecting each dyad from contamination by the other. It is hypothesized that such a split protects the dyad imbued with affection and love from invasion by the hatred contained in the opposite dyad. The hate-filled dyad is often closer to the surface, at least in the beginning of therapy. As therapy progresses, the therapist may begin to sense the patient's longing to be loved and cared for that is more fragile and hidden. Interpreting the more conscious, hate-filled dyad as protecting and defending against some underlying awareness of the possibility of love and caring gradually allows the patient to understand the defensive use of hatred as an attempt to keep the fragile longing for love and protection from the risk that it be destroyed if the splitting were abandoned.

Tactics of TFP

With these strategies as overall goals in mind, the tactics are the tasks in each session that guide the TFP therapist. These include setting and maintaining the frame of the treatment, monitoring the three channels of communication in choosing the focus of intervention, eliminating any secondary gain of the illness, and maintaining technical neutrality. Each tactic deserves explanation.

Setting and Maintaining the Treatment Frame. TFP is a treatment with a particular frame that is articulated by the therapist at the beginning of treatment. The frame describes the roles and responsibilities of both patient and therapist. It is hoped that setting the frame will contain the patient's behavioral reenactment of conflicts with the therapist, and thus optimize the possibility of examining these conflicts without dissipating them in action. The setting of the frame focuses the treatment on analysis of the transference in the here-and-now subjective experience of the therapist determined by the unconscious repetition in relationship to the therapist of pathological object relations from the past.

Once articulated and accepted by both parties, any deviations from the frame can be seen in terms of the internal world of the patient that imposes itself on the frame. The frame of the treatment includes limits on acting out by the patient, especially acting out that could destroy the patient (i.e., suicidal behavior) or behavior that could destroy the treatment itself. These limits do not necessarily eliminate these acting-out behaviors, but after the contract has been set, they provide an atmosphere in which the deviations from the contract can be examined in reference to their meaning, especially the meaning in the relationship between the therapist and the patient.

Selecting the Focus of Intervention by Monitoring the Three Channels of Communication. Every session begins with the therapist being silent and receptive to feelings, thoughts, and issues that the patient brings to treatment that particular day. As the communication from the patient unfolds, the therapist must make choices as to which particular aspects of communication, whether verbal from channel 1, or nonverbal from channel 2, is the most propitious and fruitful area of examination. Another tactic is the constant monitoring of the communication in the room. There are three major channels of communication: (1) the verbal communication from patient to therapist, which is according to the parameters defined by the contract that the patient come to the session and talk about what is on his or her mind or what comes to mind in the session; (2) the nonverbal communication coming from the patient, which is extremely important in BPO patients, who often communicate by actions (bodily expressions, etc.) rather than by words; and (3) the therapist's reaction to everything that the patient says and does. As long as therapists are aware of their own reactions and weak points, they can use internal reactions to the patient to generate more information on what is transpiring.

One consideration in terms of therapists' selection of focus as they monitor the three channels of communication is the actual content of what is being communicated, both the obvious content of the words and the implications. Because TFP is a treatment designed for BPO patients, two content themes therapists must be constantly alert for concern the patient's thoughts, feelings, and impulses for self-destruction (including suicide) and any threats to the treatment itself. A second consideration for the therapist's focus relates to the three principles of intervention: the economic principle, the dynamic principle, and the structural principle. According to the economic principle, therapists note the material in which the patient invests the most affect. Affect is often a marker of the activation of internalized object relations that are being laid out in the here and now. For example, if the patient is obviously angry, as evidenced in verbalization or facial expression, this is an indication that, at that moment, the patient's experience of self is that the therapist or other internalized object is treating him or her in such a way that he or she is angry. The dynamic principle relates to the forces of conflict and assumes that heightened affect is signaling an unconscious conflict involving a defended-against impulse. Both the impulse and the defense are represented in the internal world of the patient by object-relations dyads. The TFP therapist concentrates first on the defense that is most observable, and then on the impulse, which is often out of the awareness of the patient. Finally, according to the structural principle, the therapist struggles for an overview and perception of how the specific object-relation dyads activated in the transference are part of a larger picture. In each therapy, there are a finite and limited number of highly invested object-relations dyads. The TFP therapist soon begins to recognize and understand the repetitive dominant relationship themes that become the focus of attention with the individual patient.

Techniques of TFP

In the moment-to-moment analysis of the object relations activated in the treatment room, the TFP therapist uses the techniques of clarification, confrontation, and interpretation in the context of maintaining technical neutrality. The three techniques are different facets that can be defined separately, but form a unified approach to communications from the patient. Thus, clarification is followed by confrontation, which is then utilized in an interpretation of the here-and-now interaction.

Clarification is an invitation by the therapist to patients to amplify their communication about thoughts, feelings, behavior, and so on. Patients' responses help inform the therapist about details that have been left out or are unclear in patients' communication. Patients' responses to the clarification also enable the therapist to understand the extent of their understanding of their own feelings and thoughts. A confrontation is an invitation by the therapist for patients to clarify contradictory aspects of communication. The contradiction in patients' communication can come from incompatibility between two verbal utterances, or it can be a discrepancy between patients' verbal and nonverbal behavior. With borderline patients, who split off and isolate contradictory aspects of themselves and their experience of others, a confrontation is an attempt to see if patients can link these different aspects. Finally, an interpretation in the here and now is an attempt on the therapist's part to articulate an understanding of why patients might behave as they do in the present interaction.

The TFP therapist maintains technical neutrality by listening attentively to patients' conflicts and helping them understand the conflict without giving active advice of what they should actually do. It is from such a position of neutrality that the therapist can help patients examine their own motives and impulses. The position of technical neutrality has often been misunderstood in TFP. It does not mean that the therapist behaves as a quiet, noninvolved, affectless object.

The Progress of Treatment

The progression of TFP is discernable in reference to time (beginning, middle, and end of treatment) and in terms of the changing clinical state of the patient. The early treatment phase involves the setting of the frame of the treatment, which is often followed by some testing of the frame by the patient. The frame, combined with the interpretation of dominant object relations activated in the treatment relationship, often leads to a diminution of serious acting out, such as destruction of the patient (suicidal attempts and other self-destructive behavior) and destruction of the treatment. It is well known in the clinical and research data (Clarkin et al., 1999) that premature dropout from treatment is a major difficulty with borderline patients. In the developing treatment, the patient accepts the routine of treatment, including attendance at two sessions a week. This does not mean that the therapeutic relationship in the sessions is calm and without conflict. On the contrary, the patient decreases acting-out behavior outside of treatment and, at the same time, the internalized object relations are activated with intense affect in the treatment.

In the middle and late phases of TFP, the repetitive interpretation of the patient's internalized object relations leads to certain changes in the relationship with the therapist. Patients achieve containment and tolerance of the awareness of their own hatred. There are shifts in the predominant transference themes, progressing from paranoid and narcissistic themes to those of the depressive position, in which there is integration of affect and a capacity for experiencing guilt in reference to self and other representations.

EMPIRICAL INVESTIGATION OF TFP

Since the early 1980s, the Borderline Psychotherapy Research Project at the New York Presbyterian Hospital–Cornell Weill Medical Center, headed by Drs. John Clarkin and Otto Kernberg, has been systematizing and investigating an object-relations treatment of borderline patients. This group has articulated the use of a treatment contract (Yeomans, Selzer, & Clarkin, 1992) and an organized treatment using key strategies, tactics, and techniques. The group has generated a treatment manual (Clarkin et al., 1999) that describes a modified dynamic treatment of patients with BPO and companion volumes that detail the contract-setting phase of the treatment (Yeomans et al., 1992) and treatment complications (Koenigsberg et al., 2000).

We examined the treatment outcome for patients diagnosed with *DSM* Axis II BPD who were treated in a one-year outpatient TFP (Clarkin et al., in press). In both the intent-to-treat and treatment completion groups, borderline patients receiving TFP showed considerable improvement in a number of important symptom and behavioral areas. In this pilot study, we decided to focus on behavioral and symptom changes in the treatment. In our subsequent and current randomized trial of treatments with these patients, we are advancing our measurement to signs of both behavior change and change in the object relations and structure of the personality organization.

Subjects were recruited from all treatment settings (i.e., inpatient, day hospital, and outpatient clinics) within the New York Presbyterian Hospital–Cornell Weill Medical Center system. Written informed consent was obtained after all study procedures had been explained. After referral for evaluation, patients were interviewed and assessed by trained evaluators for inclusion in the study. Potential subjects were screened with both clinical and semistructured interviews. Women between the ages of 18 and 50 who met BPD criteria and manifested at least two incidents of suicidal or self-injurious behavior in the prior five years were eligible to participate in the study. Patients were excluded who met criteria for Schizophrenia, Bipolar Disorder, Delusional Disorder, organic pathology, and/or mental retardation. Subjects were reevaluated at 4, 8, and 12 months while participating in the study. The mean age of the patients was 32.7 years, and the majority were Caucasian (76.5%), single, and unemployed. Most subjects met criteria for more than one Axis I and Axis II disorder, the most common diagnoses being Major Depression, dysthymia, eating disorders, and Narcissistic Personality Disorder.

Retention-Attrition

For those completing the treatment contract, the one-year attrition rate was 19.1% (4 of 21 patients dropped out of treatment), and no patient committed suicide. This dropout rate compares well with previous studies (Bateman & Fonagy, 1999; Linehan, Heard, & Armstrong, 1993; Linehan et al., 1999; Stevenson & Meares, 1992), which reported a range of between 16.7 and 21.0% dropout rate. In our study, two patients dropped out early after four months of treatment, and two more dropped out after eight months of treatment. The two patients who dropped out after eight months of treatment showed improvement on both objective and subjective measures, and both felt they no longer needed the treatment. Two other subjects were administratively discharged due to protocol violations. Nine subjects declined to enter treatment during the contracting phase prior to beginning treatment. There was a tendency for the decliners to live farther from the Institute, although this difference did not reach statistical significance. Thus, 57% of the subjects completed 12 months of TFP treatment. None of the treatment completers deteriorated or were adversely affected by the treatment. Therefore, it appears that TFP is well tolerated.

Suicidal and Self-Injurious Behavior

There was a significant reduction in the number of patients who had made a suicide attempt in the year prior to treatment (53%) and those who made an attempt during the year of treatment (18%). In addition, there was a trend toward reduction in the number of suicide attempts, the medical risk of these acts, and physical condition following self-injurious behavior. Suicidal ideation did not decrease, but there was a significant increase in the reasons given for living. One possible interpretation of the combination of these data elements, which is congruent with clinical lore, is that during the first year of treatment, there is initiation of containment of action, whereas suicidal ideation remains. In this context, patients experience a growing awareness of satisfactions in life and reasons to live.

In contrast to the decline in outright suicidal behavior, self-injurious behavior did not decrease in frequency; however, the medical risk associated with this was significantly reduced, and the physical condition of the patient improved.

Symptoms

A measure of global symptoms significantly decreased, as did state anxiety. There was a trend for depression and trait anxiety to decrease. Anger, both in state and trait form, did not change.

Social Adjustment

As a group, these patients made significant changes in friendships and work. This supports the expectation that a psychodynamic object-relations treatment such as TFP would show its influence in improved relationships with significant others in the environment.

Utilization of Services

There were significant reductions in emergency room visits (55% reduction), psychiatric hospitalizations (67%), and days of inpatient hospitalization (89% reduction; 39.2 versus 4.5 days). Additionally, whereas 11 (64.7%) patients were hospitalized in the year prior to treatment, only 5 (29.4%) were hospitalized during the treatment year. This difference was significant: $X^2 (1) = 4.25, p < .04$.

Although this study was not specifically designed to examine cost-effectiveness, nor do we have data on the exact cost savings between the prior year and the treatment year, the dramatic reduction in service utilization in terms of emergency room visits, hospitalizations, and number of days in the hospital suggests a substantial cost savings associated with TFP. The results of our findings as well as those of others (Linehan et al., 1993) suggest that a longer duration of treatment appears to not only be necessary for ameliorating symptoms embedded in personality structure, but also seems to be highly cost-effective with borderline patients. A number of clinical writers have noted that patterns of short-term crisis management, brief psychotherapies, or even constant managed care review can be counterproductive and even experienced as traumatic for borderline patients.

These findings, using the patients as their own controls, are highly suggestive that extended TFP is well tolerated and may result in considerable improvement in functioning in a broad range of areas.

CASE EXAMPLE

The empirical data noted previously suggest that, as a group, patients respond to TFP with fewer symptoms and less self-destructive behavior and lower use of psychiatric emergency and inpatient services. We provide here a clinical illustration of one of these 17 cases. Individual cases provide some meaningful detail about a single person that contrasts with mean scores.

We selected the case of Amy (a false name) because she was quite disturbed at the beginning of treatment and her early treatment course in TFP was difficult, but with a persistent and consistent therapist, she began to make substantial changes on the behavioral level and in terms of her object relations. Amy was a 32-year-old married woman who entered TFP following evaluation by our research team. She had notable pathology, as indicated by Axis I disorder of Major Depression and multiple Axis II disorders, including borderline, narcissistic, and some antisocial features. Although Amy married her husband for the financial support he could provide, she viewed him as inept and someone with whom she was unable to engage in sexual relations. She had a history of being sexually preoccupied with her various psychotherapists. She manifested disdain toward her husband by overtly flaunting her affections for others. This object relation with the husband presaged a transference theme in TFP.

During the contract-setting phase and the early treatment sessions, Amy displayed the confused, fractured nature of her experience accompanied by chaotic, self-destructive behaviors. Amy's initial self and object descriptions on the Object Relations Inventory (ORI; Blatt, Chevron, Quinlan, Schaffer, & Wein, 1988) were characterized by either extreme unilateral idealization or denigration of self or other (scale point 4), or by unintegrated oscillations between positive and negative views of the other, between opposing, extreme relational and affective polarities, such as overwhelming closeness versus unbridgeable distance, invasive control versus total abandonment, and intense rage versus idealizing love (scale point 5).

For example, at the beginning of treatment, Amy's self description has a pervasive negative valence typical of scale point 4:

> Well I could give you my diagnosis. . . . I think I must be really angry . . . I'm definitely scared . . . and I sort of, I feel very, un, sort of stuck. . . . Because on the one hand, I have lots of interests and things, but at the same time, I don't seem to have any . . . ability or . . . at least not confidence in my abilities to go through with any of them. . . . I'm pretty miserable really. I don't really know how to elaborate on it.

At the beginning of TFP, the therapist's description of Amy showed the preoccupation with regulation of closeness and distance, control and connection in relationships characteristic of scale point 5. Amy's description of her therapist was:

> I like him . . . it's different from any other sort of treatment I've been in. I'm just used to people crossing more lines. . . . I worry that he doesn't see who I am . . . I mean my good qualities . . . and that he's only going to see me as a stereotypical borderline. . . . You know . . . he assumes I know less than I do. . . . I don't really need that.

During the initial contract-setting sessions, the patient articulated her essential problem: "I have hidden from people. . . . People are dangerous." For example, she talked about her feelings getting mixed messages from her former psychopharmocologist; he gave her his home number for emergency situations, and when she called him constantly in suicidal crises, terminated her treatment and referred her to the therapy project because he found her unmanageable. Reflecting on her relationship with him, she said, "I . . . feel rejected and it makes me angry and suicidal, but being treated nicely makes me encouraged and then it just gets confusing . . . I mean, not that I want to be treated not nicely, but you know what I mean." She and the therapist then talked about emergencies and how to handle them in TFP. She stated abruptly, "Feeling miserable . . . like to die," and lapsed into an unresponsive stance. "That does sound like a chronic feeling," replied the therapist, who went on to say that it must feel like she's in a state of constant emergency.

Not surprisingly, the experiencing of the therapist as a potentially fearful and dangerous object emerged quite quickly. In an early session, Amy talked about her mother's lack of concern for her, demonstrated most recently by her mother telling her that she no longer could afford to phone or visit her.

THERAPIST: Where do you imagine I'd fall on the concerned versus not concerned spectrum?
AMY: Well, you're probably about where my parents are.
THERAPIST: Your parents who don't have enough money to phone you anymore.
AMY: And my Dad who was wondering why I didn't just jump in front of a train cause

that would work (laughs). But uh, you're not that bad.

THERAPIST: Well, but it feels that way.

There is the emergence early in the transference of an object-relational pattern of a cold, abusive parent and a helpless, abused self. Conversely, at other times, Amy became the abusive and sadistic other, treating her husband and her therapist with contempt and disdain. She enacted her sadism toward these individuals whom she perceived as inadequate and behaved sadistically to demonstrate their ineptness.

A crucial moment in the early phase of the treatment came after Amy had been hospitalized for the third time and became engaged in a suicide-love pact with a man other than her husband. Using the techniques of clarification and confrontation, the TFP therapist pointed out: "You describe how the hospital staff were inept in allowing you to cut your wrists in the emergency room waiting area, and while telling me about this, you were smiling. Explain the discrepancy to me." This was followed by an interpretation linking her dissociated affect with her representations of herself and others in this narrative: "Your smiling in this context suggests to me that there is a part of you that experiences great pleasure in becoming a cold, self-destructive individual who behaves in such a way as to demonstrate the ineptness of those who are trying to care for you." It is always difficult, if not impossible, to arrive at crisp cause-and-effect understanding in therapy. However, beginning with this session, aggression and sadistic impulses could be discussed openly in the therapeutic relationship at a verbal level; concomitantly, these impulses were not acted on by the patient in the form of suicidal and other tissue-damaging behavior. Hospitalizations were no longer needed.

It was necessary to hospitalize Amy briefly on three occasions in the first six months of treatment, and at one point she engaged in an affair that escalated into a murder-suicide pact that threatened her safety as well as that of the therapist. However, this pattern of behavior changed somewhat dramatically in the face of confrontations and interpretations of the patient's dominant object-relations dyads infused with aggression and sadistic triumph. After this stormy beginning, she settled into the treatment, ceased self-destructive acting out, and became increasingly involved in and committed to the treatment. She chose to continue to participate when the research year ended. Additionally, Amy began to view her husband as less inept and a worthy partner with whom she gradually decided to have a child.

The changes Amy made in the first year of TFP were captured by changes on the ORI. After one year of TFP, Amy's self and object descriptions showed some unevenness, but in general, there was movement toward higher stages of self-other differentiation and relatedness, with rapprochement-like polarization and oscillation replaced by more integrated, modulated, and nuanced self and object descriptions. In the self description, there was tentative movement toward a more individuated and cohesive sense of self, achieved in part by trial identifications, positive self-assertion, and the expression of opinions denoting a shift toward consolidating a coherent identity (scale point 6):

> Well, I think that lately anyway, like in the last nine months, I'm an honest person. I always wanted to be. I just had a hard time. And I am very opinionated, too opinionated. . . . I still get angry too easily about strange things that just sort of escalate. And I feel actually . . . happier than I ever used to. Like just sort of in a consistently content way.

Amy's description of her therapist particularly showed not only increased modulation and integration, but also an increased appreciation for the unique qualities of the other and the specific context that may have shaped the other. Further, she showed some rudimentary understanding that one's sense of self and other is a continually unfolding narrative process (scale point 8):

> How can I describe him? ... It's just going to be something I'm attributing to him. But he seems to be a very decent person and ... I think he's sincere and is helping me very much.... I mean I've been very helped by this therapy. I think he is really interested in helping me ... but not to the point where it's, you know, at all strange, like it was with a past therapist.... I just guess, I just mean I like, I trust him, is all.

The progression of change in Amy's case was from containment of self-destructive behavior, to integration of aggressive affect, to a more cohesive sense of self, with improvement in the quality of intimate relations. Such progression is what we have begun to expect in successful TFP cases. For Amy, there was a shift in the developmental level of self and object representations from rapprochement-like polarization and oscillations to increased cohesion, integration, and modulation. These shifts represent higher levels of self-other differentiation and relatedness in self and object representations.

SUMMARY

We have traced the development of object-relations theory from Freud through Melanie Klein to Otto Kernberg. Our research group has utilized object-relations theory to articulate a manualized modified psychodynamic treatment for BPO patients that focuses on object relations and their representation as manifested in the here-and-now transference. We have presented data that indicate from pilot work that TFP results in behavioral changes having to do with a decrease in self-destructive behaviors, symptoms, and service utilization and improved social functioning. Finally, we are currently taking our research to new levels of measuring changes in the patient's object representations; this work is exemplified in the case illustration in this chapter.

REFERENCES

American Psychiatric Association. (1980). *Diagnostic and statistical manual of mental disorders* (3rd ed.). Washington, DC: Author.

American Psychiatric Association. (1994). *Diagnostic and statistical manual of mental disorders* (4th ed.). Washington, DC: Author.

Bateman, A., & Fonagy, P. (1999). Effectiveness of partial hospitalization in the treatment of Borderline Personality Disorder: A randomized controlled trial. *American Journal of Psychiatry, 156,* 1563–1569.

Blatt, S. J., Chevron, E. S., Quinlan, D., Schaffer, C., & Wein, S. (1988). *The assessment of quantitative and structural dimensions of object representations* (Rev. ed.). New Haven, CT: Yale University Press.

Breuer, J., & Freud, S. (1895). *Studies on hysteria.* New York: Basic Books.

Clarkin, J. F., Foelsch, P. A., Levy, K. N., Hull, J. W., Delaney, J. C., & Kernberg, O. F. (in press). The development of a psychodynamic treatment for patients with Borderline Personality Disorder: A preliminary study of behavioral change. *Journal of Personality Disorders.*

Clarkin, J. F., Yeomans, F. E., & Kernberg, O. F. (1999). *Psychotherapy for borderline personality.* New York: Wiley.

Freud, S. (1900). The interpretation of dreams. In J. Strachey (Ed.), *The standard edition of the complete psychological works of Sigmund Freud* (Vols. 4–5, pp. 1–715). London: Hogarth Press.

Freud, S. (1914). On narcissism. In J. Strachey (Ed.), *The standard edition of the complete psychological works of Sigmund Freud* (Vol. 14, pp. 67–103). London: Hogarth Press.

Freud, S. (1953). *On aphasia: A critical study.* New York: International Universities Press. (Original work published 1891)

Freud, S. (1957). Mourning and melancholia. In J. Strachey (Ed.), *The standard edition of the complete psychological works of Sigmund Freud* (Vol. 14, pp. 237–258). London: Hogarth Press. (Original work published 1917)

Jacobson, E. (1964). *The self and the object world.* New York: International Universities Press.

Kernberg, O. F. (1976). *Object relation theory and clinical psychoanalysis.* Northvale, NJ: Aronson.

Kernberg, O. F. (1981). Structural interviewing. *Psychiatric Clinics of North America, 4*(1), 169–195.

Kernberg, O. F. (1995). Psychoanalytic object relations theories. In B. E. Moore & B. D. Fine (Eds.), *Psychoanalysis: The major concepts* (pp. 450–462). New Haven, CT: Yale University Press.

Kernberg, O. F. (1996). A psychoanalytic theory of personality disorders. In J. F. Clarkin & M. F. Lenzenweger (Eds.), *Major theories of personality disorders* (pp. 106–137). New York: Guilford Press.

Klein, M. (1984a). *The writings of Melanie Klein. Volume II: Love, guilt and reparation and other works 1921–1945.* New York: Free Press.

Klein, M. (1984b). *The writings of Melanie Klein. Volume III: Envy and gratitude and other works 1946–1963.* New York: Free Press.

Koenigsberg, H. W., Kernberg, O. F., Stone, M. H., Appelbaum, A. H., Yeomans, F. E., & Diamond, D. (2000). *Borderline patients: Extending the limits of treatability.* New York: Basic Books.

Linehan, M. M., Heard, H. L., & Armstrong, H. E. (1993). Naturalistic follow-up of a behavioral treatment for chronically parasuicidal borderline patients. *Archives of General Psychiatry, 50,* 971–974.

Linehan, M. M., Schmidt, H., Dimeff, L. A., Craft, J. C., Kanter, J., & Comtois, K. A. (1999). Dialectical behavior therapy for patients with Borderline Personality Disorder and drug-dependence. *American Journal of Addiction, 8,* 279–292.

Luborsky, L. (1984). *Principles of psychoanalytic psychotherapy: A manual for supportive-expressive treatment.* New York: Basic Books.

Rado, S. (1928). The problem of melancholia. *International Journal of Psychoanalysis, 9,* 420–428.

Stevenson, J., & Meares, R. (1992). An outcome study of psychoherapy for patients with Borderline Personality Disorder. *American Journal of Psychiatry, 149,* 358–362.

Strupp, H. H., & Binder, J. L. (1984). *Psychotherapy in a new key: A guide to time-limited dynamic psychotherapy.* New York: Basic Books.

Yeomans, F. E., Selzer, M., & Clarkin, J. F. (1992). *The treatment contract: Framing dynamic therapy with borderline patients.* New York: Basic Books.

CHAPTER 11

A Relational Approach to Psychotherapy

J. CHRISTOPHER MURAN AND JEREMY D. SAFRAN

Our relational approach to psychotherapy emerged from our efforts to study the therapeutic alliance, to identify alliance ruptures, and to develop models of rupture resolution, which began back in the late 1980s at the University of Toronto, Clarke Institute of Psychiatry (Safran, Crocker, McMain, & Murray, 1990; Safran & Muran, 1995, 1996, 1998, 2000; Safran, Muran, & Samstag, 1994). We have defined *ruptures* as dysfluencies in relatedness, as markers of vicious cycles or enactments involving the unwitting participation of both patient and therapist, and as ubiquitous phenomena that represent windows into the relational world of the patient (as well as the therapist). We have defined *rupture resolutions* as critical change events in the psychotherapy process. Our specific aim in these efforts has been to develop metatherapeutic strategies for negotiating the therapeutic alliance, that is, strategies that at once are informed by, as well as inform, many therapeutic traditions.

We have found a conceptualization of the therapeutic alliance along the lines that Edward Bordin (1979) suggested were useful for several reasons. He defined the alliance as composed of three interdependent factors: the agreement between patient and therapist on the *tasks* and the *goals* of treatment, as well as the affective *bond* between them. This definition highlights the interdependence of relational and technical factors. It suggests that the meaning of any technical factors can be understood only in the relational context in which it is applied. It also highlights the importance of *negotiation* between patient and therapist on the tasks and goals of therapy, which is consistent with an increasingly influential way of conceptualizing the psychotherapy process as involving the negotiation between the patient's desires or needs and those of the therapist (Aron, 1996; Benjamin, 1990; Mitchell, 1993; Pizer, 1998).

In the process of pursuing this metatherapeutic initiative, we developed a short-term and time-limited model identified as brief relational therapy (BRT; Safran, in press; Safran & Muran, 2000). The development of this model took place largely in the Brief Psychotherapy Research Program at Beth Israel Medical Center in New York. In addition to being informed by results from our rupture resolution research, the BRT model is based to a great extent on principles associated with relational psychoanalysis (see Mitchell & Aron, 1999) and to a lesser extent on principles associated with cognitive (see Safran & Segal, 1990)[1] and humanistic/experiential psychotherapies (see Greenberg, Watson, & Lietaer, 1998). Some of the key characteristics of the model are as follows:

1. It assumes a two-person psychology and a constructivist epistemology (or, to be more precise, what Hoffman, 1998, refers to as a dialectical constructivist perspective).
2. There is an intensive focus on the here and now of the therapeutic relationship.
3. There is an ongoing collaborative exploration of both patients' and therapists' contributions to the interaction.
4. It emphasizes in-depth exploration of the nuances of patients' experience in the context of unfolding therapeutic enactments and is cautious about making transference interpretations that speculate about generalized relational patterns.
5. It makes intensive use of therapeutic metacommunication (defined below) and countertransference disclosure.
6. It emphasizes the subjectivity of the therapist's perceptions.
7. It assumes that the relational meaning of interventions is critical.
8. It views termination as an ultimate alliance rupture, a valuable opportunity to deal with critical issues surrounding acceptance, being alone, separation, and loss.

What distinguishes the BRT model from other short-term dynamic models is that it eschews the establishment of a case formulation during the first phase of treatment, replacing a *content* focus with a *process* focus. The emphasis in BRT is on developing a generalizable skill of mindfulness (defined below), rather than on gaining insight into and mastering a particular core theme.

In this chapter, we present the BRT model in greater detail, defining the major principles of personality and change, highlighting metacommunication as the critical principle of intervention, and outlining the treatment process from beginning to end. We provide clinical illustrations of rupture resolution that demonstrate the ongoing process in BRT and highlight the principle of metacommunication, and we present our perspective on training and supervision, with its intensive focus on therapist experience, which has been a critical part of our psychotherapy research program. Finally, we include a summary of our research regarding rupture resolution and demonstrating the efficacy of BRT.

A RELATIONAL THEORY OF PERSON

Elsewhere, we have written about the person as a relational phenomenon (Muran, 2001; Safran, 1998; Safran & Muran, 2000; Safran & Segal, 1990), describing the continuous interplay among the various processes and structures of the self. The former refers to the various cognitive and interpersonal operations that establish and protect the representational structures of the self. This refers to the self in relation to others as well as to itself. The latter refers to memory stores of multiple discrete experiences of the self in relation to significant others. These can be considered *relational schemas* that are abstracted on the basis of interactions with attachment figures (and others of interpersonal significance) to increase the likelihood of maintaining a relationship with those figures. They contain specific procedural information regarding expectancies and strategies for negotiating the dialectically opposing needs for agency or

---

[1] Saran and Segal (1990) describe a related model that is an interpersonal elaboration of cognitive therapy (see also Marcotte & Safran in Volume IV of this handbook).

self-definition and for relatedness or communion (Bakan, 1966; see Safran & Muran, 2000, for elaboration). They are also considered emotional structures that include innate expressive-motor responses, that develop from birth into subtle and idiosyncratic variations, and that serve a communicative function in that they continually orient the person to the environment and the environment to the person.

We have also described the emergence of a corresponding experience, a particular state of mind or *self-state* with the activation of a particular relational schema. Self-states are the experiential products of the various processes and structures of the self, the crystallization in subjective experience of an underlying relational schema. Different self-states can activate different relational schemas, resulting in a cycling through different states of mind. The transition points or boundaries among the various self-states that each person experiences vary in terms of seamlessness. They are naturally smoothed over, creating the illusory sense of continuity and singular identity, through the process of dissociation. The more conspicuous and abrupt the transitions between self-states, however, the more problematic the dissociative process. It is useful to distinguish between dissociation as a healthy process of selectively focusing attention and dissociation as an unhealthy process resulting from traumatic overload and resulting in severing connections between relational schemas.

Finally, a central tenet of our relational perspective is the recognition that there is an ongoing reciprocal relationship between the self-states of one person and those of the other in a dyadic interaction. This refers to the ways in which self-states are interpersonally communicated and mutually regulated in a dyadic encounter. As individuals cycle through various self-states in an interpersonal encounter, they should both influence and be influenced by the various self-states of the other. In such encounters, one is always embedded in a *relational matrix* (Mitchell, 1988) that is shaped moment by moment by the various states and implicit desires of the two individuals. Dysfluencies or ruptures in relatedness indicate the activation of dissociative processes and maladaptive schemas. We have also suggested that ruptures mark vicious *cognitive-interpersonal cycles* (e.g., Safran, 1998), which can be unduly driven by dysfunctional relational schemas of an individual, even though they invariably involve the unwitting participation of another. Relational schemas shape the person's perceptions of the world, leading to cognitive processes and interpersonal behaviors that in turn shape the environment in a way that confirms the representational content of the schemas. To the extent that they are limited in scope of internalized interpersonal experiences, they will restrict the range of interpersonal behaviors, which pull for similar responses from a range of different people, resulting in redundant patterns of interaction. Thus, they limit the possibility of new information in the form of new interpersonal experiences. In this way, the individual operates in a sense as a relatively closed system.

A RELATIONAL THEORY OF CHANGE: DISCOVERY AND CONSTRUCTION

Change is essentially understood as involving the parallel processes of increasing immediate awareness of self and other and providing a new interpersonal experience. By increasing the patient's immediate awareness of the processes that mediate a dysfunctional interpersonal pattern, change suggests not simply a correction of a distortion, but an elaboration and clarification of the patient's self-definition, in other words, expanding one's awareness of who one is in a particular interpersonal transaction. With an expansion of awareness comes an increased sense of responsibility. This translates into a greater awareness of how one constructs one's experience. It is at the more molecular level that one can begin to develop a sense of the choices one is making; thus, to develop a greater sense of responsibility and agency, one must attend to the details of experience at successive moments of perception and begin to discover the choices one is making on a moment-by-moment basis.

The clarification of the patient's self-definition invariably involves more clarification of the therapist's self-definition as well. The idea behind this is essentially twofold: first, that we are always embedded in an interpersonal field that exerts a great influence on the emergence of a self-state that we experience in a given moment (Stern, 1997); second, that greater self-definition can be achieved only by defining the edges of one self in relation to another self—in this case, the patient in relation to the therapist (Ehrenberg, 1992). This idea also invokes the notion of *intersubjectivity*, not only in terms of how the self-states of patient and therapist mutually regulate themselves, but also in terms of the clinical significance of the mutual recognition of respective subjectivities and the ongoing negotiation between the respective needs and desires of patient and therapist (Benjamin, 1990; Pizer, 1998). Thus, therapy can be understood as a process of figuring out who is speaking to whom in a given moment: Which patient self is communicating to which therapist self? With every therapeutic encounter, therapists must invariably confront themselves and expand their awareness of themselves in relation to yet another individual. Accordingly, the therapeutic process should involve change for both participants.

It is important to recognize that the psychotherapeutic process in a paradoxical sense is not only discovery-oriented, but also constructive. As Mitchell (1993) describes:

> There is no stream of experience separable from experience as accessed by someone (either oneself or someone else) at a specific time, for a particular purpose, in a specific context. Thus, experience is constructed on a moment-by-moment basis. At any given point, the patient can only report a particular construction of his experience, which may overlook or obliterate many other important constructions of his experience (which the [therapist] might be more in touch with). At any given point, the [therapist] can offer only his own construction of some aspects of the patient's experience, a construction of a construction. (p. 60)

Accordingly, self-experience does not simply flow forth without impediment but is channeled by the efforts of the individual to communicate and the other to understand. The course it takes is therefore a social or coconstruction. For example, the therapist's own experience, and articulation of that, which includes his or her theoretical orientation (Aron, 1999; Schafer, 1983), has an enormous impact on the patient's experience and articulation. This is a bidirectional and iterative process.

MECHANISMS OF CHANGE: DECENTERING AND DISCONFIRMATION

Following our relational theory of change, we have identified two specific mechanisms of change that we outline in this section: *decentering* and *disconfirmation*.

The first mechanism of change consists of inviting patients to observe their contribution to an enactment in the relational matrix of the therapeutic relationship, thus facilitating a process of decentering. The Eastern notion of *mindfulness* is particularly useful in this regard. Mindfulness consists of directing one's attention to whatever emerges in the moment, without preference, judgment, or interpretation. It is a learned skill that constitutes a central vehicle of change for the patient. A primary task for the therapist consists of directing patients' attention to various aspects of their inner and outer worlds as they are occurring, thereby promoting the type of awareness that deautomates habitual patterns and helping patients to experience themselves as agents in the process of constructing reality, rather than as passive victims of circumstances. The skill of mindfulness can be cultivated in therapy by having the therapist direct patients' attention to relevant aspects of their experience at judicious moments. Simple questions such as What are you aware of?, What are you experiencing?, and Are you aware of interfering with your experience in any way? can be very effective (if well timed) in helping patients to discover aspects of their experience and actions that normally operate out of awareness.

The principle of *metacommunication,* which was used originally in the therapeutic context by Kiesler (1996), captures the spirit of the type of collaborative exploration of what is going on in the therapeutic relationship and the essence of what we mean by decentering. Metacommunication involves an attempt to disembed from the interpersonal claim that is currently being enacted by taking the current interaction as the focus of communication. It is an attempt to bring awareness to bear on the relational matrix as it unfolds. This can be thought of as *mindfulness in action.* In a sense, all transference interpretations can be conceptualized as a form of metacommunication, insofar as they are attempts to communicate about and make sense of what is being enacted in the therapeutic relationship. The particular form of metacommunication that we discuss, however, has a number of distinctive features that set it apart from a more traditional transference interpretation. Unlike transference interpretations in which therapists offer conjectures about the meaning of the current interaction, efforts at metacommunication attempt to decrease the degree of inference and are grounded as much as possible in the therapist's immediate experience of some aspect of the therapeutic relationship (either the therapist's own feelings or immediate perception of some aspect of the patient's actions). For example, the therapist may say, "I feel shut out by you" or "I feel like it would be easy to say something that would offend you." Countertransference disclosure plays an important role in metacommunication, but other forms of feedback are used as well. For example, the therapist may say, "I experience you as withdrawn right now" or "I have an image of the two of us fencing." The objective of statements of this type is to articulate one's implicit or intuitive sense of something that is taking place in the therapeutic relationship to initiate an explicit exploration of what is being unwittingly enacted.

The second mechanism of change consists of the disconfirmation of the patient's maladaptive relational schema through the therapeutic interaction. By disembedding from a relational matrix, the therapist can provide opportunities for new learning. In practice, metacommunication about the therapeutic relationship plays a central role in facilitating the process of experiential disconfirmation, in addition to that of decentering. This perspective converges in many ways with Alexander's (Alexander & French, 1946) notion of the corrective emotional experience, as well as the Mount Zion Group's (Weiss, Sampson, & the Mount Zion Psychotherapy Research Group, 1986) view that patients unconsciously submit their therapists to "transference tests," through which the patient tests whether the therapist will confirm a pathogenic belief. For example, a patient who believes that independence will be punished speaks about quitting therapy, with the hope that the therapist will not react in a controlling fashion. If the therapist passes the test by not confirming the belief, therapeutic progress takes place. This is consistent with the tradition that originated with Ferenczi (1932), who was the first to suggest that psychotherapy involves the provision of a new or different experience.

METHOD OF ASSESSMENT AND INTERVENTION: METACOMMUNICATION

The main method of assessment and intervention in this relational model is founded on the principle of metacommunication. The following are some basic principles in the process of metacommunication. Elsewhere, we have described these and other principles in much greater detail (Safran & Muran, 2000).

1. *Start where you are.* Metacommunication should always emerge out of the inspiration of the moment. It should be based on feelings and intuitions that are emerging for the therapist in that moment. What was true one session may not be true the next, and what was true at the beginning of a session may not be true later in that same session. Furthermore, what is true for one therapist in relationship to a particular patient may not be true for another. Therapists must begin by accepting and working through their own feelings in the immediacy of the moment rather than trying to be somewhere they are not.

2. *Focus on the here and now.* The focus should be on the here and now of the therapeutic relationship, rather than on events that have taken place in the past (i.e., either in previous sessions or at different points in the same session). Commenting on what is happening now facilitates the process of mindfulness for patients. To the extent therapists are able to comment on what is happening in the moment, it will become easier for patients to develop a grounded experiential awareness of both their actions and the internal experience associated with them.

3. *Focus on the concrete and specific.* The focus should be concrete and specific, rather than general. Whenever possible, questions, observations, and comments should focus on concrete instances. This promotes experiential awareness, rather than abstract, intellectualized speculation. When patients' attention is directed to the concrete and specific, they can make their own discoveries rather than buying into the therapist's version of reality. This type of concreteness and specificity helps them to become observers of their own behavior. It thus promotes the type of mindfulness that fosters change.

4. *Explore with skillful tentativeness.* Communicate observations in a tentative and exploratory fashion. The message at both explicit and implicit levels should be one of inviting the patient to engage in a collaborative attempt to understand what is taking place, rather than one of conveying information with an objective status. It is critical to remember that relational implications of a communication are as important as, if not more important than, its content. The tentative and exploratory nature of the therapist's intervention should be genuine and not simulated.

5. *Establish a sense of collaboration and we-ness.* The implicit message should be one of inviting the patient to join the therapist in an attempt to understand their shared dilemma. During periods of therapeutic impasse, patients typically feel alone and demoralized. The therapist becomes one of an endless succession of figures who are unable to join with the patient in his or her struggle. The therapist becomes another foe rather than an ally. By framing the impasse as a shared experience, the therapist begins the process of transforming the struggle by acknowledging that therapist and patient are stuck together.

6. *Emphasize one's own subjectivity.* All metacommunication should emphasize the subjectivity of the therapist's perception. This plays a critical role in establishing a climate that emphasizes the subjectivity of all perceptions and the importance of engaging in an ongoing collaborative effort to clarify what is taking place. Emphasizing the subjectivity of the therapist's observations also helps to establish a more

egalitarian relationship. When the subjectivity of the therapist's observations is emphasized, patients are more likely to feel free to either make use of them or not and are less likely to feel a need to cling to their own perspectives and defensively reject the therapist's.

7. *Gauge intuitive sense of relatedness.* Therapists should monitor their intuitive sense of emotional closeness with or distance from patients on an ongoing basis. This continuous assessment provides one of the most important sources of diagnostic information: the quality of relatedness with patients in a given moment. This quality of relatedness reflects an ongoing interplay between interpersonal and intrapsychic dimensions. To the extent that patients are feeling safe, accepted, and validated by the therapist, they will find it easier to access their inner experience in a genuine fashion. At the same time, to the extent that patients are in contact with their inner experience, therapists will experience a greater sense of relatedness to them. A sudden shift in the direction of decreased relatedness may signal that the therapist's intervention has been hindering rather than facilitative; this indicates the need to explore the way the patient has construed or experienced the intervention. Conversely, a sudden shift in the direction of increased relatedness may signal that the therapist has developed a more attuned understanding of the patient's internal experience.

8. *Attend to patients' responsiveness to all interventions.* Therapists should continually monitor the quality of patients' responsiveness to interventions and attend to subtle intuitions about the quality of the responsiveness. If an intervention fails to deepen exploration or further inhibits it, or if the therapist senses something peculiar in the patient's response to it, it is critical to explore the way the patient experienced it. Over time, this type of exploration can help to articulate patients' characteristic way of construing interpersonal relationships and gradually lead to a fleshing out of their relational schemas. It can also lead to a progressive refinement in therapists' understanding of their own contribution to the interaction.

9. *Recognize that the situation is constantly changing.* It is important to bear in mind that the situation is constantly changing; what was true about the therapeutic relationship a moment ago is not true now. It is thus critical for therapists to use whatever is emerging in the present as a point of departure for further metacommunication. All situations are workable provided that one fully acknowledges and accepts what the situation is. Even the position of being stuck is a position that is workable once one accepts it and ceases to fight against it.

10. *Expect resolution attempts to lead to more ruptures and expect to revisit ruptures.* No matter how hard therapists attempt to follow these principles, there is always a risk that any form of therapeutic metacommunication will further aggravate the alliance rupture and perpetuate a vicious cycle. Even when the therapist is not metacommunicating defensively, there is always a risk that it will place a greater strain on the alliance by implicitly suggesting that patients should be saying or doing something other than what they are currently saying or doing. It is important for therapists to resist reluctance to metacommunicate and to recognize that it is but one step in the process of resolution, rather than an ultimate intervention. Furthermore, it is quite common for therapists to find that the same impasse is being revisited repeatedly. To the extent that therapists relate to an impasse as simply a recurrence of a previous impasse, it will be impossible to relate to it in its own terms and appreciate the unique configuration of the moment.

11. *Accept responsibility.* Therapists should accept responsibility for their contributions to the interaction. It is critical to bear in mind that as therapists, we are always unwittingly contributing to the interaction with the patient. The task is thus one of working in an ongoing fashion to clarify the nature of this contribution. Often the

process of explicitly acknowledging one's contribution to the patient can be a particularly potent intervention. First, this process can help patients become aware of inchoate feelings that they are having difficulty articulating, in part, because of a fear of the interpersonal consequences. Second, the process of explicitly acknowledging one's contribution to the interaction can validate patients' conscious and unconscious perceptions of what is taking place and help them to trust their own judgment. Third, by validating patients' perceptions through this type of acknowledgment, therapists can reduce patients' self-doubt, thereby decreasing the need for defensiveness and paving the way for the exploration and acknowledgment of patients' contribution to the interaction.

12. *Judiciously disclose and explore one's own experience.* Therapists can begin the process of working through an impasse by sharing their own experience (feelings, images, fantasies, or descriptions of their own actions) with their patients. During this process, it is important to make it clear that one's experience is not simply caused by the patient and that there is no guarantee that it will help shed light on what is going on in the current interaction. The process of articulating one's feelings to patients can begin to free one to intervene more effectively. Therapists' feelings of being stuck or paralyzed often reflect difficulty in acknowledging and articulating to themselves what they are currently experiencing. Further, the process of articulating one's contributions to the patient can play a critical role in beginning to clarify the nature of the vicious cycle. Another valuable intervention that is a variation on the theme of self-disclosure involves inviting patients to explore the therapist's contribution (see Aron, 1996). This can consist of inviting patients either to make suggestions about how the therapist's actions are contributing to the impasse or to speculate about what may be going on for the therapist internally. This type of intervention can help to clarify patients' construal of the therapist and lead to a further elaboration of their relational schemas. It can also provide new insight into the therapist's own contribution to the impasse. It is critical for therapists to be open to accepting their patient's perception and genuinely considering its truth claim.

A CHANGE EVENT: RESOLVING RUPTURES IN THE THERAPEUTIC ALLIANCE

The psychotherapy process has been described as one involving the ongoing push and pull of the respective self-states of patient and therapist and as an *intersubjective negotiation* (Pizer, 1992). As Pizer so colorfully captured, therapists in their interventions and patients in their responses are recurrently saying to each other, "No, you can't make this of me. But you can make this of me" (p. 218). This ongoing negotiation can be understood by the moment-by-moment press of *both* patient *and* therapist needs for agency and relatedness. Ruptures in the therapeutic alliance represent an interpersonal crystallization of this negotiation and, thus, an opportunity to explore the intrapsychic processes that mediate the struggle to negotiate these dialectically opposing needs in the context of a particular relational configuration.

It is useful to identify ruptures in terms of specific patient behaviors or communication and organize them into two subtypes of markers: withdrawal and confrontation. In withdrawal ruptures, patients withdraw or partially disengage from the therapist, their own emotions, or some aspect of the therapeutic process. Withdrawal markers can manifest in many different forms. In some cases, it is fairly obvious that patients are having difficulty expressing their concerns or needs in the relationship. In others, the expression is much more subtle, the process apparently seamless, whereby the patient readily complies with the perceived desires of the therapist in what can be described as a type of *pseudo-alliance*. In confrontation ruptures, patients directly express anger, resentment, or dissatisfaction with the therapist or some aspect of the therapy. These can vary in terms of how directly or indirectly the confrontation is expressed. The more indirect, the more the marker can be characterized as a mix of confrontation and withdrawal.

Withdrawal and confrontation markers reflect different ways of coping with the dialectical tension between the needs for agency and for relatedness. In withdrawal ruptures, the patient strives for relatedness at the cost of the need for agency or self-definition. In confrontation ruptures, the patient negotiates the conflict by favoring the need for agency or self-definition over the need for relatedness. Different patients are likely to experience or exhibit a predominance of one type of rupture marker over another; this reflects different characteristic styles of coping or adaptation. Nevertheless, over the course of treatment, both types of markers may emerge with a specific patient, or a specific impasse may involve both confrontation and withdrawal features. Thus, it is critical for therapists to be sensitive to the specific qualities of the rupture that are emerging in the moment, rather than to become locked into viewing patients as exclusively confrontation or withdrawal types.

We have developed two models of rupture resolution, which we describe below. They each consist of five positions, each of which includes a dyadic interaction between patient and therapist. Both models involve metacommunication about the relational matrix as the critical change process; thus, the mechanisms of decentering and disconfirmation come into play, as light is shed on the relational matrix and the beliefs and expectations of the patient's relational schema are challenged. Both begin with the vicious cycle (Position 1), which includes the rupture marker and the therapist's complementary response. Following a process of disembedding from the relational matrix (Position 2), they both include two parallel pathways of exploration: one for the vicious cycle (Positions 3 and 5), the other for various avoidant operations (Position 4). Where they differ significantly is in the nature of these exploratory pathways. The common progression in the resolution of withdrawal ruptures consists of moving through increasingly clearer articulations of discontent to self-assertion, in which the need for agency is realized and validated by the therapist (Position 5). The progression in the resolution of confrontation ruptures consists of moving through feelings of anger, to feelings of disappointment and hurt over having been failed by the therapist, to contacting vulnerability and the wish to be nurtured and taken care of (Position 5). Typical avoidant operations that emerge in these processes concern anxieties and self-doubts resulting from the fear of being too aggressive or too vulnerable associated with the expectation of retaliation or rejection by the therapist.

CLINICAL ILLUSTRATIONS OF RUPTURE RESOLUTION

In this section, we describe in greater detail the two rupture resolution models and present two clinical illustrations that elucidate the differences in the resolution process between withdrawal and confrontation ruptures (Safran & Muran, 2000).

A Resolution Model for Withdrawal Ruptures

As described above, the resolution model for withdrawal ruptures is composed of five positions. Each includes a patient state and a therapist response or intervention (see Figure 11.1). The first is signaled by the patient withdrawal marker. For example, the patient complies or defers to the therapist by agreeing with an interpretation in an acquiescent fashion. This type of withdrawal is often part of an ongoing

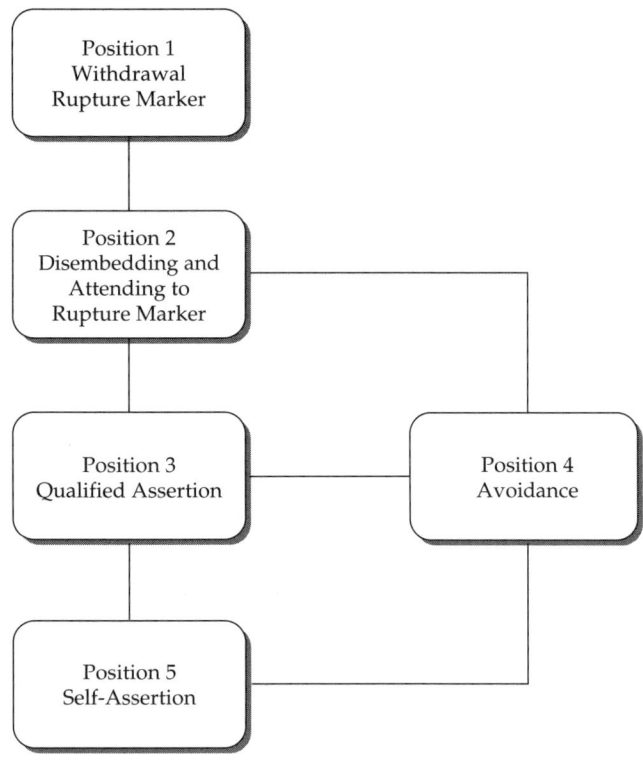

Figure 11.1 Rupture resolution model for withdrawal ruptures. From *Negotiating the Therapeutic Alliance: A Relational Treatment Guide* (p. 143), by J. D. Safran and J. C. Muran, 2000, New York: Guilford Press. Reprinted with permission.

enactment in which the therapist becomes hooked in the vicious cycle and responds to the patient's passive or submissive behavior by brushing over any subtle indications of concern or by acting in an overly active or domineering fashion.

Therapists must become mindful of their contributions to the cycle that is being enacted and be willing to explore them at any point along the way. In those situations in which the withdrawal marker is particularly subtle, therapists' awareness of their own feelings or action tendencies may be the best indicator that something is taking place that warrants exploration. For example, therapists may find themselves working harder than usual to give advice to a patient, or being less attentive to a patient's concerns than they typically would be with other patients, or they may find themselves ignoring a patient's concerns or pushing a patient to accept an interpretation or to look at things a certain way. In situations in which the patient withdraws by dissociating threatening feelings about the therapist, therapists may find themselves suddenly losing interest in the patient or becoming aware that their attention has been drifting.

Once therapists recognize the vicious cycle either by becoming aware of their own feelings or tendencies or recognizing the patient withdrawal marker, they can intervene in a number of ways. This constitutes the second position and critical stepping stone in the resolution process. It is important to direct the patient's attention to the here and now of the therapeutic relationship or to his or her experience in the context of the relationship. Common examples are statements such as "What are you experiencing?", "I have a sense of you withdrawing from me," and "How are you feeling about what's going on between us right now?" When the patient expresses negative feelings indirectly (e.g., through sarcasm), it can be helpful for the therapist to use self-disclosure to convey the impact of the patient's behavior at a personal level (e.g., "I feel judged" or "I feel criticized").

If the patient speaks about negative feelings in general terms, it is important for the therapist to explore the relevance of these feelings to the present situation. This exploration should be conducted in a noncontrolling fashion, which respects any decision on the patient's part not to discuss negative feelings toward the therapist in the present context. This is particularly important with patients who tend to be compliant, because pushing for something the patient is not ready to explore may invite more compliance. Therapists should be mindful of contributing to a new variation of an enactment through their attempts to reestablish contact with the patient who is withdrawing. Any intervention can be made in the service of perpetuating a vicious cycle. What is most important to unhooking is the ongoing struggle for patient, as well as therapist, to become increasingly cognizant of the feeling states and action tendencies that perpetuate the cycle.

Interventions that serve to unhook from the cycle typically lead to two pathways of exploration. The first involves the exploration of thoughts and feelings associated with the rupture (Positions 3 and 5). The second involves the internal processes and defensive operations that block the exploration of feelings and thoughts associated with the rupture (Position 4). The experiencing pathway can be subdivided into two successive stages (Positions 3 and 5). In the first of these (Position 3), the patient begins to express thoughts and feelings associated with the rupture experience, but these are mixed with features of the initial rupture marker. The patient begins to express negative sentiments and then qualifies the statement or takes it back.

There are a number of therapist interventions that can be helpful in the context of this type of qualified assertion and can facilitate the process to Position 5. Most important is to empathize with and display a genuine interest and curiosity in the negative sentiments that are expressed. When patients qualify their statements or indicate that they are uncertain or conflicted about their negative feelings, the therapist can acknowledge both sides of patients' perspective and then focus selectively on the concerns that patients are having difficulty acknowledging or articulating. For example, "I understand that you're uncertain about how important your concerns are. If you're willing to go into it, however, I'd be interested in hearing more." Or, "It sounds like you have two perspectives on this issue. One part of you feels that it's no big deal, but the other part has some concerns. If you're willing to pursue this a little further, I suggest that you try putting the part that feels like it's no big deal aside for a moment, and let me hear more from the part that's concerned."

Another useful intervention consists of giving patients feedback about the way they qualify or soften their statement to heighten their awareness of this process. For example, "My sense is that you start to express some negative feelings, but then you end up pulling your punch. Do you have any awareness of this?" If patients are able to become aware of this defensive or self-protective operation, the therapist can then begin to explore the internal processes associated with their avoidance. For example, "Any sense of what the risk would be of stating things in an unqualified way?"

The next position (Position 5) along the rupture experience pathway involves the patient accessing primary feelings and asserting underlying wishes or needs directly. It is critical that patients accept responsibility for their own needs or desires at this point. This implies that patients are already in a state that is somewhat individuated or autonomous with respect to the therapist. Blaming, demanding, or pleading statements, which are typical of Position 3, imply a lack of individuation. The therapist should validate and empathize with this individuated state of the patient.

In a typical resolution process, the exploration of the rupture experience pathway proceeds to a certain point and then becomes blocked. This is indicated by the patient engaging in coping strategies, defensive verbalizations, and actions that function to avoid or manage the emotions associated with the rupture experience. Examples are changing the topic, speaking in a deadened voice tone, and speaking in general terms rather than the here-and-now specifics of the therapeutic relationship. The avoidance pathway (Position 4) involves the exploration of beliefs, expectations, and other internal processes that inhibit the acknowledgment and expression of feelings and needs associated with the rupture experience. There are two major subtypes here. The first consists of beliefs and expectations about the other's response that block the exploration of the rupture experience pathway. For example, the patient who expects expressions of anger to evoke retaliation will have difficulty acknowledging and expressing angry feelings; the patient who believes that expressions of vulnerability and need will result in abandonment will have difficulty expressing such feelings. The second subtype consists of self-critical or self-doubting processes that function to block either the acknowledgment or the exploration of a rupture experience pathway. For example, patients who believe they are childish for wanting help will not be able to express their needs to the therapist; patients who believe that they are immature for being angry will have difficulty expressing angry feelings to the therapist.

As patients explore their avoidance and gain awareness of the processes interfering with their experience and more of a sense of agency or ownership of these processes, feelings associated with the rupture experience naturally begin to emerge more fully. Patients may move back to the rupture pathway spontaneously, or therapists may redirect attention to this pathway again. Typically, a resolution process involves an ongoing alternation between experiencing and avoidance pathways, with the exploration of each pathway functioning to facilitate a deepening of the exploration of the other. It is essential during the exploration of both pathways that the therapist respond in a validating and accepting fashion to whatever the patient expresses. This challenges the patient's maladaptive relational schema and provides a corrective emotional experience.

To clarify the withdrawal resolution model, each position is illustrated below with transcript material excerpted from a treatment conducted in our research program. The patient presented with bouts of anxiety and depression and with "problems in contacting, relating, and responding to others," which have debilitated him in his marriage and his work. He viewed himself as weak and incompetent and others as dominant and critical and demonstrated an avoidant, equivocating, and convoluted style of communicating.[2] In the session presented, the therapist attempted to focus the patient on a self-critical state, which emerged in an exploration of the patient's anger toward his very critical wife. The therapist was attempting to focus on such a depressive self-state to begin an exploration of its avoidant operation. What ensued was a vicious cycle in which the patient responded in cryptic ways, which served to frustrate and confuse the therapist and led to a dogged pursuit of understanding, a torturous process of cat and mouse.

Position 1: Withdrawal Marker

PATIENT: Essentially, I have such low self-esteem that I don't even pursue something basic to my well-being like getting a new portfolio to show my work in. I mean, I feel like I've deteriorated over the years. That I've . . . Presentation has never been great with me.

THERAPIST: Let me ask you to try a little exercise that's sort of different from what we did last time. I'd like you to play your really critical side. What would you say to yourself right now strictly from your critical side?

PATIENT: This is difficult. When you ask me to do something like this, I feel so hopeful. . . . It sort of triggers hope.

THERAPIST: It triggers hope?

PATIENT: Not just to be obstinate perhaps, or just to be, I don't know . . . It's often . . . I don't know why, exactly.

THERAPIST: What do you mean "obstinate"?

PATIENT: It . . . Why would I say that? Because I can't figure out why I close my eyes and feel immediately hopeful rather than feeling, uh, filled with despair. I don't know why that's the case. Why am I smiling now instead

---

[2]We present minimal information about diagnostic status, case history, and formulation because of our theoretical bias that all the necessary information about the patient becomes evident in the relational process involving the therapist.

of weeping now? I don't know why. I mean it's a certain, it's weird that I feel the opposite feeling other than what you asked me to feel. But if . . .

Increasingly, patient and therapist moved further away from the original task. The patient continued to associate to other feelings and memories, and the therapist kept in pursuit of understanding what he meant. Finally, the patient shifted into a hopeless state regarding his life situation and mused about some other solution, and the therapist became aware of their cooperative movement away from the original task. The therapist then was able to unhook from the cycle by refocusing attention on their immediate communication process.

Position 2: Disembedding and Attending to the Rupture Marker

PATIENT: That I'm stuck. This is the, this is the end, you know, I've been stuck in this so long that there's no way out of it. You know, I was thinking this morning, I mean this is a, this is an attempt to break out of whatever, whatever spot I'm in. But there are other things, I mean, too, you know, I had jokingly mentioned Dale Carnegie, or something like that, just to learn skills of presentation, might be superficial but, uh, but in conjunction perhaps with a deeper emotional restructuring of my self-esteem, some, some cosmetic, and superficial techniques might be useful as well. And I was wondering what you thought about that, I mean this is . . . I just took my son to karate last night and was looking at the catalogue for the 92nd Street Y, which has courses about things, about oh, techniques for interviews, you know. Make yourself, you know, look great. Would that be useful, do you think, I mean would that be?

THERAPIST: Well, I'll, I don't mean to ignore your question, but I'm also aware that we really shifted . . .

PATIENT: Yeah.

THERAPIST: Away from what we were doing, and I'm wondering if you're aware of what happened or how that happened?

PATIENT: Trying to put a good face on things, I guess.

The patient then began to explore why he needed to put "a good face on things," which led him to reveal his negative sentiments about the usefulness of the therapist's attempts to focus him on a self-critical state, specifically on dwelling on the negative. The therapist in turn tried to facilitate a more assertive expression of the patient's objection to focusing on his self-criticism.

Position 3: Qualified Assertion

PATIENT: Dwelling on it. You know, trying to change the image, or rebuild the image, or build a different reality is another way of stating it, but it's not . . . Another way of stating it is, of course, dwelling on it, examining the negative image is, ah, I'm not quite clear on how dwelling on this negative image is going to, is really going to lead toward, I guess, a more positive outcome eventually.

THERAPIST: So it doesn't seem very constructive to dwell on the negative.

PATIENT: I guess so.

THERAPIST: So you have some misgivings about actually doing this exercise.

PATIENT: Misgivings, I guess, maybe, a little bit, you know, maybe, I guess so, that's part of it.

THERAPIST: Can you sort of express that to me in a more direct fashion?

PATIENT: I think it was a few weeks ago, a few sessions ago, talking about, oh, examining, these, what were they? Negative? I forget what it is. I started to get really negative about it over the week. I was doing it. I felt very depressed over it, over that length of time. I was thinking a lot about my family and how that really influenced the basic way that I look at myself and the world. And just dwelling on that, on something I thought was dealt with and behind me years ago, which was quite, you know, very painful, very painful, for me until about 20 years ago when I began to be more dependent upon myself emotionally, rather than on my parents.

THERAPIST: Um hum.

PATIENT: It was the center of the pain in my life, I think this horrible relationship between my parents. Ah, um, and don't think I covered it up really because I dealt with it and talked about it with friends a lot, and really finally felt that's their problem. I've gone beyond that now. It was a big process to get to that point, and it wasn't just swept under the rug, I don't think. I think it was, was really dealt with. I think people evolve certainly, and there's still a, no doubt, that it's a big part of my basic structure of my upbringing, life, personality, and framework, emotional framework.

THERAPIST: Um hum.

PATIENT: And it might be worth considering again. It probably is, but that was my reaction to it. It felt, felt like I've dealt with this before.

THERAPIST: "Why am I doing this?"

PATIENT: Why am I doing it again?

THERAPIST: Yeah, you don't see any benefit. You just see pain, by doing this.

PATIENT: Yeah, I feel like I'm sort of stirring up things that were painful. At that time there was, ah, some resolution by being able to feel that I was getting stronger emotionally, being on my own more emotionally, having the ability to have the courage to ask girls for dates at that time. I felt that was, you know, really important stuff that I was doing at that time.

THERAPIST: So in the same sense, this exercise here doesn't seem useful to you apparently.

PATIENT: Well, I'm not sure if it feels use . . . ah . . .

THERAPIST: The costs seem to outweigh the benefits?

PATIENT: It's more, kind of, you know, talking about the reluctance or inability to get into that mode seems more like a blank wall. I mean, when I closed my eyes I didn't see black, I saw, sort of, like, a red blank wall in front of me. I mean it was like a real, real presence. I don't know, I don't know what it necessarily represents. It just wasn't black. It was something different that I saw when I closed my eyes. But there's no doubt I feel overwhelmed by these feelings.

Therapist: I'm sort of confused because on one hand, I get the sense that there's a part of you that doesn't want to do this, but then I got kind of lost in terms of that, so I don't know. Can you clarify that?

Though he expressed some of his negative sentiments, the patient's expressions were still somewhat equivocal and unclear. He engaged in extended explanations that brought him back to painful feelings regarding his relationship with his parents and that suggested he had come to some resolution of those feelings. Despite his protestations, he admitted that he can still feel overwhelmed by negative feelings, suggesting a recognition that there may be a value to focusing on them. This understandably confused the therapist, who once more encouraged a more assertive expression and finally got one.

Position 5: Self-Assertion

PATIENT: There's a part of me that doesn't want to do it. It's not an easy explanation of what that, that is. I just don't see it as useful to me. It doesn't seem to me a helpful direction to go in.

THERAPIST: How does it feel to actually say that to me?

With this question, the therapist not only demonstrated his receptivity to the assertion, but also his awareness of the anxieties that made its expression so painstakingly difficult. This led to an exploration of the avoidance to exploring the rupture experience.

Position 4: Avoidance

PATIENT: Awful. (Laughs.) I feel awful about accusing you of something like that.

THERAPIST: So . . .

PATIENT: Suggesting to you that you didn't know what you were or whatever. And it just . . . I'm sorry I said it. (Laughing.)

THERAPIST: So you're feeling apologetic and uncomfortable . . .

PATIENT: Yes . . .

THERAPIST: with saying, "I didn't find that useful"?

PATIENT: Yes, um hum. And I feel like sitting here for the next 10 minutes saying I'm sorry, you know. (Laughing.) (Long pause.) I feel so uncomfortable saying that. I could see you could see I was avoiding saying it.

THERAPIST: Right, yeah.

PATIENT: (Pause.) And that makes me then . . . I ask myself how can I get a job when my, I'm, you know, when it's so obvious what I'm saying . . .

THERAPIST: Now it sounds like you're turning self-critical. What just happened?

PATIENT: Mmhmm. (Long pause.) I guess I feel pathetic, and, and you must think I'm pathetic.

The preceeding segment illustrates the complexity of the patient's anxious world, including his fear of the condemnation of others as well as his use of self-criticism as a preemptive strike against himself. Here, the therapist facilitated the patient's awareness of the anxieties that drove his avoidant operations, whether in terms of equivocal, convoluted expressions or self-critical processes. In this particular resolution process, the avoidance stage, Position 4, emerged on the heels of Position 5, the self-assertion stage. Although one may see an oscillation back and forth between Positions 3 and 4, it is not unusual to have a resolution process without Position 4 or, in this case, to have it emerge after Position 5. In a sense, Position 4 is not a necessary element of the resolution process, but it is critical to represent in order to understand the occasional breakdown in resolution. The exploration of avoidant operations is also critical to clarifying the patient's underlying construal processes and understanding his or her representational world.

A RESOLUTION MODEL FOR CONFRONTATION RUPTURES

The resolution model for confrontation ruptures resembles the resolution model for withdrawal markers (see Figure 11.2). It begins with the rupture marker in Position 1 and continues with the disembedding process in Position 2. It includes the two parallel pathways of exploration: the experiencing and avoidance pathways. It differs, however, in a number of respects. First, to the extent that patients present with intense aggression, the processes of disembedding and of surviving the patient's aggression over an extended period of time become more central. Second, the emphasis in Position 3 is on elucidating patients' construal of the situation, rather than on helping them begin to assert themselves and individuate; for example, patients may begin to put into words that they feel let down and disappointed by the therapist. Third, the wish or need emerging in the final stage typically entails some desire for contact or nurturance rather than individuation. Fourth, we make a distinction between patients' avoidance of aggression (Position 4) and their avoidance of vulnerable feelings (Position 5).

Confrontation ruptures occur on a continuum in terms of how directly or explicitly the initial confrontation is expressed. When the initial confrontation takes place in a more direct fashion, the therapist does not need to begin by facilitating a more direct expression of the underlying demand or negative sentiments. In many cases, however, the initial confrontation is mixed with features of a withdrawal marker, and the therapist's first task is to draw attention to the

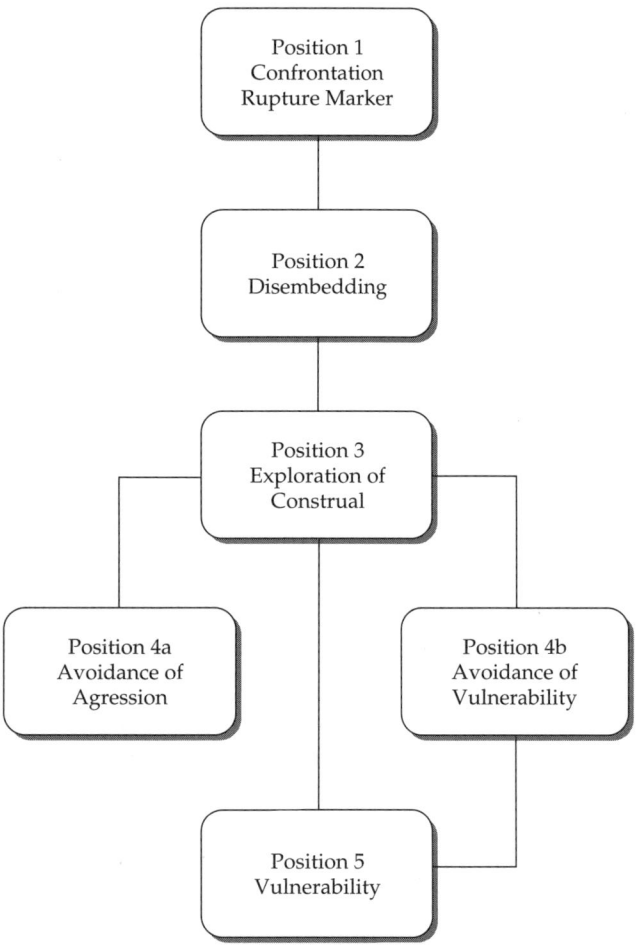

Figure 11.2 Rupture resolution model for confrontation ruptures. From *Negotiating the Therapeutic Alliance: A Relational Treatment Guide* (p. 156), by J. D. Safran and J. C. Muran, 2000, New York: Guilford Press. Reprinted with permission.

marker and to help the patient express the underlying negative feelings more directly. For example, the first step in working with patients who are expressing negative feelings toward the therapist sarcastically, but at the same time acting in a conciliatory fashion, is to help them acknowledge the angry feelings underlying the sarcasm and to express them directly. The first step with patients who are implicitly making demands of the therapist is to help them make the demands more explicitly. A useful intervention to facilitate this process is for the therapist to metacommunicate about the impact the patient is having on him or her. For example, "I feel attacked and protected at the same time" or "It feels to me like you're, in a somewhat cautious way, trying to get me to do more for you." As in the case with the withdrawal model, interventions of this type can lead to an exploration of either the experience associated with the rupture or the avoidance against that experience; this phase of the resolution process typically involves an oscillation back and forth between the experiencing and avoidance pathways.

When confrontation ruptures are taking place, it can be difficult (if not impossible) for therapists not to respond to the patient's criticism or demands defensively by justifying their actions or blaming the patient, either explicitly or implicitly. When this takes place, the process of exploring the relational configuration becomes the priority. The first step in working through a confrontation rupture (i.e., the step from Position 1 to 2) involves unhooking from the cycle of hostility and counterhostility that is being enacted by metacommunicating about the current struggle. In this process, it is often critical for therapists to acknowledge responsibility for their contribution to the interaction; for example, "I think that what's been going on is that I've been feeling criticized by you, and have responded by trying to blame you for what's going on in our interaction." It can be extremely useful for therapists to comment on the experience of a mutual struggle; for example, "It feels to me like you and I are in a power struggle right now, with me trying to hold you responsible for your frustrations with therapy, and you trying to pin the blame on me." Therapists who feel pressured to prove to the patient that therapy will be helpful can comment on their dilemma rather than responding to this pressure with ineffectual attempts at persuasion or in angry defensiveness; for example, "I'm feeling pressured to convince you that I can help you, but I have a feeling that nothing I say will seem compelling to you." Therapists who feel criticized or attacked can comment on this experience, rather than counterattacking or defending themselves; for example, "I feel wary of saying anything because I feel criticized when I try to respond to your questions or concerns."

Such metacommunication can have a number of goals. The first involves providing patients with feedback that can help them acknowledge negative feelings toward the therapist that are disowned. The second consists of helping therapists to unhook themselves from the vicious cycle to provide patients with the experience of being in a relationship in which the other person does not confirm their negative expectations about relationships. The third involves therapists disembedding themselves from the process sufficiently to begin exploring the construal processes that underlie the patient's angry and demanding actions.

Exploring the underlying construal processes (Position 3) can lead in various directions. In some cases, the patient's anger is a justifiable response to the therapist's actions; then, it is important for therapists to acknowledge their contributions to the situation. For example, when therapists cannot initially see their contribution to the situation, it can be useful to encourage the patient to spell out his or her perception of how the therapist has contributed. In this process, it is critical for therapists to be open to learning something about themselves and their contributions to the interaction, rather than think of this exclusively as a way of exploring the patient's underlying construal processes. This openness can transform the situation. At the same time, this type of genuine interest in the patient's perception will lead to an elucidation of the underlying construal processes that might otherwise not be possible. For example, in one case where the patient felt his therapist was being a bit insensitive and callous in rearranging appointment times, it was critical for the therapist to be open to that possibility to allow the exploration of the patient's concern that the therapist did not care for him and his mistrust that anyone cared for him. Similarly, in another example, where the therapist had recently had a child, it was critical for her to listen and learn about the ways she had changed in her manner toward the patient before the patient could explore fears regarding the emotional availability of others.

Although it is essential for therapists to acknowledge their contribution to the interaction, their task is not to sort out what proportion of the patient's perception is reality-based and what proportion is not. Therapists should begin with the assumption that there is a plausible basis for the patient's transference reaction in the therapist's action. Their task is to come to understand the patient's experience from an internal point of reference. For example, a patient feels outraged at his therapist because he sees her as one more in a long line of people who has failed him or will fail him emotionally. Feelings of this type in this context are secondary emotions evoked by the perception that the underlying wish to be nurtured or taken care of, once again, either has not or will not be met. Although the therapist can attempt to interpret the underlying wish for nurturance and attempt to bypass the secondary feelings of anger and disappointment, it is often prudent to first deal with the secondary feelings in their own terms. It can be important for the patient to experience the feelings of anger and disappointment as acceptable and tolerable before he can begin to acknowledge primary yearnings that have him feeling vulnerable. Moreover, bypassing the secondary feeling and interpreting the underlying emotions can be experienced as unempathic and disempowering.

To tolerate the patient's critical and angry feelings is a difficult task, and it is inevitable that therapists will respond as human beings with their own anger and defensiveness. However, to survive the patient's anger can be one of the most critical factors in negotiating an impasse. A key principle is for therapists to stay mindful of the difficult feelings that are emerging in them as they experience themselves as the object of the patient's anger and to be willing to acknowledge their ongoing contributions to the interaction. The therapist's task is not to prove to patients that he or she has no angry or defensive feelings, but rather to demonstrate a consistent willingness to stick with patients and to work toward understanding what is going on between them in the face of whatever feelings emerge for both.

It is critical for the therapist to respond in an empathic and validating way to any primary and more vulnerable feeling states that emerge (Position 5). The therapist should try to understand these feelings not as archaic infantile needs that need to be understood and renounced, nor as remobilized developmental yearnings, but rather as normal human yearnings for nurturance and support. In some cases, it can be important for the therapist to gratify the wish symbolically. For example, a patient who had traditionally had a tremendous amount of trouble acknowledging and expressing underlying needs eventually came to a point in her therapy where she began to contact some of these needs. In one session, she directly asked her therapist for some advice about how to handle a difficult situation, something she had never done before. The therapist responded by giving her advice, and then asked her how it felt. She responded by tearing up, as she contacted the relief and gratitude toward the therapist for being willing to act on her behalf in this context and the underlying yearning for nurturance that had motivated her question.

In situations where it is difficult or impossible for therapists to gratify the underlying wish, they should be empathic and understanding, while at the same time making clear what their boundaries are. The most controversial example of this involves cases where erotic feelings emerge on the part of the patient, but there are other more mundane examples. These include any request that a therapist cannot meet for whatever reason, such as extending sessions beyond the appointed time. In such instances, one should empathize with the underlying yearning and the pain and frustration that inevitably result. Through this process, patients gradually come to experience the therapist as being there for them.

In working through confrontation ruptures, it is necessary for the therapist to be sensitive to and to monitor subtle shifts in the patient's self-states. Even those patients who are most overtly aggressive or hostile toward their therapist will experience moments of anxiety or guilt about the expression of aggressive feelings and attempt to undo the harm they feel they have done, justify their actions, or attempt to depersonalize the situation to defuse the danger (Position 4). A second type of avoidance that sometimes emerges during the resolution of confrontations is the defensive withdrawal from vulnerable feeling. Sometimes, patients will contact vulnerable feelings and then shift back into a more familiar and secure state of aggression. With regard to either of these avoidant operations, it can be useful for therapists to track these subtle shifts in self-states and to help patients become aware of them as well as of the internal processes that led to them.

To illustrate the confrontation resolution process, we present the following case material. The patient presented herself as paralyzed both professionally and socially, finding herself frequently engaged in argumentative encounters that had a righteous basis for her. In these encounters, she viewed herself alternately as intolerant aggressor and misunderstood victim and considered others careless and irresponsible. It became evident that she wished for some form of supportive guidance or nurturance from others, but feared and expected disinterest and rejection. In the session presented (which was alluded to previously), the patient attacks the therapist for his nonchalant attitude toward a broken water fountain near his office. The session begins with the patient making some cryptic threats, which leave the therapist somewhat befuddled. Her caustic comments are accompanied by a smile, which the therapist notices and inquires about. This leads to a barrage from the patient and a vicious cycle in which the patient is attacking and the therapist defends.

Position 1: Confrontation Marker

THERAPIST: So, what's up for you today?

PATIENT: Nothing. (Pause.) I didn't get around to figuring what I'm gonna do about this, about this place. This week I was more or less with my mother.

THERAPIST: Ahh, I'm unclear.

PATIENT: Well, my different tactics, remember? First tactic didn't work. Second tactic didn't work. So try another one. And I said I'd think about what I was going to do.

THERAPIST: I see, so you're saying that you haven't come up with another strategy over the week.

PATIENT: Oh yes, I have. I just didn't get a chance to do it because this week has sort of been balled up with my mother, but I'll definitely be able to start my strategy and have it in place by next time. (Smiles.)

THERAPIST: Hmmm. I'm aware of your smile right now. Are you aware of that at all?

PATIENT: Oh yeah.

THERAPIST: Yeah? What's your experience behind the smile?

PATIENT: I'm telling you where it's at and putting you down at the same time. I'm letting you know you're not going to get the better of me.

THERAPIST: Uhuh. Is this . . . ?

PATIENT: The same way that, because you know that, that water fountain doesn't work. (Explodes in anger.) Why should you expose everybody to that when you know it doesn't work? You can pick up the telephone as well as anybody else and say, "Hey guys, this stupid thing hasn't worked for ages. Make it work." Why do you have to wait for someone else to do it? Why can't you do it? You live in this world. You live on this floor, even if you've got a private tap. You don't care about the public who don't have private taps in this building. You know, I really get pissed off at people. I have no use for people. How difficult is it for you? You can just tell your secretary to do it for Pete's sake if your time is too damn valuable.

THERAPIST: So you're pissed off at me right now?

PATIENT: Oh, it's just you in general. That nonsense downstairs and everything else and I didn't say anything when you made that crack about the thing. I said, "All right, I'll show you, buddy."

THERAPIST: About what thing?

PATIENT: Oh, when I said something, you made that crack about the tap. You said you knew it didn't work, so I purposely told you how I fixed the thing downstairs because . . . as a put-down to you for not doing anything about fixing the tap. That was deliberately a put-down to you.

THERAPIST: Wait a sec, when I said I knew it didn't work, you took that as being like a crack.

PATIENT: No, no, I mean you knew it didn't work. It wasn't that you weren't aware of it. You knew it didn't work, and you've done nothing about it . . . (Goes on a diatribe about people taking or not taking care of things in the world and the importance of reward and punishment.) I get fed up with people. I don't take shit like that. Sure, I was, that's what the smile was, you know.

THERAPIST: I'm kind of feeling lumped in with everybody else right now.

PATIENT: Well, why not, you're a person! You're part of humanity. Why shouldn't you be lumped in with everybody else?

THERAPIST: But I feel that I'm not being treated as a person, that you're just lumping me in with everybody else.

PATIENT: Well, look at you. You're just like everybody else. "Oh yeah, I know that thing hasn't worked for ages." Sure, you deserve to be lumped in with everybody else. You deserve it. (Launches into another diatribe.)

Although the therapist is trying to understand the patient's construal processes and describe his experience of her diatribes, he is still in a defensive position and hooked in a vicious cycle. In such transactions, survival may be all that the therapist should aim to do. Finally, the therapist discloses his reluctance to even speak and responds in a way that unhooks from the cycle and shifts the process.

Position 2: Disembedding
THERAPIST: I'm feeling reluctant to open my mouth.
PATIENT: Yeah, well, you just got one of my tirades. (Softens.)
THERAPIST: What's happening for you now?

The therapist notices a definite shift in the patient's tone and manner as she becomes more demure. At this point, she becomes anxious about her confrontation, and the therapist probes this state of mind by first focusing her attention on the physical nature of her anxiety and then exploring its meaning.

Position 4: Avoidance of Aggression
PATIENT: Now I'm all nervous. I can feel it. I feel funny, like not right, a bit nervous. I can feel I'm shaking inside.
THERAPIST: Can you dwell on this nervousness for a moment? Describe what it's like for me?
PATIENT: Well, it's physical, like I can feel sort of trembling inside, and my hands are clammy.
THERAPIST: What's your nervousness about?
PATIENT: Well, I, I know people don't like to have barrages like that.
THERAPIST: What about me?
PATIENT: Well, I don't know, I'm careful when I do it, and only do it with people I can get away with it. That's the other problem too.

THERAPIST: I want to, if possible, personalize this more. Can you say if right now you're concerned about what I might think?
PATIENT: I guess, I'm concerned that you might find this unacceptable. I don't want you to figure that I refuse to cooperate.

Here, the therapist was able to help the patient articulate her concern about what he might think, which interrupted the exploration of the rupture experience. After some exploration, she was able to return to discussing the essence of her negative sentiments.

Position 3: Exploration of Construal Processes
PATIENT: I mean, I'm getting tired of everybody. By everybody, I mean all the professionals that have been around in the last two years and a half, telling me I don't want to change and I'm not trying and all the other horseshit that they've been telling me. I'm tired of that.
THERAPIST: What are you feeling now?
PATIENT: I feel defensive a little bit. Trying to keep you and also treating you like the rest of them. Trying to make things very clear ... because, I know, this is my last chance. I can't financially fiddle around anymore, and so this is my last ditch. I've got to get something out of this therapy. This is my last opportunity.
THERAPIST: You say, "This is my last ditch chance..."
PATIENT: My last ditch chance, yeah.
THERAPIST: What are you experiencing when you say that?
PATIENT: Well, I'm feeling desperate. I don't want to waste my time anymore with more horseshit.
THERAPIST: Can you say more about the desperation?

What emerged in this exploration was a sense of gravity and desperation. The patient saw the therapy as her last chance in life. Thus, she reacted angrily to the therapist's cavalier manner with respect to the broken water fountain, fearing perhaps that he might approach her situation with the same lack of seriousness. The therapist focused her on her desperation in hope of getting her in contact with her vulnerability and underlying wish for nurturance.

Position 5: Vulnerability
PATIENT: I feel like it's the end of the line. I'm scared. (Voice breaks.) And I don't know what's gonna happen to me if this doesn't work.
THERAPIST: So, I guess, that's why you want to make sure I care as much as you do.
PATIENT: Yeah. (Tears.)

Here, the therapist makes a link between the patient's desperation and her previous barrage, which communicates both his understanding and his acceptance of her expression of vulnerability.

BRIEF RELATIONAL THERAPY PROCESS

In what follows, we present some important features and issues that have become central to the application of this treatment model in a short-term and time-limited context. In the Brief Psychotherapy Research Program at Beth Israel Medical Center, this brief relational model has been applied as a 30-session treatment protocol for outpatients presenting with longstanding difficulties. Patients included in the study typically have presented with various Anxiety or Mood Disorders on Axis I and Cluster C, or Personality Disorders Not Otherwise Specified on Axis II, according to *DSM-IV* (American Psychiatric Association [APA], 1994). The therapists have included licensed/certified psychiatrists, psychologists, and social workers, as well as psychology interns and externs, who have participated in ongoing weekly case seminars and individual supervision.

BEGINNING THE COLLABORATION

The beginning of treatment in BRT is marked by a structure to define the tasks and goals of treatment, even though this relational model remains relatively unstructured compared to other short-term dynamic models (and especially so compared to cognitive-behavioral treatments).

Establishing the Rationale for Treatment Tasks
Conveying a meaningful rationale for treatment to the patient plays an important role in establishing a therapeutic alliance. As Bordin (1979) suggested, to the extent that there is an agreement between patient and therapist about the tasks and goals of therapy, a productive working alliance will be established. This process of explicitly establishing a rationale for treatment is one that is often neglected in more insight-oriented therapies. This omission fails to recognize the crucial role that agreement about tasks and goals plays in creating an alliance. We typically give the patient concise reading material at the beginning of therapy and spend time early in treatment discussing how therapy works, with particular attention paid to the role of awareness and the use of the therapeutic relationship. It is necessary to convey a rationale for such therapeutic tasks as becoming aware of emotional experience, exploring beliefs, fantasies, and expectations, and examining what takes place in the therapeutic relationship.

Demonstrating the Task of Mindfulness
In light of the importance of establishing agreement on tasks, we also recommend the use of a mindfulness exercise to experientially demonstrate the notion of bare or nonjudgmental attention. One might ask patients to close their eyes and focus on their breath and each breathing cycle, paying attention to where their mind goes and then redirecting their attention back to their breath. There are a number of possible demonstration exercises that may be used (Kabat-Zinn, 1991). The purpose here is to

sensitize patients to attending in an accepting manner to an emerging and ongoing process, much in the same way they will be asked to attend to their feelings.

Clarifying Expectations Regarding Treatment Goals

When conveying the rationale at the beginning of therapy for short-term and time-limited therapy, it is important to begin the process of trying to establish reasonable expectations about what can take place in such a framework. Our short-term treatment is conceptualized for patients as a process of providing them a new experience, which primarily involves cultivating a new skill of attention and awareness as well as shining a beam of light on some core relational themes, such that patients can continue to grow and develop after the end of treatment. No matter how much time is spent conveying a sense of reasonable expectations at the beginning of treatment and how much explicit agreement there is by the patient about the nature of that goal, it is inevitable that there will be frustrations and disappointments by the end of treatment.

NEGOTIATING THE COURSE AND TASKS OF TREATMENT

Negotiating the course of BRT involves many tasks for the therapist. Here, we outline some of the more important ones.

Oscillating between Content and Process

A major task for therapists in this model involves oscillating their attention between the *content* and *process* of communication. As communication theorists maintain, there are always report and command aspects to any communication. The report aspect of the communication is the specific content. The command aspect is the interpersonal statement or the statement about the current relationship that is being conveyed by the patient's communication. The therapist should monitor both the content of *what* the patient says and the process of *how* the patient says it. Patients enter treatment with plenty of content regarding how they are living their lives outside of the therapy hour. A good part of treatment, including in this model, is devoted to discussing and navigating this extrasession material. Attending to content provides the therapist with insight into patients' inner experience and how they relate to themselves. Therapists typically are inclined to become too enamored with content, however, at the exclusion of being aware of the interpersonal implications of what is being said. Attending to process provides the therapist with insight into the interpersonal statement that the patient is making about the relationship with the therapist.

Observing the Interpersonal Field

The therapist should continually monitor the current interpersonal field as it shifts over time. A cue of critical importance about the interpersonal field consists of the therapist's feeling of degree of interpersonal contact or engagement with the patient. Therapists should gauge how related, connected, or disconnected they are feeling to the patient at any given moment. Moments of disconnectedness provide therapists with important information about what is presently transpiring. The feeling of disconnectedness or unrelatedness from the patient may emerge from a number of different sources. One source is when patients are currently out of contact with their inner experience. To the extent that patients are presently in contact with their inner experience and are thus related to themselves, it is more likely that the therapist will feel related to and engaged with the patient. Relatedness emerges out of affective engagement between patient and therapist. There may also be momentary shifts in relatedness or periods of unrelatedness resulting from the patient withdrawing from or avoiding some aspect of the relationship with the therapist.

Exploring the Patient's Experience

In tracking patient experience, the therapist should pay particular attention to not only the patient's emotionally salient experiential states, but also transitions in patient experience, the seams between one self-state and another. These may reflect important underlying processes that should be explored and clarified. Often, these transitions indicate an avoidance of or a defensive operation against an experience. And often, therapists find themselves losing contact with the patient as a result of this movement away. The task is to help the patient become aware of avoiding or defending against that experience, including the reasons for and ways of doing it. A number of interventions can be useful in this regard, ranging from traditional psychoanalytic interpretation of the defense to awareness-directing interventions that are more experiential in nature. By drawing the patient's attention to the avoidant operations and exploring their implications, the avoidance becomes deautomatic and subject to intentional control. It is critical in such explorations that there is a collaboration between patient and therapist in an ongoing attempt to clarify and articulate the patient's experience. The operative emphasis here is on both "coparticipatory" inquiry (Wolstein, 1977) and "detailed" inquiry (Sullivan, 1954). As for the latter, it is a respect, even a reverence, for particularity.

Exploring Self-Experience

At the same time therapists track the patient's experience, they should track their own inner experience as well. Here, it is critical to go beyond simply identifying a feeling such as sadness or anger at a more gross somatic level and to articulate the nature of one's inner experience in a more differentiated way. This process involves a movement back and forth between the level of feelings grounded in bodily felt experience and a conceptual elaboration of those feelings. This parallels the task in which we invite patients to engage. One of the great challenges for therapists is to resist the temptation to grasp onto fixed conceptions of what is taking place with their patients, to deal with their own anxiety of a complex, ambiguous, and threatening interaction by seeking the security of imposing theory on some aspect of the therapeutic interaction. Rather, therapists should try to establish an ongoing dialogue between what they are experiencing and what they are conceptualizing about their interaction with the patient. One of the obstacles is that we have been armed in our training with an impressive arsenal of theoretical concepts that ironically we can use to avoid listening to our hearts. Although therapists often recognize the importance of exploring and becoming aware of their own feelings, in practice it can be extremely difficult, especially when the therapist's feelings are threatening ones.

Oscillating between Self and Other Experience

Therapists are always directing their attention back and forth or alternating their attention between the patient's inner experience and their own inner experience. One of the primary points of orientation for therapists is their experience of contact with the patient's inner experience. Thus, the therapist's own inner experience serves as an emotional compass with which to gauge the degree of intimate relatedness or empathic contact. As long as therapists are experiencing empathic contact with the patient's inner experience, they will automatically be providing the type of therapeutic environment in which the patient needs to grow. All interventions will flow naturally out of this sense of empathic contact. Over the course of any session, however, it is common for the therapist's experience of empathic contact with the patient's inner experience to shift back and forth, with the therapist experiencing ongoing shifts in degree of contact with the patient's inner experience. When the therapist experiences a lack of contact with the patient's inner experience, the task is to reestablish that sense of contact. This can be accomplished in a number of ways, but first, therapists must realize that they have lost contact.

Hooking and Unhooking from Cycles
The course of treatment invariably involves an ongoing process of hooking and unhooking from vicious cycles, embedding and disembedding from various relational matrices. Being embedded in a relational matrix is an inevitable part of the therapeutic process. Therapists should be able to accept the fact that they will go through extended periods of being embedded without being aware of it and will also go through extended periods of feeling stuck. During these extended therapeutic impasses, it is essential for the therapist to cultivate a sense of acknowledgment and acceptance of the "stuckness." The therapist may want to speak explicitly to the patient about the fact that they are both feeling stuck, thereby acknowledging the mutuality of their experience. The experience of stuckness thus becomes a shared experience rather than a wedge between them. The therapist should have faith in the process and convey a sense of this faith to the patient. There are times when therapists feel stuck or in a rut, and all they can do is wait. During these moments, if one can cultivate a sense of openness or relaxed attentiveness, one can be open to new possibilities as they emerge. What is critical here is to be able to see each moment anew, rather than as a repetition of a previous moment. The experience of stuckness is inevitable, but what maintains this experience is the inability to distinguish between past and present. What prevents the therapist from moving through the experience of stuckness is the fear that it will never end. This fear interferes with the therapist's ability to let go and relax in the stuckness and be open to new possibilities that can emerge out of the experience of emptiness and futility. Therapists need to understand that they are always embedded in some relational matrix with their patient and are faced with the endless task of disembedding from one and embedding into another with no other place to go (Stern, 1997). The therapist's understanding of what's going on can only be partial at best.

APPROACHING THE END

The end of treatment naturally evokes certain themes, which will now be addressed. With each patient, a challenge is posed for therapists that is not unlike those they faced in working through ruptures with that particular patient throughout the course of treatment (though perhaps more intense). Thus, the termination process is considered the resolution of the *ultimate alliance rupture*.

Separation and Loss
Termination obviously involves separation and loss, and thus can evoke sadness as well as tension between the needs for individuation and relatedness. As Otto Rank (1945) suggested, the process of individuating is inherently guilt-producing and fraught with anxiety because it threatens relatedness. Paradoxically, however, true individuation and relatedness are dependent on each other. As theorists such as Margaret Mahler (Mahler, Pine, & Bergman, 1975) and John Bowlby (1973) have suggested, infants require a sense of security in relationship with the caretaker before they can engage in the type of exploratory behavior necessary to facilitate individuation. Conversely, one cannot maintain a mature form of relatedness to others until one has developed a sense of oneself as an individual. This is a critical theme that therapist and patient must negotiate as treatment comes to an end.

Acceptance
The problem of faith lies at the heart of the human change process (see Safran & Muran, 2000, for further discussion and relevant literature). At

some fundamental level, one has to have some hope that one has the ability to change and that the healer has the ability to help one change. In the final analysis, therapists need to have tolerance for their own impotence as helpers and their own inability to solve patients' problems for them or take their pain away. It is inevitable that patients will want the impossible from their therapists. They will want them to transform their lives. Therapists who have difficulty accepting their own limitations and being *good enough* as helpers will respond defensively in the face of patients' impossible demands. It is thus essential for therapists to come to terms with the fact that in the end, there is a limited amount that one human being can do for another. No matter how deeply empathic the therapist is, when the session is over, the patient goes home and the therapist goes on with his or her own life. The recognition of this limitation becomes particularly poignant when confronting treatment's end. This realization, however, must not be transformed into cavalier indifference, but rather the genuine compassion of one human being who experiences the pain of life for a fellow human being.

Being Alone
In life, we must all inevitably negotiate the fact that by the very nature of our existence we are paradoxically alone and yet in the world with others. We are alone at a fundamental level in that we are born alone and ultimately we die alone. Many of our most private experiences will never be shared with others. At the same time, we are inescapably tied to others. We are born in relationship to others and attain a sense of self only in relation to others. As human beings, we spend our lives negotiating the paradox of our simultaneous aloneness and togetherness. We begin our lives attempting to remain in proximity to attachment figures, and the pursuit of interpersonal relatedness continues to motivate our behavior through our lifetime. No matter how hard we try, we cannot, except for brief periods, achieve the type of union with others that permits us to escape from our aloneness. This theme can also become salient as the patient faces the end of treatment and the therapeutic relationship. The critical task for the therapist is to help the patient work through this disappointment in a constructive way. This involves coming to accept one's needs and desires as valid and legitimate, while at the same time living with the pain of recognizing that they will never be met in an absolute sense (Safran & Muran, 2000).

TRAINING AND SUPERVISION

In many respects, our efforts to study alliance ruptures and to develop resolution intervention strategies have led us to pay a great deal of attention to the training of therapists—specifically, to the question of how to help therapists disembed from complex relational matrices and work through therapeutic impasses. In this section, we outline some key principles and strategies that characterize our relational approach to psychotherapy supervision (Safran & Muran, 2000).

The Relational Context of Supervision
In training, as in therapy, the relational context is of upmost import. It is impossible for the supervisor to convey information to the trainee that has meaning independent of the relational context in which it is conveyed. Supervision thus needs to be tailored to the needs of the trainee. Supervisors need to recognize and support trainees' needs to maintain their self-esteem and calibrate the extent to which they have more need for support versus new information or confrontation in a given moment. Supervisors should tailor the feedback to each trainee's unique needs. Depending when on his or her developmental trajectory a particular trainee is, different lessons may be appropriate. Supervisors should monitor the quality of the *supervisory alliance* in an ongoing fashion that parallels the monitoring of the quality of

the alliance in therapy. When there is an adequate alliance, the supervisory relationship can become background and does not need to be explicitly addressed. However, when strains or tensions emerge, the exploration of the supervisory relationship should assume priority over other forms of supervision.

Experiential Focus
For many trainees, the process of establishing an experiential focus involves a partial unlearning of things they have already learned about doing therapy. Often, the training of therapists emphasizes the conceptual at the expense of the experiential. Trainees study the approaches of different psychotherapy theorists and learn to apply the ideas they are learning to their clinical experience. They learn how to develop case formulations from different theoretical perspectives and to make interpretations that are guided by their theoretical understanding of what is going on. Although this type of knowledge is essential, it can also serve a defensive function. It can help trainees to manage the anxiety that inevitably arises as a result of confronting the inherent ambiguity and chaos of lived experience and lead to premature formulations that foreclose experience. It can help them to avoid dealing with the painful, frightening, and the conflicting feelings that inevitably emerge for both patients and therapists. In some respects, this conceptual knowledge can be useful in navigating one's anxieties and therapeutic impasses; in others, it can serve to tighten the deadlock. We typically begin our training by discussing the dangers of reification and emphasizing the value of striving to develop a *beginner's mind*. In addition, we have found it useful to talk about the concept of mindfulness and the role it plays in the therapeutic process. Often, trainees have difficulty at first distinguishing between their experience and their ideas about their experience, and it can be useful to use structured mindfulness exercises to help them grasp this distinction and to develop an openness to their experience. Such exercises also help trainees sharpen their abilities to become participant-observers.

Self-Exploration
Although there are times when specific suggestions about ways of conceptualizing a case or intervening are useful, there is an overarching emphasis in our approach on helping therapists find their own unique solution to their problems. The particular therapeutic interaction that is the focus of supervision is unique to a particular therapist-patient dyad. Each therapist will have unique feelings in response to a particular patient, and the particular solution he or she formulates to the therapeutic dilemma must emerge in the context of his or her unique reactions. One therapist may respond to a patient with a desire to nurture; another may respond to the same patient with feelings of resentment. The therapist who feels resentment will inevitably have to find some way of working with these feelings, just as the therapist who feels nurturant must begin with these feelings. Ultimately, both therapists will have to harness whatever feelings they have to be used as part of the therapeutic process. An important focus of training is thus helping therapists to develop some means of dialoguing with their patients about what is going on in the moment in a way that is unique to the moment and their experience of it. Suggestions about what to say provided by supervisors or fellow trainees may look appropriate in the context of a videotape that is being viewed, but may not be appropriate in the context of the next session. The supervisor's task is thus to help trainees develop the ability to attend to their own experience of the moment and use it as a basis for intervening. At the outset, we make it clear that although self-exploration plays a central role in the training process, it is also critical for therapists to respect their own needs for privacy and their own fluctuating assessments of what feels safe to explore in front of both supervisors and fellow trainees.

Awareness-Oriented Role Plays

Awareness-oriented role plays can be a particularly useful tool for grounding the training process at an experiential level and promoting self-awareness in trainees. These consist of having therapists role-play a segment of a session that has been problematic, either with the assistance of a training group member who plays the role of patient or therapist, or themselves playing both roles (alternating back and forth between the role of therapist and of patient). Role plays of this type are particularly useful when there is no recorded material available, but can also be a useful supplement to supervision making use of recorded material. The goal of this type of exercise is not so much to practice different ways of intervening as it is to facilitate the exploration of feelings, thoughts, and fantasies relevant to the specific case. Nevertheless, it can also be an opportunity to experiment with different ways of intervening and exploring feelings that block the ability to intervene in certain ways.

Supervisors as Models

One of the most valuable learning opportunities for trainees is to see their supervisors in action. Observing an experienced therapist in action allows trainees to analyze and make sense of what their supervisor is doing in a way that the embedded perspective of the patient to some extent precludes. If videotape facilities are available, there is no substitute for observing supervisors in session with their own patients. This, of course, inevitably places supervisors in a somewhat exposed and vulnerable position, but the potential payoffs are well worth the risks. A second opportunity for observing their supervisors' clinical work is provided when supervisors help trainees engage in the process of self-exploration in either individual or group supervision. Another important opportunity is provided when strains in the supervisory alliance are explored. This exploration can range from simply checking in to see how a trainee experiences a supervisor's comment (when, for example, the supervisor has an intuition that the trainee felt criticized) to a more in-depth exploration of full-scale strains or ruptures in the supervisory alliance.

RESEARCH DIRECTIONS AND FINDINGS

On a final note, we briefly summarize the research efforts over the past 15 years that have played a central part in the development of the clinical principles described in this chapter (see Muran, in press, for an overview of our research program). Essentially, this research program has studied the process of change at two levels of analysis. At one level, we have examined the treatment efficacy of our relational model as compared to two traditional time-limited models: one ego psychological, the other cognitive-behavioral in orientation. The results have indicated (1) equal efficacy among the three models on the factors of symptomatology and personality for patients who completed treatment; (2) greater efficacy for the relational and cognitive-behavioral models for completed cases with regard to clinically significant change; and (3) a significantly lower dropout rate for the relational model over the cognitive-behavioral and ego psychological models. At a more microanalytic level of analysis, considerable effort has been devoted to the study of alliance rupture resolution as a critical change event. This effort has included the development of assessment strategies to identify psychotherapy sessions in which such change events occur (e.g., Muran et al., 1995), as well as those to define the interactional sequences of various patient states and therapist interventions in the resolution process (e.g., Safran & Muran, 1996). We have provided preliminary support for the rupture resolution models described in this chapter (Safran & Muran, 1996; Safran, Muran, & Samstag, 1994) and are currently conducting a large-scale verification study, involving a new observer-based measure that we have developed. In our research program, clinical theory, treatment development and evaluation, and the microanalysis of rupture resolution work in concert. What we have learned from the study of rupture resolution has informed the development of our treatment model as much as clinical theory has informed how we have studied rupture resolution. A working alliance among clinical theory, research, and practice is an ideal that we continuously strive to realize (Safran & Muran, 1994).

REFERENCES

Alexander, F., & French, T. M. (1946). *Psychoanalytic therapy.* New York: Ronald Press.

American Psychiatric Association. (1994). *Diagnostic and statistical manual of mental disorders* (4th ed.). Washington, DC: Author.

Aron, L. (1996). *A meeting of minds: Mutuality in psychoanalysis.* Hillsdale, NJ: Analytic Press.

Aron, L. (1999). Clinical choices and the relational matrix. *Psychoanalytic Dialogues, 9,* 1–29.

Bakan, D. (1966). *The duality of human existence.* Boston: Beacon Press.

Benjamin, J. (1990). An outline of intersubjectivity: The development of recognition. *Psychoanalytic Psychology, 7,* 33–46.

Bordin, E. (1979). The generalizability of the psychoanalytic concept of the working alliance. *Psychotherapy: Theory, Research and Practice, 16,* 252–260.

Bowlby, J. (1973). *Attachment and loss. Volume II: Separation: Anxiety, and anger.* New York: Basic Books.

Ehrenberg, D. (1992). *The intimate edge.* New York: Norton.

Ferenczi, S. (1932). *The clinical diary of Sandor Ferenczi* (J. Dupont, Ed.; M. Balint & N. Z. Jackson, Trans.). Cambridge, MA: Harvard University Press.

Greenberg, L. S., Watson, J. C., & Lietaer, G. (Eds.). (1998). *Handbook of experiential psychotherapy.* New York: Guilford Press.

Hoffman, I. Z. (1998). *Ritual and spontaneity in the psychoanalytic process: A dialectical-constructivist view.* Hillsdale, NJ: Analytic Press.

Kabat-Zinn, J. (1991). *Full catastrophe living.* New York: Delta.

Kiesler, D. J. (1996). *Contemporary interpersonal theory and research: Personality, psychopathology, and psychotherapy.* New York: Wiley.

Mahler, M. S., Pine, F., & Bergman, A. (1975). *The psychological birth of the human infant: Symbiosis and individuation.* New York: Basic Books.

Mitchell, S. A. (1988). *Relational concepts in psychoanalysis.* Cambridge, MA: Harvard University Press.

Mitchell, S. A. (1993). *Hope and dread in psychoanalysis.* New York: Basic Books.

Mitchell, S., & Aron, L. (1999). *Relational psychoanalysis: The emergence of a tradition.* Hillsdale, NJ: Analytic Press.

Muran, J. C. (2001). Meditations on "both/and." In J. C. Muran (Ed.), *Self-relations in the psychotherapy process* (pp. 347–372). Washington, DC: American Psychological Association.

Muran, J. C. (in press). A relational approach to understanding change: Plurality and contextualism in a psychotherapy research program. *Psychotherapy Research.*

Pizer, S. A. (1992). The negotiation of paradox in the analytic process. *Psychoanalytic Dialogues, 2,* 215–240.

Pizer, S. A. (1998). *Building bridges: The negotiation of paradox in psychoanalysis.* Hillsdale, NJ: Analytic Press.

Rank, O. (1945). *Will therapy and truth and reality.* New York: A. Knopf.

Safran, J. D. (1998). *Widening the scope of cognitive therapy.* Northvale, NJ: Aronson.

Safran, J. D. (in press). Brief relational psychoanalytic treatment. *Psychoanalytic Dialogues.*

Safran, J. D., Crocker, P., McMain, S., & Murray, P. (1990). Therapeutic alliance rupture as a therapy event for empirical investigation. *Psychotherapy: Theory, Research and Practice, 27,* 154–165.

Safran, J. D., & Muran, J. C. (1994). Toward a working alliance between research and practice. In P. F. Talley, H. H. Strupp, & S. F. Butler (Eds.), *Psychotherapy research and practice: Bridging the gap* (pp. 206–226). New York: Basic Books.

Safran, J. D., & Muran, J. C. (1995). Resolving therapeutic alliance ruptures: Diversity and integration. *In Session: Psychotherapy in Practice, 1,* 81–82.

Safran, J. D., & Muran, J. C. (1996). The resolution of ruptures in the therapeutic alliance. *Journal of Consulting and Clinical Psychology, 64,* 447–458.

Safran, J. D., & Muran, J. C. (Eds.). (1998). *The therapeutic alliance in brief psychotherapy.* Washington, DC: American Psychological Association.

Safran, J. D., & Muran, J. C. (2000). *Negotiating the therapeutic alliance: A relational treatment guide.* New York: Guilford Press.

Safran, J. D., Muran, J. C., & Samstag, L. W. (1994). Resolving therapeutic alliance ruptures: A task analytic investigation. In A. O. Horvath & L. S. Greenberg (Eds.), *The working alliance: Theory, research, and practice* (pp. 225–255). New York: Wiley.

Safran, J. D., & Segal, Z. V. (1990). *Interpersonal process in cognitive therapy.* New York: Basic Books.

Schafer, R. (1983). *The analytic attitude.* New York: Basic Books.

Stern, D. B. (1997). *Unformulated experience.* Hillsdale, NJ: Analytic Press.

Sullivan, H. S. (1954). *The psychiatric interview.* New York: Norton.

Weiss, J., Sampson, H., & the Mount Zion Psychotherapy Research Group. (1986). *The psychoanalytic process: Theory, clinical observations, and empirical research.* New York: Guilford Press.

Wolstein, B. (1977). From mirror to participant observation to coparticipant inquiry and experience. *Contemporary Psychoanalysis, 13,* 381–386.

CHAPTER 12

Mastering Developmental Issues through Interactional Object-Relations Therapy

CHERYL GLICKAUF-HUGHES AND MAROLYN WELLS

HISTORY OF THE THERAPEUTIC APPROACH

Although object-relations theory is becoming an influential perspective in contemporary clinical work as a means of understanding patients (particularly those with narcissistic and borderline disorders), until recently, its main impact on treatment has been limited to the modification of traditional psychoanalytic technique (Cashdan, 1988; Glickauf-Hughes & Wells, 1995). Greenson (1967), for example, posits that, whereas what is curative in treatment is the interpretation of transference, to interpret transference, a working alliance must first exist between analyst and patient. Kleinian analysts believe that the manner in which interpretations are made can transform the relationship between patient and analyst (Greenberg & Mitchell, 1983). Rucker (1968) similarly stresses that in interpreting the transference, analysts implicitly say to patients that they are not like their bad objects, but are trying to understand them and reach them. Pine (1993) believes that an "interpretation can have its maximum effect because the relationship (non-condemning) belies the patient's inner world" and that "additionally, the relationship factor has its maximum effect at precisely the moment of interpretation" (pp. 192–193).

In contrast, Sullivan (1953) de-emphasizes the value of interpretation altogether. Rather, he highlights the importance of the analyst as offering a new relationship in the patient's life. Fairbairn (1952) stresses the necessity of the analyst's being a good object in order to provide the patient with sufficient security to relinquish bad object ties. Winnicott (1965) thought that therapy should simulate a good enough maternal environment to reverse the environmental failure of patients. Likewise, Kohut (1977) believes that it is the actual interpersonal experience with the analyst that carries the treatment's therapeutic action.

Furthermore, Kohut (1997) suggests that specific analyst behaviors (i.e., empathizing, explaining, interpreting, mirroring, idealizing) are required as a corrective experience to heal the patient's developmental deficits. Guntrip (1969a) states that to help patients, therapists must actually be the kind of person with whom patients can integrate their disparate fragments. Jacobs (1993) believes that "many factors go into the development of rapport between patient and therapist, including the matching of personalities and styles, employing the correct techniques of working from the surface down, tuning into the patient's affects and interpreting these before one gets into deeper conflicts," but these factors "will not be effective or have meaning if the basic ingredient, the *mensch* factor ingredient, is not present" (pp. 4–5). Jacobs defines a mensch as a genuinely "mature individual with sound values who can relate warmly and empathically to another human being" (p. 4).

However, Renik (1993) remarked that although Jacob's (1993) concept of a therapeutic alliance was appealing, it was overly simplistic. Renik stated that what was needed was a more complex conceptualization of what type of therapeutic relationship was corrective for patients. Glickauf-Hughes and Wells addressed this issue in their 1997 book, *Object Relations Psychotherapy: An Individualized and Interactive Approach to Diagnosis and Treatment.*

The Concept of a Corrective Emotional Experience Reexamined

The concept of a corrective emotional experience, as outlined by Alexander and French (1946), has received substantial criticism in the analytic community. Alexander defined the corrective emotional experience in terms of the patient's reliving original traumatic experiences in the presence of a significant other (e.g., therapist, friend) with a more favorable resolution than in the original childhood conflict. Alexander recommended that the therapist "manipulate" the transference by assuming a role that would most readily evoke this corrective emotional experience (Horner, 1979).

Greenson (1967) cautioned against the use of essentially manipulative and anti-analytic techniques, pointing out that, when such techniques are employed, "the patient does not learn to recognize and understand his resistances, there is no premium on insight as a means of overcoming resistances, and there is no attempt to change the ego structure" (p. 136). Horner (1991) agreed, noting that "anti-analytic procedures can block or lessen the patient's capacity for insight and understanding" (p. 191).

The concept of a corrective emotional experience, however, seems to be experiencing a resurgence. Renik (1993) discusses how an analyst's countertransference enactment can provide a corrective emotional experience that helps the patient to "recreate and master crucial pathogenic experiences" (p. 142). Furthermore, Norcross (1993) and Lazarus (1993) discuss tailoring therapeutic relationship stances to the patient's needs. Dolan and colleagues (Dolan, Arnkoff, & Glass, 1993) stress the importance of making the therapist's interpersonal stance contingent on the patient's attachment style. Mahrer (1993) believes that crucial parts of the therapy relationship are uniquely tailored by and for each patient in each session. Finally, Weiss (1993) believes that patients seek corrective emotional experiences through their testing of the therapist and that therapists should provide patients with the experiences they seek. Weiss posits that providing these experiences helps patients to disprove their pathogenic beliefs and, thus, to pursue important but forbidden goals.

The therapist's offering of a corrective emotional experience is not intended to be a role manipulation or even a role assumption, but rather a genuine engagement that emphasizes the particular aspects of the parental relationship that a specific patient has insufficiently received and that are required to facilitate the patient's continued interpersonal and structural development. Much of the analytic community has recognized the validity of altering the analytic frame of therapeutic neutrality and a blank slate presentation for borderline patients who need the therapist to behave in a warm, empathic, and authentic manner as well as to provide psychic functions that these patients cannot provide for themselves (e.g., self-validation, self-soothing, self-object differentiation, reality testing). Therapists may be more effective by altering their stance with other patients (than borderlines) as well.

This proposal finds support in Lazarus's (1993) concept of the therapist as an "authentic chameleon." Lazarus thinks that "it is important for the therapist to modify his or her participation in the therapeutic process in order to offer the most appropriate form of treatment for the client being seen as opposed to the situation where the therapist fits the person to the treatment" (Dryden, 1991, pp. 17–18).

As previously stated, clinicians who utilize object-relations theories to direct psychotherapy need to develop models of treatment that go beyond the mere modification of classical psychoanalytic techniques and specify the precise way in which the therapist must be a new object for each patient, given his or her particular characterological makeup. Although Kohut (1977) has proposed such a model, self psychology best serves as a corrective interpersonal experience for individuals suffering from narcissistic disturbances (Hedges, 1983).

It is not suggested that therapists "act," "role-play," or become a "narcissistic object" for patients. What is recommended is tailoring the therapeutic relationship to the patient's developmental and interpersonal needs within the confines of what the therapist is authentically able to provide for the patient. All therapists have limits. Therapists with schizoid tendencies may not be able to help schizoid patients learn to bond. Therapists with borderline mothers may have particular difficulty containing the projective identifications of their borderline patients. What is important to note is that therapists do not help patients resolve transference feelings when they subtly behave like the patients' internal objects. It is thus helpful for therapists to be aware of their strengths and limitations, their own countertransference issues, and to know which patients should be referred to another therapist.

CURRENT INTERPERSONAL AND OBJECT-RELATIONS THEORIES OF TREATMENT

There have been several excellent models applying object-relations principles to the treatment of couples (Scharff & Scharff, 1991) and families (Slipp, 1984). The most thorough model to date of a theory of object-relations therapy that deals with varied patient problems has been proposed by Cashdan (1988). The basic tenets of Cashdan's model are that (1) emphasis in treatment is placed on the therapist-patient relationship; (2) the therapist focuses on the therapist-patient relationship in the here and now rather than on transference, defense mechanisms, and insight; and (3) the goal of therapy is to use the therapist-patient relationship as a vehicle for the patient's developing both healthier object relations and a more positive sense of self. Cashdan believes that interpersonal psychopathology is expressed through different projective identifications (e.g., dependency, power, sexuality, ingratiation) and that therapists can understand patients' pathology as well as derive a therapeutic strategy for treating that pathology by understanding their own countertransference reactions to patients' projective identifications. Once therapists understand the patient's metacommunicative demands (e.g., "Take care of me," "Do what I say"), they can treat the patient's interpersonal pathology by refusing to concede or conform to the metacommunicative demand, while helping to raise the patients unconscious motives to the level of awareness and providing an alternative and healthier way of relating.

This strategy is similar to that proposed by interpersonal therapists who stress the importance of the therapist not responding in a complementary fashion to the patient, but providing the patient with an "asocial response" (Beier, 1966). The basic modes of the asocial response are (1) delay of response, (2) reflection of content and feeling, (3) labeling the style of interaction, and (4) making a paradigmatic response (Young & Beier, 1982).

Although it is recommended that therapists not make complementary, social responses to the patient's pathological and interpersonally self-defeating behaviors, and although alternate behaviors are recommended, the primary limitation of this approach is that a model of variable therapeutic response for treating patients with different interpersonal pathology (e.g., behaving in a more spontaneous, emotional way with obsessive-compulsive patients and facilitating logical connections with hysterical patients) has not been articulated.

Alternative strategies have been proposed by Leary (1957) and Benjamin (1996). In Benjamin's structural analysis of social behavior (SASB) model, the therapist both refrains from complementary behaviors and attempts to do the antithesis with the patient. For example, if the patient whines, defends, and justifies, the therapist confirms that the patient is acceptable just as he or she is. Through confirmation, it is hoped that the patient's defensiveness will give way to free and enthusiastic disclosure.

Benjamin (1996) recommends therapeutic strategies tailored to modify particular maladaptive behaviors of patients, yet this approach does not specifically address the more complicated remediation of developmental deficits, including the building of new psychic structures (e.g., cohesive sense of self, good observing ego). Thus, the issue of increasing the development of an integrated sense of self is not addressed in the differential treatment of the dependent behavior of the hysteroid borderline patient (who requires greater therapist involvement, limits, and support) from that of the hysterical neurotic patient (who requires therapeutic abstinence and the promotion of regression while recognizing the patient's real capabilities).

Developmental issues are more clearly addressed in the model of psychotherapy (based on object relations and ego psychology principles) used by Althea Horner (1979, 1991). Horner does not specifically systematize the particular therapeutic behaviors appropriate for the resolution of specific developmental failures (and their resultant character pathology), but she does discuss different treatment implications relevant to patients with differential pathology. For example, in discussing the tasks of treatment in working with a schizoid patient (whose developmental failure is seen as stemming from the symbiotic stage and the hatching phases of separation-individuation), Horner (1979) states: "One must provide a matrix of relatedness so that, as differentiation proceeds, it is not equated with object loss, with its danger of dissolution of the self" (pp. 92–93). In contrast, Horner discusses a borderline patient with rapprochement issues who expressed a premature wish to leave treatment. Horner believes that the appropriate stance in this case was to support the patient's separation-individuation striving symbolized in the wish to leave, rather than confronting the wish as a resistance to treatment.

In her discussion of treatment for these two patients, Horner (1979) implicitly suggests that different types of corrective interpersonal experiences are needed for personality disorders that have developmental arrests at different stages. For the schizoid patient who received an inadequate symbiotic experience and consequently struggles with painful underattachment, Horner's therapeutic strategy is one of emotional availability. For the borderline patient who was not permitted to separate during rapprochement and consequently struggles with painful overattachment, the appropriate therapeutic strategy is one of supporting the patient's attempts at separation. Horner's (1991) most recent book, *Psychoanalytic Object Relations Therapy,* considers the application of object-relations theory to the general themes and phases of the treatment process as applied to patients with various developmental deficits. However, she only briefly refers to therapeutic issues that are differentially relevant to patients with various character disorders (e.g., narcissistic, schizoid, depressive, paranoid).

In this chapter, an extended model of object-relations therapy developed by Glickauf-Hughes and Wells (1995, 1997) is presented. This model (1) gives greater specificity to the concept of providing patients with a new object or corrective interpersonal experience than previously described by Fairbairn, Guntrip, Sullivan, or Alexander and French; (2) takes developmental deficits and structural change into account more than does Benjamin's SASB model; (3) discusses proactive strategies for dealing with particular character disorders more than does Cashdan's model; (4) further expands on the therapeutic strategies for rectifying developmental deficits as articulated by Horner (1979, 1991); and (5) is applicable to a broader range of disorders than Kohuts (1971, 1977) model.

THEORETICAL CONSTRUCTS

Interactional object-relations therapy is based on six fundamental assumptions:

1. Personality and psychopathology are influenced by relationships with significant others during critical stages of social and emotional development.
2. Hypothetical psychic structures (e.g., the self, the ego, the superego) that perform critical mental functions (e.g., reality testing, the ability to self-observe, the capacity to have concern for the wellbeing of others) normally develop in relationships with others during these periods.
3. One's early formative relationships are affected by ones innate temperament as well as the character style and current life status (e.g. health, marital satisfaction) of one's childhood caretakers.
4. One's early interpersonal experiences are internalized and become organized into a mental template of relationships (i.e., an image of oneself interacting with an image of an object/other) that determines one's perceptions of and behavior with others.
5. Psychopathology is a function of inaccurate and maladaptive mental templates.
6. One's mental template can be changed in psychotherapy through interpretations leading to insight about oneself and one's relationships, along with a corresponding corrective interpersonal experience.

Psychotherapy thus provides individuals with the opportunity for a developmental second chance. These principles are further elaborated next.

THE INTERPERSONAL INFLUENCES ON EARLY CHARACTER DEVELOPMENT

In contrast to the biological emphasis of Freud (1959), Fairbairn (1952) and Sullivan (1953) believed that personality was formed in relationships with other people. Glickauf-Hughes and Wells (1995, 1997) place particular importance on relationships with caretakers during critical periods of social and emotional development, as described by theorists such as Bowlby (1973), Erikson (1950), and Mahler, Pine, and Bergman (1975). When caretakers provide children with appropriate interpersonal experiences, children sufficiently master major developmental tasks or phases such as basic trust, attachment, separation, object constancy, individuation, autonomy, initiative, and intimacy. If, for example, a mother (or primary caretaker) is physically or emotionally unavailable to her child, particularly in the first year of life, and this is not rectified by later experiences, the child may become an adult who has great difficulty making attachments to others. Alternatively, if parents are not attuned to the child's needs, impinge on the child when the child is not needful, do not see and understand the child's basic nature, but rather expect his or her behavior to conform to parental expectations, the child does not develop an authentic sense of self (Winnicott, 1965). As an adult, he or she has great difficulty articulating needs and tends to behave in a reactive way to the perceived expectations of others (Miller, 1981).

The Importance of Early Relationships on the Development of Psychic Structures

Horner (1979) believes that the development of psychic structures (such as the ego, which performs such functions as reality testing, the capacity to self-observe, and the ability to tolerate frustration) is not a mere function of age and brain development. Rather, these structures and their functions evolve in the context of interpersonal relationships. For example, if children become overwhelmed by affect and are unable to maintain an objective perspective, they can temporarily "borrow" the caretaker's ego functions (e.g., the ability to assess the situation realistically). Gradually, in optimal circumstances, these caretaker functions are internalized by the child.

Additionally, Horner (1979) maintains that to be truly autonomous, one must first be dependent. She believes that the structural development that occurs outside the context of a relationship (i.e., is self-taught) is often compensatory and therefore both rigid and fragile. If, for example, children lack a realistic role model for being objective, they may develop unrealistic standards for objectivity and may attempt to be perfectly objective, thereby losing information provided by their feelings. Furthermore, when ego functions are not learned through modeling, practice, and adult assistance, individuals often feel like an imposter (i.e., feel like a child "acting" like an adult while remaining unsure of their real capacity for competent, independent functioning).

The Interaction of Nature and Nurture

We believe that individuals are not born a tabula rasa. Experiences, particularly ones with significant others, are crucial in character formation, but they account for only a portion of the variance. We think that infants are born with different temperaments that predispose them to respond to the world in particular ways. Some examples of traits that are likely to be innate are sensitivity, adaptability, activity level, regularity, emotional intensity, and persistence (Kurcínka, 1991). These traits can be reinforced or modified by the environment. For example, one child, who was not affectionate by nature, became so in a nonintrusive, affectionate family. Another child, who was sensitive, intuitive, and perceptive, developed those traits further as they were reinforced by his therapist-parents.

Having established the importance of the child's innate temperament, both parents' temperaments, and their current life circumstances, we now wish to underscore the equal importance of the temperamental fit between the child and his or her parents. Each of these factors contributes to the general adjustment and particular character formation of an individual. For example, a young, sensitive, insecure mother with little environmental support and high need for control may find it easier to accept the true self of her firstborn, low-energy, adaptable child than her second-born, strong-willed, active child who has difficulty getting on a regular schedule or adjusting to change. In addition to their being a nonoptimal fit, the mother now has two children to raise. In such a case, the first child is more likely to develop a sense of self and self-esteem than the second. Likewise, the extroverted, other-oriented child of a withdrawn mother may be more able to turn to others and thus learn to form secure attachments than an innately introverted child in the same family.

Both narcissistic and masochistic character pathology can arise in a family with narcissistic dynamics. Factors such as physical appearance, innate talents and abilities, resilience, gender, sexual preference, and birth order are variables that contribute to the development of masochistic versus narcissistic character traits (Glickauf-Hughes, 1999). For example, one client's family consisted of a narcissistic mother; an older son who physically and temperamentally resembled the idealized but absent father; a gay son who early on exhibited gender-nonconforming behaviors; and an adaptable, attractive, extroverted daughter. The mother had an enmeshed relationship with her older son, spoiled and infantalized him, and used him to meet her emotional needs. She used her daughter as an idealized self-object; in return for being her mother's ego-ideal, she received her mother's attention and approval. Neither the older son nor the daughter separated or individuated from the mother. In contrast, although the gay son did not have high self-esteem, he was the highest functioning, most mature and well-adjusted member of the family, in spite of being relatively neglected and scapegoated (i.e., shamed and physically abused). Although he suffered from low self-esteem due to his mother's prejudice against homosexuality, she nevertheless allowed him to separate and individuate. Thus, by default, he developed a sense of self. Furthermore, his intelligence and resilience allowed him to gain objectivity about his family, imagine a different world, and actively create one.

THE EFFECT OF EARLY RELATIONSHIPS ON ADULTS' COGNITIVE TEMPLATE OR MENTAL MAP OF THEMSELVES IN RELATION TO OTHERS

Through the following process, people tend to develop cognitive maps of their experience of the world that are used to guide their decision making and actions. Through the process of internalizing their experiences with significant others, particularly during critical stages of social and emotional development, these mental images become organized into a mental template of a representation of one's self in relationship to other people. This template influences the individual's perceptions and interpersonal behavior. For example, one client's intrusive, manipulative mother was so involved in a fundamentalist Christian church that she was unaware of the norms and customs of social reality. On one occasion, the client had been asked the time by another passenger on the train on the way to therapist's office. When she arrived, she was feeling irate and said: "What made that person think that it was okay to ask me for the time?" An individual's mental template also predisposes him or her to assume a particular attachment style (e.g., anxious attachment, dismissive attachment) or interpersonal stance, such as moving toward, away from, or against others (Horney, 1939), or friendly dominance, hostile dominance, friendly submission, or hostile submission (Leary, 1957). From this perspective, personality disorders are viewed as a manifestation of a dysfunctional mental template of interpersonal relationships resulting from specific developmental deficits causing the individual to behave in an inflexible, maladaptive fashion that does not take the realistic components of the current situation into account.

THE USE OF INSIGHT AND A CORRECTIVE INTERPERSONAL EXPERIENCE TO PROVIDE CLIENTS WITH A DEVELOPMENTAL SECOND CHANCE

Object-relations therapy attempts to provide patients with the opportunity for a corrective interpersonal experience geared to help them to (1) modify their mental template of self and objects, (2) better master unresolved developmental issues, (3) assume more varied and flexible interpersonal stances that are more appropriately attuned to their current social reality, and (4) remedy deficient psychic structures. By offering patients opportunities for corrective experiences, this therapy thus gives these patients "a developmental second chance" (Greenberg & Mitchell, 1983, p. 356). The kind of corrective interpersonal relationship that a given patient requires varies with his or her particular developmental impasse, structural deficits, interpersonal stance, and resulting character disorder.

For example, the primary developmental failure of clients with obsessive character occurs at what Freud (1908) refers to as the anal stage, Mahler et al. (1975) term the late rapprochement subphase of development, and is popularly referred to as "the terrible twos." During this period, children need to feel like the "acter," not just the "acted upon." They frequently use the word "no." "No" means " I don't know what I want yet, but I don't want what you want me to want." The good-enough parent needs to appreciate the budding of the child's independence and avoid control struggles with the child. The child must be allowed to win some battles (i.e., ones in which the child's safety is not endangered).

Parents of obsessive-compulsive clients are often obsessive-compulsive too. As they do not have a clearly established sense of autonomy, they are threatened by the child's acts of defiance and are often excessively controlling with the child. Furthermore, as they are conflicted about their own feelings of aggression, they either excessively or insufficiently contain the child's aggression. They are generally rigid in their beliefs and are excessively moralistic. As children tend to internalize both their parents' values and the manner in which their values are organized and expressed, the obsessive develops an overly harsh, rigid superego.

Parents of clients with obsessive character are typically high-functioning, repressed individuals who are usually more comfortable, emotionally expressive, and affectionate with infants than with toddlers. Furthermore, although they have difficulty with the child's oppositional behavior, they are able to tolerate the child's separation from them and their wish to control the child does not include a total lack of recognition of the child's innate nature. Thus, while the obsessive-compulsive has problems with autonomy and a harsh superego, he or she generally has basic trust, a sense of self, object constancy, and well-developed ego functions (e.g., reality testing, observing ego).

In treating the client with obsessive character, the developmental goal is to help the client to become more autonomous; the structural goal is to soften the superego; and the interpersonal goal is to help the client become more active (rather than reactive) and more spontaneous and engaged with people. As previously described, a corrective interpersonal experience for this client is most likely achieved when the therapist behaves in a manner that enables clients to master those tasks that they were unable to complete with parents. Thus, as parents of clients with obsessive character were concerned about power, control, and doing things right, therapists are advised to be concerned about the quality of the relationship rather than establish a pattern of nitpicking and having power struggles with the client. Therapists must celebrate clients' oppositionalism as a way of saying "I exist. I'm a person who has impact. I am in control of myself," as their parents were unable to do. This must be done before confronting them about the negative impact that their oppositional and controlling behavior currently has in their life. Because an obsessive client's parents were typically rigid and emotionally contained, it is very helpful when therapists are warm, flexible, spontaneous, and affectively expressive.

Due to limitations of space, this is an incomplete description of what constitutes a corrective interpersonal experience for clients with obsessive character structure. However, it is intended to demonstrate how, in understanding developmental principles and the client's personal history, the therapist is less likely "to repeat it" with the client.

In general, when making decisions about what constitutes a corrective interpersonal experience for a given client, therapists are advised to understand the principles used by good-enough parents to help children with particular developmental tasks and adapt these principles to the therapeutic situation (Glickauf-Hughes & Wells, 1997). The therapist must be careful not to behave in an infantilizing or condescending way to the adult patient or create or collude with the patient's fantasy about having a second childhood.

In truth, the goal of a good-enough parent (and the therapist utilizing this approach) is to help clients grow up and to render oneself obsolete. Bowlby (1973) believes that a mother helps her child separate from her by serving as a secure base from which to explore the world and get refueling. One of the authors used this principle as a guideline with a client who had difficulties with both separation and individuation. His parents were extremely narcissistic. They manifested their narcissism with the client both by being possessive and by insisting that he act like them, agree with them, and feel and think the same things they did. As his partner had recommended that he go to therapy, the client was, thus, unsure if he was going to therapy for her, for the therapist, or for himself. He also resisted becoming involved in therapy, as he feared that becoming attached to the therapist would make him unable to leave her. At the beginning of treatment, he tended to abruptly leave in the middle of the session. The therapist neither stopped him nor processed it (which would, in effect, be stopping him from leaving), but warmly said, "Goodbye. I'll see you next week." After nine months, he decided to terminate treatment. The therapist did not analyze the resistance. However, in the process of termination, she told the client that she thought it was very important to the client that he know he could leave when he wanted to and that he was in treatment by choice. One year later, he returned to therapy and remained for three years. This time, the therapist processed his occasional desires to leave prematurely. He became attached to the therapist during this treatment and was more conscious of and talked about his feelings of separation anxiety before vacations. The therapist used a variety of methods to help him with these feelings in her absence (e.g., use of journals, small symbolic transitional objects). When he terminated after three years of treatment, he did so with appropriate feelings of loss and gratitude, but not panic.

METHODS OF ASSESSMENT AND INTERVENTION

In interactional object-relations psychotherapy, through the use of interpretations leading to insight and a corresponding corrective interpersonal experience, therapists attempt to help clients master their unresolved developmental issues, modify their maladaptive interpersonal stances, and develop psychic structures that are weak or lacking. For treatment to be successful, it is extremely important for therapists to begin by making a discerning differential diagnosis that evaluates both the client's overall character style/disorder and the underlying issues that are the focus of this form of psychotherapy.

An Ego-Structural Model for Making Differential Diagnoses

Our model for making differential diagnoses (Glickauf-Hughes & Wells, 1997; Wells & Glickauf-Hughes, 1993) is a modification of Kernberg's (1975) ego-structural paradigm. These models differ from the atheoretical approach exemplified by the *Diagnostic and Statistical Manual of Mental Disorders* (*DSM-IV*; APA, 1994), as etiology, psychopathology, and treatment are directly related to diagnosis. In essence, the very factors that the model proposes to treat are assessed in each diagnostic category (i.e., unresolved developmental issues, structural deficits, interpersonal functioning). Level of ego functioning is differentiated from personality style and criteria for differentiating one diagnostic category from another are articulated.

Kernberg's Diagnostic Model
Briefly, Kernberg's (1975) diagnostic model specifies four levels of ego development: normal,

neurotic, borderline, and psychotic. *Normal* individuals generally use secondary process thinking. In essence, their thought processes are rational and reality-based and intervene between impulse and action. When they are under stress, they primarily utilize mature defenses (i.e., ones that are more adaptive and reality-based) such as sublimation, suppression, and humor. In addition, they have the capacity for self-observation and the ability to delay gratification and tolerate frustration and to integrate and differentiate. In particular, they can integrate good and bad interpersonal experiences and differentiate self from others. They have firmly developed object constancy (i.e., an internal representation of a predominately good other that can be used for security and self-soothing) and an integrated, separate, well-developed sense of self. They have the capacity for basic trust, love, commitment, and reciprocity in their relationships. They have a superego (i.e., conscience, set of moral values) that is well balanced and realistic. They thus are able to conform when necessary to societal standards without giving up pleasurable experiences.

Individuals at the *neurotic* level have fairly similar ego development to normal individuals. Two primary differences prevail. Neurotic individuals rely primarily on repression and associated middle-level defenses (including intellectualization, rationalization, isolation of affect, reaction formation) to cope with stress and conflict. They also tend to either overuse or underuse their superego or ego functions in their tendency to repeat unresolved, repressed conflicts from childhood. Individuals at the neurotic level of ego development have a fairly well-developed observing ego and typically view their psychopathology, or at least some part of it, as ego-alien or odd.

Individuals at the *borderline* level of ego development have a tendency to use primary process thinking under stress or when using drugs and alcohol. In addition, they frequently use primitive defenses that are highly maladaptive and significantly distort reality. For example, they often use splitting (i.e., the complete emotional separation of good and bad experiences) so that when frustrated, they experience themselves and/or others as "all bad." In addition, they use projection, introjection, derealization, depersonalization, acting out, and projective identification. The last defense refers to an unconscious process in which an individual projects unacceptable aspects of the self onto another and then behaves in such a manner as to induce the receiver into experiencing or acting out the projected, disowned aspects of self. Borderline individuals are not able to separate self from others and lack a cohesive sense of self and object constancy. Thus, they have problems in tolerating frustration and deferring gratification, and have great difficulty trusting other people. They generally relate to others at the need-gratifying level of object relations (i.e., they use other people for what they provide). Their relationships tend to be intense and short-lived. They have little capacity for objective self-observation and often have quite compromised social reality testing.

Finally, *psychotic* individuals rely on lower-level defenses such as derealization, depersonalization, hallucinations, severe dissociation, and delusions. They predominantly use primary process thinking and have extremely impoverished or barely discernable relationships with others. They have a vague, undefined sense of self with a contradictory set of self representations that are poorly integrated and actively kept apart. There is no objective self-observation and extremely poor reality testing.

An important characteristic of Kernberg's diagnostic model is that the term borderline is used to describe a level of ego development that includes a number of personality disorders rather than to designate a particular personality disorder. Thus, the hysterical neurotic and hysteroid borderline may initially appear similar due to stylistic or superficial similarities such as acting seductive or looking helpless.

However, their underlying structure, functioning, and consequent treatment goals are quite different.

Wells and Glickauf-Hughes's Modification of Kernberg's Model

Wells and Glickauf-Hughes (1993) have altered Kernberg's model in two ways. First, we added and more elaborately defined the category "preneurotic," which was very briefly mentioned by Horner (1979) as a fifth level of ego development. Individuals at the preneurotic level predominantly use higher- and middle-level defenses and occasionally use lower-level defenses such as introjection, projection, delimited, specialized (i.e., masochistic or narcissistic) splitting, and acting out. They primarily use secondary process thinking, can delay gratification, and have a cohesive sense of self. However, they have not fully achieved object constancy. Although they are usually able to integrate good and bad experiences of self and other and refrain from reliance on splitting, particularly in its traditional (i.e., global) form, they have never fully internalized the comforting, soothing functions of their ambivalently held, childhood caretakers. They are thus overly reliant on others for self-esteem, internal security, and soothing. They also manifest a weakened sense of basic trust, and although their social reality testing is predominantly sound, it can be compromised in areas that threaten their primary attachment relationships. Finally, under stress in intimate relationships, they can have great difficulty with objective self-observation.

Second, we categorize the personality disorders at each level of ego development in regard to their predominant attachment/interpersonal style. In our 1997 book we described personality disorders that represent three different attachment styles (moving toward or being attached to people, moving away from or dismissing others, and moving against others); we focused on the first two styles at the neurotic, preneurotic, and borderline levels of ego development. Individuals at the so-called normal level presumably do not require extended treatment, and psychotic and aggressive borderlines (e.g., antisocial, aggressive-sadistic, paranoid) are not (or, at least, are much less) amenable to this form of treatment. Therefore, we articulated only the specific form that interactive object-relations therapy would assume for treating six personality disorders (one fundamentally preoccupied and one fundamentally dismissive type) at the neurotic, preneurotic, and borderline levels of ego development.

SUMMARY OF MODEL FOR OBJECT-RELATIONS PSYCHOTHERAPY FOR SIX PERSONALITY DISORDERS WITH FUNDAMENTALLY PREOCCUPIED OR DETACHED STYLES AT THE BORDERLINE, PRENEUROTIC, AND NEUROTIC LEVELS OF EGO DEVELOPMENT

Treatment of Neurotic Clients

At the neurotic level of ego development, the preoccupied type is the hysterical personality. The level of developmental arrest of this disorder is at the late Oedipal stage. Parents of hysterics tended to discourage appropriate aggression and rewarded helpless, passive, and seductive behavior. Frequently, the opposite-sex parent triangulated the child against the same-sex parent and was seductive when the child expressed dependency needs. Their primary developmental failure is the inability to take initiative. They also have problems experiencing and expressing sexual and aggressive impulses, and have a proclivity to confuse their dependency needs with their sexual needs. Their resulting interpersonal stance is pseudodependent, attention seeking, and seductive. Generally, hysterical individuals have relatively healthy, well-developed psychic structures. Their major problem in this area is some proclivity to act out. Interpersonal treatment goals include developing (1) appropriate self-assertion, (2) initiative and awareness, and (3) direct expression of dependency needs.

Structural goals include increasing frustration tolerance by learning to self-reflect, think through, or objectively observe before acting out. Therapists of hysterical clients are generally advised to be warm and nondirective, to clarify emotions and ask for factual details, and to support strength and competence and not dominate, get seduced, or foster too much dependency (Mueller & Anischewitz, 1986).

The detached type at the neurotic level is the obsessive-compulsive personality (OCP). The stage of developmental arrest is the late rapprochement/anal period. Historically, the OCP received excessively harsh discipline. Parents tended to overcontrol the child's impulses and emotions and restricted autonomous actions. The primary developmental deficit is in the area of autonomy versus shame and doubt. Interpersonally, the OCP tends to be reserved, self-contained, and overly serious and frequently engages in power struggles with others. They have well-developed and adaptive psychic structures with the exception of their superego, which is overly harsh and tends to dominate the individual's overall personality. Interpersonal treatment goals include increasing the importance of relationships with others over having control or being right and increasing playfulness, emotional expressiveness, and spontaneity. The predominant structural goal is softening the superego. The corrective interpersonal experience in psychotherapy for the OCP includes being warm, emotionally expressive, and spontaneous; acknowledging therapeutic errors; empathizing with clients' shame or guilt about making mistakes; modeling appropriate risk taking (Wells, Glickauf-Hughes, & Buzzell, 1990); and assuming a nondirective, nonauthoritarian approach.

Treatment of Preneurotic Clients
The fundamentally preoccupied client at the preneurotic level is the masochistic or self-defeating personality. The masochist's primary developmental arrest is at the "on-the-way-to-object-constancy" phase of separation-individuation (Horner, 1979; Johnson, 1985). The etiology of this disorder includes intermittent abuse, neglect, and reinforcement of dependent behaviors; scapegoating and/or parentification; squelching the child's will (Johnson, 1985); and being overcontrolled by parents who themselves lack self-discipline. Their resulting interpersonal stance reflects an anxious attachment characterized by a preoccupied, counterdependent style. They use compensatory caretaking to indirectly meet their own dependency needs while maintaining a relatively mobilized and dominant position relative to needed others. They are overtly compliant and are covertly defiant. Structurally, although they have a sense of self, it lacks complete integration, so their self-esteem is not resilient. Furthermore, object constancy is incomplete due to a deficiency of transmuting internalizations (Horner, 1979) of the caretaker's soothing, empathy, and respect. Interpersonal goals in therapy include (1) further developing basic trust, (2) resolving preoccupied and counterdependent attachment, (3) increasing appropriate self-assertion, and (4) mastering separation and loss. Structural goals in treatment include completing object constancy by developing reality-based transmuting internalizations of self-soothing and self-esteem and resolving masochistic splitting, a process whereby the individual experiences the self as "all bad" (Meyers, 1988). A corrective interpersonal experience for masochistic clients includes (1) being constant, dependable, nonreactive, and empathic; (2) having genuine positive regard for the client; (3) being emotionally available without being possessive, controlling, or infantalizing; and (4) acknowledging relational mistakes.

The dismissive client at the preneurotic level is the narcissistic personality. The narcissist's stage of developmental arrest is the rapprochement subphase of separation-individuation (Johnson, 1987). The historical experience of narcissists is having their true selves rejected by significant others (Miller, 1981); being used as mirroring or idealized self-objects (Kohut, 1971, 1977); and being admired rather than loved. Consequently, they lack an authentic sense of self and resilient self-esteem and have difficulty soothing themselves and loving rather than using other people. Interpersonally, they relate to others as self-objects, act pseudoindependent, and are idealizing, devaluing, and manipulative. Structurally, they have a grandiose rather than realistic sense of self and a somewhat weakened ego so that they are very sensitive to slights (resulting in feelings of envy, shame, and rage). Interpersonal goals in treatment include developing the ability to love realistically perceived, whole others, and learning to be authentic with others. A corrective interpersonal experience for narcissistic clients includes (1) being sensitive, nonimpinging, and attuned; (2) providing an empathic, optimally frustrating environment (Kohut, 1971, 1977); and (3) supporting strengths and empathizing with vulnerabilities (Johnson, 1987).

Treatment of Borderline Clients

The fundamentally preoccupied client at the borderline level is the hysteroid personality. The level of developmental arrest of this disorder is the practicing and rapprochement subphases of separation-individuation. The most important factor in the etiology of the hysteroid borderline is the withdrawal of the caretaker's attention, love, support, and approval when the child begins to separate and individuate (Masterson, 1981). The resulting developmental failure is insufficient separation and individuation. Interpersonally, hysteroid borderlines alternate between clinging and rage. Their structural issues include a lack of object constancy, identity diffusion, and vulnerability to brief psychotic episodes. In psychotherapy, interpersonal goals include supporting separation and fostering individuation. Structural goals include developing object constancy, resolving splitting (Kernberg, 1975), developing an integrated sense of self, and increasing frustration tolerance. To provide a corrective interpersonal experience in therapy for hysteroid borderlines, therapists are advised to (1) set appropriate limits, (2) support genuine self-expression, (3) refrain from revenge and retaliation (Wells & Glickauf-Hughes, 1986), and (4) balance the client's need for autonomy and support by being a secure base from which to explore.

The dismissive client at the borderline level is the schizoid personality. The stage of developmental arrest of this disorder is autistic and early symbiotic (Johnson, 1985). Historically, schizoid clients were treated by the significant others in their lives with profound neglect and rejection (Guntrip, 1969a). Their developmental failure is the lack of an adequate symbiotic attachment. The resulting interpersonal stance of the schizoid personality is a defensive withdrawal from others. The structural issues of this disorder include a detached self that fears regressive self-fragmentation, rigidly maintained self-other differentiation, and a lack of object constancy. Interpersonal treatment goals thus include preventing the client from gross anxiety and establishing an attachment from which the client can separate. Structural goals include developing a cohesive sense of self that is not defensively based (Guntrip, 1969b), integrating cognitive and affective part self-representations, and establishing object constancy. To provide a corrective interpersonal experience for the schizoid client, the therapist must establish a safe relationship and be available, contactful, present, and congruent.

SYNDROMES TREATED BY THIS APPROACH

As previously stated, this model of treatment is generally not recommended for psychotic clients and clients at the borderline level of ego development whose attachment/relational style is what Horney (1939) describes as moving against others (e.g., aggressive-sadistic, psychopathic, paranoid). In the former case, psychotropic medication is generally more effective and less costly; in the latter case, the client's primary motivation is often antithetical to insight-oriented, relational therapies.

We conceptualize clients in this category as being in what Klein (1957) describes as the paranoid position. Very briefly, individuals in the paranoid position have not developed a cohesive, integrated picture of themselves or others. They have difficulty maintaining a predominantly positive, integrated picture of significant others when their needs are frustrated. In general, other people tend to be used for need gratification and clients have little concern for them as people in their own right, with separate needs and feelings.

When individuals in the paranoid position are in relationships with significant others, they are vulnerable to feeling shamed, engulfed, and powerless. To avoid these painful experiences, they use defenses such as splitting, projection, and projective identification. The objective of these defenses is to get the experience of feeling bad, powerless, or afraid out of the self and into the other. The individual thus accomplishes his or her primary goal (i.e., to protect one's self-cohesion and self-esteem); however, as these defenses are often hurtful to others, what suffers is the relationship.

Due to their propensity to shore up their fragile self-esteem when it is injured by directing the problem outward, individuals in the paranoid position tend to be externalizers. They typically have little motivation for psychotherapies that emphasize relationship and focus on self-awareness.

We do believe that, at times, clients in this category with better functioning who are sufficiently motivated are treatable, particularly if they have a mixed personality disorder. In addition, although we have categorized the personality disorders using variables such as attachment style and level of ego development, in some instances, such distinctions are not entirely clear. For example, the sadistic individual is categorized as falling in the "against others" or aggressive position. However, in contrast to the psychopath, the sadist is often intensely attached to significant others (Lansky, 1980), and the fear of losing the other can be a motivating variable for treatment.

Furthermore, being in a category described as potentially treatable does not ensure a good prognosis. Making an appointment with a therapist does not necessarily indicate that individuals want psychotherapy. Many people are not knowledgeable about what psychotherapy is, requires, or can and cannot accomplish. Additionally, some people seek treatment for reasons other than obtaining insight about themselves or making characterological changes. They may wish to use the therapist to gratify their emotional needs. They may feel quite angry about past or present injustices and seek symbolic reparation by defeating a representative authority figure (i.e., the therapist). They may want a magic cure or may simply want to feel better without doing anything difficult to bring about that change. As these wishes are unrealistic and serve as a resistance to treatment, people with these types of motivations are generally not good candidates for this form of treatment.

People have defenses for good reasons. Many do not want to acknowledge or experience the feelings associated with painful memories. It is often frightening to face the unknown. Change may evoke feelings of separation anxiety or threaten one's sense of identity. To change means to grieve the life that one has, and grief is difficult. Furthermore, it is almost impossible for some people to acknowledge their responsibility for their current problems because of their defensive avoidance of shame. We believe that clients must be educated at the beginning of treatment about what types of problems an interactional object-relations therapy can and cannot help with. From this discussion, therapists and clients are advised to collaboratively make a reasonable therapeutic contract with realistic treatment goals.

In our 1997 book, we noted that, "while therapists differ in their notion about which patient problems are treatable and which problems are not or how explicit a therapeutic contract needs to be, there are some implicit treatment contracts that all therapists are advised to be aware of and cautious about making with patients" (pp. 102–103). These include: (1) using the therapist as the solution to the client's problems (e.g., requesting unconditional support or someone to just listen as a way to avoid self-awareness or change); (2) impossible contracts with which the therapist cannot directly help clients (e.g., finishing their dissertation for them); (3) covert contracts where what the client really wants (and the therapist would be unlikely to agree to do) is different from what the client overtly requests (e.g., wanting the therapist to be a parent, wanting to defeat the therapist as a representative of all authority figures); and (4) no contract (e.g., coming to therapy for the experience). In the last example, clients are often unaware of what they need from the therapist for reasons such as lack of self-awareness or excessively shamed needs. In such instances, when that is made explicit, a workable treatment contract can be formed. This is also true for other unworkable contracts, which can sometimes be transformed by the therapist into ones that are more realistic, workable, and useful.

MAKING A WORKABLE TREATMENT
CONTRACT IN INTERACTIONAL
OBJECT-RELATIONS PSYCHOTHERAPY

Therapists using interactional object-relations therapy make an initial evaluation of each client's developmental, interpersonal, and structural issues and motivation for treatment. They then work with clients to determine if a mutual understanding and treatment contract can be made in which presenting problems that are not treatable by this form of psychotherapy are translated into problems with which the therapist can help the client. Some clients are quite unaware of what is truly wrong in their lives and what is involved in changing. They require considerable effort from the therapist to achieve this goal. In contrast, clients who are more self-aware, make internal attributions, and are more relational tend to be more informed about what they need from the therapist. Some examples of the latter are wanting to feel close to others, wanting to feel better about themselves, and wanting to be more assertive. Such problems are more easily translated into developmental, interpersonal, or structural goals.

For example, the therapist might inquire what makes it difficult to feel close to others or what the client would most fear in trying to be close to people. If the client replies, "People might hurt me," the client's developmental issue might be basic trust. The therapist would want to follow up this response by asking how the client was afraid that people could hurt him or her and if that experience was a familiar one. In contrast, if the client responds, "People might control me," the client's issue would likely be autonomy. Furthermore, if the client responds, "I am afraid I could lose myself," one would hypothesize that the client might be struggling with issues of separation-individuation (particularly individuation) and that his or her self structure needed to be developed.

For clients who simply want to feel better about themselves, the central developmental issue may revolve around deficiently resilient self-esteem (resulting from an impaired self-structure and ego functioning). One might further inquire about what these clients' opinion of themselves was and who else had that opinion of them. If clients describe a history of being criticized or even verbally abused, they might also have the developmental issue of basic trust. If clients describe a history of being the good child who had to be what their mother wanted to be loved and they no longer wanted to do that, they might have a developmental issue of individuation and a structural issue of developing an authentic sense of self. If clients add that they are still trying to be perfect, as they had always been told that they were "special" and could accomplish whatever they put their mind to, they might have the issue of "undeflated grandiosity," reflecting a developmental impasse at the rapprochement subphase.

In healthy development, the parent helps children as their grandiosity from the practicing subphase is deflated, empathizing with them to cushion their disappointments. As much as possible, the parent would also resist putting children in situations where this process occurs too fast (e.g., putting them in a preschool class with much larger children). If the parent has a narcissistic character and his or her own undeflated grandiosity and is using the child as an ideal object or trophy to enhance his or her self-esteem, then the parent is unlikely to help the child successfully master this stage. Instead, the parent is likely to expect too much of the child and be critical or unempathic when the child fails. As a consequence, the child will have unrealistic ideals and goals and lack resilient self-esteem.

Finally, if clients want to be more assertive, they could be dealing with autonomy or initiative. The therapist would need to clarify whether they are overcompliant and unable to say no to other people (autonomy) or had difficult taking action to pursue their goals and interests (initiative). In some cases, it might be both. In either case, these clients are likely to have a submissive interpersonal style. One would then want to investigate whether they are generally successful in their work and relationships and were liked and helped by others (friendly submission), or never quite succeeded, were often late, and irritated people without intending to do so (hostile submission). The therapist can also assess this by clients' in-session behavior (e.g., is the client evasive, or does the client directly answer the therapist's questions; does the client seem able to receive help, or is the client a help-rejecting complainer). In both instances, clients' interpersonal goal would be to learn to be more appropriately dominant. In the maladaptive use of friendly submission, clients with autonomy issues would particularly need to work on expressions of dominance in unfriendly situations. A good example is Clint Eastwood's film character, Dirty Harry, who says "Make my day" to criminals who are attempting to kill him. In the maladaptive use of hostile submission, clients with autonomy and initiative issues (i.e., passive-aggressive clients) need to learn not only positive forms of direct aggression but the ability to submit or receive help from others appropriately when it is in their best interest to get help.

More commonly, however, clients' presenting problems require more work on the therapist's part to translate them into workable treatment goals. For example, a client might come to therapy requesting help completing his or her dissertation. It has been our experience that many trainees with a lack of a sufficient theoretical background to guide them take this as a literal goal and begin to unsuccessfully help clients to resolve the literal problem. Previously, we categorized this particular problem as an impossible contract, because unaddressed intractable developmental conflicts underlying the literal problems mean there is no way that the therapist could have a desirable impact. Furthermore, problems such as "I should do X but I'm not" or " I shouldn't do X but I am" are usually "superego contracts" (e.g., the therapist becomes allied with the client's superego to make the client do something about which the client has ambivalent feelings). Such contracts are destined to fail, as they mitigate against a therapeutic alliance and the therapist becomes identified with the authority figure that needs to be defeated.

Although it may seem like an overwhelming task, particularly for the beginning therapist, to translate a contract like this into one with developmental, interpersonal, and structural goals, it has been our experience that when given sufficient models and examples, most therapists have reasonably good intuition about the underlying problems that can guide them in this task. It is particularly helpful for therapists to give themselves permission to ask the client questions until both therapist and client are clear about the nature of the client's problems. Therapists may empathize with clients' sense of urgency about resolving their problems, but they are advised to resist being so influenced by the sense of urgency that they make premature, inaccurate treatment contracts. In fact, a corrective experience for the client may well entail the therapist's demonstrating how to contain a sense of urgency to gather needed information, center oneself, and gain perspective before making any decisions regarding the "urgent" issue at hand. Differentiating between an urgent feeling and a true emergency or crisis may also prove helpful with some clients who confuse feeling with being and feeling with behavior.

More specifically, in this last example, the therapist might ask what the client's difficulty is in completing his or her dissertation. If the client answers, "I can't seem to get past the first page," the therapist might ask the client to elaborate on this process. One client seen by one of the authors rewrote the first page 40 or 50 times until it was perfect. When she asked the client where she learned that things must be perfect, the client talked about how hard it was being a minister's daughter in a small town where she could never make a mistake without being judged. She talked about all the expectations that people had of her throughout her life and how no one ever asked her what she wanted to do. Her father had always wanted to be a philosophy professor, which is why she was getting her Ph.D. in that field. She eventually expressed that although she was a good student in philosophy, she did not really enjoy it. When the therapist asked her what interested her, she said that she loved gardening and was fascinated by plants. She loved to dig in the ground, watch plants and flowers grow, and appreciate their beauty. In high school, she actually started a small business to raise money for the school by taking cuttings from plants and flowers and growing them. She raised a record amount of money for the school. Furthermore, throughout undergraduate school, she enjoyed working for a nursery and was so competent that she was promoted to a managerial position.

This client could be conceptualized as functioning at the preneurotic level. She had a narcissistic personality style and used some obsessive-compulsive defenses. She had a proclivity to idealize, but she related to others, including the therapist, as a separate person and did not use primitive defenses such as splitting and projective identification. She had a sense of self but gave it up to please significant others. She had unrealistic standards for herself, was overly influenced by the opinions of others, and required the approval of others to maintain a sense of self-esteem. She particularly wanted her father's approval, which is why she pursued a Ph.D. in philosophy. However, she was not out of touch with her genuine wishes, feelings, values, interests, and competencies. The developmental goals for this client included completing individuation and object constancy by helping her see and accept the differences between herself and others (including her family and the therapist), as well as encouraging her evolving sense of individuated and authentic selfhood. The structural goal for this client was to help her to internalize the positive regard and empathy of the therapist and develop realistic goals and ideals so that she had resilient self-esteem. The interpersonal goal was to help this client be more assertive (i.e., to say no to things that she did not want to do and to initiate things that were important to her). This client resolved her problem about not finishing her dissertation by dropping out of her philosophy program and getting a small business loan to start a nursery.

We have presented an interactional object-relations model that focuses on assessing the level of ego-object relations and the character organization of clients. Based on these evolving assessments, the model provides therapists with specific corrective relational experiences and insights aimed at helping clients to resolve developmental impasses and rectify structural deficits.

CASE EXAMPLE

The following case study of a male patient with Schizoid Personality Disorder is presented to illustrate how treatment is individualized to address structural, developmental, and interpersonal issues. We discuss (1) the client's presenting problems; (2) etiology, particularly the manner in which the client was treated by significant others during his formative stages of development; (3) the resulting developmental arrest; (4) structural issues; (5) treatment goals; (6) the type of corrective relational experience required to provide a developmental second chance; and (7) the treatment process and outcome, including transference and countertransference issues. In particular, this case demonstrates the treatment of a patient with a Schizoid Personality Disorder organized at the borderline level of ego-object relations.

General Description and Presenting Problem

At the time he began therapy, John was a 29-year-old, intelligent, Caucasian single male. Although he realized he was underemployed as a jewelry maker for a small shop, he said he was usually content to sit all day in his cubicle making earrings and "letting my mind wander" as long as he was "left alone." He described himself as a loner with a vivid imagination who spent much of his time daydreaming. He said he did not date ("I don't know how") but had one superficial, role-related friendship with a coworker. John said he did not consider himself spiritual or shy, but "simply unable to do life or relationships," lacking any real life purpose, having no idea who he was, and sometimes finding himself fascinated with death, because he thought he "could do that and thus accomplish something." He described a chronic experience of "living in a bubble where I can see everyone but cannot touch or be touched." He had come to therapy to find out if there was any meaning in life for himself and clarify "whether or not I can really do life."

Etiology

John's family-of-origin environment was best characterized by massive neglect punctuated by unattuned impingements and rejection. John was the fourth of four siblings, raised in the urban Northeast. His parents divorced when he was 2 years old. Each of the children had a different father. His mother dated several men and remarried twice during John's childhood.

Relationships within the family appear to have been largely remote. His older sister, Anna, was the primary caretaker of John's physical needs (e.g., making sure he was dressed for school and had breakfast). He remembered one time when she held his hand, when he was 3 and his mother was having a nervous breakdown and being taken to the hospital by her brother. After that, he remembered his mother focusing her attention on going back to school to get her degree, dating, and dealing with her generally chaotic life, which left her with little energy for raising her children. John described his mother as "the nonmotherly type. She never really parented any of us." John's other siblings were older and in and out of the house. John described a predominant "sense of vacancy, nothingness, going through motions," with no parental guidance or presence.

John noted that when his mother's attention periodically turned toward him, she invariably "got on my nerves" and was unattuned to his needs. He said she "used whatever information she got about me against me." For example, when his mother discovered that John was the only one in the family who had seen his biological father cry, she "relentlessly" asked John to tell her all about it. When he finally got her to promise to stop asking him and not bring it up again, she still did at the next family gathering. When John reminded her that she had agreed not to bring it up, she laughed and pressed him for further details. She did this at every family gathering for the next five years, which John found humiliating and felt helpless to prevent.

John reported that his mother's boyfriends and husbands "ran the gamut," usually ignoring him, but sometimes treating him as their "personal slave" (e.g., "Hey kid, go grab me a beer"). In contrast, John noted that his biological father "wanted to parent, he just didn't know how," and so remained a peripheral figure in John's life. Because John's peer relationships were also remote, his most positive relationships were with Anna and his dog, about whom he said he felt "sentimental."

Resulting Developmental Arrest

As a result of his caregivers' largely neglectful, impinging, and rejecting parenting styles, John's basic trust in the world of human relations was severely compromised, leaving him afraid of both engulfment and annihilation. Without basic trust in others to respect his boundaries or be even roughly attuned to his needs, John never achieved a stable intimate attachment from which he could separate and individuate. As a result, John's pseudoindependence was fragile and compensatory.

Fortunately, John had been able to develop a nascent sense of related self through his mother's early enjoyment of breast-feeding and his older sister's substitute mothering during his first years of life. This nascent sense of related self was later reinforced by his relationship with the family dog and a phone relationship with his father. John's symbiotic attachment needs were thus only partially met, his physical needs largely met, and his separation-individuation needs never met. He sensed "something profound was missing" and sometimes felt intense existential aloneness along with a "gut-wrenching yearning" for a nonspecific connection. However, he felt safe from impingement only when he was emotionally or physically distanced from others.

John struggled with shame (versus autonomy) to the extent that his compromised self-definition permitted. At times, he struggled unsuccessfully to express himself out of intense fears of exposure and humiliation. To avoid need-shame, John defensively viewed people as computers or objects to be contended with for survival.

Structural Issues

As a result of John's developmental failures in basic trust and stable attachment, his object relations were severely compromised and he primarily developed his ego functions outside of relationship. In particular, his synthetic function remained limited, resulting in split object relations, identity diffusion (severely limited core sense of self), and poor object constancy (self-soothing). He defended against his basic engulfment and cosmic void anxieties by vacillating between polarized self-object representations. On one side of the split, John saw himself as a dependent slave or loyal pet in relationship with a demanding, sadistic other who simply took him over. On the other side of the split, John saw himself as a totally self-sufficient aesthetic who felt safe but alone, exiled into the cosmic void.

John thus demonstrated little ability to maintain an integrated view of self or other, to empathize with self or other, or to value self or other as more than a set of functions. He entered therapy at the need-gratifying level of ego-object relations. His vague, diffuse self-identity resulted in a sense of having no rudder, and so having no unambivalent direction in life or a sense of purpose. When he entered therapy, he described his world as one primarily composed of empty space, "a garden never planted and so dead or lying fallow, which is the question."

John had little observing ego and practically no ability to soothe himself beyond distracting himself in his art, computer activities, reading, TV watching, or fantasies. In his most secret fantasies, he became possibly worthy of existence by becoming the perfect aesthetic, with no interpersonal needs, a successful artist who would provide the world pure creative genius. His perfectionism over his creativity made these efforts very painstaking pursuits, however.

Resulting Interpersonal Stance

As a result of John's developmental and structural failures, his interpersonal stance primarily focused on moving away from others, isolating or exiling himself emotionally, psychologically, and physically (e.g., he spent a lot of time alone reading, daydreaming, or working on jewelry). To protect himself from the pain of neglect and controlling impingements, he had learned to practice the art of evasion, avoidance, and emotional detachment. He learned to hide his reactions and try his best to make himself invisible to others. Specifically, he learned to control his affective responses by focusing his mental attention on a riddle or a fantasy. He interacted with others through the assumption of roles (e.g., coworker, employee), which helped him to structure relationships and maintain a built-in distance from people. He did not look to others for admiration or narcissistic supplies, but rather, for the right to exist as a separate person and so hold onto his own thoughts and feelings. John's fragility and his proclivity to split his object relations and thus project sadistic, conquering motives onto others was always right underneath the surface. Interpersonal tensions would propel him into further social isolation, where he could find at least temporary relief before his aching sense of aloneness and his negative introjects would eventually propel him back into peripheral relating.

Treatment Goals

Interpersonal treatment goals included (1) developing John's sense of interpersonal safety; (2) developing a working alliance with his nascent real self; and (3) resolving his need-fear dilemma and his "in and out" program with others; these goals in turn were aimed at helping John (4) establish a stable attachment relationship with the therapist, from whom John could then nondefensively separate. To accomplish these relational goals, the therapist had to help John contain his gross anxieties so that the world and his experiences did not seem so overwhelming. Structural treatment goals included (1) developing Johns noncompensatory ego functions (e.g., frustration tolerance, reality testing, synthesis, self-soothing, self-observation, self-reflection) and (2) resolving his reliance on splitting and projective identifications to (3) further his experience of an integrated sense of authentic related self and other. Developmentally, treatment goals included increasing (1) John's sense of basic trust in self and others, (2) his basic sense of purpose and meaning in life, and (3) his range of satisfactions in relationship with others.

TREATMENT APPROACH

First Phase of Treatment: Establishing Safety and a Working Alliance

In the initial phase of treatment, the therapist focused on developing an alliance with John's central ego or nascent real self, by joining with John first intellectually and then emotionally. Because of John's basic mistrust and strong detachment tendencies, this alliance was built slowly through the establishment of an evolving contract, an explicit focus on being a team together to examine and work on issues as they arose in the therapeutic relationship, the use of countertransference reactions to process John's primitive defenses, and the creation of a measure of interpersonal safety through a year-long testing phase. In general, to counter John's experience with parenting styles marked by neglect and impingement and thus provide a corrective relational matrix to help him work through his attachment fears, the therapist remained emotionally available in a "stand still" posture, so that John could exercise control over the interpersonal distance in the relationship. Giving John as much control as he needed over his "in and out" process was designed to help him build trust in the therapist that she would follow John's agenda rather than imposing her own on him. She consistently attempted to be emotionally and psychologically available to him without prodding or neglecting him. When distant relating was all John could tolerate, the therapist let him set the pace and stayed connected through the judicious use of metaphors and story sharing.

The issue of working together as part of a team was both a foreign and corrective experience for John, who had never been part of a working team with anyone and had no idea how to relate with another person in that manner. The therapist empathized with how completely John felt either "it was up to me" or "it was up to others." Sharing responsibility and working out plans for communicating nonverbally and verbally about the meaning of different silences provided a vehicle for developing relational skills and exploring the issues around how to involve someone else in his process.

The underlying aim of this phase of treatment was to establish a relatively stable attachment relationship between John and the therapist as well as develop John's ego functions. In particular, the therapist and John focused on developing his observing ego, self-empathy, and synthetic functions. John initially experienced great difficulty accepting even intellectual empathy from the therapist and demonstrated no self-empathy. Basically, he believed he did not deserve empathy, even though he could sometimes see how others might. Over time, it became clear that he fundamentally believed that he did not have a right to exist as a separate person and that connections were dangerous, including connections to the therapist as well as to his own affective experiences and memories. Out of these discussions, John and the therapist were able to identify the goal of working together to create enough safety so that he could risk telling his story and experiment with internalizing the therapist's empathy as well as activating his own.

Throughout this phase, the therapist focused primarily on the here-and-now therapeutic relationship with John, using her countertransference reactions to inform her interventions and activate exploration of the patterned ways of relating between them that indicated the use of primitive splitting and projective identification defenses. Through empathy and invitations to put words to the story enacted between them, she was able to help John gain insight into his use of schizoid splitting to protect his right to exist and not be taken over or engulfed by her. Specifically, the therapist helped John recognize how he tended to relate to her, with himself emotionally detached or dismissive (i.e., she was only a piece of furniture) but feeling safe, or with himself in relationship with her but feeling potentially enslaved or entrapped by her agendas, as if she were trying to conquer him by wanting to know him. Over time, the therapist was able to help John make the connection between his fears of the therapist as a powerful, demanding, self-involved puppet-master and his experience of his mother when she relentlessly pursued him.

Each time the therapist and John confronted his use of defensive splitting, the therapist invited him to entertain more complex, more realistic alternatives to his primitive self-object template. He began to see how he defensively simplified the therapist to avoid the interpersonal and internal anxieties he experienced and gain a sense of clarity in the midst of ambiguity.

The therapist tracked both John and herself, particularly attuning herself to his need-fear patterns around connecting and disconnecting. During long silences, the therapist tried to pay attention to and track whatever feelings or fantasies were stimulated within her. She reflected on what they might mean about John and what he was struggling with through testing or projective identification. Sometimes, the feelings engendered in the therapist turned out to reflect some aspect of Johns experience: feeling tested, ignored, dismissed, exiled, banished, helpless, comforted, safe, relieved, reflective. The therapist thus concentrated on the quality of the experience to potentially understand more about John's internal world. For example, the therapist used her countertransference feelings and fantasies of being bored and cut off as a signal to check out if John was feeling particularly detached or self-protective and investigate what he was responding to. At times, these investigations led John and the therapist to understand his silence to reflect his need to test the therapist's willingness to follow his agendas and not impose her own. At other times, they understood that John needed the experience of being together in nondemanding silences to internalize the safety of the therapeutic relationship. At still other times, they understood John's silences as reflecting his struggles to communicate (i.e., to overcome fears of exposure or shame). In the second phase of treatment, they would begin the work of helping John find a viable process of authentic self-expression.

Second Phase of Treatment:
A Nascent Self Is Nurtured
The first phase of treatment focused on developing a safe relationship, identifying and empathizing with the obstacles and resistances that John experienced that prevented him from expressing his needs or feelings and connecting with others, and developing the beginnings of basic trust. The second phase focused on interesting John in deeper explorations and self-reflections. The therapist tried to elicit his interest in exploring and understanding himself, in large measure by expressing her own genuine interest in knowing him to whatever degree he could allow. When John would become lost for words, the therapist would point out how their job together was to help him find a way to express himself. To counter the pervasive lack of guidance he had received historically, the therapist would sometimes inform him of different milieus of self-expression, in menu fashion, so that he could experiment with one that interested him if he so chose. As a result, John discovered that creating sculptures that represented some aspect of his self-experience was genuinely satisfying to him.

John also discovered that he could feel for himself by finding quotes that resonated with his internal experience. The first one he shared with the therapist was: "The price of dreams among the powerless." Through this process, John was eventually able to access his feelings during the therapy hour and thus began developing his affects and integrating them into his central self-experience.

During this phase of treatment, the therapist worked with John to further identify his fears and wishes, his authentic interests, strengths, and dependency needs. She empathized with his vulnerabilities and disappointments, while expressing interest and nonimpinging support for his authentic self-expressions. Where previously, John had told the therapist he would not let himself have any expectations, desires, or wishes of the therapist and so could not be disappointed by her, he now allowed that he could feel himself depending on her reliable presence in his life and his dependency "unnerved" him. He was afraid his dependencies would get out of hand and devour them both. The therapist told him that all indications were that, although he might feel overwhelmingly needy at times, feeling that way did not mean he was overwhelming. The therapist also noted that they would work together to help him develop ways of taking care of himself better over time. In addition, the two of them would work on pacing so that he could be in touch with his needs and feelings in manageable doses. Finally, they would work on developing his support network, perhaps by adding group therapy to his individual therapy experience at some point.

With a working alliance and a more defined sense of self, John and the therapist were able to identify shame as one of the fundamental affects underlying his need-fear dilemma that often prevented him from being able to express himself. To avoid the intolerable feelings of shame and exposure he felt on expressing any vulnerability or need for others, John automatically "hit a wall and stifled myself." If he began to feel shame, he would look down or off into space and play with a riddle in his mind. The therapist's expression of interest, patience, and gentle questioning around the need to resist the shamed or feared construct sometimes helped John find a pathway of expression. The therapist would observe his tendency to manage his feelings and sometimes invite him to look at her to register her nonverbal interest and understanding. John noted that one of the most healing experiences was when the therapist had obviously been thinking about an issue important to him in between sessions or in session was obviously struggling to understand something that puzzled John himself. At these times, he experienced the therapist behaving toward him in a way that demonstrated he was worth her thoughtful reflection and best efforts to understand him. This approach helped John counter his internal self-criticisms and led him to feel he deserved to exist.

Third Phase of Treatment: Individuation Is Fostered
In the third phase, John joined an adjunct group therapy, further developing his support system and his sense of autonomous selfhood. The group provided John with an authentic relational matrix, which showed him what he was still missing in terms of individuated selfhood, companionship, and intimacy with others. Group members modeled relationship skills, which inspired John to practice relating to others in a safe, supportive context. He still retreated to the sanctuary of his own mind when overwhelmed, but he was gradually able to tolerate more interpersonal tension without splitting his object relations. He decided to develop his artistic talent and eventually had a successful showing of his work. He took a hiatus from individual treatment at this point, saying he knew he "was becoming, like the weeds growing in the sidewalk cracks." He noted, "My life is still limited by the cement laid down in my childhood, but I have found my inner roots and can feel them steadily growing."

During termination with his therapist, John noted several aspects of their work together that he felt were particularly helpful to him. He commented most on the quality of the relationship that had developed between him and the therapist. In particular, he noted the safety and acceptance he had felt because of the therapist's genuine interest in him, her thoughtful struggle to understand him and help him to understand himself, her patience over the long haul, and her relaxed, friendly, unimposing style. He said he had slowly been able to believe in her good intentions and develop enough faith to risk staying connected "way more than I was comfortable with." He could now identify the experience of an "I" and empathize with himself (and with others), even when he felt scared. He felt the power of the therapist's empathy, and then his own, had mitigated some of his shame so that it was not nearly so intense, and he no longer struggled with an urgent need to avoid other people out of "fear of being taken over."

SUMMARY

Through John's case study we have illustrated the application of interactive object relations therapy to the treatment of a patient diagnosed with schizoid personality organization. We focused on how the therapist crafted an evolving, corrective relational matrix specifically designed to address the patient's particular developmental arrests and structural deficits. For example, because John's basic mistrust, intense need-fear dilemmas, and strong detachment tendencies, the therapist initially focused on developing an interested and emotionally available, but nonimpinging, therapeutic relationship designed to provide a quality of relating that fostered attachment so that John's psychic differentiation could then proceed buffered against the experience of total object loss or the dissolution of John's self. In order for John to master the subsequent developmental tasks related to individuation, the therapist had to match her approach to John's evolving psychic needs, balancing mirroring and empathy for his developing personhood with supportive invitations to take reasonable risks, while maintaining the priority of nonintrusive emotional availability.

Overall, this chapter has described an object relations treatment model that uses insight and corrective interpersonal experience to give clients a developmental second chance. More specifically, object relations therapy aims to provide clients with an interpersonal experience designed to (1) correct defects in their mental template of self and other, and (2) facilitate mastery of unresolved developmental tasks so as to increase their self-efficacy, flexibility, resilience, and general life satisfaction. In this manner a client's derailed development is put back on track. In this chapter we have specifically described the quality of corrective interpersonal relating that patients require given their particular developmental impasse, structural deficits, interpersonal stance, and resulting character disorder.

REFERENCES

Alexander, F., & French, T. M. (1946). *Psychoanalytic therapy*. New York: Ronald Press.

American Psychiatric Association. (1994). *Diagnostic and statistical manual of mental disorders* (4th ed.). Washington, DC: Author.

Beier, E. G. (1966). *The silent language of psychotherapy: Social reinforcement of unconscious processes*. Chicago: Aldine.

Benjamin, L. (1996). *Interpersonal diagnosis and treatment of personality disorders*. New York: Guilford Press.

Bowlby, J. (1973). *Attachment and loss. Volume II: Separation: Anxiety and anger*. New York: Basic Books.

Cashdan, S. (1988). *Object relations therapy*. New York: Norton.

Dolan, R., Arnkoff, P., & Glass, C. (1993). Client's attachment style and the therapist's interpersonal stance. *Psychotherapy, 30*(3), 408–412.

Dryden, W. (1991). *Therapists dilemmas*. London: Harper & Row.

Erikson, E. H. (1950). *Children in society*. New York: Norton.

Fairbairn, W. R. D. (1952). *An object relations theory of the personality*. New York: Basic Books.

Freud, S. (1959). Character and anal eroticism. *The standard edition of the complete psychological works of Sigmund Freud* (Vol. 9, pp. 169–175). London: Hogarth Press.

Glickauf-Hughes, C. (1999). The etiology of masochistic and narcissistic personalities. *American Journal of Psychoanalysis, 2*, 13–20.

Glickauf-Hughes, C., & Wells, M. (1995). *Treatment of the masochistic personality: An interactional-object relations approach to diagnosis and treatment*. Northvale, NJ: Aronson.

Glickauf-Hughes, C., & Wells, M. (1997). *Object relations psychotherapy: An individualized and interactive approach to diagnosis and treatment*. Northvale, NJ: Aronson.

Greenberg, J. R., & Mitchell, S. A. (1983). *Object relations in psychoanalytic theory*. Cambridge, MA: Harvard University Press.

Greenson, R. (1967). *The technique and practice of psychoanalysis*. Madison, CT: International Universities Press.

Guntrip, H. (1969a). *Personality structure and human interaction: The developing synthesis of a psychodynamic theory*. New York: International Universities Press.

Guntrip, H. (1969b). *Schizoid phenomena, object relations, and the self*. New York: International Universities Press.

Hedges, L. (1983). *Listening perspective in psychotherapy*. New York: Aronson.

Horner, A. (1979). *Object relations and the developing ego in psychotherapy*. Northvale, NJ: Aronson.

Horner, A. (1991). *Psychoanalytic object relations therapy*. Northvale, NJ: Aronson.

Horney, K. (1939). *Neurosis and human growth*. New York: Norton.

Jacobs, T. (1993, August). *On beginnings: Alliances, misalliances and the interplay of transference in the opening phase*. Paper presented at the American Psychoanalytic Seminar for Clinicians, Atlanta, GA.

Johnson, S. (1985). *Characterological transformation*. New York: Norton.

Johnson, S. (1987). *Humanizing the narcissistic style*. New York: Norton.

Kernberg, O. (1975). *Borderline conditions and pathological narcissism*. New York: Aronson.

Klein, M. (1957). *Envy and gratitude and other works: 1946–1963*. New York: Delacorte Press.

Kohut, H. (1971). *The analysis of the self*. New York: International Universities Press.

Kohut, H. (1977). *The restoration of the self*. New York: International Universities Press.

Kurcínka, M. S. (1991). *Raising your spirited child*. New York: HarperCollins.

Lansky, M. (1980). On blame. *International Journal of Psychoanalytic Psychotherapy, 8*, 429–456.

Lazarus, A. (1993). Tailoring of the therapeutic relationship, or being an authentic chameleon. *Psychotherapy, 30*(3), 404–407.

Leary, T. (1957). *Interpersonal diagnosis of personality*. New York: Ronald Press.

Mahler, M., Pine, F., & Bergman, A. (1975). *The psychological birth of the human infant: Symbiosis and individuation*. New York: Basic Books.

Mahrer, A. (1993). The experiential relationship: Is it all purpose or is it tailored to the individual client? *Psychotherapy, 30*, 413–416.

Masterson, J. F. (1981). *Narcissistic and borderline disorders: An integrated developmental approach*. New York: Brunner/Mazel.

Meyers, M. (1988). A consideration of treatment techniques in relation to the function of masochism. In R. Glick & D. Meyers (Eds.), *Masochism: Current psychoanalytic perspectives* (pp. 175–188). Hillsdale, NJ: Analytic Press.

Miller, A. (1981). *The drama of the gifted child*. New York: Basic Books.

Mueller, W., & Anischewitz, A. (1986). *Psychotherapeutic intervention in hysterical disorders*. Northvale, NJ: Aronson.

Norcross, J. C. (1993). Tailoring relational stances to clients' needs: An introduction. *Psychotherapy, 30*(3), 402–403.

Pine, F. (1993). A contribution to the analysis of the psychoanalytic process. *Psychoanalytic Quarterly 2*, 185–205.

Renik, O. (1993). Countertransference enactment and the psychoanalytic process. In M. Horowitz, O. Kernberg, & E. Weinshel (Eds.), *Psychic structure and psychic change*. New York: International Universities Press.

Rucker, H. (1968). *Transference and countertransference*. New York: International Universities Press.

Scharff, J. S., & Scharff, D. E. (1991). *Object relations couple therapy*. New York: Aronson.

Slipp, S. (1984). *Object relations: A dynamic bridge between individual and family treatment*. New York: Aronson.

Sullivan, H. S. (1953). *The interpersonal theory of psychiatry*. New York: Norton.

Weiss, J. (1993). *How psychotherapy works*. New York: Guilford Press.

Wells, M., & Glickauf-Hughes, C. (1986). Techniques to develop object constancy with borderline clients. *Psychotherapy, 23*(3), 460–468.

Wells, M., & Glickauf-Hughes, C. (1993). A psychodynamic object relations model for differential diagnosis. *Psychotherapy Bulletin, 28*(3), 41–49.

Wells, M., Glickauf-Hughes, C., & Buzzell, V. (1990). Treating obsessive-compulsives in psychodynamic-interpersonal group therapy. *Psychotherapy, 27*(3), 366–370.

Winnicott, D. W. (1965). *The maturational process and the facilitating environment*. New York: International Universities Press.

Young, D. M., & Beier, E. G. (1982). Being asocial in social places: Giving the client a new experience. In J. C. Anchin & D. J. Kiesler (Eds.), *Handbook of interpersonal psychotherapy*. New York: Pergamon Press.

CHAPTER 13

The Activation of Affective Change Processes in Accelerated Experiential-Dynamic Psychotherapy (AEDP)

DIANA FOSHA

THEORETICAL CONSTRUCTS

Accelerated experiential-dynamic psychotherapy (AEDP) is a model of psychotherapy that integrates psychodynamic and experiential elements, and does so within a relational framework (Fosha, 2000a, 2000b, 2001b; Fosha & Osiason, 1996; Fosha & Slowiaczek, 1997). The fostering and provision of new emotional experiences is its method and its aim. This is achieved through harnessing the transformational power of the core affective experiences associated with naturally occurring change processes involving *emotion, relatedness, the self, the body,* and *the process of transformation itself.* In optimal circumstances, these processes develop in the context of affect-regulating attachment relationships with caregivers; they are blocked or derailed when psychopathology-engendering life experiences prevail. It is precisely these naturally occurring affective change processes that AEDP seeks to reactivate.

The notion of a *state transformation* is fundamental to AEDP. A particular emotional state has a characteristic organization of arousal, attention, motivation, affect, cognition, and communication; the principles by which these psychological functions operate differ from one state to another. For instance, different principles underlie the neurophysiological and psychological functions characteristic of sleeping and waking states, or of states of trauma-induced shock and relaxation. A state transformation refers to a change that is neither gradual nor graded, but rather involves a quantum leap; there is a qualitative change to an altogether different organization that is discontinuous with the one that preceded it. Deep and direct emotional experiencing activates a state transformation, in which the body landscape and the concomitant psychic functions are organized according to a different principle. It is not just that the individual is feeling more or less: in this new state, body physiology, information-processing, affect, memory, cognition, and communication, as well as subjective self-experience, are organized to be optimally conducive to effective therapeutic work. The work proceeds differently, and better, than it does in states in which emotional experiencing is not in the visceral foreground or is actively blocked off.

The key mutative agent in AEDP is the state transformation leading to the visceral experience of core affective phenomena within an emotionally engaged dyad (Fosha, 2000b; Fosha & Slowiaczek, 1997). In turn, the visceral accessing of core affective experiences leads to a *further state transformation:* In the new state, referred to as the *core state,* intense, rapid, and mutative work readily takes place. The therapy goes faster, deeper, better; the patient has a subjective sense of "truth" and a heightened sense of authenticity and vitality; very often, so does the therapist (Fosha & Osiason, 1996). When we are outside these transforming affective states, therapeutic activities aim at getting access to them; when we are "there," therapeutic activities aim to make the most of the healing opportunities inherent within them. It is these state transformations the AEDP therapist seeks to bring about from the initial moments of the first therapeutic encounter and, from then on, moment-to-moment throughout the entire course of the therapy.

AEDP is rooted in the tradition of the experiential short-term dynamic psychotherapies (STDPs; Alpert, 1992; Coughlin Della Selva, 1996; Davanloo, 1990; Fosha, 2000b; Magnavita, 1997; Malan, 1976; Malan & Osimo, 1992; McCullough Vaillant, 1997; also see Fosha, 2000b, appendix, and Osimo, in Chapter 9 of this volume, for a history of the experiential STDPs). A deceptively simple schematic representation, *the triangle of conflict* (Malan, 1976, 1979), captures the psychodynamic basics at the heart of the experiential STDPs (see Figure 13.1). The individual's experience and expression of basic impulses and feelings lead to conflict and become associated with anxiety. Defense mechanisms are instituted to ward off the negative emotional consequences associated with the direct experience of impulses and feelings, and of anxiety. However anxiety-relieving in the short-run, long-term reliance on defense mechanisms restricts and

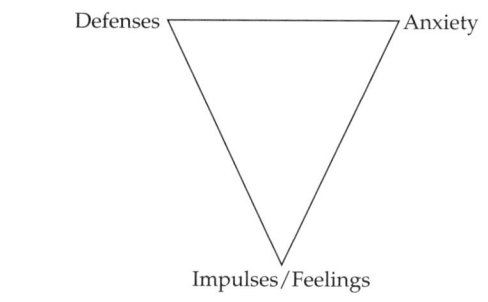

Figure 13.1 The triangle of conflict.

distorts the personality, causing the life problems and psychopathology for which the patient seeks help.

The experiential STDPs have been distinguished by innovations in stance and technique to rapidly overcome defenses, minimize the impact of anxiety, and facilitate direct and visceral access to the experience of previously defended-against feelings and impulses in the here and now relationship with the therapist. The acceleration of the experiential STDPs is not achieved through selecting a focus à la Malan (1976) or Sifneos (1987); identifying a core theme, à la Luborsky (Luborsky & Mark, 1991) or Mann (1973); or setting a time limit in advance, à la Malan (1976) or Mann (1973). Rather, accelerated change results from the deep and rapid transformations that occur in the wake of affective breakthroughs and the full processing of viscerally experienced emotion.

A model of therapy needs in its essence to be a model of change. The metapsychology of the therapeutic process should not be derivative from a theory of psychopathology, but rather should function as a strong explanatory framework in its own right. However, because the psychoanalytic/psychodynamic tradition from which the experiential STDPs emerged did not do justice to the rapidly transformational phenomena yielded by the application of their innovative techniques, for many years the experiential STDPs were a therapy without a theory.

Traditional psychoanalytic theory has been unequaled in its understanding of the processes through which psychopathology develops and is maintained. However, this depth of understanding of psychopathology has not been matched by a depth of understanding of the phenomena of healing. Whether explicating therapeutic change or developmental change, the psychoanalytic theory of change remains wedded to pathology. For example, in the Kleinian tradition, stages of normal and universal development are given clinical names (e.g., the *schizoid* and *depressive* positions), and the depressive position is seen as being as good as it gets. A transformational model rooted in pathology is much better at explaining how and why things do not change (or get worse) than it is at explaining how and why things get better.

The deep and rapid transformations that can be observed in the wake of the affective breakthroughs of the experiential STDPs push us to develop a model for therapy that can explicate the phenomenology and dynamics of change. Several bodies of theory and research have proven useful in helping to restructure traditional psychodynamics. AEDP has evolved a model that integrates their findings and insights on (1) emotion, (2) the regulation of infant-caregiver affective interactions, (3) the empathic reflection of the self, (4) somatic focusing, and (5) transforming experiences so as to be able to account for the therapeutic phenomena that emerge when the techniques of the experiential STDPs are applied.

1. *Emotion. Emotion theory and affective neuroscience* offer an account of change intrinsic to the experience of the categorical emotions (Damasio, 1994, 1999; Darwin, 1872/1965; James, 1890; Lazarus, 1991; LeDoux, 1996; Siegel, 1999; Tomkins, 1962, 1963), universal phenomena characterized by specific neurophysiological and body signatures, and by the state transformations and adaptive action tendencies released on their experience and expression.

2. *The regulation of infant-caregiver affective interactions. Attachment theory and the work of clinical developmentalists on moment-to-moment mother-infant interaction* document how optimal development and life-long resilient functioning have their roots in child-caregiver dyadic processes, highlighting the changes that occur as the result of the processes by which infants and caregivers moment-to-moment mutually regulate affective states (Beebe & Lachmann, 1988, 1994; Emde, 1981, 1988; Schore, 1994; Stern, 1985; Trevarthen, 1993; Tronick, 1989, 1998) and achieve safety and resonance despite the vicissitudes of attachment and relatedness (Ainsworth, Blehar, Waters, & Wall, 1978; Bowlby, 1982, 1988; Fonagy, Steele, Steel, Moran, & Higgitt, 1991; Main, 1995, 1999).

3. *The empathic reflection of the self. Empathy-based philosophical and therapeutic approaches* (Buber, 1965; Greenberg, Rice, & Elliott, 1993; Kohut, 1984; Rogers, 1961), *attachment theory* (Fonagy, Steele, Steele, Higgitt, & Target, 1994; Main, 1995), and *affective neuroscience* (Schore, 1994; Siegel, 1999) all document the transformational impact of self-reflective processes (the capacity to reflect on one's self born out of engaging in a reflective relationship with an other) on optimal development in general and emotional resilience in particular. The resulting high self-reflective capacity is a powerful protective factor against the development of trauma and has been shown to be one of the most powerful agents in stopping the intergenerational transmission of psychopathology.

4. *Somatic focusing. The somatic focusing experiential tradition* has documented a process where the psyche is transformed through the simple shifting of focus away from in-the-head cognition and toward moment-to-moment in-the-body sensing and feeling, a process that restores access to natural healing processes rooted in the body's basic adaptive mechanisms (Gendlin, 1981, 1991; Kurtz, 1990; Levine, 1997).

5. *Transforming experiences. A study of experiences that lead to rapid and profound change* (see

James, 1902, on religious conversions; Person, 1988, on intense love experiences; Buber, 1965, on authentic mutual communication) reveals that a focus on the experience of change itself triggers a deep transformational process with far-reaching consequences.

These works offer ample evidence of the mechanisms through which naturally occurring affective phenomena lead to rapid, deep, and long-lasting change. By going back and forth between clinical process and experience, on one hand, and the empirical literature, on the other, a first approximation of a metapsychology of therapeutics emerges.

AFFECTIVE CHANGE PROCESSES AND OPTIMAL DEVELOPMENT

AEDP has elaborated five affective change processes that, when harnessed in the therapeutic process, lead to powerful therapeutic results: (1) the experience and expression of core emotion; (2) the dyadic regulation of affective states, where the experiential focus is on the relational process; (3) the empathic reflection of the self, where the focus of both partners is on the experience of the self (of the patient); (4) somatic focusing, where the experiential focus is on the body; and (5) the activation of metatherapeutic processes, where the focus is on the very experience of transformation itself. All the change processes documented here are dyadically constructed and regulated. The hallmark of each process is a characteristic *core affective experience,* associated with a transformation of state specific to its mode of action. These change processes operate moment to moment; have clear-cut affective markers; operate through transformations of state, in which the new state is characterized by greater access to emotional resources to promote higher adaptive functioning; and thus, operate in quantum leaps rather than in a gradual and cumulative fashion.

A direct consequence of the focus on change and the study of affective change processes is an appreciation of the crucial role of positive emotional experiences in therapy. Because much of what has to be renegotiated in the course of treatment are difficult, painful experiences, at times of feared-to-be-unbearable proportions, therapy is commonly assumed to focus, of necessity, on the bad stuff; positive affective experiences are seen as the outcome of therapy, not inherent in and integral to the processes of therapy. There is no denying that the in-depth exploration of painful overwhelming matters is often excruciating, but the study of the features of processes of change has alerted us to previously ignored or misinterpreted phenomena. Not only are positive affective experiences part and parcel of the *moment-to-moment process* of transforming suffering, they are integral to a therapy that places a premium on effectiveness and efficiency, along with depth and thoroughness.

Naturally occurring affective change processes assume an affect-regulating emotional environment; they are rooted in an attachment matrix. The self's relationship with a caregiving other leads to the creation of the safe, affect-facilitating environment. Such an emotional environment allows these affective change processes to unfold, release their adaptive consequences, and access resources that are at the foundation of optimal functioning. Thus, the foundations of AEDP are in attachment theory. The attachment figure functions as a safe base (Ainsworth et al., 1978), a protection against danger, a presence that obviates fear. Alone, the immature organism is in danger, its very survival at stake. With a safe base, instead of aloneness and fear, there is the feeling of safety. The attachment relationship becomes internalized; the child can maintain the feeling of safety even when the caregiver is not physically present. The greater the feeling of safety (i.e., the greater the security of attachment), the wider the range of exploration and the more exuberant the exploratory drive (i.e., the higher the threshold before novelty turns into anxiety and fear).

In optimal development, an affect-facilitating environment supports the unfolding of core affective phenomena, thereby releasing adaptive processes that are fundamental to our optimal functioning and well-being. Viscerally experiencing deep emotion within an affect-facilitating relationship induces a state transformation that helps patients master vital psychological processes with profound implications for their life. The affect-facilitating environment is dyadically constructed, internalized, recreated, and reconstructed throughout the life span. The attachment relationship is negotiated and becomes established, elaborated, and differentiated through the engagement of both partners in the crucial processes by which transformation (i.e., growth, development, and learning), takes place through the interaction of self and environment. And those crucial processes are the naturally occurring change processes detailed below.

Applying the attachment model to the therapy situation, it is essential to establish a patient-therapist relationship in which the patient feels safe. From within an attachment perspective, emotional safety is defined as not being alone with frightening experiences. The safer the patient feels with the therapist, the greater will be that patient's capacity to explore the inner worlds of disturbing, frightening, and painful emotional experiences. In AEDP, we seek to proceed from a position of safety so as to be able to explore what is frightening, shameful, painful, and problematic. In both development and therapy, in a safe, affect-facilitating environment, affective change processes can be harnessed for the optimal adaptation of the individual. AEDP seeks to harness the power of these natural affective change processes to effect therapeutic results.

Therapeutic work with the affective change processes is thus a two-stage process, involving three states (defense, core affect, and core state) and two state transformations (from defense-dominated state to core affect, and from core affect to core state):

The full visceral experience of a specific core affective phenomenon constitutes the first state transformation. When interventions aimed at counteracting defenses, anxiety, and shame are effective, *core affective experience* is accessed. The state that occurs under the aegis of *direct and visceral core affective experience* is discontinuous with the defense-dominated state that precedes it. There is deep access to experiences that are crucial to adaptation and the characteristic processing is right-brain mediated [i.e., largely sensorimotor, image-dominated, visceral, nonlinear (Siegel, 1999, 2001)]. There is also much greater access to previously unconscious material (i.e., emotionally laden material previously inaccessible for dynamic reasons), a phenomenon referred to in the experiential STDP literature as "unlocking the unconscious" (Davanloo, 1990).

The shift from core affect to core state represents the second state transformation. This shift is invariably accompanied by positive affects. Thus, the full experience of core affect, unhampered by defense, culminates in the activation of another state, the *core state*, in which therapeutic work is at its most effective. In the core state, there is also no anxiety or defensiveness. The body is not rocked by any particular emotion. Instead, there is openness, vitality, relaxation, ease, and clarity. Working through, integration, and therapeutic consolidation optimally occur in the core state; here, therapeutic changes take root.

Core affect is like a spotlight, intensely illuminating a previously obscured segment of the emotional landscape that requires our attention. Once we attend to that segment, we gain a new perspective on our emotional life. In the core state, the entirety of the emotional landscape is visible, and it is evenly illuminated.

The following example illustrates the difference between core affect and core state: In working with a patient whose presenting problem involved anxiety-driven inhibitions in major areas of her life, experientially focusing on some current inhibitions led to memories, visual and somatic, of an earlier trauma. The patient became deeply immersed in the terror and grief associated with an accident she had been involved in when she was a teenager. The full experience of terror and grief (core affects) associated with the accident was followed by the visceral experience of rage (core affect) at her parents for dismissing her distress in their eagerness to restore the appearance of normality. Through completing the full experience of grief, terror, and rage together with a supportive other (the therapist), the patient accessed a core state, in which—with feeling and emotional conviction—she articulated her newly emergent understanding: the events that led to the accident, the accident itself, and its aftermath, were a microcosm of a lifetime of parental neglect and a childhood where a "road map" was always lacking. Freely and meaningfully roaming between the past and the present, the patient was able to articulate with startling clarity her lifelong emotional experience, making sense of her current difficulties and putting them in perspective (core state). Furthermore, she was able to do so with greater self-empathy than she had ever been able to muster toward herself prior to this work.

The phenomenology characteristic of each affective change process is described in Table 13.1. These change processes require an affect-facilitating emotional environment to support and emotionally engage the person who is activating, experiencing, and processing these phenomena and their sequelae.

The Experience of Core Emotion as a Process of Change

The experience and expression of emotion is a profound transformational experience. As William James (1902) wrote:

> Emotional occasions . . . are extremely potent in precipitating mental rearrangements. The sudden and explosive ways in which love, jealousy, guilt, fear, remorse, or anger can seize upon one are known to everybody. Hope, happiness, security, resolve . . . can be equally explosive. And emotions that come in this explosive way seldom leave things as they found them. (p. 198)

Emotions are crucial vehicles for adaptation (Damasio, 1994; Darwin, 1872/1965; Fosha, 2000b; Greenberg & Paivio, 1997; Lazarus, 1991; Tomkins, 1962, 1963). Being aware of, in touch with, and able to express emotions help individuals access biologically adaptive information that can assist them in negotiating life (Greenberg & Safran, 1987). Emotions convey information about the individual's appraisal of the environment, focus attention on what is most important to him or her, and thus motivate actions (in self) and responses (in others). Mediating interactions between self and environment, emotions are sources of information and personal meaning, and underlie experiences of authenticity and liveliness. The full cycle of experience and expression of emotion involves attention, appraisal, experience, information processing, expression, and communication (Fosha, 2000b).

Categorical, or core, emotions are deep-rooted bodily responses with their own specific physiology and arousal pattern (Ekman, 1983; Zajonc, 1985). Fear, anger, sadness, joy, disgust, all core affective phenomena, are each characterized by their own "distinctive biological signatures" (Goleman, 1995, p. 6). Two state transformations emerge from the process of fully and viscerally experiencing core emotion in the absence of defenses, anxiety, or shame:

1. *The direct and visceral experience of core emotion involves a state transformation.* Fully accessing a particular full emotion puts the spotlight on an area that requires the individual's heightened attention. The emotion is both spotlight and perceptual filter. The individual can thus

Table 13.1 The phenomenology of affective change processes.

Process	State Transformations		Consequences
Affective Change Process	Core Affective Phenomena	Core State Phenomena	Adaptive Consequences
Experience and Expression of Core Emotion	Core emotions: anger, sadness, joy, fear, disgust.	Adaptive action tendencies associated with each emotion; core state experiencing.	Emotional resources associated with each adaptive action tendency; unlocking unconscious material; new cycle of transformation activated.
Dyadic Regulation of Affective States: Attunement, disruption, and repair, leading to reestablished coordination.	Core relational experiences; affective resonance, "in sync" feelings in response to attunement; reparative tendencies in response to disconnection.	Feelings of intimacy and closeness; trust; core state experiencing.	Secure attachment; resilience; capacity to move easily between self-attunement and other-receptivity; unlocking unconscious material; new cycle of transformation activated.
Empathic Reflection of the Self: Empathy, validation, "going beyond mirroring."	Receptive affective experiences of feeling known, seen, and understood; having the sense of "existing in the heart and mind of the other."	"True self" experiences of feeling "alive," "real," "like myself"; core state experiencing.	Secure attachment; resilience; reflective capacity; self-esteem; consolidation of the self; empathy and self-empathy; unlocking unconscious material; new cycle of transformation activated.
Somatic Focusing: Shifting from in-the-head thinking to in-the-body sensing and feeling.	*The felt sense;* embodied experiencing.	*The body shift;* bodily states of relaxation, openness, and being in touch; core state experiencing.	Activation of self-righting tendencies; ease, calm, flow, energy, vitality, joie de vivre; unlocking unconscious material; new cycle of transformation activated.
Focus on the Experience of Transformation: The activation of the metatherapeutic processes: mastery; mourning the self; and affirming the self and its transformation.	Transformational affects: joy and pride; emotional pain; the healing affects of (a) feeling moved and emotional within oneself; (b) love, gratitude, and tenderness toward the other.	Adaptive action tendencies associated with each emotion; core state experiencing.	Self-confidence and exploratory zest; clarity, perspective, acceptance; empathy and self-empathy; unlocking unconscious material; new cycle of transformation activated.

address, appraise, become aware of, and understand the meaning of the situation arousing the emotion, and process its unique salience. Core emotions are also powerful motivators for action. Finally, core emotion constitutes a royal road to the unconscious (Fosha, 2000b, 2001a).

Through the specific emotion, the individual gains access to the previously unconscious network of feelings, thoughts, memories, and fantasies associated with the emotion. This is what allows the deep working through of dynamic material related to the roots of the patient's pathology. Thus, the experience of core affect reliably actualizes the fundamental psychoanalytic agenda of gaining access to the unconscious.

2. *The second state transformation, from core affect to core state, is marked by the release of adaptive action tendencies.* The very experience of the emotion activates emotional resources within the individual, essential to the resolution of the problem requiring heightened attention. Each emotion is associated with an adaptive action tendency: "Each emotion offers a distinctive readiness to act; each points us in a direction that has worked well to handle the recurrent challenges of human life" (Goleman, 1995, p. 4). With the release of the adaptive action tendencies, the individual (re)gains access to deep emotional resources, renewed energy, and an adaptive repertoire of behaviors, leading to enhanced functioning. The individual's new responses reflect access to new emotional information—about the self, the other, and the situation—that was not accessible prior to the full experience of the emotion. Even when the categorical emotion is itself negative and/or painful, as in the case of anger or grief, the core state that follows the release of the adaptive action tendencies is experientially highly positive. The adaptive action tendencies released by fully experienced anger often include a sense of strength, assertiveness, and power, which lead to the rediscovery of psychic strength, self-worth, and affective competence.

In normal development, and throughout the life cycle, emotions are regulated in a dyadic fashion. Through the dyadic process, the individual is able to emotionally process what he or she was not able to process alone, thus gaining access to the state-transformational potential of the core emotion described above (Fosha, 2001a, 2001b). Moreover, the dyadic process of affective regulation is a source of change in its own right; through coordinating emotions together, both partners are transformed. And this takes us to the second process of change, the dyadic regulation of affective states.

The Dyadic Regulation of Affective States as a Process of Change

Dyadic regulatory processes are involved in the optimal transformation of both relatedness and emotion, and thus of the self. As with emotion, adaptation is a central concept in understanding the function of dyadic regulatory processes.

The dyadic regulation of relatedness involves the attainment of coordination and collaboration between partners, allowing the simultaneous maintenance of connection and autonomy. Through emotional communication, we achieve equilibrium between self-regulation and mutual regulation. The regulation of affective states, when optimal, involves a moment-to-moment psychobiological process of *attunement* (the coordination of affective states), *disruption* (the lapse of mutual coordination), and *repair* (the reestablishment of coordination under new conditions). The coordinated state has positive affective markers and motivational properties; both partners experience pleasure on achieving coordination, strive to maintain it, and work hard to restore it when it is disrupted. The disruption of coordination is associated with negative affect; in healthy dyads, it activates reparative tendencies, which kick into gear until the disruption and its negative affects are repaired and coordination and positive affects are regained. Countless repetitions of the sequence of attunement, disruption, and repair lead to an affective competence, as the individual internalizes the affect-managing strategies of the dyad (Beebe & Lachmann, 1988, 1994; Fosha, 2000b, 2001a, 2001b; Tronick, 1989).

Experiences of attachment, connection, and mutuality lead to feelings of affective resonance, "in sync" states, and experiences of trust, intimacy, and closeness. These, in turn, promote further security of attachment, feelings of safety, and trust. The experience of being able to repair the stress of disrupted relatedness (i.e., transform negative affects into positive affects and disconnection into reconnection), leads to the individual's confidence in his or her own abilities and trust in the capacity of others to respond (Tronick, 1989). Success with efforts to repair dyadic disruptions leads to a certain emotional stick-to-itiveness which is at the heart of *resilience* (Fonagy et al., 1994) and *affective competence* (Fosha, 2000b). The process of moment-to-moment mutual coordination and affect regulation is considered to be the fundamental mechanism by which attachment is established (Schore, 2000). Furthermore, the maintenance of positive affective states associated with dyadic experiences of affective resonance has been shown to be crucial to optimal neurobiological development (Schore, 1996, p. 62; Siegel, 1999; Trevarthen & Aitken, 1994).

Here too we encounter the two-stage process of transformation:

1. The core affective experiences associated with the achievement of mutual coordination are affective resonance and "in sync" states, the "we" affects (Emde, 1988). Mutually acknowledging such experiences can "crescendo higher and higher," leading to *peak experiences of resonance, exhilaration, awe and being on the same wavelength with the partner* (Beebe & Lachmann, 1994, p. 157; italics added).
2. In the wake of these kinds of relational experiences—matching, affect sharing, and resonance—the core state comes to the experiential fore. Relational experiences of openness, closeness, intimacy, and mutuality, as well as an intensified sense of self, predominate.

Thus, the dyadic regulation of both ordinary and intense affective experiences produces the changes that are essential for optimal development. This has uncannily precise parallels in treatment (Fosha, 2000b, 2001b). Research shows that the therapist's attunement to the patient's affective state and the patient's experience of feeling safe, understood, and affectively resonated with are probably the most powerful contributors to the achievement of positive therapeutic outcome (Rogers, 1957; Rosenzweig, 1936; Truax & Carkhuff, 1967). When both partners feel in sync—the experiential correlate of the coordinated state—and engage around their respective experiences, the individual feels deeply understood and mutative therapeutic work can take place.

The Empathic Reflection of the Self as a Process of Change

Reflecting the self through the empathy of the other is the next process of change and resource for deep therapeutic transformation that will be examined. Experiencing one's self reflected through the empathy of the other (Kohut, 1977, 1984) evokes change; making authentic contact with another, *a moment of meeting* (Buber, 1965), allows one to go to a deeper place, where something new and different happens (Stern et al., 1998) and the self is transformed.

Though this, too, is a dyadic process, here the focus is on the experience of the *self*, which both dyadic partners are engaged in fostering and elaborating. The dyadic process is in the background, the self is in the foreground, and the vehicle of transformation is the other's empathic reflection, mirroring, and understanding of the self's experience (Kohut, 1977, 1984). Openly exposing a self state to someone who meets it and welcomes it with understanding can indeed transform it (Rice & Greenberg, 1991). For example, the patient who can speak of his or her sense of inferiority to an empathic other end up feeling less inferior. In being responded to by an other who is empathically attuned to the self, the individual changes, paradoxically becoming increasingly himself or herself (Fosha, 2000b).

Empathically reflecting the self is yet another affective transformational process, with powerful affective markers for its two characteristic stages of transformation:

1. The experience of receiving empathy and having one's self-experience mirrored, reflected, and empathically elaborated by the other gives rise to yet another class of core affective experiences, *receptive affective experiences,* the experiential correlates of feeling known, seen, loved, understood. Seligman (1998) notes: "Understanding is not *about* experience. It is itself an experience, and this experience involves the crucial presence of another person with whom one feels secure, in part by virtue of feeling understood by that person" (p. 84). McCullough Vaillant (1997) writes: "The receptive capacity is the substrate for vulnerability, openness, emotional connection, empathy, and intimacy" (p. 294). The individual develops a deep sense of "existing in the heart and mind of the other" (Fonagy & Target, 1998; Fosha, 2000b). The therapeutic consequences of these receptive affective experiences of feeling deeply understood are profound: In addition to promoting authentic self experiences, such experiences are believed to be at the roots of secure attachment and emotional resilience (Fonagy et al., 1994) and to function as a major protective factor against the development of trauma (Main, 1995, 2001; Siegel, 2001).

2. Fully experiencing and experientially processing receptive affective experiences facilitates the advent of the next stage, the emergence of *true self experiences.* True self experiences involve feeling "real," "alive," "authentic," and "like myself." Aspects of the core state, true self experiences may be accompanied by feelings of happiness, well-being, and relaxation, and by an almost aesthetic sense of simplicity, ease, and grace. One patient likened the true self experience to the sound of "a flute in a brass band." The experience of joy, authenticity, and aliveness, what the novelist Josephine Hart refers to as "the dazzling explosion into self" (1991, p. 41), echoes Fritz Perls's "explosion into joy, laughter, *joie de vivre* ... [that] connect[s] the authentic personality with the true self" (1969, p. 60). The individual's sense of self is accompanied by vitality affects (Stern, 1985).

The therapeutic consequences of empathically reflecting the self and the affective transformations it elicits include a strengthening and consolidation of the sense of self; enhanced and more solid self esteem, and augmented empathy toward the self. When the individual's attention is focused on his or her self through the empathic understanding and resonance of the other, the individual is presented with new opportunities for coping, mastery, and growth. Informed by growing self-empathy and self-acceptance, *adaptive self-action tendencies* are released: the individual realizes the nature of his or her basic needs and become committed to their realistic fulfillment.

Attachment research has shown that the parent's reflective ability is the key factor in the interruption of the intergenerational transmission of trauma (Fonagy et al., 1991, 1994; Main, 1995). Just one relationship with an attachment figure capable of engaging in a reflective relationship with the child promotes the child's development of his or her own reflective ability, which in turn is a major protective factor against the development of trauma (Fonagy & Target, 1998). These data provide empirical support for a core assumption of AEDP: The ability to process experience, together with an understanding other, is mutative; it transforms the experience, the self, and most likely the other (cf. Beebe & Lachmann, 1994; Beebe, Lachmann, & Jaffe, 1997; Tronick, 1989). There is also convincing evidence that it transforms what is interactionally communicated and intergenerationally transmitted.

Somatic Experience as a Process of Change
Somatic focusing theory also zooms in on adaptation and the organism's adaptive potential to self-regulate. Experiential clinicians, such as Eugene Gendlin (1981, 1991, 1996) and Peter Levine (1997), have documented the phenomenological

shifts that occur when the focus moves from in-the-head cognition to in-the-body sensing (see also Kurtz, 1990). They argue that eons of evolution have built into the body the capacity to right itself, what is referred to in the vernacular as the wisdom of the body. As with processes of core emotion and core relatedness, natural bodily processing of overwhelming events contain the seeds of healing within them (see Emde, 1981, on self-reparative tendencies, and Winnicott, 1960, on the dogged search of the true self for conditions right for its emergence). *The sense of what is wrong carries with it, inseparably, a sense of the direction toward what is right* (Gendlin, 1981, p. 76).

The evolutionary development of, and human beings' increasing reliance on, the neocortex has led to the cortical overriding of more instinctual mechanisms in situations requiring reactions and skills that the cerebral cortex is not optimally suited to handle (LeDoux, 1996). Somatic experiencing aims to change the focus from intellectual and cognitive processes, and their experientially alienating consequences, to activating somatic processes by fostering a process of moment-to-moment tracking of the body's shifting experiences. Changes that involve shifting focus from the head (cognitive, intellectual, verbally dominated) to the body (somatic, sensory, visual) also lead to deep experiential results. Key to this is the *felt sense*, "the experience of being in a living body that understands the nuances of its environment by way of its responses to that environment" (Levine, 1997, p. 69).

The process of somatic focusing—where there is an oscillation between experience and reflection, each feeding on the other—is a stepwise process.

The Felt Sense. The first state transformation involves finding *the felt sense*, "a bodily sense of some situation, problem, or aspect of one's life.... [A] felt sense must first be allowed to come; it is not already there. A felt sense is new.... It *comes* freshly, in something like tearfulness or yawning *come* in on us" (Gendlin, 1996, p. 20; italics in original text).

The Body Shift. The next state transformation is brought about through finding a *handle* (i.e., the verbal expression that does justice to that felt sense). The joining of the experience with the label that accurately describes it, an invariably idiosyncratic and highly personal term, is accompanied by a *body shift,* a relaxation, a letting go, a release of tension.

> With the emergence of such a single bodily sense comes relief, as if the body is grateful for being allowed to form its way of being as a whole.... When a step comes from a felt sense, it transforms the whole constellation ... in such a step or shift one sense oneself differently.... When one has a felt sense, one becomes more deeply oneself. (pp. 20–21)

The body shift, the state transformation associated with somatic focusing, is always in the direction of well-being.

Here, too, we see adaptive processes moving toward healing and positive changes, and the association of such processes with positive affective markers:

> The irony is that the life-threatening events prehistoric people routinely faced molded our modern nervous system to respond powerfully and fully when we perceive our survival threatened. To this day, when we exercise this natural capacity, we feel exhilarated and alive, powerful, expanded, full of energy and ready to take on any challenge. Being threatened engages our deepest resources and allows us to experience our fullest potential as human beings. In turn, our emotional and physical well-being is enhanced. (Levine, 1997, pp. 42–43)

Thus, by focusing on the sensations of the body with no agenda, another positive transformational process is activated in that a bodily core state marked by openness and relaxation is accessed. Even if the problem remains, the body is now in an optimal state where its capacities, its adaptive action tendencies, are maximally engaged. Furthermore, the very process of change itself, and not only its outcome, feels good. Therapists would do well to heed Gendlin's (1981) radical point, all the more profound for its simplicity: "Nothing that feels bad is ever the last step" (pp. 25–26).

Affective neuroscience provides further support. By having a process where there is an alternation of body-focused somatic experiencing (subcortical, right-brain mediated), with reflection on the somatic experience (cortical, left-brain mediated), there is the opportunity for a comprehensive bilateral integration based on harnessing the information-processing potential and abilities of both sides of the brain, as well as of lower and higher brain functions deemed essential to optimal health (Schore, 2000; Shapiro, 2001; Siegel, 1999, 2001).

Metatherapeutic Processes and the Focus on Transformation Itself as a Process of Change
In the last change process to be examined, it is precisely the experience of healing and therapeutic success that becomes the experiential focus of the work. What is usually the end point of the therapeutic road is the starting point of this investigation. When successful therapeutic experiences become the focus of therapeutic inquiry and work, it becomes possible to deepen and broaden the treatment's effectiveness (Fosha, 2000a).

The systematic exploration of the patient's experience of having a therapeutic experience activates highly reparative *metatherapeutic processes* associated with characteristic *transformational affects* (Fosha, 2000a). They are: (1) the *affective mastery process* and the transformational affects *of joy* and *pride*; (2) the *mourning-the-self process* and the transformational affect of *emotional pain*; and (3) the process of *affirming-the-self-and-its-transformation* and the transformational *healing affects* (i.e., feeling *moved, touched,* or *emotional,* and feeling *gratitude, love,* *tenderness,* and *appreciation* toward the affirming other). Thus, the very focus on the transformation in the context of the here-and-now of the therapeutic relationship releases mastery, mourning, and receptive affirming experiences.

The transformational affects associated with the metatherapeutic processes—joy and pride, emotional pain and the healing affects—are all core affective phenomena. It is here that AEDP's specific therapeutic technique is most evident. Once these experiences emerge, they are privileged, focused on, enlarged, and explored with the same thoroughness and intensity as any of the other core affective experiences. The visceral experience of core affect produces a state transformation. In these cascading state transformations, the deep experiential processing of one state becomes the trigger for the next wave. As in all other phases of AEDP, alternating waves of experiential and reflective work characterize the work with the metatherapeutic processes and their affective markers (Fosha, 2000b).

A focus on the process of transformation can be the catalyst for further transformations; experientially focusing on change that has already occurred activates further powerful changes. The process of transformation and healing is never-ending. The achievement of resolution at one level establishes a new plateau, which rapidly becomes the baseline from which the next cycle of transformation proceeds. By focusing on the patient's therapeutic experiences, we activate the metatherapeutic processes and their affective markers, the transformational affects. When fully experienced, these processes and affects in turn effect profound and beneficial transformations in our patients, consolidating and deepening already obtained therapeutic gains.

Summary of Change Processes: The Expansion of the Domain of Core Affective Experiences
AEDP focuses not only on the core emotions (labeled impulses/feelings in other experiential STDPs), but also includes the core affective

phenomena associated with the affective processes of change and the phenomena characteristic of core state functioning (see Figure 13.2).

The *core affective phenomena*, the results of the first state transformation, include: (1) *core emotions*, such as sadness, anger, fear, joy, disgust; (2) *core relational experiences* of and strivings for attachment, connection, intimacy, and closeness, including the "we" affects of affective resonance and in-sync experiences; (3) *vitality affects, self states, and receptive affective experiences* of feeling seen, cared about, and understood; (4) *bodily states* marked by the *felt sense*; and (5) the *healing affects* (i.e., experiences of feeling moved, emotional, and touched).

The introduction of the concept of the core state has led to the phenomenological articulation of another set of affective experiences, all positive, that occur in the absence of defenses as well as of anxiety, fear, or shame. *Core state phenomena* include but are not limited to (1) the sense of strength, clarity, and resourcefulness associated with the release of *adaptive action tendencies*; (2) *core relational experiences* of love, tenderness, compassion, generosity, and gratitude, relational experiences emergent from a state of *self*-possession; (3) *core self experiences* of what individuals subjectively consider to be their "true self;" (4) *core bodily states* of relaxation, openness, and vitality that emerge in the wake of the *body shift*; and (5) *states of clear and authentic knowing and communication* about one's subjective "truth."

Access to core affective phenomena provides the conditions necessary for thorough therapeutic exploration and working through, and leads to the release of the enormous healing potential residing within these experiences. The core state that follows the experience of core affect is optimally suited for the therapeutic integration and consolidation that translate deep in-session changes into lasting therapeutic results.

THE DEVELOPMENT OF PSYCHOPATHOLOGY

In AEDP, adaptation is the central motivational construct, equally relevant to understanding pathology, as to understanding optimal development. Different emotional environments give rise to optimal and psychopathological developments. When emotional experience can be dyadically regulated, optimal development takes place; an affect-facilitating environment is co-created and it eventually becomes part of the individual's internal attitude toward emotional experience. Pathological development occurs when emotional experience cannot be dyadically regulated and has to be excluded to preserve the attachment bond. The co-created affect-intolerant emotional environment also becomes internalized eventually. These formulations are schematically depicted in Figure 13.3. One version of the expanded triangle of conflict represents the structure underlying the self-at-best functioning characteristic of optimal development (see Figure 13.3a). The other version of the expanded triangle of conflict represents the structure underlying the self-at-worst functioning characteristic of psychopathology (see Figure 13.3b).

In optimal development, affective change processes naturally unfold and the individual

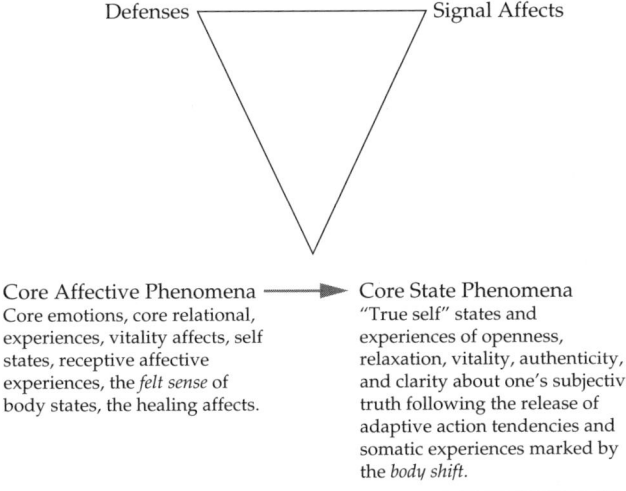

Figure 13.2 The expanded domain of core affective experiences.

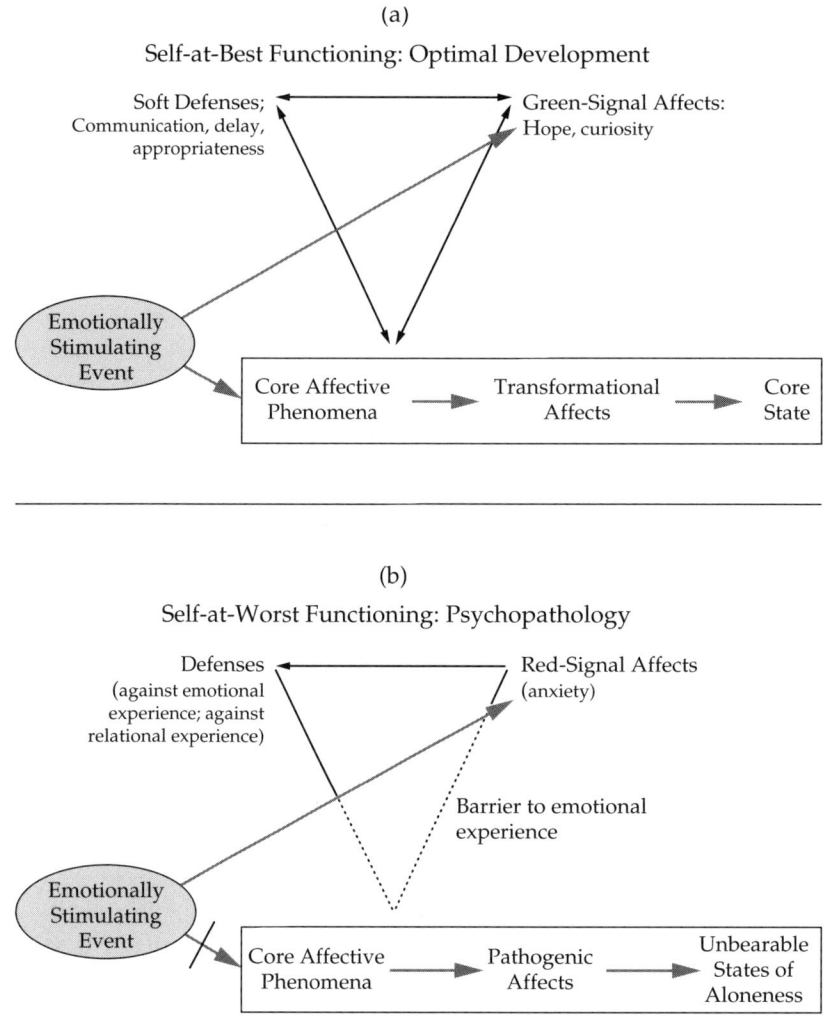

Figure 13.3 The two versions of the revised triangle of conflict.

can reap their adaptive benefits. Deep emotional experiences—occurring in the presence of a supportive, affect-facilitating other—become associated with feeling good. To authentically and deeply express oneself feels good as does feeling emotionally connected with someone. To feel understood feels good as does being understanding toward someone else who can receive it and be touched by it. Expressing painful feelings to a receptive partner also feels good. Positive affective states, markers for highly adaptive processes and experiences, ensures that we pay attention to and keep engaging in psychic activities that foster our development, growth, and expansion.

In optimal emotional environments, where the attachment figure is essentially accepting and supportive of the individual's emotions, core affective phenomena are paired with the *transformational affects*, positive experiences that mark the state transformation to the core state. The individual comes to expect that core emotional experience will lead to enhanced functioning, strengthening the integrity of self and/or of attachment ties. Over time, situations likely to arouse emotion will trigger the *green signal affects*, the signal version of the transformational affects. The green signal affects communicate essential safety and the go-ahead to feel. This is the self-at-best configuration that underlies optimal functioning represented in Figure 13.3a.

In pathogenic environments, the affective change processes, instead of bringing psychic gains, bring aversive results: The experience and expression of core affective phenomena meets with disruptive, nonfacilitating responses from attachment figures. The caregiver is unable to maintain coordination in the face of the child's spontaneous emotional experience; some aspect of the child's emotional being triggers profound discomfort in the caregiver, who responds either inadequately, with errors of omission (e.g., withdrawal, distancing, neglect, denial), or aggressively, with errors of commission (e.g., blaming, shaming, punishing, attacking). The expression of distress meets with the other's disdain or anxiety. The desire for contact meets with rejection or withdrawal. The offering of love is met with indifference or tension. Authentic self-expression meets with the other's anger or ridicule. These disruptive reactions on the part of the attachment figure (i.e., the errors of commission or omission), elicit a second wave of emotional reactions: fear and shame, *the pathogenic affects* (Fosha, 2001a). What should feel good ends up feeling bad; whereas transformational affects motivate further emotional experience, the pathogenic affects spur the exclusion of emotional experience.

Pathogenic affects arise when the response of the attachment figure to the individual's core affective experience is disturbing and disruptive. The disruption in mutual coordination caused by core affect cannot be dyadically repaired. The individual has to contend not only with the initial emotion-stimulating event and the overwhelming affective experiences it elicits; now he or she also has to contend with a second emotion-stimulating event, namely, the reaction of the figure of attachment, and the fear and/or shame it elicits.

There is a crucial distinction to be made between fear and shame as categorical emotions and fear and shame as pathogenic affects. As a categorical emotion, fear provides important adaptive information about the dangerous aspects of the situation that elicits it and kicks in the adaptive action tendencies associated with it. Fear triggers flight, immobility, but also notably, attachment-seeking behaviors. A child whose fear of a dog or of a stranger is overwhelming can seek out the caregiver for assistance. Similarly, shame as a categorical emotion about a specific event or behavior is an essential tool for social learning. That kind of shame can be metabolized in the context of an affect-facilitating environment (Hughes, 1998; Schore, 1996). Handling disruptive emotions is the essence of the process of attunement, disruption, and repair (Fosha, 2001a).

Fear and shame become problematic only when they occur in reaction to the attachment relationship itself. It is then that they function as pathogenic affects. Fear about the very person who is supposed to be the safe base disrupts the attachment relationship and its essential protective function (Hesse & Main, 1999). Shame that is not about a specific behavior but which, instead, is about the essential nature of the self disrupts the very integrity of self-experience and of the individual's ongoing sense of being (Hughes, 1998; Schore, 1996). When shame and fear are elicited by disruptive experiences with attachment figures and cannot be dyadically repaired, individuals find themselves alone, emotionally overwhelmed, unable to be real and unable to count on the safety of the emotional environment. Highly aversive, the hallmark of the pathogenic affects is that they are experienced by an individual who is alone, as the affect-regulating attachment relationship has collapsed.

The combination of (1) interrupted core affective experiences, (2) compromised self-integrity and disrupted attachment ties, and (3) the overwhelming experience of the pathogenic affects in the context of unwilled and unwanted aloneness lead to *unbearable emotional states:* these include experiences of helplessness, hopelessness, loneliness, confusion, fragmentation, emptiness, and despair, the "black hole" of human emotional experience. Hence, disrupted attachment and the compromised integrity of self result in unbearable emotional states that are to be avoided at all costs. If in the core state we encounter the *self-at-best*, in the unbearable emotional states, we have the *self-at-worst*: this is the individual at his or her most depleted, the sense of self essentially compromised, with no safety and thus no access to emotional resources. No wonder individuals will literally do anything to escape these states! The attempts to escape the excruciating experience of these unbearable emotional states become the seeds for defensive strategies that, when chronically relied on, culminate in the development of psychopathological conditions (see Table 13.2).

In disrupted attachments, core affect becomes paired with pathogenic affects and the unbearable emotional states. The individual comes to expect that core emotional experience will be catastrophic, threatening the integrity of self and/or of attachment ties. Over time, any situation that threatens to arouse emotion will trigger the *red signal affects*, the signal version of the pathogenic affects. The red signal affects automatically trigger the institution of defense mechanisms that preclude the experience of core affects and their feared-to-be-unbearable emotional consequences. The red signal affects communicate the same information as the pathogenic affects, without full-blown psychic pain: They signal that feelings are quite dangerous in the current conditions and thus to be warded off through the application of defenses. This is the self-at-worst configuration which underlies pathological functioning (see Figure 13.3b).

The patient comes to rely on defenses, denying, avoiding, numbing, or disavowing the affectively laden experiences that wreaked such havoc in the past and are expected to do so again. Psychic survival and a kind of secondary security (Main, 1995; Sandler, 1960) can be achieved only through the *defensive exclusion* (Bowlby, 1988) of the very processes that constitute optimal psychic health. Core affective experiences and their adaptive consequences are preempted, leaving the individual with terribly reduced resources to face the challenges of the world.

Some defenses are aimed at bodily experience, others at self or dyadic experiences, still others at particular emotions. A full taxonomy of the specific defenses associated with each change process is beyond the scope of this chapter. Some examples are: formal defenses, such

Table 13.2 Affect regulatory difficulties and the development of psychopathology.

Core Affective Phenomena	→	Failures of Dyadic Regulation	→	The Pathogenic Affects	→	Unbearable States of Aloneness	→	Consequences
Core emotions; core relational experiences; reparative tendencies in response to disconnection; "true self" experiences; spontaneous bodily states; the realization of emotional truth; the healing affects.		Misattunement and the failure to repair: *errors of omission* (withdrawal, avoidance, denial, neglect); *errors of commission* (criticism, humiliation, punishment, ridicule).		Fear, shame.		Loneliness, despair, helplessness and hopelessness, emptiness; sense of self as "bad," "defective," "worthless"; fragmentation, loss of control, falling apart, confusion, panic.		The institution of defenses against experiencing and/or relatedness.

as isolation of affect or denial, that prevent the experience of the categorical emotions; defenses in the realm of dyadic regulation that involve a hyperfocus on self or other and are reflected in the types of insecure attachment; defenses against receptive affective experiences, the other side of the interpersonal wall, that are usually accompanied by denial of, or hypofocus on, the self; defenses against somatic processes that include numbing, body armoring, mannerisms, and postural distortions; and the denial of change, the failure to register it, and such phenomena as false modesty or hypernegativity that can be manifestations of defenses against the healing affects and the underlying vulnerability. However, once a defense becomes entrenched in the individual's repertoire, it can function against any aspect of emotional experiencing that might be threatening to the individual, regardless of the initial dynamic realm in which it arose.

These formulations are schematically represented in the two versions of the triangle of conflict represented in Figure 13.3, showing the interrelatedness of core affective experiences, signal affects and defenses in affect-facilitating and affect-inhibiting emotional environments.

THE AIM OF TREATMENT

Treatment aims to undo the chronic reliance on defenses against core affective experiencing, thereby restoring the patient's natural healing and self-reparative tendencies. *The ultimate goal of therapy is to change the structure of the patient's experience of what feels good.* We do this by restoring the association between safety and emotional experiencing.

In AEDP, the goal is *to lead with* (Fosha, 2000b) a corrective emotional experience (Alexander & French, 1946). The therapist seeks to create an affect-facilitating environment from the get-go and to activate a patient-therapist relationship in which the patient is in touch with his or her resources as much as possible. If this is accomplished, from the beginning, the patient will feel sufficiently safe to be willing to take the risks involved in doing deep and intensive emotional work (Fosha & Slowiaczek, 1997). The theory behind the stance of the AEDP therapist is grounded in attachment theory, whereby the function of the therapist is to counteract the patient's aloneness by being a safe base so that exploration can begin. Pathogenic affects and previously unbearable emotional states become more tolerable and are eventually transformed as they are explored together with an other, from the position of the safe base. AEDP treatment seeks to (1) counteract the patient's aloneness and transform the experience of unbearable states; (2) minimize the impact of defenses and of the pathogenic affects of fear and shame; (3) restore access to core emotions, and thus to the wellspring of adaptation and well-being; and (4) facilitate the emergence of the core state.

The four steps to restore access to core affective experiencing are:

1. Through a *therapeutic stance* that is actively and explicitly empathic and actively and explicitly emotionally engaged. The therapist facilitates the patient's affective experience through being affirming, supportive, and authentic. There is a high premium on the use of the self in the form of making use of the therapist's authentic emotions.
2. Through active, specific, and systematic therapeutic activities designed to *melt or break through defenses*.
3. Through active, specific, and systematic therapeutic activities aimed at countering the pathogenic affects.
4. Through active, specific, and systematic therapeutic activities aimed at *facilitating core affective experiences*, releasing adaptive action tendencies, and allowing the seeds of healing contained within the visceral

experience of core affect to come to the fore, thus activating the core state, where maximal therapeutic healing takes place.

Essential to the carrying out of AEDP is the grounding in the phenomenology of affective experience. Therapists' familiarity with the phenomena associated with change processes and pathological processes will enable them to be firmly grounded in the patient's experience, using that experience as a constant guide regarding the state of the patent, the state of the relationship, and the state of the therapeutic process. Through a moment-to-moment immersion in experience and its fluctuations, patient and therapist are able to engage in what is the hallmark of AEDP: an experiential dyadic process informed by an affect-centered psychodynamic understanding devoted to promoting full visceral experience of core affective phenomena, thus unleashing the transformational power of the processes of change.

HISTORY OF THE THERAPEUTIC APPROACH

Because history of the experiential STDPs is discussed elsewhere (see Osimo, this volume), this section only briefly highlights the differences between AEDP and the other experiential STDPs that emerge as a result of the theoretical framework outlined. Healing processes, rather than psychopathology, are at the very center of the affective model of change, the metapsychology that informs AEDP (Fosha, 2000b).

1. There is an expansion of the phenomenological realm of core affective phenomena as a result of the theoretical grounding in multiple processes of change (and thus not just one change process). This includes core affective phenomena associated with each affective change process, core state phenomena, and the affective experiences that arise in nonaffect-facilitating environments (i.e., the pathogenic affects and the unbearable emotional states).

2. The emphasis on the differential nature of the co-constructed environment in optimal and pathogenic development has led to the awareness of multiple configurations of core affect, signal affect, and defense within the same individual underlying quite different levels of functioning. This has led to the elaboration of different versions of the triangle of conflict—the self-at-best and self-at-worst configurations—and the respective role of positive and negative environmental experiences, which become differentially encoded in the form of signal affects—green or red.

3. In AEDP, the therapeutic stance is seen as a dyadic construction and thus unique to each dyad. Although empathy, compassion, and affirmation always characterize the genotype of the AEDP therapist's stance, its phenotype is always unique and idiosyncratic, inasmuch as it is a stance grounded in dyadic construction (Tronick, 2001).

4. From within an affirming and emotionally engaged stance, the AEDP therapist seeks to lead with a corrective emotional experience, aiming to engage the patient's least defensive, most emotionally resourceful self-state, represented by the self-at-best configuration. Through the process of mutual coordination of affective states, patient and therapist coconstruct an affect-facilitating therapeutic environment in which the defended against painful and intense core affective experiences, encoded in the self-at-worst configuration, can be accessed, experienced, worked through, and reintegrated within the personality in a more adaptive fashion.

The techniques that follow assume all of these developments.

METHODS OF ASSESSMENT AND INTERVENTION

THE TRIAL THERAPY

The trial therapy (Davanloo, 1990; Malan, 1976) is the major assessment tool in AEDP, as it is in the other experiential STDPs. The therapist is primed to cocreate an affect-facilitating environment and a corrective relationship within which to begin the therapeutic work. The AEDP therapist does not wait for the material to unfold but actively fosters the kind of interaction the model defines as optimal. As the patient begins to tell the therapist his or her story (or not tell it), the therapist has access to two potent sources of dynamic and diagnostic information: the content of the story, manifest and latent, and the interactive process between patient and therapist. Taking whatever the patient offers, the therapist uses it as starting point for an affective experiential interaction. At the first sign of affect, the therapist stops the action and shifts the focus to the affect; the message is: This is what we do here. The moment-to-moment experiential tracking of the flow of the session has begun. Severity of functional disturbance, chronicity of the problem, or the point in development at which the problem is thought to have arisen in the patient's genetic past do not play an automatic role in determining suitability for AEDP. Showing a capacity to engage and work experientially augurs well and is heavily weighted against other factors. The patient's capacity to respond affectively and engage relationally is a major selection criterion, as it indicates the patient's capacity to make use of the therapy being offered.

AEDP trial therapy always begins with the present situation: "The precipitating event is, in truth, the final blow that simply cannot be tolerated" (Mann & Goldman, 1982, p. 24). In the presenting complaint and the specific example are the patient's response to the therapist's first and second questions: What brings you here now? followed by Can you give me a specific example? The presenting complaint represents a "final common pathway" (p. 20) of core conflicts, anxieties they elicit, defenses deployed, and consequences of those defenses. The request for a specific example announces the departure from vagueness: The work of therapy has begun. The emotionally charged atmosphere of the first minutes of the first session offers tremendous opportunities as the first set of dynamics that underlie the suffering the patient is seeking to remedy is exposed. Two further explorations are a desired feature in every trial therapy: There needs to be a somatic/experiential/affective exploration (grounded in a specific example: How do you feel? How do you experience that? Where in your body?), as well as a relational exploration of the here-and-now experience with the therapist: What is it like for you to do this with me? How do you feel when you have eye contact [or avoid eye contact] with me?

By following the patient's affect, it is possible to see how it links present and past and how it becomes manifest in the evolving patient-therapist relationship. The relationship with the therapist evokes intense feelings; from the first minutes of the first session, the therapist declares that he or she wishes to relate to the patient. By focusing on the patient's feelings, asking for specifics, and responding empathically and emotionally, the therapist activates the patient's complex feelings about intimacy and closeness.

That the first session presents a unique opportunity is recognized by many STDP therapists (e.g., Coughlin Della Selva, 1996; Davanloo, 1990; Magnavita, 1997; Malan, 1976, 1979; Mann & Goldman, 1982; McCullough Vaillant, 1997). Gustafson (1986) writes about the "sacred nature of the first session" and how important it is to focus on what brought the patient to treatment. If the precipitating event is a "common pathway," hope and dread inspired by the encounter with the therapist shape the dyadic interaction, making their encounter the second common pathway.

The greater the crisis, the greater the opportunity. Affective charge creates an intrapsychic crisis and therefore fluidity (Lindemann, 1944); the result is an unmatched opportunity to get past the patient's customary defenses. During such a crisis, the patient's customary ways of handling intense feelings becomes evident, as does his or her ability to respond differently as the therapist engages the patient in new ways of relating.

In this first session, patient and therapist, as members of a brand-new dyad, are creating their own unique patterns. As both bring best and worst configurations, much is possible and nothing is yet determined. Such a fortuitous chance for creation might never arise again in the course of their relationship. Another source of dynamic information is the moment-to-moment therapeutic process. Making interventions and observing their impact is a form of hypothesis testing.

In keeping with AEDP's healing-centered orientation and adaptation-based framework for understanding psychopathology, the therapist is always on the lookout for evidence of strength, ease, and resourcefulness. Areas of psychic health are as important to a thorough psychodynamic assessment as areas of difficulties. The following are some questions for therapists to ask themselves during the initial interview:

Has contact been made? If the therapist thinks so, does the patient? If the patient thinks so, does the therapist?

What are areas of defensiveness and areas of ease? What are areas of difficulty in the patient's life and areas of pleasure?

What defenses does the patient use, and what resources are available?

What makes the session flow? What makes the session get stuck?

How does the patient respond to empathy, validation, and support? To confrontation?

How does the patient respond to his or her own emotionality, or to the lack thereof?

What are the patterns of relational repetition, and what kinds of environments trigger them? What are the exceptions?

What feelings are difficult for the patient, and what feelings not so hard? Can the patient experience, for example, sadness but not anger, or anger but not vulnerability? Are positive feelings more difficult than negative feelings (or vice versa)? Are all feelings difficult?

How does the patient handle negative feelings such as anger, pain, and disgust? How does the patient handle positive feelings such as joy, love, pleasure, and tenderness?

Can the patient tolerate negative aspects of the session, that is, areas of stuckness, disagreement, confrontation, or disappointment? Can the patient tolerate positive aspects of the therapeutic interaction, that is, empathy, collaboration, closeness, contact, and hope?

What brings out the worst in the patient? What is he or she like at worst? What brings out the best in the patient? What is he or she like at best?

The first interview has several purposes: to establish contact with the patient; to learn the story of what brings the patient to treatment; and to uncover the way the patient's seemingly excessive or incomprehensible reactions make complete sense. The most important goal for the first session, however, is that *the patient should have a therapeutic experience,* a visceral feeling for at least a moment of self-at-best in the context of a dyadic relationship. From the beginning, the therapist begins to share with the patient his or her empathic understanding of the patient's experience and of the therapeutic interaction. A therapeutic aim is to give the patient experiential access to healing affects that unlock access to other corrective affect-facilitating experiences, which, for whatever dynamic reason, were relegated to marginality or to dynamic oblivion, or have been accessible but robbed of their reparative restorative potential. If, in the initial session, the patient has some moments of core affect and then core state experiencing, he or she will have had a taste of the freedom that comes with emotional access and will have had a visceral experience of their own resources and positive qualities. Such experiences are intensely motivating (Davanloo, 1990). This is why we seek to proceed from strength to face vulnerability and seek to lead with a corrective emotional experience.

METHODS OF INTERVENTION

Essential to all AEDP methods of intervention is the moment-to-moment experiential tracking of the patient's state in the context of the dyadic interaction. It is what determines and guides the selection of interventions, what gives the therapist precise feedback about the patient's response to each intervention, and what provides the precise raw data necessary for an accurate and thorough psychodynamic understanding both of the moment-to-moment therapeutic process and of the patient's personality organization as a whole. The work is approached from a stance of affirmation and empathy and support and valuation of the patient: The understanding of clinical phenomena is informed by an adaptation-focused and healing-centered approach.

The phenomenology of the states of defense, core affect, and core state, and the therapist's ability to read and interpret them correctly are crucial because the entire AEDP approach is rooted in the patient's experience. What strategies the therapist uses at any specific time depends on being able to accurately sense the patient's state, for each state is characterized by a different therapeutic goal.

1. In a state where defenses predominate, the goal is to help patients relinquish their defensive reliance. Unless transformed, in the top of the triangle of conflict state, nothing deeply therapeutic happens. There are highly confrontational ways to work with defenses and there are deeply accepting, removing-the-pressure, paradoxical ways to proceed (little-step-by-little-step attunement). Enhancing the patient's experience of safety and thus rendering defenses vestigial is another strategy. But the goal of all interventions aimed at defense is the same: to foster the state transformation from top of the triangle of conflict functioning to core affect in which the impact of defenses is neutralized (i.e., the state transformation from defensive functioning to core affective experiencing).

2. When dealing with the affective phenomena represented at the bottom of the triangle of conflict, a major focus is the promotion of embodied, visceral experiencing. There are different goals and thus different therapeutic interventions tailored to the different types of affective phenomena represented at the bottom of the triangle of conflict. *Core affective experiences* require a type of therapeutic work different from that needed for the *pathogenic affects* and *unbearable emotional states*. All three are categories of affective experience that come to the fore in the absence of anxiety and defense, yet there are different therapeutic goals with each.

With the pathogenic affects and the unbearable emotional states, the goal is to ultimately eliminate these from the patient's emotional repertoire. They serve no adaptive function for the individual. In fact, they both reflect, and are a consequence of, the disintegration and depletion of adaptive resources. Merely reexperiencing them proffers no therapeutic benefit (see also Levine, 1997, on this point). Therapeutic benefits accrue only if the patient's emotional aloneness is counteracted. Originally, the pathogenic affects and unbearable states arose in an individual deprived of the benefits of dyadic regulation when sorely in need of help, and further overwhelmed by the onslaught of aversive affects associated with attachment disruptions. What is transformational and therapeutic here and now is the sharing of these experiences with a supportive, helpful, emotionally engaged other. At stake here is restoring the matrix of affect-regulating attachment. It is not enough for the therapist to "be with" the patient; active therapeutic work *also* needs to take place to make sure that the patient takes in (i.e., registers and processes) the therapist's presence and involvement (see Fosha, 2001b, for elaboration of this point). In order for the experience of emotional aloneness to be therapeutically transformed, it is essential that defenses against receptive affective experience not be in operation.

The work with core affective phenomena is different from the work with the pathogenic affects and the unbearable states. Emotional access to these phenomena assumes an affect-facilitating environment already in place. It is either internalized and reflected in the affective competence of the individual, and/or is being actively coconstructed dyadically and is operating in the background at that moment. Given a solid affect-regulating attachment environment, it is the therapeutic and adaptive benefits that emerge on the full visceral experiencing of core affects themselves that are the therapeutic goal. When the adaptive action tendencies kick in, the next experiential depth level is activated and the transformation to core state is under way.

3. The most important therapeutic goal in working with the third state, the core state, is for the therapist to recognize it and promote its unfolding. Once core state is achieved, the therapy runs itself. With patients in core state, the therapist's activities can be reflective, collaborative, experiential, mirroring, or witnessing. The therapist can validate and receive and participate in deep collaborative dialogue that is simple, essential, and "true." Just being present and listening deeply is sometimes precisely what is needed. Often, the most powerful work can be done when both patient and therapist are in core state (which is not unusual). At those peak moments, characterized as I-Thou relating (Buber, 1965) or true-self/true-other relating (Fosha, 2001a), some of the deepest therapeutic work can take place.

Technically, all AEDP techniques aim to (1) undo emotional aloneness, (2) bypass defenses, (3) neutralize and reverse the inhibiting impact of the pathogenic affects, and (4) promote visceral embodied experience of core affect and core state. There are specific techniques that focus on getting there (i.e., effecting the state transformations) and specific techniques for doing the therapeutic work once one actually does get there (i.e., regulating, deepening, and working through techniques for working with core affect and core state). These techniques are outlined in Table 13.3. A detailed discussion of each technique is beyond the scope of this chapter. (For a more detailed discussion, see Fosha & Slowiaczek, 1997; Fosha, 2000b, Chaps. 10–13.)

With an understanding reflecting the integration of the psychodynamic, relational, and experiential therapeutic traditions, the therapist's activities are rooted in the moment-to-moment tracking of the patient's experiential access to these sources of transformation. The AEDP therapist helps the patient bypass defenses (psychodynamic contribution) and enhance embodied visceral experience (experiential contribution) in the context of an affirming affect-facilitating relationship (relational component). AEDP treatment harnesses the transformations arising from (1) the experiencing of core emotion, (2) the dyadic regulation of affective states, (3) the empathic reflection of the patient's self experience, (4) somatic focusing, and (5) a focus on the very experience of transformation. Focusing on affect

Table 13.3 AEDP intervention techniques.

Relational Strategies

Facilitating patient-therapist relational experiences: Moment-to-moment tracking and focusing on relational engagement; engaging authentically and using one's experience; leading with affirmation, support, and encouragement; exploration of experience of relatedness.

Expression of therapist's support and affirmation: Making the nonspecific factors of treatment treatment-specific: Validating, affirming, and appreciating patients and their experience: expressing care, compassion, and concern; offering encouragement and being helpful; acknowledging, validating, and amplifying healthy responses; recognizing, validating, and appreciating self-empathy and self-care; exploring patients' reaction to support and affirmation.

Expression of therapist's empathic response: Explicit expression of empathy; empathic elaboration; exploring patients' reactions to empathy.

Expression of therapist's affective experience: Affective self-disclosure; self-disclosure; acknowledging errors, vulnerability, limitations; disclosure of therapist's experience of and responses to the patient; receptiveness to patient giving and acknowledgment of impact; self-disclosure to counteract therapeutic omnipotence; exploring reactions to therapist's self-disclosures.

Promoting intimacy and closeness through little-step-by-little-step attunement and coordination, and repair of lapses of attunement and coordination: Sharing, reflecting, and participating in patients' moment-to-moment experiences; becoming aware of the rhythms of attunement, disruption, and repair; initiating reparation in the face of disruption; being responsive to and acknowledging patients' reparative attempts; reactions to therapeutic intimacy.

Collaborative work with patient: Reciprocal monitoring of nonverbal communication; comparing views; recognizing and making use of patients' psychological expertise.

Restructuring Strategies

Tracking moment-to-moment fluctuations in openness versus defensiveness: Encouraging patients' awareness of fluctuations; encouraging patients to explore the differential experiential correlates of states of open and blocked states.

Working with defensive responses: Identification, labeling, and clarification of defenses; validation of adaptive function of defenses in the past; experientially focused defense work and evocative shorthand; appreciative reframing; cost-benefit analysis; removing the pressure.

Working with red-signal affects of anxiety and fear: Exploration of physical concomitants of anxiety; exploration of cognitive, fantasied, and experiential aspects of anxiety; finding meaning and making sense; reassurance, reframing through accurate labeling, education; removing pressure and appreciating patients' hard work and accomplishments.

Working with red-signal affect of shame: Validating patients' emotional experience; exploration of physical concomitants of shame; exploration of cognitive, fantasied, and experiential aspects of shame; shifting shame focus from self to specific behaviors, understood empathically; not throwing out the baby with the bathwater; normalizing, praising, valuing; helping patients tolerate the experience of pride.

Working with green-signal affects: Focusing and tracking affects; familiarizing patients with affects and their informational significance; counteracting denial through amplification.

Affect restructuring: Exploring differences between the experience and the expression of affect; feeling and dealing; exploring the difference between defense mechanisms and socially appropriate mechanisms of delay, modulation, and discrimination in the expression of relational experience; looking at core affect from the perspective of core state.

Tracking moment-to-moment fluctuations in positive versus negative aspects of self and relational experience: Coming to understand how self, other, and emotion are interdependent; juxtaposing good and bad states; understanding dyadic nature of self-at-best and self-at worst states.

Experiential-Affective Strategies

Facilitating genuine affective experience: Direct moment-to-moment tracking of affect; translating ordinary language into language of feelings, motivation, and desire; encouraging patients to stay with and tolerate deepening emotional experience; sharing in the emotional experience.

Mirroring: Mirroring patients' affect; affective resonance; anticipatory mirroring; amplifying affect.

(continued)

Table 13.3 *(Continued)*

Going beyond mirroring: Complementary coordination (e.g., responding to patients' fear with reassurance, to patients' anger with acknowledgment); helping in the bearing and processing of overwhelming emotion; the coach approach (i.e., encouraging patients to persist and affirming the value of trying to do so).

Sharing in the bearing of pathogenic affects and unbearable states: Framing patients' experience in adaptive context; validating and affirming essential aspects of patients' experience and refuting pathogenic spin on it; explicitly sharing in the painful experience; focusing on patients' experience of therapist's emotional engagement and affirmation (see Going beyond mirroring; Working with defenses against receptive experience).

Naming and acknowledging affective experience.

Somatic focusing: Focusing on body-rooted correlates of experience: Direct tracking of bodily sensations and fluctuations therein; attending to felt sense and body shift experiences; teaching the somatic monitoring of experience; experimenting with being active in transforming somatic experience; exploring somatic and visceral correlates of triangle of conflict categories.

Portrayals: Imagined interactions and their dynamic-experiential correlates: Portrayal; completion of portrayal; affective portrayal to complete interrupted affect sequences; internal dialogue portrayals (to help with issues of shame, guilt, ambivalence, and dissociation); impulse, affect, and interpersonal desensitization portrayals; reparative portrayals.

Reflective-Integrative Strategies

Metaprocessing of affective-relational experience (end of episode of experiential work; end-of-session processing; end of treatment processing): Alternating waves of reflection and experience and reflection on experience.

Comparing repeating versus emergent reparative patterns of interaction: Comparing relationship patterns; sensitizing patients to repetitions of interpersonal patterns, both painful and affirming; sensitizing patients to "new" patterns, or departures from repetitions, both painful and affirming; exploring the role of self and other in the construction of interpersonal patterns, while exploring their consequences for self experience.

Integrative processing: Creating a new, psychodynamically informed autobiographical narrative from the perspective of core state.

---

transformation helps patients heal, thrive, and increasingly approach becoming who they are.

MAJOR SYNDROMES, SYMPTOMS, PROBLEMS TREATED USING AEDP

AEDP can be utilized with a wide variety of outpatients. It is suitable for patients presenting with Axis I symptomatology (i.e., anxiety disorders, dysthymia, etc.) as well as for patients with Axis II personality disorders (e.g., Avoidant, Dependent, and Histrionic personality disorders). AEDP is particularly suited to pathology where issues of loss (e.g., pathological mourning) are central. Exclusion criteria include all psychotic disorders, bipolar disorders, Major Depression, impulse disorders, marked acting-out behavior, and substance abuse disorders. Generally, disorders resulting from the overregulation of affect are more suitable for AEDP than disorders resulting from its underregulation.

For more severely disturbed patients, such as those with Somatoform, Dissociative, and/or Borderline Disorders, rather than rigid selection/exclusion criteria, the trial therapy plays a major role in determining suitability for treatment. Response to trial therapy is weighed heavily against other considerations. If the patient responds to the trial therapy with deepening rapport and increased motivation resulting from affective engagement, the patient is likely to be taken into therapy even in the face of other concerns. However, if in the course of the trial therapy, the patient exhibits disorganizing anxiety, fragmentation, identity confusion, paranoid ideation, thought blocking, and/or other signs of a fragile personality structure, even in the absence of other exclusion considerations, AEDP is not the treatment of choice. A less affectively arousing and relationally stimulating treatment approach, such as cognitive or supportive therapy, would be recommended.

There is, however, one diagnostic group usually considered difficult to treat that AEDP has had success with: patients with Narcissistic Personality Disorder (see also Trujillo, this volume). They often present with subclinical Axis I disorders of anxiety and/or depression (dysthymia). Stress-related somatic disorders (Somatoform Disorders) are common, as are substance abuse tendencies (though that is not the primary diagnosis). Their disorder of self experience can be severe and quite debilitating. Though these patients often work, have relationships, families, and *appear* high functioning, they are propelled into treatment by frightening dysphoria, emptiness, despair, and deadness (Eigen, 1996). These latter experiences are the long-term legacy of the personality disorder and where AEDP interventions can be quite effective.

Included here under the rubric of disorders of the self are both frank Narcissistic Personality Disorders and personalities constructed around significant narcissistic vulnerabilities, usually referred to as disorders of the self. These two subgroups are referred to by Magnavita (2000) as patients manifesting either *the narcissistic dysfunctional personologic system* or *the covertly narcissistic dysfunctional personologic system*. According to Magnavita's description, the patient manifesting a *narcissistic personologic system*

> manifests a reversal of the parent-child subsystem, with either spouse or children catering to the unmet needs of one or more family members. A sense of entitlement often predominates the family system and an air of superiority covers an essential emotional defect. Members of these systems appear to "have it all" and elicit admiration from those who are not too close to them. Achievement is expected of all members regardless of cost. This description fits families in American society that have been placed on a pedestal, but whose succeeding generations manifested a litany of substance abuse, unethical conduct, and so forth that indicated a deep emotional void. (p. 135)

The patient manifesting a *covertly narcissistic dysfunctional personologic system*

> is characterized by narcissistic dynamics but in a more hidden fashion than the [covertly narcissistic dysfunctional personologic system]. The reversal of the parent-child subsystem has a much more subtle feel to it; it is not out in the open. The basic dynamic is that the children, but most often one child, becomes a mirror for the incomplete identity of a parent. This process is discussed in the writings of Miller (1981) and Kohut (1977) who [spoke of the] "not good enough mother" to refer to *a maternal-child relationship that does not sufficiently fulfill the needs of the child. There is a deficiency in the nurturing, mirroring capacity of the parental figures and an expectation that the child will inordinately satisfy the validation needs of the parental figures.* Some members of these systems may appear to be highly functional and productive members of society; others, however, may function only marginally and are often described as the black sheep of the family. *Emotion, if recognized, is not adequately processed or assimilated* so that family members seem emotionally underdeveloped or with well-developed false selves. (p. 138; italics added)

Noteworthy in the histories of patients manifesting covertly narcissistic personologic systems is a parent with a history of major trauma, unresolved loss, or often undiagnosed but significant metal illness. The impact on the second generation of unresolved loss and trauma in the parent is currently the focus of intensive empirical investigations (Hesse & Main, 1999; Lyons-Ruth, 2001; Main, 2001). These patients also have recently been characterized as manifesting a disorganized attachment style, which overlaps with or is identical to dissociative disorders (Liotti, 1995, 1999). In these parent-child constellations, those aspects of the child's emotional experience that serve the parent's well-being are highlighted and co-opted for the parent's self-regulation; those that fall outside it are ignored or ridiculed. Usually, the child's needs heighten the parent's own anxiety, shame, and feelings of inadequacy, triggering the parent's need to defend against these aversive affects and the traumatic experiences in which they are rooted. Thus, the child is shamed and humiliated for needing what the parent is incapable of providing. Adaptive, healthy aspects of the self become not only excluded, but drenched in shame.

For patients with narcissistic vulnerability, basic adaptive functions, including needs and yearnings for contact and attachment, are rejected and cast in shame, thus the narcissist's defensive self-reliance. The apparently high functioning of these patients is deceptive: the high functioning is compensatory. Its aim is to regulate self-cohesion, self-vitality, and self-esteem. Without consistent success, or in the face of ordinary setbacks or ups and downs, these strategies collapse. When external buttressing of the self fails, there is tremendous shame, and many aspects of the previously high functioning collapse.

Patients manifesting covertly narcissistic personologic systems have been described by Eigen (1996), Ferenczi (1931, 1933), Guntrip (1969), Kohut (1977), Alice Miller (1981), Winnicott (1949, 1960), and others. As Ferenczi, Winnicott, and Miller note, these patients are often encountered in the caregiving professions. At the mild end of the continuum, we see narcissistic vulnerabilities in the regulation of self-esteem; at the severe end, there are more severe dissociative disorders, with self-cutting, sexual perversions, and other acting-out behaviors as pathological means of self-care and maintaining aliveness and integrity of self. Attempts to regulate self-experience and self-esteem through dysfunctional self-other interpersonal patterns result in phenotypes that can appear as grandiose, (defensively) self-sufficient, or else self-effacing and overly dependent. The pathogenic affect of shame plays a major role in these patients, and defensive self-reliance is often the result of the massive dissociation of needs, vulnerabilities, and yearnings that are too drenched in shame to be tolerated and thus need to be disowned. The result is the depletion, flatness, and deadness that bring patients into treatment.

CASE EXAMPLE: THE TRAPPED SELF

Diagnosis and Assessment

Yves, a 55-year-old account executive, entered treatment after his wife's discovery of his extramarital affair. In the marital crisis that ensued, the patient and his wife sought couples therapy; Yves was referred for individual therapy by the couples' therapist, a referral he readily accepted. His presenting complaint, uttered in despair, was "I feel trapped." He presented with acute and intense depression, an exacerbation of a chronic depression he had had for most of his adult life. Suicidality was carefully assessed, as the patient's father suicided when in his 60s. Although passive suicidal ideation was present, the patient was not and had never been actively suicidal. In addition to the chronic, unaddressed marital difficulties that exploded to the forefront, the patient had a multitude of difficulties: deep dissatisfaction with a job that did not engage his considerable intelligence and talents, accompanied by an inability to mobilize resources to find a different job, despite a humiliating demotion; a sense, dating to his 20s, of being adrift and "at a loss" about what to do with his life; and a proneness to verbally losing control of his temper with his children, which was deeply distressing to him, as he perceived it as damaging to them. He met *DSM-IV* criteria for Dysthymic Disorder (Axis I) and for Passive (or Passive-Aggressive) Personality Disorder (Axis II) and showed a pronounced tendency to somatization. Using Magnavita's (2000) diagnostic system, the patient's personality organization is best described as a *covertly narcissistic dysfunctional personologic system.*

Yves evidenced a profound dissociation between his "true self" experience and his day-to-day experience. He covered up his anger but also his needs, yearnings, and painful disappointments. His passive-aggressive interpersonal style came to the fore in situations of conflict, most blatantly so in his relationship with his controlling, dismissive wife. At work, he was in a similarly submissive relationship with an irascible, demanding boss, with whom he felt unable to assert himself. He felt trapped by obligations, duties, and unsatisfactory relationships. Seeing himself as "a hopeless underachiever," he felt distressed, ashamed—and yet resigned—that he had never been able to do justice to his talents. However, in isolated areas of his life, he felt alive and engaged: this was true in his love of jazz, in his deep commitment for over 20 years to the study, practice, and teaching of chess, and in his occasional affairs, which were invariably with warm, sensitive women. He also enjoyed "hanging out" with good friends. In music, chess, affairs, and occasionally with friends, he felt himself, he felt free, and he experienced a sense of ease.

Case Formulation

Yves grew up in an intact middle-class family with a deep commitment to education, radical causes, and the arts. Very loving with his son, Yves's father had nevertheless been a highly ineffective man. His outbursts of temper were frightening and destabilizing to his son, though he was invariably remorseful and concerned with reparation afterward. Yves's father was dominated by his wife, who ran over him with her words. To escape her, he immersed himself in increasingly quixotic causes, until he committed suicide in his 60s.

Yves's mother had been supportive, involved, and emotionally engaged with Yves; however, she had to be in control and she was always right. Yves never heard her say "I'm sorry" or admit to making a mistake, particularly in the emotional realm, where she was very proud of her prowess in reading and understanding people. In subtle and not so subtle ways, Yves's mother sought to control his every emotional tremor. She took over at the slightest sign of trouble. Yves came to rely on her and submitted to her agenda for how he should proceed, relinquishing his autonomy.

His difficulties began after he left home. Previously an excellent student, at college he felt "lost" and performed poorly. Despite graduating with a degree from one of the nation's top universities, he moved from job to job, unable to devote himself to any particular career. He was attracted to his wife in part because of how structured, definite, and down-to-earth he perceived her to be. In spite of her having a tin ear for emotional nuance and dismissing his emotional concerns as evidence of wanting to be pampered, in her contempt for an emotional inner life, she was refreshingly unlike his mother, and in her practical engagement in real-world matters, she was most unlike his father. But the unconscious is not so easily fooled. Yves replaced his mother with his wife, and he became his father.

In his parents, Yves had two models of dyadic regulation, neither of which included empathic reflection of *his* self. With mother, there was no room for his autonomous authentic experience; she behaved as if his emotional reactions were valid only when she deemed them to be so.

Although his mother did acknowledge his qualities and talents, these were co-opted in the service of her narcissistic needs. His wonderfulness reflected *her*. Though there was genuine and mutual love in Yves's relationship with his father, his father was too preoccupied with his struggle to maintain his own self to have much energy to attend to his son's experience. Furthermore, in that model of dyadic regulation, the capacity to metabolize and modulate emotions was clearly compromised.

As a result, from an early age, Yves learned to dissociate major aspects of his real self. He thus protected those very precious aspects of himself (Winnicott, 1960), yet, in his actual existence, he lost access to vital resources, energy, and thus direction. His actions required effort, and nothing flowed; thus the despair of feeling trapped in a life robbed of joy. The depletion he experienced became overwhelming in the crisis precipitated by the discovery of his affair; he needed to make a choice he felt incapable of making. The acuteness of the situation so stressed his already anemic resources that he yearned for the peace that death would bring.

Treatment Approach and
Rationale for Its Selection

Yves was all too good at attacking himself for all his personality flaws. He had genuine remorse and guilt for causing his wife pain; capable of deep empathy, the distress he felt about the suffering he would bring on his children if the family were to dissolve approached the unbearable (it was something he literally could not bear to think about prior to treatment, and so he did not). What was almost completely absent was any empathy for himself.

From the beginning, starting with the trial therapy, the therapist validated the importance of the patient's needs and framed the current crisis as an opportunity to understand and eventually restore access to dissociated aspects of his emotional experience. The AEDP therapist's actively and explicitly empathic, affirming, and nonjudgmental stance had an immediate impact on the patient: He felt deeply understood. He was all the more moved as he had expected the condemnation he felt he deserved. The focus on the patient's *experience* of being heard and understood (receptive affective experience) and then of feeling deeply himself (core self experience) here and now with the therapist led to a breakthrough of healing affects, a phenomenon the patient, in the initial trial therapy, dubbed "truth tears."

With the therapeutic alliance strong and the patient's emotional resources activated, the current crisis and the patient's chronic difficulties could now be dealt with from a position of resourcefulness. Together with the therapist, Yves was now in a position where he could experientially explore the various life options available to him. A portrayal was used to explore his feelings about saying goodbye to his family, were he to choose to end his marriage. The deepest feelings, a major breakthrough of grief, occurred as he imagined saying goodbye to Matthew, his oldest son. Previously unconscious material flowed; deeply identified with this child, the overwhelming grief he had about how hurt Matthew would be, accessed previously unprocessed grief and fear about his own experiences as a boy with his own father. In the core state that followed, strengthened by having borne the grief he had been so afraid of being destroyed by, he felt increasing clarity about what he needed and wanted to do. And he started to feel compassion for himself.

The AEDP aim of leading with a corrective experience and viscerally accessing core affective experiences so that the patient could benefit from the emotional resources accessed through the emergent state transformations was met. From the first session on, Yves had visceral access to a "new experience," a deep resonant sense of "true self," a state in which he felt strong, vital, feelingful, relaxed, clear, and in touch with his own subjective "truth." From that point on and throughout the therapy, the patient had a visceral knowledge of the state that he was striving for. The patient's deep response during the trial therapy suggested that AEDP had the potential to be of substantive help.

THE COURSE OF THERAPY

The patient was seen weekly, for sixty minute sessions. During the course of the AEDP therapy, *all five affective change processes* were activated. *Work with the core emotions* of fear, grief, and rage in the context of Yves's relationships with his mother, father, and wife allowed Yves to relinquish his habits of passivity (defenses). His passivity diminished in direct proportion to the satisfaction he experienced in speaking directly. It became clear that his explosiveness with his children covered up intense feelings of helplessness and being at a loss (unbearable states). As his extensive shame about his helplessness diminished, he came to realize how linked it was with his (defensive) attempts to deal with his experiences with his father, whom he had deeply loved; that, in turn, led him to recover the enormous fear he experienced in reaction to his own father's loss of control, which inhibited the development of his own aggression. This work led to an extensive phase of mourning; he mourned the damage he had done to his children and he mourned for himself— what he had lost out on as a result of his father's difficulties. *The exploration of interpersonal patterns of dyadic regulation* showed them to be severely skewed in the direction of his accommodating to the other and letting go of his own experience. This work was also crucial in undoing his lifelong passivity and promoting the development of his self-assertion. *The path of somatic experiencing* was relatively undefended; leading from strength, the patient's easy access to his bodily experience helped the experiential work. But the aspects of the work the patient deemed most mutative involved *the empathic reflection of his self* and the *activation of the metatherapeutic process of affirming the (transformation of) the self.*

A few weeks into the treatment, Yves decisively ended his affair and recommitted himself to his marriage and to working out the difficulties in it. The therapeutic goal was to replace his seeming acquiescence to his wife with honest communication about his dissatisfaction in the marriage, as both sexually and emotionally, he felt quite unresponded to. Renouncing his previous strategy of seemingly capitulating to his wife's forceful point of view while seeking responsiveness elsewhere, he became increasingly assertive and declarative. Time and again, he discovered how well he felt when he declared openly what he thought and felt, independent of the interpersonal consequences of his declaration. Experientially focusing on the positive sequelae of often difficult instances of self-assertion solidified his gains. The patient eventually became quite able to take responsibility for his behavior, owning the damaging impact it had on his wife's ability to feel safe with him, and at the same time, not lose sight of his own experience. It became of paramount importance to Yves that he betray neither his wife (outside of the marriage) nor himself (within the marriage relationship). Similar issues around declarative self-assertion were also worked on in the context of his relationships at work.

After 15 months, Yves terminated his treatment (the couple therapy had ended approximately six months before). The communication between him and his wife was excellent. With visceral access to his authentic self experience, he had much more energy in his daily life; the feelings of despair and feeling trapped disappeared as his actual lived life increasingly reflected *his* choices. His passive-aggressive personality was largely restructured, and those patterns largely disappeared from his repertoire. The key to the treatment was the visceral experiencing of the true self state (core state). That became the experiential guide both in and outside of sessions. Even when his behavior fell short, he always knew whether he was being true to himself or whether his determination was slipping and he was at-risk for resorting to old patterns (i.e., hiding behind passivity and seeming compliance instead of directly dealing with what he thought and felt).

POSTTERMINATION SYNOPSIS AND
EFFECTIVENESS DATA

The patient has been seen for yearly follow-ups since his treatment ended four years prior to this writing. He has maintained his gains. His relationship with his wife continues to be based on a high level of communication. The marriage remains a difficult one for the patient, but he feels unconflicted, having discovered a deep commitment to making it work as best he can. No longer ashamed of his needs and yearnings for greater responsiveness and intimacy, he has become increasingly aware of how his wife's inability to respond to his yearnings for contact are rooted in her own painful history (e.g., two mentally ill parents). This represents ongoing work for him, and being able to feel the validity of his own experience has made him much more able to deal with the frustrations in his marriage. At work, he has been increasingly assertive, gaining greater recognition. His demotion was rescinded and he has received further promotions. Like his marital situation, his situation at work is far from ideal; yet within the situation, his affective competence is high. In addition to the fading of his passive-aggressive patterns, Yves's depression has lifted. The remaining area of difficulty is that of occasional somatic difficulties, which the patient has framed as his body's way of reminding him when he is not taking care of emotional business; these disappear as soon as he attends to the emotional matters requiring his attention.

The following vignette comes from a session that took place a few weeks prior to termination. It is a beautiful example of core state (and true self) experiencing, gracefully captured in the idea of "the unencumbered moment." The experience of being unencumbered is all the more significant in light of the patient's having come into treatment "feeling trapped." I chose this passage because the patient so eloquently articulates the nature of core state experiencing and contrasts it with the defense-dominated state. Very different ways of being oneself in the world emerge from those different orientations.

The patient's italicized words capture the essence of his in-the-moment core state experiencing. In parentheses are the descriptions of the nonverbal aspects of the communication, and in brackets are my moment-to-moment microprocessing comments.

PATIENT: *There are no miracles, there's just this . . . that there's not really that much that's disturbing me. . . .*
THERAPIST: Yes.
PATIENT: There's nothing really bothering me about the way things are at home . . . because I used to come in and invariably some aspect of Patti's [his wife] behavior would upset me. Either something we went through. Or something we didn't go through . . .
THERAPIST: Uh huh.
PATIENT: . . . or something that bothered me that I either didn't bring up with her or did bring up with her and . . .
THERAPIST: Right.
PATIENT: You know, one of those little cobwebs and stuff. I don't really feel that . . . *there doesn't seem to be any lingering unfinished business.* ["Cobwebs": a symbolic expression of the consequences of defense-based living.]
THERAPIST: Wow.
PATIENT: (Sigh, pause.) So . . . I don't feel as if things haven't been taken care of . . . There is always something that worried me, whether it's money or this or that . . .

THERAPIST: Right.
PATIENT: ... or my mother, you know, things with that. I don't know, things seem to be ... pretty good actually.
THERAPIST: Mmm. (Pause.) What's that like, internally? [Encouraging exploration of the somatic/visceral correlates of emotional experience.]
PATIENT: It's just grrreat!
THERAPIST: Hmmmm.
PATIENT: (Hand over solar plexus, over the center of his being.) It reminds me of this habit of mine of carrying around little pieces of paper with notes about various things I have to do, you know. There are not too many notes in my pocket ... [Another metaphor for the simplicity of core state functioning.]
THERAPIST: Uh huh.
PATIENT: But I don't feel like there is all this unfinished business ... around me (Expansive gesture), so *I feel kind of clean.*
THERAPIST: Uh huh.
PATIENT: You know, *feels kind of good ... Feels clean.* That's really what it is.
THERAPIST: Hmm.
PATIENT: *Unencumbered, no strings.* (Brushes imaginary stuff off him, reference to the cobwebs.)
THERAPIST: I love the way you said "feels grreat."
PATIENT: Did I say it that way? (Laughs.) I thought I said it very quietly, in my usually subdued manner. [Reparative efforts: patient is correcting the therapist's mirroring, which in fact was slightly off.]
THERAPIST: You're right, it was quiet, but with a whole lot of "oomph." [Acceptance of patient's reparative efforts and reestablishment of coordination after minidisruption.]
PATIENT: Yeah, you know, it's not as though I was thinking about this before I came in or even in the last few days or anything like that ... But that's the truth. There aren't any kind of things that really left me disturbed. I can't remember yelling at the kids in a while ...
THERAPIST: Uh huh.
PATIENT: Patti and I are very similar in certain respects, although we have very different styles. I think we're very critical people ... I think in certain areas we demand a lot from ourselves.
THERAPIST: Mm hmm.
PATIENT: And we demand a lot from each other. Demand ... well, we expect ...
THERAPIST: Expect.
PATIENT: Expect a lot from each other. And ... hm, it's funny, she called me up yesterday and said (Gives example of wife confronting him about a particular incident with one of their children, and his directly describing what happened without being either defensive or self-derisive). So Patti said, "Oh, I see," and that was basically it. It didn't leave any kind of aftertaste ... There is nothing left over about that thing.
THERAPIST: Uh huh.
PATIENT: There would be times when Patti would call me and afterward I would be stewing that whole day and come home and have an attitude and maybe not say anything ... just ...
THERAPIST: This time it got taken care of.
PATIENT: Yeah, and I probably thought "Why is she calling me about *that*?" but it didn't really bother me ... it didn't take hold, inside, you know ... because little things like that, I would say, in the past ... in the past we both would have remembered something of it ... So I think these things haven't taken hold anymore, these negative accusatory things, or critical things or stuff like that ... We seem to be working pretty well, you know ...
THERAPIST: Mmmm. (Very affirming noise, with wonder.) [Empathic affirmation and amplification; admiring.]
PATIENT: ... and a lot of the same things may be happening.

THERAPIST: Just with a different spirit inside. And very different ways of dealing. [Empathic elaboration.]

PATIENT: Yeah ... yeah ... yeah ... (Pause.) A lot of the old language of criticism, of accusation is withering away ... and life seems a lot more normal, you know?

THERAPIST: Wow. It's strange to think it was only a year ago that things were so different ... and how it must feel to you now to feel like this. [Explicit focus on the process of change.]

PATIENT: Yeah. Well, last November ... we were in the thick of it. That wasn't an easy time. It was very uncomfortable then, so ... that might be another reason why I have *this feeling of being clean*, like I do.

THERAPIST: Yes.

PATIENT: It has so many implications in light of what happened in the last year, that, given our whole history, that I can go through days and times like this and *feel the vitality of the moment, unencumbered ... The unencumbered moment*, you know. [Core state: the straightforward declaration of subjective emotional truth.]

THERAPIST: Hmmm. [Appreciation.]

PATIENT: It's really terrific. *In a way, that's all I want*. I'm not that ambitious.

THERAPIST: That's so beautiful, the unencumbered moment ... [Empathic reflection.]

PATIENT: But because things happen, I guess, again, it's been such a short time but ... But one can tend to forget how close it all was, how nearby all this bad feeling and difficult living and all this encumbered living used to be ... just how close it really was ... it was here so recently ... (Pause.)

THERAPIST: (Sigh.)

PATIENT: I don't need any great charge or any great high ... this is fine ... (Pause.) That's right, that's all that's really needed. Obviously, there are also joyful moments ... *but this is joyful as it is*. [Positive affects as markers of core state experience.]

Thus, from the patient who described the healing affects accompanying the recognition of change as "truth tears," now comes yet another phrase capturing an experiential essence: the "unencumbered moment," the moment of feeling free of the sticky cobwebs of defense-driven living, a perfect characterization of the subjective simplicity of core state experiencing. This material comes from the session in which the patient and I set the termination date for our treatment; it seems a fitting way to end this chapter on AEDP, a treatment whose goal is to create opportunities for unencumbered moments from which a patient can experience and examine the emotional truth of his or her existence.

REFERENCES

Ainsworth, M. D. S., Blehar, M. C., Waters, E., & Wall, S. (1978). *Patterns of attachment: A psychological study of the strange situation.* Hillsdale, NJ: Erlbaum.

Alexander, F. G., & French, T. M. (1946). *Psychoanalytic therapy: Principles and application.* New York: Ronald Press.

Alpert, M. C. (1992). Accelerated empathic therapy: A new short-term dynamic psychotherapy. *International Journal of Short-Term Psychotherapy, 7*(3), 133–156.

Beebe, B., & Lachmann, F. M. (1988). The contribution of mother-infant mutual influence to the origins of self- and object representations. *Psychoanalytic Psychology, 5,* 305–337.

Beebe, B., & Lachmann, F. M. (1994). Representation and internalization in infancy: Three principles of salience. *Psychoanalytic Psychology, 11*(2), 127–165.

Beebe, B., Lachmann, F. M., & Jaffe, J. (1997). Mother-infant interaction structures and presymbolic self and object representations. *Psychoanalytic Dialogues, 7,* 133–182.

Bowlby, J. (1982). *Attachment and loss. Volume I: Attachment* (2nd ed.). New York: Basic Books.

Bowlby, J. (1988). *A secure base: Parent-child attachment and healthy human development.* New York: Basic Books.

Buber, M. (1965). *The knowledge of man: Selected essays.* New York: Harper Torchbooks.

Coughlin Della Selva, P. (1996). *Intensive short-term dynamic psychotherapy.* New York: Wiley.

Damasio, A. R. (1994). *Descartes' error: Emotion, reason and the human brain.* New York: Grosset/Putnam.

Damasio, A. R. (1999). *The feeling of what happens: Body and emotion in the making of consciousness.* New York: Harcourt Brace.

Darwin, C. (1965). *The expression of emotion in man and animals.* Chicago: University of Chicago Press. (Original work published 1872)

Davanloo, H. (1990). *Unlocking the unconscious: Selected papers of Habib Davanloo.* New York: Wiley.

Eigen, M. (1996). *Psychic deadness.* New York: Aronson.

Ekman, P. (1983). Autonomic nervous system activity distinguishes among emotions. *Science, 221,* 1208–1210.

Emde, R. N. (1981). Changing models of infancy and the nature of early development: Remodeling the foundation. *Journal of the American Psychoanalytic Association, 29,* 179–219.

Emde, R. N. (1988). Development terminable and interminable. *International Journal of Psycho-Analysis, 69,* 23–42.

Ferenczi, S. (1931). Child analysis in the analysis of adults. In (M. Balint, Ed. & E. Mosbacher, Trans.), *Final contributions to the problems and methods of psychoanalysis* (pp. 126–142). New York: Brunner/Mazel.

Ferenczi, S. (1933). Confusion of tongues between adults and the child. In (M. Balint, Ed. & E. Mosbacher, Trans.), *Final contributions to the problems and methods of psychoanalysis* (pp. 156–167). New York: Brunner/Mazel.

Fonagy, P., Steele, M., Steele, H., Higgitt, A., & Target, M. (1994). The theory and practice of resilience. *Journal of Child Psychology and Psychiatry, 35,* 231–257.

Fonagy, P., Steele, M., Steele, H., Moran, G. S., & Higgitt, A. (1991). The capacity for understanding mental states: The reflective self in parent and child and its significance for security of attachment. *Infant Mental Health Journal, 12,* 201–218.

Fonagy, P., & Target, M. (1998). Mentalization and the changing aims of child psychoanalysis. *Psychoanalytic Dialogues, 8,* 87–114.

Fosha, D. (2000a). Metatherapeutic processes and the affects of transformation: Affirmation and the healing affects. *Journal of Psychotherapy Integration, 10,* 71–97.

Fosha, D. (2000b). *The transforming power of affect: A model of accelerated change.* New York: Basic Books.

Fosha, D. (2001a). Core affect and its dyadic regulation. In A. Guerini & F. Osimo (Eds.), *Core factors in experiential short-term dynamic psychotherapy: Quaderni di Psichiatria.*

Fosha, D. (2001b). The dyadic regulation of affect. *Journal of Clinical Psychology/In Session: Psychotherapy in Practice, 57*(2), 227–242.

Fosha, D., & Osiason, J. (1996). *Affect, "truth" and videotapes: Accelerated experiential/dynamic therapy.* Presented at the spring meeting of Division 39 (Psychoanalysis) of the American Psychological Association, New York.

Fosha, D., & Slowiaczek, M. L. (1997). Techniques for accelerating dynamic psychotherapy. *American Journal of Psychotherapy, 51,* 229–251.

Gendlin, E. (1981). *Focusing.* New York: Bantam New Age Paperbacks.

Gendlin, E. (1991). On emotion in therapy. In J. D. Safran & L. S. Greenberg, (Eds.), *Emotion, psychotherapy and change* (pp. 255–279). New York: Guilford Press.

Gendlin, E. (1996). *Focusing-oriented psychotherapy: A manual for the experiential method.* New York: Guilford Press.

Goleman, D. (1995). *Emotional intelligence: Why it can matter more than IQ.* New York: Bantam Books.

Greenberg, L. S., Rice, L. N., & Elliott, R. (1993). *Facilitating emotional change: The moment-by-moment process.* New York: Guilford Press.

Greenberg, L. S., & Safran, J. D. (1987). *Emotion in psychotherapy.* New York: Guilford Press.

Guntrip, H. (1969). *Schizoid phenomena, object relations and the self.* New York: International Universities Press.

Gustafson, J. D. (1986). *The complex secret of brief psychotherapy.* New York: Norton.

Hart, J. (1991). *Damage.* New York: Columbine Fawcett.

Hesse, E., & Main, M. (1999). Second-generation effects of unresolved trauma in nonmaltreating parents: Dissociated, frightened, and threatening parental behavior. *Psychoanalytic Inquiry, 19*(4), 481–540.

Hughes, D. A. (1998). *Building the bonds of attachment: Awakening love in deeply troubled children.* Northvale, NJ: Aronson.

James, W. (1890). *The principles of psychology* (Vol. 2). New York: Dover.

James, W. (1902). *The varieties of religious experience: A study in human nature.* New York: Penguin Books.

Kohut, H. (1977). *The restoration of the self.* New York: International Universities Press.

Kohut, H. (1984). *How does psychoanalysis cure?* Chicago: University of Chicago Press.

Kurtz, R. (1990). *Body-centered psychotherapy: The Hakomi method.* Mendocino, CA: LifeRhythm.

Lazarus, R. S. (1991). *Emotion and adaptation.* New York: Oxford University Press.

LeDoux, J. (1996). *The emotional brain: The mysterious underpinnings of emotional life.* New York: Simon & Schuster.

Levine, P. (1997). *Waking the tiger: Healing trauma.* Berkeley, CA: North Atlantic Books.

Lindemann, E. (1944). Symptomatology and management of acute grief. *American Journal of Psychiatry, 101,* 141–148.

Liotti, G. (1995). Disorganized/disoriented attachment in the psychotherapy of the dissociative disorders. In S. Goldberg, R. Muir, & J. Kerr (Eds.), *Attachment theory: Social, developmental and clinical perspectives* (pp. 343–363). Hillsdale, NJ: Analytic Press.

Liotti, G. (1999). Disorganization of attachment as a model for understanding dissociative psychopathology. In J. Solomon & C. George (Eds.), *Attachment disorganization* (pp. 291–317). New York: Guilford Press.

Luborsky, L., & Mark, D. (1991). Short-term supportive-expressive psychoanalytic psychotherapy. In P. Crits-Christoph & J. P. Barber (Eds.), *Handbook of short-term dynamic psychotherapy* (pp. 110–136). New York: Basic Books.

Lyons-Ruth, K. (2001). The two-person construction of defenses: Disorganized attachment strategies, unintegrated mental states and hostile/helpless relational processes. *Psychologist/Psychoanalyst, 21*(1), 40–45.

Magnavita, J. J. (1997). *Restructuring personality disorders: A short-term dynamic approach.* New York: Guilford Press.

Magnavita, J. J. (2000). *Relational therapy for personality disorders.* New York: Wiley.

Main, M. (1995). Recent studies in attachment: Overview with selected implications for clinical work. In S. Goldberg, R. Muir, & J. Kerr (Eds.), *Attachment theory: Social, developmental and clinical perspectives* (pp. 407–472). Hillsdale, NJ: Analytic Press.

Main, M. (1999). Epilogue. Attachment theory: Eighteen points with suggestions for future studies. In J. Cassidy & P. R. Shaver (Eds.), *Handbook of attachment: Theory, research and clinical applications* (pp. 845–888). New York: Guilford Press.

Main, M. (2001). *Attachment disturbances and the development of psychopathology.* Paper presented at conference on Healing trauma: Attachment, trauma, the brain, and the mind, University of California at San Diego, School of Medicine.

Malan, D. H. (1976). *The frontier of brief psychotherapy.* New York: Plenum Press.

Malan, D. H. (1979). *Individual psychotherapy and the science of psychodynamics.* London: Butterworth.

Malan, D. M., & Osimo, F. (1992) *Psychodynamics, training, and outcome in brief psychotherapy.* London: Butterworth-Heinemann.

Mann, J. (1973). *Time-limited psychotherapy.* Cambridge, MA: Harvard University Press.

Mann, J., & Goldman, R. (1982). *A casebook in time-limited psychotherapy.* New York: McGraw-Hill.

McCullough Vaillant, L. (1997). *Changing character: Short-term anxiety-regulating psychotherapy for restructuring defenses, affects, and attachment.* New York: Basic Books.

Miller, A. (1981). *Prisoners of childhood: The drama of the gifted child and the search for the true self* (R. Ward, Trans.). New York: Basic Books.

Perls, F. S. (1969). *Gestalt therapy verbatim.* Lafayette, CA: Real People Press.

Person, E. S. (1988). *Dreams of love and fateful encounters: The power of romantic passion.* New York: Norton.

Rice, L. N., & Greenberg, L. S. (1991). Two affective change events in client-centered therapy. In J. D. Safran & L. S. Greenberg (Eds.), *Emotion, psychotherapy and change.* New York: Guilford Press.

Rogers, C. R. (1957). The necessary and sufficient conditions of therapeutic personality change. *Journal of Consulting Psychology, 21,* 95–103.

Rogers, C. R. (1961). *On becoming a person.* Boston: Houghton Mifflin.

Rosenzweig, S. (1936). Some implicit common factors in diverse methods of psychotherapy. *American Journal of Orthopsychiatry, 6,* 412–415.

Sandler, J. (1960). The background of safety. *International Journal of Psychoanalysis, 1,* 352–356.

Schore, A. N. (1994). *Affect regulation and the origin of the self: The neurobiology of emotional development.* Hillsdale, NJ: Erlbaum.

Schore, A. N. (1996). The experience-dependent maturation of a regulatory system in the orbital prefrontal cortex and the origins of developmental psychopathology. *Development and Psychopathology, 8,* 59–87.

Schore, A. N. (2000). Attachment, the right brain, and empathic processes within the therapeutic alliance. *Psychologist/Psychoanalyst, 20*(4), 8–11.

Seligman, S. (1998). Child psychoanalysis, adult psychoanalysis, and developmental psychology: An introduction. *Psychoanalytic Dialogues, 8,* 79–86.

Shapiro, F. (2001). *EMDR: Basic uses and future applications.* Paper presented at conference on Healing trauma: Attachment, trauma, the brain, and the mind, University of California at San Diego, School of Medicine.

Siegel, D. (1999). *The developing mind: Toward a neurobiology of interpersonal experience.* New York: Guilford Press.

Siegel, D. (2001). *Attachment, the brain and the developing mind.* Paper presented at conference on Healing trauma: Attachment, trauma, the brain, and the mind, University of California at San Diego, School of Medicine.

Sifneos, P. E. (1987). *Short-term dynamic psychotherapy: Evaluation and technique* (2nd ed.). New York: Plenum Press.

Stern, D. N. (1985). *The interpersonal world of the infant: A view from psychoanalysis and developmental psychology.* New York: Basic Books.

Stern, D. N., Sander, L. W., Nahum, J. P., Harrison, A. M., Lyons-Ruth, K., Morgan, A. C., et al. (1998). Non-interpretive mechanisms in psychoanalytic psychotherapy: The "something more" than interpretation. *International Journal of Psychoanalysis, 79,* 903–921.

Tomkins, S. S. (1962). *Affect, imagery, and consciousness. Volume I: The positive affects.* New York: Springer.

Tomkins, S. S. (1963). *Affect, imagery, and consciousness. Volume II: The negative affects.* New York: Springer.

Trevarthen, C. (1993). The self born in intersubjectivity: An infant communicating. In U. Neisser (Ed.), *The perceived self: Ecological and interpersonal sources of self-knowledge* (pp. 221–273). New York: Cambridge University Press.

Trevarthen, C., & Aitken, K. J. (1994). Brain development, infant communication, and empathy disorders: Intrinsic factors in child mental health. *Development and Psychopathology, 6,* 597–633.

Tronick, E. Z. (1989). Emotions and emotional communication in infants. *American Psychologist, 44*(2), 112–119.

Tronick, E. Z. (1998). Dyadically expanded states of consciousness and the process of therapeutic change. *Infant Mental Health Journal, 19*(3), 290–299.

Tronick, E. Z. (2001). Emotional connections and dyadic consciousness in infant-mother and patient-therapist interactions: Commentary on paper by Frank M. Lachmann. *Psychoanalytic Dialogues, 11*(2), 187–194.

Truax, C. B., & Carkhuff, R. R. (1967). *Toward effective counseling and psychotherapy: Training and practice.* Chicago: Aldine.

Winnicott, D. W. (1949). Mind and its relation to the psyche-soma. In *Through paediatrics to psychoanalysis* (pp. 243–254). New York: Basic Books.

Winnicott, D. W. (1960). Ego distortion in terms of true and false self. In *The maturational processes and the facilitating environment* (pp. 140–152). New York: International Universities Press.

Zajonc, R. B. (1985). Emotion and facial efference: A theory reclaimed. *Science, 228,* 15–22.

CHAPTER 14

Short-Term Dynamic Psychotherapy of Narcissistic Disorders

MANUEL TRUJILLO

The term narcissism and its multiple derivatives have progressively pervaded popular culture and the sociological and psychiatric clinical literatures for many decades. As such, the term has been used broadly and imprecisely. When used colloquially, the term may depict the increasing individualism of post–World War II urban Americans and be extended as well to the more affluent citizens of other developed countries. Sociologically, as Christopher Lasch (1979) and others have abundantly demonstrated, many features of our contemporary culture mirror the narcissistic traits of some individuals. A value orientation dominated by materialistic cravings, the seeking of success for success's sake to the detriment of values such as integrity, and the pursuit of pleasure rather than the realization of ideals draw the picture of an ecology where narcissistic personality traits may be valued, adaptive, and, therefore, preferentially selected.

When used clinically, the term is equally broad and its boundaries similarly diffused. Freud (1914/1957) first referred to narcissism to describe a libidinal position in which cathexes were invested in the subject's own ego and not in objects. Under those conditions, true transferences could not develop, making these patients ineligible for psychoanalysis. The clinical expression of nonobject libidinal cathexes included psychotic processes.

Following Freud's initial description, advances on the clinical relevance of narcissism were slow and proceeded along two relatively separate tracks: the descriptive and the dynamic. Descriptively, the efforts of many clinicians and clinical investigators led to the phenomenological delineation of the Narcissistic Personality Disorder (NPD) in the American Psychiatric Association's (APA; 1994, 2000) *Diagnostic* and *Statistical Manual of Mental Disorders IV* and *IV-TR* as an Axis II disorder. Dynamically, significant advances have been made in the clarification of the metapsychological dimensions of narcissistic disorders. Two authors, Otto Kernberg (1984, 1986, 1998) and Heinz Kohut (1971, 1977), have advanced well-developed metapsychologies for these disorders and proposed comprehensive techniques for their treatment through appropriately modified psychoanalytically based interventions. In both cases, treatment is deemed to be plagued by problems, to last long, and to result in uncertain outcomes. The metapsychological clarity achieved by authors such as Kohut and Kernberg has so far not generated a proportionate therapeutic optimism.

In particular, few authors have attempted to apply to patients suffering from self-disorders techniques of short-term dynamic psychotherapy, which have demonstrated respectable efficacy in the treatment of patients suffering from complex psychoneurotic disorders, select Axis II personality disorders, and Axis I disorders such as Anxiety and Depressive Disorders (Trujillo & McCullough, 1985; Winston et al., 1991). Patients meeting criteria for these disorders have been shown to make rapid and impressive gains, as long as their dynamic problems are related to difficulties in the management of sexual and/or destructive impulses, problems in the regulation of object loss, or complex combinations of both types of pathology.

In this chapter, a review is presented of the current status of the outcome of the treatment, through short-term dynamic psychotherapy, of a spectrum of psychoneurotic disorders, with special emphasis on the treatment of patients suffering from syndromes that reflect complex dynamic constellations resulting from the interaction of impulse problems and problems of object loss at key developmental moments, which affect the patient's relationships with developmentally key objects. These genetic-developmental pathologies cause patients who suffer from them considerable impairment of normative character development, significant distortions of ego functions (largely through hypertrophy of defensive operations), and much personal suffering and interpersonal dysfunction. Also presented are techniques derived from this framework for the treatment of patients suffering from a range of narcissistic disorders, including NPD, as well as innovative techniques designed by the author to meet the unique treatment needs of self-disordered patients in shorter time frames than are common in the classically open-ended psychodynamic technique.

HISTORY OF THE THERAPEUTIC APPROACH

A significant shift in the deep psychological understanding of narcissistic disorders is represented by the work of Kohut (1971) and summarized in his book *The Analysis of Self*. Kohut advanced a complete metapsychology of self-disorders, including (1) the supraordinate position of the self as a whole-system organizer to which other mental agencies (e.g., drives, ego, and superego) and mental capacities (e.g., motivation, vitality, goals, and values) are, to different degrees, subordinate; and (2) the relative independence—but rich interdependence—of the development of the self from the development of the other components of the mental apparatus (e.g., drives, id, ego, and superego).

The key pathogenetic phenomenon in the mental apparatus proper is interagency conflict and the articulation of repression and other defenses against forbidden impulses. The affect of anxiety signals, in these cases, the inability of the mental apparatus to cope with conflict. In the area of the self, the key pathogenic phenomenon is lack of integration, that is, the inability of the organism to maintain a sense of wholeness. The signal of failure to maintain self-homoeostasis is the affect of shame. Its presence indicates the inability of the self to maintain sufficient wholeness and fullness. In cases of more severe pathology, fragmentation anxiety denotes the organism's fear for its own basic integrity.

A very important theoretical and practical construct in self psychology is the developmental process that, when successful, promotes the maintenance of a coherent, whole, optimally altruistic persona. When "good enough" environmental fit is present, this process, fraught with complexities and opportunities for derailment, facilitates vital human functions: (1) the slow maturation of a primal boundaryless, grandiose self, into realistic, enduring, and resilient self-esteem and personal identity; and (2) the gradual transformation of undifferentiated, global, idealizing needs into values and ideals that color and mediate each person's investment in and involvement with external social systems of beliefs, meaning, and action.

Narcissistic psychopathology occurs via two interrelated mechanisms:

1. Failure to complete key developmental steps along the pathway delineated previously. Lack of maturation, integration, and realization of large segments of grandiose self (or idealized object image) create split-off (or dissociated) self-object representations, which entail potential problems of identity formation, maintenance of self-esteem, and/or development of an appropriate and satisfying system of values, ideals, and accomplishments for the patient.
2. Pathological interrelatedness of self-development with drive-developmental processes. In this regard, the presence of significant, unresolved self-developmental pathology may color drive-developmental and interpersonal processes such as separation-individuation, the ability to cope with object losses, and the resolution (or lack thereof) of triangular Oedipal pathology. Kohut (1971), in fact, stated unequivocally that clinically significant Oedipus complexes occurred because the developing child's normal drives and conflicts were disturbed and intensified by unempathic parental responses.

Once consolidated, narcissistic psychopathology is expressed via:

1. Frequent experience of the affect of shame and/or fragmentation anxiety, a terrifying experience that signals the fear of the self for its imminent loss of integrity. Patients may experience unbearable feelings of identity confusion and identity loss. Subjectively, they may fear losing their mind. Terrifying feelings of emptiness and unreality may also appear.
2. The presence of extreme intrapsychic defenses (e.g., splitting and cognitive-affective dissociation) and interpersonal defenses (e.g., distancing, feeling extreme superiority or inferiority, intense neediness, or equally unyielding indifference).
3. Symbolic or manipulative behaviors designed to restore the integrity of self-experience by procuring soothing or vicarious experiences of wholeness via symbiotic fusion. Various addictions, compulsive use of people, compulsive sexuality, and certain forms of self-mutilation such as cutting may, at times, serve this function.

Clinically, symptomatic behavior follows two distinct pathways:

1. Actual behavior designed either to "enact" some version of the patient's subconscious grandiose self-image or to hide it, if revealing it would cause unbearable shame and anxiety. In the latter case, patients hide behind a self-effacing exterior and avoid exposure and self-revelation. In the former, patients enact a script of grandness and perfection, attempting to depict and maintain the image of total control over their personal and nonpersonal environment.
2. Subjective states related to the experience of narcissistic trauma and rejection. These subjective states, intensely painful, range from fragmentation anxiety and Panic Disorder to disorganizing primitive rage and

depression often related to emptiness and meaninglessness.

THEORETICAL CONSTRUCTS

ORIGINS AND DEVELOPMENT OF THE METHOD

This method emerged in the author's clinical practice as a result of the confluence of three developments. First, the author was influenced by clinical and research exposure to the theories and clinical practices of noted clinicians and theoreticians such as Sifneos (1987), Malan (1976), and Davanloo (1978, 1979, 1980), which were presented in detail in a series of studies and reports to the literature in the 1970s and 1980s. Second, the author observed increasingly frequent manifestations of narcissistic features, traits, and conflicts (both in the overt and covert forms) in patients suffering from intense and extensive multifocal psychoneurotic psychopathology. Although for these patients, Davanloo has developed a series of techniques, which he calls intensive short-term dynamic psychotherapy (ISTDP), these techniques so far have not been expanded to encompass the treatment of these patients' specific narcissistic vulnerabilities. Third, the author repeatedly observed the responsiveness of these patients to the therapist's clinical attention to their narcissistic conflicts and problems. Under certain conditions, described later, these patients are fully capable of the intense reactivation of primal aspects of the self and of achieving a clinically satisfactory, relatively rapid, reintegration of these formally dissociated aspects of self.

Because the author's techniques are related to those developed by Sifneos, Malan, and Davanloo on the one hand, and to the metapsychology of self-disorders proposed by Kohut and Kernberg on the other, both developments are summarized.

INTENSIVE SHORT-TERM
DYNAMIC PSYCHOTHERAPY

Davanloo (1980) labeled as ISTDP a series of psychoanalytically based psychodynamic techniques designed to deal with the problems of patients whose pathology is generated by multiple genetic foci of Oedipal psychopathology and object loss, but who manifest extensive defensive structures (including character defenses), which render their unconscious conflict practically inaccessible to dynamic techniques based on free association. His techniques have been reported to best reach patients suffering from Axis I syndromes of anxiety and depressive disorders and/or Axis II Cluster C disorders such as Avoidant, Dependent, Obsessive-Compulsive, and Passive-Aggressive Personality Disorders (APA; *DSM-IV-TR*, 2000).

Authors such as Sifneos and Malan had already developed such features of short-term techniques as (1) high activity of the therapist, (2) development and maintenance of a focus (or foci), and (3) early use of transference among others. But it is to Davanloo's credit that he elegantly systematized the techniques required to obtain an early breakthrough into the unconscious of highly resistant patients. Thus, Davanloo was able to reach directly, and make available for psychotherapeutic work, highly defended painful feelings related to interpersonal conflict and loss. Davanloo's techniques unfold through two steps: an evaluation phase and a therapy phase. The evaluation phase is considered successful if it leads to a breakthrough into patients' repressed unconscious feelings and/or impulses through their multilayered defensive barrier. When successful, this phase leads to intense derepression of feelings, enhanced motivation for further therapeutic work, a positive feeling toward the therapist, and a concomitant productive rise in the conscious and unconscious therapeutic alliance.

The treatment phase also makes extensive use of many of the techniques of the initial evaluation. This phase can be conceptualized by two triangles: the triangle of conflict, described by Menninger (1958; Figure 14.1) and the triangle of the person, proposed by Malan (1976; Figure 14.2). Using short-term dynamic psychotherapy with various nonpsychotic depressive and other psychoneurotic disorders, Malan reported empirical evidence supporting the finding that the higher the number of interpretations that link transference, past figure, and present figure (TCP interpretations), the better the outcome of the treatment.

Treatment can be conceptualized as an ongoing and repeated working through in an atmosphere of heightened emotions and repressed impulses and/or feelings (I/F). This working-through process is leveraged by active use, detection, and clarification of the transference and encompasses repeated visits to all the problems and foci delineated in the initial psychodynamic evaluation.

At the end of initial evaluation, the therapist should have a global picture of the patient's functional problems, their dynamic sources, and the core genetic determinants of both. This assessment can be portrayed using what the author calls the psychodynamic hologram (Figure 14.3).

The top portion of the hologram represents the patient's adaptive problems. All problems

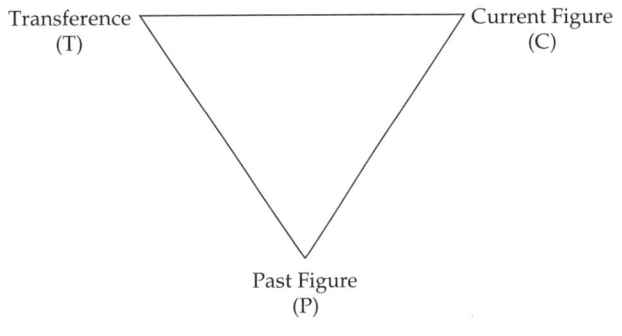

Figure 14.2 Malan's (1976) triangle of the person.

($1 \to n$), that represent sources of suffering and/or functional impairment are recorded here. These may include symptoms of anxiety or depression, interpersonal problems at work or at home, and other problems of adaptation. The second level of the psychodynamic hologram depicts the large dynamic force (or forces) that accounts for the problems recorded in the first level. Such dynamic forces as ongoing self-sabotage leading to repeated failures at work, or the ongoing rage-fueled need to destroy people in positions of authority, need to be carefully noted and delineated here. It is important to try to account for as many of the problems identified in the initial evaluation as possible. The third level of the hologram is constituted by the core pathogenic I/F constellation(s). Through

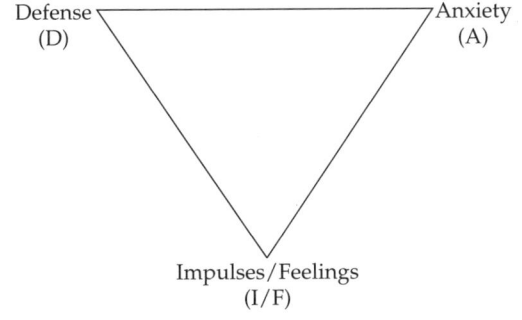

Figure 14.1 Menninger's (1958) triangle of conflict.

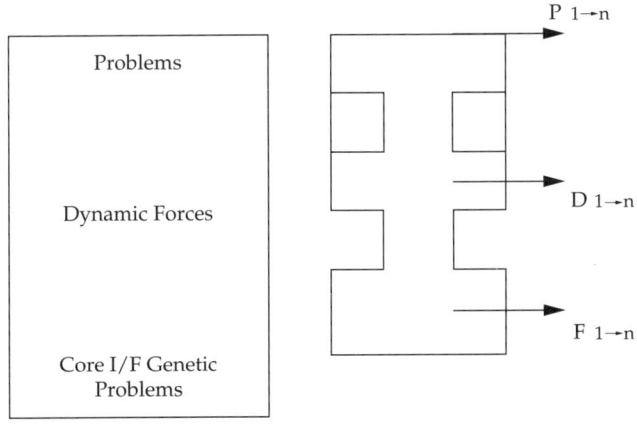

Figure 14.3 The psychodynamic hologram.

the activation of dynamic forces, these generate the patient's symptomatic, functional, or interpersonal psychopathology. Issues such as repressed and/or pathological grief reactions for one or more key developmental figures, repressed impulses such as destructive aggression, and sexual impulses or fused sexual and aggressive impulses need to be uncovered and denoted here.

The therapist aims for as complete a picture as possible of the genetic → dynamic → problems constellation. Problems that are not delineated adequately in the initial evaluation may constitute hidden sources of resistance and/ or negative transference reactions and transference neurosis as the therapy goes on. The therapy aims for as complete a resolution as possible of the patient's pathogenic foci. This is achieved through repeated access to all pathogenic foci of I/F, the working through of grief and ambivalent feelings toward developmentally significant objects, and the repeated, full experiencing of aggressive feelings and their sadistic destructive derivatives leading to reduction of superego-based self-sabotaging tendencies.

Magnavita (1997) has presented an application of ISTDP to narcissistic disordered patients and has demonstrated the critical role of patients' self-destructive behavioral repertoire in the creation of their resistance to treatment. Self-destructive behavior must be controlled if intense derepression of affect is to be promoted in search of optimal resolution of core pathology.

Self Psychology

Kohut (1971) advanced systematic descriptions of self-disorders and proposed principles for their metapsychological understanding and techniques for their treatment. He has described the relatively independent developmental line of the self and various disordered responses to failures of environmental support, including parental mirroring. The central expression of these failures is registered through deficits and distortions of the perception of self (affecting self-esteem), the relative lack of integration of ambitions and capacities (creating grandiosity, self-effacement, and/or underachievement), or the incomplete development of appropriate, socially accepted values and ideals. For Kohut, the reparation of these deficits requires the development of a reparative transference of either of three types: (1) mirror transference proper, involving the use of the therapist as an admiring self-object and/or the interpretation of perceived failures via empathic interpretations; (2) idealizing transference, involving the acceptance by the therapist of the patient's unconscious needs to see him or her as a quasi-omnipotent object, capable of soothing and consoling and (transferentially speaking) worthy of emulation; and (3) twinship transference, which allows the patient to feel like others and develop a sense of connectedness.

Self psychologists may conceptualize therapy as a process that allows the patient—via the development, experience, verbalization, and resolution of intense transferences—to reactivate primitive, dissociated, anxiety-provoking self and object perceptions and structures. Once activated, a more normal developmental pathway can be resumed, where primitive self-perceptions mature and become more integrated and healthier.

The paradigmatic intervention for self-problems is empathic understanding and empathic interpretation. In this realm, empathy involves an accurate grasp, both cognitive and affective, of what others experience. This commitment to empathic understanding creates a supportive milieu in which the patient can either bask in the utilization of the therapist as an optimum self-object, or bitterly, but safely, complain about the therapist's failure while benefiting from the healing effects of resolving the damage caused by that failure.

To accomplish this task in a relatively short-term period of 50 sessions or less requires:

1. An accurate—empathically mediated and shared—grasp of the patient's core narcissistic vulnerabilities. For many patients, these problems are hidden behind a well-defended wall of character defenses; thus, these narcissistic vulnerabilities are apparent only after significant breakthroughs into the patient's unconscious rage and/or grief. For this part of the process, the ISTDP techniques reviewed previously are crucial.
2. Active and early attention to the development of various forces of self-object transferences.
3. Early detection and reactivation (largely through active inquiry) of primitive, dissociated, grand, or grandiose self-images and the containment of defensive affects, such as dissociative anxiety, fragmentation anxiety, and a pervasive sense of embarrassment and shame.
4. A special form of corrective emotional experience that I call imaginary reconstruction. This involves the healing of a narcissistic wound by the imaginary reconstruction, following the experiencing of painful moments of self-object failure, of an imagined optimum (not perfect, but not wounding) self-object interaction. (A few of these interventions are discussed later.)

Just as the course of an episode of ISTDP treatment can be depicted by allusion to the two triangles, the course of an episode of treatment of a (pure or mixed) self-disorder problem can be depicted as shown in Figure 14.4.

Feelings

The typical therapy process focuses repeatedly on the overt manifestations of defensive activities, such as character defenses buttressed by splitting and cognitive-affective dissociation. Subsequent and repeated therapeutic challenges to the defenses may prompt the emergence of anxiety or paralyzing shame and finally lead to the reactivation of formerly repressed and distorted self-representation. Distorted negative self-images are deactivated via this exposure, as they can be seen more realistically and as the attendant grief is experienced and resolved. Positive self-images are allowed again to flow through the barriers of dissociation and are reactivated (experienced by patients as rightfully belonging to them) and appropriately linked to hopes, dreams, skills, and values. This way, profoundly personal projects of much meaning to the patient can reemerge as valued blueprints for purposeful and meaningful life plans and actions.

MAJOR SYNDROMES, SYMPTOMS, AND PROBLEMS TREATED

Though clinicians have learned to recognize several presentations of patients suffering from NPD, only one distinct syndrome has found its

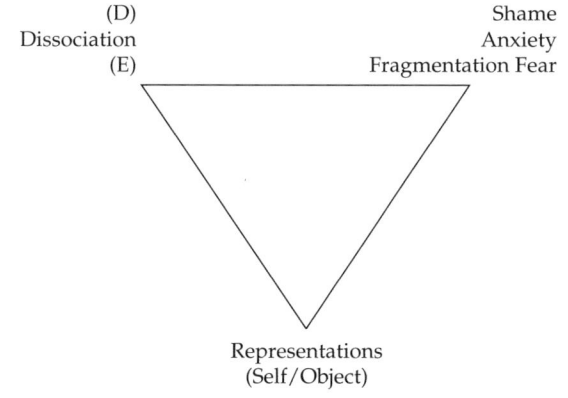

Figure 14.4 Triangle of the self.

way into the *DSM-IV* (APA, 1994). Experienced self psychologists recognize the following additional syndromic presentations:

Primary self-disorder:

1. NPD proper, as defined by *DSM-IV-TR* (see Table 14.1).
2. Covert NPD represents a mirror image of NPD. Features that are overt in NPD proper are often covert here, but can be detected either in fantasy or hiding behind considerable resistance (see Table 14.2).

Table 14.1 Diagnostic criteria for Narcissistic Personality Disorder 301.81.

A pervasive pattern of grandiosity (in fantasy or behavior), need for admiration, and lack of empathy, beginning by early adulthood and present in a variety of contexts, as indicated by five (or more) of the following:

1. Has a grandiose sense of self-importance (e.g., exaggerates achievements and talents, expects to be recognized as superior without commensurate achievements).
2. Is preoccupied with fantasies of unlimited success, power, brilliance, beauty, or ideal love.
3. Believes that he or she is "special" and unique and can only be understood by, or should associate with, other special or high-status people (or institution).
4. Requires excessive admiration.
5. Has a sense of entitlement, for example, unreasonable expectations of especially favorable treatment or automatic compliance with his or her expectations.
6. Is interpersonally exploitative, for example, takes advantage of others to achieve his or her own ends.
7. Lacks empathy; is unwilling to recognize or identify with the feelings and needs of others.
8. Is often envious of others or believes that others are envious of him or her.
9. Shows arrogant, haughty behaviors or attitudes.

DSM-IV-TR, APA, 2000.

Table 14.2 Diagnostic presentation for Narcissistic Personality Disorder (covert type).

A pervasive pattern of grandiosity (in fantasy, *not* in overt behavior), need for admiration, excessive sensitivity to judgment and opinion of others, beginning by early adulthood and present in a variety of contexts, as indicated by:

1. A covert grandiose sense of self-importance, though may compulsively minimize achievement.
2. Fantasies of unlimited success, power, brilliance, beauty, or ideal love often hidden under considerable shame.
3. A craving to be noted as special but fears automatic rejection by other high-status people or institution.
4. Need for excessive admiration.
5. Behavior as if driven by a sense of entitlement, for example, easily hurt and disappointed when high expectations for favorable treatment or automatic compliance are not met.
6. Compulsively seeking others as admiring objects.
7. Excessively focused on the behavior of others but unwilling to recognize other's independent needs.
8. Often envious of others or believing that others are envious of him or her.
9. Hidden arrogant behavior or attitudes.

Mixed self-disorders:

3. Reflect a mixture of narcissistic traits and conflict/drive problems. Narcissistic vulnerabilities and traits may appear through Axis I disorders, such as anxiety disorders, depressive disorders, and eating disorders.
4. Mixed with Axis II disorders. Pronounced self-disorder traits may color the clinical presentation and outcome of Axis II disorders, such as Avoidant and Dependent Personality Disorders.

Secondary self-disorders:

5. Self-esteem and self-representation may be impaired, reflecting the impact

6 Self-esteem and self-representation may be impaired, reflecting the impact of structural, biologically based, disorders such as Attention-Deficit/Hyperactivity Disorder in the normal process of development of the self.

of functional, biologically based illnesses such as schizophrenia and bipolar disorders in the normal development of self.

The importance of secondary self-disorders lies in the fact that unattended, their presence may complicate the treatment and outcome of the primary disorder and force the patient to live with unresolved unconscious, defective, and pathogenic self-images. Each clinical presentation requires different interventions, priorities, and techniques.

CASE EXAMPLES

The following are vignettes about patients who exemplify the descriptions listed in Tables 14.1 and 14.2. These are illustrative of relevant aspects of evaluation and treatment.

Patient 1: NPD Proper

G.R. is a 44-year-old unmarried professional man who first consulted because of unbearable anxiety, depression, and loneliness. Though periodically present throughout his life, these feelings appeared in a clinically explosive form at the end of a troubled six-month relationship with Ms. B., a divorced professional woman who was the mother of a 10-year-old girl. Ms. B. ended the relationship after a few months of goodwill efforts on her part to please him and cater to his many needs and demands. His escalating and sometime frantic demands reflected a craving for perfectly attuned attention and responsiveness to the endless flow of his physical and emotional needs. Despite all Ms. B.'s efforts (now painfully recognized by the patient), he usually treated her with a mixture of cruel devaluation and condescension, forcing her to admit, in practically every encounter, her incredible luck at being with a man with his "unique" capacity for sensitivity and passion and her pitiable incompetence at "adequately" responding to him.

Dynamically, his conscious life was dominated by the need to enact scenarios of uniqueness and specialness in search of boundless confirmation from whoever was chosen to function as confirming self-object. Failures in this regard met with a cascade of subjective effects such as unbearable anxiety, and/or pervasive rage and fury, which often led to prolonged, sadistic devaluing and attacks on the hapless offender. When such a person left his presence, his affect shifted to intense loneliness and profound depression, often requiring immediate medical attention.

The dynamic picture for patients like this can be represented as follows:

- Ongoing, somewhat unstable conscious experience of entitled grandness or frank grandiosity, with large segments of the patient's adaptive behavior devoted to seeking opportunities for confirmation and to searching for, and holding onto, complementing, confirming self-objects.
- Storms of primitive anxiety and despair often accompanying the experience of the effect of narcissistic traumas and self-object rejections. This may include painful episodes of fragmentation anxiety, depression, and self-devaluation, and prolonged experiences of emptiness.
- An unconscious life dominated by negative self-images and experiences of rejection and devaluation or anticipation of such states. These experiences color patients' conscious fears and frequently populate their dreams.

Patient 2: Covert NPD

I.G., a businessman in his mid-30s, first consulted when, repeatedly confronted by his first serious and long-term girlfriend (whom he had dated for a few months), he realized "I have very few opinions about anything . . . I don't have any strong feelings, any clearly discernible passions. . . . It's difficult for me to know my likes and dislikes."

Mr. G. was unaware of any strong feelings or defining personal goals and passions. He skated the surface of life behind a facade of quiet amiability and easy accommodation. He abhorred interpersonal conflict, fearing and avoiding the searing power of anger. He craved to fit in and be left alone. At deeper levels, behind several layers of repression and dissociation, lay powerful undercurrents of resentment and personally shaming yearnings for power and radiance as well as for recognition. Dynamically, his conscious life was dominated by the search for harmony, fairness, and acceptance at any price. Interpersonal conflict and challenge were carefully avoided, as they elicited painful anxiety. He had experienced what he called a "low-grade depression" for "as long as I can remember." At times, he suffered bouts of meaninglessness and disconnection from others, which made him feel "transparent" and utterly alone.

The dynamic picture of this type of patient can be represented as follows:

- An ongoing conscious resignation to a life devoid of entitlement to experiences of grandeur, power, joy, and other powerful emotions. Life is to be endured and lived on a palette of grays. Disrupting emotional colors must be avoided. Personal ambitions, recognition, and rewards bring about painful shame and the subjective conviction of not being entitled to or worthy of their fulfillment ("I don't deserve it").
- Underneath hide deeply dissociated longings for grandness, power, and joy, protected by a barrier of numbness and shame.

Patient 3: Self-Disorder and Axis I Disorder

L.G., a single woman in her late 30s who had immigrated to the United States about two years prior to her initial consultation, first sought psychiatric help for a panic attack disorder. Her first episode occurred while her mother was visiting her in New York. One night during the visit, she woke up from a dream full of fear, drenched in sweat, flooded with nausea, and terrified at the thought that she was about to lose her mind. In her dream, she saw herself hovering over her mother's bed holding a huge knife and about to plunge it into her mother's body. The dream held for her a quality of total reality and left her to wonder in terror whether she would always be able to prevent the actual enactment of such a scene. She had many such attacks in the succeeding weeks and was plagued by the conviction that it was a matter of time until she completely lost control of her mind to end up in a long-term psychiatric hospital or in jail. L.G. is strikingly beautiful and highly talented. As her treatment went on, she expressed some of her talent in creative paintings and designs. At the same time, she has been utterly impractical in the conduct of her daily affairs, displaying a phobic avoidance of such practicalities as stocking her refrigerator and keeping personal papers such as passports, tax returns, and immigration documents.

Dynamically, Ms. G.'s conscious life was dominated by fear and frequent running away. She ran away often from self-created crisis situations, which typically arose after her having phobically neglected a significant reality demand. Once, she ran out of money and was evicted. Another time, she lost her job as an assistant in an architectural firm when she neglected to complete and present an important proposal. These episodes of frantic running away were punctuated by other periods, lasting for weeks or even several months, of relative tranquility and peace of mind. The occurrence of such periods seem related to the presence of a benign person who took an interest in her, provided some form of holding, a modicum of soothing and nurturance, and—just as important—a reality anchor. During her late college years, a placid, middle-age, encouraging female teacher played that role and allowed Ms. G. to complete a college education. Later, some of her boyfriends stepped in, seeming to provide succor and continuity of self-experience more than an adult sexual and emotional partnership.

As treatment went on, it became clear that Ms. G.'s mental life contained the following:

- The ongoing, conscious subjective experience of fear, which could be triggered either by an awakening of rage or by experiences of isolation and emptiness. In the former case, anxiety became an alarm signal of the reactivation of overwhelming anger; in the latter, the fear was linked to experiences of self-fragmentation in relation to abandonment.
- A profound lack of self-esteem a very tenuous experience of self manifested by constant numbness and emptiness. Beyond that numbness, the patient was occasionally flooded by distorted and negative self-images. At times, she saw herself as irreparably deformed and repugnant. In a parallel and dissociated fashion, images of unparalleled grandness and beauty occasionally broke through; she dreamed of herself as a painter as grand as Picasso, a philosopher capable of an unusual understanding of life and the universe.
- Under the surface, disruptive floods of rage plagued the patient when she perceived herself abandoned (or rejected) by anyone she had selected as a protective self-object. These episodes of rage were very disruptive to the patient. They created considerable anxiety and/or prompted poorly integrated responses of "fight" (at times, prolonged and vicious) or "flight," and dissociated episodes of running away. Though descriptively the patient met the full criteria for a panic attack disorder, the predominant dynamic diagnosis was a self-disorder with additional areas of psychopathology reflecting foci of loss, pathological grief reactions, and complex Oedipal triangular relationships.

PATIENT 4: SELF-DISORDER AND
AXIS II DISORDER

O.F., a married female professional in her mid-40s and the mother of a teenage boy, exhibited profound narcissistic vulnerabilities, conflict, and problems that are the features of an Axis II disorder. Mrs. F. emerged from a stormy adolescence largely out of contact with personally felt hopes and ambitions. Extremely intelligent but equally insecure, she completed a professional doctoral degree but was unable to practice because of feelings of inadequacy and intense sensitivity to criticism and fear of rejection. This avoidance also extended to the area of friendship and even to the friend of her only son, who was carefully scrutinized for his potential to be critical or act "superior."

Clinically, O.F. met full criteria for Avoidant Personality Disorder. At other times in her life, she had received such Axis I diagnoses as Generalized Anxiety Disorder and Dysthymia.

From the dynamic viewpoint, this patient can be described as follows:

- Her ongoing conscious experience was dominated by her need to avoid encounters in which she might feel rejected. She avoided encountering schoolmates who had continued with their career aspirations; she avoided socializing with other parents in her child's school who had achieved a higher social standing. When she feared that such encounters might be inevitable, she secured the company of one of her few "unconditional friends" (really, trusted self-objects) to help her avoid the anticipated sense of rejection.
- Below this surface self-experience, she was subject to many experiences of rage

and sadness. The rage, often denied and repressed, exploded at times in relation to the perceived disloyalty or indifference of a trusted friend. The most intense and disorganizing bouts were directed at "cruel" people who dared to snub her or—exquisitely more painful—snub and reject her child. Sadness and depression followed either rage of a certain intensity or unavoidable exposure to more successful, self-affirming peers.

- At a deeper level, and well defended by layers of anger and grief as well as through vicarious projection onto her son, lay self-images of grandness, power, and entitlement.

DIAGNOSIS AND ASSESSMENT

PATIENT I

Initial Evaluation

Like other forms of complex ISTDP, the treatment of self-disordered patients, whether they present in relatively pure, covert, or mixed form, requires a rather extensive initial evaluation or trial therapy phase. The aim of this phase of treatment is to gain access to one, and optimally more than one, core conflict focus and its associated repressed impulses and painful affects. When the barrier of defense is immobilized access to impulses such as anger restores in the patient's subjective experience the continuity of the psychophysiological, emotional, and cognitive dimensions of emotions with a concomitant gain in the sense of mastery. For patient 1, this phase was rather dramatic and occurred early in the initial session while trying to describe his anger toward Ms. B., who had recently left him. This sequence of therapy required an initial clarification that what he experienced when she announced the end of the relationship was indeed anger.

When asked the paradigmatic initial evaluation question, "How did you experience your anger toward Ms. B.?", the patient resorted to a sequence of well-developed automatic defenses: "I didn't know. [helplessness] How do you experience anger?" [directed at the therapist in defiance]. These defenses were complemented by the extensive use of nonverbal defensive behaviors, such as a rather passive body posture and avoidance of eye contact, constituting a formidable barrier. After considerable clarification and challenges to his defenses, the patient was able to experience more of his anger toward Ms. B. in a freer form. He felt his rage, deeply in his stomach as a violent "surge of adrenaline" moving upward toward his chest and into his arms. This provoked an almost compulsive urge to hit and destroy; he had an image of holding a knife and repeatedly plunging it into her chest cavity, bringing about her death. This image linked with a "flash-like" image of his father who died, chest cavity open, eight years earlier while undergoing coronary by-pass surgery. When asked to focus and stay with this linked image, the patient was suddenly flooded by rhythmic waves of profound sobbing, expressing repressed grief and sadness for his father. He became aware (arising from his intense feelings without much need for interpretation) of his complex ambivalent feelings toward his father, his habitual way of defending himself, and his pathological identifications with the failed aspects of his father's life and experience. A flood of memories ensued, including a forgotten dream of the very early years of his life where he saw himself as a naked and fragile premature infant. In the dream, his father grabbed him and put him in his coat pocket; he fell through the pocket, in terror that his father would trample him underfoot. Flooded with anxiety, he woke up. Talking about this dream gave way, in turn, to another layer of grief, this time for his self. It became apparent that, underneath his often conscious experiences of grandeur lay a terrifying self-image of utter helplessness and fragility that necessitated ongoing ministration by an abundance of self-objects, lest the experience of helplessness overwhelm him. In fact, he was practically unable to be alone, and any form of questioning of his human potency and capacities, however slight, evoked crippling anxiety and self-doubt, often covered by explosive bursts of rage.

Case Formulation

At the end of the evaluation phase, G.R.'s dynamic hologram appeared to have the following configuration:

Problems:

1. Inability to channel professional activities to reasonable success despite evident intellectual assets.
2. History of stormy failed relationships with multiple females despite craving to achieve stability, be married, and have a family.
3. Chaotic life dominated by a craving for emotionally intense professional and emotional relationships (self-object like).

Dynamics:

1. Ongoing need for outside emotional supplies. The need to search for the perfect (i.e., all-admiring, all-giving, and nurturant) partner dominated his life to the practical exclusion of more mature relatedness.
2. Primitive rage and vindictiveness triggered by perceived or actual failure of partners.
3. Ongoing professional and personal self-sabotage.

Core Conflicts:

1. Profound repressed, primitive, ambivalent feelings toward the maternal object, resulting in an insoluble tension between libidinal investment and sadistic-destructive derivatives, in his actual relationships with women. Thus, his relationships with women typically started on a high of idealization and, just as often, crashed in a low of violent recriminations.

Impulse/Feeling:

2. Ambivalence toward paternal object complicated by unresolved pathological grief, with consequent disruption in the formulation of dynamically equivalent actual relationships.

Self-Representations:

3. Split-off primitive unintegrated self-images. The grandiose self-images are acted out in consciousness in the form of demands to be met by partners; the helpless self feeds enormous self-doubts and constant neediness.

Treatment Approach and Rationale for Its Selection

Working-through and Termination. The dynamic hologram depicted previously was obtained, in the process of the initial evaluation. During this time, the patient was suffused with anger, grief, and other painful feelings. The hologram represents a roadmap for the unfolding of the therapeutic experience. For patient 1, therapy will proceed through repeated runs around the triangle of impulses, person, and self. The two key pathogenic foci for him are the focus of self and the focus of pathological grief reaction for the death of his father. The pathogenic capacity of each foci reinforces the pathogenic capacity of the other. The images of helplessness and utter fragility derived from his repressed disturbed negative self-images are reinforced by identification with the failed aspects of his father's life as a way to maintain some bond with the father, charged again by his need to expiate guilt for his unconscious murderous impulses toward him. The trigger for such destructive feelings relates to his father's failure to act as an adequate narcissistic self-object (optimum mirror).

The working through of these problems will require revisits to the experience of anger and destruction in relationship to the people in his current life (C) or toward the therapist (T) and subsequently toward his father (P). Multiple T C P interpretations were made before a sense of peace and emotional understanding and a modicum of closure and closeness obtained for the patient in relationship to memories of his father. Simultaneously expressed and covert demands for closeness, support, feedback, extra time, and extra resources, showed up in the therapeutic situation. The slightest disappointment in the therapist evoked feelings of desolation and devastation in the session.

A technique I call imaginary reconstruction allowed the patient to evoke emotionally satisfying moments of optimum mirroring following the expression of anger toward the perceived failure. After one episode when the patient bitterly berated the therapist for not responding the way he "needed" during a telephone interchange, the following dialogue ensued:

THERAPIST: You were obviously very disappointed with my response. What would you have wished me to say?
PATIENT: You know—something warm, something supportive, like "Of course, Gerry, she should have agreed with you."
THERAPIST: And how would you have felt if I said that?
PATIENT: Relaxed, accepted, or, like I have value.
THERAPIST: And how do you imagine I feel toward you?
PATIENT: Never thought of that—I think you want me to succeed, I think (With emotional conviction) you love me!
THERAPIST: And how do you feel about that?
PATIENT: Warm—great . . . it makes me think of my father. I think that if he would have been able to, he definitely would have loved me . . . how sad!
THERAPIST: What would he have loved especially about you?
PATIENT: That I am sensitive, that I am creative, that I am funny.

THERAPIST: Because—how do you see yourself as a person now?
PATIENT: Just like that: funny, creative.

The ultimate goal of the therapy is the rapid reactivation of formerly dissociated positive self-images and their reintegration with such sectors of the self and the mental apparatus as hopes, dreams, and aspirations for the future and such means of self-realization as skills and capacities. This aim may be succinctly expressed by paraphrasing Freud's well-known dictum "Where id was, there ego shall be" (S. Freud, 1933/1964) as "Where emptiness is, there self will be."

For this patient, the reactivation of affectively lived images of joy, increasing potency, and optimism continued during the midphase of treatment. In parallel, there was a deactivation of fragile self-images and destructive impulses, as exemplified in the following dream: "I am sitting in a car. A couple of Nazis move rather menacingly toward the car, and as they pass next to it, they scratch the side of my car with a set of keys."

The core conflict configuration, as portrayed in the psychodynamic hologram, provides a rough map to the unfolding of the working through and termination phases. The successful positive therapeutic alliance, both conscious and unconscious, generated in the evaluation phase permits the patient to attempt to complete the following pieces of unfinished business:

1. Bring into the focus primitive sadistic feelings directed toward his father. Concomitant with such feelings is an unconscious identification with, and attachment to, the father strengthened by the presence of pathological grief.
2. Confront, experience, and resolve profound destructive impulses toward the mother.
3. As 1 and 2 achieve some resolution, they facilitate the reactivation of repressed grand and grandiose self-images and positive self-experiences. Gradually, painful

experience of loneliness, emptiness, and shame lessen.

The task of focusing on and resolving sadistic ambivalence toward objects, which were experienced largely as self-objects, is difficult and may meet with considerable resistance. For example, this patient's conviction of his father's utter lack of value or any redeeming human feature was absolute. The radical logic of the self required as much. Seeing his father as a total failure as a father and as a person in a strange way absolved him of any responsibility for his own imperfections and limitations. Unconsciously, he seemed to cling to the idea that "I would have been perfect were it not for my parent's total helplessness and incompetence."

Working through of Rage. Only after the patient experienced hope of adequate mirroring via the transference could he reevaluate his view and experience of his father and bring into consciousness his profound sadness for his father's rather tragic and failed life experience.

As in the initial evaluation, the technique of working through of narcissistic rage requires a sequence of interventions that achieve (1) maintenance of the focus; for example, a specific memory of rage in his interaction with his father; (2) reactivation of the physiological-emotional-cognitive continuum; (3) pressure and challenges to the defenses against rage; and (4) pressure and challenges to the defenses against interpersonal closeness and, especially, closeness toward the therapist. As the therapist acquires via the transference a certain standing in the patient's emotional life, the attachment to the therapist heightens the patient's ambivalent attachment to the primary object and intensifies his unconscious conflict of emotional loyalty. This is yet another source of considerable resistance and active therapeutic work. Rage toward the therapist may reach murderous proportions.

Pathological Grief Work. For patient G.R., the sequence of therapeutic work described previously led to a rather sudden recognition and explosive surrender to a frenzy of murderous impulses toward his partner. This rage was felt as a jolt of electricity running through his body and imaginatively acted out in the form of repeatedly plunging a knife into her heart. All it took was a simple allusion by the therapist to the father's life-long existential tragedy ("But in a way, we know he actually died a heart-broken man") to release a flood of sobbing sadness for his father and longing for an optimal and tender father-son relationship.

This emotional explosion opened the door to a fuller exploration of grief for the father and for the self and to a lessening of the pathological, guilt-driven identification with the "failed father." Repetition of this sequence in regard to this and other foci allows for a progressively clearer reactivation and ownership of positive self-images and emotions such as joy, hope, and ambition.

Reactivation and Reintegration of Self. As patients gain mastery and knowledge of their own experience of rage and the pathological grief is lessened, they are ready to reactivate grand and grandiose self-images and complete the process of reintegration of such self-images with both reality and their own unique set of skills and personal capacities.

For G.R., this sequence of the work started when he began taking seriously a significantly ambitious creative project that he had embarked on. As he very tentatively started to discuss his project, he scrutinized the therapist's face and demeanor in search of any trace of disapproval (which would lead to considerable defensive rage) or approval (which would lead to a mixture of shame tinged with self-doubt). For this phase, techniques such as the imaginary reconstruction provide for the patient a corrective emotional experience without fostering any violation of therapeutic boundaries. The following interchange took place after the patient described his pride and pleasure at a recent piece of work he did that was rather well received by the intended audience:

THERAPIST: You look at me as if you expect me to . . .
PATIENT: (With anger.) Of course I want your approval! What is wrong with that!!!
THERAPIST: Specifically what would you want me to feel and say?
PATIENT: This is a great piece of work, Gerry! Go on with it. I am proud of you, you'll make it.
THERAPIST: And if I felt exactly that, how would that make you feel?
PATIENT: (Blushing.) Wow! . . . Maybe I could believe that I am entitled to that.

The work of reactivation of primal, dissociated self-images also requires clarification and correction of multiple self-distortions. For example, for G.R., a rather large, athletic, and physically powerful man, the self-image described earlier of utter fragility of a premature, inhumanly small baby in danger of being trampled underfoot at any moment actually contaminated the way he saw his self physically. He carried himself hunched over, making himself appear considerably smaller than he actually was. As the therapy advanced, he derived considerable pride in his body and his physical prowess, as well as in his sense of style, for which he often sought the therapist's admiration and approval. Increasingly, his dreams and fantasy life filled with images of grandness ("I feel like the captain of my own ship"), pride, and pleasure at his own physical, mental, and emotional characteristics. The resolution and integration of this sequence of work require a process akin to a recapitulation of the developmental work of adolescence. Much as in late adolescence, through newly developed capacities for introspection one takes some ownership and responsibility for one's self and destiny.

This sequence of the work often brings about a minirecapitulation of the developmentally appropriate sequence. There is often a lessening of the earlier dependence on external mirroring, and a sense of pride and pleasure at defining and taking responsibility for unique subjective aspects of each person. For G.R., there was a growing pleasure at discovering and following "my own path": an autonomy that earlier could be experienced only through rebellious anger, which often brought about catastrophic failure.

PATIENT 2

Initial Evaluation
The trial therapy phase in the evaluation of patient I.G. yielded significant breakthrough into two Oedipally flavored foci of severely repressed rage. After confronting a bland, unerringly polite character defense structure, the initial interview focused his anger in the present. He reported that he was indignant at the "predatory" behavior of another colleague at work, who acted as if he could "take whatever he wanted," his own capriciousness appearing as his only moral compass. Following the arduous work of defense clarification, confrontation, head-on collision and challenges and appeals to the ego-syntonic nature and the emotional toll of his passivity, a breakthrough was made into a large pool of repressed rage, alternatively felt toward his colleague and toward the therapist. Powerful surges of murderous rage were experienced and imaginatively carried through. After a few such bouts, the link to the past became unmistakable; the patient could see behind the image of the "capricious colleague" the largely repressed representation of a family friend, "a charming rogue," with whom the patient's mother may have had a brief affair when the patient was 12. His pent-up rage was structured in multiple levels: (1) toward his mother, for "betraying" his father and (subjectively speaking) him; (2) toward the "charming

rogue," for endangering the family unit and robbing him and his father of the presence of the mother; (3) toward his father, for his passive inability to deal forcefully with the situation; and (4) toward himself, for secretly envying the freedom and obvious pleasure-seeking nature of the "charming rogue." Below the surface there were painful ambivalent feelings toward both parents: toward his mother, for her inability to mirror him and for setting the "bar of approval" ever higher, so that he could never be quite "good enough"; toward his father, for his passively driven inability to allow the patient to idealize him, his passive handling of the mother's affair representing one more example of such unavailability for idealization.

The core conflict component of the dynamic hologram for patient I.G. can be represented as follows:

Core Conflict:
1   Murderous impulses toward three members of the Oedipal triangle, leading to deep character defenses of bland amiability.

Impulse/Feelings:
2   Guilt-provoking identification with the apparent grandness of the Oedipal victor.

Self-Representations:
3   Guilt-guided identification with parental failures: the father to triumph over rivals, the mother for excessive perfectionism interfering with basic simple pleasures.
4   Loss of contact with primal grand(iose) self-images and derailment of idealization.

Reactivation of the Grand(iose) Self
The working through phase has two differentiated segments: (1) the resolution of Oedipally tinged destructive impulses and their aftermath (superego pathology, self-sabotage, self-destruction, phobic avoidance of conflict passivity) as core character constituents; and (2) the reactivation of primitive self-structures whose optimum development was derailed and interrupted. In this regard, a series of highly emotional breakthroughs into his murderous impulses toward his mother were followed by great sadness on realizing the painful personal origins of his mother's injurious perfectionism. As these layers of grief for mother, for father, and for self were sequentially worked through, they gave way to a period of mild euphoria, punctuated by repeated floods of early childhood memories and images suffused with feelings of incredible power and well-being. He was able to hold onto one memory of great impact: He is at home, at that time, temporarily in a Caribbean country, watering a luxuriantly verdant lawn, the sun high in the sky. While holding a powerful hose, he feels flooded with the pleasure of action, competence, power, and joy. This memory unleashed a torrent of equally pleasurable memories, some of which were reflected in photographs taken in diverse settings throughout his early childhood. His obvious pride while sharing pictures of celebrated aspects of his being with the therapist solidified in increasing ownership of pride and pleasure at his own being as well as ownership of some uniquely personal features of that being.

Reintegration of Self and Ego
To the degree that core narcissistic psychopathology involves abundant dissociation of self with other mental agencies, the therapeutic process requires healing that rift by building bridges between the different mind structures. Of great value is the reintegration of grand ambitions with actual ego skills and capacities, a process fraught with pain and disappointment that must be endured. For I.G., a large part of this process of reintegration was accomplished via dreams. Many adventures were replayed night

after night, action-oriented scenarios that required tolerance for failure, imaginative attempt at mastery, and, on achieving some mastery, the capacity to celebrate and accrue a lasting sense of power and well-being. His telling these "large tales" in the therapy room accrued additional therapeutic value because it allowed him to "brag a bit" about his adventures, to command the therapist's attention in rapture, and when (at least in the patient's subjective experience) his large tales met with empathic failure, to feel and master the sadness and the fury of the disappointment.

PATIENTS 3 AND 4

Grief for Lost Self
The case of L.G. illustrates the need for ongoing grief work in many patients suffering from self-disorders. Her experiences at the hands of her rather wounded, incompetent, and lost parental caretakers involved lack of provision of basic safety and mirroring in the early stages, and abandonment, abandonment threats, and physical and emotional neglect at a second stage. Physical, and possibly sexual, abuse in her prepubertal years was also part of her traumatic development. The cumulative subjective experiences of such development involves additional pockets of grief for the self that (despite its innocence) is neglected, abandoned, not provided with mirroring, and later abused. This aspect of grief for self was responsible for R.G.'s pervasively distorted images, where she saw herself in reveries and dreams as irreparably deformed and repugnant. It is as if the patient blamed herself rather than her parents for the catastrophic outcome of her care: "If they treated me like that, how good can I possibly be?" The sadness derived from statements like this must be identified, empathically brought out, and allowed to flow while the self distortions are questioned and corrected.

POSTTERMINATION SYNOPSIS AND EFFECTIVENESS DATA

Mutually agreed termination of therapy with patients suffering from NPD or substantive narcissistic traits requires the fulfillment of the following criteria:

1. Significant reduction of Axis I symptoms and substantive lessening of the interpersonal and work dysfunctions that typically bring these patients into treatment. If the treatment is monitored through the use of symptoms scales such as the Hamilton Depression Scale (Hamilton, 1960) or the Beck Depression Inventory (Beck, Ward, Mendelsohn, Mock, & Erbaugh, 1961), clinicians may use as criteria for improvement the ones often used in the research literature (e.g., a preselected score; a 50% reduction from baseline score).
2. Evidence of significant reactivation of the grand(iose) self: increasing acceptance enjoyment of aspects of self, and the experience of feelings of vitality and well-being independent of the approval of an admiring self-object. Often, patients experience wonder and pleasure on reflecting, or discovering, self-functions such as imaginativeness and playfulness. It is as if they say to themselves: "This is who I am and I like it." As this function grows and expands, patients come to expect that a large part of the pleasure of living will come from the exercise of these self-functions and from their ability to develop life projects—and build human relationships—from this deep source of being. As pleasure and pride accrue from the exercise of these self-functions, tyrannical perfectionistic demands on self or others lessen, and empathy may appear in intimate relationships, together with tolerance for the self-object shortcomings of others.

3. Significant resolution of pathological grief reaction for others and for self. A patient whose treatment the author supervised epitomized the process of pathological grief resolution while describing a particular moment of well-being achieved while hiking:

> I came to this point on the road where I could see the whole valley down the road; struck by the beauty of the place, I had what I would call an epiphany: for the first time in a long time I felt totally at peace with myself and, I guess with life: there was no anxiety, no fear, no guilt. I thought about my wife, I thought about my mother and my father, and I could imagine the three of them looking at me and I could see [tears streaming down his face] that they were pleased with my success, that they were proud of me.

This experience summarizes several features present in the resolution of pathological grief reactions: objects for whom the patient has felt ambivalently alienated are restored to an optimal, emotionally meaningful contact; anxiety and guilt disappear from those relationships and are replaced by peace and harmony.

The closer the process comes to the fulfillment of these criteria, the better the outcome and the easier the termination process. Active work on the transference can solidify the process. When the patient was asked by his therapist "And where would I be in that picture?" he answered, "You made it possible. You created the peace treaty. You gave them all back to me." The patient thus indicated the termination of the therapist function as a self-object who functions in lieu of the parental self-objects; they are now restored to their sublimated self-object function in memory. The transference can now be deactivated and the therapist becomes the real object who mediated and facilitated the changes in the patient's subjective emotional life.

The outcome of the treatment of these disorders has not as yet been tested through appropriately designed research studies. Clinicians treating many of these patients report substantial gains in symptoms, interpersonal function, personal integrity, and object-relatedness. Characteristics of the treatment process, such as short duration, enhanced activity of the therapist, development of treatment foci, use of transference, and mobilization of intense affects, have been satisfactorily researched in many studies of efficacy and effectiveness of short-term dynamic psychotherapy in the treatment of severe psychoneurotic and personality disorders (Trujillo & McCullough, 1985; Winston et al., 1991). These studies represent a good background for the design of future studies of the treatment of self-disorders.

SUMMARY

In this chapter, the ISTDP approach to the treatment of a rising number of patients presenting to clinics and practices suffering from various forms of self-disorders has been described and elucidated. Prior efforts to extend the applications of these techniques to patients suffering from relatively uncomplicated psychoneurotic disorders (Sifneos) and to complicated multifocal psychopathology (Davanloo) required the honing and refinement of the psychotherapeutic techniques needed to break through complex characteriological barriers. The application of these techniques to self-disordered patients requires their adaptation to the metapsychology of self and self-development (as distinct from the metapsychology of impulse/feeling, derived conflict). The aim is similar: to achieve rapid access to unconscious pathogenic structures and their attendant repressed feelings and to promote rapid healing through early, active, and abundant recourse to the transference.

It is the author's hope that the successful marriage between well-established short-term techniques and the emerging metapsychology of self-disorders will yield increasingly effective treatments for these patients.

REFERENCES

American Psychiatric Association. (1994). *Diagnostic and statistical manual of mental disorders* (4th ed.). Washington, DC: Author.

American Psychiatric Association. (2000). *Diagnostic and statistical manual of mental disorders* (4th ed., text rev.). Washington, DC: Author.

Beck, A. T., Ward, C. H., Mendelsohn, M., Mock, J., & Erbaugh, J. (1961). An inventory for measuring depression. *Archives of General Psychiatry, 4*, 561–571.

Davanloo, H. (Ed.). (1978). *Basic principles and techniques in short-term dynamic psychotherapy.* New York: SP Medical and Scientific Books.

Davanloo, H. (1979). Techniques of short-term dynamic psychotherapy. *Psychiatric Clinics of North America, 2*, 11–22.

Davanloo, H. (Ed.). (1980). *Short-term dynamic psychotherapy.* New York: Aronson.

Freud, S. (1957). On narcissism. In J. Strachey (Ed. and Trans.). *The standard edition of the complete psychological works of Sigmund Freud* (Vol. 14, pp. 69–102). London: Hogarth Press. (Original work published 1914)

Freud, S. (1964). New introductory lectures on psychoanalysis. In J. Strachey (Ed. and Trans.), *The standard edition of the complete psychological works of Sigmund Freud* (Vol. 22, p. 80). London: Hogarth Press. (Original work published 1933)

Hamilton, M. (1960). A rating scale for depression. *Journal of Neurology, Neurosurgery and Psychiatry, 23*, 56–62.

Kernberg, O. (1984). *Severe personality disorders: Psychotherapeutic strategies.* New Haven, CT: Yale University Press.

Kernberg, O. (1986). Further contributions to the treatment of narcissistic personalities. In A. P. Morrison (Ed.), *Essential papers on narcissism* (pp. 245–292). New York: New York University Press.

Kernberg, O. (1998). Pathological narcissism and Narcissistic Personality Disorder: Theoretical background and diagnostic classification. In E. F. Ronnigstam (Ed.), *Disorders of narcissism: Diagnostic, clinical and empirical implications* (pp. 29–51). Washington, DC: American Psychiatric Press.

Kohut, H. (1971). *The analysis of the self.* New York: International Universities Press.

Kohut, H. (1977). *The restoration of the self.* New York: International Universities Press.

Lasch, C. (1979). *The culture of narcissism: American life in an age of diminishing expectations.* New York: Norton.

Magnavita, J. J. (1997). *Restructuring personality disorders: A short-term dynamic approach.* New York: Guilford Press.

Malan, D. H. (1976). *The frontier of brief psychotherapy.* New York: Plenum Press.

McCullough, L., Trujillo, M., & Winston, A. (1985). *A video-coding manual of psychotherapy process.* Unpublished manuscript, Beth Israel, Department of Psychiatry.

Menninger, K. (1958). *Theory of psychoanalytic technique.* New York: Basic Books.

Sifneos, P. E. (1987). *Short-term dynamic psychotherapy: Evaluation and technique* (2nd ed.). New York: Plenum Press.

Trujillo, M., & McCullough, L. (1985). Research issues in short-term dynamic psychotherapies: An overview. In A. Winston (Ed.), *Clinical and research issues in intensive short-term dynamic psychotherapy.* Washington, DC: American Psychiatric Press.

Winston, A., Pollack, J., McCullough, L., Flegenheimer, W., Kestenbaum, R., & Trujillo, M. (1991). Brief psychotherapy of personality disorders. *Journal of Nervous and Mental Diseases, 179*, 188–193.

CHAPTER 15

A Relational-Feminist Psychodynamic Approach to Sexual Desire

M. SUE CHENOWETH

HISTORY OF APPROACH

Although researchers and clinicians have made significant progress in the study and theoretical understanding of human sexuality (Basson, 2000, 2001; Kaplan, 1979, 1995; Kinsey, Pomeroy, Martin, & Gebbard, 1953; Levine, 1984, 1987, 1988, 1995; Masters, Johnson, & Kolodny, 1994; Masters & Johnson, 1966, 1970; Tiefer, 2001), in many ways, this field remains in its infancy (Levine, 1988, 1995; Tiefer, 1995; Weis, 1998a, 1998b). For example, hypoactive sexual desire is a complex disorder that has proven difficult to treat (Beck, 1995; Hawton, 1995; O'Carroll, 1991; Rosen & Leiblum, 1995a, 1995b). Whereas treatment outcomes for some sexual dysfunctions (i.e., premature ejaculation, inorgasmia, and vaginismus) are excellent, the therapy outcome for the sexual desire disorders remains satisfactory to poor for many individuals (Beck, 1995; Hawton, 1995; Hawton, Catalan, & Fagg, 1991; O'Carroll, 1991; Wiederman, 1998).

A review of the literature on sexual desire disorders shows that Inhibited Sexual Desire (ISD), now known as Hypoactive Sexual Desire Disorder (HSDD), is the most prevalent sexual disorder among adult women, accounting for 33 to 62% of sexual difficulties in women (Hawton, 1995; Kohn & Kaplan, 1999; O'Carroll, 1991; Rosen & Leiblum, 1995a). Yet, ISD/HSDD remains the most resistant sexual disorder to treatment interventions (Hawton, 1995; Kaplan, 1979; MacPhee, Johnson, & Van Der Veer, 1995; Rosen & Leiblum, 1995a, 1995b; Schreiner-Engel & Schiavi, 1986). The treatment of sexual disorders in adult women have been especially fraught with complexity and confusion, leading to modest (MacPhee et al., 1995) to poor long-term treatment outcome (Hawton & Catalan, 1986; O'Carroll, 1991). Hawton (1995) states that "success of treatment of disorders of female desire seems to be associated particularly with the couple's general relationship, interpersonal communication and attraction, sexual ease and confidence, and the male partner's motivation" (p. 310). Rosen and Leiblum (1995a) state that although treatment interventions for sexual desire disorders vary widely, "presently, there is no standardized or generally accepted format for treatment, nor is there agreement regarding the likely prognosis" (p. 115).

Multiple complex factors contribute to these variations in treatment outcome. Currently, there is a "good understanding of the sexual dysfunctions that respond best to this treatment and the couples most likely to benefit" (Hawton, 1995, p. 307). However, many previous outcome and comparative studies suffer from methodological difficulties and inadequate control groups, which result in incomplete and/or misleading data. Examples of these methodological difficulties are different types of sexual dysfunctions combined across treatment groups; prognostic factors that are not matched across treatment groups; poor outcome criteria; and lack of long-term outcome data (Hawton, 1995).

Additional factors that may explain differences in outcome data include changing incidence and prevalence rates for specific types of sexual dysfunctions over the past 20 to 50 years. Consequently, researchers have refocused their attention on new sexual dysfunctions not previously studied and may have only minimal outcome data for these recently investigated disorders (Donahey & Carroll, 1993; D. P. Spector & Carey, 1990). Recent changes in nomenclature and additions of new diagnostic categories in the past two editions of the American Psychiatric Association's *Diagnostic and Statistical Manual of Mental Disorders* (*DSM-III-R*, APA, 1987; *DSM-IV*, APA, 1994) have contributed to the lack of consistent outcome data. An example of a newly investigated sexual disorder is HSDD (Seagraves & Seagraves, 1991).

The scientific study of human sexuality and sexual behavior has developed mainly through four separate traditions: "the case study method; the use of normative survey research; the laboratory physiological approach; and behavioral assessment and treatment studies" (Rosen & Beck, 1988, p. 4). Many late nineteenth- and early twentieth-century writings on sexuality and sexual behavior were based on motivation, instinct, and/or a developmental stage model (Rosen & Beck, 1988). In the latter half of the twentieth century, psychoanalytic case analyses and biological/behavioral studies of sexual behavior by Kinsey and colleagues (1953), Masters and Johnson (1970), Kaplan (1979), and LoPiccolo and Friedman (1988) have served as a foundation for the diagnosis and treatment of sexual dysfunctions.

Sigmund Freud was the first theorist to propose a model of human sexuality from a scientific and psychoanalytic perspective. Before the 1950s, Freud's *Three Essays on the Theory of Sexuality* (1905/1953) was the touchstone use almost exclusively by other clinicians and theorists as a basis for treatment of clients' psychosexual difficulties. The traditional Freudian psychoanalytic model is predicated on the male Oedipal conflict as the basis for normal psychosexual development. Female sexuality is presented from the perspective of a biological deficit based on the female gender position as a castrated male.

William Masters and Virginia Johnson's (1966) research was based on clinical observation and direct measurement of physiological responses to sexual stimuli. Masters and Johnson's results (1966, 1970) unequivocally added to the knowledge of the physiological aspects the human response to sexual stimuli. On the basis of their research, Masters and Johnson defined and described a four-stage sexual response cycle for both males and females. This model is predicated on a biologic-based understanding of sexual drive and discrete physiologic responses. It includes the following stages: (1) excitement, (2) plateau, (3) orgasm, and (4) resolution. Each stage has specific and unique physiological aspects that are observable and measurable. In 1980, Masters and Johnson's model became the basis for nomenclature, classification, and diagnosis of sexual dysfunctions in the third edition of the APA's *DSM* (Tiefer, 1988).

As a result of Masters and Johnson's findings, researchers developed specific sex therapy techniques for treating sexual dysfunctions related to performance anxiety, particularly the inability to reach orgasm in women and premature ejaculation in men. If no physical reason could account for the patient's dysfunction, then psychological/behavioral treatments were assumed necessary to treat such sexual dysfunctions (Masters & Johnson, 1966, 1970). Therefore, specific methods such as "sensate focus" exercises were devised.

Masters and Johnson's approach and techniques were met with much enthusiasm in the 1970s (Hawton & Catalan, 1986). Originally, many clinicians thought their approach would become the panacea for couples with sexual difficulties. However, Hawton and Catalan state: "Claims for the effectiveness of sex therapy have become more cautious. While it is clear that sex therapy can be extremely effective for some couples, failures are also relatively common and often difficult to predict" (p. 377). Despite these more cautious claims, Masters and Johnson's approach continues to be the basis of treatment for many sexual dysfunctions. Today, however, sex therapy is usually combined with psychoeducation, marital therapy, homework assignments, medical treatments (e.g., use of Viagra), and/or individual and group treatment interventions (Hawton, 1995).

It is the long-term failure outcomes of traditional sex therapy (Hawton, 1995; Hawton, Catalan, Martin, & Fagg, 1986; O'Carroll, 1991), particularly in cases of low sexual desire, that raise the question of possible limitations in Masters and Johnson's understanding of the human sexual response cycle. It is noted that Masters and Johnson's (1966, 1970) original work did not include a sexual dysfunction category for decreased sexual interest (i.e, hypoactive sexual desire). Hawton et al. (1991) state, "There is little evidence for a biological basis for this problem in healthy pre-menopausal women.... However, a wide range of psychological factors and social factors can impair sexual interest" (p. 217). Therefore, it is important to review and expand our knowledge in this area, particularly because hypoactive sexual desire continues to be both prevalent and difficult to treat (Hawton, 1995; Rosen & Leiblum, 1995a; D. P. Spector & Carey, 1990).

Later models of sexuality, and specifically sexual desire, focus on the psychological factors influencing sexual behavior (Kaplan, 1979; Levine, 1984, 1987). Kaplan (1979, 1995) notes that Masters and Johnson's model ignores the "motivational" aspects of the human sexual response cycle. Kaplan's (1979) model begins with desire and follows with excitement (arousal) and orgasm. Levine's (1984, 1987) model of sexual desire is a detailed description of three aspects of sexual desire: drive, motivation, and aspiration.

Kaplan (1979, 1995) hypothesized that sexual desire is a distinct stage in the sexual response cycle and is considered to be physiological as well as psychological in nature. The remaining two stages, excitement and orgasm, are viewed similarly to Masters and Johnson's physiological stages. Kaplan (1979) defined sexual desire as the experience of "specific sensations which move the individual to seek out, or become receptive to, sexual experiences. These sensations are produced by the physical activation of a specific neural system in the brain" (p. 10). On the basis of her findings, the diagnostic category of HSDD was added to later versions of the *DSM*'s list of sexual dysfunctions (Kaplan, 1995). She also found that, despite hypoactive sexual desire, the individual might not experience inhibition of either the arousal or the orgasm cycles.

Kaplan was the first clinical researcher to understand the connection between the biological/physiological sexual response cycle and the interpersonal, psychological factors affecting desire. She states that one learns to suppress or to allow sexual desire based on past relational events and the social context (Kaplan, 1979). Her focus, however, remained biologically based and performance-minded. Her explicit goal for the new sex therapy model was "to teach them [clients] how to maneuver their sexual desire in an upward direction" (Kaplan, 1995, p. 6).

In Levine's (1984) classic essay on sexual desire, he conceptualized sexual desire as follows: "Sexual desire is not the discrete entity it has seemed to be. Sexual desire is semantic shorthand for the interaction of at least three other variables—'drive,' 'motivation,' 'aspiration'" (p. 85). Of these three variables, Levine proposed that it is the motivational component that is the most important in a clinical context. This conceptualization, though traditional, is more inclusive. Although Levine addresses the importance of biological sex drive, he places the emphasis on motivation or "willingness" of the individual to engage in sexual activity. Motivation can be induced by both intrapsychic and/or external stimuli. Aspiration or "wish," the cognitive element of sexual desire, plays an important role. An individual may not have a drive or motivation/willingness for sex, but may cognitively wish for sex because it is expected. Aspiration/wish acts as the "gating mechanism" that either allows the system to operate freely or, in its absence, inhibits it. Normal healthy sexual desire means that all three systems—biologic drive, motivation/willingness, and aspiration/wish—are working and interacting together. Within this system, sexual desire fluctuates and its sources can be baffling (Levine, 1984, 1987).

Recent clinical research on the role of desire in the female sex response describes sexual desire as more responsive to sexual stimuli rather than a spontaneous event that precedes sexual activity (Basson, 2000, 2001). Although Basson (2000) states that women may have spontaneous desire, this may be more common for new relationships. In long-term relationships, sexual desire is more often motivated for reasons of sharing "emotional closeness, bonding, commitment, desire to increase a sense of attractiveness and attraction to a partner, and desire to share physical sexual pleasure" (Basson, 2001, p. 34) rather than a "sexual hunger."

Basson also states that sexual desire is greatly impacted by fatigue, distractions, and marital and relational difficulties.

Within the past 10 years, some theorists and clinicians have incorporated the traditional models of approaching human sexuality utilizing systems theory to determine the role the marital system contributes to the etiology and maintenance of the sexual dysfunction (LoPiccolo & Friedman, 1988; MacPhee et al., 1995; Verhulst & Heiman, 1988). The integration of systems theory with both behavioral and psychodynamic theory has greatly enhanced the effectiveness of both the assessment and treatment of sexual dysfunctions, particularly the complex problems related to sexual desire. LoPiccolo and Friedman recommend that couples develop experiential/sensory awareness of their emotions and insight into the etiology of their individual as well as relationship problems. This is to be followed by cognitive restructuring and, finally, behavioral interventions. Further, they suggest that the etiology of sexual dysfunction is broad-based and highly individualized depending on the couple's relational patterns. Relational issues of power and the ability to maintain intimacy, control, trust, and vulnerability are key variables to be addressed in the couple system.

Verhulst and Heiman (1988) conceptualize sexual desire problems as a complex dysfunction of the "synchronization or coordination of the sexual rhythms in a relationship" (p. 243). These clinical theorists take an important step in assessing the "subjective nature of the complaint" (p. 243). Although the addition of systems theory is an important advance in the treatment of sexual dysfunctions, none of these theorists specifically addresses the relationship between sexual desire and the impact of psychodynamic relational patterns, such as sexual objectification.

Up to the present there has been no theoretical construct that adequately explicates the complexities of female sexual desire, nor is there currently a thorough understanding of the etiologic factors that contribute to sexual desire dysfunction. Weis asserts there are two reasons for this: (1) that "relatively little sexuality research is oriented to testing theoretical hypotheses" and (2) "few empirically tested theories with conceptual precision have yet to emerge" (Weis, 1998a, p. 1, 1988b).

Recent contemporary object-relations and feminist theory (Benjamin, 1988, 1995; Chodorow, 1994; Jordan, 1987) have suggested that traditional psychodynamic constructs and biological/physiological processes may not adequately represent aspects of female sexuality and sexual desire. Although Kaplan (1979), Levine (1984, 1987), and Basson (2000, 2001) attempted to integrate the psychological aspects of human sexuality with biological/physiological processes, and LoPiccolo and Friedman (1988) developed a systems approach in assessing sexual dysfunction, there still remains an inadequate theoretical understanding of just how human sexuality might be impacted by interpersonal interactions and sociocultural factors.

By the late 1980s, clinicians began to see couples with more complicated sexual dysfunctions. Couples seeking treatment were no longer seen as simply lacking technical skills and/or sexual information (Wiederman, 1998). These couples presented with multiple sexual dysfunctions and, in many cases, one or both partners experienced long-term difficulties in their sexual lives. It was found that these more complicated cases did not respond well to previously established treatment protocols, especially when one or both partners had low sexual desire (Beck, 1995; Hawton, 1995; Wiederman, 1998).

The high prevalence rate of sexual desire disorders in women combined with poor long-term treatment outcome suggest that further clinical and theoretical analyses and studies are needed. This chapter describes and discusses the role of the psychodynamic relational pattern of sexual objectification, which may be a key component of HSDD.

THEORETICAL ORIENTATION

Existing models of treatment based exclusively on either traditional psychoanalytic theory or biological/behavioral principles are particularly problematic. The biases and assumptions found in these traditional models fail to represent women's experience of sexuality and, thus, may be partly responsible for poor outcome results. There are a number of ways in which these models may appear to inadequately account for all the relevant factors associated with female sexuality.

First, many research studies have focused exclusively on ability to reach orgasm and the frequency of this event as indicators of sexual health. Sex therapy treatment outcome goals have implicitly and primarily focused on increasing the frequency of sexual behavior between individuals (Masters & Johnson, 1966, 1970; Masters et al., 1994), rather than the quality of that sexual experience. In part, this may be due to the difficulty of measuring intrapsychic experiential phenomena such as perceptions, images, and personal meanings of sexuality and sexual desire. However, when researchers include the category of sexual satisfaction along with these factors, some studies show that attaining orgasm may not be synonymous with sexual satisfaction (Beck, Bozman, & Qualtrough, 1991; LoPiccolo & Stock, 1986). This finding suggests that focusing primarily on a traditionally recognized sexual expression, such as orgasm, may be too simplistic and limiting. The exclusion of intrapsychic experiential phenomena may ignore important aspects of the woman's sexual experience.

Second, within the traditional biological/behavioral models, emphasis is placed on the primacy and end goal of heterosexual intercourse (Masters et al., 1994; Rich, 1980; Stock, 1988; Tiefer, 1995). Gavey (1992) states, "The standard heterosexual narrative seems to dictate the situations in which sex is required as well as the form it will take...we are all familiar with the dominant assumption that heterosexual intercourse (coitus) is synonymous with 'real' sex" (p. 332). This bias leaves a whole segment of women, including lesbians and bisexuals, adrift. When sexual preferences and diversity are ignored, it becomes possible to imply psychopathology and/or to isolate those individuals who are outside the dominant assumption that coitus is "real sex."

Finally, the traditional Freudian psychoanalytic model is a biased polarization of gender (i.e., male sexuality as normative, and female sexuality as deficient). This has been so deeply embedded within our culture, it is no longer noticed or questioned. Benjamin (1988) argues that when the phallus is idealized, woman is subsequently repudiated. When the phallus assumes "the power to represent her sexuality as well as his, it denies women's independent sexuality. Thus, masculinity is defined in opposition to woman, and gender is organized as polarity with one side idealized, the other devalued" (p. 168). From the perspective of some feminists, the psychoanalytic model dangerously defines the sociocultural presumption of male superiority and subsequent female inferiority.

The model of sexual objectification and the loss of subjectivity presented here is structured within a framework comprised of contemporary psychodynamic, object-relations, and self psychology theory, and feminist perspectives of gender-role socialization. The integration of these different theories provides the structure to explain and understand the complex stepwise process of sexual objectification, loss of subjectivity, and possible subsequent impairment in the woman's felt experience of sexual desire. The ultimate goal in the integration of contemporary psychological theory with feminist psychology is to account for complex interactions between "internal psychological processes and the external social forces" in the environment (J. Freyd, personal communication, POWR-L, February 24, 1998). The following discussion outlines the basis for the theoretical concepts and the terms that will be used to elaborate the stepwise psychodynamic process of sexual objectification and loss of subjectivity.

The framework used for understanding heterosexual female sexual desire in this chapter includes the inter- and intrarelationships of (1) sexual behavior; (2) the sexual self image (e.g., perceived body image and personal meanings of the sexual self); (3) psychosexual functioning (e.g., internal emotional affect that results in either sexual satisfaction or dissatisfaction); (4) dyadic influences between self and other (e.g., intersubjective processes); and (5) external stimuli (e.g., context, identified gender roles, and social pressures) that result in the experiential (i.e., subjective) state of desire (Chenoweth, 1993). The remainder of this chapter focuses on these last two aspects of female sexual desire, that is, dyadic influences between self and others, and external stimuli as they impact felt desire.

In the context of sexual relationships, *intersubjectivity* is best characterized by the capacity for experiencing oneself as a desiring subject and as one who is desired by another (Benjamin, 1988, 1990, 1995; Jordan, 1987, 1991). The contemporary relational view of intersubjectivity asserts that the role of the object is both an intrapsychic phenomenon and an interpersonal and reciprocal relationship between a self and a real other (Benjamin, 1995; Mitchell, 1988, 1991.) A specific example of the second aspect of female sexual desire occurs in the sexual socialization process, in which women in our society are often sexually objectified (Bartky, 1990; Daniluk, 1993; Fredrickson & Roberts, 1997). It is hypothesized that sexual objectification that is nonmutual and unbalanced between couples may contribute to HSDD in women. Rosen and Leiblum (1995a) state that couples with a significant discrepancy in desire states may experience sexual desire problems, and that, "in such cases, the inhibitory effects of sexual coercion, either overt or covert, by the 'high desire' partner should always be taken into account" (p. 108). Sexual objectification may have a direct, potentially harmful impact on dyadic interactions, which may result in alteration of women's subjective experience of sexual desire and arousal. Further research is needed to adequately ascertain the specific subjective effects of sexual objectification on the woman's sexual response cycle.

Sexual objectification of another individual can be viewed as an intersubjective dyadic stepwise process. The process of viewing an individual as a sex object has been criticized by some feminist theorists as a negative process embedded in our male-dominated society (Bartky, 1990; Fredrickson & Roberts, 1997). It is argued that these theorists may be referring to a negative sexual objectification process that includes the loss of subjectivity in the sexual object. However, sexual objectification need not be viewed solely as an intrinsically negative experience. It can be part of the normal mutual identification process between individuals who are attracted to each other. In other words, attraction for another person at times may in fact involve viewing each other as sexual objects. According to Lothstein (1997, personal communication), sexual objectification may in fact be "a more universal phenomenon than otherwise assumed," especially when viewed from an object-relational and intersubjective perspective. The following discussion identifies different factors present in positive and negative sexual objectification processes.

Several factors characterize the intricate and interactive process of positive sexual objectification that, at the same time, emerge from and effect the self and the other. There is an internal process of identification that results in a projection onto the object. The projection is what the objectifier perceives the other to be for the subject/self. It involves an intrapsychic relationship with the self, both as a subject and as an internalized version of the other as a part of the self (i.e., self/object). If the objectification process is reciprocal and desired by both individuals, there must be a conscious awareness on the part of both individuals that the other is also an external, independent object and subject with a separate and different subjective experience (Chenoweth, 1998). This interactive dyadic (intersubjective) system is "formed by the reciprocal interplay between worlds of experience" (Stolorow, 1997, p. 338).

The process of sexual objectification is *balanced* when it includes a conscious awareness that each is an independent *other* with his or her own separate and private subjective state. Only when the subject acknowledges the possibility of discrepancy in desire states between the two internal experiences is sexual objectification mutual and balanced. For the relationship to feel mutual, both individuals must feel enhanced by the experience and expression of desire (Jordan, 1987).

Therefore, when mutuality is present, one is consciously aware of one's subjective duality of experience: that of having desire as well as being desired (Benjamin, 1995; Jordan, 1987, 1991). Both individuals remain consciously aware that the *other* possesses this same subjective duality of experience, and that the independent other's subjective experience of sexual desire may be discrepant from one's own subjective experience of desire (Benjamin, 1988, 1995). The dyadic interchange mutually influences the other (i.e., affective attunement). This means that the relational experience is both behaviorally and subjectively desirable by both subjects, albeit the levels of desire are not necessarily quantitatively or qualitatively the same. This is a bidirectional process whereby the intersubjective dyadic experience is desired by both (mutuality), and the discrepancies between level and quality of sexual desire are acknowledged as different but sufficiently similar. In other words, each individual views the self as an object and a subject experiencing desire and being desired simultaneously in the affectively attuned and mutual relationship (Chenoweth, 1998).

The process of sexual objectification may play a positive role in sexual attraction and desire. However, it has the potential for becoming a negative intrapsychic and intersubjective experience. A negative sexual objectification process, although still bidirectional, is defined as *unbalanced* and *nonmutual*. This means that the relational experience is not mutually desired by both subjects. It includes the loss of subjectivity on the part of the objectified other. Therefore, what determines a negative outcome from sexual objectification is when the response to sexual objectification is the loss of subjectivity in the objectified person. This is not to say that the objectified person is responsible for this negative outcome, but that loss of subjectivity results from a failed attunement with the object, a lack of recognition or denial on the part of the objectifier that a discrepancy exists between the two individuals' internal worlds. In the case of negative sexual objectification and the subsequent loss of subjectivity, it is proposed that each dyadic participant remains in only one position. This means that one person is the subject, the other is the object. This process involves the initiation of objectification by one individual and the relinquishing of subjectivity by the other. What has not been sufficiently addressed in the literature thus far is the response of the objectified individual and the subsequent loss of one's subjectivity when the *objectified individual* perceives and accepts the self as the projected object of the other (Chenoweth, 1998).

Negative sexual objectification is a process whereby an individual is reduced to some extent to a "thing" or object by another person. The objectified individual is split and fragmented because various parts are sexualized and emphasized at the expense of the whole. The objectified individual's subjectivity, to some harmful degree, is ignored and/or denied. Mutuality between the individuals and a true consent by the objectified recipient are neither required nor present. The loss of subjectivity is a process whereby the view of self is limited to being an object of gratification for the other, and without a conscious awareness of a subjective wish, motivation, or desire separate from the objectifier. The individual relinquishes the self-perception as a subject with the potential for an experience different from that of the objectifier (Chenoweth, 1998).

The components of negative sexual objectification include (1) an intrapsychic process whereby the subject identifies with the *object/other* as an integral part of the self, a self/object; (2) views the object/other as the only possible gratifier of needs; (3) projects his or her subjective experience of sexual desire onto the *object/other* and perceives the object's states as the same as that of the self; and, most important, (4) denies that the subjective experience of the *object/other* may be (and is in most cases) different from that of the self/subject. The objectifier is not consciously aware of the intersubjective process wherein the objectified person may not experience reciprocated sexual desire. The objectifier may even deny the possibility of discrepancy in desire between the two. This demonstrates a distortion in the objectifier's perception of the self as a desired object. This distortion can be defined as a false state of objectivity as a desired object, when in fact the opposite is true. The objectifed person does not desire the objectifier. The primary element of negative sexual objectification is the absence of relating to and interacting with the other as an independent *external other* with separate needs, wishes, and desires.

Completing the intersubjective dyadic cycle of negative sexual objectification, the loss or impairment in the subjectivity of the objectified other ensues. From this author's perspective, the relinquishing or denial of a separate and different internal experience results in the loss of subjectivity in the *objectified other* that is a similar, but reverse, process of the intrapsychic and intersubjective process of the objectifier.

Loss of subjectivity may well begin as an internal process of identification with the external objectifier. The objectified person most likely internalizes the external objectifier, creating a self-representation as the objectifier. The *objectified other* then responds by accepting the projection of the objectifier as the gratifier of needs, regardless of either a conscious or a partially unconscious momentary wish to do otherwise. At this juncture, the *objectified other* views the self as *only an object* for the objectifier and subsequently loses perspective of the self-as-separate-subject with separate needs, wishes, and desires. According to Fredrickson and Roberts (1997), taking an observer's perspective of the self, that of viewing the self as an object, "can profoundly disrupt a woman's flow of consciousness" (p. 180). This impairment of the individual's subjectivity creates a whole array of lost emotional experiences for the self but, most important, leads to the impairment of the elemental subjective experience of female sexual desire.

Specific Consequences of the Loss of Subjectivity

The consequences of the loss of one's subjectivity are varied, multidetermined, and far-reaching. A complete discussion of origins and ramifications related to this loss is beyond the scope of this chapter. However, an elaboration of impairment in the felt experience of sexual desire is the focus of the following discussion. The specific expressions of and outcomes from the loss of subjectivity combine both intrapsychic and intersubjective forces, as well as influential sociocultural imperatives (Benjamin, 1988, 1990, 1995; Chodorow, 1994; Fredrickson & Roberts, 1997; Jordan, 1991) that increase the likelihood of a state of self-alienation (Bartky, 1990). One of the ways individuals make sense of who they are is by attaching meaning to both internal and external events through language (Mitchell, 1991; Stern, 1997; Wrye, 1994). If there is a loss of meaning in either the internal or external world, confusion and alienation are possible.

There appear to be two specific areas affected by the impairment and/or loss in the subjective domain: first is the distortion of reality related to the integrity of the whole self—a discontinuity between self-states and actual denial of the mental content; second is the loss of integration between mental representations of the whole self and the representation of the body/self—a disembodied self. Loss of subjectivity creates a disjointed and skewed perspective of the "real me" related to the "real body" and what is "really happening" (Grand, 1997; Zegans, 1987). Not only is there a disavowal of self related to one's body and between one's internal world and the external world, but a disengagement among the real self, the body, and one's subsequent actions actually occurs. Thoughts, feelings, and behaviors become a "not me" phenomenon. Grand states that inherent in the loss and impairment in subjectivity is "the destruction of linkages between self-states" and "the loss of the senses of agency and of the embodied self" (p. 471). Therefore, the loss of the felt experience transforms and distorts the perception of a "real body" as it relates to the internalized body-self. The split is complete. The dissociation of the self-states combines with the disembodied self, which may lead one to conclude that *I am not really who I am, my body is not me, and my actions are not mine* (Grand, 1997). When this occurs, one might ask, What happens to the experience of sexual desire?

First, however, what does it mean to experience reciprocal sexual desire? How does the felt experience affect perception of the self and others? Unfortunately, these questions are difficult to answer and, in some cases, impossible to describe. Many times, the true meaning of the experience is difficult to articulate. In part, this may be due to the limitations of language or to the inability to translate deep unmodulated thoughts and feelings from the unconscious mind. Hurston (1990, as cited in Burack, 1994) states, "There is a depth of thought untouched by words, and deeper still is a gulf of formless feelings untouched by thought" (p. 26). Feelings of deep love, passion, and desire possess qualities that many times defy description.

To experience sexual desire means to feel alive, excited, potent, and connected with one's mind and body (Levine, 1995). Most important, when another reciprocates sexual desire, one feels deeply understood as an individual (Jordan, 1987) and one's spirit is repaired and renewed (Khan, 1979). In more technical terms, one's self-identity and experience of one's body are integrated as an embodied self with the capacity to own one's thoughts, feelings, and behaviors (Benjamin, 1988, 1990, 1995; Dio Bleichmar, 1995; Jordan, 1987; Young, 1992).

Person (1980) proposes that an adequate theory of sexuality and sexual desire must include the conscious subjectivity of that state of being and that one's perceptions of sexuality are intrinsically intertwined with one's identity and relationship with others. Jordan (1987) states that sexual desire plays an integral part in "attaining a sense of clarity in knowing ourselves" (p. 1). Thus, the loss of the felt experience (subjectivity) of sexual desire has the potential to alter one's perceived experience of sexual identity, sexual potency, agency, autonomy, efficacy, and one's own bodily reactions and behaviors. A powerful disconnection can occur between the self and the body, which may be exhibited as an absence of intention, motivation, and knowledge of the ability to feel sexual desire. One becomes a disowned passive self that is *done to* instead of realizing the capacity for *doing with* an other. To make sense out of confusing and contradictory data belonging to a true self-state that ultimately becomes dissociated, one may conclude that *this body* and *this self* do not have the capacity to want, feel, or have sexual desire. One is bereft of any sensations of one's own and is vulnerable to the possibility that the only satisfaction is that of being an *object* to the *other*. When satisfaction is derived only from being an object to the other, it may appear to render some sense of control, but it could prove to be a hollow victory, because only the other's intention, motivation, and desire are at play. The self sees the self from only an observer's perspective. The perception of a different subjective experience of sexual desire in the self may now be blocked when one no longer views the self as a subject.

Fredrickson and Roberts (1997) hypothesize that continued "sexualized evaluation" of women has profound psychological effects on a woman's sense of self and increases her risk for eating disorders, depression, and sexual difficulties. They suggest that, at the psychological level, sexual objectification generates negative emotions of shame and anxiety, interferes with "peak motivation states," and encourages a loss of awareness of internal physiological states. Lacking a conscious awareness of a separate self-state or separate felt experience outside of the objectifier's perspective, the objectified individual has unconsciously accepted the position (projection) as the gratifying self/object of the objectifier's needs. This impairment of the subjective self most likely plays an important role in the destruction and/or repression of any conscious awareness of important affective differences in felt experience (Chenoweth, 1998).

Factors That Maintain the Process of Sexual Objectification and Loss of Subjectivity

The loss of subjectivity due to objectification is influenced and maintained by a complex interchange of intrapsychic, intersubjective, and sociocultural factors that impede an integrated sense of self-experience and self-embodiment (Bartky, 1990; Fredrickson & Roberts, 1997;

Khan, 1979; Zegans, 1987). The goal is to understand the factors that maintain the process of sexual objectification and subsequent loss of subjectivity in the woman. Particular attention is paid to psychodynamic intrapsychic processes (e.g., organizing fantasies and defense strategies), poor interpersonal communication strategies that impede mutuality and attunement, and sociocultural influences that alter and/or impact the felt experience of sexual desire.

When there is negative sexual objectification, the objectifier perceives and projects only his or her own felt experience onto the woman. The objectifier ignores her perceived experience and this can elicit in the objectified woman intrapsychic defensive reactions of denial, dissociation, and disavowal. Such reactions stem directly from the misattunement and absence of mutuality in the relationship. Dissociation and disavowal appear to play an important role in the loss of subjectivity and impairment in the felt experience under specific conditions of sexual objectification. Dio Bleichmar (1995) explains this defensive process as follows: "If the body possesses an attribute of sexual meaning that does not arise from one's own subjectivity, mechanisms of disavowal and dissociation must be brought into play in order to free oneself of that intrusive meaning" (p. 340).

The process of viewing oneself as an object is not only influenced by one's intrapsychic processes and dyadic interchanges, but also is externally framed by the cultural and linguistic milieu in which women are socialized (Bartky, 1990; Sheinberg & Penn, 1991; Van Buren, 1994). Fredrickson and Roberts (1997) state "that the cultural milieu of objectification functions to socialize girls and women to...treat themselves as objects to be looked at and evaluated. In other words...women often adopt an observer's perspective on their physical selves" (p. 177). This means that not only the individual looking at the woman will see her in culturally prescribed ways, but that the woman who views herself as an object will claim "ownership of socialized values and attitudes, often by incorporating them into [her] sense of self" (p. 177). Examples of this socialization process include pressures to maintain standards of beauty and thinness sanctioned by society, as well as expectations to behave sexually in gender-specific roles (e.g., woman as passive, submissive, or nurturing; Tiefer, 1995).

The expressions of sexuality—sexual desire, function, and actual behavior—are inextricably linked with one's context and culturally derived sex and gender roles (Chodorow, 1994). Therefore, when a woman perceives and views herself as a culturally derived object to be looked at and evaluated, one might presume that she is less aware of or may deny her own subjective experience, particularly if that felt experience is different from a prescribed gender role. For example, a woman's experience of sexual desire may be less than or more than the assumed norm as culturally prescribed. Not surprisingly, one makes assumptions about *normal* sexual behavior and expression based less on facts than on cultural or religious mores and political mandates (Tiefer, 1995).

The situation becomes even more complex when these culturally prescribed roles are aligned within the dyadic interactions of a significant other's socialized intentions, motivations, and desires. A woman's felt experience of sexual desire is impacted and, in many cases, altered by the sociocultural and interpersonal context.

METHODS OF PSYCHOSEXUAL ASSESSMENT AND INTERVENTION

The psychosexual clinical interview is the most important assessment tool for evaluating the psychological etiology of hypoactive sexual desire. Although there are several objective self-report sexuality assessment measures, many are one-dimensional. Outcome is based on overt behaviors, frequency, and performance indicators (Talmadge & Talmadge, 1990). One difficulty in measuring only overt behavior is that sexual behavior can occur without sexual desire and vice versa (Beck et al., 1991). In addition, most sexuality assessment tools do not measure cognitive, emotional, contextual, and relational factors, which may contribute to hypoactive sexual desire. And there is significant difficulty in measuring an internal subjective experience such as desire: "Sexual desire is *not* a behavior" but a feeling about and/or "*interest in* sexual activity" (I. P. Spector, Carey, & Steinberg, 1996, p. 178). Therefore, an extensive psychosexual clinical interview is the primary assessment tool for determining the psychological factors of hypoactive sexual desire.

Prior to beginning psychological treatment for hypoactive sexual desire, it is important for the woman to have a recent medical/sexual workup by her physician. This examination may include a thorough medical history, an internal and external physical exam, lab work, and possible blood flow studies of the genitals. If the patient has not had a recent medical/gynecological exam, it would be prudent to do so to rule out any major illnesses, physical pain, or anatomical or physiological component of hypoactive sexual desire (e.g., surgery, illness, or menopausal status).

Prior to evaluating the specific sexual difficulties, the clinician takes a thorough psychiatric and medication history because disorders such as depression, schizophrenia, posttraumatic stress, and medication side effects have been associated with hypoactive sexual desire (Rosen & Leiblum, 1987). The psychosexual section of the interview includes details of the couple's sexual history, current problems, and current sexual behaviors. The clinician obtains a detailed sexual history of the individual's and/or couple's sexual behavior (see Table 15.1) and must thoroughly evaluate and assess the interpersonal communication style of each individual. Most important is to observe interactions and verbalizations

Table 15.1 Psychosexual clinical interview for female sexual dysfunction.

Prior to the formal psychosexual history:
   Reason for referral and presenting problem.
   Assess for level of anxiety about discussing sexual issues.
   Briefly explain the psychosexual evaluation process.
   Discuss confidentiality and patient's right not to answer sensitive sexual questions.
   History of psychiatric, medical, and medication history.

1. *Psychosexual History*
   First sexual experience.
   Current and past relationships.
   Masturbation practices.
   Sexual trauma/domestic violence/rape.
   Unusual sexual practices/fetishes.

2. *Sexual Functioning in Current Relationship/ Self and Partner*
   Description of behaviors.
   Frequency of behaviors.
   Level of desire, arousal, and orgasm.
   Subjective experience/satisfaction.
   Psychological issues/anxiety/depression.

3. *Sexual Self-Image and Sexual Self-Esteem Issues*
   Identity.
   Orientation.
   Body image.
   Sexual efficacy.
   Sexual knowledge.
   Sexual autonomy within the relationship.
   Awareness of subjective experience, feelings, thoughts, and fantasies.

4. *Sexual Attitudes and Hidden Assumptions*
   Basic attitudes.
   Family values.
   Cultural and religious values.
   How values differ from partners and/or family.

5. *Sexual Fantasies*
   Awareness.
   Frequency.
   Sexual themes.
   Ability to discuss with partner.

6. *Sexual Communication Styles*
   Ability to communicate needs, feelings, and thoughts with partner.
   Comfort level with self and partner.
   How couple manages sexual disagreements.
   Level of disclosure.

between the couple or by the individual wherein evidence of sexual objectification may be embedded. For example:

WOMAN/COUPLE: I don't feel any sexual desire, ever, but I know he needs to have it.
MALE/COUPLE: She used to have sex all the time. I know if she just tried, it would work.

In the treatment of couples, it is important to identify, challenge, and change the unconscious process of negative sexual objectification to a more conscious positive sexual objectification process. The goal of treatment is to facilitate the identification and resolution of the imbalances and nonmutual relational interactions that are maintained by negative sexual objectification. To accomplish these goals, the following steps are recommended:

1. Identify and define the process of negative sexual objectification.
2. Encourage each partner to describe his or her subjective experience preceding and during intimate interactions.
3. Identify the conditions wherein one partner denies subjective differences between them and the other dissociates or disavows his or her different felt experience.
4. Increase understanding of the consequences and maintenance of negative sexual objectification within the relationship.
5. Develop strategies and capacities so that each partner remains both a subject and an object within the intimate relationship.

Treatment needs to address the multiple etiologic factors, including the intrapsychic, interpersonal, and sociocultural, that contribute to the maintenance of negative sexual objectification.

It is posited that these changes will promote mutuality and balance between partners, thus increasing the capacity of individuals to view themselves as both a subject and an object. It is believed that when one is able to see both perspectives, psychological health is improved and one's capacity is increased for experiencing oneself as simultaneously having desire and being desired (Benjamin, 1995).

MAJOR PROBLEMS TREATED

SEXUAL TRAUMA HISTORY

Obvious examples of negative sexual objectification are situations of rape, childhood sexual abuse, domestic violence, and sexual harassment. The empirical literature is replete with examples of individuals with histories of sexual trauma who experience sexual difficulties, particularly problems with sexual desire (Becker, 1989; Beitchman et al., 1992; Chenoweth, 1993; Finkelhor, 1990; Maltz, 1991; Tharinger, 1990; Westerlund, 1992). It is important for the clinician to specifically address the impact of negative sexual objectification in this patient population. Although the long-term treatment goal is to treat specific sexual sequelae in this patient population, treatment should first focus on crisis stabilization, posttraumatic stress, depression, anxiety, self-image, and loss of control issues.

INDIVIDUALS AND COUPLES WITH HYPOACTIVE SEXUAL DESIRE

The impact of negative sexual objectification and loss of subjectivity in the experience of female sexual desire may involve other types of situations aside from sexual traumatization, domestic violence, and harassment. Less obvious examples of negative sexual objectification and loss of subjectivity also occur in adult sexual relationships in which the mutuality and balance between individuals has been lost. It has been established that hypoactive sexual desire is the most prevalent sexual disorder for adult women

(Hawton, 1995; O'Carroll, 1991), as well as being quite difficult to treat (Beck, 1995; Levine, 1995; Rosen & Leiblum, 1995a).

Couples or individuals presenting with marital stress and hypoactive sexual desire in the woman may benefit from treatment that focuses specifically on the impact of negative sexual objectification. It is argued that the dyadic process of sexual objectification and loss of subjectivity may be partially responsible for the lack of sexual desire in some women. For example, what originally begins as a simple discrepancy in sexual desire levels between the couple over time may develop into problematic dyadic interactions of misattunement, imbalance, and lack of mutuality. The sexual objectification by one individual, the loss of subjectivity in the other, and the subsequent impairment of female sexual desire may be factors in the development of hypoactive sexual desire disorder.

CASE EXAMPLE

The following case was referred to a private practice setting. Initially, the wife, Linda, was seen in a women's sexual health clinic for low sexual desire. A physical exam, hormonal studies, and blood flow studies were completed prior to beginning therapy. Although the lab studies showed that Linda was perimenopausal, no significant physical evidence was found to explain her loss of sexual desire. Linda called requesting couples therapy and stated, "I'm basically calling because my husband wants me to do something. If I had my way, I wouldn't really care if I ever had sex again. It's just not important to me anymore, but I know I need to do something to save my marriage. I really do love him." This case illustrates the process and ramifications of how negative sexual objectification and loss of subjectivity impair sexual desire in the objectified individual in adult sexual relationships.

DIAGNOSIS AND ASSESSMENT

David and Linda have been married for eight years. David is 48 years old and Linda is 45 years old. This is the second marriage for both individuals. Each has teenage children from their former marriages, no children from this marriage. David's two girls live with his former wife; however, they spend most of the summer with David and Linda. Linda's twin teenage sons live with them full time, except for one month during the summer when they visit their father. David is a financial planner for a large brokerage firm and Linda is an attorney with a large law firm. Both are avid hikers, when time permits. David and Linda describe a whirlwind affair during their courtship, when they traveled and exercised together from the beginning. They initially experienced an active sex life; however, both agree that they did not discuss this much and assumed that each was happy with the "way things were." They reported having sexual relations three to four times per week until approximately two years ago. However, David did state that he was the initiator of sexual intimacy most of the time. For the past two years, the couple's sexual relationship has become increasingly sporadic and less satisfying for both. For the most part, they describe the rest of their lives as "good"; however, they have both noticed that they argue about small things more than usual.

David reports that he believes "Linda is playing a game with him." He states, "I know she really wants to have sex. She wants sex as much as I do. I know when she has sex, she loves it, just like I do. We probably have sex only every other week now. I know this sounds crazy, but sometimes I feel like I have to have more sex, the more she avoids me." He reports that he asks Linda every morning and evening if she wants to have sex. He describes feeling unwanted and misunderstood when Linda says no. He withdraws in silence and anger.

Linda reports that she feels anxious or "numbed out" at times. Mostly, she tries to "forget" what is happening in her sexual relationship with David. She states, "Mostly, I just try to avoid him. I don't know why I try to avoid him so much, but it just seems like all he wants is sex. I don't feel like having sex at all anymore. He is not interested in how I feel, so I just keep my feelings to myself. Well, actually, I'm not sure how I really feel. When I do have sex, it's like my body works, but my heart doesn't."

The information from the initial intake demonstrates that David and Linda are experiencing a significant discrepancy in their levels of perceived sexual desire. David is frustrated and angry that Linda does not respond to him as he wishes. He believes he knows what her internal experience of desire is more than she does (e.g., "She wants sex as much as I do"). Linda is unable to access sufficiently her internal experience (e.g., feels numbed). Under these conditions, David cannot see Linda as having a separate experience from him, and Linda is unable to access her separate experience.

CASE FORMULATION

Linda's defensive process of numbing places her in the position of being an object of desire to David and prevents her from taking a proactive (subjective view of self) versus a passive (objective view of self) position; thus, she relinquishes her separate subjectivity. At this juncture, Linda identifies herself as an object only or as the other (David) perceives her. She will have sex to please David, but her experience of sex provides her with no satisfaction or sense of intimate connection. Her motivation is to manage her "anxiety" and defend against the fear of loss of the relationship were she to continue to deny David or to voice her own different level of desire. From Linda's perspective, the interaction is not mutual or balanced. She is not viewing herself as a subject who experiences desire as well as an object of desire. She is not acting from her own experience of desire, but from David's projection of desire and her reflected sense of being an object.

From David's perspective, Linda's rejection of him increases his internal experience of desire for her. His increase in perceived desire and projection of desire onto Linda may be a defensive strategy to manage his fear that he is unlovable. David's repeated requests for sexual behavior is an example of his inability to view Linda as having a separate internal experience of desire as different from his own. He believes that if he could just get her to "stop playing a game," she would recognize her desire for him as equal to his for her. David projects onto Linda his own internal state of desire as a defense against his fear of rejection and that he may indeed be unlovable. He needs Linda to view him as a desirable sexual object. His projection that Linda really "does want to have sex" with him every time he wishes defends against a narcissistic injury and rejection of him as lovable.

TREATMENT APPROACH AND
RATIONALE FOR ITS SELECTION

The treatment of low sexual desire disorders is a complex psychotherapy task, involving individual and couple psychodynamics, systems change, and behavioral issues combined with family of origin and gender-role socialization. The model of sexual objectification and loss of subjectivity presented here combines contemporary psychodynamic, object-relations, and self psychology theories with feminist perspectives of gender-role socialization. The integration of these theories provides the structure to explain, understand, and treat some of the complex processes that might maintain and exacerbate decreased sexual desire in a woman in an adult relationship. Psychodynamic object-relational couples therapy was the therapy of choice to treat low sexual desire in this couple.

The couple was seen initially together and then individual sessions were scheduled with each. It is important to establish rapport with both individuals at the onset, before interviewing each. David originally did not want to attend couples therapy. He felt the problem was Linda's and that she should "fix it." He stated at the first session, "I really don't think this is my problem. I'm not the one who doesn't want to have sex. Why can't you just talk with her? She's always been able to do whatever she wants before. She should just fix it."

The initial joint session was used to assess the level of sexual difficulties, but most important was to obtain cooperation and motivation for couples treatment. Although Linda could choose individual treatment for her difficulties, this might prove to be more difficult, longer term, and perhaps more disruptive to the integrity of the couple. When only one individual changes within the dyad, dissatisfaction and resistance can ensue, both on the part of the individual in treatment and the partner who has refused to change. After the first session, Linda and David chose to proceed with couples therapy.

The individual sessions were scheduled to give each a chance to discuss problems they currently perceived to be too difficult to discuss in front of each other. This allowed the therapist to assess for issues that may prevent couples therapy from progressing (e.g., a secret affair or trauma or specific wish to separate or divorce that has not been discussed). The individual sessions allowed each partner to discuss family history and personal history not previously discussed in detail with each other. It turned out that both were committed to saving the marriage.

During Linda's individual session, she revealed a history of date rape at the age of 15. She never disclosed this information to anyone. At the time of the session, she believed David would not understand. She described her mother as quite passive and dominated by her father, a successful physician in the community. She has two older brothers who also believe that women should remain in the home. She learned at a young age that feelings "were of no use." Linda's professional success has never been positively acknowledged by anyone in her family; in fact, her decision to become an attorney was actively discouraged by her father. She moved away from her family as a way to avoid their criticism. Linda acknowledged that she wants to learn about herself, but described this process as terrifying. Feelings mean "chaos."

David's individual session revealed a history of a borderline/narcissistic mother who left the family when David was 6 years old. He was told by his father that his mother simply "couldn't deal with the family and that she had to do her own thing." He has had no communication with her for 20 years. He states that he does not "think about her much anymore" and in fact "hates her." He believed he has dealt with her disappearance and that it did not affect his feelings now. David indicated that he really loves Linda. He wants to "work on things"; however, he continued to believe that Linda needed to stop playing the "sexual game."

REFERENCE TO EXISTING TREATMENT PROTOCOLS

There are no specific psychotherapy protocols for treating sexual objectification and loss of subjectivity related to low sexual desire. Use of traditional sex therapy, which incorporates sensate focus techniques and focuses on increasing sexual behavior, is limited and would not address the psychodynamic intra- and intersubjective processes of sexual objectification and loss of subjectivity that may lead to low or absence of sexual desire. However, Magnavita's (1997, 2000) approach of integrative relational therapy, designed to address the restructuring of defenses and personality issues, provides the framework to interpret and intervene in the ongoing intra- and intersubjective process of sexual objectification of one partner. The use of Magnavita's approach actively challenges the couple to examine and modify unhealthy defense strategies, disruptive patterns of emotional responses, and the legacy of family patterns of relating in their present relationship.

The addition of an analytic relational feminist perspective (Benjamin, 1990, 1995; Jordan, 1987) provides a theoretical structure to examine in detail the intersubjective processes of a self-other perspective. In treating low sexual desire and possible sexual objectification of the partner, the development of a self-other perspective becomes vital to managing and incorporating discrepant levels of desire and differences in internal experience. As stated earlier, for a relationship to be mutual, balanced, and intimately connected, the partners need to view the self as both an object and a subject experiencing desire and being desired simultaneously. This bidirectional process allows for the individual experience of sexual desire, which includes discrepancies between level and quality of sexual desire. The differences in sexual desire can then be experienced without threat of rejection on the part of the objectifier or the need to eradicate the self-experience on the part of the objectified other.

POSTTERMINATION SYNOPSIS AND EFFECTIVENESS DATA

Linda and David remain in couples treatment. At present, they have completed 10 sessions. At this juncture, Linda continues to experience significant anxiety about expressing her internal experience; however, she has progressed to the point where she is consciously aware of her internal state and is no longer numbing. She continues to feel frightened of her emotions, especially those that feel negative and chaotic. Nonetheless, she is developing the capacity to tolerate and identify these feelings. This new capacity has allowed her to begin to express her sense of self as a woman with desires of her own, including having a level of sexual desire separate from David's. She has begun to understand that her family experience was one of forcing her to repress her anger at her father's dominance over women. She has gained an understanding of what it means to be passive versus proactive in establishing and verbalizing her needs.

David continues to be somewhat skeptical about Linda's "sexual game." He has made progress in understanding his feelings of rejection when Linda does not exactly mirror his needs. He struggles with tolerating his perceived sense of rejection. He has begun to understand and examine his feelings of abandonment by his mother and how these feelings relate to his fear of Linda's rejecting him sexually. Although David and Linda need continued treatment, both feel that the therapy has been positive for their relationship. Linda has experienced periods of feeling renewed sexual desire; David feels encouraged by her response to him.

Linda's struggles with accessing and expressing her subjective experience without overwhelming anxiety and David's feelings of rejection and abandonment have presented challenges to this couple. At one point during treatment (sessions 6 to 8), David became extremely angry and considered leaving therapy. Linda experienced renewed fears that if she were to express herself, David would want to leave the relationship as well as therapy. Identifying each partner's defensive strategies for managing their overwhelming fears adequately allowed the couple to gain understanding of their vulnerabilities. This provided the framework to tolerate separate internal experiences without destabilization. David was able to allow Linda to experience her separate level of desire without assuming it meant a rejection of him sexually.

Linda developed a capacity to access and express her separate subjective experience without numbing.

REFERENCES

American Psychiatric Association. (1980). *Diagnostic and statistical manual of mental disorders* (3rd ed.). Washington, DC: Author.

American Psychiatric Association. (1987). *Diagnostic and statistical manual of mental disorders* (3rd ed., rev.). Washington, DC: Author.

American Psychiatric Association. (1994). *Diagnostic and statistical manual of mental disorders* (4th ed.). Washington, DC: Author.

Bartky, S. L. (1990). *Femininity and domination: Studies in the phenomenology of oppression.* New York: Routledge.

Basson, R. (2000). The female sexual response: A different model. *Journal of Sex and Marital Therapy, 26,* 51–65.

Basson, R. (2001). Human sex-response cycle. *Journal of Sex and Marital Therapy, 27,* 33–43.

Beck, J. G. (1995). Hypoactive Sexual Desire Disorder: An overview. *Journal of Consulting and Clinical Psychology, 63,* 919–927.

Beck, J. G., Bozman, A. W., & Qualtrough, T. (1991). The experience of sexual desire: Psychological correlates in a college sample. *Journal of Sex Research, 28,* 443–456.

Becker, J. V. (1989). Impact of sexual abuse on sexual functioning. In S. R. Leiblum & R. C. Rosen (Eds.), *Principles and practice of sex therapy* (pp. 298–318). New York: Guilford Press.

Beitchman, J. H., Zucker, K. J., Hood, J. E., DaCosta, G. A., Akman, D., & Cassavia, E. (1992). A review of the long-term effects of child sexual abuse. *Child Abuse and Neglect, 16,* 101–119.

Benjamin, J. (1988). *The bonds of love: Psychoanalysis, feminism, and the problem of domination.* New York: Pantheon.

Benjamin, J. (1990). An outline of intersubjectivity: The development of recognition. *Psychoanalytic Psychology* (Suppl. 7), 33–46.

Benjamin, J. (1995). *Like subjects, love objects: Essays on recognition and sexual difference.* New Haven, CT: Yale University Press.

Burack, C. (1994). *The problem of the passions: Feminism, psychoanalysis, and social theory.* New York: New York University Press.

Chenoweth, M. S. (1993). *Lack of sexual desire and arousal in adult heterosexual women survivors of childhood sexual abuse.* Unpublished masters' thesis, Pacific University, Forest Grove, OR.

Chenoweth, M. S. (1998). *Female sexual desire, subjectivity, and the problem of negative sexual objectification.* Unpublished doctoral dissertation, Pacific University, Forest Grove, OR.

Chodorow, N. J. (1994). *Femininities, masculinities, sexualities: Freud and beyond.* Lexington: University of Kentucky Press.

Dio Bleichmar, E. (1995). The secret in the constitution of female sexuality: The effects of the adult's sexual look upon the subjectivity of the girl. *Journal of Clinical Psychoanalysis, 4,* 331–342.

Donahey, K. M., & Carroll, R. A. (1993). Gender differences in factors associated with hypoactive sexual desire. *Journal of Sex and Marital Therapy, 19,* 25–40.

Finkelhor, D. (1990). Early and long-term effects of child sexual abuse: An update. *Professional Psychology: Research and Practice, 21,* 325–330.

Fredrickson, B. L., & Roberts, T. (1997). Objectification theory: Toward understanding women's lived experiences and mental health risks. *Psychology of Women Quarterly, 21,* 173–206.

Freud, S. (1953). Three essays on the theory of sexuality. In J. Strachey (Ed. and Trans.), *The standard edition of the complete psychological works of Sigmund Freud* (Vol. 7, pp. 135–230). London: Hogarth Press. (Original work published 1905)

Gavey, N. (1992). Technologies and effects of heterosexual coercion. *Feminism and Psychology, 2,* 325–351.

Grand, S. (1997). The paradox of innocence: Dissociative "adhesive" states in perpetrators of incest. *Psychoanalytic Dialogues, 7,* 465–490.

Hawton, K. (1995). Treatment of sexual dysfunctions by sex therapy and other approaches. *British Journal of Psychiatry, 167,* 307–314.

Hawton, K., & Catalan, J. (1986). Prognostic factors in sex therapy. *Behavior Research Therapy, 24,* 377–385.

Hawton, K., Catalan, J., & Fagg, J. (1991). Low sexual desire: Sex therapy results and prognostic factors. *Behavior Research Therapy, 29,* 217–224.

Hawton, K., Catalan, J., Martin, C., & Fagg, J. (1986). Long-term outcome of sex therapy. *Behavior Research Therapy, 24,* 665–675.

Jordan, J. V. (1987). *Clarity in connection: Empathic knowing, desire and sexuality.* Wellesley, MA: Wellesley College, Stone Center.

Jordan, J. V. (1991). The meaning of mutuality. In J. V. Jordan, A. G. Kaplan, J. B. Miller, I. P. Stiver, & J. L. Surrey (Eds.), *Women's growth in connection* (pp. 81–96). New York: Guilford Press.

Kaplan, H. S. (1979). *Disorders of sexual desire.* New York: Simon & Schuster.

Kaplan, H. S. (1995). *The sexual desire disorders: Dysfunctional regulation of sexual motivation.* New York: Brunner/Mazel.

Khan, M. M. R. (1979). *Alienation in perversions.* New York: International Universities Press.

Kinsey, A. C., Pomeroy, W. B., Martin, C. E., & Gebbard, P. H. (1953). *Sexual behavior in the human female.* Philadelphia: Saunders.

Kohn, I. R., & Kaplan, S. A. (1999, September). Female sexual dysfunction: What is known and what remains to be determined. *Contemporary Urology,* 54–72.

Levine, S. B. (1984). An essay on the nature of sexual desire. *Journal of Sex and Marital Therapy, 10,* 83–96.

Levine, S. B. (1987). More on the nature of sexual desire. *Journal of Sex and Marital Therapy, 13,* 35–44.

Levine, S. B. (1988). Intrapsychic and individual aspects of sexual desire. In S. R. Leiblum & R. C. Rosen (Eds.), *Sexual desire disorders* (pp. 21–44). New York: Guilford Press.

Levine, S. B. (1995). What is clinical sexuality? *Psychiatric Clinics of North America, 18,* 1–6.

LoPiccolo, J., & Friedman, J. M. (1988). Broad-spectrum treatment of low sexual desire: Integration of cognitive, behavioral, and systemic therapy. In S. R. Leiblum & R. C. Rosen (Eds.), *Sexual desire disorders* (pp. 107–144). New York: Guilford Press.

LoPiccolo, J., & Stock, W. E. (1986). Treatment of sexual dysfunction. *Journal of Consulting and Clinical Psychology, 54,* 158–167.

MacPhee, D. C., Johnson, S. M., & Van Der Veer, M. M. (1995). Low sexual desire in women: The effects of marital therapy. *Journal of Sex and Marital Therapy, 21,* 159–173.

Magnavita, J. J. (1997). *Restructuring personality disorders: A short-term dynamic approach.* New York: Guilford Press.

Magnavita, J. J. (2000). *Relational therapy for personality disorders.* New York: Wiley.

Maltz, W. (1991). *The sexual healing journey: A guide for survivors of sexual abuse.* New York: HarperCollins.

Masters, W. H., & Johnson, V. E. (1966). *Human sexual response.* Boston: Little, Brown.

Masters, W. H., & Johnson, V. E. (1970). *Human sexual inadequacy.* Boston: Little, Brown.

Masters, W. H., Johnson, V. E., & Kolodny, R. C. (1994). *Heterosexuality.* New York: HarperCollins.

Mitchell, S. A. (1988). *Relational concepts in psychoanalysis.* Cambridge, MA: Harvard University Press.

Mitchell, S. A. (1991). Contemporary perspectives on self: Toward an integration. *Psychoanalytic Dialogues, 1,* 121–147.

O'Carroll, R. (1991). Sexual desire disorders: A review of controlled treatment studies. *Journal of Sex Research, 28,* 607–624.

Person, E. S. (1980). Sexuality as the mainstay of identity: Psychoanalytic perspectives. *Signs: Journal of Women in Culture and Society, 5,* 605–630.

Rich, A. (1980). Compulsory heterosexuality and lesbian experience. In C. R. Stimpson & E. S. Person (Eds.), *Women, sex, and sexuality* (pp. 62–91). Chicago: University of Chicago Press.

Rosen, R. C., & Beck, J. G. (1988). *Patterns of sexual arousal: Psychophysiological processes and clinical applications.* New York: Guilford Press.

Rosen, R. C., & Leiblum, S. R. (1987). Current approaches to the evaluations of sexual desire disorders. *Journal of Sex Research, 23,* 141–162.

Rosen, R. C., & Leiblum, S. R. (1995a). Hypoactive sexual desire. *Psychiatric Clinics of North America, 18,* 107–121.

Rosen, R. C., & Leiblum, S. R. (1995b). Treatment of sexual disorders in the 1990s: An integrated approach. *Journal of Consulting and Clinical Psychology, 63,* 877–890.

Schreiner-Engel, D., & Schiavi, R. C. (1986). Lifetime psychopathology in individuals with low sexual desire. *Journal of Nervous and Mental Diseases, 174,* 646–651.

Seagraves, K. B., & Seagraves, R. T. (1991). Hypoactive sexual desire disorders: Prevalence and comorbidity in 906 subjects. *Journal of Sex and Marital Therapy, 17,* 55–58.

Sheinberg, M., & Penn, P. (1991). Gender dilemmas, gender questions, and the gender mantra. *Journal of Marital and Family Therapy, 17,* 33–44.

Spector, D. P., & Carey, M. P. (1990). Incidence and prevalence of the sexual dysfunctions: A critical review of the empirical literature. *Archives of Sexual Behavior, 19,* 389–408.

Spector, I. P., Carey, M. P., & Steinberg, L. (1996). The sexual desire inventory: Development, factor structure, and evidence of reliability. *Journal of Sex and Marital Therapy, 22,* 175–190.

Stern, D. B. (1997). *Unformulated experience: From dissociation to imagination in psychoanalysis.* Hillsdale, NJ: Analytic Press.

Stock, W. (1988). Propping up the phallocracy: A feminist critique of sex therapy and research. *Women and Therapy, 7,* 23–41.

Stolorow, R. D. (1997). Dynamic, dyadic, intersubjective systems: An evolving paradigm for psychoanalysis. *Psychoanalytic Psychology, 14,* 337–346.

Talmadge, L. D., & Talmadge, W. C. (1990, Spring). Sexuality assessment measure for clinical use: A review. *American Journal of Family Therapy, 18,* 80–104.

Tharinger, D. (1990). Impact of child sexual abuse on developing sexuality. *Professional Psychology: Research and Practice, 21,* 331–337.

Tiefer, L. (1988). A feminist critique of the sexual dysfunction nomenclature. *Women and Therapy, 7,* 5–21.

Tiefer, L. (1995). *Sex is not a natural act and other essays.* Boulder, CO: Westview Press.

Tiefer, L. (2001). The "Consensus" conference on female sexual dysfunction: Conflicts of interest and hidden agendas. *Journal of Sex and Marital Therapy, 27,* 227–236.

Van Buren, J. (1994). The engendering of female subjectivity. *American Journal of Psychoanalysis, 54,* 109–125.

Verhulst, J., & Heiman, J. R. (1988). A systems perspective on sexual desire. In S. R. Leiblum & R. C. Rosen (Eds.), *Sexual desire disorders* (pp. 243–267). New York: Guilford Press.

Weis, D. L. (1998a). The use of theory in sexuality research. *Journal of Sex Research, 35,* 1–9.

Weis, D. L. (1998b). Conclusion: The state of sexual theory. *Journal of Sex Research, 35,* 100–114.

Westerlund, E. (1992). *Women's sexuality after childhood sexual abuse.* New York: Norton.

Wiederman, M. W. (1998). The state of theory in sex therapy. *Journal of Sex Research, 35,* 88–99.

Wrye, H. K. (1994). Narrative scripts: Composing a life with ambition and desire. *American Journal of Psychoanalysis, 54,* 127–141.

Young, L. (1992). Sexual abuse and the problem of embodiment. *Child Abuse and Neglect, 16,* 89–100.

Zegans, L. S. (1987). The embodied self: Personal integration in health and illness. *Advances, Institute for the Advancement of Health, 4,* 29–45.

SECTION FOUR

PSYCHOTHERAPY WITH FAMILIES AND COUPLES

Chapter 16   Object-Relations Couples Therapy

Chapter 17   Self-Object Relationship Therapy with Couples

Chapter 18   Relational Psychodynamics for Complex Clinical Syndromes

CHAPTER 16

Object-Relations Couples Therapy

MARION F. SOLOMON AND RITA E. LYNN

An object-relations approach to understanding intimate relationships helps to illuminate the treatment of patients with a history of traumatic attachments. Often, inter- or intrapsychic turmoil interferes with the therapist's ability to sort out exactly what is occurring with a couple. The goals of this chapter are fourfold: (1) to contextualize the application of object-relations theory in the treatment of couples; (2) to clarify the diagnosis of underlying dynamics between partners; (3) to suggest a treatment method that can help couples stop recreating early object relations with their current partners; and (4) to establish means of identifying which couples may benefit from this approach to treatment.

OBJECT-RELATIONS THEORY AND COUPLES PSYCHOTHERAPY

The application of object-relations concepts to the problems of couples has a history at least 60 years long. After individual analysis was firmly established as an effective way of unraveling intrapsychic processes, innovative thinkers began to consider treating patients in different permutations and combinations: parent-child dyads, spouses seen during the same period but in separate sessions, and group therapy.

It did not take long for those interested in psychoanalysis to bring couples into the consulting room. Adler (1924) initiated the practice of having one therapist see parents and child in separate sessions. The parents' sessions generally focused on counseling them in dealing with the child. Because the parents were usually seen together, however, this was among the earliest forms of couples therapy. In 1931, Carl Oberndorf (1938) presented the first paper on marital therapy to the American Psychiatric Association. At the 1936 9th International Congress of Psychoanalysis, Rene Laforge described his experience analyzing both members of a marital couple concurrently (during the same period, but in separate sessions). He demonstrated that each spouse unconsciously communicated in ways that tended to support the other's neurosis. At the same conference, Leuba presented his attempts to develop a system of family diagnosis (Slipp, 1984, p. 9).

At roughly the same time, a series of advances in looking at the family as a unit strongly affected psychodynamic theory. In 1937, Ackerman published his work on the family as a system, and in 1940, he took the revolutionary step of bringing whole families together in treatment. He wrote that psychotherapists should treat the whole family as a unit, viewing the family as the patient because its members are inextricably interrelated. He described work with the family as a treatment modality in its own right, rather than as simply a technique for treating an individual. Mittelman (1948) reported on the individual psychoanalyses of 12 married couples treated concurrently. As part of his treatment regime, Mittelman conducted several joint sessions to resolve conflicting issues. At the Tavistock Child Guidance Clinic in London, Bowlby (1969) employed family interviews to understand and supplement studies of childhood attachment and separation.

In the first explicit application of object-relations theory to the treatment of married couples, Dicks (1967) established a family psychiatric unit at the Tavistock Clinic and attempted to reconcile couples referred from the divorce court. He noted that one basis for mate selection is that the other's personality unconsciously meets split-off aspects of the self. Dicks wrote that members of dysfunctional couples, permitting unacceptable aspects of the self to be externalized and acted out by the partner, frequently employ projective identification. Thus, dysfunctional marriages seemed to depend on an unconscious complementarity. In an observation made frequently by subsequent generations of couples therapists, Dicks noted that even when the partners hated each other and the relationship had assumed an explicitly sadomasochistic aspect, many of the couples he saw had difficult divorcing.

Although the family therapy field shed psychodynamic theory to emphasize a systems approach, a number of current theorists seek a reintegration of family systems and psychodynamic thinking. The movement in psychodynamic thinking toward object-relations theory, with its emphasis on connection, provides a major point of convergence between the family systems and psychodynamic approaches (Fairbairn, 1954; Scharff & Scharff, 1987; Slipp, 1984; Sutherland, 1980; Winnicott, 1965). Indeed, a rapprochement between the two schools is fitting, especially given the number of psychoanalytically trained therapists important to the field of family therapy, including Boszormenyi-Nagy and Spark (1984), Framo (1982), Paul (1967), Satir (1988), and Wynne (1987). A quarter-century ago, Skynner (1976) presented a model integrating general systems theory and object-relations theory as they apply to the institutions of marriage and family.

The introduction of an object-relations perspective to couples therapy paved the way for attention to narcissistic disturbances and Borderline Personality Disorder and provided a framework for describing and understanding the effect of narcissistic issues on relationships. For example, Lansky (1981) described the underlying shame and humiliation of those who are narcissistically vulnerable and suggested that vulnerable couples use each other to avoid dealing with the emergence of guilty feelings. He demonstrated that couples form collusive bonds to defend against fragmentation when feelings of shame arise. Instead of helping each other grow and mature, the partners may use each other to reinforce a distorted view of reality. Instead of changing and adapting, the relationship relies on defensive strategies, and the collusive contract is maintained because each partner needs to keep destructive forces at bay. In such relationships, communication is not viewed as a way to improve a problematic situation, but as a dangerous weapon that might expose the underlying fear of humiliation (Lansky 1987). Both partners may think of their relationship as a disaster and may not be able to explain even to themselves why they remain attached to someone who is so despicable. Yet, through the years, even decades of unremitting misery, these attacking relationships endure. Lansky suggests that by helping each partner to reclaim his or her own cut-off, disowned parts, a couples therapist can, in turn, help to break disruptive patterns.

Schwartzman (1984) described the contributions of self psychology to the treatment of five couples. She noted the differences in the transference that distinguish the severely disturbed person who lacks functional boundaries between self and other from the merely neurotic patient who is capable of viewing others as distinct and separate. Schwartzman suggests that the therapist may have to perform needed functions temporarily for one or both partners to provide the essential self-cohesion necessary to enable the couples therapy to effectively proceed.

Scharff and Scharff (1987) elaborated on the ways that each partner, carrying an internalized exciting or frustrating object, uses marital and family relationships to contain intolerable affect and anxiety. Couples therapy, they propose, requires a secure treatment environment with a focus on understanding beyond language, the ability to tolerate and contain each partner's anxieties and make interpretations, carefully noting the response: "to look us back in the eye, and to set us straight.... They need to be able to do this with [the therapist] if they are to manage to do it with each other." (p. 30)

Solomon (1989) focused on the range of needs, from healthy to pathological, that arise in couples therapy, and on the effect that early, unmet dependency needs have on adult intimate relationships. She offers strategies for understanding the connection between presenting and underlying problems and described how various forms of acting out are based on lifelong relationship issues. When stressful conditions cause emotions to well up, defensive patterns acquired in infancy or early childhood reemerge in adult behavior. Solomon differentiated among healthy narcissism, narcissistic disorders, and severe personality disorders, including psychotic and autistic states. Her description classifies different types of boundaries, levels of object relations, types of anxieties, ability to give and take emotional support, self-image, awareness of emotions, and defensive patterns in terms of their roots in infancy and their effect on adult relationships.

THEORETICAL CONSTRUCTS

Object-relations theory provides both a normative model of healthy and adaptive functioning and a way of understanding small, repetitive attachment failures that cause disruptions in normal growth and development. Parental sensitivity to a baby's signals results in a sense of trust and confidence in the availability of the caregiver, an increased capacity for exploration and self-confidence, open communication between parent and child, development of awareness of others, and reflectivity about the feelings and needs of others. With what object-relations theorists would call "good-enough parenting" (Winnicott, 1958), the child feels safe in the world of self and other and learns to perceive situations based on both internal experience and the messages of others. This enhances the capacity to maintain cooperative communication, negotiate goals and conflicts, and self-regulate emotions. The inability to perform such functions may result from a poor match between the needs of the developing child and the ability of caretakers to meet those needs adequately.

Primary Affects as Precursors of Lifelong Emotions

All babies are born with the capacity for primary affects such as joy, excitement, fear, and rage

(Tomkins, 1980). Emotions and feelings become more complex as development adds new experiences and the ability to think about events as they occur. A spectrum of emotions and defenses emerges throughout life as anxiety-provoking situations reminiscent of early life experiences increase in intensity and complexity.

As described by Fairbairn (1954), frustrating experience is created by inadequate response to the infant's need for attachment. The infant, for instance, is either uncomfortably rejected or overstimulated to the point of distress. The more intolerable the anxiety resulting from experience with the mother, the more intense the repression. As a result less of the ego is left to relate freely. With "good-enough mothering" (Winnicott, 1958, 1965, 1971), enough central ego in relation to an ideal object is left so that adaptation to the environment is possible. If there has been an open system, both flexible and adaptable, it tends to fashion future relationships in a form resembling satisfying aspects of the primary relationship. Even then, however, there is always some experience that has been repressed and defended against.

Because primary defenses do not include a component of verbally mediated thought, the earlier in life these defenses are imprinted, the more firmly entrenched they are. Lacking words, the infant experiences traumatic pain in the body and wards off the intense discomfort with a series of primal, preverbal defenses and somatic reactions. There are often no conscious memories or words to describe the trauma of failed attachments, nothing to differentiate the representation of this early trauma from memories of natural disaster, physical attachment, or sexual abuse (in which the person knows what happened, but dissociates emotions related to the experience). Therefore, in the wordless infant, the brain registers the experience, the body may remember, but the mind carries no accessible thoughts forward for recapitulation later through the medium of language (Schore, 1997).

PRIMARY AFFECTS AND COUPLES

To understand how these dynamics apply to couples, it may be helpful to see where in the developmental sequence the damage took place (Solomon, 1989). Figure 16.1 indicates when in the developmental sequence an attachment trauma or threat to security causes the erection of defenses as a protection against overwhelming emotions.

The early relationship with parents largely determines the nature and form of the defensive structures maintained throughout life. In adult relationships, patterns learned early in life are reenacted because the internalized object-relationships formed through repetition are so familiar that the adult is attracted to the familiarity, even if it is painful. Consequently, the greater the intimacy with another person, the more likely that archaic emotions and their associated defenses will reemerge.

Early self-other experiences, positive and negative, imprinted in the developing psyche are projected onto significant others in adult life, a process observed repeatedly in psychotherapy and in marriage relationships. Through close observation of couples' dynamics, it is possible to understand how the different internal object-relationships of each partner are played out in the marriage. Self-other representations brought into a relationship are central in giving meaning to the relational experience. Individuals work hard to maintain and defend their preexisting models for interacting, and these organize expectations, interpretations, and response patterns. The need to preserve the representational model strongly conditions every relationship into which the individual enters. Two people will not form a relationship unless the partnership appears to preserve an internal structure that for each of them recapitulates experiences that are familiar and, in fact, are object-relationships. In this way, the internal object-relationships of each partner, developed

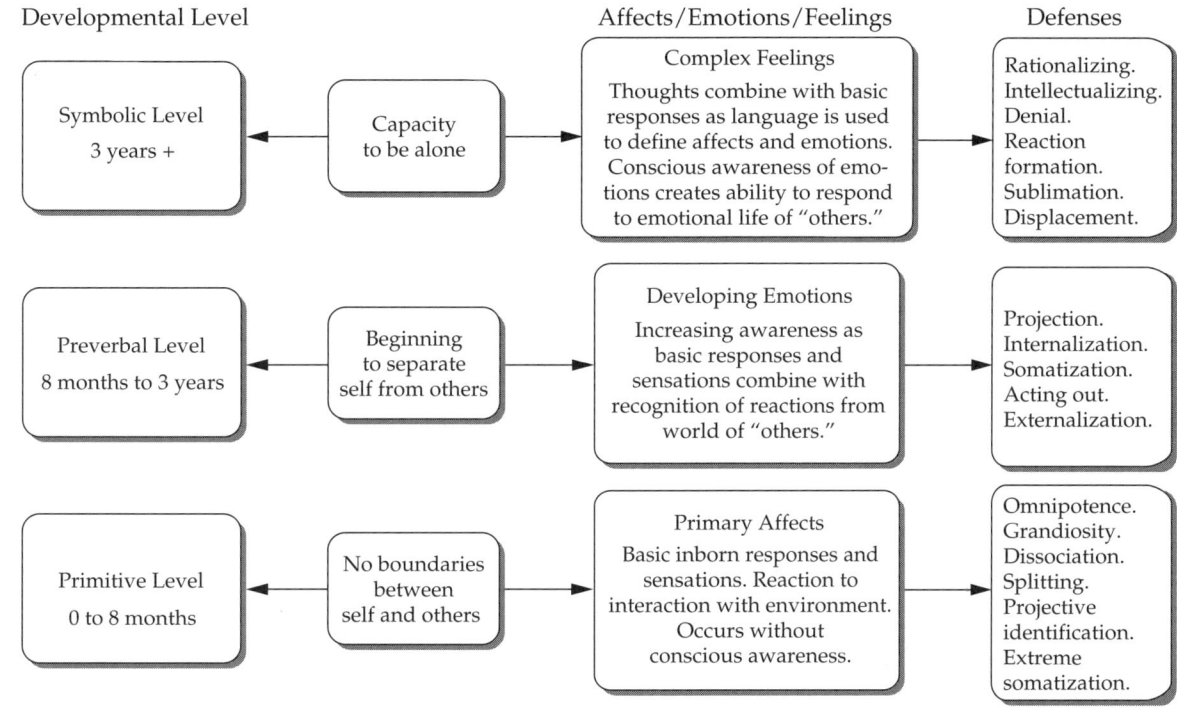

Figure 16.1 Emotions and defenses.

early in life with members of the family of origin, become the pattern of intimate adult relationships.

APPLICATION OF OBJECT-RELATIONS THEORY TO COUPLES THERAPY

The infant's relationship with the primary caregiver works well as a framework for understanding couples' dynamics. Because the core self derives from a history of intersubjective transactions, the concept of an isolated individual mind is a theoretical fiction (Stolorow & Atwood, 1992). Individual experience always manifests itself through relationships with others. The earliest representations shared by mother and infant are structures of interaction, an emergent dyadic phenomenon that cannot be described from the perspective of either partner alone. Consequently, the intimate relationships of adulthood tend to reproduce not only the external features of early dyadic encounters, but also the internal experiences that accompanied those first interactions.

A host of presenting problems may have a narrow range of causes. Underlying many problems that couples identify are issues of power and control, independence and dependence, closeness and distance, and injuries to areas of narcissistic vulnerability. More often than not, couples at first do not even recognize issues other than the crisis that has brought them to treatment. Deeply hidden wounds may make it impossible for the partners to reach agreement about anything. These are the couples most in need of an object-relations approach to treatment.

It is basic to object-relations theory that adults seek outlets through repetition of their infantile experience in the here and now. They project their infantile object-relationships onto those they love, and fear retaliation. The addition of this concept of projection is what makes object-relations theory so helpful in working with couples because it gives the therapist a way of thinking about why individuals in couples, groups, and families treat each other as they do. In couples therapy based on object-relations theory, internal models of relationships that develop in infancy and continue into adult life are explored, confronted, and modified.

Object-relations couple therapy connects intimate relationships between adults with the early attachment of a child with the object of his or her love. In applying such an approach, the therapist helps the partners to recognize that complaints they have about the relationship are probably based on the dysfunctional patterns of interaction learned early in life. Marital problems often begin because most people unconsciously look for a match to their own early object-relations patterns, unconsciously hoping that what went wrong in the past will be healed with a new partner, who is expected to represent an improvement over the original caretaker. The very same defenses and resistances developed in infancy operate in any close relationship as the exquisite vulnerability of emotional injury and fear of one's own rage and aggression, becoming the foundation of relational impasses.

The goal of therapy is to increase the partners' reflective functioning by promoting the acceptance of previously unacceptable feelings about closeness and distance, connection and differentiation, trust and anxiety. By encouraging and empathizing with the true self of each partner, therapy provides a secure base, which opens the door to mutual communication, reduces reactivity to negative behavior, and enables partners to initiate repair processes. The therapist monitors interactions and reflective functioning for signs of movement toward more open and cooperative communication, greater confidence on the part of each, greater care for each other, and a greater sense of competence and efficacy on the part of each.

METHODS OF ASSESSMENT AND INTERVENTION

Because an object-relations approach to couples therapy does not apply to everyone, it is important to understand the scope of this form of treatment and to make a differential diagnosis to determine who can benefit from this approach. Table 16.1 is a schema for understanding relationships from an object-relations perspective. It is an overview of the kinds of imprinted patterns of relating between intimate partners that are seen in couples therapy and includes a range of disturbance and defense that fits most couples. The entries in the chart should not be understood as firm diagnoses, but rather are intended to summarize the kinds of observations and impressions the therapist may take away from one or a few early sessions with a particular couple.

THE NONENMESHED COUPLE

The terms in the first column of the chart characterize those whose relationship problems are not the outgrowth of old family traumas, attachment failures, or cultural crises (war, famine, etc.) These are nonenmeshed persons, often with a single focus of conflict. When each member of the couple has a mature, adaptive self-organization, the partners benefit from an approach that emphasizes straightforward communication. Because clarification of motives will usually help to eliminate simple misunderstandings, they will benefit from partnership education and homework assignments. They are easily helped when they receive sexual counseling and education in marital or parenting skills.

Table 16.1 Degree of relational dysfunction.

	Relatively High Functioning	Moderate Disorder	Severe Personality Disorder
Functioning	Adequately functional.	Ambivalently resistant.	Impairment in self-care.
Anxiety level	Anxiety appropriate to situation.	Anxiety emerges in emotional situations.	Anxiety with thought disruption.
Self-other development	Resilient self.	Impaired self-other attunement.	No boundaries between self and other.
Defenses	Higher-level defenses: Intellectualization. Rationalization. Sublimation. Displacement. Reaction formation.	Mixed repressive and regressive defenses: Idealization. Projection. Internalization. Somatization. Acting out.	Regressive defense: Splitting.
Impulse control	Good impulse control.	Fluctuating impulse control.	Repeated loss of impulse control.
Capacity for intimate relationship	Capacity for emotional closeness. Adaptive in relationships. Ability to love and work.	Moderate level of defense against emotional closeness. Ambivalent about relationships in love, work, and friendship.	Significant defense against closeness. All relationships very compromised.
Motivation for treatment	Motivation for treatment.	Resistant to treatment process.	Treatment marred by fragile ego and fragmentation.

The following case illustrates treatment of couples who are relatively high functioning.

Julie and Ed had been dating for two years and were engaged to marry when Julie discovered she was pregnant.* Ed was not thrilled. Both were angry and disappointed: Julie with Ed's reaction, and Ed with the disruption to his plans. They each thought of themselves, and the impasse brought them to therapy. Their wedding was set for June, and by that time, Julie would be eight months pregnant. "I love you and want us to marry and have children together," Ed said. "But we have planned everything so carefully: our work, saving money for a house, starting a family in a couple of years. This isn't the time to have a baby."

"I know," Julie replied. "I was on the pill. I shouldn't have gotten pregnant. I don't know how it happened. But I'm pregnant with your child. I can't bear the thought of aborting our baby. I'm afraid of what it would do to us the rest of our lives if we always had the memory of this child between us." For some women, this would not be a major issue, as it was for Julie. For some men, having a baby with the woman they love would take precedence over plans for a well-ordered, well-timed life.

Although Julie and Ed had strongly opposing feelings, they were able to communicate their

---

*A longer version of this case was described in a chapter of *Short Term Therapy for Long Term Change* (2001) Eds. M. Solomon, R. Neborsky, L. McCullough, M. Alpert, F. Shapiro, and D. Malan, New York, Norton.

needs and wishes and were lovingly attuned to each other. Therefore, they were able to resolve their conflict and did not get caught in a blame or shame syndrome, as couples with a collusive resistance pattern so often do.

Ed said that to have the baby would disrupt his plans, that they would have to pare down their expectations about where they would live, but that in 30 years it probably wouldn't make much difference in their lifestyle. He did not want to put Julie or himself in the position of wondering who their child might have become. "I'm still not crazy about it, but I would hate to have the big house we dreamed of, filled with ghosts and an unhappy wife."

They made a decision that they both could live with. Nevertheless, when Ed said to Julie, "You owe me big," in a kidding tone, the therapist knew it was not a joke. The quid pro quo of the relationship requires that, when there are differences and decisions must be made, each will hear the other out fully, and in things that are a high priority for one of them, his wishes will be considered as often as hers. The treatment for Julie and Ed was short term, but their Christmas cards come each year with pictures of Jenny, now 6, accompanied this year by a picture of twin sons. Couples like this are not stalemated, and they do not need to expend their energy defending against the attachment trauma.

Moderately Vulnerable Couples

In the middle range of the spectrum of relationship and individual psychic health (represented in the second column of the table) are those most frequently seen by couples therapists. They present a wide range of problems connected to "real-life" issues. Those who fall into this category often come into therapy with high levels of anxiety. Fear of the outcome of seeing a marital therapist is added to fears deriving from unconscious emotions. These couples—and individuals—may begin using repressive defenses almost as soon as the opening session begins, denying that there is any problem, projecting problems on the other, and explaining that a busy schedule precludes regular sessions together with their mate.

When this happens, it is quite common for one partner or both to resort to regressive defenses such as acting out and externalization. In therapy, the partners may quickly erect a barrier to meaningful communication, just as they have done in their marital relationship. At the same time, their symptoms may cause significant personal distress, and the viability of their relationship may be severely impaired. The impending demise of the relationship, whether it is fully recognized or not, often forms the basis for the therapeutic alliance, motivating the couple to endure the discomfort necessary to make a true change in themselves and their relationship.

Members of these couples have well-integrated psyches, but require some work at the unconscious level to overcome collusive patterns of relating to each other. The partners have good boundaries, but one or both of the members of the dyad may be depressed, emotionally distant, overly demanding, or *parentifying* the other, thus sabotaging the growth of the relationship. Although the issues with which such a couple presents often at first seem to be about power and control, they more likely reflect some form of punishment to atone for guilt for feelings of primitive rage arising from early childhood experience.

A Moderately Disturbed Couple
Hugh and Lori came into therapy because, although they love one another, they were unable to tolerate each other's behavior. Hugh complained that Lori was never symptom-free, something was always hurting, and Lori complained that Hugh never listened to her but

tried to "fix" her and then shouted at her in frustration if he was unable to do so.

Lori was in her late 50s and Hugh in his late 60s when they came for treatment. Hugh did not believe in therapy. This was his second marriage and Lori's first. They had been married for 10 years.

Their issues were clearly based on experiences in early childhood, and yet neither wanted to make those connections in their thinking about the problems of the relationship. Yet, as the therapist started to look at their dynamics, it was evident that Lori never felt seen or understood by her mother and Hugh had always been expected to fix things and be extremely self-sufficient.

Lori's Dynamics. Lori had been in individual therapy for several years and was very psychologically astute. However, she had never gotten in touch with her extreme sadness and the rage caused by her mother's behavior. In Lori's earliest memories, her mother was pathologically depressed and it was Lori's job to fill her mother's life and to be completely under her control. Her mother constantly screamed at her, did not allow her any autonomy or privacy, and threatened to die if her wishes were not minutely observed. Lori grew up terrified that she would kill her mother and was filled with rage at the ludicrous constraints put on her. This lasted well into young adulthood. Her internal object experience consisted entirely of experiencing her mother's needs and wishes, with a dreadful consequence if she did not comply.

She complied, was enraged, and felt enormous guilt as a consequence. At an early age, she figured out that if she was physically ill, she would be taken to a doctor, even though her mother felt that Lori was being ill to spite her. The doctor, however, would occasionally listen to her, and she derived great comfort from this. Her father was too passive and too frightened to protect or defend her. If it were not for her maternal grandmother, who validated her experience and indicated that her mother was being unreasonable, she would have "gone under." When she was in her 20s, Lori left home and traveled as far away as she could, to live an independent life, on the advice of her psychiatrist. The internalized mother came with her and she spent years self-medicating with alcohol and food. Whenever she felt controlled and enraged by her mother, who continued to persecute her by phone and in person, she would eat and drink to excess to stifle those feelings, and the intense feelings of rage would subside temporarily. But more and more, food and alcohol became necessary to achieve this state of relief. This went on until her mother died. Almost immediately, Lori went to Alcoholics Anonymous and stopped self-medicating. She continues to be sober, her eating is controlled, and she still attends AA meetings every week.

Although Lori understood a great deal about her history, she was constantly surprised by rages that would burst out of her and that she would then regret. However, she did not make the connection between suppressing her rages and the physical symptoms that were erupting.

Hugh's Dynamics. As Lori's story emerged in joint sessions, Hugh would listen with enormous interest and would point out how different his childhood was from Lori's. When he was 12, he was living an affluent and secure life in Europe, which was violently overtaken by the Second World War. He was put on a boat for America, sent to live with a distant relative, and did not see his parents again for 15 years. As a child, he dissociated from his vulnerable feelings in order to survive. Feelings were not a currency that he could afford, so he functioned by always looking forward, never back. Solving problems became his strength and his compulsion; he became very successful professionally, but not personally. His first marriage broke down, but he dealt with it in the same manner as usual. He left his wife, never looking back, only moving forward. So this extremely self-controlled man who could fix most things met and married this extremely emotional woman and both were frustrated.

The Couple's Dynamics. In first hearing and then learning about each other's early internal worlds, the partners were able to accept each other in a different way. Lori was able to express her needs differently so that Hugh was not so compelled to solve her problems, and Hugh was gradually able to recognize and then express his true feelings of pain, anger, and loss. Lori lost her persistent symptoms of itching skin, headaches, and pains and, becoming more and more aware of her "child" bursting out of her, she was increasingly able to control and care for herself. Hugh was able to listen to Lori without feeling impotent if he did not solve everything. He also was able to acknowledge his feelings more and more to Lori, and the marriage became strong enough that when real health issues arose for them both, each was able to care for the other with love and understanding.

Before this change occurred, the therapist had to examine the early object-relationships of both Lori and Hugh. This was not an easy task as both had repressed and forgotten many of their early childhood experiences because of the painful feelings those experiences produced. Initially, both insisted that they had gotten over their early childhood traumas and that those wounds had healed. Then memories started to trickle back; gradually, the trickle became a flood.

Lori's memories came back without the emotions attached. She would tell horrible stories about a little girl (herself) who, when she broke her arm falling off her bike, was punished, screamed at, and yanked about by her broken arm for causing trouble to her mother. Lori had no sympathy for the little girl and no sadness as she told the story. She laughed at her. She became her mother. When the therapist reacted with sadness at the plight of the child, Lori was shocked. Then, very gradually, she became able to recall more appropriate feelings of pain, sadness, and care for the abused and abandoned child. The more appropriate the feelings for the wounded child appeared, the more the present physical symptoms receded.

Hugh's memories were even harder for him to recall as his stoic presentation of the brave little boy waving good-bye at the rail of a ship did not contain any feelings of pain or fear at the separation from his parents. This time, it was not the therapist but Lori who made the imaginative leap and felt immense pain at Hugh's loss, and only then was Hugh able to cry about his feelings for the first time. As a child, he felt so out of control that he vowed never to allow himself to feel that pain again. So he split it off. Lori sought the good mother in Hugh, looking for the care and sympathy that was lacking originally and that she could not give herself. Hugh was incapable of sympathy because he had none for himself; he saw it as soft: One should just move on. Over time, Lori increased her symptoms, and Hugh increased his stoicism. Lori projected the unsympathetic mother onto Hugh, and Hugh was incapable of expressing sympathy because no one had ever expressed any to him.

The result of both partners' being able to experience their own and each others' pain and to allow the original emotions to emerge and be accepted in the here and now gave tremendous relief and a very strong bond to this couple. The marriage remains strong because they have recognized their own and their partner's internal worlds and have detoxified the projections that each placed on the other. Without this recognition, their internal object-relationships would have been played out with no comprehension of their origins or meaning. They continue to work on these issues; it is not all roses, but they can now truly see and hear each other.

Therapy for such a couple might include education, clarification with extensive cognitive input, and gentle confrontation through light pressure on the cut-off feelings and maladaptive behavior. The purpose is to lead each of the partners through an exploration of affect, present and past, putting them in a position to make their own interpretations. Throughout the process, it is necessary for the therapist to remain vigilant for countertransference feelings that emerge in sessions and explore with the partners their experience of any similar feelings during the session or in their past relationships.

SEVERLY DISTURBED COUPLES

In the third column of the chart are the terms that describe those people who are most in need of an object-relations approach. These are patients with extreme ego fragility leading to severely disordered relational functioning. These people, whose personality style falls in the borderline-narcissistic continuum, are likely to develop collusive relationships with others who have complementary defenses. Their presenting issues may vary, but the underlying dynamics are similar. They form unconscious love bonds that help them ward off painful or frightening emotions and draw other members of their family into dysfunctional dynamics to defend a vulnerable inner core. Although they sometimes are successful in other aspects of their lives, these people have fragile egos and their relationships are almost invariably quite troubled.

In stressful situations, they tend to display some thought impairment and resort to primitive defenses such as splitting, projective identification, psychosomatic illness, or dissociation. Lacking the ability to distinguish between feelings and the defenses against those feelings, they often experience states of chaos in their relationships. They tend to deny differences between self and other and are prone to encourage obliteration of boundaries, thereby adding confusion about who, in fact, holds the feelings. Thus, anxiety, feelings, and defenses are all confused and lack clarity.

Working with a couple when one or both partners has an extremely fragile ego and is highly defended presents a unique dilemma to the marital therapist. The traditional modes of treatment designed to improve communications, change dysfunctional behavioral patterns, and enhance positive aspects of the relationship may seem to work for a time, but therapeutic efforts are destined to fail because of the partner's regressive pull to return to the old dynamics.

The most difficult couples to treat are those who are in collusive deadlocks in which effective treatment may be seen as dangerous to the relationship. Fear of the unknown may feel more dangerous than the pain experienced in the relationship. There is always an unconscious pull to revert to the entrenched pattern.

Over time, each shapes the other until the partners have no way of breaking the deadlock of their collusive resistance to change. This is the toxic cycle of projective and introjective identification. By the time they seek help in couples counseling, the pattern is solidly entrenched. Rarely is there ever a way to establish who started it. Close inspection of the dynamic of borderline-narcissistic collusions reveals that both partners are heavily invested in their enmeshment. Each subtly pushes the other to fulfill unconscious needs, at the same time generating conditions that make such fulfillment impossible.

The constant failure provokes previously repressed unconscious rage. At the deepest level, this rage feels so dangerous and destructive that it must be projected out of the self onto the other, or it will be introjected in shame and depression. Each may encourage the other to act in ways that project the problem outside him or her. In that way, each can limit access to aggressive impulses toward the other, impulses that are transferred from a parent, where they originated. The behaviors of both maintain a cycle of sadomasochistic activity that stems from unconscious attachment to a parent. Thus, a circular attack-and-defend pattern becomes established. Commonly, one partner seems to choose the role of victim, receiving the other's sadism and feeling tortured in the relationship, but it is not surprising to see them change roles, with the victim gaining strength and becoming the rageful tormentor. Each partner feels trapped in a state of permanent isolation, hopeless about positive change, because unconscious forces sabotage every attempt to extricate oneself from this self-made system. The known terror of daily torture in the relationship feels less dangerous than the terror of the unknown.

Object-relations therapists working with couples who have such issues know all too well the strong emotions that define the relationship. These couples enter treatment presenting conflict around surface issues—money, work, sex, in-laws—whereas the underlying battle revolves around separation, autonomy, dependence, and validation, or the still deeper fear of rejection and abandonment, guilt and punishment. Often, there is a marital history of threats to divorce or actual separations. Reconciliation may lead to a period of peace, only to be followed by new battles, demonstrating to them that they can live neither together nor apart.

A couple with such a history will come into the early counseling sessions with specific identified problems. On close observation, they demonstrate a level of aggression toward each other vastly out of proportion to the problems they describe. Not only are they suffering because of deep structural divisions, but they have no empathy for each other and are angry at each other for the mutual lack of attunement.

Richard and Eileen had been married for 20 years and had been talking about divorce for almost half of that time. "He is not there for me at all," she complained. "His work always comes first. He is almost nonsocialized. He doesn't know how to be in a relationship," and on and on. Richard, a very talented and extraordinarily successful man in his career, acknowledged that he had difficulty in his personal relationships. Eileen put much energy into focusing the problems on Richard, who seemed overly willing to accept them. He went into therapy on several occasions trying to resolve the issues that he brought into the marriage. But no matter what he did or how he tried to change, it became more ammunition to be used against him the next time a problem arose. Eileen seemed very well "put together" and saw herself as kind and generous. She was extremely charitable and very generous with gifts to all of her friends. It was only Richard who saw the wrath that lay below the surface of her perfect facade.

Their interactions were marked by fluctuating, disturbing, contradictory messages. Sometimes, Richard became like a small child desperately trying to please mother. At other times, Eileen was like a tiger, suddenly springing up to attack, pacing around the office, upset that the therapist was not telling Richard to grow up. She said that his parents caused all the problems. As a result, she wanted nothing to do with his family because she was forced to live with the damaged man they had raised.

They said their problems began when they were on their honeymoon. Richard arranged a Hawaiian honeymoon at a resort that was supposed to be elegant and secluded. Instead, it was barren and isolated. She became very upset and he felt mortified, a failure; his weakness was exposed. Instead of complaining to the management and getting them out of there, he tried to placate her but would not act, and forced her to stay in an uncomfortable place for two weeks.

Eileen could not tolerate any examination of her part of the marital problem. She said that she, of course, knew that both are part of the problem. When I asked what her part was, she said that it was her staying in the marriage even though she never got what she wanted.

Richard continued his search for help with his unhappiness. He tried individual therapy and realized that he felt intense rage at his parents and also at his wife. He said that he wanted to resolve the problems with his parents before they became too old and infirm.

At points like this, major changes can occur in a long-term relationship. When one partner becomes aware of the deep unconscious emotion that is driving current relationships and can separate past from current relationships, a shift out of the collusive deadlock is possible. When anxiety emerges signaling a defense, the therapist can assist in refocusing on the feeling that is avoided. Cognitive, emotional, and interpersonal strategies are meant to keep anxiety-provoking thoughts and feelings out of conscious awareness. By exploring the defenses and physiological responses, cognitive recognition of emotion comes into play. If cut-off emotions are freed to come into conscious awareness, the person is helped to connect the impulses and feelings to the appropriate person in earlier life and begins to connect past figures with current relationships. Each of the partners is helped to recognize how current life figures have taken on aspects of people from the past. In concurrent couple sessions, it is possible to see how behaviors developed in the past as protection against being injured in a relationship are affecting the current partner and molding the partner's responses.

Richard was helped to recognize how his parents' unhappiness with each other, and his mother's anxieties about being judged negatively by others, caused him to withdraw into a shell in adolescence. Always wanting to please and always afraid of doing something wrong, he found it hard to join the world of his peers during the revolutionary 1960s. He has continued to feel like a child, even after years of marriage. His wife, like his mother, put much energy into teaching him how to behave appropriately. Of course, nothing he did was right enough.

Despite her underlying disturbance, Eileen appeared on the surface to be an extraordinarily capable woman who set out to accomplish many things and often succeeded in her endeavors. She had learned early in life that her job was to stay on top of everything she undertook. She came from what she described as a very loving family. Nevertheless, her father became permanently disabled just at the time she was born. One can imagine the fear and despair experienced by Eileen's mother, with two young children at home, a newborn baby, and an incapacitated husband. Eileen, however, described a happy, loving family. She also described her ability to stay calm and take charge whenever crises in her family arose. "What happens when the pressure gets too great?" I asked. "I don't let it," she responded.

In the joint sessions, however, the pressure did build up, and Eileen demonstrated what happens when she becomes overwhelmed with emotion. As her anger burst forth, she threw her open purse across the room, scattering her belongings, screaming that Richard was a liar. He frantically attempted to calm her down, apologizing for whatever he did wrong, and begged her not to leave the therapy office. She walked out, but 10 minutes later returned to retrieve her keys and appointment book. When the therapist offered her the chance to talk about what had happened, she seemed totally changed. She calmly explained that what Richard had said could not be true, because she had been monitoring his activities and his phone calls. She seemed totally to dissociate her raging behavior of a few moments before and wanted to clarify her position in a way that put her in the best possible light.

During the following week, Eileen called to tell me that Richard had hit her and she told him to move out. When I asked her to tell me what happened, she explained that they had one of their many fights. Richard had too much to drink, which is what usually causes their fights, she said. She got angry and hit him, and this time he hit her back. "You hit him?" the therapist asked. "Of course," she said. "I don't know any woman who doesn't hit her husband when they fight. But men are not supposed to hit back. Richard is big and he can hurt me. I am afraid now that he will lose control and do something dangerous. I can't have him live in our home until he learns to change his behavior." She asked him to move out.

Eileen's description was evidence of unconscious projective identification, turning him into the one who could lose control. Richard agreed with Eileen that his behavior was inappropriate and dangerous: "I am afraid it's getting out of control." He intensified his individual therapy, entered a program to deal with his drinking problem, and continued to try to make his relationship work. He asked Eileen to go into therapy also. She at first said that therapy wasn't doing much for Richard, so why should she go; besides, she added, the problem isn't hers. Ultimately, she went to a psychotherapist with whom she spent almost a year talking about what was wrong with Richard. Because she didn't believe that she had any problem, she saw no need to change.

This is the point in many marriages where the change in one partner either forces changes in the other, or the marriage is no longer viable and the couple divorce. For many years, both had agreed that the entire problem between them was Richard's and was caused by the dysfunctional family in which he had grown up. When therapy helped him uncover the unconscious forces that kept him in distress most of his life, he began to change. Richard was no longer engaged in their collusive pattern. When emotions arose and Eileen's anxiety felt intolerable, she could no longer induce shame and guilt in Richard. She subsequently dropped out of the therapy when confronted with her own resistance.

Eileen, who blamed Richard's dysfunctional behavior for all of her painful, unhappy feelings, had to face her own pathology. She tried unsuccessfully to pull him back into his old behavior patterns: drinking too much, losing his temper and screaming at her, feeling ashamed and apologetic for his actions. For her to change and for the marriage to reconstitute at a different level, Eileen would have to look at how the qualities that she sees as her strengths are also well-entrenched defenses. This results in her walling off from other people and from her own defenses. She remains totally in control by being ever competent and generous with money and gifts to family and friends. There is a brittle, frightened quality that emerges whenever confronted about her defenses. When intense emotion takes over, her fear of losing control is realistic. She then dissociates and fears that she is losing her mind.

Richard continued his own growth process and remained very connected to Eileen. But he realized that his work included maintaining his own autonomy and separate boundaries. When he and Eileen met to discuss his moving back into their home, he no longer engaged in the battles of the past. When she berated him for all his past failures as a husband and all of his mother's terrible behaviors, Richard refused to be drawn in. When she threatened divorce, as she so often did in the past, Richard said that as much as he would hate it, he could survive even divorce.

THE SPECTRUM OF PATHOLOGY AND DIFFERENTIAL TREATMENT

The members of many couples that present for therapy exhibit Axis II disorders, which can range from mild to very severe. When horrific external and internal experiences occurred before language and symbolic development, narcissistic and borderline defenses may emerge to protect a vulnerable self from being overwhelmed by feelings. As we have already seen, during the first months of life, overwhelming negative affective experiences become precursors of the most severe disorders in individuals and their relationships.

The techniques used in object-relations couples' therapy verbally and nonverbally demonstrate interest in the partners' ways of handling their most painful emotions. There is a fine attunement, not to the anger, but to the pain and sadness associated with the loss or anticipated loss of connection with an intimate other. The therapist establishes a therapeutic alliance in which each member of the relationship feels supported and cared for. The therapeutic milieu becomes a transitional space, giving the couple enough of the therapist to allow them to wait for the transformations to occur in their partner. The therapist can then help them to adjust to the transformations and to see that it will be better than the old collusive structure. The therapist is the advocate for the couple.

Without stigmatizing, and without stimulating shame or guilt in either of the partners, the therapist helps them to repair breakdowns in empathy. The therapist supports and produces a holding environment in which it is possible to focus on the negative constellation of parental introjects each partner has brought into the marriage. Each partner is seen as having a separate existence, and when defenses do arise, the couple and the therapist are in a position to examine any resistance to this process of individuation. Sometimes, the resistance continues, and no amount of effort on the part of the therapist will break it. Ultimately, it is up to the partners to decide the fate of the marriage.

Using Empathic Attunement in the Treatment of Couples

Goals are determined by the assessment of the couple. If the couple is not particularly resistant to therapy, the work is on the level of communication enhancement and education. If they are moderately resistant, work includes reframing and clarifying the interaction to help them achieve a more accurate perspective on the situation that is causing them so much misery, so they can find their way out of the toxic interaction. If the couple is highly resistant, the way to create the holding environment is by empathizing with the wound that causes the perpetrating behavior. Empathy with the pain of each is not the change agent, but is designed to help partners communicate and express the underlying wound, to reclaim projections, and to accept the other qualities and characteristics they hate in themselves.

In an object-relations approach, attunement to the suffering each feels produces pressure to face the damage inherent in their collusion to protect their vulnerabilities. The therapist must be prepared to contain toxic feelings, translating attack and defense patterns and communicating to each partner that these patterns remain because they were once necessary for psychic (and sometimes physical) survival. Each partner is encouraged to describe the wishes and fears that emerge almost simultaneously. One or both are likely to draw on memories of early wishes for closeness and recount disappointing, painful encounters that led to the development of defenses against being hurt.

When they achieve a familiarity with the nature of the defenses that are at work, partners are then encouraged to recall the pain of the early failures, the effect on the body and the emotions, and the ways they have responded in the past when there were no words to describe their feelings. As issues arise that cause strong feelings to manifest during the session, space is made to hold and contain the emergence of emotion. There is often an opportunity to explore physical reactions and any images of which either partner becomes aware. The greater the couple's ability hear and understand the reasons behind the reactions that arise, the more they are able to modify their interactions. The more they are able to feel in the sessions and overcome shame of what had been, the greater the chance of healing symptoms of old pathological defenses such as dissociation, toxic projection, and denial of others as separate individuals.

With partners who are well defended against repeated attachment failures, the soothing interaction may allow a relinquishment of defenses and a translation of anger and control into a need for love and connection (Solomon,

2001). Verbally, the therapist keeps them focused on the pain of the loss, empathizing, keeping them in the experience without inducing shame and guilt. The destructive behavior can then be examined while the pain is tolerated, thereby enhancing the transmutation of the self-structure.

CONTRAINDICATIONS TO OBJECT-RELATIONS COUPLES THERAPY

Although an object-relations approach to couples therapy can be used to address most of the problems presented by couples, there are some for whom it is much more difficult to effect lasting change. If a couple is functioning at a paranoid-schizoid (Klein, 1946) level with part-object relationships, lack of ego boundaries, and extensive use of denial, splitting, and projection, then defensive barriers will inevitably reemerge to maintain the status quo of the relationship.

Couples who have not yet mastered the depressive position (Klein, 1946) fear and resist change in the relationship. They experience deep anxiety when there are signs of emergence of rage and destructiveness. The rage resulting from the frustration of intense emotional hunger or from actual abuse is felt to be too threatening to allow it to come to the surface. If these intense, mutually dependent ties are threatened by an arousal of hostility, disagreement, or even an awareness of separate identity, all of which represent separation or loss that had once occurred in the primary love relationship, intolerable depressive anxiety is generated.

Because boundaries are diffuse and defenses high, it is contraindicated for the therapist to arrange both individual and conjoint sessions with the partners. The danger is that therapy itself can become a tool used by each to attack and protect against each other. It is very often the case that both members of these "difficult to work with" couples are at the more regressed end of the borderline spectrum.

The therapist must be prepared to be a container for toxic emotions and to maintain a position equidistant from both. There is competition to be the favored one, resulting in anxiety, shame, and rage when the therapist does not accurately attune to deep, powerful, dangerous feelings. Although both individuals experience distinct psychological functions, with separate impulses and controls located in each partner, they may surprise the therapist by shifting pathology from one to the other. The functional unit is not the individual but the couple. The unconscious processes revolve around permeable boundaries and psychic fusion. They are lost without each other, in treatment as in other activities.

The Reparative Process

If therapy is to be successful, the goal is to help each reclaim split-off parts and, without shame, recognize the defenses used to hide these split-off aspects of self. There is often a period of guilt and shame that must be expressed and passed through. When each is able to develop more solid self-boundaries, the relationship begins to grow and change. This is the result of a new awareness of the partner as separate and unique, along with a sadness for the damage that had been done to each other. The wish to repair and make right replicates the process Klein (1946) described in young children who reach the depressive position. Object-relations therapists believe that the possibility of repair of early damage can occur in later relationships throughout one's life; it is simply more difficult than the repair of failure in normal early development.

SUMMARY

The bonds of love in adults are an accumulation of the loving attachments developed early in life.

When there is interference in early connection with the object of a child's love, the frustration and pain are diminished through emotional defense mechanisms. Once such defenses are imprinted, they become firmly entrenched modes of relating. Therapists treating adults who are having problems in relationships must determine whether the issues pertain only to the current relationship or there are archaic relational imprints that may be creating turbulence in the present. In the latter case, the treatment methods require a change in the early blueprints for relationships.

People are used to what is familiar and resist change. Often, when therapeutic treatment begins to have an effect and one of the individuals begins growing, the therapy is experienced as a threat to the equilibrium of long-established family patterns. Thus, a partner may sabotage therapy by pushing to get the relational bonds back on the old footing. Sometimes, couples therapists believe that they are helping by encouraging partners to strive for autonomy and a separate identity without recognizing the systemic repercussions and the unconscious battle to maintain the homeostasis of even a painful equilibrium. Both partners must grow and change or the development of one is perceived as a danger to the relationship. The change is perceived as a threat to the partner who continues to utilize a collusive relationship to ward off awareness of core psychopathology. Object-relations couples therapists recognize that any change creates anxiety, mobilizing regressive defenses. This is no time to resent the partner's resistance. It is most important to understand what the defense is used for and where it was developed as a useful tool for survival of the self, and to maintain connection with important others.

When something went wrong in early bonding relationships, there is always the wish to repair. When people with a history of failed attachments marry, there is a belief that it is never too late to have a happy childhood: "Perhaps with this person I will be known, accepted, and loved." On rare occasions, this is indeed the result; the intimate partnership becomes a corrective emotional experience and both partners are secure to grow together. More often, as therapists so often see, there is a re-creation of the initial painful relationships and a downward spiral of anxiety, anger, and defense.

If the pathology is at a high level, it is very difficult to create a mutually nurturing safe space in which to heal the depth of the pain. In treatment, a painstaking examination of early objects has to be undertaken for the couple to see why the vulnerability is so intense in certain areas. The steps of treatment include de-escalation of the negative cycle, change in interactional patterns, and consolidation and integration of new object relations into the couple's relationship.

The therapist takes in the communication of information, integrates it, and returns it in such a way that it accomplishes the strategic goals of treatment. Therefore, the therapist provides a transitional relationship that gives each partner enough attunement to allow him or her to wait for the transformations to occur in the other. At first, they need help adjusting to the transformations and in believing that it will be better than the old collusive structure. Then the challenge to the dysfunctional patterns is possible without the partners' feeling shamed or blamed.

The result is a technique that helps the partners communicate and express the underlying wound; in that process, the soothing interaction allows a dominating or demanding partner to relinquish the "power position" and to translate anger and control into a need for love and connection. Clinical observation and reports from couples indicate that the process of doing this decreases the frequency of controlling behavior outside therapy in the spousal relationship. Without the behavior's being labeled bad, it tends to decrease in frequency, and the individuals themselves become more motivated to do exploratory work on their own to examine the origins of their vulnerabilities.

REFERENCES

Ackerman, N. (1937). The family as a social and emotional unit. *Bulletin of the Kansas Mental Hygiene Society, 12.*

Ackerman, N. (1940). *The psychodynamics of family life: Diagnosis and treatment of family relationships.* New York: Basic Books.

Adler, A. (1924). *Understanding human nature.* London: Allen & Unwin.

Boszormenyi-Nagy, I., & Spark, G. M. (1984). *Invisible loyalties: Reciprocity in intergenerational family therapy.* New York: Brunner/Mazel.

Bowlby, J. (1969). *Attachment and loss. Volume I: Attachment.* New York: Basic Books.

Dicks, H. (1967). *Marital tensions.* New York: Basic Books.

Fairbairn, W. R. D. (1954). *An object relations theory of personality.* New York: Basic Books.

Framo, J. (1982). *Explorations in marital and family therapy: Selected papers of James L. Framo, PhD.* New York: Springer.

Klein, M. (1946). Notes on some schizoid mechanisms. *International Journal of Psychoanalysis, 27*(3), 99–110.

Lansky, M. (1981). Treatment of the narcissistically vulnerable marriage. In M. Lansky (Ed.), *Family therapy and major psychopathology* (pp. 163–182). New York: Grune & Stratton.

Lansky, M. (1987). Shame and the families of borderline patients. In J. Grotstein, M. Solomon, & J. Lang (Eds.), *The borderline patient: Emerging concepts in diagnosis, etiology, psychodynamics and treatment* (Vol. 2, pp. 187–200). Hillsdale, NJ: Analytic Press.

Mittelman, B. (1948). The concurrent analysis of married couples. *Psychoanalytic Quarterly, 17,* 182–197.

Oberndorf, C. P. (1938). Psychoanalysis of married couples. *Psychoanalytic Review, 25,* 435–475.

Paul, N. (1967). The role of mourning and empathy in conjoint marital therapy. In G. Zuk & I. Boszormenyi-Nagy (Eds.), *Family therapy and disturbed families.* Palo Alto, CA: Science and Behavior Books.

Sandler, J. (1987). *Projection, identification and projective identification.* Madison, CT: International Universities Press.

Satir, V. (1988). *The new peoplemaking.* Palo Alto, CA: Science and Behavior Books.

Scharff, D., & Scharff, J. (1987). *Object relations family therapy.* Northvale, NJ: Aronson.

Schore, A. N. (1997). Early shame experiences and the development of the infant brain. In P. Gilbert & B. Andrews (Eds.), *Shame: Interpersonal behaviour, psychopathology and culture.* Oxford, England: Oxford University Press.

Schwartzman, G. (1984). Narcissistic transferences: Implications for the treatment of couples. *Dynamic Psychotherapy, 2,* 5–14.

Skynner, A. C. R. (1976). *Systems of family and marital psychotherapy.* New York: Brunner/Mazel.

Slipp, S. (1984). *Object relations: A dynamic bridge between individual and family treatment.* New York: Aronson.

Solomon, M. (1989). *Narcissism and intimacy: Love and marriage in an age of confusion.* New York: Norton.

Solomon, M. (2001). Breaking the deadlock of marital collusions in couples therapy. In M. Solomon, et al. (Eds.), *Short term therapy for long term change.* New York: Norton.

Stolorow, R. D., & Atwood, G. E. (1992). *Contexts of being: The intersubjective foundations of psychological life.* Hillsdale, NJ: Analytic Press.

Sutherland, J. D. (1980). The British object relations theorists: Balent, Winnicott, Fairburn, Guntrip. *Journal of American Psychoanalytic Association, 28,* 4.

Tomkins, S. S. (1980). Affect as amplification: Some modifications in theory. In R. Plutchik & H. Kellerman (Eds.), *Emotion: Theory, research and experience* (pp.141–164). New York: Academic Press.

Winnicott, D. W. (1958). Pediatrics and childhood neurosis. In D. Winnicott (Ed.), *Collected papers: Through pediatrics to psychoanalysis* (pp. 316–321). London: Tavistock. (Original work published 1956)

Winnicott, D. W. (1965). *The maturational process and the facilitating environment: Studies in the theory of emotional development.* New York: International Universities Press.

Winnicott, D. W. (1971). *Playing and reality.* New York: Basic Books.

Wynne, L. (1987). Mutuality and pseudomutuality reconsidered: Implications for therapy and a theory of development of relational systems. In J. L. Sacksteder, D. S. Schwartz, & Y. Akabane (Eds.), *Attachment and the therapeutic process: Essays in honor of Otto Allen Will, Jr.* (pp. 81–98). Madison, CT: International Universities Press.

CHAPTER 17

Self-Object Relationship Therapy with Couples

MICHAEL D. KAHN

It has often been said that couple therapy is the most difficult of all the forms of psychotherapy, neither focusing exclusively on the therapy of two closely linked but nonetheless distinctly separate individuals, nor treating the couple per se as a systemic unit. It can also take the form of always including, and reaching for, issues within the couple that were derived by each individual from his or her family of origin. The focus for the therapist may occur at many levels: the microlevel of intrapsychic process, the interpersonal level of transactions and meaning making between the individuals, or the systemic level in working with the broad sweep of family-based ritual, memory, and activity. Sometimes, these areas of inquiry and intervention are in direct conflict with one another; speaking about one's parents or the partner may be antithetical to a felt desire to speak about oneself, and usually, Rashamon-like, each person's view of reality differs from the other's. Sometimes these different areas integrate well. Along with questions of theory, many questions of technique arise. Does or should the focus remain entirely in one domain, or can it jump back and forth, orchestrated by the therapist as a conductor or manager of the process? Who sets the tempo and pace of the therapy, the necessary content to be covered? Which member of the couple receives more attention, who sets the emotional pitch and tone of the work that has to be done, and who determines the length of the therapy (managed care notwithstanding)?

After many years of working with couples, many of us come to realize how powerful the therapist can be in determining such factors, for reasons that may be unconscious—as a countertransference reaction to the tremendous number of issues we are dealing with, or as a manifestation of the dynamic processes that are swirling around the consulting room. A psychodynamic or behavioral or communications-based set of theories can rarely be justified as the single best way of proceeding simply on the basis of the elegance of the theory. Nor does the amount of overt pathology, or diagnostic makeup of the individuals needing treatment, dictate that one approach should take precedence over another. Furthermore, the couple usually has little idea of what approach or theory or techniques would work best with them. The couple seldom "owns" the therapy at its initial stages, usually arriving distraught, despairing, and demoralized. Although therapists can fit a couple to a predetermined format by asking certain diagnostically important questions, the disjunctive narratives that emerge between the couple regarding each person's view of the problems often reveal the tension, ambivalence, and hostility that exists between them. This is sometimes displaced onto the therapist.

In the face of what often rapidly emerges as a complex agenda for the therapeutic contract, many couple therapists will attempt to maintain control of the process by one of three defenses. They may hold to a position of "expert," displaying a somewhat grandiose, knowing superiority with their interpretations throughout the length of the psychotherapy. They may exhibit "flight-fight," shutting down emotionally, feeling fatigued and overwhelmed, and become less active. Or they may begin to give excessive advice around the practical matters the couple raises while they themselves feel hypomanic or fragmented. Becoming uncomfortable when the participants begin to assert their point of view in a sometimes heated, impassioned way, and establish their own rules for the conduct of the therapeutic process is an inevitable by-product for therapists in the process of doing couple therapy. How the therapist deals with these tensions becomes crucial to the therapeutic outcome. Now that we are beginning to learn more about the actual conduct of all kinds of therapy, we can appreciate the subjectivity that often guides the course of any therapeutic endeavor. Wachtel (1993), for example, quotes Wile (1984) in illustrating how a renowned psychoanalyst, while guided by his theory in the interpretations he made, exhibited a tendency to make a set of accusatory interpretations to the expressions of resistance by a patient in individual therapy.

Recognizing the difficulties of doing psychotherapy with couples, this chapter attempts to broaden the basis on which therapists can deal more effectively with the intense affects and disruptive disjunctions couples bring to the therapeutic endeavor. It builds on the emerging theories of hermeneutics, unformulated experiences, constructivism, social construction, narrative epistemologies, dialectics, and language formation. It utilizes the blending of both recent self-psychology concepts and object-relations theories. And it formulates a basis for allowing the couples involved to be thought of as co-equal to the therapist in the construction of their narrative reality. The dominant themes are the emphasis on development, progressive structuralization of mind, the intersubjective experience of people in sustained intimate relationships, and the advantage to the self of establishing a durable set of relationships that will facilitate the sense of cohesiveness and integrity the individual experiences of the world and of the self. The name, self-object relationship therapy (SORT), seems most apt to describe this type of approach.

THE PHILOSOPHICAL SETTINGS FOR THE WORK

Often, therapists reach judgments as to what should be the overarching focus of work with couples (especially early in their careers), due to having been exposed to one school of therapy or another. Followers of Murray Bowen (1978) always look at triangles and levels of differentiation; those who studied Salvador Minuchin (1974) consider family structure; those who value Jay Haley (1976) emphasize power and hierarchy; and followers of Carl Whitaker (1976) take an experiential approach. Or therapists have been influenced and energized by one expert, supervisor, or group, who espoused their way as the "best possible way" in a kaleidoscope of difficult, even imponderable choices. It soon becomes clear that as valuable as these perspectives are, no one approach suffices, that working with couples and families is not only demanding, but the therapist is often forced to make clinical decisions and interventions without necessarily knowing all the parameters and dimensions of what they are asked to deal with or whose description to believe. Making clinical decisions on the basis of obvious presenting problems, such as alcoholism, spousal abuse, depression, or an extramarital affair, is but the first small step in a series of possible therapeutic openings. Therapists often feel less sure of the territory they need to cover as they hear more and more of the "double-descriptions" of the couple's realities (Dym & Glenn, 1993).

Most therapists have attended at least a few brief workshops on couple or marital therapy, but this is usually insufficient preparation for work with couples in distress. If, in addition, therapists adopt a stance of listening closely and respectfully, if they suspend relying exclusively on their cherished theories, appreciating initially how much they do not know of the individuals and the complexity of their shared, mutually influential lives, they can set a climate for work in which more of the intimate, more guarded aspects of each individual can come to the fore. Donnel Stern (1997) points out that what we know, and how we come to know it, is a function of the interpersonal field. The assumption that the patient has an emergent self, a predisposed self, eager, albeit anxious, to create a larger landscape of meanings about the self, is a guiding assumption of constructivist-influenced therapists.

Meaning, some believe, is made; it is not a given, rendered true by the endorsement of a higher authority. Stern (1997) points out that all language is hermeneutic, yet to be discovered. Meaning, and the symbols we help to create of the phenomenological world of each person who comes to see us for help, has the nascent potential to be understood with ever greater certainty and conviction. Contemporary psychoanalytically informed couple therapists, influenced by contributions from self psychology and object-relations theory, emphasize a respect for the dialectical and collaborative effort with their patients toward creating an even-handed, nonpejorative, subjectively constructed reality. If I think of a man as "domineering" toward his wife, I have foreclosed other possible ways of seeing him, as, for example, being appropriately assertive, or disturbed by what she has cumulatively done to him over many years (and he to her), or as compensation, in a strident way, for the humiliation and shame that he may have experienced with his parents at a crucial, earlier period in his life. These recrudescences, and our capacity to hear them, I believe, is what Jerome Bruner (1990), Roy Schafer (1978, 1983), and Donald Spence (1982), each in his own way, meant in part when they described a respect for the primacy of "narrative truth" over historical truth, or what fits patients' perceived sense of what they often already know from past experience, but have never quite been able to express in a way that finds a willing audience. It is not necessarily just discovering what has been "repressed," but also validating what remains "unknown" to others. Because we now realize that all language is social in origin, lacking a good-enough language to describe what an individual senses to be true prevents that person from building a representation of reality that does justice to the essence of his or her important developmental experiences. If we can deal with some of our own anxieties that are stimulated by not completely knowing the material that patients' bring forth, we have a good chance of creating a useful collaboration. In the process, we have to be willing to constantly review and revise the cluster of meanings we help the couple bring forth. Part of the work of this type of therapy is to facilitate the couple's capacity to do this for one another.

THE CHALLENGES OF AN INTEGRATIVE ATTITUDE

This chapter is written from the perspective of a psychoanalytically informed individual, couple, and family systems therapist who, in 35 years of clinical practice, has had the privilege of working with many sensitive, caring, committed, and, in many instances, professionally successful adults, primarily in outpatient clinics and private practice. In spite of their individual triumphs and accomplishments, some of these individuals have been unable to achieve any stable or satisfactory relationship with a partner, or they may come to treatment as a couple at a certain phase, such as after an affair has been discovered, when the children have left home, when a business is failing, when a parent has just died, when the marriage has reached some intolerable level, or when, in a remarried family, the effectiveness of the parenting framework has broken down. Sometimes they have been referred by their individual therapist, who may have seen the couple once or twice, particularly when the dominant and recurrent complaints by the individual patient have been about the partner, or when the referring therapist construes that the patient's condition is worsening due to the dynamics between the couple. When the couple come in for treatment, they often appear to have failed in their holding capacity for each other; their ability to tolerate the aggressive and masochistic drives in themselves and the other is usually marginal; sexual intimacy and nurturance is usually minimal or routinized; and communication is typically restricted, guarded, or accusatory. Rarely do couples accept fully their own personal contributions to the impasse, instead expressing enormous dissatisfaction with the partner, as viewed from a blaming position. Seldom do they use representative language about their collective dysfunction, which is of equal magnitude (an exception was one woman saying in the first diagnostic session: "We're both stubborn, proud, and if hurt, we both act vindictively"). Instead, one partner typically assigns more blame to the other. Often, they reveal that they are concurrently having serious difficulties with or disruptive ties to one or more members of their family, and report narcissistically frustrating or aggressive and fractured interactions with significant others in childhood and adolescence. (It is always important to ask detailed questions about relationships other than with parents and grandparents, such as with siblings; see Bank & Kahn, 1982, 1997; Kahn & Lewis, 1988.) Thinking systemically, we are often left wondering whether these are a cause or effect of the couple's difficulties. These couples are no different from individuals presenting for therapy, but often use the relationship impasse as their "calling card" for help. Looking at them as a mutually regulating, systems-determining unit or in terms of individual personality strengths and weaknesses is a delicate balance. Tipping too much to one side or the other may prejudice the whole process, blinding us to many important matters. Given the myriad issues a couple can present (and they often compete for the therapist's attention and Solomon-like approval for what they choose to bring up), we need to maintain a heightened sensitivity at the most delicate stage of our encounters with each of these couples, the initial meetings when we set the frame for whether we are going to have a collaborative exchange of meanings and work. And we need to know how to maintain that sensitivity and empathy as the therapy unfolds and intense affect spills out.

It appears to this clinician that both family systems perspectives and contemporary psychoanalytic perspectives have enormous epistemological value for an integrative effort. It helps the therapist move back and forth from the clients' worlds of their self systems and their relationship systems. Yet, as I have previously pointed out (Kahn, 1986, 1989), integration of such seemingly radically differing epistemologies rarely occurs, because clinicians tend to be too heavily influenced by their professional and guild associations and the attendant conceptual foundations to feel comfortable embracing both psychoanalytic thinking and family systems thinking. Each is viewed as antithetical to the other. The pragmatics of clinical practice and each clinician's personal orientation and background cause most therapists to work either chiefly from the outside in (family systems), focusing primarily on the couple as a unit and helping them find new patterns and rules of behavior, or from the inside out (psychoanalytic), focusing on the vicissitudes of the self or selves. The language of each emphasis manifestly differs; the focus on the problems certainly differs, and the lengths of the therapies are usually at extremes from one another. The couples work qua family systems is often under 10 to 15 sessions duration (e.g., Johnson, 1996), whereas that with a more psychoanalytic cast is likely to be of considerably greater length (more than one year, often two to four; e.g., D. E. Scharff & Scharff, 1987). Such vast differences in the length of treatment may too easily reflect a subtle but powerful coercive economic, moral, and political reality created largely by the culture and reflected in the values of the therapist (Cushman, 1995). Nonetheless, some clinicians have written about the merits of integration, difficult as that may be to bring about (Feldman, 1992; Kahn, 1986; Kirschner & Kirschner, 1986; Moultrup, 1986; Nichols, 1988; Norcross & Goldfried, 1992; D. E. Scharff & Scharff, 1987; Slipp, 1984; Sugarman, 1986; Wachtel & Wachtel, 1986).

Many pragmatic questions arise as a function of the philosophical and economic tenets held by therapists. Does the therapist communicate that faster is better, or that longer is deeper? Does the influence of the competitive, industrialized therapeutic marketplace, controlled by third-party payers and the managed care industry, turn the patient into a "consumer" and the therapist into a "provider," shifting the focus away from the psychological maturation, complexity, and development of the self or the couple? Most therapists, no matter their orientation, would agree that it does. Stabilization of symptoms or symptom relief, not the intense, deeper work of personality change, relinquishing of primitive defenses, conflict resolution, working through of narcissistic and archaic needs, and development of empathy, takes precedent in a climate of managed care. Furthermore, the fourth edition of the *Diagnostic and Statistical Manual of Mental Disorders* (*DSM-IV*; American Psychiatric Association [APA], 1994) does not even recognize the validity of a couple-based, systemically interactive problem, except as a nonreimbursable V-code. Instead, to be paid by third-party payers, couple therapists are sometimes forced to lie about the focus of their work, applying an often pejorative or inaccurate Axis I diagnostic label arbitrarily to one member of the couple. The politically and economically driven decision of who gets diagnostically labeled, even if left entirely up to the couple, inevitably supports the fantasy that one person is more "damaged" than the other.

In addition, as Cushman and Gilford (2000) eloquently warn, the very nature of self becomes reconstructed when managed care organization-generated treatment reports, filled out by the therapist, and consumer satisfaction scales determine the efficacy of treatment. Therapists are forced to prove their worth not through the criteria of their training, licensure, board certification, professional accreditation, and impartial peer review, but by the dictates of who controls the consumer marketplace. One result is the proliferation of extravagant claims by some therapists of success with the most difficult personal and relationship problems. The planned application of briefer and briefer therapies—fewer than 10 sessions and even single sessions—as described by Talmon (1990), undocumented by rigorous research, is now routine for some therapists. Such therapists, not of psychoanalytic persuasion, primarily overemphasize competence and skill building in their approach, block the expression of painful affects, and steer the therapeutic dialogue prematurely to strengths and successes.

These types of approaches intentionally prevent clients (note: not patients) from discussing and reflecting on the less adequate or more unhappy aspects of their relationship and themselves. Externalizing the problem may provide relief for some who are obsessively guilt-ridden or prone to an excessive, superego-driven self-reproach. But these positively skewed approaches often do little to undo past hurts from significant others, or to build an enhanced, complex, and durable sense of self, or to locate part of the problem as lying within the person's own realm of responsibility. It should be noted, however, that there is a burgeoning body of theory and research in American psychology emphasizing optimism (Seligman, 1991), happiness (Lyubomirsky, 2001), and resiliency (Mastin, 2001), which hold that focusing on positive attributes can counteract a person's proclivity to become mired in despair. We should not ignore that restoration of hope has always been a desirable goal in therapy (Frank, 1973; Mitchell, 1993). In couple therapy, externalizing the responsibility for a person's dilemma (White & Epston, 1990) by understanding socially constructed, oppressive elements in the patient's world, for example, due to burdensome gender politics, can relieve despair, unrequited yearning, and grieving about perceived failures in the self. The goal in a self-object relational approach, in contrast, is to not preclude viewing, no matter how distressful, any aspect of the participants' lives. An adequate course of therapy, with sufficient attention to detail, gives us a much better chance of establishing a framework for empathy and nonjudgmental collaboration.

When one approaches work with a couple, one needs to understand when the shifts in the therapy should occur. These shifts are from focusing on external dilemmas and forces to internal forces of feelings and conflicts, or vice versa. Questions we can ask ourselves as we use our "internal supervisor" (Casement, 1985) include: Are these vicissitudes between the inner and outer world of the participants a function of political and moral imperatives of the patient and the therapist, and from where are they derived? Are they residues and derivatives of previous unhappy experiences and powerful psychological forces in either of the participants? What do I need to know about the histories of these people? If they are not ready to tell me, how much do I need to know? Can I contain the corrosive affect between them, or will I become defensively oriented, shifting the topics out of my needs, not theirs? How can a dialectic between them be created that is mutually satisfying, not regressive, aggressive, or persecutory?

One of our goals is to provide a greater sense of clarity and definition to the experience of patients with their inner and outer worlds, but always modifying and propelling that sense of reality forward, so that it can evolve further. In older language, we want to help create a better observing ego in each; in newer language, we wish to create the possibilities for ever-widening dialectical interchange between the couple, a larger scale of open-ended narrative realities, a "scaffolding" (Wood, 1988) of meanings. Both senses of the language seem appropriate.

Deciding how deeply we should delve into long-standing personality issues with couples impacts the amount of time the therapy will take. Few couples, in the author's experience, are willing to come in more than once weekly, except under emergency conditions. In addition, unlike individuals undergoing psychoanalytic treatment, couples can seldom articulate, nor can we forecast, the length of time they wish to commit to the therapeutic process. What has become clear to me is that if we work effectively and comprehensively, not excluding anything of what they speak about at the most evident level of the presenting distress, the couple will inevitably stay to do more salient work. They will be more willing to take on the level of undiscovered, unknown, or repressed emotional material, gaining an increased understanding that "it takes two (or more) to tango." Whereas the sense of the known self provides an individual psychological cohesiveness and self-certainty (however misguided), the dialectics of psychological and behavioral interaction as reflected in cultural and social embeddedness—this "dialogic" self (Bakhtin, 1973, Hermans, Kempen, & van Loon, 1992), this "What do people think of me, Why don't people respond to me as I think they should, Why is he or she so unhappy when what I do is so logical and right" self—are usually much less well-known or vague or remains inarticulated by the individuals before they have entered the therapist's office. Being in a successful intimate relationship requires much more effort and psychological maturity than being alone.

If we accept the premise (a healthy one for therapists) that the human species has a self-actualizing tendency (Maslow, 1962), or destiny drive (Bollas, 1989), we are often pushed by the couple's wish for healthy change, this crying out for a relief from their psychic distress, to take on the larger agenda of being in a satisfying relationship, which most therapists begin to appreciate is always there, waiting for us. This second stage of the work often takes at least four to six months before we can get to it, following a first stage of crisis management and dealing with the more obvious pathological patterns of behavior they bring in. Then, after the initial stage, how expansive should our role as the therapist with couples become? The therapist's office becomes a space for many of their difficulties to be worked on, and the issues can be quite comprehensive. The self-object relationship therapist will be asked to help them increase their sensitivities to one another, "save the marriage," prevent a potentially disastrous divorce, help resolve issues with family members, create a favorable emotional climate where each partner can flourish and emotionally grow, prevent unchecked and unanalyzed expressions of anger, or help liberate them from the oppressive roles and damaging, repetitive interactions they help perpetuate with their family of origin. Who will set the kind and complexity of the agenda? Some couple therapists work only with the presenting, manifest, and mutually agreed upon problem (e.g., "Our son is in difficulty again"; "We're having a miserable marriage that we want to fix"). Jay Haley, with whom the author studied in the 1970s, often said that therapy ought to be a set of renewable options, and that once the presenting problem is dispatched, the therapy should end. But it is not that simple; often, the agenda rapidly shifts, or unfolds to reveal more and more material, or one partner has an entirely different perspective from the other partner on the same phenomenon, or the partners are at markedly different levels of psychological sophistication or capacity for insight. These are the difficult kinds of issues we continue to struggle with.

LOVE AND THE CULTURAL CHALLENGES OF WORKING WITH COUPLES

The difficult task of couple therapy comes as no surprise given the complexities underlying falling in and out of love, dealing with disillusionment (Mitchell, 1997), staying with the relationship for gratification of our most basic needs, the passion and agonies of being attracted to and then being in love with someone, the concerns and conflicts that culminate in the frequent occurrence of divorce, and the challenges of raising children in difficult times (Spock, 1974). Miller (1989) contends that modern psychotherapy has not been very successful in helping men and women deal effectively with the anxieties of loving one another. We put out the fire of an immediate crisis, but the consensus in the field is that many couples often leave therapy before the harder work of characterological and existential change can take place. Perhaps, as Mitchell (1997) pointed out, couples sense that love is a dangerous form of illusion, and that the reawakening of idealization of the partner and, with it, the reawakening of passion always runs the risk of a new loss.

Inevitably, there will be some aggression, and with it, de-idealization. I sense that premature termination obviates the fear that the safety and security that people wish for in a relationship will not be able to be reconciled with the passion and romance they are also seeking. Such matters need to be discussed.

Couple therapists often have to deal with the serious entry-level problems presented by the couples; the emotional hazards of infidelities, the emotional and physical abandonment by significant partners, sexual impasses, substance and physical abuse, all kinds of emotional distress, the problems within a relationship affected by difficulties with children, and, though not having the crisis proportions of some issues, the deadened quality of the relationship of some couples who have stayed together for a long time in a devitalized marriage. Rarely do couples now arrive for therapy just seeking "marital enrichment," "enhancement," or "fine tuning." People's schedules are too crowded, the proliferation of self-help and pop psychology's remedies too ubiquitous, the expectations of feeling loved too diminished or too quickly demolished. Men and women are continuously told how different they are from one another, in such books as *Men Are from Mars, Women Are from Venus* (Gray, 1992). Such perspectives do little to enhance the trust between the genders and only increase the sense of oppressive power differentials for men and women (Zimmerman, Haddock, & McGeorge, 2001). In fact, many more women now speak openly about the abuse they have suffered in past relationships with men.

Western culture is simultaneously harsh and seductive (Kegan, 1994; Slater, 1970), making everyone still feel, slightly or to a greater degree, that in spite of intellectually knowing better, we will feel complete, beautiful, contented, or fortunate only if we are loved by an equally charming and charmed partner. The operative assumption is that all we are supposed to be will eventuate in such a relationship. Universally, those who are single or who choose not to become part of a life-long couple arrangement often are made to feel disadvantaged, or are expected to be always working on or evolving toward couple status. Individuals who are not able to achieve coupledom are perceived as incomplete, and receive scorn, pity, or other forms of rejection. As therapists, we often have to ameliorate the internalized, projected denigrations individuals carry as a result of society's collective harsh judgment of those who do not stay coupled, or who eventually are deemed to have "failed" everyone by becoming divorced. Some couples are indeed not well suited for each other. Working on articulating the critical differences and understanding their importance to the individual is just as important a piece of the therapeutic process as attempts to reconcile those differences. In addition, Kantor (1989) points out how the myths of sexual and emotional contracts between men and women and the journey they embark on to fulfill such fantasies are like that of Odysseus and Penelope in Homer's *Odyssey*, marked by high ideals of valor and sacrifice but filled with tragedy and disappointment. The pure and chaste woman, Penelope, the besieged but valiant adventurer/wanderer man, Odysseus are celebrated for the gender-role arrangements they hold to throughout Odysseus' 10-year-long wanderlust (many modern sailors have completed Odysseus' voyage in less than 30 days of sailing!). The expectation for modern couples that the woman should always be a noble, faithful sufferer who tends to her mate when he is present, while the man keeps his distance, fulfilling his destiny through his triumphs at work, war, or sports, dooms many couples to relationships of acrimony or sterile emotionality (not to mention the deleterious effects on children observing their parents in such arrangements). The culture at large, and families and friends, continually project these primitive and archaic images of love, loss, danger, and attachment. These become internalized by many, compounding the already held fantasies of persecutory and idealized object relations, a recrudescence and reenactment of infantile dependence, yearning, and frustration (Kernberg, 1995) that people hold onto while growing up.

Given these conditions, we know that many individuals often engage in self-defeating behaviors with significant others, in spite of claiming and valuing otherwise. Under such circumstances, the therapist often has to serve as an educator, weaving in questions and explanations that may allow the couple, at their most tenuous and initial stage of the therapeutic work, to be able to offset these deleterious projections of beauty and power, which are explicitly expected to be the ongoing result of being in a couple relationship. Sadomasochistic derivatives of childhood experiences and the perceived sense of inequality of power and fairness carried from childhood and adolescence rapidly emerge. But when we explain too much about this or do it too quickly, and then try to soothe the couple with an unacknowledged self-certainty about our premises (for we often are working with incomplete information), we can easily trigger a good deal of transferential anxiety. Loyalty to parents and family and defensive alignments about the self should not be quickly undone merely because the couple are at an impasse or in distress. Conversely, if we offer advice, we run the risk of presenting ourselves as just one more expert in an ocean of experts. Other resources are usually available to the couple that are less intimidating than our interpretations. Psychological Band-Aids or instant panaceas that preclude insight, such as the overreliance on antidepressants and anti-anxiety psychotropic medications, are increasingly promoted and are appealing to many people. As therapists, we have to be knowledgeable about these cultural matters, staying informed, balancing advice, reassurance, and careful questions with a continual leading edge of inquiry about the couple's less apparent psychological worlds. We have to appreciate how elaborate and self-sustaining their psychological constructions are and yet be willing to risk incurring some of the transferential anxiety in them, and countertransferential anxieties in ourselves, as we move forward. As Greenberg & Johnson (1988) point out, we must be prepared to work with intense emotions.

Our culture's love messages and solution messages are often both explicitly and subliminally defined by powerful commercial interests; mass media and technology are now the foremost creators of cultural norms for many individuals. The couple's families of origin, ethnic traditions and customs, and even the structural components of the post-Oedipal and postadolescent self, which permit reflection and introspection, are increasingly submerged under a layer of postmodern impressions. Thus, the information and communications that many people receive about love relationships, partnering, and marriage are often overly simplistic, contradictory, reductionistic, but nonetheless powerful and ubiquitous. Television shows seem to have become the mother for many, providing scenarios and templates that distort reality. These days, individuals appear to be swimming upstream against an ever increasing torrent of information from articles, the Internet, brief how-to books, talk shows, movies, music lyrics, and advertising, in the hope that there are quick-fix solutions to some very serious personal and relationship problems. Simultaneously, because these images and ephemeral messages of love and happiness are constantly being replaced by new ones, individuals engage in a plaintive search for more durable ones. Many excellent movies, plays, and writings of the past 50 years have dwelt on the tension between old culture and new culture, of the search for authenticity, durability, inner, and outer cohesiveness. Under these conditions, most people become disappointed in the way an intimate relationship unfolds. There is a paradigm clash between those inner states of affect, which rely on continuity, durability, coherence, integrity, fairness, loyalty, and contentment to remain effective and resilient, and externally created states of affect, which are shaped by excitement, stimulation, disruption, innovation, and tension, what Rabkin described as the clash between *Inner and Outer Space* (Rabkin, 1970).

DIFFICULT COUPLES

Since the 1950s and 1960s (see Lasch, 1977), American families pursuing the ideals of freedom, change, and happiness, have often become isolated "havens in a heartless world," cut off from the spiritual and community roots that characterized previous ties between the individual self and the family or the community. Couples have become more alone or have relied excessively on their children to give themselves a sense of purpose. Modernization and increasingly rapid technological change have helped to create conditions for the emergence of what Kohut (1977) once called "tragic man," supplanting "guilty man." Tragic man, in Kohut's eyes, was somewhat like Reisman's (1973) earlier view of outer-directed man, someone who was forced into narcissistic retreat, unable to cope with the harsh realities of the modern world, unable to find and be nourished by committed caregivers and cohesive ideologies, and therefore, unable to rely on personal emotional resources. Kohut often pointed to "disintegration" anxiety as a feeling state prevalent in many individuals and axiomatic of our times. This "threat of the destruction of the nuclear self" (p. 117) that some people carry threatens the stability of any intimate relationship.

Increasingly, many therapists see couples for treatment who, in their emotional isolation, splitting, and denial, have overloaded their emotional expectations of what their partner can provide them. Such couples may have little to do of emotional importance with other people, or experience disintegration anxiety, phobias, fragmentation, and culturally promoted dissociative episodes through alcohol, drugs, sex, the Internet, extramarital affairs, and spending binges, when they cannot get what they think they need from their partner, and so look to others for a quick fix. Diagnostically, they can be viewed as narcissistic or borderline, and there appear to be many more such individuals than 30 or 40 years ago. Affective storming often occurs in their relationships: idealization, followed by disappointment, followed by rage. Years of substance abuse, constant threats of abandonment or divorce, acting out through sexual escapades, excitement seeking, or financially risky behavior, or the making of poor choices in their work world can also occur. On presentation, the couple may appear beleaguered but united in their desire to work together on their problems; there can also be a powerful undercurrent of disturbed characterological processes, which makes an initial focus on only the couple unit a serious clinical error.

Psychotherapy with couples where one or both have a narcissistic, borderline, or antisocial personality disorder due to long-standing issues of abandonment, developmental disruptions, and neglect is becoming more common (Nichols, 1996; Solomon, 1996). Solomon, drawing on the consensus of those who, like Kernberg (1995) and Kohut (1977), have attempted to work with borderlines without much success, warns of the difficulties the clinician faces in treating couples who are organized and function emotionally at that level. Solomon stresses that it behooves every clinician to pay close attention to the intrapsychic processes of each of the individuals in therapy. If this does not occur, the couple may quickly terminate therapy, never pursue further exploration of their difficulties, and/or condemn the whole spectrum of psychotherapies. The "We tried to see a therapist once, and went for four sessions, but it didn't help" lament has been heard countless times by many clinicians in early introductory meetings with couples. On exploration, this often is due to the previous therapist not paying close attention to the personality variables, the developmental histories of interactions with important family figures, the derivatives of fragmented emotional experiences, and the previous attempts at restitution and resolution that failed. Many couples also lack an understanding of normal developmental stages and family processes over time (Wynne, 1984).

Finally, in spite of the hazards described, most people still long to be in a relationship that fills their needs, but not if it totally subordinates or obliterates their definition of themselves. People usually understand that there has to be a quid pro quo between giving and receiving, a "50-50" arrangement. How to achieve that balance, both with their own views of themselves and what is needed by the partner, is a universal challenge from which none of us are exempt. But the risk is psychological pain. One patient, who is described in more detail later, existed barely, with back pain and chronic fatigue syndrome, in an excruciatingly symbiotic tie with her husband, from whom she later separated. In the past few years, she had begun projecting all of her rage and sense of annihilation onto him, cursing him with every foul name, but she nonetheless would keep calling him at all hours of the night and depended on him to drive to their home, tend the garden, pay the bills, repair the house, drive her to appointments, and accompany her to social events. Most such occasions were followed by rage reactions: screaming and sometimes physically attacking him. She was torn between the fear of abandonment, the state of utter aloneness, and a morbid fear of closeness. She certainly had never achieved the sense of contentedness and self-composure we equate with psychological well-being. In her family, she believed she had been a persecutory hate object for a vengeful mother, a target of abuse by a vindictive older sister, and an idealized but absent father who never spoke up to protect his children or have any meaningful influence through play, conversation, or interaction. She always lived in fear of ridicule and hate, and there was never, throughout childhood and adolescence, a sense of security or psychological safety. People in that family appeared to exist only to survive or endure, and no one, outsider or family member, was ever trusted. By adulthood, this woman was fearful, malignantly paranoid, and pessimistic of any future. The husband was faithful, but masochistically aligned with the sadistic side of her character. He remained subservient to her, yet each felt that the other had failed him or her. Neither had been able to achieve a sense of security with each other, but she had clung to the delusion that her life with him would ameliorate all the hurts and shame she felt about all others in the world. The wife, projecting her grandiose expectations onto the husband and for many years unable to metabolize or work through her rage, seemed to have exaggerated the essence and importance of what the poet Rainer Maria Rilke once stated in the following way: "I hold this to be the highest task of a bond between two people; that each should stand guard over the solitude of the other" (1954). In this case, the wife's solitude was depressive, corrosive, and experienced as endangering. Left alone, she would psychologically crumble. She had no friends. Conversely, when she was with her husband, she was chronically dissatisfied and rageful. But she would plaintively ask me and the husband in a bewildered way: "I have been a good wife. Don't I deserve to have a good husband?"

TECHNICAL CONSIDERATIONS

We now know that contemporary psychoanalytic theories, though elegant and extremely useful for the treatment of individuals, are often insufficient for practice with couples and extended family systems. Relatively few papers and books have been written about couple therapy from this perspective, although many clinicians agree on the appropriateness of viewing couples this way. Yet, the intensity of the projective processes between couples, the reigniting of primitive affects within them by being in a dependent relationship, and the usual unwillingness, culturally promoted, to come to therapy more than once a week render much of psychoanalytic technique elusive and difficult to apply. I have proposed that restoration of the self is at the heart of most couple distress, and that psychoanalytic insights from a self-object relationship perspective are the richest source for successful work with couples. A difficult epistemological problem occurs, however, when we attempt to move from theory to practice. Too often, sophisticated theories about individual behavior and development are difficult to fathom in the realm of interactive and systemic behavior, and we come to realize that, as Willi (1982) points out, couples act collusively to maintain the regressive aspects of their personalities. Some authors have provided us with insights from the more traditional psychoanalytic perspective, which we can find useful.

Willi (1982) describes four types of collusion he believes are present in every married couple relationship. Each couple, he posits, will find the resolution of these themes difficult, particularly if there have been deeper conflicts around these matters with their parents in early childhood. Adult partners, Willi states, metamorphize earlier yearnings for gratification in the relationship along the following collusive, interactive lines:

1. The narcissistic relationship, centering on the question: How much does love and marriage demand that I sacrifice myself for my partner and how much can I be myself? To what extent do we need to set limits for each other and to what degree can we become one with each other? ...
2. The oral relationship, focusing on: How far should one be concerned with helping and supporting the partner in love and marriage? How much right do I have to expect that my partner will care for me like a mother, without expecting the same treatment in return? ...
3. The anal-sadistic relationship: How much can I be the autonomous leader ... to whom my passive partner submits? How passively dependent on my partner can I become without fear of manipulation? Do I have the right to possess my partner completely and to control all their thoughts and actions, or do I have to allocate autonomous areas to them?
4. The phallic-oedipal relationship: ... As a woman, how much should I deny the development of "masculine" characteristics for the sake of my partner, be passive, and lean on him in weakness? As a man, am I always obliged to show male strength or can I also sometimes give in to passive tendencies? (p. 58)

Although Willi's language is a bit outdated, we still can appreciate the interactive dynamics he outlines as germane to many relationships. The therapist's stance, he cautions, must be even-handed; insight is stressed, and side-taking through acting out of the countertransference is guarded against scrupulously. Unfortunately, he gives us comparatively little description of the clinical techniques he uses with couples to help break them out of their relationship impasse and to move the collusive elements from the level of toxic disturbance to that of enjoyable and productive interaction.

Kernberg (1995) has written extensively about love relations, both normal and pathological. Building on earlier work by Dicks (1967) and Stoller (1979, 1985), he, like Willi, attempts to understand the unconscious motivations that occur in love relationships as a function of disturbed object relations, and the predominant reliance by the individuals on splitting and projective identification. Kernberg expands on Dicks's work to include the actual sexual relations of the couple, their consciously and unconsciously predominant object relations, and their establishment of a joint ego ideal. Kernberg stresses the importance of integrating libido and aggression and the predominance of love over hatred in all three of these areas of influence. He points out the enormously crucial role the superego has in the governance of relationships, in which an individual may experience the inevitable disillusionment and deidealization of the partner as a betrayal and, splitting the object, may devalue the partner or seek revenge. Infidelities or other forms of disturbed acting out can unbalance the defenses against sadomasochistic impulses in either individual and, according to Kernberg, may be further inflamed by projective identification by either or both partners. The aggression and persecutory fantasies that may then appear, particularly with borderline and narcissistic individuals, can often destabilize the relationship further. In all cases, Kernberg emphasizes that the therapist explore fully the Oedipal relations of each participant, the degree of transference to the therapist, the capacity for eroticization to sustain love, and the ability to tolerate aggression. Mature love can result in working through these issues, generally in psychoanalytic treatment of each individual, with integration of pre-Oedipal and Oedipal levels of superego formation. Kernberg describes a "neutralization" of primitive idealization and the persecutory fantasies in successful treatment as giving way to the emergence of the capacity for gratitude and authentic forgiveness to those from whom the individual previously felt slight or damage. A healthy balance between narcissistic self-love and love of the important object is also crucial to stable adjustment.

Kernberg (1995) emphasizes the important distinction that must be made diagnostically regarding the level of pathology of each member of the couple. He gives examples of obtaining a history and diagnostic impression by seeing couples in the first phase of treatment conjointly. However, he appears more comfortable referring one member to another therapist and engaging the other to then undertake psychoanalytic treatment with him. It appears he does not see couples in ongoing treatment and he has written little about the actual process of seeing couples together.

Solomon (1989, 1996), on the other hand, using object-relations theory, has given us some very useful guidelines when working with fragile couples who rely on borderline and narcissistic defenses. She emphasizes rigorous self-observation and self-control in the face of the intense affects displayed by such couples and urges therapists to be aware of their countertransference reactions when faced with the participants' defenses of projection, introjection, splitting, and projective identification. She advocates a stance of empathic attunement while maintaining neutrality, allowing the observing ego of each patient to align with and identify with the healthy parts of the therapist. Therapists can be selectively transparent, sharing some aspects of their lives, as stimulated by the material revealed in the couple therapy, and need to be psychologically present and preoccupied with what is occurring during the therapeutic hour.

Solomon (1989, 1996) anticipates that in the midphases of treatment, more of the regressive material will emerge and that therapy will be turbulent. The couple now feels freer to express all their hurt and loathing, and frequently, dysfunctional patterns of attack and counterattack, blame and refutation, hurt and defense will take place. Analogs to the feelings they have to one another are now more readily felt toward the therapist, who, as an ambivalent object, may be alternately idealized (listened to) and reviled (overtly criticized). Together, and repeatedly, the couple and therapist work through the aspects of each partner's sense of being hurt and the disappointments that then result in recurring regressive sequences. She helps the couple track their cycles of perceived narcissistic loss, regression, and then retaliation. She seems keenly aware of the couple's need for empathy and support, and is verbally active in her expression of describing these impasses to them, attempting always to give the support needed by the individuals to help them work through the issues. She appears more inclined when working with those with borderline and narcissistic personality disorders to stay in the here and now, rather than uncover primitive material from the pre-Oedipal and early Oedipal phases of their life.

David Scharff and Jill Scharff (D. E. Scharff, 1992; D. E. Scharff & Scharff, 1987; J. S. Scharff & Scharff, 1991), by leaning heavily on the insights of the British object-relational theorists, particularly Bion (1961, 1970), Fairbairn (1952), Winnicott (1958, 1965), and Klein (1948, 1957), have made important contributions in their emphasis on early life experiences in working with couples and families. For the Scharffs, establishing a safe, holding environment for a couple is the sine qua non for effective treatment. Within such a framework, the customary transferential material that is projected and introjected between the couple, is also experienced by the therapist. This shared experience occurs in the form of focused transferences, akin to the central experiences the individuals had with their mothering object, and contextual transferences, which are a reprise of many of the feelings incurred in the shared space of mother and father (and, I might add, with siblings, nannies, and other important family figures). The valued objects in the individual's early life are experienced as libidinal (exciting and gratifying) and antilibidinal (frustrating and/or intrusive); reconciliation of these contrasting experiences follows Kleinian theoretical lines of reconciliation and reowning of the projected bad feelings.

In couple sessions, the Scharffs (D. E. Scharff & Scharff, 1987; J. S. Scharff & Scharff, 1991) contend, the focused transferences and contextual transferences are more blurred than they would be in individual therapy and less intense than in psychoanalysis. Nonetheless, they are present, and alternate from each of the participants and what they collectively create in their attitude and associations to the therapist. The couple's basic wish to be understood and "held" by the therapist creates ample opportunities for splitting, projective identification, and introjection to occur among all the participants, including the therapist (focused and contextual countertransferences). By speaking selectively about what he or she is experiencing, the therapist not only models a desirable attitude for the patients but, like a good parent, helps detoxify or metabolize the previously disowned material. Integration of previously repressed, dissociated, feared, or split-off parts is a central goal of treatment. Although the Scharffs do not totally eschew giving advice, their experience with young children and adolescents and their comfort with dream material and play sometimes lends itself to also offering helpful suggestions and directions with couples who are having difficulties with their children, while the other intense transferential and interpretive work is concurrently taking place.

In an excellent guide to viewing family therapy with a psychoanalytic lens, Gerson (1996) offers a useful framework with which to compare the obvious and essential differences between the psychoanalytic tradition and foundation theories of family therapy that emerged 30 to 40 years ago. She points out that the actual practices of both approaches have begun to look somewhat similar in some of their essential curative factors. Although the essence of psychoanalysis remains the power of interpretation of unconscious material,

Other significant aspects of the analyst's presence identified in the literature include a faith in the restorative function of empathy (Atwood & Stolorow, 1984), containment of the patient's projections and anxieties (Bion, 1961; Winnicott,

1958), and a commitment to honestly examine how participation is shared in reenacting the patient's disowned experience (Hoffman, 1991). (p. 161)

Gerson points out that relationship enhancement and the analyst not holding to a rigid frame are becoming more acceptable in analytic practice, although she underscores that this is controversial and that many in the psychoanalytic community still emphasize the centrality of the analysis of resistance. An appreciation of the importance of mutuality and the understanding of countertransference dynamics appear similar to what was central to the approaches by Willi, Solomon, and the Scharffs in their work with couples.

Conversely, Gerson (1996) cites the family systems therapeutic stance as active, intentional, often explicitly experimental, and playful. Working with concepts of ritualized behavior, stages of development, homeostasis, complementarity, symmetry, family rules, power, heirarchy, and relationship configurations, rich unconscious material can often be overlooked or intentionally ignored by the systems-minded couple therapist who, rather than only interpreting, will attempt to move the couple out of their dysfunctional and redundant patterns of behavior. Systems-oriented couple therapists often assign homework to a couple or stop one member of the pair from destructive behavior detrimental to their partner. Such direct interventions are anathema to most psychoanalysts. But, Gerson points out, family therapists are utilizing "liminal" experience (a concept she borrows from anthropology) when they create a suspension of the usual order of things in time and space, setting forth a more magical, plastic play of ideas, words, and behaviors. Although psychoanalysis would appear to have a more rigorous way of working (some critics, Gerson states, would say ponderous or overbearing), there is a growing appreciation of the play of language in analysis, the mutual, interactive influence, not easily put into words, of the intersubjective process, and an awareness that unconscious or preconscious material, understood and metabolized by both therapist and patient, can often hold the key to breaking the rigid and unhappy ways individuals experience themselves (see Winnicott, 1971). This too, without Gerson saying so explicitly, is "liminoid."

Rather than characterize certain behaviors and feelings that emerge in therapy as necessarily regressive, Gerson (1996) prefers to examine the notion of playfulness in its various guises in family and analytic therapy, as more growth-enhancing for the possibilities of therapeutic change. She also skillfully compares authoritativeness and honesty in both modalities. Finally, in her examples of work with couples, she allows us to more fully understand the complexities of working conjointly in analytic and family systems venues, how and when referral from one modality to another might best occur, and how therapists can appreciate the conceptual struggles they face as they attempt to use the best of both traditions or integrate sometimes disparate bodies of knowledge.

AN INTEGRATIVE PERSPECTIVE ON TREATMENT

The self-object relationship therapist, by paying attention to both inner and outer states of tension, structure, and organization, and staying continuously informed about the vicissitudes of culture, can offer participants a safe environment in which to feel appreciated and understood. As therapists, we have to create a delicate but enduring balance for the emergent selves of the individuals to unfold. But so often with couples, due to the complexity of two interactive individuals blending and clashing in what they present, we cannot afford the pragmatic, technical luxuries of the individual therapist, psychodynamically informed, who can reflect on the dynamics in the room between analyst and patient, as the transferential elements slowly build. (The author, who is also a professional jazz musician, is reminded of the French composer Nadia Boulanger, who once said, "To begin to play music, one must read the notes; to become a virtuoso, one must forget the notes.") Reflection by the clinician on what has occurred in session and what the associated thoughts and evocations are can usually occur only postsession, when we are by ourselves, hopefully not crowded by the next clinical case. In the author's view, this is indispensable. This reflective process becomes internalized, if we "practice," and is carried internally by the clinician and then, we hope, by the participants, through the duration of the therapy. Like the accomplished musician, the insights can then be operative and can often be shared as the session occurs without our stopping to think about them for too long. Having a cotherapist also helps enable this more spontaneous, reflective way of working.

The intensity of the processes among couples mandates that we be verbally active, informative to the participants, and intuitive about when to offer interpretations. We usually have to offer solace, but not be patronizing. We often have to offer caution about acting impulsively, but not ignore the emergencies of the situation, as when there is suicidal danger or physical abuse. By being active, we run the risk of being seen as partial to one participant or the other, transference and countertransference can run rampant, and there is usually some competition for our judgments between the couple members. We have to be self-reflective, but usually most of this occurs after the white-hot heat of the session has passed. We have to take care of ourselves psychically and not be ground up by the intensity of the cumulative affects we are dealing with. We have to deal with the surface structure and the interpersonal and behavioral world of the participants, while trying to gain access to the innermost feelings of each. This is not an easy task when the couple are hurling ferocious invectives at one another, creating jarring, even inchoate narratives, feel entirely misunderstood or betrayed by their partner, or sit in silent scorn, projecting every scintilla of unarticulated, primitive affect to their significant other in our consulting room. It is not surprising, in this light, that many psychoanalysts who embrace self psychology and object-relations theories and have made significant contributions regarding technical considerations in the therapy of individuals have, up to now, eschewed working with couples.

This author works with couples at all levels of experience, but always within the province of informed consent and by listening at the intuitive level, with the "third ear" (Reik, 1948). I explain where I am heading and why I have chosen that path. I alert the couple to when and why I am shifting focus, and will sometimes ask their cooperation in bringing the focus back to where we had left off, either in that same session or in subsequent sessions. Do they agree? Do they take exception? Do they wish to modify the course of the therapy, or change direction? I trust, as they do, that we are working with the best of intentions, and that listening for the clues to unconscious, unclarified elements of their lives (Reik, 1948) earns their respect. As Atwood and Stolorow (1984) point out, the exploration of disjunctions between therapist and participants, and explanations of why we spoke as we did, often prove the best way to clinically proceed. The easier flow of exchanged meanings, irrespective of content, is therapeutic for some people who have persistently destroyed the other's efforts at meaning making. Our attitude is consciously to help, yet this does not preclude our sometimes feeling despairing or frustrated or angry or any of myriad other feelings. I have shared with couples stories about my parents, or instances from my own professional work in institutions or with other patients in the past (carefully chosen to delete any deleterious comparisons) and the dilemmas or insights that were triggered by the associative processes going on in the therapy on that particular occasion. Such revelations by analog generally helped illuminate aspects of their own projective and introjective processes. There certainly have been times when, on first mention, they didn't "get it," and I subsequently would worry that my own narcissistic issues were emerging for reasons I was not aware of. But if the associations in me again occurred, I would bring up another analog and refer to the previous occasion. Usually, the couple would then seriously attempt exploring to see whether it fit their own dynamics.

The idea is now becoming prominent in contemporary psychoanalysis that we learn from the patient and the patient learns from us in mutual, interactive ways (Casement, 1985). Note the spirit of this in what Lewis Aron (1996) has written recently:

> A broader notion of mutuality emerges from the idea that both patient and analyst participate in the analytic process, that they mutually regulate or mutually influence each other both consciously and unconsciously. From a relational perspective, who the analyst is and his or her personal contributions to the analytic process are fundamental to the psychoanalytic investigation. The analytic method cannot be considered as isolated from the personal variables and immediate affective experience of the individual analyst. From this point of view, countertransference is not an occasional lapse that intermittently requires investigation and elimination, but rather is a continual and central element of the investigation. The analyst as a person, and his or her shifting affective experience is both a major component of the analytic method and a primary variable in what is being investigated. (p. 125)

The dominant ideology and practice of both object-relations and self psychology psychoanalysts is to attempt to maintain a desirable focus and facilitate the opportunities for microanalysis, affective attunement, empathy, and transference reenactment and interpretation. Such conditions are considered the sine qua non for the development of the emergent self, yet, with couples, with their often disjunctive, conflicted interpersonal processes, such stormy matters are often experienced by many analytic practitioners as difficult and counterproductive. They must become active. The treatment of couples regarding their relationship to one another is, almost by definition, choppy, chaotic, and disruptive, and may be inimical to arriving at a satisfactory and cohesive resolution. Spouses interrupt each other, tell the stories of their lives in ways the other protests, edit the past selectively, leaving it to the other to fill in or correct, and forget things that are vital. Referral to an outside therapist for one member of the couple can sometimes seem warranted and clinically justifiable (Gerson, 1996; Slipp, 1984). It is as if the therapist is forced to choose between the couple and the individuals. Indeed, creation of a safe holding environment as the sine qua non for treatment of the self can be seriously contaminated by the affective disruptions of two individuals in a couple relationship who are engaged in serious splitting, projection, blaming, and projective identification. Nor do they have to suffer from a borderline personality disorder for such phenomena to occur and be collusively maintained. But in the process of dealing with their difficulties by setting them apart, the entity known as the couple may become set aside. When faced with such a quandary, it is best to consult with the couple about the dilemma of the self versus the system. Usually, by having this question raised, the couple will then be willing to bend to the task of subordinating some of their individual differences in the interests of working to improve the relationship. Inevitably, we will still have to help at the individual level.

An elderly but vital couple, who were still sexually active, had good relations with their children, and knew how to have fun to the envy of their friends, separated when the wife felt she had had enough of her husband of 50 years. After six months of therapy with the author, they resolved enough of their problems for the wife to decide not to renew her six-month lease out of town and to begin to make plans to rejoin the husband. Although we had worked assiduously on resolving some of the major differences each found upsetting in the other, the wife's ambivalence resurfaced when, at my urging, she spent a "trial" three days with him in their home, a month before the scheduled rejoining. Although he had been neat and habitually very well organized, the wife felt compelled to clean the house, straighten up, and get to her list of unfinished chores, while he arranged a surprise dinner party with guests for which he prepared the entire meal. He repeatedly urged her to take a rest and not do anything. The wife came to the subsequent therapy session with a splitting headache, a backache, and a worried frown. We explored her dutifulness, her lack of protest, her being the "good girl" who went along with what was expected (rejoining the husband and acting the gracious hostess), and her status as an only child. Hearing about the demands her parents had made of her, her old problems as a student, her not learning the subjects that her father, a teacher known for his strictness, taught, and the "can do" manner of her mother uncovered how this woman's husband unconsciously slipped into the role of efficient, expectant parent, and the wife's silent, somaticized protest. One form of her transference was to come to my office and, like a good student, take notes about the forthcoming week's "assignment." I chose to interpret some of her contained ambivalence toward her parents, and how, while seeming compliant, she consistently "misunderstood" some of my explanations, and the need for her to suppress more of what she undoubtedly still disliked about her spouse. Noteworthy was how she spoke in a girlish manner, constantly relying on the husband, an accomplished person, to explain things to and for her. I needed to speak about the collusive aspects of their relationship, my concern that she was denying the ambivalence, and her self-perception that she was "inadequate." I reflected on my concern, that the rejoining might not work. Was this only her projected worry, or his as well? The husband admitted that he too was worried, and began describing afresh the sources of his own anxiety, including the domination and humiliation he had always experienced from his severe and entitled matriarch of a mother, whom he still faithfully visited weekly. Would his wife, no matter how well managed, break out of control and, like his mother, hurt him severely again? Both expressed relief at my containing their projected anxieties and were more readily able to express some of their ambivalence and hesitation in their own right.

Conversely, the more purely family-systems-oriented approaches may miss some of these important nuances of development and the intertwining of the self, language, and affect. The self-object relationship therapist will also work with the couple on shared goals, shared assumptions, and shared identities. Systemic thinking demands it. But how much is enough? Thirty years ago, one of my esteemed teachers, the late Virginia Satir (personal communication, 1972), stated that she would start every new therapy with a couple with the question: "How, of all the people in the world, did the two of you manage to find each other and get together?" Satir's question was filled with irony and pointedness, but also with an emphasis, continued throughout the therapy, on the difficulty of joining and sharing by two different individuals into a new subidentity called couple and their attempts to stay together in satisfying ways. The question always arises, however, if we strengthen the couple, do we lose the importance of the self? (a question George Bernard Shaw seems to have repeatedly asked.) Today this is a particularly important question in light of feminists' concern about the usual disadvantage to women that occurs in more traditional male-female social arrangements. Should we sequence the work from couple to individual, or work prospectively in collateral fashion? If we accept the couple for treatment, do we know how and when to shift our focus from couple to individual, to the individuals, and back to the couple in the session? What does it mean when we hear of many couples who complain that their selves are being stifled, crippled, or severely damaged "by the relationship"? We need to explore their cultural norms, their stages of development, their histories of loss and gain, their talents and strengths, the complementarity of their lives and roles and efforts. What are the dialectics of self, change, and relationships we should pay attention to? The rhythm and pace of their interchanges are all-important. When we see a couple, is there such a thing as or is it even desirable to have "therapeutic neutrality," as Freud (1915) long ago extolled analysts should have when working with patients? This hardly seems possible and may be detrimental, particularly if, as Aron (1996) and Atwood and Stolorow (1984) point out, we avoid exploring our subjectivity.

Feminist critics such as Goldner (1985) and Luepnitz (1988) have pointed out how much of family and couple therapy has not been neutral and objective. As practiced by some of the leading founders in the field, who were men, their assumption of neutrality was belied by their actual way of practicing: an overvaluing of traditional patriarchal values of detachment and rationality and a selective disavowal of nurturance. It has been increasingly clear that we carry our own perspectives, biases, values, and experiences into the therapeutic consulting room. Couples seen together often trigger the enactment of those therapist-held attributes faster, and often unconsciously, than the slower, more reflective pace of individual work. Should we share these emotional reactions with the couple, and to what degree? Boundary maintenance is often more difficult in couple and family work. Do we know when it is therapeutic for the patient if we share

aspects of our own lives, as many family therapists do (see Minuchin & Fishman, 1981; Minuchin & Nichols, 1993; Whitaker, 1976), and/or should we risk rupturing the therapeutic bond (Levinson, 1993)? These and many other questions abound as we consider how to work with relationship problems in couples.

The author believes that working analytically within the couple relationship is often, but not necessarily always, the best way to proceed. Other therapists of integrative persuasion have written similarly (Dicks, 1967; Gerson, 1996; Kantor, 1989; Sander, 1979; D. E. Scharff & Scharff, 1987; Stierlin, 1977; Wachtel & Wachtel, 1986). Proceeding with both perspectives allows us the enormous advantages of seeing the intimate world each of our patients lives in, challenges some of the transference and countertransference induction that might become distorted and overly prolonged, strengthens the alliance between the intimate partners, deepens their understanding of each other, demonstrates the parallel and intertwining trajection of their lives, and prepares each to have a more intimate understanding of the other. But each case requires a differently formed dialectical matrix. Being able to work in both domains requires discipline, informed by the interchanges with the couple. I have been borrowing from the best of both the analytic and family systems traditions, showing how there may be more overlap and isomorphism between the best of these dominant practices than we have realized. The goal is to try to remove clinicians from the constraints of any one system, to a sounder, more integrated level of therapeutic work. Admittedly, there are times when I am not sure how to make the best of choices. Hoffman (1998) points out that dialectical thinking prompts certain kinds of therapeutic action that may be spontaneous and crucial to an individual patient's search for authenticity. Hoffman writes from the perspective of an analyst, yet his views seem quite apt for work with couples as well.

THE PROBLEMS OF LANGUAGE

In the past 15 years, many psychotherapists have moved from a predetermined position of expert, which invites abuses of power and judgment, to an appreciation of therapy as a hermeneutic science, where meaning is often socially constructed (Anderson & Goolishian, 1988; Gergen, 1985; Goolishian and Anderson, 1987). The phenomenology of the patient is respected and a collaboratively determined language system is maintained throughout the course of the therapy. Self psychologists Atwood and Stolorow (1984) have called this creation the intersubjective matrix, the space between patient and therapist, maintenance of which requires the therapist to be listening closely to nuance and subtlety and facilitating previously unexpressed or long-repressed affects to become noticed, named, and socially constructed. Errors of emphasis or interpretation are readily admitted by the therapist, and there is an interplay, a dialectic where a scaffolding of meaning occurs, more and more elaborated and understood (Atwood, Stolorow, & Trop, 1987). A family therapist, Anderson (1993), has written similarly:

> Although all hermeneutics and social constructionist concepts cannot be lumped onto one, they do share a common thread: They emphasize meaning as an intersubjective phenomenon, created and experienced by individuals in conversation and action with others and with themselves. This assumes that human action takes place in a reality of understanding that is created through social construction and dialogue and that we live and understand our lives through socially constructed narrative realities, that is, that we give meaning and organization to our experiences and to our self-identity in the course of these transactions. (p. 324)

Whereas both of these views mirror a similar basic assumption of respect for the client-therapist world of constructed meaning, the family systems therapists and psychoanalysts we have been describing differ markedly in their work with couples in their focus on locating the sources of meaning. Contemporary object-relations and self psychologists always give more time for latent meaning to emerge, tied to earlier developmental events with their attendant affect, and to be collaboratively constructed as more and more of the nuances of meaning show themselves without undue pressure. Family therapists often engage rapidly, help define problems quickly, and use the readily available language of therapist and couple alike, what Noam Chomsky (1972) once called surface structure, to ask for observable change, more in the here and now. An important and perennial question we seem to be constantly reviewing is whether a therapist applies undue pressure for patients to comply with; ergo, whose meaning will be dominant?

From either perspective, we should never overlook what is readily available and predominant, often necessitated by the emergencies and despair that motivated the couple to seek help in the first place. This includes the premise that, while constantly open to new understanding and revision, we still hold to an expert position that we can help ameliorate their presenting problems, that our objectivity is an advantage, and that our questions need to be responded to. In that vein, it is important to construct a contract of engagement as the work begins. The expectation that we will work together toward effective solutions permits us to ask the couple very direct questions at the beginning and sets an agenda for the subsequent work. These include asking the couple their respective views on how bad the problems are, what solutions or previous therapies have been tried, how they have conceptualized the origin(s) of their difficulties, what aspects of the self are compromised or damaged by the continuance of the problems, who else is involved, and what the satisfactory goals for therapy should be. It is rare that we can obtain a consensually arrived at, coherent picture, but creating such a contract of engagement is useful to refer back to as a touchstone when the process becomes more intense, complex, and obscure and seems to reflect the couple's central concerns. (It is also remarkable how many issues central to the understanding of the problems are present in the initial sessions, for which therapists cannot initially formulate the words.) Establishing a respectful framework allows us to pursue additional avenues of information, and we listen carefully much like a jazz performer who improvises while remaining cognizant of the original chord structure, melodic line of the tune selected, and the mutually regulating influence of the others in the musical group. Knoblauch (2000) has labeled such a process as "simultaneous conconstruction."

For example, a couple in their 40s began therapy after a failure to work cooperatively with a female therapist, who, continuing to see the wife, referred the husband to a male therapist for individual therapy. Each spouse continued to berate the behavior and attitude of their partner; it was decided to augment the weekly individual sessions with every-other-week conjoint couple therapy with both therapists present. After obtaining the partners' respective views, which were filled with disagreement, the cotherapists noted how each spouse continued to belittle the other, cutting off meanings, overlapping, changing the subject, turning to his or her individual therapist for a coalition partner, in a cycle of attack-defend-attack. Self-definition was so obscured, with each person claiming he or she could not be authentic in this relationship, that the therapists asked them to do a traditional communications exercise. They were to take turns for an uninterrupted three minutes, each explaining himself or herself to the other, followed by one minute of responding to what they had heard. The couple was unable to do this in the conjoint session, nor, after coaching, could they accomplish this at home by themselves. In the individual sessions, the therapists heard of the beleaguered childhood each had suffered from a domineering, intrusive parent, he at the hands of his mother, she at the hands of her father. In spite of interpretations and explanations of the obvious perverse complementarity of their childhoods for the marriage, they continued to fight and attack. Only after hearing of the man's life-long restitutional efforts to make himself into someone of worth and dignity could the male therapist appreciate how the husband exerted control and closure in the way he too eloquently attempted to communicate to his wife, complete with historical, social, and political analogs to bolster his rationalizations. He was simply too much for her in his comprehensiveness. Her desperate attempts to be on an equal plane, she confided to her therapist, revived her haunting memories of herself as inarticulate, squashed, inadequate; when her husband filibustered, she either dissociated on the spot or lashed out viciously. Hearing of these mutual deprivations in the couple sessions softened their antagonism. The communications exercise had been doomed to failure, but now could be reexamined as an example of how the foundation work in many individual sessions needed to be done well for orderly meaning making to occur when they were together. Failures at the exterior, interpersonal level can be understood only by delving into what is experienced at the interior level. Only after the individual work could attempts to fulfill a contract of engagement be adequately honored.

Stern (1997) points out how people create narrative rigidities, applying selective attention to the details of their lives to convey a continuous and coherent identity. But details are always left out, others would (and do) tell the story in a different way, and each storyteller, when pressed, usually admits there is a "marginal, shadowy, not-quite-complete" aspect to the experience that he or she cannot, as yet, formulate. The therapist influenced by self-object relational and social constructivist awareness takes this into account, asking for specificity

("In this situation, what happened, and then under those circumstances, what then happened?"), not generality. Generalities exclude awareness about the other and about oneself. The previously mentioned couple fought desperately to maintain their stereotype of the other and of themselves; the therapists enlarged the stories to include parents and the memory of each as a dominated child, and then embedded those narratives in the new construction of the interactive unit of multiple selves: the couple.

Hoyt and Berg (1998), in describing their form of constructive therapy, describe three forms of narratives: "progressive narratives that justify the conclusion that progress is being made; stabilizing narratives that justify the conclusion that life is unchanging; and digressive (or regressive) narratives that justify the conclusion that life is moving away from goals" (p. 318).

Constructivists emphasize the importance of progressive narratives and focus their efforts on the here and now; psychoanalysts like Stern always regard the regressive and digressive narratives as the bridge toward the unfolding of a more complex future. A view that encompasses and integrates both perspectives is offered by Watson and Greenberg (1996) as experiential therapy. They state that clients face two tasks to construct new meanings: to symbolize inner subjective experience, and to reflexively examine that experience. Both involve dialectical integration of different processes. Symbolization, they state,

> involves a dialectic between experience (the automatically synthesized levels of information that create a bodily felt sense) and the representation of that experience . . . in language. Reflexive self-examination involves a dialectic between symbolized experience and its examination and evaluation in the light of current needs, goals, and values, in order to create new meaning and plans for future action. Both dialectical processes result in newly synthesized experience. (p. 254)

CASE EXAMPLE

The patients previously described in the section on Difficult Couples, who had separated after a long and painful marriage, had only pseudo-relationships with others. Sally and Jim had never told anyone of their problems, she because her mother had always explicitly demanded secrecy, he because his wife expected him to obey her principles. Each insisted on seeing me, not another therapist, and she insisted that I see them separately. Only a few times was I successful in getting Sally to agree to joint sessions, at which she either sulked and sat stolid, rigid, and off to the side, or screamed at Jim for being a neglectful husband and for not having sex with her. Although I had tried to refer him, he wanted to see me and not another therapist, partly as a bridge to experiencing his estranged wife's presence. Although I was very mindful of the dangers of unintentionally breaching confidentiality, I agreed to keep working with each of them because they seemed so desperately overinvolved with one another. I was the container, holding all their split-off, projected feelings, better I hoped, than they or their parents had been able to metabolize all that they felt. He and she were both the youngest children and had been compliant, loyal, and filled with unexpressed anger. His parents always fought, as Jim later was fighting with Sally, and he was the "good" child, always trying to ameliorate their arguments and, in contrast to his two older siblings, never giving them any additional troubles. But a toll was taken; while crying out for attention from his father, who called him "my little buddy," he identified with the depression and anguish of his mother, who saw herself trapped in a failed marriage of diminished gratifications. Now the good son was in a failed marriage with a depressed, angry wife with whom he could only be dutiful, like a child who brings his mother flowers to cheer her up. Bringing his wife breakfast in bed and doing household chores were dismissed by Sally as superficial, devious, and a cover-up for his "evil" nature. His reluctance to leave her in spite of her physical and verbal abuse of him reflected his compassion that she was a desperate person, alone in the world, in physical and emotional pain, but also that he had a passive-dependent personality with severe masochistic tendencies. From the beginning, he was passive-aggressive; they had had no sex for the whole year of their engagement (they had been in their early 30s) and had fought constantly. Once married, they had gone seven years without sexual intimacy. For Sally, this barren existence only emphasized how doomed her life was to be. She explained that she had married him only "out of obligation"; she had never expected to marry, have children, or obtain any pleasure out of life. She exhibited much of the personality configuration of someone of strict Irish Catholic upbringing: deprived, constrained, reconciled to seeing life "through a veil of tears."

I felt that Sally had a borderline personality disorder of a very severe nature. There was no evidence of early sexual abuse, but she definitely seemed a trauma victim. Her father was an immigrant from Ireland who never saw or spoke to any of his family members again, lived in the house of his in-laws, whom he resented, and stayed away from his wife and two children, working double-shift six days a week. His youngest daughter idealized him, as is often the case with an absent parent when the child has an angry, intrusive parent close at hand. In her marriage, she could only hold onto a rigid narrative that husbands and wives have sex and always talk about their relationship. But she had married a man who would never state his own position on matters, went along with whatever she wanted, but could never deliver the essence of a good marriage, whatever that was supposed to be. Sally had no template for a good marriage. She had never known anyone with one, she could never learn from friends or even from literature, and so internalizing a wide range of affect seemed impossible; indeed, she seemed alexythymic except for the anger, which energized and excited her. Affects had to be labeled for her by me, and my countertransference reactions were crucial to her beginning to experience emotions of a sort different from anger. People were categorical for Sally; husbands were supposed to act in certain ways, administrators in certain ways, friends in certain ways, doctors and therapists as well. Sally distrusted her body; she had little skin sensation and little capacity for sexual excitement.

This very rich case deserves a much longer exposition, which space does not permit. At the time of this writing, the couple is still seeing me, she three times weekly, he once weekly. They may divorce in the next year, but each, now in their early 50s, realizes that they would be alone in the world and have to rebuild their entire lives. Though they have seen me now for three years, they appear willing to not push for the divorce process to begin, so long as they continue to make progress on the rest of their relationships and on their attitudes about themselves. This is happening, with Jim becoming more self-reliant, making more friends at work, confiding in people, coming to their house for circumscribed hours after seeing me, and arranging to do so when Sally is not there. Although very sad that he is no longer with her, he is proud of the progress Sally is making. Sally feels physically better, is speaking to her mother and sister more directly, has made a better adjustment with work colleagues and administrators, whom she now eats lunch with, and struggles more successfully to not think of Jim as an "evil" person who "stole" her birthright from her. She views reality as multi-determined and historically driven, with interpersonal processes as dialectical and redundant and with a trajectory that reaches across space and time. That they see me separately illustrates several important principles:

1. The self-object relationship therapist can see couple members individually, so long

as he or she is committed to an in-depth analysis of each person's emotional and cognitive way of organizing the self.
2. Confidentiality can be maintained if the therapist commits to constant self-scrutiny, attempting to understand his or her own wide range of emotions in the face of transference and countertransference reactions.
3. Narrative construction must be dialectical and expansive. Each person's self-system is capable of being reorganized, differentiated, made more complex, and understood to be social in origin.
4. A spirit of empathy must be maintained. By reaching to understand previously unformulated experience, the therapist helps the participants discover themselves, a process that ultimately produces the joy of surprise and revelation that every individual can delight in, and provides them with clarity and authenticity.
5. Such processes of self-discovery enhance intimate relationships. For some individuals, the pathology that marked their earlier lives cannot be undone while focusing on the needs and reactions of the other. Time and space for self-discovery has to be protected and maintained.
6. Planning the structure for couple therapy requires ongoing consideration. Seeing the participants separately, together, alternately, or with another therapist is still couple therapy, so long as there is constant attention to how boundaries are maintained, how the effects are being assimilated, and how the self-structures of the therapist and the patients can be best accommodated.

SUMMARY

In examining the literature on communication from infant-parent and neurobiological research, Siegel (1999) proposes that two systems, two human beings, can become functionally linked or integrated in a manner that produces a single, more complex system. Maximal complexity occurs by combining individual differentiation and interpersonal integration. Being independent from one's partner in adult life through avoidance decreases complexity through stable but excessive internal continuity. Being too tightly enmeshed or coupled risks being paralyzed by being a mirror of the other and reduces complexity by reducing the variability between systems. It appears we need an optimal balance of being by ourselves *and* being with the significant other. Siegel adds that people connect across important interpersonal space by means of energy and information from both sides of the brain. He states: "Emotional attunement, reflective dialogue, co-construction of narrative, memory talk, and the interactive repair of disruptions in connection are all fundamental elements of secure attachment and of effective interpersonal relationships" (p. 336).

Couple therapy approached from the perspective of self-object relationship theory is inclusive and respectful of who each person is and is striving to be. It requires a therapist to be aware of the power of narrative construction, hermeneutics, and the sharing of the privilege of how individuals ultimately come to see themselves. It recognizes, as Siegel (1999) states, that interdependence can be hindering as well as facilitative. It requires that the therapist eschew a single theory for an integrative view that incorporates the best findings from the analytic tradition and the family systems tradition, and more. Couples, as they remind us in our offices, are changing as quickly as our theories change, maybe faster. Western culture puts enormous strains on the capacity for sustained intimacy, while stretching our imaginations and horizons. Most of us have no idea what our world will be like in 20 years. What we can know is that if we immerse ourselves in emotional and intellectual communities, where others are considerate (not ideological) and stay informed, allowing cross-correspondence of ideas and affects, we will be more able to deal with whatever comes our way. The couples we see demand no less from us, and will respect us all the more.

REFERENCES

American Psychiatric Association. (1994). *Diagnostic and statistical manual of mental disorders* (4th ed.). Washington, DC: Author.

Anderson, H. (1993). On a roller coaster: A collaborative language systems approach to therapy. In S. Friedman (Ed.), *The new language of change*. New York: Guilford Press.

Anderson, H., & Goolishian, H. A. (1988). Human systems as linguistic systems: Preliminary and evolving ideas about the indications for clinical theory. *Family Practice, 27*(4), 374–394.

Aron, L. (1996). *A meeting of minds: Mutuality in psychoanalysis.* Hillsdale, NJ: Analytic Press.

Atwood, G. E., & Stolorow, R. D. (1984). *Structures of subjectivity.* New York: Erlbaum.

Atwood, G. E., Stolorow, R. D., & Trop, J. L. (1987). Impasses in psychoanalytic therapy: A royal road. *Contemporary Psychoanalysis, 25,* 854–873.

Bakhtin, M. (1973). *Problems of Dostoevsky's poetics* (R. W. Rostel, Trans.). Ann Arbor, MI: Ardis. (Original work published 1929)

Bank, S. P., & Kahn, M. D. (1982, 1997). *The sibling bond.* New York: Basic Books.

Bion, W. R. (1961). *Experiences in groups and other papers.* London: Tavistock.

Bion, W. R. (1970). *Attention and interpretation: A scientific approach to insight in psychoanalysis and groups.* London: Tavistock.

Bollas, C. (1989). *Forces of destiny: Psychoanalysis and human idiom.* London: Free Association Books.

Bowen, M. (1978). *Family therapy in clinical practice.* New York: Aronson.

Bruner, J. S. (1990). *Acts of meaning.* Cambridge, MA: Harvard University Press.

Casement, P. J. (1985). *Learning from the patient.* New York: Guilford Press.

Chomsky, N. (1972). *Language and mind* (Enlarged ed.). New York: Harcourt, Brace Javanovich.

Cushman, P. (1995). *Constructing the self, constructing America: A cultural history of psychotherapy?* Reading, MA: Addison-Wesley.

Cushman, P., & Gilford, P. (2000). Will managed care change our ways of being. *American Psychologist, 55*(9), 985–986.

Dicks, H. (1967). *Marital tensions.* New York: Basic Books.

Dym, B., & Glenn, M. L. (1993). *Couples: Exploring and understanding the cycles of intimate relationships.* New York: HarperCollins.

Fairbairn, W. R. D. (1952). *Psychoanalytic studies of the personality.* London: Routledge & Kegan Paul.

Feldman, L. B. (1992). *Integrating individual and family therapy.* New York: Brunner/Mazel.

Frank, J. D. (1973). *Persuasion and healing.* Baltimore: Johns Hopkins University Press.

Freud, S. (1915). Observations on transference-love. In *The standard edition of the complete works of Sigmund Freud* (Vol. 15, pp. 157–171). London: Hogarth Press.

Gergen, K. (1985). The social constructionist movement in modern psychology. *American Psychologist, 40,* 266–295.

Gerson, M. J. (1996). *The embedded self: A psychoanalytic guide to family therapy.* Hillsdale, NJ: Analytic Press.

Goldner, V. (1985). Feminism and family therapy. *Family Process, 24*(1), 31–48.

Goolishian, H., & Anderson, H. (1987). Language systems and therapy: An evolving idea. *Psychotherapy, 24*(35), 529–538.

Gray, J. (1992). *Men are from Mars, women are from Venus: A practical guide for improving communication and getting what you want in your relationships.* New York: HarperCollins.

Greenberg, L. S., & Johnson, S. M. (1988). *Emotionally focused therapy for couples.* New York: Guilford Press.

Haley, J. (1976). *Problem-solving therapy.* San Francisco: Jossey-Bass.

Hermans, H. J. M., Kempen, H. J. G., & van Loon, R. J. P. (1992). The dialogical self: Beyond individualism and rationalism. *American Psychologist, 47*(1), 23–33.

Hoffman, I. Z. (1991). Discussion: Toward a social-constructivist view of the psychoanalytic situation. *Psychoanalytic Dialogues, 1,* 74–105.

Hoffman, I. Z. (1998). *Ritual and spontaneity in the psychoanalytic process.* Hillsdale, NJ: Analytic Press.

Hoyt, M. F., & Berg, I. K. (1998). Solution-focused couple therapy: Helping clients construct self-fulfilling realities. In M. F. Hoyt (Ed.), *The handbook of constructive therapies* (pp. 314–340). San Francisco: Jossey-Bass.

Johnson, S. M. (1996). *The practice of emotionally focused therapy: Creating connection.* New York: Brunner/Mazel.

Kahn, M. D. (1986). The self and the system: Integrating Kohut and Milan. In S. Sugarman (Ed.), *The interface of individual and family therapy* (pp. 50–64). Rockville, MD: Aspen Press.

Kahn, M. D. (1989). Through a glass brightly: Treating sexual intimacy as the restoration of the whole person. In D. Kantor & B. F. Okun (Eds.), *Intimate environments: Sex, intimacy and gender in families* (pp. 54–73). New York: Guilford Press.

Kahn, M. D., & Lewis, G. K. (Eds.). (1988). *Siblings in therapy: Life-span and clinical issues.* New York: Norton.

Kantor, D. (1989). Mythic contracts and mythic journeys into intimate, sexual relationships. In D. Kantor & B. F. Okun (Eds.), *Intimate environments: Sex, intimacy and gender in families* (pp. 243–291). New York: Guilford Press.

Kegan, R. (1994). *In over our heads: The mental demands of modern life.* Cambridge, MA: Harvard University Press.

Kernberg, O. F. (1995). *Love relations: Normality and pathology.* New Haven, CT: Yale University Press.

Kirschner, D., & Kirschner, S. (1986). *Comprehensive family therapy: An integration of systemic and psychodynamic treatment models.* New York: Brunner/Mazel.

Klein, M. (1948). *Contributions to psychoanalysis, 1921–1945.* London: Hogarth Press.

Klein, M. (1957). *Envy and gratitude.* London: Tavistock.

Knoblauch, S. H. (2000). *The musical edge of therapeutic dialogue.* Hillsdale, NJ: Analytic Press.

Kohut, H. (1977). *The restoration of the self.* New York: International Universities Press.

Lasch, C. (1977). *Haven in a heartless world: The family besieged.* New York: Basic Books.

Levinson, E. (1993). Shoot the messenger: Interpersonal aspects of the analyst's interpretations. *Contemporary Psychoanalysis, 29*(3), 383–396.

Luepnitz, D. (1988). *The family interpreted.* New York: Basic Books.

Lyubomirsky, S. (2001). Why are some people happier than others? The role of cognitive and motivational processes in well-being. *American Psychologist, 56*(3), 239–249.

Maslow, A. H. (1962). *Toward a psychology of being.* Princeton, NJ: Van Nostrand.

Mastin, A. S. (2001). Ordinary magic: Resilience processes in development. *American Psychologist, 56*(3), 227–238.

Miller, M. V. (1989). Transference and beyond. In D. Kantor & B. F. Okun (Eds.), *Intimate environments: Sex, intimacy and gender in families* (pp. 93–107). New York: Guilford Press.

Minuchin, S. (1974). *Families and family therapy.* Cambridge, MA: Harvard University Press.

Minuchin, S., & Fishman, H. C. (1981). *Family therapy techniques.* Cambridge, MA: Harvard University Press.

Minuchin, S., & Nichols, M. P. (1993). *Family healing.* New York: Free Press.

Mitchell, S. (1993). *Hope and dread in psychoanalysis.* New York: Basic Books.

Mitchell, S. (1997). Psychoanalysis and the degradation of romance. *Psychoanalytic Dialogues, 7*(1), 23–41.

Moultrup, D. (1986). Integration: A coming of age. *Contemporary Family Therapy, 8,* 157–167.

Nichols, W. C. (1988). *Marital therapy: An integrative approach.* New York: Guilford Press.

Nichols, W. C. (1996). Persons with antisocial and Histrionic Personality Disorders in relationships. In F. W. Kaslow (Ed.), *Handbook of relation diagnosis and dysfunctional family patterns* (pp. 287–299). New York: Wiley.

Norcross, J. C., & Goldfried, M. R. (Eds.). (1992). *Handbook of psychotherapy integration.* New York: Basic Books.

Rabkin, R. (1970). *Inner and outer space: Introduction to a theory of social psychiatry.* New York: Norton.

Reik, T. (1948). *Listening with the third ear: The inner experience of a psychoanalyst.* New York: Farrer, Straus and Giroux.

Reisman, D. (1973). *The lonely crowd: A study of the changing American character.* New Haven, CT: Yale University Press.

Rilke, R. M. (1954). *Translations and considerations of Ranier Marie Rilke* (John L. Mood, Trans.). New York: Norton, 1975.

Sander, F. (1979). *Individual and family therapy: Toward an integration.* New York: Aronson.

Schafer, R. (1978). *Language and insight.* New Haven, CT: Yale University Press.

Schafer, R. (1983). *The analytic attitude.* New York: Basic Books.

Scharff, D. E. (1992). *Refinding the object and reclaiming the self.* Northvale, NJ: Aronson.

Scharff, D. E., & Scharff, J. S. (1987). *Object relations family therapy.* Northvale, NJ: Aronson.

Scharff, J. S., & Scharff, D. E. (1991). *Object relations couple therapy.* Northvale, NJ: Aronson.

Seligman, M. E. P. (1991). *Learned optimism.* New York: Knopf.

Siegel, D. J. (1999). *The developing mind: Toward a neurobiology of interpersonal experience.* New York: Guilford Press.

Slater, P. (1970). *The pursuit of loneliness: American culture at the breaking point.* Boston: Beacon Press.

Slipp, S. (1984). *Object relations: A dynamic bridge between individual and family treatment.* New York: Aronson.

Solomon, M. (1989). *Narcissism and intimacy: Love and marriage in an age of confusion.* New York: Norton.

Solomon, M. (1996). Understanding and treating couples with borderline disorders. In F. W. Kaslow (Ed.), *Handbook of relational diagnostic dysfunctional family patterns* (pp. 251–269). New York: Wiley.

Spence, D. P. (1982). *Narrative truth and historical truth.* New York: Norton.

Spock, B. (1974). *Raising children in a difficult time.* New York: Norton.

Stern, D. B. (1997). *Unformulated experience: From dissociation to imagination in psychoanalysis.* Hillsdale, NJ: Analytic Press.

Stierlin, H. (1977). *Psychoanalysis and family therapy.* New York: Aronson.

Stoller, R. J. (1979). *Sexual excitement.* New York: Pantheon.

Stoller, R. J. (1985). *Presentations of gender.* New Haven, CT: Yale University Press.

Sugarman, S. (Ed.). (1986). *The interface of individual and family therapy.* Rockville, MD: Aspen Press.

Talmon, M. (1990). *Single session therapy: Maximizing the effect of the first (and often only) therapeutic encounter.* San Francisco: Jossey-Bass.

Wachtel, P. L. (1993). *Therapeutic communication: Principles and effective practice.* New York: Guilford Press.

Wachtel, P. L., & Wachtel, E. F. (1986). *Family dynamics in individual psychotherapy.* New York: Guilford Press.

Watson, J. C., & Greenberg, L. S. (1996). Emotion and cognition in experiential therapy: A dialectical constructivist perspective. In H. Rosen & K. T. Kuehlwein (Eds.), *Constructing realities: Meaning-making perspectives for psychotherapists* (pp. 253–274). San Francisco: Jossey-Bass.

Whitaker, C. (1976). The hindrance of theory in clinical work. In P. J. Guerin (Ed.), *Family therapy* (pp. 154–164). New York: Gardner Press.

White, M., & Epston, D. (1990). *Narrative means to therapeutic ends.* New York: Norton.

Wile, D. B. (1984). Kohut, Kernberg and accusatory interpretations. *Psychotherapy, 21,* 353–364.

Willi, J. (1982). *Couples in collusion.* New York: Aronson.

Winnicott, D. W. (1958). *Collected papers: Through paediatrics to psychoanalysis.* London: Tavistock.

Winnicott, D. W. (1965). *The maturational processes and the facilitating environment: Studies on the theory of emotional development.* London: Hogarth Press.

Winnicott, D. W. (1971). *Playing and reality.* New York: Tavistock.

Wood, D. (1988). *How children think and learn: The social contexts of cognitive development.* Cambridge, MA: Blackwell.

Wynne, L. C. (1984). The epigenisis of relational systems: A model for understanding family development. *Family Process, 23,* 297–318.

Zimmerman, T. S., Haddock, S. A., & McGeorge, C. R. (2001). Mars and Venus: Unequal planets. *Journal of Marital and Family Therapy, 27*(1), 55–68.

CHAPTER 18

Relational Psychodynamics for Complex Clinical Syndromes

JEFFREY J. MAGNAVITA

HISTORY OF THE THERAPEUTIC APPROACH

This chapter presents a form of relational psychodynamic therapy termed integrative relational therapy (IRP; Magnavita, 2000c), which uses an integrative psychodynamic model (Magnavita, 1997) as its foundation and blends a systemic perspective to broaden the reach. A significant leap was originally made in this respect by Wachtel (1977), who developed his "cyclical psychodynamic" model that initially integrated both psychodynamic and behavioral approaches and later was expanded to include a systemic component, further broadening its application and theoretical potency (Wachtel, 1997). The author's IRP is not meant to be a new form of psychotherapy, as the field does not need more acronyms, but is used to refer to the author's model, which places the greatest emphasis on the combination of the psychodynamic and systemic theories.

AN EMPHASIS ON CLINICAL UTILITY

A relational dynamic model offers the clinician the flexibility to move between the microscopic lens of the intrapsychic model to the wider lens of the interpersonal and, finally, the widest magnification of the systemic. This enables the clinician to intervene at various fulcrum points in a system, shifting the focus of intervention among individual, dyad, triangles, and larger system. Relational psychodynamics is rooted in psychodynamic theory with a careful blending of other valuable approaches; much of this is presented in this volume and also in Wachtel's *Psychoanalysis, Behavior Therapy, and the Relational World* (1997), a classic in the field that cannot be extensively reiterated in this format.

INTRAPSYCHIC AND INTERPERSONAL COMPONENTS

Contemporary psychodynamic theory has multiple perspectives that can be clustered into four main trends: (1) structural drive theory, (2) object-relations theory, (3) ego psychology, and (4) self psychology. Each of these offers the clinician a perspective useful for conceptualizing various components of the clinical phenomenon. There is much to be said for the use of a multiperspective approach, as no one theory can adequately explain the range and diversity of human experience and expression of psychopathology. Pine (1990) recommends, and most clinicians, out of necessity, synthesize these derivative psychoanalytic models. These essential ways of understanding the complex syndromes that are seen in clinical settings are briefly summarized, and readers can refer to many other excellent chapters in this volume to deepen their understanding.

Structural Drive Theory
The structural drive approach offers an explanation for the way intolerable impulses and feelings generate anxiety and how defensive functioning moderates this anxiety. Regardless of one's primary orientation, an understanding of the interplay among various intrapsychic structures enhances assessment and orients the clinician to the way the individual is experiencing or repressing affect.

Object-Relations Theory
A major advancement in psychoanalysis was achieved when theorists and clinicians expanded the domain of inquiry away from the intrapsychic and moved toward the dyadic relationships between parent and child. This perspective afforded an opportunity to understand the patient in relationship with the therapist (see Glickauf-Hughes & Wells, this volume).

Ego Psychology
Hartmann's (1958, 1964) ego psychology emphasized the problem of adaptation. He elaborated various aspects of what constitutes ego-adaptive capacity, essential in assessing all patients but especially so when the clinician is considering offering a brief treatment approach that may tax the defense system of the individual (see Osimo, this volume).

Self Psychology
This theoretical model and approach, developed primarily by Kohut (1971), has particular application for treating narcissistic disorders (see Trujillo, this volume). Kohut emphasized the importance of healthy and pathological narcissism and the critical function of experiencing a relationship with a responsive mirroring figure who provides adequate affirmation and admiration. The core affects of shame and rage emerge when sufficient mirroring is not provided, leading to the development of the false self, which serves as a protection against further injury. Kahn (1986) wrote: "The Kohutians and self-psychologists have tightened their focus to earlier and earlier stages of development and to the therapist as an all-important narcissistic mirror with whom the patient experiences the opportunity for transmutting internalizations and restructuralization of mind" (p. 52). Contemporary feminist theorists have also expanded on and emphasized the roll of empathy in maintaining connections essential for the reparative work of psychotherapy (Jordan, 2000).

EXPANDING THE FRAME—TOO FAR?

These psychodynamic models offer the clinician a rich and fertile theoretical map with which to make sense out of mental disturbance, symptom complexes, interpersonal difficulties, and maladaptive character styles, emphasizing primarily the intrapsychic matrix. However, until the development of the interpersonal and systemic perspective, personality was viewed more like an onion than "a complex set of feedback processes in which the cooperation of other people is essential" (Wachtel, 1997). As mentioned, Wachtel (1997) has been one of the most prominent theoreticians in the integration of psychodynamic and systemic models of treatment. His efforts and those of others before him, like Ackerman (1958), have bridged the long-standing schism between psychoanalytic and family systems approaches. Wachtel makes a crucial point that "the essence of the family system perspective is that however close or distant family members may appear to be, however much they may either ignore or interfere excessively, they are inevitably part of a network of relationships that plays a crucial role in the lives of all network members" (p. 380). This movement from the intrapsychic to the relational matrix represented a paradigmatic shift pioneered by interpersonal or dyadic theorists such as Sullivan (1953) and later Benjamin (1993) and triadic theorists such as Bowen (1976) and Minuchin (1974). Diamond, Diamond, and Liddle (2000) comment on the dialectic process in the evolution of psychotherapy:

> In the 1950's, family systems therapies redefined the meaning of relationship-based therapy. The innovation was not only in bringing family members together in one room but also in clarifying how we understand psychopathology and change. Pathology was no longer seen as driven solely by intrapsychic forces but also by interpersonal functioning. The focus of treatment shifted from internal representations to real relationships. Change was no longer thought to occur via the transference relationship but through improving communication or behavior between family members. Unfortunately, in their revolutionary fervor, radical constructivist family systems theorists went too far in ignoring individuals' cognitive and emotional functioning. (p. 1038)

Although intrapsychic structure is an essential component in conceptualizing human psychic functioning, there is ample evidence accruing from neuroscience that the structure and function of the brain is stimulated by interpersonal and attachment experience (Siegel, 1999). This is likely the merger point where psychotherapy and neuroscience will intersect and provide improved treatment protocols with empirical documentation.

RELATIONAL-SYSTEMIC COMPONENTS

The development of relational therapy involves various evolutionary branches: "(a) the intersubjectivity of the dyadic relationship, (b) the development of triadic theory, (c) the centrality of relationships in women's development, (d) the therapeutic alliance, and (e) a new model of relational diagnosis and treatment" (Magnavita, 2000b, p. 999). This chapter focuses on these developments, with the exception of c.

THE INTERSUBJECTIVITY OF THE
DYADIC RELATIONSHIP

The development of relational psychodynamics began with the pioneering work of Sandor Ferenczi (Ferenczi & Rank, 1925), who dramatically diverged from Freudian-based structural/drive theory, which emphasized the intrapsychic self, to a model emphasizing the self in relationship. Muran and Safran present a comprehensive overview of their work on relational phenomena in Chapter 11 (this volume). They suggest that "relational schema" are derived from significant interactional patterns with major attachment figures and that the self is formed as a by-product of these dyadic interactions.

THE DEVELOPMENT OF TRIADIC THEORY

The development of general systems theory (von Bertalanffy, 1968) has had a remarkable impact on a number of disciplines, including psychotherapy, which were radically altered by this model of how systems operate. This development, representing a sudden jump from previous theoretical formulations, was what Kuhn (1970) describes as a paradigmatic shift. This new perspective offered an alternative way of looking at the world as a mixture of interrelated variables that were governed by complex feedback systems in constant motion. Instead of emphasizing the variables or components themselves, it was the relationships among them that were considered central. Bateson (Bateson, Jackson, Haley, & Weakland, 1956) and his research team, which developed the double-bind theory of schizophrenic family communication, achieved the earliest application of this model. Although double-bind communications was later rejected as the cause of schizophrenia, clinicians continue to find the description relevant in many dysfunctional families (although clearly, schizophrenia is best understood using a stress-diathesis model: biological vulnerability that may be triggered by stress). Bowen (1978) developed the most comprehensive theoretical system, introducing constructs such as triangulation, differentiation (self-other and emotional), dysfunctional family systems, family projection process, and multigenerational transmission process.

THE THERAPEUTIC ALLIANCE

Without a therapeutic alliance, there is no opportunity to use any method or intervention. Certain technical interventions can enhance the therapeutic bond, such as deepening the emotional experience or altering defenses, but the alliance is the container that provides the crucible for the therapeutic process. The maintenance of the therapeutic alliance is considered to be the central issue of most forms of therapy and is especially emphasized in relational psychodynamic models; techniques and methods are secondary to its establishment and maintenance. This crucial alliance is actively strengthened and enhanced by various methods. Critical to the therapeutic alliance is affective contact (see Fosha and Osimo, both in this volume) and appropriately responding to fluctuations in the relational matrix.

RELATIONAL DIAGNOSIS

The field of family therapy exploded on the clinical landscape in the 1970s as a number of pioneering clinical theorists (Ackerman, 1958; Bowen, 1976, 1978; Minuchin, 1974) began to apply systemic principles to the field of psychotherapy. As early as the 1950s leaders such as Ackerman began questioning taboos against interviewing or treating family members together. He stated:

> The task of therapy cannot be simplified by the magic device of avoiding contact with other family members. Life is not simple, nor are the problems of family relationships simple. When a therapist refuses to see other family members, he has not thereby reduced the complexity of his position. He is a silent presence in the patient's family life anyway. Even though the therapist rejects face-to-face contact with other family members, he is a live image to them. He is a psychic force in the day-to-day emotional interchange among family members. In this sense, the therapist can no more avoid relatedness to the family group than can the patient cut off relations with his family while undergoing therapy. The real question is not the artificial control

of the simplicity or complexity of the therapeutic situation, but rather the need to explore the dynamic implications of different methods. Does one deal with these family members *in absentia,* through a medium, or does one deal with them directly? The position of the therapist cannot be an easy or simple one with any approach. It is conceivable that a therapist who deals with one patient faces one set of complications, whereas a therapist who deals with multiple family members faces another. (p. x)

As the pendulum swung in reaction to the individualist model of psychopathology to the systemic one, much of the diagnostic nomenclature was also dismissed as being too "pathology-oriented" and nonsystemically informed. This created an opportunity to fill the vacuum that occurred when those who ascribed to the systemic school realized that a new diagnostic model based on systemic assumptions was called for. Thus, a movement to develop a diagnostic system more in tune with the core beliefs of the systemic model was initiated (Kaslow, 1996). One aspect of this development was to formulate various components of a relational diagnostic model.

Ackerman (1958) noted: "The pathology of some families is such that it makes much the same kind of person of all family members and produces essential similarities in the manifestation of psychiatric illness. In other families, the opposite is true" (p. 103). Further, he commented:

> But whatever the pattern—and we recognize countless patterns of family behavior—it is useful in a basic sense to think of the family as a kind of carrier of elements predisposing both to mental illness and mental health.... Why does one type, generation after generation, multiply the crop of mentally sick people? Why does another produce a sturdy lot?
> It is not the individual personality of the parent alone, mother or father. It is a paradox that certain pairs of neurotic parents, despite distortions of individual personality, interact in such a way as to create emotionally healthy children. Other pairs, in which the man and woman are apparently healthy persons, produce disturbed children. (p. 104)

Although Ackerman laid the foundation for a relational diagnostic system, it was not until much later that this movement gained momentum.

Kaslow's (1996) volume, *Handbook of Relational Diagnosis and Dysfunctional Family Patterns,* was a major effort to begin to remedy the lack of a relational diagnostic system. Of particular interest is her relational perspective on personality disorders and their variants. The more difficult cases are those in which there is multisystemic disturbance that is extant over successive generations. In an effort to begin to categorize some of the common systems that produce and maintain personality pathology and the complex clinical syndromes often encountered in difficult cases, the term dysfunctional personologic system (DPS) was coined (Magnavita, 2000c). It is imperative for clinicians evaluating family systems to be cognizant of cultural differences that are normal variants of culturally adaptive patterns. It is also essential that clinicians be aware of the sociopolitical influences that may shape patterns of adaptation. For example, "paranoid" systems may be adaptive in repressive and authoritarian political systems. Sue and Sue (1999) warn, *"ethnocentric monoculturalism"* itself "is dysfunctional in a pluralistic society like the United States" (p. 32). The following ten DPSs were identified:

1. *The Addicitive DPS*
   This system revolves around addictive process. There is a reversed assumption that without substances, survival is threatened. Codependency is a substitute for intimacy. A negative feedback loop produces marginally functioning

systems; members may gravitate toward substances as a way to buttress fragile defense systems.

2. *The Narcissistic DPS*

   This system's major theme is false protection and avoidance of the vulnerable self. Donaldson-Pressman and Pressman (1994) describe these families in their book *The Narcissistic Family: Diagnosis and Treatment,* which provides useful reading for many patients. In these families, public images must be maintained. Children's achievement that reflects favorably on the parents often becomes a substitute for core affirmation and validation.

3. *The Covertly Narcissistic DPS*

   Another system identified by Donaldson-Pressman and Pressman (1994) is the covertly narcissistic family. This system, more subtle than the previous type, creates chronic feelings of not being understood or affirmed. There is pressure to compensate for deficits in members. Affirmation is provided for emotional caretaking, often taken on by children. This reversal is often seen in parent-child interactions and, though subtle, is nonetheless pervasive and limits full development of the child.

4. *The Psychotic DPS*

   The theme of this system is adaptation to chaos. Family members struggle with feelings of severe insecurity and fragmentation. Autonomy is severely threatened and may be seen in fused relationships and, in some cases, shared psychosis. Basic attachment is attempted by assuming caretaking functions for disabled figures or by sharing psychotic behavior.

5. *The Developmentally Arrested DPS*

   The theme of this system is inability to tolerate individuation. Separation is viewed as dangerous to family survival and cohesion. The relational dynamic is differentiation versus fusion. It should be noted that this system may be culturally determined and therefore not considered pathological (e.g., as in some Asian or Afro-American families).

6. *Physically/Sexually Traumatizing DPS*

   The theme in this system is accommodation to chronic abuse patterns. Family members are viewed as objects to be dominated by the "powerful" members. Relational themes are "use and abuse" dynamics. Violence, emotional abuse, and neglect predominate family communication patterns.

7. *The Depressigenic DPS*

   Insufficient emotional resources typify this system. There is typically a history of untreated affective disorder, influencing parenting style/attachment systems and marital function. In depressed systems, the quality of attachments does not generally provide a solid base for security and emotional growth (Diamond et al., 2000). The dominant fear is that there are not enough resources to meet members' needs. Family development is stunted due to the chronic emotional insufficiency.

8. *The Chronically Medically Ill DPS*

   The theme in this system is the domination of family functions with the business of medical illness, which dictates family communication and relationships. There may be a history of genetic predisposition for chronic illness. The chronic stress of coping may lead to emotional disturbance, which, if left untreated, can consolidate into personality disturbance.

9. *The Paranoid DPS*

   The theme in this system is an "us versus them" dichotomy. Family members feel compelled to protect themselves from intrusion from outsiders and/or from other family members. Cohesion is maintained through a sharing of this paranoid view. Clinicians must be alert to the possibility that the social milieu may engender this reaction, as in cases of subjugation or discrimination.

10. *The Somatic DPS*
    The theme of this system is the substitution of somatic for emotional expression. The only "valid" and safe form of affective communication is through somatic language and expression. Nurturing is elicited through "illness" and psychosomatic complaints. There is usually an extreme demand placed on primary care providers by these systems. "Among the most challenging patients presenting in medical contexts are those with somatoform symptoms" (Watson & McDaniel, 2000, p. 1068).

THE BIOPSYCHOSOCIAL MODEL: MICROSCOPIC VERSUS MACROSCOPIC VIEW OF THE CLINICAL PHENOMENA

The biopsychosocial model developed by Engle (1980) was a major conceptual advance that is often cited as a metamodel for understanding human mental and physical disorder. From a psychotherapeutic vantage point, exclusive focus on any one level in the hierarchy is limiting. Most therapists learn to "oscillate" among various levels (Sugarman, 1986). Psychodynamic therapy offers a microscopic view of human mental functioning and understanding of psychopathology; using a narrowly focused lens, a great deal of magnification of the intrapsychic phenomena is possible. Thus, we can focus on the impulses and feelings, manifestations of anxiety, and defensive organization. When the view is widened and the magnification reduced, an interpersonal focus is encompassed; these interactions are observed and processed in countertransference and transference transactions and object relations. We can also witness and empirically measure the complementary transactions that occur in an interpersonal dyad (Benjamin, 1993). We witness "downward spirals" in couple sessions when each member of the dyad reactivates increasingly more regressive defensive responding. However, in traditional intrapsychic/interpersonal approaches, the broader system is often ignored. When we reduce the magnification and widen the lens even further, we can view the triadic configurations and overlapping triangles often created in dysfunctional systems (Guerin, Fogarty, Fay, & Kautto, 1996). For example, each member of a downward spiraling couple can be observed to be triangulated with a parental figure with whom he or she has unresolved issues.

THEORETICAL CONSTRUCTS

Sugarman (1986, p. 1) writes: "The individual and family perspectives are arbitrary areas of the biopsychosocial continuum of a general systems theory" as proposed by Engle (1980). A comprehensive theory of psychotherapy must account for and allow flexible movement among the various biopsychosocial factors. Frances, Clarkin, and Perry (1984) were innovators in their development of "differential therapeutics," which offered suggestions for selecting and combining modalities of treatment for enhanced effectiveness. In their personality-guided therapy, Millon, Grossman, Meagher, Millon, and Everly (1999) similarly propose blending modalities in a "synergistic" fashion. Personality disorders demand comprehensive integration and blending of treatment modalities for enhanced effectiveness (Magnavita, 1998).

DEPICTING THE THERAPEUTIC PROCESS WITH THE TRIANGLE

Triangular configurations have proved to be a useful way to visually represent various psychological constructs. A number of theorists have conceptualized aspects of the psychotherapeutic process using triangles. Menninger (1958) originally offered the *triangle of insight* to depict interpersonal patterns, and Ezriel (1952) the *triangle of conflict* to describe the intrapsychic matrix. Malan (1963), in a major conceptual leap, brought these together, renaming Menninger's the *triangle of persons*. Bowen (1976) also used the triangle to show, through a broader systemic perspective, how three-person units function. Guerin et al. (1996) calls these "relationship triangles" and, for consistency, this will be referred to as the *triangle of relations*. Combining these triangular configurations in one theoretical model allows the therapist to conceptualize treatment and flexibly move from one perspective to another. Integrative relational therapy blends two main theoretical models, psychodynamic and systemic, using these three essential triangular configurations that can be used to depict (1) intrapsychic, (2) interpersonal-dyadic, and (3) triadic relationships.

Intrapsychic Matrix
Psychodynamic constructs provide clinical utility for conceptualizing the way in which affect, anxiety, and defense create internal feedback loops. If the feedback loops are not working effectively, personality pathology and recognizable symptoms emerge (Millon, Grossman, Meagher, Millon, & Everly, 1999). This can be

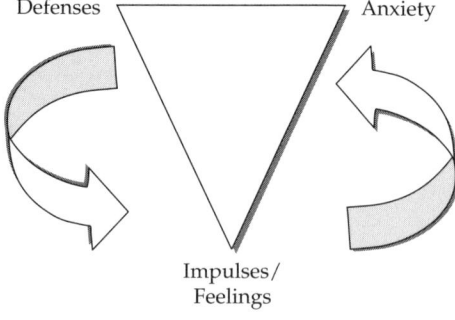

Figure 18.1 Triangle of conflict: Interrelationship among impulses/feelings, anxiety, and defense.

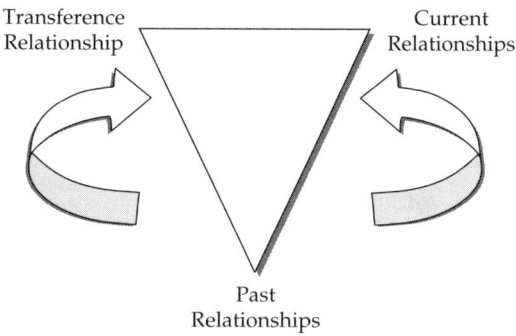

Figure 18.2 Triangle of persons: Influence of past relationship patterns on current and transference relationships.

visually depicted by the *triangle of conflict* or intrapsychic view (Figure 18.1).

Interpersonal-Dyadic Matrix
The *triangle of persons* or interpersonal view depicts three essential interpersonal transactional patterns (Figure 18.2). The current corner depicts the current relationships that generally compel the patient to enter treatment because of conflict such as marital problems or issues with peers. The transference corner represents the manner in which the patient recapitulates his or her relational schema onto the therapist. The bottom corner of the triangle signifies the past relational schema, which contains the unprocessed cognitive/affective elements of the

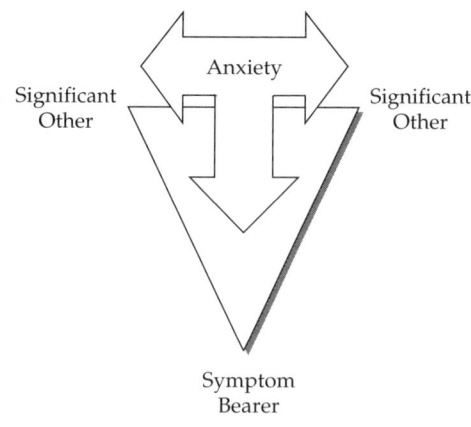

Figure 18.3 Triangle of relations: The dispersion of anxiety from a conflicted dyad to a symptom bearer.

core traumata. This comprises the core conflict(s) that need resolution.

Triadic Relationships

The *triangle of relations* is a systemic construct that depicts the way anxiety in an unstable dyadic relationship is channeled to a third person, such as in an affair, that stabilizes a dysfunctional marriage, or an addiction such as gambling that can serve the same function (Figure 18.3).

METHODS OF ASSESSMENT AND INTERVENTION

A comprehensive assessment is required when working with complex clinical syndromes, especially when attempting to accelerate the treatment process. A full discussion of this vital topic is beyond the scope of this chapter. (See Shea's, 1998, *Psychiatric Interviewing: The Art of Understanding,* for an excellent compendium on the topic.) There are four major categories of assessment: (1) structural interview and history, (2) psychological testing, (3) family genogram, and (4) relational processing. Each of these can be useful alone, but a multilevel assessment is more beneficial (Synder, Cavell, Heffer, & Mangrum, 1995); these include "(a) individuals, (b) dyads, (c) nuclear families, (d) extended families and related systems interfacing with the immediate family, and (e) community and cultural systems" (p. 164). Multilevel assessment combines aspects of various categories and levels of the biopsychosocial matrix.

When evaluating an individual, ego functions that include relation to reality, object-relatedness, maturity and flexibility of defenses, psychological-mindedness, and ability to contain impulses are assessed. Assessment can be made through clinical interview and history or through a combination of interview and psychological testing. Probably the most effective form of individual assessment is a structured interview where the way in which anxiety is channeled and managed is observed and titrated by exploring anxiety-laden material (Davanloo, 1980; Kernberg, 1984).

When evaluating a couple, the clinician also should complete an assessment of the dynamic pattern, communication style, and capacity for intimacy that occur in the dyad as well as a basic assessment of each member's individual ego functions. The clinician should carefully ascertain the level of differentiation evident in the couple and the emotional differentiation each is capable of achieving.

Family evaluation must utilize a number of techniques, which may include meeting with subsystems and evaluating and assessing triangular patterns. The use of a family genogram is one of the most effective ways in which to begin to see multigenerational transmission patterns and intergenerational coalitions and triangles. Readers not familiar with doing genograms should refer to McGoldrick and Gerson's (1985) *Genograms in Family Assessment,* a classic work on this topic.

Treatment Stance and Methods

Similarities in Flexible Stance

Both systemic and short-term dynamic therapists show a degree of flexibility in the way they approach the therapeutic process. There are striking similarities between the early family therapists and short-term dynamic therapists in the manner in which they conduct their work. Kahn (1986) comments: "The early family therapists, such as Satir, Ackerman, and Whitaker were celebrated in the 1950s for being humane in attitude, verbally confrontative, and emotionally involved in the therapeutic process" (p. 53). Short-term dynamic therapists, beginning with Ferenczi (Ferenczi & Rank, 1925) and proceeding to Alexander (Alexander & French, 1946), Davanloo (1980), Sifneos (1987), and current-day therapists, emphasize confrontation of defenses when appropriate, emotional engagement, and affective experience (see Osimo, this volume). Both approaches allow for and encourage emotional experiencing but also provide "mirroring, comforting and empathizing that the patient's family had previously failed to provide" (Kahn, 1986, p. 62).

Emphasis on Restructuring Methods
A notable similarity among many family systems (Minuchin, 1974) and short-term dynamic therapists (Davanloo, 1980), as well as experiential (Greenberg, Rice, & Elliott, 1993) and cognitive therapists (Beck, Rush, Shaw, & Emery, 1979), is the shared emphasis and the use of the term "restructuring" to capture the process of therapy. In a literal way, restructuring may capture the process by which the brain is reorganized, strengthening certain neural connections and weakening others through the process of psychotherapy. Restructuring also describes what occurs when relational patterns are systematically modified. In their book *Neurodynamics of Personality*, Grigsby and Stevens (2000) write:

> Behavior change is an emergent property of change in the synaptic structure of the brain. The changes characteristic of learning appear to be robust, so that once learned, it may be that most things cannot be completely unlearned. Subsequent learning from experience thus involves the reorganization of neural networks and a resetting of the probabilities of activation. This process is facilitated by the fact that different aspects of memories change over time as a function of state, the environment, and the specific way in which one experiences the memory on any given occasion. Such changes may be temporary, reflecting only brief neurochemical influences, but they also may be long lasting. The later type of change may be especially likely under conditions of high levels of arousal. (p. 373)

Restructuring may be seen as a group of procedures by which cognition schema, affect schema, and relational schema are reorganized. The following methods of restructuring are a component part of many types of therapy and technical interventions.

Defense restructuring is a method by which the defenses are catalogued and a defense constellation is developed (Davanloo, 1980; Reich, 1945). Unique for each patient, the defense constellation is brought to attention by increasingly building awareness of how the defenses are manifested in the triangle of persons (Magnavita, 1997) as well as in the relational triangle. It is also an essential method for increasing awareness of the manner in which defensive responding prevents more open and intimate responding. The basic goal is to activate the cognitive/affective matrix so that previously unconscious feelings, memories, and schema can be processed. Defense restructuring can be utilized in various degrees and titrated at various levels based on the patient's specific requirements (Magnavita, 1997; McCullough Vaillant, 1997). It is generally used for individuals such as those described by Reich (1945), who have "character armor" or are what is termed egosyntonic. These individuals are so identified with their defenses that they cause little anxiety and when pointed out say "I am who I am" suggesting there is little potential to change. They also tend to externalize by blaming others for their troubles.

Affective restructuring is a method for accessing and opening up the emotional channel that has been partially sealed from full experiential contact (Greenberg et al., 1993; McCullough Vaillant, 1997). The goal of most forms of reconstructive or depth therapy is to encourage as much affective experience as possible so that emotions can be metabolized and traumatic experiences processed and let go (see Fosha, this volume). Affective restructuring uses techniques of mirroring and affirmation and is highly effective with higher-level patients, although Fosha (2000) uses it with a broad spectrum of patients. McCullough (1998) has coined the term "affect phobia" to describe the process in which patients who are afraid of their emotional responses undergo desensitization through emotional experiencing.

Cognitive restructuring refers to two approaches. The first emerged from Beck's (Beck & Freeman, 1990; Beck et al., 1979) groundbreaking work in cognitive therapy and operates by identifying and making conscious dysfunctional beliefs. Once this has been accomplished, a restructuring of the cognitive matrix can occur. Young's (1990) cognitive approach, which is highly integrative, focuses on early maladaptive schema. The second type of cognitive restructuring, emerging from Davanloo's (1980, 1990) groundbreaking work in short-term dynamic psychotherapy, is a process by which differentiation of feeling, anxiety, and defense (triangle of conflict) is attempted using specific incidents in the patient's current life. This process strengthens and builds ego-adaptive capacity and can set the stage for more intense emotional experiencing later on.

Dyadic restructuring is a method by which the interpersonal space in a dyadic relationship is defined through mutual relational experiences (Bowen, 1976). Bowen's systemic model described two essential aspects of differentiation: self/other and emotional. Self/other refers to the ability to maintain one's sense of identity in the relational matrix. Emotional differentiation refers to what Goleman (1994) calls "emotional intelligence": the capacity to sense emotions, see them in others, and label them appropriately. In dyadic or family relationships in which there are low levels of differentiation, family members become entangled in the emotional force field. There is a high level of reactivity and difficulty tolerating separateness. In these systems, members have difficulty striking a balance between needs for affiliation/closeness and growth/separation.

In a parallel development but separate theoretical model, McCullough Vaillant (1997) has developed effective strategies for what she has termed self/other restructuring. She has developed a number of specific technical advances that enable the therapist to strengthen the self system of lower-functioning patients. Her method "most often employs exposure of the client to positive feelings associated with self/other relationships, and the prevention or resolution of negative feelings. This objective is often necessary when a client is too impaired to proceed with either defense or affect work" (McCullough, 1998, p. 40).

When trying to select from these methods, the therapist should remember to apply dyadic restructuring occurring in the framework of a couple's session and self/other in the therapist-patient dyad.

Triangular-relational restructuring is a method whereby triangular relationships are modified so that anxiety can be better tolerated in dyadic relationships and no longer must seek expression in a third person, as in an extramarital affair, or activity, such as workaholism or gambling (Bowen, 1976, 1978; Guerin et al., 1996; Minuchin, 1974). Minuchin writes: "In all cultures, the family imprints its members with selfhood. Human experience of identity has two elements: a sense of belonging and a sense of being separate. The laboratory in which these ingredients are mixed and dispensed is the family, the matrix of identity" (p. 47). Triangular relationships are quite commonly expressed in symptomatic parent-child configurations and unstable marriage and affair configurations. Relational restructuring aims to resolve intolerable anxiety in the dyad so that a third member does not need to be drawn in to stabilize the relationship.

MAJOR SYNDROMES, SYMPTOMS, AND PROBLEMS TREATED

Integrative relational therapy was developed especially for personality disturbance and for complex clinical syndromes evidenced by those often described in the literature as "difficult patients." Complex clinical syndromes are those in which one or more comorbid symptoms are expressed in the setting of various types of personality pathology (Magnavita, 2000a). This can be understood using a stress-diathesis model, which posits that all people have a particular vulnerability to stress, which can be expressed physically or emotionally. Personality can be thought of as the psychic equivalent of the physical immune system (Millon et al., 1999). This is depicted in Figure 18.4. Stress impacting an individual can be absorbed to some degree by the personality. Individuals with personality pathology or vulnerability, reflected by poor adaptive capacity and insufficient defensive functioning in the triangle of conflict, may become symptomatic. For example, as illustrated in the figure, the father, who has an obsessive-compulsive personality, may experience generalized anxiety and, if the stress continues unabated, may develop intermittent explosive reactions. The mother, with a histrionic personality adaptation, may develop major depression as her predominant symptomatic outbreak. The marital dyad may experience stress by developing sexual dysfunction related to unresolved issues of intimacy and closeness, which may increase the level of marital dissatisfaction. The marital dyad may also deflect

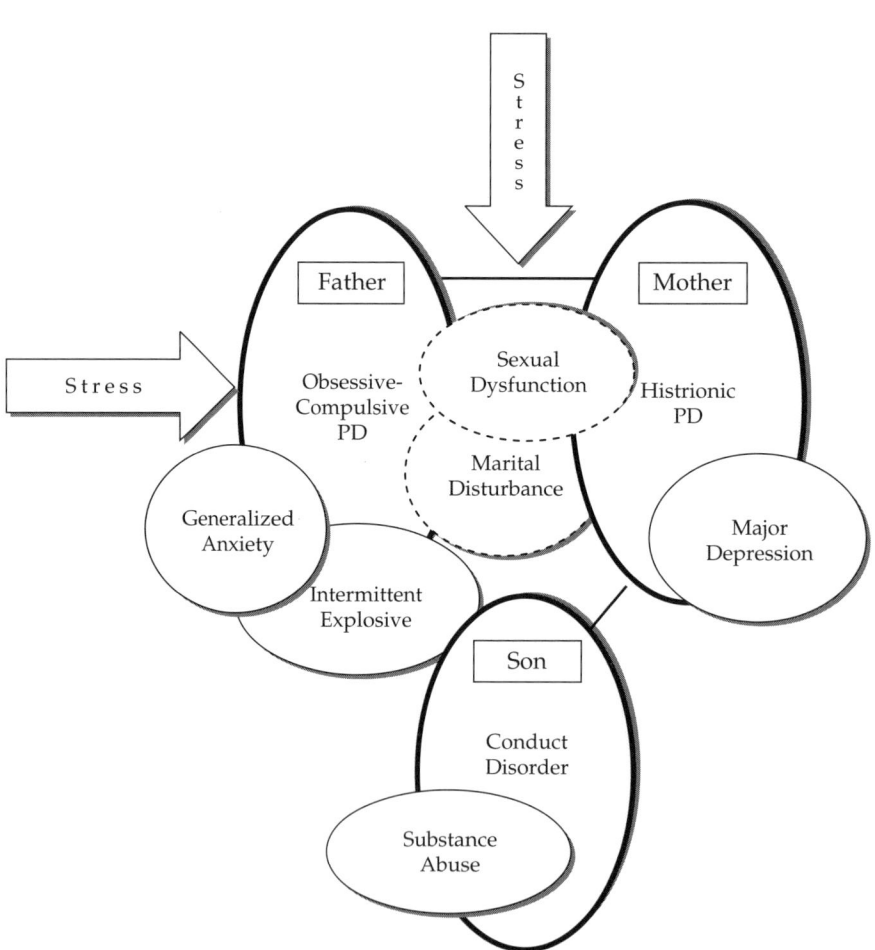

Figure 18.4 Using the stress-diathesis model: Psychological stress on the personality, marital dyad, and triadic relationship with son and the outbreak of symptoms.

some of the anxiety generated by unresolved tension to a third party, in the example, their son, who develops Conduct Disorder with secondary symptom pattern of substance abuse (triangle of relations). One can see how the complexity multiplies; trying to find the fulcrum point to begin to shift the system and the individuals within it can easily overwhelm the clinician. In addition, one can focus on the intrapsychic triangle of each family member or on the interpersonal or the relational triangle.

FINDING THE FULCRUM

One of the main challenges when working with complex clinical syndromes and the dysfunctional systems in which they occur is to find the fulcrum or the point where the most leverage can be applied to shift an individual, dyad, or triad. The fulcrum is usually determined by conducting a comprehensive assessment in which ego-adaptive capacity, motivation, will to change, and level of emotional suffering are evaluated at the individual, dyadic, and triadic levels. Determining the type of dysfunctional personologic system, if applicable, can alert the therapist to relevant themes, such as addiction or abuse, that need to be addressed. If one member of the family is motivated and the others are not, a shift in the motivated individual may set in process a pattern of positive change. On the other hand, growth of one member may threaten the homeostasis of the system and create negative reverberations. For example, an alcoholic partner may increase his or her drinking or substance abuse or workaholic pattern. Relational restructuring can be effected by strengthening a subsystem by creating boundaries or offering a block of treatment for an unstable marriage or for a parent-child dyad in a single-parent family using the therapist as a partner for addressing parenting deficiencies. In the example illustrated in Figure 18.4, the fulcrum might be the marriage, which, if enhanced, would reduce the overall stress level and allow the parents to address their son's difficulties more effectively, instead of triangulating him.

CASE EXAMPLE

In this complex case, the patient was a 23-year-old male who was referred to treatment by his sibling. John came for the initial session with a great deal of anxiety and self-consciousness. He reported that he was feeling depressed, but clearly, anxiety was also a significant problem. His eye contact was poor and he appeared much younger than his chronological age. In fact, he reported that many people thought he was only 14 or 15 years of age. Since he had graduated from high school, he had been employed only one week; he was asked to leave because he wasn't keeping up with the job requirements. He spent most of his time watching television and sleeping.

DIAGNOSIS AND ASSESSMENT

The initial individual diagnostic formulation was (1) Generalized Anxiety Disorder, (2) Agoraphobia, (3) Avoidant and Dependent Personality Disorders, and (4) Dysthymia. A family genogram and history were quite revealing. There were three siblings ranging from 23 to 30, two of whom were still residing at home with the parents. Using a relational diagnosis, the family system seemed to be best described as a *developmentally arrested DPS*. It seemed that there was a high incidence of dependent and avoidant personalities manifesting over the course of three generations. John seemed to be extremely dependent and relied on his parents to accomplish most tasks for him. He was clearly developing agoraphobia; his parents did all tasks outside the home, which further reinforced the patient's dependency and avoidance.

Case Formulation

The initial case formulation involved addressing what appeared to be the patient's severely stunted personality development. John was functioning on the level of a preadolescent. The lack of differentiation emotionally and in terms of identity consolidation was quite troubling. John realized that he was delayed but did not seem to have a clear perception of the extent of developmental fixation.

Treatment Approach and Rational for Its Selection

The initial course of treatment was a phase of individual therapy on a bimonthly basis because of financial limitations and low motivation. This phase of treatment lasted about 14 months. The focus was to address the developmental fixation by helping John to see that his pattern of avoidance and dependency was creating difficulties for him exponentially: The more he avoided, the more he missed his developmental opportunities. His anxiety would increase and self-confidence erode, creating a negative feedback loop. A typical individual session would include the following dialogue:

THERAPIST: But John, if you continue to avoid leaving your house and venturing out to look for a job, you will remain stuck.
PATIENT: No one will give me a chance!
THERAPIST: You sound angry.
PATIENT: I am! They never gave me a chance at my job and then asked me to leave.
THERAPIST: Tell me what the anger is like? (The therapist used defense analysis to increase John's awareness of his self-defeating pattern, often present in personality pathology. Affective responding was also encouraged to help begin to get at the emotion underneath John's chronic anxiety, which itself became a defense against his true feeling.)

John had frequent episodes of temper tantrums at home. He would become furious when his parents gave him advice about getting a job or tried to push him to greater responsibility for himself. The initial phase of therapy alternated between defense and cognitive restructuring in an attempt to help John contact his emotions and use less regressive defenses in his reactions to others. He was able to contact intense feelings of anger and rage primarily directed toward his father, whom he experienced as controlling and abandoning. His ability to face his feeling in the session resulted in his becoming somewhat more assertive at home and less likely to rely on temper tantrums.

Extratherapeutic Effort

It was also suggested that John contact the Department of Rehabilitation, and he finally did so, attaining an entry-level job at 30 hours per week. John seemed to stagnate at this level and did not want to discuss the possibility of attending community college or entering technical training. His avoidant and dependent pattern began to emerge at work; when he was not busy, he would read books because his boss "didn't tell me what to do." This resulted in a gradual scaling back of John's hours to part time. At this point, the therapist asked John if his family could come in for a consultation. He agreed and a family session was scheduled.

The Macroview: Widening the Lens to Include the Family System

This phase of therapy consisted of five family sessions with various members present. On the surface, John's family seemed responsive and concerned about his developmental arrest; paradoxically, they were severely enabling and undermining. Although John was the most obviously stuck, his siblings also had major difficulties establishing independent lives. They all nagged John about finding a job and getting on with his life, but they actually gave mixed messages. They would tell him to "get any job" but then add "but your eye contact is so poor you will have difficulty in interviews." The degree with which John was infantalized is reflected in the following dialogue from the second family session:

THERAPIST: It seems that John serves a vital function for maintaining the family cohesiveness and that, on one hand, members want him to become independent and, on the other, they support dependency.
MOTHER: I have stopped making lunches for John!
THERAPIST: You make lunch for John?
MOTHER: Up until the last session, I made lunch for John every day.
THERAPIST: John, how does it feel to have your mother stop making lunches?
PATIENT: Good, although it was nice.

It soon became clear that John was bearing the symptoms for a system that was not functioning adequately. He was very enmeshed with his mother, who viewed him as the emotionally sensitive child with whom she could talk. His father was quite distant and had little interaction with John aside from nagging him and becoming upset when he would watch an R-rated movie because of the sexual content John would be exposed to.

Initially, the focus in treatment was on restructuring two obvious triangles: John/father/mother and John/sister/brother. The brother had assumed a pseudoparental function with John. Other issues in the family emerged. In individual sessions, John often complained about his father and the way he treated his mother. John's father had refused any couples therapy, even though his wife was in favor of trying it. In the family session, the children mounted a confrontation toward the parental system, saying that their marital problems were affecting everyone and they were really the ones who needed therapy. At this point, the parents were invited in for a couples session and agreed.

Narrowing the Focus to the Marital Dyad
The parents' marriage was severely dysfunctional. The wife evidenced signs of being very dependent and was furious at her husband, who had joined a social club and for the past five years had spent most of his time there helping those he felt were less fortunate. In a retaliatory strike, the wife had stopped having sexual relations, which further drove him from his house. She acknowledged in one session that she stayed only because of financial reasons and because it was better than being alone. It also became apparent that the father had significant characterological disturbance and became highly controlling and pedantic when his motives were questioned, as manifested by the following interaction:

THERAPIST: It seems that the marriage is in severe distress.
WIFE: Yes, for the last five years since he got involved in the social club our relationship has worsened.
THERAPIST: How has it worsened?
HUSBAND: We are no longer intimate in the way husband and wife should be. According to the Bible, a wife's duty is that she . . .
WIFE: This is exactly why I don't have any feeling toward him and am not at all interested in sex! He is emotionally absent and unavailable for us [grown children] but is always talking on the phone to people from the social club who think he is great.

The couple seemed locked into a hostile homeostatic balance that neither seemed prepared to disrupt. The couple made some progress in treatment in that they clearly defined the stalemate. The wife said there was no love left and she stayed only because it was easier than leaving and she was comfortable in her house, which she would lose if she divorced. The husband said that he would be patient and she would come around.

Reference to Existing Treatment Protocols
In addition to the modalities of individual, family, and couples therapy for the parents, John was referred for psychopharmacological treatment and was placed on an antidepressant with anxiety-reducing properties. His problems are generally treated with standard treatment formats, which can include cognitive, behavioral, psychodynamic, and integrative treatment.

Termination
As is the case with many dysfunctional families, termination was not planned, and the couple, after a number of rescheduled appointments, did not return. At this point, the prognosis seemed poor, with no evidence of significant change.

Posttermination Synopsis and Effectiveness Data
The family was contacted one and a half years after treatment by telephone. The patient's father was interviewed and was pleased to receive the call. He was happy to report that John, although still living at home, had attained another 20-hour-a-week job with benefits and would be moving into a full-time position. He was driving outside of his pretherapy comfort zone of about 5 miles to 15 miles in another town. John's father did report that he accompanied him the first time so he would be familiar with the route. He also noted that John now went out to dinner with the family on a frequent basis, which he did not do before. Also of great significance was that his father reported that John had started to date a girl he had met on the Internet, but he said that she was "too fast for John" and "a little too forward." When asked what he meant, he replied, "She didn't get what she wanted" (alluding to sexual involvement). When asked about his marriage, he replied "reasonably well," although there was "no intimacy yet."

Often, when working with complex clinical syndromes, the therapist feels demoralized by the lack of apparent results. However, follow-up, which is an important therapeutic tool, often suggests that therapy may have planted the seeds of change or opened up a new developmental pathway that will continue to benefit the system and individuals within it posttreatment.

EMPIRICAL SUPPORT OF TREATMENT APPROACH

Because IRP is not a model that has been empirically researched, evidence of effectiveness comes from the two domains that constitute the treatment approach: psychodynamic therapy, specifically, accelerated forms, and systemic-relational therapy. It is far beyond the scope of this chapter to present a comprehensive review of the research, so a brief, focused one is offered.

The effectiveness of short-term dynamic therapy for what are usually considered the most challenging patients to treat has been robust for Cluster C (Avoidant, Dependent, and Obsessive-Compulsive) and some Cluster B (Histrionic, Narcissistic, and Borderline) Personality Disorders (Horowitz, Marmar, Weiss, Kaltreider, & Wilner, 1986; Winston et al., 1991, 1994). Lebow (2000) addressed the question of effectiveness of relational-based therapy: "An overwhelming body of evidence indicates that the outcomes of these therapies are primarily positive, achieving rates of success in improvement of general functioning and in achieving treatment goals that are similar to the rates of individual therapy as well as to other interventions in the health sciences" (p. 1087). Also, according to Lebow, the research findings do not support the efficacy of one model of relational therapy over another.

SUMMARY

Psychodynamic therapy has been influenced and shaped by many innovative pioneers over the century since Freud discovered the unconscious. Blending various theoretical components of the psychodynamic model, such as structural-drive, ego psychology, object relations and self psychology, has expanded the domain of treatment of a wide spectrum of patients. Combining the psychodynamic model with a systemic model that was initially viewed as incompatible has broad appeal for the clinician who is looking for a flexible approach that can be used with individuals, couples, and families. Using a relational psychodynamic model, one can flexibly conceptualize and navigate the biopsychosocial matrix that best accounts for complex clinical syndromes.

REFERENCES

Ackerman, N. W. (1958). *The psychodynamics of family life: Diagnosis and treatment of family relationships.* New York: Basic Books.

Alexander, F. G., & French, T. M. (1946). *Psychoanalytic therapy: Principles and applications.* New York: Ronald Press.

Bateson, G., Jackson, D., Haley, J., & Weakland, J. (1956). Toward a theory of schizophrenia. *Behavioral Science, 1,* 251–264.

Beck, A. T., Freeman, A., & Associates. (1990). *Cognitive therapy of personality disorders.* New York: Guilford Press.

Beck, A. T., Rush, A. J., Shaw, B., & Emery, G. (1979). *Cognitive therapy of depression.* New York: Guilford Press.

Benjamin, L. S. (1993). *Interpersonal diagnosis and treatment of personality disorders.* New York: Guilford Press.

Bowen, M. (1976). Theory in the practice of psychotherapy. In P. J. Guerin (Ed.), *Family: Theory and practice* (pp. 42–90). New York: Gardner Press.

Bowen, M. (1978). *Family therapy in clinical practice.* New York: Aronson.

Davanloo, H. (Ed.). (1980). *Short-term dynamic psychotherapy.* New York: Aronson.

Davanloo, H. (1990). *Unlocking the unconscious.* Chichester, England: Wiley.

Diamond, G. M., Diamond, G. S., & Liddle, H. A. (2000). The therapist-parent alliance in family-based therapy for adolescents. *Journal of Clinical Psychology/In Session: Psychotherapy in Practice, 56*(8), 1037–1050.

Donaldson-Pressman, S., & Pressman, R. M. (1994). *The narcissistic family: Diagnosis and treatment.* New York: Maxwell Macmillan International.

Engle, G. L. (1980). The clinical application of the biopsychosocial model. *American Journal of Psychiatry, 137,* 535–544.

Ezriel, H. (1952). Notes on psychoanalytic group therapy: Interpretation and research. *Psychiatry, 15,* 119–126.

Ferenczi, S., & Rank, O. (1925). *The development of psychoanalysis.* New York: Nervous and Mental Diseases.

Fosha, D. (2000). *The transforming power of affect.* New York: Basic Books.

Frances, A., Clarkin, J., & Perry, S. (1984). *Differential therapeutics in psychiatry: The art and science of treatment selection.* New York: Brunner/Mazel.

Goleman, D. (1994). *Emotional intelligence.* New York: Bantam Books.

Greenberg, L. S., Rice, L. N., & Elliott, R. (1993). *Facilitating emotional change: The moment-by-moment process.* New York: Guilford Press.

Grigsby, J., & Stevens, D. (2000). *Neurodynamics of personality.* New York: Guilford Press.

Guerin, P. J., Fogarty, T. F., Fay, L. F., & Kautto, J. G. (1996). *Working with relational triangles: The one-two-three of psychotherapy.* New York: Guilford Press.

Hartmann, H. (1958). *Ego psychology and the problem of adaptation.* New York: New York University Press.

Hartmann, H. (1964). *Essays on ego psychology: Selected problems in psychoanalytic theory.* New York: New York University Press.

Horowitz, M. J., Marmar, C. R., Weiss, D. S., Kaltreider, N. B., & Wilner, N. R. (1986). Comprehensive analysis of change after brief dynamic psychotherapy. *American Journal of Psychiatry, 143*(5), 582–589.

Jordan, J. V. (2000). The role of mutual empathy in relational/cultural therapy. *Journal of Clinical Psychology/In Session: Psychotherapy in Practice, 56*(8), 1005–1016.

Kahn, M. D. (1986). The self and the system: Integrating Kohut and Milan. In S. Sugarman (Ed.), *The interface of individual and family therapy* (pp. 50–63). Gaithersburg, MA: Aspen.

Kaslow, F. W. (Ed.). (1996). *Handbook of relational diagnosis and dysfunctional family patterns.* New York: Wiley.

Kernberg, O. (1984). *Severe personality disorders: Psychotherapeutic strategies.* New Haven, CT: Yale University Press.

Kohut, H. (1971). *The analysis of the self.* New York: International Universities Press.

Lebow, J. (2000). What does the research tell us about couple and family therapies? *Journal of Clinical Psychology/In Session: Psychotherapy in Practice, 56*(8), 1083–1094.

Magnavita, J. J. (1997). *Restructuring personality disorders: A short-term dynamic approach.* New York: Guilford Press.

Magnavita, J. J. (1998). Challenges in the treatment of personality disorders: When the disorder demands comprehensive integration. *Journal of Clinical Psychology/In Session: Psychotherapy in Practice, 4*(4), 50–17.

Magnavita, J. J. (2000a). Integrative relational therapy of complex clinical syndromes: Ending the multigenerational transmission process. *Journal of Clinical Psychology/In Session: Psychotherapy in Practice, 56*(8), 1051–1064.

Magnavita, J. J. (2000b). Introduction: Advancements in relational therapy. *Journal of Clinical Psychology/In Session: Psychotherapy in Practice, 56*(8), 999–1004.

Magnavita, J. J. (2000c). *Relational therapy for personality disorders.* New York: Wiley.

Malan, D. H. (1963). *A study of brief psychotherapy.* London: Tavistock.

McCullough, L. (1998). Short-term psychodynamic therapy as a form of desensitization: Treating affect phobias. *Journal of Clinical Psychology/In Session: Psychotherapy in Practice, 4*(4), 35–53.

McCullough Vaillant, L. (1997). *Changing character: Short-term anxiety regulating psychotherapy for restructuring defenses, affects, and attachments.* New York: Basic Books.

McGoldrick, M., & Gerson, R. (1985). *Genograms in family assessment.* New York: Norton.

Menninger, K. (1958). *Theory of psychoanalytic technique.* New York: Basic Books.

Millon, T., Grossman, S., Meagher, S., Millon, C., & Everly, G. (1999). *Personality-guided therapy.* New York: Wiley.

Minuchin, S. (1974). *Families and family therapy.* Cambridge, MA: Cambridge University Press.

Pine, F. (1990). *Drive, ego, object, and self: A synthesis for clinical work.* New York: Basic Books.

Reich, W. (1945). *Character analysis* (3rd ed.). New York: Noonday Press.

Shea, S. C. (1998). *Psychiatric interviewing: The art of understanding* (2nd ed.). Philadelphia: Saunders.

Siegel, D. J. (1999). *The developing mind: Toward a neurobiology of interpersonal experience.* New York: Guilford Press.

Sifneos, P. E. (1987). *Short-term dynamic therapy: Evaluation and technique* (2nd ed.). New York: Plenum Medical.

Sue, D. W., & Sue, D. (1999). *Counseling the culturally different: Theory and practice.* New York: Wiley.

Sugarman, S. (1986). Individual and family therapy: An overview of the interface. In S. Sugarman (Ed.), *The interface of individual and family therapy* (pp. 1–16). Gaithersburg, MA: Aspen.

Synder, D. K., Cavell, T. A., Heffer, R. W., & Mangrum, L. F. (1995). Marital and family assessment: A multifaceted, multilevel approach. In R. H. Mikesell, D. Lusterman, & S. H. Daniel (Eds.), *Integrating family therapy: Handbook of family psychology and systems theory* (pp. 163–197). Washington, DC: American Psychological Association.

von Bertalanffy, L. (1968). *General systems theory: Foundations, development, application.* New York: Braziller.

Wachtel, P. L. (1977). *Psychoanalysis and behavior therapy: Toward an integration.* New York: Basic Books.

Wachtel, P. L. (1997). *Psychoanalysis, behavior therapy, and the relational world.* Washington, DC: American Psychological Association.

Watson, W. H., & McDaniel, S. H. (2000). Relational therapy in medical settings: Working with somatizing patients and their families. *Journal of Clinical Psychology/In Session: Psychotherapy in Practice, 56*(8), 1065–1082.

Winston, A., Laikin, M., Pollack, J., Samstag, L., McCullough, L., & Muran, C. (1994). Short-term psychotherapy of personality disorders. *American Journal of Psychiatry, 151*(2), 190–194.

Winston, A., Pollack, J., McCullough, L., Flegenheimer, W., Kestenbaum, R., & Trujillo, M. (1991). Brief psychotherapy of personality disorders. *Journal of Nervous and Mental Diseases, 179*(4), 188–193.

Young, J. E. (1990). *Cognitive therapy for personality disorders: A schema-focused approach* (Rev. ed.). Sarasota, FL: Professional Resource Exchange.

Section Five

GROUP PSYCHOTHERAPY

Chapter 19 Psychodynamically Oriented Group Therapy

Chapter 20 Psychodynamic/Object-Relations Group Therapy with Schizophrenic Patients

Chapter 21 Group Therapy Treatment of Sex Offenders

CHAPTER 19

Psychodynamically Oriented Group Therapy

WILLIAM E. PIPER, JOHN S. OGRODNICZUK, AND SCOTT C. DUNCAN

The topic for this chapter is psychodynamically oriented group therapy (POGT) with an interpretive (expressive) emphasis. POGT can be provided in different forms; these differ on such characteristics as their interpretive versus supportive emphasis, structure (e.g., length), objectives, and group composition. In this chapter, two specific forms of interpretive POGT are highlighted: open-ended, long-term group therapy with a heterogeneous patient composition (LTG), and time-limited, short-term group therapy with a homogeneous patient composition (STG). Before focusing on these two forms, the historical origins of group psychotherapy and the development of POGT are reviewed. Next, some basic principles (assumptions) and concepts associated with psychodynamically oriented therapy in general are addressed. Four theoretical schools are also briefly considered: drive theory, ego psychology, object relations theory, and self psychology. Then, the features that characterize the optimal process for POGT are described. Subsequently, the focus of the chapter shifts to differentiating the long-term and short-term forms of POGT; this is done in reference to the structure and objectives of the groups. Methods of assessment and intervention, including a discussion of pretherapy training, are considered, as well as selection of patients for POGT. The two forms are further differentiated through the use of clinical illustrations. Finally, some concluding comments are provided.

HISTORY OF THE PSYCHODYNAMIC APPROACH

ORIGINS OF GROUP PSYCHOTHERAPY

Life progresses through groups. We mature and develop through a series of different groups, for example, family groups, school groups, peer groups, work groups, and recreational groups. The types of experiences we have in these various groups have a profound impact on our functioning, our self-image, our self-esteem, and our health (Rutan & Cohen, 1989). Although psychotherapy in groups is a relatively new phenomenon, tapping the motivational forces inherent in cohesive groups for therapeutic purposes has been practiced throughout the ages

(Scheidlinger, 1993). Speculation about the curative factors of the group include the concepts of universality, which refers to individuals' experience of relief that they are not alone in their struggles; altruism, which refers to how individuals often feel better about themselves when they can help another person; and interpersonal learning, which refers to how the group allows for a unique opportunity to work out interpersonal relationships (Yalom, 1975). The group setting for psychotherapy offers the opportunity for purposefully created, closely observed, and skillfully guided interpersonal interaction that capitalizes on these and other factors (Alonso & Swiller, 1993). Group psychotherapy is emerging as a powerful, appropriate, and cost-effective modality for treating a wide spectrum of patient problems. In groups, patients enjoy a range of resources beyond those that can be provided by a single therapist, namely, the pooled efforts, experiences, associations, and goodwill of all the participants in resolving the difficulties that limit all the members' lives (Alonso & Rutan, 1984).

During the past eight decades, there have been widespread refinements in both theory and practice of group treatments. The field has moved from a comparatively narrow range of theoretical formulations regarding the principal dimensions of group interactions to a profusion of treatment models (Dies, 1992). Our focus here is on the developments within one particular branch of group psychotherapy: the psychodynamically oriented approach. Psychodynamically oriented therapies are steeped in the psychoanalytic theory that was pioneered by Sigmund Freud.

Historical Developments of POGT

S. Freud's *Group Psychology and the Analysis of the Ego* (1921/1967) contributed significantly to our understanding of groups. He reasoned that a collection of individuals is not a group unless clear leadership and a sense of purpose develop. He viewed the role of the leader as critical and placed the process of identification at the heart of group formation (Rutan, 1993). Despite his interest in and impressive writings about group psychology, Freud never conducted a therapy group.

As the efforts of Freud and other pioneer theorists and practitioners (e.g., Edward Lazell, Gustav LeBon, William McDougall, and Joseph Pratt) became more widely known, others soon began to experiment with treating emotional and mental problems in group settings. In the late 1920s, Trigant Burrow, a founder of the American Psychoanalytic Association, began to see neurotic patients in groups. His key contributions included an emphasis on the here and now and a refusal to polarize the group into a sick patient–well therapist situation (Anthony, 1971). Others who were in the forefront of invoking psychoanalytic principles in group therapy were Alfred Adler, whose concern about the social context of human behavior led naturally to his use of groups as early as 1921; Louis Wender, whose work with inpatient and outpatient populations involved interpretations of family transferences in the group transactions; Paul Schilder, who pioneered analytic group therapy through systematic reliance on both transference and dream interpretations; and Jacob Moreno, whose psychodramatic approach emerged in the United States in the mid-1930s (Rutan, 1993; Scheidlinger, 1993).

Samuel Slavson deserves special recognition for his role in the founding of the American Group Psychotherapy Association. Slavson adapted a classical, individual psychoanalytic model for his group psychotherapy, conducted primarily with children and adolescents. He devised the term "group dynamics," but believed that such phenomena interfered with treatment, where the emphasis should remain on the individual patient. Slavson stressed that a permissive group climate promotes a benign regression in which early conflicts can be expressed in the context of a stable and accepting environment (R. Klein, Bernard, & Singer, 1992).

The use of group psychotherapy was greatly expanded during and following World War II due to the limited supply of mental health professionals and the increased need for psychiatric services. Developments in psychodynamically oriented group treatments continued with the works of many distinguished writers, such as S.H. Foulkes, Henry Ezriel, Florence Powdermaker, Jerome Frank, and Wilfred Bion. Alexander Wolf and Emanuel Schwartz, who in 1962 wrote *Psychoanalysis in Groups*, emphasized a focus on individuals in group therapy. They believed that the goal of the group analyst was to guide patients to fuller awareness and social integration. They suggested that this goal is reached through analysis of the transferences that individual members have toward the analyst and other members of the group (Rutan, 1993; Scheidlinger, 1993). In contrast, Ezriel, Bion, and Foulkes believed that the group therapist's task resides essentially in confronting the group as a whole with its shared unconscious fantasy themes (Rutan & Stone, 1993; Scheidlinger, 1993).

More recent advances in psychodynamically oriented group treatments are provided in the works of Henriette Glatzer and Helen Durkin. They sought to integrate individual psychoanalytic theory with group theory and practice by focusing on the use of group interactions as a means of clarifying individual as well as group transferences and resistances (R. Klein et al., 1992). Leonard Horwitz (1977) developed a group approach that begins with an initial focus on individual contributions and ends with group-level interpretations. Otto Kernberg (1980) proposed a model of group therapy in which group-level interventions are used to address problems that stem from early developmental issues (e.g., pre-Oedipal), and more individual-focused interventions are used to address the transferences and resistances that stem from conflicts in later development (e.g., Oedipal) (Rutan, 1993). Saul Scheidlinger has written extensively about identification and regression in group therapy and how, on archaic symbolic levels, the group represents the nurturing mother with whom members wish to restore an unconflicted state of psychological unity (R. Klein et al., 1992).

The practice of psychodynamic group psychotherapy began on a trial-and-error basis, with practitioners trying to meld the individualized psychoanalytic theories of Freud with the observations of LeBon, McDougall, and others on how groups functioned. Clinicians and theorists varied in their emphasis as they worked toward an optimal integration; some focused on the individual, others examined groupwide phenomena (Rutan, 1993). The different theories, however, shared the belief that multiple-person interactions within the group could illuminate the individual's inner conflicts.

THEORETICAL CONSTRUCTS

Under the psychodynamic umbrella there reside many complex theoretical approaches to understanding the patient and the therapy process. Despite such diversity, however, there are some core principles that underlie the theory and practice of all forms of psychodynamic psychotherapy. These principles or assumptions have remained relatively constant from Freud's earliest theories. These include the conviction that (1) there is psychological determinism, (2) there are unconscious processes, (3) human behavior is dynamic and goal-oriented, (4) development is epigenetic, and (5) functions of the mind are at work at any given point in time (Rutan, 1992). We also review two other key concepts of psychodynamic theory and practice: transference and resistance.

Psychological Determinism

Psychological determinism is the assumption that every manifestation of the human mind is lawfully connected with every other manifestation of the mind (Rutan, 1993). That is, there is a rational explanation for human behavior and all human behavior makes sense. Even behavior that may appear accidental, irrational, or self-defeating follows the rule of psychological determinism. This notion suggests that even the most bizarre behavior serves some purpose.

Unconscious Processes

To explain the logic underlying the apparent illogic in human behavior and thought, Freud introduced the concept of unconscious process. For efficient mental functioning, the mind selects those thoughts and feelings that will serve the present needs of the individual and deletes from present awareness those thoughts and feelings that threaten to disequilibrate and interfere with the goals of the moment (Gabbard, 1990). The unconscious is the term used to describe a process of storing out of awareness all the data that are not relevant or tolerable; it is not a place or an anatomic structure of the mind. Through the defense mechanism of repression, events, feelings, and traumas that threaten to overwhelm the individual are relegated to this unconscious realm. The goal of psychodynamic therapy is to help the patient gain awareness of those parts of the unconscious that result in destructive distortions in present-day perceptions.

Dynamic and Goal-Oriented Behavior

Psychodynamic theory posits that all human behavior, including pathological behavior, is goal-directed. Instead of being a mistake, pathological behavior involves the ineffective pursuit of goals that are concealed from the patient in the unconscious. The goal of treatment is not to expunge the behavior, but to identify the underlying goal and bring it into the open. When the goals of pathological behavior become known to the patient, the patient is freer to integrate them with the rest of his or her life, and their maladaptive impact is diminished.

Epigenetic Development

According to psychodynamic theory, personality is formed developmentally. An epigenetic model of development is one in which each stage of development builds on the prior stage, and each developmental stage affects the subsequent one. In this sense, it can be said that the past is prologue; the earliest infantile experiences are the foundations of all later experiences (Gabbard, 1990). Important for treatment is the assumption that flaws in early stages of development can be repaired if that stage is recalled, relived, and corrected in the here and now of the treatment situation.

Functions of the Mind

Psychodynamic theory assumes that there are distinct functions of the mind that may be in conflict. These functions are managed by internal structures that have been postulated to explain the process of how the mind works in the here and now. Structures refer to heuristic divisions of the mind that are responsible for organizing and managing conflicting ideas and competing impulses (Alonso, 1989). They are a way of explaining simultaneous and opposing thoughts and impulses in an individual. A primary tenet of this assumption is that psychological distress occurs subsequent to unconscious conflict between structures of the mind.

Transference and Resistance

Because of the basic assumption that patients are unaware of important internal events that are responsible for their distress, the internal events must be inferred from patients' overt expressions (feelings, thoughts, and behaviors). In the therapy session, the therapist relies on such material as patients' dreams, fantasies, slips of the tongue, verbal associations, and nonverbal behaviors to make inferences about patients' internal events. In addition, a great deal of importance is attributed to patients' reactions to the therapist. A central concept is that of transference. Although many different definitions of transference have been offered in the literature, it generally refers to the patient's subjective response to a present person, which is based on the patient's previous experiences with other people who are perceived as similar. It is viewed as a displacement, that is, a repetitive inappropriate response to the present person. The other people are often parental figures. In individual therapy, the therapist is the transference object. In group therapy, the therapist, other patients, and even the group as a whole can be transference objects. It is part of the therapist's task to interpret (i.e. attribute meaning to) transference. Because transference is often intense, affect-laden, and immediate, it is seen as a prime opportunity for analysis that leads to learning and dynamic change. However, because the internal events of the patient are often disturbing and threatening, the patient frequently resists the interpretation of transference. This highlights another central concept: resistance. In general, this refers to the process of opposition to insight and change in dynamic therapy. Resistance, too, is often the object of therapist interpretation. It is probably fair to say that, over the years, interpretation of transference and interpretation of resistance have served as hallmarks of dynamic psychotherapy.

FOUR SCHOOLS OF PSYCHODYNAMIC THEORY

The theoretical concepts outlined above are shared by several schools of psychodynamic theory, with the major differences residing in the relative emphases given to different themes. In the following, four major schools of psychodynamic theory are briefly reviewed. Each takes a somewhat different perspective on human psychological functioning, emphasizing somewhat different phenomena. Although the four certainly overlap, each adds something new to our theoretical understanding, and each has significant relevance in the clinical situation by alerting us to different facets of the processes of change.

Drive Psychology

Drive psychology is based on S. Freud's (1949/1964) structural theory of the mind. Freud postulated that there are three structures: id, ego, and superego. The id contains all the sexual energy in primitive form. The dual instincts of libido and aggression are located in the id and propel (drive) the individual through life. These drives take shape as wishes that are embodied in actions and in conscious and unconscious fantasies. The superego develops as an accommodation to the civilizing influences of the parents and the culture. As a result of the internalization of parental and societal constraints, the wishes come to be experienced as unacceptable and dangerous. The ego modulates the expression of the drives by generating defenses that function as a compromise between the unacceptable wishes of the id and the constraints of the superego, so that the individual can continue to function and grow (Alonso, 1989). But the ego is always only partially successful at this compromise. The instinctual press may be too intense because of earlier trauma, genetic endowment, or present stress coming from within or outside of the individual. Hence, the conflict remains in part irreconcilable and generates anxiety, shame, inhibition, and pathological character traits.

From the perspective of drive psychology, which calls attention to the taming, socialization, and gratification of drives, the group therapist is alert to the wishes that are being expressed and how they relate to consciousness; the underlying fantasies and how they emerge as a compromise among wish, defense, and reality; and which defenses are employed against the wishes and how effective they are. The goal of treatment is to restore equilibrium among the psychic structures so that the ego is able to maintain a comfortable compromise among instinctual drives, superego requirements, and the demands of reality. According to Alonso and Rutan (1984), however, the highly individualistic, conflict-based structural theory of drive psychology has never fit entirely well into the interpersonal matrix of the therapy group.

Ego Psychology

Ego psychology is an early modification of classical drive psychology that expanded and elevated the role of the ego and of reality (A. Freud, 1936; Hartmann, 1939). The ego is defined as having both conscious and unconscious aspects and having at its disposal a host of defenses. It is the incompatibility of the demands of the id with the demands of the environment that necessitates the formation of ego defenses. All the defenses are in the service of allowing the individual to function and adapt. Adaptation is primarily a reciprocal relationship between the individual and the environment, with each having the capacity to change the other. Ego psychology emphasizes the individual's capacities for adaptation, reality testing, and defense and the availability of these capacities for dealing with the inner world of drives and the outer world of reality demands. Psychopathology is thus postulated to be a function of inadequate, disturbed, or otherwise defective ego functioning (Gabbard, 1990).

Kauff (1993) suggests that the larger the window into the ego in action, the more varied the opportunities to observe and the more productive treatment can be. Group therapy provides just such an expanded window through which to view ego functioning. The group therapist working from the ego psychology perspective likely would consider what defenses are operative against the drives and how effective they are, how affects are being defended against, and what tools of adaptation have failed to develop or have developed aberrantly (Pine, 1988). Essentially, the core of the therapeutic work is the rigid, malfunctional, ineffective, and outdated defenses of the individual. Thus, the goal of therapy is to help the individual gradually bring conflict to awareness and modify inflexible modes of defense.

Object Relations Psychology

Object relations psychology stresses the importance of internal and partial representations of the important people in a child's early environment (Fairbairn, 1952; M. Klein, 1964; Winnicott, 1965). Object relations refer to the partially incorporated parental images that reside in the individual's mind in the form of split-off and incomplete memories. For example, the remembered mother of the adult often bears little resemblance to the white-haired elderly lady of the present. Instead, she lives in the mind of the adult in caricature and undigested fantasy that bears some truth and some distortion. We react to people on the basis of these internal and partially fantastic emotional memories (Gabbard, 1990).

From this perspective, the experiences of early childhood with primary objects become part of an internal drama that is carried in the mind as memory and is subsequently reenacted. In the repetition of these internalized family dramas, propelled by efforts at attachment or mastery or both, the individual plays one or more of these roles (Pine, 1988). New experiences, rather than being fully experienced in their contemporary form, are assimilated into the templates created by old dramas. Pathology thus stems from the individual's being constrained by early conflictual experiences that cause the individual to absorb new experiences into the old drama of historically based object relations (R. Klein et al., 1992).

Thus, in the context of the group, these unconscious reenactments result in individuals playing out particular roles and selecting and inducing others to assume the necessary reciprocal roles to permit the externalizing of their internal dramas. The group setting provides the interpersonal stimulus that evokes the unconscious paradigms that underlie each individual's internalized relationships. The work of the psychotherapy group is to establish a safe environment that will enable its members to reenact and to examine their distorted internal dramatizations. When the group serves as an effective container, the primitive, disowned, distorted aspects of the self can be recovered and the restrictive grip of archaic family dramatizations can be loosened (R. Klein et al., 1992).

Self Psychology

Self psychology views the self as the fundamental and supraordinate structure in mental functioning (Kohut, 1971). The central concept of self psychology theory is the development of a stable, coherent, and accurately perceived sense of self as the center of experience that initiates action and inspires the individual toward higher levels of development throughout the life cycle (Pine, 1988). The crucial issues in the continuing development of the individual include continuity, cohesion, differentiation, regulation, and esteem. These issues are initially mediated by the parent, who, through empathic attunement, integrates and modulates for the baby. Because the parent is an object who performs these self-modulation functions on behalf of the infant, the parent is construed as a self/object. Kohut (1971) coined the term self/object to describe the child's internal perception of those people in his or her environment who serve functions that will later be performed by the individual's own psychic structure.

At the core of self psychology theory is the experience of the relation between the self and the empathic self/object (Alonso, 1989). The presence, availability, consistency, and responsivity of self/objects profoundly affect the individual's development. According to the self psychology perspective, the primary determinants of anxiety and pathology derive from disturbances in self-self/object relationships. Individuals unconsciously seek what they previously missed, in the form of mirroring, idealizing, and alter-ego functions, to permit the development of a vital, cohesive self (Gabbard, 1990).

Patients experience current self/object failures in the psychotherapy group as echoes of unresolved past disappointments. Therapy involves working through self/object failures and disruptions, thereby restoring and/or creating what is needed for further development. According to self psychology theory, the provision of necessary, phase-specific, legitimate but previously unavailable self/object functions by an experience-near, empathic therapist and group will promote change. Via the process of transmuting internalization, individuals gradually take over the necessary functions initially provided by others outside of the self (R. Klein et al., 1992).

Each of these four psychodynamic schools of thought has a somewhat different conception of the individual (Pine, 1988). Drive psychology emphasizes the socialization and gratification of drives. Ego psychology emphasizes the development of defenses with respect to the internal world of the individual and adaptation to the external world. Object relations psychology focuses on the task of simultaneously carrying within us the record of the history of our significant relationships and freeing ourselves from the constraints of those relationships so that new experiences can be responded to on their own contemporary terms. Self psychology focuses on the diverse tasks of forming a differentiated and whole sense of self, of establishing the self as the center of initiative, and of developing an ongoing sense of subjective worth.

GROUP PROCESS

A defining feature of POGT is the type of group process the therapist attempts to facilitate. Initially, the therapist attempts to create a climate of safety and trust that will promote cohesion (bonding) and strong working alliances among members of the group. To a large extent, the therapist achieves this by being familiar with typical concerns and issues that preoccupy patients during early sessions and gently but firmly addressing them as they arise. These often include experiencing fear of exposure, criticism, attack, rejection, and being overwhelmed emotionally; searching for commonalities among other patients; and wishing for reassurance from and protection by an all-knowing therapist. By encouraging patients to address these issues in the here and now, the therapist demonstrates that affective and conflict-laden topics can be worked on safely in the group. This process requires time and effort, given the number of people that are involved. When that is accomplished, a number of patient and therapist behaviors are evident. Patients disclose private material, react affectively and verbally to each other, give and receive feedback in a nondefensive manner, accept and work with therapist interpretations, analyze group events, and provide interpretations to themselves and others regarding their problems. The therapist primarily facilitates clarification and interpretation of how long-standing conflicts and trauma are related to present problems. There are attempts to link events across different people and times (e.g., patients' problems and relationships with past figures, current figures outside the group, and members of the group). There are also attempts to understand events in terms of intrapsychic, interpersonal, and group processes. As the group develops, the therapist encourages patients to perform these functions.

To some extent, each session begins anew. There is no preset agenda of specific topics to be covered during a particular session; there are only general objectives and guidelines. The patients, rather than the therapist, assume responsibility for choosing how to begin and what to discuss as the session proceeds. The therapist intervenes from time to time, primarily to clarify and interpret events. The patients are granted the immediate choice of either working with the therapist's offerings or avoiding them. However, if resistance to explore certain topics continues, the therapist confronts the group about the defensive pattern and provides interpretation. In this type of unstructured group situation, some regression occurs and unconscious processes, including transference phenomena, are allowed to freely emerge. Through the processes, patients reveal much about their personalities, their interpersonal styles, and the problems that brought them to therapy. These are conveyed as much by their behavior in the group as by what they describe about current and previous events in their lives. The fact that their present behavior is immediate and available for all group members to observe makes it compelling material for analysis and understanding, which is encouraged.

The optimal process of POGT can be viewed as comprising a set of three group processes that reoccur repeatedly. They often, but not always, occur in the following sequence. For each patient, there is the process of *experiencing*. This refers to attending to the group process and allowing oneself to be influenced both emotionally and cognitively. Thus, the patient is fully present. Next, there is the process of *investing*. This refers to offering something of value to receive something of value. In the group, something of value may include feelings, ideas, memories, dreams, and interpersonal feedback. Investing carries the risk of not receiving anything in return or experiencing something negative. Patients vary considerably in how soon and how much they are willing to invest in the group. Then, there is the complementary process of *examining*. This involves exploring and reflecting on what has been experienced and invested by members of the group. It includes the three subprocesses of describing (specifying), interpreting (attributing meaning to), and evaluating (determining the value of) what has occurred in the group. The three group processes are prerequisites for *patient change,* which begins in the group. This includes acquiring insight and knowledge, new coping mechanisms, new skills, and new reactions and approaches to one's problems. Engaging in each of the processes affects the nature of subsequent processes.

In summary, the patient's task is to attentively immerse himself or herself in the group, engage in the processes of investing and examining, and eventually work toward changing long-standing conflictual and traumatic patterns. The patient is also asked to help other patients do the same. The therapist's task is to facilitate a group process that encourages psychodynamic work; this is sometimes referred to as establishing therapeutic norms. In part, this is accomplished by providing useful interventions during the sessions. These have the direct effect of addressing important issues associated with patients' problems and the indirect effect of demonstrating to patients how to analyze and work toward changing their problems. In addition, the therapist's efforts toward facilitating psychodynamic work begins well before the first session of the group. It involves the appropriate assessment, selection, and preparation of patients. Before addressing these procedures, the major differences in structure and objectives between LTG and STG are addressed.

STRUCTURE AND OBJECTIVES

Long-Term Group Therapy

In LTG, the expectation is that the patient will belong to the group for an extended period of time (e.g., for a minimum of two years). New patients may arrive after the group is formed. If the patient is considering leaving, he or she is asked to discuss this in the group and if there is a decision to leave, a departure date is set that permits an unhurried termination. The extended period of time allows the patient to experience a full range of events both internal (e.g., arrivals and departures of other patients) and external to the group (e.g., anniversaries, holidays, life events, work decisions, relationship decisions) that can be integrated with his or her work in the group. It also provides an opportunity to engage in the process of working through while still being a member of the group. Working through refers to applying one's insights and changes to a variety of situations. In regard to objectives, Rutan and Stone (1993) have accurately stated that the goal that is primary to most patients in long-term group therapy is to achieve more mutually gratifying and authentic interpersonal relationships. Patients manifest many different types of interpersonal problems, but they usually share the common goal of improving their relationships with other people. That is the goal that LTG appears best suited to achieve. Other goals, such as obtaining relief from specific symptoms (e.g., anxiety or depression), are also important, but are usually regarded as secondary. Over time, benefit regarding specific symptoms is usually achieved. If such symptoms are initially precipitating a crisis, LTG is not the treatment of choice. However, once the crisis has remitted, LTG may very well be the treatment of choice. Despite having a common interpersonal goal, patients in long-term groups are usually regarded as being relatively heterogeneous. Their symptoms, interpersonal styles, interpersonal difficulties, and underlying conflicts differ.

Short-Term Group Therapy

In STG, the expectation is that the patient will belong to the group for a short period of time (e.g., 12 weeks). New patients will not be added and all patients have the same termination date. The short period of time creates pressure on all group members to work quickly and efficiently. The therapist is usually quite active. Because of the preset time limit, the therapist cannot wait for substantial evidence to accumulate before making interpretations. Skill as a therapist requires familiarity with typical themes and roles, early recognition of their presence in the group, and appropriate interventions to heighten patient awareness. For example, the preset time limit inevitably heightens tensions concerning separation and loss. The short-term group therapist must be well primed. Therapists who have had experience with both long-term and short-term group therapy typically report that the latter is more exacting. Working through mainly occurs after the group has ended. In regard to objectives, the primary goal is usually limited to making progress in a specific area (e.g., adaptation to loss or adjustment to other traumatic events such as physical abuse, sexual abuse, or exposure to life-threatening situations). Because of the specificity of the area, the commonality of associated symptoms, and the limited range of associated conflicts, patients in short-term groups are regarded as being relatively homogeneous. This is considered to be useful to the necessary tasks of establishing cohesion, strong working alliances, and optimal psychodynamic process in a short period of time. Obviously, patients in crisis would be unable to accomplish these in STG.

METHODS OF ASSESSMENT AND INTERVENTION

Useful selection decisions are dependent on valid assessments. A recent research review of the predictive ability of interpersonal selection criteria revealed that the best assessment method (i.e. the most predictive of desirable process and outcome) was direct observation of the patient's behavior in a previous therapy group (Piper, 1994). Although this opportunity is available in many clinics, it is not available to most private practitioners. The most common method of assessment is, of course, the dyadic clinical interview. The review findings indicated that the dyadic interview method is useful when used to assess interpersonal traits and problems, but not when used to rate the actual interview behavior of the patient. The implications from the review are fairly clear. If possible, observe the patient's group behavior directly; if not, inquire about the patient's previous experiences in therapy groups or previous interpersonal behaviors from the patient in the clinical interview or from the referral source. Finally, do not be misled by the patient's dyadic interview behavior. In regard to LTG and STG, it would probably be most informative to inquire about the patient's previous therapy or other group experiences that resembled the structure and objectives of the group for which the patient was being considered. For example, did the patient have any previous experience in a time-limited, intensive group that had a specific focus and an active leader?

There is one issue concerning patient selection that deserves emphasis. Given our current state of knowledge, selection criteria are not powerful predictors of patient success in therapy groups. Research reviews of predictor variable studies typically indicate that many predictor variables are investigated, but only a few emerge as statistically significant. Of these, most associations are of small magnitude and have not been replicated. Aside from our limited state of knowledge, therapists may wish to provide one or more "high-risk" patients with an opportunity to have a valuable experience in a therapy group. Risky patients sometimes pleasantly surprise us. We may not want to deprive all risky patients of an opportunity to benefit even if we know that a number will not.

Having only one or two risky patients in a therapy group is very different from having five or six.

PRETHERAPY TRAINING: THE IMPORTANCE OF CAREFUL PATIENT PREPARATION

A method of reducing the risk for failure for all patients entering group therapy is careful preparation, also known as pretherapy training (PT). PT refers to any procedure conducted prior to therapy that attempts to prepare patients for the task of working in a therapy group. The ultimate objectives of PT include facilitating attendance, remaining for the duration of the group, desirable group process, and favorable outcome. More immediate objectives include creating accurate expectations about desirable patient behavior, customary therapist roles, typical therapy events, and realistic outcomes; reducing anxiety; establishing positive bonds; and increasing participation, self-disclosure, and interpersonal feedback. In most cases, PT occurs as a natural part of the initial interviews between patient and therapist. Many therapists find it useful additionally to present the patient with a brief set of written guidelines, often covering such topics as commitments to the group (e.g., attending, remaining), responsibilities inside the group (e.g., self-disclosing, working), and responsibilities outside the group (e.g., confidentiality). Research reviews (Piper & Perrault, 1989; Yalom, 1995) suggest that careful preparation by means of PT procedures is a good investment of resources.

Much of the information concerning commitments to the group and responsibilities inside and outside the group is similar for the two forms (LTG, STG) of POGT. Information about the structures and objectives of the groups are, of course, different. Also different is information about the topics covered (more focused in STG), the pace of the group process (quicker in STG), and the role of the therapist (more active in STG).

MAJOR SYNDROMES, SYMPTOMS, AND PROBLEMS TREATED

Patient selection involves making decisions about whether particular patients are included in or excluded from various groups. The aim is to avoid such events as premature termination and treatment failure. Selection is determined, in part, by the group therapy process that is required to achieve therapy objectives. Over time, the patient must be able to engage in optimal psychodynamic group processes (i.e., experiencing, investing, and examining). A number of common selection criteria have been suggested for the different forms of POGT. These include motivation for treatment, motivation to change, interpersonal skill, psychological mindedness, ability to form give-and-take relationships, susceptibility to group influence, ability to tolerate the group situation, and willingness to help others. It has been suggested that minimum levels of these criteria are required, although the specification of what constitutes a minimum level has rarely been provided. Given that Axis I disorders of the *Diagnostic and Statistical Manual of Mental Disorders* (*DSM*; American Psychiatric Association, 1994) focus on symptoms rather than interpersonal behaviors and problems, the *DSM* is not particularly helpful in contributing to selection decisions regarding POGT. Many patients with Axis I disorders (e.g., mood disorders, anxiety disorders, adjustment disorders, posttraumatic stress disorders) may benefit from POGT. More relevant are Axis II disorders (i.e., the personality disorders), which typically manifest themselves in interpersonal dimensions. For example, Borderline Personality Disorder patients have tumultuous interpersonal relationships related to feelings of dependency and hostility. They tend to distort their relationships by putting people into either an all-good or an all-bad category. They also tend to perceive people as either nurturing and secure attachment figures or hateful and sadistic persons who deprive them of security needs and threaten them with abandonment. As a result of such splitting, the good person is idealized, and the bad person is devalued. Shifts of allegiance from one person or group to another are frequent. Furthermore, some borderline patients cannot tolerate being alone; to assuage loneliness, if only for brief periods, they sometimes accept strangers as friends or can be promiscuous. Many patients who participate in POGT have borderline or other Axis II disorders. Exclusion criteria for patients who are unable to engage in optimal psychodynamic group processes have also been offered. These include patients who are in crisis, acutely suicidal, psychotic, organically dysfunctional, antisocial, and engaged in active substance abuse.

Selection is also determined by the particular structure and objectives of the group. In LTG, patients must have the ability to work over a long period of time; they should also have salient problems involving interpersonal relationships. In STG, patients must have the ability to bond and work in a short period of time and to tolerate the preset termination date; they should also have the specific problem (e.g., difficulty adapting to loss) that is common to all patients in the group.

CLINICAL CASE EXAMPLES

Next, clinical examples of an LTG and an STG are presented. In each case, information about the background of the group and a focal patient in the group precedes presentation of a session vignette. Commentaries are made throughout the vignettes; these are indicated in italics.

Then, some observations about the vignette are made. The LTG is presented first. The specific area of focus of the STG is loss. Each of the patients had experienced difficulty adapting to the loss of one or more significant persons through death. Since 1986, we have conducted over 60 such groups in a clinical program developed to treat patients with complicated grief (Piper, McCallum, & Azim, 1992).

LONG-TERM PSYCHOTHERAPY GROUP

Background

Originally, there were 10 patients in this open-ended, long-term psychotherapy group led by a male therapist. As in most new groups, there was a period of initial adjustment. Three patients dropped out of the group in the first few months; one new member was added after 11 months. The group composition (8 patients, 1 therapist) remained stable for the next 7 months. At 18 months, a female cotherapist joined the group. She was completing her requirements for professional registration as a psychologist; the male therapist was her supervisor. A number of significant changes followed. One patient moved to another city. A second patient dropped out after 26 months in the group; the departure was hasty and premature. This left six patients in the group. Three new patients were subsequently added; the group was informed of the addition of the new patients two months prior to their arrival. The following vignette is an excerpt from a session that occurred two weeks after their arrival. The interaction begins with people talking about Carla, a new group member. The work of Ellen is the focus of the vignette. She sorts out her reactions to Carla's arrival and, in particular, her sense of Carla's capacity to express her emotions.

Diagnosis and Assessment

Ellen was a 36-year-old single woman who presented to an outpatient psychiatric clinic with complaints of "loneliness and worthlessness." She had few friends, was socially isolated, and had an unfulfilling relationship. Ellen was the only daughter in her family. Her family showed little affection for one another, which contributed to her feelings of loneliness as a child. Ellen's father was described as "controlling" and "rejecting." Ellen perceived her mother as being afraid of her father, which left her feeling distanced from her mother. She noted feeling hurt that her father could not appreciate her. Ellen was diagnosed with Dysthymic Disorder and referred to long-term group psychotherapy. Throughout the course of the group, Ellen was relatively quiet, often silenced by her shame of making her needs known.

ANNE: Carla, I find you more threatening than Bob—just because of your personality. (Silence.)

THERAPIST: What is it that threatens you about Carla? (Pause.) You said it almost... (Silence.) Is it because she came in and sort of tried to take over the group?
(Therapist is focusing on current interpersonal interaction.)

ANNE: Um hmm. More domineering. The way that she's, um, she's dominating you, I guess. She's... uh, she's, yeah, she's consuming a lot of your attention right now.

CARLA: That's the first time I ever heard anything like that. It's funny because when you say that I get this feeling it's almost like happy like, oh my god—you actually think I'm dominating, oh my god—thank you, haha, I want to bow down like you're so great ha, like so you think that way but I'm really not, ha. On the other hand, I'm just—I—I'm—I'll just shut up, I'm sorry.

THERAPIST: What is it Anne? Can you put your finger on what's...
(Therapist attempts to clarify the dynamic issue.)

ANNE: She's trying too hard or something...

THERAPIST: There's something scaring you, though.

ANNE: Her aggressiveness.

THERAPIST: You mean she's aggressive as in you're afraid she's going to be angry...

ANNE: No, no, no. Her aggressiveness for attention bothers me.

THERAPIST: It seems to me that, although Carla can keep up with the rest of you when she doesn't want to admit she's having a feeling, when she gets into her feelings, she leaves everybody in the dust. I think you're reacting to the possibility that you might think because she's so emotional that she's going to seduce me somehow—get all my attention and leave you sitting out there somewhere.
(Therapist interprets the group's fear of being abandoned.)

DORIS: You're in a dream world. (Anxious laughter in the group.) To say to all of us that you're going to seduce her into getting all her attention. I mean...

THERAPIST: That *I'm* going to?

DORIS: Yeah. Well—that she's going to...

ELLEN: But that has crossed my mind. Carla, you're able to open up just like that and it takes me—I've been here for how long and, um, I envy you for that.
(Ellen confirms the therapist's interpretation.)

THERAPIST: Well, to be fair, um, the anger that you have—that you're talking about, you old group members—really belongs toward the therapists and you can't really deal with us. I think it's easier to take it out on Carla at the beginning even though I know you have feelings of anger just because they [the new members] are here. We brought them here. I think all the swearing in the room and all that stuff is because of anger toward the therapists.
(Transference interpretation.)

ELLEN: We feel that maybe we—or maybe I'm just not good enough for you—you had to bring somebody else in.

THERAPIST: Well, you must have a lot of feelings toward us about that if that's how you feel you're being treated.

ELLEN: Yeah. I wasn't good enough, you had to abandon me almost and go on with somebody else.
(Ellen identifies theme of abandonment.)
THERAPIST: Who is it you feel is abandoning you, Andrea [cotherapist] or me?
(Clarification of transference dynamic.)
ELLEN: Oh, it's definitely you.
FRANCES: Why did you say that? Because I feel that it's Andrea who's abandoning us by the fact that she's leaving [upcoming maternity leave].
ELLEN: I'm sorry?
FRANCES: I said why is it you feel that Scott [therapist] is abandoning us, because Andrea already is abandoning us? And I've been feeling like that since you announced you were having a baby—three weeks ago—two weeks ago.
ELLEN: I think it's because Scott is the more dominant one. I see him as having more authority and it's him that I look for more approval from than Andrea.
FRANCES: And that's how I thought I was until I realized how angry I was—because you're leaving [to Andrea]. I felt abandoned there, you know—so—strange.
(Confirms therapist's references to abandonment.)
THERAPIST: So, Ellen, in your heart of hearts it feels like Carla is the one that I'm more interested in now than you.
ELLEN: (Silence, tears.) Well, I felt there was a bond and it's been taken away—that somebody newer and better has come along.
THERAPIST: Can you put that bond into words—of what was it made?
ELLEN: Accepting, mutual respect. (Silence.) Almost like a friendship a little bit. (Silence.) That's pretty much it.
CARLA: I envy you.
ELLEN: In what way?
CARLA: I envy you that you have control over your emotions.
ELLEN: (Silence.) It's funny—while I'm envying you, you're envying me. (Silence, tears.)
THERAPIST: What are you feeling, Ellen?

(Therapist attempts to deepen Ellen's emotional experience.)
ELLEN: Sad.
THERAPIST: It might be good to say more about that.
ELLEN: I'm feeling a bit more bonded to Carla now, but sad. (Pause.) Sorry for myself. (Pause, tears.)
COTHERAPIST: It's a way of chasing away the sadness—you have things to feel sorry for. What's the sadness?
(Cotherapist gets Ellen to clarify her feelings and defensiveness.)
ELLEN: (Sobs, tears.) I think all my inadequacies—my inability to let my emotions go—to express myself. [To Carla] It's funny that you say that you envy that because I wish I could be freer with them. It's very frustrating that I can't express myself the way I'd like to.
CARLA: Did you ever have those feelings that you had to be perfect?
ELLEN: Always. (Pause.) Perfect was not showing emotions.
THERAPIST: Now you're feeling that I'm throwing you over for a woman who is full of emotions and you can't figure out why I'd be doing that when you've been so good for all this time . . .
ELLEN: (Tears.) Yeah . . . (Silence, tears.) I just keep relating it to my father, feeling I had been thrown over for my brothers. (Pause, tears.) Because I wasn't a boy.
(Ellen makes link to past genetic system.)
THERAPIST: It's been your attempt to be someone your father could love more when you try not to have your own feelings—you tried not to have your own feelings—not to show them.
(Therapist interprets Ellen's chronic suppression of feelings as a way to gain her father's approval.)
ELLEN: Yeah. (Tears, silence.)
GEORGE: I couldn't figure out why I was reacting to Carla and I just made the connection. She reminds me so much of my mom. You're very vocal. (Pause.) Loud, and my reaction is because I just feel like cringing. My mom was always very expressive and loud. I found that

very hard to take. It was almost like a verbal assault. Whereas the rest the rest of my family were more like Ellen, quiet and not expressive. I still find that anyone who is like that—loud and overly emotional, very boisterous or anything—I tend to back away. I have a sort of built-in dislike for type As I guess. (Pause.) I have a perception of myself that I can be very much like that at times and I didn't like it and so I become very cautious about how I express myself.

(Peer transference. George makes a link between Carla and his mother.)

FRANCES: (Silence.) Are you like that with type As that are males or just type As that are females?

GEORGE: I don't know.

CARLA: (Tears.)

THERAPIST: Can you put it into words?

CARLA: Thank you for being honest. (Silence.) What do you mean by loud?

GEORGE: (Ahem.) Very strong feelings. You really project how you feel—if you're nervous it really shows, if you're happy you're laughing, if you're angry you say so, and I'm personally not very comfortable with that because I tend to restrain all that. Maybe I think I'd be able to be comfortable with doing that myself but I'm not. (Pause.) In the past few weeks I've been talking about harder situations that have been happening at work—being criticized for being very opinionated and, well, basically I've been called an asshole numerous times. I think that it's because of that—because of how I conduct myself. Maybe there's a lot of negative undertones to it, a lot of anger behind it. I'm not really sure but people seem to take me the wrong way sometimes. (Pause.) I'm struggling with saying what's on my mind but still trying not to be offensive.

(George comes close to linking his parental family, his workplace, and the therapy group.)

COTHERAPIST: You said when your mom was boisterous you would cringe. What were you cringing from?

GEORGE: (Sigh.) I'm not sure. It wasn't always happy boisterous. It was—if I can use the expression—more PMS. When I was younger she was pretty bitchy and she seemed like she was angry all the time and I didn't like her like that at all. As I grew older, I noticed how patient my dad would be with her. She would sometimes beat on him. She never really did it a lot with me but she did it a lot to him and I always felt like I wanted to defend my dad or protect him from that. I grew to dislike her because of that. I didn't say anything but I still definitely noticed it—maybe I was afraid she would turn on me.

COTHERAPIST: Maybe you felt it was wrong to have your feelings. I mean, here you often talk about wanting . . .

GEORGE: I don't think there was much room for anybody to have their feelings except for her. She was extremely strong at times. I mean, at the dinner table sometimes you could hear a pin drop.

ELLEN: That's how it was with my dad too. You weren't allowed emotions very much but he was certainly allowed his anger.

DORIS: That's how my mom was too.

ELLEN: When he'd come home from work you weren't allowed to talk to him until he had taken his nap, until he had read his paper, until he had had his dinner, until after he had watched the news, or otherwise you'd really get it. "Do you mind. I'm trying to read the paper or watch the news—I don't have time for you."

GEORGE: I remember the same kind of thing. When she came home from work we were all at home sitting around the kitchen table. She walked in, put a couple of groceries in the fridge, and said "Why is everybody here so goddamn bitchy?" and kinda stomped out of the room. Nobody had said a word.

ELLEN: My mom and I would be sitting talking at the table and my dad would come in and say to her, "What's she bitching about now?" There were times when I'd just get really depressed and I'd be crying and crying and crying. I'd just want to close myself off because I would get hurt if they found me—"Smarten up, you're just looking for attention." They'd say all these things because they didn't want to deal with it. Which of course would set me off more because I was just looking for comfort.

GEORGE: I got comfort from my mom. She could actually be very loving, but you were always kinda wondering when she'd snap.

ELLEN: I feel that too much of my life was spent trying to gauge my dad's moods. Trying to . . . he was totally unpredictable. I felt too much time was spent tiptoeing around him. I really resented that he had so much control over us and I resented the rest of the family for never challenging that. They'd be mad at me when I did.

Theoretical Approach and Rationale

This vignette demonstrates many characteristics of optimal group process for POGT. The group is very much in the throes of adapting to the recent addition of three new patients. This is in the context of having experienced five dropouts, one previous patient addition, and one cotherapist addition in its life of just over two years. The "old" patients likely have a good sense of what such disruptions can mean; nevertheless, they are a mature group and waste no time in working on the problem. The vignette begins with a self-disclosure by one of the old patients (Anne) about her reactions to one of the new patients (Carla). Carla's initial reaction is to ramble regressively. This is the beginning of a whole series of examples of the patients reacting affectively and verbally to each other. For the most part, they receive peer feedback in a nondefensive manner. Similarly, their responses to therapist interventions are receptive. In one instance, after some initial resistance voiced by Doris, Ellen confirms the therapist's interpretation concerning the group's fear that Carla will consume all his attention. In another instance, Frances confirms the therapist's reference to abandoning but applies it to the cotherapist. In both instances, the patients not only confirm the therapist's input but attempt to work with it.

The focal patient, Ellen, was particularly work-oriented. It was she who originally identified the theme of abandonment. Later, she made the link between the therapist and her father. In the same tearful statement, she also mentioned the role of her brothers, thus clarifying the theme of sibling rivalry in the group. This seemed to inspire George to make a link between Carla and his mother, an example of referring to a horizontal (peer) transference in the group. George also disclosed material about work and came close to linking three different situations: his parental family, his workplace, and the therapy group. In an affectively charged sequence, both Ellen and George traded memories about one of their expressive parents who was also controlling and blaming. With assistance from both the other patients and the therapists, Ellen, in particular, was able to understand her current behavior in the group in terms of a long-term pattern consisting of unsuccessful attempts to gain recognition, suppressed feelings, and self-blame. What is especially notable about the vignette is how much the patients assisted each other in understanding their conflicts and offered useful interpretations to each other and themselves. Clearly, the patients were experiencing, investing, and examining.

Next, let us consider the role of the therapist and cotherapist in the group. The therapist initially restricted his interventions to requests that patients clarify their use of words (e.g., threatening, aggressiveness). Then, he made a transference interpretation to the entire group about getting all his attention, thus connecting the tension in the group to himself. He soon followed this with a second transference interpretation to the subgroup of old patients about their anger toward both therapists and its displacement from the therapists to Carla. The therapist was persistent in attempting to get the patients to clarify their reactions, particularly their feelings toward each other and the therapists. The focus was very much on the here and now. In addition to making interventions to the entire group, the therapist eventually focused on Ellen, the focal patient. The cotherapist assisted in getting Ellen to clarify her feelings and defensiveness. The therapist then made an individual interpretation to Ellen about her chronic suppression of feelings to win her father's approval. For the remainder of this part of the session, the group required only minimal facilitative comments and questions by the therapists to sustain an active working process that involved five of the patients. The therapists wisely let the patients make many of the connections and links to other people and situations. Once primed by the therapists, they worked nearly independently.

SHORT-TERM PSYCHOTHERAPY GROUP

Background
The group is composed of patients who are experiencing difficulties associated with complicated grief. Treatment consists of 12 90-minute sessions, once per week. Eight patients started therapy together; one patient dropped out after three sessions and seven patients completed therapy. There is a male therapist. The vignette is from the final session, which is typically intense. The focus of the vignette is on Ed as he struggles to accept and express ambivalent feelings about his losses and the loss of the group.

Diagnosis and Assessment
Ed is 43 years old. Ten years earlier his only son, age 4 years, died of cancer after a prolonged illness. Four years after their son's death, Ed divorced his wife. He struggled with the losses and drank considerably on a daily basis. A year before he entered therapy, Ed's mother passed away, also of cancer. Ed attempted to bury his feelings by helping other family members with their grief. It was clear that his mother's death had forced unresolved feelings about losing his son to come to the surface. Ed used an overly intellectual approach to deal with his emotional difficulties. He was diagnosed with a severe major depressive episode. Throughout the group, Ed continued to avoid his feelings. He seemed to become quite attached to other group members and the therapist. In each of the three sessions leading up to the final session, he had asked the therapist if what the group was going through was "normal." He was unable each time to work with the meaning of his inquiry.

ALICE: If we don't get our daily—our weekly—here—where are we going to get it—our—for me a crying jag—for anyone else . . . (Pause.) The interaction with people that understand. *(Alice begins the session by expressing fear of the group ending.)*

THERAPIST: Yeah, the fear is there that, uh, the thing that people have a hard time embracing are the feelings around the disappointing group or the bad group—the ending group. You don't really want to deal with these except by trying to make me answer questions or force me to do this or that. (Pause.) And you're still holding onto something for everyone. Ed, you're the most—you've been pushing for this for four weeks in a row now. I think you owe it to yourself to give up your stubbornness and try to get into what it is you're trying to get from me. What is it about me that's been frustrating you—the me that hasn't been enough for you—that might be related to how stuck you got after losing your son and your mom?
(Interpretation of the group's fear about termination and expressing negative feelings. Transference interpretation directed at Ed.)

ED: I don't know.

THERAPIST: You gotta go farther than that . . .

ED: I just don't know.

THERAPIST: What is it—it's about emotions—what you're feeling. Try to put them into words. (Silence.)

ED: (Looking stricken.) It's not going to come. (Pause.) It's not going to come.

THERAPIST: This is everybody's dilemma, not just Ed's. Brenda, you're the second most pushy in terms of asking questions—trying to get something—so my guess is you're also in touch with the same thing this guy's in touch with. If only somebody could start putting it into words. What's behind all this pressure on me?
(Therapist expands transference interpretation to include the whole group.)

BRENDA: Well, my feeling is that our conditions are hopeless—this didn't help . . .

THERAPIST: That's definitely the feeling.

BRENDA: We had high expectations—I did.

GLORIA: Maybe Ed felt hopeless when he lost his son and he lost his mom. He was his son—he couldn't save him. Being a parent you think that you're supposed to be able to protect your children from all the bad in the world. That's gotta be a helpless feeling to not be able to help them. (Pause.) You have no control over your circumstance. When I look at Ed I get so anxious for some reason. Fiona and Ed both have so much pain. They can't let go. I worry about Fiona because she said if this didn't work she didn't know what she'd do.
(Gloria provides an interpretation for Ed.)

THERAPIST: It's going on inside of you as well—the very same thing . . .

GLORIA: Maybe . . .

THERAPIST: You're on the verge of tears too—it's all about you. All of you are in the same boat.

HELEN: You feel like they do, so you can relate to the same pain.

GLORIA: I guess I feel for them.

THERAPIST: And for yourself.

GLORIA: Getting up in the morning and seeing hope for the future, not just getting through another day. (Silence.)

ALICE: But isn't that why we're asking Where do we go from here? Because we know we're not whole yet? (Silence.)

THERAPIST: Can you speak for yourself? Do you know you're not whole?

ALICE: Yeah!

THERAPIST: And what does that feel like?

ALICE: Well—frustrating, for one thing. After putting in this period of time I know I'm better, but I'm still not whole.
(Alice identifies feeling frustrated.)

THERAPIST: Maybe people just cannot admit at this point that you're feeling a lot of anger that this thing's coming to an end.
(Therapist asserts that the patients are angry.)

BRENDA: I think the way we feel is that we could almost start all over again. (A few people laugh.)

THERAPIST: Well, it's a nice fantasy you could use to try to cope with what you're feeling now. (Pause.) But you're angry.

ED: Well, I'm not happy.

THERAPIST: You're angry.

ED: Um hm.

THERAPIST: You're angry with me.

ED: Not really. (Silence.)

IRENE: Nothing personal but . . .

ALICE: I have a hard time dealing with anger.

THERAPIST: You can join the club today.

ALICE: When I get upset and angry with somebody I end up in tears, even when I'm giving them a piece of my mind. I will cry through the whole thing. I can't handle my anger or anger from anyone else. More often than not I end up crying. (Pause.) Unless I completely block it out. (Silence.)
(Alice acknowledges her defense of becoming tearful when feeling angry.)

THERAPIST: Ed, when you ask "Is this normal?", I think you're trying to avoid how angry you are. (Silence.)

ED: I don't know what's wrong. (Silence.)
(Ed continues to resist acknowledging anger.)

GLORIA: Try to get it out. (Silence.)

THERAPIST: [To the group] Does he look happy with me to you?

IRENE: No. I can feel his anger from here. (Silence.)

ED: I respect you.
THERAPIST: Is that easier to say than . . .
ED: I don't know you that well . . .
THERAPIST: Do you like me? You know, whatever "liking" means in this context?
ED: Yeah. (Silence.)
THERAPIST: So you don't know what to do with liking me and hating me at the same time because you're losing me—hating me because you don't feel I've been enough for you. (Silence.) What do you feel? You're feeling something, very powerful. So is everybody. (Pause.) You loved your mother.
(Therapist interprets Ed's ambivalence.)
ED: A lot.
THERAPIST: You couldn't possibly be angry at her for leaving you, could you? (Silence.) You loved your son.
ED: Mm hm. (Pause.) You're trying to get me to go to a place I don't want to go.
THERAPIST: I'm not trying to—you're already there. (Pause.) You couldn't possibly feel angry with him for leaving you. (Pause.) You couldn't possibly be angry at me for how you see me as responsible for ending this group, not answering questions and all that stuff. (Pause.) You're all in the same boat, by the way, with your attempts not to deal with that part of the group. (Silence.)
(Therapist links Ed's ambivalence toward the people he lost and Ed's ambivalence toward him.)
ED: I don't want to go there. (Pause.)
THERAPIST: No. You can't go there with me. You can't go there with your mom. You can't go there with your son. (Silence.)
ED: No. (Silence.)
GLORIA: What if you know it would make you feel better to let go?
ED: It doesn't. It hurts too much.
THERAPIST: You're not angry at those people?
GLORIA: I don't know if I'm angry—I don't think I am. (Pause.) Let's talk about Ed, haha.
THERAPIST: You see what I am getting at? (Pause.) I think in your own ways—in the ways things come about in groups like this— you've come to love this group and love each other and I guess love me. You just don't seem to be able to handle being furious with group—with me—for its frustrating parts.
(Therapist broadens interpretation to include the whole group.)
ALICE: I don't know how you can be angry at someone for leaving you—for dying when they didn't have a choice. If they had had a choice, they wouldn't have. (Pause.) So how could you possibly be angry?
THERAPIST: Nice try.
ALICE: Well rationalized, eh?
THERAPIST: For all the good it does you . . .
ALICE: Yeah. (Pause.)
(Alice concedes the possibility of feeling angry toward the lost person.)
THERAPIST: Just check out your feelings. You'll know you can be. (Silence.)

Theoretical Approach and Rationale

This vignette also demonstrates aspects of optimal group process, although there is considerably more evidence of resistance as well. This group is in the throes of experiencing their last session together. The vignette begins with a patient's (Alice) direct reference to fear about one consequence of the ending of the group (loss of people who understand). In response to the therapist's questioning, some of the patients disclose other feelings: Brenda adds feeling "hopeless"; Gloria adds feeling "helpless," although nonverbally she also communicates sadness. Her statement also provided a sensitive interpretation for Ed. Also in response to the therapist's questioning, Alice eventually identifies feeling frustrated. The patients have a much more difficult time acknowledging anger. Finally, Alice acknowledges her defense of becoming tearful when she is really angry. Perhaps the most resistant patient is Ed, the focal patient. Despite a concerted effort by the therapist to spell out the possibility that he is angry, he steadfastly resists acknowledging anger. Although in part a defensive action to divert attention away from herself, Gloria assists the therapist in encouraging Ed to get in touch with his feelings. As the vignette comes to a close, Alice's resistance to accepting the possibility of feeling angry toward people whom one has lost melts away as she concedes the point in response to the therapist's brief comments. Clearly, the women in the vignette were engaged in experiencing and investing and, to some degree, examining. Although Ed was very much engaged in experiencing, his investing appeared to be minimal. How much he was able to take in from the therapist and other patients regarding examining is not evident from his behavior in the vignette.

The therapist assumed an active role, which is typical for STG. Because there is a specific area of focus, in this group's case, difficulty adapting to the experience of loss, the therapist expects certain conflicts and themes to emerge. In this sense, the therapist is primed. Thus, with minimal prompting from Alice, the therapist provided a rather substantial dual interpretation: The first part addressed the group's fear about termination and their difficulty in expressing their feelings; the second part was an individual transference interpretation directed to Ed. When Ed resisted, the therapist again broadened the interpretation to include the entire group. In a directive style, he urged the patients to clarify their feelings and many did. Without much delay, he pointedly asserted that the patients were angry and that they were angry with him. After refocusing on Ed, he solicited the group's assistance in confirming the impression that Ed was angry. As the session continued, the therapist clearly laid out an interpretation about ambivalence, a common theme in loss groups. He made the link between Ed's ambivalence toward the people he had lost and Ed's ambivalence toward him. Then, once again, which is very common in STG, the therapist broadened the interpretation to include the rest of the patients. Such interpretations are based on the assumption that many of the patients share similar conflicts and on evidence from the group process.

POSTTERMINATION SYNOPSIS AND EFFECTIVENESS DATA

The therapist's impression regarding the groups just illustrated is that the patients who remained and worked clearly benefited from the experience. Although clinical impressions of patient progress in therapy groups can be informative, controlled, or comparative, outcome studies are required to confirm the efficacy of the group therapy approaches. Unfortunately, in the case of long-term therapy, such studies are extremely rare. Ethical considerations prohibit long-term control groups and resource limitations tend to prevent long-term comparative studies. An exception was a comparative outcome study carried out a number of years ago in Montreal by our research team (Piper, Debbane, Bienvenu, & Garant, 1984). The study compared the outcomes of four forms of time-limited therapy (short-term individual, short-term group, long-term individual, and long-term group) for a diagnostically mixed sample of psychiatric outpatients. The short-term therapies were of six months duration and the long-term therapies were of two years duration. The outcome results favored long-term group therapy and short-term individual therapy over long-term individual therapy and short-term group therapy. According to the impressions of the therapists, long-term group therapy was characterized by a high degree of involvement and attentiveness by both patients and therapists. In contrast, both the patients and therapist experienced difficulty in short-term group therapy. The absence of a particular problem focus may have contributed to the apparent lack of cohesion and sense of direction. Initial anxiety about working on sensitive issues in the presence of others was soon replaced by anxiety about ending the group.

The short-term group that was illustrated in this chapter differed from those of the comparative study described above by having a specific focus. All of the patients joined the group to work on difficulties related to complicated grief. Having a specific focus appears to be a decided advantage for short-term therapy groups. Accordingly, since 1986, we have provided time-limited short-term therapy groups for patients with complicated grief (Piper et al., 1992). Sixteen of the groups in our program (154 patients) were studied in a randomized outcome study involving immediate treatment versus delayed treatment (control) conditions. Treated patients improved significantly more than control patients on 10 of 16 outcome variables, including grief symptoms, general symptoms, interpersonal functioning, self-esteem, and life satisfaction. The improvements were clinically significant and were maintained at six-month follow-up. The findings from this randomized clinical trial clearly supported the efficacy of short-term group therapy for complicated grief and suggested that the treatment may have initiated therapeutic processes that continued well beyond the end of the groups.

SUMMARY

There are many forms of POGT; this chapter has focused on two in particular. LTG, with precursors in the late 1920s, has been valued by clinicians for many years. These clinicians shared the belief that multiple-person interactions could illuminate patients' inner conflicts and that group therapy could provide unique therapeutic factors. STG, which has evolved during the past 25 years, is a much more recent technical adaptation. It arose out of the belief that important objectives could be achieved in specific areas in a short period of time and out of societal pressure to develop more cost-efficient forms of therapy. Common to both forms of POGT are certain principles (assumptions) and concepts that have characterized psychodynamic theory for most of the twentieth century. Examples are psychological determinism and unconscious processes. A number of different schools have proliferated and differentiated under the umbrella of psychodynamic theory; these include drive, ego, object relations, and self psychologies.

Despite the differences in theoretical schools, most therapists attempt to facilitate a similar type of psychodynamic process in their therapy groups. This begins prior to the group's onset by means of careful assessment, selection, and preparation of patients for group therapy. After the group has begun and cohesion and strong working alliances have been achieved, both patients and therapists engage in a number of work-oriented behaviors. Patients engage in the processes of experiencing, investing, and examining. Therapists primarily clarify and interpret events in the group in relation to the patients' problems; this involves linking the problems to long-standing conflicts and trauma. Therapists also must attend to management issues to ensure that the structure of the group is conducive to optimal group therapy process.

Although LTG and STG share a similar theoretical framework and many features of optimal therapy process, there are important differences that should not be overlooked. These are most apparent in their differing objectives and structure. In LTG, the diminishment of interpersonal distress and the improvement of interpersonal relationships are primary. LTG provides an ideal structure for slowly but surely identifying patients' interpersonal problems and their bases, and promoting adaptive interpersonal changes. Given the length of time, working through is facilitated by the ongoing group process; as life events occur, they can be examined in the group and integrated with the group's work. In contrast, the objectives of STG are more focused and limited in scope. When interpersonal insights and changes occur in STG, they usually refer to a specific area of focus and the associated set of relationships (e.g., those who have lost loved ones and those who are grieving). There is an acute time pressure in STG, which is very different from LTG; this creates a productive pressure to work, yet, only so much material can be covered before the group ends. Thus, opportunities for working through and bringing about characterological changes in patients in STG are inevitably more limited and narrower in scope.

In the current era of health care reform, there is much pressure, primarily for economic reasons, to develop short-term forms of therapy. Many third-party payment sources restrict their coverage to brief treatments. In such a climate, there is obviously an opportunity for short-term forms of POGT such as STG to provide useful treatment to patients. However, they should not be viewed as a substitute for long-term forms of therapy such as LTG. Each type of group pursues and achieves different objectives. In addition, the point is often overlooked that the cost per patient of treatment in LTG is often similar to the cost per patient of treatment in short-term individual therapies. It appears that advocates of STG and LTG will have to continue to expend considerable energy in informing the various parties in health care systems of the nature and benefits of these useful therapies if they wish them to remain viable and available.

REFERENCES

Alonso, A. (1989). The psychodynamic approach. In A. Lazare (Ed.), *Outpatient psychiatry: Diagnosis and treatment* (2nd ed., pp. 37–58). Baltimore: Williams & Wilkins.

Alonso, A., & Rutan, J. S. (1984). The impact of object relations theory on psychodynamic group therapy. *American Journal of Psychiatry, 141,* 1376–1380.

Alonso, A., & Swiller, H. I. (1993). Introduction: The case for group therapy. In A. Alonso & H. I. Swiller (Eds.), *Group therapy in clinical practice* (pp. xxi–xxv). Washington, DC: American Psychiatric Press.

American Psychiatric Association. (1994). *Diagnostic and statistical manual of mental disorders* (4th ed.). Washington, DC: Author.

Anthony, E. J. (1971). The history of group psychotherapy. In H. I. Kaplan & B. J. Sadock (Eds.), *Comprehensive group psychotherapy* (pp. 4–31). Baltimore: Williams & Wilkins.

Dies, R. R. (1992). Models of group psychotherapy: Sifting through confusion. *International Journal of Group Psychotherapy, 42,* 1–17.

Fairbairn, W. R. D. (1952). *An objects relations theory of the personality.* New York: Basic Books.

Freud, A. (1936). *The ego and the mechanisms of defense.* New York: International Universities Press.

Freud, S. (1964). An outline of psychoanalysis. In J. Strachey (Ed.), *Standard edition of the complete psychological works of Sigmund Freud* (pp. 1–87). London: Hogarth Press. (Original work published 1949)

Freud, S. (1967). *Group psychology and the analysis of the ego.* New York: Liveright Press. (Original work published 1921)

Gabbard, G. O. (1990). *Psychodynamic psychiatry in clinical practice.* Washington, DC: American Psychiatric Press.

Hartmann, H. (1939). *Ego psychology and the problem of adaptation.* New York: International Universities Press.

Horwitz, L. (1977). A group-centered approach to group psychotherapy. *International Journal of Group Psychotherapy, 27,* 423–440.

Kauff, P. F. (1993). The contribution of analytic group therapy to the psychoanalytic process. In A. Alonson & H. I. Swiller (Eds.), *Group therapy in clinical practice* (pp. 3–28). Washington, DC: American Psychiatric Press.

Kernberg, O. (1980). *The internal world and external reality.* New York: Aronson.

Klein, M. (1964). *Contributions to psychoanalysis: 1921–1945.* New York: McGraw-Hill.

Klein, R. H., Bernard, H. S., & Singer, D. I. (1992). *Handbook of contemporary group psychotherapy.* Madison, CT: International Universities Press.

Kohut, H. (1971). *The analysis of the self.* New York: International Universities Press.

Pine, F. (1988). The four psychologies of psychoanalysis and their place in clinical work. *Journal of the American Psychoanalytic Association, 36,* 571–596.

Piper, W. E. (1994). Client variables. In A. Fuhriman & G. M. Burlingame (Eds.), *Handbook of group psychotherapy* (pp. 83–113). New York: Wiley.

Piper, W. E., Debbane, E. G., Bienvenu, J. P., & Garant, J. (1984). A comparative study of four forms of psychotherapy. *Journal of Consulting and Clinical Psychology, 52,* 268–279.

Piper, W. E., McCallum, M., & Azim, H. F. (1992). *Adaptation to loss through short-term group psychotherapy.* New York: Guilford Press.

Piper, W. E., & Perrault, E. L. (1989). Pretherapy preparation for group members. *International Journal of Group Psychotherapy, 39,* 17–34.

Rutan, J. S. (1992). Psychodynamic group psychotherapy. *International Journal of Group Psychotherapy, 42,* 19–35.

Rutan, J. S. (1993). Psychoanalytic group psychotherapy. In H. I. Kaplan & B. J. Sadock (Eds.), *Comprehensive group psychotherapy* (3rd ed., pp. 138–146). Baltimore: Williams & Wilkins.

Rutan, J. S., & Cohen, A. (1989). Group psychotherapy. In A. Lazare (Ed.), *Outpatient psychiatry: Diagnosis and treatment* (2nd ed., pp. 645–654). Baltimore: Williams & Wilkins.

Rutan, J. S., & Stone, W. N. (1993). *Psychodynamic group psychotherapy* (2nd ed.). New York: Guilford Press.

Scheidlinger, S. (1993). History of group psychotherapy. In H. I. Kaplan & B. J. Sadock (Eds.), *Comprehensive group psychotherapy* (3rd ed., pp. 2–10). Baltimore: Williams & Wilkins.

Winnicott, D. W. (1965). *The maturational process and the facilitating environment.* New York: International Universities Press.

Wolf, A., & Schwartz, E. K. (1962). *Psychoanalysis in groups.* New York: Grune & Stratton.

Yalom, I. D. (1975). *The theory and practice of group psychotherapy.* New York: Basic Books.

Yalom, I. D. (1995). *The theory and practice of group psychotherapy* (4th ed.). New York: Basic Books.

CHAPTER 20

Psychodynamic/Object-Relations Group Therapy with Schizophrenic Patients

José Guimón

Though the theoretical orientation of psychiatrists has been altered throughout the past 20 years because of the impressive advances in the biological model, most mental health professionals continue to be interested in eclectic or generic approaches, which have frequently been called dynamic (Guimón, Fischer, Zbinden, & Goerge, 1998).

For psychiatry to be considered dynamic, it must take into account the importance of the unconscious and of transference. In addition, dynamic psychiatry has traditionally been linked to the concept of conflict arising between desire and defensiveness, between different components of the personality, and between instincts and external reality. It also takes into account concepts such as psychological determinism, deficits in intrapsychic structures, and internal object relations. Dynamic psychiatry is focused more on desires, fantasies, dreams, and self-image than on a meticulous description of the behavior observed. Nevertheless, it incorporates conceptions and procedures emanating from nonanalytical psychotherapeutic models (behaviorism, cognitivism, and general systems theory; von Bertalanffy, 1968), which have shown their efficacy in the treatment of certain disorders.

The procedures described herein for treatment of schizophrenic disorders can be characterized as dynamic rather than analytical psychotherapies. They also make use of object-relations theory. Among the psychoanalytical orientations, object-relations theory has offered, both to professionals treating these patients and to the institutions with which they are associated, the most interesting insights into the treatment of schizophrenic patients.

HISTORICAL ASPECTS OF GROUP ANALYTICAL PSYCHOTHERAPY

Techniques for use in groups have modified the traditional dyadic relationship of psychiatric treatment. Over the past decades, psychotherapists have had to take an interest not only in intrapsychic phenomena but also in the phenomena arising from groups and their interaction.

FREUDIAN CONCEPTIONS OF GROUPS AND INSTITUTIONS

Freud mainly expressed his concepts on groups in *Totem and Taboo* (1913) and *Group Psychology and Analysis of the Ego* (1922). The ideas that he presented therein are clearly related to those of several of his contemporaries. Le Bon (1896, 1952) spoke of certain precise phenomena arising in crowds: outbursts of unconscious phenomena and massive contagion of affects among individual members of the crowd. McDougall (1920) spoke of "disorganized" and "organized" masses of people; the latter were characterized by the existence of a common goal and convergent affects. Crocter (1921) pointed out the existence, within the individual, of a "gregarious instinct" that he defined as a natural tendency to join groups. These ideas were taken up later by authors associated with the object-relations approach of some members of the British school of psychoanalysis.

Freud established psychoanalytical technique as a verbal process to resolve unconscious conflicts through the analysis of transference created between two persons. Psychoanalysis carefully distanced itself from methods of suggestion. Nevertheless, in 1918, in Budapest, Freud had already recognized that, in the future, to make psychoanalysis accessible to a greater proportion of the population, it would be necessary to ally the "pure gold of analysis" with the "copper of suggestion." In the years that followed, Freud's disciples continued to interpret psychoanalysis as opposed to suggestion. However, by the 1950s, they were forced to recognize that other specific techniques, such as those derived from behaviorism, had a place in psychotherapy. Psychoanalysis also had to make room for numerous categories of psychoanalytical psychotherapy practiced individually or in groups.

It became obvious that groups do not offer the ideal setting for analysis because of multiple transferences and the impossibility of practicing free association. However, since the early 1930s, a strong analytical group psychotherapy has developed, based on different theoretical approaches (object relations, ego psychology, and self psychology) and techniques of group process pioneers at Tavistock Clinic in London.

FROM THE COUCH TO THE CIRCLE

At the end of the 1920s, Tringant Burrow (1927) became interested in the application of individual psychoanalysis to small groups. At the same time, group psychotherapy benefited from the support of distinguished psychiatrists such as Paul Schilder (1936), who, stimulated by the effects of unstructured discussion on the conflicts of seriously ill patients at Bellevue Hospital in New York, made the decision to undertake the same experience with small groups of patients suffering from neuroses. He favored interaction among members of the group. He considered them to be elements of one "body"—a concept similar to the one that would be developed later by Foulkes (1969), who, like Schilder, was under the influence of the "holistic" outlook of Kurt Goldstein on the functioning of the brain. Schilder maintained a strict attitude of neutrality and analyzed transference and resistance according to classical psychoanalytical methods.

Wender (1940) noticed that, during his hospital visits, psychotic patients' replies were more often appropriate when he had an open and frank discussion with them about their psychodynamic problems. Encouraged by this observation, he began to organize therapeutic groups. Adler underlined the importance of a social atmosphere of equality and mutual support in groups, and he insisted on the fundamental importance of these aspects in the therapeutic process.

THEORETICAL CONSTRUCTS

Wilfred Bion (1959), who had been analyzed by John Rickman and Melanie Klein, proposed some very original ideas based on his experiences in the recruitment units of the British army. He established an analogy between the child-mother relationship and that of the "group as a whole" with the leader. He considered that (1) the emotional situation of the group showed a regression to the first steps in development of the ego (schizoparanoid and depressive positions), and (2) the group's reactivation of psychotic anxiety and of primitive defenses (projective identification and splitting) against those steps was characteristic of childhood development in accordance with the theories of Klein. Bion identified what he called "the group mind" (a functional unit of members of a group arrives at a determined goal, whether consciously or unconsciously) of the "group culture" (the combination of the group mind and the individual feelings of each group member).

Bion (1946, 1959, 1962, 1965, 1970, 1972, 1977, 1989; Bion & Rickman, 1943) distinguished between two stages in the evolution of groups. In the first stage, the group functions according to "basic assumptions"—three primitive emotions that are always present in each individual and each group:

1. *Dependency*, especially when the therapist is considered to be the provider and nurturer of all that is good.
2. Paranoid tendencies of *fight/flight* toward internal or external enemies.
3. *Pairing* tendencies directed at the therapist or another member of the group. In fantasy, the fruit of this union can give birth to a "messiah" who resolves all difficulties.

In the second stage, "group work," what is dominant in the mentality of the group is the attainment of an outcome or a goal. In therapeutic groups, the goal is cure. Conscious cooperation among members of the group favors its realization and *valency*, but an instinctive process is opposed to it and complicates it.

For Bion, the interpretation carries the name *new idea*. He considers that the interpretation may lead the basic-assumptions group toward the *working group*. Faced with the new idea, the group reacts in particular ways (changing the leader, changing the group's basic position, or exhibiting "aberrant" reactions and "catastrophic" reactions). The group calls the person who brings the new idea a "genius" or "mystic" (or messiah).

With regard to the techniques of the group itself, it must be noted that Bion treated groups only from 1947 to 1949. He did not systematically write about group therapy, and his approach was implemented only after important modifications. Henry Ezriel, at the Tavistock Clinic, contributed the most to the development of the method of group psychoanalysis; however, Malan et al. (1975) obtained only meager clinical results for such groups. These methods are still in use at the Tavistock Clinic and in the Scottish Institutes of Human Relations, but are mainly used to train organization administrators who must frequently face primitive group processes.

METHODS OF INTERVENTION

Syndromes and Situations in Schizophrenic Patients

In this chapter, we refer to schizophrenic and schizophreniform patients as well as patients presenting schizoaffective disorders, short-term psychotic reactions, and schizoid and severe schizotypal personalities. For schizophrenic patients, numerous studies have underlined the better prognosis of certain paranoid features when compared to other, nonparanoid ones; thus, a better prognosis and a better response to phenothiazines are shown for patients presenting "positive" symptoms as compared to patients presenting mainly "negative" symptoms. Among the latter, it has been theorized that there is a loss of encephalic substance and a greater deterioration in cognitive function.

Furthermore, a survey of the literature provides some spectacular portraits of psychotic patients whose illnesses were documented as beginning suddenly and evolving in a positive fashion after psychotherapeutic treatment. To identify the illnesses, certain authors used the term "hysterical psychosis" (Pankow, 1969). Most authors consider that this type of patient is diagnosed as having a Brief Psychotic Disorder as described in the *Diagnostic and Statistical Manual of Mental Disorders* (*DSM-IV*; APA, 1994).

A large proportion of schizophrenic patients present a chronic deteriorating course even with new pharmacological procedures. Schizophrenic deterioration includes some cognitive difficulties and a lack of interest and energy, and these lead the patient to avoid the efforts of daily life. Under the heading "lack of social skills," a series of characteristics has been described that renders the chronic schizophrenic less apt to live in the community, at least in Western societies. It is well-known that, among the factors contributing to social ineptitude, the role played by hospitalization has been factored into the equation for several years. Because the traditional psychiatric institution represents a source of chronic illness and therefore of iatrogenic pathology, it produces an "institutional syndrome" (Barton, 1959; Goffmann, 1961) characterized by apathy, loss of initiative, disappearance of interest, inability to plan for the future, and disappearance of feelings of individuality.

For this reason, several authors have had a tendency to differentiate between the concepts of "clinical remission" and "social remission."

THE LARGE VARIETY OF GROUPS FOR
PSYCHOTIC PATIENTS

The developments described in group psychotherapy and the different syndromes covered in schizophrenia explain the great diversity in group therapy activities that can be observed in the treatment of schizophrenic patients. A distinction can be made among psychotherapeutic groups (those directed by professionals with the objective of treating dysfunction in patients); group therapy activities—"group work" in Foulkes's terminology (1969)—aimed at occupying, amusing, or increasing social interaction for participants; and didactic groups that train persons charged with the care of psychotic patients.

From the point of view of their composition, these groups are heterogeneous as to sociodemographic characteristics but homogeneous in the diagnosis of schizophrenia because this type of patient is very rarely included with patients who have other diagnoses. Two exceptions are: (1) the groups of staff and patients in the short-stay units of the general hospitals and (2) some long-term analytical heterogeneous groups in which very well-compensated schizophrenics are occasionally included.

Most of the groups that include schizophrenics are directed by two leaders. They may act as cotherapists, or one may be an observer who remains a "silent witness."

The groups are referred to as "closed" if they do not allow entry of new members once they have been set up (e.g., time-limited skill rehabilitation programs). They are "open" if new members may freely join (e.g., staff-patient groups in short-stay units) and "partially open" if one or more patients may enter when the leader judges it necessary (long-term outpatient groups). Differences exist among the durations of the groups. As with individual psychotherapy, until recently group psychotherapy generally had been considered a long-term treatment, limited to the psychoanalytic model. This orientation was later widened to encompass a psychodynamic orientation that incorporates learning techniques and systems theory. Furthermore, because of managed care, the need for short-term group psychotherapies has increased over recent years. The maximum is now 70 sessions. Criteria are: a predetermined time limit and a well-defined focus aiming for the shortest duration possible. The goals of short-term group therapy should be clear and limited, and the therapist must be active.

We shall now briefly describe some of the main types of groups formed with schizophrenics.

GROUPS WITH SCHIZOPHRENIC PATIENTS IN ACUTE EPISODES

In most Western countries today, schizophrenic patients tend to be admitted into the psychiatric units of general hospitals. These patients' short stay in these units encourages the use of biological rather than psychodynamic treatments. To minimize this bias, group analytical programs have been established at some short-stay units. In a previous study, the results of the program organized at Bilbao University Hospital, in Spain, during the past 17 years, were viewed as positive from a clinical standpoint (Guimón, Sunyer, Sanchez de Vega, & Trojaola, 1992). The researchers believed that these positive effects were the result of the atmosphere created in the wards.

Staff Group
This group meets early every weekday morning, for half an hour. All available personnel are in attendance. The goals are: to gather and to share information on the evolution of patients and on problems that have arisen in the ward since the previous meeting. Occasionally, interpersonal problems among members of the staff are also taken up. This agenda makes for a better understanding of the ward atmosphere and a more comprehensive approach to the patient. Interpersonal difficulties and interprofessional competitiveness are often dealt with under the guise of theoretical disagreement and appear at times in the form of tardiness, absence, or rationalizations.

Staff-Patients Group
This group is held early on weekday mornings for 45 minutes. All patients are urged to attend and do so, except under exceptional circumstances. The sessions are conducted by a skilled group analyst. Approximately 40 chairs are arranged in a circle, and the conductor is always seated in the same position. Most of the personnel attend; they usually sit close to the more disturbed patients. The goals of this "rapid medium-size open group" are: facilitate the integration of the incoming patients into this new environment, discuss the situation of the outgoing patients, and encourage patients' active involvement in their therapeutic plans. Although a psychoanalytical reading of the communication is undertaken later by staff, the interventions are carried out in a psychopedagogical vein.

The conductor actively encourages each patient to participate in an open discussion. Patients are asked to talk about the tensions and conflicts arising among them and with the staff. Attempts are also made to show them how these reactions are often distorted by their psychopathology. They are invited to talk about their general condition and to contrast their assertions with those of the other patients. They share objective and subjective feelings about their symptoms. The therapist in charge bears in mind some ubiquitous topics: reluctance to take medication, side effects, unawareness of the illness, and fears of being discharged.

Suggestions, protests, and patients' initiatives are worked out in the group by giving responsibilities to the members. Thus, once a week, the meeting takes the form of an administrative session wherein patients elect a president and a secretary from among themselves, and a plan of activities (plays, mural work, and so on) is organized. All this contributes to the development of healthy and creative tendencies among patients.

Within this group, the effort is to guide patients along the path from the abstract to the actual, from the delusional to the real. We foster communication and interpersonal relationships and try to involve patients in a setting that provides information concerning the many aspects of their lives, family, and friends. The presence of staff members in these groups enables patients to have a closer relationship with them. This dispels persecutory feelings and resolves conflicts that otherwise would persist. This atmosphere fosters openness and directness for the patients and the therapeutic team. Resistance arising in the patients, such as fear of criticizing others or of being punished, tends to rapidly disappear.

Irregular attendance on the part of doctors, which arises during certain periods under the pretext of overwork, reflects a devaluation of the group approach that can spread to the rest of the team. Nursing staff rotation also results in sporadic attendance and a lack of commitment to the group. Institutions that are reluctant to have their auxiliary personnel involved in these kinds of "specialized" activities often foment this response. These problems are best worked out through the participation of the staff in the postgroup meeting created for this purpose. In addition, this meeting provides a valuable means of sharing information about the patients.

Short-Term Verbal Group Psychotherapy
In units for short-term hospitalization where the goal is to improve communication, patients who have retained their verbal ability, and are neither too regressive nor too agitated, form a small group that meets five times a week for one hour. This is called a verbal session, and the leaders are very active. Certain conductors, in accordance with Yalom's (1983) precepts, put "game" or "go around" techniques into play. Others (such as those in Bilbao) have evolved toward more open meetings by instigating conversations in which the focus tends toward the usual recurring themes in these groups (e.g., circumstances that resulted in destabilization, problems caused by hospitalization, and the effects of medication).

To constantly stimulate verbal communication, the leader encourages patients to take advantage of these sessions to voice their preoccupations and vent their frustrations and complaints. This type of intervention commonly suits the state and personality characteristics that most often are dominant in this type of patient: oral gratification (often devouring and destructive); hostility (passively self-directed and/or destructive to others); the important deficits insofar as defense of the ego is concerned; and problems in adaptation and refusal and/or flight when faced with reality.

Leaders attempt to convey to patients a psychopedagogical understanding of the meaning of their symptoms and their relationship to situations in real life. One of the principal objectives is to render the patient sensitive to the possibility of following psychotherapeutic treatment after discharge from the hospital.

In accordance with Yalom (1983), we initially tried to conceive of each session as an independent unit. Eventually, we arrived at the conclusion that this tendency toward discontinuity is a defense against the spontaneous appearance of relatively profound dynamic elements that are continually in play from one session to the next. This obliges us to keep a certain analytical attitude. Concurrently, the appearance of intense transference that cannot be handled must be avoided.

Short-Term Group Work

In short-term hospitalization units, this type of group is organized in an informal manner. The intent is to keep up psychomotor activities in patients while promoting the possibilities of improving orientation and interaction with different members of the group. For patients who are suffering from severe mental disorganization and are incapable of maintaining a sufficient attention span, the verbal groups described previously are not suitable. Instead, they take part five times a week, for one hour, in what Yalom (1983) termed a "low group." (We call it a "focus" or "structuring" group.) This group may include patients who are not cooperative, hallucinating psychotics, patients suffering from delirium and severe regressive states, and patients who, though not psychotic, are too anxious or phobic to take part in groups functioning at a high level.

The session is organized, according to Yalom (1983), into several stages:

1. Orientation lasts 2 to 5 minutes. Therapists introduce themselves, explain what the group is, and describe its utility to patients.
2. Warm-up lasts 5 to 10 minutes. Staff members prepare several structured exercises (simple games) and comment on participants' physical and mental states, or feelings, in accordance with the group's situation in each session.
3. Structured activities last 20 to 30 minutes. One or two activities are chosen, in accordance with the group's daily needs: partial sentences to complete, lists of values, and exercises intended to increase empathy.
4. Review of the session is followed by a quick conclusion that covers the activities carried out.

Patients who take part in these groups are allowed to leave them when they wish. The atmosphere of each session must be reassuring and show empathy for the patient. Therapists focus their activities on helping patients to identify their problems, promote relationships among patients, and decrease levels of anxiety. All activities are centered on the here and now.

Patients who take part in this group sometimes perceive, in a negative manner, how it is different from the verbal group. Some therapists prefer to introduce patients into the different groups, not because of any diagnostic criterion, but in relation to their ability to communicate at the time of their arrival. This explains the existence of heterogeneous groups at the level of diagnosis, and relatively homogeneous groups when the possibility of establishing relationships with others is concerned. As already stated, interventions address problems in daily life, not unconscious conflicts.

Medication Information Group

Among the factors that influence negative attitudes toward psychotropic drugs, especially among narcoleptics, are cognitive, affective, and behavioral elements. Public awareness campaigns that focus on the indications for these products and the precautions to take against possible drug interaction and side effects could help decrease negative bias, which is especially prevalent (Guimón, Eguiluz, & Bulbena, 1993) among persons coming from more modest cultural and educational backgrounds. However, we are more pessimistic about the possibility of influencing all the other aspects based on affective elements, which are often unconscious and very difficult to change. In this connection, it is useful to recall that a campaign addressed to the inhabitants of a North American city, and waged through various media, did not, after several months, succeed, in any appreciable manner, in improving the attitudes of the population. Rather, it finally annoyed the very people it was meant to influence. Attempts to modify attitudes with regard to psychopharmacological substances demand, in addition to public educational programs, that campaigns be directed at specific target populations—for instance, the physicians who prescribe these drugs, the patients who take them, and their families.

A program intended to modify the negative attitudes of schizophrenic patients and their families toward medication has been ongoing since 1987 at the Civil Hospital of Bilbao (Eguiluz, González Torres, & Guimón, 1999). Patients took part in eight groups and their families in two groups. Each group lasted 90 minutes. The first 45 minutes were given over to a theoretical explanation of schizophrenia as an illness and information about neuroleptics and their collateral effects. The second part of the session was an open discussion. Patients who took part in this program have shown better compliance and fewer hospitalizations than those who did not. This kind of group is also employed, with some modifications, in the management of chronic schizophrenic patients.

GROUP PSYCHOTHERAPY FOR CHRONIC SCHIZOPHRENIC PATIENTS

Outpatient Programs
Our group therapy with schizophrenic outpatients in Geneva, Switzerland, is conducted in an outpatient facility. A cohort of 170 patients is treated continuously. The psychiatric hospital of Belle-Idée ensures, if necessary, short-term or longer-term treatments. Protected housing is also available to provide, in the medium term, space and extended therapeutic care for patients undergoing difficulties in daily life. In a recent survey, 45 patients who took part in the program presented expected risk factors: The majority were unmarried, more than half had no professional training, and two-thirds were living on disability benefits. From a clinical point of view, 15% had been in treatment for over 2 years, and more than half had been treated for more than 10 years. The social functioning of 75% of this group was poor or very poor.

The care program (Eiselé & Zannelo, based on Brenner, Hodel, Roder, & Corrigan, 1992) includes control over medication, individual help, social orientation, and a cognitive therapeutic program. This individually adapted program includes five subprograms (modules), all intended to remedy the patients' dysfunctional cognitive mechanisms and social and behavioral deficiencies. Groups of five to eight patients meet with one or two therapists for 30 to 40 minutes two or three times a week. The modules are organized in a hierarchical fashion and cover tasks circumscribed in increasing complexity. The initial interventions are aimed at improving attention span, concentration, and the patient's skills in social perception. Next, the interventions become centered on verbal and social responses, and, finally, activities are proposed that will teach patients to solve more complex interpersonal problems.

The first two modules directly address the vicious circles where dysfunction in elementary cognitive components is observed. Stimulation, represented by an improvement in cognitive skills, will increase the capacity to acquire social and adaptation skills. In the succeeding modules (from verbal communication to solving interpersonal problems), the behavioral repertoire of the patients increases; they become less vulnerable to social stresses, and the impact of cognitive dysfunction on their interpersonal abilities to adapt is reduced. After the first module, cognitive skills improved in a significant manner for one-third of the patients. The improvement in response in adapting to the stress of daily life could contribute to preventing hospitalization and decreasing the risk of backsliding in psychosocial stabilization, synonymous with chronic and definitive deterioration. The dynamics introduced by these modules gave most patients the impression that they had acquired control over their illness; they appreciated the defined nature of the program with regard to objectives and length of the sessions. Those who were less motivated could receive objective information about their disorder and improve the therapeutic alliance; they could also make progress in adopting self-help strategies, with an improved acceptance of the therapeutic programs.

Short-Term Groups

Among the important changes brought about by health insurance companies, short-term therapy of proven effectiveness has become the norm. But, in general, this form of treatment, which can be practiced only with patients presenting acute decompensations in short-stay units, is not applicable to chronic mental patients, who often require treatment for life. However, some time-limited approaches have also been tried with these patients.

Daniels (1998) proposed a short-term group treatment that can help to fill the breach existing between the quality of help and the ideal financial allocation of mental health care services for persons suffering from chronic mental illnesses. The results of this model of group psychotherapy, which combines active cognitive-behavioral and object-relation techniques, may bring about, according to the author, important benefits for persons who suffer from chronic social discrimination and negative symptoms. Because of the pioneering work of Liberman at Cammarillo and the Brentwood Hospital in Los Angeles, this type of technique already has shown its effectiveness with patients who were hospitalized for long periods.

Long-Term Psychoanalytically Oriented Groups

Analytical group psychotherapy with mentally ill patients suffering from chronic psychoses has often been an exasperating and sterile experience (Frankel, 1993) that creates intense emotional responses in leaders, and simultaneously reinforces a spiral of repetitive failures. As "prototypes" of the chronically ill, whether schizophrenic patients or others, different group models have been put forward. Among them is a program we developed and have implemented for more than 20 years at the Departments of Psychiatry of Bilbao and Geneva mainly in collaboration with Dr. Alerra.

The objectives of this type of dynamic group are: to promote the mechanisms that will contribute to structuring, in a progressive manner, the ego of the schizophrenic, while allowing the errors in the patient's perception to be addressed. Simultaneously, recourse to self-evaluation is stimulated to promote the reentry of patients into the objective "real" world, thereby facilitating the patient's processes of intrapsychic and interpersonal communication.

The technique implements the dynamics inherent in the present moment and in the comprehension of current relationships. The use of free association remains at a secondary level, having been replaced by techniques of maintenance and discussion. Without abandoning interpretation, the therapist does not build the transference around himself, but rather links it to the development of relationships of support with other members. Insofar as transference reactions are concerned, therapists try to redirect them into socially useful channels, while advising against any attitude that might provoke regressive tendencies and dependency on the therapist or on other members of the group.

It often happens, especially during acute manifestations, that the patient becomes verbally inhibited and displays confused attitudes of withdrawal and negativism. This set of behaviors must be considered as analytical raw material and accorded a much greater significance than traditionally has been given in the analysis of neurotics (Rosenfeld, 1976).

The world of schizophrenia allows certain behaviors to emerge. They act as compensatory defense mechanisms for an insufficiently formed ego that has been crushed by anxiety, and for the pressures of an archaic id that nourishes serious consequences and taboos (Searles, 1977). Accordingly, these groups try to favor mechanisms that contribute to structuring the ego of the schizophrenic in a progressive manner, and facilitating the processes of communication. This does not mean that the psychotherapist should call for intervention that might be completely superficial. These mechanisms need to be balanced with ego-adaptive interventions. Immediate and direct approaches to the genital and Oedipal elements contained in patients' illness are avoided because they generally provoke (Rosenfeld, 1976), in these patients, fantasies that further increase their psychotic compulsions.

Many authors, such as May and Simpson (1990), are very skeptical about the value of dynamic interpretations and "insight" for the chronic schizophrenic patient. We do not share this pessimism, although we cannot give any proof of our favorable impressions. For instance, a recent study failed to show any modification of the Karolinska Psychodynamic Profile after a group psychotherapy program with schizophrenics. However, it is well known that the benefits of therapies with an analytical orientation are not measured merely in percentages of reintegration or on scales of social rehabilitation. Their benefits are sometimes felt by patients themselves, in the form of emotional modifications that are difficult to gauge in an objective manner.

Several more or less active techniques have been proposed to improve the response of this type of patient to group psychotherapy. Correale and Celli (1998) describe a technique fostering the idea, particularly endorsed by ego psychologists, that the group may represent an a self-object of the ego (Kohut, 1977), and therefore has a value and particular powers. This theory may represent a useful perspective for studying the therapeutic factors offered by group psychotherapy with chronic psychotic patients (Klein, Bernard, & Singer, 1992). It is based on the creation, by the patient and the therapist, of "imaginary scenarios" that are reminders of the emotional resonance of a type of relationship that the patient experienced with a caregiver. These reminders would allow us to circumvent the mechanisms of separation, projection, and emotional self-mutilation, and to integrate the dispersed and fragmented mental elements.

These authors described a group of seven outpatients who were under pharmacological care at the same time. They had all previously suffered from serious psychotic disorders that affected their self-image and their ability to have affective relationships in a harmonious and satisfying fashion. Among other objectives, the leader tried to create an affective atmosphere capable of containing and allowing a prudent stimulation of the emotions, progressively activating confidence, and forming attachment to the group. Each member could experience the group as an object of his or her ego while finding the means of identifying with a collective entity; in consequence, the interpretations were addressed in an individual manner, and personal references were avoided. The authors favored an approach that was centered on the group but allowed interventions that implicated the patient's environment as a whole. By utilizing the model scenario as a theoretical framework, they admitted this hypothesis: Numerous interventions could not be considered to be complete in and of themselves, but could be considered as part of a web or scenario drawn together from several elements. The configuration of the scenario may result from the integration of slowly emerging elements of the narrative, so the stage cannot be entirely set from the very beginning of the group's work. Its explanatory value may emerge for the therapist only after a long period of time.

Other techniques based on analytical approaches have been used. Stone (1998) described a dynamic group treatment model that allowed chronic patients to determine the frequency of assistance. In this context, absences are formulated as acts of self-protection and self-stabilization rather than as resistance. Other authors say they have obtained good results with psychodramatic techniques, and the author has occasionally introduced a certain number of activation techniques of this type, based on analytical models (O'Donnell, 1983; Rodrigué, 1965) or systemic ones.

Rehabilitation Techniques for Deteriorated Patients: An Object-Relations Point of View

In addition to techniques based on psychoanalysis, the necessity of introducing group activities to increase the social abilities of patients and their adaptation to the community, became apparent in recent years. Most useful was a behavioral approach derived from the pioneering work of Liberman (1982)—in Cammarillo and in the Brentwood Hospital in Los Angeles—with patients who had been hospitalized over long periods. Some of these techniques have been integrated into psychodynamically oriented programs.

However, given the increased knowledge of symptoms of deficiency, it became apparent that even these simple learning activities were difficult to respond to because of cognitive deficits in certain patients. Some authors therefore tried to ameliorate basic deficits (e.g., Eckman et al., 1992). These authors described a technique for teaching skills in self-management of the illness through the use of cognitive methods—a technique that has been useful in overcoming or compensating for deficits in processing information and long-lasting cognitive deficits that are commonly found in schizophrenia (Eckman et al., 1992). Other studies have shown that good results were obtained with stress management techniques (Borelli & DeLuca, 1993; Starkey, Deleone, & Flannery, Jr., 1995).

Overall, the relatively few controlled trials on group psychotherapies have revealed serious methodological problems that limit the extent to which they can be generalized. Scott and Dixon (1995) surveyed the literature for clinical results of dynamic and supportive psychotherapies (both individual and for groups) and training programs in psychosocial skills. They found that the approaches oriented toward real-life situations seemed to be preferable to those of dynamic psychotherapies, in which orientation favors insight. They underlined the importance of targeting the acquisition of psychosocial skills that can be learned and maintained over time.

Multifamily Groups

Experiences in extended groups (more than 40 members, and sometimes up to several hundred members) are not easily carried out (Roberts, 1995) but can constitute a strong incentive for personal and social change. The extended group, as described and implemented by Kreeger (1975), de Mare (1983), and Ayerra (1997; Ayerra & Lopez Atienza, 1993), provides what initially would seem to be a disagreeable experience. Participants are allowed to experiment with "psychotic" symptoms, primal defense mechanisms, and insight into the political process (Roberts, 1995), through which they can create a veritable microcosm of life outside the family circle. For over 20 years we have included groups of this type in our seminars on block group training and specific seminars on extended groups. For those working with schizophrenics, these groups are remarkably useful sources for first-hand experience of psychotic feelings.

The objective of the groups is to provide support to families by offering a differentiated interpretation of the phenomena experienced in the family circle. They begin as psychopedagogical groups and are frequently transformed, little by little, into groups for open discussion. The multifamily group tries to overcome resistance arising not only from the patient, but also from within the families themselves. When they find common ground with other families going through the same difficulties, they can identify with their ongoing struggles.

In the experience of Garcia Badarracco (1990) and Ayerra and Lopez Atienza (1993), families take part, with patients and professionals, in groups of 30 to 35 people. The weekly sessions last 90 minutes. The members of the team sit next to patients or families who are undergoing the most delicate situations. Patients can choose to sit in "protected" locations according to their condition; very often, they are seated next to the group's therapists. In these sessions, fantasies arising from the subconscious or from transference are not interpreted; in contrast, anxieties, desires, and defense mechanisms are confirmed. Behaviors and interpersonal relationships are analyzed in an attempt to highlight the positive aspects and deep-seated affective needs that are often hidden beneath each conflict. The objective is to help patients find a path that lies between the rational and the irrational, and to go beyond it, to the emotional stage. When patients are confronted with the most primal anxieties, their responses take the form of more intensive investment and greater self-control. Prolonged silence is considered to be counterproductive. One characteristic of the group's therapeutic team is the spontaneity of its intervention. Team members renounce omnipotence and absolute knowledge; they prefer to appear simply as fellow human beings who furnish daily examples intended to promote trust. Over time, members of the group become the true cotherapists; they treat aspects that they have slowly succeeded in resolving. The presence of family members who have had positive experiences of this process is invaluable; they can guide others and give them hope.

The multifamily group is also useful when important decisions must be made regarding hospitalization, a possibly ill-considered and premature decision to leave the hospital, or changes in therapeutic projects. Such groups also help to prevent legal difficulties that could arise from these decisions.

Little by little, the group becomes more homogeneous and progressively leaves behind the dissociated pedagogical group (families/patients, sick/healthy, people who are knowledgeable/those who are uninformed). Families start to recognize that the same problems can be encountered in their children. In couples, conflictual situations start to appear. When it is understood that all group members are in the same predicament and have similar experiences, and that members cannot save themselves without help, acceptance crystallizes. This principle also applies to institutions and to society. Garcia Badarracco (1992) developed these groups to act as exceptionally useful instruments in treating patients with schizophrenia and other serious illnesses within the context of their "multifamily, psychoanalytical therapeutic community."

CASE EXAMPLE

Pierre was born in 1946, in Lausanne, Switzerland, the second child in his family. He had one brother and one sister. At the age of 4 years, because of frequent asthmatic bronchitis episodes, he was home-schooled by a private tutor. At the age of 6 years, he withdrew from his mother and attended school.

At the age of 7, he went to a religious school. He finished his baccalaureate at the age of 17. He has some memories of a homosexual teacher who sexually abused him. He was introverted, and said he had always wanted to be an artist or a movie director. As an adolescent, he was very religious and a perfectionist; he repressed his sexuality.

He described his father as a very rigid man who was always absent—a handsome man "whom women were attracted to." He had married at age 38 because his wife "chased after him, otherwise he wouldn't have." He had a job in which he had to change residences frequently, so the children remained with the mother. He wrote very often to the mother (never to the children), and when he came home on holiday, he would side with her in any disputes. The mother was described as very beautiful, authoritarian, "hysterical," ambitious, worried about money, always saying that she was going to have a heart attack ("which she never had"). She did not have a sense of humor.

When he was 16, Pierre had an infection of the penis, and he believed he had homosexual tendencies; he also had erotic fantasies about his aunt, and mild delusional thoughts about a friend who he thought was making homosexual advances to him. He went to a psychiatrist who told him he had obsessional-compulsive neurosis. Having interrupted his studies, he began to work at transient jobs but was not able to keep them.

At the age of 20, just around the time his father retired, he decompensated with agitation and paranoid ideation. At his arrival in an emergency service, an interview could not be carried out because he was aggressive with the staff and his movements had to be restrained. In an ulterior evaluation in a short-stay unit of that general hospital, he was disoriented, uncooperative, and reticent, and had delusional interpretations. At the beginning of his hospitalization, he was aggressive, agitated, and incoherent, and experienced auditory hallucinations and blockages in thought processes. After a few days spent with neuroleptics, he showed himself to be cooperative, correct, and adequate, and he referred to delusional ideas and interpretations that had existed in varying degrees of intensity over the prior four years. The delusions centered on a supposedly incestuous relationship between his brother and sister, around which he had organized his whole theory of human sexuality. Hallucinations and delusional interpretations disappeared progressively, although the nucleus of the delusion persisted. After some weekend leaves, he was discharged, although he still had a subdepressive mood. He then was followed by a psychiatrist with neuroleptic treatment and support therapy.

His sister, Marie, left the family's home for one year. During that time, Pierre was better psychologically and gained 10 kg in weight. When Marie came back, his problems reappeared. He began to tell her that he loved her, and he chased after her for six months, so she told these facts to her parents. Pierre thought Marie had denounced him because he *didn't* do anything with her. He then had to be hospitalized again, and he improved for one year with medication.

After his discharge, when he began again to harass his sister, he was placed in a halfway house for one year. While there, he began to be very delusional and had to be hospitalized. There he met Jeanne, who had been a patient there for three years. He related: "She was the 'Queen of the Hospital' and everybody was around her, to prevent her from committing suicide. I fell in love with her and, once, we escaped from the hospital and went to my place to make love, but I was impotent."

He continued to be with Jeanne, but he remained impotent. He then began psychoanalytically oriented individual psychotherapy (two sessions a week with one psychiatrist, and biological treatment with another). He found it difficult to speak about his impotence in psychotherapy; he feared sexual advances from the therapist. In addition, the therapist told him once that his apartment surely looked like a garbage dump. Pierre felt this wasn't acceptable, so he left the treatment and went to a female therapist.

In 1986, Jeanne left him, and he became very depressed. He came back to his family's home, and his sexual desire for his sister began again.

He thought she had agreed to have relations with him, but later thought it could be a delusion. When he thought she had accepted, he became terrified: "What can I do with my sister? I phoned Jeanne and I thought she had committed suicide because she didn't answer me, and I went to her place and found her in the kitchen with an overdose and carried her to the hospital. We began to be together again, but I was now in love with my sister and I didn't want to live with Jeanne. I began to be jealous of my brother because I thought he was interested in Marie and I thought they had a sexual relationship."

Then, Jeanne committed suicide. Pierre left his home and reproached his sister and mother for Jeanne's death. He stopped medication, went to a boarding house, and had ideas of killing his brother and sister. In a delusional state, he bought medication to kill them. He began to fantasize having sadomasochistic relations with his sister, and he did "crazy" things in the streets "as an anarchist." The police sent him to another hospital, but he escaped, went to the halfway house, and began to be depressed with delusional ideas.

At age 41, he again had sadomasochistic fantasies about his sister. He left the house again, stopped taking medication, and became aggressive. He broke down the entry door at the house of a friend and beat the man's wife. He had to be hospitalized, but, after a few days, he went to Marie's house and beat her and her boyfriend. He was then hospitalized for two months. From then until May 1988, at age 42, he had four hospitalizations and established a paranoid transference with his therapist. In June 1988, he abandoned his individual psychotherapy.

When his father died, in November 1988, Pierre was put into group psychotherapy, where he began to elaborate his grief at the death of his father. He participated very well in the group; for example, he told the others: "We speak here about personal relationships with very simple explanations. Everything that is considered mysterious in psychoanalysis is normal here. We speak about jealousy, anger, and madness, and not about strange words." In the group, he explained some dreams and distortions, idealizations, and projections. He doubted he would be able to love anyone after so much time without loving. He talked extensively about his delusions. His perfectionism, rigidity, and grandiosity were confronted by the other members of the group. He began to have emotional reactions when he spoke about abandonment, separations, and losses. In 1989, he was working well in the group, living in the apartment of a friend, and beginning to think about working.

In 1991, he was very well adapted to the group and had worked on the separation from his mother. He exhibited good participation in the group, and a part of his neurotic structure appeared. He spoke about his latent homosexuality, began to fantasize about making love with a transvestite, and said he dreamed of making love with a man. He had an internal dialogue with the leader of the group and thought about him when he was in need of something. He contested his previous grandiosity and omnipotence, and he accepted his limitations. In 1993, after five years in the group, he was psychologically stabilized.

When his mother developed dementia, Pierre began to be delusional and had sadomasochistic fantasies about his sister. While he was living with some friends in an apartment, he gave up medication. He went to a neighbor's house, was verbally abusive, and was hospitalized. After neuroleptic treatment, his aggressive behavior diminished, and he spoke about the delusional ideas that he had always had. He was discharged on Haldol.

He was next hospitalized for 10 days for psychomotor agitation. He was uncooperative, but after taking medication and speaking with his new girlfriend, he was more cooperative. His delusional ideas persisted. In July 1993, he had an agitation crisis and needed to be hospitalized for a few days. In July 1994, he began to live with a female who was a recovered cocaine addict who had a high suicidal risk and a previous pathology of anorexia nervosa. For the first time, Pierre was able to make love and established a relationship.

In December 1995, he joined a theater group. His girlfriend, who was less prone to suicidal ideas, went to psychotherapy. When he was assessed in January 2000, Pierre appeared integrated. His ego-adaptation capacity was higher, and recent stressful situations (always involving his girlfriend) had not produced new psychotic disorganizations. He acted in several plays with a theater group. He was very thankful to his therapist. When Pierre was alone and had difficulties, he established a vivid (almost hallucinatory) "inner dialogue" with the therapist. When he didn't want to go to the group, he asked that his chair be maintained in the group.

He recently had a dream:

> I dreamed that I would like to make a theater play about the day center where the group takes place. You may know that Arrabal was interested, in fact, in doing a play on schizophrenia, a theme that has been very seldom treated. I know this project of a theater play could be done with our therapist's help and the participation of the other members of the group, but, of course, I see the difficulties. I don't know if you would like to, but I could give you my impressions of the contacts I have. If you want, I can give you my ideas.

EFFECTIVENESS

This dream was symbolic of a degree of homeostasis and of reintegration of defense mechanisms that had resulted from the therapeutic process.

GROUP ANALYSIS AND INTERACTION

The first studies involving groups with a dynamic orientation but without a set time limit for schizophrenic patients hospitalized for long periods underlined the weak results of this therapeutic approach. In the same way, studies with schizophrenics in posthospitalization phases could not show that group therapy decreased the percentage of rehospitalization, nor that, more than other methods, it further improved the patient's capacity to adapt to society.

In contrast, certain studies showed positive effects with regard to variables on socialization and interpersonal skills (B. Levine & Postom, 1981; H. Levine, 1980; O'Brien et al., 1972). Subsequent studies (Gunderson, 1983; Mosher & Keith, 1980; Mosher, Vallone, & Menn, 1995) have shown that the results were positive when not only was the goal to be reached well defined—e.g., "interaction," in the work of Corder, Corder, and Hendricks (1971)—but specific activities ("motivational therapy" and "feedback through videotape") were set up to obtain this result. Furthermore, it was shown that group psychotherapy, when associated with pharmacotherapy, is more comprehensive, and the efficacy of medication improves treatment, even for profoundly affected patients.

Most authors agree that group psychotherapy benefits a large proportion of schizophrenics on an outpatient basis—80% according to Kanas (1986)—but studies analyzing its global effectiveness with hospitalized schizophrenics are inconclusive. However, in an overall evaluation of the literature, Kanas (1986, 1991) found that group therapy was effective in two-thirds of the inpatient studies.

May and Simpson (1990) stated that they obtained good results when psychotherapy was centered on daily activities, on difficulties in social relationships, on cooperation in taking medication, and on recreational activities. The bases for the focal programs, which were structured and generally of limited duration, were established.

Interaction-oriented groups were more effective than those using insight orientation (Kanas, 1991), which could even be harmful for schizophrenics. In our present study, items that were rated higher in our wards referred to aspects that could be enhanced by interaction. This favorable effect of groups on patient interaction is probably more evident in cases that require prolonged treatment.

The inpatient literature indicates that therapy groups that lasted longer than three months were more likely to be successful than those conducted for shorter periods of time. Only five of the studies favored the use of short-term group programs with schizophrenics.

Kanas (1991) also favors homogeneous groups for schizophrenics because they enhance cohesiveness and offer protection from the anxiety-provoking discovery techniques (long silences, emphasis on past conflictual events) frequently used in groups where other kinds of patients (borderline, neurotic, and so on) are present.

In our units, we prefer to assign patients to one of the two small groups in existence—not in accordance with their diagnosis, but in relation to the severity of the impairment of their overall orientation. This gives rise to groups that are heterogeneous in diagnosis but relatively homogeneous in their ability to relate to others. Of course, intervention does not address unconscious conflicts, but it can resolve questions of everyday life in a supportive vein.

One study we conducted (Guimón et al., 1992) showed that a comprehensive group-analytic program resulted in the use of lower doses of medication and fewer serious disturbances (aggressions, attempts at suicide, and runaways) in the wards. Moreover, patients tended to seek psychotherapeutic help more frequently when discharged.

SHORT-TERM DYNAMIC GROUP PSYCHOTHERAPY

In the 1990s, good results were shown in studies that introduced certain modifications in short-term dynamic group psychotherapy for schizophrenic patients. However, there has been a recent upsurge of interest in time-limited therapy groups with these patients. Kanas (1991) developed a model (9 discussion-oriented inpatient group sessions, and 12 closed outpatient group sessions) that has shown empirical evidence of efficacy when used in conjunction with antipsychotic medication. Stone (1998) reformulated a hypothesis that patients' absences from group were, in fact, acts of self-defense and self-stabilization rather than resistance, and this improved the results of the groups. Daniels (1998) proposed a technique, interactive behavioral learning, that actively combines cognitive-behavioral and dynamic techniques.

Nevertheless, even if the controlled studies of group psychotherapies for schizophrenics show serious methodological problems that limit their ability to be generalized (Scott & Dixon, 1995), the reality-oriented approaches seem to be superior to psychotherapies oriented toward insight. Research on models for learning psychosocial skills (both in individual conditions and in a group) shows that the skills targeted can be learned and maintained over time. However, a study by Hayes (1995) did not find a better evolution for schizophrenic patients who had followed training in psychosocial skills than for those placed in the control group. Mader et al. (1996) found modest results in absolute terms, and these results were limited to certain subgroups of patients, such as a group dedicated to schizophrenic patients' acquisition of social skills.

On the other hand, many psychoeducational attempts have been made in groups dealing with individuals (North et al., 1998) or families (Elmore & Young, 1996; Nightingale & McQueeney, 1996). A particular technique is aimed at attenuating "the expressed emotion" (Brown, Monck,

Carstairs, & Wing, 1958; Leff, 1994) of families, thus improving the outcome of schizophrenic patients. Most of these approaches have a cognitive-behavioral orientation. However, conducting this kind of group can be facilitated enormously by a thorough understanding of object-relations issues.

SUMMARY

The application of psychodynamic and object-relations theory to group therapy offers powerful insights to understanding and treating schizophrenic disorders. Group therapy has expanded the domain of the intrapsychic and dyadically oriented approach of early psychoanalysis, significantly broadening the reach to more disturbed populations. Although Freud outlined his concepts on groups, Bion made a paradigmatic shift in his new conceptualizations of group process. There are a variety of applications of group models to a broad spectrum of treatment needs for the schizophrenic patient. They can be used to help chronically hospitalized patients adapt to the community, change negative attitudes and increase medication compliance, and to learn psychosocial skills. Groups can be offered both in short- and longer-term formats and can be applied in outpatient, partial, and inpatient settings. In spite of methodological difficulties in many studies, the effectiveness of group therapy appears to be rather robust in that it seems to benefit a large number of both inpatients and outpatients.

REFERENCES

American Psychiatric Association. (1994). *Diagnostic and statistical manual of mental disorders* (4th ed.). Washington, DC: Author.

Ayerra, J. M. (1997). Grupo grande. *Boletin, 7,* 28–46.

Ayerra, J. M., & Lopez Atienza, J. L. (1993). *Grupo multifamiliar.* Paper presented at the Congreso Nacional de Psiquiatria, Bilbao.

Barton, R. (1959). *Institutional neurosis.* Brisstol: John Wright.

Bion, W. R. (1946). The leaderless group project. *Bulletin of the Menninger Clinic, 10,* 77–81.

Bion, W. R. (1959). *Experiences in groups and other papers.* New York: Basic Books.

Bion, W. R. (1972). *Volviendo a pensar.* Buenos Aires, Argentina: Paidos.

Bion, W. R., & Rickman, J. (1943). Intra-group tensions in therapy. *Lancet,* 678–681.

Bion, W. R. (1962). *Learning from experience.* New York: Basic Books.

Bion, W. R. (1965). *Recherche sur les petits groupes.* Paris: Presses Universitaires Françaises.

Bion, W. R. (1970). *L'attention et l'interprétation [Attention and interpretation].* Paris: Payot.

Bion, W. R. (1977). *Group dynamics: New directions in psycho-analysis.* London: Maresfield Reprints.

Bion, W. R. (1989). *Experiencias en grupo [Experience in groups].* Buenos Aires, Argentina: Paidos.

Borelli, M. D., & DeLuca, E. (1993). Physical health promotion in psychiatric day treatment. *Journal of Psychosocial Nursing and Mental Health Services, 31*(3), 15–18.

Brenner, H. D., Hodel, B., Roder, V., & Corrigan, P. (1992). Treatment of cognitive dysfunctions and behavioral deficits in schizophrenia. *Schizophrenia Bulletin, 18,* 21–26.

Brown, G. W., Monck, E. M., Carstairs, G. M., & Wing, J. K. (1958). The posthospital adjustment of chronic mental patients. *Lancet, 2,* 658–659.

Burrow, T. (1927). The group method of analysis. *Psycho-Analytic Review, 22*(10), 268–280.

Corder, B. F., Corder, R. F., & Hendricks, A. (1971). An experimental study of the effect of paired-patient meetings on the group therapy process. *International Journal of Group Psychotherapy, 21*(3), 310–318.

Correale, A., & Celli, A. M. (1998). The model-scene in group psychotherapy with chronic psychotic patients. *International Journal of Group Psychotherapy, 48*(1), 55–68.

Daniels, L. (1998). A group cognitive-behavioral and process-oriented approach to treating the social impairment and negative symptoms associated with chronic mental illness. *Journal of Psychotherapeutic Practice Research, 782,* 167–176.

de Mare, P. (1983). Michael Foulkes and the Northfield Experiment. In M. Pines (Ed.), *The evolution of group analysis*. London: Routledge.

Eckman, T. A., Wirshing, W. C., Marder, S. R., Liberman, R. P., Johnston-Cronk, K., Zimmermann, K., et al. (1992). Technique for training schizophrenic patients in illness self-management: A controlled trial. *American Journal of Psychiatry, 149*(11), 1549–1555.

Eguiluz, I., González Torres, M. A., & Guimón, J. (1999). Psychoeducational groups in schizophrenic patients. In J. Guimón, W. Fischer, & N. Sartorius (Eds.), *The image of madness: The public facing mental illness and psychiatric treatment* (pp. 208–216). Basel, Switzerland: Karger.

Elmore, J. L., & Young, D. M. (1996). Modular group therapy in a community mental health center. *Psychiatric Services, 47*(12), 1390–1391.

Foulkes, M. (1969). *Therapeutic group analysis*. London: Wheaton.

Frankel, B. (1993). Groups for the chronic mental patient and the legacy of failure. *International Journal of Group Psychotherapy, 43*(2), 157–172.

Freud, S. (1913). *Totem und tabu*. Paris: Payot.

Freud, S. (1922). *Group psychology and analysis of the ego*. London: International Psychoanalytic Press.

Garcia Badarracco, J. E. (1990). *Comunidad terapeutica psicoanalitica de estructura multifamiliar* [Psychoanalytical multifamily therapeutic community]. Madrid, Spain: Tecnipublicaciones, S.A.

Garcia Badarracco, J. E. (1992). Psychic change and its clinical Evaluation. *International Journal of Psycho-Analysis, 73*(Pt. 2).

Goffmann, E. (1961). *Asylums: Essays on the social situation of patients and other inmates*. New York: Doubleday.

Guimón, J., Eguiluz, I., & Bulbena, A. (1993). Group pharmacotherapy in schizophrenics: Attitudinal and clinical changes. *European Journal of Psychiatry, 7*(3), 147–154.

Guimón, J., Fischer, W., Zbinden, E., & Goerge, D. (1998). Therapeutic practice profiles, theoretical models and representations of the psychiatry of Swiss psychiatrists. *Schweizer Archiv fur Neurologie und Psychiatrie, 149*, 41–50.

Guimón, J., Sunyer, M., Sanchez de Vega, J., & Trojaola, B. (1992). Group analysis and ward atmosphere. In F. P. Ferrero, A. E. Haynal, & N. Sartorius (Eds.), *Schizophrenia and affective psychoses: Nosology in contemporary psychiatry*. London: John Libbey.

Gunderson, J. G. (1983). An overview of modern milieu therapy. In J. G. Gunderson (Ed.), *Principles and practice of milieu therapy*. London: Aronson.

Hayes, J. A. (1995). Countertransference in group psychotherapy: Waking a sleeping dog. *International Journal of Group Psychotherapy, 45*(4), 521–535.

Kanas, N. (1986). Group therapy with schizophrenics: A review of controlled studies. *International Journal of Group Psychotherapy, 36*, 339–351.

Kanas, N. (1991). Group therapy with schizophrenic patients: A short-term, homogeneous approach. *International Journal of Group Psychotherapy, 41*, 33–48.

Klein, R. H., Bernard, H. S., & Singer, D. L. (Eds.). (1992). *Handbook of contemporary group psychotherapy*. Madison, CT: International Universities Press.

Kohut, H. (1977). *The restoration of the self*. New York: International Universities Press.

Kreeger, L. (Ed.). (1975). *The large group: Dynamics and therapy*. London: Constable and Company.

Le Bon, G. (1896). *Psychologie des foules [The psychology of crowds]*. Paris: PUF.

Le Bon, G. (1952). *The crowd*. London: Benn.

Leff, J. (1994). Working with families of schizophrenic patients. *British Journal of Psychiatry* (Suppl. 23), 71–76.

Levine, B. E., & Postom, M. (1981). A modified group treatment for elder narcissistic patients. *International Journal of Group Psychotherapy, 30*(2), 153–168.

Levine, H. B. (1980). Milieu biopsy: The place of the therapy group on the inpatient ward. *International Journal of Group Psychotherapy, 30*(1), 77–93.

Liberman, R. P. (1903). Research on the psychiatric milieu. In J. G. Anderson (Ed.), *Principles and practice of milieu therapy*. New York: Aronson.

Liberman, R. P. (1982). Assessment of social skills. *Schizophrenia Bulletin, 8*(1), 62–84.

Mader, S. R., Wirshing, W. C., Mintz, J., McKenzie, J., Johnston, K., Eckman, T. A., et al. (1996). Two-year outcome of social skills training and group psychotherapy for outpatients with schizophrenia. *American Journal of Psychiatry, 153*(12), 1585–1592.

Malan, D. (1976). Group psychotherapy: A long term follow-up study. *Archives of General Psychiatry, 33,* 1303–1315.

May, P. R., & Simpson, G. M. (1990). Schizophrenia: Evaluation of treatment methods. In H. I. Kaplan, A. M. Freedman, & B. J. Sadock (Eds.), *Comprehensive textbook of psychiatry* (Vol. 2, pp. 1240–1275). Baltimore: Williams & Wilkins.

McDougall, W. (1920). *The group mind.* New York: Putnam.

Mosher, L. R., & Keith, S. J. (1980). Psychosocial treatment: Individual, group, family and community support approaches. *Schizophrenia Bulletin, 6*(1), 10–41.

Mosher, L. R., Vallone, R., & Menn, A. (1995). The treatment of acute psychosis without neuroleptics: Six-week psychopathology outcome data from the Soteria Project. *International Journal of Social Psychiatry, 41*(3), 157–173.

Nightingale, L. C., & McQueeney, D. A. (1996). Group therapy for schizophrenia: Combining and expanding the psychoeducational model with supportive psychotherapy. *International Journal of Group Psychotherapy, 46*(4), 517–534.

North, C. S., Pollio, D. E., Sachar, B., Hong, B., Issenberg, K., & Bufe, G. (1998). The family as caregiver: A group psychoeducation model for schizophrenia. *American Journal of Orthopsychiatry, 68*(1), 39–46.

O'Brien, C. P., Hamm, K. B., Ray, B. A., Pierce, J. F., Luborsky, L., & Mintz, J. (1972). Group vs individual psychotherapy with schizophrenics: A controlled outcome study. *Archives of General Psychiatry, 27*(4), 474–478.

O'Donnell, P. (1983). *Teoria y tecnica de la psicoterapia grupal* [Theory and techniques of group practice]. Buenos Aires, Argentina: Amorrortu.

Pankow, G. (1969). *L'homme et sa psychose* [Man and his psychology]. Paris: Aubier.

Roberts, J. P. (1995). Group psychotherapy. *British Journal of Psychiatry, 166*(1), 124–129.

Rodrigué, E. (1965). *Biografia de una Comunidad Terapeutica* [Biography of therapeutic communities]. Buenos Aires, Argentina: Eudeba.

Rosenfeld, H. A. (1976). *Etats psychotiques* [Psychotic states]. Paris: Presses Universitaires Françaises.

Schilder, P. (1936). The analysis of ideologies as a psychotherapeutic method, especially in group treatment. *American Journal of Psychiatry, 93,* 6601–6617.

Scott, J. E., & Dixon, L. B. (1995). Psychological interventions for schizophrenia. *Schizophrenia Bulletin, 21*(4), 621–630.

Searles, H. (1977). *L'effort pour rendre l'autre fou* [The effort to make the other work]. Paris: Gallimard.

Starkey, D., Deleone, H., & Flannery, R. B., Jr. (1995). Stress management for psychiatric patients in a state hospital setting. *American Journal of Orthopsychiatry, 65*(3), 446–450.

Stone, W. N. (1998). Affect and therapeutic process in groups for chronically mentally ill persons. *Journal of Psychotherapeutic Practice Research, 7*(3), 55–68.

von Bertalanffy, L. (1968). *General systems theory.* New York: Braziller.

Wender, L. (1940). Group psychotherapy: A study of its application. *Psychiatric Quarterly, 14,* 708–718.

Yalom, I. D. (1983). *In-patient group psychotherapy.* New York: Basic Books.

CHAPTER 21

Group Therapy Treatment of Sex Offenders

LESLIE M. LOTHSTEIN AND ROSEMARIE LAFLEUR BACH

HISTORY OF THE THERAPEUTIC APPROACH

Group therapy has been advocated as the treatment of choice for sex offenders (B. Schwartz, 1995a) and for sexually compulsive, addictive offenders and victims of sexual crimes (Anderson, 1969; Ganzarain & Buchele, 1990; Goodman, 1998; Lehne, Kate, & Berlin, 2000; Lothstein, 1979; Peters, Pedigo, Steg, & McKenna, 1968; Peters & Roether, 1972; B. Schwartz, 1995a, 1995b, 1995c; Slater, 1964).[1] Treating men who sexually offend in a homogeneous group therapy format (Yalom, 1975) allows them to benefit from treatment, as this heals their "vertical splits" in ego development (Goldberg, 1995, 1999, 2000) that led to their sexual acting out and dissociated shame. In homogeneous group therapy, sex offenders can experience feelings of acceptance and universality and reduce shame, and thereby cope with their superego deficits while they

---

[1] The term *sex offender* is a forensic term, not a clinical description or a diagnostic label. Individuals who are arrested for violating legal statutes governing criminal sexual behavior are a diverse group in terms of self-experience, psychogenetic precursors to their disorder(s), defensive strategies, and personality development. In addition to being described as sex offenders, many of them may have one or more *DSM-IV* diagnoses (including a paraphilia) or are dually diagnosed. In this chapter, we refer to sex offenders as males because the research findings suggest that there are approximately 10 times as many male sex offenders as female. Sex offenses may involve a whole range of behaviors, some of which have been catalogued as paraphilias by *DSM-IV* (American Psychiatric Association, 1994) while others are not formally diagnoses by *DSM-IV* standards and have been labeled as nonparaphilic sexually compulsive and addictive disorders (Kafka, 1997). More recently, the terms "sex addiction" and "sexually compulsive disorder" have been applied to describe the latter group of men and women who need treatment to control sexual urges that may be relentlessly enacted on a daily basis (Carnes, 1983; Coleman, 1988; Schneider, 1991). The terms "compulsive" and "addictive" have been used interchangeably despite challenges from dynamic theorists that the term "compulsive" refers to a specific type of behavior that represents a defensive compromise to ward off anxiety associated with a wish and one's conscience. Additionally, medical specialists in addiction want to limit the term "addiction" to drugs and alcohol addiction (despite the fact that sexual behavior disorders may involve tolerance and cravings that respond to a relapse model). The recent publication of the *Journal of Sexual Addiction and Compulsivity*, vol. 1(2), 1994, 99–184, points to the use of an addiction model in the field of sexuality.

work on the self-deficits, developmental arrests, and neurotic conflicts that led to their sexual problems in a supportive, nonjudgmental group therapy environment.

Homogeneous group therapy for sex offenders is helpful because the members share a basic sexual fault that is not usually accepted in mixed groups. For paraphiles, especially child molesters, the self-image of a monster pervades the self and prevents disclosure of the behavior and fantasies for fear of being rejected, hated, and expelled from the group. In a homogeneous group of sex offenders, everyone shares intense shame for sexually acting out their impulses. Sharing the details of the paraphilia may be less difficult in such a homogeneous group because of the common link that brings the patients together. For example, in an outpatient group supervised by Lothstein, a patient announced that he had molested a child. One woman threw up; others became agitated and angry. Eventually, the group insisted that he terminate his involvement in the treatment. The group members felt unsafe with their impulses toward him and feared his presence. The fragility of group cohesion secondary to aggression in the early stages of group development has been previously noted (Lothstein, 1979).

Many members in sex offender groups have offended, been arrested, had their pictures and stories appear in the newspaper and other media, and experienced intense humiliation and ongoing social isolation. They share the devastation of the shame that follows from such public disclosure, and they share society's view of them as monsters. Whereas individual therapy may be helpful regarding privacy issues, secrecy and shame issues are best managed in a group setting.

The basic rule in a psychodynamically oriented group therapy is that the members not judge another individual's paraphilic behavior. The group therapy is directed toward understanding, not judging, the individual's sexual behavior and fantasies. With this rule in place, group members may begin to disclose sexual details about themselves that would otherwise remain denied, disavowed, suppressed, or split off from the self and acted out dissociatively in a hypnoticlike state.

In a behaviorally oriented treatment, a patient may be forced or compelled to reveal private details of the self that may prevent a trusting relationship, which is necessary for sex offenders to develop genuine responsibility and empathy for their victims. A psychodynamically oriented group therapy facilitates disclosure via the group culture. The dynamics of group process also facilitate the penetration of defensive denial without sacrificing trust (Lothstein, 1979).

Group therapy for sex offenders and sex addicts has generally been behaviorally or cognitive-behaviorally based, and the model is primarily used for an incarcerated population. A hybrid psychodynamically oriented group therapy model is advocated in this chapter to deal with the large number of sex offenders who are not incarcerated. Such a model increases the likelihood of an individual's developing the self-regulatory control processes necessary for deviant behavior to stop entirely.

The application of group therapy to sex offenders uses theory and research from cognitive-behavioral therapy (B. Schwartz, 1995d), relapse prevention models (Laws, 1989; Marques & Nelson, 1989; Twerski, 1997), harm reduction models (Milton & McLean, 1999), psychoeducational models (Green, 1995), programs involving 12-step techniques (Sex and Love Addicts Anonymous, 1964), abstinence models (Sexaholics Anonymous, 1989),[2] or a combination of psycho-

---

[2]Because of the evolution and the wiring of the human brain for sex and reproduction, the abstinence model is not the primary recommendation for sex offenders (though abstinence of the deviant behavior is a goal). Sexual desire is a primary behavioral mode built into the hardware of the brain. Any attempt to apply a model of sexual abstinence will meet with harsh resistance from the brain. In his analysis of celibacy (i.e., abstinence) and

educational techniques (Sex Addicts Anonymous, 1986). Although there may be important insights to be gained from a behavioral model and cognitive-behavioral techniques, almost all sex offender outcome research is based on treating incarcerated populations.

However, the majority of sex offenders and those patients with sexually compulsive and addictive sexuality are not incarcerated. Indeed, the vast majority are living in the community and are under some form of supervision. The Bureau of Justice statistics for criminal sex offenders reported that for any given day in 1997, "there were approximately 234,000 offenders convicted of rape or sexual assault under the care, custody, or control of corrections agencies; nearly 60% of these sex offenders are under conditional supervision in the community" (Bureau of Justice Statistics, 1997). These statistics do not include those sex offenders who either did not come before the criminal justice system or who were sexually compulsive and addicted and voluntarily sought therapy for their disorders. Many of these sexually compulsive or addicted individuals are classified as nonviolent. In seeking out treatment, they are attempting to live fuller, healthier, and safer lives. These individuals are treated in a variety of ambulatory settings, and the research on sex offenders in prison may not apply to their problems. Newer models of treatment need to address the specific problems of those who sex-offend or are sexually compulsive or addictive and live outside a controlled environment.

---

the Catholic priesthood, Sipe (1990) reported that only 2% of American Catholic priests are genuinely celibate and another 18% strive for celibacy but are not successful. About 80% of Catholic priests are not celibate (which does not mean that they are always acting out sexually). That is, even for those individuals who choose sexual abstinence (celibacy) for moral and theological reasons, it is difficult to remain abstinent. Sexual urges and behaviors are intimately involved in the development of affectionate relationships. When individuals fail to establish healthy sexual relationships, paraphilic behavior may ensue.

This chapter goes beyond the purely behavioral model of sex offender treatment and focuses on a novel hybrid psychodynamic group therapy model that integrates insights from a cognitive-behavioral model with insights from psychoanalysis, ego psychology, self psychology, and perversion theory (Chassequet-Smirgel, 1986; Goldberg, 1995; Kaplan, 1991; Khan, 1974, 1979, 1983; Lothstein, 2001; Socarides, 1988; Stoller, 1975, 1979, 1985, 1991). This hybrid treatment model is viewed as providing a more comprehensive framework for recognizing and treating the deeper psychological structures of individuals who sexually act out their psychic conflicts as a result of a developmental arrest, childhood trauma, or structural ego deficits and neurotic conflicts.

The underlying assumption of this hybrid psychodynamic model comes from over 25 years of treating a wide range of sex offenders and sexually addicted or compulsive individuals in group therapy. As a result of this experience, we found that these patients suffer from core disturbances in attachment, dread and fear women, and experience intense abandonment and separation anxiety that led to their being alienated from themselves and their social networks. Consequently, these men were unable to form appropriate attachments or need-satisfying relationships necessary for healthy object relationships. They are intensely lonely, angry, and needy men who cannot be alone and have sexualized their intimacy needs. As a result of individual and family dynamics, these men have learned to establish some type of relationship and attachment through deviant sexual behaviors and perverse symptom formation. For them, it is better to have a deviant sexual relationship than to be lonely, angry, and alienated and have no contact with others.

Group therapy allows these men the possibility of dealing with their childhood sexual trauma, developmental arrests, and gender and masculinity conflicts while attaining genuine intimacy and reconnecting to their failed self-identities. In the context of group therapy, they can focus on these issues along the lines of the four pillars of their sexual lives: sexual arousal, core gender identity, sexual orientation, and love relationships. A dynamically oriented group therapy allows them to express their innermost fantasies and disavowed affect and develop a level of trust and honesty to overcome their arrested social development and learn to engage in meaningful and gratifying relationships with real people (Lothstein & Zimet, 1988; Rutan & Stone, 1984).

The cognitive-behavioral model de-emphasizes the importance of emotion and affect because most of the patients are incarcerated. Prison environments discourage affective and emotional displays because these can destabilize an individual or group. However, without an emphasis on experiential or emotional learning, no real change can take place. In a dynamic group context, these men are able to connect to their dissociated emotions and experience the real pain in relationships that they avoid through their perverse symptoms. Subsequently, they come to understand that their perverse symptom is based on an illusion that some type of meaningful relationship is possible through a fetishistic or part-object relationship. Only through the establishment of genuine whole-object relationships can caring and concern for others develop, the deviant sexual enactment be controlled, and the perverse symptom be resolved. Psychodynamic group therapy allows for such processes to occur and change to take place.

For the psychodynamically oriented group therapist, sexually errant behavior is viewed as stemming from early childhood self-deficits that can be repaired only when deficits in self-structure have been recognized and treated (Goldberg, 1995, 1999, 2000; Lothstein, 1997). A purely cognitive approach to treatment is inadequate because of the failure to identify and treat these deeper self structures that are impaired. Although cognitive-behavior therapists correctly emphasize the need to control deviant behavior, learning the appropriate social skills is insufficient and no substitute for the internalization of genuine object relationships and the self-regulation of affect necessary for genuine self-control. Moreover, true empathy must be experientially, not cognitively, learned, otherwise, behavioral methods may actually enhance some perpetrators' skills in controlling and grooming victims. Psychodynamic group therapy emphasizes the need to socialize and demystify the underlying secrets of the sexual self by verbalizing these secrets in an accepting, nonjudgmental and nonblaming group atmosphere.

In this chapter, we review the current status of the behaviorally oriented group therapy model for sex offenders (primarily developed from work with prison populations), discuss the psychodynamic model, and introduce the use of a hybrid psychodynamic model of group therapy emphasizing an integration of cognitive-behavioral therapy with a broad-based psychodynamic theory involving attachment theory, self psychology, and object-relations theory, and informed by psychoanalytic theory. We identify what assessment methods are important to diagnose these conditions, identify who can benefit from these interventions, and provide some rich clinical examples of how the hybrid model is put into action and the therapy is carried out (Quinsey, Lalumiere, Rice, & Harris, 1995; Quinsey, Rice, & Harris, 1995).

THEORETICAL CONSTRUCTS

Most sex offender treatment models emphasize using behavioral therapy, which is based on learning theory. More recently, these treatment methods have been informed by cognitive-behavioral treatment emphasizing cognition, skills training, and symptom removal. Cognitive-behavioral sex offender group therapy stresses skills development to repair the patient's deficits.

Smith (1995) emphasized that sex offenders need to participate in and successfully learn specific skills around the following issues: sex education, victim empathy, drug and alcohol education, social and interpersonal training, anger management, relapse prevention, assertiveness training, stress management, dating skills, and self-esteem building. In addition, treatment should focus on distorted cognitions or thinking errors that lead to denial, rationalization, and minimization as excuses for sexually acting out. Some individuals may also need a concurrent residential placement to ensure compliance with treatment and safety for the patient and the community.

Green (1995) suggested a number of interventions for sex offenders, including psychoeducational modules (e.g., focusing on sex offender dynamics, anger management, and relapse prevention); interpersonal techniques; psychological and behavioral diaries; assignments (reading books on incest, rape, anger management); reconditioning (overt or covert methods of counterconditioning, behavioral rehearsal, and/or masturbatory reconditioning); cognitive-behavioral techniques (relapse prevention methods, identification of the deviant cycle, evaluation of incorrect assumption and perceptions); pharmacological treatments (neuroleptics and antiandrogen medication); and aftercare needs.

For Green (1995), sex offender treatment involves the offender's admitting guilt, accepting responsibility, identifying the deviant sexual cycle, and making restitution. In some cases, where notification and registration statutes are in place and civil commitment is a possibility, it may be difficult to achieve these goals.

Travin and Protter (1993) identified five major categories of sex offender treatment: (1) self-control techniques aimed at helping the offender to gain control over his "deviant fantasies, urges and activities"; (2) stress management aimed at eliminating sources of stress that fuel paraphilic acting out; (3) cognitive restructuring aimed at correcting erroneous thought patterns that contribute to and sustain paraphilic behavior; (4) empathy training; and (5) social rehabilitation techniques aimed at treating client's social and interpersonal deficits (e.g., assertiveness training). They also recommended psychoeduational/sex education to provide patients with accurate information about both normal sexuality and abnormal sexual functioning. They emphasized that psychoeducational techniques may be utilized throughout therapy as an adjunct to any of the five cognitive-behavioral techniques. They believe that it is important to "demystify and correct distortions about sexual functioning" that may contribute to a paraphilic's "stress, frustration, and low self esteem regarding his sense of manhood" (p. 147).

All cognitive-behavioral treatment models for sex offenders employ relapse reduction and/or prevention techniques that reinforce therapeutic gains and shore up a person's defenses against recidivism. The sex offender learns to anticipate, and cope with, the problems of relapse from the outset of treatment (Becker, 1996; Laws, 1989; Travin & Protter, 1992, 1993). By helping an offender identify the microbehavioral events preceding a relapse (an actual episode of acting out), he can control his sexual behaviors.

Carnes (1983) believed that deviant arousal patterns need to be interrupted for the paraphilic ritual to lose its ability to excite and to consume one's thoughts and behaviors. Whereas initial approaches to deviant arousal in sex offender treatment involved using aversive conditioning behavior therapy techniques, therapists now employ a broad range of integrative techniques that are more inclusive (Becker, 1996; Marshall, 1994; M. Schwartz & Brasted, 1985; Travin & Protter, 1993). Moreover, cognitive behaviorists emphasize observable, measurable responses, and their techniques lend themselves well to the scrutiny of outcome studies (Marshall & Barbaree, 1988).

Arguments against a behavioral approach include the following:

1. It does not promote in the offender an ability to experience and express affects appropriately.
2. The method may teach antisocial individuals about victim empathy and give them another tool to exploit vulnerable individuals.
3. Teaching some offenders about assertiveness training and anger management may provide them with the tools to further manipulate others.
4. Teaching about sex education may excite their interest and lead to acting out.
5. Behavioral group therapy may have a tendency to diffuse responsibility and enable the sex offender to avoid focusing on very embarrassing and important details about his sexual fantasizing that are necessary to prevent relapse.
6. Behavioral group therapy may reinforce defenses supporting denial, rationalization, and minimization of the sexual acting out.

A major criticism of the multiskills approach to the cognitive-behavioral model is that it seems to propose a tandem series of treatment recommendations that are not integrated.

The goals of psychodynamically oriented treatment are similar to those of cognitive-behavior therapy but is based on a recognition that the sexual or aggressive symptoms are viewed as secondary and as an expression of a damaged or traumatized self. Unless the individual's self-deficits are treated, he will periodically resort, under stress or during periods of self-fragmentation or decompensation, to errant sexual behaviors.

The psychodynamic group therapy model emphasizes a developmental psychological approach to treatment using transference and countertransference issues and ego and self psychological perspectives and is informed by classical and neopsychoanalytic theory. This model facilitates an enriched understanding of the sexualized symptom as part of the individual's massive self-deficits and lack of self-cohesion. In cognitive behavior therapy models, treatment focuses on cognitive scripts alone and not on the developmental issues from the individual's past that contributed to the development of a sexualization.

Because individuals who engage in sexually offending or compulsive and addictive sexual behavior often report the onset of their sexual misbehavior as preceded by abandonment fears, depression, surfacing rage and other negative affects secondary to frustration of loss of gratification, and separation anxiety, it would seem that a psychodynamic model would be best suited to treat the underlying issues driving the paraphilic and nonparaphilic behavior. Sex offending behaviors can be brought under "real" control only when the internal mechanisms for self-regulatory processes of control are in place.

Psychodynamic group therapy emphasizes experiential learning, affect modulation, emotional expression, and insight into early childhood experiences as necessary for change to occur and destructive acting out to cease. Psychodynamic therapists have advocated that the treatment factors that must also be considered (in addition to mental illness or brain damage) should include the following list of nonexhaustive factors: family, religion, societal and personal factors, developmental age level, ethical issues, underlying erotic fantasies, use of alcohol or drugs, factors related to sexual abuse, ethnicity, and an understanding of the specific sex offender typology that applies to a given patient.

Psychodynamic group therapy methods may help offenders to neutralize guilt, shame, and self-hatred and control their addictive sexual cycles. The aim of this type of group therapy is to help sex offenders control their deviant sexuality through increased awareness and insight and repair of self-deficits through the development of self-object transference that led to the sexualization in the first place.

To ensure that all treatment providers, regardless of theoretical orientation, have a common or core knowledge of sex offender treatment goals, B. Schwartz (1995b) concluded that all therapists should consider focusing on the following in their group therapy approaches (as part of setting up guidelines for treatment and the licensing of sex offender treatment providers):

- Address the client's deviant sexual urges and recurrent deviant sexual fantasies as necessary to prevent sexual reoffense.
- Educate clients and the individuals who are part of their support systems about the objective risk of reoffense.
- Attempt to teach clients how to use self-control methods to avoid sexual reoffending, where applicable.
- Consider the effects of trauma and past victimization as factors in reoffense potential, where applicable.
- Address the client's thought processes that facilitate sexual offense and other victimizing or assaultive behaviors.
- Modify the client's thinking errors and cognitive distortions where possible.
- Attempt to ensure that clients have accurate knowledge about the effects of sexual offenses on victims, their families, and the community.
- Assist clients to develop a sensitivity to the effects of sexual abuse on their victims.
- Address the client's personality traits and deficits that are related to their reoffense potential.
- Address the client's deficits in coping skills in present life situations.
- Include and integrate the client's family into the therapy process, where appropriate.
- Attempt to maintain communication with client's spouse and family, where appropriate, to assist in meeting treatment goals (pp. 13–14).

Schwartz (1995a) noted that some sex offenders who engaged in extremely disorganized, chaotic, and shameful sex offending may need long-term individual therapy before they are ready for a group. She viewed these individuals as too narcissistically damaged and self-focused and with little available ego capacity to work in a group therapy setting. Some of these men cannot benefit from group therapy until they have undergone many months of individual therapy.

Cognitive-behavioral approaches to the treatment of paraphilias are generally more symptom-focused than insight-oriented (Becker, 1996; Travin & Protter, 1993). However, the use of a psychodynamic perspective allows the self's integration of the emotional and cognitive deficits. Without such integration, no real change in the self can occur. Clinicians who treat sex offenders in a primarily behavioral-oriented mode are aware of the phenomenon of individuals who, after treatment, can "talk the therapy talk" but are still vulnerable to acting out. Whereas cognitive-behavioral treatment micromanages the sex offender's behavior, a psychodynamic approach provides comprehensive understanding of why the behavior occurs and gives the individual more control over his "fate."

Although behavioral therapists have noted that the treatment of sex offenders must be tailored and focused according to the various characteristics and typologies of sex offenders (Dougher, 1995; Lothstein, 1996; Pithers, 1994; Pithers & Cummings, 1995; Pithers, Kashima, Cumming, Beal, & Buell, 1998), there is a tendency for those using this model to treat the symptoms without integrating them into the person's life. That is, although cognitive-behavioral therapies for sex offenders are espoused as the gold standard, how all of the tandem rehabilitative techniques are integrated into a coherent treatment program is a matter of mystery, if not debate.

Sexually addicted and compulsive individuals stress the importance of emotional and sexual arousal in their enactments. Powerful emotions drive aberrant sexual behavior and these emotions need to be an important part of treatment. Emotional and sexual arousal are critical psychobiological components that must be addressed in treatment. Employing aversive therapies to eliminate the emotion and deviant erotic images or arousal misses the point of how entrenched and important the arousal and the fantasy basis are for self-survival. Once these images are addressed psychodynamically in the group process, they can be defused and increase the offender's control over his impulses. To extinguish emotion rather than understanding its meaning and relevance for the individual seems gratuitous.

As a result of 25 years of experience treating sexual offenders, we are advocating a hybrid psychodynamic model informed by behavioral therapy as the treatment model of choice. This hybrid model of group therapy for the paraphilias (sex offenders and compulsive and addictive sexuality) is based on the assumption that paraphiles experience profound deficits in their self-experience. A deficit model supports treatment attempts to repair self-deficits, integrate impulse and defensive processes, and help individuals develop insight into their behavior and work through and rehabilitate their self structures through a hybrid model of psychodynamic group therapy. The healing process is facilitated through the following: use of transference phenomena; using other group members and the group as a whole as factors in repairing developmental arrests regarding one's history of being sexually abused; being over- and understimulated; and being sexually reactive in response to disorganizing anxiety and the surfacing of core self-conflicts (cf. Ganzarain & Buchele, 1990; Travin & Protter, 1993).

Work with sex offenders suggests how themes of attachment deficits, alienation, and loss and abandonment (and the attendant affects of shame, humiliation, and primitive narcissistic rage) may lead to sexualization as a defense against massive fragmentation anxiety. Only psychodynamically oriented group therapy can address their early childhood attachment conflicts.

The dynamic forces in the group allow for attachment and relational deficit issues to emerge in a safe environment in which other individuals share the same basic structural deficits, developmental arrests, and underlying conflicts over abandonment anxiety, depression, and rage. Therapists serve as transference objects to work through these structural deficits and core conflicts. Moreover, the sex offender's loss of control over his sexual symptoms (a dynamic that intensifies feelings of shame) can be worked on effectively in a group therapy setting in which these issues are shared by all group members. If these issues were raised in individual therapy, there might be too much opportunity for keeping secrets that could lead to further defensive denial, splitting, disavowal, and other primitive defensive maneuvers to keep the shame, or basic fault in the self, hidden even from the therapist. However, in the group, all members are operating within the same framework of guilt, shame, humiliation, and blame.

It is our experience that sex offenders perceive themselves as monsters who cannot control themselves and are regarded by society as evil. Working with the patient's self-image as a monster, in the context of a group in which all of the patients share the monster label, eventually allows for the diffusion of the intense shame and the powerful evil social role with which these patients identify. This process enables group members to tolerate their shame and avoid suicidal depressions, dissociative ego states, or heightened aggression and overwhelming feelings of helplessness that may led to self-fragmentation and, perhaps, psychosis. Unless shame is experienced and worked through in the group, genuine change cannot take place. The group as a whole acts as a container, a safe place, a holding environment and a "good-enough parent" (Winnicott, 1965), making the sex offender feel safe and contained so that change can take place.

Psychodynamically oriented group therapy encourages the phenomenon of narcissistic mirroring to occur. This allows the impaired narcissism of each group member to surface without having devastating effects as ego strengths. This is critical because not all patients are low functioning. Sexually aberrant behavior knows no educational or social status limits; many patients who seek treatment are high functioning, intelligent, and employed as professionals and clergy. In a homogeneous group of sex offenders, issues of self-worth and acceptance are heightened and allow each person to face his shame and repair his structural ego deficits. The function of the group as a self-object for the sex offender has been highlighted by Coleman (1998) and Travin and Protter (1993).

Every paraphilia involves some type of deficit around core gender identity (Goldberg, 1995; Lothstein, 1979). For male paraphiles, the gender identity conflicts usually take the form of a damaged masculinity and a fear that they are not manly enough and too feminine. This has little or nothing to do with homosexuality, but with core issues of self-identity as a male and masculinity. As a group, paraphilic males share conflicts around the following issues: they may perceive their genitals as defective and childlike; they may experience their masculine self as failing; they may believe that their lack of control of their urges is associated with feelings of gender confusion; they may believe they are damaged males who are like females (a derogatory assignment of gender that equates damaged masculinity with a failure at male differentiation); and they may reveal envy and hatred toward females.

Issues of damaged ability in self-assertion, narcissism, aggression, and separation conflicts are all embedded in the sense of damaged masculinity. Some of these men cross-dress, and some develop a circumscribed fetish (female shoes, undergarments, clothes) or live out private sexual fantasies in which they see themselves as women in the sex act and being penetrated by phallic females. All of these confused but excited enactments keep alive the damaged secret self. The female identifications and secret female longings allow some aspects of their dependency needs to be gratified. Many of these men are very angry and have chaotic and aggressive marriages. Unless these issues are addressed in therapy, no real change in the self can occur. Only a psychodynamically oriented group therapy allows such shameful material to be discussed and worked through so that structural change can occur.

Once the unconscious conflicts surface and the defensive adaptations are identified, the rehabilitation of self structures can take place. Otherwise, the self may further isolate, compartmentalize, deny, rationalize, disavow, or dissociate intense feeling and appear to be "normal" while secretly carrying out the paraphilia with greater intensity but hidden from the family, the therapist, and the self. Most clinicians are familiar with patients who, because of the intensity of pleasure associated with defensive sexualization, are unable to give up their sexual symptoms. These symptoms are the person's only source of gratification, contentment, soothing, and pleasure. Many of these individuals exhibit behaviors that mimic frontal disinhibition and a frontal lobe syndrome (involving impulsivity, lack of organization and integration, poor judgment, limited insight, and lack of recognition of consequences). Some of these men may exhibit an identifiable neuropsychological deficit (Lothstein, 1999).

One group of understimulated and depressed men (especially exhibitionists) may experience themselves as sexually "dead." They may fuel their exhibitionism by using chemicals such as cocaine to intensify their feeling of excitement while alleviating their depression and making them feel alive. For them, the sexual acting out is an antidote to depression and their understimulated self system. Men who are alienated from themselves because of severe early childhood trauma are among the most difficult to treat because they aggressively ward off all help that threatens to annihilate their pleasure system.

In a psychodynamically oriented group, members with similar problems may identify with each other and develop self-object transferences that Kohut (1977) labeled twinship transferences. Group members may pair with one another in a way that allows their damaged narcissism to be repaired and appropriate ambitions and goals to be established. The twinship transference overcomes the isolation and alienation that cripple the self system and provides an idealized other with whom the self can identify. The group culture allows transferences to develop and be more effectively identified. The ability to tolerate intense shame and develop appropriate ego mechanisms governing self-observation, and victim and self empathy and to foresee the consequences of one's behavior are facilitated in psychodynamic group therapy.

The assumption underlying a psychodynamic treatment perspective is that to effectively rehabilitate the sex offender's structural ego deficits and repair unconscious conflicts, the sex offender has to feel safe from damaging criticism and aggression that activates his split-off self and can lead to further defensive sexualization and destructive behavior.

The ability to experience guilt and tolerate shameful feelings through open disclosure in a safe environment is the immediate goal of psychodynamic group therapy (Buchele, 1994; Catherall & Shelton, 1996; Friedman, 1994; Ganzarain & Buchele, 1990; Goldberg, 1995; McCarthy, 1994; Travin & Potter, 1993). According to Goldberg, "Nothing seems to highlight a perverse activity so much as a feeling of alienation and difference; nothing seems to relieve it more than a feeling of acceptance" by the therapist, group members, and the group as a whole. This sense of alienation was explained by Kaufman (1992) as being born of the rigid defenses employed by the paraphile against experiencing shame. Consequently, these individuals fail to develop adequate relationships and feel alienated from others. For the alienated sex offender, the possibility of building a corrective "interpersonal bridge" and healing damaged relationships is sworn off. Consequently, there is no possibility of trust. According to Kaufman, it is only through open and constructive relationships that the rift in the self-other matrix can be healed. The psychodynamically oriented therapy group acts as an experimental social field in which reparative work can be done.

A few studies focusing on a homogeneous group of sex offenders helps to illuminate the curative factors in such group therapy. Ganzarain and Buchele (1990) described a long-term outpatient psychodynamic group therapy model for incest perpetrators, most of whom were court-ordered to treatment. For these patients, shame and guilt were externalized and blame was routinely assigned or projected onto everyone outside the self. Initially, these patients focused on themselves as victims of a legal system, unsympathetic parents, and lying therapists (who are really angry with them, or at least disappointed) whom they could not trust. The ability to move from a paranoid perspective to a relational-trusting perspective was the goal of the initial stage of group therapy.

Ganzarain and Buchele (1990) noted how the group as a whole functioned as a benign superego allowing for a nonjudgmental and accepting environment in which a patient's lying, manipulation, and exploitation (i.e., antisocial tendencies) could be analyzed. Group members' low self-esteem reflected their developmental deficits of being raised in an unempathic and destructive family environment. The group therapy environment, however, functioned as a benign and accepting surrogate family that allowed the paraphile to talk about his inner experience and sexualized behaviors in an empathic and constructive manner. This is especially important for patients who are employed as professionals or clergy, who may have entered their vocations to be looked up to as responsible, caring, morally virtuous, and ethically impeccable individuals. Essentially, their choice of vocation may have been a defense against early childhood developmental deficits related to shame and feelings of inadequacy secondary to childhood trauma, abandonment, and depression.

Caffaro (1991) described a homogeneous psychodynamic group treatment program for incestuous men (all of whom were fathers). Using an object-relations framework, Caffaro observed that all of these men harbored intense rage and "unfinished business" with their own fathers, who were uniformly missing, inadequate, or aggressively damaging to their children. He proposed that treatment needed to take the patients back in time where their problems began, in the early parental and family-of-origin relationships. He believed that if they were able to work through these issues, significant change could occur in their object-relationships such that they would not have to resort to paraphilic or sexually offending behavior. In an all male therapy group, the patients had the opportunity to establish a variety of possible solutions to their damaged selves via healthy self-object relationships in which empathic mirroring and idealizing self-object transferences were possible. In addition, Caffaro believed that the exclusively male environment "provided an area of safety to withdraw into when working through the shameful feelings associated with longing for the absent father" (p. 37).

The all-male group was also endorsed by Sternbach (1996) as a unique opportunity for men to nurture other men, and to represent the "fathering that all men wish for: fathering that rests on mutuality, relational authority, openness to feedback and vulnerability" (p. 37). Sternbach agreed with Caffaro's (1991) viewpoint that to expose feelings of shame, weakness, and lack of masculinity is very difficult for men and the presence of women during this process may enhance men's feelings of defect or weakness.

When females are in the group, the issue of gender must be addressed directly. Having a female cotherapist may arouse intense pain for some men, as they fear the judgment of the "woman-as-mother." Also a female's presence can reinforce their self-concepts as monsters. The male-female cotherapy model, however, may lead to the optimum transference situation in which exploration of the early parental relationships that were damaging may be more easily facilitated. For Buchele (1994) and Ganzarain and Buchele (1990), a male-female cotherapy pair enhances transference issues focused on relating to the opposite sex, dealing with Oedipal and primal scene issues, and developing a capacity for telling their story to the "mother" and repairing their damaged narcissism. Pietz and Mann (1989) suggested that a male and female coleadership pair in a group of male pedophiles can model appropriate ways of relating to the opposite gender and enable the sex offender to experience a respectful male-female relationship in which differences do not have to lead to murder or abandonment.

For many paraphiles, there is both fear and dread of the female and a wish for identification and fusion with the female that leaves them in a state of confusion. Working through their female issues (related to their damaged masculinity) with a female group leader can have an enormous therapeutic benefit. In a group led by Lothstein primarily involving Catholic clergy, patients rejected the idea of a female coleader. A few group members threatened to quit the group if a female was present. For these Catholic clergy, women were feared and dreaded and could not be tolerated in the group. The dread of the female involved a fear of the mother that was defended against through a superficial expression of "love" from the pulpit. In one group with a female cotherapist, two of the patients (nonclergy) attempted to cross boundaries with her (either through exposure or touching), and it was the intervention of the other group members that led to boundary maintenance and interpretation of the dynamic.

Many men who sexually abuse have also been sexually abused (between 15% and 35% of perpetrators have been abused; Schwartz, 1995d). The trauma of being sexually victimized during childhood can lead to a defensive disengagement from developing close relationships secondary to a fear of being sexually retraumatized (most perpetrators know their victims). Stoller (1975) believed that all perversion was the result of a reenactment of a childhood trauma and represented a derivative of hatred now experienced as "love" but with the inability to develop typical love relationships. To prevent further acting out of the early trauma, an ego function needs to be developed that allows the sex offender to empathize with his victim. This can come about only through an affective experiencing of empathy in the transference.

Empathy cannot be taught as a cognitive construct with the idea that intellectual knowing will act prophylactically against further victimization. Unless the empathic link is made affectively, no real emotional learning can take place. This issue has been raised by Mark Schwartz (1995) and more recently by Barbara Schwartz (1995a). They recognized that unless emotion was addressed, no substantive change in victim empathy could occur. Unfortunately, many sex offender programs avoid treating perpetrators' own sexual victimization in depth for fear that they will develop an excuse for their behavior. However, unless such treatment take place, how can we expect the perpetrator to fully emotionally understand his behavior toward his victims? A psychodynamically oriented group therapy can more effectively "teach" empathy for the victim through experiential and emotional learning.

A hybrid psychodynamic model of treatment for sex offenders moves from the surface issues of symptoms (i.e., sexual enactments) to deeper psychological structures that have been damaged and are in need of repair. Unless therapy addresses the profound need to rehabilitate impaired self structures and confront the individual's abandonment anxiety, depression, trauma, and damaged masculinity, no real change in intimacy relationships will occur. When stresses impinge on the self and negative emotional states prevail (anger, abandonment anxiety, rage, loneliness), it is likely that sexual enactments will be repeated. This is part of the deviant sexual cycle that sex offenders and sexually compulsive and addictive individuals find themselves stuck in, unable to extricate themselves. Until these individuals learn to tolerate anxiety and learn how to comfort themselves when alone, abandoned, or angry, they will always be at risk for sexually acting out. Fear of punishment and a cognitive awareness of deviant thought structures cannot act as an effective barrier against sexual acting out. Combining the behavioral and psychodynamic models into a hybrid model allows the therapist to understand the points of weakness of self-expression and how to integrate them on various levels of understanding and rehabilitation.

METHODS OF ASSESSMENT AND INTERVENTION

To be effective, psychological treatment must always proceed from accurate diagnosis. In the absence of a thorough evaluation and diagnosis, treatment will be haphazard. Moreover, psychological treatment must be tailored for each individual. Labeling a person a sex offender does not imply a specific type of treatment. Sex offending is a final common pathway for a wide range of possible disturbances and treatment must be tailored for each individual. A hybrid psychodynamic model of group therapy for sex offenders is a powerful method, but it does not work for all individuals.

Sex-offending behavior may be a symptom of many psychological disturbances or cerebral abnormalities, including mental retardation, temporal lobe epilepsy, Pervasive Developmental Disorder or Asperger's syndrome, the result of a traumatic brain injury or other cerebral abnormality, the result of an Antisocial Personality Disorder, the result of acute mania secondary to a Bipolar Disorder, behavior following from a schizophrenic episode in which sexual delusions and hallucinations lead to sexual acting out, or the result of acute brain intoxication secondary to alcohol, cocaine, or other psychostimulants. Although this list is not exhaustive, it points to the need to know what kinds of underlying diagnostic issues need to be addressed in the treatment of the sexual behavior part of the disorder. To know what kind of treatment a sex offender may benefit from and whether specialized sex offender therapy techniques are necessary, it is important that accurate diagnosis be an integral part of the evaluation process.

Assessment methods should include, but not be limited to, the following:

- Neuropsychological testing.
- Projective testing, including the Rorschach. (Self-report measures and an array of sexual symptom inventories are generally useless.)
- Objective psychological testing.
- Medical and neurohormonal evaluation.
- EEG, fMRI, CT scan, and other neuroimaging where relevant.
- Complete chemical dependency profile.
- Complete psychosexual and psychosocial history with third-party confirmation of findings (complete school records).
- Review of all police and court records and prior history of offending.

Accurate diagnosis involves extensive clinical interviewing of the patient and his family. In some cases, it is only when the psychobiological components of sexually compulsive and aggressive behavior are addressed and sexually suppressant drugs employed that the individual is able to settle into treatment and address the core conflicts that are driving his deviant sexual behavior (Lothstein, 1996). Programs that do not incorporate psychobiological, neurohormonal, and pharmacological perspectives (tailored for each person) may fail to deal with the individual's propensity for hyperarousal that does not respond to behavioral or psychodynamically oriented treatment strategies. The potential effectiveness of neurohormonal and psychological medication for reducing sexual and aggressive deviant arousal must not be discounted (Berlin, 1983). The psychobiology and psychodynamics of sexually deviant behavior are complementary (and competing) processes that must become a part of their sex offender treatment program (Lothstein, 1995). It is our experience that about 60% of sex offenders and sexually compulsive individuals are on some form of psychotropic or neurohormonal medication to reduce their sex drive.

There is a tendency in the mental health field to encourage the development of treatment guidelines, if not standards, for the treatment of certain mental illnesses. The establishment of guidelines for the treatment of sex offenders has been supported by the Association for the Treatment of Sex Offenders (ATSA, 1996) and through legislative enactments in a few dozen states. These recommendations by ATSA are only guidelines and do not reflect the final view on this matter, as there is considerable disagreement among clinicians regarding what works, with whom, and when. There are no research findings using control groups and double-blind studies that provide definitive results as to which treatment method works best for sex offenders.

As an example of the difficulty of defining treatment protocols, consider a group of pedophiles who are genuinely attracted to prepubescent children. Some may be aroused by sensory modalities (i.e., sight, smell, touch); others by a core masturbatory fantasy that is sexually arousing (involving small genitals and lack of pubic hair, and arousal to a child's small, smooth, body); others by primary identifications with the developmental level of the child and with that stage of development in their own lives; others by a repetition compulsion to enact something that happened to them in their youth; and others by a sadistic need to control and overpower a helpless object (stemming from identification with the aggressor as a defense mechanism). The treatment for each of these conditions is different, as the various psychogenetic precursors need to be addressed uniquely for each sex offender.

Child molesters pose a unique treatment problem because of the risk they pose to their innocent victims, and this hybrid model has been effective in their treatment (Lothstein, 2001). Some of the particular problems involved in treating child molesters have been described by Finkelhor and Araji (1986). They posited a four-factor model to examine the child molester's interest in children: emotional congruence, sexual arousal, blockage, and disinhibition. Each of these issues must become a focus of treatment for the child molester, yet, unless a psychodynamic approach to treatment is instituted, he will never understand how to identify and control the triggers and motivations for his sexual enactments. Additionally, there always remains the possibility of an as yet undetected age-specific biological marker for an adult's interest in a specific age group.

For many sexually offending men, it is only during the group therapy experience that they are able to connect their intense unmet longings for intimacy with the defensive sexual acting out they employ (Alonso & Rutan, 1988). Prior to treatment, it was only the experience of ejaculation that brought an end to a sexually deviant cycle. However, though ejaculation may provide an immediate sense of relief, it also may eventuate in a sense of despair; the relief is associated with the pleasure of orgasm, but the despair is associated with the recognition that the fundamental problem has not been resolved, as the individual is aware of mounting anxiety as the sexual cycle begins again. In a homogeneous psychodynamic group therapy setting where all participants understand the role of shame in their disorders, shame is dealt with openly and regularly throughout treatment (Wright, 1994).

MAJOR SYNDROMES, SYMPTOMS, AND PROBLEMS TREATED

To benefit from this hybrid model of group therapy, individuals diagnosed with the following sexual acting-out disorders *should not* be referred to this type of treatment: individuals with traumatic brain injuries; hypersexuality secondary to a medical condition, Bipolar Disorder, or schizophrenia; individuals with mental retardation or verbal expressive disorders; or individuals with severe personality disorders who will thwart treatment (e.g., antisocial and psychopathic individuals or individuals with malignant narcissism and paranoia). Individuals with severe drug and alcohol addictions should have those disorders treated and in remission before starting the program of treatment we are advocating.

All forms of disorganized and chaotic, disinhibited, and deviant sexual behavior and compulsive or addictive sexuality need to be completely evaluated for possible causes before treatment is instituted. This is especially true given the large number of elderly men arrested for sex offending behavior that is part of their medial illness (Lothstein, Fogg-Waberski, & Reynolds, 1997). The presence of a chemical addiction or alcohol problem may further impair and disinhibit one's self system and lead to sexual acting out. The mix of severe psychopathology with alcohol and/or drugs can be sexually lethal. Moreover, many sex offender programs do not recognize severe mental illness as organizing or activating the commission of sexual crimes. Many sex offender treatment programs either exclude individuals with severe psychopathology from their treatment protocols or fail to diagnose and treat an Axis I disorder because they presume that all sex offenders are Axis II disordered. However, once an individual's psychosis is managed or his medical condition treated, he may be eligible for beginning this type of group therapy.

One pilot program has been reported (Brown & Lothstein, 1996) involving a long-term group therapy project in which a group of severely mentally ill sex offenders in a state hospital system participated in a twice-weekly group psychotherapy using a multimodal approach to treatment. Although progress was slow, the group setting allowed these severely impaired men to talk about their sexual behavior disorders in a group where fear of censure and ridicule were absent. Treating their sexual issues in a homogeneous group allowed these men to better understand how their isolation, lack of relationships, and loneliness led to a deviant sexual drive that dovetailed with their Axis I illness. This pilot study illuminated how individuals with severe psychopathology may be eligible for treatment in a hybrid psychodynamic group therapy model.

There are only a few reported ambulatory programs that employ the type of hybrid model advocated herein. The Berkeley Group (Cook, Fox, Weaver, & Rooth, 1991) reported on the success of using an outpatient treatment model for nonviolent sex offenders. The use of an ambulatory model of care is consistent with current mental health models of a continuum of care and a focus on treatment in least-restrictive settings. Bach (2000) and Lothstein (2001) have provided additional research on the success of using an ambulatory treatment model with sex offenders.

Psychodynamic group therapy requires that a person be of sufficient intellectual capacity to understand complex group and individual dynamics. Individuals with below-average intelligence, borderline personality, or mental retardation are not referred for a psychodynamic group therapy. Some of these men cannot even manage the cognitive parts of a cognitive-behavioral therapy. Patients who are acutely psychotic or depressed cannot benefit from this form of treatment until their illness has been stabilized. Once their psychosis and depression has lifted, they may be evaluated for inclusion in psychodynamic group therapy. Individuals with traumatic brain injury or organic brain syndromes that impair insight and judgment are not referred to a psychodynamic group because it may be too overstimulating for them. Patients with traumatic brain injury may become so disorganized in a psychodynamic group that they may misinterpret communications and become flagrantly disorganized and/or paranoid. Patients who have engaged in different types of paraphilias can function in the same group, yet it is our experience that child molesters experience a particularly vulnerable narcissistic threat to their self systems and benefit from a group experience in which other child molesters are present. The point of exclusion from a psychodynamic group has more to do with timing and acuity of illness than with diagnosis.

Of all the sex offenders, the child molester poses one of the highest sexual risks to society and the family. They are difficult to identify and profile (Knight, 1992; Knight, Carter, & Prentky, 1989). Some are sexually attracted only to children; others may engage in a single episode of sexually acting out with a child (though they primarily identify as heterosexual, are married, and father children). Lanyon (1986) stated that the child molester may escape detection because he "is most commonly a respectable, otherwise law abiding person" (p. 176). In the past decade, a new phenomenon of adult sexual interest in teenagers (ephebophilia) has challenged our notions of pedophilia (sexual interest and arousal in prepubescent minors). The law, however, typically views any minor under the age of 15 as a child and treats pedophilia and ephebophilia as identical legal problems, though treatment may differ for each group.

The majority of child molesters who are evaluated and treated are incest perpetrators. A second group involves professionals (e.g., lawyers, physicians, engineers, dentists, teachers, coaches, or clergy) who act out with someone under their care (typically, a teenager). The myth that the child molester or paraphile is likely to be a stranger, uneducated, of a lower social class, homosexual, unemployed, and older was dispelled by Abel et al.'s study (1987). Indeed, child molesters are found in all sectors of society. The prototypical child molester is known to the victim, Caucasian, well educated, employed, heterosexual, and married. Because of the special problems that child molesters have, it is common practice to try to put them in a homogeneous group with other child molesters to deal with the intense shame of having disgraced themselves with a child or minor.

Another group of sexual offenders are those men and women who have a *DSM-IV* diagnosis of paraphilia or who have a nonparaphilic sexually addictive or compulsive sexual disorder. These individuals pose a unique threat to others because of their hypersexuality and their secretive means of acting out. It is our experience that most of these individuals can be helped by assigning them to a hybrid psychodynamic group therapy. Paraphilias have been variously explained by appeals to cerebral abnormality, constitutional issues, arrested psychosexual development, trauma and sexual abuse, and embeddedness in early family psychodynamics (Goldberg, 1995, 1999; Litin, Giffin, & Johnson, 1956; Stoller, 1995). B. Schwartz (1995a) has summarized the extant literature on the characteristics and typologies of sex offenders per the current research and concluded, "The characteristics of sex offenders can become a meaningless list of traits . . . typologies may be reduced to labels that do more harm than good" (p. 31).

Individuals who engage in compulsive, addictive, anonymous sex, who cruise, and who expose their unknowing partners, in marriage or relationship, to STDs and HIV are a special subgroup of paraphiles or potential sex offenders who may benefit from a hybrid model of psychodynamic group therapy treatment. Included in this group are voyeurs, exhibitionists, and those who commit noncontact paraphilias or sexual offenses that do not attract police or community notice. This group may also include some incest child molesters and the full range of sexual offenders who are not sentenced to jail because they evade detection. Most compulsive or sexually addicted sex offenders never come into contact with the courts (Abel et al., 1987). Indeed, their "crimes" may go unnoticed by the judicial system. However, their victims are often unaware that they were even perpetrated against (e.g., the wife of a compulsive cruiser who is exposed to HIV because of her husband's cruising, which he has not shared with her).

To illustrate the approach to treatment advocated, clinical vignettes of typical cases are presented and then a clinical example from one session in a long-term therapy group is presented.

CASE EXAMPLES

Harvy, a 58-year-old, married with two grown children, had sexually molested three latency-age boys, whom he coached. For years, he avoided intimacies with his wife. When he experienced his first erectile dysfunction, he isolated himself and felt like a child. He could not see how he could satisfy his wife or any other woman. He felt unmasculine. During his coaching, he genitally fondled the three boys (on different occasions) and had no understanding of what his behavior meant. The group helped him to set limits and avoid contact with boys and forced him to address his lack of emotional awareness. At times, he acted as if he had no control over any of his actions: Things just happened to him. Over time, he was able to give words to vague feeling states and identify his feelings that preceded acting out.

Samuel, a 30-year-old, told the group that his 5-year-old female neighbor was very sexy. He reported that he could tell from her eyes that she wanted him and that she excited him. When he was arrested for having oral sex with her, he was shocked, because "she wanted it and seduced me." His cognitive distortions were addressed in many ways: learning about the needs of a 5-year-old and developmental issues related to sexuality; affirming that the feelings were really coming from within his body and not from the girl; developing the social skills necessary to form age-appropriate relationships with women, who he feared would reject him; and learning to have better self-confidence and increased self-esteem in his relationships with peers. Issues of loneliness, anger, and abandonment anxiety were integral parts of his treatment.

David, a 43-year-old professional, was a compulsive cruiser. He told the group that he would enter a trance-like state in which "I found myself going to the bookstores" (i.e., pornography bookstores), where he would meet other men for casual sex. The group focused on his lack of awareness of how he made decisions that had serious consequences for him. He experienced his cruising as involving an ego state in which he lacked a connection between his feelings and behavior and entered into a "hypnoticlike state" where "I found myself at a bookstore." Whenever David felt rejected, abandoned, hurt, angry, or lonely, he bottled up those feelings and then acted out sexually. During these dissociative episodes, he experienced himself at the level of a 6-year-old child. In group therapy, he became aware of how his cruising was a reenactment of the disappearance of his mother, who was taken away and died of a terminal illness when he was 6 years of age. His need for connection and attachment was so painful that he could not bear to reexperience the trauma of his childhood loss but recreated the situation with a new twist: Now he was sexual and triumphant and felt ecstatic as opposed to helpless, powerlessness, and grief-stricken. In the group, he was able to link his aggressive feelings as a child to his mother's death and understood how his shameful behavior was a punishment for his earlier transgressions.

Andy, a 36-year-old, was in a crazed state of exhibitionistic frenzy when he was arrested. When he relapsed, he drove across state lines and exposed himself to the police while he was being arrested for exhibitionism. His untreated mania led to a frenzied episode of exhibitionism that was chaotic, bizarre, and disorganized. Once back on medication, he was contained, but the episode cost him his freedom, as he was arrested and incarcerated. During the group, the focus was on helping him to track his feelings of low self-esteem and masochistic submission and identify negative emotions to prevent acting out. In group, he presented as a glib, social, interpersonally warm individual who was an organizer and manipulator. Unfortunately, Andy's self-defeating personality traits and masochism won out before he was able to fully make use of the gains he made in therapy.

The use of the group as a "family" is exemplified in the following vignette. Three of the group's 10 members shared a common identity through multiple addictions involving eating disorders, chemical dependency and drug addiction, and sexually compulsive and addictive sexuality. Frequently, they talked about problems they were having with their children, who served as symbolic aspects of their past family issues. One of the group members said he felt like an outsider and didn't belong in the group because his sexual behavior problems were not as serious as those of the members of the "triad." In actuality, he had had intercourse with his daughter, whereas the triads sexual acting out was limited to pornography and prostitutes. Howard's feelings of an outsider paralleled his history of being adopted and having an identity as an outsider. The group raised the issue of how disturbed one can be and still be accepted by the group in terms of inclusion, norms, and group culture. Jack was struck by the fact that his son had grown up to be just like him. Being a sexual addict, he felt he had no leverage in convincing his son to give up his addictions. The group functioned as a surrogate family, with subgroups, jealousies, envies, rivalries, and favorites. Group members began to see how the group process brought up the old issues in a disguised form and allowed them some emotional distance as they discussed their core relational problems of not being attached to anyone.

As can be seen from these vignettes, a hybrid psychodynamic group therapy focuses on treating the person as a whole and not just as an array of symptoms. However, during periods of crisis and destabilization, the symptom of sexual acting out often took center stage. In the group, an individual's behavior, emotions, and decisions were highlighted while focusing on issues of dampening arousal and changing fantasy content. Group members benefited from the group via the following methods: The leader was active and established a plan of treatment that was carried out in the group; patients were treated within the group, with attention paid to transference, self-object transferences, group process, group as a whole, and a systems approach; the group served as a matrix for socializing and developing the capacity for genuine caring and empathy for other group members; and when interpretations were given, timing was of the essence so the patient could hear the interpretation without becoming too anxious and more susceptible to acting out.

The following vignette illustrates how the psychodynamic approach to sex offender group therapy was applied in one session of a long-term group. This vignette occurred during the eighth year of the group and has been cited elsewhere (Lothstein, 2001).

CASE EXAMPLE

All nine men were present. The group began with Sandy, a 66-year-old grandfather, in his fourth year of group, who had molested the teenage daughter of his woman friend, reporting on his visit to his probation officer. The probation officer was upset and angry at Sandy's plan to go overseas to marry an Asian woman. Sandy characterized her as hostile. She refused to give him permission to go to Asia and marry, yelled at him, called him a sex offender in front of other clients, and said, "Why can't you marry an American woman?" He was intimidated by her caustic remarks.

The group listened to Sandy's concerns, clarified his perceptions, and identified his distortions in communication. While they empathized with Sandy's "pain," they sided with the probation officer and confronted Sandy directly about his decision to go to Asia to find a bride.

At the previous session, Sandy announced that his 29-year-old son, who had gone to Florida, had been missing for several weeks. He did not appear concerned. The group was alarmed for his son's safety and Sandy's lack of interest in finding his son. At this group, Sandy did not make a link between his desire to travel to Asia to meet a strange woman with his lack of interest in finding his son locally. The group wondered about Sandy's capacity for empathy. They insisted that Sandy tell his "fiancée" that he had sex-offended against a minor and served time in jail.

Eric, a 38-year-old with a prior history of exhibitionism, had molested his children. He had been silent in the group for several weeks. For two years, he was separated from his children; currently, he had supervised visits with them. Both Eric and his ex-wife were each romantically involved with new partners. Eric wanted to know what psychological effects their new partners might have on their children. Eileen, his new partner, was putting pressure on him to meet his children. However, Eric wanted the group's advice as to whether it was a good idea and what effect it might have on his children. His oldest son, Richard, was depressed and suicidal and expressed a wish to join grandma in heaven. A link to Sandy's missing son was made. Eric was resistant to the idea of Richard taking antidepressant medication. Eventually, he supported such medical treatment for his son; however, his son's depression persisted.

Eric's ex-wife had already introduced her male companion to the children. The group wondered if Richard wasn't afraid of losing his dad again and perhaps being molested by another man. Steve wondered whether Richard's depression might be related to the introduction of a new dad and whether Eric ought to discuss this with his ex-wife or Richard's therapist. The group supported Eric's decision to call his son's therapist and make this a therapeutic issue. For the first time, Eric began to understand the internal conflicts he caused in his children. His anguish suggested an ability to empathize with his son's conflicts.

Arnold began to talk about his parent-child relationship. A sexual compulsive, Arnold had been in the group 3½ years. He had a recurrent memory that began around the time of his mother's death, when he was about 6 years old. The memory was of a hand going up his shorts and touching his penis. There was no person attached to the hand or arm. Arnold was visibly shaken. He had no idea what the memory meant. The group leader recalled that Arnold's mother became ill when he was 4 years old. When Arnold was 5 years old, his mother's arm was amputated. Arnold's oldest child was now the same age (5 years old) that Arnold was when his mother died. Was this anniversary reaction the trigger of his anxiety memory? He was preoccupied with obsessional thoughts about his own children being harmed. One group member wondered whether the image of a disembodied arm might not relate to Arnold's paraphilic symptoms of exposing his penis to strangers while cruising. The group leader wondered whether Arnold was trying to integrate his mother's mutilation and his abuse through this body image memory. The material was also linked to Sandy's lack of concern for his missing son. Arnold was relieved at having shared his memory with the group. He understood that the multiple meanings of his sexual disinhibition were probably rooted in very early childhood experiences.

Peter, divorced and 40 years old, was raising one of his two sons. He was cross-addicted, diagnosed as a binge eater, alcoholic, compulsive exerciser, and sex addict. He spent enormous sums of money on prostitutes and phone sex. He had been in the group two years. After his mother and brother died of leukemia, Peter, from age 7, was raised in foster care. He was emotionally cold as a result of his childhood history of abandonment, loss, death, and being raised in a foster care environment. He looked sullen, pouted, and was withdrawn, empty, and alone. Prior to acting out, Peter felt bored, depressed, and empty. His son, Greg, who had been living with him for the past year, was 17 years old. Peter described Greg as angry, rebellious, abusing drugs, staying out all night, conduct disordered, and engaging in manipulative and sadomasochistic relationships with both parents. Greg had been impulsively suicidal and was recently admitted to an inpatient psychiatric unit. He had spent some time in jail for dropping out of a drug treatment program and having an "attitude" with the judge.

Peter's father-son relationship paralleled that of Sandy and his son. Serendipitously, the female cotherapist had been on call in the emergency room when Greg was in a psychiatric crisis. She perceived Greg as a "softy," a compliant, frightened, insecure youngster who was tearful and quite different from Peter's image. The group wondered if Greg's behavior wasn't a reflection of his father's defective masculine self. Did Greg need to present himself as a "bully" to compensate for his father's masculine inadequacy and impaired male self-image?

Peter responded by recalling traumatic images of sexual victimization at the hands of his older brother, Matt (who died from cancer when Peter was 7 years old). Matt climbed into Peter's bed and forcibly put his penis in his mouth. Peter struggled to get away. The image of forcible oral sex became a trigger for Peter's anxiety about his masculinity and his adult addictive, compulsive paraphilic behavior. Matt's death intensified Peter's ambivalence. When Peter's mother died of cancer, his father farmed out the children to various foster homes. Peter felt isolated, lonely, despairing, depressed, angry, and numb. He vowed never to establish any meaningful emotional connections to a woman. When Peter found a woman who loved him, he lost interest in her. He pursued only women who were cold and rejecting. Talking about these conflicts lessened Peter's anxiety. The group interpreted Peter's multiple addictions as attempts to repair early self-deficits around loss, separation, and death. Peter's drinking, drugging, sexual addiction, using pornography and prostitutes, and schizoid self system were interpreted as compensatory reactions and defenses against his self-deficits and early object losses.

At the end of the group, one member recalled that Sandy, who had started the group session, had not been appropriately anxious over the disappearance of his 29-year-old son. The therapist interpreted Sandy's anxiety as having been projectively identified onto the group and emerging in the content of the group's discussion. Sandy's indifference to his son's loss became a symbolic representation of the group's identity as lost children whom no one searched for. Moreover, it appeared as if their unconscious paraphilic compulsions may have been "communicated" to their children, who, like their fathers, were acting out sexually and aggressively. Issues of object loss, which had been sexually acted out, were now identified as unpleasant feelings that could be consciously recognized and not sexualized. As a result of sharing intensely intimate material, some of the men's desire to sexualize their pain decreased.

This group vignette is characteristic of the way a broad-based psychodynamic method was employed in a sex offender group, emphasizing a self psychological and object-relations theory that was blended into an integrated model of care. For sex offenders to develop the internal mechanisms to self-regulate their sexual behavior, they have to affectively integrate all aspects of their experience, using the group process as a screen to reenact and work through their childhood anxieties.

The following are some of the curative and rehabilitative group dynamics at work in a hybrid psychodynamic sex offender group therapy:

1. Group process may dilute the intensity of the transference and allow patients to disclose personal material at a faster rate.
2. Group therapy may lessen the effects of the superego on the patient's shame as other sex offenders who share a self-identity as a "monster" begin to mobilize healthy, nonshameful aspects of self in the curative process.
3. Group therapy may blunt the negative effects of defensive denial, minimization, rationalization, and projection through group members' confrontation of these defenses and allow for the exposure and elimination of cognitive distortions.
4. Group therapy allows empathy to develop as the group members develop the emotional capacity to relate to real human beings (i.e., allowing for real person-victim empathy versus a memorized cognitive script of quasi-empathy statements).
5. Group therapy may help patients to develop real connections to other human beings through the power of the self-object transferences that emerge in the group process that are then generalized to interpersonal relationships outside the group.

The psychodynamic group focus on emotional learning and the need to link affects, internal representations, and object-relationships are necessary to help prevent the sex-offending individual from sexualizing his conflicts. Moreover, these methods make the sex offender more aware of what his offending means on a deep intrapsychic and intrapersonal level. At this stage, a capacity for depression may develop that allows the perpetrator to understand the emotional basis for his victim's pain. The sine qua non for group leadership is the capacity to tolerate and support strong affective expression in the group.

Psychodynamically oriented groups typically meet for longer periods of time than psychoeducational or support groups (90 minutes versus 45 minutes to an hour). In psychodynamic groups, there is no weekly agenda; it is left up to the patients to bring material into the group. However, in open-ended groups, it is typical to introduce new members by going around the group and asking the old members to introduce themselves and describe their core sexual problems and goals for treatment. At the end, the new member introduces himself, his symptoms, and his goals for treatment. During periods of stress, the group leader(s) in a psychodynamic group may ask members to talk about any acting out during the prior week. The group culture, dynamics, and process of working through individual and group issues and termination in these groups are in keeping with current thinking in the group therapy field.

The importance of group dynamics becomes a centerpiece of the group's work as patients come to recognize that only through long-term group work can their shame-based acting out be demystified, secrets dispelled, interpersonal isolation and loneliness addressed, and the development of healthy attachments become a reality.

POSTTERMINATION SYNOPSIS AND EFFECTIVENESS DATA

Most of the research on sex offenders (e.g., recidivism rates; whether treatment is effective in controlling sexual behavior; and how to assess risk for acting out sexually in a violent way) has typically focused on a heterogeneous group of sexually violent individuals who are incarcerated (B. Schwartz, 1995c). Incarcerated sex offenders are a very specialized group of sex offenders who are under state or federal custody and may already be in specialized sex offender treatment programs.

In most studies, the recidivism rate is the main outcome measure or dependent variable for assessing the cost-benefit ratio of group therapy for incarcerated sex offenders (Prentky, Lee, Knight, & Cerce, 1997). Although researchers have provided a number of tools for predicting risk of recidivism (Epperson, Kaul, & Hesselton, 1998; Hanson, 1997; Hanson & Thornton, 2000), all of these risk assessment tools are based on studies of incarcerated sex offenders and cannot be used with a nonincarcerated population. In this sense, we do not have any reliable risk assessment tools for the vast numbers of individuals who may have severe sexual acting-out problems but have never been arrested.

Unless all incarcerated violent sex offenders are civilly committed after serving their jail sentences, we can expect that the vast majority of them will leave institutional care and be maintained in outpatient, ambulatory treatment settings. Most will be mandated to continue their therapy on an outpatient basis. In many cases, the recommendations for treatment will be court-ordered as part of probation.

Prior to 1980, the majority of men (and women) who committed nonviolent sexual crimes spent little, if any, time in jail. Typically, they were put on probation and assigned to individual psychotherapy. Recent changes in sentencing guidelines and the effect of public opinion on the judiciary have changed this pattern. Now, it is more common for sex offenders to receive lengthy jail sentences and have probation requirements, long-term supervision, and referral for sex offender treatment postincarceration. Essentially, no matter how lengthy the prison sentence, the overwhelming majority of sex offenders will be returned to society and outpatient treatment. As clinicians, we must ask ourselves whether we have treatments that work, and if so, what are they and how should they be administered?

Despite a spate of studies suggesting statistically acceptable low recidivism rates for sex offenders who have undergone treatment (Hanson & Bussiere, 1998), the public is very wary of whether sex offenders can benefit from treatment. It has been difficult to change public attitudes toward the treatment of sex offenders (who are all associated with child molesters). Indeed, despite a number of studies highlighting the effectiveness of specialized sex offender treatment, the public perception is that it does not work. Most clinicians treating individuals with Axis I pathology aspire for an 80% rehabilitation (not cure) rate, yet the findings of an average rate of 86% for sex offenders is not accepted as high enough because there is zero tolerance among the public for any form of relapse when sex is concerned.

Over the past two decades, state and federally funded treatment programs have designed specialized approaches to the treatment of sex offenders that proved the efficacy of such treatment. Although specialized approaches for treating incarcerated sexual offenders have been proposed that suggest promising results on follow-up (Hanson & Bussiere, 1998), all studies are subject to methodological criticism.

Many states have implemented specialized sex offender treatment programs into their prison system rehabilitation programs (Pithers, 1990), but none of these programs are standardized and treatment outcome variables across programs cannot be adequately assessed. Moreover, the staffs at the different penal institutions differ as to level of training, professional education, and degree of supervision in treatment techniques. There is no coherent nationwide policy for employing the same standards for selection of staff and the utilization of treatment protocols. All of these points have been used as criticisms against an array of very good programs from a clinical perspective.

The efficacy of group therapy for paraphilic behavior has been demonstrated by outcome studies that revealed a 14% relapse rate with treatment (Hanson & Bussiere, 1998) compared with a relapse rate of about 25 to 50% without treatment over an extended period of time (Marshall & Barbaree, 1988). Despite quite low recidivism rates (about 14%) for all the paraphilias and a 3% rate for incest perpetrators (and 25 to 50% relapse after 10 years for untreated sex offenders), society does not appear willing to tolerate any relapse risks when it comes to the safety of children and other high-risk vulnerable populations. A continuous focus on relapse prevention, however, may help paraphiles break the shaming cycle of acting out sexually preceded by intense negative emotions that are too painful to bear.

In evaluating outcome, each sex offender treatment program must be assessed for the unique context in which treatment is administered and the effects of the context of treatment (i.e., the environment in which treatment takes place). The effect of context is so important that programs from different contexts cannot be compared (in terms of treatment efficacy and outcome) with one another. This does not mean, however, that the results of their studies cannot be used in policymaking decisions.

In a recent study by Lothstein (2001), 109 consecutive sex offenders and sexually compulsive and addictive men (and 1 woman) were treated in the hybrid model advocated in this chapter. The average age was 50.7 years, with 57% of the sample having been arrested and 50% on probation. The relapse rate for all patients was 21% (range = 3% to 52%). The higher relapse rates were for exhibitionists and nonparaphilic behaviors (cruising, fetishism, compulsive masturbation, pornography and Internet use). The lowest relapse rate was for incest perpetrators. The results of the study are consistent with other research and suggest that a psychodynamic group therapy model can address successfully the complex issues of sex-offending behavior.

It is our hope that clinicians will see the value in using a hybrid psychodynamic model of group therapy for sex offenders and compulsive sexual addicts. Unless we treat the deeper psychological structures of individuals who sexually abuse, both the individual and society will continue to be at risk.

REFERENCES

Abel, G., Becker, J., Mittelman, M., Cunningham-Rathner, J., Rouleau, J., & Murphy, W. (1987). Self reported crimes of nonincarcerated paraphilias. *Journal of Interpersonal Violence*, 3–25.

Alonso, A., & Rutan, J. (1988). The experience of shame and the restoration of self respect in group therapy. *International Journal of Group Psychotherapy*, 38, 3–27.

American Group Psychotherapy Association. (1995). *Certified group psychotherapist: National Registry of Certified Group Psychotherapists: Promoting quality of care and standards of practice for group psychotherapy.* (25 E 21st St., New York, NY 10010)

American Psychiatric Association. (1994). *Diagnostic and statistical manual of mental disorders* (4th ed.). Washington, DC: Author.

Anderson, R. (1969). The exchange of tape recordings as a catalyst in group psychotherapy with sex offenders. *International Journal of Group Psychotherapy*, 19, 214–217.

Anonymous. (1987). *Hope and recovery: A twelve step guide for healing from compulsive sexual behavior.* Minneapolis, MN: CompCare.

Association for the Treatment of Sex Abusers. (1996). *Reducing sexual abuse through treatment and intervention with abusers* [Policy statement].

Bach, R. (2000). *Issues of shame in the etiology and treatment of non-violent paraphilias: A group therapy model.* Doctoral dissertation, University of Hartford, West Hartford, CT.

Becker, J. (1996). Outpatient treatment of adolescent male sexual offenders. In M. Andronico (Ed.), *Men in groups: Insights, interventions, and psychoeducational work.* Washington, DC: American Psychological Association.

Berlin, F. (1983). Sex offender: A biomedical perspective and a status report on biomedical treatment. In Greer & Stuart (Eds.), *The sexual aggressor: Current perspective on treatment* (pp. 83–123). New York: Van Nostrand-Reinhold.

Brown, T., & Lothstein, L. (1996, September). *An innovative program to treat sexual offenders with severe mental illness in a state mental health facility.* Paper presented to the Forensic Directors meeting, San Antonio, TX.

Buchele, B. (1994). Innovative uses of psychodynamic group psychotherapy. *Bulletin of the Menninger Clinic*, 58(2), 215–223.

Bureau of Justice. (1997, April). *U.S. Department of Justice.* Retrieved from www.ojp.usdoj.gov/bjs

Caffaro, J. (1991). A room full of fathers. *Journal of Psychotherapy*, 24(4), 27–40.

Carnes, P. (1983). *Out of the shadows: Understanding sexual addiction.* Minneapolis, MN: CompCare.

Carnes, P. (1989). *A gentle path through the twelve steps.* Minneapolis, MN: CompCare.

Catherall, D., & Shelton, R. (1996). Men's groups for posttraumatic stress disorder and the role of shame. In M. Andronico (Ed.), *Men in groups: Insights, interventions and psychoeducational work.* Washington, DC: American Psychological Association.

Chassequet-Smirgel, J. (1986). *Sexuality and mind: The role of the father and the mother in the psyche.* New York: New York University Press.

Coleman, E. (1988). Sexual compulsivity and treatment considerations. In E. Coleman (Ed.), *Chemical dependency and intimacy dysfunction* (pp. 189–204). New York: Haworth Press.

Cook, D., Fox, C., Weaver, C., & Rooth, G. (1991). The Berkeley Group: Ten years' experience of a group of non-violent sex offenders. *British Journal of Psychiatry*, 158, 238–243.

Dougher, M. (1995). Behavioral techniques to alter sexual arousal. In B. Schwartz & H. Cellini (Eds.), *The sex offender: Corrections, treatment, and legal practice.* Kingston, NJ: Civic Research Institute.

Epperson, D., Kaul, J., & Hesselton, D. (1998). *Final report on the development of the Minnesota Sex Offender Screening Tool-Revised* (MnSORT-R).

Presentation at the 17th annual research and treatment conference of the Association for the Treatment of Sexual Abusers, Vancouver, British Columbia, Canada.

Finkelhor, D., & Araji, S. (1986). Explanations of pedophilia: A four factor model. *Journal of Sex Research, 22,* 145–159.

Friedman, R. (1994). Psychodynamic group therapy for male survivors of sexual abuse. *Group, 18*(4), 225–234.

Ganzarain, R., & Buchele, B. (1990). Incest perpetrators in group therapy: A psychodynamic perspective. *Bulletin of the Menninger Clinic, 54*(3), 295–310.

Goldberg, A. (1995). *The problem of perversion: The view from self psychology.* New Haven, CT: Yale University Press.

Goldberg, A. (1999). *Being of two minds: The vertical split in psychoanalysis and psychotherapy.* Hillsdale, NJ: Analytic Press.

Goldberg, A. (Ed.). (2000). *Errant selves: A casebook of misbehavior.* Hillsdale, NJ: Analytic Press.

Goodman, A. (1998). *Sexual addiction: An integrated approach.* New York: International Universities Press.

Green, R. (1995). Psycho-educational modules. In B. Schwartz & H. Cellini (Eds.), *The sex offender: Corrections, treatment and legal practice.* Lexington, NJ: Civic Research Institute.

Hanson, R. (1997). *The development of a brief actuarial risk scale for sexual offense recidivism RRASOR* (User Rep. No. 97–04). Ottawa: Department of the Solicitor General of Canada.

Hanson, R., & Bussiere, M. (1998). Predicting relapse: A meta-analysis of sexual offender recidivism studies. *Journal of Consulting and Clinical Psychology, 66,* 348–362.

Hanson, R., & Thornton, D. (2000). Improving risk assessments for sex offenders: A comparison of three actuarial scales. *Law and Human Behavior, 24,* 119–136.

Kaplan, L. (1991). *Female perversions: The temptation of Madame Bovary.* New York: Doubleday.

Kaufman, G. (1992). *Shame, the power of caring* (3rd ed.). Rochester, UT: Schenkman Books.

Kaufman, G. (1996). *The psychology of shame* (2nd ed.). New York: Springer.

Kendricks vs. Kansas Nos. 95–1649/95–9075. U.S. Lexis 3999. (June 23, 1997).

Khan, M. (1974). *The privacy of the self.* New York: International Universities Press.

Khan, M. (1979). *Alienation in perversions.* New York: International Universities Press.

Khan, M. (1983). *Hidden selves: Between theory and practice in psychoanalysis.* New York: International Universities Press.

Knight, R. (1992). The generation and corroboration of a taxonomic model for child molesters. In W. O'Donohue & J. H. Geer (Eds.), *The sexual abuse of children: Theory, research and therapy.* Hillsdale, NJ: Erlbaum.

Knight, R., Carter, D., & Prentky, R. (1989). A system for the classification of child molesters: Reliability and application. *Journal of Interpersonal Violence, 4,* 3–23.

Kohut, H. (1977). *The restoration of the self.* New York: International Universities Press.

Lanyon, R. (1986). Theory and treatment in child molestation. *Journal of Consulting and Clinical Psychology,* 176–182.

Laws, R. (Ed.). (1989). *Relapse prevention with sex offenders.* New York: Guilford Press.

Lehne, G., Kate, T., & Berlin, F. (2000). *Treatment of sexual paraphilias: A review of the 1999–2000.*

Litin, E., Giffin, M., & Johnson, A. (1956). Parental influences in unusual sexual behavior in children. *Psychoanalytic Quarterly, 25,* 37–55.

Lothstein, L. (1979). Group therapy with gender-dysphoric patients. *American Journal of Psychotherapy, 33,* 67–81.

Lothstein, L. (1995). An olfactory perversion (osmophilia) successfully treated with Depo-Provera and then psychotherapy. *Sexual Addiction and Compulsivity, 2,* 40–53.

Lothstein, L. (1996). Antiandrogen treatment for sexual disorders: Guidelines for establishing a standard of care. *Sexual Addiction and Compulsivity, 2,* 20–53.

Lothstein, L. (1997). Pantyhose fetishism and self cohesion. *Gender and Psychoanalysis, 2,* 103–121.

Lothstein, L. (1999). Neuropsychological findings in clergy who sexually abuse. In J. Plante (Ed.), *Bless me Father for I have sinned: Perspectives on sexual abuse committed by Roman Catholic priest.* Westport, CT: Praeger.

Lothstein, L. (2001). Treatment of non-incarcerated sexually compulsive/addictive offenders (SCAO) in an integrated/multimodal and psychodynamic group therapy model. *International Journal of Group Psychotherapy.*

Lothstein, L., Fogg-Waberski, J., & Reynolds, P. (1997). Risk management and treatment of sexual disinhibition in geriatric patients. *Connecticut Medicine, 61,* 609–618.

Lothstein, L., & Zimet, G. (1988). Twinship and alter ego self object transferences in group therapy with the elderly: A reanalysis of the pairing phenomenon. *International Journal of Group Therapy, 38,* 303–317.

Marques, J., & Nelson, C. (1989). Understanding and preventing relapse in sex offenders. In M. Gossop (Ed.), *Relapse and addictive behavior* (pp. 96–106). London: Tavistock/Routledge.

Marshall, W. (1994). Treatment effects on denial and minimization in incarcerated sex offenders. *Behavior, Research and Theory, 5,* 559–564.

Marshall, W., & Barbaree, H. (1988). An outpatient treatment program for child molesters. *Annals of the New York Academy of Sciences, 528,* 205–214.

McCarthy, B. (1994). Sexually compulsive men and inhibited sexual desire. *Journal of Sex and Marital Therapy, 20,* 200–209.

Milton, J., & McLean, P. (1999). Treatment of heroin use and deviant sexual thoughts: Harm reduction or collusion? *Journal of Forensic Psychiatry, 10,* 679–686.

Peters, S., Pedigo, J., Steg, J., & McKenna, J. (1968). Group psychotherapy of the sexual offender. *Federal Probation, 32,* 41–46.

Peters, S., & Roether, H. (1972). Group psychotherapy for probationed sex offenders. In H. Resnick & M. Wolfgang (Eds.), *Sexual behaviors: Clinical and legal aspects.* Boston: Little, Brown.

Pietz, C., & Mann, J. (1989). Importance of having a female co-therapist in a child molesters' group. *Professional Psychology: Research and Practice, 20*(4), 265–268.

Pithers, W. (1990). Relapse prevention with sexual aggressors. In W. L. Marshall, D. Laws, & H. Barbaree (Eds.), *Handbook of sexual assault.* New York: Plenum Press.

Pithers, W. (1994). Process evaluation of a group therapy component designed to enhance sex offenders' empathy for sexual abuse survivors. *Behavior Research and Therapy, 32,* 565–570.

Pithers, W., & Cummings, G. (1995). Relapse prevention: A method for enhancing behavioral self-management and external supervision of the sexual aggressor. In B. Schwartz & H. Cellini (Eds.), *The sex offender: Corrections, treatment and practice* (Vol. 1). Livingston, NJ: Civic Research Institute.

Pithers, W., Kashima, K., Cumming, G., Beal, L., & Buell, M. (1988). Relapse prevention of sexual aggression. In R. Prentky & V. Quinsey (Eds.), *Human sexual aggression: Current perspectives* (pp. 244–260). New York: New York Academy of Science.

Prentky, R., Lee, A., Knight, R., & Cerce, D. (1997). Recidivism rates among child molesters and rapists: A methodological analysis. *Law and Human Behavior, 21,* 635–659.

Quinsey, V. L., Lalumiere, M. L., Rice, M. E., & Harris, G. T. (1995). Predicting sexual offenses. In J. C. Campbell (Ed.), *Assessing dangerousness: Violence by sexual offenders, batterers, and child abusers* (pp. 114–137). Thousand Oaks, CA: Sage.

Quinsey, V. L., Rice, M. E., & Harris, G. T. (1995). Actuarial prediction of sexual recidivism. *Journal of Interpersonal Violence, 10,* 85–105.

Rutan, S., & Stone, W. (1984). *Psychodynamic group psychotherapy.* Lexington, MA: Collamore Press.

Schneider, J. (1991). How to recognize the signs of sexual addiction. *Postgraduate Medicine, 90,* 171–182.

Schwartz, B. (1995a). Characteristics and typologies of sex offenders. In B. Schwartz & H. Cellini (Eds.), *The sex offender: Corrections, treatment, and legal practice.* Lexington, NJ: Civic Research Institute.

Schwartz, B. (1995b). Decision making with incarcerated sex offenders. In B. Schwartz & H. Cellini (Eds.), *The sex offender: Corrections, treatment, and legal practice* (pp. 1–15). Lexington, NJ: Civic Research Institute.

Schwartz, B. (1995c). Group therapy. In B. Schwartz & H. Cellini (Eds.), *The sex offender: Corrections, treatment, and legal practice.* Lexingston, NJ: Civic Research Institute.

Schwartz, B. (1995d). Theories of sex offenses. In B. Schwartz & H. Cellini (Eds.), *The sex offender: Corrections, treatment, and legal practice* (pp. 2–28). Kingston, NJ: Civic Research Institute.

Schwartz, M. (1995). In my opinion: Victim to victimizer. *Sexual Addiction and Compulsivity* (2), 81–88.

Schwartz, M., & Brasted, W. (1985). Sexual addiction. *Medical Aspects of Human Sexuality, 19*(10), 103–107.

Sexaholics Anonymous. (1989). International Central Office, P. O. Box 300, Simi Valley, CA 93062.

Sex and Love Addicts Anonymous. (1964). Boston, MA 02105

Sexual Addicts Anonymous. (1986). Twin Cities Sexual Addicts Anonymous, P. O. Box 3038, Minneapolis, MN 55403.

Sipe, R. (1990). *A secret world: Sexuality and the search for celibacy.* New York: Brunner/Mazel.

Slater, M. (1964). *Sex offenders in group therapy.* Los Angeles: Sherbourne Press.

Smith, R. (1995). Sex offender program planning and implementation. In B. Schwartz, & H. Cellini (Eds.), *The sex offender: Corrections, treatment, and legal practice.* Kingston, NJ: Civic Research Institute.

Socarides, C. (1988). *The preoedipal origins and psychoanalytic therapy of sexual perversions.* Madison, CT: International Universities Press.

Sternbach, J. (1996). The father theme in group therapy with men. In M. Andronico (Ed.), *Men in groups: Insights, interventions and psychoeducational work.* Washington, DC: American Psychological Association.

Stoller, R. (1975). *Perversion: The erotic form of hatred.* New York: Pantheon Books.

Stoller, R. (1979) *Sexual excitement: Dynamics of erotic life.* New York: Pantheon Books.

Stoller, R. (1985). *Observing the erotic imagination.* New Haven, CT: Yale University Press.

Stoller, R. (1991). *Pain and passion: A psychoanalyst explores the world of S&M.* New York: Plenum Press.

Travin, S., & Protter, B. (1993). *Sexual perversion.* New York: Plenum Press.

Twerski, A. (1997). *Addictive thinking: Understanding self deception.* Minneapolis, MN: CompCare.

Winnicott, D. W. (1965). *The maturational processes and the facilitating environment.* New York: Hogarth Press.

Wright, F. (1994). Men, shame and group psychotherapy. *Group.*

Yalom, I. (1975). *The theory and practice of group psychotherapy.* New York: Basic Books.

Section Six

SPECIAL TOPICS

Chapter 22   Groups in Therapeutic Communities

Chapter 23   Psychodynamic Treatment for Cardiac Patients

Chapter 24   Race, Gender, and Transference in Psychotherapy

Chapter 25   Contemporary Psychodynamics: Major Issues, Challenges, and Future Trends

CHAPTER 22

Groups in Therapeutic Communities

José Guimón

THERAPEUTIC GROUPS: HISTORY

From the Circle to the Institution

Several experiments that were undertaken in the period between World Wars I and II showed that some group techniques, as well as more global interventions in certain institutions, could be very effective. For instance, in the early 1930s, the Spanish psychiatrist Mira y Lopez began to form groups and, at the beginning of the Spanish Civil War, he took steps to ensure that the 1,300 patients in the Hospital of San Baudilio (Barcelona) could learn to manage, to some extent, their own therapy. This made him a forefather of therapeutic communities.

During the Second World War, the sudden increase in psychiatric illnesses due to stress led to the utilization of therapeutic group techniques and to the employment of nonmedical personnel. These innovations yielded important savings in time and money. Similarly, group treatment (in inpatient and outpatient settings) of veterans presenting mental disorders became necessary. Halfway houses and clubs were then created to promote the veterans' readaptation into society.

The Northfield Experiments (Bion, Rickman, Foulkes)

In 1942, during the Second World War, Wilfred R. Bion was sent as a psychiatrist to the Northfield Military Hospital in England. There, with John Rickman, he promoted a very interesting program, "the first Northfield experiment," an effort to modify the functioning of the institution "as a whole" by forming various groups. However, conflicts with the military administrators of the hospital led to a premature ending of the experiment after six weeks.

The second experiment was more the result of a team effort and lasted until the end of the war. One month after Bion's departure, Foulkes arrived. He was able to continue and enlarge the movement during a four-year period that has been called "the second Northfield experiment." The account of the first trial, published in the

Bulletin of the Menninger Clinic (Menninger, 1942), and the ensuing comments by Foulkes (1948) and other participants (Anthony, 1983; de Mare, 1983; Main, 1946, 1977) are of great value in helping us to understand the genesis of therapeutic communities. Foulkes, the only psychoanalyst at Northfield, brought knowledge and skill from his experience as a leader of small therapy groups, which he had previously developed in a psychiatric service in Exeter (Foulkes & Lewis, 1944).

At the same time, Maxwell Jones (1952, 1968, 1972) initiated, at the Mill Neurosis Center, a program that was based on the same principles as Northfield (with whose leaders he was in contact), although its orientation was more sociotherapeutic than psychoanalytical. His therapeutic approach became very popular; the term "therapeutic community" is commonly associated with Jones, who later specialized in the treatment of delinquents presenting what today would be diagnosed as personality disorders (especially Borderline and Antisocial Personality Disorders).

Therapeutic communities were, thus, originally used for the treatment of neurosis and personality disorders. Only later, principally after Main's experiences at the Cassel Hospital in London, were they used for schizophrenics.

From Therapeutic Communities to Milieu Therapy

After the Second World War, there was a veritable explosion in group psychotherapy. Some psychiatrists—in the United Kingdom, at the Tavistock Clinic and Cassel Hospital (the resettlement units); and in the United States, particularly among the Menninger Clinic's Group for the Development of Psychiatry (Menninger, 1939, 1942)—felt the need to break out of their traditional isolation from the public by adapting these authors' wartime group experiences to the needs of daily practice. These ideas, which inspired the work of others in several countries (Rees & Glatt, 1955; Rickman, 1935; Sivadon, Davies, & Baker, 1963; Sivadon, Follin, & Tournaud, 1952), showed the usefulness of open rooms and more open communication links between patients in psychiatric hospitals and those persons responsible for their treatment.

THEORETICAL BASIS OF THERAPEUTIC COMMUNITIES

United Kingdom: From Bion to Foulkes

The first "holistic" approach to groups, and its early application to the understanding of institutions, was the responsibility of Wilfred Bion, who described "group analysis" as the self-analysis of the group by its members and its leader. The theoretical foundations of this procedure (based on neurophysiology, psychoanalysis, medicine, neurology, psychiatry, Gestalt psychology, and sociology) have not yet been well developed (Roberts, 1995), even if significant work has been accomplished by authors such as Malcolm Pines (1976, 1994, 1996).

Foulkes's most original concept was the "group matrix," which presupposes that an individual mind might not exist at all but is, in fact, an illusory concept derived from the dialogue between two or more members of a group. In the case of a person alone, the participants in the dialogue would have been internalized. For Foulkes, mental illness results from a perturbation in communication and an excessive attachment to the family. These difficulties are further reinforced in the various social groups to which the subject belongs. Foulkes referred to this process as the reticular theory of neurosis. The result is that therapy for adults is best undertaken in a group.

In interpreting group phenomena, all kinds of communication (whether in words or gestures) must be taken into account, as should the fact that any kind of communication coming from a single individual represents, in a certain manner, communication with the group as a whole. Although mainly used for neurotic patients, Foulkes's techniques were also employed—at the Institute of Psychiatry in London and, later, in many parts of Europe—with psychotic patients.

Other authors extended Bion's theories on the regressive phenomena in small groups to the study of group processes, the definition of the role of a leader, and the authority and structure of great social organizations. A "systemic" approach to analysis of organizations was developed. Later, Kernberg (1975) applied these contributions by integrating object-relationships into the understanding of hospitals' organizational problems.

FRENCH INSTITUTIONAL PSYCHOTHERAPY

In France (Chanoit, 1995), the Center for Treatment and Social Readaptation of the City of Evrard (Sivadon et al., 1952), some facilities within the 13th arrondissement of Paris (Diatkine, 1958; Diatkine, Socarras, & Kestemberg, 1959; Lebovici, 1953; Racamier, 1979, 1980, 1983), and the Delaborde Clinic developed new therapeutic approaches with an orientation that was both sociological and psychoanalytical. This was called "institutional psychotherapy."

Coming from the field of sociology, Tosquelles (1995) stated that institutional psychotherapy was based on the techniques that underline the singularity of illness, teamwork, the system of meetings, and active therapies. Meetings are planned to facilitate the transmission of information among technicians, patients, and directing teams, while reducing the intensity of corridor noises. Active therapies, such as occupational therapy and social therapy, are based on methods of eliciting group participation. The therapeutic group, created to promote autonomy in occupational therapy (Tosquelles, 1995), and directed by patients, also has a therapeutic function.

On the psychoanalytical side, the movement toward institutional psychotherapy was enriched by the contributions of authors in three categories (Chanoit, 1995): (1) psychoanalysts, who tried to apply analysis to the group situation (Diatkine, 1958; Kestemberg & Decobert, 1964; Lebovici, 1953); (2) psychiatrists, who tried to understand psychoses through psychoanalysis (Racamier, 1979); and (3) psychotherapists, who tried to define mental illness and social alienation (Oury, 1976; Tosquelles, 1995). These authors were interested in the analysis and interpretation of transference on the personnel in the hospital, which develops in a fashion somewhat different from dual transference.

However, the concepts of individual institutional transference and countertransference have been challenged. Some authors of psychoanalytical persuasion demand that these concepts be used with caution. In any case, thanks to these approaches, progress has been made in our knowledge of the therapeutic function of the institution. Specifically, we have learned which modifications of the institutional setting are necessary to put into action psychoanalytic treatments for seriously ill patients and, through certain modifications in psychoanalytic theory, for those with psychoses as well. For instance, because the patient is connected to the institution only for the duration of hospitalization, a differentiation is made between psychoanalytic interpretation of individual patients and the psychoanalytic understanding that the therapist acquires of the phenomena of the group and the institutional relationship. Therefore, for psychotic patients, Racamier (1979) proposed a "bifocal" treatment: a psychiatrist would take charge of aspects centered on reality, and a psychoanalyst would work at the level of unconscious fantasy.

A law enacted in France in 1985 established sectorization to ensure continuity of care in various settings, over different periods of time. This strategy for the continuity of care permits the same team to follow up the patient at the hospital and in outpatient care, and favors a better and more dynamic care program.

Other Theoretical Approaches

In the United States, the liberalization of the hospital environment was already active in the 1950s. Woodbury's therapeutic team started a study in a ward, Chestnut Lodge, at St. Elizabeth's Hospital in Washington, DC. It became the first experiment with community therapy in the United States. The most complete program of community therapy was organized at the Menninger Clinic (Menninger, 1942), in Topeka, Kansas.

Following those experiments, therapeutic communities were created in other parts of the world. In Latin America, the first communities were established mainly in the private sector—for example, in Buenos Aires, Argentina, at the clinic of J. Garcia Badarracco (1990). In Italy, Franco Basaglia (1970), at the Hospital of Gorizia, criticized the concept of community therapy and proposed a program of treatment based on large groups called "community meetings." All patients in the hospital were followed via meetings with personnel and leaders. The objective was to exchange ideas about the preceding session.

METHODS OF INTERVENTION

Therapeutic Mechanisms in Communities

According to Gunderson (1983), in the treatment programs proposed by Menninger (1939) and Bettelheim (1950), two factors present in the course of treatment in certain psychiatric hospitals were recognized. *Containment* (in Bion's sense) furnishes a feeling of security in the face of infantile pain, rage, and despair, which frequently are reexperienced in the therapeutic community. *Structuring the environment* makes the therapeutic environment less ambiguous and chaotic and facilitates modifications in ill-adapted behaviors in the patient. Activities ranged from organizing hierarchical systems of reward and privilege to using contracts, setting up meetings, and issuing guidelines for patients' daily routine and hygiene. Menninger and Bettelheim set up programs that offered structure through the organization of space, activities, certain privileges and contracts, and the planning of daily activities.

Other factors entering into the efficacy of a therapeutic milieu have been described. Most notable is the *support* of anything that might foster patients' personal investment in a treatment plan for fighting against passivity and for promoting acceptance of the expression of their pathology ("validation"), which allows them to assume their individuality. In these programs, it is stipulated that patients' desire for solitude, their need to keep secrets, and their disabilities and symptoms must also be respected. *Implication* is the mechanism through which patients are encouraged to interact with their environment as a way of escaping from passivity and to collaborate with treatment staff.

These mechanisms have specific effects for different patients. Thus, containment can be necessary for a schizophrenic who is in an acute phase and exhibits confusion and impulsiveness, but may have a negative effect on chronic patients. Support can be very useful for depressed or frightened patients, but may be harmful for paranoid or borderline patients. Providing structure can also be useful for chronic schizophrenics, whereas an active psychotic may be overwhelmed by the demands of community inclusion. Validation can be very useful for paranoid and borderline patients, but may be dangerous for suicidal patients and may lead to the neglect of certain passive or verbose patients.

In the developmental sequence articulated by Haigh (1999) and Hinshelwood (1999), several therapeutic ingredients were described, the first of which was attachment. The theory of attachment posits that if the link with the mother has not been reassuring, the adult will lack confidence in himself or herself, which is notable among some patients who suffer from personality disorders. The therapeutic community creates a culture in which belonging is highly prized and members are validated. This culture is reassuring, but, for an individual to develop, he or she must be able to confront other complex experiences such as love, hate, anger, frustration, sadness, attack, defense, and comfort. In this sense, the therapeutic community offers experiences of inclusion (a process of derivation and evaluation) and of departure (rituals of leaving). A fundamental therapeutic factor of development (Haigh, 1999; Hinshelwood, 1999), already mentioned, is containment, which relates to the "mothering element" of these institutions. There is also a "paternal element," that establishes limits and rules and reinforces boundaries.

When the therapeutic community has mastered primitive preverbal work with a patient, another fundamental challenge looms: establishing "communication" in the form of contacts with other patients and caregivers. These contacts encourage mutual understanding through the use of "symbolic representations" and the process of "identification." But first there must exist a "communal identity" (Rapaport, 1974)—a set of intimate relationships that are forged when all members participate in the therapeutic, social, and informal activities that form a "culture of inquiry" (Main, 1977). Stable, protected groups with well-defined boundaries encourage this process.

Another factor specific to therapeutic communities is the stipulation that all interpersonal interaction belongs to all members of the community; that is, everything that goes on in the community can be utilized from a therapeutic point of view, and this leads to an inseparable union between "living and learning" (Jones, 1968). At the same time, there is a basic belief that the patient's unconscious is the best judge of the direction therapy should take. This brings into play the notion that the most important therapeutic effect is brought into being by the patient, not the therapist. The lack of symmetry between the therapist and the patient is accepted, but any automatic assumption of the therapist's superiority is rejected. This attitude fosters accountability in patients. By assuming responsibility for their own therapeutic process, they facilitate its improvement. However, the process can be a source of ambivalence—for example, it may engender feelings of guilt.

The majority of severely disturbed patients have a fragmented internal world; their identity and mental processes are disorganized. Disorganized institutions threaten to increase disorganization in their members, who, in turn, will disturb the institution. In other words, patients project their difficulties onto the community that surrounds them, and they introject elements from that community. The concept of "internalization of object relations" thus is relevant in most therapeutic communities.

The life of a community is in constant evolution because of the curiosity of its members. This is evident in patients' search for self, which constitutes a "culture of inquiry" (Main, 1977). Bion (1962) referred to relations of curious inquiry in psychoanalysis as K relations of knowing. The K approach is the equivalent of the attitude of community inquiry that, at each step, seeks to know why certain things are done. If we do not call things into question, memories disappear and are replaced by a moralist tone: "We do this like that." As a result, rules are made by the superego rather than the ego (Main, 1977). However, even this culture of inquiry can become ritualized and it is necessary to have a sort of "metavigilance" to avoid that outcome (Levinson, 1996).

WARD ATMOSPHERE AND TEAMWORK

Ward Atmosphere
In the psychiatric units of general hospitals, patients have to deal with a high degree of stress arising from short stays, acute symptomatology, auto- and heteroaggression, a rapid turnover in patients, and limited space. Group analytical

programs of the type described above, which place particular emphasis on the here and now and on intermember cohesiveness, have been shown to be useful stabilizing ("buffer") tools because they foster involvement and support and allow controlled expressions of anger and aggressiveness.

The patients/staff group is the key holding element of our group analytical program because of its basic contribution to the creation of a "container" (Bion's (1962) term; Winnicott (1971) calls it a "holder") for the anxieties arising in the ward. It is also valuable because it provides information on each patient. Other groups also offer patients orientation and emotional support.

On the staff side, tensions among members of the therapeutic team are reduced by initiating group discussions; for example, nursing personnel find that their previous fears and apprehensions diminish. On the whole, despite a staff shortage, a pleasant and supportive atmosphere was created in the wards by emphasizing support and appropriate expressions of feeling. Moreover, the variety of groups of patients and staff, together with those in the outpatient clinic and in the day hospital (Guimón, Luna, Totorika, Diez, & Puertas, 1983), constitutes a group analytical network that encourages more harmonious communication among the various units of the hospital. This systemic vision of the institution greatly increases understanding and detection of the organizational problems and internal struggles. This provides the input for the "healthy anticipatory paranoia" needed (Kernberg, 1979) in the management of these organizations.

Staff Vicissitudes

It is assumed that the therapeutic team should play the role of an *alter familia,* thereby enabling patients to have a "corrective emotional experience" of all those events that might have been at the root of their troubles. In our study, the staff tended to overevaluate the items of the scale supposedly related to the "maturational" qualities of the relationships in the ward: involvement, spontaneity, autonomy, personal problem orientation, expression of anger, and aggressiveness. However, in reality, various difficulties arise in therapeutic teams that are working with psychotic and borderline patients. Some of these difficulties come from very real problems: work-related stress, professional rivalry, therapeutic frustration, and so on. Others arise from projective identifications of patients by the staff. The role of the staff should be to receive these projections, work through them, and, after they have been transformed, allow the patient to introject them. However, therapists frequently feel compelled to act transferentially, as if they were moved by the projective identifications of the patients (Grinberg's "projective counteridentification," 1962). These projections can acquire an independent life for therapists if they are not able to perceive, work through, and transform them.

As Racamier (1983) states, the therapeutic team can become dissociated because of these projections. Tension rises while team members pretend to maintain a perfect understanding among themselves—an image of an ideal family, an adequate container in which patients can grow. As a consequence, through a splitting mechanism, therapists identify their patients with some aspects of sickness that they reject in themselves. A "loving therapeutic team"— one that parallels Winnicott's (1971) "loving mother"—would be able to take on the needs of the patients and avoid having patients assume the difficulties of staff members. Rarely does a team have enough flexibility to adapt to the variable needs of patients. The groups that personnel encounter in the wards seem to be of great help in this sense.

Personnel tend to idealize some characteristics of the ward atmosphere, but they show a disparaging attitude toward others. Thus, they value the concepts of staff control and practical orientation significantly less than the patients do, and they consider it undesirable to introduce restrictions in these wards. However, we know that being a "loving mother" is not, according to Winnicott (1971), the only function of the "good-enough mother." A "good-enough team" is similarly required for adequate handling of reality in the care of self and others, and that includes setting certain limits. This function may have to be ascribed to the qualities of a "good-enough father," still to be described.

EXAMPLES OF CLINICAL PROGRAMS

Therapeutic communities have had difficulty surviving in the medicalized atmosphere wrought by the managed-care strategies that are prevalent in most Western countries (Schimmel, 1997). However, this type of approach should be utilized for managed care. Patients who have serious psychiatric illnesses (incompetence, suicidality, dependency) and suffer from a feeling of profound insecurity will continue to need long-term, intensive therapy, and the clinical community should display reticence when faced with attempts to reduce or dilute the current services (Campling & Dixon Lodge, 1999a, 1999b; Campling & Haigh, 1999). A training process that corresponds to therapeutic community principles should encourage the growth and differentiation of patients, and, as Campling and Haigh warn, avoid the indoctrination and infantilization that are typical of medical and psychoanalytical training. As pointed out earlier, although the philosophy of therapeutic communities has become especially widespread in halfway institutions during recent years, the hospital-based therapeutic community will continue to justify itself. It combines sociotherapeutic treatment, psychotherapeutic treatment, and the advantages of a hospital context (Schimmel, 1997), and it has shown itself to be useful in the treatment of Borderline Personality Disorder and the rehabilitation of some delinquents. Progress in research is needed before we can evaluate its efficacy for other diagnostic groups, but it seems that the intensive approach—permitting carefully monitored therapeutic regression within a safe environment—can be very appropriate for psychotic patients who have been resistant to treatment by other means (Nieminen, Isohanni, & Winblad, 1994).

Access to quality therapeutic community treatment represents, therefore, an important element in furnishing complete psychiatric service. But *quality* must be a main component of care (Isohanni & Nieminen, 1992). Patients' lack of participation, or their passiveness, is principally linked to certain aspects of the program, such as ward policy; when a program is good, participation and commitment grow. Thus, it is necessary to improve therapeutic programs and the skills of their leaders. In a study by Nieminen et al. (1994), patients who achieved better immediate results generally stayed 10 to 20 days longer in the hospital.

Over the past 30 years, whether with the more social approach of the British or the more dynamic one of the Americans and the French, many traditional psychiatric hospitals and halfway institutions (day hospitals, protected living quarters, workshops, and so on) have adopted this philosophy to varying degrees. However, they have also modified it. Much of its effective force, especially insofar as psychoanalytical elements are concerned, is gone. The idea of a therapeutic community was adopted by residential and day units assisted by social services and volunteers who, because they lacked the necessary training, contributed to its loss of credibility (Roberts, 1995).

With the dramatic shortening of the hospital stays of mental patients over the past decades, the usefulness of milieu therapy has been contested. However, in the United States and some other Western nations, therapeutic community ideas have inspired the organization of many day hospitals and some short-stay units.

Over the past 20 years, in Spain and Switzerland, we have developed a number of group programs in many psychiatric units. An orientation toward community therapy can be found in various care units: short-stay accommodations in general hospitals, rehabilitation units, and day hospitals (Guimón, 1998, 2001). At a minimum, the programs include a daily medium-size group of patients and staff, and a small group of patients with a dynamic orientation but with occasional cognitive-behavioral techniques as well as group activities (group work, in Foulkes's sense).

FORMAT FOR PSYCHOTIC PATIENTS

Day Hospitals

Now that the optimism born 30 years ago from the efficacy of neuroleptic treatment has diminished, much of the general public considers the deinstitutionalization of schizophrenic patients a threat to the security and well-being of the population, thus further increasing opposition to their release from hospitals. Nevertheless, serious studies (Dolan, Warren, Menzies, & Norton, 1996; Kruisdljk, 1994) show that, at the clinical, social, and economic levels, the costs of the efforts to deinstitutionalize are financially viable for a great number of schizophrenic patients, as long as an appropriate outpatient structure exists to lend assistance. Day hospitals and other halfway houses are indispensable structures for maintaining schizophrenics in the community. In a day hospital, group psychotherapy is the basic therapeutic approach.

At some day centers, treatment of patients begins at the very first manifestations of their disorder and continues until remission. Others focus on rehabilitation following treatment in a hospital. A day hospital in Geneva, where both types of patients are accepted in different but complementary programs, is described next. The first therapeutic function of this day hospital is to offer patients an environment that allows them to shore up internal checks and balances and to receive psychiatric attention. A second function is to furnish emotional support to reinforce their self-esteem. To do this, the hospital offer a whole set of possibilities based on groups where "pathogens and pathogenic ties" can be displayed and therefore addressed and modified.

Sample Day Program. The Day Program in Geneva University Hospitals (Guimón et al., 2001) is planned for a maximum of 20 patients five days a week, seven hours a day. On average, it handles 15 patients at a time. Patients' average age is 26.5 years ± 7.8 years. An average hospital stay is 9.9 months ± 7 months. Diagnoses mainly reveal schizophrenic disorder. Because this unit offers a range of corrective group experiences, it allows modification of patients' clinical symptomatology, social adaptation, and relationship structures.

The program includes prescription and control of medication, organization of psychotherapeutic activities based on the dynamic factors that intervened in triggering, and techniques to combat symptoms characteristic of schizophrenic deterioration: intellectual difficulties, apathy, libidinal object withdrawal, and isolation in the patient's introverted world. The days begin with a coffee break and include lunch. Three small groups are convened each day. They focus on verbal psychotherapy (dynamic and cognitive) twice a week; introduce group activities and discussions (on medication, social information, and daily life); and encourage various activities: artistic expression, theater and video, body movement, cooking, and games. Additional groups are: a general assembly that unites all caregivers and patients once a week, and a multifamily convocation that unites all patients, families, and caregivers once a month.

The therapeutic team includes psychiatrists, psychologists, social workers, occupational therapists, psychomotor therapists, and others. In general, these professionals have received training in individual and group psychoanalysis.

They possess certain expertise in family therapy and social networks. Communication among therapists is facilitated by holding meetings of working groups.

Short-Term Units

It has been generally concluded that short-stay units constitute a totally inadequate setting for psychotherapy and for organizing the systems of assistance oriented on the model of the therapeutic communities. It was believed that the serious symptomatology of patients and the heterogeneity of diagnoses were not conducive to the fluctuating and variable settings of short stays, which would undermine and make impossible the usual psychotherapeutic approaches. In addition, the care required for patients placed in these facilities by a court ruling—patients who pose a threat to themselves and to others—necessitates the establishment of a closed system and obliges personnel to act in a sometimes overly authoritarian manner. Such conditions are effectively an obstacle to the establishment of a therapeutic community.

In spite of this, within the framework of various short-stay units for patients with acute illness, it has been possible to show the efficacy of psychotherapy and the value of the introduction, into the organization itself, of certain elements that are characteristic of the philosophy of community therapy.

Sample Short-Term Unit. Since 1980, Bilbao University Hospital in Spain (Guimón et al., 1983), has operated a standard program in Bilbao's Civil Hospital. This is a closed unit with 20 beds; it receives between 350 and 450 patients each year. The average stay is 20 days, and the most frequently encountered disorders are schizophrenia and schizophreniform, neurotic and personality disorders, and affective psychoses. The clinical state of these patients is characterized by poor functioning on any level of reality testing, varying degrees of mental regression, and a predominance of primal defense mechanisms and thought processes. In these circumstances, the environment becomes an essential support for the mental process and an important therapeutic tool.

In 1984, we introduced a group therapy program (Guimón, based on Yalom) of participation in a medium-size group of all patients with staff, preceded by and followed up with two short meetings of the personnel. As described earlier, two types of small groups have been organized, in accordance with the patients' levels of mental disorganization. Once or twice a week, we organize group art therapy (participation is voluntary), and occupational therapeutic groups meet several times a week.

From a clinical point of view, the program results have been very positive. The setting is a key element. It has created a "home" within the consulting room and the group assigned communicates valuable information to patients. The other groups also give patients orientation and emotional support. Dosages of medication have decreased in this setting, as have the number of negative patient incidents (aggression, suicide attempts, runaways) and tensions within the therapeutic team. In this study, researchers noted that specialized groups, in addition to the community groups of the day hospital (Guimón et al., 1983) and the outpatient consultation at the university hospital, constitute a network for group analysis that encourages harmonious communication among the various units of the Department of Psychiatry and the rest of the hospital. This systemic approach is conducive to detecting problems and conflicts more easily and more quickly. All these elements furnish the input that feeds "healthy precursor paranoia" (Kernberg, 1979, p. 29), an indispensable element in managing these organizations.

Rehabilitation Units

A number of psychotic patients, most of whom are schizophrenic, need long-term hospitalization because their symptoms do not respond to treatment, or for social or legal reasons. An adequate ward atmosphere created via a milieu therapy approach is essential if a rehabilitation program is to be successful.

Sample Rehabilitation Unit. A rehabilitation unit for 12 psychotic patients has been set up in the psychiatric hospital of Belle-Idée, Department of Psychiatry of Geneva University (Guimón, 2001). The average stay is 51 to 61 days; the mean is 20 days. The average age is 38 years, and the median is 35 years. The care program for patients includes individual and group activities, and each professional category takes part in both aspects of treatment. The multidisciplinary team includes psychiatrists, psychologists, nurses, social workers, and psychomotor therapists.

In general, the patients are low functioning. This results in social and family problems, especially resistance to a care program in an outpatient setting. For younger patients and those with a more recent onset of illness, the work is focused on: integration and acceptance of the illness itself, the meaning of the illness for each patient, daily maintenance, and the possibility that skills may be regained or improved.

The individual care program is characterized by discussions with doctors and nurses, sessions with occupational and psychomotor therapists, and social services interventions. At their arrival, patients receive a welcoming brochure that lists the ward rules, the daily schedule, the names of medical nurses, and descriptions of activities.

A complete group program has been developed during the past few years. The 30-minute program, attended by patients and staff (the ward group), takes place daily except on weekends. A group for the rehabilitation of cognitive deficits (in accordance with Brenner methodology) is led by an occupational therapist and a nurse. The group meets four days a week, for 20 minutes each day. A psychoeducational group for medication is conducted by a medical resident and two nurses once a week, for 30 minutes. A group on social skills (Liberman type) is led by two nurses once a week, for 45 minutes. A family group, under the direction of a physician and with the participation of a representative from each professional category, meets once a month, for 90 minutes. Three recreational/occupational groups (storytelling, sports, creativity) are conducted by nurses once a week, for one hour.

FORMAT FOR BORDERLINE PERSONALITY PATIENTS

Day Centers

Dawson's (1988) Managing Emotions program insists that patients accept responsibility for regulating their emotions. Therapists facilitate by not being overly controlling, though acting out is forbidden. Regular attendance at meetings is not obligatory, which means that only 30% of patients come regularly. They form the nucleus of active patients; this number is more or less constant. A much larger group of patients may show up from time to time, in search of occasional help.

Sample Day Center. The cognitive-behavioral approach of Linehan (1987) was initiated for young women who were parasuicidal. Later, she widened it to include persons who are unable to resolve problems because of so-called dialectic failure—inability to bring into opposition poles such as emotional vulnerability versus invalidation, passiveness versus competency, or demonstrative crises versus emotional inhibition.

These programs combine individual and group approaches in problem solving and skills training. In the psychoeducational groups, patients are taught skills in regulating emotion, interpersonal functioning, and stress tolerance. Patients take part in these groups for at least one year, and then join help groups that reinforce the application of the learned skills. In individual and concomitant therapy, which lasts at least one year, patients are taught to integrate these skills into their daily life. The leaders propose rules to generalize the apprenticeship to the outside world, and they establish a follow-up, sometimes by telephone. The group is closed or, at most, opened gradually.

Sample Day Center. The psychoanalytical approaches to day treatment of borderline patients are based on object-relations theory. Most programs have been developed in hospital environments or in halfway houses. Kernberg (1980) is the approach's principal theorist.

In the psychoanalytical model of object relations, the focus is on increasing the fortress of the ego and improving adaptive function as part of an attempt toward internal reconstitution. From a technical point of view, the splitting mechanism is reinforced rather than struggled against. Therapists encourage open expression of anger, and group interpretation based on the here and now, which favors cohesion.

In comparing Linehan's (1987) cognitive-behavioral and Kernberg's (1980) object-relations models, some authors point to their main differences. Therapists using Kernberg's approach are neutral in their emotional stance toward patients, whereas those following Linehan actively reinforce patients. The expression of anger is encouraged by Kernberg, whereas Linehan does not encourage it. Unlike Kernberg, Linehan is not interested in the here and now of the group nor in group phenomena.

Finally, with a perspective which is just as dynamic, recent work by Bateman and Fonagy (1999) shows good results in a program developed in a British day hospital.

Sample Day Center. Bateman and Fonagy (1999) studied the evolution of 19 patients who were treated in a British day hospital. The group treatment was partially based on a psychoanalytic approach and outcomes were compared with those 19 patients who had received a general psychiatric treatment. In the group model, self-mutilating behavior and suicide attempts decreased during the 18-month program, and the average hospital stay was shorter than for those who received the general treatment.

Hospital Programs
In the hospital milieu (and also in halfway institutions), the treatment is carried out in settings where several caregivers interact. Adshead (1998), in light of the theory of attachment, reported that the hospital milieu provides security only if caregivers are capable of tolerating both the external demands of the system and the internal demands of patients. He pointed out that therapeutic relationships between staff and patients are repetitions and re-creations of internal object relations, and the team's responses to splitting and projective identification can sometimes be negative. He describes how certain negative reactions can be detected because of the patronizing and contemptuous way caregivers sometimes express themselves to the patients. Adshead theorizes that some excessive reinforcement of the regulation of services (e.g., the inappropriate use of restriction on movement) may result from the contrary attitude exhibited by some personnel. He also remarks that the conflict between therapist and patient, particularly in the managed care system, can be traced to the interference of insurance companies. Finally, he recalls that problems affecting the organization of the unit—inadequate accounting practices, lack of leadership, difficulties in communication, and violation of boundaries—can seriously aggravate the condition of patients.

Sample Hospital Program. The patients of Francis Dixon Lodge are generally hospitalized because of their destructive ways of expressing mental pain. After three weeks of hospitalization, patients receive psychodynamic treatment focused on predicting transferential reactions that are attempts to cover self-aggressive behavior (e.g., feelings of abandonment, trigger situation). Therapists try to create a therapeutic relationship in which patients feel sufficiently reassured to explore avenues of new relationships, while allowing them access to past horrors that may carry so much negative emotion that mere recollection could endanger the relationship. Therapists regard acting out as an expressive and defensive function. They warn that more self-destructive behavior may be the patient's way of avoiding another catastrophe (e.g., psychosis, heteroaggression) that is regarded as more destructive to his or her own integrity.

These patients, because of their poor self-esteem, do not know how to ask for help in an appropriate manner; instead, they provoke crises, causing the therapeutic team to counterreact. The team explains to patients that they must learn to talk about their suicidal feelings or their inclinations toward self-mutilation. Therapists explain that, though tolerant, they expect patients to modify their own behavior. The therapists also try to avoid any feeling of omnipotence over patients when their own behavior triggers self-aggressive reactions. Their response to phenomena of hostile and envious dependency consists of trying to avoid or to manage negative therapeutic reactions.

Springer (Springer & Silk, 1996), building on existing literature, proposed a framework in which an effective short-term group treatment is organized. Discussed in particular are the advantages and disadvantages of adapting Linehan's (1987) dialectical behavior therapy for short-term use with hospitalized patients. Dolan, Warren, and Norton (1997), working with 137 hospitalized patients, evaluated the impact of psychotherapeutic treatment on the principal symptoms of these patients' personality disorder. They noted a significantly greater improvement in those treated. Hafner and Holme (1996) conducted a similar prospective study with 48 residents of a therapeutic community, all of whom were diagnosed with Borderline Personality Disorder. The goal was to determine which elements of the program were most useful. A reduction in significant symptoms on the Brief Symptom Inventory was noted at discharge after an average stay of 64 days, and the rates of readmission to the hospital fell significantly during the year after discharge. Patients rated group therapy as the most useful element of the program. A study by Sabo, Gunderson, Navajavits, Chauncey, and Kisiel (1995) followed prospectively, for five years, 37 hospitalized patients suffering from Borderline Personality Disorder. The goal was to evaluate the changes in two forms of self-destructiveness. Schimmel (1997) underlined the efficacy of therapeutic community treatment for patients suffering from Borderline Personality Disorder.

FORMAT FOR PATIENTS WITH
AFFECTIVE DISORDERS

Hospital Program
In Geneva University Hospital (Guimón, 2001), a unit with 10 beds has been designated for patients suffering from resistant or recurrent depression. The length of hospitalization is 28 to 78 days on average, with a median stay of 15 days. The patients' average age is 44 years; 42 years is the median. Care of patients is accomplished in individual and group treatment. Multimodal with patients' pharmacological needs are evaluated, and a crisis intervention unit assesses the impact of depression on cognitive and relational skills. Individual activities include medical nursing discussions, sessions in occupational therapy and psychomotor therapy, evaluation, and social follow-up. Upon arrival, a brochure that stipulates ward rules is distributed to each patient.

The program offers eight groups: A staff group assembles all personnel daily, except on weekends, for 15 minutes. A social skills group, led by a nurse and a psychologist, meets two hours per week. A verbal group, led by two physicians, meets one hour per week. A medication group, led by a resident and two nurses, meets once a week for 30 minutes. A family group, led by a physician with participation from each professional category, meets once a month for 90 minutes. Three recreational-occupational groups ("inside-outside" games and sports) led by occupational therapists and nurses, meet for several hours a week.

FORMAT FOR SUBSTANCE ABUSE PATIENTS

For patients who abuse substances, the group format is used throughout the world—in outpatient and halfway programs, and during short or medium stays in hospitals. Long-stay, more or less structured programs, are sufficiently specific for substance abuse patients. The approach they offer ranges from very firm restrictions on freedom to a progressive autonomy. Total freedom is acquired through successive steps during periods ranging from a few months to several years. Some of these programs are carried out in centers that are directed in accordance with therapeutic community principles.

Fisher (Fisher & Bentley, 1996) studied two models of group therapy for patients presenting a dual diagnosis of substance abuse and personality disorder. This semi-experimental study was led in a facility that treated substance abuse on an outpatient and a hospital basis. Three groups were developed in each context. Two groups were formed for the integral treatment of patients with a dual diagnosis (substance abuse and personality disorder); the third, used as a control group, received the usual treatment.

One of the experimental groups was developed in accordance with the illness-and-cure approach. Its objective was acceptance of substance abuse as a chronic, progressive, and possibly fatal illness. In a similar fashion, although mental illness (personality disorder, for example) is not necessarily fatal, its evolution is typically considered to be chronic and progressive. This approach is based on an assumption that patients have an underlying biological vulnerability, characterized by a loss of control over substance abuse and mental disorders. After the start of treatment, the number of patients was set at seven or eight members. The groups were led in cotherapy by a principal investigator and another clinician. The immediate objectives in the illness-and-cure treatment model include the development of an identity as an alcoholic or an addict, recognition of a loss of control over substance abuse and the effects of personality disorder, acceptance of abstinence as a treatment objective, and participation in a self-help group such as Alcoholics Anonymous.

A second experimental group was developed in each location. This group used a cognitive-behavioral approach and results were comparable to the approach described previously.

EFFECTIVENESS

Silberstein et al. describe therapeutic communities' programs of residential assistance for recovering addicts; the personnel in the traditional communities are recovered addicts. Recently, the therapeutic community model has been modified to treat persons for substance abuse and severe mental illness. In these programs, the staff is made up, to varying degrees, of mental health professionals. Patients are often placed in institutions where the model of assistance is based on service to patients rather than patients' self-help. Conflicts are inherent in the modified therapeutic community, which is a hybrid of these two treatment approaches. This section explores questions relative to the roles of patients, mental health professionals, and the parent institution when a therapeutic community is modified to provide treatment for substance abusers.

The therapeutic community's approach has been used for a multiplicity of diagnoses, but with varying results. For some authors (Early, 1971; Van Putten & May, 1976), the usefulness of creating such environments in psychiatric hospitals has not been clearly proven. They pointed out that some research projects that attempted to show the efficacy of therapeutic communities did not render conclusive results because of differences among patients, varying lengths of hospitalization, and differing techniques. More recently, an important body of work demonstrated the therapeutic value of programs based on group techniques.

The best early studies are those of Rapaport (1974) and Whiteley (1980), conducted at the Henderson Hospital, in the UK, and the findings of the Association of Therapeutic Communities Research Group. More recently, other studies have been conducted in the UK. The methodologies used to carry out these studies are descriptive or evaluative, ideographic or nomothetic, sociological or psychological, or a combination of the above.

A controlled experimental study at Kingswood House, in the UK, concluded that it was almost impossible to link effect to cause when evaluating multidimensional treatments such as those offered in a therapeutic community (Clarke & Cornish, 1972). An alternative method to experimental design is represented by a cross-institutional design, which can be completed by using one of several quantitative methods. An example of this methodology was proposed by Moos (1987, 1997), who used the "ward atmosphere scale" to evaluate the social and physical atmospheres of treatment units within therapeutic communities (Guimón, 2001).

Several studies have focused on a single therapeutic community (e.g., Clark & Yeomans, 1969). Some used simple measures such as rehospitalization or penal relapse (Whiteley, 1980; Whiteley & Collis, 1987). Others had a psychological orientation (De Leon, 1997; Dolan et al., 1997) or centered on economical aspects showing a good relationship between cost and efficiency (Dauwalder & Ciompi, 1995).

Psychotic Disorders

Several studies, of variable methodological quality, saw a favorable result with a therapeutic community approach in psychotic patients. De Hert, Thys, Vercruyssen, and Peuskers (1996), who followed up 120 young chronic patients who took part in the rehabilitation program at the Night Hospital in Brussels, showed that most of them maintained the level of adaptation obtained, continued to live in the community, and engaged in useful pursuits, posttreatment. Dauwalder and Ciompi (1995) showed the efficacy, in the long term, of a community-based program for chronic mental patients. A great number of the patients had jobs and were living independent lives, even if most of them still needed professional help. Jin and Li (1994) observed that the number of suicides decreased and the active participation increased at Yanbian Community Psychiatric Hospital after its transformation (from a residential facility for chronic psychiatric patients) into a therapeutic community. Coombe (1996), in an account of principles and treatment practices given to the therapeutic community at the Cassel Hospital in London, underlined the ability of the therapeutic network to be successful in the treatment of families and individuals suffering from serious disorders.

Mosher (Mosher & Feinsilver, 1971) compared the treatment program for young schizophrenic patients in the Soteria project with that of a small social environment, generally without neuroleptics. The atmospheres of treatment settings were evaluated using the Moos (1997), Community-Oriented Programs Environment Scales (COPES), or WAS scales. Using a similar approach, the two systems managed to reduce the serious psychotic symptomatology in six weeks—generally, without antipsychotic medication. The method was as effective as the normal hospital treatment, which routinely used neuroleptics. Shepherd, Muijen, Hadley, and Goldman (1996) presented the benefits and limitations of a new type of institutional solution, the unit in a home, for patients suffering from severe disorders who came forward in a health sector (Cambridge) in the United Kingdom. Another study (Nieminen et al., 1994), was carried out in a therapeutic community unit for severely affected patients. The average hospital stay was 40 days, but the study reported that patients who obtained a better immediate result had stayed in the hospital 10 to 20 days longer than did those who had an inferior result. A longer stay was associated with a younger age, a diagnosis of psychosis, and active and motivated participation in individual and milieu therapy.

BORDERLINE DISORDERS

The best results for therapeutic communities were obtained with borderline and delinquent patients. Dolan et al. (1997) evaluated the impact of psychotherapeutic treatment on the principal symptoms of 137 hospitalized patients with Borderline Personality Disorder. A significantly greater symptom reduction was noted in treated patients, compared to those in the non-hospitalized control group. The changes were significantly and positively correlated to the length of treatment.

Hafner and Holme (1996) carried out a study on 48 residents of a therapeutic community (most of whom had Borderline Personality Disorder; N = 34). A reduction of significant symptoms was observed after an average stay of 64 days. The rates of readmission to the hospital fell significantly during the year following these patients' discharge. Clients' evaluations indicated that group therapy was the most useful element of the program. Sabo et al. (1995) followed up—in a prospective fashion, over a five-year period—37 hospitalized patients suffering from Borderline Personality Disorder. Their purpose was to evaluate the changes in two forms of self-destructiveness. They noted that suicidal conduct diminished significantly, self-aggressive conduct presented a certain tendency but not a significant decrease, and aggressive ideation (both suicidal and self-harming) did not decrease in a notable fashion.

Schimmel (1997) concluded that empirical studies relied on treatment efficacy in the therapeutic community for patients suffering from Borderline Personality Disorder, and that further research was necessary to evaluate its value for other diagnostic groups. In principle, this intensive treatment approach was appropriate for patients who are resistant to other treatment.

VARIABLES ASSOCIATED WITH EFFICACY

Regarding variables associated with therapeutic results (Guimón et al., 2001), Holmqvist (1998) found no important differences in an analysis of the relationship among psychiatric diagnoses of patients, their self-image, and the feelings of personnel toward patients in 17 treatment units for psychiatric patients presenting severe disorders. Werbart, using the COPES, studied the exploratory factors and those that supported insight-oriented milieu therapy in three Swedish therapeutic communities with psychotic patients. The study showed that a beneficial psychotherapeutic environment needs an organization and a setting that correspond to a well-defined treatment philosophy. Several structured studies that have been carried out showed that community meetings had the effect of reducing unfavorable ward incidents—in particular, incidents that had an aggressive character (Ng, 1992).

Regarding the value of specific techniques used in the programs, Winer and Klamen (1997) presented a model of community relations for hospitalized patients. Its key element was a large-group interpretative psychotherapy that centered on the examination of here-and-now relationships between patients and personnel. This model is useful even for short-term hospital stays and with seriously ill patients. It can provide a gauge of the milieu, throw light on undesirable conduct of staff and patients, discover antitherapeutic attitudes in personnel, help to improve patients' compliance with treatment, and reduce tension in the unit.

Several studies indicated the fundamental value of group therapy in these programs. Kahn, Sturke, and Schaeffer (1992) compared the group dynamics that took place in a short-term hospital unit and the atmosphere in the unit, and found very clear parallels between the process of group therapy and that of the ward. Isohanni and Nieminen (1990, 1992) studied the degree of participation in group psychotherapies in a therapeutic community for severe patients, and observed, for example, that the lack of participation (4% in all episodes) or passiveness (14%) was associated with an inferior therapeutic result and depended principally on program characteristics (ward policy, short treatment times) and diagnoses of personality disorder. The results suggested that participation in the group, type of therapeutic program, patient characteristics, and success of treatment are interrelated.

Concerning the efficacy of the different therapeutic mechanisms, Holmqvist and Armelius (1994) proposed a method for following the development of relations and studying their usefulness or lack of usefulness. A recapitulative list of words is given to nurses; this list permits measurement of the quantity of emotional arousal in a reliable manner. Holmqvist and Fogelstam (1996) studied therapists' feelings of countertransference toward patients in 21 small treatment houses and their influence on the psychological climate in the unit (Guimón, 2001).

SUMMARY

Over the course of the twentieth century, various interdisciplinary approaches combining aspects of psychoanalysis with novel developments in understanding group process has led to the development of an array of programs with which to more effectively treat severe mental disorders. Therapeutic communities offer a potentially viable modality for a variety of severe and chronic patients with substance abuse, affective illness, severe personality and psychotic disorders, who are often refractory to other treatments. The therapeutic community offers a powerful format in which integrative psychodynamic approaches can be delivered in various treatment formats to a spectrum of challenging patients. In various parts of Europe and North and South America, therapeutic communities were established in an attempt to offer a corrective emotional experience by using healing elements of the social system. This type of community affords the opportunity to experience a culture of belonging while both staff and patients together process the powerful communal forces and underlying dynamics in an open and constructive fashion. This model offers the possibility of containing the affects associated with severe mental illness and structuring the environment so that chaos is reduced and more adaptive patterns can be learned.

REFERENCES

Adshead, G. (1998). Psychiatric staff as attachment figures: Understanding management problems in psychiatric services in the light of attachment theory. *British Journal of Psychiatry, 172,* 64–69.

Anthony, E. J. (1983). The group-analytic circle and its ambient network. In M. Pines (Ed.), *The education of group analysis.* London: Routledge & Kegan Paul.

Basaglia, F. (1970). *L'institution en négation.* Paris: Edition du Seuil.

Bateman, A., & Fonagy, P. (1999). Effectiveness of partial hospitalization in the treatment of Borderline Personality Disorder: A randomized controlled trial. *American Journal of Psychiatry, 156*(10), 1563–1569.

Bettelheim, B. (1950). *Love is not enough.* New York: Free Press.

Bion, W. R. (1962). *Learning from experience.* New York: Basic Books.

Campling, P., & Dixon Lodge, F. (1999a). Boundaries: Discussion of a difficult transition. In P. Campling & R. Haigh (Eds.), *Therapeutic communities: Past, present and future.* London: Jessica Kingsley.

Campling, P., & Dixon Lodge, F. (1999b). Chaotic personalities: Maintaining the Therapeutic alliance. In P. Campling & R. Haigh (Eds.),

Therapeutic communities: Past, present and future. London: Jessica Kingsley.

Campling, P., & Haigh, P. (1999). Introduction. In P. Campling & R. Haigh (Eds.), *Therapeutic communities: Past, present and future* (pp. 12–17). London: Jessica Kingsley.

Chanoit, P. S. (1995). *La psychothérapie institutionnelle* [Institutional psychotherapy] (Vol. Que sais-je N° 2999). Paris: Presses Universitaires de France.

Clark, A. W., & Yeomans, N. J. (1969). *Fraser House: Theory, practice and evaluation of a therapeutic community.* New York: Springer.

Clarke, R. V. G., & Cornish, D. B. (1972). *The controlled trial in institutional research.* London: HMSO.

Coombe, P. (1996). The Cassel Hospital, London. *Australian and New Zealand Journal of Psychiatry, 30*(5), 672–680.

Dauwalder, J. P., & Ciompi, L. (1995). Cost-effectiveness over 10 years: A study of community-based social psychiatric care in the 1980s. *Social Psychiatry and Psychiatric Epidemiology, 30*(4), 171–184.

Dawson, D. F. (1988). Treatment of the borderline patient, relationship management. *Canadian Journal of Psychiatry, 33*(5), 370–374.

De Hert, M., Thys, E., Vercruyssen, V., & Peuskers, J. (1996). Partial hospitalization at night: The Brussels Night Hospital *Psychiatric Services, 47*(5), 527–528.

De Leon, G. (1997). *Community as method: Therapeutic communities for special populations and special settings.* Westport, CT: Praeger.

de Mare, P. (1983). Michael Foulkes and the Northfield Experiment. In M. Pines (Ed.), *The evolution of group analysis.* London: Routledge.

Diatkine, R. (1958). Activité de psychothérapie de groupe et de psychodrame [Group psychotherapy and psychodrama]. *Group Psychotherapy, Psychodrama and Sociotherapy, 11,* 187–188.

Diatkine, R., Socarras, F., & Kestemberg, E. (1959). Le transfert en psychothérapie collective [Transfer in group psychotherapy]. *Encephale, 39,* 248–274.

Dolan, B., Warren, F., & Norton, K. (1997). Change in borderline symptoms one year after therapeutic community treatment for severe personality disorder. *British Journal of Psychiatry, 171,* 274–279.

Dolan, B. M., Warren, F. M., Menzies, D., & Norton, K. (1996). Cost offset following specialist treatment of severe personality disorders. *Psychiatric Bulletin, 20,* 413–417.

Early, D. F. (1971). Rehabilitation des schizophrènes [Rehabilitation techniques for schizophrenic patients]. *Information Psychiatrique, 47*(4), 327–332.

Fisher, M. S., Sr., & Bentley, K. J. (1996). Two group therapy models for clients with a dual diagnosis of substance abuse and personality disorder. *Psychiatric Services, 47*(11), 1244–1250.

Foulkes, S. H. (1948). *Introduction to group-analytic psychotherapy.* London: Heinemann.

Foulkes, S. H., & Lewis, E. (1944). Group analysis: A study in the treatment of groups on psychoanalytic lines. *Journal of Medical Psychology, 20,* 1.

Garcia Badarracco, J. E. (1990). *Comunidad terapeutica psicoanalitica de estructura multifamiliar [Psychoanalytical multifamily therapeutic community].* Madrid, Spain: Tecnipublicaciones, S.A.

Grinberg, L. (1962). On a specific aspect of countertransference due to the patients projective identification. *International Journal of Psychoanalysis, 43,* 436–440.

Guimón, J. (1998). Thérapie groupale dynamique intensive et brève [Brief, therapeutic, dynamic group psychotherapy]. *Psychothérapies, 18*(1), 15–21.

Guimón, J. (2001). *Introduction aux thérapies de groupe* [Textbook of group psychotherapy]. Paris: Masson.

Guimón, J., Erhensperger, S., Weber, A., Fredenrich, A. L., Vucetic, V., Zanello, A., et al. (2001). Evaluación de la psicoterapia grupal en la asistencia psiquiátrica: la Batería "Bel-Air" [The evaluation of group psychotherapy: The Bel-Air Battery]. *Psiquis, 21*(6), 9–21.

Guimón, J., Luna, D., Totorika, K., Diez, L., & Puertas, P. (1983). Group psychotherapy as a basic therapeutic resource in psychiatric community care from the general hospital. In J. J. L. Ibor & J. M. L. Ibor (Eds.), *General hospital psychiatry.* Amsterdam: Excerpta Medica.

Gunderson, J. G. (1983). An overview of modern milieu therapy. In J. G. Gunderson (Ed.), *Principles and practice of milieu therapy.* London: Aronson.

Hafner, R. J., & Holme, G. (1996). The influence of a therapeutic community on psychiatric disorder. *Journal of Clinical Psychology, 52*(4), 461–468.

Haigh, R. (1999). Psychotherapy for severe personality disorder. Evolution is part of the therapeutic process of therapeutic communities [Letter].

British Medical Journal (England), 319(7211), 709–711.

Hinshelwood, R. D. (1999). Psychoanalytic origins and today's work: The Cassel heritage. In P. Campling & R. Haigh (Eds.), *Therapeutic communities: Past, present and future*. London: Jessica Kingsley.

Holmqvist, R. (1998). The influence of patient diagnosis and self-image on clinicians' feelings. *Journal of Nervous and Mental Disease, 186*(8), 455–461.

Holmqvist, R., & Armelius, B. A. (1994). Emotional reactions to psychiatric patients: Analysis of a feeling checklist. *Acta Psychiatrica Scandinavica, 90*(3), 204–209.

Holmqvist, R., & Fogelstam, H. (1996). Psychological climate and countertransference in psychiatric treatment homes. *Acta Psychiatrica Scandinavica, 93*(4), 288–295.

Isohanni, M., & Nieminen, P. (1990). Relationship between involuntary admission and the therapeutic process in a closed ward functioning as a therapeutic community. *Acta Psychiatrica Scandinavica, 81*, 240–244.

Isohanni, M., & Nieminen, P. (1992). Participation in group psychotherapy in a therapeutic community for acute patients. *Acta Psychiatrica Scandinavica, 86*(Suppl. 6), 495–501.

Jones, M. (1968). *Social psychiatry in practice*. London: Penguin Books.

Jones, M. (1972). *Therapeutic communities*. Villeurbanne: Simep Editions.

Jones, M. S. (1952). *Social psychiatry: A study of therapeutic communities*. London: Tavistock.

Kahn, E. M., Sturke, I. T., & Schaeffer, J. (1992). Inpatient group processes parallel unit dynamics. *International Journal of Group Psychotherapy, 42*(3), 407–418.

Kernberg, O. F. (1975). A systems approach to priority setting of interventions in groups. *International Journal of Group Psychotherapy, 25*, 251–276.

Kernberg, O. F. (1979). Regression in organizational leadership. *Psychiatry, 42*, 24–39.

Kestemberg, J., & Decobert, S. (1964). Approche psychanalytique pour la compréhension de la dynamique des groupes thérapeutiquesm [Psychoanalytic approach to therapeutic groups dynamics]. *Revue française de Psychanalyse, 28*, 393–418.

Kruisdljk, F. (1994). Substituting 24-hour therapeutic communities by 8-hour day hospitals: A sensible alternative to accepting budgetary cuts. *Therapeutic Communities, 15*(3), 161–171.

Lebovici, S. (1953). A propos de la psychanalyse de groupe. *Revue Française de Psychanalyse, 17*, 266–268.

Levinson, A. (1996). The struggle to keep a culture of enquiry alive at the Cassel Hospital. *Therapeutic Communities, 17*, 47–57.

Linehan, M. M. (1987). Dialectical behavior therapy for Borderline Personality Disorder: Theory and method. *Bulletin of the Menninger Clinic, 51*(3), 261–276.

Main, T. F. (1946). The hospital as a therapeutic institution. *Bulletin of the Menninger Clinic, 10*, 66–70.

Main, T. F. (1977). The concept of the therapeutic community: Variations and vicissitudes. *Group Analysis, 10*(Suppl.), 2–16.

Menninger, W. C. (1939). Psychoanalytic principles in psychiatric hospital therapy. *Southern Medical Journal, 32*, 354–384.

Menninger, W. C. (1942). Experiments and educational treatment in a psychiatric institution. *Bulletin of the Menninger Clinic, 6*, 38–45.

Moos, R. H. (1987). *The social climate scales: A user's guide*. Palo Alto, CA: Consulting Psychologists Press.

Moos, R. H. (1997). *Evaluating treatment environments: The quality of psychiatric and substance abuse programs* (2nd ed.). New Brunswick, NJ: Transaction.

Mosher, L., & Feinsilver, D. (1971). *Special report on schizophrenia*. Mestaesda: National Institute of Mental Health.

Ng, M. L. (1992). The community meeting: A review. *International Journal of Social Psychiatry, 38*(3), 179–188.

Nieminen, P., Isohanni, M., & Winblad, I. (1994). Length of hospitalization in an acute patients' therapeutic community ward. *Acta Psychiatrica Scandinavica, 90*(6), 466–472.

Oury, J. (1976). *Psychiatrie et psychothérapie institutionnelle* [Psychiatry and institutional psychotherapy]. Paris: Payot.

Pines, M. (1976). *The evolution of group analysis*. Author.

Pines, M. (1994). Borderline phenomena in analytic groups. In V. Schermer & M. Pines (Eds.), *Ring of fire—Primitive affects and object relations in group therapy*. London: Routledge.

Pines, M. (1996). She self as a group: The group as a self. *Group Analysis, 29*, 183–190.

Racamier, P. C. (1979). *De psychanalyse en psychiatrie* [On psychoanalysis in psychiatry]. Paris: Payot.

Racamier, P. C. (1980). *Les schizophrènes* [The schizophrenic patients]. Paris: Payot.

Racamier, P. C. (1983). *Le psychanalyste sans divan—la psychanalyse et les institutions de soins psychiatriques* [Psychoanalysis without a coach]. Paris: Payot.

Rapaport, R. N. (1974). *La communauté thérapeutique* [Therapeutic communities]. Paris: François Maspéro.

Rees, T. P., & Glatt, M. M. (1955). The organization of a mental hospital on the basis of group participation. *International Journal of Group Psychotherapy, 5*, 157–161.

Rickman, J. R. (1935). *A study of Quaker beliefs, the Lister Memorial Lecture given to the Quaker Medical Society*. Unpublished paper.

Roberts, J. P. (1995). Group psychotherapy. *British Journal of Psychiatry, 166*(1), 124–129.

Sabo, A. N., Gunderson, J. G., Navajavits, L. M., Chauncey, D., & Kisiel, C. (1995). Changes in self-destructiveness of borderline patients in psychotherapy: A prospective follow-up. *Journal of Nervous and Mental Diseases, 183*(6), 370–376.

Schimmel, P. (1997). Swimming against the tide? A review of the therapeutic community. *Australian and New Zealand Journal of Psychiatry, 31*(1), 120–127.

Shepherd, G., Muijen, M., Hadley, T. R., & Goldman, H. (1996). Effects of reversal in health services reform in clinical practice in the United Kingdom. *Psychiatry Service, 47*(12), 1351–1355.

Sivadon, P., Davies, R. L., & Baker, A. (1963). *L'hôpital psychiatrique public, n° 1* [The public psychiatric hospital n° 1]. Genève, Switzerland: OMS.

Sivadon, P., Follin, S., & Tournaud, S. (1952). Les clubs sociothérapiques à l'hôpital psychiatrique [Sociotherapy groups in a psychiatric hospital]. *Annales Medico-Psychologiques, 110*.

Springer, T., & Silk, K. R. (1996). A review of inpatient group therapy for borderline personality disorder. *Harvey Review of Psychiatry, 3*(5), 268–278.

Tosquelles, F. (1995). *De la personne au groupe: à propos des équipes de soins* [From person to the group: The therapeutic team]. Ramonville Saint Agne: Erès.

Van Putten, T., & May, P. R. A. (1976). Milieu therapies of the schizophrenias. In L. J. Wets & D. E. Flinn (Eds.), *Treatment of schizophrenia, progress and prospect* (pp. 217–243). New York: Grune & Stratton.

Whiteley, J. S. (1980). The Henderson Hospital: A community study. *International Journal of Therapeutic Communities, 1*(1), 38–57.

Whiteley, J. S., & Collis, M. (1987). The therapeutic factors in group psychotherapy applied to the therapeutic community. *International Journal of Therapeutic Communities, 8*, 21–32.

Winer, J. A., & Klamen, D. L. (1997). Interpretive psychotherapy in the inpatient community meeting on a short-term unit. *Psychiatric Services, 48*(1), 91–92.

Winnicott, D. W. (1971). *Playing and reality*. London: Tavistock.

CHAPTER 23

Psychodynamic Treatment for Cardiac Patients

ELLEN A. DORNELAS AND PAUL D. THOMPSON

HISTORY OF THE THERAPEUTIC APPROACH

The literature on psychotherapeutic approaches to alter lifestyle or improve psychological adjustment to cardiac disease is limited. Heart disease is the leading cause of death in the United States and a large proportion of cardiac patients experience psychological distress that is significant enough to warrant treatment. Psychological factors can impede recovery from cardiac illness (Rozanski, Blumenthal, & Kaplan, 1999), but few psychotherapists specialize in treating patients with heart disease. Some risk factors for heart disease cannot be altered (e.g., family history, gender, and age), but the majority are modifiable conditions that respond to intervention (cigarette smoking, hypertension, hyperlipidemia, physical inactivity, diabetes, obesity, lack of social support, depression, hostility, and anxiety). Almost half of the individuals are diagnosed with coronary heart disease (CHD) before age 65, when it is most likely that risk factor modification will improve their prognosis, but many people find it difficult to alter long-standing behaviors on their own.

From the perspective of the cardiologist, motivating patients to change behaviors (quitting smoking, modifying diet, increasing physical activity, taking medications as prescribed) is essential to cardiac risk factor reduction. In addition, depression, anxiety, and chronic stress are common patient problems encountered by the average cardiologist. Our health care systems do not routinely employ mental health professionals to treat medical patients, and a referral for psychotherapy is often viewed by physicians as a last-resort measure.

The relationship between heart disease and psychological functioning is multidimensional. Significant psychological stress reduces the likelihood that patients will be able to successfully modify their lifestyle and increases the probability of noncompliance with treatment, factors that, in turn, lead to more heart disease. Not only does poor psychological functioning present a significant barrier to behavior change, but there have also been repeated demonstrations indicating a direct pathophysiological link between stress and increased heart rate, coronary vasoconstriction, propensity for arrhythmia, and increased tendency for thrombosis (Allan

& Scheidt, 1996). In a study of airline pilots subjected to regular proficiency exams, chronic stress was related to significant increases in cholesterol (Stoney, Bausserman, Niaura, Marcus, & Flynn, 1999). Both life stress and hostility are predictors of coronary heart disease (Manuck, Kaplan, & Matthews, 1986; T. Miller, Smith, Turner, Guijarro, & Hallet, 1996). Depression is an independent risk factor for death after heart attack (Frasure-Smith, Lesperance, & Talajic, 1993). Thus, psychological factors impact on heart health through both indirect and direct pathways.

Recognition of a link between cardiac function and the mind is not new. Type A behavior pattern was described by M. Friedman and Rosenman in 1959 in the *Journal of the American Medical Association*. Health psychologists have been focused primarily on the study of coronary prone behavior and the psychological sequelae of heart disease during the past four decades. Between 15% and 30% of cardiac patients are severely distressed after the precipitating event, according to a meta-analysis of psychoeducational programs for coronary heart disease patients (Dusseldorp, van Elderen, Maes, Meulman, & Kraaij, 1999). The same meta-analysis did not find an effect of such programs on depression or anxiety, but the authors noted that the program components were not well described. Terms such as health education, stress management, group psychotherapy, and counseling are often used interchangeably when describing psychological care of the cardiac patient. Of the 37 studies included in Dusseldorp et al.'s meta-analysis, only 17 included a psychologist, psychotherapist, or psychiatrist on the treatment team. The lack of precision in describing interventions designed to alter psychological factors in cardiac patients is evidence that this is a field still early in its development.

The best descriptions of large-scale lifestyle intervention trials have been written by Allan and Scheidt (1996) in their edited book *Heart and Mind: The Practice of Cardiac Psychology*. The Lifestyle Heart Trial (Billings, Scherwitz, Sullivan, Sparler, & Ornish, 1996), the Recurrent Coronary Prevention Project (Bracke & Thorensen, 1996), and Project New Life (Burell, 1996) have all involved the use of group therapy in the context of multifaceted lifestyle intervention trials. Quinn (1999) reviewed 12 articles assessing the impact of family relationships on cardiovascular health, but few marital or family interventions have been tested with cardiac patients. Currently, the multicenter study Enhancing Recovery in Coronary Heart Disease (ENRICHD, 2000), funded by the National Institute of Health, is evaluating the effect of individual and group cognitive-behavioral therapy on cardiac patients with depression and low levels of social support.

Health psychology has emerged in the past two decades as a field devoted to applying the science of psychology to problems of health and illness. There are increasing numbers of health psychologists who work with cardiac patients in inpatient, outpatient, and rehabilitation settings. As a health psychologist and a cardiologist, respectively, we often encounter patients who can benefit from psychotherapeutic intervention. This chapter describes psychodynamic issues relevant to the treatment of the cardiac patient.

THEORETICAL ORIENTATION

The preponderance of clinical treatment models described in health psychology settings are cognitive-behavioral in nature, reflecting the prevailing theoretical orientation of pioneers in health psychology. Integration of psychodynamic psychotherapy into the practice of clinical health psychology has been slow, but short-term dynamic psychotherapy can play an important role in the psychological care of the cardiac patient. Models for short-term dynamic psychotherapy have been described by Sifneos (1972), Mann (1973), Malan (1976), and

Davanloo (1980). Each of these is characterized by selection of a focus that is maintained throughout each session, an active stance on the part of the therapist, time limitations, and elicitation of intense affect. Each of these, in turn, has particular salience for the clinician treating the cardiac patient.

Thomas Mann (1973) is credited with the development of a 12-session model. Mann "contrasts the reality of finite time with the allegedly universal unconscious fantasy of timelessness, unlimited nurturance, gratification and immortality" (Weston, 1986, p. 502). Time-limited psychotherapy for cardiac patients can be useful because it capitalizes on the existential crisis that is precipitated by a heart attack or hospitalization. The stages of psychotherapy have been described as (1) engagement, (2) clarification of patterns of dysfunction, (3) alteration of those patterns, and (4) termination (Beitman, Goldfried, & Norcross, 1989). Only a minority of cardiac patients will self-select to be treated with outpatient psychotherapy, but properly timed intervention can intensify the impact of the intervention, thus speeding up progression through those stages. For example, a single bedside session in the period of hospitalization after a cardiac event can have a more dramatic impact than multiple outpatient psychotherapy sessions due to the setting and the proximity to the medical crisis. The psychotherapist who provides bedside counseling is uniquely positioned to help the patient clarify problematic behaviors that contribute to heart disease (e.g., smoking, not taking medications) in relation to other life stressors (e.g., a conflicted marriage). Thus, time-limited therapy with cardiac patients is often brief but intense, because the medical crisis can serve to soften psychological defenses. For example, a 48-year-old construction worker with a myocardial infarction was hospitalized for angioplasty and referred by his cardiologist for smoking cessation. The patient complained of a great deal of pain following the catheterization procedure. Upon questioning, he indicated that he had been depressed and drinking heavily prior to the hospitalization. The therapist used two 30-minute bedside sessions and six brief postdischarge telephone follow-up calls to treat the patient. The therapist used motivational interviewing (W. R. Miller & Rollnick, 1991) to increase the patient's belief that it would be worthwhile to radically alter his lifestyle. The possibility of more intense treatment was broached with the patient, but his psychological well-being improved steadily in the months following discharge. At six-month follow-up, he had stopped drinking and smoking. He was asked to complete an outcome evaluation, where he wrote, "It really helped to talk to the counselor in the hospital because I realized I had to change my life. It wasn't as hard as I thought it would be. The phone calls helped because I felt someone cared about how I was doing." Thus, people who might not ordinarily seek counseling are often receptive to intervention following a life-altering medical event. Even very brief interventions can have an impact when properly timed.

Peter Sifneos (1972) developed short-term anxiety-provoking therapy, designed for high-functioning patients to learn emotional problem-solving skills that will generalize to other areas of life following the termination of therapy. In the decades that followed, McCullough (1997) described a method of regulating, rather than provoking, anxiety. In contrast to supportive forms of therapy that seek to reduce anxiety, many forms of short-term dynamic therapy seek to elicit as much anxiety as the patient can tolerate (Magnavita, 1997) but then to explore and resolve anxious feelings so that the patient becomes comfortable with more intense affect. The ultimate goal is to increase the patient's ability to discern and master the emotional conflict hidden behind the anxiety. Anxiety-regulating techniques are extremely helpful to the clinician treating people with heart disease. For example, at one end of the continuum might be those patients who are overly anxious and come to the emergency room with chest pain, only to have their symptoms dismissed as psychogenic in nature. At the other end of the continuum might be the stoic, highly defended patient who is transported to the hospital via helicopter, survives a serious coronary event, yet seems unfazed. A 48-year-old accountant, whose father died of a heart attack at age 45, was hospitalized for a severe myocardial infarction. A two-pack-per-day smoker, he mused, "They tell me this is very serious, but I have to be honest, I've felt worse pain. It is very hard to believe I had a heart attack." A mix of defense-challenging techniques coupled with strategies to increase motivation and rapport can be an effective method of engaging such patients. In this case, the therapist responded, "So what is your understanding of what happened to your heart?" The patient recounted the course of the day leading up to his heart attack, the ambulance ride to the hospital, and the emergency angioplasty. He noted that the angiographer provided detailed information on the catheterization procedure and extent of the myocardial damage. The cardiologist, whom the patient met for the first time that day, had subsequently drawn a diagram of the patient's heart and outlined a plan following discharge from the hospital. Featured prominently in the plan was the expectation that the patient quit smoking. Having established an initial rapport with the patient by taking time to hear his story, the therapist was then able to help the patient acknowledge his shock at having a heart attack and come to the realization that his smoking was his most serious risk factor, but one over which he could exercise control.

Habib Davanloo (1980) developed intensive short-term dynamic psychotherapy. Davanloo is credited with developing techniques to confront psychological defenses in such a way that the therapist "unlocks the unconscious." Later generations of short-term dynamic therapists have refined these techniques and refer to methods of clarifying, rather than confronting, defenses (McCullough, 1997). Defense analysis is a central aspect of short-term dynamic psychotherapy and can be an important technique that allows the therapist to work with cardiac patients who present as unable or unwilling to attempt lifestyle changes, even when their survival is threatened. A 43-year-old woman working in customer service was seen at our cholesterol management clinic for extremely high triglyceride levels. She reported being unable to make any dietary changes and used her nutritional counseling sessions to vent her anger about her job stress. Thus, she was referred for psychotherapy by the clinic nutritionist. After several therapy sessions, she noted that she had stopped taking her medication, failed to get her blood drawn at the laboratory, and essentially, was taking a hiatus from medical treatment. Defense analysis was used to confront and challenge her seemingly impregnable defense system. Eventually, the anger that had been defensively avoided emerged, permitting therapist and patient to pinpoint the etiology of her affect. After the initial medical intake, the patient had been given a copy of a letter from the cardiologist to her primary care physician that described her diet as "atrocious." The patient said nothing but took offense and, in her anger, stopped medical treatment altogether. With the patient's permission, the wording of the letter was discussed with the clinic nurse, the patient made a new appointment for treatment, and the cardiologist was able to resolve the situation easily. Upon analysis, the intensity of the patient's anger and the self-destructiveness of her response surprised her. She spontaneously made reference to her own father and her tendency to view male authority figures as powerful, uncaring, and demeaning of woman. Defense analysis succeeded with this patient where supportive counseling and nutrition education from the dietitian had made little or no impact on her ability to adhere to the medical regimen.

METHODS OF PSYCHOLOGICAL ASSESSMENT AND INTERVENTION

In our hospital setting, the psychologist may assess the patient via clinical interview at bedside during hospitalization, in the cardiac rehabilitation program, or in an outpatient setting. Each of these settings lends itself to a different interview format. Bedside counseling is typically brief (20 to 30 minutes). The patient enrolled in cardiac rehabilitation is referred by the nurse following intake and the 45-minute interview takes place in a section of the gym partitioned by room dividers. The outpatient interview lasts 45 to 90 minutes and takes place in a therapist's office in the multidisciplinary Department of Preventive Cardiology.

In the inpatient hospital setting, patients are seen for a single session; thus, assessment and intervention are combined. The purpose of the clinical interview is to gather information about the patient's psychological status and inform the patient about the impact of psychological factors on his or her physical health. Most frequently, patients have already been asked by their physician to make one or more behavioral changes following discharge from the hospital. At the end of the interview, patients should have a clearer understanding of their major sources of life stress and how these may impact on their ability to make behavioral changes. The therapist's job is to clarify the patient's readiness to change and to leave the patient more motivated and informed about how to do so than before the session.

In our clinical experience, many cardiac patients minimize the significance of the presenting complaint. A 56-year-old man whose adult son died in an auto accident two months prior to his heart attack reported, "This has been a tough year for me. I don't know why I can't snap out of it." Recently diagnosed heart disease is stressful in itself. Many cardiac patients also have additional sources of stress that impede their ability to make lifestyle changes and form the basis of their presenting complaint. Evaluation of the nature of the stress and its history constitutes the bulk of the assessment process (see Table 23.1). Medical history, mental health history, substance abuse history, living situation, and other demographic variables are always assessed through clinical interview and/or chart review.

The Brief Symptom Inventory is a 53-item psychological inventory that has been widely used with many types of medical patients, including cardiac populations (Deragotis, Dellapietra, & Kilroy, 1992). We routinely assess all outpatients using this measure. Many domains of interest are covered in the nine subscales, including depression, anxiety, hostility, and somatization. We are aware of few widely used cardiac-specific psychological measures validated for people with heart disease. Common psychological factors that are relevant for cardiac patients include depression, anxiety, hostility, and lack of social support.

Up to 25% of patients recovering from heart attack or coronary artery bypass surgery meet diagnostic criteria for Major Depression and an additional 40% to 65% of patients experience depressed mood immediately after the event (Taylor & Cameron, 1999). In particular, prior history of depression, rather than first onset, is an indicator of poorer prognosis (Lesperance, Frasure-Smith, & Talajic, 1996). We typically assess for depression via clinical interview but weigh the import of the somatic symptoms against the proximity of the cardiac event. For example, difficulty sleeping and appetite disturbance is very common following a heart attack but typically improves steadily in the weeks after the patient is discharged home. Hopelessness is a predictor of cardiac morbidity and mortality and should be assessed routinely in this population (Anda et al., 1993). Most patients with cardiac illness experience

Table 23.1 Psychological assessment of the cardiac patient.

1. Presenting problem.
2. Physical functioning:
   a. Current medical problems.
   b. Recent hospitalizations or exacerbations of illness.
3. Current psychological functioning:
   a. Review of the Brief Symptom Inventory results.
   b. Past history of treatment for mental health problems.
   c. Current pharmacological or behavioral treatment for mental health or substance abuse problems.
4. Living situation:
   a. Who lives at home.
   b. Quality of patient's relationships with partner and family members.
   c. Sexual functioning.
   d. Quantity and quality of social support network.
5. Employment:
   a. Formal education.
   b. Work history.
   c. Current employment; level of stress.
   d. Relationship of the medical illness to work (medical leave, etc.).
6. Family of origin:
   a. Status of parents/siblings (alive, cause of death if deceased).
   b. Major medical problems of parents/siblings.
   c. Major psychological difficulties of parents/siblings.
7. Risk factors for cardiovascular disease:
   a. Smoking: stage of readiness to change.
   b. Sedentary lifestyle: stage of readiness to change.
   c. Poor diet: stage of readiness to change.
   d. Nonadherence to medical regimen: stage of readiness to change.
   e. Drinking/drug use: stage of readiness to change.
8. Personality factors:
   a. Characterological traits.
   b. Coping style.
9. Readiness to change:
   a. Motivation.
   b. Self-efficacy.

increased levels of anxiety. Because worry, nervousness, and other anxiety symptoms are often commingled with symptoms of depression and are prominent features of the adjustment following a cardiac event, we always include these as part of the initial interview.

Hostility is a risk factor for coronary heart disease among both men and women. Hostility is a construct comprising three specific factors: anger, aggression, and cynicism (Sotile, 1999). We ask questions about how the patient responds when angered; problems in expressing anger effectively are ubiquitous, and cardiac patients are no exception. Many people with heart disease are under the assumption that they may have a heart attack if they "blow their stack," and thus they work harder to suppress their anger. We typically ask patients to give a recent example of something that made them really angry and describe in detail how they handled it to determine whether this is an area of difficulty.

Low levels of perceived social support are linked to poor recovery from heart attack and coronary artery disease (Pitula, Burg, & Froelicher, 1999). We ask patients about the people with whom they live, the organizations to which they belong, and the quantity and quality of relationships in their social network. We also assess the quality of their relationship with spouse or partner and sexual functioning. Following heart attack, 30% to 44% of patients report decreased sexual activity (Rankin-Esquer, Deeter, & Taylor, 2000). Few patients receive any information about sexual functioning following a cardiac event from their health care provider.

We do not typically conduct an in-depth assessment of the patient's functional status beyond the domains already discussed, but there are disease-specific self-report inventories that measure functional status. For example, the Seattle Angina Questionnaire (Spertus et al., 1995) is a 19-item self-report inventory that measures functional status in five domains:

physical limitations, angina stability, angina frequency, treatment satisfaction, and disease perception. Although these domains have clinical relevance, this type of questionnaire is less helpful to the clinician intent on discerning whether the patient has noteworthy psychiatric symptomotology. To evaluate functional status, we typically ask questions about the degree to which the patient's day-to-day life, in terms of work, relationships with others, and health, has been affected by the medical event.

MAJOR PROBLEMS TREATED

In the outpatient setting, patients are self-referred or referred by a health care provider. The majority of patients treated in our outpatient clinic fall into one of three categories.

Adjustment Problems

Diagnosis of heart disease is unnerving at any age. Even those patients with a family history of cardiac problems who have a fatalistic sense that they, too, will eventually develop the disease are often in shock with an initial diagnosis of CHD. Uncomplicated adjustment problems are relatively easy to treat. Factors such as patient's age, nature and severity of the CHD, and the degree to which the risk factors are under the patient's control impact on psychological adjustment. Many patients who have had a parent die prematurely due to heart disease become preoccupied with the notion that they will die at the same age. Loss of body integrity and impact of the illness on the patient's job, family dynamics, sexual functioning, and overall satisfaction with life are common themes. The primary goal for an otherwise well-functioning patient with adjustment difficulties is to explore and come to terms with feelings of anger and grief about the illness. Exploration of the meaning of the illness in the patient's life can result in improved quality of life and an increased sense of meaning in day-to-day living. Though many cardiac patients face adjustment problems, these rarely occur in isolation, and the majority of individuals diagnosed with CHD need to make lifestyle changes to reduce their cardiovascular risk.

Lifestyle

Following a heart attack, the typical cardiac patient is advised to engage in moderate walking, reduce dietary fat, take a series of new medications, and, above all else, quit smoking. Making changes of this magnitude is difficult. The theoretical framework for understanding how individuals change smoking behavior is found in Prochaska and DiClemente's (1983) transtheoretical model. This model suggests that behavior change involves a nonlinear progression through the stages of precontemplation, contemplation, preparation, action, and maintenance. Using cardiac inpatient smokers as an example, those who report that they are not considering quitting are at the precontemplation stage. Those who are ambivalent but seriously considering quitting in the next six months are at the contemplation stage. Patients who report that they do not plan to resume smoking upon discharge from the hospital are at the preparation stage, and those who had quit smoking within a few months prior to hospitalization are at the action stage. The transtheoretical model integrates motivational, cognitive, and behavioral variables to explain the process of behavior change. Motivation and confidence typically increase linearly with each successive stage, suggesting the need for individually tailored interventions aimed at the stage on the continuum of preparedness to change. In clinical practice, patients often present with the desire to make lifestyle changes, as well as a variety of life stresses that make it difficult to do so.

Our practice of psychotherapy typically emphasizes altering the patient's characteristic patterns for coping with life stressors (Dornelas & Magnavita, 2001). A smaller portion of the session is devoted to actual behavioral change strategies, such as coping with nicotine cravings, substituting heart-healthy food choices, or mapping out a walking route. We provide a variety of educational materials and go over any questions about how to accomplish their goal of altering the behavior, but overall, we believe that the most effective behavioral change strategies are those elicited from the patient rather than prescribed by the provider. Most people find it easiest to change behavior when they are feeling emotionally healthy. The patient's ability to quit smoking, increase physical activity, or reduce dietary fat is an excellent marker of the success of therapy. In our clinical experience, most behavior change is accompanied by an overall improvement in quality of life.

CORONARY-PRONE PERSONALITY

The evidence supporting the validity of a coronary-prone personality has been mixed, but there is a plethora of data demonstrating that anxiety and anger are associated with increased cardiovascular reactivity, as well as impaired immune functioning and susceptibility to pain (Suinn, 2001). Although these negative emotions are not specific to coronary artery disease, there is substantial evidence that a *generic* "disease-prone personality" exists (H. S. Friedman & Booth-Kewley, 1987). Negative affects, such as anger and anxiety, are associated with autonomic nervous system arousal. Our clinical experience suggests that psychotherapeutic techniques designed to elicit emotional arousal are effective methods for altering ego-syntonic personality traits (Magnavita, 1997). For example, a self-employed 53-year-old man with a history of severe CHD described a long-standing pattern of ripping his telephone out of the wall when dealing with customers who irritated him. The therapist asked the patient to recount, in as much detail as possible, the most recent experience of ripping the telephone out of the wall. The patient protested, insisting that he didn't really get mad and would never hurt anyone. He went on to describe his experiences of intense rage. His emotional engagement in the session was dramatic. In the weeks following the session, he described instances of becoming angry without either suppressing or venting his anger on others. Altering this pattern had a profound influence on the patient's interpersonal relationships with both family members and customers.

In summary, most patients treated in our clinic have a mix of adjustment difficulties, unhealthy lifestyles, and various maladaptive personality traits. Under the stress of the medical illness, psychological defenses break down, and thus many patients present with symptoms of depression, anxiety, or panic. We believe that focusing treatment on these three areas, rather than the quest for symptom relief, results in enduring change.

CASE EXAMPLE

This case describes the treatment of a 70-year-old cardiac patient seen at our clinic. Through the case study, we illustrate many of the concepts described in this chapter.

DIAGNOSIS AND ASSESSMENT

The patient was treated by the first author (Dornelas). Mr. C. was referred by his wife, who had seen media coverage of the program. She described her husband as having a difficult time adjusting after his heart attack, which occurred four weeks prior to her phone inquiry. She explained that both she and her husband were retired and had recently received a clean bill of health from their physician on routine examination. Two weeks later, the patient felt chest pain, went to see his cardiologist, and was hospitalized immediately for coronary catheterization. Catheterization revealed a significant coronary stenosis, which was successfully treated with angioplasty. Mr. C. was reassured by his cardiologist that his heart was actually healthier now than prior to intervention. Following his discharge from the hospital, he became increasingly irritable and despondent by turns. His wife of 25 years and their two adult children became increasingly concerned that his depressed mood was not remitting as quickly as they had anticipated.

During the initial telephone inquiry, the patient's wife made it clear that Mr. C. would be unlikely to be receptive to psychotherapy. Instead, she preferred that he think of the initial consultation as an assessment for "stress management." I concurred, and suggested that I would spend 30 minutes with the patient alone and 15 minutes with both the patient and his wife.

Mr. C., a tall, spare septuagenarian with a warm smile and intense blue eyes, appeared neatly dressed in a suit for the initial interview. He had worked in sales for more than 30 years and approached the world with relaxed confidence. Contrary to his wife's concern, he was open to psychotherapy and proceeded to review a litany of physical complaints during the initial interview: "See, I was only discharged last month. My cardiologist told me to take an aspirin every day. But I have an enlarged prostate. The aspirin gives me blood in the urine and my other doctor said I shouldn't take it. Frankly, it scares the hell out of me to see that blood, and I don't know which one to believe."

Mr. C. had had a heart attack 10 years before, just after his retirement, but had been treated successfully with a combination of angioplasty and lipid-lowering medications. He was diagnosed by the therapist as having an Adjustment Disorder with depressed mood. His most prominent symptoms included worry about dying, problems falling asleep, sadness, and feeling tense. On the Brief Symptom Inventory he reported feeling easily annoyed, having uncontrollable temper outbursts, and getting into frequent arguments. His clinical profile on the Brief Symptom Inventory was not noteworthy in other respects, and during the clinical interview he revealed that his arguments and temper outbursts were primarily related to disagreements with his wife.

After meeting his wife in the waiting area, the therapist agreed to meet with the patient for 30 minutes and to use the last 20 minutes of the session to meet with the couple together.

PATIENT: Honestly, I still can't believe it. I went to see my doctor. Two weeks later, I'm in the hospital, tubes sticking out all over. Now I'm doing everything, everything they tell me to do. But still I'm not back on track. I'm really down about the whole situation. I can't sleep at night and I'm getting irritated with my wife. Sometimes I just don't feel like doing anything at all. It seems completely unfair. I was already having these prostate problems and now the heart attack. I was doing everything the doctor told me to do. Everything! I just don't understand it. (Emits a deep sigh.)

THERAPIST: You sound pretty angry.

PATIENT: Angry? No, I'm not angry. I'm aggravated is what I am. The heart doctor, he says, take an aspirin every day. So, I take an aspirin and it makes the bleeding from the prostate worse. It's terrible getting old.

THERAPIST: So you are doing everything right and still you get this heart attack?

PATIENT: Exactly. That is exactly right.

THERAPIST: So what do you make of that?

PATIENT: I don't know. I didn't expect to live forever. But I was feeling really good until this. We go to Florida every winter. We are due to leave in two months. Right now, I don't even want to go.

Mr. C. related easily to the therapist and was comfortable expressing his sadness and anger during the interview. He had never had any history of mental health treatment nor any significant

558 SPECIAL TOPICS

medical history other than that already described. Mr. C.'s wife expressed concern about his health. She worried that he was not sleeping well and that they argued frequently.

SPOUSE: He gets really angry with me. For instance, today, I didn't want him to drive here. I said I would drive.
PATIENT: The doctor didn't say I couldn't drive!
SPOUSE: (Ignoring the patient.) He gets tired from the driving and the walking over from the garage.
PATIENT: I tell her, stop treating me like an invalid. I know whether I can drive or not!
THERAPIST: So the two of you have been arguing with each other about this type of thing? How much his activity is restricted and so on?
SPOUSE: I'm just worried about him! He's stubborn!
THERAPIST: Its sounds like the two of you are talking about control.
PATIENT: (Looks delighted.) You hit the nail on the head. She is always trying to control me!

CASE FORMULATION

Mr. C. was an only child who was orphaned at age 11. Following the death of his parents, he went to live with an aunt, who raised him. Mr. C. lived with his aunt until he went to college at age 18. He expressed a great appreciation for his aunt, but noted that "It was really hard. My aunt had other kids. She took me in and was really good to me. Still, it is not the same, though. Not the same as having your own mother."

THERAPIST: Do you ever talk about it [death of patient's mother] with your family?
PATIENT: Not much, but my wife has always been close with my aunt. My wife and I are really close. Yesterday, I was trying to get some things done for our trip to Florida next month, and my mother—I mean my wife! [Interrupts himself, starts to laugh.] Now where did that come from? I meant to say my wife.

With unconscious material so close to the surface, the therapist wondered out loud whether Mr. C.'s recent hospitalization for his heart attack stirred up some old memories about losing his mother.

PATIENT: It might be. I just feel sad and down in the dumps.
THERAPIST: You look sad right now.

Mr. C. expressed a profound appreciation for his wife's caretaking but also felt extremely annoyed by what he perceived as her attempts to control him. The therapist formulated the following preliminary case conceptualization. Mr. C. was a man who had lost his parents early in life. Growing up, he didn't feel as though he rightfully belonged in his home with his aunt and learned to avoid conflict out of fear of being abandoned. His second heart attack triggered both existential anxiety about his own mortality and his concerns about becoming increasingly dependent on his wife.

Mr. C. and his wife reported that they were both invested and satisfied with their marriage, but his wife felt that Mr. C. was taking out his anger about the heart attack on her. According to the couple's report, they argued with each other, then avoided talking about the confrontation until it blew over. Although this pattern of interaction was characteristic of their relationship during the course of the marriage, it was markedly worse since Mr. C.'s second heart attack. Mr. C. expressed anger at his wife's overprotection but also described many instances of dependent, care-seeking behavior on his part.

TREATMENT APPROACH AND RATIONALE FOR ITS SELECTION

Short-term treatment involving both the patient separately and the couple conjointly was the therapy of choice for this patient. His departure for Florida provided a clear termination point. In addition to the initial session, he was treated with four 45-minute individual psychotherapy sessions and three 45-minute conjoint sessions with his wife. The majority of patients who self-refer for anxiety or depression following hospitalization for a cardiac event are treated in 12 or fewer sessions. We commonly include the spouse or partner in one or more of the sessions.

Mr. C. noted consistent improvement between each session. His sleeping difficulties and worry about the blood in his urine remitted by the third session.

PATIENT: (Beginning of the session, looks anxious.) I'm sleeping better but I'm not quite right this morning. Rachel and I had a tiff. We are trying to get things packed for Florida this last week and I said, "Don't pack my things, I'll do it myself." So she goes ahead and packs my things anyway. And this morning, I can't find one of my shirts that I want to wear today. So she's downstairs and I say to her, "Where are my shirts?" She tells me where they are, and I can't find them. So I tell her "Well, I can't find them!" Then she says, in that loud voice of hers, "Well, open your eyes and look for them!" So then I said something I really shouldn't have said.

THERAPIST: What did you say?

PATIENT: I told her, "Shut up!" Just like that. And that's something I never say. I feel bad about it.

THERAPIST: What were you feeling at that time?

PATIENT: Mad! She packs up my things after I told her not too. And I know she is a little busy, doesn't have time to come upstairs and help me. But if she would just leave my things alone, I could do it myself. (He hits the edge of the seat.)

THERAPIST: What does your anger feel like, inside your body?

PATIENT: Like Pow! I feel like popping something!

THERAPIST: Who do you feel like popping?

PATIENT: Well, her I guess [referring to his wife]. But that's awful. I would never hit a woman. Especially not my wife. That's a terrible thing to even think.

THERAPIST: What happened next?

PATIENT: Nothing. I was so mad I didn't talk to her. I came here to this appointment. My wife, she has a strong personality. Do you know in all these years she has never once said that she was sorry to me? Not once. Now we are on top of each other all the time and she is getting on my nerves.

THERAPIST: So it sounds like you experience your wife as being controlling. Not letting you pack your things or drive your car. You get angry and hopeless that she won't change and then you get depressed. On top of that, since you haven't been feeling well, you seem to be less tolerant of your wife's strong personality.

PATIENT: (He cocks his head to one side, considering the implications, and nods his head.) Damned if that's not right on the mark.

Mr. C. went on to relate another story of how he continually gets on his wife's case about her weight. "She has put on about 20 pounds and I keep after her to stay away from the sweets. In fact, at one of those bridge games, I took the candy dish away from her. Boy, was she mad!" He told the story with obvious relish at the memory of his wife's wrath.

The therapist pointed out that he was humiliating his wife in front of her friends and Mr. C. took umbrage.

PATIENT: *Never*, never would I do that! I tell her "No one cares more about your health than I do." I don't care about her weight, it's the fact that it is bad for her health. She is younger than me but she'll have worse health problems.

THERAPIST: I agree, I don't think you are consciously trying to humiliate her. But she controls a lot of aspects of your life, especially since you got sick. Do you think you might be trying to get her back?

PATIENT: (Appearing puzzled but intrigued, and leaning forward in his seat.) Uh, I think I'm helping her.

THERAPIST: One of you is always trying to control the other, like a parent and child. Your wife tells you to take your medicine, packs your clothes, and won't let you drive the car. You in turn, try to control what she eats. Both of you get angry with each other and you don't resolve the real problem.

PATIENT: (The interpretation clearly resonated with Mr. C. and he began to laugh.) That is exactly what we do! But, heavens, I don't know whether we can change just like that!

The dialogue in future sessions continued to focus on multiple examples of similar incidents, and over time, Mr. C. became more emotionally connected with and accepting of his anger. The argument over packing clothes was a good example of the dysfunctional communication pattern in the relationship and Mr. C.'s characteristic pattern of burying his anger. The intensity of his anger surprised the patient and then triggered guilt feelings, a classic example of the type of conflicted feeling that often responds well to affect restructuring (Magnavita, 1997; McCoullough, 1997). The therapist's goals were to encourage greater emotional expression and to elicit the patient's wish for caretaking, anger at his wife, fears about dying, and grief.

Throughout therapy, Mr. C. expressed his ambivalence about getting older. He was shocked that he had suffered a heart attack, particularly because he had been feeling fine in the months prior to the event. His sadness at reaching the latter part of his life was poignant. At times, he made reference to the therapist's age by noting "that was probably before your time." Initially, during the first session, Mr. C. seemed somewhat taken aback by the therapist, but by the end of the session he related easily to her.

PATIENT: (End of first session.) So, how long have you been at the hospital, doctor?

THERAPIST: (Mentally calculating that her age is the same as his daughter's.) Seven years.

PATIENT: How do you pronounce your last name?

THERAPIST: (Pronounces it for him.)

PATIENT: I see. (Tries out the pronunciation.) I should call you Dr. Dornelas.

THERAPIST: (Unclear about whether he is making a statement or a question.) Whatever you are comfortable with.

PATIENT: No, I prefer to call you Doctor. (The therapist gets the sense that he is trying to educate her.) I'll tell you a story. Years ago, there was a rabbi in our synagogue and he was a young man. Everyone else used to call him David. That was his name. But I never did. I didn't think it was right. I used to call him Rabbi, because that's what he was. So I'll call you Doctor, because that's what you are.

THERAPIST: (Smiling.) Okay. When would you like to come back?

REFERENCE TO EXISTING TREATMENT PROTOCOLS

There are few psychotherapy protocols for treating the psychological distress of cardiac patients. Those discussed below are specific to cardiac patients but are still in the early stages of outcome evaluation. Our approach shares some common elements with the Relationship Support Program, designed for patients with heart disease (Rankin-Esquer et al., 2000). The Relationship Support Program is designed to complement medical interventions and to help couples examine how relational issues impact and are impacted by the cardiac event. Recognizing the literature that points to lack of social support as an important prognostic indicator of cardiovascular morbidity and mortality, this model adapts cognitive-behavioral marital therapy to the needs of the couple affected by cardiovascular disease.

The ENRICHD (2000) study tests a cognitive therapy intervention for depressed cardiac patients, and outcome data from that study are forthcoming. The ENRICHD treatment protocol is designed to provide behavioral activation, encourage active problem solving, and alter dysfunctional automatic thoughts. The research protocol for ENRICHD allows up to 6 months of individual psychotherapy, with up to 3 months of group psychotherapy and up to 12 months of adjunctive pharmacotherapy, making it a particularly intensive form of treatment.

Richard Suinn (2001) has described Anxiety-Anger Management Training (AAMT), designed to deactivate the emotional arousal caused by anger and anxiety through relaxation training. AAMT consists of six to eight individual psychotherapy sessions that expose the patient to the stressor through visualization followed by relaxation. Homework, self-monitoring, and teaching of self-control skills are also included in this cognitive-behavioral model. There are outcome data to support that this treatment model is effective at reducing symptoms of anxiety, depression, and road rage (Suinn, 2001).

POSTTERMINATION SYNOPSIS AND EFFECTIVENESS DATA

This patient was treated with four sessions of individual therapy and three conjoint sessions with his wife. Six months following treatment, both Mr. C. and his wife were contacted by the therapist by phone. Mr. C. reported that his mood was much improved and he thought that counseling had been very helpful to him. His wife agreed that they rarely argued and were enjoying more activities together than ever before. Mr. C.'s cardiac health was stable, and he enjoyed a variety of outdoor activities. Based on the report of the patient and his wife, the most significant change occurred in their communication patterns. All of Mr. C.'s symptomatic complaints had remitted by the end of treatment. Prior to treatment, the patient had reported worry about dying, problems falling asleep, sadness, tension, being easily annoyed, having uncontrollable temper outbursts, and getting into frequent arguments with his wife. None of these were evident at follow-up.

This treatment model uses many of the same therapeutic strategies as the Relationship Support Program and AAMT but is different in its emphasis on eliciting emotional response and relating it to unresolved core issues. In contrast to many stress management programs offered in clinical health psychology settings, this model does not seek to *deactivate* emotional arousal by teaching patients various methods of inducing the relaxation response. Instead, the experience of emotional arousal is intensified in vivo, with the goal of making the patient more comfortable with intense negative affect. The importance of working in the psychotherapy session with a patient's emotionally laden material has long been recognized (Goldfried & Hayes, 1989). Learning that takes place in the context of emotional arousal might be viewed as the essential change agent in psychotherapy.

This treatment model is evolving. We evaluated an earlier version of this model with smokers who had experienced myocardial infarction. Long-term follow-up indicated that brief intervention at bedside following heart attack is an effective treatment to help smokers quit (Dornelas, Sampson, Gray, Waters, & Thompson, 2000). There is a critical need to evaluate psychotherapy outcomes (Dornelas, Correll, Lothstein, Wilber, & Goethe, 1996). Research to determine the long-term outcomes of cardiac patients treated with psychodynamic pychotherapy is currently underway in our clinic.

SUMMARY

There are few psychotherapists who specialize in the psychological care of the cardiac patient, yet heart disease is the leading cause of death in the United States; thus, there is a great need to develop psychotherapy services specifically tailored to this population. It is currently in vogue for psychotherapists of all orientations to note that they have become interested in mind-body medicine or health psychology. The movement toward greater recognition of the biopsychosocial aspects of physical illness is a very positive step. However, there is still a need to apply what works from psychodynamically oriented psychotherapy to problems of health and illness. Although mind-body medicine workshops and training centers have become increasingly popular, mind-body medicine as practiced today often does not meet the psychological needs of the medical patient. Stress-reduction techniques can induce short-term improvement in symptomatic distress; however, as a health psychologist (Dornelas), I have found stress management techniques to be helpful but not sufficient to address the psychological needs of most cardiac patients. Stress management is not of much help in clarifying the existential issues faced by people with cardiac disease, in restructuring their relational patterns, or in helping clients achieve greater levels of emotional maturity, yet these are the salient issues for people with heart disease. Generations of clinicians and researchers have refined the practice of psychodynamically oriented therapy. Applying these treatment models to problems of health and illness is the logical next step. Treating cardiac patients with psychotherapy is a rare privilege as well as a unique learning experience, and we encourage more clinicians to consider working in this rewarding area.

REFERENCES

Allan, R., & Scheidt, S. (1996). *Heart and mind: The practice of cardiac psychology*. Washington, DC: American Psychological Association.

Anda, R., Williamson, D., Jones, D., Macera, C., Eaker, E., Glassman, A., et al. (1993). Depressed affect, hopelessness and risk of ischemic heart disease in a cohort of U.S. adults. *Epidemiology, 4*, 285–294.

Beitman, B. D., Goldfried, M. R., & Norcross, J. C. (1989). The movement toward integrating the psychotherapies: An overview. *American Journal of Psychiatry, 146*, 138–147.

Billings, J. H., Scherwitz, L. W., Sullivan, R., Sparler, S., & Ornish, D. M. (1996). The Lifestyle Heart Trial: Comprehensive treatment and group support therapy. In R. Allan & S. Scheidt (Eds.), *Heart and mind: The practice of cardiac psychology*. Washington, DC: American Psychological Association.

Bracke, P. E., & Thorensen, C. E. (1996). Reducing Type A behavior patterns: A structured-group approach. In R. Allan & S. Scheidt (Eds.), *Heart and mind: The practice of cardiac psychology*. Washington, DC: American Psychological Association.

Burell, G. (1996). Group psychotherapy in Project New Life: Treatment of coronary-prone behaviors for patients who have had coronary artery bypass graft surgery. In R. Allan & S. Scheidt (Eds.), *Heart and mind: The practice of cardiac psychology*. Washington, DC: American Psychological Association.

Davanloo, H. (1980). *Short-term dynamic psychotherapy*. Northvale, NJ: Aronson.

Deragotis, L. R., Dellapietra, L., & Kilroy, V. (1992). Screening for psychiatric disorder in medical populations. In G. Fava, G. Rosenbaum, & R. Birnbaum (Eds.), *Research methods in psychiatry*. Amsterdam: Elsevier.

Dornelas, E. A., Correll, R. E., Lothstein, L., Wilber, C., & Goethe, J. W. (1996). Designing and implementing outcome evaluations: Some guidelines for practitioners. *Psychotherapy, 33*, 237–245.

Dornelas, E. A., & Magnavita, J. J. (2001). High impact therapy for smoking session. *Journal of Clinical Psychology*.

Dornelas, E. A., Sampson, R., Gray, J., Waters, D., & Thompson, P. D. (2000). A randomized controlled trial of smoking cessation counseling after myocardial infarction. *Preventive Medicine, 30*, 261–268.

Dusseldorp, E., van Elderen, T., Maes, S., Meulman, J., & Kraaij, V. (1999). A meta-analysis of psychoeducational programs for coronary heart disease patients. *Health Psychology, 18*, 506–519.

The ENRICHD Investigators. (2000). Enhancing recovery in coronary heart disease patients (ENRICHD): Study design and methods. *American Heart Journal, 139,* 1–9.

Frasure-Smith, N., Lesperance, F., & Talajic, M. (1993). Depression following myocardial infarction: Impact on 6 month survival. *Journal of the American Medical Association, 270,* 1819–1825.

Friedman, H. S., & Booth-Kewley, S. (1987). The disease-prone personality: A meta-analytic view of the construct. *American Psychologist, 42,* 539–555.

Friedman, M., & Rosenman, R. H. (1959). Association of specific behavioral pattern with blood and cardiovascular findings. *Journal of the American Medical Association, 169,* 1286–1296.

Goldfried, M. R., & Hayes, A. M. (1989). Can contributions from other orientations complement behavior therapy? *Behavior Therapy, 12,* 57–60.

Lesperance, F., Frasure-Smith, N., & Talajic, M. (1996). Major depression before and after myocardial infarction: Its nature and consequences. *Psychosomatic Medicine, 58,* 99–110.

Magnavita, J. J. (1997). *Restructuring personality disorders: A short-term dynamic approach.* New York: Guilford Press.

Malan, D. H. (1976). *The frontier of brief psychotherapy: An example of the convergence of research and clinical practice.* New York: Plenum Medical.

Mann, J. (1973). *Time-limited psychotherapy.* Cambridge, MA: Harvard University Press.

Manuck, S., Kaplan, J., & Matthews, K. (1986). Behavioral antecedents of coronary heart disease and atherosclerosis. *Arteriosclerosis, 6,* 2–14.

McCullough, L. (1997). *Changing character: Short-term anxiety-regulating psychotherapy for restructuring defenses, affects and attachment.* New York: Basic Books.

Miller, T., Smith, T., Turner, C., Guijarro, M., & Hallet, A. (1996). A meta-analytic review of research on hostility and physical health. *Psychological Bulletin, 119,* 322–348.

Miller, W. R., & Rollnick, S. (1991). *Motivational interviewing: Preparing people to change addictive behavior.* New York: Guilford Press.

Pitula, C. R., Burg, M. M., & Froelicher, E. S. (1999). Psychosocial risk factors: Assessment and intervention for social isolation. In N. K. Wenger, L. K. Smith, E. S. Froelicher, & P. M. Comoss (Eds.), *Cardiac rehabilitation: A guide to practice in the 21st century.* New York: Marcel Dekker.

Prochaska, J. O., & DiClemente, C. C. (1983). Stages and processes of self-change of smoking: Toward an integrative model. *Journal of Clinical and Consulting Psychology, 51,* 390–395.

Quinn, M. H. (1999). Family relationships and cardiovascular health: A review with implications for family psychology. *Family Psychologist, 15,* 10–13.

Rankin-Esquer, L. A., Deeter, A., & Taylor, C. B. (2000). Coronary heart disease and couples. In K. B. Schmaling & T. G. Sher (Eds.), *The psychology of couples and illness: Theory, research and practice.* Washington, DC: American Psychological Association.

Rozanski, A., Blumenthal, J. A., & Kaplan, J. (1999). Impact of psychological factors on the pathogenesis of cardiovascular disease and implications for therapy. *Circulation, 99,* 2192–2217.

Sifneos, P. (1972). *Short-term psychotherapy and emotional crisis.* Cambridge, MA: Harvard University Press.

Sotile, W. M. (1999). Psychosocial risk factors: Overview, assessment, and intervention for anger and hostility. In N. K. Wenger, L. K. Smith, E. S. Froelicher, & P. M. Comoss (Eds.), *Cardiac rehabilitation: A guide to practice in the 21st century.* New York: Marcel Dekker.

Spertus, J. A., Winder, J. A., Dewhurst, T. A., Deyo, R. A., Prodzinski, J., McDonell, M., et al. (1995). Development and evaluation of the Seattle Angina Questionnaire: A new functional status measure for coronary artery disease. *American College of Cardiology, 25,* 333–341.

Stoney, C., Bausserman, L., Niaura, R., Marcus, B., & Flynn, M. (1999). Lipid reactivity to stress: II. Biological and behavioural influences. *Health Psychology, 18,* 251–261.

Suinn, R. M. (2001). The terrible twos—anger and anxiety: Hazardous to your health. *American Psychologist, 56,* 27–36.

Taylor, C. B., & Cameron, R. P. (1999). Psychosocial risk factors: Assessment and intervention for depression. In N. K. Wenger, L. K. Smith, E. S. Froelicher, & P. M. Comoss (Eds.), *Cardiac rehabilitation: A guide to practice in the 21st century.* New York: Marcel Dekker.

Weston, D. (1986). What changes in short-term dynamic psychotherapy? *Psychotherapy, 23,* 501–512.

CHAPTER 24

Race, Gender, and Transference in Psychotherapy

MARY F. HALL

Much has been made of the fact that people of color—First Nation people, African Americans, Latinos, Asian and Pacific Islanders—will eventually comprise the largest segment of the population in the United States during this century (Fong & Furuto, 2001). In the process, many questions have been raised about the generalization of psychodynamic theoretical models beyond their original patient populations, for example, primarily educated persons of European descent. Can this diversity be accommodated (Altman, 1996)? How universal is the psychoanalytic self (Roland, 1996)? What is a multicultural perspective for psychodynamic psychotherapies (Adams, 1996; Jackson & Greene, 2000)? Is it for everyone or are there any limitations on who is an appropriate candidate (Moskowitz, 1996)? What constitutes culturally competent practice (Foster, 1996; Helm & Cook, 1999)?

Roland (1996) maintains that as psychodynamic models expand to work with persons from increasingly diverse cultures, they will have to incorporate a much more detailed consideration of social, cultural, and historical factors within a psychoanalytic framework of the self. He suggests that a cultural self will need to be posited that is profoundly linked on all levels of self-experience, developmental stages, earlier and later object and selfobject relationships, inner structures, and normality/psychopathology within the sociocultural milieu(s) in which a person has grown up and/or currently lives. Fulani (1988) asserts that a historical self will also need to be posited because all societies are simultaneously making and adapting to history at any point in time. These historical processes also have implications for an individual's internal world that may be conscious or unconscious. Adams (1996) notes the more general problem that psychodynamic models, which are distinguished by their emphasis on the unconscious, have never adequately taken into account the social and cultural dimensions of the psyche; with few exceptions, the tendency to regard social and cultural variables as "extrapsychic" continues into the present.

When issues of race, gender, or culture have been given attention, the tendency has been to view these socially constructed groupings as homogenous populations and to ignore the multiple layers of complexity that can exist within and between these social constructions. This trend too has received increasing criticism from many quarters in recent years (Atkinson, Morten, & Sue, 1993; Jackson & Greene, 2000; Roland, 1996). For example, there has been a strong feminist critique of most psychodynamic theories as being patriarchal, ethnocentric, and claiming a universality that does not allow for the uniqueness of women's voices (Gilligan, 1982; Jordan, 1997). In turn, Comas-Diaz (1988) notes how many ethnic minority women have questioned the relevance of feminism and feminist therapies to their group. She suggests that most ethnic minority women tend to view their ethnicity and feminism as opposing forces; or, due to survival issues, they tend to be more committed to their ethnic identity than their political identity as women. Historically, minorities of color have also tended to feel alienated by the feminist movement because of its early emphasis on the paid labor force and escaping the confines of home, as these were not their issues (Comas-Diaz, 1988; Greene, 1994b). Tatum (1997) notes how Black women cannot separate their Blackness from their femaleness, that they are always simultaneously both.

In general, African American psychotherapists (Daniel, 2000; Greene, 1994a, 2000; Jackson, 2000) have been particularly strong voices in challenging feminist psychotherapies to answer the question, Which women are you talking about anyway? Jessica Daniel's critique (1994) of Judith Herman's book *Trauma and Recovery* (1992) is a good illustration. In this classic work on violence and its associated trauma, Herman (1992) asserts how the need to come face-to-face with the capacity for evil in humans is inherent in the study of psychological trauma. She stresses how the perpetrators of atrocities will do everything in their power to promote the forgetting of their transgressions with arguments that frequently prove irresistible. If secrecy and silence fail, the perpetrator will attempt to discredit the victim. Herman allows how the study of psychological trauma must constantly contend with this tendency to discredit and/or render the victim invisible. To illustrate, she notes three times during the past century that she considers a particular form of psychological trauma to have surfaced into public consciousness and flourished briefly primarily because of its association with a political movement: hysteria and the oppression of women; the shell shock or combat neurosis affecting veterans from World War I; and the extent of sexual and domestic violence brought to light by the feminist movement.

Daniel (1994), in turn, challenges Herman (1992) to task for having written a book on trauma that is hailed as a classic yet renders invisible the unique potential for intrapsychic trauma among African Americans resulting from societal violence and racial oppression. She observes how the Civil Rights Movement, with its freedom marches, bombings, assassinations, and so on, is noticeably absent from Herman's list of psychological trauma brought to light by a political movement in the past century. Daniel finds it equally insidious that the one reference to African Americans in the entire book has to do with the potential for violence toward White women by Black men.

In reality, there are tremendous sociopolitical, historical, and cultural differences between and within racial groups that could influence transference and an individual's internal perception of objects in the clinical situation (Cornacchia & Nelson, 1992). For example, Vickerman (1999) notes how African Americans of West Indian descent, in contrast to other African Americans, have constructed a unique identity for themselves. That emphasizes achievement and success over racial solidarity. However, he does not connect this observation to the significant differences historically in the systems of slavery that produced these two groups of African descent. African Americans of West Indian descent were, for the most part, never subjected to chattel slavery. This was a system of slavery that was uniquely American and distinguished by its legalized attack on the family structure of African Americans (Higginbotham, 1978).

The need to be particular rather than general becomes even more pertinent when discussing psychodynamic theories and concepts such as transference and object relations. In the clinical situation, both transference (Esman, 1990) and object relations (Summers, 1994) are particular to an individual's experiences and the persons that have been or currently are significant in that individual's life. African American and Asian women who were immigrants may have been subject to sexual exploitation in the United States. However, there were significant differences between the sexual exploitation of Asian women, in the form of mail-order brides, for example, and the historical sexual exploitation of African American women as legal and chattel slaves. There are also major differences in the accompanying stereotypes these two groups have had to confront, that is, Asian women as exotic sexual objects (Chan, 1988) versus African American women as amoral, loose, and hypersexual (West, 1995).

Finally, the need to be specific rather than general about the particular object-relations perspective one employs in any given case must be noted. The closing decades of the twentieth century were witness to tremendous theoretical ferment in the field of psychoanalysis and psychoanalytic psychotherapies. This has resulted in multiple and frequently competing perspectives on object relations (Greenberg & Mitchell, 1983; Pine, 1990; Schafer, 1992; Summers, 1994). The impetus for this development has been diverse. First and foremost was the dialectical tension within psychoanalysis that generated multiple models of object relations. Equally important were the pressures of external funding sources making their demands for briefer and less costly therapeutic interventions with a wider range of patients diagnostically. The demand to treat more seriously ill patients than had previously been thought possible led to an increased emphasis on the developmental theory that was implicit in each psychoanalytic model and how this knowledge could inform therapists' clinical transactions with such populations (Blanck & Blanck, 1986; Horner, 1984, 1995; Kohut, 1984; Pine, 1985). The demand for more cost-effective therapies led to increased theoretical ferment about short-term models of therapy (Davanloo, 1980; Horner, 1994; Levenson, 1995; Magnavita, 1997; Mann & Goldman, 1982). Simultaneously, the demand for psychoanalytic therapies to expand their theoretical boundaries and articulate how the existing social order is reproduced in the individual has continued to grow (Foster, Moskowitz, & Javier, 1996; Jackson & Greene, 2000). Race, gender, and, to a lesser degree, class identities have been of particular interest (Adams, 1996; Fong & Furuto, 2001; Fulani, 1988; Jordan, 1997; Mathura & Baer, 1990).

This chapter seeks to make its contribution to this ferment by an exploration into the interface between race and object relations as this is manifested in the transference during treatment. This is a topic that has received scant attention in the literature. To meet the editorial request to be particular, a case is used to illustrate some of the issues that have been identified in the literature on race and transference. Because Ms. A. is an African American woman, the interface between race and gender in the transference can also be explored. Given the complexity and heterogeneity of models explicating object relations, the developmental object-relations lens of ego psychology (Blanck & Blanck, 1986; Horner, 1994, 1995) has been adopted in this case. There is no intent to privilege this model above others. Rather, this selection was made based on the utilitarian criterion that it effectively structures the discussion of assessment and treatment.

PSYCHOANALYTIC DEVELOPMENTAL OBJECT-RELATIONS THEORY MODEL

Gertrude and Rubin Blanck (1986) offered the term psychoanalytic developmental object relations (PDOR) to distinguish the view of object relations that grew out of ego psychology. Ego psychology builds on the drive/structure model postulated by Freud. It is distinguished by a shift from Freud's id psychology, with instinctual drives and libidinal stages as superordinate organizers of mental structure, to a psychology of the ego (Blanck & Blanck, 1974, 1979). Herein, the ego becomes the superordinate structure that mediates the development of both an individual's internal structure and external adaptation in the world. From a dynamic point of view, developmental lines replace libidinal stages as the epigenetic model of structure development in the ego. Psychoanalytic developmental object-relations theory (PDORT), in turn, builds on ego psychology. The shift from ego psychology to an object-relations theory reflects the emphasis on the central role of object relations in the overall structuring of the ego (Horner, 1984, 1995). As such, the development line of object relations as explicated by Mahler, Pine, and Bergman (1975) performs the function for the ego that libidinal stages performed for the id in the drive/structure model. In PDORT, the instinctual drives transition to become one of the developmental lines to be organized within the context of object relations. (Readers interested in a more in-depth treatment of this evolution in theory are referred to the classic trilogy by Blanck & Blanck, 1974, 1979, 1986.)

In PDORT, object relations includes both the structural and dynamic relationships between internal mental representations of the self and objects. From a structural point of view, Mahler (1975) and her colleagues postulated that the infant's mental representation of self and objects are essentially merged at birth. From this undifferentiated state, the developmental line of object relations proceeds in consecutive steps of increasing differentiation that culminate in the state of libidinal object constancy. The hallmark of this latter achievement is the separation of self and object mental representations and the ability to tolerate (i.e., sustain this separation of self and object mental representations) loving and hostile feelings simultaneously experienced toward a valued object. In terms of an individual's adaptation in the external world, we assume this milestone has been achieved when a person demonstrates the capacity to stay in a relationship with a valued object when it does not gratify a wish or need.

From a dynamic perspective in PDORT, developmental arrest before libidinal object constancy is achieved sets the stage for personality disorders that are considered understructured (Blanck & Blanck, 1986) or narcissistic (Horner, 1984; Kohut, 1984). In broad strokes, Psychotic, Borderline, and Narcissistic Personality Disorders would be included in this category. In the drive/structure model, these personality disorders would be considered pre-Oedipal structures. Because a developmental arrest in object relations has occurred before psychic differentiation of self and object mental representations could take place, the mental representation of self and object remain merged and are activated according to the need state of the mental representation of self. Splitting (Kernberg, 1975), or the tendency to relate to objects based on the current state of need of the self, continues as a major defense in such disorders. Under stress, these need states tend to be sharply divided into feeling all good or all bad, and, similarly, experiencing objects as either all good or all bad.

The transference of personality disorders in this group is considered narcissistic because it seeks to fulfill early object needs that have not been met (all good object) or replicates the experience with overly frustrating, prior objects (all bad object). Such transferences do not respond well to interpretation aimed at insight. Insight-oriented interpretations are at high risk to flood the person with bad feelings in the moment and trigger regression and/or the defense of further splitting. In the PDORT model, the transference is used to identify the level of developmental arrest on the developmental line of object relations as explicated by Mahler (1975) and her colleagues, and advance the goal of treatment. The goal of treatment is to help the understructured personality resume the development of ego structure within the context of object relations and with the goal of restructuring the personality (Blanck & Blanck, 1986; Horner, 1995; Magnavita, 1997).

Should further developmental arrest occur once libidinal object constancy has been achieved, the stage is set for the neurotic disorders (Horner, 1994). Such personalities are considered structured. Libidinal object constancy is considered a prerequisite for transference in the classical sense (i.e., feelings, attitudes, and behaviors first experienced with a primary object are transferred into the present). Because the mental representation of self and object are separate and have achieved constancy, it is possible for the self to experience internal conflict with a whole object. In clinical work with persons who have achieved this level of structure, transference can be interpreted and insight can be useful.

It is to be noted that the developmental diagnosis is frequently difficult to make and there are dangers in diagnosing too high and too low (Blanck & Blanck, 1986). If the diagnosis is too high and insight-oriented interpretations are made, one would anticipate regression and the increased use of splitting as a defense. This was the experience Kohut (1968) initially set out to understand in his narcissistic patients who frequently looked neurotic but responded to an insight interpretation with rage and regression.

In practice, this error tends to be more serious than making the developmental diagnosis too low. Here, the risk is to infantilize a structured personality that may be engaged in defensive regression to avoid higher-level conflicts when the structure is in place to do this work (Horner, 1995). Such persons are capable of responding to insight interpretations. Other markers of the understructured personality as compared to the structured personality include a dyadic versus triadic mode of relating to objects; whether the level of developmental arrest affects all functioning or there are some conflict-free spheres of functioning; and whether there are any higher-level defenses in place.

CRITIQUE OF PDORT MODEL

It is significant to note that PDORT has been subject to both severe criticism (Atwood & Stolorow, 1984; Gilligan, 1982; Jordan, 1997; Stern, 1985) and praise (Horner, 1994, 1995; Pine, 1990; Shorter-Gooden & Jackson, 2000; Thompson, 1996) over the years. Criticisms include it being an overly simplistic, linear, and hierarchical theory; the fact that it is culture-bound, pathologizes lesbians and gays, and makes claims to universality that it cannot sustain; and that it advances a mother-blaming, gender-stereotyping, approach to women. In spite of this substantive criticism, clinicians continue to find clinical utility in this model into the present (Horner, 1994, 1995; Pine, 1990; Shorter-Gooden & Jackson, 2000; Thompson, 1996). There is a certain paradox in the fact that what these clinicians find most useful about the model are the same elements that have received most of the criticism. Specifically, the model is simple, easy to understand and, as such, offers tremendous clinical utility in helping to reduce very complex clinical material for assessment and treatment planning. Although raising serious challenges to the validity of Mahler's work, even Daniel Stern (1985) noted this clinical utility.

Some of this paradox appears to be a result of criticism that has a goal of weaving psychoanalytic discourse into modern trends in intellectual history. Linguistic and hermeneutic approaches to interpretation are particularly prominent (Schafer, 1976, 1992). Such criticism raises very different questions from those that inspired the original work and shift the nature of the criticism away from the replication logic of the scientific movement that gave birth to PDORT. Instead, the language of psychoanalytic discourse as a narrative that "stories" lives becomes the focus of attention rather than the scientific explanatory power of metapsychology, developmental lines, and object-relations theory. In the process, concepts with specific intrapsychic meanings in PDORT, such as separation, individuation, and autonomy, become increasingly relational and cultural.

There is no question about the need to more fully articulate the role of culture and social identities in this paradigm, yet it is important to remember that in PDORT, object relations refers to an aspect of ego organization that is intrapsychic. It does not refer to the objective reality of external personal relationships and/or social oppression. PDORT postulates the course of development in the mental representation of self and objects given an average expectable environment and endowment. We infer the steps in this developmental line based on what we see in the individual's growing capacity for adaptation. In this paradigm, concepts such as separation, individuation, and autonomy refer to the mental representations of self and objects. They do not seek to explain the social and spatial relationships for which all societies and cultures have norms. Rather, this theory seeks to answer such questions as how an infant comes to know and a schizophrenic does not seem to know that his or her body, thoughts, and feelings are separate and may be different from those of other important objects in the environment.

Schizophrenia has been found in all types of societies (American Psychiatric Association, 1994; Goodwin & Guze, 1996). The rates of schizophrenia are also relatively uniform worldwide. Loss of reality testing and other manifestations of the underlying structure of this disorder have consistently been observed across all types of sociopolitical societies that espouse vastly different cultural norms. Culture is thought to determine the specific and manifest form this illness takes (e.g., paranoid, catatonic, hebephrenic, etc.; American Psychiatric Association, 1994). For example, the catatonic form of schizophrenia is far more prevalent in other parts of the world than in the United States. Similarly, culture would also determine norms of what is considered best care for this population and what options are made available (Castillo, 1997). Persons with this illness in remission can be supported to live on their own, return to their family, or live in a group home. Similarly, a young adult that has successfully completed the separation-individuation subphases and achieved libidinal object constancy can choose to continue to live at home or move away. Culture will establish norms for such behavior and a "structured" personality can choose to act in a manner that is cultural or countercultural.

PDORT PERSPECTIVE ON RACE, GENDER, AND OBJECT RELATIONS IN THE TRANSFERENCE

Given the assumption that the developmental line of object relations structures ego development in the PDORT paradigm, there is the expectation that all transference material will be expressed in a way that reflects this developmental level. This includes transference content related to race and gender. Thus, we would expect the defense of splitting—all-good, all-bad self and object mental representations—to become increasingly prominent in the content on race and gender the earlier the developmental arrest in object relations when working with an understructured personality (Horner, 1984; Kernberg, 1975). In neurotic structures, which presuppose the achievement of object constancy, we would anticipate race and gender content manifestations to be increasingly connected with the internal and intrapsychic conflicts that are associated with the mother and father identifications postulated for that level of structure (Blanck & Blanck, 1986; Horner, 1994).

Whereas a developmental line for gender development has been proposed (Tyson, 1982) in the PDORT model, this does not appear to be the case for race. Significant strides have been made regarding the process of racial identity development in adulthood and how this content can be used in treatment (R. Carter, 1995; Helm & Cook, 1999). Although these formulations are stage theories, they do not constitute a developmental line because they do not begin at birth or deal with life cycle development. Thus, the work of elucidating a developmental line that incorporates a life span perspective for racial identity development remains to be done.

Thompson (1996) notes that the treatment of African Americans and women has been remarkably similar in the psychoanalytic literature. Most often, issues for both groups have been ignored. On those occasions when race and gender have been given attention, this attention has tended to be negative and stigmatized. For example, women have been seen as castrated men who could not achieve the same level of superego development as men. Although it is generally accepted that both men and women can develop a mother and a father transference in treatment regardless of the sex of the therapist, questions have been raised about whether men can develop a full paternal transference with a female therapist (Kulish, 1986; Lester, 1985). The parallel question has not been raised about male therapists.

Historically, African Americans have been underrepresented in the psychoanalytic movement (Thompson, 1996), both as providers of services and as recipients. Questions have been raised as to whether African Americans are appropriate candidates for interpretive psychodynamic therapies, or whether they have the capacity for insight (Holmes, 1992; West, 1995). Given this limited historical attention, Adams (1996) notes the irony that the first psychoanalytic journal in America (*The Psychoanalytic Review*, 1914) had three articles about African Americans. One article was on dreams, the second on schizophrenia, and the third was about the "color complex" of African Americans. Prominent themes in these articles all identified deficits in African Americans (e.g., low self-esteem and the assertion of a universal "color complex"; Adams, 1996, p. 120).

Three themes have tended to dominate the sparse psychoanalytic literature that does exist on race and treatment. First is the question of the impact of similarities and differences in the race of the therapist and patient (Altman, 1996; Calnek, 1970; Griffith, 1977; Schachter & Butts, 1968). The second centers on the internalization of racial oppression, as expressed most often in the transference around color, and self-esteem (Greene, 1996; Shade, 1990; Williams, 1996). The third major theme encompasses issues of transference and countertransference (J. Carter & Haizlip, 1972; Greene, 1985; Holmes, 1992; Owens-Patterson, 2000; Schachter & Butts, 1968). Collectively, this literature suggests that race can have multiple unconscious meanings in the transference that can change over the course of treatment. This is true for the client as well as the therapist. Although the source and content may differ, therapists can experience countertransference difficulties with clients whether they are of the same or a different race.

For example, Calnek (1970) notes two potential countertransference reactions when both client and therapist are African American: denial of identification and overidentification. Denial of identification occurs when the therapist seeks to avoid acknowledging that the client is Black. Here, the therapist may engage in a pretense that the therapy situation is unique and race does not matter. Calnek suggests that the therapist, in essence, engages in a pretense that he or she and the client are both White. When the threat is overidentification, the therapist feels a strong bond to the client based on common racial experiences. However, the bond is used primarily to achieve personal satisfaction. Daniel (2000) notes the need for all therapists to have the courage to hear the memories of racial trauma that African American women have experienced. Therapists avoid this content for multiple reasons: Some fear the anger of their clients, some wish to avoid feeling guilt, some worry about their own personal pains being stirred up, exacerbated, and so on.

If not acknowledged and discussed, race can cause a spectrum of negative effects on treatment. Most often, patients terminate their treatment feeling that the therapist did not understand them as patients and individuals (Brantley, 1983). But the issues that can emerge around race are not always negative. Schachter and Butts (1968) discuss how differences in race can also have a catalytic effect on treatment. Leary (1997) presents clinical material from an interracial treatment in which the content around race deepened the clinical process. To help sort through the multiple transference/countertransference issues that inevitably emerge, it is important for the therapist to have good supervision available (Holmes, 1992; Owens-Patterson, 2000).

PSYCHOTHERAPY WITH AFRICAN AMERICAN WOMEN

There is growing scholarship that speaks specifically to issues for African American women in treatment that is particularly gratifying (Greene, 1994a; Jackson & Greene, 2000; Leary, 1997; Thompson, 1996; Turner, 1997a). All too often, the unique minority experience of these women has been overlooked, ignored, or stereotyped in the literature (Jackson & Greene, 2000). It could be argued that, as a group, African American women represent the interface between racism and sexism in their most pernicious forms. This group's experience is both historical and cultural, and has been unique among minorities of color. Although the number of minority mental health therapists is increasing, there are and will be for the foreseeable future more White professionals than Black and the White therapist–Black patient dyad will continue to be the most common (Greene, 1985). Whereas White mental health professionals see the majority of African American patients, the reverse is not true for White patients. Further, African Americans are forced to have some understanding of the workings of the mainstream if they are to survive. Therefore, it is considered critical that majority mental health professionals know more about the cultural and historical differences between Black and White Americans.

Most Americans do not seem to be aware that the first African immigrants in America entered as indentured servants and had the same social and economic status as most of the first White immigrants (Bennett, 1970; Higginbotham, 1978). For a 40-year period, from 1619 to about 1660, African immigrants accumulated property and participated in the public life of this country on a basis of substantial equality. Here, the facts in American history are eminently clear: Racism grew out of the economic base of slavery and not the reverse. Cotton was king, there was a tremendous demand for labor, and Africans were an easily exploited group because they were cut off from Africa.

Tannenbaum (1977) notes that the English had no legal tradition affecting slavery and did not initially know what to do with slaves. Most slaves were baptized Christians and English law in the early seventeenth century did not permit the enslavement of baptized Christians. Chattel slavery, a peculiarly American invention unique in the slave practices of the so-called civilized world, was the solution to this dilemma. The

Constitution legitimized this institution by allowing Southern states to count each slave as three-fifths of a human in determining their congressional representation and by supporting the enactment of a fugitive slave law. Eventually, legislation was drafted making Negroes slaves for life, and the Church took steps to reconcile slavery and Christianity by decreeing that conferring baptism did not alter the person's condition in regard to bondage and freedom. As such, African Americans became the only racial minority group for whom immigration was forced. This forced immigration lasted over 200 years.

African women as slaves did not own their own bodies. In the broader American culture, the highest value was placed on African female slaves with the greatest breeding capacity. Children were routinely conceived as a result of forced sexual relations with slavemasters or other male slaves. The children of African women were sold without consideration for their maternal preferences. Slaves were not allowed to legally marry and stable unions between slaves could be disrupted at the whim of owners. In contrast to most other immigrant women, African females labored outside the home from the onset. Most often, this work was in the fields alongside African men. As such, African American women have always been exempted from the observance of the traditional gender roles in American society.

Far more pernicious for women (and men) of African descent is the fact that their essential humanity was challenged. The legal and categorical social construction of African slaves as chattel was unique and distinguishes the historical and cultural oppression of African Americans from that of all other racial and ethnic groups. Women of African descent were not just the legal property of white men, as was the case in the parallel oppression of women. Their oppression also went beyond just being discriminated against and denied full access to the social and economic resources of this nation; or stereotyped as culturally deprived as was the case in the parallel oppression of each new immigrant group to this nation. The "animalization" of the African slaves as chattel was the bedrock of their oppression and justified their inhumane treatment. It made invisible the atrocities being perpetrated against them (Herman, 1992); and, the metaphor of African Americans as animals continues into the present as a significant sustaining mechanism in dominant-minority relations.

The sociology of dominant-minority relations (Kendall, 1997; Yetman, 1999) instructs that for a group to maintain dominance, specific actions and attitudes must be incorporated into the social system and achieve taken-for-granted status. As such, they ensure that minorities will not achieve positions of power or fully compete for available resources. They also relieve dominant individuals from feeling responsible or even recognizing that their attitudes and actions are repressive. As Herman (1992) so eloquently notes, the perpetrators of atrocities will do everything in their power to promote the forgetting of their transgressions. Similarly, a public that does not wish to come face-to-face with humankind's capacity for evil has been all too willing to engage in the conspiracy of secrecy and silence about these transgressions and watch, if not actively support, the discrediting of the victim. Stereotypes and metaphors are manipulated so that victims are blamed for their condition in the public perception.

Thus, in the scholarship on psychotherapy with African American women, a good deal of attention is paid to stereotypes. This group is considered to have more negative cultural stereotypes than any other racial minority group of women. West (1995) identifies the three historical images/stereotypes of Mammy, Sapphire, and Jezebel and the considerable role strain connected with each. Jenkins (2000) adds three additional images: the matriarch, the superwoman, and the she-Devil. These stereotypes are subsequently manipulated in the public's perception and African American women are discredited as victims and become the active architect of their fate. At times they are even made the scapegoat for the plight of the African American community. For example, African American women have been accused of: (1) being hypersexual and amoral, (2) being irresponsible breeders who have too many children out of wedlock, (3) taking jobs away from Black men, and (4) being too matriarchal, which in turn has led to the breakdown in the African American family, and so on (Jenkins, 2000; Turner, 1997b; West, 1995). Forgotten in the process are the perpetrators of a violent forced migration, a more than 200-year history of institutionally legalized physical and sexual abuse based solely on race, and a persistent attack on the African American family that continues into the present under the guise of a grossly ineffectual "war on drugs" (Tonry, 1995; Zimring & Hawkins, 1992).

For example, Hall (1997) maintains that a deconstruction of this nation's war on drugs suggests it has served as a far more effective vehicle to update the system of chattel slavery than it has to control drugs (Hawk, 1994; Tonry, 1995). In the war on drugs, African American men and women are disproportionately criminalized and incarcerated for the abuse of crack, a cheap derivative of cocaine that has been the drug of choice among African Americans until quite recently. In this update, mandated sentencing replaces slave codes as the legal underpinnings for the restriction of movement of African American men, and the prison system replaces the plantation system. Through imprisonment, racism, and poverty, African American males are denied access to gainful employment; this results in their leading lives that are marginal to African American women and their children. In turn, the women and their children are increasingly forced into poverty and dependency on a welfare system that does not promote family preservation. With the ever increasing trend over the past decade toward criminalizing substance-abusing pregnant women (Hawk, 1994; Kandall, 1996), the legal authority over the process of reproduction and the right to separate women and children at the discretion of the state is reinstated and the update is complete. African American women have been disproportionately reported for substance abuse during pregnancy and disproportionately incarcerated rather than treated for substance abuse during pregnancy (Kandall, 1996; Tonry, 1995). This latter practice has continued even though we do not have scientific evidence to support the adverse developmental outcomes in children whose mothers were abusing cocaine.

Given the enduring primacy of race in American culture, it is always a factor in any psychotherapy situation with African Americans (Holmes, 1992). The experience of African American women in this culture has been unique along several dimensions and culturally imposed stereotypes may influence this group in ways that are different from the experience of women of other racial groups. A therapist needs to be aware of these historical and cultural differences and be alert to ways in which this content can effectively be addressed throughout the treatment process. Issues of race and racism are omnipresent for African American women; if they are not discussed in treatment, the therapist is unaware of a significant and substantial portion of the patient's life. If clients seem to have achieved a positive regard and sense of self-esteem in regard to their racial identity and physical characteristics, the therapist can learn a lot about their strengths and social supports by exploring how this was achieved. On the other hand, clients may not be aware of how external forces connected with race and racism, both cultural and historical, are impacting their internal world; as with any other unconscious material, the therapist will have to be prepared to take responsibility for initiating this discussion and integration of clients' life story.

CASE EXAMPLE

Presenting Problem

A fair-skinned, 30-year-old, college-educated African American woman sought treatment for problems she was experiencing establishing a committed relationship with a man. Ms. A. was well-spoken, slightly obese, and quite fashionably dressed. She had specifically sought treatment with an African American therapist because she felt issues for women of color were different from those confronted by White women.

She indicated that she had had brief affairs with African American men over the years. She made a point that they were usually dark-skinned men and that they usually were the ones that ended the relationship. She had to admit, however, that she had not considered any of these men good candidates for a long-term relationship or marriage. Although she was sexually attracted to these men and things generally went well in that arena, they had little else in common. In each of these relationships, she had more education and made more money. On the other hand, her most recent and long-term relationship was with an educated White man who treated her better than any of her previous relationships. She was in some conflict, however, because this was an interracial relationship. She noted the significant critical mass of African Americans in the city where she lived and felt a strong undercurrent of censure of interracial relationships within the African American community.

Although she never seemed to attract them, she had to acknowledge that there were educated African American men around with good jobs, and that other African American women whom she knew had been successful in attracting them and establishing long-term relationships, if not marriage. She noted the irony that though she has been quite successful competing in the work sphere, she had never been successful competing with other Black women for available Black men, "and we won't even talk about the White women who are after our Black men!" On the other hand, she felt there was something wrong with her current relationship with a White man, even though intellectually she felt she should feel free to date whomever she wanted. When asked, she indicated that she had never been interested in or experimented with having a sexual relationship with a woman. She noted that this was a shame because she knew so many more interesting Black women than men.

Significant history included her being the youngest of three children from a working-class family. Although her father did not complete high school, he had worked as a laborer in a unionized job for many years, where he made a good hourly wage. Her mother had completed high school; she was a stay-at-home mom devoted to raising the children until Ms. A. entered junior high school. At that time, Ms. A.'s mother secured part-time office work to supplement the family income. She loved her mother dearly, but she was quite critical of her passivity in her relationship with her father. Her father had had repeated affairs over the years and eventually abandoned the family when she was in early adolescence. Although her parents were still married "on paper," her father had moved on to establish another family. Her father's support, both financial and emotional, of her and her siblings once he abandoned the family had been sporadic at best. When Ms. A. entered treatment, all contact between her and her father had ceased. Although she knew where he was, "I have nothing to say to him . . . if he has something to say to me, he knows where I am. . . . He's the one that left." This was significant because the client acknowledged that to the extent that "someone like him could have a favorite, I guess I would have been it." Also, she was aware that her siblings did have some contact with their father, but "that is their business."

On the other hand, she had praise for her mother, who she thought was "very smart" and "knew how to manage." To her mother's credit, she did not fall apart when her father left. She increased her employment to full time, and the family had scraped by. They were very close to her mother's side of the family and maternal kin had been supportive in various ways over the years. They had food on the table and she and her siblings had all finished high school and attended some college. She was the only sibling to finish college, and she had done the best careerwise. Both of her siblings now worked at white-collar jobs and were married. Although she personally would not be satisfied with either of their relationships, she was aware that the relationships worked for her siblings and she took pleasure in her role as aunt to her two nieces and a nephew.

Initial Themes about Race in Treatment

Two themes dominated the beginning of treatment. The first was the larger theme of the plight/multiple levels of oppression that Black women had to contend with in their search for an acceptable mate. Specific topics were far-ranging: the shortage of men on the same level and the sense of entitlement of the few educated and eligible men who were left; the number of Black men in jail or on drugs; violence against women and the number of single-parent Black women who were receiving no child support; and the multiple ways the courts were used as an instrument of oppression against Black men and women. The second theme had to do with problems in the relationships between men and women in her immediate and extended family and the messages they conveyed to her about Black male-female relationships growing up. She emphasized that all of the women in her family suffered at the hands of men in ways she could not accept. She was most impassioned when she spoke about her parents' marriage. She felt her mother should have been far more aggressive in putting her foot down with her father when they were together and should have taken him to court when he abandoned the family. Instead, her mother had always been like a "doormat" when it came to her father and suffered in silence.

A third theme emerged early on that had to do with skin color. Ms. A. acknowledged but was somewhat derisive about messages in the family about skin color, that is, that she should not get involved with and definitely not marry a dark-skinned man; the children would have bad hair and a harder time in life. She ridiculed the fact that her family (particularly her mother) had criticized her about the African American men she had dated more for their dark-skinned complexions and hair (kinky or straight) than how they had treated her as a woman, or what they did for a living. She noted that both of her siblings had married partners with similar complexion and, for the most part, her nieces and nephew met the "brown paper bag" test. She identified herself as having the lightest complexion in her immediate family and her father the darkest, even though "he would be considered a good-looking medium-brown-skinned man."

When asked to reflect on what she considered the major messages to her from society and her family about male-female relationships among African Americans, Ms. A. had nothing to say spontaneously about messages or stereotypes from society. She had much to say and with a good deal of affect about the messages from her family. It angered her that none of the women in her family seemed to even expect loyalty or fidelity from their men. Her mother even went so far as to say that Ms. A. was setting her "standards too high as far as a Black man is concerned" and was just "setting herself up for disappointment." This only infuriated Ms. A. all the more. She had decided that she would never be in that position, that is, in a relationship with a man who ran around on her while she suffered in silence. She noted that the women in her family did seem to have greater expectations around financial support from their men; however, there were strong messages to her that this, too, was fragile and that "even a good Black man" could be irresponsible with money from time to time. So there were very strong family messages as far back as she could remember that in marriage, a "Black woman never puts all her eggs in one basket," and that when she is dealing with a Black man, she should "always put a little money aside for a rainy day" and should not tell her husband about it or he would always be after her for it.

Ms. A. also spoke about how different her life was from her siblings' and how she had some guilt that she was the only sibling to complete college. She had always been the best student in the family and had received substantial scholarship assistance to complete her undergraduate degree. All things being equal, she would probably earn more money in her lifetime than either of her siblings, their spouses, or her parents. This would be true whether she continued on for graduate training or not. Although she felt some guilt about her success relative to her siblings, she was glad that she was financially independent and that she would not have to depend on anybody to support her. The only reason to be in a relationship with a man would be because she "wanted" to be there, not "had" to be there. She would always be able to take care of herself, with or without a man.

PDORT ASSESSMENT OF MS. A.'S
OBJECT RELATIONS

From a PDORT perspective, it seemed clear early on that object constancy had been achieved. Specifically, the client had developed the capacity to tolerate good and bad feelings in the same person and did not relate to people based solely on what she might be feeling in the moment. In general, the people or objects in her world were not split into categories of all-good and all-bad, although it was clear that her relationship with her father was a conflicted sphere. This remained true in sessions where she was impassioned and expressing strong affect, as well as when she was being more reflective and analytical about her dilemma. It also seemed clear that the conflicts she experienced were internalized and that she had some observing ego about this. For example, she was self-referred and able to distinguish both external stressors and internal conflicts connected to her past relationships with Black men and her current relationship with a White man. In terms of external stressors, Ms. A. was very much aware of oppression against African Americans at the broader society level and the contribution this makes to the challenge of finding an acceptable mate. In terms of internal conflict, she was able to observe at intake the irony that she has been very successful competing at work but has not done well competing for available Black men like other Black women she knows.

DYNAMIC PDORT ASSESSMENT OF
RACE AND GENDER ISSUES

The client has achieved object constancy and is struggling with neurotic conflicts associated with an unresolved Oedipal complex (Horner, 1994). Ms. A.'s adaptation is characterized by conflicted and conflict-free spheres. She was a good student, and has been a high achiever in the work or instrumental sphere. Her intimate relationships with men and including her father are an area of conflict; in this arena, her internal experience of her past and current relationships with men is that of "forbidden fruit." Additional themes in treatment to support a neurotic level of austerity included her assessment that she is losing in a competition for men, that she does not want to be like her mother (competition and refusal to identify), her repressed rage toward her father who leaves her (the favorite) and "chooses" another family competition (triangles), the guilt she feels about doing better than her siblings (possible displaced anxiety about being her father's favorite and possible Oedipal victor), and anxiety about her current and past relationships with men, whether White or Black (theme of anxiety/guilt associated in her mind with transgressing family and community taboos).

Major defenses include reaction formation, intellectualization, doing and undoing, denial, and repression of both libidinal and aggressive/competitive strivings. Defenses of repression and reaction formation seemed most pronounced in Ms. A.'s narrative about her father. We are struck by her lack of anger toward her father, who abandoned her and the family, and her lack of interest in a relationship with him in the present, particularly when she was his favorite historically. The fact that she gets involved with dark-skinned African American men (her father was the darkest in the family) to whom she is sexually attracted but does not consider appropriate mates appears to be an acting out of her unconscious and forbidden libidinal/Oedipal strivings toward her father. The fact that she perceives dark-skinned men to be forbidden by her mother and that these men subsequently leave her is seen as both defense (doing and undoing) against these strivings and repetition compulsion of her losing the competition for her father. In contrast, we are struck by the intense affect Ms. A. directs toward her mother for having acted as a dishrag, and the inference that she would have done better (competition). At the same time, she is able to credit her mother for having been quite strong in her management of the family without father (ambivalence). It is striking that she does not see the similarity between her mother's adaptation and her own. Both are strong women in the work sphere who get involved with men who leave them.

PDORT Model of Brief Treatment with Structured (Neurotic) Personalities

Horner (1994), building on the work of Sifneos (1979), identifies four phases in short-term work with a structured personality such as Ms. A.'s: uncovering, working through, resolution, and termination. In an optimal situation, the uncovering, working through, and beginnings of resolution can be completed in 40 sessions. It is only in long-term follow-up that one can tell how much has actually been achieved. In the uncovering phase, the goal is to help the patient acknowledge the wishes and fears of the mother and father identifications and their associated affect. In the working-through phase, focus shifts to how these conflicts are played out in everyday life and in the transference with the therapist. As this occurs, the parents should increasingly be seen as real people. The resolution phase speaks to the neutralization of both sexual and aggressive drives toward the goal of pursuing success and achievement without feeling unduly aggressive and to reunite libidinal strivings with affection without feeling guilty and anxious. Termination addresses the resolution of the transference. The goal here is for the therapist to be experienced in realistic terms as an adult equal. Full resolution and termination in this sense most frequently occur during the follow-up process. Horner notes that no treatments are quite this neat and orderly; however, she found that therapists can select issues of focus more freely if they hold a conceptualization of the overall process.

A Transference and Countertransference Enactment

During the uncovering phase, the therapist addressed the mother and father identifications by raising with Ms. A. certain themes she was hearing in her "story" that puzzled her. On the one hand, she expressed admiration for her mother, particularly how she had carried on after her father's abandonment. At the same time, she continued to feel very angry with her over her passivity in connection with her father and how she felt her mother had allowed herself to be treated "like a doormat" by him. Also, she seemed to have little or no anger toward her father, who had abandoned her family and chosen another. This was particularly striking because she had suggested that she was probably his favorite. In a sense, she too seemed to be suffering in silence. The therapist also reflected on her surprise that Ms. A. had so little empathy for the way her mother had allowed herself to be treated by her father because it was similar in many ways to what she appeared to have experienced in her relationships with African American men. Ms. A. was initially annoyed at the suggestion that she might be like her mother and, by inference, "a doormat." However, in the following sessions after this was first suggested, she acknowledged some truth to this observation. The therapist then inquired whether Ms. A. thought her mother might have been experiencing any of the pressures she first talked about at the beginning of treatment concerning the problems of finding an acceptable mate. Ms. A. was able to observe that it had never occurred to her that her mother would have experienced the same kinds of challenges she now faced because "my mother was always bigger than life to me." She noted that she knew nothing of her mother's history of dating and she actually knew little about her parents' marriage. During this period, she did begin to acknowledge that there were some financial gains for her mother in remaining married. For example, the family had remained on her father's health insurance plan; in fact, her mother was still covered by his plan.

As Ms. A. began to reflect on these issues, the theme of her competitive strivings became more pronounced in sessions. However, she was most comfortable talking about this in the work arena, where she felt she was not allowing herself to fully compete for a job she was qualified to do because she was worried about the problems it would cause with colleagues she considered friends. She described one such colleague, Dorothy, who "has real issues around everything, but especially color!" On multiple occasions, Dorothy had intimated that Ms. A.'s career success was because of her lighter skin color. This infuriated Ms. A. because she felt it denigrated her hard work and, "if the truth be told, I not only work harder but I am brighter than she is!" When the therapist inquired about Dorothy's complexion, Ms. A. indicated that she was darker-skinned. In an attempt to be more specific she noted, "She is about your complexion." Ms. A. noted that she had a gut feeling that she would lose Dorothy as a friend if she found a man she could be happy with or got promoted. She added that Dorothy had also been married and was now divorced, "like you," and that this experience had resulted in Dorothy's becoming quite bitter toward men. When asked how she knew about the therapist's divorce, Ms. A. indicated that this was information that had been shared with her when she was searching for a woman therapist of color.

The therapist was struck by the fact that she did not consider Ms. A. to be that much lighter than she. As the session was ending, the therapist returned to the issue of skin color. She reminded Ms. A. that she had suggested on several occasions that color had been a real issue in her family. The therapist identified this as a topic to be further explored and suggested that she bring in pictures to help facilitate their discussions. Ms. A. agreed.

Subsequent to the session, the therapist found herself feeling uncomfortable about having made the suggestion that Ms. A. bring in pictures and sought consultation. During the consultation, the therapist admitted to feeling exposed and as though she had failed when Ms. A. indicated that she knew that she was divorced. She was even more surprised at the strong feelings invoked in her when Ms. A. indicated that Dorothy was darker-skinned than she and that

Dorothy was about the same complexion as the therapist. She had felt like saying "You may be light, but you're not as light as you think you are!" It was clear to the consultant that the therapist had heard it as dark-skinned, not darker-skinned.

When the consultant inquired about the request for family pictures, the therapist acknowledged some uneasiness and wondered whether she was doing something that could be therapeutic or was "acting something out." On the one hand, she felt a case could be made for seeing the reality of color differentials within the family. However, she was aware that she fully expected the objective reality of the pictures would reveal distortions in Ms. A.'s subjective experience of color in the family similar to that in the transference. She would then have the opportunity to make the point that "she is not as light as she thinks she is." The therapist recognized this as countertransference and questioned if she could make therapeutic use of the pictures, as she had already asked for them.

The consultant indicated that it was important that the therapist be aware of her feelings on this issue first. This led to a discussion of just how subliminal messages about color had been in the therapist's family growing up. She had been surprised how intensely felt her emotions had been when the client suggested that she was dark-skinned. The therapist indicated that she could not remember many overt discussions about color in her family. However, growing up she had always felt as though she was the darkest when compared with her siblings. In recent years, the therapist had been seeing more of her siblings and liking them a lot better. In the process, she had become increasingly aware that "she wasn't as dark as she thought she was" and that they all had about the same skin color. The consultant suggested that this might be why the therapist had suggested that Ms. A. bring in pictures.

When the consultation returned to Ms. A., the therapist could immediately see how her feelings had gotten in the way and that many of the themes prompting Ms. A. to seek treatment were being expressed in the transference. For example, Ms. A. had induced in the therapist feelings of being a failure in her marriage and how she had handled her husband. Ms. A.'s constriction of her competitive strivings and her worry about being the Oedipal victor appeared to be projected onto her colleague at work (e.g., her worry that she would lose the relationship with Dorothy if she beat her in competition at work or in love). The therapist was able to see that all of the issues Ms. A. raised around Dorothy, including the issue of color, were unresolved issues she had with her mother. Similarly, in associating the therapist with Dorothy, she had transferred them into treatment.

SUMMARY

This chapter has presented a Psychoanalytic Developmental Object Relations Theory (PDORT) perspective on the interface between clinical manifestation of race, gender, and object relations in the treatment transference. The PDORT model builds on the developmental line of object relations explicated by Mahler and her colleagues. It assumes a positive correlation between the developmental stage of object relations a subject has achieved and the process of psychic structuring. In this model, the level of object relations an individual has achieved structures the quality of the treatment relationship and all transference material. This would include content on race and gender. Persons who complete this developmental line and achieve object constancy are considered to have structured personalities. In situations where earlier developmental arrest has occurred, the personality is considered unstructured.

Psychodynamic models, which have never adequately taken into account the social and cultural dimensions of the psyche, have been challenged in recent years to expand and accommodate persons from increasingly diverse cultures. In the process, the need to become more culturally specific rather than all-inclusive (e.g., minorities of color) when discussing such socially constructed categories as race has received increasing emphasis. Racial minority groups can have vastly different sociopolitical and cultural histories and be subjected to qualitatively different cultural stereotypes, opportunities, and constraints. These differences have significant implications for conscious and unconscious transference content. The case of an African American woman who sought treatment for struggles around intimacy was adopted to particularize the discussion in this chapter.

Salient in the particular sociopolitical history for African Americans is a violent forced migration from Africa and over two hundred years under a system of "chattel slavery" that gave legal sanction to this population's physical and sexual abuse, and economic exploitation. Most pernicious by far was the legal and categorical social construction of African slaves as chattel in the Constitution. This social construction challenged the essential humanity of African slaves, distinguished it from all other minority groups, and justified their inhuman treatment to the public at large. This "animalization" of the African American continues into the present as a metaphor and is a significant sustaining mechanism in dominant-minority relations for this group.

Women of African descent were exempted from the observance of traditional gender roles from the very beginning and forced to work outside the home and in the fields with men. Thus, in terms of the interface between race and gender, it has always been more difficult for this group to separate their Blackness from their femaleness. The dominant culture valued African women most highly for their capacity to breed. Marriage was illegal, intimate associations could be interrupted at the discretion of slave owners, and they had no discretion over their children.

The dominant culture has done everything in its power to promote a forgetting of these transgressions in the public perception. It has generated and skillfully manipulated more negative stereotypes and metaphors about the African American woman than any other group of minority women. In the process, the African American woman has been discredited as a victim (e.g., Jezebel); or she becomes the active architect of her fate and that of the African American family (e.g., matriarch) in the public perception. In fact, the public has been all too willing to join this conspiracy of silence.

These processes have tremendous implications for the subject and the therapist when an African American woman presents for treatment. There is an enduring primacy to race in America that the African American woman can never escape. If the ramifications of race in her life are not discussed in treatment, the process is incomplete and the therapist is in the dark about a substantial and significant portion of her life.

In culturally competent work with African American women, a therapist needs to be prepared to listen to stories of racial pain and trauma. A therapist also needs to be prepared to initiate such discussion when an African American woman appears to be unaware of the cultural, historical, and political forces that are impacting her internal world and presenting problems. In the PDORT model, the level of object relations the subject has achieved would guide the selection and timing of specific content addressed and the goals of such interventions. This would be true in the structured and unstructured personality.

Being prepared means more than just being well informed about the culture and history of a racial population. Being prepared requires a well-developed capacity for self-reflection and flexibility on the part of the therapist, which can be achieved only through considerable self-study into one's own social identifies and associated values, biases, and potential countertransference vulnerabilities. This is important and challenging work that should not be underestimated or ignored.

REFERENCES

Adams, M. V. (1996). *The multicultural imagination: Race, color and the unconscious.* New York: Routledge.

Altman, N. (1996). The accommodation of diversity in psychoanalysis. In R. P. Foster, M. Moskowitz, & R. A. Javier (Eds.), *Reaching across boundaries of culture and class: Widening the scope of psychotherapy* (pp. 195–209). Northvale, NJ: Aronson.

American Psychiatric Association. (1994). *Diagnostic and statistical manual of mental disorders* (4th ed.). Washington, DC: Author.

Atkinson, D. R., Morten, G., & Sue, D. W. (1993). *Counseling American minorities: A cross-cultural perspective.* Madison, WI: Brown & Benchmark.

Atwood, G., & Stolorow, R. (1984). *Structures of subjectivity.* Hillsdale, NJ: Analytic Press.

Bennett, L., Jr. (1970). *Before the Mayflower: A history of the Negro in America 1619–1964.* Baltimore: Penguin Books.

Blanck, R., & Blanck, G. (1974). *Ego psychology: Theory and practice.* New York: Columbia University Press.

Blanck, R., & Blanck, G. (1979). *Ego psychology II: Psychoanalytic developmental psychology.* New York: Columbia University Press.

Blanck, R., & Blanck, G. (1986). *Beyond ego psychology: Developmental object relations theory.* New York: Columbia University Press.

Brantley, T. (1983). Racism and its impact on psychotherapy. *American Journal of Psychiatry, 140*(12), 1605–1608.

Calnek, M. (1970). Racial factors in the countertransference: The Black therapist and the Black client. *American Journal of Orthopsychiatry, 40*(1), 39–46.

Carter, J. H., & Haizlip, T. M. (1972). Race and its relevance to transference. *American Journal of Orthopsychiatry, 42*(5), 865–871.

Carter, R. T. (1995). *The influence of race and racial identity in psychotherapy: Towards a racially inclusive model.* New York: Wiley.

Castillo, R. J. (1997). *Culture and mental illness.* Pacific Grove, CA: Brooks/Cole.

Chan, C. S. (1988). Asian-American women: Psychological responses to sexual exploitation and cultural stereotypes. In L. Fulani (Ed.), *The politics of race and gender in therapy* (pp. 33–38). New York: Hawthorne Press.

Comas-Diaz, L. (1988). Feminist therapy with Hispanic/Latina women: Myth or reality? In L. Fulani (Ed.), *The politics of race and gender in therapy* (pp. 39–61). New York: Hawthorne Press.

Cornacchia, E. J., & Nelson, D. C. (1992). Historical differences in the political experience of American Blacks and White ethnics: Revisiting an unresolved controversy. *Ethnic and Racial Studies, 15*(1), 102–124.

Daniel, J. H. (1994). Exclusion and emphasis reframed as a matter of ethics. *Ethics and Behavior, 4*(3), 229–235.

Daniel, J. H. (2000). The courage to hear African American women's memories of racial trauma. In L. C. Jackson & B. Greene (Eds.), *Psychotherapy with African American women: Innovations in psychodynamic perspectives and practice* (pp. 126–144). New York: Guilford Press.

Davanloo, H. (Ed.). (1980). *Short-term dynamic psychotherapy.* New York: Aronson.

Esman, A. (Ed.). (1990). *Essential papers on transference.* New York: New York University Press.

Fong, R., & Furuto, S. B. C. L. (2001). *Culturally competent practice: Skills, interventions and evaluations.* Boston: Allyn & Bacon.

Foster, R. P. (1996). What is a multicultural perspective for psychoanalysis? In R. P. Foster, M. Moskowitz, & R. A. Javier (Eds.), *Reaching across boundaries of culture and class: Widening the scope of psychotherapy* (pp. 3–20). Northvale, NJ: Aronson.

Foster, R. P., Moskowitz, M., & Javier, R. A. (Eds.). (1996). *Reaching across boundaries of culture and class: Widening the scope of psychotherapy.* Northvale, NJ: Aronson.

Fulani, L. (1988). Poor women of color do great therapy. In L. Fulani (Ed.), *The politics of race and gender in therapy* (pp. 111–120). New York: Hawthorne Press.

Gilligan, C. (1982). *In a different voice: Psychological theory and women's development.* Cambridge, MA: Harvard University Press.

Goodwin, D. W., & Guze, S. B. (1996). *Psychiatric diagnosis* (5th ed.). New York: Oxford University Press.

Greenberg, J. R., & Mitchell, S. A. (1983). *Object relations in psychoanalytic theory.* Cambridge, MA: Harvard University Press.

Greene, B. (1985). Considerations in the treatment of Black patients by White therapists. *Psychotherapy, 22*(Suppl. 2), 389–393.

Greene, B. (1990). What has gone before: The legacy of racism and sexism in the lives of Black mothers and daughters. *Women and Therapy, 9*(1/2), 207–230.

Greene, B. (1994a). African American women. In L. Comas-Diaz & B. Greene (Eds.), *Women of color: Integrating ethnic and gender identities in psychotherapy.* New York: Guilford Press.

Greene, B. (1994b). Diversity and difference: The issues of race in feminist therapy. *Women in context: Toward a feminist reconstruction of psychotherapy* (pp. 333–351). New York: Guilford Press.

Greene, B. (1996). African-American women: Considering diverse identities and societal barriers in psychotherapy. *Women and Mental Health, 789,* 191–209.

Greene, B. (2000). African American lesbians and bisexual women in feminist-psychodynamic psychotherapies: Survival and thriving between a rock and a hard place. In L. C. Jackson & B. Greene (Eds.), *Psychotherapy with African American women: Innovations in psychodynamic perspectives and practice* (pp. 82–125). New York: Guilford Press.

Griffith, M. S. (1977). The influences of race on the psychotherapeutic relationship. *Psychiatry, 40,* 27–40.

Hall, M. F. (1997). The "war on drugs": A continuation of the war on the African American family. *Smith College Studies in Social Work, 3*(67), 609–621.

Hawk, N. M. (1994). How social policies make matters worse: The case of maternal substance abuse. *Journal of Drug Issues, 24*(3), 517–526.

Helm, J. E., & Cook, D. A. (1999). *Using race and culture in counseling and psychotherapy: Theory and process.* Boston: Allyn & Bacon.

Herman, J. L. (1992). *Trauma and recovery.* New York: Basic Books.

Higginbotham, A. L., Jr. (1978). *In the matter of color: Race and the American legal process.* New York: Oxford University Press.

Holmes, D. E. (1992). Race and transference in psychoanalysis and psychotherapy. *International Journal of Psycho-Analysis, 73*(1), 1–11.

Horner, A. J. (1984). *Object relations and the developing ego in therapy.* New York: Aronson.

Horner, A. J. (Ed.). (1994). *Treating the neurotic patient in brief psychotherapy.* Northvale, NJ: Aronson.

Horner, A. J. (1995). *Psychoanalytic object relations therapy.* Northvale, NJ: Aronson.

Jackson, L. C. (2000). The new multiculturalism and psychodynamic theory: Psychodynamic psychotherapy and African American women. In L. C. Jackson & B. Greene (Eds.), *Psychotherapy with African American women: Innovations in psychodynamic perspectives and practice* (pp. 1–14). New York: Guilford Press.

Jackson, L. C., & Greene, B. (Eds.). (2000). *Psychotherapy with African American women.* New York: Guilford Press.

Jenkins, Y. M. (2000). The Stone Center theoretical approach revisited: Applications for African American women. In L. C. Jackson & B. Greene (Eds.), *Psychotherapy with African American women: Innovations in psychodynamic perspective and practice* (pp. 62–81). New York: Guilford Press.

Jordan, J. (Ed.). (1997). *Women's growth in diversity: More writings from the Stone Center.* New York: Guilford Press.

Kandall, S. R. (1996). *Substance and shadow: Women and addiction in the United States.* Cambridge, MA: Harvard University Press.

Kendall, D. (1997). *Race, class and gender in a diverse society.* Boston: Allyn & Bacon.

Kernberg, O. (1975). *Borderline conditions and pathological narcissism.* New York: Aronson.

Kohut, H. (1968). The psychoanalytic treatment of narcissistic personality disorders: Outline of a systematic approach. *Psychoanalytic Study of the Child, 23,* 86–113.

Kohut, H. (1984). *How does analysis cure?* Chicago: University of Chicago Press.

Kulish, N. M. (1986). Gender and transference: The screen of the phallic mother. *International Review of Psycho-Analysis, 13,* 393–404.

Leary, K. (1997). Race, self-disclosure, and "forbidden talk": Race and ethnicity in contemporary clinical practice. *Psychoanalytic Quarterly, 66,* 163–189.

Lester, B. M., & Tronick, E. Z. (1994). The effects of prenatal cocaine exposure and child outsome. *Infant Mental Health Journal, 15*(2), 107–120.

Lester, E. P. (1985). The female analyst and the erotized transference. *International Journal of Psycho-Analysis, 66,* 283–293.

Levenson, H. (1995). *Time-limited dynamic psychotherapy: A guide to clinical practice.* New York: Basic Books.

Magnavita, J. (1997). *Restructuring personality disorders: A short-term dynamic approach.* New York: Guilford Press.

Mahler, M. S., Pine, F., & Bergman, A. (1975). *The psychological birth of the human infant: Symbiosis and individuation.* New York: Basic Books.

Mann, J., & Goldman, R. (1982). *A casebook in time-limited psychotherapy.* New York: McGraw-Hill.

Mathura, C. B., & Baer, M. A. (1990). Social factors in diagnosis and treatment. In D. S. Ruiz (Ed.), *Handbook of mental health and mental disorder among Black Americans* (pp. 167–179). New York: Greenwood Press.

Moskowitz, M. (1996). The end of analyzability. In R. P. Foster, M. Moskowitz, & R. A. Javier (Eds.), *Reaching across boundaries of culture and class: Widening the scope of psychotherapy* (pp. 179–193). Northvale, NJ: Aronson.

Owens-Patterson, M. (2000). The African American supervisor: Racial transference and countertransference in interracial psychotherapy supervision. *Psychotherapy with African American women* (pp. 145–165). New York: Guilford Press.

Pine, F. (1985). *Developmental theory and clinical process.* New Haven, CT: Yale University Press.

Pine, F. (1990). *Drive, ego, object, and self: A synthesis for clinical work.* New York: Basic Books.

Roland, A. (1996). *Cultural pluralism and psychoanalysis: The Asian and North American experience.* New York: Routledge.

Schachter, J. S., & Butts, H. F. (1968). Transference and countertransference in interracial analyses. *American Psychoanalytic Association, 19,* 736–745.

Schafer, R. (1976). *A new language for psychoanalysis.* New Haven, CT: Yale University Press.

Schafer, R. (1992). *Retelling a life: Narration and dialogue in psychoanalysis.* New York: Basic Books.

Shade, B. J. (1990). Coping with color: The anatomy of positive mental health. In D. S. Ruiz (Ed.), *Handbook of mental health and mental disorder among Black Americans* (pp. 273–289). New York: Greenwood Press.

Shorter-Gooden, K., & Jackson, L. (2000). The interweaving of cultural and intrapsychic issues in the therapeutic relationship. In L. P. Jackson & B. Greene (Eds.), *Psychotherapy with African American women: Innovations in psychodynamic perspectives and practice.* New York: Guilford Press.

Sifneos, P. E. (1979). *Short-term dynamic psychotherapy.* New York: Plenum Press.

Stern, D. A. (1985). *The interpersonal world of the infant.* New York: Basic Books.

Summers, F. (1994). *Object relations theories and psychopathology.* Hillsdale, NJ: Analytic Press.

Tannenbaum, F. (1977). Slavery in America. In L. Broom & P. Selznick (Eds.), *Sociology: A text with adapted readings* (6th ed., pp. 449–452). New York: Harper & Row.

Tatum, B. D. (1997). Racial identity development and relational theory: The case of Black women in White communities. In J. Jordan (Ed.), *Women's growth in diversity* (pp. 91–106). New York: Guilford Press.

Thompson, C. L. (1996). The African-American patient in psychodynamic treatment. In R. P. Foster, M. Moskowitz, & R. A. Javier (Eds.), *Reaching across boundaries of culture and class.* Northvale, NJ: Aronson.

Tonry, M. (1995). *Malign neglect: Race, crime, and punishment in America.* New York: Oxford University Press.

Turner, C. W. (1997a). Clinical applications of the Stone Cienter theoretical approach to minority women. In J. Jordan (Ed.), *Women's growth in diversity* (pp. 74–90). New York: Guilford Press.

Turner, C. W. (1997b). Psychosocial barriers to Black women's career development. In J. Jordan (Ed.), *Women's growth in diversity* (pp. 162–175). New York: Guilford Press.

Tyson, P. (1982). A developmental line of gender role, and choice of love object. *Journal of American Psychoanalytic Association, 30,* 6–86.

Vickerman, M. (1999). *Crosscurrents: West Indian immigrants and race.* New York: Oxford University Press.

West, C. M. (1995). Mammy, Sapphire, and Jezebel: Historical images of Black women and their implications for psychotherapy. *Psychotherapy, 32*(3), 458–466.

Williams, A. L. (1996). Skin color in psychotherapy. In R. P. Foster, M. Moskowitz, & R. A. Javier (Eds.), *Reaching across boundaries of culture and class.* Northvale, NJ: Aronson.

Yetman, N. R. (Ed.). (1999). *Majority and minority: The dynamics of race and ethnicity in American life.* Boston: Allyn & Bacon.

Zimring, F. E., & Hawkins, G. (1992). *The search for rational drug control.* Cambridge, MA: Cambridge University Press.

CHAPTER 25

Contemporary Psychodynamics: Major Issues, Challenges, and Future Trends

JEFFREY J. MAGNAVITA

HISTORICAL BACKGROUND AND FACTORS THAT SHAPED PSYCHODYNAMIC PSYCHOTHERAPY

The second century of contemporary psychodynamic psychotherapy promises to be an exciting one for the field. Psychodynamic therapy holds a place of prominence in this century as in the past century, despite controversy over its use and relevance (Magnavita, 1993, this volume). As the new century unfolds, will psychodynamic psychotherapy remain relevant, or as Dumont (1993) believes, will Freud "be viewed as a popularizer of 19th century psychiatric concepts that are seen in many instances to be increasingly antiquated, if not as impediments to a more contemporary science of the mind"? (p. 197). Judging from the innovative contributions presented in this volume, one would claim that psychodynamic models remain effectual, fertile, and ever evolving. Psychodynamic formulations continue to influence contemporary models of the mind and theories of personality. This chapter first considers some of the main assaults that have helped shape psychodynamics and then reviews current and future trends, calling for a new contemporary era of "scientific psychodynamics."

Psychodynamic psychotherapy has come under attack at various junctures throughout the past century; the most threatening criticism concerned Freud's rejection of the seduction theory (Magnavita, this volume). Other influences also have substantially affected the evolution of contemporary psychodynamics. The first came from the behaviorists and the second from the managed care industry.

WATSON'S ATTACK ON PSYCHOANALYSIS

The first credible attack on psychodynamic psychotherapy was launched by the behaviorists, who rightly challenged the "ungrounded" theoretical system of the psychodynamic model. One of the early attacks was initiated by James Watson, a major figure in academic psychology, who ridiculed psychoanalysis for many of its notions that lacked empirical support. Rilling

(2000) points out: "The paradox of *Behaviorism* was that one of the paths by which Freud's ideas made their way into American popular culture was through Watson's anti-Freudian declarations" (p. 302). Watson (Watson & Rayner, 1920) demonstrated that neurosis could be induced using principles of classic conditioning in the famous Little Albert experiment. He first conditioned the 9-month-old to be frightened of a white rabbit; the rabbit was then paired with a loud sound, and the fear became generalized to other stimuli. Watson and Rayner were not subtle in their somewhat tongue-and-cheek contempt for psychoanalysis:

> The Freudians twenty years from now, unless their hypothesis changes, when they come to analyze Albert's fear of a seal skin coat—assuming that he comes to analysis at that age—will probably tease from him the recital of a dream which upon their analysis will show that Albert at three years of age attempted to play with the pubic hair of the mother and was scolded for it. (p. 14)

This challenge raised questions about the effectiveness and pertinence of psychoanalysis. If psychoanalytic concepts could be explained more parsimoniously using principles of learning, then maybe the system was overly complex and was actually being used to create an esoteric, hermetic language to obscure a flawed model.

Later, Dollard and Miller (1950) published their classic *Personality and Psychotherapy: An Analysis in Terms of Learning, Thinking, and Culture*, a highly integrative work that underscored their position that although two different languages were used by the psychoanalyst and the behaviorist, they were describing similar phenomena. According to Rilling (2000):

> Despite the weakness identified by historians, Watson and Rayner's (1920) study remains a classic, a benchmark against which the theoretical questions, methods, and psychological limitations of the past anchor us to the same psychological questions about emotional learning and psychopathology that we are considering today with better methods and theories than were available to Watson and Rayner. (p. 310)

As can be seen from the contributions in this volume, Watson's (1924) prediction "that 20 years from now an analyst using Freudian concepts and Freudian terminology will be placed in the same category as a phrenologist" (p. 243) has not come to fruition. In fact, many of Freud's theories and suggestions are finding support in neuroscience. Many of his notions are antiquated and no longer useful, but this does not negate his entire model, which is continually evolving.

Eysenck's Attack on the
Field of Psychotherapy

Eysenck (1952) launched the most notorious initial attack on the effectiveness of psychotherapy. He, like Watson before him, expressed dissatisfaction with psychoanalysis. His assault on the field was a much-needed tonic to reawaken interest. Presenting his findings, he argued that after two years, two-thirds of those who receive other than behavioral therapy, along with those who received no therapy, significantly improved. Psychotherapy owes much to Eysenck for challenging the field to begin to provide empirical validation of efficacy. Later, other researchers, sparked by Eysenck's challenge, demonstrated the effectiveness of psychotherapy (Smith, Glass, & Miller, 1980).

The Impact of Managed Care and the
Cost-Containment Era

In the United States, a major effort at cost containment in health care was undertaken beginning in the 1980s. Although medicine first came under scrutiny, mental health was soon under the cost-cutting knife of policy planners and third-party payors. Inpatient mental health care, the most expensive of the mental health services, was the first to experience the effects of the knife; outpatient mental health services soon followed. The toll on inpatient treatment programs throughout the country was enormous: The length of hospitalization was dramatically reduced. Training and education programs for the clinical staff of these facilities were among the first to be jettisoned by institutions struggling to stay afloat in the new health care environment, which was more concerned about the bottom line than quality of care.

The managed care movement has been judged by many to have been a failure, combining as it does the worst aspects of a national heath care system and the worst aspects of a privatized one. The impact on the field of psychotherapy has been particularly profound; some positive trends have been stimulated, but many setbacks have resulted. For example, psychotherapy is now viewed as a commodity by third-party payors, one that can be provided by anyone holding a treatment manual. In the next section, I address some noteworthy positive and negative aspects of this movement and then discuss future implications.

Pros and Cons of the Challenges

The attacks and challenges to psychodynamic psychotherapy and the field of psychotherapy in general have had both positive and negative results. Prior to the cost-containment era, some psychotherapists viewed patients with good insurance as cash cows, expecting third-party payors to provide "unlimited" benefits. Some insurance plans even covered psychoanalysis. There was little appreciation for the call for cost containment and treatment protocols. When one consulted with a psychoanalyst or psychodynamic psychotherapist, long-term treatment was generally recommended as the treatment of choice. Brief dynamic therapy was considered by all but a few as palliative at best, and supportive therapy was derided as less than the pure gold of analysis. Psychotherapists were strongly identified with their schools and little thought was given to what was later termed differential therapeutics—applying various treatments to specific disorders (Frances, Clarkin, & Perry, 1984). As the field advanced, those outside of the field were asking for proof of effectiveness and research evidence that various models of treatment were truly change-promoting.

THE STRUGGLE TO ESTABLISH AN EMPIRICALLY BASED SCIENCE OF PSYCHODYNAMICS

The Eschewing of Empirical Findings by Psychoanalysis

According to Schut and Castonguay (2001), "The failure of the analytic community to provide scientific support for its concepts or treatment methods threatens to render psychoanalytic psychotherapy a nonreimbursable form of therapy and push it toward the realm of an outdated psuedoclinical science" (p. 41). Whereas behavior therapy had its roots in the empirical movement and experimental psychology, empiricism for the most part did not exert a strong influence on psychoanalysis. This is interesting in light of Freud's scientific training, background, and interest in neuroscience. According to Strupp (1986) Freud "had little patience with this kind of inquiry and was openly disdainful of efforts to study the nature of the psychological influence on psychotherapy by means other than the therapist's clinical observations" (p. 121). Unquestionably, psychoanalysis did not lend itself to simple empirical validation. Part of the problem was the length of treatment, which made it inordinately complex to test the theoretical propositions and to carry out controlled studies. Another problem was that many of the tenets of the analytic model were reified to the point of becoming taboo (Fosha, 1995). For example, the sanctity of the analytic relationship was used to dismiss anything that might interfere with or contaminate the process. To many, psychoanalysis seemed more like a religion with an esoteric and complex language that could be used to explain any contradictions, very different from the assumptions of the scientific method. Schut and Castonguay believe that a "disregard for the scientific tradition by individuals within the analytic community reflects a breakdown in the graduate training and education process" (p. 45).

Audiovisual Technology and the Advancement of the Science of Psychotherapy and Psychodynamics

The use of audiovisual recording was eschewed by mainstream psychoanalysis and considered a severe intrusion that could not be condoned. Yet, some psychotherapists had a different perspective: "The advent of videotape has revolutionized evaluation, technique, and outcome research in the whole field of psychotherapy" (Sifneos, 1984, p. 479). The importance of audiovisual technology was a major advance offering a new tool that Sifneos (1990) likened to the discovery of the microscope in biology and, a more current analogy, the PET scan in neuroscience. Alpert (1996) writes:

> Psychotherapy has long been a private affair. However, by keeping their therapeutic work so private, therapists have decreased the ability of others to objectively evaluate their work. Videotapes of psychotherapy sessions provide the data necessary for the objective evaluation of psychotherapy. (p. 93)

Why was this cost-effective tool not heartily embraced by the psychotherapeutic community at large? The answers are complex and beyond the scope of this chapter to consider in depth, but it is a compelling question. One noteworthy exception to rejection of this technology has occurred in the family therapy movement, whose early practitioners embraced videotaping sessions as well as using one-way mirrors to observe the therapeutic process. The use of videotapes is a major asset for researchers, offering a treasure trove of information. The lack of utilization of such techniques curtailed the process of empirical validation of psychodynamics.

In one major branch of psychodynamics, the disparagement of research and outcome findings has not occurred: short-term dynamic psychotherapy (STDP). Sifneos (1984) comments: "Research work, particularly involving long-term follow-up interviews, has always been emphasized by short-term dynamic investigators and has demonstrated the efficacy of their treatment with selected neurotic patients" (p. 480). Interestingly, most of the pioneering figures of STDP were trained analysts who were considered renegades, notably Sandor Ferenczi and Franz Alexander, whose efforts at empirical investigation and results were not widely accepted by the analytic community (Eisenstein, 1986). Other notables, such as Davanloo (1980), Malan (1963; Malan & Osimo, 1992), and Sifneos (1972), were also very interested in examining the process by videotaping sessions and doing follow-up to determine outcome. Certainly, brief dynamic psychotherapy was far easier to study than psychoanalysis, but the short-term analysts were also more willing to challenge the status quo. They considered themselves to be scientists and their subject amenable to scientific investigation.

Time-Tested Psychodynamic Postulates

The practice of scientific research involves testing theories that have been formulated using empirical methods; over time, unsubstantiated theories (such as phrenology) fall by the wayside (Hunt, 1993). "Fortunately, however, over the last two-and-a-half decades, a contingent of psychoanalytic psychotherapy researchers has begun to generate a substantial body of empirical research on the analytic encounter, breathing new life into the psychoanalytic approach and reaffirming its position as a worthy clinical and scientific enterprise" (Schut & Castonguay, 2001, p. 40). Although much of psychodynamic theory remains empirically unsubstantiated, Westen and Gabbard's, (1999) review of the empirical data suggests that important "postulates of contemporary psychodynamic thinking have withstood the test of time" (p. 74). These include:

1. Much of mental life is unconscious, including thoughts, feelings, and motives.
2. Mental processes, including affective and motivational processes, operate in parallel, so that individuals can have conflicting feelings toward the same person or situation that motivate them in opposing ways and often lead to compromise solutions.
3. Stable personality patterns form an important role in personality development, particularly in shaping the ways people form later social relationships.
4. Mental representations of the self, others, and relationships guide people's interactions with others and influence the ways they become psychologically symptomatic.
5. Personality development involves not only learning to regulate sexual and aggressive feelings but also moving from an immature, socially dependent state to a mature, interdependent one. (p. 74)

THE USE OF EMPIRICAL FINDINGS BY PSYCHODYNAMIC CLINICIANS

A major impediment to the advancement of the science of psychodynamics and psychotherapy in general is that empirical findings are not always known to, or considered by, the clinicians. Traditionally, psychotherapists and psychotherapy researchers have not communicated, and for the most part, each read separate publications (Shea, Benjamin, Clarkin, & Magnavita, 1999). Although most clinicians would agree that psychotherapy research is important, few apply these findings to their clinical work (Morrow-Bradely & Elliott, 1986), and clinicians report that a discussion with colleagues is generally more valuable to them than are articles (Cohen, Sargent, & Sechrest, 1986). Unfortunately, it has also been difficult to apply the findings of psychotherapy research to clinical populations. One problem is that psychotherapy researchers tend to write their articles for other researchers and many clinicians are frustrated with the need to wade through complex statistical and methodological material to find the gem of information that will provide clinical utility. Another problem has been that patients treated in research/academic settings are not always the type of patients seen by clinicians. Research settings typically look for uncomplicated clinical presentations that are the focus of their studies, such as anxiety or depression, and reject the more complicated comorbid cases commonly seen in clinical practice.

Another obstruction is that clinicians do not generally read psychotherapy research findings reported in scientific publications. At a National Institute of Mental Health (NIMH) workshop, the participants concluded: "Findings from psychotherapy research have had limited influence on clinical practice, and, ultimately on public health" (Street, Niederehe, & Lebowitz, 2000, p. 128). Recent attempts have been made to bridge this gap with, for example, the founding of the journal *In Session: Psychotherapy in Practice*, edited by Marvin Goldfried, whose mission is to provide clinicians with current, clinically relevant research findings.

THE CHALLENGE TO PROVIDE EFFECTIVE BRIEF PSYCHOTHERAPY

One of the few positive outcomes from the recent cost-containment era is in the new accountability and pressure to accelerate the course of treatment without the loss of effectiveness. "As in all matters psychoanalytic, the history of brief therapy starts with Freud" (Messer, 2001, p. 5), when he shifted his attention from the technique of catharsis to free association (Eisenstein, 1986). However, Freud soon lost interest in this treatment approach, as well. Over the past 20 years, there has been a major renewal of interest in the field of psychodynamic therapy in accelerated forms of brief psychodynamic therapy (BPT) that were first pioneered by Ferenczi (Ferenczi & Rank, 1925), who developed his active therapy. Later, Alexander (Alexander & French, 1946) revitalized interest in the accelerated treatment model of Ferenczi. According to Messer (2001):

> The strong negative reaction of the psychoanalytic establishment to Alexander's ideas led to a lull in the development of BPT until the 1960s and 1970s, when a second cohort of therapists took up the cause. Three psychoanalytic psychiatrists, Malan (1963), Davanloo (1978), and Sifneos (1972), established a foothold for BPT based on traditional models of drive/defense or drive/structural (id/ego/superego) constellations and their active confrontation by the therapist. (p. 6)

Most therapy is time-limited, and the greatest impact seems to accrue fairly early in the process and wanes as time passes. Empirical studies have shown that most improvement in psychotherapy comes by the 26th session (Howard, Kopta, Krause, & Orlinsky, 1986). Providing effective brief therapy remains a challenge to the field, in particular in application to a full range of personality disorders (Magnavita, 1999a), including the "silent sufferers" (Magnavita, 1999b), the severe disorders, and the complex clinical syndromes (Magnavita, 1999c, 2000). Over a decade ago, Marmor (1989) predicted:

> There is little doubt that the future of psychotherapy in the United States as well as elsewhere, for cogent cultural reasons, lies with the further development of short-term therapeutic techniques. Only short-term approaches provide a reasonable hope for dealing economically and effectively with the deluge of emotional and behavioral problems that our complicated society seems to be spawning in ever-increasing numbers. (p. 557)

Based on the number of new works that have been published in this area, his prediction seems to be holding up.

TREATMENT MANUALS AND EMPIRICALLY VALIDATED TREATMENT

A trend to manualize treatments has been undertaken in an effort to standardize the application of various treatment models for both research and clinical purposes. Many forms of brief dynamic therapy have been manualized for research and training (Binder, 1993). Practical in design, these manuals cannot serve as a substitute for training in such a complex process as psychotherapy. They are, however, vital to research and useful for training (Shea et al., 1999). Similar to treatment manuals, empirically validated treatments (EVTs) are those methods that are considered to have attained a currently acceptable standard of empirical support for their efficacy for a particular disorder.

Psychodynamic clinicians/researchers have demonstrated that manualized treatments developed for personality disorders are effective forms of psychotherapy and that psychodynamic psychotherapy can be empirically validated (Winston et al., 1991, 1994). Undoubtedly, the future of psychodynamic psychotherapy necessitates the judicious use of manuals, not as a replacement for clinical judgment, flexibility, and intuition, but to advance research and enhance effectiveness through the scientific method. Luborsky (1993), the consummate scientist-practitioner, summarizes: "Experience in the use of the manual typically leads to the realization that in dynamic therapy particularly, only broad guidelines are possible and that the therapist is really not constrained but rather helped in applying clinical understanding in timing and content of interventions" (p. 579).

Is Psychodynamic Psychotherapy Effective?

Although a comprehensive review of the effectiveness data for psychodynamic psychotherapy is beyond the scope of this chapter, Gabbard (1997a, pp. 540–541), in his excellent review of the empirical literature, concludes:

- Dynamic therapy is in general no better and no worse in benefits than other therapies.
- Very few studies involve randomized, controlled designs of extended dynamic therapy or of psychoanalysis.
- A good deal of research on dynamic therapy has appeared in recent years to support its efficacy.
- Extended psychodynamic therapy for suicidal patients may be cost-effective in preventing suicide.
- Extended psychodynamic therapy for borderline patients may be cost-effective when comparing the cost of health care provision, such as high rates of emergency room usage, consulting specialists, and recidivism in psychiatric hospitalization.

Clarkin (1999) adds some other findings from his review of the literature on personality disturbance:

- Seriously disturbed patients generally fare better when they receive a combination of supportive and expressive dynamic therapy.
- Patients with primarily neurotic personality disorders treated with brief dynamic therapy had moderate improvement in symptoms as compared to a control group.

Toward the Convergence of Theories: Achieving Consilience

One clearly positive outcome of the cost-containment era is that it stimulated practitioners from various schools to look outside of their own model for effective treatment techniques and helpful theoretical constructs. This development has had a significant influence on the field of psychotherapy. Within psychoanalysis, the impact of integration has been somewhat less evident, though more evident in contemporary psychodynamics, many models of which are presented in this volume. However, psychoanalysts/psychodynamic therapists remain somewhat iconoclatrous and isolated. Alpert (1996) describes the situation in this way:

> Just as it is hard to see one's own defensiveness, it is also hard to see the weaknesses of cherished theories. We are likely to protect our theories. They may be a personal creation and a source of pride. They may be the badges of membership in a select fraternity. To abandon a theory may mean that we must admit we have been wrong, but also face the resistance and rejection of teachers and peers. (p. 102)

The cross-fertilization that is possible when integration is considered advances the field immensely:

> Even within the more restricted domain of individual interventions, growing recognition of unique strengths and limitations of competing theoretical approaches has fueled a burgeoning movement towards psychotherapy integration.... For example, advocates of various integrative models of psychotherapy have emphasized the strengths of psychodynamic approaches for identifying enduring problematic interpersonal themes, the benefits of experiential techniques for promoting emotional awareness, gains from cognitive interventions targeting dysfunctional beliefs and attributional processes, and advantages of behavioral strategies for promoting new patterns of behavior. (Snyder, 1999, p. 349)

This convergence has led various competing schools of psychotherapy to arrive at similar conclusions about many aspects of the process shared by all psychotherapies. For example, in other models of psychotherapy, such as behavioral, there is a recognition that emotion is not to be rejected as being unworthy of attention. Samoilov and Goldfried (2000) announce: "As we are entering the 21st century, the decade of affect in CBT [cognitive-behavioral therapy] is yet to come" (p. 373). Further, they write, "We suggest that in-session emotional activation has the potential for enhancing the long-term effectiveness of CBT interventions" (p. 373). Their conclusion emphasizes the role of affect: "With the growing interest in the role of affective processes in cognitive and behavioral change, and with the emerging attempts to incorporate them into behavior therapy, the decade of affect in behavior therapy is finally beginning to emerge" (p. 382). This type of talk would have been heresy in behavioral camps formerly. Clearly, there is a convergence among various models of psychotherapy; as volume 4 of the *Comprehensive Handbook of Psychotherapy*, which is devoted to the integrative/eclectic model, indicates, the integration movement has been influential for many psychodynamically grounded theorists/clinicians as well as for those of all the other theoretical persuasions.

A PARADOX: REDUCTION OF OPPORTUNITIES FOR TRAINING AND THE PRESSURE FOR RESULTS

Psychodynamic psychotherapy, regardless of the model, is not easily or quickly mastered. Training inevitably takes a long time and often requires personal psychotherapy, extensive study, and supervision. Eisenstein (1986) describes why many thought Franz Alexander was so effective as a psychotherapist: "It was said of him by some that his patients made much progress because he was so charismatic, so impressive, so well known, and that they could only improve and give up their neurosis. He used to laugh at this assertion, saying that anyone can learn this science provided he has the empathy, the intuition, and the curiosity to look at the human condition" (p. 189). Apparently, "He had all these traits" (p. 189). Unfortunately, a direct result of the cost-containment era was the reduction in training opportunities and supervision for psychotherapists. Many programs that offered advanced training in psychodynamic and other models of psychotherapy were abandoned. Now they exist only in major metropolitan areas where there is a large enough pool of mental health professionals from which to draw attendees.

With the advent of managed care, biological psychiatry was promoted and psychotherapy correspondingly discredited. Many psychiatry residence programs stopped offering training in psychodynamic psychotherapy. Over the past 10 to 15 years, there have been progressively fewer training programs available for those studying all forms of psychotherapy. Psychoanalysis, previously one of the most sought-after forms of training, now finds there are few trainees willing to spend the necessary time and financial resources on a pursuit that few are able to practice in this era of cost containment. This has resulted in a generation of psychotherapists who have not been afforded the opportunity to have a century of verbal and written clinical tradition and knowledge passed on to them.

Many new trainees have been burdened with medical and graduate school loans in the pursuit of a career in a field with decreasing salaries and opportunities. The loss of training opportunities has probably been one of the most insidious, indirect influences of the cost-containment era. The transfer of knowledge about the practice of psychotherapy was severely disrupted as a survival mentality took hold and supervision and training ceased to be considered essential. This phenomenon has been described by the author (Magnavita, 1997):

> Effective psychotherapy does not take place when the clinician is worried about paying the rent. I think that active studying as a psychotherapist is very difficult, especially in the current sociopolitical and economic atmosphere where

issues of survival seem to dominate everyone's thinking. I am discouraged when I see endless conferences on marketing and business practices, where in the past one would have seen clinically stimulating topics. I think psychotherapists need to have opportunities to think about their work and confer with others.... In the former Soviet Union psychotherapy was banned by the communist movement... those who wanted to keep the practice alive would occasionally plan conferences in the mountains, literally in tents. (pp. 313–314)

In the remainder of the chapter, current challenges and future trends are discussed and a summary of what this means for the future of scientific psychodynamics is presented.

CURRENT CHALLENGES AND FUTURE TRENDS

The Emergence and Relevance of Neuroscience for Psychodynamics

In *The Story of Psychology*, Hunt (1993) describes Freud as "the would-be neuroscientist," spending his early years of training "at laboratory tables, dissecting fish and crayfish, tracing their nerve pathways, and peering at nerve cells through a microscope" (pp. 169–170). Although on an intellectual level, he was committed to physiological psychology (one of the precursor disciplines of neuroscience), as a Jew, he could not achieve an academic position and financial security and was advised against continuing that pursuit.

A leader in contemporary psychodynamic psychotherapy, Glen Gabbard (1997b), stated at a conference entitled *Dynamic Therapy in the Decade of the Brain*: "We cannot artificially separate the mind and the brain." Contemporary psychotherapy requires models of the mind and an understanding of how the brain works and how the two interrelate. The growth of the field of neuroscience has major implications for advancing the field of psychotherapy. Gabbard (1997a) believes that just as "psychoanalytic reductionism" took place in the first half of the twentieth century, contemporary psychiatry is in danger of "biological reductionism" (p. 537). As Gabbard (1997a) underscores: "The integration of the psychosocial and biological is the essence of psychiatry... psychotherapy must be effective by changing brain function" (p. 537).

In the last decade of the twentieth century, a stream of books grappled with what many consider the last mystery of science: understanding consciousness (Damasio, 1999; Dennett, 1991). The 1990s have been referred to as the "decade of the brain" because of increasing interest and focus on this and other topics within the discipline of neuroscience. Consciousness is the state of personal awareness that is derived from our ability to think, feel, perceive, sense, and dream (Magnavita, 2002). Understanding states of consciousness can only add to our understanding of how to go about altering disturbed or troubled states of consciousness. Neuroscience, an interdisciplinary science, has much to offer the relatively young field of psychotherapy. For psychodynamic psychotherapy to continue to advance and hold a place of prominence, there needs to be a convergence of scientific evidence that validates many of the underlying assumptions that have been accepted by the field. Neuroscience offers a variety of scientific tools for exploring the brain-mind connection: magnetic resonance imaging, positron emission tomography, near-infra-red spectroscopy, and magnetoencephalography (Carter, 1998).

Learning and Neural Structure
Learning strengthens neuronal connections. Kandel (1979, 1989), the Nobel prize-winning neuroscientist, in his often cited studies demonstrated the effect of simple learning on synaptic connections. His findings show that neural structures can be modified and strengthened through the process of learning.

These findings support Hebb's (1949) original brilliant contention that firing of a neuronal system increases the probability of that system's firing in the future. According to Gabbard (1997a): "Kandel has suggested that similar mechanisms must be involved in psychotherapeutic work. He compares the psychotherapist to a teacher who helps the individual learn new ways of thinking about self and others" (p. 538).

The Neurobiology of Attachment and Interpersonal Experience

Contemporary psychodynamics are based on the assumption that relationships are the primary vehicle to shape personality and influence the expression of biological vulnerabilities (see diathesis-stress model, below). Siegel (1999), in his synthesis of neuroscientific findings, proposes "that the mind develops at the interface of neurophysiological processes and interpersonal relationships" (p. 21). Harry Stack Sullivan's (1953) interpersonal psychiatry proposed the interpersonal experience as the formative influence on personality; neuroscience is validating this connection (Grigsby & Stevens, 2000). Siegel suggests that the neuroscientific findings support the contention that attachment systems are likely implicated in the development of the brain. There appear to be critical periods for attachment when the individual is especially sensitive to stimulation or neglect. Although there appears to be plasticity of the neuronal systems, attachment disturbances at critical periods may leave a lifetime imprint: "The individuals at greatest risk of developing significant psychiatric disturbances are those with disorganized/disoriented attachments and unresolved trauma or grief" (p. 119). Greenspan and Benderly (1997) describe how the interpersonal experience affectively primes growth:

> Without some degree of this ecstatic wooing by at least one adult who adores her, a child may never know the powerful intoxication of human closeness, never abandon herself to the magnetic pull of human relationships, never see other people as full human beings like herself, capable of feeling what she feels. Whether because her nervous system is unable to sustain the sensations of early love or her caregiver is unable to convey them, such a child is at risk of becoming self-absorbed or an unfeeling, self-centered, aggressive individual who can inflict injury without qualm or remorse. (p. 51)

The findings from neuroscience strongly support the contention that experience shapes and organizes the brain, and that psychotherapy restructures/reorganizes neuronal networks (Grigsby & Stevens, 2000). Neuroscience is an interdisciplinary science that draws from various sources, including animal behavior. Victoroff (2000) summarizes an exciting neuroscientific finding about neurogenesis—how brain cells rejuvenate themselves—as well as how stress impacts this process:

> The investigators moved several of the marmoset monkeys into a cage with another adult for one hour, a notoriously stressful situation in which the adult with a sense of cage ownership reliably becomes aggressive toward the newcomer. This single stressful event was enough to significantly decrease the rate of neurogenesis, a contribution to the accumulating evidence that psychological stress can cause lasting injuries to brain and cognition. This conceivably helps explain why major depression is associated with an increased risk for late-life cognitive deficits, hinting that these deficits may not just be a matter of cellular injury, but perhaps a matter of failed cellular renewal. (p. 17)

Positive experiences seem to build neuronal connections and enhance conductivity, whereas stress and trauma may prune connections. Greenspan and Benderly (1997) contend that the quality of affective relationship with the primary attachment figure exerts a substantial influence on how the mind grows: "Support for the link between affects and intellect comes from a number of sources including neurological research, which has found that early experiences influence the very structure of the brain itself" (p. 7).

The Neurobiology of Affect

> Rapid developments in our understanding of emotion, mood, and affective style have come from the study of the neural substrates of these phenomena. The identification of the brain circuitry responsible for different aspects of affective processing has helped to parse the domain of emotion into more elementary constituents in a manner similar to that found in cognitive neuroscience, where an appeal to the brain has facilitated the rapid development of theory and data on the subcomponents of various cognitive processes. (Davidson, 2000, p. 1196)

There are many aspects of affective style that are influential in the subjective experience of emotion (Davidson, 2000). These include "threshold to respond, magnitude of response, latency to peak of response, and recovery function" (p. 1197). Accumulating evidence suggests that the prefrontal cortex and amygdalar activation are related to affective style as well as emotional regulation. Susceptibility to activation may be one factor in developing psychopathology. In the stress-diathesis model, stress such as trauma may cause undue activation and shape the neuronal networks. There is evidence to suggest that voluntary emotional regulation may indeed alter neuronal connections. Davidson cites the Dalai Lama (Dalai Lama & Cutler, 1998):

> The systematic training of the mind—the cultivation of happiness, the genuine inner transformation by deliberately selecting and focusing on positive mental states and challenging negative mental states—is possible because of the very structure of the brain.... But the wiring in our brains is not static, not irrevocably fixed. Our brains are also adaptable. (pp. 44–45)

Evidence is accruing that supports the notion that affective arousal is necessary for change (Fosha, this volume). We know from clinical and animal research that the highly emotionally activating states that occur from trauma are very difficult to deal with, seemingly trapped in the patient's neural networks, prone to reactivation from external or internal cues. Siegel (1999) writes: "The relationship between emotion and memory suggests that emotionally arousing experiences are more readily recalled later on" (p. 48). Various emotionally charged traumatic events might alter neuronal receptivity. According to Stern (1985): "The sharing of affective states is the most pervasive and clinically germaine feature of intersubjective relatedness" (p. 138).

THE NEW SYNTHESIS: BUILDING INTERDISCIPLINARY BRIDGES

Contemporary psychodynamic psychotherapy, as we have seen in this volume, is increasingly being strengthened from interdisciplinary (assimilating other theoretical perspectives within psychotherapy) and intradisciplinary (using models and empirical findings from related disciplines) integration, which enriches the theoretical model and broadens the potential for research. One exciting area where this trend is emerging is in the area of neuroscience, another, to be discussed shortly, is personality theory and research. Productive collaboration often occurs when interdisciplinary bridges are built. An exciting new book, *Neurodynamics of Personality* (Grigsby & Stevens, 2000), is an example of the collaborative efforts between a research scientist and a psychologist and psychoanalyst.

In a recent volume, *Theories of Personality: Contemporary Approaches to the Science of Personality* (Magnavita, 2002), the author predicts that the component systems will continue to shape our understanding of personality, psychopathology, and psychotherapy. Important new scientific disciplines that have emerged in the last half of the twentieth century are offering exciting new vantage points and data sets to add to our understanding and theoretical modeling. These include:

- *Cognitive science:* A scientific revolution was created when cognitive science emerged from behaviorism, using computer models to understand cognitive processes (Gardner, 1985).
- *Neuroscience:* One of the most exciting new disciplines emerging from a combination of related disciplines such as physiological psychology, genetics, and medicine. Neuroscience is primarily concerned with understanding consciousness (Dennett, 1991).
- *Affective science:* Emerging from Darwin's (1872) seminal work, which was the first scientific examination of emotion, and furthered in the 1960s by Silvan Tomkins (1962), the topic of emotion was downplayed by academic psychology and was later rediscovered and energized by the work of Ekman and Davidson (1994), two pioneers of the new field of affective science.
- *Developmental science:* E. Mavis Hetherington (1998) defined the term developmental science, which is the study of development over the life span.
- *Relational science:* Berscheid (1999) wrote of the birth of relational science: "Today, if you squint your eyes and cock your head just so, you can see the greening of a new science of interpersonal relations" (p. 79). Relational scientists emphasize the study of what transpires between and among individuals.
- *Sociobiology/evolutionary science:* Evolution has been a powerful model that has been applied to various disciplines. Evolutionary psychology and sociobiology have applied the principles of natural selection and survival of the fittest to understand behavioral patterns and social structures (Buss, 1984; Wilson, 1975).
- *Clinical science:* Contemporary clinical sciences have offered remarkable advances in knowledge of psychopathology, epidemiology, psychopharmacology, and statistical methods/research design and a rich heritage of clinical observation for over 100 years.

Diversity and Multicultural Challenges

All models of the mind and psychopathology as well as the theories of psychotherapy that emerge from these evolve from cultural and sociopolitical forces. The impact of this fact is inescapable for an increasingly pluralistic and multicultural world. Upper-middle-class European males developed most of the accepted theories of personality, psychopathology, and psychotherapy. They viewed clinical phenomena through the lens of their own cultural and political experience, deriving their theories to account for what they saw.

Psychopathology, personality theory, and psychodynamic therapy have evolved considerably from the time of Freud and continue to do so. Societal changes that are occurring throughout the world as a result of the global economy, ease of transportation, and almost instant communication are rapidly altering sociopolitical systems and draw ever greater attention to sociocultural factors. Hickling (1988) poses the question: "Do political issues affect the presentation and diagnosis of mental illness, and therefore influence the nature of the psychotherapy interventions directed toward the relief of psychological suffering?" (p. 91). The answer to this rhetorical question is clearly yes! Gender (Minas, 1993), ethnicity, socioeconomic status, religion, migration, and political ties are all influential in determining cultural/sociopolitical variability (McGoldrick, 1982). Twenty years ago,

McGoldrick, Pearce, and Giordano (1982) assessed the situation:

> The United States is the most ethnically diverse nation in history, but this fact has not increased our ability to tolerate differences. We have regarded our society as a melting pot and have blinded ourselves to its inherent diversity. Our wish to forget cultural variations and to encourage common norms, though understandable, has been an idealistic and fallacious goal. (p. xv)

Hickling (1988) writes: "The individual transformation process cannot be divorced from the social process, and psychotherapy therefore must seek to link with social activity and to potentiate social change through some form of systematic group action" (p. 108). Clearly, as psychodynamic science evolves, greater attention needs to be paid to the new plurality that is emerging and shaping the world.

Personality Theory, Psychopathology, and Psychotherapy

Personality theory, psychopathology, and psychotherapy are the three sisters of effective clinical practice (Magnavita, 2002). Each of these disciplines is subsumed under Freud's metapsychology, which provided the first flexible and broad-ranging model for explaining personality development, expressions of psychopathology, and methods for ameliorating emotional disorders, considered to be the expression of psychopathological dynamic forces. Alexander and Selesnick (1966) describe the significance of Freud's work:

> This advancement was in large part the fruition of thousands of years of study of the human psyche, but it became possible only after Freudian discoveries transformed psychiatry and penetrated medical thought.... Freud's method made it possible to bring the first comprehensive theory of personality based on an effective method of scrupulous, systematic observation and interpretation to the study of the human mind. (p. 5)

Fawcett (1999) posed the age-old question that has held particular interest to psychodynamic theorists over the past century: "What actually determines our personality and by what mechanisms can it change?" (p. 684). Personality theory has a close tie to clinical practice as well as empirical research and is, at the turn of the century, an interdisciplinary science (Magnavita, 2002). Personality theory during the twentieth century was a guiding light for those who embarked on the murky journey of depth therapy in an effort to achieve personality/character change. Many theoretical models that have recently been developed have broadened immensely our dynamic understanding of personality development, disorder, and change. I briefly summarize four of these that have particular significance for psychotherapy because of their theoretical power and clinical utility: diathesis-stress model, biopsychosocial model, general systems theory, and chaos theory.

The *diathesis-stress model* (Monroe & Simons, 1991) is an important development in understanding the relationships among genetic vulnerability, psychological vulnerability, and the point at which stress can result in symptom complexes or personality disturbance. "The diathesis-stress model provides a general theory of the etiology of most mental disorders" (Paris, 1999, p. 696).

The *biopsychosocial model* is a remarkable, parsimonious framework with which to understand both physical and emotional disorders (Engle, 1980). Its use highlights the infinite and complex substrates, from the cellular to the ecosystem, that shape personality and social systems.

The development of *general systems theory* (von Bertalanffy, 1968) has been an intellectual milestone of the twentieth century with multidisciplinary impact. In part, it gave rise to the development of family systems theory. General systems theory has broad application for understanding how any complex system interrelates and emphasis the rules and processes over static variables.

Another fairly new theoretical development is *chaos theory* (Gleick, 1987), which is beginning to be applied to understanding complex natural phenomena:

> In the last few years, a scientific theory of change has emerged from the study of dynamic, nonlinear, self-organizing, chaotic, and complex phenomena in the physical, biological, and social sciences. The theory articulates a set of universal principles that describe how living systems of all kinds self-organize into stable, ordered states and how these states change over time. (Miller, 1999, p. 356)

Gleick writes of the explanatory power of chaos theory:

> In science as in life, it is well known that a chain of events can have a point of crisis that could magnify small changes. But chaos meant that such points are everywhere. They were pervasive. In systems like the weather, sensitive dependence on initial conditions was an inescapable consequence of the way small scales intertwined with large. (p. 23)

Chaos theory has multiple applications. For example, a personality disorder is a disorder of complex systems that can be set in motion by the introduction of fluctuations of small events that reverberate through the biopsychosocial system (Magnavita, 2002). Evolution may be an example of chaos in operation. Chaos has four dynamic states: (1) stable, (2) bifurcation, (3) chaos/complexity, and (4) a complex new, more adaptive order (Butz, 1997). Within these states there appears to be a model that may possibly be applied to understanding human change and growth.

These powerful models, when blended with contemporary psychodynamic models, offer the possibility of a new, stronger science of psychodynamics.

PSYCHOTHERAPY TRAINING AND SUPERVISION

The field of psychotherapy is an enormously complex one to absorb and challenging to master. It is unlikely that future psychotherapists can be trained in abbreviated training programs; the delivery of effective psychotherapy requires the development of advanced training programs that emphasize a blend of scientific knowledge and clinical skills. Given the extremely high cost of graduate education in psychiatry, psychology, social work, and marriage and family therapy, it is unclear how this will be funded.

SPECULATION ABOUT THE FUTURE OF PSYCHODYNAMICS AND MODELS OF THE MIND

Psychodynamics has been refining a theory of the mind and an evolving psychotherapy for over a century. Fawcett (1999) writes:

> What is the future of the mind in the next millennium? Will minds be "permanently" altered by technical interventions that become possible as neuropsychopharmacology, genetics, neurophysiologic conditioning, and computer technology continue to develop at lightning speed and intersect in their applications? Will our minds be able to live "forever" by downloading our consciousness to a more lasting vehicle than our frail bodies, such as a bionic megachip with a nuclear power source? Will science fiction continue to become reality? Will our innocent, unborn generations have the courage and wisdom to handle such technical possibilities? (p. 684)

Clearly, rapid advances in science, technology, and sociocultural forces will have major impact on the evolution of psychodynamics in the twenty-first century. The future trends are likely to include some of the following:

- Greater emphasis in psychodynamics on empirical investigation and effectiveness.
- Continued growth toward an interdisciplinary science of psychodynamics, borrowing from other disciplines such as neuroscience, cognitive science, and relational science.
- Absorption of relevant aspects of psychodynamics into an overarching science of psychotherapy. In some fashion, this may represent an abandonment of the various school models of psychotherapy prominent in the twentieth century and a convergence of the field into one system.
- Continued growth of forms of brief integrative psychodynamic psychotherapy, with an emphasis on research and use of audiovisual technology.
- A realization of the necessity for advanced training to become effective and a renewed commitment to provide comprehensive training to psychotherapists.
- Increasing use of technological advances such as those now available in neuroscience and computer technology.
- An emphasis on developing culturally relevant models of psychopathology, personality theory, and psychotherapy.
- Increased emphasis on and blending of the systemic model.
- Psychoanalysis and long-term psychodynamic psychotherapy will continue to have a limited role in the new century. Psychoanalysis will probably be sought by those interested in training and in long-term treatment for the patients that are unresponsive to shorter-term treatment formats.
- An emphasis on developing effective methods and techniques for treating personality disorders and complex clinical syndromes that plague modern societies.

SUMMARY

Current and future models of the mind will continue to evolve and be shaped by cultural, societal, and technological forces. Will psychodynamics continue to provide fertile models for interdisciplinary thought? I think the answer is yes! Will psychodynamic psychotherapy remain a separate school of psychotherapy? The answer to this question is more tentative. It may be more likely that there will be a convergence of all the models of psychotherapy presented throughout *The Comprehensive Handbook of Psychotherapy*. In the future, this convergence will likely validate methods common to all forms of psychotherapy, a continual blending of techniques that work and abandonment of those whose effectiveness fails to demonstrate clinical utility and/or be empirically validated. I concur with Judd Marmor (1989), the Franz Alexander Professor Emeritus of Psychiatry at the University of Southern California, who wrote:

> My own hope is that psychotherapists of the future will become more systems-oriented, always aware of the total bio-psycho-social field, and flexibly able to do whatever necessary in any of these spheres for the best interest of their patients. Within that orientation, short-term dynamic psychotherapy will continue, I believe, to be one of our major resources for unlocking the unconscious intrapsychic forces that are at play in the psychopathology of our patients. (p. 257)

This, combined with the new era of scientific psychodynamics, holds much excitement and potential to further help those suffering from emotional disorders and the effects of social ills.

REFERENCES:

Alexander, F., & French, T. M. (1946). *Psychoanalytic therapy: Principles and application.* New York: Ronald Press.

Alexander, F. G., & Selesnick, S. T. (1966). *The history of psychiatry.* New York: Harper & Row.

Alpert, M. C. (1996). Videotaping psychotherapy. *Journal of Psychotherapy Practice and Research, 5*(2), 93–105.

Berscheid, E. (1999). The greening of relationship science. *American Psychologist, 54*(4), 260–266.

Binder, J. L. (1993). Observations on the training of therapists in time-limited dynamic psychotherapy. *Psychotherapy, 30*(4), 592–598.

Buss, D. M. (1984). Evolutionary biology and personality psychology: Toward a conception of human nature and individual differences. *American Psychologist, 39,* 1135–1147.

Butz, M. R. (1997). *Chaos and complexity: Implications for psychological theory and practice.* Washington, DC: Taylor & Francis.

Carter, R. (1998). *Mapping the mind.* Berkeley, CA: University of California Press.

Clarkin, J. F. (1999). Research findings on personality disorders. *In Session: Psychotherapy in Practice, 4*(4), 91–102.

Cohen, L. W., Sargent, M. M., & Sechrest, L. B. (1986). Use of psychotherapy research by professional psychologists. *American Psychologist, 41*(2), 198–206.

Dalai Lama, & Cutler, H. C. (1998). *The art of happiness.* New York: Riverhead Books.

Damasio, A. (1999). *The feeling of what happens: Body and emotion in the making of consciousness.* New York: Harcourt Brace.

Darwin, C. (1872). *The expression of the emotions in man and animal.* London: John Murray.

Davanloo, H. (Ed.). (1978). *Basic principles and techniques in short-term dynamic psychotherapy.* New York: Spectrum.

Davanloo, H. (Ed.). (1980). *Short-term dynamic psychotherapy.* New York: Aronson.

Davidson, R. J. (2000). Affective style, psychopathology, and resilience: Brain mechanisms and plasticity. *American Psychologist, 55*(11), 1196–1214.

Dennett, D. C. (1991). *Consciousness explained.* Boston: Little, Brown.

Dollard, J., & Miller, N. E. (1950). *Personality and psychotherapy: An analysis in terms of learning, thinking, and culture.* New York: McGraw-Hill.

Dumont, F. (1993). The Forum: Ritualistic evocation of antiquated paradigms. *Professional Psychology: Research and Practice, 25*(3), 195–197.

Eisenstein, S. (1986). Franz Alexander and short-term dynamic psychotherapy. *International Journal of Short-Term Psychotherapy, 1*(3), 179–191.

Ekman, P., & Davidson, R. J. (Eds.). (1994). *The nature of emotion: Fundamental questions.* New York: Oxford University Press.

Engle, G. L. (1980). The clinical application of the biopsychosocial model. *American Journal of Psychiatry, 137,* 535–544.

Eysenck, H. J. (1952). The effects of psychotherapy: An evaluation. *Journal of Consulting Psychology, 16,* 319–324.

Fawcett, J. (1999). Editorial: What will happen to our minds in the next millennium? *Psychiatric Annuals, 29*(12), 684.

Ferenczi, S., & Rank, O. (1925). *The development of psychoanalysis.* New York: Nervous and Mental Diseases.

Fosha, D. (1995). Technique and taboo in three short-term dynamic psychotherapies. *Journal of Psychotherapy Practice and Research, 4,* 297–318.

Frances, A., Clarkin, J., & Perry, S. (1984). *Differential therapeutics in psychiatry: The art and science of treatment selection.* New York: Brunner/Mazel.

Gabbard, G. O. (1997a). Dynamic therapy in the decade of the brain. *Connecticut Medicine, 61*(9), 537–542.

Gabbard, G. O. (1997b). Dynamic therapy in the decade of the brain. *The C. Charles Burlingame Award Lecture—1997.* Hartford, CT: Institute of Living.

Gardner, H. (1985). *The new mind's science: A history of the cognitive revolution.* New York: Basic Books.

Gleick, J. (1987). *Chaos: Making a new science.* New York: Viking/Penguin Books.

Greenspan, S. I., & Benderly, B. L. (1997). *The growth of the mind: And the endangered origins of intelligence.* Reading, MA: Perseus Books.

Grigsby, J., & Stevens, D. (2000). *Neurodynamics of personality.* New York: Guilford Press.

Hebb, D. O. (1949). *The organization of behavior: A neuropsychological theory.* New York: Wiley.

Hetherington, E. M. (Ed.). (1998). Special Issue: Applications of developmental science. *American Psychologist, 53*(2), 89–272.

Hickling, F. W. (1988). Politics and the psychotherapy context. In L. Comas-Diaz & E. E. H. Griffith (Eds.), *Clinical guidelines in cross-cultural mental health* (pp. 90–111). New York: Wiley.

Howard, K. I., Kopta, S. M., Krause, M. S., & Orlinsky, D. E. (1986). The dose-effect relationship in psychotherapy. *American Psychologist, 41*(2), 159–164.

Hunt, M. (1993). *The story of psychology.* New York: Doubleday.

Kandel, E. R. (1979). Psychotherapy and the single synapse: The impact of psychiatric thought on neurobiological research. *New England Journal of Medicine, 301,* 1028–1037.

Kandel, E. R. (1989). Genes, nerve cells, and remembrance of things past. *Journal of Clinical Neuroscience, 1,* 103–125.

Luborsky, L. (1993). Recommendation for training therapists based on manuals for psychotherapy research. *Psychotherapy, 30*(4), 578–580.

Magnavita, J. J. (1993). The evolution of short-term dynamic psychotherapy. *Professional Psychology: Research and Practice, 24*(3), 360–365.

Magnavita, J. J. (1997). *Restructuring personality disorders: A short-term dynamic approach.* New York: Guilford Press.

Magnavita, J. J. (1999a). Challenges in the treatment of personality disorders: When the disorder demands comprehensive integration. *In Session: Psychotherapy in Practice, 4*(4), 5–17.

Magnavita, J. J. (1999b). Introduction: Advancements in the treatment of personality disorders. *In Session: Psychotherapy in Practice, 4*(4), 1–4.

Magnavita, J. J. (1999c). Methods of restructuring personality disorders with comorbid syndromes. *In Session: Psychotherapy in Practice, 4*(4), 73–89.

Magnavita, J. J. (2000). Integrative relational therapy of complex clinical syndromes: Ending the multigenerational transmission process. *Journal of Clinical Psychology/In Session: Psychotherapy in Practice, 56*(8), 1051–1064.

Magnavita, J. J. (2002). *Theories of personality: The contemporary science of personality.* New York: Wiley.

Malan, D. H. (1963). *A study of brief psychotherapy.* New York: Plenum Press.

Malan, D. H., & Osimo, F. (1992). *Psychodynamics, training, and outcome in brief psychotherapy.* Oxford, England: Butterworth-Heinemann.

Marmor, J. (1989). The future of dynamic therapy. *International Journal of Short-Term Psychotherapy, 4,* 253–258.

McGoldrick, M. (1982). Ethnicity and family therapy: An overview. In M. McGoldrick, J. K. Pearce, & J. Giordano (Eds.), *Ethnicity and family therapy* (pp. 3–30). New York: Guilford Press.

McGoldrick, M., Pearce, J. K., & Giordano, J. (Eds.). (1982). *Ethnicity and family therapy.* New York: Guilford Press.

Messer, S. B. (2001). What makes brief psychodynamic therapy time efficient? *Clinical Psychology: Science and Practice, 8*(1), 5–22.

Miller, M. L. (1999). Chaos, complexity, and psychoanalysis. *Psychoanalytic Psychology, 16*(3), 335–379.

Minas, A. (Ed.). (1993). *Gender basics: Feminist perspectives on women and men.* Belmont, CA: Wadsworth.

Monroe, S. M., & Simons, A. D. (1991). Diathesis-stress theories in the context of life stress research. *Psychological Bulletin, 110,* 406–425.

Morrow-Bradely, C., & Elliott, R. (1986). Utilization of psychotherapy research by practicing psychotherapists. *American Psychologist, 41*(2), 188–197.

Paris, J. (1999). A diathesis-stress model of personality disorders. *Psychiatric Annals, 29*(12), 692–697.

Rilling, M. (2000). John Watson's paradoxical struggle to explain Freud. *American Psychologist, 55*(3), 301–312.

Samoilov, A., & Goldfried, M. R. (2000). Role of emotion in cognitive-behavior therapy. *Journal of Clinical Psychology: Science and Practice, 7*(4), 373–385.

Schut, A. J., & Castonguay, L. G. (2001). Reviving Freud's vision of a psychoanalytic science: Implications for clinical training and education. *Psychotherapy, 38*(1), 40–49.

Shea, M. T., Benjamin, L. S., Clarkin, J. F., & Magnavita, J. J. (1999). Personality disorders: A discussion of current status and future directions for research, practice, and policy. *Journal of Clinical Psychology/In Session: Psychotherapy in Practice, 55*(11), 1371–1384.

Siegel, D. J. (1999). *The developing mind: Toward a neurobiology of interpersonal experience.* New York: Guilford Press.

Sifneos, P. E. (1972). *Short-term psychotherapy and emotional crisis.* Cambridge, MA: Harvard University Press.

Sifneos, P. E. (1984). The current status of individual short-term dynamic psychotherapy and its future: An overview. *American Journal of Psychotherapy, 38*(4), 472–483.

Sifneos, P. E. (1990). Short-term anxiety-provoking psychotherapy (STAPP): Termination outcome and videotaping. In J. K. Zeig & S. G. Gilligan (Eds.), *Brief therapy: Myths, methods, and metaphors* (pp. 318–326). New York: Brunner/Mazel.

Smith, M. L., Glass, G. V., & Miller, T. I. (1980). *The benefits of psychotherapy.* Baltimore: Johns Hopkins University Press.

Snyder, D. K. (1999). Affective reconstruction in the context of a pluralistic approach to couple therapy. *Clinical Psychology: Science and Practice, 6*(8), 348–365.

Stern, D. N. (1985). *The interpersonal world of the infant: A view from psychoanalysis and developmental psychology.* New York: Basic Books.

Street, L. L., Niederehe, G., & Lebowitz, B. D. (2000). Toward greater public health relevance for psychotherapeutic intervention research: An NIMH workshop. *Clinical Psychology: Science and Practice, 7*(2), 127–137.

Strupp, H. H. (1986). Psychotherapy: Research, practice, and public policy (How to avoid dead ends). *American Psychologist, 41*(2), 120–130.

Sullivan, H. S. (1953). *Interpersonal theory of psychiatry.* New York: Norton.

Tomkins, S. S. (1962). *Affect imagery consciousness. Volume I: The positive affects.* New York: Springer.

Victoroff, J. (2000). Brain and behavior: Fresh horses. *Psychiatric Times, 27*(1), 16–17.

von Bertalanffy, L. (1968). *General systems theory: Foundations, development, application.* New York: Braziller.

Watson, J. B. (1924). *Behaviorism.* New York: Norton.

Watson, J. B., & Rayner, R. (1920). Conditioned emotional reactions. *Journal of Experimental Psychology, 3,* 1–4.

Westen, D., & Gabbard, G. O. (1999). Psychoanalytic approaches to personality. In L. A. Pervin & O. P. John (Eds.), *Handbook of personality: Theory and research* (2nd ed., pp. 57–101). New York: Guilford Press.

Wilson, E. O. (1975). *Sociobiology: The new synthesis.* Cambridge, MA: Harvard University Press.

Winston, A., Laikin, M., Pollack, J., Samstag, L. W., McCullough, L., & Muran, C. (1994). Short-term dynamic therapy of personality disorders. *American Journal of Psychiatry, 151*(2), 190–194.

Winston, A., Pollack, J., McCullough, L., Flegenheimer, W., Kestenbaum, R., & Trujillo, M. (1991). Brief psychotherapy of personality disorders. *Journal of Nervous and Mental Diseases, 179*(4), 188–193.

Author Index

Aalberg, V. A., 5
Abel, G., 516
Abraham, K., 109
Abram, J., 49
Abrams, S., 114, 116
Achenbach, T. M., 51, 118
Ackerman, N. W., 388, 437, 438, 439
Adams, M. V., 565, 567, 571
Adelson, E., 81, 90
Adler, A., 387
Adshead, G., 539
Agras, W. S., 147, 148
Ahern, C., 85, 93
Ainsworth, M. D. S., 107, 108, 311, 312
Aitken, K. J., 84, 317
Akman, D., 376
Alexander, F., 8, 208, 209, 215, 233, 257, 284, 287, 325, 443, 592, 599
Allan, J., 51
Allan, R., 549, 550
Allen, F., 47
Allport, G. W., 9
Alonso, A., 458, 460, 461, 462, 463, 514
Alpert, M., 207, 208, 310, 590, 593
Altman, N., 110, 565, 571
Alvarez, A., 120
Anda, R., 553
Anderson, H., 426
Anderson, R., 501
Andrews, B., 144
Angyal, A., 163, 166
Anischewitz, A., 294
Anthony, E. J., 458, 530
Appelbaum, A. H., 246
Araji, S., 514
Archer, J., Jr., 162
Armelius, B. A., 544
Armstrong, H. E., 247, 248
Arnkoff, P., 284
Aron, L., 253, 254, 256, 260, 423, 425
Asnis, L., 106
Atkinson, D. R., 566

Ato, G., 54
Atwood, G., 4, 5, 391, 420, 422, 425, 426, 569
Auerbach, A., 191
Austin, S. B., 134
Axline, V. M., 47, 48
Ayerra, J. M., 491, 492
Azarian, K., 192
Azim, H. F., 477

Bach, R., 515
Baer, M. A., 567
Bakan, D., 255
Baker Miller, J., 134, 137
Baker, A., 530
Baker, L., 142, 146, 149
Bakhtin, M., 413
Balint, E., 208, 209
Balint, M., 209
Bank, S. P., 410
Barbaree, H., 505, 522
Barber, J. P., 183, 184, 185, 186, 188, 189, 190, 191, 192, 203
Baron, J., 106
Bartky, S. L., 370, 371, 373, 374, 375
Barton, R., 484
Basaglia, F., 532
Bass, D., 110
Basson, R., 365, 368, 369
Bateman, A., 247, 539
Bateson, G., 438
Battle, C., 186
Bausserman, L., 550
Bay, L., 135, 151
Beal, L., 507
Beaumont, P., 151
Beck, A. T., 192, 362, 444, 445
Beck, J. G., 365, 366, 369, 376, 378
Becker, J., 377, 505, 507, 516
Becvar, D. S., 135
Becvar, R. J., 135
Beebe, B., 84, 311, 316, 317, 318
Beier, E. G., 285
Beitchman, J. H., 377

Beitman, B. D., 551
Belsky, J., 107
Benderly, B. L., 596
Benedict, H., 53, 54
Benjamin, J., 253, 256, 369, 370, 371, 373, 374, 377, 381
Benjamin, L., 286, 437, 441, 591
Bennett, L., Jr., 572
Bentley, K. J., 541
Berg, I. K., 428
Bergman, A., 3, 24, 35, 48, 54, 276, 287, 290, 568
Berlin, F., 501, 513
Bernard, H. S., 458, 459, 462, 463, 490
Bernheim, H., 2
Berscheid, E., 598
Bettelheim, B., 532
Beutler, L. E., 140
Bibring, E., 183
Bienvenu, J. P., 476
Billings, J. H., 550
Binder, J. L., 166, 239, 592
Bion, W. R., 109, 420, 483, 533, 534
Birch, M., 85, 93
Bird, H. R., 69
Bischof, L. J., 2
Blaine, J., 192
Blakely, E. H., 69
Blanchard, M., 144
Blanck, G., 48, 567, 568, 569, 571
Blanck, R., 48, 567, 568, 569, 571
Blatt, S. J., 249
Blehar, M. C., 107, 311, 312
Bleiberg, E., 113, 117, 118, 120
Blos, P., 163
Blumenthal, J. A., 549
Bollas, C., 413
Bolton, A., 119
Book, H. E., 183, 187, 203
Booth, P. B., 51
Booth-Kewley, S., 556
Bordin, E., 253, 273
Borelli, M. D., 491

605

606 AUTHOR INDEX

Boris, N. W., 70
Boston, M., 119
Boszormenyi-Nagy, I., 388
Bowen, M., 9, 138, 408, 437, 438, 442, 445
Bower, T. G. R., 83
Bower, T. R., 107
Bowlby, J., 48, 49, 82, 107, 108, 111, 138, 210, 276, 287, 291, 311, 324, 388
Bozman, A. W., 369, 376, 377
Bracke, P. E., 550
Bradburn, I. S., 151
Brandt, M., 83
Brantley, T., 572
Brasted, W., 505
Bravo, M., 69
Brazelton, T. B., 83
Bredekamp, S., 40
Brenner, C., 106, 111
Brenner, H. D., 488
Breuer, J., 105, 240
Bristol, M., 36
Brody, V., 47, 48
Brook, C., 119
Broughton, J. M., 83
Brown, G. W., 496
Brown, T., 515
Brumberg, J. J., 137
Bruner, J. S., 409
Bryant-Waugh, R., 149
Buber, M., 311, 317, 330
Buchele, B., 501, 508, 510, 511
Buckley, P., 3
Buell, M., 507
Bufe, G., 496
Bulbena, A., 487
Burack, C., 374
Burell, G., 550
Burg, M. M., 554
Burrow, T., 482
Bus, A. G., 107
Buss, D. M., 598
Bussiere, M., 522
Butts, H. F., 571, 572
Butz, M. R., 600
Buzzell, V., 294

Cacciola, J., 183, 184, 185, 186, 188, 189, 190, 191, 192, 203
Caffaro, J., 511
Calnek, M., 571
Cameron, R. P., 553
Campling, P., 535
Canino, G. J., 69
Cantor, S., 120
Caplan, G., 83

Carew, J. V., 36
Carey, M. P., 366, 367, 376
Cargo, M., 134
Carkhuff, R. R., 317
Carlson, V., 107
Carnes, P., 505
Carroll, R. A., 366
Carson, M., 54
Carstairs, G. M., 497
Carter, B., 148
Carter, D., 515
Carter, J. H., 571
Carter, R., 571, 595
Casement, P. J., 412, 423
Cashdan, S., 283, 285
Cassavia, E., 376
Cassidy, J., 108
Castillo, R. J., 570
Castonguay, L. G., 589, 591
Catalan, J., 365, 367
Catherall, D., 510
Cavell, T. A., 443
Celli, A. M., 490
Cerce, D., 521
Chaloner, D., 144
Chambers, C. L., 51
Chan, C. S., 567
Chanoit, P. S., 531
Chapin, H. D., 82
Chase, N. D., 54
Chassequet-Smirgel, J., 503
Chauncey, D., 540, 543
Chavez, D., 53
Chenoweth, M. S., 370, 371, 372, 374, 377
Cherniss, D. S., 94
Chethik, M., 116
Chevron, E. S., 120, 249
Chittams, J., 192
Chodorow, N. J., 369, 373, 375
Chomsky, N., 426
Christie, D., 145
Cicchetti, D., 49, 106
Ciompi, L., 542
Clark, A. W., 542
Clarke, R. V. G., 542
Clarkin, J., 108, 140, 239, 246, 247, 441, 589, 591, 593
Cloninger, C. R., 141
Cohen, A., 457
Cohen, D., 36, 113, 120
Cohen, L. W., 591
Cohen, R., 119
Coleman, E., 509
Coleman, R. W., 82
Coles, R., 9
Colligan, R., 151

Collis, M., 542
Comas-Diaz, L., 566
Comtois, K. A., 247
Connolly, M. B., 190, 192
Cook, D., 515, 565, 571
Coombe, P., 542
Cooper, A., 185
Cooper, S., 162
Copple, C., 40
Corder, R. F., 495
Cornacchia, E. J., 566
Cornish, D. B., 542
Correale, 490
Correll, R. E., 561
Corrigan, P., 488
Costello, A. J., 51
Costello, J., 36
Coughlin Della Selva, P., 207, 212, 213, 214, 310, 327
Craft, J. C., 247
Cramer, P., 5
Crisp, A. H., 138, 140
Crits-Christoph, K., 191, 192, 195
Crits-Christoph, P., 183, 184, 185, 186, 189, 190, 191, 192, 195
Crocker, P., 253
Crow, S. J., 147
Crowther, C., 135
Cruickshank, R. M., 83
Cumming, G., 507
Cummings, E. M., 107
Cummings, G., 507
Cummings, N., 8
Cunningham-Rathner, J., 516
Cushman, P., 411
Cutler, H. C., 597

DaCosta, G. A., 376
Dalai Lama, 597
Damasio, A., 311, 314, 595
Daniel, J. H., 566, 572
Daniels, L., 489, 496
Dare, C., 135, 146, 148, 150
Darwin, C., 6, 311, 314, 598
Dauwalder, J. P., 542
Davanloo, H., 166, 207, 208, 209, 212, 213, 216, 310, 313, 327, 329, 348, 443, 444, 445, 551, 552, 567, 590, 592
Davidson, R. J., 5, 6, 597, 598
Davies, P. T., 107
Davies, R. L., 530
Davis, M., 3, 4
Dawson, D. F., 538
De Hert, M., 542
De Leon, G., 542

de Mare, P., 491, 530
Debbane, E. G., 476
Decobert, S., 531
Deeter, A., 554
DeFolch, T. E., 109
DeGangi, G., 36, 45
Delaney, J. C., 246
Deleone, H., 491
Dellapietra, L., 553
DeLuca, E., 491
Denckla, M., 36
Dennett, D. C., 595, 598
Deragotis, L. R., 154, 553
Deveraux, G., 133
Dewhurst, T. A., 554
Deyo, R. A., 554
Diamond, D., 246
Diamond, G. M., 437, 440
Diamond, G. S., 437, 440
Diatkine, R., 531
Dicks, H., 388, 418, 425
DiClemente, C. C., 555
Dies, R. R., 458
Diez, L., 534
Dignon, A., 144
Diguer, L., 183, 184, 185, 186, 188, 189, 190, 191, 192, 203
Dimeff, L. A., 247
Dio Bleichmar, E., 374, 375
Dixon Lodge, F., 535
Dixon, L. B., 491, 496
Dolan, B., 536, 540, 542, 543
Dolan, R., 284
Dollard, J., 9, 588
Donahey, K. M., 366
Donaldson-Pressman, S., 440
Dornelas, E. A., 556, 561
Dougher, M., 507
Dryden, W., 285
Dumont, F., 2, 587
Duncan, M. K., 51
Dusseldorp, E., 550
Dye, H. B., 82
Dykens, E. M., 113
Dym, B., 409

Eaker, E., 553
Early, D. F., 541
Eckberg, T., 36
Eckman, T. A., 491, 496
Edelbrock, C. S., 51
Edgcumbe, R., 113
Eguiluz, I., 487, 488
Ehrenberg, D., 256
Eigen, M., 333, 334
Eisenstein, S., 590, 592, 594
Eisler, I., 140, 142, 143, 146, 148, 150

Ekman, P., 5, 6, 314, 598
Elliott, R., 311, 444, 591
Elmore, J. L., 496
Emde, R. N., 84, 107, 124, 311, 317, 319
Emery, G., 444, 445
Engle, G. L., 140, 441, 599
Engleman, D., 69
Epperson, D., 521
Epston, B., 149
Epston, D., 412
Erbaugh, J., 362
Erhensperger, S., 536, 543
Erikson, E. H., 83, 287
Escalona, S. K., 82
Esman, A., 567
Estes, L. S., 134
Everly, G., 441, 442, 446
Eysenck, H. J., 588
Ezriel, H., 442

Fagg, J., 365, 367
Fairbairn, W. R. D., 3
Fairbairn, W. R., 3, 48, 49, 107, 138, 241, 283, 287, 388, 390, 420, 462
Fairburn, C. G., 147
Fantz, R. I., 83
Farber, B., 208
Farnsworth, D. L., 162, 168
Faude, J., 183, 187, 192
Fawcett, J., 599, 600
Fay, L. F., 441, 442, 445
Feinman, S., 105, 106
Feinsilver, D., 542
Feldman, L. B., 411
Feldman, S. S., 151
Fenichel, H., 6
Fenichel, O., 183
Ferenczi, S., 7, 8, 209, 257, 334, 437, 443, 592
Ferlinande, R., 151
Feuerstein, R., 36, 39
Fichter, M., 145, 183, 191
Finkelhor, D., 377, 514
Fischer, W., 481
Fisher, M. S., Sr., 541
Fishman, H. C., 137, 425
Flannery, R. B., Jr., 491
Flegenheimer, W., 346, 363, 450, 592
Flynn, M., 550
Foelsch, P. A., 246
Fogarty, T. F., 441, 442, 445
Fogelstam, H., 544
Fogg-Waberski, J., 514
Follin, S., 530, 531

Fonagy, P., 113, 117, 118, 119, 120, 122, 124, 247, 311, 317, 318, 539
Fong, R., 565, 567
Fosha, D., 207, 208, 209, 225, 309, 310, 314, 315, 316, 317, 318, 320, 323, 325, 326, 330, 444, 589
Foster, R. P., 565, 567
Foulkes, M., 482, 484
Foulkes, S. H., 530
Fox, C., 515
Fraiberg, L., 81, 85, 94
Fraiberg, S., 81, 85, 94, 95
Framo, J., 388
Frances, A., 441, 589
Frank, A., 192
Frank, G., 4
Frank, J., 186, 412
Frankel, B., 489
Frasure-Smith, N., 550, 553
Fredenrich, A. L., 536, 543
Fredrickson, B. L., 371, 373, 374, 375
Freeman, A., 445
French, T. M., 8, 208, 209, 215, 233, 257, 284, 287, 325, 443, 592
Freud, A., 5, 47, 82, 106, 109, 110, 212, 462
Freud, S., 2, 84, 91, 96, 109, 183, 184, 240, 241, 287, 290, 345, 358, 366, 425, 458, 461, 482
Freyd, J., 370
Friedman, H. S., 556
Friedman, J. M., 366, 368, 369
Friedman, M., 550
Friedman, R., 510
Froelicher, E. S., 554
Fulani, L., 565, 567
Furman, E., 84
Furman, R. A., 84
Furuto, S. B. C. L., 565, 567

Gabbard, G. O., 3, 6, 183, 460, 462, 463, 591, 593, 595, 596
Gaenbauer, T., 84
Ganzarain, R., 501, 508, 510, 511
Garant, J., 476
Garcia Badarracco, J. E., 492, 532
Gardner, H., 598
Gardner, R. A., 47
Garfinkel, P. E., 140
Garner, D. M., 140
Garside, R. F., 119
Gaul, R., 5
Gavey, N., 369
Gebbard, P. H., 365
Gendlin, E., 311, 318, 319, 320
Gergely, G., 107
Gergen, K., 426

Gerson, M. J., 420, 421, 423, 425
Gerson, R., 443
Giffin, M., 516
Gil, E., 53
Gilford, P., 411
Gilligan, C., 566, 569
Giordano, J., 599
Glass, C., 284
Glass, G. V., 588
Glassman, A., 553
Glatt, M. M., 530
Gleick, J., 600
Glenn, J., 113
Glenn, M. L., 409
Glickauf-Hughes, C., 48, 49, 54, 283, 284, 286, 287, 288, 290, 291, 293, 294, 295
Goerge, D., 481
Goethe, J. W., 561
Goffmann, E., 484
Goldberg, A., 501, 503, 504, 509, 510, 516
Goldfried, M. R., 411, 551, 561, 594
Goldman, H., 542
Goldman, R., 9, 327, 567
Goldner, V., 425
Goldsmith, B., 191
Goleman, D., 314, 316, 445
Goli, M., 163
Golinkoff, R. M., 107
González Torres, M. A., 488
Goodman, A., 501
Goodwin, D. W., 570
Goolishian, H., 426
Gordon, R. A., 133
Gotlib, I. H., 69
Gowers, S., 140
Grainger, E., 119
Grand, S., 373
Grandison, C., 85, 93
Granger, D., 119
Gray, J., 414, 561
Grayson, P. A., 164
Green, R., 502, 505
Greenberg, J. R., 283, 289, 567
Greenberg, L. S., 254, 311, 314, 317, 415, 428, 444
Greene, B., 565, 566, 567, 571, 572
Greenson, R., 185, 283, 284
Greenspan, S., 15, 16, 18, 19, 20, 31, 36, 39, 44, 84, 596
Griffith, M. S., 571
Grigsby, J., 6, 444, 596, 597
Grinberg, L., 534
Grossman, S., 441, 442, 446
Grossmann, K., 107
Gruen, R., 106

Guerin, P. J., 441, 442, 445
Guerney, B., 48
Guijarro, M., 550
Guimón, J., 481, 485, 487, 488, 496, 534, 536, 537, 538, 540, 542, 543, 544
Gunderson, J. G., 495, 532, 540, 543
Gunnar, M. R., 106
Guntrip, H., 283, 287, 295, 334
Gustafson, J. D., 327
Guze, S. B., 570

Haddock, S. A., 414
Hadley, T. R., 542
Hafner, R. J., 540, 543
Haigh, P., 535
Haigh, R., 532, 533
Haizlip, T. M., 571
Halek, C., 140
Haley, J., 136, 408, 438
Hall, H., 69
Hall, M. F., 574
Hallet, A., 550
Halmi, K. A., 147
Hambridge, G., 47
Hambright, A. B., 135, 140
Hamilton, M., 362
Hamilton, N. G., 69, 70
Hamm, K. B., 495
Han, S., 119
Hanfmann, E., 163, 169
Hanson, R., 521, 522
Hardig, C. B., 107
Harmon, R. J., 84
Harris, G. T., 504
Harrison, A. M., 317
Hart, J., 318
Harter, S., 54
Hartmann, H., 3, 106, 436, 462
Hastings, L., 54
Havens, L. L., 2, 4, 8
Hawk, N. M., 574
Hawkins, G., 574
Hawton, K., 365, 366, 367, 369, 378
Hayes, A. M., 561
Hayes, J. A., 496
Head, S. B., 152
Heard, H. L., 247, 248
Hebb, D. O., 596
Hedges, L., 285
Heffer, R. W., 443
Heiman, J. R., 368
Heinicke, C. M., 119
Helm, J. E., 565, 571
Hendricks, A., 495
Herman, J., 7, 91, 566, 573
Hermans, H. J. M., 413

Herscovici, C. R., 135, 136, 147, 151
Hersh, J. B., 163
Herzog, D. B., 150, 151
Hesse, E., 323, 334
Hesse, P., 106
Hesselton, D., 521
Hetherington, E. M., 598
Hewitt, K., 84
Hickling, F. W., 598, 599
Higginbotham, A. L., Jr., 567, 572
Higgitt, A., 311, 317, 318
Hinshelwood, R. D., 532, 533
Hodel, B., 488
Hodes, M., 150
Hoehn-Saric, R., 186
Hoek, H. W., 134
Hoffman, I. Z., 254, 421, 425
Hoffman, L., 113
Hoffman, M., 39
Hole, A. V., 183, 191, 192
Holi, M. M., 5
Holmberg, J., 53
Holme, G., 543
Holmes, D. E., 571, 572, 574
Holmqvist, R., 544
Hong, B., 496
Honig, P., 150
Hood, J. E., 376
Horner, A., 3, 284, 286, 287, 288, 293, 294, 567, 568, 569, 571, 577, 578
Horney, K., 6, 289, 295
Hornik, R., 106
Horowitz, M. J., 450
Horvath, A. O., 185
Horwitz, L., 459
Howard, K. I., 592
Howells, K., 144
Hoyt, M. F., 428
Hsu, G. L. K., 140, 146
Hug-Helmuth, H., 109
Hughes, D. A., 323
Hull, J. W., 246
Hunt, M., 590, 595
Huxley, G., 106
Hynan, L., 53

Imber, S., 186
Irving, L. M., 134
Isohanni, M., 535, 543, 544
Issenberg, K., 496

Jackson, D., 438
Jackson, L., 565, 566, 567, 569, 572
Jackson, S. W., 2
Jacobs, T., 284
Jacobson, E., 106, 241

Jaffe, J., 84, 318
James, W., 9, 314
Javier, R. A., 565, 569
Jenkins, Y. M., 573, 574
Jernberg, A. M., 47
Jin, K., 542
Johnson, A., 516
Johnson, S., 294, 295, 365, 366, 367, 368, 369, 411, 415
Johnson, V. E., 369
Johnston, K., 85, 496
Johnston-Cronk, K., 491
Jones, D., 553
Jones, M., 530, 533
Jordan, J., 369, 371, 373, 374, 381, 436, 566, 567, 569

Kabat-Zinn, J., 273
Kahn, E. M., 543
Kahn, M. D., 410, 411, 436, 443, 444
Kalas, R., 51
Kallen, R., 36
Kalmanson, B., 85
Kaltreider, N. B., 450
Kamp, J., 151
Kanas, N., 495, 496
Kandall, S. R., 574
Kandel, E. R., 595
Kanter, J., 247
Kantor, D., 414, 425
Kaplan, H. S., 367, 368
Kaplan, J., 549, 550
Kaplan, L., 503
Kaplan, N., 108
Kaplan, S. A., 365
Kashima, K., 507
Kaslow, F. W., 136, 439
Katan, A., 84
Kate, T., 501
Katz, C., 119
Kauff, P. F., 462
Kaufman, G., 510
Kaul, J., 521
Kautto, J. G., 441, 442, 445
Kazdin, A. E., 110
Kegan, R., 414
Keith, S. J., 495
Keller, M. B., 150, 151
Kelly, F. D., 51
Kempen, H. J. G., 413
Kendall, D., 573
Kennedy, H., 112, 113, 117
Kennedy, R., 117
Kernberg, O., 6, 108, 111, 115, 117, 118, 139, 239, 241, 242, 246, 291, 295, 345, 415, 416, 418, 419, 443, 459, 531, 534, 537, 539, 568, 571

Kernberg, P., 48, 50
Kestemberg, E., 531
Kestemberg, J., 531
Kestenbaum, C., 120
Kestenbaum, R., 346, 363, 450, 592
Khan, M. M., 365, 366, 367, 369, 374
Khan, M., 503
Kiesler, D. J., 257
Kilroy, V., 553
King, P., 111
Kinsey, A. C., 365
Kirkby, R. J., 119
Kirschner, D., 411
Kirschner, S., 411
Kisiel, C., 540
Klamen, D. L., 543
Klaric, S., 51
Klein, M., 3, 8, 47, 107, 109, 120, 138, 241, 296, 402, 420, 462
Klein, P. S., 39
Klein, R. H., 458, 459, 462, 463, 490
Klein, R., 458, 459, 462, 463
Klerman, G. L., 120
Klimes-Dougan, B., 69
Knell, S. M., 48
Knight, R., 183, 515, 521
Knoblauch, S. H., 427
Koenigsberg, H. W., 246
Kohn, I. R., 365
Kohut, H., 4, 107, 108, 139, 209, 283, 285, 287, 295, 311, 317, 333, 334, 345, 350, 416, 436, 463, 490, 510, 567, 568, 569
Kolbo, J. R., 69
Kolodny, R. C., 365, 369
Kolvin, I., 119
Kopta, S. M., 592
Kottman, T., 48
Kraaij, V., 550
Kraemer, G. W., 48
Kraemer, H. C., 147
Krakauer, I., 192
Krause, M. S., 592
Kreeger, L., 491
Kris, E., 82
Kruisdljk, F., 536
Kulish, N. M., 571
Kurash, C., 139
Kurcias, J. S., 185
Kurcínka, M. S., 288
Kurtz, A., 119
Kurtz, R., 311, 319

Lachmann, F. M., 84, 311, 316, 317, 318
Laikin, M., 208, 450, 592

Lalumiere, M. L., 504
Langford, W. S., 83
Langs, R., 8
Lansky, M., 296, 388
Lanyon, R., 515
Lasch, C., 345, 416
Lask, B., 145
Lavori, P. W., 151
Laws, R., 502, 505
Lazarus, A., 284, 285
Lazarus, R. S., 6, 314
Le Bon, G., 482
Le Grange, D., 148, 150
Le Grange, P. D. F., 146
Leary, K., 572
Leary, T., 286, 289
Lebovici, S., 531
Lebow, J., 450
Lebowitz, B. D., 591
LeDoux, J., 319
Lee, A., 521
Lee, C. M., 69
Leff, J., 497
Lehne, G., 501
Leiblum, S. R., 365, 367, 370, 376, 378
Leigh, T., 117
Leitch, I. M., 119
Leitch, M., 82
Lennerts, W., 151
Leon, G., 151
Lesperance, F., 550, 553
Lester, B. M., 571
Lester, E. P., 571
Levenson, H., 567
Levine, B. E., 495
Levine, H. B., 495
Levine, M. P., 134
Levine, P., 311, 318, 319, 329
Levine, S. B., 365, 367, 368, 369, 374, 378
Levinson, A., 533
Levinson, E., 425
Levis, N. B., 84
Levoy, D., 69, 70
Levy, D., 47
Levy, K. N., 246
Levy, R. J., 82
Lewis, E., 530
Lewis, G. K., 410
Lewis, H., 39
Lewis, M., 83
Li, K., 542
Liberman, R. P., 491
Liddle, H. A., 437, 440
Lieberman, A. F., 70, 85, 86, 93, 94, 95

Lietaer, G., 254
Lindaman, S. L., 51
Lindemann, E., 83, 328
Linehan, M. M., 247, 248, 538, 539, 540
Links, P. S., 106
Liotti, G., 334
Lipsett, L., 83
Lipton, R., 82
Litin, E., 516
Lock, J., 148
Lopez Atienza, J. L., 491, 492
LoPiccolo, J., 366, 368, 369
Loranger, A., 106
Lothstein, L., 371, 501, 502, 503, 504, 507, 509, 513, 514, 515, 518, 522, 561
Lourie, R., 84
Lowenfield, M., 47
Luborsky, L., 166, 183, 184, 185, 186, 188, 189, 190, 191, 192, 203, 239, 310, 495, 592
Lucas, A., 134, 151
Luepnitz, D., 425
Luna, D., 534, 537
Lush, D., 119
Lynch, M., 50
Lyons-Ruth, K., 317, 334
Lyubomirsky, S., 412

Macera, C., 553
MacMillan, A., 119
MacPhee, D. C., 365, 368
Mader, S. R., 496
Maes, S., 550
Magnavita, J., 1, 2, 5, 6, 7, 8, 9, 135, 137, 154, 207, 208, 310, 327, 333, 335, 350, 380, 435, 437, 439, 441, 444, 446, 551, 556, 560, 567, 569, 587, 591, 592, 594, 595, 597, 599, 600
Mahler, M., 3, 24, 48, 106, 138, 209, 276, 287, 290, 568, 569
Mahrer, A., 284
Main, M., 108, 311, 318, 323, 324, 334
Main, T. F., 530, 533
Malan, D. H., 166, 185, 208, 209, 210, 212, 310, 327, 348, 349, 442, 550, 590, 592
Malan, D. M., 310, 483
Maltz, W., 377
Mammen, O. K., 70
Mangrum, L. F., 443
Mann, J., 9, 164, 310, 327, 511, 550, 551, 567
Manuck, S., 550
Marcus, B., 550

Marder, S. R., 491
Mark, D., 183, 187, 191, 192, 310
Marmar, C. R., 450
Marmor, J., 592, 601
Marohn, R. C., 117
Marques, J., 502
Marshall, W., 505, 522
Martin, C., 365, 367
Maslow, A. H., 413
Masson, J. M., 7
Masters, W. H., 365, 366, 367, 369
Masterson, J. F., 106, 139, 295
Mastin, A. S., 412
Mathura, C. B., 567
Matthews, K., 550
Mattoon, G., 117, 122
Matzko, M., 69, 70
May, P. R., 490, 495, 541
May, R., 163
Mayes, L., 113
McCallum, M., 477
McCarthy, B., 510
McClain, J., 53
McCullough, L., 207, 208, 209, 213, 214, 215, 218, 310, 318, 327, 346, 363, 444, 445, 450, 551, 552, 560, 592
McDaniel, S. H., 441
McDonell, M., 553
McDougall, W., 482
McGee, W., 53
McGeorge, C. R., 414
McGinnis, M. A., 83
McGoldrick, M., 443, 598
McGuire, J., 69, 70
McKenna, J., 501
McKenzie, J., 496
McLean, P., 502
McLellan, A. T., 192
McLellan, T., 192
McMain, S., 253
McQueeney, D. A., 496
McWilliams, N., 166
Meagher, S., 441, 442, 446
Meares, R., 247
Medalie, J., 162
Mendelsohn, M., 362
Menn, A., 495
Menninger, K., 349, 442
Menninger, W. C., 530, 532
Menzies, D., 536
Merikangas, K. R., 6
Messer, S. B., 9, 592
Meulman, J., 550
Meyers, M., 294
Miller, A., 287, 295, 333, 334
Miller, M. L., 588, 600
Miller, M. V., 413

Miller, N. E., 9, 588
Miller, R., 39
Miller, T., 550, 588
Miller, W. R., 551
Millon, C., 441, 442, 446
Millon, T., 6, 441, 442, 446
Milton, J., 502
Minas, A., 598
Mintsker, Y., 39
Mintz, J., 191, 495, 496
Minuchin, S., 136, 137, 142, 146, 149, 408, 425, 437, 438, 444, 445
Mitchell, J. E., 147
Mitchell, S., 253, 254, 255, 256, 283, 289, 370, 373, 412, 413, 567
Mittelman, B., 388
Mittelman, M., 516
Mock, J., 362
Monck, E. M., 496
Mongoven, L. B., 53
Monroe, S. M., 599
Moore, M. K., 83
Moos, R. H., 542
Moran, G., 113, 117, 119, 311
Moras, K., 183, 184, 185, 186, 188, 189, 190, 191, 192, 203
Moreau, D., 120
Morgan, A. C., 317
Morgens, R., 39
Morrow-Bradely, C., 591
Morse, J. Q., 192
Morten, G., 566
Morton, T., 119
Mosher, L., 495, 542
Moskowitz, M., 565, 567
Moultrup, D., 411
Mueller, W., 294
Mufson, L., 120
Muijen, M., 542
Munster, P. K., 162, 168
Muran, C., 450, 592
Muran, J. C., 253, 254, 255, 258, 261, 276, 277, 279, 280
Murphy, W., 516
Murray, E., 119
Murray, P., 253

Nahum, J. P., 317
Narcavage, C. J., 53
Narcavage, D., 53
Nash, E., 186
Nash, M., 54
Nasserbakht, A., 151
Navajavits, L. M., 540, 543
Neiderman, M., 151
Nelson, C., 502
Nelson, D. C., 566
Nemiah, J. C., 34

Ng, M. L., 543
Niaura, R., 550
Nichols, M. P., 135, 425
Nichols, W. C., 411, 416
Nicol, A. R., 119
Niederehe, G., 591
Nieminen, P., 535, 542, 544
Nightingale, L. C., 496
Norcross, J. C., 284, 411, 551
North, C. S., 496
Norton, K., 140, 536, 540, 542,543
Nover, R. A., 84

Oaklander, V., 48
Oberndorf, C. P., 387
Oldham, J., 106
Onken, L. S., 192
Oppenheimer, R., 144
Orange, D. M., 4, 5
Orlinsky, D. E., 592
Ornish, D. M., 550
Ornstein, P., 209
Osiason, J., 309, 310
Osimo, F., 207, 208, 209, 210, 211, 212, 213, 215, 310, 590
Ott, I. L., 151
Oury, J., 531
Owens-Patterson, M., 571, 572
O'Brien, C., 192, 495
O'Brien, J., 119
O'Carroll, R., 365, 367, 378
O'Connor, K., 48, 50, 51
O'Donnell, P., 491
O'Shaughnessy, E., 109

Paivio, 314
Palmer, R. L., 144
Pankow, G., 484
Papp, P., 146, 148
Paris, J., 599
Paul, N., 388
Pavlov, I. P., 2
Pawl, J., 85, 86, 88, 94, 95
Pearce, J. K., 599
Pearson, G. S., 113, 120
Pedigo, J., 501
Pekarsky, J., 85, 88, 94
Peller, J. E., 170
Penn, P., 375
Perls, F. S., 318
Perrault, E. L., 467
Perry, S., 441, 589
Person, E. S., 312, 374
Peters, S., 501
Petti, T. A., 120
Peuskers, J., 537, 542
Piaget, J., 31
Pierce, J. F., 495

Pietz, C., 511
Pine, F., 9, 24, 35, 48, 54, 110, 112, 166, 276, 283, 287, 290, 436, 462, 463, 567, 568, 569
Pines, M., 530
Pinsof, W. M., 135, 140
Piper, W. E., 466, 467, 476, 477
Piran, N., 134
Pithers, W., 507, 522
Pitula, C. R., 554
Pizer, S. A., 253, 256, 260
Pollack, J., 208, 346, 363, 450, 592
Pollio, D. E., 496
Pomeroy, W. B., 365
Popp, C., 191
Porter, F., 208
Postom, M., 495
Prentky, R., 515, 521
Pressman, R. M., 440
Prior, S., 47, 48, 50, 69, 70
Prochaska, J. O., 555
Prodzinski, J., 554
Protter, B., 505, 507, 508, 509
Provence, S., 82
Puertas, P., 534

Quadflieg, N., 145
Qualtrough, T., 369
Quinlan, D., 249
Quinn, M. H., 550
Quinsey, V. L., 504

Rabkin, R., 416
Racamier, P. C., 531, 534
Rachman, A. W., 7
Radke-Yarrow, M., 69
Rado, S., 241
Ramsey-Klee, D. M., 119
Rand, Y., 36, 39
Rank, O., 8, 207, 209, 276, 437, 443, 592
Rankin-Esquer, L. A., 554, 560
Rapaport, D., 6
Rapaport, R. N., 533, 542
Rastam, M., 151
Ratnasuriya, R. H., 140
Rauss-Mason, C., 151
Ray, B. A., 495
Rayner, E., 3
Rayner, R., 588
Rees, T. P., 530
Reich, A., 3, 6
Reich, W., 444, 609
Reik, T., 422
Reinhold, J. E., 161
Reisman, D., 416
Renik, O., 284

Rexford, E., 84
Reynolds, P., 514
Rice, L. N., 311, 317, 444
Rice, M. E., 504
Rich, A., 369, 376
Rickman, J., 483, 530
Rilke, R. M., 417
Rilling, M., 587, 588
Rinsley, D. B., 106, 117
Rio, A., 119
Rivas-Valquez, A., 119
Rivinus, T. M., 69, 70
Robbins, L., 183
Roberts, J. P., 491, 530, 535
Roberts, T., 371, 373, 374, 375
Robinson, M., 84
Roder, V., 488
Rodrigué, E., 491
Roether, H., 501
Rogers, C., 47, 311, 317
Rogers, S., 35, 36
Roland, A., 565, 566
Rollnick, S., 551
Romney, P., 163
Rooth, G., 515
Rosen, R. C., 365, 366, 367, 370, 376, 378
Rosenblatt, B., 106, 114, 117
Rosenblum, L. A., 83
Rosenfeld, B. A., 83
Rosenfeld, H. A., 489, 490
Rosenman, R. H., 550
Rosenzweig, S., 317
Rosman, B. L., 142, 146, 149
Rouleau, J., 516
Rounsaville, B. J., 120
Rovine, M., 107
Rozanski, A., 549
Rubio-Stipec, M., 69
Rucker, H., 283
Rudick, D., 183, 191
Rush, A. J., 444, 445
Russell, G. F. M., 140, 146, 148
Rutan, J., 457, 458, 459, 462, 465, 504, 514
Rutan, S., 504

Sabo, A. N., 540, 543
Sachar, B., 496
Safran, J. D., 253, 254, 255, 258, 261, 276, 277, 279, 280, 314
Sammallahti, P. R., 5
Samoilov, A., 594
Sampson, H., 257
Sampson, R., 561
Samstag, L., 253, 279, 450, 592
Sanchez de Vega, J., 485, 496
Sander, F., 425

Sander, L., 84, 317
Sandler, J., 5, 106, 107, 110, 112, 113, 114, 117, 324
Sands, S. H., 143
Sargent, H., 183
Sargent, M. M., 591
Satir, V., 388
Sayama, M., 7, 8
Sayers, J., 8, 12
Schachter, J. S., 571
Schaeffer, J., 543
Schafer, R., 1, 5, 166, 256, 409, 567, 570
Schaffer, C., 249
Scharff, D., 285, 388, 389, 411, 420, 425
Scharff, J., 285, 388, 389, 420
Scheidlinger, S., 458, 459
Scheidt, S., 550
Scherwitz, L. W., 550
Schiavi, R. C., 365
Schilder, P., 482
Schimmel, P., 535, 540, 543
Schmidt, H., 247
Schmidt, K., 183, 184, 185, 186, 188, 189, 190, 191, 192, 203
Schmidt, U., 144
Schneider, J., 514
Schore, A., 48, 49, 84, 311, 317, 320, 323, 390
Schreiner-Engel, D., 365
Schut, A. J., 589, 591
Schwartz, A. J., 169
Schwartz, B., 501, 502, 507, 512, 516, 521
Schwartz, E. K., 459
Schwartz, J., 2, 7
Schwartz, M., 505, 512
Schwartz, R., 135
Schwartzman, G., 389
Schwitzer, A. M., 163
Scopetta, M., 119
Scott, J. E., 491, 496
Seagraves, K. B., 366
Seagraves, R. T., 366
Searles, H., 490
Sechrest, L. B., 591
Segal, Z. V., 254
Seidel, R., 151
Selesnick, S. T., 599
Seligman, M. E. P., 412
Seligman, S., 85, 86, 318
Selzer, M., 246, 247
Sexton, M. E., 107
Shade, B. J., 571
Shapiro, F., 320
Shapiro, J., 84

Shapiro, V., 81, 90, 94, 95
Shappell, S., 190, 192
Shaw, B., 444, 445
Shea, M. T., 592
Shea, S. C., 443
Shea, M. T., 591
Sheinberg, M., 375
Shelton, L. E., 53
Shelton, R., 510
Shepherd, G., 542
Shepherd, R., 3, 4
Shisslak, C. M., 134
Shorter-Gooden, K., 569
Shure, M., 82
Siegel, D., 48, 49, 311, 313, 317, 318, 320, 430, 437, 596, 597
Siegel, T., 110
Sifneos, P., 164, 310, 348, 443, 550, 551, 578, 590, 592
Silk, K. R., 540
Silverman, R., 85, 93, 94, 95
Silverstein, O., 148
Simons, A. D., 599
Simpson, G. M., 490, 495
Singer, D., 458, 459, 462, 463, 490
Siqueland, L., 192
Sivadon, P., 530, 531
Skeels, H. M., 82
Sklar, I., 207, 208
Skynner, A. C. R., 388
Slater, P., 414, 501
Slimak, R. E., 163
Slipp, S., 285, 387, 388, 411
Slowiaczek, M. L., 309, 310, 325, 330
Smith, C., 151
Smith, M. L., 588
Smith, R., 505
Smith, T., 550
Smyrnios, K. X., 119
Snyder, D. K., 593
Socarides, C., 503
Socarras, F., 531
Solnit, A. J., 82
Solomon, J., 47
Solomon, M., 389, 390, 401, 416, 419
Sotile, W. M., 554
Spangler, G., 107
Spark, G. M., 388
Sparler, S., 550
Spector, P., 366, 367, 376
Spence, D. P., 409
Spertus, J. A., 554
Spitz, R., 82, 89, 138
Spock, B., 413
Springer, T., 540

Sroufe, L. A., 106
St. John, M., 85, 88, 94, 95
Starkey, D., 491
Steele, H., 117, 311, 317, 318
Steele, M., 117, 311, 317, 318
Steenbarger, B. N., 163
Steg, J., 501
Steiger, H., 151, 152
Steinberg, L., 376
Steiner, H., 151
Steiner, M., 106
Steiner, R., 111
Steinhausen, H. C., 140, 151
Stern, D. A., 569
Stern, D. B., 256, 276, 373, 409, 427
Stern, D. N., 48, 49, 84, 89, 95, 108, 311, 317, 318, 597
Sternbach, J., 511
Stevens, D., 6, 444, 596, 597
Stevenson, J., 247
Stierlin, H., 425
Stock, W., 369
Stoller, R., 418, 503, 512, 516
Stolorow, R., 4, 371, 391, 420, 422, 425, 426, 569
Stone, A., 186
Stone, L., 183
Stone, M. H., 246
Stone, W., 459, 465, 490, 496, 504
Stoney, C., 550
Stotland, S., 151, 152
Strachey, J., 116
Street, L. L., 591
Strober, M., 141, 151
Strupp, H. H., 166, 239, 589
Sturke, I. T., 543
Sue, D., 439, 566
Suess, G., 107
Sugarman, A., 139
Sugarman, S., 411, 441
Suinn, R. M., 556, 561
Sullivan, H. S., 4, 275, 283, 287, 437, 596
Sullivan, P. F., 133
Sullivan, R., 550
Summers, F., 567
Sunyer, M., 485, 496
Sutherland, J. D., 388
Swiller, H. I., 458
Symonds, B. D., 185
Synder, D. K., 443
Szapocznik, J., 119
Szmukler, G. I., 140, 146

Talajic, M., 550, 553
Talbot, P., 151
Talmadge, L. D., 376

Talmadge, W. C., 376
Talmon, M., 411
Tannenbaum, F., 572
Target, M., 113, 117, 118, 119, 120, 122, 311, 317, 318
Tatum, B. D., 566
Taylor, C. B., 553, 554, 560
Taylor, D. G., 107
Terr, L. C., 106
Tharinger, D., 377
Thomas, C., 110
Thompson, C. L., 569, 571, 572
Thompson, P. D., 561
Thorensen, C. E., 550
Thornton, D., 521
Thys, E., 542
Tiefer, L., 365, 366, 369, 375
Tiller, J., 144
Tomkins, S. S., 6, 314, 390, 598
Tonry, M., 574
Tosquelles, F., 531
Toth, S. L., 49
Totorika, K., 534
Tournaud, S., 530, 531
Touys, S., 151
Towbin, K. E., 113, 120
Travin, S., 505, 507, 508, 509, 510
Treasure, J., 144
Trevarthen, C., 84, 311, 317
Trojaola, B., 485, 496
Tronick, E. Z., 311, 316, 317, 318, 326, 571
Trop, J. L., 426
Truax, C. B., 317
Trujillo, M., 346, 363, 450, 592
Tullis, E., 106
Turner, C., 550, 572, 574
Twerski, A., 502
Tyson, P., 112, 118, 571
Tyson, R., 110, 112, 113

Unzner, L., 107

Vaillant, G. E., 5, 212, 218
Vallone, R., 495
Van Buren, J., 375
van der Ham, 151
Van Der Veer, M. M., 365, 368
van Elderen, 550
van Engeland, 151
van Furth, 150, 151
van Hoeken, 134
van Ijzendoorn, M. H., 107
van Loon, R. J. P., 413
Van Putten, T., 541

van Strien, 151
Vandereycken, W., 144, 146
Vanderlinden, J., 144, 146
Vaughn, W. T., Jr., 83
Vela, R. M., 120
Velleco, A., 183, 192
Vercruyssen, V., 542
Verhulst, J., 368
Vickerman, M., 566
Victoroff, J., 596
Volkmar, F., 113, 120
von Bertalanffy, L., 1, 438, 599
Vucetic, V., 536, 543

Wachtel, E. F., 408, 411, 425
Wachtel, P. L., 190, 408, 411, 425, 435, 437
Waldstein, A., 85
Walker, L., 137
Wall, S., 107, 311, 312
Waller, G., 144
Wallerstein, R. S., 124, 183
Walsh, B. T., 147
Walter, J. L., 170
Walters, M., 148
Ward, C. H., 362
Warren, F., 536, 540, 542, 543
Warshaw, S. C., 110
Waters, D., 561
Waters, E., 107, 108, 311, 312
Watkins, B., 145
Watson, J. B., 588
Watson, J. C., 254, 428
Watson, W. H., 441
Weakland, J., 438
Weaver, C., 515
Webb, R. E., 163
Weber, A., 536, 543
Wein, S., 249
Weis, D. L., 365, 369
Weiss, B., 119
Weiss, D. S., 450
Weiss, J., 257, 284
Weissman, M. M., 6, 120
Weisz, J. R., 119
Wells, M., 48, 49, 54, 283, 284, 287, 290, 291, 293, 294, 295
Wender, L., 482
West, C. M., 567, 571, 573, 574
Westen, D., 3, 6, 591
Westerlund, E., 377
Weston, D., 551
Whitaker, C., 408, 425
White, M., 137, 138, 149, 412
Whiteley, J. S., 542

Widseth, J. C., 163
Wieder, S., 16, 36, 39, 44
Wiederman, M. W., 365, 369
Wilber, C., 561
Wile, D. B., 408
Willi, J., 418
Williams, A. L., 571
Williamson, D., 152, 553
Wilner, N. R., 450
Wilson, E. O., 598
Wilson, G. T., 147
Winblad, I., 535, 543
Windauer, U., 151
Winder, J. A., 554
Winer, J. A., 543
Wing, J. K., 497
Winnicott, C., 3, 4
Winnicott, D. W., 48, 49, 55, 82, 88, 89, 107, 110, 111, 209, 283, 287, 334, 336, 388, 389, 390, 420, 421, 462, 509, 534, 535
Winston, A., 208, 346, 450, 592
Wirshing, W. C., 491, 496
Wishart, J. G., 83
Wolf, A., 459
Wolf-Palacio, D., 183, 191
Wolstein, B., 275
Wolstenholme, F., 119
Wood, D., 412
Woody, G., 183, 192
Wooley, L. M., 53, 69
Wright, F., 514
Wrye, H. K., 373
Wynn, L. C., 135, 140
Wynne, L., 388, 417

Yalom, I., 458, 467, 486, 487, 501
Yeomans, F., 108, 239, 246
Yeomans, N. J., 542
Yetman, N. R., 573
Young, D. M., 285, 496
Young, J. E., 445
Young, L., 374

Zajonc, R. B., 314
Zanello, A., 536, 543
Zbinden, E., 481
Zeanah, C. H., Jr., 70
Zegans, L. S., 373
Zetzel, E., 185
Zimet, G., 504
Zimmerman, T. S., 414
Zimmermann, K., 491
Zimring, F. E., 574
Zucker, K. J., 376

Subject Index

Abuse:
   child, 7, 71, 144
   substance, 192, 332, 541
Accelerated experiential-dynamic psychotherapy (AEDP), 309–343
   assessment, 327–329
   case example ("the trapped self"), 334–340
   experiential-affective strategies, 331–332
   intervention methods, 329–332
   phenomenology of affective change processes, 315
   reflective-integrative strategies, 332
   syndromes/symptoms/problems treated, 332–334
   theoretical constructs, 309–326
   treatment aim, 325–326
   trial therapy, 327–329
Addictive dysfunctional personologic system (DPS), 439–440
ADHD, 71, 120, 121
Adolescents. *See* College psychotherapy; Eating disorders in adolescence
Adults, psychotherapy with:
   activation of affective change processes in accelerated experiential-dynamic psychotherapy (AEDP), 309–343
   borderline patients (object-relations approach to treatment), 239–252
   brief psychodynamic therapy, 207–237
   developmental issues, and interactional object-relations therapy, 283–307
   narcissistic disorders (short-term dynamic psychotherapy), 345–364
   relational approach to psychotherapy, 253–281
   sexual desire disorders (relational-feminist psychodynamic approach), 365–384
   supportive-expressive psychotherapy, 183–205
Affect:
   neurobiology of, 597
   regulatory difficulties and the development of psychopathology, 324
Affective change processes, 315
   activation of, accelerated experiential-dynamic psychotherapy (AEDP), 309–343
   dyadic regulation of affective states, 315, 316–317
   and optimal development, 312–313
Affective competence, 317

Affective disorders, and therapeutic communities, 540–541
Affective phenomena, core, 321, 324
Affective restructuring, 444–445
Affective science, 6–7, 598
Affective states, dyadic regulation of, 315, 316–317
African Americans, 565–585
   case example, 575–580
   countertransference reactions (African American client and therapist), 571
   feminist psychotherapies and, 566
   psychoanalytic developmental object-relations theory (PDORT) model, 568–570
   women (historical sexual exploitation of), 567
   women (in psychotherapy), 572–574
Agoraphobia (in case example), 447
Anal-sadistic relationship, 418
Anorexia nervosa, treatment for, 146–147. *See also* Eating disorders in adolescence
Anxiety-Anger Management Training (AAMT), 561
Anxiety disorder, and eating disorders, 151
Anxiety regulation (AA) (in E-STDP), 214–215
Attachment:
   accelerated experiential-dynamic psychotherapy (AEDP) and, 312–313
   eating disorders and, 138
   infant need for and early trauma of failed, 390
   neurobiology of, 49, 596–597
   object relations and, 49
   research, 318
   theory, 108, 532–533
Audiovisual technology, 590
Autism, infantile/normal, 48–49
Autistic spectrum disorders, 36–44
   case example, 42–44
   components/steps, comprehensive DIR (developmental, individual-difference, relationship-based) program, 40–42

Beck Depression Inventory, 362
Behavioral organization (developmental level), 22–23
Behaviorist attack on psychoanalysis, 587–588, 589
Biopsychosocial model (microscopic *vs.* macroscopic view of clinical phenomena), 441, 599
Bipolar disorder, and object-relations play therapy, 71
Body shift, 319

Borderline (one of four levels of development, Kernberg's diagnostic model), 291–292
Borderline personality disorder (BPD):
  accelerated experiential-dynamic psychotherapy (AEDP), 332
  child sexual abuse and, 7
  couples therapy, 388
  experiential short-term dynamic psychotherapy (E-STDP), 218
  interactional object-relations therapy, 295
  object-relations approach to treatment of borderline patients, 239–252
  psychoanalytic developmental object-relations theory (PDORT), 568
  psychodynamically oriented group therapy (POGT), 468
  self-object relationship therapy (case example), 429
  therapeutic community (day centers/hospital programs), 532, 538–540, 543
Borderline personality organization (BPO), defined, 239
Boundaries, 136
Brief psychodynamic therapy. *See* Experiential short-term dynamic psychotherapy (E-STDP); Short-term therapies
Brief relational therapy (BRT), 253–281
  acceptance, 276–277
  assessment methods, 258–260
  being alone, 277
  clarifying expectations, 274
  clinical illustrations, 261–273
  cognitive-interpersonal cycles, 255
  content *vs.* process focus, 254, 274
  demonstrating task of mindfulness, 273–274
  establishing rationale for treatment tasks, 273
  exploring patient/therapist experience, 275
  key characteristics of model, 254
  observing interpersonal field, 274–275
  process, 273–279
  relational matrix, 255
  relational schemas, 254–255
  relational theory of change: discovery and construction, 255–256
  relational theory of person, 254–255
  research directions and findings, 279–280
  self-state, 255
  termination, 276–277
  training/supervision, 277–279
Brief Symptom Inventory, 553
Bulimia nervosa, treatment for, 147–148. *See also* Eating disorders in adolescence

Cardiac patients, psychodynamic treatment for, 549–563
  Anxiety-Anger Management Training (AAMT), 561
  assessment/intervention methods, 553–555
  case example, 556–561
  coronary-prone personality, 556
  history of therapeutic approach, 549–550
  lifestyle, 555–556
  posttermination synopsis and effectiveness data, 561
  problems treated, 555–556
  Relationship Support Program, 560, 561
  theoretical orientation, 550–552
Caregiving relationship, primary (and infant mental health), 81–83
Causation, psychological, 111
Change, 255–258
Chaos theory, 600
Child Behavior Checklist, 51
Child molesters. *See* Sex offenders, group therapy for
Children, 8
  developmental basis of psychotherapeutic processes, 15–45
  infant mental health, 81–104
  object-relations play therapy, 47–80
  psychodynamic approaches to child therapy, 105–129
    assessment methods, 113–114
    case study, 120–123
    disorders of mental processes, 117–118
    disorders of mental representation, 114–117
    evolution of technique, 108–110
    evolution of theories, 105–108
    internalizing-externalizing dichotomy, 119
    intervention methods, 114–117
    problems for which expected to be efficacious, 118–120
    shortcomings, 124
    termination, 117
    theoretical constructs, 110–113
  sexual abuse as, and eating disorders, 144
Chronically medically ill dysfunctional personologic system (DPS), 440
Clinical programs, examples, 535–541
Clinical science, 598
Cognitive-behavioral therapy (CBT), bulimia nervosa, 147
Cognitive-interpersonal cycles, 255
Cognitive restructuring, 445
Cognitive science, 598
Cognitive templates, 289
College psychotherapy, 161–179
  assessment methods, 169
  brief therapy and its variants, 163–165
  case study, 175–178
  history, 161–162
  mental health services *vs.* counseling services, 162
  nondirective responses, 173
  nontraditional attendance patterns, 164–165
  pathology level/type, 168
  patient diversity, 167–168
  precounseling, 169–171
  problem areas and diagnosis, 174–175
  psychodynamic opportunities, 165–166
  theoretical constructs, 163–168
  theoretical orientation, 162

College psychotherapy (Continued)
  therapeutic relationship, 166
  transference, countertransference, and termination, 173–174
  treatment, 169–174
Communication, developmental level, 21–22
Communities, therapeutic, 529–547
  affective disorders, 540–541
  borderline disorders, 538–540, 543
  day centers/hospitals, 536–537, 538–539
  effectiveness/efficacy, 541–544
  examples of clinical programs, 535–541
  French institutional psychotherapy, 531–532
  intervention methods, 532–535
  milieu therapy, 530
  Northfield Military Hospital experiments, 529–530
  psychotic disorders, 536–538, 542–543
  rehabilitation units, 537–538
  staff vicissitudes, 534–535
  structuring environment, 532
  substance abuse patients, 541
  theoretical basis of, 530–532
  ward atmosphere and teamwork, 533–535
Community-Oriented Programs Environment Scales (COPES), 542, 543
Conduct disorder, 71, 120
Conflict:
  child therapy and intrapsychic, 111
  core conflictual relationship theme (CCRT), 184, 195 (see also Supportive-expressive (SE) psychotherapy)
  "ghosts in the nursery" and the walking wounded: the unharmonious cohabitation of conflict and trauma, 90–92
Confrontation ruptures, resolution model for, 267–273
Constructive therapy narratives, 428
Containment, 532
Contract, treatment, 297–300
Core conflictual relationship theme (CCRT), 184, 195. See also Supportive-expressive (SE) psychotherapy
Corrective emotional experience, 284–285
Corrective interpersonal experience, 289–291
Countertransference. See also Transference/countertransference:
  disclosure, and metacommunication, 257
  reactions (African American client and therapist), 571
Couples therapy, object relations, 387–405. See also Self-object relationship therapy with couples
  assessment/intervention methods, 392–402
  contraindications, 402
  degree of relational dysfunction, 393
  emotions and defenses, 391
  empathic attunement, 401–402
  moderately vulnerable couples, 394–397
  nonenmeshed couple, 392–394
  primary affects, 389–391
  reparative process, 402
  severely disturbed couples, 397–400
  spectrum of pathology and differential treatment, 400–402
  theoretical constructs, 389–392
Covertly narcissistic dysfunctional personologic system (DPS), 335, 440
Cultural love/solution messages, 415
Cybernetic epistemology, 135

Decentering, 256–258
Defense, 111–112
  analysis, 552
  cataloguing and empirical support of, 5
  developmental perspective, 20
  emotions and, 391
  interpretation of, 115, 116
  restructuring, 209, 212–214, 444
Dependency, 483
Depressigenic dysfunctional personologic system (DPS), 440
Depression, 33–36, 553
Determinism, psychological, 459–460, 481
Development, levels of (four, in Kernberg's model), 291–295
Developmental, individual-difference, relationship-based (DIR) model, 15–45
  autistic spectrum disorders and, 36–44
  case examples, 17–18, 32–36
  constructing developmental profile, 16–17
  principles, 28–32
  psychotherapeutic process (with children and adults), 18–27
  schematic outline of functional developmental levels, 36, 37–39
Developmentally arrested dysfunctional personologic system (DPS), 440, 447
Developmental profile, 16–18
Developmental science, 598
Diagnostic Interview Scale for Children, 51
Diathesis-stress model, 446, 599
Digressive/regressive narratives, 428
Disconfirmation mechanism, 256–258
Dissociative disorders, 7, 332
Diversity:
  challenges of, 598–599
  impact of on college psychotherapy, 167–168
Drive psychology/theory, 108, 436, 461–462, 463
Dyadic restructuring, 445
Dyadic terms, 136
Dynamic psychiatry, 481. See also Psychodynamic theory/approaches to psychotherapy
Dysfunctional personologic system (DPS):
  addictive, 439–440
  chronically medically ill, 440
  developmentally arrested, 440
  paranoid, 440–441
  physically/sexually traumatizing, 440

somatic, 441
term coined, 439
Dysthymic disorders (in case examples), 335, 447

Eating disorders in adolescence, 133–159, 218
    anorexia nervosa treatment, 146–147
    assessment methods, 145–146
    attachment theory, 138
    biopsychosocial paradigm, 140–143
    body in, 143–144
    bulimia nervosa treatment, 147–148
    case example, 152–156
    challenges of puberty, 141–142
    child sexual abuse and, 144
    comorbid psychopathology, 151–152
    context of dysfunctional family system, 135
    epidemiology, 134
    experiential short-term dynamic psychotherapy (E-STDP), 218
    family context, 142–143
    hermeneutics, 134–135
    history of therapeutic approach, 133–140
    hostility and, 144–145
    object-relations theory, 138–139
    outcome, 150–151
    personality traits, 141
    psychodynamic frame, 138–140
    psychotherapeutic process, 148
    self psychology theory, 139–140
    systemic paradigm, 135–138
    theoretical constructs, 140–145
    therapeutic alliance, 146
    treatment stages, 149–150
Ego psychology, 105–106, 436, 462, 463
    adaptation emphasis, 3
    and object relations, 286
    and psychoanalytic developmental object-relations theory (PDORT), 568
Ego-structural model for differential diagnoses, 291–293
Emotion(s):
    activation of unconscious/conflicting, 211–212
    core, 314–315
    defense and, 391
    fear and shame as pathogenic affects (*vs.* categorical emotions), 323
    stage in evolution of groups, 483
    theory, and affective neuroscience, 311
Emotional maieutics (XA) (E-STDP), 215–216
Empathic attunement, couple therapy, 401–402
Empathic reflection of self, 311, 315, 317–318
Epigenetic development, 460
Epistemology, cybernetic, 135
Experiential short-term dynamic psychotherapy (E-STDP), 207–237. *See also* Accelerated experiential-dynamic psychotherapy (AEDP)
    activation of unconscious/conflicting emotions, 211–212
    anxiety regulation (AA), 214–215
    assessment, 216–218
    case example, 218–236
    characteristics, 209–210
    defense restructuring (DA), 212–214
    dynamic activities, 209
    fear of expression and emotional maieutics (XA), 215–216
    flexible format, 217–218
    history, 207–209
    mirroring function, 209, 211
    syndromes/symptoms/problems treated, 218
    theoretical constructs, 209–216
    therapeutic alliance, 213
    trial relationship, 216–217
    triangles of conflict/person, 209, 210–211

Family, 136
    eating disorders and, 135–138, 142–143
    object-relations couples therapy, 387–405
    relational psychodynamics for complex clinical syndromes, 435–453
    self-object relationship therapy with couples, 407–433
    system, 135–138
Fear and shame as pathogenic affects (*vs.* categorical emotions), 323
"Felt sense," 319
Feminist:
    criticism of family/couple therapy, 425
    model of family therapy, 148–149
    perspective on family therapy and eating disorders, 137, 148–149
    psychotherapies, and African Americans, 566
    relational-feminist psychodynamic approach to sexual desire, 365–384
Fight/flight, 483
Free association, 1–2, 109
Functional developmental levels, schematic outline of, 36, 37–39
Future trends, 600–601

Gender:
    identity deficit, 509
    issues in family therapy (feminist perspective), 148–149 (*see also* Feminist)
    race and (transference in psychotherapy), 565–585
Generalized anxiety disorder (GAD), 191–192, 447
General systems theory, 599–600
Genogram, family, 443
"Ghosts in the nursery," 90–92
Global Assessment of Functioning (GAF), 218
Green signal affects, 322
Group therapy:
    psychodynamically oriented (POGT), 457–479
    psychodynamic/object-relations, with schizophrenic patients, 481–499
    for sex offenders, 501–526
    therapeutic communities, 529–547

Hamilton Depression Scale, 362
Histrionic personality disorder, 218
Hologram, psychodynamic, 349
Home visiting, 86–88
Hospitalization. *See* Communities, therapeutic
Hostility in eating disorders, 144–145
Human sexuality. *See* Sexual desire disorders
Hysteroid personality, 295

Id/ego/superego, 105
Infant mental health, 81–104
   assessment, 92–93
   case example, 97–100
   conflict/trauma ("ghosts in the nursery"), 90–92
   contemporary approaches, 84–85
   development (infant/parent) within relational matrix, 88–90
   history of therapeutic approach, 81–85
   home visiting (theory/practice/reality), 86–88
   infant capacities, 83
   Infant-Parent Program, 85–86
   intervention, 94–97
   maturational processes and facilitating environment, 88–90
   parameters of infant-parent psychotherapy, 85–86
   primary caregiving relationship, 81–83
   social environment intervention, 83–84
   syndromes/symptoms/problems treated, 97
   theoretical constructs, 86–92
Inhibited sexual desire (ISD), 365. *See also* Sexual desire disorders
Insight, 184, 289–291
Institutional psychotherapy, 531–532
Integrative relational therapy (IRP), 435–453
   affective restructuring, 444–445
   assessment/intervention methods, 443–445
   biopsychosocial model (microscopic *vs.* macroscopic view of clinical phenomena), 441
   case example, 447–450
   clinical utility emphasis, 435–436
   depicting therapeutic process with the triangle, 441–443
   dysfunctional personologic system (DPS) (term coined), 439
   ego psychology and, 436
   empirical support, 450–451
   fulcrum, 447
   history, 435–441
   interpersonal components, 436
   interpersonal-dyadic matrix, 442–443
   intersubjectivity of dyadic relationship, 437–438
   intrapsychic components/matrix, 436, 442
   object-relations theory and, 436
   relational diagnosis, 438–441
   relational-systemic components, 437
   self psychology and, 436
   stress-diathesis model, 446
   structural drive theory and, 436
   syndromes/symptoms/problems treated, 445–447
   theoretical constructs, 441–443
   therapeutic alliance, 438
   treatment stance and methods, 443–445
   triangular-relational restructuring, 445
Integrative theory and multiperspective approach to psychotherapy (trend toward), 9
Intelligence, development of (and affect and interaction), 31–32
Intensive short-term dynamic psychotherapy (ISTDP), 348–450, 552
Interactional object-relations therapy, 283–307
   assessments/intervention methods, 291–295
   case example (schizoid personality disorder), 300–305
   corrective emotional experience (concept reexamined), 284–285
   current interpersonal and object-relations theories of treatment, 285–287
   and developmental levels, 291–295
   ego-structural model for making differential diagnoses, 291–293
   history, 283–287
   syndromes treated, 295–300
   theoretical constructs/fundamental assumptions, 287–291
   treatment of borderline clients, 295
   treatment of neurotic clients, 293–294
   treatment of preneurotic clients, 294
   workable treatment contracts, 297–300
Internalizing-externalizing dichotomy, 119
Interpersonal-dyadic matrix, 442–443
Interpersonal experience, neurobiology of, 596–597
Interpersonal field; observing, 274–275
Interpersonal interactions, 111
Interpersonal psychiatry, 4–5
   current theories of treatment, 285–287
   intersubjectiveness, 4–5
Interpretation:
   addressing repudiated wishes, 115, 116
   child's deep anxieties, 109
   of defenses, 115, 116
   maximum effect of, 283
   "new idea," 483
   reconstructive, 115–116
   supportive-expressive psychotherapy, 184–185
Intersubjectivity, 256, 370, 426, 437–438
Intrapsychic matrix, 442

Language system in therapy, 426–428
Learning and neural structure, 595–596
Long-term therapy:
   efforts to accelerate psychodynamic treatment, 8 (*see also* Short-term therapies)
   group, 465, 468–473, 489–491
   traditional psychoanalysis, 8
Love (couple therapy), 413–416

Managed care, 588–589, 594
Marshak Interaction Method, 51

Matrix:
    group, 530
    interpersonal-dyadic, 442–443
    intersubjective, 426
    intrapsychic, 442
    relational, 88–90, 255, 257
Medication information group, 487–488
Metacommunication, 257, 258–260, 285
Milieu therapy, 530, 535
Mind, functions of, 460
Mindfulness, 256–257, 273–274
Mirroring function, 209, 211
Mood/anxiety disorders, 71, 467
Motor tone/planning, 19–20

Narcissistic disorders:
    accelerated experiential-dynamic psychotherapy (AEDP) and, 333
    couples therapy, 416
    covertly narcissistic dysfunctional personologic system (DPS), 333
    expressions of, 347
    interactional object-relations theory, 283, 294–295, 299
    mechanisms of, 347
    narcissistic dysfunctional personologic system (DPS), 440
    narcissistic personality disorder, covert type (diagnostic presentation), 352
    narcissistic personality disorder (diagnostic criteria), 352
    narcissistic personologic system, 333–334
    narcissistic relationship, 418
    psychoanalytic developmental object-relations theory (PDORT) and, 568
    short-term dynamic psychotherapy and, 345–364
        case examples, 353–364
        covert NPD, 354, 360–362
        diagnosis and assessment, 356–362
        feelings, 351
        history, 346–348
        intensive short-term dynamic psychotherapy (ISTDP), 348–450
        NPD proper, 353, 356–360
        posttermination synopsis and effectiveness data, 362–363
        self psychology, 350–351
        syndromes/symptoms/problems treated, 351–353
        theoretical constructs, 348–353
    symptomatic behavior, two pathways, 347–348
Narrative rigidities, 427–428
Nature/nurture interaction, 288–289
Neuroscience, 595–597, 598
    affect, 597
    attachment and interpersonal experience, 596–597
    learning, 595–596

Neurosis/neurotic level of development, 118, 120, 291–292, 293–294
Normal (one of four levels of development: Kernberg's diagnostic model), 291–292

Object relations theory, 240–242, 436, 462–463
    couples therapy, 387–405
    current theories of treatment, 285–287
    disordered (conceptualization of developmental level), 54–69
    eating disorders and, 138–139
    emphasis on attachment, 3–4
    Freud and, 240–241
    general model of, 242
    reformulation (Kernberg), 241–242
Object relations therapies:
    borderline patients, and transference focused psychotherapy (TFP), 239–252
    interactional object-relations therapy (mastering developmental issues through), 283–307
    play therapy, 47–80
    psychoanalytic developmental object-relations theory (PDORT) model, 568–570
    psychodynamic/object-relations group therapy with schizophrenic patients, 481–499
Obsessive-compulsive, 151, 218, 290, 294
Oppositional Defiant disorder, 71, 121
Oral relationship, 418
Orgasm, 369
Outpatient programs, 488–489

Pairing tendencies, 483
Paranoid dysfunctional personologic system (DPS), 440–441
Paraphilia. See Sex offenders, group therapy for
Passive-aggressive personality disorders (case example, AEDP), 335
Personality disorder, 5–6
    accelerated experiential-dynamic psychotherapy (AEDP) and, 332
    brief psychodynamic therapy, 208–209
    eating disorders, 151–152
    experiential short-term dynamic psychotherapy (E-STDP) and, 218
    interpersonal and object-relations theories, 286–287
    psychodynamically oriented group therapy (POGT) and, 467–468
    psychodynamic approaches to child therapy, 120
    transference, and psychoanalytic developmental object-relations theory (PDORT), 568–569
Personality theory (and psychopathology and psychodynamic therapy), 5–6, 598, 599–600
Personality traits, and eating disorders, 141
Phallic-oedipal relationship, 418
Physically/sexually traumatizing dysfunctional personologic system (DPS), 440
Play therapy, object relations, 47–80
    assessment methods, 50–51

Play therapy, object relations (Continued)
　case examples, 71–78
　components (three essential), 52–53
　compromised rapprochement, 55, 60–61, 75–78
　conceptualizations of developmental level of disordered object relations, 54–69
　effectiveness data, 78
　intervention, 51–69
　late separation-individuation presentations, 65–66
　"on the way to object constancy" presentations, 62–64
　post-oedipal presentations, 67–68
　practicing and rapprochement presentations, 58–59
　presymbiotic and early symbiotic presentation, 55, 56–57, 72–75
　"secure base" relationship, 52
　six childhood patterns, 54–55
　syndromes/symptoms/problems treated, 69–71
　theoretical constructs, 48–50
　types of, 47–48
Posttraumatic stress disorder, complex, 91
Preneurotic clients, treatment of, 294
Presymbiosis, 49, 55, 56–57, 72–75
Profile, developmental, 16–18
Progressive narratives, 428
Projective testing, 51
Pseudo-alliance, 261
Psychiatric hospitalization. *See* Communities, therapeutic
Psychoanalytic developmental object-relations theory (PDORT) model, 568–570
　case example, African American woman, 575–580
　model of brief treatment with structured (neurotic) personalities, 578
　object relations assessment, 577
　perspective on transference, 570–572
　race/gender issues assessment, 577–578
　transference/countertransference enactment, 578–580
Psychodynamically oriented group therapy (POGT), 457–479
　assessment/intervention methods, 466–467
　epigenetic development, 460
　ethical considerations, 476
　history, 457–459
　long-term group therapy (LTG), 465, 468–473
　posttermination synopsis and effectiveness data, 476–477
　pretherapy training (importance of careful patient preparation), 467
　process, 464–465
　psychological determinism, 459–460
　short-term group therapy (STG), 465–466, 473–476
　syndromes/symptoms/problems treated, 467–468
　theoretical constructs, 459–461
　transference and resistance, 460–461
　unconscious processes, 460

Psychodynamic theory/approaches to psychotherapy:
　convergence (achieving consilience), 593–594
　current challenges, 595–601
　empirically based science (struggle to establish), 589–595
　four schools of:
　　drive psychology, 108, 436, 461–462, 463
　　ego psychology, 3, 105–106, 286, 436, 462, 463, 568
　　object-relations psychology, 3–4, 436, 462–463
　　self psychology, 4, 436, 463
　future trends, 600–601
　history, 1–12, 587–589
　training/supervision, 600
Psychopathology, 5–6, 321–325
Psychotherapy, 1–2, 9, 551
Psychotic dysfunctional personologic system (DPS), 440
Psychotic patients, therapeutic communities, 536–538, 542–543
Puberty, and eating disorders, 141–142

Race:
　college psychotherapy, 167–168
　impact of similarities and differences, therapist/patient, 571
　and transference in psychotherapy, 565–585
Rapprochement, 55, 58–61, 75–78
Reconstructive interpretations, 115–116
Reflective-integrative strategies (AEDP), 332
Rehabilitation:
　techniques for deteriorated schizophrenic patients (object-relations point of view), 491
　therapeutic communities, 537–538
Relational diagnosis, 438–441
Relational matrix, 88–90, 255, 257
Relational schemas, 254–255, 257
Relational science, 598
Relational theory, 254–256
Relational therapies:
　brief relational therapy (BRT), 253–281
　relational-feminist psychodynamic approach to sexual desire, 365–384
　relational psychodynamics for complex clinical syndromes (*see* Integrative relational therapy (IRP))
　strategies in accelerated experiential-dynamic psychotherapy (AEDP), 331
Relationships Anecdotes Paradigm (RAP), 186
Relationship Support Program, 560, 561
Restructuring methods/strategies, 331, 444–445
Rorschach, 51
Ruptures, 253, 259, 260–273
　resolution model for confrontation, 267–273
　resolution model for withdrawal, 261–267

Schizoid personality, 295, 300–305
Schizophrenia:
　psychoanalytic developmental object-relations theory (PDORT) model critique and, 570

psychodynamic/object-relations group therapy, 481–499
  acute schizophrenic patients, 485–488
  case example, 492–495
  chronic schizophrenic patients, 488–491
  diversity of groups for psychotic patients, 484–485
  effectiveness, 495–496
  Freudian conceptions of groups and institutions, 482
  historical aspects of group analytical psychotherapy, 481–483
  interpretations, 483
  intervention methods, 483–492
  long-term psychoanalytically oriented groups, 489–491
  medication information group, 487–488
  multifamily groups, 491–492
  open/closed groups, 484
  outpatient programs, 488–489
  rehabilitation techniques for deteriorated patients (object-relations point of view), 491
  short-term groups, 486, 487, 489
  staff-patients group, 485–486
  syndromes/situations, 483–484
  theoretical constructs, 483
therapeutic mechanisms in communities, 532
Science, empirically based, 589–595
  audiovisual technology and the advancement of science of psychotherapy and psychodynamics, 590
  challenge to provide effective brief psychotherapy, 591–592
  convergence of theories (achieving consilience), 593–594
  eschewing of empirical findings by psychoanalysis, 589–590
  paradox: reduction of opportunities for training and pressure for results, 594–595
  struggle to establish psychodynamics as, 589–595
  time-tested psychodynamic postulates, 590–591
  treatment manuals and empirically validated treatment, 592–593
  use of empirical findings by psychodynamic clinicians, 591
"Secure base" therapeutic relationship, 49–50, 52
Seduction/trauma theory, 7
Self-at-best/self-at-worst, 324
Self disorder(s), 333, 352–353
Self-object relationship therapy with couples, 407–433
  case example, 428–430
  collusion (four types) present in every married couple relationship, 418
  culture's love messages and solution messages, 415
  difficult couples, 416–417
  difficulties of couple therapy, 407–408
  feminist critics, 425
  integrative perspective on treatment, 409–413, 421–425
  language system in therapy, 426–428
  philosophical settings, 408–409
  technical considerations, 417–421

Self psychology, 4, 350–351, 436, 463
  couples therapy, 389
  eating disorders and, 139–140
Self-regulation, developmental level, 19–20
Self-state, 255
Sensory reactivity, 19
Separation-individuation, 49, 65–66, 286
Separation and loss, 276
Sex offenders, group therapy for, 501–526
  assessment/intervention methods, 512–514
  behavioral approach, arguments against, 505–506
  case examples, 516–521
  categories (five) of treatment, 505
  female cotherapist, 511
  gender identity deficit, 509
  history, 501–504
  hybrid psychodynamic model, 508, 512
  posttermination synopsis and effectiveness data, 521–523
  syndromes/symptoms/problems treated, 514–516
  theoretical constructs, 504–512
Sexual desire disorders, 365–384
  assessment/intervention methods, 375–377
  case example, 378–382
  four-stage sexual response cycle, 366
  history of therapeutic approach, 365–369
  hypoactive sexual desire (individuals/couples), 365, 377–378
  intersubjectivity, 370
  objectification model, 370–375
  orgasm, 369
  problems treated, 377–378
  protocols, 380–381
  psychosexual clinical interview for female sexual dysfunction (outline), 376
  relational-feminist psychodynamic approach, 365–384
  study of human sexuality (four traditions in), 366
  subjectivity, specific consequences of loss of, 373–374
  supportive-expressive (SE) psychotherapy (in case study), 194
  theoretical orientation, 369–375
Sexual dysfunction, stress-diathesis model and, 446
Sexual lifestyle (college psychotherapy), 168
Short-term therapies:
  anxiety-provoking, 551
  challenge to provide effective brief therapy, 591–592
  dynamic, 310, 496–497, 551, 590
  dynamic psychotherapy of narcissistic disorders, 345–364
  efforts to accelerate psychodynamic treatment, 8
  experiential short-term dynamic psychotherapy (E-STDP), 207–237 (*see also* Accelerated experiential-dynamic psychotherapy (AEDP))
  group, 465–466, 473–476, 486, 487, 489, 496–497
  variants, 163–165
Simultaneous conconstruction, 427
Sociobiology/evolutionary science, 598
Somatic dysfunctional personologic system (DPS), 441

Somatic experience as process of change, 318–319
Somatic focusing, 311, 315
Somatoform disorders, 332, 333
Stabilizing narratives, 428
State transformation, 309–310, 313–315
Stress-diathesis model, 446, 599
Structural analysis of social behavior (SASB) model, 286, 287
Structural drive theory, 436. *See also* Drive psychology/theory
Substance abuse, 192, 332, 541
Superficiality, hypothesis of, 208
Supportive-expressive (SE) psychotherapy, 183–205
    assessment, 185–186, 192–193
    case example, 192–202
    core conflictual relationship theme (CCRT), 184, 195
    expressive techniques, 188–191, 194–195
    generalized anxiety disorder, 191–192
    history, 183–184
    interpretations, 184–185
    intervention, 186–191
    supportive techniques, 188, 190–191, 194
    syndromes/symptoms/problems treated, 191–192
    termination, 191
    theoretical constructs, 184–185
    therapeutic alliance/relationship, 185, 188, 194
    transference, 184
    wish (W), response of other (RO), response of self (RS), 184, 185, 187, 195
Suppression, 7
Symbiosis, normal, 49
System(s):
    dysfunctional personologic system (DPS) (term coined), 439
    general systems theory, 599–600
    systemic paradigm, 135–138

Therapeutic alliance:
    brief relational therapy, 253
    college psychotherapy, 166
    eating disorders, 146
    experiential short-term dynamic psychotherapy (E-STDP), 213
    integrative relational therapy, 438
    interactional object-relations therapy, 284, 300–305
    supportive-expressive psychotherapy, 185, 188, 194
Therapeutic communities. *See* Communities, therapeutic
Therapist:
    countertransference reactions (African American client and therapist), 571
    exploring self experience, 275–276, 278
    with schizoid tendencies, and schizoid patients, 285
Training/supervision, 277–279, 600
    awareness-oriented role plays, 279
    experiential focus, 278
    paradox: reduction of opportunities for training and pressure for results, 594–595
    relational content of supervision, 277–278
    self-exploration, 278
    supervisors as models, 279
Transference/countertransference:
    college psychotherapy, 173–174
    dynamic psychiatry, 481, 482
    individual institutional, 531
    object relations, 567
    psychodynamically oriented group therapy (POGT), 460–461
    psychodynamic therapy with children, 109, 112, 116
    race/gender and, 565–585
    supportive-expressive psychotherapy, 184
Transference focused psychotherapy (TFP), 239–252
    assessment, 242–243
    case example, 248–251
    empirical investigation of, 246–248
    intervention, 243
    object-relations theory and, 240–242
    progression of, 246
    retention-attrition, 247
    strategies of, 243–244
    suicidal and self-injurious behavior, 247–248
    tactics of, 244–245
    techniques of, 245–246
    utilization of services, 248
Transformation experiences, 311–312, 315
Trauma, 7
    of failed attachment, 390
    "ghosts in the nursery" and the walking wounded: the unharmonious cohabitation of conflict and trauma, 90–92
    physically/sexually traumatizing dysfunctional personologic system (DPS), 440
    sexual trauma history, 377
Trial therapy, 327–329
Triangulation:
    depicting therapeutic process, 441–443
    eating disorders, 136
    experiential short-term dynamic psychotherapy (E-STDP), 209, 210–211
    interpersonal-dyadic matrix, 442–443
    intrapsychic matrix, 442
    relational restructuring, 445
    triadic theory, 438
    triangle of conflict, 210–211, 310, 321, 322, 329, 349, 442, 446
True self experience, 318
Type A behavior pattern, 550

Unconscious processes, 111, 460, 481

Ward atmosphere and teamwork, 533–535
WAS scales, 542
Whole person perspective, 112–113
Wish(es), interpretation, 115, 116, 184, 185, 187, 195
Withdrawal ruptures, resolution model for, 261–267